FDR

THE BECKONING OF DESTINY

THE FRANCIS PARKMAN PRIZE

The Society of American Historians was founded in 1939 by Allan Nevins and others to stimulate literary distinction in historical writing. In its early years, the Society sought to create a magazine for popular history; this effort culminated in the establishment of *American Heritage* in the early 1950s. The Society then resolved to advance its mission by offering an annual prize for the best-written book in American history. To name the prize after Francis Parkman seemed nearly a foregone conclusion.

Parkman was born in 1823, the grandson of one of Boston's wealthiest merchants. Throughout his life, Parkman was plagued with nervous disorders and problems with his eyes. Yet he loved the outdoors and exulted in sojourns into the wild. "I was haunted with wilderness images day and night," he recalled, one reason why his evocations of frontier life were so powerful.

But he also was drawn to history. As a sophomore at Harvard he resolved on his life's work—a history of the struggle between France and Britain for mastery of North America. But first he trekked to the West and wrote *The Oregon Trail* (1849), a youthful work that exhibited the masterful writing that became his hallmark. The first volume of *France and England in North America* was published in 1865, the ninth and final volume in 1892.

Some of Parkman's judgments have been superseded by modern scholarship, and, in matters of style, he overused the concept of opposition (the most significant being the contrast between authoritarian and Catholic France, and democratic and Protestant Britain). Henry Adams was a more sophisticated thinker, and perhaps a more profound writer, but Parkman was the great American historian of the nineteenth century.

The first Parkman Prize was awarded in 1958 to Arthur M. Schlesinger, Jr., for his *Crisis of the Old Order*, published the previous year. And now the Society of American Historians is pleased to be working together with History Book Club to develop their exclusive new editions of Parkman Prize winners from the past—allowing readers to rediscover what many consider to be some of the best writing on the American story.

Mark C. Carnes
Executive Secretary
The Society of American Historians

FDR

THE BECKONING OF DESTINY

1882—1928
A HISTORY

Kenneth S. Davis

Introduction by
Geoffrey C. Ward

FRANCIS PARKMAN PRIZE EDITION
HISTORY BOOK CLUB
NEW YORK

Again
To Flo
With all my love

Contents

CONTENTS

Introduction to the Francis Parkman Prize Edition

by Geoffrey C. Ward

W HAT'S TO become of us?" *Fortune* magazine asked its readers in December 1933. "Roosevelt only knows. Who is Roosevelt?" Franklin Delano Roosevelt had been president for just nine months. The nation was still mired in the worst depression in its history. Not since the Civil War had ordinary Americans felt themselves so dependent on the actions of a single man, and yet no one seemed to know how much substance lay beneath that man's glossy surface.

All great political leaders possess complicated personalities; seeming to be all things to all men is part of the job description. But, as his friend the playwright Robert Sherwood wrote, FDR's personality was so mercurial, so filled with paradox, it was "multiplex"; even those who worked with him most closely, he said, were barred from the President's "thickly forested interior." According to the *Fortune* article, a White House correspondent claimed to have caught a glimpse of the authentic Roosevelt the previous June while covering the President's visit to his family's summer home on Campobello Island. One afternoon, he and a young woman reporter had been strolling through the stunted fog-shrouded woods "looking for a quiet place," when they'd suddenly come upon the President's Ford parked beneath a tree, his bodyguard asleep behind the wheel. "And there beside the car was the President . . . sitting on the trunk of a tree, his legs folded out in front of him, his hands over his face. And suddenly, before [the couple] could move, the hands came down and there were his eyes looking straight into their eyes just a few steps off and not seeing them at all . . . there was a kind of drawn grimace over his mouth and over his forehead like a man trying to see something in his mind and suffering. And then all at once they could see his eyes focusing and it was like a shutter clicking down on a camera the way the smile came back . . . and he called out: 'Hello there, Billy. Picking flowers?' They turned and got out of there. They could hear his big laugh back of them in the spruce."

For more than seven decades, biographers have been trying to understand the private man behind that big laugh. Kenneth S. Davis worked at it for nearly thirty years. For him, history really was biography and the lives of those who sought to lead us mattered most. Of his seventeen books, ten were biographies: *Soldier of Democracy: A Biography of Dwight Eisenhower* (Davis had been a correspondent attached to Eisenhower's headquarters during the Second World War); *A Prophet in His Own Country: The Triumphs and Defeats of Adlai E. Stevenson; The Hero: Charles A. Lindbergh and the American Dream; The Politics of Honor: A Biography of Adlai E. Stevenson; Invincible Summer: An Intimate Portrait of the Roosevelts, Based on the Recollections of Marion Dickerman*; and the five-volume *FDR*, for which *FDR: The Beckoning of Destiny, 1882-1928* provides the vivid opening chapter.

Davis was a storyteller—a novelist as well as an historian—and he brought to the Roosevelt story a novelist's sense of drama. The book opens with a lyrical prologue about the Hudson River that was the great constant flowing through its subject's life, and it ends with the telephone call from New York Governor Al Smith that lured Roosevelt back into the sweaty world of politics and away from the serene pampered life along that river to which his crippling once seemed permanently to have doomed him.

Throughout the book, FDR remains at center stage, where he always insisted on being. But the members of Roosevelt's large supporting cast all have their time in the spotlight, as well: his mother, Sara Delano Roosevelt, whose celebrated hauteur disguised the fact that it was she who had instilled in her son her own belief in his potential greatness; his wife, Eleanor, whose unsteady progress from unloved orphan to public figure Davis traces sensitively but without sentimentality; Louis Howe, the ugly little political operative whose savvy counsel helped transform FDR from a genial dabbler in politics into the ablest politician of his age; Secretary of the Navy Josephus Daniels, whose near-saintly forbearance kept his young assistant's overweening ambition from destroying his career during World War I; Woodrow Wilson, whose example helped make

Roosevelt understand American responsibilities overseas, but also demonstrated to him the perils of venturing too far ahead of public opinion; his wife's social secretary Lucy Mercer, with whom he developed the relationship that nearly destroyed both his marriage and his career; and Missy LeHand, the loyal secretary whose hopes to grow still closer to her boss were crushed when he returned to public life.

Davis has high standards for his subject: For every strength with which FDR emerges from these pages—charm, quick wits, eagerness for action—there is a concomitant flaw: deviousness, shallowness, inconsistency. But even he cannot fault the gallantry of Roosevelt's struggle against infantile paralysis or the ability to inspire those less fortunate than he that it reinforced. "Of greater life-affirming courage and fortitude in a political leader of first rank, all history affords few examples . . . ," Davis writes. "He was at ease in the world. He made others feel at ease. And often in hours of gloom, when dark clouds lowered ominously and every breath stank of despair, his effect on those around him was a burst of sunlight, a cleansing sweep of wind off sea or prairie. Become a hero, he would bring many gifts to his fellowmen. Some would prove worthless or worse in the end. But in this first gift of all—his laughter in the face of doom, his gay defiance of all dire adversity, his constant implicit insistence on life against death and that life is meant to be lived to the utmost—this gift was a priceless boon."

Nearly three decades is a long time for anyone to labor in any vineyard, and in Davis's case, familiarity with his elusive subject would eventually breed something close to contempt. By the time he reached his fifth and last volume, *FDR: The War President, 1940-1943* (published after his death in 1999), his disappointment at what he saw as Roosevelt's excessive caution had eclipsed his earlier admiration for his courage, and Roosevelt's obvious delight in maneuver seemed more threatening to him even than the turbulent seas through which the President charted his sinuous course.

But at the end of this first volume destiny still beckons and everything seems possible, for the country, for the world, and for the multiplex man who did so much to transform them both.

Prologue

❯❯❯❮❮❮

HOUSES BESIDE A RIVER

Prologue: Houses Beside a River

THE river that flowed through his life—beside which he was born, beside which he is buried—has its main source in a small wilderness lake high in the Adirondacks. Its early career is southeasterly as a slender winding mountain stream. Soon, however, continuously fed by springs and frequently by tributaries, it grows into a full-sized river which assumes noble proportions forty miles north of Albany, where it makes a sharp turn southward. Thereafter it is the lordly Hudson, monarch of a fertile glacier-terraced valley which, below Albany, reaches between the erosion-carved Catskills in the west and the Taconics, a once-mighty mountain range now worn down to rolling hills, in the east. The river is peculiar geographically in that it is an estuary through most of its length, one of the longest in the world. After the Mohawk flows into it, its bed becomes the floor of a geologically ancient gorge lying well below the level of the sea. In consequence it measurably rises and falls with the ocean tides as fresh waters flowing down it meet and mingle with the salt of the Atlantic far above its mouth.

The river is also peculiar historically. It has been the central theme of the most aristocratic community ever established in America. When the Dutch West India Company ruled the valley, early in the seventeenth century, it issued a Charter of Privileges to Patrons, whereby anyone who brought fifty settlers to New Netherland was granted a feudal estate with a fifteen-mile front on the Hudson. Over this vast tract and its people, the patron had the despotic powers of a medieval baron: he held exclusive hunting and fishing rights; he decreed laws; he dispensed justice; he exacted tribute from all who labored. And the feudal land system thereby established was but slightly modified when the British conquered New Netherland; the Dutch patroonships were simply transformed into English manors, defined and protected by English law. To them were then added immense new land grants along the river made by corrupt Crown governors to their favorites usually in return for substantial private gains.[1] Thus palpable dishonesty nourished aristocratic pride. New York became the most Tory of all the colonies.

But key members of the Hudson Valley aristocracy were shrewd enough to leave the sinking loyalist ship during the political storms of the 1770's. Scions of the Livingstons and Van Rensselaers, two of the richest manor families, did so. They became moderating leaders of the independence movement; they helped shape the new Republic in ways that ensured a continuation not only of their own privileges, but also of those of less prescient neighbors. The aristocracy continued to function, only mildly diluted by the rising streams of democracy.

Not until the bloodless but bitter Rent War of the 1840's did the inherited feudal rights of the oldest river families come at last to an end, followed by an accelerated breaking up of the largest holdings into smaller but still large estates fronting on the river.[2] Social privilege, nevertheless, remained. The attitudes, the customs and habits of the great English landed families of the eighteenth century remained, all up and down the middle Hudson, long after their principal economic support had been shifted away from the land to shares in banks, railroads, mills, mines, and factories. Side by side with them were the very different attitudes, customs, habits nourished by the Puritanism of New England, the natural rights doctrines of Jefferson, and the liberalizing insurgency of the Jacksonians.

Hence there was a meeting and mingling of traditions (democratic, aristocratic) along the river's bank as there was of waters (fresh, salt) within its channel.

The actual social classes, however, remained distinct and separate as the waters could never be. Class distinctions were maintained as high stone walls with few gates in them. Social intercourse between the proprietors of the riverfront estates and the farmers, artisans, and tradesmen of the immediate hinterland was slight indeed and never on the basis of equality. In sharp contrast was social intercourse among the river families themselves. These, gentleman and ladies living lives of ample leisure in their private parks, were in constant and often intimate communication with one another. They continuously exchanged visits, entertaining one another with teas, dinners, evening parties, and occasional great formal balls in houses always large, sometimes palatial. They shared out-of-doors recreations, riding, picnicking, boating, sleighing, and playing games together. They went, year after year, to the same summer resorts, maintaining second (or third) homes there (they also generally had houses in New York), and whether or not they traveled together, they were constantly meeting one another abroad, for they sailed on the same luxury ships, toured Europe by the same routes, and stopped in the same fashionable places. Inevitably they intermarried generation after generation until, by the 1880's, many, if not most, of them were at least distantly related to one another.[3] The son of one family courting the daughter of another would discover, if he had not known before, that the two had ancestors in common. Married, they became husband and wife while remaining cousins, ensuring blood ties among their children and grandchildren so complicated as to defy any easily comprehended exposition.

Change came slowly along the river. The river families were generally satisfied, as well they might be, with things as they were; technological innovation did not per se intrigue them as it did most Americans. They were less worshipful of material progress than most, somewhat slower than most who could afford them to buy for their personal use such newfangled devices as telephones, gramophones, and automobiles.[4] Yet they did not oppose change blindly. During the transition from an agrarian society toward an industrial one in post-Civil War America, they protected their privileged social and economic positions in essentially the same shrewd way as they had during the transition from aristocracy toward democracy at the time of the Revolution—that is, they joined, to at least the minimum necessary degree, the forces that threatened to overwhelm them. Members of the same exclusive clubs in New York City, the landed gentry also often became fellow directors of large industrial organizations headquartered there or in other seaboard cities, and while none among them, if one excepts the Astors, who had large riverfront holdings, amassed a fortune comparable to the greatest among the *nouveaux riches* (the Vanderbilts, Rockefellers, Carnegies), a disproportionate share of the new wealth created by the continuing Industrial Revolution poured into their coffers.

They had little personal liking for the sights and sounds and odors of the industry that enriched them. The landscapes they preferred, and did all they could to preserve along the Hudson, contained no ugly sprawling factories, no giant heaps of slag, no barren acres of warehouses and railroad freightyards. It was, for those living on the Hudson's left bank (which was the generally "right" side to live on), a landscape of civilized natural beauty, its organic forms shaped to the needs of men but harmonious with the rises and dips and curves of geologic structure upon which they were imposed. The great shimmering river was in the foreground. Rolling meadow and field and wood, all neatly bounded, were in the middle distance, with a scattered farmstead or small village adding to the overall impression of fertility and prosperity. In the background, blue-misty with distance, were the Catskills. The sky that arched overhead was unstained by hugely smoking chimneys, and the soft breezes that flowed through the open windows of the river mansions during the warm seasons carried no acrid odor of sulfur. A thin drift of smoke across the autumn valley came from burning leaves of grass and trees: the sweet pungency of this and of flowers and new-mown hay was the odor breathed by river families as they lounged at ease upon their terraces.

Almost the only visible and audible thrust of the age of iron and steam into the valley came up or beside the flowing body of the river. The *Clermont,* Robert Fulton's steamboat, made its first triumphant run up the Hudson on August 17, 1807, and by October of that year it was making regularly scheduled trips between New York and Albany, carrying from eighty to ninety passengers each day.[5] Before long steamboats were almost constantly in view along the stretch of river to be seen from any river mansion, the number increasing year by year until the latter part of the nineteenth century. Steam engines on the river's water were paralleled by steam engines at the water's edge. In the 1840's the Hudson River Railroad laid lines along the east bank, one section being built down from Albany and another up from New York, the two joining in 1850 just below the village of Hyde Park. Soon thereafter, as a result of Commodore Vanderbilt's manipulations, the line became part of the New York Central, one of the most heavily trafficked roads in the nation. Thus a faint clatter of iron wheels on iron rails and the lonely cries of steam whistles on river and shore became a frequent part of the valley's music, heard on the crests of the river hills.

Book One

≫≫≪≪

BEGINNINGS

One

>>><<<

The House at Crum Elbow

I

WHERE the first rail lines met and joined in 1850, the river flows more narrowly than it does either above or below while bending slightly to the east. The bend is labeled Crum (or Krum) Elbow on some local maps.

Above its left bank, up a long steep wooded slope climbed by a winding dirt road, there stood in 1880 a red clapboarded house with green shutters that had been built more than a half century before and was of the general architectural style known in later years as Hudson River Bracketed because of the brackets under the eaves.[1] The house, large by ordinary standards, was of moderate size if compared with the average river mansion. Containing some seventeen rooms, of which many were small, it stood two and a half stories high in its main portion but had at its south end a square tower of a full three stories, with a narrow balcony along the twin tall windows of its third floor, facing south. The tower commanded a wide view of the wooded slope down to the river and of the river itself. The east-facing front commanded a view of graveled driveway and extensive tree-shaded bluegrass lawn beyond which lay level acres of cultivated field reaching toward the Post Road from New York to Albany. Across the front and around the south side of the house was a wide, open veranda of which the pillars were thickly intertwined with ivy. Tall chimney pots extended above both chimneys on the roof ridge of the main portion.

The owner of this house was representative, if not typical, of the river gentry. Nearly all that has been here said of their general attitudes, their way of life, their family histories applies directly to him.

His name was James Roosevelt, and he was, in 1880, fifty-two years old—an erect figure of middle height whose bearing and facial expression were of a virtually unbroken sobriety, benign, yet with an aloofness that repelled easy intimacies. His mouth, though wide enough for generosity, had a tucked-in look. His nose had, somehow, the appearance of having been much looked down by one who held his head high, proudly. His hazel eyes, below a round forehead from which his once-abundant dark hair (now streaked with gray) had receded, looked out in calm, secure appraisal of a world that was his oyster. He wore mutton-chop whiskers. But it is significant that these, which were often deemed comic appurtenances even in 1880 (witness their name), detracted not at all from his dignity. Perhaps nothing could have done so. He seemed to possess—a considerable number of his nonintimate acquaintances who regarded him as a snob were convinced he possessed—an invincible belief in his personal and class superiority to most of mankind. He knew himself to be a gentleman and "of the old school," as his father had been, and his paternal grandfather, each so described in obituary notices.[2]

In only one respect did he differ markedly from others of his class along the river. He was a Democrat. They, almost to a man, were Republicans. Many of them had been Democrats prior to the Civil War, when Democracy was a national political expression. Even when it became increasingly identified with the Southern sectional interest, as the slavery issue split the Republic, it claimed the allegiance of not a few of the Hudson River aristocracy. These, in their affinity with the British aristocracy, in their general outlook and way of life had had a good deal in common with Southern planters—more than they had had with Northern farmers and mechanics and tradesmen—and the commonalities had often outweighed the differences over slavery and the tariff. But the Civil War and the emergence of the Republican Party as the political organ of large-scale business and industry, nearly all of it in the North, had changed everything. Virtually all the river families save the Roosevelts and the Newbolds, who lived next door to them, became Republicans as a matter of course. The Roosevelts, after temporarily forsaking Democracy during the war, for some reason returned to what had then become and would remain in Dutchess County a small minority party. Not that James Roosevelt differed radically from his friends and neighbors on the major national issues of his time. He shared with them a strong opposition to bimetallism and every other form of currency inflation, despite the fact that Westerners and Southerners of his own party pressed with increasing fervor for these. He was a sound money man. He clung to the gold standard as he did to family tradition.

And as regards family he was certainly an ardent traditionalist. He had studied well his family's ancestral records—the letters, the diaries, the books of genealogy—and was thoroughly knowledgeable concerning the springs and tributaries that had fed the vital river, the bloodstream, of which he was a part.

II

He was the sixth in direct line of descent from one Claes Martenszen Van Rosenvelt (Nicholas* the son of Martin of the Rose Field) who came from Holland to New Amsterdam early in the seventeenth century, married sometime before 1650 a girl named Jannetjke, the daughter of a Thomas Samuels, and became the farmer-owner of forty-eight acres on lower Manhattan which, perhaps in nostalgia for his birthplace in Zeeland, he called Rose Hill.[3] Claes had six surviving children but only one surviving son. This last, Nicholas, born in 1658 and orphaned as an infant, took for himself his father's name, but partly in deference to practicality after his homeland became an English colony and partly, no doubt, through misspellings and illegible writing on official documents, he modified it. He also dropped the "Van" to which many of his compatriots clung as a badge of class superiority. He called himself simply Roosevelt; he became the first of that name in America.

Nicholas also became the first of his line to live on the middle Hudson, not far from where his descendant James lived in 1880. When twenty-four, he married nineteen-year-old Heyltje Jans Junst and took her from New York to the small trading post of Esopus, near the site of present-day Kingston. There he engaged in fur trapping and barter with the Indians along the river for eight years. Evidently he prospered. For in 1690, when he was thirty-two and the father of several children, he returned to New York and established a grain-grinding mill on or near the waterfront. His prosperity continued; he became a man of weight in New York's commercial and political affairs, serving as alderman in the early 1700's. But through all his long life (he lived to be eighty-four) he maintained friendships, if not business connections, with families on both sides of the Hudson where he had adventured as a young man.[4]

Two of Nicholas' nine children were destined to be singled out for special historical attention two centuries later. One was Johannes, born in Esopus in 1689. The other was Jacobus, born in New York in 1692. Both married young (Johannes married Heyltje Sjoerts; Jacobus, Catherine Hardenbroeck). Both were men of immense energy and business shrewdness who, building on inherited property, established substantial

* Claes was a contraction of Nicholas.

fortunes. (They engaged in a wide variety of enterprises: linseed oil manufacture, chocolate processing, flour milling, general contracting and building, and extensive real estate speculations.) Both were devout church members. Both were active in civic affairs, and Johannes took a leading part in the establishment of a library in City Hall. But it was not for these reasons that the two later figured in biographies. Rather was it because Johannes' direct descendants became the so-called Oyster Bay branch of the Roosevelt family while Jacobus' became the so-called Hudson River branch.

Jacobus, who came increasingly to be called James (Johannes became John) as the Dutch language fell into disuse in New York, had eleven children. Of these, his sixth, a son named Isaac, born in 1726, became the most distinguished of all the Roosevelts during the first two centuries of the family's existence in America.[5] It was through him that his branch of the family became rooted in Dutchess County and that the bloodstream of this branch, hitherto exclusively Dutch and German, was first intermingled with Swedish, Finnish, English, probably Scotch as well, becoming a typically American admixture.

For when he was twenty-six years old—having used inherited money to establish the first large-scale sugar refinery on Manhattan Island, having already become a business and civic leader in the city—Isaac Roosevelt took for wife a Dutchess County girl, eighteen-year-old Cornelia Hoffman. Her paternal grandfather, Martinus Hoffman I,[6] had served as a Finnish-Swedish soldier in the Swedish Army before coming to New Netherland in 1657, settling first in Albany. Hoffman had greatly prospered in his adopted land; he acquired vast landholdings on both sides of the middle Hudson. His namesake son, Colonel Martinus Hoffman II, thus became one of the wealthiest men in Dutchess County, and his daughter Cornelia brought a fortune of her own into the Roosevelt family.

It has been suggested by some historians,[7] and indeed it is obvious, that Isaac Roosevelt's sugar business could not possibly have prospered as it did had Isaac obeyed the Molasses Act of 1733 and the Sugar Act of 1764. These acts, designed by the British Parliament to protect the planters of the British West Indies from competition with planters in the French and Spanish West Indies, imposed a prohibitive tax on the importation of rum, molasses, and sugar from any but the British islands. Yet without such imports from the foreign-owned islands no large-scale refinery could have operated at a profit on Manhattan, nor could profits have been made there from trade (as Isaac traded) in molasses and rum. His prosperity was therefore a fruit of illegality, as well as of shrewdness and industry; it was part and parcel of a growing colonial rebellion against the economically depressing effects of the mercantile theory as applied by Crown and Parliament. And the fact that his personal economic interests were more heavily weighted on the side of independence from Britain than were those of most New York merchants is at least a partial explanation of his becoming a Patriot whereas they remained Tory when the political storms of the 1770's culminated in Lexington, Concord, and the Declaration of Independence.

He became celebrated in family histories and widely known among his contemporaries as Isaac the Patriot. He served as an elected member of the Provincial (not the Continental) Congress in 1775, signing a letter from that body to the British government asserting that "the horrors of Civil War will never compel America to submit to taxation by Parliament." When the British forces occupied New York, he moved with his family to his wife's family estate in Dutchess County, where, aged fifty, he enlisted in the Sixth Regiment of the New York Militia. He fought in no battles. But at the behest of the Provincial Committee of Safety which sat during the adjournment of the Provincial Congress he supervised an emission of paper money whereby 55,000 pounds of hard currency was transformed into 213,400 bills of various denominations—a complex operation which temporarily helped relieve New York's desperate shortage of money.[8] He was a delegate to the convention in Kingston which drew up the first state constitution of New York, in 1776–77. He was elected state senator under that constitution and served continuously in the Senate until the peace treaty with Britain had been signed in 1783.

His patriotism, however, was of a quality different from Tom Paine's or Sam Adams': he was motivated by no immoderate passion for human freedom and equality. During the turbulent years preceding Lexington, he was a Whig, who defined "freedom" primarily in private-prosperity terms; he was never a Son of Liberty, who defined it primarily in private-personal terms. After Lexington, when a rising tide of radicalism threatened to engulf New York City, he joined a group of conservative men who issued an appeal to the people to preserve "peace and good order and the safety of individuals and private property" while opposing Parliament's oppressive acts and awaiting "a reconciliation between Great Britain and America." The state constitution he helped shape and fervently supported was as conservative an instrument as the leveling temper of the times would permit. It imposed a property qualification upon voting and upon membership in the Senate, though not in the lower house. It permitted slavery. It concentrated more power in the executive than was pleasing to democratic minds, permitting the governor to appoint many officials who, in the democratic view, should

have been popularly elected. In short, it was a constitution carefully designed to protect the economic and political interests of such as Isaac
Roosevelt against the radical notions of unpropertied men, and since
the government established under it was limited to upstate New York,*
particularly the Hudson and Mohawk valleys, it "instilled upon that region the political conservatism and deep respect for property" that characterized it a century and a half later.[9] The fact might temper with irony
a twentieth-century Roosevelt's grateful memory of his most distinguished paternal ancestor.

Isaac returned to New York when the British withdrew. With him
came his eldest surviving son, Jacobus (James), born in 1760, who in his
teens had attended the New Jersey College at Princeton, graduating in
1780—the first of his Roosevelt line to obtain a college degree. Isaac
took his son into partnership with him in the sugar refinery, thereafter
known as Isaac Roosevelt & Son. He, with William Walton and others,
established in 1784 the Bank of New York—the first bank to be established in that city, the second in the country—becoming its second president in 1786 and holding that office until 1791. He continued active in
politics, was a delegate to the state convention called in 1788 to ratify
the Constitution of the United States (he strongly supported ratification), and naturally gravitated toward Hamilton's Federalists, the forerunners of today's Republicans, as opposed to Jefferson's Republicans,
the forerunners of today's Democrats, when repercussions of the French
Revolution precipitated a two-party system in this country. He died in
1794, leaving to his partner-son James a considerable fortune, a firm
basis for pride of ancestry, and his portrait painted by Gilbert Stuart.[10]

The portrait shows him as a handsome and polished aristocrat—urbane, outgoing, immensely self-confident, firmly self-controlled, proud,
and obviously accustomed to command. Of all of Stuart's works, it was
destined to be one of the most widely reproduced in the 1930's and '40's.
And in these latter years it would be compared with the portrait expertly
painted of Isaac's son James and with that painted equally expertly of
Isaac II, the Patriot's grandson, all three portraits having been done
when their subjects were well into middle age. The comparison of them
is interesting and instructive; it seems to measure a marked decrease in
forcefulness from one generation to another, with an equivalent increase
in tendencies toward introversion and withdrawal.

James' career followed the pattern established by his father's but was
in every way less distinguished. He profitably continued the sugar refinery without initiating any large new enterprise. He was an officer in the

* Because the British held New York City.

Bank of New York, but never its president. He was active in Federalist politics, serving in the State Assembly but never in the Senate. In 1786 he married Maria Eliza Walton, daughter of Abram Walton, a nephew of William and a close friend of the Patriot's despite having become one of New York's most notorious Tories during the Revolution.[11] By Maria Eliza, James fathered eight children before she died in 1810, whereupon he took as his second wife Catherine Eliza Barclay, by whom he had two more children before she, too, died. In 1821, when he was sixty-one, he married a third time, his bride being Harriet Howland of a *Mayflower* family that had grown rich and powerful in the shipping trade. By her he had no children. He greatly increased his inherited wealth, or it was increased for him by the growth of the city, and lived with his large family in more than comfort, first in a house on the waterfront near his refinery and then, after his third marriage, in a much larger, more fashionable home on Bleecker Street in Greenwich Village.

His only important deviation from the career pattern of his father was determined by a greater love of country life than his father had ever manifested. He purchased a rocky, picturesque tract of land lying between what is now 110th and 125th streets in Harlem, extending from what is now Fifth Avenue to the East River—some 400 acres in all—and tried hard to make a going farm of it. He had little success. Timber covered a large part of the purchased acreage; much of this he cut and profitably sold as lumber and fuel. But the soil thus cleared was too infertile and poorly drained to be successfully cultivated—it was good only as pasturage for the fine horses he raised and loved—and eventually he sold the entire acreage for $25,000, much of it to John Jacob Astor, whose descendants immensely profited from it as the city, growing northward, covered it with no fewer than 130 densely built-up city blocks.[12]

James himself turned northward from Harlem. He bought in 1819 a large tract of land, many hundreds of green acres fronting on the Hudson, in the Dutchess County where his Hoffman mother had been so richly born and reared and where he himself had lived long before as an exile from British-occupied Manhattan. There, in the town of Poughkeepsie, but just across the Albany Post Road from the town of Hyde Park, he built a large house on a hill he called Mount Hope. And there, until he died in 1847, he lived the pleasant, quiet life of a country gentleman for as much of his time as his city business interests would permit.

These facts confirm the impression conveyed by his painted portrait. Where Isaac the Patriot looks out boldly from the canvas, James—bald, thin-cheeked, tight-mouthed—looks out diffidently, almost timorously through weak eyes slightly squinted behind steel-rimmed spectacles.

Where Isaac seems poised and relaxed, James appears tense, as if he habitually forced himself to do what must be done by sheer willpower, against his natural desire. It is easy to imagine the owner of such a face retreating gratefully at every opportunity from the hurly-burly of city business to the quiet, the solitudes of the country.

And this tendency of his is even more evident in the portrait of his son, the Patriot's namesake grandson. Isaac II's is the face of an introvert.[13] His heavy-lidded, light-colored eyes, strikingly resembling those in the portraits of Jefferson, have a dreamy look.

He, this second Isaac Roosevelt, born in 1790 as the first of all of James I's many children, would seem to later generations a strange anomaly in the Roosevelt family. Did he "take after" his mother's people, the proud, aloof, self-centered Waltons? Or did he suffer at a tender age some traumatic experience, unrecorded, which turned him inward, away from the world? Whatever the reason, he *did* turn inward and away: he displayed none of the exuberance, the venturesomeness, the ambition, the tremendous vital energy that had characterized his forebears and would come in succeeding generations to be regarded as characteristically Rooseveltian.

Like his father, he attended Princeton, graduating in the class of 1808, but unlike his father, he declined to enter the business world or take any part in public affairs. Instead, he enrolled in Columbia's College of Physicians and Surgeons, becoming a doctor of medicine who, however, never practiced. He confessed he couldn't bear the sight of blood or the sound of a human in pain! He became a dilettante of science, continuing his studies for a while under Dr. David Hosack, physicist and botanist, who had botanical gardens on the site of present-day Rockefeller Center. Later he interested himself in the history of medicine. He studied and acquired something of a library in all these fields but produced no published work of his own. Then, when his father's house at Mount Hope was completed in 1820, he forsook city life altogether and forever; he made Mount Hope his permanent home, devoting himself thereafter in a desultory way to gardening and breeding of cattle and fine horses.

He was thirty years old when he came to Mount Hope—a man of far from robust constitution, a hypochondriac, seemingly a confirmed bachelor, almost a recluse. And so he remained for seven more years. Then, to the astonishment of his contemporaries and to the further complication of an already complicated Roosevelt genealogy, he married an eighteen-year-old girl, Mary Rebecca Aspinwall, a niece of the Harriet Howland who, with his father's third marriage, had become his stepmother.

The Aspinwalls, like the Howlands, were a seafaring family—hearty, adventurous, acquisitive—who had greatly prospered in shipping enterprises based first in Massachusetts (the earliest Aspinwall in America, settling in Dorchester in 1645, became a founder of Brookline) and later in New York.[14] They and the Howlands were two of the wealthiest merchant families in that city when, in 1803, an Aspinwall son, John, Jr., married a Howland daughter, Susan. Mary Rebecca (she called herself by the latter name) was a daughter of this marriage.

She had been described in memoirs as vigorous, amiable, gentle, and loving—qualities perhaps equal to one another in their importance to her husband's marital happiness.[15] But it was her vigor, which she evidently instilled into the thinning Roosevelt bloodstream, that would seem of all her qualities the most important to future historians of the family.

Her family's vitality was especially manifest in Rebecca's brother, William Henry, two years her elder, whom Dr. Isaac recognized as head not only of his in-law family but also in a sense of his own. For he consulted his brother-in-law on all important worldly matters and was more frequently a guest in his brother-in-law's town and country homes than his brother-in-law was at Mount Hope.

William Henry Aspinwall became a partner in the Howland firm when he was twenty-five.[16] When he was thirty, he and his cousin William Edgar Howland became joint heads of the firm, now named Howland & Aspinwall, the largest importing, exporting, and general trade merchants in the Port of New York, with a fleet of clipper ships, including the record-breaking *Rainbow,* sailing all the seven seas. Nor did the replacement of sail by steam reduce his profits and prestige in the world of commerce as it did those of many a Yankee trader. On the contrary, he greatly increased his fortune after he had resigned as active head of Howland & Aspinwall in order to become a director of the initially highly speculative but ultimately hugely successful Pacific Railroad and Panama Steamship Company. He formed a new corporation, Panama Railroad, which built a rail line across the Isthmus of Panama to link up with the Pacific Mail Steamship Company, which he, the Howlands, and others had formed a few years before. The accelerated growth of the West Coast that followed the California gold rush of 1849 greatly favored these interlinked ventures: Aspinwall and his colleagues held a virtual monopoly of the carrying trade between the East and West coasts, a trade which multiplied through two decades, until the first transcontinental railroad was completed in the late 1860's.

Aspinwall became, for his time, immensely wealthy—"one of the merchant princes of New York," whose home at 33 University Place was among "the palaces which have been lately erected in this part of the city," according to an 1846 entry in Philip Hone's celebrated diary.[17] "A more beautiful and commodious mansion, or in better taste in every particular, I have never seen," wrote Hone, whose own taste in such matters was snobbishly fastidious. As his country home, Aspinwall maintained another "palace" on a huge acreage at Barrytown, just north of Rhinebeck, overlooking the river.

Far different from the bustling life of these mansions, whence energies radiated to the remotest part of the globe and into which poured treasure from distant lands, were the passivity and quietude of the Mount Hope to which Dr. Isaac Roosevelt brought his bride in 1827. New life, however, was promptly generated there.

In late 1828, Rebecca Aspinwall Roosevelt gave birth to a son. On December 2 of that year the child was baptized in the Dutch Reformed Church at Poughkeepsie. He was the James Roosevelt, second of that name in his line (or third, if one counts the Jacobus born in 1692), who in 1880, aged fifty-two, would be the master of the clapboarded house on the hill at Crum Elbow, on the Hudson.

III

Significant of his father's ineffectuality was the fact that the house where James was born was not at that time his father's property but remained, still, his grandfather's. Not until James was four did Dr. Isaac, at the age of forty-two, establish a home of his own, and one suspects that the doctor's young and vigorous wife may have had more to do with instigating this rare enterprise than did the doctor himself.

If so—if she was anxious to loosen in-law ties—she did not move her husband far. He bought a considerable acreage in Hyde Park town, immediately north and across the Post Road from Mount Hope. He built upon it a commodious but exceedingly plain gabled house from whose spacious but heavily shaded porches a wide view of the river was rendered narrow by groves of trees.[18] Soon planted shrubbery grew thick where open sunlit spaces would otherwise have been. All in all the house and grounds expressed their owner's temperament and tastes. Only its name Rosedale (and this was evidently determined by its owner's family name and the history of his forebears), was suggestive of gaiety and bright colors.

Of James' early boyhood there are few authentic records and virtually no character-revealing anecdotes survive. Since he was the only child of a father who every year had less concern with the world and more with his own health, who looked upon this life as but a preparation for the next and had the possibility of sudden death constantly on his mind ("'Be ye also ready' is the warning voice," Dr. Isaac said often to his son[19]), James' early life can hardly have been characterized by buoyant enthusiasms or riotous exuberance. His was evidently a placidly happy existence (his mother's influence upon him seems to have been thoroughly healthy), but it must also have been an unusually solitary one— at least until, at age nine, he was entered in the then newly established and exclusive Poughkeepsie Collegiate School (only "gentlemen's sons" went there), where, it has been significantly said, his classmates never called him Jim but always and only James.[20] He continued to live at Rosedale. When he was twelve—suddenly, unexpectedly—he found himself no longer an only child. John Aspinwall Roosevelt, Dr. Isaac's second and last child, was born in 1840. The new life arrived too late, however, to mitigate such loneliness as James may have felt as a boy or to provide him with any close fraternal companionship during his adolescence.

This adolescence was spent, for the most part, as a preparatory school and college student. In the fall of 1841, he was sent away from home for the first time to attend a school conducted by a Mr. Alexander Hyde in his home in Lee, Massachusetts. Dr. Isaac's letters to his son at Lee are revealing.[21] In mid-July, 1842, he wrote of his brother James' death by accidental drowning in the Hudson. "How uncertain our lives," he commented. ". . . I am now without a Brother. Seven are in the land of Spirits. The places which once knew them know them no more. How important my dear Son that we should make it the great business of our lives to be prepared for another and a better world, where there is no sin or death or sorrow. Repent, believe in the Lord Jesus and lead a life of holy obedience to his commands. Strive to correct your faults—in your intercourse with your companions be gentle and mild—obtain the command of your temper. Be not discomposed by trifles." He added cryptically, perhaps in reference to an experience which had directed him away from the world: "I should have had much less trouble to govern myself if when your age I had practiced more self-discipline."

During Christmas week of 1842 the pious doctor wrote Mr. Hyde to express his satisfaction with the tutelage James had been receiving "in your family school." He worried lest his son's health be "injured by study," hoping that "in the intervals of study he will read instructive books, especially history. I have not sent him the New World etc. lately on account of the works of fiction so frequently published," he went on. "I have no objection to his reading *occasionally* a well-written and moral or religious work of fiction." In the spring of 1843, he worried about his son's selection of New York University as the college he wished to at-

tend, giving his reluctant consent (". . . I should have preferred the retirement of a country village") only because "you [James] will be the
greater part of the time in my Father's family and near your other relations." He wrote: "I trust you will never become a Dandy or an Idler.
Your Uncle G. Howland said to me—'Send James to the University of
New York and he will become a Dandy and will walk Broadway with
his cane.' You know you were created for better things. We live for
God—for the good of our fellow men—for duty—for usefulness."

Two months later, on July 21, 1843, he wrote his son in alarm over the
"dangers and disagreeables [sic] of a freshman class in the University of
N.Y. They tell me the boys have much to encounter which is mortifying
to the feelings—and puts their temper as well as their principles to a severe test," he continued, urging James to consider spending another
year with Mr. Hyde and enter the university as a sophomore. "In
making the proposition to wait another year," he said, "I only discharge
my conscience of a weight of responsibility, casting it all upon yourself
—so that if you find our predictions verified in regard to the disadvantages of the freshman year, you may be the more able to bear it without
complaint. . . . Do not be hasty in answering this letter, consult your
excellent friend Mr. Hyde and carry your cause to a still higher course,
dear James—ask counsel of One who is wise to direct and kind to
choose in all the difficulties of His weak shortsighted child."

But James had evidently learned by that time to discount his father's
timorousness. He entered New York University that fall. He remained
only one semester. During it he continued in the bosom of family, for he
lived in his Grandfather Roosevelt's Bleecker Street home and was
closely watched by both his father and mother's people (his Aspinwall
grandparents also lived on Bleecker Street) for signs that he was being
dandified or otherwise corrupted by the wicked city. They saw none. He
comported himself as a singularly sober and industrious youth who did
his classwork conscientiously, joined a debating society, and won a gold
medal in debate. In early 1845 he returned to Rosedale, received special
tutelage for a time in the Poughkeepsie school, and soon thereafter was
enrolled in Union College, Schenectady, which was then headed by one
of the most famous educators of his day, Dr. Eliphalet Nott.[22]

On October 2, 1846, Dr. Isaac wrote to his son at Union College,
saying he was "both grieved and astonished by the reception of a letter
from Dr. Knott [sic] respecting your membership of a secret society contrary to the laws" of the college. "I mean the Society which holds its
meetings in a tavern. I must request you to dissolve all connection immediately with this Society. . . . Remember, my dear Son, your promise
that while at College, you would not give your Mother or me the least

anxiety on your account." Presumably James did as he was told, for in July of the following year, 1847, he was graduated from Union.[23]

He then went abroad. From November, 1847, until May, 1849, having (with the help of his mother) overcome his father's morbid fears for him, James Roosevelt, aged nineteen and twenty, made that "grand tour" then customary for young Americans of his class. He traveled in an exciting time. All Western Europe seethed with the Revolutions of 1848. And it became family legend that for one of the eighteen months he was abroad he himself—this staid, sober, eminently respectable youth— donned a red shirt, shouldered a gun, and served as a soldier of revolution!

Nearly a century later, James' youngest son would tell the tale in a White House memorandum.[24] Having become the close friend (so the memorandum says) of a "mendicant priest," with whom he conversed exclusively in Latin, young James set off with him on a walking tour of Italy. "They came to Naples and found the city besieged by Garibaldi's army." The two "enlisted in this army" but, after a month of inaction, "went to Garibaldi's tent and asked if they could receive their discharge. Garibaldi thanked the old priest and my father and the walking tour was resumed by them." But alas for one's belief in this account, whose veracity would seem attested to by its very lack of heroic quality, the family records show young James to have been in Naples in March, 1840, while history records that Garibaldi was at that time at Rieti, some forty miles northeast of Rome. Certainly James displayed no yearning for martial adventures when Civil War came to his own country a dozen years later. Thousands of other men his age (he was thirty-two in the spring of 1861) then enlisted in the Union Army, but he did not. Nor did he actively serve the Union cause in any other recorded way, though it was later claimed by his family that he had been involved in the work of the Sanitary Commission.[25]

Upon his return from Europe, James Roosevelt, in the fall of 1849, entered Harvard Law School, receiving his LLB on his twenty-third birthday. Admitted to the New York bar, he entered the firm of a distinguished New York City lawyer, Benjamin Douglas Silliman, as a law clerk in 1851. He thus followed in the footsteps of his namesake grandfather, who had also studied law and been admitted to the bar.

The earlier James had never practiced law, yet had never regretted his legal training, for it had proved of immense value to him in business. It proved valuable in this way to the later James also. The Silliman firm, which practiced common, equity, and admiralty law, numbered among its clients many of the greatest corporations that were then newly formed or (often with the Silliman firm's legal assistance) in process of formation. One of these was the Consolidated Coal Company of Maryland. James Roosevelt became a director of it within a year after entering the Silliman firm. Not long afterward he abandoned the practice of law altogether and forever. He became from then on a financier, a capitalist, and one not averse to taking large risks. On the contrary, he employed inherited wealth to buy (with partners) a controlling interest in highly speculative corporate endeavors which, had they succeeded, would have made him by 1880 one of the richest men in America.

But they did not succeed. Indeed, his two most ambitious ventures prior to 1880—daring and grandiose beyond anything Dr. Isaac, who died in 1863, would have dreamed of for himself—failed lamentably.

One of these stemmed in part from his first directorship, in part from his family relationship with the redoubtable William Henry Aspinwall. He joined with his Uncle William in the formation of the Consolidation Coal Company, which by 1868, when he became a director, was already the largest bituminous coal enterprise in the country and well on the way toward an absolute monopoly of the coal mines in the Cumberlands of Kentucky and Tennessee.[26] The other ambitious venture, engaged in almost simultaneously, was an attempt to bring into one centralized system all the rail lines in the war-ravaged southeastern United States, then suffering under Reconstruction. James Roosevelt had an inherited interest in railroads. His namesake grandfather in 1847, the last year of his life, had joined with Matthew Vassar and others in Poughkeepsie to promote construction of the Hudson River Railroad. He had bought stock in it. So had Dr. Isaac. And the latter also had bought a substantial block of stock in the Delaware and Hudson, much or most of which was bequeathed to his son James. Of the Southern railway enterprise, young James was not the initiator: the original idea for it came from a vice-president of the Pennsylvania Railroad, but he invested heavily in it and, in 1872, was elected president of the Southern Railway Security Company, a holding company (then a novel device) whereby the Pennsylvania, whose executive agent James became in effect, achieved a virtual monopoly of all rail transport in an area extending south from Washington through Georgia and west from the Atlantic into Tennessee.[27]

From both these monopolistic enterprises, untold riches seemed about to pour into the Roosevelt coffers. But then came the Panic of 1873—heralded by a collapse of stock prices on the Vienna exchange, initiated by the failure of the great banking house of Jay Cooke and Company in New York, and followed by a decade and a half of deep economic depression. Factories closed down by the hundreds, railroad construction virtually halted, rail traffic was drastically reduced, and so was the demand for bituminous coal. In 1875 a revolt of disappointed stockholders deprived Aspinwall, James Roosevelt, and their colleagues of control of the Consolidation Coal Company (the Baltimore and Ohio Railroad bought a controlling interest in it and, within a few years, made great profits from it). The Southern Railway Security Company struggled on longer but returned to its investors no dividends and was finally liquidated, with heavy financial loss to James Roosevelt and the other New York investors.

But he was far from ruined financially by these failures. He continued active in railroads and coal. In the very year he and his group were forced out of control of Consolidation Coal he became a member of the board of the Delaware and Hudson (Cornelius Vanderbilt and J. Pierpont Morgan were fellow members), a company that derived a major portion of its substantial profits (it paid a 10 percent dividend year after year) from the anthracite coal mines it owned outright or in which it held a controlling interest.[28] Nor would he be deterred from future grandiose ventures by the failures of his past. As a matter of fact, the most grandiose of all was, in 1880, yet to come—and its ultimate failure would prove no more damaging to his personal happiness and complacency than the earlier losses had been.

He simply did not care enough for power, economic or otherwise, to be deeply hurt when it was denied him; he cared not at all for the hugely expensive ostentation so gratifying to the Vanderbilt ego and to that of his social friends, the Astors. He felt no strong vocation for business. He would have liked to be an empire builder; a creative urge in him would have been gratified by imperial conquests. But he was not willing to commit all his time and energy to the realization of such possibilities. He had other interests. So long as he retained enough financial substance to indulge these—so long as he could continue the spacious, leisurely, and mobile life to which he was accustomed—he remained only mildly perturbed by losses, even heavy losses, in what he seems to have regarded as a generally diverting game of chance, a game occasionally fascinating as the stakes were raised to gigantic heights but by no means all-absorbing.[29]

He managed to divorce his domestic life almost completely from the vicissitudes of his financial career.

In 1853, when he was twenty-three and embarking on his first business ventures, he married a Howland girl. His choice complicated the labors of future Roosevelt genealogists since his paternal grandfather's third wife had been a Howland, his maternal grandmother had been a Howland, and his bride, twenty-two-year-old Rebecca Brien Howland, was a daughter of his mother's first cousin. But for him the marriage, far from being a complication, was a felicitous simplification of life. Rebecca Howland Roosevelt in her early twenties was a pretty girl, inclined toward plumpness, vivacious and outgoing, and since she was to both the manor and manner born, she fitted easily, perfectly the role of wife of that country squire which her husband increasingly was in Dutchess County. And not only squire was he—philanthropic, literally patronizing, with an influential if not too arduous part in all local affairs of importance—he was also farmer, a gentleman farmer but a genuine one in that he aimed, successfully, to run his place at a profit. This place, at first, was Mount Hope. James had inherited it when his paternal grandfather died. And upon it he supervised the raising of crops of grain and hay for sale, as well as for feed for the dairy herd and horses that grazed his pastures.

Less than two years after the wedding, his wife gave birth to a son. Upon him was bestowed the traditional family name of James. But the elder James had heartily disliked the "Junior" appended to his own name (because of his grandfather) and was determined to avoid it for his son. He therefore gave the latter a middle name which was, strangely, the same as his last one—a choice which may have been regretted by both father and son as the years passed. For inevitably James Roosevelt Roosevelt became known as "Rosy" Roosevelt, to distinguish him from his father, and the appellation would strike most people as less dignified, more deprecating than "Junior" would have been.

Whatever hopes for a large family James and Rebecca may initially have had were disappointed as the years passed—pleasant years with a European trip in almost every one of them and long vacations in all. Rosy Roosevelt remained an only child when, in the summer of 1865, while James and Rebecca were in England, the house at Mount Hope, which had been rented to a New York City family, caught fire in the night (there was some suspicion of arson by a disaffected butler) and burned to its foundations. Most of the family papers and heirlooms were destroyed. Only a few of the furnishings—some dining-room and Duncan Phyfe chairs, a heavy silver tea service of the mid-eighteenth century (Isaac the Patriot had acquired it), a rosewood bed and bureau —were saved. But the event was not an unmitigated catastrophe in the view of James and Rebecca. The State of New York offered $45,000 for the now-houseless property, to be part of the grounds of the Hudson River State Hospital (the "Lunatic Asylum," by local usage), and James Roosevelt accepted the offer. He and Rebecca were thus free to find a home more suited to their tastes than inherited Mount Hope had ever been.[30]

IV

The home they found was the one at Crum Elbow. Springwood it was named; it was two miles north (in the town of Hyde Park) from Mount Hope and Rosedale.

James bought it, with 110 acres of land—much of it wooded, most of it unsuited to cultivation—in the spring of 1867. To it, because he wished to continue active farming, he soon added other tracts and continued to do so until, ultimately, he owned some 900 contiguous acres. Here he continued to build his herd of fine Channel Island dairy cows— Guernseys and Jerseys and Alderneys (he had established at Mount Hope one of the first Alderney herds in this country)—and built stables for his riding and driving horses and for the racing trotters which were a fashionable possession of country gentlemen in those days.[31] Here he established extensive gardens, here he raised crops, and through the sale of milk and produce, of hay and grain, he managed to make his country estate pay the considerable cost of its upkeep with something left over with which to pay at least part of the cost of a town house at 15 Washington Square, in New York City, where he and his family were accustomed to go during the coldest winter months.

Simultaneously, inevitably, he became a leader of civic affairs in Hyde Park. He was accepted by fellow citizens pretty much on his own terms, as men generally are when their terms are not too flagrantly contradicted by immediately available evidence or too ruthlessly pressed against the interests and self-esteem of those to whom they are presented. His particular terms were not onerous. He saw himself and asked others to see him as a kindly, dignified, public-spirited gentleman who had a proper respect both for his class position and for others as well, maintained a high regard for tradition, and was conscientious in fulfilling the obligations that must necessarily, in his view of the social order, accompany his privileges. He probably did not much care, if he knew, that some among his less privileged neighbors regarded his attitudes as snobbish.

He who had been baptized in the Dutch Reformed Church had become by this time an Episcopalian, the church most favored by the river gentry, as well as the one in which his wife had been raised. He became both vestryman and warden of Hyde Park's St. James Church. He was elected town supervisor for a two-year term (1871–72), he was named a member of the board of managers of the Hudson River State Hospital, and having long taken a more active interest in the Hyde Park village school than any other local taxpayer, he would in later years become a member of the school board. He was a conservative public servant, anxious to save tax dollars. Fellow town supervisors less wealthy than he and struggling contractors doing business with the town may have been something less than enthusiastic over his proposals to cut from $6 to $4 the pay of supervisors for "footing" (that is, adding up) the tax rolls, to limit per diem payments of $3 strictly to the time the board was actually in session, and to hold to a severe minimum the cost of repairs and improvements of public buildings. Yet he was not averse to public expenditures that served his conception of the general welfare. As state hospital manager he made regular personal inspection tours of the hospital buildings and grounds, visiting every ward, as well as every utility room, and writing reports which not infrequently pointed out deficiencies requiring a considerable corrective expenditure. And as a special friend of local public education he was largely responsible for the erection of a new two-story red-brick school building in the village, a model building for its day, with high-ceilinged, well-lighted, well-aired rooms. He made frequent inspections of the school, too; once a month, when he was in Hyde Park during the school term, he visited the classrooms and listened to recitations.[32]

Thus, while his pursuit of economic empire was frustrated by events in the great world, his pursuit of private happiness prospered in the small world of the Hudson River aristocracy. For eight years and more (their son Rosy growing up strong, healthy, poised, charming; becoming a student in Columbia College, making there an outstanding scholastic record; simultaneously entering New York's high society of which he became one of the most popular young members), James and Rebecca Roosevelt lived serenely pleasant, active lives at Springwood.

Then sorrow came.

Not abruptly but gradually, over a period of several months, beginning in 1875, Rebecca's health began to fail. She developed symptoms of heart disease. These grew worse. In August, 1876, James took her aboard a yacht for a voyage intended to last several days, up Long Island Sound, in the hope that the sun and sea air would revive her, but the yacht had scarcely cleared the harbor when she fell desperately ill. She was removed to the New York house on Washington Square. She died there on the last day of the month. Her body was taken to Hyde Park and buried in the churchyard of St. James.[33]

Not many days afterward, Rosy returned to New York City to enter upon his senior year at Columbia. The elder James, a middle-aged widower facing the prospect of a companionless old age, lived alone, save for servants, in Springwood, though it cannot be truly said that his life thereafter was, even temporarily, dull and empty. He continued his many and varied business and civic activities, even during the prescribed period of mourning, and after this had ended, he returned to active social life—a more active one, perhaps, than before, since his friends (he was very popular within his exclusive social circle) sought to mitigate with frequent invitations his presumed sad solitudes. In addition, he was a member of the most prestigious of New York clubs—the Century, the Metropolitan, the Manhattan—and was assured of good companionship whenever he visited them.

He took pride and pleasure in his son. Rosy was graduated with honors from Columbia in 1877, then studied law, and while doing so became engaged to *the* debutante of her year, if not, in fact, of many years. She was Helen Schermerhorn Astor. Her mother was that Mrs. William Astor who, already the fabled arbiter of New York society, was destined, with the aid of the ineffable Ward McAllister, to reign over it for decades as none other before or since.* Helen was wealthy in her own right. As Rosy's bride she contributed to their mutual well-being the income of a $400,000 trust fund and a mansion at 372 Fifth Avenue.³⁴ But she, too, had a taste for country living and happily acquiesced when her young husband proposed their purchase of an estate next door to the south of Springwood on which was built a large and comfortable but far from palatial dwelling called the Red House, because that was its color. So father and son remained in close touch with each other, and the widower father became, whenever he so chose, one of those in attendance at Mrs. Astor's spectacular dinners and balls.

V

Among the guests at some of the huge and hugely expensive evening parties which proud, power-loving Mrs. Astor presided over (diamonds glittered around her neck, on her fingers and arms, in a tiara on her head) amid a stifling bower of hothouse flowers, was a young lady named Sara (nicknamed Sallie) Delano. Her father, Warren Delano, was a longtime business acquaintance of James Roosevelt's and a member of some of the same clubs as he. Her uncle, Franklin Delano, had married William Astor's sister Laura and lived with her (they were a childless couple) on a splendid Hudson River estate called Steen Valetje, in Barrytown, twenty miles north of Hyde Park.³⁵ Thus the Delanos and Astors had long considered themselves part of that same family cir-

---

* It was Ward McAllister who named the "four hundred" socially elect, this being the maximum number of people who could be accommodated in Mrs. William Astor's ballroom. After years of excited speculation on who was on (and off) McAllister's list, he published it in 1892. Rosy Roosevelt's name was there, of course.

cle which James Roosevelt, by virtue of his son's marriage, now entered.

It was not at Mrs. Astor's, however, that widower Roosevelt first met Sallie Delano. Instead, it was at a dinner party given one soft spring evening in 1880 by the widowed Mrs. Theodore Roosevelt (her husband had died two years before) at her home at 6 West Fifty-seventh Street. Neither of her two sons was present that evening. Twenty-one-year-old Theodore, Jr., future President of the United States, was in Cambridge, Massachusetts, where he was about to be graduated from Harvard; eighteen-year-old Elliott, having suffered a nervous breakdown while a student at St. Paul's and apparently recovered from it at a military post in Texas, was busy with preparations for a hunting trip he was to take with his older brother through Iowa and Minnesota that summer. But the two daughters of the hostess—Anna (Bamie) and Corinne—were among those seated at table. Others included Sallie Delano, who had been an intimate friend of Bamie's since girlhood; a Mr. Crowninshield of Boston; and widower James Roosevelt, who, his hostess noted, gave Sallie his virtually exclusive attention. "He talked to her the whole time," said the hostess to her daughters after the guests had departed. "He never took his eyes off her!"

And indeed she was pleasant to look at—a tall, slenderly graceful, dark-eyed and dark-haired young lady of aristocratic beauty, whose lips (above a slightly heavy, stubborn-looking chin) formed an almost perfect cupid's bow, whose nose was finely chiseled, whose brows arched proudly, and whose complexion was clear and glowing with good health. Her demeanor was more grave than gay; her dignity was so immense that no trick played upon her by a mischievous younger sister had upset it when she was growing up. She could be, she often was with young men, intimidatingly haughty, aloof. Yet she remained attractive to men.

It was not for lack of suitors that, at twenty-five (she would be twenty-six next September 21), she remained unmarried. Rather was it because she was very much her father's daughter, and Warren Delano, whose paternal role was evidently in several respects classically Victorian, displaying some of the features which Freudians later deemed darkly significant, had disapproved of every young man who thus far had paid her serious attention. The story is told of a suitor with red hair to whose ardent wooing she was not, it would seem, wholly unresponsive. One day he sent her a "huge basket of flowers" from which she was stripping away the wrappings when her father entered the room. He eyed the basket with distaste. "I suppose these are from the red-haired trial," he is said to have "quietly" remarked. "Remember that I don't go for that at all." He wrote out for her to copy a coldly worded one-sentence thank-you note, tantamount to a dismissal. She dutifully copied it. She mailed it to her hapless admirer without overt protest or even, apparently, the slightest covert regret. She adored her father. She would not dream of going against his judgment on anything. He was, in her view, all-wise.[36]

It seems more than probable—the circumstances indicate a virtual certainty—that she saw in the widower Roosevelt attractive resemblances to her father. He who flattered her with his admiring attentions was twice her age, with a son barely six months younger than she. He wore gray-streaked side whiskers, as her father did, though he lacked other hirsute splendors (a heavy mustache, a tuft of beard immediately below the lips) which adorned the Delano countenance. He had a great and sober dignity, as did her father, yet had also a sense of humor and a fund of interesting stories, which he told well, as did her father; and he was obviously thoroughly well-bred—poised, urbane. She would hear her father say that James Roosevelt convinced him of a possibility he would not otherwise have known existed—namely, that a Democrat might also be a gentleman.

A few days later, in response to an invitation probably issued at Mrs. Roosevelt's dinner party, Sara Delano, with Mrs. Theodore Roosevelt and her two daughters, arrived at Springwood. The date, May 7, 1880, was forever impressed on her memory as one of the two or three most important in her life. "If I had not come then," she would write fifty-two years later in a letter to her son, "I should now be 'old Miss Delano' after a rather sad life!" [37] Thus she indicated that, by the time she met James Roosevelt, she had accepted the probability of her lifelong spinsterhood—and indicated, too, her conviction that there was no other man in the world whom she could possibly have married. For by the end of that idyllic week (spring was early that year along the Hudson; all the trees were in full summer foliage, and Springwood's flower garden was in bloom), it was clear to her that her host intended to propose marriage, subject of course to her father's approval.

This last, as might be expected, was not gained without effort. It required a full exercise of James Roosevelt's charm, a full exploitation of his assets (high breeding, the highest social standing, a sufficient fortune to absolve him of all suspicion of fortune hunting), aided by Sallie's own fervently expressed desire.

On a morning in early June, James Roosevelt left Springwood and journeyed by buggy and ferry to Warren Delano's country home. It was not a long trip. Algonac, as the Delano estate was called—a forty-room mansion with some sixty beautifully landscaped acres around it—stood on a hill two miles north of Newburgh on the west bank of the river, almost within sight of the tower room at Springwood, so that James Roosevelt was able to arrive at his destination, without hurry, well before noon. And if he was apprehensive as he rode up the long curving drive, through wide lawns with beds of flowers, on this drowsy sun-drenched morning, none could blame him. What father would not doubt the wisdom, at the very least, of marriage between his daughter and a man more than a quarter century older than she? Certainly, as Roosevelt anticipated, Warren Delano had such doubts and expressed them at the outset in tones of outright opposition. As the day wore on, however, his opposition weakened. Apart from the age difference, there could be no question of James Roosevelt's suitability as a son-in-law. Warren Delano had long liked him personally. When James Roosevelt left Algonac the following noon, he had no reason to despair of his suit.

Almost immediately thereafter Sallie's older sister Dora, with her husband, Will Forbes, came to Springwood for a visit of five days during which they presumably carefully looked over, in their host, a prospective brother-in-law. They were evidently satisfied with what they saw. At any rate, James Roosevelt had by early summer formally asked Sara Delano's hand in marriage and had received Warren Delano's blessing. An October wedding was planned.[38]

VI

Of family pride, Sara Delano had as much as, if not a good deal more than, her middle-aged fiancé. In later years she would often insist that her son was "a Delano, not a Roosevelt at all," and would sometimes irritate her daughter-in-law by reciting at slight provocation portions of the ancient and aristocratic lineage which, through her, descended to her son.[39] She knew it well. In the great house beside the river, as she grew up, she had often traced it—a noble Hudson of familial blood, herself an element of it, flowing out of misty mountains of past time through a long valley of years toward the ocean of the future.

Some among her relatives claimed to have traced it all the way back to "the Actii, a Roman patrician family of 600 B.C." [40] According to this tenuous genealogy, the Delanos descended from certain of the Actii who pushed northward from Italy and had firmly established themselves at a place called Alnetum in French Flanders, not far from Isla (now Lille), by the time the Roman power collapsed. As the centuries passed, these forebears clung stubbornly to their land whose place-name went through many modifications—from Alnotum through L'Aulney, L'Annee—until, in the eleventh century, it had become Lanney. Near the close of that century, in 1096, a scion of the family so distinguished himself as a jousting knight that he was granted a title of appellation; he became Hugues de Lanney; and from him the title descended through male heirs until, in 1300, there was none. Demoiselle de Lanney, the last of her line, then lived alone as lady of the manor. But the family title was preserved when one Jean de Franchiment married her and, in 1310, took her name. He was related to that William, bastard son of a Norman duke, who in 1066 had become William the Conqueror.

This Jean de Lanney's descendants, in the line extending to Sara, came to be called De la Noye and they were among that minority of the French nobility who became Huguenots when Calvinism swept from Geneva into France in the sixteenth century. One of them, Jean de la Noye, fled from religious persecution in France to Leyden, Holland, as the century drew to a close. He with his wife, Marie, did not leave France emptyhanded. They were, in fact, among the wealthiest residents of Leyden, living in a large house on the Clockstag which became a hospital for the aged in 1683 and was still so used when Sara Delano saw it in the late nineteenth century. Jean and Marie also established twelve houses of refuge for Puritan immigrants when a bedraggled band of these, some one hundred people in all, arrived in Leyden from Amsterdam in 1609 after they had deemed themselves harried out of their native England.

The English Puritans remained in Leyden for eleven difficult years, during which one of their number, a little girl named Priscilla Mullins (Priscilla Mullines, in the Bradford history), daughter of Puritan émigré William Mullins, grew to be an attractive young woman. Simultaneously, Jacques de la Noye, eldest son of Jean and Marie, grew to be an attractive young man. Priscilla fell in love with him. He did *not* fall in love with her. And this would have ended the matter so far as Sara's family history was concerned if Jacques had not had a younger brother, Philippe, whose desire for the fair Priscilla was as great, and initially as silent and from a distance, as that of Miles Standish and John Alden for the same girl a year or two later. It was so great, in fact, that he followed her as soon as he possibly could after she with her co-religionists had gone from Holland to England and there sailed for the New World, in the *Mayflower,* in the autumn of 1620. Thus, Philippe de la Noye, landing at Plymouth in 1621, became the first Huguenot to come to America—and also became the founder of the American family of which Sara was descended. But it was not through Priscilla that he did so. He pressed his suit. She rejected him. She married instead John Alden, after having induced that youth to "speak for himself." And proud Philippe nursed his deep hurt for many years thereafter, a lonely bachelor, before finally marrying, in 1634, Hester Dewsbury.[41]

Having married, however, he fathered many children, of whom the seventh son, Jonathan, born on a farm at Duxbury in 1647, married Mercy Warren, granddaughter of Richard Warren, who had been on the *Mayflower*. Jonathan, whose family name was variously spelled in colonial records (De Lane, Delanow, Delannoy, etc.) but was finally established as Delano, fought valiantly in King Philip's War (his father had fought the Pequots of Narragansett Bay in 1637) and, two years later (1679), was granted 800 acres near New Bedford. Geographic location determined family vocation. New Bedford became almost exclusively a seafaring town, for decades the most famous whaling port in the world, and the Delanos became seafaring men. Jonathan's son Ephraim went to sea. Ephraim's son Warren went to sea, became a sea captain who made repeated voyages 'round the Horn to China. The family prospered, each generation richer than the last. When Warren II, Sara's father, was born in 1809 at Fairhaven, just across the narrow harbor from New Bedford, he was assured of a comfortable inheritance.[42]

But he did not rest on this. He, too, went to sea. He, too, entered energetically into the China trade. He was captain of his own ship while yet in his twenties, intimately familiar with the dangerous miseries of Horn and Roaring Forties and with the peculiarities of Chinese traders. By his thirtieth birthday he had become a senior partner in Russell, Sturgis and Company, whose headquarters were in Boston but whose main enterprise was the export of tea from China. This enterprise was directed by Warren Delano at its Chinese end; he became chief of Russell, Sturgis operations in the Macao-Canton-Hong Kong area. He helped build his firm (later Russell and Company) into one of the great overseas trading empires of the world—this during that most glamorous and prosperous era of the U.S. Merchant Marine, that of the clipper ship.* He became, in his early thirties, the wealthy owner of a magnificent estate in Macao.

To this estate, when he was thirty-three, he brought his bride, née Catherine Robbins Lyman of Northampton, Massachusetts, Sara's mother, whom he married during a visit to New England in 1843. She, too, was of distinguished lineage—old American stock on her mother's (Robbins') as on her father's side. Richard Robbins, American founder of the maternal line, had settled on the bank of the Charles, about halfway between Boston town and Cambridge village, in 1639. Two of his

* The peculiar needs of the China tea trade were a principal stimulus to the development of swift-sailing ships, since tea flavor steadily deteriorated during storage in a ship's hold. Designers narrowed the hulls and increased the sail spread until, with the launching of Aspinwall and Howland's *Rainbow* in 1845 (see page 23), the ultimate in knifelike three-masted huge-sailed ships was reached. *Rainbow* was the first "true" clipper, but the term was widely used as a label for forerunners of this extreme type all through the 1830's.

grandsons had fought at Lexington; others of his descendants had become famous clergymen; one had been Speaker of the Massachusetts House; and another had been lieutenant governor of the commonwealth. Lyman ancestors, prosperous farmers in the fertile Connecticut River Valley, had been Indian fighters in the seventeenth century and soldiers of revolution in the eighteenth; they were among the founders of Hartford, Connecticut. As for the daughter of these lines, Catherine Lyman herself, she was only eighteen when she married, her husband being thus almost, but not quite, twice her age, a fact which may have helped soften his initial opposition to James Roosevelt's suit thirty-seven years later. She was dark-haired and dark-eyed and firm-chinned (Sara resembled her in appearance) and remarkable for her vivacity, stamina, energy.[43]

And of stamina and energy she needed an abundance, to keep pace with her tireless husband. The first three years of her marriage were lived in Macao, where her husband's already considerable fortune so swiftly and greatly grew that he decided to return to America and enjoy his wealth in more leisurely fashion. The Delanos did so in 1846, settling in New York City, where they bought a fashionable house (one of nine linked together to form what was known as Colonnade Row) on Lafayette Place. But neither of them liked urban life. They spent their summers in a rented house on Danskammer Point, near Newburgh, and devoted much time to looking for a river estate which they might buy as their permanent home. They found one that perfectly suited them in 1851—a fruit farm of sixty acres, most of them covered by natural forest rather than by orchards, on a point of land around which the Hudson flowed in a slow curve and from whose house could be seen mountains rising in dark grandeur against the sunsets. Meanwhile, Warren Delano, far from retiring from business, used his great capital and credit to expand and diversify, buying New York Harbor real estate, Pennsylvania coal mines, Tennessee copper mines, and various income-producing properties in Maryland. Meanwhile, too, Catherine Delano gave birth to five children—Susie (the eldest, who died in infancy) and Louise, born in China; Dora, Annie, and Warren III (who also died in infancy), born in New York City.

The house on the newly purchased estate, Algonac, was of the same general style as Springwood and, in 1851, was considerably less grand than it was when James Roosevelt first saw it. Warren Delano was rich enough to put into full effect these expensive ideas for "rural improvement" which his friend and neighbor Andrew Jackson Downing, the famous landscape architect, developed for him.* He promptly did so. By

* It was Downing who, in his highly influential *Landscape Gardening*, published in 1841, first

1852 the house had been completely remodeled and much enlarged. Towers and wide verandas had been added to take maximum advantage of magnificent vistas, of river and mountains, from Algonac's hill, and within the house itself the tall-ceilinged rooms were enlarged. The entrance hall was nineteen feet square, the drawing room eighteen by twenty-seven, a parlor sixteen by twenty, the kitchen sixteen by twenty-one, and the other rooms (library, breakfast room, bedrooms, etc.) were proportionately large. They were richly furnished, too—ostentatiously cluttered as rich Victorians liked their homes to be with heavy, carved rosewood furniture and potted plants, along with teakwood screens and tables, exquisite porcelains, Buddhist temple bells, and other Oriental objects to remind visitors of the main source of the Delano fortune.

There the family continued to grow, with a sixth child born in 1852, shortly after the move—a boy to whom they gave the same name as the dead son had been given, Warren III. Two years later came the birth of the girl who, decades later, so often traced out all these relationships. She herself, the seventh Delano child, was born at Algonac on September 21, 1854, and christened Sarah after a spinster aunt (her father's sister) who made her home at Algonac, a name from which the h was dropped (to distinguish her from Aunt Sarah) and upon which the nickname Sallie was superimposed while she was yet a small child. Not for long was she the youngest of the family. She soon had a younger brother, Philippe; and before she was well into her teens she had yet another younger brother, Fred, and two younger sisters, Cassie (Kassie) and Laura.

"I suppose it was altogether terrifying to my young mother to give up her beautiful home and its peaceful security for perhaps the rest of her life," said Sara when she had grown old, "—but in those days the older members of the family carefully kept away from the children all traces of sadness or trouble or the news of anything alarming. I often think today, when I hear money troubles, illness, or accident discussed before eager-eyed, open-eared children, how tranquil and unmarked by adult emotions our lives really were." [44]

In these words, after nearly three-quarters of a century had passed, she would indicate the general character of her childhood life—an idyllic existence, profoundly peaceful, yet intensely active and crowded with people she loved who loved her, sustained by every creature comfort and surrounded by great natural beauty whose central theme was the

---

used the term "Hudson River Bracketed." Edith Wharton used the term as the title of one of her late (and inferior) novels. Downing was himself of the river gentry, with an estate near Fishkill Landing.

river, the flowing sailboat- and steamboat-bearing river of spring and summer and autumn, the glittering ice-sheathed river of midwinter with the Delano sleigh often crossing it from Algonac to Beacon on the opposite bank. But in those same quoted words, Sara also indicated a great trouble which came to her family in 1857 and grew worse during the immediately following years.

It did not come to the Delano family alone. Millions suffered, and more severely than the Delanos, from the financial panic which began in late August, 1857, with the failure of the Ohio Life Insurance and Trust Company. By the end of October all save one of the banks in New York City had suspended specie payment, as had scores of other banks in towns large and small throughout the country. By the end of the year nearly 5,000 businesses had failed. In the following year well over 4,000 more failed, and nearly 4,000 failed in the year after that. Tens of thousands of people lost everything they had, including their homes and means of livelihood. A terrifyingly high proportion of the total labor force was unemployed. Through three bitter winters there was actual starvation and freezing to death in city streets and in the shacks of those miners of coal and copper from whose labors Warren Delano had formerly profited.

He and his family suffered no physical misery. The children suffered not at all; a sharply reduced scale of living deprived them of no comforts and few, if any, of their pleasures. But the head of the family suffered great psychological misery as, abruptly, having spread his capital too widely and thinly to bear the weight of depression, he found himself no longer wealthy but teetering instead on the verge of bankruptcy. The future loomed dark before him. He would have sold Algonac (he actually put a for sale sign on it) had he been able to find a buyer who would come anywhere near paying a reasonable price for it. He cast about with growing desperation for means of retrieving his fortune. An entry in a diary kept at Algonac in those years indicates his restless anguish; it was written by his brother Edward (Sara's Uncle Ned), who, a bachelor, made his home (like spinster Aunt Sarah) at Algonac. "Warren has various projects, mostly impractical," wrote Uncle Ned, "one of which is to go to China to do business five years and return with a fortune." [45]

Yet it was precisely this "impractical" scheme which Warren Delano, aged fifty, carried out, and with precisely the results he predicted. In 1859 he left his pregnant wife (she carried Cassie) and half dozen children at Algonac, with Aunt Sarah and Uncle Ned to look after them. He sailed for China. And in Hong Kong he entered into a business more lucrative than tea, but also far less respectable, one that would be seldom mentioned by his family in later years. This was the opium trade. It would be denied in these later years that the opium he bought and shipped was intended for the tremendously profitable market provided by addicts; stressed would be the vastly increased market for medicinal opium which the Civil War created. But undeniable was the fact that he restored his fortune, if indeed he did not increase it over its former amount, with astonishing, almost incredible speed. Within two years he was able to charter a clipper to transport to Hong Kong from Algonac (which he rented to A. A. Low) the whole of his household, including Aunt Sarah and Uncle Ned. Within seven years he was able to retire again from the China trade and return, a rich man, to Algonac, there to live out the rest of his long life.[46]   The voyage to China; her eighteen months in Rose Hill, the great house of her father's in Hong Kong; and the leisurely return journey by way of Singapore, Paris and London— these constituted the great adventure of Sara's early life. She traveled much in the years intervening between this adventure and her first meeting with James Roosevelt. In 1876 she went again to Hong Kong, via Europe and the Suez Canal (officially opened in 1869), accompanying her newly married sister Dora and husband, Will Forbes, who were to live in Rose Hill while he carried out his duties as a partner in Russell and Company. But no later travel adventure had for her the excitement of this first one. Especially was this true of the outward voyage. Often she spoke of it decades later to her son, telling him as a wide-eyed little boy how exciting it had been to sail out of the harbor on a bright June day in 1862 (Americans killed one another in battle that day in Virginia, in Tennessee); how school classes were conducted regularly for her and the other children aboard the *Surprise* during the 120 days required to sail down through the North and South Atlantic, around the Cape of Good Hope, and slant up through the Indian Ocean into the China Sea; how on September 21, twelve weeks out, she and the ship's captain, who had the same birthday as she (he was twenty-eight, she eight), celebrated it together as guests of honor at a birthday feast of roast goose, ham, vegetables, and two birthday cakes, with champagne for the adults; how a week later they all went ashore at Java Head and she made crayon sketches of strange birds and flowers; and how finally, on October 30, after weeks of still, moist heat such as the Hudson River Valley knows for only a few days at the height of summer, she saw land again and a boat being rowed out from the shore with her father in it, her father handsome and slender, clothed all in white.

VII

In early June, 1880, the Republican National Convention, meeting in Chicago, became hopelessly deadlocked between the candidacies of former President U. S. Grant and Maine's "Plumed Knight" (though his plumes were now tattered), James G. Blaine. After thirty-five ballots the delegates, on the thirty-sixth, turned to the reluctant James A. Garfield of Ohio, who thus became the first convention Presidential draftee in history. Chester A. Arthur of New York was chosen as Garfield's running mate.

In late June, 1880, the Democratic National Convention, meeting in Cincinnati, nominated handsome Civil War General Winfield S. Hancock. William H. English of Indiana was chosen as Hancock's running mate.

During the following weeks, Warren Delano contributed money to Garfield's campaign while James Roosevelt contributed to Hancock's. Roosevelt was also offered the Democratic nomination for Congress from his district, an empty honor, if an honor at all: the party, expecting defeat, obviously sought a Congressional candidate who could and would pay his own campaign expenses. James Roosevelt refused.

The summer of that year was hot and dry in the Hudson Valley, so dry that the river became brackish with tidal seawater far above its mouth, in late August. Locomotive boilers in which the river water was used became caked with salt. But as summer ended, autumn came on in a succession of lovely golden days.

Sara Delano and James Roosevelt were married at Algonac on one of them.

On October 7 the sun shone bright and warm upon leaves just beginning to turn, and the Hudson was a deep rich blue in reflection of a sky that had no clouds. The wedding was not as large and elaborate as had been originally planned. The bride's Aunt Sarah, after whom she had been named and whom she had greatly loved, had died only a few weeks before after a lingering illness; the family remained in mourning for her. Hence only members of the two immediate families and a few of their closests friends were invited to the ceremony. These, however, made an occasion large by common standards—no fewer than 125 attended—and next day's New York City newspapers, reporting the event fully, made it appear quite gala.

Mr. Delano's gardener, said the New York *World*, had decorated the house's interior "in every style of horticultural art." [47] The drawing room had been "made into a conservatory filled with the choicest plants and flowers." A "floral channel whose foundation was composed of ferns and tropical palms" rose against the "rear wall of an alcove on the west side of the room," and it was there, "under the floral canopy," that the Reverend Dr. Bellows of New York stood as he read the marriage service. "There were no bridesmaids, but the sisters [of the bride] and female relatives of the bridegroom stood with the bridal party." (Among the latter was James Roosevelt's aged mother, the widow of Dr. Isaac, clad in black silk.) The bride was radiant in pure white brocade and tulle veil, a five-strand pearl necklace given her by the bridegroom around her neck. After the ceremony everyone went into the dining room, where New York's most noted caterer, Pinard, had "laid a collation" so abundant and varied as to bely its name.

Shortly thereafter (at four twenty precisely, Warren Delano noted in his diary), James Roosevelt and his bride (she had changed to a gray dress trimmed in black) left Algonac in a Delano carriage driven by the Delano coachman, bound for Hyde Park. But it was not in the Delano carriage that the pair turned off the Albany Post Road, having crossed the Hudson on the Highland Ferry, to drive up the long treelined lane to Springwood. Halfway to Hyde Park, though still on the west bank of the river, they changed punctiliously from the Delano equipage to a T cart owned by James Roosevelt and driven to that point by his coachman. From then on the bridegroom himself took the reins.[48]

Two

>>)(<<

A Son Is Born

I

THROUGH all that October and into the first week of November the newly married couple remained on the banks of the Hudson—at Springwood most of the time, at Algonac the rest.

Every morning at Springwood the bride and her husband inspected the greenhouses, the grape arbors, the stables of fine horses, the flower gardens being prepared for winter. They rode horseback through a rustle of fallen leaves in woods that flamed with autumn's colors and across fields of brown grass and plowed earth. They went in a rowboat upon the river, going almost every day downstream to the boathouse at Rosedale, whence they climbed a steep path to the darkly shaded house where James' aged mother, Dr. Isaac's widow, still lived with her son John Aspinwall Roosevelt and his wife, Ellen, and family. They paid informal calls, were called upon. Almost daily they saw the Rosy Roosevelts. They dined (accepting their first dinner invitation after the wedding) in the palatial home of the Maturin Livingstons in Staatsburg. On another day, accompanied by the Warren Delanos, they visited in yet another splendid house in Staatsburgh, The Locusts, newly built by William B. Dinsmore.

At her leisure, the bride opened the great packages in which her wedding presents were forwarded from Algonac, distributing these around her new home. During the last week of the month she and her husband came to stay at Algonac, where they enjoyed much the same daily round as on their own estate, though somewhat less quietly, not only because so many active people were there but also because the Presidential election campaign generated in its closing days an intensification of partisan emotions.[1]

This last, the approaching quadrennial climax of the American political process, was the only intrusion from the outside upon the tiny world of immense privilege in which the bridal couple lived so happily. It served to remind them that the great world of the unprivileged by which they were surrounded was far more turbulent, far less polite and pleasing to the senses than the one they inhabited.

II

There were three emergent national issues in that election year which would affect the destinies of the Roosevelt family—in both its Oyster Bay and Hudson River branches.

One was a growing antagonism between capital and labor. In 1877, amid the economic depression which dashed James Roosevelt's hopes for a fortune from his Consolidation Coal and Southern Railway Security ventures, the Hudson River gentry had been perturbed by a series of labor strikes, more widespread and strongly organized than any before, against all the principal rail lines in the East. They were strikes marked by bloody violence. President Hayes had at last committed federal troops to the restoration of order, thereby establishing a precedent of forceful federal intervention in labor disputes which all true believers in laissez-faire government must deplore and whose effect on labor was to promote an embittered aggressive solidarity.

A second issue was that of the currency, sharpened by the hard times of 1873–79. It, too, was permeated by class bitterness. Myriads of farmers, small merchants, and urban workers constituted a debtor class whose borrowings had been of the easy money of Civil War years but whose due notes now had to be paid in money much higher in value and proportionately harder for them to obtain. These debtors were generally inclined to support the demands of Western silver interests that the government engage in a free and unlimited coinage of silver in a ratio to gold of sixteen to one, for now that sixteen ounces of silver had become worth a good deal less than an ounce of gold on the world market, the effect of this would be an inflation of the currency.

The third issue was that of federal civil service reform. Repeated instances of the most flagrant graft and corruption at every level of government had been exposed to the public gaze since the early days of Grant's administration, and reformers were convinced that a main root of the evil lay in the "spoils system" which Andrew Jackson was alleged to have introduced into national politics. In this view, the Hudson River gentry concurred. They as individuals may or may not have been aware of the wholesale bribery of lawmakers, the virtual purchase of entire

state legislatures, whereby their railroad and various other of their interests were advanced. But they certainly *were* aware of the threat presented to their world by a rampant criminality that spread through the
whole apparatus of government, and their refined personal tastes were
offended by the acts and agents of a venal politics. They therefore favored, most of them, the establishment of a federal civil service divorced
altogether from politics.

All this was given, however, only a muffled, ambiguous expression in
the Presidential campaign of 1880. By historical accident rather more
than conscious design it was by then the general practice of the American political party system to blur issues and prevent flat ideological confrontations, especially in election years. Thus there was little to choose
between the two major party platforms in that year, for each party contained factions opposed to one another on these major emergent issues.
Each had spoilsmen, as well as civil service reformers, gold standardites
as well as bimetallists, and advocates of both sides of the antagonisms of
labor and capital, of farmer and corporate industrialist. Each maintained its traditional stance on the tariff, Republicans supporting protectionism and Democrats demanding a "tariff for revenue only," but
this was no burning question that year. Otherwise, each platform was an
attempt to placate the factions in order to achieve the broadest possible
party unity.* On the currency matter alone did the Democrats show
themselves slightly more responsive than the Republicans to the demands, the felt needs of the unprivileged many as distinct from the privileged few.

III

The fact that James Roosevelt was himself opposed to his party's
fiscal policies—and that the 1880 campaign was the first since the Civil
War in which the Republicans did not "wave the bloody shirt" in an
effort to damn all Democrats as betrayers of the Union—helped him
bear with equanimity his isolation in a sea of Republicanism during the
closing days of the campaign. He alone of the gentlemen at Algonac,

* So was the choice of candidates, especially in the case of the Republicans. Hilarious to
some, infuriating to others, and outrageous to almost everyone was the spectacle of Chester A.
Arthur (like James Roosevelt, he was a graduate of Union College) running as Vice Presidential candidate on a Republican platform calling for civil service reform. For Arthur was himself among the most notorious of all spoilsmen politicians. President Hayes, with great difficulty, had removed him from his post as Collector of Customs of New York following an investigation commission's report of gross inefficiencies and wholesale fraud in New York's Customs House.

and among the men employed there only the Irish, would vote Democratic.[2] The proportions were nearly the same in the nearby town of Newburgh: when a giant torchlight parade through Newburgh's streets was held by supporters of Garfield and Arthur a few days before the election, it seemed to observers that virtually the entire population was either parading or cheering from the sidewalks. James Roosevelt may not have enjoyed this gaudy demonstration of partisanship as greatly as did others at Algonac, but he was certainly not dismayed by it. Insulated against the anxieties of public affairs by his great private happiness, he viewed the close of the political campaign with a detached good humor. And this remained his mood on election day, November 2. He and Sara left Algonac that morning and went across the river to Hyde Park. There, in the early afternoon, he hopefully cast his vote for Hancock and English.

Nor did the election's outcome seriously disturb him. As a matter of fact, any Democrat, studying the 1880 returns in the light of the events of 1876, might take heart for the future. True, James A. Garfield had won the Presidency with a decisive victory in the electoral college. But the popular vote had been close, and the winner did not have a majority of the total vote: of the more than 9,000,000 ballots cast, some hundreds of thousands had gone to James B. Weaver, the Greenback Party candidate. Four years before, the Democratic candidate, Samuel J. Tilden, had actually polled more popular votes than Republican Hayes and had clearly won 184 of the 185 electoral votes needed to place him in the White House. Only brazen skulduggery by Congressional Republicans had denied him the electoral votes of all three Southern states—Louisiana, Florida, South Carolina—where two opposing sets of returns had been filed. The 1880 returns thus confirmed the overwhelming probability, if not the virtual certainty, that the long period of Republican domination of Presidential politics (not since 1856 had a Democrat won the White House) was coming at last to an end.

A day or so after the election, in pursuance of honeymoon plans made before the wedding, the bridal couple went down to New York, where they were registered in the fashionable Brevoort House. They were visited there by the bride's parents, one of her sisters, and her Uncle Ned on November 5. Two days later they sailed for Europe on the White Star liner *Germanic*. And for ten months thereafter they did nothing but enjoy themselves as they journeyed leisurely through Italy, Spain, France, Holland, Germany, Switzerland, and across the Channel into England and Scotland. Always they traveled in the best of style; everywhere they encountered friends, relatives, acquaintances from home; nowhere did they have meaningful contacts with the classes of people whose discontents were developing dangerous pressures in every Continental country.[3]

In Spain they both fell briefly ill of a fever from which James recovered first, delighting his wife thereafter with his nursing care of her. ("James too devoted to me," she noted in her diary.) In Italy they met Dora and Will Forbes, who introduced them to several of that newly unified country's aristocratic families. In Paris, in April 1881, they became part of a gathering of the whole Delano clan for whose accommodation Warren Delano rented an entire floor of the Hôtel du Rhin. In northern France they visited the Château of Clervaux, medieval castle of the Seigneurs de Lanney, where Sara saw her family's arms carved in marble, and in Leyden they saw the house of Jean and Marie de la Noye. In Holland they visited Zeeland, seeking the "Rose Field" from which the Roosevelts derived their name. In Switzerland they were again in a Delano family group; they met there Sara's Uncle Frank and Aunt Laura (Astor) Delano.

In England they stayed with James Roosevelt's friends, Sir Hugh and Lady Cholmeley, in their "lovely old Queen Anne house" at Grantham, near Euston.

In England, too, in the home of a Madame Schwabe whom they had met in Florence, they were introduced to a Madame Goldschmidt—a memorable meeting for Sara especially.[4] Madame Goldschmidt was a dumpy little woman clothed in black taffeta, plain- though pleasant-faced, who looked every bit her age (she was sixty) and would probably have received slight attention from them had they not been told that she was the former Jenny Lind, the Swedish Nightingale, whose singing had enthralled vast audiences on both sides of the Atlantic in the 1850's.*

By then, or very shortly thereafter, Sara Roosevelt knew that she was with child. The knowledge made her and her husband anxious to return soon to Springwood. On September 1, 1881, they boarded the same liner that had taken them to Europe, the *Germanic*, and ten days later they were again in the United States.

IV

The pregnancy was, on the whole, an easy one. It did not prevent the Roosevelts from having an active, pleasant social life through the au-

* Many babies born in America in the 1850's were named after Jenny Lind, among them the second daughter of a music-loving Wall Street speculator named Leonard Jerome who made a great fortune in the fifties and sixties and lost it during the Gilded Age. Miss Jennie (as she spelled it) Jerome was a dark-haired, dark-eyed, arrogant beauty when she met and fascinated a British aristocrat, Lord Randolph Churchill, son of the seventh Duke of Marlborough. Her marriage to him was a great social event of 1874. Her first child, born in the year of her marriage, was a boy who was christened Winston Leonard Spencer Churchill.

tumn of 1881. They returned to the routine of the preceding autumn, minus the daily horseback ride for Sara. They boated every day on the river, paid almost daily visits to Rosedale, dined frequently in the Red House with Rosy and Helen Roosevelt (whose first child, James' grand-child, was born that fall; he was named James Roosevelt Roosevelt, Jr., subsequently nicknamed Taddy) and occasionally with the Archibald Rogerses, who (with Rockefeller oil money, Rogers being one of John D's top assistants) had built a mansion reputed to have cost more than $300,000 north of Springwood.[5] Now and then they lunched with the Dinsmores at The Locusts. The Delanos were often at Springwood, of course, and the Roosevelts at Algonac, where, on Christmas Day, when Sara was very big with child, they feasted on turkey and plum pudding.

The weather had turned bitterly cold by then. The river was sheathed in ice, and upon it members of the Poughkeepsie Ice Yacht Club took their dangerous pleasure, sailing their iceboats at speeds of well over a mile a minute when the wind was right. Sara, watching from an upstairs window of her home, often saw her brother-in-law John flashing by in his *Icicle*, which was not only the largest iceboat in the world, but also one of the fastest.[6] John Roosevelt (he was commodore of the yacht club) had had it built to his specifications and had made over eighty miles an hour in it. Pleasure was not all that the river's ice provided, however, nor was it the only activity that Sara saw from her upstairs window. There was work also, the hardest kind of labor, as gangs of men cut tons of river ice, sawing it into blocks and storing these for summer refrigeration in the icehouses and ice pantries of Springwood and the other river mansions. Snow fell. Almost every day Sara, care-fully bundled up against the cold, was helped by her husband into the elegant Russian sleigh he had bought for a song in Paris in 1872* and taken for a drive to the village or down to Poughkeepsie on the Post Road.

Meanwhile, a layette was accumulated—night slips, little dresses, dia-pers, cribsheets. In mid-January a trained nurse, Mrs. Carrie Lee, moved into Springwood.

Two weeks went by.

In Albany, an angry struggle between Tammany and rural Democrats postponed organization of the State Assembly in which the Democrats were in a majority. Republicans watched the altercation with under-standable glee. From Boston came news of financier Jay Gould's latest spectacular move; he had captured control of the St. Louis and San

* The sleigh had been a gift from Czar Alexander II of Russia to Napoleon III of France—and Roosevelt was able to buy it for a mere $15 in the bitter aftermath of 1870, which had brought the Second Empire to an ignominious end.[7]

Francisco Railroad. In Columbus, Ohio, the Democratic organization, smarting in the hot glare of exposures by the New York *Times*, confessed it had "been led into crooked paths by false leaders" and promised to mend its ways. In Washington, ex-Secretary of State James G. Blaine's foreign policy with regard to warring Chile and Peru was under attack, its opponents charging that a letter of instructions sent to the American envoy in Chile by Blaine had not been cleared with President Garfield. Garfield himself, alas, could neither confirm nor deny the charge. Shot by a disappointed office seeker in July, he had died last September 19 and been succeeded by Chester Arthur, who, to the amazement of everyone (including, perhaps, himself), was turning out to be an honest, hardworking, enlightened Chief Executive, committed to the general welfare against the private interests of his former spoilsmen colleagues. From abroad, the most important news story had a Paris dateline: the government of M. Gambetta (who had escaped from Paris in a balloon during the siege of 1870) had fallen; M. de Freycinet had undertaken the formation of a Cabinet.[8]

But none of these continuing stories made much impression on James Roosevelt when he read the latest installments on Sunday, January 29, 1882. It was time for the baby to come, if not more than time! Mrs. Lee agreed that it was. So did the physician, who was Dr. Edward H. Parker of Poughkeepsie. And though both assured him there was as yet no need for worry, he *did* worry as one more day was added to those that had passed since the earliest time predicted for Sallie's taking. (He always called her Sallie.) The weather's mood did nothing to lift his spirits. The day was dreary and cold, with a wind that sighed endlessly through Springwood's pines and moaned through the house's bracketed eaves.

Sallie herself seemed perfectly serene. If she had any dark forebodings, she hid them perfectly. Yet she might well have had them. Childbirth was to prove as hard for her as her pregnancy had been easy.

At seven thirty that Sunday evening, her labor pains began. All night, lying in a heavy mahogany double bed in an upstairs bedroom, she suffered recurrent pangs, her sleepless husband anxiously attending her until, on Monday morning, January 30 (a bright clear morning, though still very cold), these pangs came so regularly and close together that Mrs. Lee was called and then, at seven o'clock, the doctor. There followed for Sara a long day of agony. The child which she, in recent days, had felt to be so strong and independent and self-assertive in her womb was now reluctant to leave it. She bore down, as doctor and nurse urged her to do. She bore down and bore down, screaming. But the child would not come. At seven that evening, the train carrying her mother, who came in response to James' telegram, was met at Hyde Park station by her white-faced, distraught son-in-law.[9] The baby still had not come, and when James and Mrs. Delano arrived at the house, Sara's screams seemed louder, more agonized than ever.

Could nothing be done for her?

At eight o'clock, Dr. Parker resorted to a dangerous, if not desperate, stratagem. He administered chloroform, then more chloroform, until all at once it was evident that he had administered an overdose. Sara, sinking into complete unconsciousness, gasped for breath and turned blue. And when the infant was at last delivered at precisely eight forty-five, it, too, was blue and limp in a respiratory trance from which the traditional spanks could not awaken it. Artificial respiration was promptly resorted to, the doctor breathing into the infant's mouth until the blue skin had become red, the tiny body heaved, and the opened mouth from which the doctor removed his own omitted a surprisingly loud cry of protest at being forced into a world of strangeness, discomforts, and dangers.[10]

Before Dr. Parker left, James Roosevelt scrawled upon a telegraph blank a note to his sister-in-law Ellen, to be dropped off at Rosedale by the doctor on his way back to Poughkeepsie. "I have only a moment . . . to write you that Sallie has a bouncing boy," said the note. "Poor child, she has had a very hard time." And before he went exhausted to bed, he opened his wife's diary in which no entry had been made by her for six weeks (all the entries for those weeks were in his handwriting). Under January 30, 1882, he wrote: "At quarter to nine my Sallie had a splendid large baby boy. He weighs 10 lbs., without clothes." [11]

The next day the worst winter storm in many years swept over the Hudson River Valley. Snow began to fall in great heavy flakes shortly after sunrise. By noon the flakes were small and dry and driven in blinding white sheets by a rising wind. Dr. Parker had to wade through drifts of snow when he came to see Sara in the afternoon, finding her weak but in good condition, happily nursing her baby at her breast.

She made a quick recovery, and the baby thrived on her milk, but the doctor kept her confined in her room for several weeks, as was the custom then. He made daily visits for a time. The final doctor's bill was "$50 for confinement and 8 visits $32, total $82," but James—perhaps to pay for prenatal care, perhaps out of gratitude—sent two checks for $50 each, thus bringing the total reimbursement to $100. Mrs. Lee, whom they found "perfect as a nurse and woman," remained with them until mid-March. For these eight weeks of service she was paid $160.[12]

V

No trumpets sounded over this babe in his crib. No slightest sign was given that his destiny might be markedly different from those of a thousand other boy babies born that year into privileged American homes. Nor did his parents wish it otherwise. They were content to have him fit perfectly into the niche prepared for him by heredity and environment and would be as happy to see him developing, later on, traits and attitudes "proper" for his "position" as they would have been disturbed to see him developing marked eccentricities or any outstanding idiosyncrasy of mind, body, or personality. "I know that traditionally every American mother believes her son will one day be President," his mother said to an interviewer a half century later, "but much as I love tradition and believe in perpetuating good ones, that is one to which I never happened to subscribe. What was my ambition for him? Very simple— . . . to grow to be like his father, straight and honorable, just and kind, an outstanding American." [13]

For the first seven weeks of his life he did not even have a name. One reason for this was a disagreement between the parents, mild but real, about the name they wished to bestow. A Roosevelt family tradition had been initiated when Jacobus (James) Roosevelt, back in 1726, named his sixth son Isaac. Isaac and James had thereafter alternated as names of father and son from generation to generation in the line that descended to the present James. The latter had risked, if not broken, this tradition when he named his eldest son James (with a middle name of "Roosevelt") instead of Isaac. He wished now to restore it; he would name his second son Isaac. His proposal to do so, however, met his wife's adamant opposition. She detested the name "Isaac." It lacked "distinction." [14] Before her baby was born, she had decided that it would, if a boy, be named after her beloved father. And it is significant of her force of character (and no doubt encouraged her sense of her son as more Delano than Roosevelt) that her will prevailed over her husband's commitment to his own family tradition. James yielded, though it must not be thought that this was typical of their relationship. In general, Sara gladly deferred to her husband's judgment, gladly accepted his word as law, subordinating herself to him as she had to her father. And her father, Warren Delano II, was in this instance delighted. But then a sad complication arose. Sara's elder brother Warren III had a namesake son, Warren IV, whose death in early childhood very nearly coincided with the birth of the Roosevelt baby, and when Sara wrote her griefstricken brother to ask if he would mind their naming her child as planned, he replied that, in the circumstances, he "could not bear it." So it was decided instead to name the baby for Sara's Uncle Frank—the Franklin Delano who had married Laura Astor and, childless, lived at Steen Valetje.[15]

The christening ceremony was held in Hyde Park's St. James Chapel (not the church, which lacked heating facilities) at eleven o'clock in the morning of March 20, 1882. The rector, the Reverend Dr. Philander K. Cady, was officiating priest. Godmother to the infant was Miss Eleanor "Nelly" Blodgett of New York City, one of Sara's closest friends since childhood. There were two godfathers—Will Forbes, Sara's brother-in-law (Dora's husband), and Elliott Roosevelt, brother of Sara's close friend Bammie and of Theodore Roosevelt, Jr. Elliott, who was only twenty-one, had responded diffidently to James and Sara's invitation. Sara had known and liked him since he was a small child. During their European honeymoon she and James had seen much of him (he was on a trip around the world), and James had grown very fond of him, too. But both of them knew, of course—and Elliott knew that they knew—of his mysterious "nervous breakdown" of a few years before. This may have been why, in answer to their letter, he wrote that he felt himself "not good enough to be the godfather of such rare people" and indicated that he would have declined "the high honor you offer me" had not "my dear mother . . . persuaded me that I should accept." [16]

Thereafter Sara's diary reported for her son a standard progress through infancy, every step of which delighted her. In the autumn of his first year she wrote that "Baby . . . crows and laughs all the time," that he "went to his first party," where the sight of children dancing made him eager to dance too ("I could hardly hold him"), that in mid-November he was trying to imitate the mewing of cats and barking of the dog, and that he could then make noises that resembled "Mama" and "Papa." She continued to breast-feed him until he was nearly a year old. Some four months after his weaning, on May 17, 1883, she wrote: "Baby walked quite alone. He is quite proud of his new accomplishment."

By then he had some kind of name for almost every person and thing in his life. His nurse was Helen McRorie, "a good experienced woman and very gentle," whom Dora Forbes had hired for the Roosevelts after the first nurse, engaged by Sara before Mrs. Lee had departed, proved unsatisfactory. She came to Springwood a few days after the baby's christening. James and Sara called her Ellen. Baby Franklin, when he first began to talk, dubbed her Mamie and continued to call her so for the remainder of the nine years she stayed with the family. The housekeeper, originally engaged by Rebecca Howland Roosevelt, was Elspeth

McEachern, a Scotswoman whom her employers called Elespie. Baby Franklin dubbed her Tiddle, and this name, too, stuck.[17]

There were always at least five or six other servants at Springwood during the boy's infancy—butler, cook, maid, gardener, groom, with occasional helpers for these. There was also, and most important, the farmer, a man named John Irving who had been in James Roosevelt's employ for many years and knew precisely how James wanted him to grow the crops, care for the meadows, and tend the poultry and dairy herd and other livestock. The active presence of all these people made it unnecessary for James and Sara to curtail in the slightest their social life or travels, once the baby was weaned, and, indeed, even before his weaning, their activities were but slightly, if any, modified by his dependent existence. They took him with them when they went down to New York to spend a month with the Forbeses in 1882 and when they went, later that summer, on what had become and was to remain an annual pilgrimage to The Homestead at Fairhaven, Massachusetts—the fine old house, built in the Federal period by the first Warren Delano, where Sara's father had been reared. They, of course, took him and nurse again to New York when they moved there during the first months of 1883, into a rented furnished house at 31 West Forty-ninth Street, and his wants and needs did not deter them from a typically active city social life: opera parties, theater parties, coming-out parties, parties for celebrities from abroad, formal and informal dinners, Mrs. Astor's ball, recitals, late suppers at Delmonico's.

They returned to Hyde Park in the spring for a few months and then, in the summer of 1883, went for the first time to an island in the Bay of Fundy which, though just off the coast of Maine, was part of the Canadian province of New Brunswick. Its name was Campobello.

VI

Later generations would find it difficult to account for the attraction Campobello had as a summer residence for the wealthy in the late nineteenth and early twentieth centuries, an attraction it was just beginning to exert in 1883. The island was remote from the main centers of urban or country living in the East. A long train ride brought a summer visitor to the Maine seacoast village of Eastport, whence a ferry crossed to Welshpool, the island's principal town. The climate left much to be desired. At the height of summer the air temperature was often too chilly for comfort, and not infrequently the scenery, beautiful in places but never spectacular, was hidden from view by heavy fogs or by dark curtains of rain from clouds that hovered only slightly above the treetops. Swimming off the island's shores was a rugged, even a hazardous enterprise. The ocean waters were always cold, and the tides, among the highest in the world, ebbed and flowed within granite-walled inlets and between island and offshore islets with the speed and force of the mightiest river's swiftest rapids. Only the sailing, which was excellent, and the fishing, which was very good, could be deemed unqualified recommendations of the place as a vacation spot.

Nevertheless, a group of wealthy American businessmen had become convinced that Campobello could be developed into an excellent and exclusive summer resort and had formed for this purpose the Campobello Land Company in 1881. The company had bought much of the island and had promptly set about selling lots, each one or more acres in size, to carefully screened buyers. In 1882 a large and comfortable inn, called Tyn a Coed (Welsh for House in the Woods), was constructed. It was there that the Roosevelts stayed in the summer of 1883.

The sailing, of which he had heard glowing accounts, was what initially attracted James Roosevelt, and he found it as splendid as he had been told it would be. But he and Sara found other attractions as well. The island natives, who lived by fishing for the most part, were highly intelligent, ruggedly independent, and self-respectful, yet at the same time deferential toward their "betters," in the English tradition.* The summer weather, if imperfect, was to the Roosevelts preferable to the humid heat of the Hudson River Valley in July and August. There were lovely places for picnics in fine weather and much that was quaint and picturesque in the fishing villages. Most important of all, several of James and Sara's longtime friends had bought or were planning to buy land on Campobello on which to build summer cottages, among them the Russell Sturgises of Boston, who were fellow guests with the Roosevelts at Tyn a Coed. Obviously a very congenial summer colony, consisting of only the "right" people, was in the making. Before that summer ended, James and Sara had decided to join it; they bought four acres of seashore land and arranged to have a cottage built upon it to their specifications, in time, they hoped, for occupancy the following summer.

---

* Such attitudes had been encouraged by the island's history. Campobello was named by a Captain William Owen of the Royal Navy who had obtained legal title to it through a royal grant in 1767. Having brought over from England a colony of seventy people and settled them as he wished, the captain had returned to his naval career, from which he eventually retired an admiral. His agent on the island, ruling it as a lord, was a relative, David Owen. In 1835, Admiral William FitzWilliam Owen, son of the original grantee, inherited the island, built a large house at Welshpool, and from then on till his death in 1857 reigned over his private domain almost as a king in the days of divine right, the islanders his subjects.[18]

Thus was determined a major influence upon the future life of their infant son.

Nor was this the only such influence determined that summer.

Among the other guests at the inn were Mr. and Mrs. James Lawrence of Groton, Massachusetts. They, too, were old friends of the Roosevelts, and seated of an evening before an open fire in the inn, they spoke enthusiastically of a project then being initiated in their quiet village—a project in which they themselves were involved.[19]

A few months before, in the spring of 1883, the Lawrences had had as weekend guest at Groton a young friend named Endicott Peabody, whose eldest brother had married James Lawrence's sister. As they all talked together on Sunday morning, Mrs. Lawrence remarked that she wished a school for boys could be opened in the village under the auspices of the Episcopal Church, of which she was a devout member, because this would mean that Episcopal services would be conducted there and it would no longer be necessary, as it then was, to go all the way to Fitchburg, fourteen miles distant, to attend services. The remark was as a flint spark striking dry tinder, for young Peabody (he was then twenty-five) had recently become obsessed with the dream of establishing an American boys' school modeled on the public schools of England—particularly on Rugby as Rugby had been under the great headmaster Thomas Arnold.[20]

Some there were who thought the dream strange for one of his character, appearance, and circumstances. His mother, née Marianne Lee, was the daughter of the great Boston investment house of Lee, Higginson and Company. His father, Samuel Endicott Peabody, was a highly successful businessman who had become a member of J. S. Morgan and Company in London when Endicott was thirteen. This circumstance determined for the boy an English upper-class education: he had gone first to Cheltenham in Gloucestershire, then to Trinity College, Cambridge, where he had distinguished himself in athletics (he rowed in his college boat) and been graduated with honors in the Law Tripos. Upon his return to the United States he had entered the office of Lee, Higginson, where nepotism plus his native abilities virtually assured him an early partnership. He appeared eminently well suited to the lucrative administrative career thus opening before him. He had a commanding physical presence, being a blond Nordic type standing more than six feet tall, long-limbed and muscular, with rugged facial features dominated by piercing blue eyes. He had great force of character, felt by all who came in contact with him, compounded of a stern self-discipline, a hard quick prosaic intelligence, and an absolute confidence in the correctness of his judgments, the moral rightness of his views. His self-confidence was so immense, in fact—he so took for granted his "rightness"—that it made him less self-conscious than most and impressed others, often, as modesty.

But all these qualities had somehow become harnessed, while he was still in England, to an idealism he deemed Christian—a Christianity more muscular than spiritual, perhaps, and (despite the impression he gave of modesty) notably lacking in humility, yet nonetheless sincere. He had been driven by it to consult the great Phillips Brooks of Boston's Trinity Church on the course he should follow and, soon thereafter, had resigned from Lee, Higginson in order to enter the Episcopal Theological School in Cambridge, Massachusetts.

It was while he was serving for a few weeks as clergyman at St. Marks School, and loving the work, that the idea of starting a school of his own was suggested to him. His response was immediately and enthusiastically affirmative. From that moment on he knew precisely what he wanted to do with his life. He wanted to establish a school for upperclass American boys of which, as his prospectus later put it, the headmaster (himself, at the outset) would "be a clergyman of the Protestant Episcopal Church" and in which "every endeavor . . . [would] be made to cultivate manly, Christian character, having regard to moral and physical as well as intellectual development." Religious education would be stressed; so would athletic games and physical fitness in general, along with preparation for entrance into college and "a thorough education for those who are to enter at once upon the active work of life." [21]

He was immensely excited by what was still a brand-new idea when he arrived at Groton for his weekend with the Lawrences. His vivid excitement enhanced the personal attraction he had always had for his host and hostess; they at once took fire from that which burned so brightly in him. Before the fateful Sunday had ended, they all drove out to look over a farm two miles west of the village—a farm owned by James Lawrence and his brother Prescott which, all agreed, would be the perfect site for such a school as Peabody envisaged. A few days later, Peabody in Cambridge received a letter from the Lawrence brothers offering him the ninety-acre farm, provided he would establish his school upon it. Peabody promptly accepted.

Applying himself to the task with characteristic energy, exploiting to the full his many intimate contacts with people of great wealth, including his father, Peabody raised enough money to assure the initiation of his project and assembled a most impressive board of trustees, including Phillips Brooks, J. Pierpont Morgan, S. Endicott Peabody, and James

Lawrence himself. The latter, speaking of all this before the fireplace at Tyn a Coed, told James and Sara Roosevelt that young Peabody was already receiving unsolicited applications for enrollment in his school despite the fact no official announcement that it would be opened had yet been made.* Some fathers were trying to enter sons who would not be old enough actually to enroll for many years to come. Obviously there would be more applications than there could be acceptances during the years ahead, for Peabody was determined to limit severely the size of his school. He would make it highly exclusive. . . .

James and Sara Roosevelt were much impressed. Perhaps on the very day of this fireside conversation, certainly within a day or so afterward, through the good offices of trustee James Lawrence, the name of Franklin Delano Roosevelt was entered upon the list of those who, at the proper age, would enter Groton School.

The Roosevelts returned to Hyde Park in early September.

VII

Some three months later, on December 1, 1883, they went down to New York City to attend the wedding of their young friend Elliott Roosevelt, godfather of their child, whose elder brother Theodore, to the surprise and disapproval of many in their circle, had embarked on a political career and was now a Republican member of the legislature in Albany. (Theodore and his young wife, the former Alice Lee, of course attended the wedding.) Elliott's bride was eighteen-year-old Anna Hall—a tall, slender, graceful girl, golden-haired and blue-eyed, with a perfect complexion, famous in society for her beauty. He had become engaged to her at a house party given at Algonac by Sara's youngest sister, Laura, then nineteen, also a famous beauty.

Laura had a remarkable capacity for happiness and for spreading joy around her. All who knew her loved her, including her infant nephew Franklin, whom she adored. But she died in screaming agony barely seven months after Elliott was married.

It happened on a Sunday morning at Algonac in July, 1884. Laura's (and Sara's) older sister Annie with her husband, Fred Hitch,† had arrived the afternoon before from Shanghai, where he was a Russell and

* The official announcement was not issued until February, 1884, when it was stated that the school would open (as indeed it did) "next autumn" and that "the charge for tuition and board" would be "$500 per annum, payable half yearly in advance."
† His full name was Frederic Delano Hitch. He was a distant cousin of the Delanos.

Company associate, and they with the Warren Delanos waited for Laura to finish dressing for church. Through her bedroom window, as she heated her curling irons over an alcohol lamp, Laura could see her parents and sister strolling and talking together on the lawn. She wore a loose negligee. Perhaps it became caught in the lamp, knocking it over. At any rate, the lamp exploded, spraying burning alcohol all over the girl and abruptly transforming her flimsy negligee into a flaming shroud. She fled, mad with pain and terror, down the stairs and out into the yard, pursued by Fred Hitch, who snatched up a rug from the lower hall as she dashed by. He caught her; he smothered the flames with the rug. But it was then too late. The girl, who had been so lovely to look at only a few minutes before, was now a shrieking mass of charred flesh. She died early next morning.[22]

In general, though, Franklin was remarkably protected against tragedy or even unpleasantness during his early years. Symbolic of parental care and of maternal attitudes toward him was a tale told by his mother decades later. It concerned an episode in the first of eight European trips, each of several months' duration, made by the boy before he was fifteen.

This trip began in the fall of 1884, when the Roosevelts sailed to England. There Franklin was left, with Mamie and Tiddle, at Tunbridge Wells while his parents went on to Bad Kissingen, Bavaria. James, who was beginning to worry about his health (he had developed what his doctors diagnosed as a mild heart condition), took the water cure, as he did most years thereafter, though generally at Bad Nauheim. In early December they returned to England, where, with Franklin and his nurses, they stayed for four months before sailing for home. They embarked at Liverpool on their favorite White Star liner, the *Germanic* (they nearly always crossed on either the *Germanic* or the *Teutonic*), on Good Friday of 1885. Two days out, on Easter Sunday, they were caught in one of the worst North Atlantic storms in many years. The ship was battered by huge seas, which injured several crew members, knocked the captain unconscious, and smashed a bulkhead in the reading room, which was immediately above the Roosevelt cabin. Water poured in. And as it rose, Sara seized her fur coat hanging beside her berth and wrapped it around three-year-old Franklin.

"Poor little boy," she said to her husband, "if he must go down, he is going down warm." [23]

The ship did not go down. Instead, it put back to Liverpool, where the passengers were transferred to the *Adriatic*. And it was perhaps on the *Adriatic* sailing westward, though it may have been on the outward voyage months before, that Franklin, in another of his mother's true stories, made one of his earliest revelations of a self not wholly subordinate to his elders, a self that might resist and impose. He terrified Sara at the dinner table by biting a hunk out of a fragile glass tumbler and holding it in his mouth until she, rushing him on deck, took it out and threw it into the sea. She spoke to him sternly and warned him against a repetition of the act; he seemed properly penitent. But when he returned to the table, he promptly bit a piece out of the tumbler with which the steward had replaced the earlier one. This, too, was removed by a mother who now spoke to her son more sternly than before.

"Franklin," she wanted to know, "where is your obedience?"

"My 'bedience," replied the little boy, unsmiling, "has gone upstairs for a walk."

She shuddered for days thereafter at "the thought of what might have happened had that piece of glass punctured his little windpipe." [24]

But of dangers different in quality from this—dangers from outside the circle of self and family—he encountered few. Ease and comfort enwrapped his childhood years as thickly, softly, as his mother's fur coat had enwrapped his body on the presumably sinking ship. He could not be wholly protected against sickness. Indeed, from early infancy he seems to have been more than normally susceptible to respiratory ailments; his childhood letters and mother's diary are full of reference to his colds and sore throats, though he escaped most of the common children's diseases while a child. But when he did fall ill, the care given him was expressive of his highly privileged status.

Thus at the start of one of his European trips, in 1889, he, then seven years old, was taken aboard ship suffering from a fever. "He has been trying to learn to swim in the river lately, and Dr. Parker thinks it is malaria," wrote Sara in her diary on the day they went aboard. "James and I hate to start with the dear little man ill, but Dr. Parker says the sea voyage is the best thing to break it up. . . ." The fever worsened as they sailed eastward, however, and was diagnosed by the ship's doctor as typhoid. The sick boy received thereafter such special attention as a prince of blood might receive. He was put to bed in the captain's cabin, the captain moving elsewhere. He was met at the Liverpool dock by a Dr. Gemmell, who, a cousin of the captain's, had been summoned by the latter via a telegram from Queenstown. He was taken in an ambulance to the doctor's own home since the hospitals in those days, believing typhoid highly contagious, would not accept typhoid patients. And every day he was confined there he received flowers and milk sent by two top officials of the ship line whose coupled names had the euphony of pig latin, Ismay and Imray, both of whom were longtime friends of James Roosevelt. For convalescence, he was taken to a house in Mixbury rented by Rosy and his family that year. James and Sara left him there with Rosy and Helen while they went down to visit Sir Hugh and Lady Cholmeley at Grantham, near Euston. ("James had some good shooting with Sir Hugh," Sara noted in her diary.) [25]

Seldom and slight, save in the master-servant relationship, were the boy's contacts with people who had to earn their livings. In Europe, his parents mingled almost exclusively with the aristocracy. For instance, in mid-October, 1889, after the boy had fully recovered from his illness, he was taken by his parents to France, where they all lived for several weeks in Versailles and Paris before moving on to Pau. In Pau, James rented an apartment for the winter. They were presented to Princess Christian of Holstein, who was the former Princess Helena of England, daughter of Queen Victoria; they were in constant and intimate social intercourse with the Duke and Duchess of Rutland, Admiral of the Fleet Lord Clanwilliam, and Sir Cameron Gull, MP, among others. It was Sir Cameron who taught Franklin to swim, reportedly by tying one end of a rope around the boy's waist and the other around a long pole and then throwing the boy into the water; when the boy went under for too long, Sir Cameron hoisted him to the surface as if he were a hooked fish at the end of a rod.[26]

Similarly exalted were the Roosevelt social contacts in their own country.

In the winter of 1887 the family lived in Washington, in a house rented from the Belgian ambassador at 1211 I Street. James went there because the political signs and portents of 1880 had been proved accurate in 1884: Governor Grover Cleveland of New York, a friend of his,* had become the first Democrat since 1856 to be elected President of the United States. From this friendship and from his financial contribution to the Democratic Presidential campaign, James could have derived the conventional reward—namely, appointment to a prestigious foreign diplomatic post. Indeed, according to Sara's recollection decades later, Cleveland actually begged her husband to accept an appointment, preferably as minister to Holland. But James steadfastly refused. He was pleased to have Rosy appointed first secretary of the American embassy in Vienna in 1886 (Rosy's contribution to the campaign had been *very* heavy) while he himself, with Sara, derived compensation from their involvement in the highest circles of Washington society.[27]

They were entertained in both the town house and country place of wealthy William C. Whitney, Secretary of the Navy, a New York friend.

* When Cleveland, aged forty-nine, married twenty-two-year-old Frances Folsom in the White House in June, 1886, they received as a wedding gift from the Roosevelts an antique Dutch clock.

Often they dined in the home of John Hay, who had been Assistant Secretary of State in the Hayes administration and was now hard at work (with John G. Nicolay) on a ten-volume "history" of Abraham Lincoln, whom he had served as private secretary during the Civil War. The Hays lived next door to dour Henry Adams* directly across Lafayette Square from the White House—and in the White House, too, as well as at the country place Cleveland had bought for a private retreat after his marriage, the Roosevelts were guests on several occasions.

"Everyone is charming to us," Sara wrote happily in her diary. "Even Franklin knows everybody."

A few days before leaving Washington, James called at the White House to say good-bye to the President and to express his and Sara's regret that they would, because of their leaving town, be unable to accept an invitation to dine with the Clevelands. He brought with him five-year-old Franklin, who would remember that the President, receiving them in his study, seemed tired and depressed. And well he might be. His veto of the Dependent Pension Bill and of every other bill that (to him) smacked of "paternalism" in government, though heartily approved by his visitor of that day, had raised waves of popular wrath that threatened to swamp his bid for reelection in 1888. James did not stay long with his unhappy friend. When he rose to go, taking Franklin by the hand, Grover Cleveland also rose and put his hand on the boy's head.

"My little man, I am making a strange wish for you," he said with great earnestness. "It is that you may never be President of the United States." [28]

Even in those years when the boy was not taken abroad, he lived a highly mobile life—though, as in Europe, his travels did not provide much meaningful exposure of him to points of view and ways of life radically different from his family's.

Every year he visited for extended periods the family seat of the Warren Delanos at Fairhaven, summered on Campobello, was at Algonac for days at a time, was often at Steen Valetje, and lived for several months in New York City, where, after years of renting the furnished house at 31 West Forty-ninth Street, James rented a small apartment in the Hotel Renaissance at 10 West Forty-third. He accompanied his parents on inspection trips over the railroads in which his father had an interest—the Delaware and Hudson; the Louisville, Albany, and Chicago,

* Hay and Adams had jointly employed H. H. Richardson, the most influential American architect of his day, to build them adjoining houses in 1884. A hotel, the Hay-Adams House, now stands on the site.

of which James for a time was president—and on the boats of the Lake
George Steamship Company and the Champlain Transportation Company, which were subsidiaries of the D and H and of which James was
also, for a time, president. For his inspection trips and for other trips
over other lines in pursuit of other interests, James as a top railroad executive was provided with a private car, the Monon, which contained
luxuriously furnished bedrooms and a sitting room and which was
staffed by an excellent black cook, who served also as porter. The boy
Franklin was thus accustomed to domestic travel in the most regal style.

On one occasion he accompanied his father all the way to Superior,
Wisconsin, where James had invested heavily and, in the end, unprofita-
bly in a large business block and a group of dwellings called Roosevelt
Terrace. The trip was made especially memorable for Franklin when,
standing on a pier watching the launching of a whaleback ore boat, the
large wave raised as the boat hit the water rolled over him and swept
him into Lake Superior. Fortunately he was by then a strong swimmer
and was fished out none the worse for having swallowed a little water.[29]

On another occasion, in the fall of 1892, he accompanied his father to
Chicago. James was an alternate commissioner of the World's Fair
which would open in Chicago in 1893—the great Columbian Exposition
celebrating the four hundredth anniversary of America's discovery—
and he came to help with advance arrangements. When he stepped off
the train at the Illinois Central station, he was greeted as "Cousin
James" by a driver of a livery stable equipage. Franklin was astonished.
This driver wore the conventional costume of his occupation (top hat,
bell-shaped coat)—he was but little if any removed from what the ten-
year-old boy regarded as the servant class—yet he greeted the boy's father not merely as an equal but as a member of the family! Astonishment was not mitigated when the boy learned that this stranger really
was "a Roosevelt too"—a distant cousin—as he claimed.[30]

On that same trip or on one a few months later to Chicago, after the
fair had opened, the boy may have heard talk about a woman who had
been an intimate childhood and girlhood friend of Sara's. With Maggie
Carey, Sara had gone to school in Dresden, in Maggie's New York
home she had been a guest for months at a time, and Maggie had often
been at Algonac for extended visits. When Maggie was married in New
York to a Dutch diplomat, Alphonse De Stuers, Sara was one of the
bridesmaids. Thereafter, because Maggie's home was in Europe, the two
friends saw each other but seldom and, though they corresponded for a
time, gradually drifted apart. They were no longer in touch with each
other when Maggie divorced and remarried in circumstances deemed
scandalous by the best society of the 1890's. So it was wholly by chance

that Sara in Chicago encountered Maggie Carey De Stuers Zborowski. She was delighted, eager to restore the old intimacy; Maggie had now a great need for old friends. James, however, forbade it. He would not have his wife associate with so disgraced a woman, and there arose in Sara's breast a rare conflict of loyalties. "It is not easy to make up my mind!" she wrote in her diary. In the end, she yielded to James—and if there was a residue of resentment from the episode, she never revealed it.[31]

Three

➤➤➤⋘⋘⋘

Boyhood of a Patrician

I

BUT FOR all his frequent and prolonged absences from it during his boyhood, Springwood at Hyde Park was home for Franklin Roosevelt—the place he departed from, the place he returned to, up and down the long lane with its double row of maples and between the brownstone gate posts (moved there by his father from fire-ruined Mount Hope) at the lane's entrance. Even the cottage and seashore acres on Campobello, though he lived there for months every summer and was much molded by its island-and-sea activities, was never home as Hyde Park was.

Here were formed the most important, the most enduring of his childhood friendships. His closest friends were two sons of Colonel Archibald Rogers, whose grand neighboring estate, Crumwold, with its huge house of extremely complicated design (Victorian Loire-Château) set atop a long slope that provided the best coasting for miles around in winter, became for him a second home. After Archibald, Jr., died of diphtheria in December, 1889, Edmund P. Rogers was the boy's greatest intimate. With Edmund he dug tunnels and caves in winter snows. With Edmund he built of planks a crow's nest in a great hemlock near Springwood's kitchen garden and there played naval battles. With Edmund, when they were eleven or twelve, he chopped down trees in a cove near the Roosevelt boathouse and built of matched logs lashed together a raft beautiful to behold but one which sank beneath their feet when they launched it, for they had used green timber heavier than water. Others of his playmates were his half niece, Helen Roosevelt, a great tomboy, and his half nephew, Rosy, Jr. (generally called Taddy), a rather strange sort of boy, seemingly a throwback in some ways to Grandfather Isaac Roosevelt; Mary Newbold, daughter of Thomas Jefferson Newbold, whose home was immediately north of Springwood and who, among the Dutchess County gentry, shared with James the unique distinction of being a Democrat;* and Leonora, Mortimer, and Frederick Ashton, the three children of the Reverend Amos T. Ashton, who succeeded Dr. Cady as rector of St. James.

But as an only child on a farm he spent more of his time alone or in the company of adults than most children do and early developed adult ways of talking and acting, so that he often impressed his elders as precocious, far more serious in mien and purpose than most his age. He also impressed them from his earliest years—especially those most intimately associated with him—as more than usually "good." Seldom indeed did his " 'bedience . . . [go] upstairs for a walk." In general he was malleable, tractable, eager to please, and *did* please, learning swiftly the art of doing so if he did not already possess it by instinct. He was only four when, during lunch at Algonac, a maternal aunt remarked upon the sensitivity and adroitness with which he handled a conversational problem. "Franklin," said she, "you really have a great deal of tact." And the little boy, swelling with pride, replied: "Yes, I'm just chock full of tacks." [1]

He was encouraged toward tactfulness and other pleasing qualities by parents who, according to his mother's statement and evident belief, "never tried . . . to influence him against his own tastes and inclinations or to shape his life" [2] but who in actual fact watched and supervised him more closely than most parents do their children. Though he was seldom punished and practically never in any physically painful or spiritually humiliating way, he was left free to follow his natural "tastes and inclinations" only to the extent that they were those of a "gentleman." Any others were deemed by his parents unnatural in a son of theirs. And "gentleman" was a term having for both Sara and James a clear and definite meaning. A gentleman was polite, courteous, being sensitive to and respectful of the rights and feelings of others. He was dignified and self-controlled, maintaining always certain privacies, certain reticences (he never "gave himself away" completely), in consequence of which he was also courageous or at least clung stubbornly to the posture of courage, refusing to cringe or whine under such blows as came to him. Finally, he strove to be tolerant of the crudities, the vulgarities, the ill-bred assertiveness of those less advantaged than he and was willing to reach down a helping hand to them, that they might be raised to a level more nearly his own. In the attitudes that Sara and

* Newbold was elected state senator in 1884. He was the last Dutchess County Democrat to be elected to that office until 1910.

James maintained toward the world outside their own class, in the attitudes they instilled in their son, there was a large element of *noblesse oblige.*

Both parents, but Sara especially, were concerned to keep their son from being spoiled by too much attention, too much open adoration, and too few outer checks on the part of those employed to have charge of him. Mamie and Tiddle both so doted on him that they were sometimes protective of him even against parental corrections. One day Sara, having heard that Franklin had been misbehaving, went to Tiddle (Elespie) to ask about it. The Scots girl made evasive reply. "They tell me he has faults," she said, "but I can not see them." [3] His mother saw a few— and one fault that disturbed her was her son's insistence upon winning always when, as a small child, he played games. If he played Old Maid with his nurses and lost, he was furious until the stigma of "old maid" (though he knew not what it meant) was removed from him. If he played Steeplechase with toy horses and lost, his response was the same.

It was while he played the latter that his mother undertook to correct this fault. When he was almost four, he challenged his mother to a Steeplechase and his horse had twice been beaten when he demanded an exchange of horses because his mother's, he insisted, was "a better horse." The exchange was made, but to no avail. He lost the next race, too, and his temper with it. His mother gathered up the toys. She would not play with him again, she said, until he had learned to take a beating gracefully. The treatment was effective; no one ever again "saw a lack of sportsmanship in Franklin," according to his mother.[4]

His days were patterned by a time schedule against which a less tractable boy would occasionally have rebelled. He seems never to have done so. But one day when he was five years old, his mother found him sunk in an emotional depression out of which he could be lifted by no effort she made to amuse or distract him. This was unprecedented. She became somewhat alarmed. She finally asked him point blank if he was unhappy, and he confessed that he was; she asked him why, and he replied ("his voice had a desperate note . . .") that he longed "for freedom." She told James of this that evening, and after discussion, they agreed to give their son complete freedom for one day. The next morning Franklin was told by his mother that he was exempt from all ordinary rules, save for appearance at mealtime, until evening; he could go where he pleased, do as he pleased, and need give no accounting of his activities. The boy took full advantage of his opportunity. His parents never asked how he spent that day. They only knew that he returned in the evening much dirtier and tireder and hungrier than usual, ate heartily, and went to an early bed. On the following day, "quite of his own accord, he went contentedly back to his routine." It is probable, however, that Sara, who had been sometimes accused by her husband of "nagging the boy," was from that time forth a bit more careful than she had been to avoid excessive regulation of him.[5]

But she certainly did not consult his natural "tastes and inclinations" on such matters as dress and hairstyle as he grew out of infancy into boyhood. Sara was not immune to the virus spread by a best-selling novel of those years, *Little Lord Fauntleroy,* and her son suffered accordingly. Until he was five years old, he wore long curls and dresses. Thereafter his mother dressed him for a time in kilts, complete with a miniature sporran at his belt and a beribboned Highlander cap. Not until he was nearly eight did he wear pants; he was graduated then to cute little sailor suits. And he was nearly eight and a half when, in a brief letter to his absent father, he proudly announced that, his mother having left that morning, "I am going to have my bath alone"—evidently for the first time! [6]

Nor was it in response to any freely expressed natural inclination of his that he was required by his mother to take lessons in drawing, for which he had some but no special aptitude; dancing lessons, which he seems thoroughly to have enjoyed; and piano lessons, which he actively disliked and during which he abundantly demonstrated an almost total lack of music appreciation or performing talent. No matter. His mother's purpose was not to make an artist of him in any field but to cultivate his emotional sensibilities and refine his tastes.

She had the same purpose in mind when she read aloud to him as a little boy the stories that had moved her to tears when she was a child— stories with such titles as *Misunderstood, Alone in London,* and *Piccolomini*—as well as *Little Men* and *Robinson Crusoe* and *Swiss Family Robinson.* Years later she objected strenuously to the theory of child rearing that would keep sentimental works from the growing child because their sentimentality promoted a falseness of emotional attitudes, a weakness of character. She insisted that, on the contrary, they developed a child's capacity to feel, they stimulated an emotional development in the absence of which children grew up "like hard little apples." But it was she rather than her son who, outwardly at least, was affected by the "sad parts" of the stories she read. She choked up. Tears came to her eyes. And her son, looking up from the toys with which he played as she read, would ask in mock wonderment, "What's the matter, Mummy? Why do you speak like that?" [7] He himself showed no such feelings at all, and his mother, speaking of this to her women friends, indicated a pride in him that he did not, that he was in this respect thoroughly "masculine." For if she did not want him to grow up a "hard little apple," even less did she want him to grow up soft and mushy.

He might conceivably have done so.

He was as a small boy (the fact would seem strange to those who knew him in later years) painfully shy, and this shyness remained as he grew older, though he learned to dissemble it with increasing success. By the time he was in his teens his mother was inclined to believe that only she fully appreciated "what a time Franklin had in hiding the self-consciousness he felt when he spoke to any one other than the members of the immediate family." She recalled how, when he was four and five, he accompanied her as she made her morning rounds of the house, chattering away happily until they reached the kitchen. There, facing the cook and kitchen help, he was struck dumb.[8] He hid behind his mother's skirts, unresponsive to the cook's efforts to make friends with him. And so he was with others, including his parents' friends. Obviously within the realm of possibility for such a boy—an only child, pampered and overmothered, protected to an unusual degree against harsh competitions with his contemporaries—was a developing effeminacy.

But his mother's was not the sole parental influence upon him. As we have seen, she deferred to her husband in nearly all things, willingly subordinating herself in ways that could not but impress on her son the "proper" nature and importance of the masculine role. Moreover, James played very actively the role of father to his son while the latter was a child, despite the great difference in their ages.

Sara's diaries during the years of her son's boyhood are full of references to activities her husband and son engaged in together. Typical are entries for early March, 1888, when immense snows fell on the Hudson River Valley. "James took Franklin out ice-boating . . . ," Sara wrote. "James coasted with Franklin yesterday and the day before. . . . Franklin tobogganing with James." The two were constant companions when the father was not away on business. And most of their companionship was of a healthful, manly, out-of-doors kind. The son who when small accompanied his mother on her morning rounds of the house also accompanied his father, often sitting on his father's shoulders, as the latter made his inspections of the stables and greenhouse, of fields and woods. The boy developed a lifelong love of trees, a lifelong commitment to forest conservation.

He learned to ride at an early age. A photograph of him at the age of two and a half, his long blond curls resting on the wide lace collar of his dress, shows him seated in a wicker-basket saddle atop a donkey led by Mamie while his first pet dog, a Spitz named Budgy, trots along beside them. He was not yet seven when he was given a Welsh pony, Debby, with the understanding that he was to care for her himself, feed and water and groom her, for his father wanted to develop what the boy seems to have had to an unusual degree from the beginning—a sense of responsibility coupled with generally sober, sound judgment.

He was held responsible, too, for the care of his dog. He always had one, from the time of his earliest memory. The Spitz puppy of his babyhood was succeeded by a huge St. Bernard named Nardo and he, in turn, by a Newfoundland named Monk. Then Franklin's Uncle Warren Delano gave him a particularly fine dog, a red setter whose full name was Mr. Marksman. Marksman was always with him in Hyde Park, accompanying him on virtually every hike or ride or visit to neighbors. Twice daily he carried a plate of food from Springwood's kitchen to Marksman's bed in the stables.[9]

He developed early, and was permitted to indulge, always with the understanding that he must be careful and responsible, a passion for shooting which his mother described as "insatiable." She confessed that if she had had her way, "he should never have gotten off to such an early start, but already at eleven he had his own gun, given him by his father, and had established a reputation among his playmates for being a crack shot." [10]

He developed early, too, a passion for boats and open water. The very first letter he ever wrote (in 1887, when he was five), a few painfully scrawled lines addressed to his mother who was confined to her room in Springwood with a bad cold, had as enclosures a couple of nautical pen-and-ink drawings—one a sketch of three sailboats, the other a quite detailed depiction of a large vessel driven by both sail and steam.[11] This fascinated interest grew stronger as he grew older. To its shaping, Campobello and Fairhaven—the Atlantic as it thrust into the Bay of Fundy and New Bedford Harbor—were more important than Hyde Park, but there was much sailing on the Hudson, too, and he was making and sailing crude toy boats at Springwood and Algonac before he could read and write.

As a small child he listened for hours utterly absorbed in stories his mother told of her girlhood voyage on the *Surprise* to China, stories his maternal grandfather and uncles told of Delano whalers and China clippers and the fighting ships of the Civil War, highly imaginative stories his nurse Mamie told of allegedly true sea adventures she herself or others of her acquaintance had had. Before he himself could read, he loved to be read to out of books about the sea. When he was five and six and seven, he used often to sit upon his grandfather's stone wharf at Fairhaven looking out over the many old whaleships (they made a forest of masts and spars) still anchored in New Bedford Harbor and imagine what the harbor had been like in the old days when scores of ships sailed out every year for the farthest corners of the earth and what the ships themselves had been like, the life aboard them during voyages lasting often a year and more. In the attic at Fairhaven were canvas-bound logbooks of whaling masters of the early nineteenth century. He pored over them for hours and wrote of them when he was a man: "Stencilled whales in the margins, the speaking of other ships, the total of the catch, the visits to Fayal, to the Falklands, to Unalaska, the accountings to the owners, the lay of the crew—here was a tale." [12] And it was a tale he never tired of. He began to dream of going to sea himself, of Annapolis and a career in the U.S. Navy.

When he was nine, he happily announced in a letter to an aunt that "Papa is going to buy a cutter that will go by naphtha and we are going to sail it at Campobello and here." [13] A few months later he was photographed in a short-pants sailor suit, his little face drawn and tense as, in heavy seas off Campobello, he struggled with the wheel of the fifty-one-foot sailing yacht (it did have an auxiliary motor which "went by naphtha") that his father had bought—the *Half-Moon*, launched in July, 1891. The *Half-Moon* became for him a laboratory of sea training. Even as a boy he was a skilled sailor, remarkably knowledgeable concerning the rocks and shallows, the tides and currents of the Bay of Fundy and the coast of Maine below it, competent to navigate and handle a boat under sail or motor power. He would increase his skill and knowledge when, aged sixteen, he was given by his parents a twenty-one-foot knockabout of his own. He would name her *New Moon*. Summer after summer thereafter he would sail her at every opportunity, generally with friends aboard.

From an early age he with other neighbor boys had a weekly training session under a man competent to direct their use of carpenter's tools. They made birdhouses, toys, model boats, articles of furniture. During one period a man instructor came weekly to Springwood to teach not only manual training but also gymnastics. And Franklin responded to the training with great facility, for he loved to work with his hands, loved to work with wood and tools. Before he reached adolescence, he had developed some of a cabinetmaker's skills.

Thus was his masculinity both expressed and, by paternal and environmental influences, continuously encouraged.

Joined to it, despite his shyness, was a strong will to power, an instinct for command, and an ardent, if often masked, competitiveness. If no longer guilty of such flagrant violations of good sportsmanship as he had committed when nearly four, he lost none of his desire to win every game and be first in every group enterprise. His mother noted that, when he played with other children, he was the one who gave orders, which they "for reasons I have never been able to fathom" generally obeyed. She remonstrated with him one day when she overheard him issuing commands to a boy with whom he was digging a play fort. "But, Mummie," he replied, looking at her with perfect seriousness, "if I didn't give the orders, nothing would happen!" [14]

II

His earliest formal schooling began in October, 1888, when he went for two hours each day to Crumwold, there to be tutored with the Rogers children by their German governess. But well before this, he had learned in his own home to read and write sufficiently well to compose, with help, simple letters. Under the tutelage at Crumwold he learned the rudiments of the German language as well—lessons improved by his own German governess at Springwood, Fräulein Reinhardt. [15]

The latter—an extremely tense, high-strung, humorless woman who would ultimately be confined in a mental institution—was the first of a succession of governesses, each responsible for his schooling. One of them, when he was eight, was a Viennese woman hired sight unseen but on the basis of the highest possible recommendations while the Roosevelts were in Paris. James paid all her considerable travel expenses from Vienna to Paris, where, almost from the moment of her arrival, Sara greatly disliked her. When they all went together to London and occupied quarters smaller than those in Paris, the situation became for the mother unbearable. But Franklin, repeatedly asked for his opinion of the woman, replied merely that she was "all right." Not until his mother made it plain that she disliked the Viennese and would prefer not to take her back with them to America, though this would be done if the boy wished it—not until then did Franklin confess that he, too, disliked her intensely, that she was "perfectly awful" and had been dubbed in his own mind "the Long-legged Duckling." Why, then, had he not said so? asked his somewhat exasperated mother. Because, he replied, his father had "gone to so much trouble and spent so much money to get her." He felt "it wouldn't be right for me to complain!" [16]

While they were in London, the Roosevelts hired the woman who became, of all his governesses, the most important by far to Franklin's development. Having had bad luck with a German-speaking governess, they decided to try a French-speaking one (they were particularly anxious, in any case, to have their son perfect his French), and they communicated this decision with other specifications to an employment agency. Soon several applicants appeared in succession at the Roosevelts' London hotel suite, among them a slender slip of a girl, barely five feet tall and only nineteen years old, who had just left a post in Scotland where she had had charge of four boys and a girl and who, she confessed, was attracted by the prospect of having only a single boy in charge. She was hesitant, however, about journeying all the way to America. Her hesitancy was overcome by the boy himself—she thought him most attractive—who whispered quite loudly to his parents, "Take that one. I like her. She smiles all the time." [17]

Her name was Jeanne Sandoz. She was a native of Switzerland. She remained at Hyde Park for more than two years, during which she "more than anyone else . . . laid the foundations of my education," as Franklin himself wrote her more than forty years later.

She did not do so without initial difficulties. *"Franklin travaille bien mais l'obéissance hors des leçons laisse beaucoup à désirer,"* she wrote on her first report card to his parents.[18] For her charge was entering the age when a normal boy—at the climax of childhood, in anticipation of adolescence—is most mischievous, smart-alecky, callous in his dealings with others, and young Franklin was all these things. He was forever trying to be "funny," regaling his governess with joking riddles (Question: "What animals are always ready to travel?" Answer: "Elephants— they always have their trunks with them"). His letters of this period, sometimes signed "Nilknarf" or "Tlevesoor D. Nilknarf," were often characterized by a hyperbole he but few others could have deemed hilarious ("I am dying of school fever and you will be horrified to hear that my temperature is 150° . . . Mlle. . . . wears skirts 7 yards in circumference. I am flourishing and have only fallen 3 times from the top story window"). And since Mlle. Sandoz lacked the physical presence (she was shorter than he) which, of itself alone, would have given her frowns, her admonitions a disciplinary effect, she had to rely wholly on moral suasion, appealing to his dutifulness, his eagerness to accommodate and please his elders, and that real liking for her he sometimes showed he had. One day when he had been particularly obnoxious she issued a flat ultimatum. "Frankie," she said coldly, "your father is wasting his money and I am wasting my time. I shall leave you." The threat worked. He at once "straightened out," as she told an interviewer four decades later, and the two "became fast friends." [19]

She was an excellent teacher, capable of imparting to her pupil some of the enthusiasm she herself felt for nearly every subject in her curriculum. He became a master of the French language under her tutelage, French being not merely one subject among others for her but the language in which nearly all the others were taught. She had a rather surprising interest in natural science. Often she chose for her subject matter information out of physics and chemistry when she gave him dictation —dictation he took down in French and then translated into English. Thus his translation of the *"Dictée du 29 juillet, '92"* says among other things: "Salt disolves [*sic*] ice for this reason: Water freezes at 32 degrees but salt and water will not freeze till the air is twenty-five degrees colder. . . . Light is rapped [*sic*] undulations of a fluid eather [*sic*], made sensible to the eye by striking the optic nerve. . . ." (Each *faute* of spelling was marked by Mlle. Sandoz, Franklin being required to write each misspelled word correction twice.) Another page of translation asserts that "Chemistry is the most important science with which man is acqanted [*sic*]. The application of steam and gas to general purposes and the discovery of gunpowder which has changed the whole habits of society, are among the benefits which science bestowed on manskind [*sic*]." [20]

In all his formal schooling, the proportionate emphasis on scientific among other kinds of knowledge would never be greater than it was in the curriculum imposed by Mlle. Sandoz, and it was accompanied by a no less surprising emphasis, in her teaching, upon a concern for social welfare inspired and sustained by her Christian faith. She preached the Social Gospel, insisting that the spirit of the New Testament must permeate man's economic and political activities if these were truly to prosper. She identified not with the rich and wellborn and powerful, but with the common people, the exploited poor. She spoke out against the criminal selfishness of the "masters of money." She strove to arouse in her charge some sense of the social responsibility, the concern for those less fortunate than he, that ought in her view to accompany his abundant privileges. And some of this showed dimly through a typically hyperbolic composition entitled *"Sur l'Histoire Ancienne"* (though it dealt only with ancient Egypt) written by the boy as an assignment from his teacher. "The working people had nothing . . . ," he wrote. "The kings made them work so hard and gave them so little that by wingo! they nearly starved and by jinks! they had hardly any clothes so they died in quadrillions." Sethos, "the first king they speak of after Rameses," was, he wrote, "a negroe" and "a nasty kind . . . [who] was so cruel to the poor people that they had to die." [21]

The composition reveals not only substantive effects of Mlle. Sandoz's teaching, but also something of the pupil's personal attitude toward her. Implicit in its bantering tone, which denied any deep sympathy for the despised and injured, was a felt masculine superiority to the earnestness, the moral fervor, with which the girl expounded her social views. The absurd hyperbole was in part an assertion of male "realism"

against female "sentimentality." And he was destined to carry this attitude across nearly three decades, well into his public career, if indeed he
ever completely lost it.

As for Mlle. Sandoz's attitude toward Franklin, it was, by her own account, one of admiration, as well as affection. He charmed her with his
personality, impressed her with his mind. His *joie de vivre* seemed immense and unbroken. He seemed never to be bored. She found remarkable the range of his active interests, the quick ease with which he
learned, the swiftness with which he read (as he grew older he could
sweep up whole pages at a glance), the retentiveness of his memory. She
became convinced that he would go far. To his mother, whom she confessed she found *"très formidable,"* intimidatingly so, she often said,
"Frankie will distinguish himself." [22] She probably manifested a greater
concern that he do so than his mother did, since Sara, the *grande dame,*
continued serene in her confidence that she and hers had been from
birth at the apex of all the world that counted, that there was really no
farther Franklin could go in that direction, and that there was nothing
of value to be gained by his going far in the direction of mere popular
acclaim whereby his name (and hers) would become part of the vocabulary of the vulgar.

It was during Mlle. Sandoz's tenure that Franklin had his only experience of a public school. In May, 1891, the Roosevelts crossed the Atlantic on the White Star liner *Teutonic,* went to Bad Nauheim, and there,
while James took his annual cure, enrolled their son for six weeks in a
small Volksschule. He enjoyed it hugely. To two of his cousins he wrote:
"I go to public school with a lot of little mickies, and we have German
reading, German dictation, the history of Siegfried, and arithmetic . . .
and I like it very much." According to his German schoolmaster, the
boy was "an unusually bright young fellow" with "an engaging manner,
and he was always so polite, that he was soon one of the most popular
children in the school." His mother recorded a doubt "if he learns very
much," but certainly his command of the German language was much
improved.[23]

In early 1893, Mlle. Sandoz, who had evidently been engaged to
marry before she accepted her position with the Roosevelts, left Hyde
Park, returned to her native land, and there became Mme. Rosat-San-
doz of the watchmaking town of Le Locle, Switzerland. "Franklin's
mother gave me three dozen pieces of silver from their collection
marked with their initials, the same pattern as my new ones, and a white
silk dress for my wedding," she remembered decades later.[24] Franklin
wrote to her in her new home, in French, asking her about her voyage
and asking also questions about Swiss politics. He wanted to know,

among other things, who was the President of Switzerland, whether there was a representative of each canton in the Federal Assembly, and how many senators there were for each canton. He signed his letter

Je suis
Votre fidèle
Tlevesoor[25]

This last of Franklin's governesses was succeeded by a male tutor, Arthur Dumper of Cleveland, a personable young man, quick of mind and lively, interested in outdoor sports and nature studies, who established an immediate rapport with his charge and got on well also with his employers. The boy was eleven when the tutor came. Had his parents adhered to the general rule, he would have spent a year thereafter preparing for entrance into Groton at the normal age of twelve—an event presumably determined on Campobello when Franklin was only a year and a half. Instead, because his parents could not bear to part with him, he remained with them for three more years during which his subject matter education more than kept pace, on the whole, with that of his contemporaries in boarding school.

For this, Mr. Dumper's tutelage was only partially responsible. Of probably equal, if not greater, importance were the boy's collecting hobbies, already actively pursued when the new tutor arrived but continued thereafter with increasing ardor.

When he was nine, he started a postage-stamp collection.[26] He was no doubt stimulated to do so by his mother, who had indulged this hobby as a girl, had acquired some of the earliest issues following the adoption of adhesive stamps (by Britain in 1840, by the United States in 1847), and had added rare Hong Kong and Chinese issues during her years at Rose Hill on Macao. She had continued collecting until she was in her early twenties, her round-the-world travels giving her abundant opportunities to acquire foreign issues. She had then presented her collection to her younger brother Fred, under whom it was greatly enlarged and who now watched with approval his young nephew's increasingly serious interest in philately. He watched for a year. Then, one day, he presented his collection to the boy, who thus, at age ten, acquired a more valuable collection than many an active and affluent philatelist acquires in a lifetime. He continuously added to it (an early order from the Scott Stamp and Coin Company of New York, recorded in a school exercise book, was "*Reçu le 2 Avril 1892,*" and cost $66.14).[27] He pasted stamps into his albums with utmost care, spent hours studying them through a magnifying glass, made detailed notes upon them between the pasted rows. And from this enterprise he learned a great deal about geography, foreign affairs, and world history.

Simultaneously he began a collection of birds' eggs and nests. Leonora Ashton, daughter of the then rector of St. James, never forgot an Easter egg hunt at the Roosevelt home to which she and her two brothers were invited, a party planned for Franklin, who, however, was nowhere to be seen for some time after all the guests had assembled. Finally he appeared, walking slowly across the lawn, carrying with the greatest care a robin's egg for his collection.

But eggs and nests were no substitutes for the birds themselves. He conceived the ambitious project of shooting and mounting one of every species of bird in Dutchess County, and it was for this purpose that his father gave him, at about the time of Mr. Dumper's arrival, the gun his mother was inclined to object to, a collector's gun. His father stipulated that he not shoot during the mating season, never shoot a nesting bird, and not kill more than one of any species. The stipulation became his rule. But during the next two years he killed representatives of more than 300 species, male and female, and, moreover, mastered the technique of stuffing and mounting the specimens himself. The latter operation was significant of character. He had not realized at the outset how unpleasant, even nauseating, were initial portions of the taxidermist's techniques. His mother remembered that learning them by performing them, he sometimes "turned quite green." [28] Nevertheless, he persevered. Not until he had proved to himself that he could become a thoroughly competent taxidermist did he abandon the art and have his birds mounted thereafter by a professional in Poughkeepsie.

He had developed a professional competency as an ornithologist by the time he was fourteen. On January 1, 1893, he began to keep a bird diary which, when he ended it on August 6, 1896, contained seventy-nine pages of carefully reported sightings. In the winter of 1893, when he had his eleventh birthday, he wrote a composition on "Birds of the Hudson River Valley" which he read to the assembled family at Algonac one evening, delighting his maternal grandfather so much that Warren Delano, by then confined by a stroke to a wheelchair, presented to the boy a life membership in New York's Natural History Museum. It was as a member, therefore, that Franklin gave the museum's bird department a vireo's nest in 1895 and ten pine grosbeak study skins in 1896. In the latter year he also presented three starfish and four *Astrophyton agassiz* to the invertebrate section.[29] Meanwhile, his collection of Hudson River birds became the most comprehensive ever made.

Nor was knowledge and pleasure all the boy gained from his hobby. He gained also in social poise, for his ornithological interest grew great enough to overcome on occasion the shyness that continued, throughout his boyhood, to inhibit his relations with people outside his immediate circle.

A few months after his grandfather's gift of the museum membership he was with his parents in England, where they all were invited to visit a country house reported to contain the finest stuffed bird collection in Europe. When his parents were forced by business to decline the invitation, eleven-year-old Franklin astonished them by asking if he might make the visit without them, though he had not then even met his prospective host and hostess. His mother, incredulous, asked him if he was sure he really wanted to. He was. "I'd go anywhere to see those birds," he said flatly. Permission granted, he took a train by himself from London to the country place in Nottinghamshire, spent hours studying the collection, and had altogether a grand time, marred only by his being returned to London, at his visit's end, in the company of his hosts' housekeeper. The evinced lack of confidence in his ability to take care of himself was, as his mother surmised, a blow to his pride.[30]

On this trip he carried with him the engraved, elaborately gold-decorated card which betokened his membership in the Natural History Museum. He carried it with him everywhere. And it proved useful in the summer of his fourteenth year, when he and his tutor went one day in London to see the great bird collection in the South Kensington Museum. Their visit happened to coincide with that of the Prince of Wales, later Edward VII, who was dedicating a new wing of the building. Entrance to the museum was by invitation only. But a determined Franklin took out his Natural History card and handed it to Mr. Dumper to present to the liveried doorman, who, after perusing it and consulting top-hatted officials beside him, gave it back and bowed them in as a couple of distinguished American scientists.[31]

The South Kensington Museum episode took place during the closing months of Mr. Dumper's stay with the Roosevelt family, in the summer of 1896—a summer during which Franklin visited Holland for the first time (his parents had not been there since their honeymoon) and, after his parents had settled in Bad Nauheim for his father's annual cure, made with his tutor a highly educative bicycle tour through western Germany on an allowance of four marks (then about a dollar) a day for each of them. He was forcibly impressed by the Teutonic passion for imposed order, for coercive authority. He and Dumper were arrested four times in one day—for picking cherries from an orchard along the road, for taking their bicycles into a railway station, for riding into Strasbourg in the evening (it was illegal to enter "a fortified city of the

Empire on, with, or in a wheeled vehicle after nightfall"), and for running over and killing a goose. Franklin's mastery of German, coupled with his winning ways, freed them from fines for the first three of their transgressions, but for killing the goose they were fined five marks. They returned to Bad Nauheim with a considerable portion of their allowance still in their pockets, having made many of their meals of black bread and cheese and slept for the smallest of fees in peasants' cottages.[32]

Not long thereafter they all sailed for America, each acutely aware that they approached a season of endings and beginnings. In early June, immediately before leaving for Europe, Franklin had taken the prescribed examinations for entrance into Groton's III Form (Peabody's school employed the British classification of forms, of which there were six) and had easily passed them. In early September, immediately after their return to Hyde Park, Mr. Dumper left the family, his tutorial duties ended.

There followed for the Roosevelt mother and son a day whose every hour ached with farewell, whose every act and sensation were characterized by finality: this is the last, never again can we be as we are now. They spent the whole of that day together. "We dusted his birds and he had a swim in the river," wrote Sara into her diary that evening. "I looked on. And with a heavy heart." [33]

The next day, with his parents and half nephew Taddy, who had already been in boarding school for three years, and with Mrs. Rogers and Edmund, who was to enter II Form, he made for the first time a journey he was to take over and over again during the next four years. By train (the Boston and Maine) they went to Ayer, and by horse and buggy they went from Ayer to Groton, a few miles distant. He put up a brave front, so did his parents, as he was introduced to the headmaster. And the following morning he maintained this brave front as his mother kissed him and his father shook his hand and he watched their buggy down the drive and out of sight. His face was pale, however, and his lips trembled.

As for his parents:

"It is hard to leave our darling boy . . . ," wrote Sara in her diary. "James and I both feel this parting very much." [34]

III

He came now to the first great change in his life and the first great challenge. How would he fare, what were his qualifications for success, in the small but highly competitive world into which he was now being thrust?

Physically and in certain basic emotional ways he was, at fourteen, less mature than most boys his age. He *seemed* in general much more mature than he actually was, for he was abnormally sensitive to the effect he produced on others and many of his words and deeds in relation to adults were those of an actor responding to the mood and demands of an audience rather than true expressions of an inward self.[35] His voice had not yet begun to change; he would sing soprano in the Groton choir all through his first year in the school and into the autumn of his second year, when he was well on the way to his sixteenth birthday. He was slightly built, very far from his full growth. He stood only three inches above five feet in height and weighed only a little more than 100 pounds. He lacked the heft, the hard bulk of muscle required for success in football or other contact sports of which, up till that time, he had played virtually none at all. His health was generally good; his complexion was clear; his blue eyes were bright. But his general appearance —his posture and facial expression—was characterized by a certain delicacy and fastidiousness.

He took many photographs of himself that year, less from vanity, one suspects, than from a desire to experiment with his expensive camera's self-timer, then a new device. The resultant pictures appear to contradict the general impression he made on family and friends and sustained in his letters that he was always self-assured and cheerful and "never bored," a far happier adolescent on the whole than most, emerging thus from a remarkably privileged, carefree, happy boyhood. He has in the photographs a rather supercilious, sullen look, hinting at inward insecurities. His mouth is always tight and small, seemingly clamped hard upon the symbolic silver spoon, and there is no more of a smile in his eyes than on his lips. He is dressed always as a dude, wearing what for a middle-class boy would be party or Sunday clothes, but it is evident that even were he wearing the roughest garb, none could mistake him for a callus-handed farm boy or a tough child of the city streets. He was indubitably a young patrician, perhaps (even thus early) "different from you and me," as F. Scott Fitzgerald later claimed the "very rich" to be, in that he was "soft where we are hard, and cynical where we are trusting. . . ."[36]

He had developed, by age fourteen, a mind extraordinarily facile, able to acquire and retain factual information with far more ease than most can do. The increasing speed with which he read has already been noted; the amount he had already read, considering the demands made on his time by his many other interests, was equally remarkable. He evinced relatively little interest in fiction, after having read the standard works for boys. He was much more interested in history. When in his early teens, he raced through historical works that would have bored most his age: Parkman's *Montcalm and Wolfe*, for one; Mahan's epoch-making *The Influence of Sea Power upon History*, for another. Among magazines, though he had reveled in *St. Nicholas* as a child, his favorites by the time of his departure for Groton were the *Illustrated London News*, *Survey Graphic*, and *Scientific American*, then a magazine considerably less "scientific" in content than it is today. His appetite for facts appeared insatiable. His mother had once found him in bed with Webster's *Unabridged Dictionary* propped open against his knees, he having carried it up from the stand which normally held it in the library. When she asked him "what on earth" he was doing with the huge tome, he replied that he was reading it because "there are lots of words I don't understand," and that he was "almost half way through." [37]

But reading was by no means the whole, it was not even the most important, source of his general information. He fed his appetite for facts through unusual powers of observation, unusual abilities to listen, and active experience. He, more than most, learned by doing. He was able to operate mentally on two levels simultaneously, with surprising efficiency. Often as a boy he had worked with his stamp collection while his mother read to him, and one day he had seemed to her so utterly absorbed in them and so deaf to her reading that she became annoyed. "I don't believe you are hearing a word," she said irritably. Whereupon, looking up at her with a grin, he had repeated verbatim the whole of the last paragraph she had read, adding by way of explanation that he would "be ashamed if I couldn't do at least two things at once." [38]

In consequence of all this he had already packed into his brain, by the fall of 1896, an unusual quantity and range of information. About ornithology, philately, photography, carpentry, navigation, seamanship in general, naval architecture, world geography, political and military and naval history, foreign languages, foreign customs, forest conservation, animal husbandry, agronomy (especially pasture management and field crops), horticulture, agriculture in general—about these the sum total of his information, at age fourteen, exceeded what many acquire in a lifetime.

It was not, however, connected-up information forming, then or perhaps ever, a truly organized body of knowledge. His mother once described him as being, when he was very young, "a rather introspective little fellow," but this assessment of him is borne out by no other observation. On the evidence—though he had certainly his secret life, more so than most—he was among the least introspective of boys, with no natural bent toward self-examination. His mental interests were turned almost wholly outward; the facility of his mind was purchased, at least in part, at the price of profundity. For he probably could not have gathered up facts and ideas so swiftly, so easily, had he possessed or been inclined to develop overall conceptions into which these must be integrated. There might then have been resistance to the inward flow of more information than could be digested. As it was, he collected and classified facts and ideas in much the same way as he collected and classified stamps, birds, historical memorabilia, and naval books and prints. They did not become integral parts or illustrative examples of any basic (if necessarily, at fourteen, rudimentary) philosophy; they were never inwardly related aspects of an overall system of meaning. They seem to have remained, simply, collections.

What he had in lieu of a philosophy was a certain kind of faith. At fourteen it was certainly no profound religious faith. His religious belief, indeed, was of the simplest. He believed in a loving God who had created and now ruled a world which must therefore be essentially or at least mostly good and in Jesus Christ as the Son of God who had preached the Word of God and whose earthly sufferings had redeemed a sinful mankind. He believed in the immortality of the soul and that a good life is rewarded by heaven. This faith was fused with the music and ritual and formal doctrine of the Episcopal Church, whose teachings he accepted quite literally (he would never have the slightest interest in theological complexities, any more than he had in other abstract theorizing) and whose services he enjoyed. It is true that he had sometimes faked little illnesses on Sunday mornings, when his parents were away, to avoid attending St. James' at Hyde Park or St. Anne's on Campobello, but he had not done so often. In general, he *wanted* to worship in the Sunday congregation. He derived from worship an inner peace.

An effect of his faith was a profoundly optimistic attitude toward the world and its challenges. He had at the core of him a serene unexamined confidence in the beneficent ongoingness of the universe. He was convinced that however bad things might be at the moment, they were bound to come right in the end and that his own enterprise, however frustrated at the moment, must ultimately prosper, if only he and others played their proper parts, were patient, and placed their trust in God. Indeed, there were times when he seemed perfectly assured that he himself was a special favorite of the Lord's. One day he had come up from the river woods to the house at Springwood, not running or even walking particularly fast, to get his bird gun. He told his mother he had sighted a winter wren in a great tree beside the river, several hundred yards from the house, and was going to shoot it for his collection. His mother laughed at him. Did he really think that wren was going to oblige him by waiting in the tree to be killed? "Oh, yes," the boy replied with confidence, "he'll wait." And he went back down the hill with his gun, still in no hurry. A little while later, to his mother's astonishment, he returned to the house with the tiny wren dead in his hand.[39] There were other instances of this sort, seeming to manifest his power of positive thinking, his special stand-in with God.

Joined to his optimistic faith and sustained by it was a rare physical courage, a rare ability to bear pain stoically. One morning aboard the private car *Monon,* as the boy arose from his berth, a heavy steel curtain rod fell upon his forehead. He called to his mother, who, having just awakened him, was only a step away with her back turned. She turned to see a huge ugly bump rising just below her son's hairline with a bloody gash across it that widened as the bump swelled. Alarmed, she moved to call his father, who was at breakfast with friends at the other end of the car. The boy wouldn't let her. He insisted that she patch him up with court plaster and say nothing to anyone, and he spent most of that day on the observation platform so that he could hide his wound under his cap.[40]

On Campobello in the summer of 1896 (we anticipate a bit), he was walking with his friend Joe Lovering, each boy striking at pebbles with a long heavy stick, when the stick in Joe's hand slipped at the end of a wide swing and struck Franklin in the mouth with great force. One tooth was broken off, another chipped, and his lip was cut inside and out. The nerve of the broken tooth hung down, nakedly exposed. The boy was in excruciating pain when he came up to the house. Nevertheless, he attempted to hide the extent of his injury from his mother, who discovered it only after she took note of his pale, drawn face and of his reluctance to answer her questions about his cut and swollen lip in other than closed-mouth monosyllables. A considerable time was required to get him to the dock at Welshpool and ferry him across to Eastport, where their summer dentist, a Dr. Hodgkins, extracted the nerve under gas. He bore this long anguish, as his mother proudly recorded, "without fuss." [41]

Evident in both these displays of stoicism is that thoughtfulness of others, that dutiful concern for their rights and sensibilities, which he had manifested when asked his opinion of the Viennese governess whom he had privately labeled the "Long-legged Duckling."

Also evident in all three cases and of great significance in terms of his future was an unusual ability to hide his true feelings. At age fourteen he had already raised a wall of reserves around his essential self where dwelled his anxieties, his instinct for power, his driving need to excel and command. He had also begun to paint upon this wall a smiling mural depicting sunlit open spaces which, when completed, was destined to be viewed by millions as the landscape of his interior being.

Four

→>><<<←

The Great World and Groton

I

DECADES later, an astute politician* who was also a man of liberal views and who had a good deal to do with launching Franklin Roosevelt in national politics made a list of the major handicaps his sometime protégé had had to overcome to achieve success.[1] The first of these was Franklin's patrician birth and upbringing. The second was his Groton education. And certainly, despite the stress which the headmaster and some other masters in the school placed on the duties of citizenship and the need for Grotonians and Groton "ideals" in political life, the insular Groton world would seem in retrospect a poor preparation for rough-and-tumble democratic politics in the then-emerging great world.

Devised for the rich and wellborn, Groton was naturally dedicated to the preservation of the existing social order in all essential respects. It was naturally loath to admit the possibility of approaching social upheaval. Nor could Groton be severely blamed for not recognizing that this possibility existed. It was not widely recognized in the world at large. Marxists, Christian Socialists, syndicalists peaceable and violent, anarchists godly and atheistic—all these stressed the need for social change as they did battle with conservatives and with one another for men's minds. In the intellectual community there was a good deal of talk about incipient or impending crisis, cultural as well as social and economic. Some intellectuals, measuring the need for wisdom and moral goodness against what seemed to them a palpable lack of these among the generality of mankind, were profoundly pessimistic as they looked toward the future. Others, greater in number, were equally pessimistic for a different reason: they had a despairing sense of man's loss of control over his own destiny, of his having become the helpless puppet

* Josephus Daniels.

of historical energies he himself had released or of a machine environment he himself had made. In Germany, Schopenhauer, who spoke almost as contemptuously of history as he did of women, had become in certain quarters a fashionable philosopher. In Austria, Oswald Spengler was shaping dark word pictures of civilizations as living and dying organisms, ideas that would issue, two decades later, in his somberly prophetic *The Decline of the West*. In France and England, in the arts, a continuing alienation from the persons, ideas, and values of the bourgeoisie was colored, as the century drew toward its close, by a mood of *fin de siècle* decadence. In America, Brooks Adams' gloomy essay on economic determinism, *The Law of Civilization and Decay* (1895), found a receptive audience, if in part because it seemed to support the political aims of silverites. But these voices of gloom and doom were a discordant minority of a chorus that, as a whole, sang in a very different key. Groton, for all its insularity, sounded the dominant conscious note of the time far more accurately than they.

This note was one of optimism.

The prevailing secular faith among the educated classes—even in backward czarist Russia, even among the great majority of social reformers in Western Europe and the United States—was in an orderly evolutionary progress toward a world of material abundance, perpetual peace, and increased freedom for all men. The congenitally melancholy Henry Adams was not immune to it. Beneath his surface pessimism lurked the optimistic notion that if he and his two best friends were permitted to return to earth for their centenary in 1938, they might find "for the first time since man began his education among the carnivores, . . . a world that sensitive and timid natures could regard without a shudder." [2]

And indeed evidence of progress toward such a world could be seen on all sides.

During the years that Franklin Roosevelt was at Groton a future college professor of his, Silas M. MacVane of Harvard's History Department, edited a translation into English of Charles Seignobos' *Histoire Politique de l'Europe Contemporaine*.[3] Professor Seignobos of the University of Paris had a pedestrian academic mind; his ideas, his portrayals were for the most part flat representations, mirrorlike, of the prevailing views of his time. But for that very reason his book, which was widely circulated in American colleges and which Franklin was probably required to read, would prove useful to those who, in later years, strove to understand how educated men saw their world at the close of the nineteenth century.

The good professor, much admired by MacVane for "his steady inter-

est in the welfare of the common mass of men," presented statistics on
the multiplication of the annual production of economic goods that resulted from the application of machinery and scientific method to industry and agriculture; spoke of advances in the biological sciences that
"have transformed the practice of medicine"; stressed the "revolution in
methods of communication" effected by "the telegraph, railroads, and
newspapers"; and evinced not the slightest doubt that the total effect of
all this was to increase the individual liberties and well-being of the
masses while promoting the growth of political democracy. He wrote
that "everywhere the increase in commodities has penetrated to the
masses and relieved their condition," that "filthy ways of living no
longer exist in Europe except in the south or east or in the poorest portion of the community," that a "public feeling of disgust and shame has
compelled the clearing away of infected dwellings and alleys in which
the poor of the great cities had been allowed [sic] to bury themselves,"
and that, as regards "enjoyment and mental culture," the manual laborer now had "as many opportunities" for them "as the lower middle
class had in 1814." The laborer had thus "been enabled to take part in
politics without causing the reaction of barbarism which . . . [had been]
predicted and which seemed an invincible argument against universal
suffrage." Of major importance to the latter development was the press,
"revolutionized by machinery." Cheap newspapers and magazines
"made it possible to introduce into . . . [the hitherto] inert mass [of peo-
ple] a current of propagandism and opposition, which aroused the political life of the people and started the evolution of politics in the direction of democracy."

Even the development of "new means of destruction" terrible beyond
any dreamed of in earlier ages (he spoke of new explosives many times
more powerful than gunpowder, of guns vastly "more efficacious than
the old ones," and of the consequent transformation of "the conditions
of warfare"), even this seemed to the professor more hopeful than otherwise. The very idea of a war between "two great European powers" in
which this new weaponry would be employed had become "so frightful
that it is enough to keep every government from taking the responsibility for it. The progress of the art of war has made war so hideous that no
one dares to bring it on. The chemistry of explosives has worked in
favor of peace." [4]

And this was the general mood, this the conception of history as progress, which permeated the teaching minds at Groton during Franklin's
four years there. It was generated by precisely the kind of externalism—
the refusal of introspection, the unquestioning acceptance of a simplistic

faith and ethic, the virtually exclusive emphasis thereafter upon environmental factors—which characterized Groton's headmaster *in toto* and the adolescent Franklin in large part. Its tacit assumption was that men of power and privilege, rather more than the commonality of mankind, would act as rational creatures animated by generous emotions, dedicated to humane values, and with clear conceptions of the general good, when faced with unprecedented historic challenges that seemed to threaten them personally.

But there was in reality an alternative possibility. There was the possibility that men of power and privilege might at decisive moments prove to be willful, perverse, terror-stricken, sentimentally tied to the past, passionately attached to their own narrowly conceived interests, even viciously cruel and destructive. And it would become clear in retrospect that this alternative possibility, largely ignored by Franklin's teachers, was the one that was being increasingly actualized as the rulers of the old order strove to maintain it against the accelerating onrush of scientific technology. In consequence, new and powerful social forces, created or released by new forms and combinations of physical energy, pressed ever more dangerously, ever more explosively against the confinements of a class structure and political system whose essentials had been determined in the eighteenth century.

II

Consider what was happening on the surface of European politics by that autumn of 1896 when Franklin Roosevelt entered Groton's III Form. Focus on Germany, for it more than any other European power was calling the tune to which others danced in the last decade of the nineteenth century.

For twenty years—from 1870, when a unified Germany was born of the Franco-Prussian War whereby the Empire of Napoleon III was destroyed, until 1890, when the architect of this Germany was dismissed from office—Germany's position as the dominant power on the Continent had not been seriously challenged. Its domestic and foreign affairs had been managed by a statesman of authentic, if limited, genius, for though Chancellor Otto von Bismarck was a thoroughgoing reactionary, an exponent of "blood and iron" as a means of political decision, adamant in his hostility to parliamentarianism (if he had generous emotions and humane values he hid them well), he was also a man who very carefully and accurately measured the extent of his own power over domestic affairs and of his country's power in world affairs. He did not often try to go beyond this measure. He knew when and how to make concessions.

He had come to power at a time (1862) when the Prussian emperor, Wilhelm I, was being worsted in a dispute with the Chamber of Deputies on the question of which, Crown or Parliament, under a newly adopted constitution, had control of national defense. The emperor had been on the point of abdicating when Bismarck as his freshly appointed minister saved him by simply ignoring the claims of the deputies and asserting those of the Crown. And the domestic politics that Bismarck had pursued thereafter had increased the prestige and authority of the Crown while stunting the growth of parliamentarianism, rendering Germany, with a divine right sovereign, an anachronism among West European powers.* He had not achieved this end by consulting only his political emotions—his contempt for the common man, his hatred of democracy. He was no *blind* reactionary. He saw clearly enough the growing strength of Socialism and some of the reasons for it. He responded with severely repressive measures against German Socialists. But he also responded by pushing through a reluctant Reichstag social legislation (a sickness insurance law in 1883, accident insurance laws in 1884 and 1885, an old age insurance law in 1889) which made Germany the most advanced welfare state in the world. These were effective in reducing internal class antagonisms and thereby increasing Germany's military might, the latter being also important to Bismarck's management of domestic affairs. For he, perhaps more consciously and deliberately than any other leading Continental statesman of his time, made use of militarism and the kind of emotional patriotism it engendered to reduce the effectiveness of demands for more social and political democracy.

In foreign affairs, Bismarck's policy was as aggressive as it could be within his conception of the possible. But this latter conception was realistically limited. Faced by a resurgent, implacably hostile France, whose rapid economic and military recovery from the debacle of 1870 astonished everyone, the Iron Chancellor in 1875 prudently refrained from a "defensive war" when he saw that England and Russia would in that case probably come to France's aid. He turned instead to the formation of military alliances—first with Austria (1879), then with both Austria and Italy in the Triple Alliance of 1882—whereby Germany's position would be so strengthened that France, without firm allies,

---

* Austria-Hungary was a constitutional monarchy (or dual monarchy) over which the emperor, Franz Joseph, had far less authority than the Kaiser had over Germany.

would not dare make war upon his country. His policy further aimed to deprive France of such allies. He strove hard to bring Russia into his military combination, to shape an alliance of the three emperors of Germany, Austria, Russia. When this effort failed, because Austria and Russia had flatly opposing interests in the Balkans, he entered into a treaty with Russia to relieve the latter of fears of an Austro-German combination in the Balkans and to reassure Germany that a Franco-Russian combination would not be formed. Dread of the latter possibility was a major determinant of Bismarck's conduct of foreign affairs after his Triple Alliance was formed. He saw only too clearly that this possibility, if realized, would dangerously weaken Germany's position. It would no longer be clearly predominant on the Continent. There would be established instead a precarious balance of hostile powers so arranged as to threaten Germany with a two-front war. Bismarck's policy called, finally, for friendly relations with England. For if France and Germany clashed again or *when* they did (France's passionate determination to recover Alsace and Lorraine made the clash seem to him almost inevitable), Germany's interest obviously required an at least neutral Britain.

But in 1890 Bismarck had become the victim of a historic irony, with fateful consequences for Franklin Roosevelt's future and for that of the world at large. By the political system he as Chancellor had preserved and strengthened against a hated parliamentarianism, he held his office at the exclusive pleasure of the emperor. The arrangement had worked well for him so long as Wilhelm I was on the throne. The effect then had been that Bismarck ruled while the emperor reigned. But when Wilhelm I died in March, 1888, and was succeeded three months later by his twenty-nine-year-old grandson Wilhelm II (the interim was filled by Wilhelm I's son Friedrich III, who died of throat cancer), all this was changed. The Iron Chancellor found himself at the mercy of a brash, impetuous, excessively self-confident and egotistical and ambitious young man who had no intention of yielding one iota of his imperial power to anyone and who bitterly resented the vast fame and prestige that Bismarck had achieved. The young Kaiser had quickly made it clear that he wished the old Chancellor to resign. When he did not, Wilhelm II, after two years of increasingly acrimonious quarrel, demanded his resignation.

Nor was this all. Partly as a puppet of socioeconomic forces he never understood, partly in expression of a national psychology that mingled brutal authoritarianism and cringing servility in equal parts and was characterized by an overweening egotism, partly through the compulsive behavior dictated by his hysterical temperament, Wilhelm II abruptly set about weakening or destroying virtually every external prop and safeguard which Bismarck had arranged around Germany's greatness. The spirit of moderation was not in him. Where Bismarck would have remained discreetly silent, the new emperor must shout at the top of his shrill voice about German superiority, Germany's right to "a place in the sun," the "destiny" of Germans to rule over others, simultaneously rattling with his healthy hand (one was withered) the saber he wore always at his side. There was an abrupt increase of aggressive militarism, a renewed push for expansion abroad, as he gave free rein to forces within Germany which Bismarck had tried with considerable success to keep in check. Franklin Roosevelt experienced a manifestation of this during his brief attendance at a Volksschule in the late spring of 1891. He was there exposed to courses in map reading and military topography that had been introduced into all German schools by the new Kaiser, courses that made a lifelong impression upon him and which he cited long afterward as an example of Germany's thorough preparation for military conquest.

A year later, or two years after Bismarck's dismissal, came the event the Iron Chancellor had most feared. France and Russia drew together in military combination. The whole power structure of Europe was drastically altered.

And two years after that, in 1894, the young Kaiser, alas, read a book —the same book Franklin Roosevelt was to read a little later, Captain Mahan's *The Influence of Sea Power upon History.* Wilhelm claimed, indeed, that he was "devouring" it and "trying to learn it by heart," for it was "first class" and "classical in all points." [5] He ordered a copy of it placed on every ship in the German Navy, which, he abruptly decided and loudly proclaimed, was much smaller than it should be. For Germany was not merely a Continental power, but a world power. It had entered late into the race for colonies, but it had run strongly and now possessed a colonial empire of respectable proportions. No longer, therefore, could it be content with an inferior navy. It must and would have a navy second to none. Such talk was of course alarming to the English, whose very existence on a crowded island required open sea lanes and whose development as a sea power, whose acquisition of a vast overseas empire, had been initially and remained largely determined by their insular position.

The generally friendly feelings that had theretofore existed between Germany and England and that Bismarck had been at considerable pains to cultivate began swiftly to fade. So far as the general publics of both countries were concerned, they virtually disappeared and were replaced by feelings of hostility in early 1896. For in January of that year, in the aftermath of Dr. Leander Starr Jameson's ill-starred raid into the Transvaal, the Kaiser sent a telegram to President Paul Kruger of the South African Republic congratulating him on the defeat of the raiders. The obvious implication was that in case of war between the British and the Boers, a conflict that appeared increasingly likely, imperial Germany would aid the Boers. The anger of the British public was augmented when it was learned that Germany's purpose was to *frighten* the British into friendlier relations with it! England at once acted to remove a major obstacle to friendlier relations with France; it abandoned claims in Siam which conflicted with those of France. It even made approaches to Russia, another traditionally hostile power, though nothing came of these.

Yes, Germany was calling the tune in that last decade of the nineteenth century. Retrospection would make it ever more clear that what other European powers did in their management of foreign affairs was then very largely a response to German initiatives. The character, the temperament of the German people and of their rulers was, therefore, an important determinant of history.

But in a yet more distant retrospect it would seem equally clear that the ultimate, the basic determinant of European politics, in those as in later years, was a combination of forces, rooted in science and flowering in technology, that were indefinable in terms of national sovereignty, were inhibited and distorted by these, and pressed with an increasingly explosive energy toward new forms of human association on earth or toward the death of all.

III

They were operating in America, too, these forces, though with differences determined by historical and environmental circumstances peculiar to the United States.

The chief historical circumstance was the creative evolution of the U.S. Constitution with its incorporated Bill of Rights, along with the institutions and procedures of government that were specified or implied by the written document. The chief environmental circumstance was the existence to begin with of a vast empty wilderness of forest, plain, and mountain lying west of the colonial settlements out of which the Republic was initially made. The effect of both circumstances was to inhibit the development of a rigidly stratified society such as characterized European nations and to mitigate the struggle between those classes which nevertheless did form, classes that were more open than Europe's. For one thing, there did not develop in the United States to anything like the degree that there did in nineteenth-century Europe an urban-industrial proletariat having a sense of class solidarity whereby it was enabled to act as a single cohesive political force. The trade union movement, crossing the Atlantic, was enfeebled by its passage; it remained a negligible factor among those determining U.S. national politics.

The American conflict between exploiter and exploited, or haves and have-nots, as it had developed by 1890 under the impact of the advancing technology, was given in politics a very blurred definition. It was generally viewed as Agriculture vs. Industrial Monopoly or Farmer vs. Financier, with only a passing reference to Labor vs. Capital. There was no widely recognized identity of political interest between farmer and urban-industrial worker; if both suffered at the same hands and would benefit in the long run from the same governmental measures, neither was sufficiently aware of it to enable the two of them to work closely, effectively together. And this initially blurred definition of conflict was yet further blurred by the identification of its oppositions with geographic regions—the agrarian West and South vs. the industrial and financial East—and by its expression through national political parties that had themselves no clear definition, being conglomerates (each of them) of every sectional, economic, and sociocultural interest. Only the proportions differed between them.

But in 1890 and the immediately following years there was a clarification of issues and a drastic realignment of political forces. The farmer's grievances remained the same in essence as they had been a decade before, when James Roosevelt married Sara Delano. They had, however, grown greater, and the popular conception of their nature had become more sharply and consistently defined. The farmer had to buy his processed goods from corporate trusts (the Barbed Wire Trust, the Harvester Machinery Trust, etc.) that were powerful enough to control production and fix prices and that were, in addition, protected against foreign competition by tariff walls which, in 1888, were raised by the McKinley Tariff Act to the highest peacetime level in history (an average of 48.8 percent on dutiable goods). He was himself unable to raise prices by limiting production, he had to ship his goods to central markets via railroads whose rates were deliberately discriminatory against him, and he had to sell, unprotected, on a highly competitive world market, since he produced more than the domestic market could absorb. He was in consequence chronically in debt, and because of the deflationary fiscal politics of both Republican and Cleveland Democratic administrations, he had to make his mortgage payments in dollars that were worth considerably more, as a general rule, than those he had originally borrowed. Nor could he take his case to court or plead his cause in existing legislative halls with much hope of success. The courts, whose judges were in high proportion former corporation lawyers, almost always ruled against him, and the rich lobbies of the railroads and trusts were in effective control of many, if not most, state legislatures and hence of the U.S. Senate, whose members these legislatures then elected.

Some recent economic historians, notably Douglass C. North,* cast doubt upon the validity of this diagnosis of the farmer's ills. North cites statistical evidence that farm prices in actual fact "fell less than all prices" between 1865 and 1890, that railroad rates fell *more* than all prices during this period, and that, considering the loud complaints about farm mortgages, there was a surprisingly small percentage of them (29 percent, to 35 percent of their value) in the country as a whole. Even in the Midwest, only 38.7 percent of the farms were mortgaged in 1890, though well over half were mortgaged in both Nebraska and Kansas, and since the average life of a mortgage was four and one-half years in the Midwest as a whole (3.6 percent for Kansas, 3.7 for Nebraska), the complaint that the farmer had borrowed cheap money but was required to pay back expensive money was invalid. The real cause of the farmer's distress, suggests North, was his dependence on a world market "in which fluctuations in price made no sense to him."

However this may be, and whether or not farmers of the West and South had accurate perceptions of the causes of their troubles, they *were* in trouble. They felt that they were held in economic bondage by the capitalistic East. They became convinced that the only solution for them was intensive and extensive political organization. And in the last years of the 1880's they began to engage in it on an unprecedented scale. The Farmers' Alliance movement gained power, establishing marketing and processing cooperatives of various kinds and entering elective politics aggressively. Alliance members captured control of the local Democracy in much of the South in 1890, blacks and poor whites actually joining together to do so in a linkage that was, however, very brief and destined to be succeeded by Jim Crowism.† In Kansas that same year, Alliance members met in convention to form a People's (Populist) Party and sent around the state Mary Elizabeth Lease, dubbed "the Kansas Pythoness" or "Mary Yellin" by her foes, who made about 160 speeches attacking government "of Wall Street, by Wall Street, for Wall Street" and urging farmers to "raise less corn and more hell." That fall, Kansas

* In his *Growth and Welfare in the American Past* (Englewood Cliffs, N.J., 1966), Chapter 11, pp. 137–48.
† The poor whites and the Populism they espoused became the authors of a racism more virulent than had theretofore existed in the South.

Populists swept the legislature, elected one of their number to the Congressional House, and sent another to the U.S. Senate.

Two years later, in a theretofore unprecedented joining together of farmer and labor organizations (though labor was distinctly a junior partner), a convention of Alliance members, in which representatives of the Knights of Labor participated, established a national People's Party with a platform calling for government ownership of railroads, telegraph, and telephone; a graduated income tax; an eight-hour day for wage earners; the Australian (secret) ballot; the initiative and referendum; direct election of U.S. Senators; restriction of immigration; and (particularly interesting in terms of Franklin Roosevelt's future) the establishment of so-called produce subtreasuries wherein farmers could deposit produce in return for U.S. Treasury notes. Thus was vaguely defined for America the issue between Socialism and free enterprise. But this was blurred almost out of recognition in the public mind by two other convention actions: first, the adoption of a platform plank which called for the free and unlimited coinage of silver in the ratio of sixteen to one; second, the nomination for the Presidency of General James B. Weaver of Iowa, who had run as the Greenback Party candidate in 1880 and remained convinced that present social justice and future social progress required above all an inflation of the currency through a repudiation of the gold standard.

In the election that followed, the Populists made an impressive showing. Weaver polled more than 1,000,000 popular votes, about 9 percent of the total, and carried six Middle Western and Western states with a total of 22 electoral votes. In four of these states the Populists captured control of state governments (in Kansas, Populists elected a governor while strengthening their hold on the legislature). The alarming effect of this was heightened for conservative sound money men in proportion to their realization that a significant segment of Grover Cleveland's winning vote as Democratic candidate (he ran against Republican incumbent Benjamin Harrison) came from Populists in the South who had fought the campaign under the Democratic banner and that he could not have run as well as he did among rank-and-file Democrats had not his party convention offset his fiscal conservatism by nominating as his running mate a notorious silverite, Adlai E. Stevenson of Illinois. All in all, to those with eyes to see, there was evident a ground swell of revolt against the order that had prevailed virtually unchallenged since 1870.

Events of the next four years did nothing to reduce this ground swell.

Cleveland was inaugurated at a time of deepening financial crisis for the federal government. The Treasury's gold reserves, normally held at

$100,000,000, were becoming so depleted that the gold standard was threatened. There were several closely linked causes. One was a panic in London which forced the liquidation of American securities there. Another was the legally required purchase of silver by the Treasury at an exorbitant price in gold. A third, and most important of all, was the legally required redemption in gold of greenbacks (paper currency) presented to the Treasury and the immediate reissue of these greenbacks for redemption again in gold if their holders so desired. This last became, in the journalism of the day, an "endless chain" for conveying gold from the United States to Europe and into private hoards at home.

The President moved vigorously against a threat which he, in common with all other conservatives, regarded as the most serious to the Republic since the Civil War. He called a special session of the Congress in the late summer of 1893 and, after breaking a silverite filibuster through a judicious, if ruthless, use of his patronage powers, obtained repeal of the Sherman Silver Purchase Act. He tried also to obtain repeal of the requirement that redeemed greenbacks be promptly reissued —he wished instead to retire them—but in this he failed. And so the "endless chain" continued to operate (two large government bond issues were rendered futile by it) until the President in desperation, when the reserves were down to a mere $41,000,000, called J. P. Morgan to the White House and begged the banker's help. Morgan undertook to save the country—at a price. He formed a syndicate of international bankers which lent the government some $65,000,000 of gold and took other steps to prevent a further excessive gold drain. Before Cleveland's term had ended, confidence in the dollar had so far returned that a bond issue to raise $100,000,000 was offered directly to the public and taken at a substantial premium.

This success, however, was purchased at the price of Cleveland's political power and prestige. The repeal of silver purchasing alienated a large majority of his own party, and the negotiations with the much-feared and hated "Jupiter" Morgan alienated almost everyone outside the financial community itself. For simultaneously with the gold crisis and causally linked with it, but partially caused also by glaring malpractices on the part of railroad and other corporation entrepreneurs (the issuance of heavily watered stock to benefit speculators at the expense of the investing public was then standard operational procedure), came financial panic, followed by the deepest, widest, most prolonged economic depression since the 1850's. There were three times as many failures of commercial enterprises in 1893 as there had been in 1873, nearly all of them having much larger liabilities, and banks by the hundred, a high proportion of them in the West and South, closed their doors. Virtually every railroad—169 of them with 37,855 miles of track and a total capitalization of nearly $2.5 billion—went into receivership.

The event had direct effects upon James Roosevelt's fortunes and hence upon Franklin's: it frustrated the most grandiose of all of James Roosevelt's financial ventures.[6] In the late 1880's he had joined with other capitalists to form a Maritime Canal Company of Nicaragua, whose act of incorporation was pushed through Congress and promptly signed by President Cleveland during that winter of 1887 which the James Roosevelts spent in Washington. The company's purpose was to dig across Nicaragua a canal that would run through Lake Nicaragua and link the Atlantic and the Pacific for oceangoing vessels. The project was originally competitive with an effort being made by a French syndicate headed by Ferdinand de Lesseps of Suez Canal fame, but the De Lesseps enterprise had failed by the time the Maritime Canal Company, having obtained valuable concessions from the Nicaraguan government, began preliminary construction in 1890. Maritime's prospects had then seemed bright. Many additional millions of dollars would be needed to complete the canal, but these, it appeared, could be quickly and easily obtained through stock sales and, probably, substantial U.S. government subsidy. Then came the panic and depression. Sources of credit dried up in America and abroad. The company, whose success would have made James Roosevelt immensely wealthy, was ultimately liquidated at, presumably, a considerable loss to its originators.

But such misfortune had no dire effect on the Roosevelts' private lives, whereas the effects of the depression on the lives of millions of common folk were dire indeed. Industrial unemployment mounted. So did the number of strikes and lockouts, with the workers losing in almost every case. So, too, did the wrath of farmers as farm prices sank below the cost of production and mortgages were foreclosed by the thousand. Neither farmer nor laborer was disposed to look with favor upon a President who moved boldly to aid capitalists at the expense of debtors (this was deemed the effect of Cleveland's fiscal measures) and who made use of federal troops and court injunctions to break strikes and destroy unions (Cleveland did so in the case of the great Pullman strike in Chicago in 1894), while claiming he was utterly powerless to aid common people who had lost jobs and savings through no fault of their own.

Thus the way was prepared for the Presidential election of 1896, the most crucially important to the Republic since that of 1860 and of even greater significance than that of 1860 if measured in terms of world-historical trends. It was made so in large part by the fact that the Western frontier, which had psychologically cushioned the impact upon American society of the accelerating Industrial Revolution, had now disappeared—a fact whose importance was popularly recognized.* Americans had to face squarely for the first time some of the social and economic problems that had been determinants of European politics for decades. Of course, these problems were defined in different terms from those in Europe. The monetary issue, on which centered most of the sound and fury, continued to confuse everything; both major political parties were split by it while Populism was wholly dominated by silverites. But silverites remained a distinct minority among Republicans and a distinct majority among Democrats so that, despite the confusion, there emerged in unprecedentedly clear outline the larger, deeper issue of economic classes struggling for power within the framework of the American Constitution.

The Republican candidate was Ohio's William McKinley of McKinley Tariff fame, who was easily persuaded to renounce his earlier bimetallist views (he had voted for free coinage of silver while a Congressman) in return for big business support, though he did so as softly and equivocally as possible in order to lose a minimum of silverite votes. His principal backer, Mark A. Hanna of Cleveland, who had grown rich in the iron business and who sincerely loved McKinley as a person, was convinced that the businessman was the author of all prosperity and that the primary function of government was to aid business. Largely because of Hanna's skill and ruthlessness as a political organizer who made lavish use of his own and other people's money to promote his candidate, McKinley was nominated at the convention in St. Louis, in June, on the first ballot.

The Democratic candidate was a thirty-six-year-old Nebraska newspaperman and lawyer named William Jennings Bryan, who had gained brief national prominence in 1893, while serving his single term in the Congress, through his eloquent defense of the Silver Purchase Act against Cleveland's effort to repeal it, but who was otherwise unknown outside the Middle West. His nomination by the Chicago convention in July was totally unexpected. He stampeded the convention with a sensational address in which every social ill was linked to the gold standard, itself allegedly a device of the plutocracy for robbing and enslaving common men. Bryan's peroration became one of the most famous in all American political oratory. "Having behind us the producing masses of

* Farmers' Alliance members sang a song entitled "Where Will the Farmer Be?" which contained the following lines:

  Free lands will be gone and naught else can I do
  But be the rich man's slave.

this nation and the world," he cried, "supported by the commercial interests, the laboring interests, and the toilers everywhere, we will answer their demand for a gold standard by saying to them: '*You shall not press down upon the brow of Labor this crown of thorns; you shall not crucify mankind upon a cross of gold.*'" He was then nominated on the fifth ballot. A few weeks later he also received the nomination of the People's Party; Populism and Democracy became that year a single national political force.

In the campaign that followed, Bryan confounded Mark Hanna's plan to make the tariff the principal issue. Free silver became the issue. But in his "Cross of Gold" speech Bryan had made it abundantly clear that silver vs. gold was for him agent and symbol of the larger, deeper issue of plutocracy vs. democracy. "The sympathies of the Democratic party . . . are ever on the side of the struggling masses . . . ," he had said. "There are two ideas of government. There are those who believe that, if you will only legislate to make the well-to-do prosperous their prosperity will leak through on those below. The Democratic idea, however, has been that if you legislate to make the masses prosperous, their prosperity will find its way up through every class which rests upon them." He reiterated these sentiments as he traveled 18,000 miles through twenty-seven states, preaching the silver gospel with a religious fervor. He made nearly 600 speeches altogether, 36 of them in a single day.

McKinley, on the other hand, traveled not at all. He conducted a relaxed campaign from his home in Canton, Ohio, where he daily made innocuous little speeches from his front porch to small crowds brought to visit him via railroads which gave special reduced rates for such travel. There was nothing relaxed, however, about the campaign that Mark Hanna waged on his candidate's behalf. Hanna formed the largest and most efficient national campaign organization ever seen till then, financing it by levying what amounted to a "campaign tax" upon the wealthy individuals, the trusts and corporations that had most to fear from Bryan's election. He raised in this way about $16,000,000 as compared with the $1,000,000, at most, which the Democrats managed to gather. The Republicans sent hundreds of trained speakers around the country, distributed tens of millions of pamphlets and leaflets and posters, and flooded the press with propaganda, all of it designed to arouse and play upon fears of renewed financial panic, Socialism, and even Red Revolution should Bryan be elected. Factory owners put slips into pay envelopes informing workers that their jobs depended on a McKinley triumph. Not untypical was the president of a large factory in Steinway, New York, who on election eve told his assembled workers, "Men, you may vote as you please but if Bryan is elected tomorrow the whistle will not blow on Wednesday morning." [7]

Bryan was not elected. McKinley won by 7,107,822 of the popular vote, compared to 6,511,073 for Bryan, and by 271 to 176 in the electoral college. In what seemed to many a Republican and nearly all Democrats a head-on collision between plutocracy and democracy, with control of the Republic at stake, it was democracy that had been knocked down. But analysis revealed that McKinley's seemingly substantial victory was actually a narrow one. Most of the McKinley majority had been piled up in the three highly industrialized states most favorable to Hanna's campaign tactics, those of New York (where James Roosevelt voted for McKinley that year), Pennsylvania, and Illinois, and Hanna himself realized that a shift of fewer than 20,000 votes in states narrowly won by the Republicans would have given the prize to Bryan.

Thus, the threat which Bryan represented to such as Hanna was by no means ended. The Great Commoner and Peerless Leader, as Bryan came to be called, might well be elected President in 1900. And the response of many conservatives to this challenge during the immediately following years was an American variant of a classic pattern. A rising tide of imperialist sentiment began to sweep over the United States. There were renewed demands for the annexation of Hawaii, for the liberation of Cuba from the misrule of Spain, for the planting of the American flag on islands in the far Pacific.

IV

Of all this, only muffled echoes were heard within the confines of Groton School.

V

"I am getting on finely, both mentally and physically." Thus did Franklin Roosevelt begin his first letter from Groton to "Dear Mommerr & Popperr," dated Friday, September 18, 1896. And the letters that followed maintained a uniformly cheerful tone. "I am getting on very well . . . ," he wrote on September 20. "I am getting on very well . . . ," he wrote on September 21. "I am getting on very well so far," he wrote on September 27. "I am getting on very well with the fellows although I do not know them all yet," he wrote on October 1. There is a certain suspicious insistence in the refrain, as if it expressed his wish with a greater accuracy than it did the reality of his experience.[8]

Others would remember that so far as full acceptance by "the fellows" was concerned, he was severely handicapped by his having entered the school two years later than all his classmates save one. The eighteen others had found their niches and come to know one another well as first and second formers. They entered the III Form as members of a close-knit, fiercely conformist group, such a group as is typical of fourteen-year-olds in a boarding school but was especially encouraged at Groton by the rector's emphasis on group rather than individual activity and upon those character traits which form the common denominators of a Christian community as he conceived it. These others had already formed their personal friendships; they had no strongly felt need for another. Franklin was an outsider. So was the only other new boy in III Form, whose name was James L. Goodwin and who, as a fellow sufferer, became Franklin's first new friend in the school. These two, simply because they were late, must somehow overcome a covert, if not overt, group hostility before they could themselves become truly of the group.

For Franklin there were other handicaps. In the IV Form was half nephew Taddy, whom others in the school called Rosy—a boy now so markedly "different" that he was regarded as something of a joke by his contemporaries. It did nothing for the new boy's prestige to be known as Rosy's "Uncle Frank" (". . . but I would sooner be Uncle Frank, than Nephew Rosy . . . ," he wrote home[9]). Nor did it help that he who had lived so much abroad, who had habitually spoken German with a German governess and French with a French-speaking one, spoke English with an accent strange to his contemporaries. He was ridiculed for it. It seemed to them affected. And he promptly endeavored, with ultimate success, to cultivate an accent in keeping, if not actually identical, with that of his schoolfellows. Finally, there was his shyness. He had learned to dissemble it, but it remained a factor inhibiting to his relations with new acquaintances or with anyone whose good opinion he particularly valued.

The school's physical setting was not dissimilar to what he was accustomed to in Hyde Park. The apparent seclusion, the seeming remoteness from the world of men, was considerably greater. Red-brick buildings— a new dormitory known as Hundred House because it could sleep about one hundred boys, a classroom building called Brooks House (after Phillips Brooks, who died in 1893), a gymnasium and fives-courts building,* and a chapel—were arranged around a greensward shaded by great elms on a wide ridge whose wooded sides sloped down, northward and westward, to the Nashua River. Beyond the river rolled ridge after wooded ridge ascending to the foothills and ultimate peaks of Wachusett in Massachusetts, of Monadnock and Pac Monadnock in New Hampshire. In all the wide, long landscape in that direction there was no town or village to be seen, no hint at all of human habitation. The view to the east was only slightly less empty of the works of men. A few of the houses of Groton village, two miles away, could be glimpsed through the trees, and that was all. It was a beautiful setting whose solitudes were not strange to one reared in the open country of the Hudson River Valley.

But the self-contained world of the school itself and the life he was required to live as one of a family (for the school was run so) of a hundred boys were widely different in many respects from any he had known before.

He had been accustomed at Springwood to a comfortably large bedroom with a large, if plain, brass bed in it, and a heavy hugely mirrored bureau, and tables large and small across which he spread his belongings; its colorfully papered walls were cluttered with framed historical memorabilia and award certificates and pictures. He was now required to sleep in a six-by-ten cubicle whose walls were wholly bare save for hooks on which suits could be hung. In shape and size and furnishings, this cubicle was identical with a hundred others. It provided a severely limited privacy. The walls were only seven feet high; atop them was empty space reaching to a tall ceiling. And there was no door which could be closed; there was only a curtain which might be drawn, to shut off the cubicle from the traffic of a wide corridor. It was furnished with the bare necessaries—a plain bureau, a table, a chair, a rug, and a narrow, hard-mattressed bed.

At the end of the corridor was a lavatory with showers and long sinks of black soapstone with tin basins in them. It was there that the daily regimen began, a regimen considerably more restrictive and rugged than that Franklin had known at home. He arose with the others shortly before seven each morning and trooped with them to the lavatory, where, under the watchful eye of a prefect, he took a cold shower. This was a sufficiently Spartan test in a New England autumn; it would become excruciating in the depths of winter. Face scrubbed, teeth brushed, hair combed, he went to a breakfast served promptly, after the saying of grace, at seven thirty. Morning chapel was at eight fifteen, and classes

* Fives in a British handball game of which Peabody had become fond during his English school and university days.

began at eight thirty, continuing uninterrupted till noon. The main meal, dinner, was served at noon. In the afternoon were two forty-five-minute classroom sessions.

Franklin Roosevelt's classes were fairly representative of Groton's curriculum as a whole, so far as relative emphasis on different subjects was concerned. He took Latin, Greek, algebra, English literature (Shakespeare, Grey's *Elegy*, Goldsmith's *Deserted Village*, etc.), English composition, French (both literature—De Maupassant, Montaigne, Dumas—and composition), history (Greek and Roman), science, and sacred studies. The latter, taught by the rector himself, consisted for III Form of Bible history and the history of missions. (The rector's famed traditional command to nearly every pupil at the opening of nearly every sacred studies class is revelatory of the man and his pedagogy. "Nails and notebook, boy!" Peabody would cry, whereupon the pupil must show that his fingernails were clean and his notebook ready to receive jottings down of the rector's wisdom.) Franklin's 1896 science course—the only one he took during his four years at Groton, for none was offered in IV, V, and VI forms—was in zoology, a study of invertebrates, with laboratory work. It was such science as Aristotle might have taught, being primarily, if not exclusively, concerned with descriptive classification. Franklin answered a typical examination question in this subject by explaining that animals "are classified according to homology and not analogy, thus a bird and butterfly are not classed together" despite the fact that both "have organs of flight" because their wings are "analogous not homologous." [10] He did well in his classes. On the first report sent his parents, October 17, 1896, his grades averaged 7.79 out of a possible 10.00 (he had a perfect score for Punctuality, one of 9.68 for Neatness) and the rector noted in a hasty scrawl under Remarks: "Very Good. He strikes me as an intelligent & faithful scholar & a good boy." He stood fourth in a class of nineteen; he would continue to stand in the upper fourth or fifth of his class throughout his four years.

But it was not through intellectual competitions and attainments that the path to glory lay at Groton. Of no less importance than formal studies in the school's overall program, and of far greater importance to the gaining of personal prestige among masters and boys, were the athletic games that followed the afternoon classes. Every boy was expected to participate in them unless physically incapacitated or so hopelessly inept as to destroy the sport of others, and Franklin did so with ardor but, alas, no success that autumn. It was football season. The student body was divided into eight eleven-man teams graded from best to worst. Franklin, after an afternoon or two, was placed on the next to worst team. "Poor Taddy" was on "the lowest team" when he could have been "on a much higher one if only he kept his wits about him!" So wrote Franklin to his parents on October 1.[11]

After football, each afternoon, came another cold shower, again under the supervising eye of a prefect. Then, before supper, he, like every other boy, donned for the evening a stiff collar and patent-leather dress shoes. Evening chapel followed supper, and a study period followed chapel. The traditional close of the day was a good-night visit to Rector and Mrs. Peabody in their house. The boys filed past the headmaster and his wife, who shook hands with each of them and bade each good-night by name, the rector adding, in most cases, some personal word.[12]

This nightly ritual was doubly important. It was important as a means of instilling in every boy a sense of Groton as family—the rector a strict but lovingly concerned father; Mrs. Peabody a mother unfailingly kind and sympathetic. It was important also as a means of discipline. With an unsmiling handshake and a curt good-night the rector could register his disapproval of a boy—of that boy's conduct and general tone—in a way that was perfectly plain not only to the boy himself, but to those around him. A sensitive lad could be cast into the deepest slough of despond by this public rebuke, all the more effective for being implied rather than directly expressed. Even the rector's failure to speak the boy's name or to substitute for it the "my-dear-boy" with which he sometimes covered his inability to remember it at the moment (such memory lapses were rare), even this could hurt terribly, though doing so might not be any part of the rector's intention. Contrariwise, such a boy might be raised to seventh heaven by a special cordiality in the rector's handshake and a word of praise accompanying the good-night—and this, too, was sometimes inadvertent on the rector's part.

VI

He, Endicott Peabody, was the god (god the creator, god the father) of this world he had made. His impact on every boy was direct and personal and very great; he inspired love, hate, fear, but always a profound respect more than tinged with awe.

He was one of those rare men, their judgments swift and uncompromising on every issue presented to their decision, who know from early manhood precisely who they are, what they mean, and where they stand. In consequence, he had a rock-hard integrity and was thrust up as a rock, seemingly unchangeable, amid a turbulent sea of change. Others, storm-tossed upon the sea, sometimes wrecked themselves against him or clung to him as a refuge; in any case they could count on him to be always there, exactly there, an eternal feature solid and incorruptible in a generally fluid and dissolving temporal scene. They could orient themselves in relation to him. And all "his boys" did so orient themselves, not only while under his supervision but throughout their lives, doing so from points of view that varied considerably less widely than they would have in the absence of a common Groton experience of him.

He was thirty-nine years old in 1896. He looked little, if any, older, he certainly *seemed* little older in his essence, than he had a dozen years before when he first opened his school. His blond hair was somewhat thinner than it once had been; there were a few hollows and lines in his ruggedly honest, open countenance. But the gaze of his blue eyes was as straight and piercing, as little inhibited in its outward thrust by doubts and hesitations, as that of a boy of ten. And he remained an erect figure, physically fit, energetic, zestful, radiant of vitality, boyish in his enthusiasms. In many ways he could be described in negatives: he was *not* a great classroom teacher, *not* an educational theorist, *not* a great preacher, *not* a creative intellect. But these negatives were peripheral to what he centrally, positively *was*—to wit, a powerful and even overwhelming personality. The force of his personality, his authoritarian moralistic temper sustained by a simple unquestioning faith in "his particular God" [13] and in Jesus Christ as the Supreme Gentleman—these had been great in the spring of 1883 when he first spoke to Mrs. James Lawrence of his schoolmaster's ambition. They had grown immense as his ambition was realized. Perhaps this was the only change in him of any importance, and it was a change of quantity rather than quality: there was simply more of him, he bulked larger, than before.

He was as happy in his personal family life as in his work—and indeed, as headmaster of so small a school, run on familial lines, the two were necessarily fused. He had married at the close of Groton's first school year, in June, 1885, a first cousin of his, Frances "Fannie" Peabody of Danvers, Massachusetts, who was a little more than three years younger than he. It was in every sense a fruitful marriage. The Peabodys had in 1896 four children, three girls (one born that year) and a boy; two more were destined to be born to them. This, however, was not the limit of their family which, in her conception as in his, included all the boys in the school and all of the school's alumni. (Once, on a crowded Fifth Avenue bus in New York, Fannie Peabody pushed her way up to a dignified gentleman who had never seen her before, saying to him eagerly, "Pardon me, but aren't you the father of one of my boys?"—then backing away red-faced from his obvious astonishment.[14]) She was in every way her husband's helpmate; without her he could not have shaped Groton so successfully as he did.

Her qualities were in many respects complementary and corrective of his. Maintaining the feminine principle at its "highest" and "purest" (as one of her eulogists put it) amid the prevailing masculinity, she loved the school and its boys more gently, selflessly than he. The rector sometimes fell short of grace, becoming harsh and unjust in his anger, for he was a notably quick-tempered man, whose wrath, provoked by any threat to his or the school's dignity, was literally awful. ("You know," wrote W. Averell Harriman [Groton, '09] to his father a few years later, "he [Peabody] would be an awful bully if he weren't such a terrible Christian." [15]) On such occasions his wife strove to mitigate his harshness and often succeeded. She had sensitivities he lacked and was even inclined to laugh a little at his fervent guardianship of what she deemed the "minor morals." He had little patience with such ills as homesickness, for instance, whereas she, serving tea in her parlor or presiding there over evening games, eased many a boy through the painful transition from home to school life. (Franklin wrote his parents of "Mrs. Peabody's Parlor" in capitals; it was a formal Groton institution.) For the rending pangs of an awakening sexuality, for the guilt feelings they inevitably aroused in a closed society that deemed the sex drive shameful save in holy wedlock, for these the rector's cures were the standard ones of a muscular Christianity—namely, hard physical exercise, cold showers, and prayer. Every year he chose as one of the "texts for the week" the Biblical prayer "Make me a clean heart, O God, and renew a right spirit within me." He preached that week against the unholy trinity of Gambling, Drinking, and Impurity.[16] His wife had a larger sympathy. It appears that boys made confessions to her they could never have made to the rector and received from her such absolution as kindness to those in trouble can give, though there is no evidence and every unlikelihood that Franklin Roosevelt, whose sexual development was obviously slower than most, ever did so.

The Peabodys, man and wife, were of course not the only influential factors in the Groton world. There were other masters, especially the two men who had joined with Peabody to open the school in 1884 and who made it as much their lifework as he did—two men approximately as different from the rector as it was possible for men to be. All that the three had in common was their Episcopalian affiliation and Christian faith and a passion, differently aimed and expressed among them, for the education of boys.[17]

Sherrard Billings, three years younger than Peabody, a native of

Quincy, Massachusetts, was a very small man with a very black beard who was intensely conscious of his lack of physical size and inclined to compensate for it with an even greater insistence upon masculine toughness and courage, upon rugged outdoorsmanship and bold skill in contact sports, than the rector found necessary to his *amour propre.* He was more of a martinet in the classroom than Peabody was. He was also more sensitive in ways that made him a better classroom teacher. He was, indeed, an excellent teacher (Latin his favorite subject) who taught outside the classroom as well as in, by example as well as precept. He was a fine preacher, too—an ordained minister of the Episcopal Church who engaged in as much parish work as his Groton duties would permit. And whatever his subject matter, formal or informal, secular or religious, he stressed always and strongly the importance of good form, in the British meaning of that phrase. "He never ceased to insist that there is always a correct way of doing things, whether of speaking, or shaking hands, or parsing a Latin sentence," wrote a pupil of his in a later year, adding that Billings further demanded that a man "be a good . . . , informed, and active citizen," concerning himself with public affairs. In this he and the rector were at one ("If some Groton boys do not enter political life and do something for our land it won't be because they have not been urged," wrote Peabody to a friend in 1894[18]); the fact was of some importance in Franklin Roosevelt's prep school education. So was Groton's emphasis on public speaking and debate, for which Billings was more responsible than anyone else.

William Amory Gardner (the "William" was seldom used), a cousin of the rector's, was the youngest of the three original masters of Groton.[19] He had been barely twenty-one and just graduated *magna cum laude* from Harvard when the school opened; he was only thirty-three when Franklin first met him. A Boston native, the son of wealthy parents, he had been orphaned at the age of twelve and reared thereafter in the fabulous home of his fabulous aunt by marriage, Isabella Stewart Gardner, "Mrs. Jack," patroness of the arts and (particularly) of John Singer Sargent. He was nearly unique at Groton in that he took no part in athletics, being far from strong physically and often unwell, though he was an enthusiastic spectator of sports, a good horseman, and an active yachtsman. He was altogether unique at Groton, and would have been anywhere, in his character and personality. He was highly eccentric: the boys called him Uncle Billy Wag with mingled affection and amusement, and the nickname suited him. A lifelong bachelor, he was a great knitter of socks in which he often used yarns of widely differing hues, with results, when he wore them, that startled beholders. He was also a great talker, an excitable bridge player, a linguist, an amateur sculptor, a knowledgeable lover of music and, indeed, of all the arts. Most important, he was a truly brilliant teacher, able to illuminate his subjects (mathematics and Greek) from many points of view. He was thoroughly progressive, wholly committed to general education, in his pedagogical theories. "Let the best men, if they are to teach physics and chemistry, be men who know a good deal about Homer, Beethoven, Dante, and Velasquez," he once wrote. "If they are to teach classics and history, let them know something of business, trigonometry, how long it takes a hen's egg to hatch, etc." Franklin wrote to his parents of Gardner's Greek class, "I can learn better & quicker with him than anyone else." [20]

No more than in the case of Billings was Amory Gardner's influence on the boys limited to the classroom. He was an extremely wealthy man, and a generous one. The Tudor-styled timber and plaster chapel was his gift to the school. So would be the magnificent new stone chapel, designed by Henry Vaughan in the Gothic manner, which would rise during Franklin's last year at Groton. For himself, Gardner built at the school a luxurious mansion, staffed with many servants. To it he attached a large building of strange design "containing a stage, a swimming pool, a squash court, and a maze, which was known as the 'Pleasure Dome' " and which was, certainly, a great pleasure center for the boys. "We go to Mr. Gardner's on Sunday afternoons and have cake and google," wrote Franklin to his parents on October 4 of his first year, "google" being a cloyingly sweet lemonade served in two colors at the Pleasure Dome.[21]

Gardner was the only master in the school who deviated at all widely from the pattern imposed by the conceptions, the peculiar piety, the imperious will of the rector, who sometimes evinced a Puritan's disapproval of the younger man's sybaritic tastes and habits. The two men had in common a strong religious faith, but Gardner's was much more lyrically, much less dogmatically expressed than Peabody's. They often disagreed on curricular matters. In faculty meetings, Gardner grew used to standing alone in opposition to policies the rector proposed and the others accepted. But he seldom prevailed (it was a standard complaint of his that nobody paid the slightest attention to anything he said) and never did so save when he managed, somehow, to win the rector to his view.

For Groton, to repeat, was Peabody's world, conceived by him, ruled by him.

He it was who developed the disciplinary system whereby masters and prefects assigned black marks for misconduct. In the English public schools after which he modeled Groton each mark would have required for its removal a specified number of strokes with a cane across the miscreant's bottom. Peabody's system was healthier. It required a boy to work off each black mark with some assigned task—a half hour of leaf raking or lawn mowing or snow shoveling or a certain number of briskly walking turns around the campus. Black marks could be and often were awarded in clusters of from two to five. On rare occasions a block of six, the maximum, was given, requiring the culprit to visit the rector in the latter's study for a justifiably dreaded interview, the rector in wrath being a towering, terrifying figure. Most boys received two or three black marks a week. Franklin Roosevelt received none at all during the whole autumn and winter and early spring of his first year. Not until mid-May of 1897 would he "serve off" his first black mark, for talking in the schoolroom—"and I am very glad I got it, as I was thought to have no school spirit before," [22] he would confess in a letter to his parents. Thereafter he saw to it that he received enough black marks to prevent his being deemed a goody-goody by his fellows.

Fagging was another English public school feature which Peabody wisely avoided at Groton. But he permitted to develop, instead, without giving it official sanction or even openly admitting it existed, a system whereby boys in the upper forms imposed traditional punishments on boys in the lower forms who conspicuously violated the Groton code (by cheating, for instance) or who were simply deemed "too fresh" and in need of humbling. The punishments were of two kinds. The milder, "boot-boxing," consisted of being placed, painfully doubled up and cramped, in the basement locker assigned each boy as a depository for the boots he wore outdoors. The more severe was "pumping." It consisted of being called out by name before one's schoolmates, generally in study hall, and taken to a lavatory, where one's face was held under an open spigot for a long enough period to induce the sensations of drowning.

Franklin Roosevelt seems never to have questioned the justice of these painful humiliations. Never did he show any sympathy for the sufferers. Quite the contrary. "The Biddle boy [Moncure Biddle] is quite crazy, fresh and stupid, he has been boot-boxed once and threatened to be pumped several times," he wrote to his parents on September 27, 1896. Three months later he wrote: "A new kid has come from Fitchburg whose name is Crocker [Alvah Crocker, Jr., Groton, '01, of the paper-manufacturing family] and we hope he will turn out better than Biddle!" Alas, he did not. "The new Crocker kid had 8 blackmarks & 1 lateness last week & was pumped yesterday," wrote Franklin on December 13.[23]

As for Franklin himself, he was not so much as threatened with "boot-boxing" or "pumping" that autumn. He would never be. He seemed to have no rebellious instincts which, expressed in acts or attitudes, required to be suppressed by coercion. At no point would he exert an individuality that varied markedly from the norm. He evinced, instead, a veritable passion for conformity—an almost pathetic eagerness to be accepted and to "succeed" according to the standards of Groton's world. Nor would he at any time afterward indicate that in retrospect, he in any way regretted this or suspected that the code that the Groton boys developed under the aegis of Peabody's will, Peabody's ideas was less than perfectly right. Others did so, though they were surely a small minority of the Groton alumni. Among them was the artist George Biddle (Groton, '04), younger brother of Moncure and elder brother of Francis (Groton, '05), who became convinced that the school's "effect was to stifle creative impulse" and that Groton's code was in several ways morally contemptible and, insofar as it was ostensibly sustained by the professed standards of a church school, intellectually dishonest. He came to regard Peabody personally as a seriously flawed monolithic character, "a somewhat great man, whom I find incompatible with my conception of the adequate," and passed upon the headmaster the judgment Delacroix once made of Ingres' "Odalisque" in the Louvre as Delacroix's students filed past it: " '*Messieurs, le chapeau dans la main mais les yeux fixés à terre*'—Gentlemen, your hats in your hands, but turn your eyes the other way." [24] Franklin Roosevelt's later judgment was wholly different; throughout his life he would express his profound admiration for the rector, his gratitude for educative experience of him, and would never so much as hint that the rector's educational views and conceptions of Christianity and right conduct could be validly questioned. "As long as I live, the influence of Dr. and Mrs. Peabody means and will mean more to me than that of any other people next to my father and mother," [25] he would publicly testify nearly forty years after he first met the headmaster.

The nature of this influence can be indicated by a couple of quotations. Peabody once said: "It used to bother me when I made mistakes and I wasted a lot of time fretting. Now I have learned that if one does the best he can in the light of all his available knowledge and judgment then that is all he can do or could have done and there is no use grieving about it. I do the best I can under the circumstances and go on to something else. One thing at a time, that is the great thing." [26] He also once said: "I am not sure I like boys to think too much. A lot of people think a lot of things we could do without. Manifestly the world is full of evil and we all encounter it as we go along. Nobody denies that. But why emphasize it ahead of time?" [27] Peabody himself had been so greatly in-

fluenced intellectually by Professor A. V. G. Allen of the Episcopal Theological School in Cambridge, Massachusetts, that he could not but
transmit this influence—modified by his own mentality, of course—to
his pupils. He quoted Allen directly in some memoirs he once wrote of
his days as a theological student: "History is not merely a collection of
facts to be learned by heart but a revelation of the working of God
through the ages. . . . I am always moving underground, beneath institutions and customs and formulas of thought, and trying to get at some
deeper meaning. To study history is to bring one near to the process of
God, that is, the study of it upon a large scale, which takes in great
reaches of events. The undevout astronomer is mad. The same might be
said of the undevout historian." [28]

Franklin Roosevelt would gladly lend his persuasive prestige to an
effort to obtain for Peabody an honorary degree from his English alma
mater, Cambridge, in 1935, writing the U.S. ambassador in London that
Peabody was "the unquestionably outstanding private school Head
Master in the United States." [29] To Peabody himself he would write in
1936 in thanks for a birthday card, adding, "Do you know that I have
every one of them that you have sent me since the earliest days after I
was graduated?" Also to Peabody he would write: "More than forty
years ago you said, in a sermon in the Old Chapel, something about not
losing boyhood ideals in later life. These Groton ideals—taught by you
—I try not to forget—and your words are still with me." [30]

It would be a mistake to assume, however, that he told the literal truth
(though probably he believed he did) when he indicated that the Peabody influence was one of two major determinants of the self he ultimately became or of the acts he would perform in the position of supreme power he ultimately achieved.

It is true that his parental relationships had developed in such a way,
by the time he came to Groton, as to make him peculiarly susceptible to
the rector's massive paternalistic authority. James Roosevelt was then
sixty-eight years old and ill of heart disease. He had not for some time
been able to play a strong fatherly role in his son's life. Indeed, mother
and son had been and continued to be at great pains to protect the husband and father from cares, worries, shocks that, in the precarious state
of his health, might prove fatal. Hence there was a vital gap which the
rector could fill, and all the more effectively because the boy had certain
natural similarities to the rector as regards character traits and intellect,
such similarities as a son might inherit from such a father. Like the rector, he directed his conscious energies outward; they became activities
that made changes in the physical environment, to a more than usual

degree. Like the rector, he had no inclination toward introspection or abstract theorizing. Moreover, his parental circumstances increased his susceptibility to the rector's religious message. Franklin had by then embraced, as has been said, a Christianity sustained by Episcopalian ritual which had as its essence a pure, simple, unquestioning and unquestioned belief in God as a loving Father and in the consequent ultimate beneficence of universal processes. This faith was essentially the same, in substance and mood, as the rector's and was doubtless increased, and rendered less vulnerable to inward doubts, by the rector's preaching of it.

But if Franklin Roosevelt had close similarities to the rector, he had also marked differences from him. What the rector was as a whole (this constituted his rare integrity), Franklin was only in part. Peabody had nothing to hide and hid nothing—what he seemed to be he really essentially was—whereas Franklin's outward seeming, even at age fourteen, was in many respects a deceptive appearance. Thus, in his letters home, Franklin wrote flat news reports of what he had been doing, what was happening in the school, how he was faring in classroom and extracurricular activities. He expressed only orthodox sentiments, conventional emotions, attitudes consistent with Groton's conception of good form. But behind the outward seeming, this façade which Groton helped him shape in ways that would gain favor or win approval, were reserves that would widen and deepen with the years—reserves in which several selves with different interests operated on different principles toward different ends. The ultimate harmonization of these selves, the fitting or fusing of them into a single effective community, required an inner politics. It required a full inward exercise of the art of creative compromise.

VII

No mention was made of the Presidential election campaign in the letters Franklin Roosevelt wrote home that autumn of 1896. On the Sunday before election day, as political excitement rose to fever pitch all across the nation, Franklin's excited anticipation was focused on a football game to be played between Groton and the school which was its chief traditional rival. "We play St. Marks next Wednesday and if we win I shall telegraph you," he wrote his parents that day. "We expect the game to be very close. . . . I will tell you all about [it] . . . on Thursday." And on Thursday, November 5, he did so in a letter which bore no salutation but began instead in newspaper headline style:

Hurrah,   Hurrah,   Hurrah
GROTON
46
St. Marks
0

He had lunched with the James Lawrences the day before and had then gone with them to a game in which "our fellows played without a fault. . . . I am hoarse, deaf, and ready to stand on my cocoanut!" [31] He said nothing whatever about the triumph at the polls, two days before, of sound conservatism (gold) over dangerous radicalism (silver).

But the significance of what had occurred, as viewed by the orthodox, was certainly impressed upon him during a lecture and discussion course he took that year in political economy. He made very full notes of the lectures he heard. All buying and selling, he recorded, are "in reality only an exchange of one commodity for another" effected by use of money; that "gold and silver are used as money because . . . they are durable, portable, divisible without loss of value, can be stamped and have intrinsic value." The value of money must itself be stable, however. "Gold is stable, silver is unstable, therefore gold is the only suitable standard of value." The essential absurdity and dire consequence of the Silver Purchase Acts, as viewed by the teacher, were pointed up. "It is a fact, proved by history, that with a depreciated currency prices rise much faster than wages. In silver-using countries the rate of wages and the standard of living are much lower than in gold-using countries." He further recorded that the "more capital in a country, the greater will be the employment of labor, or in other words, the more wealth that is used to produce further wealth, the more will be the labor employed"; that "capital is the result of saving"; and that a "glut of capital is impossible until everyone has everything he wishes, but there may be too much capital invested in a particular business," in which case "capital will be withdrawn and will seek investment elsewhere." [32]

In that same spring he was a member of the Junior Debating Society. Through this involvement came to him further muffled echoes of events in the great world—of the growing agitation for U.S. intervention on the side of Cuban insurrectionists against Spanish tyrants; of the demand, voiced by McKinley himself, for the annexation of Hawaii in the wake of a bloodless revolution (in 1893) which had deposed Queen Liliuokalani; of demands for colonial acquisitions in the Far East. All these had their impress when he was assigned the affirmative side of a debate on the question "Resolved, that the United States increase the Navy." He and his partner, Casper Goodrich, prepared carefully and, on the evening of the debate, March 22, scored a great victory when one of their opponents "got very confused" and had to "quit." Franklin's speech of some six minutes' duration had been thoroughly memorized and "came out without a hitch." Out of thirty votes cast by listeners, Franklin and his partner received all but three.[33]

"Last Monday was a red letter day for me," wrote Franklin to "Dear Papa and Mama" on March 24, reporting his debating triumph along with another which to him seemed much more important (he reported it first and at much greater length than he did his debate). This was the III Class High Kick, an athletic competition so painful and even dangerous to participants that it was discontinued a few years later. A tin pan was suspended by cord from the gymnasium ceiling, at first only about three and a half feet from the floor, in such a way that it could be raised to a new height following each round of kicks. In each round, each contestant was permitted three tries in which at least to touch with his kicking foot the suspended pan. As this became raised well above the height of the tallest boy and most of the contestants were eliminated, each kick required of each boy a leap in the air and, his kick completed, a heavy fall to the floor. Franklin managed, in the third of three tries, to kick 7 feet $3\frac{1}{2}$ inches, which was 2 feet over his head. This was as great a test of stoic courage as it was of physical prowess. "At every kick I landed on my *neck* on the left side," he wrote, "so the result is that the whole left side of my body is sore and my left arm is a little swollen!"[34] His arm continued to bother him for several months, reducing his effectiveness on the baseball diamond that spring. And this effectiveness would not have been great in any case; when he put his name down for baseball in mid-April, he informed his parents, who were about to sail to Europe for James Roosevelt's annual cure at Bad Nauheim, that he expected to be placed on a junior team "as I do not play well."[35]

He played so badly, in fact, that in early May he became a member of "a new team which is called the BBBB or Bum Base Ball Boys" and was "made up of about the worst players in the school." Another team of poor players was called the "Carter's Little Liver Pills" and was the opponent of the BBBB team in a mid-May game which Franklin reported with burlesque humor to his parents. "The only ball I received, I nobly missed," he wrote, "and it landed biff! on my stomach, to the great annoyance of that intricate organ, and to the great delight of all present. The walls of my tummy caved in and a great panic ensued inside. . . . Excuse all this tummy rot, but I have no larger change."[36] Other spring activities were reported: canoeing and rowing on the Nashua and its tributaries, swimming in the river, tennis, golf, drilling for the Decoration Day parade, in which the boys, wearing blue coats, white ducks, and straw hats, would march in formation behind the rector, mounted on his huge white horse.

In early June came yet another muffled echo of the great world, cloaked in laughter and bearing with it personal prestige for Franklin. On the first Friday of that month, Theodore Roosevelt, the boy's "Cousin Theodore," then the newly appointed Assistant Secretary of the Navy and long a favorite of the rector's (Peabody had wanted Theodore to become a master at Groton), came to the school to speak to the boys. He did so after supper that evening, giving "a splendid talk on his adventures when he was on the Police Board [in New York City]. He kept the whole room in uproar for an hour, by telling us killing stories about policemen and their doings. . . ." During this visit, Franklin learned, if he had not known before, that Sherrard Billings had been a classmate of Theodore Roosevelt at Harvard; he may well have learned from Billings that Roosevelt as college undergraduate had been unpopular with other students (though elected to the best clubs) because he was so aggressively enthusiastic in a time and place where the fashionable attitude was one of careless indifference. When "it was not considered good form to move at more than a walk, Roosevelt was always running," Billings said.[37]

During this visit, too, "Cousin Theodore" invited Franklin to come stay over July 4 at the Roosevelt home in Oyster Bay, Long Island—an invitation the boy promptly accepted. His doing so was part and parcel of a virtually unprecedented self-assertion in defiance of his mother's wishes. Earlier, Mrs. Anna "Bamie" Roosevelt Cowles, sister of Theodore, had asked the boy to Oyster Bay for the Fourth, evidently also asking the boy's mother, then in Europe, if his acceptance of the invitation met with parental approval. For some reason it did not. The boy had rebelled. "I am very sorry to hear that you refused Cousin Bammie's [sic] invitation for the 4th and as you told me I cd make my own plans and as Helen writes me there is to be a large party & lots of fun on the 4th, I shall try to arrange it with Cousin B. next Wednesday," he wrote. "Please don't make any more arrangements for my future happiness." Thus his acceptance of Theodore Roosevelt's invitation, which he flatly announced to his parents on June 8 ("I am going to Oyster Bay to stay with the Theodore Roosevelt's on Friday July 2nd & shall stay there all Monday"), was a stubborn continuation of his rebellious stance. Nor did later communications of censure from abroad force a retreat. "I am sorry you didn't want me to go to Oyster Bay for the 4th but I had already accepted Cousin Theodore's invitation & I shall enjoy it very much," he wrote firmly on June 13, adding the next day: "I am so sorry you have refused Cousin Bammie's [sic] invitation and I wish you had let me make my own plans as you said. As it is, I have accepted the Theodore's invitation and I hope you will not refuse that too." [38]

A few weeks later came Prize Day, Groton's graduation ceremony, at which Franklin received the medal for his high kick triumph and the first of the three Punctuality Prizes he would win before his graduation. His last grade report for the year was of an average of 7.86, placing him fourth in a class of seventeen and earning from the rector a scrawled "Very satisfactory."

VIII

In general, his last three years at Groton followed the pattern established in the first.

When he returned to the school to enter IV Form, after a summer of much outdoor exercise at Hyde Park and Campobello, he was markedly taller and heavier than he had been the spring before. He weighed "116 lbs. with my clothes on, or about 112 without, which is a considerable gain," he reported to his parents—and in later letters he reported in considerable detail on his physique, its growing size and strength. He was enabled to do so by an elaborate system of physical measurements instituted at Groton, that fall of 1897, by a new gymnasium instructor, a Swede named Skarström ("Cigar Stump," the boys promptly nicknamed him). Skarström recorded some fifty different measurements for each examination, doing so on an "Anthropometric Chart, showing the Relation of the Individual in Size, Strength, Symmetry and Development to the Normal Standard." Wrote Franklin on October 7, 1897: "I was measured two days ago, by Herr Cigar Stump & it was a very interesting process. I was done all over & in every conceivable position, lying down, standing up & kneeling. Mr. Skarström said I was well developed & proportioned & that I did not need special exercises. . . ." Later measurements revealed a satisfactory development but also, perhaps owing to the rapidity of his growth, a certain weakness of his heart. Or so Skarström insisted. In late September, 1898, the youth's examination indicated that "my heart is still a little weak, and I must be careful in playing football not to get too tired." But when, in the following spring, "Old Cigar Stump" again insisted upon a heart weakness, his diagnosis was challenged by the patient. "I told him that he was a liar (not quite in those words)," wrote Franklin in a letter home. He was sufficiently concerned, however, to follow Skarström's advice that he not try out that spring for one of the rowing crews, as he had planned to do. "I suppose it would be on the whole safer not to," he said, adding that he would instead "do my best at base-ball and golf." No further mention was made of a heart condition in his letters from Groton. Evidently the "weakness," if any, was thereafter overcome.[39]

His health during the remainder of his prep school years was considered good on the whole, though he continued to have frequent head colds, had at least one quite severe bout with the grippe which left him weak and depressed for several days, was seriously ill with scarlet fever in the spring of his IV Form year, and had a normally light case of the mumps at the close of his V Form year—a dangerous age for this glandular illness, which seems, however, to have produced no permanent ill effects in his case. He had considerable trouble with his teeth, in consequence not only of the injury he had suffered on Campobello but also of having inherited the irregular, uneven teeth characteristic of the Delanos. (He suffered much discomfort from his dentist's efforts to straighten his teeth; to replace the tooth destroyed on Campobello, his dentist gave him one which could be removed, then screwed back in place.) In the spring of his last year in the school an eye examination revealed that he was somewhat nearsighted and should, the doctor said, wear glasses to avoid increasing the weakness. "I ordered a pince-nez, & spectacles . . . ," he wrote home on April 10, 1900. Two days later he informed his parents that he was "writing in 'specks'! It seems so strange. . . ." [40]

Since his increase in height and weight was no greater, relatively, than that of his contemporaries, it gave him no advantage over them in contact sports, and he continued to manifest no remarkable athletic prowess. He was on the third football twenty-two during his IV Form year; he managed to make only the second twenty-two in his last football season at Groton; and while his letters recorded many football injuries suffered by him, painful if minor, they told of no personal football triumphs. He fared no better in the boxing ring after taking up boxing in the IV Form. Entered as a lightweight in the "winter Sports meeting" in March, 1898, he had "two three minute rounds with Fuller Potter," from which both emerged "with bloody noses and cut lips." The match was decided in Potter's favor. "I did not much expect to win," said Franklin, "as this is the third year he has boxed and even then we were quite close." He didn't expect to win the high kick during that meeting, either, "as I am in the 2nd class instead of the 3rd [where he'd won last year] and several boys in it are better kickers than I am." Through a supreme effort combined with characteristic stoic courage he managed to place second, kicking eight inches higher than he had the year before and within an inch of the winning kick. ("I hurt my elbow in the same way as last year, but I do not think I will have any trouble with it, as I rub it and put vaseline on every day." [41]) On the baseball diamond he remained a mediocre player.

He continued eager to conform, and he succeeded in fitting almost perfectly, so far as outward appearance and expressed attitude were concerned, into the Groton mold. A letter he wrote home on October 21, 1897, showed how well he had learned the importance of "school spirit" and how willing he was to manifest it to the discomfiture of a new master, Julian L. Coolidge, who (said Franklin) "talks just like a baby pronouncing all his 'r's like 'w' & 'th' like 'z.' " When Coolidge was in charge of study hall for the boys of the III and IV forms, some of his charges started whistling, and Franklin promptly began to sing "Yankee Doodle in a high falsetto key." Coolidge ordered the whole IV Form to stand. "That did not do much good, & we all sat down again & the 3rd Form stood up. Then paper & ink & nutshells flew thick & fast, and the old man got perfectly wild. He called up the wrong boys & for ten minutes he yelled at a boy who really was not in the room, while he really wanted me, but the end of the period came just in time to save me from a large number of Black-marks." [42]

He was properly patronizing of the boys in the lower forms; properly protective, in big-brotherly fashion, of his cousin Warren Delano Robbins who entered I Form in the fall of '97; and also properly disapproving, even priggishly so, of his "Nephew Rosy" (or Taddy, as Franklin called him in letters), who so conspicuously failed to "come up to the mark" of a proper Grotonian in his studies or in his extracurricular activities. Poor Taddy did not leave his troubles behind when he was graduated from Groton and, during Franklin's VI Form year, became a Harvard freshman; nor did Franklin cease his disapproval of him. "I was not very much surprised to hear that he [Taddy] had been put on probation," wrote Franklin to his mother on June 13, 1900, "as I had heard from *all* our graduates that he was not doing well. . . . I do not know what the direct cause has been . . . , but I think I should tell you that I *know* that Taddy has been on to N.Y. several times without letting anyone know of it. . . . I think the very strictest measures sh'd be taken, but of course Papa must not worry in the least, as after all it is no affair of ours." (His worry about Papa's worrying was by then a standard feature of his correspondence.) Franklin recommended that Taddy's allowance be drastically cut next year "as even this year he has had just *twice too much*." [43]

His eagerness to conform and to please, however—his seemingly unquestioning acceptance of Groton's standards of "good form"—did not wholly prevent the development of overt traits of personality which occasionally grated on others. James Goodwin, who had been the only other "new boy" in III Form when Franklin came to Groton, would remember that in the fourth and fifth and sixth forms, "Franklin D. . . . developed an independent, cocky manner and at times became very argumentative and sarcastic." It was Goodwin's impression that Franklin in an argument "always liked to take the side opposite to that maintained by those to whom he was talking" and that this "irritated the other boys considerably." [44] But his developing individuality seems to have involved no marked change in his attitude toward girls, which remained remarkably boyish for a youth of sixteen and seventeen and eighteen. The evidence of his letters requires interpretation on this point, of course. Allowance must be made for the fact that nearly all of them were addressed to his mother, to whom he would have been unlikely to reveal the scope of his sexual interests had these been great. But even so, it is surprising that he, entering into his late teens, never indicates that any girl is positively attractive to him but only that some are not unattractive while most are boring or irritating "brats." Often he expresses indifference to whom he should escort to a holiday dance, just so he does not "get left" with someone like so-and-so, "as I did two years ago to my great and everlasting regret!" Thus, when he was nearly sixteen, having accepted a dance invitation in New York, he wrote that he had been "in a quandary as to whom to ask [as his date] . . . , and not caring at all, I drew lots and . . . the fateful die fell on Mary Newbold." A year later he reports that he has asked a certain girl to accompany him to "the Dodworth dance, not being able to think of anyone else." On another occasion he writes his mother: "I wish you would think up some decent partner for me for the N.Y. dance, to which I suppose I will be invited, so that I can get somebody early, and not get palmed off on some ice-cart like the —— girl!" [45]

Increasingly, in his letters home, he assumed the role of man-of-the-family, a role his aging father was no longer able adequately to fill. The salutation of these letters was habitually "My dearest Mama and Papa," but in the body of his communications his mother was always "you," his father always "Papa," and to his mother he often gave advice, even instruction, on practical matters, admonishing her directly or by implication to protect his father from anxiety. The *Half-Moon*, his father's yacht, was being towed up the Hudson in early October, 1898, when the naphtha in her fuel tank exploded. The boat was a total loss. Franklin, shocked and dismayed, promptly wanted to know "how it was that *none of the men were on board,*" for he had supposed the yacht wouldn't "tow unless there was someone to steer her and it was very dangerous to leave her alone, in case she might have broken adrift." He simply could not understand how the fuel could have been ignited "as the tank was surrounded by water and nothing short of a great blaze all over the boat could have set fire to the engine-pipes." He said that his own boat, the *New Moon*, was theirs to sell to help pay for building a new *Half-Moon*, an offer not accepted. The original *Half-Moon* was replaced in the spring of 1900 by a sixty-foot eighteen-ton auxiliary schooner which had been launched three years before James Roosevelt's purchase of it and which became *Half-Moon II*. Franklin gave his mother instructions concerning her. "I *don't like* the idea of a flush deck as they are not comfortable in any kind of a breeze and you would feel always insecure, unless you have a rail. You must have all rigging renewed as by all accounts it is unsafe." Later he wrote he was "glad you are to have an enlarged cockpit, instead of a flush deck," and instructed his mother to have the *Half-Moon* "flag *red* with a white half-moon instead of *blue*," evidently because crimson was the college color of Harvard, where he was to enroll a few months later.[46]

In his V Form year, his interest in charitable activities stimulated by Sherrard Billings, he became a member of Groton's Missionary Society, which conducted religious services in various localities near the school, actively aided the work of the Boys' Club of Boston, and ran the Groton Summer Camp on Lake Asquam, New Hampshire. Of the latter, which was for "poor boys" ten to fourteen years old, mostly from Boston, Franklin in the summer of 1900 was a director, one of a five-man Camp Committee, and devoted two weeks of his summer vacation to service as member of the camp's "faculty." (This consisted regularly of a master, two graduates, and two or three undergraduates and was changed every fortnight.) Another Missionary Society activity of Franklin's was, with another student, the care of an eighty-four-year-old black woman, widow of a Civil War drummer, who lived in a small house near the school and was a permanent object of society charity. "We are to visit her a couple of times a week," explained Franklin to his mother in late January, 1899, "see that she has coal, water, etc, feed her hens if they need it, and in case of a snow-storm we are to dig her out & put things ship-shape." He thought this would be "very pleasant as she is a dear old thing, and it will be a good occupation for us." [47]

He became more concerned, though by no means abnormally so, with current events in the great world as these continued to be echoed within Groton's walls. On January 19, 1898, two days after the death of his Grandfather Warren Delano II at age eighty-nine ("I know you are heart-broken," he wrote his mother, "but we must remember that he has gone to a better place than this earth, and will be far happier there"),[48] Franklin argued the assigned negative side of the Groton debate on the question "Resolved, that Hawaii be promptly annexed." The nub of his argument was that by taking over the islands, the United States would for the first time present to a hostile naval power a "really vulnerable point" (the United States and Russia were thus far "the only two countries no part of whose territory can be cut off by a naval enemy") whose defense would require vast expenditures for island fortification, the maintenance of armed forces there, and enlargement of our Navy. To his opponent's assertion that "we need a coaling-station for our ships" he replied that, though it was "not generally known," a port "in one of the islands," called Pearl Harbor, already "belongs to the United States"; with "a little inexpensive dredging" at Pearl Harbor we would acquire a coaling station "without annexation." He also expressed moral scruples: "Why take away the nationality of a free people? Why meddle with this land thousands of miles away whose inhabitants are so different from us in every way?" [49]

In the following year there was much talk throughout America, throughout the world, about an impending "breakup of China" into bits and pieces imperfectly controlled by Western powers unless these powers joined together to establish and maintain an Open Door policy there. The question was debated at Groton: "Resolved, that the United States and England should guarantee the integrity of China." Franklin was assigned the con side. In the fall of 1899 came the long-anticipated war between the British and the Boers, with the latter winning all the initial battles. "Hurrah for the Boers!" Franklin wrote home. "I entirely sympathize with them." When his mother, an ardent Anglophile, protested his anti-British sentiments, he compromised his original position. "I think you misunderstand . . . ," he wrote. "I cannot help feeling convinced that the Boers have the side of right and that for the past ten years they have been *forced* into this war. I am sure you will feel this if you only read up the Boer case. *However,* undoubtedly, now that the war is actually on, it will be best from the humanitarian standpoint for the British to win speedily and civilization will be hurried on, but I feel that the same result would have been surely obtained without war." [50]

Yet other echoes of the great world reached his ears. In the same letter in which he explained his stand on the Boers he wrote that Jacob Riis (soon to add to his fame with his autobiography, *The Making of an American*) had spoken before the Missionary Society "and told stories of his experiences with 'Teddy' [Roosevelt] on the police-force in N.Y." [51] (In point of fact Riis was never on the Police Board; he was only a good friend of "Teddy.") Professor Edward S. Morse, curator of the Peabody Academy of Sciences in Salem, Massachusetts, and founder and editor of the *American Naturalist,* lectured the boys on Japan, then on China, the latter lecture being "most interesting," according to Franklin, "although I rather thought he ran down the poor Chinamen a little too much and thought too much of the Japs." He was a great Orientologist, was Professor Morse; it was as a result of his talks on Oriental art that "Uncle Billy Wag's" aunt, Mrs. Jack Gardner, initiated what was to become her world-famous Oriental collection. But his greatest influence on Franklin was as a naturalist, "a wonderful naturalist" with whom a hike in the woods was a fascinating experience and under whose impetus Groton revived a moribund Natural History Society, of which Franklin became one of the most enthusiastic members.

On a single occasion during Franklin's Groton years did a historic event have direct impact on his personal life. This was during the second half of his IV Form year when the long agitation over Cuba, immensely heightened by the blowing up of the U.S. battleship *Maine* in Havana Harbor, culminated in war with Spain.

Franklin's closest friend at Groton by that spring of 1898 was Lathrop Brown, a fellow member of the class of 1900, and as war fever swept the school, the two friends, with a third member of their class, laid plans to run away and enlist in the U.S. Navy. A pieman came to the school twice each week to sell cookies and pies. From him the boys learned that the Navy was accepting enlistments on the Long Wharf in Boston. With him they arranged that he smuggle them off the school grounds in his horse-drawn cart in the early afternoon of the last Sunday in April. They assumed that by the time they were missed they would have been inducted into the Navy, having of course lied about their ages and perhaps (this is unrecorded) given false names and addresses. But alas for the success of this venture, war fever was not the only fever then sweeping the school. A scarlet fever epidemic was on. And on the Sunday when the escape to glory was to have been made all three boys were ingloriously detained in Groton's infirmary with sore throats, temperatures, and scarlet-marked skins.

Franklin's case of scarlet fever was initially a mild one. There seemed at first no need for serious worry on the part of his parents, who were on the high seas bound for James Roosevelt's Bad Nauheim cure when the illness struck. But then complications in the form of a kidney infection developed. Franklin's fever mounted; he became very sick indeed. His parents hurried home, his mother establishing her semi-invalid husband at Hyde Park and then coming to Groton to be near her son. He was in an isolation ward where no visitors were permitted, but the imperious Sara Delano Roosevelt circumvented this strict rule, at some cost to her dignity, by placing a stepladder outside her son's second-story window and mounting it daily to see him, talk to him, read to him. "He was dreadfully wan . . . ," she later remembered, "and so thin that a neighbor called him my little *reconcentrado,* a term applied in those days to groups of starving Cubans." * As soon as he was out of quarantine, he was taken to Hyde Park, then to Campobello, where he gradually recovered his strength.[52]

It was as a convalescent, therefore, comforted and comfortable amid scenes of peaceful beauty, that he followed the martial exploits of Cousin Theodore who, having resigned his post as Assistant Secretary of the Navy and become colonel of a volunteer cavalry regiment called the Rough Riders, gained fame and glory on July 1, 1898, by leading his regiment in a charge up Kettle Hill at San Juan, Cuba, and personally killing a Spaniard. (He was proud of this killing; he spoke with evident delight of how the enemy soldier had doubled up in mortal agony when the bullet hit him.) Seldom has a single exploit of so little intrinsic importance been more successfully exploited for political profit. "Teddy" blew his own horn with gusto in tones a sensation-hungry public was eager to hear. He came home a national hero, promptly got himself nominated as Republican candidate for governor of New York, and won the election handily. He was cheered by Groton fifth former Franklin as he did so and was voted for by Franklin's father, despite the latter's normally rock-ribbed Democracy.

Thereafter New York politics and national politics had for Franklin an enhanced personal interest. On an October evening in 1897 he had heard Dr. William S. Rainsford, rector of St. George's Church in New York and a noted political reform leader in that city, talk "on the present political crisis in New York"—a talk in which the good doctor had used "pretty strong language against the Platt & Tammany machines & especially against the *former.*" [53] He had therefore a frame of reference through which to view Cousin Theodore's struggle for power against Republican "Boss" Thomas C. Platt and by which to measure the governor's success and failures. Theodore Roosevelt, as man and example, was of major importance in Franklin's education. The boy's admiration of the colorful "Teddy" became a motivating force: his identification of himself with his famous distant cousin bolstered his self-confidence and suggested, albeit vaguely, a possible career. Why should not he, a Democratic Roosevelt (he seems not to have considered switching parties), emulate the Republican Roosevelt and enter elective politics, as the rector and Theodore Roosevelt himself urged Groton boys to do?

* Actually the term applied to Cubans released from Spanish concentration camps.

IX

During his last year in the school, Franklin became a dormitory prefect and was assigned a study of his own, which he deemed "one of the five best single studies" available, but this was no outstanding distinction since nearly half the sixth formers became dormitory prefects. The great distinction was to be named a senior prefect, and this he never was. He became manager of the baseball team in the spring of his VI Form year, having been assistant manager the year before, but this was an office rich in responsibility and drudgery, relatively poor in prestige and glory.

A curious unevenness in his personal development became evident. He appeared in general every bit as mature as the average sixth former, if not more so. He demonstrated sound judgment in his handling of his duties as prefect; he was both admired and respected, he was liked too, by the boys in his charge. He was of great help as guide and mentor of young Warren Delano Robbins. In his advice and judgment on family matters he seemed often to manifest a stability and wisdom beyond his years. He performed conscientiously and efficiently his demanding tasks as baseball team manager and was proud of the fact that when his work was "over, & over successfully" there had been not "a single complaint." [54] His elders did not hesitate to assign to him posts of adult responsibility: he became a leading member of the Campobello Golf Club and, in the spring of 1900, accepted the position of club secretary and treasurer, which required him to supervise the physical care of the course and to collect dues and special contributions from other members. In sharp contrast with Poor Taddy, who was headed for personal tragedy, he seemed to have no wayward tendencies whatever. All the more surprising, therefore, were some other of his attitudes and interests as he approached and passed his eighteenth birthday.

That year's school play was *The Wedding March* by W. S. Gilbert, an adaptation of a French comedy entitled *Le Chapeau de Paille d'Italie.* Franklin, goaded by a strong element of the histrionic in his makeup (this was perhaps the earliest clear and definite manifestation of it), wanted a part in this play desperately and thought after the first tryout that he had won one. He wrote home excitedly about this, impressing on his parents the importance not only of the role he thought he had won but also of keeping the presumed fact "secret." ("*Mum's* the word. Impress the importance of it on Papa, as it would spoil *everything to have it known.*") But the part went to another. He then tried out for another part, a woman's (Grotonians played both male and female roles), "but shall not have it as it is being saved for Kerr Rainsford," who had been forced to leave school for an operation but would be back in February. "I think it rather hard," added Franklin with rare bitterness, "as there are so few girls and I am sure I could do as well as Kerr. As it is now I doubt if I get a good part at all, and Mr. Cushing [the director] is being bullied by his Boston friends (!) to give *them* all the best parts!" This was in mid-January, 1900. His letters make no more mention of the play until February 11, a dozen days after he had turned eighteen, when he wrote the "joyful news" that he was to have "a part in the play at last." A boy named Jimmie Jackson had been assigned "the part of an old hayseed countryfied uncle of the bride," but poor Jimmie had become "sick in Boston with rheumatic fever & water on the knee so won't be back again this term. I suppose it is criminal to rejoice," he went on, "but I can't help it! I've got his part, and it's one of the best in the play!!!!" [55]

No other activity of his in the whole of his Groton career so engaged him as this. He begged his parents for clothes suitable to his role (each actor must provide his own costume) and was delighted by the choices given him in two large boxes that arrived from Hyde Park a few days before dress rehearsal. He found "the dress coat . . . simply perfect, and I am learning how to manipulate the tails when I sit down. Don't tell anyone, however what I am to wear." Both his parents came with the James Lawrences (whose house guests they were) to the performance in the school gymnasium on Thursday evening, February 22, 1900. His Aunt Kassie came also with friends. And his parents stayed over to witness the play's second and final performance in Groton's Town Hall on Saturday evening, February 24. His relatives were all agreed, and contemporary news accounts concurred in the judgment, that F. D. Roosevelt in the role of "Uncle Bopaddy, a deaf gentleman" who generally managed to hear whatever he was not supposed to, was very funny.[56]

During that last year at Groton, Franklin was not only a sixth former, but also, to all intents and purposes, already a college freshman.

President Charles Eliot's famous "elective system" was then in its fullest flower at Harvard: students were required to take certain basic subjects during their first year, but after these were out of the way, they had almost unlimited freedom of choice among the courses offered. And at Groton, most of whose graduates automatically went on to Harvard, a so-called anticipatory plan had been initiated whereby a boy who passed his college preliminary examinations in his V Form year was permitted during his VI Form year to take examinations in the courses required of Harvard freshmen. If he passed these, he could complete work for a Harvard degree in just three years after coming to Cambridge instead of the customary four. Franklin was taking advantage of this opportunity.

He anticipated Harvard in other ways also. In the fall of 1899 he and Lathrop Brown decided to room together at college; they went to Cambridge in January to look for rooms in one of the Gold Coast dormitories on Mount Auburn Street—private dormitories which, for a price far beyond what the average college student could pay, offered much more luxurious accommodations than did the college-owned student houses in the Yard. They decided upon a first-floor corner suite (Number 27) in Westmorly Court, a spacious and well-lighted brick structure which had been completed the year before. The suite consisted of two bedrooms, sitting room, bath, and entrance hall. "The sitting room is large enough for two desks, & the bedrooms & bath room light & airy," Franklin wrote home enthusiastically. "The ceilings are very high." The rent, $400, seemed to him remarkably low.[57]

On the evening of the first Thursday in June, Cousin Theodore made the second of his two visits to the school during Franklin's enrollment there. The governor of New York was then being much talked of as a probable Republican candidate for Vice President of the United States, though he himself was far from enthusiastic about the movement to "draft" him as President McKinley's running mate. Theodore Roosevelt was only too well aware that Boss Platt, among others, was anxious to get him out of the state by sidetracking him into a position of impotent obscurity. In any case, it was not as future Vice President but as past Rough Rider that Teddy appealed most strongly to Groton boys, and he delighted them by opening his talk with references to that famous cavalry regiment. According to the *Grotonian*, the governor said that Westerners in the regiment at first "looked down" on Easterners but changed their minds after a couple of fistfights won by the latter. He also "showed the absolute uselessness of a weak-minded officer" by citing the case of a captain who tried to curry favor with his men by permitting breaches of discipline to go unpunished. "After a couple of weeks that captain was more despised than any officer in camp."

Prize Day that year was June 25. Franklin was surprised and delighted to find he had won the Latin Prize, which consisted of a forty-volume set of the Temple Shakespeare. On his final grade report, which maintained the average of earlier ones, the rector made a last comment to the graduate's parents: "He has been a thoroughly faithful scholar & a most satisfactory member of this school throughout his course. I part with Franklin with reluctance." Many years later Endicott Peabody made retrospective comment: "There has been a good deal written about Franklin Roosevelt when he was a boy at Groton, more than I should have thought justified by the impression that he left at the school. He was a quiet, satisfactory boy of more than ordinary intelligence, taking a good position in his Form but not brilliant. Athletically he was rather too slight for success. We all liked him." [58]

Five

※》※《※

Harvard

I

THERE had been a sharp break in Franklin's life when at age fourteen he left his home to enter Groton. No such break occurred as, aged eighteen, he moved from Groton to Harvard, he having in several respects become a Harvard man while yet a Groton schoolboy. And in Cambridge he remained distinctly Grotonian, part of a school community that had been transplanted virtually intact within the college and maintained its identity there.

Differences there were in the manner, the style of his living. When in late summer of 1900 he came with his parents and Lathrop Brown to Boston, there to choose and buy furnishings for their rooms, he did not stint himself; he had no intention of continuing in college the Puritan austerities that had characterized his prep school life. He would live in true Gold Coast style, not ostentatiously but in quiet luxury; he thoroughly enjoyed deciding how the furniture should be placed and what should be hung upon bedroom and sitting-room walls in the suite in Westmorly Court. By late September, when they were finally settled into their quarters, these quarters were assertively Grotonian. Groton pennants, Groton certificates, Groton photographs (including one of the 1900 baseball team, Franklin its manager), Groton mementos of all kinds, decorated the walls and study tables.

And he continued through his first year, if not through all his Harvard years, to feel more intimately identified with his prep school than with his college. Most of his Groton classmates remained his close neighbors, ensconced in Westmorly and the other three Gold Coast dormitories on Mount Auburn Street—Randolph, Claverly, and Russell. He and his roommate ate breakfast, lunch, and supper, not in commons, but at a Groton table in a Cambridge eating house, a table he described as "great fun & most informal." For evening recreation they went often to Sanborn's billiard parlor on Massachusetts Avenue where they found "most of the Groton, St. M[ark's], & St. Paul's and Pomfret fellows." He returned to Groton often for visits.

He was there on Saturday and Sunday, October 14 and 15, 1900, when Consecration Service for the magnificent new chapel was held, an event "most impressive . . . which none of us will ever forget," as he wrote his "dearest Mama and Papa" upon his return to Cambridge.[1] He heard there two sermons, one by Episcopal Bishop William Lawrence of Massachusetts, the other by Peabody, of which, when he later read them in the ceremony's printed program booklet, he marked the passages that had most impressed him. Of Bishop Lawrence's sermon was singled out a portion that described Christ as "no thoughtless quixotic, no unenlightened fanatic" but one who came to earth "that He might lead men to truth." The marked portion went on: ". . . with sublime courage He lived out His life and died the death He most dreaded. Surely, my friends, in the presence of that life, we cannot encourage the thought that in order to know evil, a young man must for a while experience evil. . . . No! It is the part of parents and of this School to cultivate in youth that sensitiveness to evil, which causes a shrinking from sin. . . . This is spiritual culture. . . ." Of the rector's sermon was marked a passage saying: "For life—which is in any way worthy, is like ascending a mountain. When you have climbed to the first shoulder of the hill, you find another rise above you, and that achieved there is another, and another still, and yet another peak, and the height to be achieved seems infinity: but you find as you ascend that the air becomes purer and more bracing, that the clouds gather more frequently below than above, that the sun is warmer than before and that you not only get a clearer view of Heaven, but that you gain a wider and wider view of earth, and that your horizon is perpetually growing larger."

Of such was made the living faith he carried from adolescence into his dawning manhood.

II

The transition from prep school to college was relatively smooth and easy for him, but this was not because Harvard as educational process was a simple continuation of Groton. There were great differences in mental and spiritual climate, a radical difference in educational aims, between the university headed by Charles W. Eliot and the school dominated by Endicott Peabody. By these, no member of the transplanted Groton community could fail to be affected.

The differences can be indicated in part by comparing Harvard with Yale, the only other college for which Groton at that time specifically prepared (there were "Yale" as distinct from "Harvard" courses in the VI Form), for though the number of Grotonians going to New Haven was small compared to the number going to Cambridge, Yale far more than Harvard could be accurately described as a continuation of Groton's educational methods and purposes. Like Groton, Yale's student life, both curricular and extracurricular, was rigidly routinized, systematized; almost alone among America's major institutions of higher learning, Yale had refused to succumb to Eliot's persuasive, though much criticized, example of "free electives." Like Groton, Yale laid great stress on a ruggedly competitive individualism, not only in athletics, but in all other endeavors. Like Groton, Yale emphasized traditions and traditional values against which victories and defeats were generally graded. Part and parcel of this was an insistence upon "spirit"—team spirit, patriotism, school spirit. Once accepted into the community, neither family nor wealth counted for much in determining a student's classroom success or extracurricular prestige; the competition was as free as it was fierce. Yet the overall tendency of this intense competitive individualism was to develop not individuals but, instead, easily identifiable types—a paradox for which the explanation becomes obvious at a close look. Competition, after all, is itself a kind of conformity: it is an effort by the competitors to conform as precisely as possible to some single standard of excellence by which all their efforts are graded. He who most precisely conforms is adjudged the winner.

Harvard, on the other hand, though an even more historical institution than Yale, had relatively few active traditions and was inclined to take a certain pride in its careless lack of them. The pride was not strong. Indeed, Harvard men in the early 1900's, like those of Henry Adams' college days a half century before, were inclined to regard strong emotions of any kind with suspicion; a certain skepticism was as characteristic of them as enthusiasm was of the typically hearty Yale man. Harvard "indifference" had been proverbial since the 1870's. There were competitions at Harvard, certainly—intense competitions into which Franklin Roosevelt as a transplanted Grotonian dutifully entered and within which he strove with all his might to excel—but the competitive spirit did not dominate the college community. And as competition counted for less, wealth and family counted for proportionately more in all extracurricular activities save team sports; as a matter

of fact, such activities as college politics and theatricals were largely organized on the basis of social class, with members of certain private
clubs in positions of power. Nor did the college administration pay
much heed to such activities so long as they were confined within quite
broad limits of permitted conduct. Harvard on the administrative level
defined "education" almost exclusively in intellectual terms and had little active concern for character development or the protection of private
morality among its enrollees. It felt it did its full duty by offering the
best of mental fare, insofar as it could discern and obtain the best; it
was up to the individual student to decide how much of this offer to accept or reject beyond the minimum required to pass examinations. And
the student must for the most part shift for himself outside the classroom, unrestrained and unsustained by such institutional disciplines as
hedged about the activities of Groton schoolboys and Yale underclass-
men. In consequence, Harvard's influence on those who gained most
from it was an encouragement of genuine individuality and flexibility of
mind and of a tolerance, if not an actual appreciation, of honest eccentricities, coupled with a profound contempt for all that was bogus,
fraudulent.

Such gains were necessarily balanced, to an indeterminate degree, by
risks, by losses. George Santayana, a junior member of Harvard's philosophy faculty during Franklin's college years, conceded that Yale near
the turn of the century had "more unity, more energy, and greater
fitness for our present conditions" than Harvard, yet believed these advantages to be more than offset by Harvard's greater "freedom, both
from external trammels and from the pleasant torpor of too fixed a tradition," and by its "single eye for truth." [2] But this same Santayana, decades later, recognized that the "single eye" was the very opposite of a
unifying vision; he noted that "Harvard liberalism tended . . . to encourage dissolution." [3] And with this dictum the critics of Charles W.
Eliot, who were many and vociferous, wholeheartedly agreed.

Eliot had been a center of controversy and had had to make his way
against strong opposition from the moment he assumed his duties as
Harvard's president in 1869—a "bland, grave young man" of thirty-five
with "a placid smile on his face that looks as if it might mean a deal of
determination, perhaps of obstinacy," as Dr. Oliver Wendell Holmes,
then a professor in Harvard's Medical School, wrote to John Lothrop
Motley in early 1870.[4] He was not personally an attractive, likable man;
unequipped by nature for the arts of popularity, he disdained to cultivate them. Most of the right side of his face was covered by a particularly ugly birthmark, a huge livid welt extending from temple to mouth
that had subjected him to cruel ridicule from boys in Boston Common

when he was growing up and forced him to build around his sensitive self a protective shell which thickened and hardened as he grew older. Few ever penetrated it. His manner was cold, aloof, austere, forbidding. He seldom smiled. Notorious were his seeming snubs of students and faculty members as he strode across the Yard looking to neither the right nor the left and acknowledging no salutations. It was said of him that the only time he ever spoke to students was at commencement. But he had immense courage, tenacity, and strength of mind and will; he was a forceful and persuasive advocate of his views; and from the outset he knew precisely what he wanted Harvard to be and never wavered in the slightest from this initial purpose. He had spent two years abroad, before his appointment, studying the curricula and administrative structure of European institutions of higher learning. He had measured the Harvard of the 1860's against German universities and found it sadly wanting. Harvard had become a stagnant backwater of Yankee gentility, a pool of complacency into which new ideas fell and were drowned with scarcely a ripple, and he was determined to make of it a vibrant center of culture and learning, a true university on the German model. He would abolish the old narrow, rigid, almost exclusively classical curriculum prescribed willy-nilly for all undergraduates; he would substitute flexibility, variety, freedom of choice, and the mental excitement that accompanied these. He would radically reform the Law School, the Medical School, and add to them a Graduate School second to none. Much money would be needed. He would raise it, if sometimes after he spent it, for he refused to be deterred by annual deficits from what he regarded as crucially important projects.

In the event, he did almost precisely what he initially set out to do. His success, measured in terms of his purpose, was immense; it was undeniable when measured in any valid overall terms by the time Franklin Roosevelt entered college. This, however, had not silenced criticism.

For in 1900, as in 1890 and '80 and '70, Eliot's academic critics were convinced that his radical transformations had dissolved ancient and valuable disciplines, had shattered into unrelated fragments what should have remained unities of truth and knowledge, and had "dissipated the atmosphere of humanistic culture" (as one critic put it), thereby destroying the very possibility of a Harvard student's acquiring "a well-ordered general culture"—all this in service of a false notion of freedom and a mistaken theory of education.[5] The theory had been explicitly stated by Eliot in a famous address on "Aims of Higher Education" in which he flatly asserted: "There is today no difference between the philologist's method of study and the naturalist's, or between the psychologist's method and the physiologist's. Students of history and natural history, of physics and metaphysics, of literature and the fine arts, find that, though their fields of study are different, their methods and spirit are the same. This oneness of method characterizes the true university." On this shaky foundation (dubious is the alleged "oneness of method," even more so the implication that all knowledge is of equal value) had been erected the system of free electives, which, as its critics were quick to point out, was not really a system at all but an institutional technique inimical to systematization. Encouraged was a proliferation of highly specialized courses (information formerly incorporated in chemistry was detached and developed into a full-blown course in theory of photography, for example), and between these ever-narrower specialties were ever-fewer bridges of communication. Encouraged, too, was an extreme of individualism among student minds, an individualism hostile to community. The fact that free electives had become widely popular and had been adopted by colleges all across the land only multiplied the evil: where formerly had been order, there now was chaos.

Nor was this all. The process of fragmenting and dissolving old unities was not confined to curricular matters. It had operated also upon the extracurricular life of the student body—that portion of the total college experience which would prove more important to Franklin Roosevelt's education than his formal studies.

Before the "bland, grave young man" took office, the vital center of Harvard had been the Yard, where nearly all students and many of the unmarried faculty lived in dormitories interspersed among lecture halls, classrooms, and laboratories. Students and teachers had had abundant personal as well as professional contacts. Social and intellectual life had been interpenetrative in a community animated by a single, if relaxed, college spirit. But Eliot's system of priorities was allegedly such as to deny to the Yard the money needed for repair and modernization of its ancient dormitories, several of which predated the Revolution. Improved student housing had in his view to await the acquisition of the most brilliant faculty in America, the development of a great library (only the Library of Congress and Boston Public, among American libraries, had more volumes than Harvard in 1900), and the provision of the teaching and research facilities necessary to the functioning of a graduate school of the highest quality. In consequence, the Yard as a place to live failed to keep pace with nineteenth-century ideas of sanitation. Long after shower baths and bathtubs, once luxuries, had become necessities of civilized life, there were few bathtubs or showers in the Yard, and since the university administration was loath to supply the deficiency, private enterprise moved to do so outside the Yard. There arose on Mount Auburn Street one after another of those luxurious private dormitories into which moved the affluent, the socially prestigious, so that the majority who remained in the Yard had to add to their relative physical discomfort the psychological discomfort of being unfashionable. And the social gap thus opened was widened by the growth of the elite private clubs—a growth encouraged, certainly, by the development of private dormitories. Eliot was severely blamed in some quarters for permitting, if not promoting, the erection of an artistocratic society on ruins of the democratic community he had allegedly inherited.

But in this last charge, in the judgment of those well acquainted with Harvard's history, the critics of Eliot were less than fair. The college as a whole was barely if any larger than the Yard in 1869; it was clear at that time that the institution Eliot took hold of, if it were to survive and prosper, had to outgrow the Yard. And of course, the kind of community that obtained in a college of a few hundred was impossible in a university of several thousand.

As for the student "democracy" that Eliot's policies had allegedly destroyed, it was largely a myth. In point of fact Harvard's student society had always been among the most rank-conscious in America, reflecting in this the caste system of the Boston society whose leaders have historically dominated Harvard's affairs. In the mid-eighteenth century the college president personally listed students, when they enrolled, in order of their social rank or, to be precise, according "to the Dignity of the Familie whereto the students severally belonged"—a list that was printed in the college catalogue and that determined precedence in such matters as table seating and service, position in academic processionals, even recitation in class. The practice was officially abandoned in the latter part of the century, but not because it was undemocratic; it had become uncomfortable for the president, who was increasingly harassed by irate parents who thought their sons ranked "too low." Long after the official list ceased to be kept, however—and indeed well into the nineteenth century—an unofficial unpublished list was maintained in the president's office for his guidance in dealings with undergraduates. It must be added that Eliot himself had none; he was personally opposed to the whole idea.[6]

But by his time the Harvard clubs, which multiplied after the Civil War, were performing with harsh efficiency the same function as the former listings. They did so through their peculiar and complicated system of selecting members, a system that would have what some would claim to be a profound psychological effect on Franklin Roosevelt. Its workings should therefore be understood.

The first sifting out of the socially eligible few from the ineligible many took place in the autumn of the sophomore year when the oldest and largest of the clubs, the Institute of 1770, chose one hundred students for membership. This amounted to something over 20 percent of Franklin's class. Elections were in groups of ten each, the most eligible being in the first group chosen and the barely eligible in the last. When Franklin was in college, it was still the practice to print in Harvard and Boston newspapers the names of the elected in the precise order of their election, thereby providing Boston society with a list as determinative of social rank as ever the president's list had been.* The first several groups elected not only dominated institute affairs but were also automatically members of a "secret" fraternity, Delta Kappa Epsilon (D.K.E. or Dickey), whose initiations, known as "running for Dickey" or "the Agony," involved the performance of all manner of humiliating stunts in public, around Harvard Square and sometimes in Boston. It was from the Dickey that the so-called final clubs made their selections—clubs whose houses were generally unpretentious on the outside but often luxurious inside. Membership in one of them assured and was essential to one's social success in college, gave entrée to Boston and New York debutante society, and also led to membership in the most prestigious Boston and New York clubs after graduation and to employment, for those who wanted it, by the best financial houses.

But these final clubs were by no means all on the same level of social prestige. Among them, too, was a hierarchy of social value, so that their elections to membership constituted a final sifting process. At the very top, recognized by everyone as the elite of the elite, was the Porcellian, eldest of them all (it was founded in 1791 as the Pig Club†), model for them all. Following in generally recognized order were A.D., Alpha Delta Phi (the Fly), Zeta Psi (the Spee), Delphic (the Gas), and five others.[7]

Several factors operated to determine whether or not a student was "club material" and, if he were, what his ultimate social standing, as manifested through the elective process, would be. The chief determinant was, of course, family prestige and inherited wealth, the two being generally coincident. It was highly important, if not essential, that the student be a graduate of one of the "right" preparatory schools, the most "right" being the five Episcopal Church schools of New England: Groton, St. Mark's, St. Paul's, St. George's, and Middlesex. It was also important that one have the proper manners and attitudes, a working knowledge of what was "done" and "not done" by clubmen—manners

---

* The practice was discontinued in 1905.
† The name was bestowed because of the fondness of certain of the founders for roast pig.

and knowledge which a graduate of the right prep school was almost sure to have. It helped if one was personally attractive and socially adroit; it hurt if one was too conspicuous—if one called attention to oneself by unusual dress, by too strong an advocacy of controversial opinions (indeed, of any opinions), or by overassertiveness in any direction—and it hurt badly if the conspicuousness was due to scandal.

Franklin Roosevelt, was, of course, club material from the outset, preeminently so. Even as a freshman he was a welcome guest in the most prestigious of Beacon Hill and Back Bay homes. He could count, and did count, upon being elected to the Porcellian, as Cousin Theodore had been (despite personal unpopularity owing to a consistent flouting of certain taboos) and as any bearer of the Roosevelt name might legitimately aspire to be.

III

Only a few weeks after his freshman year began, however, there occurred an event which may have had some depreciating effect on Franklin's social standing—how much, if any, it is impossible to say.

Not all who entered Harvard were capable of bearing the burden of freedom it imposed, and one who could not was Taddy "Rosy" Roosevelt, Franklin's half nephew. The dissolute Taddy, at the start of his second Harvard year, continued along the downward path that Franklin had deplored the year before. He had not had his allowance cut in half, as Franklin had said it should be the preceding spring. Instead, he had become the recipient of an income of $40,000 a year in August, 1900, when he achieved his majority. Two months later he married a girl named Sadie Meisinger. He could not have made a less suitable match. His bride had been a frequenter of the Haymarket Dance Hall, long the most notorious house of assignation in New York City, where girls were often openly auctioned off to the highest bidder and where she was known to all as "Dutch Sadie." Franklin was personally embarrassed and disgusted. "It will be well for him . . . to go to parts unknown . . . and begin life anew," he wrote home.* Certainly it would be well for Franklin's social prestige at Harvard that the scapegrace do so. The mésalliance was front-page news in the sensational press all across the country, Taddy being identified as not only a Roosevelt but also a grandson of *the* Mrs. Astor.[8]

---

* Taddy and his bride soon fled under assumed names to Florida, where their marriage turned out as disastrously as Taddy's distraught father had predicted it would. Eventually he returned to New York and, resuming his name, did penance by devoting much of his energy and resources to the Salvation Army.

No further reference was made to the matter in Franklin's letters home.

He himself found Harvard's freedom much to his liking. He used it profitably, if in ways different from those he would have used had he possessed strong intellectual interests.

The Harvard faculty of those years included many great names. In philosophy were William James, George Herbert Palmer, Josiah Royce, Santayana. Young Hugo Müsterberg, called from Germany to Harvard by William James, was in the process of transforming psychology from a branch of speculative philosophy into an experimental science; his psychology course was already becoming famous. In English were George Lyman Kittredge, the great Shakespearean scholar; Barrett Wendell, who had been one of the founders of the *Harvard Lampoon* and remained a famous wit; William Allan Neilson, later president of Smith; George Pierce Baker, who would later provide laboratory training in the drama to Eugene O'Neill and Thomas Wolfe, among others; Charles Townsend Copeland, master of classroom histrionics; and Le Baron Russell Briggs, dean of Harvard College during Franklin's freshman year, who resigned this post in 1901 to accept the Boylston Professorship of Rhetoric and Oratory. Teacher of what he called the "Science of Government" was A. Lawrence Lowell, who in 1909 would succeed Eliot as president of Harvard. In economics were Frank W. Taussig and Abram Piatt Andrew—the latter a brilliant young instructor who had entrée into the best Boston society and, of all the faculty, seems to have made the strongest personal impression on Franklin. In natural science was Nathaniel S. Shaler, America's preeminent geologist, dean of the Lawrence Scientific School. In history were Albert Bushnell Hart, Edward Channing, and Archibald Cary Coolidge, who would later become famous as Harvard's great librarian and was a brother of the Julian Coolidge who had been one of Franklin's teachers at Groton. And these were but a few of the most brilliant names among many hardly less so.

Thus a great and various intellectual feast was spread before all, and hungry minds were free to partake of it according to their various tastes, with a minimum of outward coercion. There were inevitably some enrollees, especially on the Gold Coast, who regarded college as merely a pleasant interlude, chose only snap courses, and relied upon tutoring and trots to get them through examinations with passing grades. Franklin was not one of them. His faculty adviser during his freshman year was Archibald Coolidge, with whom he spent most of a Wednesday afternoon in late September, 1900, mapping out a year's classroom work which contained not a single notably "easy" subject. It was decided between them that history and political science would be his major field of study, with English composition and literature (including public speaking) his minor, and in the event every one of his classes during four years at Harvard was within these fields, save for courses in Latin literature, French literature (Irving Babbitt was an instructor), and geology (under Dean Shaler) in his first year; a course in general paleontology (also under Shaler) in his second year; and a brief exposure to logic under Royce in his third year, the latter being part of a general introduction to philosophy which, by his own account, he dropped after three weeks. During these years his teachers included virtually all the great Harvard names of his time in English, history, government, and economics. In addition to these already mentioned were Silas MacVane, Hiram Bingham, Jr., Roger Bigelow Merriman, William Z. Ripley, and Frederick Jackson Turner, author of *The Frontier in American History,* who came to Harvard for a year as visiting professor from the University of Wisconsin and under whom Franklin took a half-year course in "The Development of the West." * 9

At Harvard as at Groton he was, in Peabody's phrase, a "thoroughly faithful scholar." On one occasion he with everyone else in the class escaped by a rear window and down a fire escape from one of MacVane's lectures in English history, MacVane being notoriously nearsighted and unconscious of his audience (it is said that the good professor, absorbed in his subject as his pupils could never be, continued his lecture to the end that day, unaware that he had no listeners). But such behavior was exceptional for Franklin. He was the very opposite of Taddy in that he never forsook his studies for the fleshpots of Boston or New York but, on the contrary, declined proffered pleasures whose acceptance would unduly interfere with classroom work. Typical was his refusal of an invitation from Alex Forbes "to go to Naushon [an island in Buzzards Bay privately owned by the Forbes and Russell families] for Sunday" early in his first year because if he had accepted "I should have had to take 3 cuts." He very seldom took cuts. One of his instructors (an assistant to George Pierce Baker in the latter's course on "The Forms of Public Address") would remember that Franklin "regularly attended the lectures and always appeared to give close attention and to take notes." This same instructor would further recall that young Franklin, notably courteous, was "never jocose, and perhaps . . . a little austere." 11

Conscientiousness is not enough, however, to make a brilliant scho-

* Many later assumed that Turner's frontier thesis, forcibly impressed by its author upon student Roosevelt's mind, was important to the latter's conception of America as a "mature economy," a conception determinative of several New Deal measures. The assumption is rendered somewhat dubious by the fact that Franklin, because of travel, missed the first six weeks of Turner's course.10

lastic career, and Franklin Roosevelt's would be far from that. None of his teachers, with the possible exception of Andrew, struck fire from his mind; none of his formal courses deeply stirred his interest, engaging the major part of his attention. His normal grade for a course would be a C or low B, with more of the former than the latter—a respectable average in view of his extremely heavy load of extracurricular activities but far inferior to the requirements of membership in Phi Beta Kappa.

Franklin himself would become increasingly dissatisfied with his Harvard classroom experience—as Theodore Roosevelt had been with his, a quarter century before. Looking back over four years of it, at the close of his last college year, Franklin was sure that he had not learned or (as he no doubt would have put it) been taught all that he should have. He complained to roommate Lathrop Brown that his studies had been "like an electric lamp that hasn't any wire. You need the lamp for light but it's useless if you can't switch it on." [12] His implication was that Harvard and its faculty, by failing to provide needed stimulation and guidance, were to blame. And perhaps they were in part; Eliot's critics would have insisted that they were.

But surely the failure to "connect up" and "switch on" was also and probably largely the student's own. Learning is no less an active process than teaching is, and if Harvard had indeed given this student a lamp of knowledge by the close of his fourth year, it had done most of what could be legitimately expected of it. It was largely up to him to provide the wire, to supply the current. Franklin Roosevelt's mind seems to have remained at eighteen and twenty-two essentially what it had been at age fourteen, namely, a collector's mind almost exclusively, quick to grasp and classify bits and pieces of information, but unresponsive to the challenge of the abstract. Having no interest in the generalizing conceptions that were presented to him, he was unwilling, if not unable, to develop generalized conceptions of his own. Perhaps he came closest to doing so in his studies of history. There is no evidence that he ever developed, at Harvard or later, anything that could properly be called a philosophy of history, but he certainly did develop what might be called a habit of historicity. Encouraged in him was a tendency to view contemporary events and people in historical perspective, and since this was linked up with his unexamined faith in God as a beneficent process continuously at work throughout the universe, it might become, in time, a not wholly inadequate substitute for a philosophy.

IV

His father died early in his freshman year.

The event was not unexpected. For years James Roosevelt had been fading gradually out of life, becoming steadily weaker, frailer. One by one he had given up the physical activities he had once enjoyed—first, tennis and mountain climbing, then riding, then long walks, and finally even casual strolls around his estate. In one of the last, if not actually the last, photograph taken of him, on a bright autumn day in 1900, he stood with Franklin, neither of them smiling, under the nearly naked boughs of an elm (only a few withered leaves still clung to twigs above their heads)—a very erect and dignified old gentleman clad in funereal black who appeared to be what in fact he was, a relic of a bygone era who, endeavoring to deal with contemporary business complexities (chiefly those of "the everlasting D. & H.," as Franklin complained), found these too much for his waning strength.

Yet he had seemed that fall to be in better health than he had been for some time before. He made business trips to New York, though Franklin was sure he should not; he went driving with Sara; he attended St. James Church and "handled the plate as usual, but he looked very delicate as he did so." [13] Then, in late October, came "another attack in the night," as Franklin (on October 23) reported himself "distressed" to hear. The mother sought to reassure her son: the attack was a mild one; James was making satisfactory recovery. Nevertheless, she made arrangements to take her husband to Aiken, South Carolina, for complete rest; she rented a cottage there, and Franklin was "delighted . . . to hear about it." On Saturday, November 17, came yet another attack. Wrote Franklin from Cambridge two days later: "I am sure the Doctor ought to absolutely forbid his [father's] going to N.Y. I hope that you will get off by *Dec. 15th* for Aiken, as that will be the only way Papa can have absolute rest. . . ." His mother tried again to reassure him. "I am so glad Papa is really better," wrote Franklin on November 23, "and I only hope he will . . . not go to New York again, for it is not *necessary* I am quite sure, and is bound to be bad for him, no matter how quietly he takes it. I feel it is most important that Papa should realize this, even if he has to be forbidden by the Doctor." He reiterated his hope that his parents would "start for Aiken by the middle of December." [14]

Franklin went down to New Haven next day "in a car of 50 other Freshmen" to see the Harvard-Yale football game, then went on to Hyde Park to spend Sunday, November 25, with his mother and failing father. "James is happy to have his two sons," wrote Sara in her diary that night. "Rosy came over to lunch and to our surprise James came

down in the lift and sat with us, and then he and Franklin and I sat together in the South Parlor all afternoon and until F. left at 9 P.M. James
very delicate and tired looking in a velvet coat, but it was sweet just to
be together." By that time Sara, who had hurt her knee in a fall on the
stairs as she hurried to her husband's sickroom, had been compelled to
hire a full-time nurse for him.[15]

A few days later, in early December, James felt well enough to go
down with Sara to their apartment in the Renaissance Hotel in New
York. But there he had yet another attack, and it became obvious that
the end for him was very near. Franklin was sent for; he and his half
brother Rosy were both at the bedside to bid farewell to their father on
Friday, December 7. Early next morning, James Roosevelt, aged sev-
enty-two, breathed his last. He died without fuss. "At 2:20 he merely
slept away . . . ," wrote his heartbroken widow into her diary, later on
that December 8, 1900. "As I write this I wonder how I lived when he
left me. . . ." [16]

Yet live she must.

She was only forty-six years old. Her health was unusually good. She
came of notably long-lived stock.

And as she lived, or through the way she had now to live, she tested
her son's character, encouraging the development in him of certain natural tendencies.

She had long focused on her son forces of love which in different circumstances—if James had been as young and vigorous as herself—she
would doubtless have focused on her husband. On the latter, her "beloved invalid," she had lavished a love that was in many respects maternal. She now inevitably focused *all* her forces of love on her son. Most
of her meaningful life would from now on be lived through him; to as
large an extent as possible she would make his life and activities her
own. Not that she had any conscious intention of dominating him, absorbing him. Indeed, she would have vehemently denied such a thought,
insisting that what she wanted him to be and do was what he himself, in
his deepest nature, really wanted, and that her whole aim was to help
him become in every respect a strong and free individual. But hers was
an imperious nature and not a notably generous one. It imposed on her
son a necessity to steel his will against hers. He must insist on his independence; he must even, on occasion, fight for it; and because he truly
loved his mother, profoundly respected her character, and dreaded hurting her, he must do this in ways that required an exercise of the politician's art. He must often *seem* to yield, *seem* to concede positions which
were in fact stubbornly, if disguisedly, maintained. Only when this

"seeming" failed of its deceptive purpose would the conflict of wills become overt. When this happened, it would generally be his will, not hers, that prevailed.

He remained with his mother as long as he possibly could after his father's funeral and interment in the St. James burial lot James had purchased at Hyde Park long ago. He did not return to Cambridge until after New Year's Day, 1901. He saw his mother several times during the second semester of his freshman year. Once, in early March, he had a weekend with her at Fairhaven and Cambridge. And he wrote to her often, if less often than she wished he would, telling her—in letters as dryly factual, as conventional in expressed attitudes, as unrevealing of inner feelings as those from Groton had been—about the classes he was taking and the extracurricular activities in which he was engaged.

V

His emphasis was on the latter, in his letters as in his actual life.

In the fall of his freshman year he went out for football. At eighteen he was six feet one inch in height, taller than the average of his contemporaries and considerably taller than his father. He was well coordinated and well muscled. He tried for an end position on the freshman team. But his weight of 146 pounds (he never weighed more than 150 while in college) was not commensurate with his height. It was easy for blocking or running backs little heavier than he, but compactly built, to take him out of plays. He did not survive the second pruning of the squad, on October 13, 1900. He then, as at Groton, joined a scrub team so that he might continue playing. His team was called the Missing-Links, was one of eight "which are to play till November 5 for a Cup," and was the only one of these to be composed wholly of freshmen. He was elected captain of it, a fact possibly indicative of a personal impressiveness he had lacked at Groton. He was evidently surprised and certainly proud of this honor; at least twice he reported to his parents that he was "the only Freshman Captain." He had also to report that his team, "being by far the lightest of the eight," had no chance to win the cup and that he himself suffered, as at Groton, minor but painful injuries on the field. Thus on October 23: "I have had most of the skin of my left hand kicked off in football. . . ." A week later he wrote that "we [the team] have made a very good showing & won two & lost two," that he was "pretty well banged up with football," but that "it will be over in a couple of days" when the series came to an end. He would "then golf or row," he said.[17]

He did row, though he was destined to have little more success in this sport throughout his college career than he had had in freshman football. Failing to win a place on the Harvard crew, he had to content himself with stroking an intramural crew in the fall of his sophomore year, and when (in June, 1904, as he completed his last year at Harvard) he became one of a crew of Groton alumni rowing against the Groton varsity, the latter won.

For him, the path to the greatest distinction he was to win at Harvard lay through yet another activity whose initiation he announced to his parents in the letter that first told of his football captaincy. "I am . . . trying for the 'Crimson' & if I work hard for two years I may be made an editor," he wrote (he was one of eighty-six candidates for a mere handful of these prestigious, influential posts). "I have to make out notices & go to interviews so I am very busy." [18]

The *Crimson* was Harvard's student newspaper, a morning daily whose editors were trying at the turn of the century to transform it from a lackadaisical, obviously amateurish operation into a truly professional publication, competitive to a degree with the Boston dailies. To this end the *Crimson* paid attention to national politics as reflected in Harvard that election year. Franklin did also, and in ways that might seem strange in retrospect. He joined the Harvard Republican Club; he engaged enthusiastically in local campaign activities on behalf of the Republican Presidential ticket. The explanation was that Cousin Theodore, despite his initial reluctance and Mark Hanna's antipathy to him, had become the Republican candidate for the Vice Presidency and now waged a strenuous, hard-hitting campaign against the Democratic opposition, as Hanna had told him he would have to immediately after the convention (he had replied in a typically exuberant letter [June 25, 1900] that he was "as strong as a Bull Moose and you can use me up to the limit"). William McKinley, on the other hand, running for his second term as President, remained as passive as he had been in 1896.

Bryan, the Peerless Leader, threatful still to the special interests which Hanna represented and identified as the whole interest of the country, had been the inevitable Presidential candidate of the Democratic Party that year. The discovery of new goldfields and of the cyanide process for extracting gold from crude ore had so cheapened gold that free coinage of silver was no longer a viable party issue. Against the reluctance of other party leaders, Bryan had forced a silver plank into the Democratic platform and weakened it thereby. But the underlying social forces of which silver had been merely a misleading symbol continued their surge and thrust, and Bryan continued to be their most eloquent political spokesman. He had supported the administration's war policy in 1898—had indeed served as colonel of the Third Nebraska Volunteer Regiment (it never left the United States) which he organized. But he broke with the administration when it decided to retain U.S. sovereignty over the Philippines after the war ended, despite the necessity this imposed of bloody, dirty fighting (torture interrogations of prisoners were employed) against Filipino insurrectionists under Emilio Aguinaldo. Bryan, with the Democratic platform, proclaimed imperialism the "paramount issue" of the campaign.

And as he did so, he ran head on into Teddy, the Rough Rider, imperialism's flaming apostle. Cried Bryan: "Behold a republic standing erect while empires all around are bowed beneath the weight of their armaments. Behold a republic whose flag is loved while other flags are only feared. . . . Behold a republic gladly but surely becoming the supreme moral factor in the world's progress and the accepted arbiter of the world's disputes—a republic whose history, like the path of the just, is as the shining light that shineth more and more unto the perfect day." To which the colorful Teddy made simple reply. Touring the country with revolver-toting and shooting cowboys, he bared his big teeth and raised his clenched fist against all cowardly weaklings who, in service of a sissy sentimentalism, would give up conquests made in valor and blood by America's fighting men. Over and over again he cried: "Don't haul down the flag!"

On this issue, in the era of Kipling and the White Man's Burden, it was Teddy who exerted by far the more potent popular appeal. Franklin Roosevelt succumbed to it, along with the great majority of his fellow students. The issue, however, was one on which Charles Eliot had recently differed sharply, publicly with Theodore Roosevelt. In 1895, TR, having become famous as head of the New York Police Board, was calling vociferously for the annexation of the Hawaiian Islands and for war with Britain over the latter's threat to collect by force debts owed its nationals by a revolution-torn, criminally misgoverned Venezuela. The Monroe Doctrine was being flouted! cried Teddy. American security was in jeopardy! On May 28 of that year he told the National Republican Club, in a nationally publicized speech, that "the Venezuela question" would be settled by the United States "in Canada" and that Canada (to quote the newspaper account) "would surely be conquered, and once wrested from England it would never be restored." Eliot was outraged. He said so publicly. Nothing could be more offensive "than this doctrine of Jingoism, this chip-on-the-shoulder attitude . . . of a ruffian and a bully," he asserted; he branded both Theodore Roosevelt and fellow Jingoist Henry Cabot Lodge as "degenerated sons of Harvard."

TR's public response was on the order of his angry, contemptuous private comment to Lodge that Eliot, whom he had personally disliked since his college days, was at one with "the futile sentimentalists of the international arbitration type" whose effect was to develop "a flabby, timid type of character, which eats away the great fighting qualities of our race." [19] Nor was this acrimony between the two men lessened in the slightest degree during the years immediately following, when TR did all in his considerable persuasive power to scuttle every attempt at peaceful settlement of the Cuban dispute and to foment a war with Spain.

Hence, during the fall of 1900, there was a large question in the public mind about whom Harvard's president would vote for that year. The question was increased in urgency when Eliot published in *Outlook* magazine an article that *seemed* to support the Republicans on most issues but was critical of U.S. imperialism, Bryan's "paramount issue." [20] When reporters put the question to him, however, Eliot refused to answer it. The *Crimson* editors were therefore justifiably proud of a news story they printed on the front page of their October 29 issue under the heading "President Eliot Declares for McKinley"—a story saying, "President Eliot gave the Crimson the following statement last night concerning his article in the Outlook about which there has been so much discussion: I intend to vote for President McKinley, Governor Roosevelt, and Representative McCall, and I have never had any other intention." This was a major reportorial scoop. It was picked up, with credit to the *Crimson,* by newspapers all over the country.

The surprise news value of the scoop gained from the fact that Eliot had long maintained an iron rule against granting personal interviews to *Crimson* reporters. Who had managed to obtain an exception to this rule? And how had he done it?

Thirteen years later Franklin Roosevelt answered these questions in circumstantial detail during an interview with a reporter for the New York *Telegraph* (November 30, 1913). He himself had done the deed, he said. Ignorant of Eliot's rule, he had come of an evening to the president's house, had identified himself by name in response to the frosty Eliot's curt "Who are you?," and had then without more ado blurted out the reason for his visit: "I came to ask you, Mr. President, whether you are going to vote for McKinley or Bryan?" The sheer effrontery of it took Eliot aback. He glared at the trembling freshman, who for the first time realized that he had broken a taboo and who "wished the floor might open and let me through to any kind of darkness that would hide me." Nevertheless, Franklin stood his ground, and in the end, Eliot, for whatever reason, gave him the requested statement.

Thus the story. It was destined to become an integral part of the FDR legend, having allegedly gone far to assure victory in his competition with other candidates for a *Crimson* editorial post. It would be referred to as fact in an annotation in the carefully edited *F.D.R., His Personal Letters: Early Years,* published in 1947—though the annotator remarks that there "is surprisingly no mention of the event" in any of the letters, a circumstance he ascribed to the probability that some letters of this period are missing. The real explanation is that the story is untrue. This triumph of reportorial enterprise was won not by Franklin Roosevelt, but by Albert W. De Roode, as Franklin himself would privately confess in a letter written in 1931 but, for some reason, not included in his published *Personal Letters* for that year.*

Two days after the famous scoop was printed, Franklin wrote home: "Last night there was a grand torchlight Republican parade of Harvard and Mass. Insti. of Technology. We wore red caps & gowns and marched by classes into Boston & thro' all the principal streets. . . . The crowds to see it were huge all along the route." On the following Tuesday he wrote: "You wouldn't know that this is an election day, all is so quiet, we haven't heard any returns yet, but I think there can be only one outcome." [21]

The outcome immensely pleased him. The McKinley-Roosevelt ticket won a plurality of 849,000, receiving 292 electoral votes to 155 for Bryan.

VI

Meanwhile, and through the months that followed, the competition among candidates for *Crimson* editorships absorbed more and more of Franklin's time and energy. He demonstrated no remarkable journalistic talent: his writing was undistinguished; his ideas were unoriginal; his sense of news values was no more accurate than another's. But by hard work and a full exploitation of his high social connections to obtain

* Frank Freidel, the first writer to expose the falsehood, quotes the letter, to Michael E. Hennessy, October 22, 1931, in his *Franklin D. Roosevelt: The Apprenticeship* (Boston, 1952), p. 56. "In some way I was a number of years ago given credit for getting a scoop from President Eliot in regard to the way he was going to vote in the autumn of 1900," wrote Franklin then. "The real man who got that scoop was . . . DeRoode, now a lawyer in New York City, and he should have the credit and not I." The strangeness of Roosevelt's falsehood is augmented by the fact that he was in continuous contact with De Roode through the 1910's. He formed with Langdon P. Marvin and Henry S. Hooker, in 1911, the firm of Marvin, Hooker, and Roosevelt, Counsellors at Law, 52 Wall Street. The firm's stationery listed two junior partners, one of them Albert W. De Roode. Did the latter explicitly agree, in 1913, to Roosevelt's laying claim to the "scoop"?

news he managed to survive the ruthless eliminations whereby only a fraction of the number of original candidates was retained as *Crimson* staff members in the spring of 1901. By that time he was averaging about six hours a day on the paper.

And in that spring of his freshman year he *did* manage to score a scoop, quite a large one.

This was in late April, when the newly inaugurated Vice President of the United States—the most popular, newsworthy Vice President in the nation's history—came to Cambridge as house guest of Professor Lowell, in whose constitutional government course Franklin, with distant cousin Theodore Douglas Robinson (himself a nephew of TR*), was enrolled. Franklin phoned the Vice President to ask when he and Robinson might see him. Cousin Theodore replied that he was lecturing before Lowell's class the next morning and would be delighted to see the two after the class ended. The fact that the Vice President was to lecture at Harvard was news indeed: Lowell was anxious to keep it a secret, and no hint of it had appeared in the Boston papers. Franklin rushed to the *Crimson* offices with the story which, the next morning, appeared on the front page under a four-column heading. "Vice-President Theodore Roosevelt, '80, will lecture this morning at 9 o'clock in Sanders Theater before the class in Government I," the story said. "Mr. Roosevelt will speak on his experiences as Governor of New York."

Professor Lowell was surprised and distressed to find a crowd of 2,000 struggling to get into the lecture hall (capacity 500) when he and his guest arrived at Sanders. He phoned the *Crimson* as soon as he could demanding to know who was responsible for the unwelcome publicity. But of course, Franklin, far from being penalized by his superiors on the paper, was rewarded by them. In mid-June the *Crimson* announced that he was one of five newly appointed editors.[22]

As soon as school was out, he hurried home to his mother at Hyde Park.

They did not go to Campobello that summer. Instead, with Teddy Robinson (the aforementioned nephew of the Vice President), they sailed on the *Deutschland* for Europe in early July. In Hamburg they were joined by Mrs. Alfred Pell and her daughter Frances and sailed with them for Norway. From Norway, the Roosevelt mother and son went to Berlin, Dresden (she showed her son the school she and Maggie Carey had attended when she was a girl), Munich, Zurich, Geneva, Paris.

* Theodore Douglas Robinson's mother was Mrs. Douglas Robinson, who was TR's sister Corinne.

And in Paris, on the morning of Saturday, September 7, they learned that President McKinley had been shot and dangerously wounded in Buffalo, New York, the preceding afternoon.

Avidly thereafter they read every news bulletin that was published in Europe before they sailed for home. They learned that the President, on a ceremonial visit to the great Pan-American Exposition in Buffalo, had been at a reception shaking hands with a long line of people when one of them, Leon Czolgosz, an anarchist, obviously mentally ill, shot him with a .32 revolver wrapped in a handkerchief. He had been immediately operated upon, and the operation was pronounced a success by the doctors. The bullet had not been found, they admitted (several reporters promptly warned of possible peritonitis), but the danger this presented was discounted. In the immediately following days, the official medical bulletins were determinedly, extravagantly optimistic. When the Roosevelts sailed for home, it was with the belief that the President was well on the road to recovery.

All the greater was the shock to them, therefore, when, landing in New York on September 18, they learned that McKinley had died four days before.

Sara Roosevelt, herself so recently bereaved, felt for the "poor wife." McKinley's widow "seems much the same," wrote Sara to a sister who was abroad, adding, as if from her own experience: "I do not believe that grief ever kills. . . . She *may* live on for a long time . . . without his devotion which seemed to be her life." [23]

But her son's excited attention focused at once on McKinley's successor in the White House. The Vice President had been so far taken in by the false optimism of the medical bulletins that having postponed his expedition for several days, he had felt safe in setting off on a mountain-climbing trip into the Adirondack wilderness. On Friday the thirteenth he had climbed Mount Marcy, the highest mountain in New York, and was descending when, in late afternoon, he was met by a panting guide with a sheaf of telegrams for him; they told him the President had suffered a relapse and was sinking fast. He had almost run the rest of the way down the mountain, had then ridden all night in a buckboard, with three relays of horses, to the nearest railway station, and there, as dawn was breaking on Saturday the fourteenth, he had been met with the news that McKinley was dead. A special train had taken him to Buffalo, where, in the library of a private home, a dozen hours after McKinley's death, he had taken the oath of office and solemnly pledged himself "to continue, absolutely unbroken, the policy of President McKinley for the peace, the prosperity, and the honor of our beloved country."

Cousin Theodore was now President of the United States.

* * *

So it was that Franklin Roosevelt returned to Cambridge in late September, 1901, with the prestige value of his name and family connections yet further and greatly enhanced. From this point on in his college career, whenever his activities were reported in the Boston press (and they were much more fully reported than they would otherwise have been), he was invariably identified as a blood relation of the President, and generally as a far closer one than he actually was.

Such articles "make me excessively 'tired,' " he complained to his mother in the fall of 1902. And well they might. When he was named secretary of the *Crimson*, this in the spring of 1902, one Boston paper, identifying him as a "cousin of President Roosevelt," stressed that he, "like the President," was "thoroughly democratic" and that his winning high office on the college paper against stiff competition "shows the kind of stuff that is in him. . . ." Not long afterward he was in the news again as "a nephew of President Roosevelt" who was heading up a fund drive for relief of the Boers. He had been thoroughly aroused by tales of British mistreatment of Boer women and children herded into concentration camps in the aftermath of the Boer War. With two other students he organized the money-collecting movement ($336 was cabled to Capetown in May) whose "promoters," said the news story, were among "the wealthiest and most prominent men in the university." The story continued: "Young Roosevelt has many of the qualities that have put his uncle at the front. He is a hard worker, thoroughly democratic . . . and with him at the head [of the movement] there is every reason to believe that it will go through with a rush." [24] The fawning, the snobbery manifested in such writings were offensive to their squirming subject's Grotonian (and innate) sense of good form and good taste. They also constituted a hazard to the success he was pursuing in college insofar as this depended on the goodwill of fellow students. No "democracy" so blatantly proclaimed could fail to impress his fellows as other than spurious; it must encourage in them a mingled envy and resentment of him.

And this was rendered all the more likely by the fact that his way of life during his last three years at Harvard, as regards personal concerns (food, shelter, sociability), remained as thoroughly aristocratic, in the precise meaning of the word, as it had been during his first year.

The new Harvard Union was opened on October 5, 1901, in "a most impressive ceremony," which Franklin attended. It was a magnificent building with game rooms, reading rooms, rooms for dining and discussion, a library, etc., and was designed to be a club inclusive of the whole student body and faculty. But its success, measured in terms of this intention, was limited. A distinct social gap continued to divide the gilded few who inhabited the Gold Coast dormitories from the many who lived in the Yard. And Franklin made no serious effort to bridge this gap. He was affable; he was never deliberately intimidating of those who lacked his advantages, he consciously snubbed no one. If he carried over into Harvard something of that rather cocky, argumentative manner—a manner defensive in motivation but sometimes offensive in effect— which Goodwin had found irritating during Franklin's last Groton years, it operated only when he was among those in his own social circles, which included the elite of Cambridge, Boston, New York, and Washington. And even by their standards his social life was remarkably brilliant. A notable instance of it was his going down to Washington on the first weekend of January, 1902, to attend the most glamorous, prestigious society event of the year, perhaps of the decade, the debut in the White House of Alice Roosevelt (Princess Alice), daughter of the President. On a Friday night he went to the coming-out party proper, in the White House's East Room—an event which Alice enjoyed only "moderately" because it was "just a dance without a cotillion" and "punch was provided instead of champagne," according to her later remembrance, but which Franklin found to be "the most glorious fun." On Saturday he toured the new Library of Congress building, had tea at the White House, and attended a reception given by the Austrian ambassador. On Sunday he was again at the White House immediately before leaving Washington.[25]

The view of him as a thoroughgoing aristocrat was further encouraged when his mother, lonely at Hyde Park, took a furnished apartment in Boston to be near him during the winter months of 1902 and again in 1903—at 333 Commonwealth Avenue the first winter, at 184 Marlborough Street the second. She was content to move exclusively in the highest Boston society and to know virtually no one there outside it; her participation in it inevitably frequently involved her son. In her apartment she often entertained him and his friends with teas, suppers, dinners, and occasionally overnight. It became clear to their social friends that mother and son were unusually close and that the relationship between them was in part one of psychological dependence, though even an intimate observer might at this time have been hard put to determine which of the two actually leaned more heavily on the other. It was clear also, even glaringly so, that this mother would exert no democratizing influence on her son. (Something of Sara's now-hardened social attitudes is revealed by her diary comments on servants who displeased her during these years immediately following her husband's death: "My old cook is horrid and Elespie gets excited. . . . I got a new cook, French, fat and ugly, called Marie Premault. . . . Sent off cook, Marie. She is too coarse and careless. . . . Had to dismiss caretaker. She is a disgusting old creature. . . . Sellers is impertinent and contradicted my orders.

I shall not keep him." [26]) She continued to be as Mlle. Sandoz had found her, *très formidable*. No longer slender, she was still physically attractive, proud of bearing, her brilliant eyes looking out commandingly upon *her* world from beneath highly arched brows, her mouth set firmly upon having her way. She made her presence felt in any gathering. Self-centered, she was a concentrated force that radiated force, and her generosities outside her social class, which she very precisely and narrowly defined, were never of a kind that would reduce in the slightest her pleasures and privileges. Her son's detractors might well have said that he was tied to her apron strings, save that the metaphor itself seemed unsuitable: it was as hard to imagine the aristocratic Sara in a kitchen apron as it was easy to conceive of her son's being (unless one knew him extremely well) completedly under her domination.

In view of all this, if he was not among the most popular of Harvard students—and his classmates later agreed that he was not—the fact is not surprising. He often seemed to want to be, but this helped not at all; it even aroused contempt for him in some quarters, where he was regarded as a false smiler, "two-faced" and not to be trusted.[27] In his own social circles were a few who thought him immature for his age and circumstances and that his enjoyment of high society, an excessive enjoyment in their view, manifested this. There were girls, attracted by his lithe handsomeness and social prestige, who were put off by what they deemed an all-too-smug awareness of these on his part and by a personality that seemed to them shallow, trivial, timidly conventional beneath a superficial self-assurance. They told one another that he was a lightweight with many of the attributes of a prig. They dubbed him "the featherduster." [28]

But such denigrating estimates of him did not go unchallenged, even at the time; they were offset by estimates that were sincerely admiring—estimates made by students and faculty members associated with him in one or another of his numerous activities. And the most solid factual evidence is that far from being frivolous, he was a more serious young man than most, worked harder than most, and, despite his sometimes irritating manner of personal superiority, was generally truly democratic in his attitudes. He was wholly committed to democracy in theory.

There was much kindness in him—a generosity of spirit and a concern for the feelings and rights of others, especially the less fortunate, that were notably lacking in his mother—and this was joined to concepts of Duty and Obligation and Responsibility which his father had evidently instilled in him as a child and which Mlle. Sandoz, Peabody, Billings, and the whole Groton experience had encouraged in him. He sincerely wanted to be and do good in the world. He was quickly active in sympathy for underdogs and victims of injustice, if often unclear in his perception of the latter. His response to the plight of the Boers in British concentration camps was typical of him. He continued at Harvard certain Missionary Society activities begun at Groton, spending hours with poor boys at St. Andrews Boys Club in Boston, helping them with their entertainments, teaching a class now and then, and joining in their sports. He became an active member of the St. Paul's Society, the Social Service Society. He sought to justify through work in the public interest that "good position" into which he had been born and of which he spoke in a paper written for an English composition class in the first semester of his sophomore year.

This paper, carefully researched and annotated, was on "The Roosevelt Family in New Amsterdam Before the Revolution" and in it he pointed to the many once-great and -famous Dutch families who had gone into decline in America. He opined that they had done so because "they lack progressiveness and the true democratic spirit." The Roosevelts, on the other hand, had still great "virility" as a family because of their "very democratic spirit." He went on: "They [the Roosevelts] have never felt that because they were born in a good position they could put their hands in their pockets and succeed. They have felt, rather, that being born in a good position, there was no excuse for them if they did not do their duty by the community. . . ." [29]

VII

Such attitudes and this view of the Roosevelts were encouraged in him by the highly educative example of Theodore Roosevelt in the White House.

The "damn cowboy" who was "now President of the United States" (the words were those of an appalled Mark Hanna), though he had solemnly promised to continue McKinley's policies and had retained the McKinley Cabinet intact, promptly broke all precedent in his personal conduct of the office. He had been barely a month in the White House when he invited Booker T. Washington, the black leader, founder of the Tuskegee Institute, to lunch there, provoking a storm of angry outrage expressed in ugly reprisals against helpless blacks on the part of Southern whites. Soon the whole world was astonished witness to the "strenuous life" as TR took foreign diplomats on long hard hikes along Rock Creek, engaged in all manner of violent exercise, including boxing (he lost the sight of one eye from a blow, though this was unknown to the public), and managed to invest his almost every official act with a dramatic combativeness. Nor did he pursue McKinley's policies for long. "Speak softly and carry a big stick," he said, and strove through military and naval preparedness to obtain the "big stick." But in neither foreign nor domestic affairs was his voice notably soft. Actually the word was often more forceful than the deed—though of forceful deeds he performed what most observers deemed a sufficiency.

Franklin at Harvard watched with fascinated attention as Cousin Theodore evolved, in *ex post facto* justification of his acts (". . . he was," wrote Henry Adams, "pure act"), a "stewardship theory" of the Presidency whereby the President might do anything that was not explicitly forbidden by the Constitution if it seemed to him clearly in the national interest, evolved also a Roosevelt Corollary to the Monroe Doctrine whereby the United States was deemed to have the "duty" of interfering in the affairs of countries in the Western Hemisphere which incurred foreign debts they refused to pay or engaged in "brutal wrongdoing." He repeatedly involved himself in Latin American affairs: he forcibly collected from Santo Domingo debts owed foreign creditors; he fomented a bloodless revolution in Panama against Colombia in order to facilitate the building of the Panama Canal. To obtain from Canada a disputed strip of coast extending down from the main body of Alaska, he threatened war. And in domestic affairs he was no less high-handed. He was temperamentally incapable of being as pliant a servant of anyone or any interest as McKinley had been of big business. He soon exerted federal power over giant corporations, notably in the case of the Northern Securities Company, which was organized by J. P. Morgan on behalf of James Hill to establish a railroad monopoly in the Northwest and against which TR instituted an unprecedented government suit under the Sherman Antitrust Act; the combination was dissolved by Supreme Court decision in 1905. He also, and without precedent, intervened in a great labor dispute. In May, 1902, the United Mine Workers called a strike which closed down the anthracite coal fields after the mineowners refused to grant the union the recognition that was a prerequisite to a negotiation of demands for a 10 percent wage increase and the alleviation of a number of serious grievances. The strike continued through a long summer, by the end of which the shortage of coal was acute and its price rising sharply. TR finally ended the strike, in October, by threatening government operation of the mines, using the U.S. Army to mine coal, unless the operators would accept the decisions of an arbitration commission appointed by him, as the United Mine Workers had already agreed to do.

Franklin Roosevelt's personal reaction to all this was not uncritical. He had especially grave doubts about Cousin Theodore's handling of the coal dispute—in part, perhaps, because a good portion of his family's wealth derived from anthracite. "In spite of his success in settling the trouble," Franklin wrote his mother from Cambridge on October 26, 1902, "I think that the President made a serious mistake in interfering—politically, at least. His tendency to make the executive power stronger than the Houses of Congress is bound to be a bad thing, especially when a man of weaker personality succeeds him in office." [30]

VIII

Midway through his sophomore year, not long after his return from Alice Roosevelt's White House debut, Franklin Roosevelt had that experience of the workings of the Harvard club system to which reference has been made—an experience which may well have deepened and widened his democratic sympathies while strengthening his commitment to democracy in theory.

None in his position could avoid entering the competition for membership in one of the elite clubs; he did so without perturbation in the fall of 1901. Some slight perturbation is hinted at in late November, however, when he wrote his mother, after having been passed over in the first tens selected for the Institute of 1770, that his roommate Lathrop Brown had "made the last ten & is running now, a physical wreck" and that he felt he himself might have "a ghost of a show" for the next ten or, as he put it, "for the D.K.E. which begins Thursday." He didn't make it then, however. Not until January 9, 1902, could he write his mother that he had been chosen as "the first man on the next ten of the Institute . . . & the D.K.E." and that, though he was "about to be slaughtered," he was "quite happy." [31] He began "running for Dickey" on the next night and continued to do so until the following Wednesday, when the initiation ordeal at last ended. There began then the ordeal of waiting for the final club selections in which he certainly hoped, if he did not still confidently expect, to be elected to the Porcellian.

He wasn't, however! The gilded youths of Porcellian did not want him!

He never knew why—and we may be sure he pondered the matter. Was it because of Taddy's disgrace? Was it because he had given offense, inadvertently and unwittingly, through some specific word or deed? Was it because he was in general, by his very nature, irritating and obnoxious or at least unattractive and unimpressive? Whatever the reason, he had been weighed and found wanting on scales whose accuracy he had not theretofore questioned, and the knowledge that this was so came to him as a severe blow. It constituted "the bitterest moment in . . . [his] life" up till then, in the words of one of his relatives; it gave him an "inferiority complex," in the opinion of the remarkable woman who later became his wife; and he learned from it (this also was the opinion of his wife)—learned something of how it feels to be among the despised and rejected, a helpless victim of injustice. And if the importance thus assigned to this exclusion from a college club seems absurd today, it accords perfectly with the importance that Cousin Theodore, all his life long, assigned to his own *in*clusion in this same club. Theodore Roosevelt was President of the United States when, writing to Kaiser Wilhelm II of his daughter Alice's engagement to Nicholas Longworth, he remarked that "Nick," like himself, was a member of the Porcellian, the "oldest club" at Harvard.[32]

But though the blow staggered Franklin, it did not fell him. Porcellian's rejection of him was by no means tantamount to expulsion from that society in which he was accustomed to move. When offered membership in Alpha Delta Phi, popularly known as the Fly Club, he promptly accepted, and though Fly was distinctly inferior to Porcellian in prestige, and was generally rated slightly lower than A.D., it was superior on the prestige scale to all others.* It thereafter loomed large and happily in Franklin's college life. He spent much of the little leisure time he had in the unpretentious red-brick, white-porticoed clubhouse at 2 Holyoke Place, just off Mount Auburn Street.

His fellow club members evidently regarded him from the outset as a bookish intellectual, for they placed him on the library committee a few weeks after he had joined and, in the following year, made him the club's head librarian. The choice was a happy one. He may or may not have been "intellectual," as clubmen used the term, but he certainly was, or quickly became, "bookish" in the sense of loving books as objects, and to so widely recognized a degree that other organizations took advantage of it. He was elected to the library committee of the Harvard Union during his third year. In that same year he became a member of the Hasty Pudding Club, as did (automatically) all juniors and seniors who were in the Institute of 1770.† The Hasty Pudding, whose principal activity was the annual production of a musical show, maintained a

---

* As for the exact origin and hence age of the Fly, there is some disagreement. The club claimed descent from a chapter of the national Greek-letter fraternity, Alpha Delta Phi, established at Harvard in 1836, which would make it the second oldest of the final clubs. Harvard's official historian, Samuel Eliot Morison, casts doubt upon this claim, however. In his *Three Centuries of Harvard* (Cambridge, 1942), p. 203, Morison writes of the chapter of AΔΦ "from which the A.D. stems and the Fly claims to. . . ."

† The Institute and Hasty Pudding were merged in 1926.

clubhouse in which was a library, and in his last college year Franklin Roosevelt became the Hasty Pudding's librarian while retaining his post as librarian of the Fly. His librarianships opened up new avenues for active expression of his collector's instinct. He began to haunt bookshops, especially those dealing in secondhand books and in old, rare editions, his eye increasingly trained to recognize market bargains by a Mr. Chase, a "rare and delicious man" employed by N. J. Bartlett and Company of Boston. He was soon buying not only for his club libraries, but also for his own collection. "I . . . went to Bartlett's to see about some Club books, with the sad result that I invested in a few volumes myself," ran a typical letter to his mother. "They are to be sent home and you can open them. The Smollett is a very nice old edition, as are the Junius letters and the Dryden's Virgil." Also at Bartlett's, on another occasion, he bought "the best possible set of Morte d'Arthur & very hard to get." [33] He was soon persuaded, however—no doubt by "old man Chase"—that book collecting would be more fun, and his collection become more valuable, if he specialized. He focused thereafter on Americana. But he soon found that this was much too broad a field for anyone of limited financial resources, and so he chose from within it a specialty in which his natural interest was intense and in which relatively few other collectors were buying—namely, naval history. He was enabled to acquire quite rapidly and cheaply the nucleus of what would ultimately become one of the finest collections in the country of naval books, manuscripts, pamphlets, articles, and prints, a collection worth many times its initial cost. He also began collecting books, manuscripts, and prints on the Hudson River Valley, early American children's books, and miniature books.

His librarian's activities, joined to his *Crimson* editorship, ensured his election, late in the first semester of his third year, to the Signet, a literary society of which several of the stars of Harvard's English faculty were active members and which maintained a clubhouse on Mount Auburn Street. Late the following spring he was elected to the Memorial Society ("on the first ten—it is a good thing to make," he wrote his mother)—an organization dedicated to perpetuating "a knowledge of the history of the University" and to commemorating "the great men who have been students or teachers here." [34]

Thanks to Groton's "anticipation plan," Franklin Roosevelt had completed his requirements for an AB degree by June of 1903. He chose, however, to remain another year in Harvard. On the advice of his professors, he entered the Graduate School, ostensibly in pursuit of a Master of Arts degree, taking that year advanced courses in history and economics, plus a half-year three-hour course in Francis Bacon, in the English Department. "I do not in the least expect to get the degree," he wrote his "Dearest Mama," "but the training will be excellent." He had seriously considered entering the Law School, instead, but was told by "many Law School men" that he would "regret it" if he did; embryo lawyers were required to work hard at their studies if they were to receive passing grades, and young Roosevelt, whose "every spare moment" was "taken up with the paper," had "little time to think about courses." [35]

IX

It was "the paper," in fact, which decided him to remain for a fourth year in the university—a year during which he thought of himself as a senior rather than a graduate student. In the second semester of his third year he was managing editor. This meant that in June, 1903, he would become president of the *Crimson* for the first half of the 1903–04 school year, the president being actually the paper's editor-in-chief—director of its news policy, author of all its editorials. Having thus achieved the height of the ambition that had inspired his principal extracurricular activity since early in his freshman year, he had no intention of stepping down without enjoying it.

In the summer of 1903 he sailed on the *Celtic* for Europe, with Charles B. Bradley, a Harvard classmate, as his traveling companion. This was the first extended vacation he had ever had away from his mother, who went that summer as usual to Campobello, and the decision to take it had not been easy for him to make. Indeed, he required his mother to make it. ". . . I really want you to tell me what you want me to do," he wrote her in late April, 1903. "I have told you what I feel about it: that it would in all probability be good for me, and a delightful experience; but that I won't want to be away from you . . . ; also that I don't want to go unless you could make up your mind not to care at all. I feel that really it would be a very thoroughly selfish proceeding on my part." His mother—with what reluctance, we may imagine—then urged him to go, and something of the wrench this parting cost them, something of the guilt feelings he continued to have about it, was revealed in the letter he wrote from the ship before the pilot was dropped at Sandy Hook. Three huge baskets of fruit had been given him—two from aunts of his, one from his mother—and he told his mother how much he and his companion would enjoy the gifts from his aunts. But "*your* basket," he added, "I am going to eat *all alone* & give none of it to

C.B.B.!" His letter closed: "Goodbye dear Mummy I am longing for Aug. 25. Don't worry about me—I always land on my feet—but wish so much you were with me." Thereafter he wrote her very full accounts of his activities abroad—in England (he was a house guest of the Cholmeleys at Grantham), Switzerland, France—conventional activities, nearly all in the company of British aristocrats and wealthy Americans, which he reported in wholly conventional terms.[36]

But he did not forget on his holiday that he was president of the *Crimson*. He took with him a file of the preceding year's editorials, studied them carefully, and, aboard ship, as he wrote his mother, did "a lot of work" on his own editorials for next fall. He did still more work on them and on plans for the paper as a whole after he rejoined his mother in late August.

It was not innovative work. He felt no compulsion to upset apple carts or set houses afire. He made no striking changes in the paper's format or typography or news emphases, introduced no outstanding new features, and was content on the editorial page to operate wholly within traditional patterns of thought and attitude, revealing as he did so no particular genius for pungent, vivid expression. Indeed, many a future student of his life would wonder how a young man of nearly twenty-two, obviously more intelligent than the average and having had every advantage of formal education and wide travel, could so wholeheartedly identify himself with the fortunes of Harvard's football team and so earnestly chide the student body for "listless cheering" at the games. He was, however, more energetic than the average *Crimson* editor had been. He produced more editorials than most. And he was perhaps justified in regarding some of his editorial stands as, for their time and place, rather daring.

He lectured the incoming freshman class on "responsibility" in the *Crimson* for September 30, 1903, saying that "this idea of responsibility" was one "which every Freshman should keep constantly before him—responsibility to the University, to his class and to himself; and the only way to fulfill this is to be always active." He asserted that the "opportunities are almost unlimited: There are athletics—a dozen kinds—and athletic managements, literary work on the University publications and the outside press, philanthropic and religious work, and," he added lamely, "the many other interests that are bound to exist." He made no mention of scholarship as a possibly worthy "interest," though he may have meant to indicate that a certain amount of study was worthwhile when he wrote that "every man should have a wholesome horror of . . . doing nothing but enough classroom work to keep off probation." Not too much was required in the way of scholarship, however. "It is not so much brilliance as effort that is appreciated here—determination to accomplish something," he wrote.

His roommate, Lathrop Brown, was manager of the football team that year, and it was perhaps because of this that he devoted so much editorial attention to football, notably in a surprisingly angry attack on the team for its play in a game with the Carlisle Indians,* a game Harvard won 12-11. "Of course, the team was satisfied with so excellent a showing. What did it matter that the Indians, some twenty or twenty-five pounds lighter to a man, had literally run over them in the first half? What did it matter that, after Harvard had gained the lead, the Indians were again on the way to Harvard's goal when time was called? . . . What did it matter?—Harvard won. No wonder the team was satisfied!" The "undergraduates watching the game were not so well satisfied," however. "They are weary of a spirit that will not awake till the team is in a desperate crisis, and goes to sleep again when the crisis is fancied to be past. They are weary and angry—why?—because they know there is no reason why the team should not be powerful, aggressive, and, withal, successful if it wills to be. . . . How much longer must the University wait?" This provoked what Franklin admitted to his mother was a "row," one he somewhat regretted. "*Something* of the kind was indeed necessary but *I* shouldn't have made it quite so strong." He added that the effect on the team had been salutary; the players were "angry and they are playing all the better for it." [37] (He led the cheering for the team when it left for a game in Philadelphia on Thursday, November 5, 1903, and was head cheerleader at the game itself, November 7.)

The team's play did not improve enough to conquer Yale—Yale (as usual) won, 16-0—but editorialist Roosevelt was not displeased with Harvard's showing in the great game of the year. ". . . not all the plaudits and honors go to Yale . . . ," he wrote for the following Monday morning's paper. The next day he looked anxiously into the football future. "Why has the captain of next year's football team not yet been elected?" he wanted to know. "We feel very strongly that the work of producing the next eleven should begin, not sometime next spring, but now."

Other editorials, fewer in number and less vehement in tone than those on football, exhorted students to take an active interest in politics and government, particularly municipal government. In an early October editorial he commended the university's Political Club for "ar-

* This was the famous game in which a Carlisle player caught a Harvard kickoff and tucked the football up the jersey of a fellow player, who then calmly walked down the sidelines for a touchdown while the Harvard men tried frantically to find the ball.

ranging . . . talks on politics" but suggested an expanded program, one that would not only "open the talks to the whole University" but also "attempt . . . to give a practical idea of the workings of the political system—of the machinery of primary, caucus, convention, election and legislature. With such a large city as Boston close at hand," he went on, "it would be easy to send in parties, under the guidance of some experienced man, which in one day could learn more than through the means of lectures. There must be many among us who . . . would be glad to gain knowledge by actual experience of the intricacies of Federal, State and Municipal politics." Another editorial commented on an address on "Opportunities for Political Influence" to be given by President Arthur Twining Hadley of Yale in the Harvard Union. The address, wrote Franklin Roosevelt, was on a subject "of interest to every man who intends either directly or indirectly to enter the field of politics or who hopes to aid in other ways the welfare of the country." Yet another editorial, though not dealing directly with politics, revealed a politician's approach to human relations. "In looking back over the college careers of those who for various reasons have been prominent in undergraduate life in the University, one cannot help noticing that these men have nearly always shown from the start an interest in the lives of their fellow students," he wrote. "A large acquaintance means that many persons are dependent on a man and conversely that he is himself dependent on many. Success necessarily means larger responsibilities, and responsibility means many friends." He added that the "man who makes a success of his college career like the successful man of business makes his friends not after the hard work is over, but while it is going on. . . ."

He also editorialized on undergraduate politics at Harvard as the Senior Class Day elections approached, subsequently claiming somewhat dubious credit for having effected a major reform, in the direction of greater democracy, in the university's student elective processes. "There is a higher duty than to vote for one's personal friends," he wrote in an editorial published December 15, 1903, "and that is to secure for the whole class, leaders who really deserve the positions." What he here opposed was slate-making by elite clubs, each of whose members was then pledged to support the slate agreed upon. He may well have felt more strongly on the subject than he would otherwise have done because he himself was one of a half dozen nominees for the exalted position of class marshal, only three of whom could win election, and had good reason to believe that a club combine had put up a ticket for this on which his name did not appear. (" . . . I don't stand a show of being elected," he wrote his mother, "—though I am pleased at the honor of the nomination.") Election day was Wednesday, December 16. He wrote his mother that day, repeating his pessimistic estimate of his chances: ". . . I don't stand the least show—in fact will get less votes than any of the others for marshal—but may do better if nominated for a Committee to be voted on next Friday." [38] He did better that day than he expected, or *said* he expected, however: he was fourth in the balloting, and very close to third, in an election in which a vote pool was obviously operative. As for the "committee" to which his letter referred, it was the 1904 Class Committee, and in the election to it, on Friday, December 18, there was evidently no club slate. Franklin Roosevelt won the post of permanent chairman, gaining 168 votes out of 253. It was the first elective victory he had ever gained—and he gained it just a little over six weeks after he had voted for the first time in Hyde Park Town Hall, where he would cast all his ballots for the rest of his life, his first vote being in an off-year New York State election. ("Hooray for the Dimocrats of Hoide Park!" he wrote his mother after being informed of the local election's outcome.[39])

He closed his term as *Crimson* president creditably by campaigning editorially for a boardwalk across the Yard from the then-new Union to Gore Hall and for greater fire protection for Yard dormitories. The latter campaign's initial editorial appeared in late December, 1903, and its persuasive force was immediately thereafter increased by a horrible fire (December 30) in the Iroquois Theater in Chicago, where public officials had neglected to enforce adequate fire protection and where 588 people attending a holiday matinee, most of them women and children, lost their lives. A few days later an irate letter writer to the *Crimson*, commenting on Franklin's editorial in the lurid light of the Iroquois tragedy, sarcastically implied that the Harvard Corporation (President Eliot and the university fellows) was guilty of criminal negligence on the order displayed by Chicago's public officials. Franklin demurred, perhaps because he had concluded that a reform is more easily achieved if aspersions are not cast by reformers upon the motives and personal quality of those in a position to make it. At any rate, his editorial comment on the letter was that "its sarcasm . . . seems to us in rather bad taste." At the same time he expressed again and yet again his conviction that new fire protection facilities must indeed be installed. Five months later they were.*

* Forty years later, Compton Mackenzie, the British author, told of reading at Oxford, where he was editor of one undergraduate paper and on the staff of another, exchange copies of the *Crimson* edited by Franklin Roosevelt and of being impressed by "the way it [the *Crimson*] interested itself in the material administration of the university. That seemed extraordinary to Oxford undergraduates," he went on, "who always accepted their own university as a changeless and unchangeable medieval relic." [40]

If the episode, just in itself, seems to manifest political talent, it certainly does so when viewed as an integral part of his general management of the paper. Consider especially his working relationship with the printers. The time pressure under which a printer must perform painfully precise operations with small pieces of metal and intricate machinery, joined perhaps to the kind of temperament generally attracted to such enterprise, seems to breed irritability, cantankerousness, even a species of paranoia. Any student editor soon learns, therefore, that getting along with printers is as difficult as it is necessary to his happiness, if not his overall success. It requires an art of cajoling persuasiveness, rare good humor and self-control, firmness of decision, and not a little boldness. In Franklin's case the situation was not eased by the fact that the printers he must deal with ("Mac" and "Ed") were Scotsmen and that their busy shop handled several printing jobs in addition to the daily *Crimson*; they had good reason to resent a student editor's request that forms already locked and on the press be taken off and made over to accommodate late copy. Yet Franklin had no trouble with them. They responded "with alacrity and complete approbation" to his every wish.[41] The same was true of his relations with his editorial staff and reporters. His managing editor, due to succeed him the following semester as president, was W. Russell Bowie, destined to become rector of Grace Church in New York City, and Bowie immensely admired his superior's leadership qualities and administrative talents. Bowie found in Franklin Roosevelt's "geniality . . . a kind of frictionless command." [42]

There is little other testimony from his contemporaries to the developing, toughening instinct for power which young Roosevelt certainly had. There is much testimony to the smoothness of manner, the social poise and adroitness in which this instinct was enveloped as he approached and passed his twenty-second birthday.

He completed his term as *Crimson* president at the end of his first semester, and with it he ended, to all intents and purposes, his student career. He knew by then that he had no chance of winning an MA degree in the spring: he had failed during the first semester to maintain the B average required for this, and he was so little concerned with scholarship as such that he did not hesitate to accept his mother's offer of a vacation cruise in the Caribbean which delayed for six weeks his first attendance of second-semester classes. Nor did his studies occupy a major portion of his attention upon his return. He entered upon a swirl of social activities in Boston and New York, as well as Cambridge. He was often at Groton. He helped reorganize the *Crimson* in such a way as to relieve the president of sole responsibility for the editorials, shifting this responsibility, instead, to a board of which the president was a member. He judged a track meet on Soldier's Field. In early May he was usher at the wedding of a fellow member of Fly, Herbert Burgess, to a Brookline girl.

The wedding reception provided a particularly notable instance of his smoothness. Without prearrangement he assumed the task of introducing to the bride's mother all the club members present, easing what might otherwise have been a somewhat awkward situation—a feat for which the groom was forever grateful. "Mrs. Kay [the bride's mother] was much impressed by his savoir faire," Burgess later recalled. "His charm and easy manner were apparent in those early days." [43]

X

By this time Franklin Roosevelt habitually measured himself and his progress against the personality and career of his famous Cousin Theodore. A comparison of the two men as they were at age twenty-two is therefore interesting and may even be helpful toward a definition of Franklin's developing character.

To begin with, there are several similarities between the events and activities of Franklin's college years and those of TR's a quarter century before. Like Franklin, TR entered Harvard as an outwardly conforming member of the elite and subsequently made virtually no social contacts outside his clubs and the larger society to which the clubs gave entrée. Like Franklin, TR lost his father to death early in his college years: he was nineteen when the elder Theodore Roosevelt died, Franklin nearly nineteen when James Roosevelt died. Like Franklin, TR participated enthusiastically but without much success in athletics, was librarian of his chief club, and was active in undergraduate publications—though TR did not make the latter a major concern, as did Franklin. Like Franklin, TR by the close of his last college year had become one of the most prominent members of his class without becoming truly popular and, again like Franklin, was highly critical of the kind of education he had obtained from Harvard. Both as young men manifested an amazing energy and range of interests, an amazing capacity for concentrated work.

But as regards total mind, character, personality, the differences between the two were many and wide.

Young Theodore, before he received his diploma from President Eliot's hand, had demonstrated intellectual abilities far beyond any Franklin had shown he possessed at the same stage of life. Devoting no larger portion of his total attention to formal studies than Franklin had done, TR nevertheless was graduated twenty-first in a class of 177—high enough to qualify for Phi Beta Kappa—and had by then initiated a project of historical research and writing massive enough, difficult enough to constitute the major portion of a whole career for a better-than-average professor of history. Having learned that no satisfactory history of the naval side of the War of 1812 existed, he had set about supplying the deficiency, and when the project was completed two years later (he completed it while a full-time law student), its result was a book of more than 500 pages, *The Naval War of 1812*, which at once became the standard work on its subject and would remain so more than eighty years later. TR had actually written a chapter or two of this his-tory while still an undergraduate, he being then precisely as old, or young, as the Franklin Roosevelt who wrote such earnest editorials about Harvard's football team and the urgent need for more and better cheering from the stands.

As regards character and personality, there were differences so strik-ing as to amount to contrasts.

The young Theodore Roosevelt was a remarkably frank and open youth, whose social relationships were characterized by blunt forthright-ness and tense enthusiasm. He was capable of showmanship, certainly, and often inclined to practice it, but he was not inclined at all to the kind of role playing designed to give false impressions of his real self, his actual feelings, his true intentions. Rarely, if ever, did he resort to guile in pursuit of ends that might be achieved by direct assault; he preferred face-to-face combat, he reveled in it, and his motives were for the most part transparent. Franklin seemed sometimes, even as a young man and increasingly as the years passed, to indulge in deviousness and indirec-tion for the sheer fun of it. TR never did—and none therefore called him "two-faced" or charged him with other forms of calculated deceit.

Nor did any speak of the young TR as a notably smooth, urbane, graceful, charming, poised young man, possessed of unusual *savoir-faire*. None described his leadership qualities as being so lubricated by "gen-iality" as to issue in a "kind of frictionless command." Classmates spoke instead of his assertive argumentativeness and "boyish positiveness," of his being "a bundle of eccentricities" and "a little bumptious," or even *very* bumptious. When a girl who had known him well while he was at Harvard was asked years later how he had been as a dancer she replied that he "danced just as you'd expect him to dance . . . ,—he hopped." [44] Franklin didn't; he was an excellent dancer.

What these differences, these contrasts seem to add up to is the classic difference or contrast between the masculine and the feminine principle, with TR as embodiment of the former, Franklin of the latter. This is not to say that Franklin was effeminate in his overall character, his total personality, but it *is* to say that there was a strong element of the feminine in his makeup and that this was the principle difference, so far as character and personality were concerned, between himself and his famous distant cousin. He had much and TR little of the kind of sensitivity, empathy, intuitiveness, and involuted guile that are generally deemed characteristic of women. He had, on the other hand, relatively little while TR had much of the kind of hardness, bold ruthlessness, joy in killing, and love of physical combat that are generally deemed characteristic of the warrior male, the wilderness huntsman.

Consistent with this, if not actually explanatory of it, is the fact that the dominant figure in young Theodore's life was his father, whom he both feared and loved (all his life he consciously measured himself by his father's standards), whereas the dominant figure in young Franklin's life was his proud, imperious mother, with whom his relationship was abnormally close and against whom he was required to exert himself in firm, yet subtle ways in order to achieve his independent manhood.

He was so exerting himself, unprecedentedly, that very spring of his last Harvard year.

Again there was a similarity of outward event, joined to sharp contrasts of inward experience, between young Franklin and TR at the same stage of life. Franklin as Harvard upperclassman, like young Theodore a quarter century before, had fallen in love, proposed marriage, and been accepted. On Commencement Day of 1904 he could look down from the ceremonial platform and see seated beside his mother the tall, slender, willowy girl who would become his bride, just as Theodore Roosevelt had looked down on Commencement Day of 1880 upon his beloved Alice Lee, whom he married four months later and who became the mother of the "Princess Alice" of Franklin's generation.

The 1904 commencement was not actually Franklin's graduation day; he had received his bachelor's degree the year before, marching then in cap and gown across the stage of Sanders Theater to receive his diploma. But it marked the formal close of his Harvard years, was deemed his actual commencement by himself and others (he was always listed as an alumnus of the class of '04), and was attended by his mother and numerous relatives, including the distant cousin whom he would marry. He gave a tea for them following the last baseball game of Harvard's 1904 season. And the next day they watched and listened with close attention as the Ivy Orator, W. Russell Bowie, whom they knew as

Franklin's good friend on the *Crimson*, addressed sundry "witty parting words" to his classmates, as tradition required the Ivy Orator to do, and heard Arthur Davison Ficke, as class poet, read the traditional "heroic part of considerable length." This was during the formal Class Day ceremonies, in the stadium, ceremonies in which Franklin himself had no active role but in which he was nonetheless prominent, for as an officer of his class he sat in cap and gown upon the stage. Later, during informal festivities of the day, he was presented with a policeman's uniform and required to don it and then arrest the captain of the baseball team on a charge of stealing bases.[45]

He personally was far less impressed by his college commencement than he was by the twentieth Prize Day at Groton, whence he hurried after the Harvard ceremonies had ended. Groton's Prize Day speaker that year was none other than Theodore Roosevelt, President of the United States, whose address had as its central theme words closely similar to those Franklin had himself employed in his Harvard essay on the Roosevelt family in America. "Much has been given you," said President Roosevelt to the sons of privilege in his audience, as reported in the *Grotonian*; "therefore we have the right to expect much from you." [46]

Book Two

✦⋙⋘✦

THE GREEN, YET RIPENING YEARS

Six

-->>><<<-

Enter, Eleanor

I

B Y NO strange quirk of fate, no unlikely chance or mysterious destiny, were these two brought together in casual acquaintanceship. Even had they been wholly without ties of blood and family tradition, unsharing of the same family name and distant ancestry, the strangeness would have been in their *not* meeting as they pursued their highly mobile physical lives within that small social world, close-knit and rigidly exclusive, which both of them inhabited. As it was, several special circumstances conspired to ensure their meeting on the easiest, most familiar of terms. Thus:

Her beloved "Auntie Bye" was the Anna "Bamie" Roosevelt (later the wife of Admiral Sheffield Cowles), who had been among the closest of Sara Delano's friends from early girlhood. Her paternal grandmother, Bamie's mother, was Mrs. Theodore Roosevelt, Sr., in whose New York City home Sara and James Roosevelt first met. Her father was the Elliott Roosevelt, Theodore, Jr.'s younger brother, who had been so much with James and Sara during their European honeymoon and had so diffidently consented to become godfather to their newborn child, Franklin. Her mother, born Anna Hall and grown into a lovely blue-eyed golden-haired girl, famous as a society beauty, had been a good friend of Sara's younger sister Laura, who had died so tragically; it had been at one of Laura's house parties at Algonac that Anna and Elliott Roosevelt had become engaged. James and Sara had been among the principal guests at the wedding of Elliott and Anna in New York City on December 1, 1883. Hence, even before she was born, in 1884, and christened after her mother, Anna Eleanor, this in the house her Grandfather Hall had built a generation before at Tivoli-on-the-Hudson, some twenty miles up the Albany Post Road from Hyde Park (the occasion of her birth elicited heartiest congratulations to her parents from Spring-wood), even before this it had been determined that she and the son of the James Roosevelts were bound to meet, bound to know each other as friends.

And in actual fact they did meet for the first time when she was only two years old. On a day in 1886 her parents came to Hyde Park as house guests of James and Sara, bringing her with them—a plain-visaged, re-markably solemn little girl whom her mother called Granny and her fa-ther Little Nell and who stood around in doorways with her finger in her mouth, excessively shy, silently withdrawn, until four-year-old Franklin set about entertaining her. And himself. He (her distant cousin, her fa-ther's godson, her future husband) took her into the nursery to play "horsey"; she sat astride his back as he romped joyously around the room on his hands and knees. She herself had no later recollection of this, but she would learn of it from her mother-in-law.[1]

But she remembered meeting him again when she was in her early teens and was forced to attend dances at which she was miserable while he was perfectly at ease and thoroughly enjoyed himself. One such occa-sion was, for her, especially memorable. It was during the Christmas holidays, the only time of the year when she was permitted to see boys her own age. All the other guests knew one another well; she alone was a stranger, an outsider, with nothing about her that in her eyes could at-tract anyone's favorable attention, much less actively interest a boy. Al-ready she was taller than most grown women, and since she was, by her grandmother's decree, inappropriately dressed in a little-girl's skirt that reached barely to her knees, her height became an exaggeration, a kind of vertical elongation, of her natural awkwardness. She was rigid with embarrassment. She knew herself to be a poor dancer, and so she watched in helpless envy as other girls danced, one after another, and flirted, too, with her handsome cousin Franklin, an urbane Harvard man who was evidently admired by all. Then he spied her. He came to her. He asked her to dance with him, and asked, moreover, as if he re-ally wanted her to! She was almost tearfully grateful to him![2]

The next encounter, so far as either of them could later recall, was on a New York Central train. She was then eighteen and had just returned from schooling in Europe. She was on her way from New York to Tivoli to spend the summer in her grandmother's house when he, sauntering through the day coach in which she sat, recognized her and took her back to talk to his mother who, despite the shortness of the ride, occu-pied a pullman seat. She would never forget how formidably beautiful his mother had seemed to her that day. James Roosevelt had died only six months before. Sara (Eleanor's "Cousin Sallie") was still in mourning, clad all in black, with a heavy veil that fell from hat to feet, and the somberness of her attire somehow accentuated the brilliance of her eyes and the classic purity of her features. She appeared at least a decade younger than her actual years.[3]

A few months later, Eleanor Roosevelt was introduced to New York society at an Assembly Ball where she knew only two unmarried men and suffered again agonies of humiliation over her lack of popularity or, as she profoundly believed, the means of ever achieving it. She fled the ballroom as early in the evening as she possibly could. But not long afterward her Aunt Tissie and Uncle Stanley (Mr. and Mrs. Stanley Mortimer) gave a large party for her—theater, late supper at Sherry's, followed by dancing—which went very well, and from then on the season proceeded for her more smoothly, less unhappily, through a crowded sequence of luncheons, teas, dinners, suppers, dances where, inevitably, she met her fifth cousin Franklin from time to time. She continued to meet him the following autumn (1903) after her Grandmother Hall had decided not to open the old Hall family brownstone on West Thirty-seventh Street (the cost of doing so was too great), but instead to permit Eleanor to live with her Cousin Susie and Susie's husband, Mr. and Mrs. Henry Parish, in the city. She and Franklin became good friends that fall, then better friends as the holidays came and passed. Once she was asked to a house party at Hyde Park where nearly every guest was a cousin of his, and a much closer one than she. She rather felt at that time that his mother was sorry for her.[4]

All of which, as regards their relationship, was in general outline predictable.

The event emergent from it, however—the intimacy that grew up, that ripened into love—seemed to most observers no fruit of the inevitable. Indeed, there was about it, if not an actual strangeness or mystery, then at least an improbability, an unlikelihood that bred surprise. Few could have foreseen it, and this few emphatically did *not* include Sara Delano Roosevelt. Franklin's mother was more than surprised; she was initially shocked. And when the shock wore off, she was deeply hurt, with a hurt that contained a sense of outrage and insult.

First the shock.

It came to her in the great white house her Grandfather Warren Delano had built in Fairhaven, the house now legally owned by all the Delano brothers and sisters but actually managed, along with the trust fund that accompanied it, by Sara's elder brother Warren III. The Delano clan had gathered there for Thanksgiving, 1903, and it was during that weekend, in a room containing mementos of the old China trade and, upon one wall, the coat of arms of Jean de Lannoy, Knight of the

Golden Fleece, that Franklin told her as tactfully as possible, after a considerable verbal preparation, that he had fallen in love with Eleanor Roosevelt, had proposed marriage to her, had been accepted.

His mother was visibly staggered. She could not at first believe her ears. Her handsome son "had never been in any sense a ladies man," according to her recorded belief. "I don't believe I remember ever hearing him talk about girls. . . ." she later wrote.[5] Certainly he had betrayed no slightest romantic interest in any girl. Yet here he was, a college student who had cast his first ballot less than three weeks before, who had yet to earn a dollar of his own or decide definitely upon a career, here he was, not seeking her advice, much less her permission, but simply flatly informing her, as of an accomplished and irrevocable fact, that he was going to be married! And to Eleanor Roosevelt! Of the girl's suitability in terms of family and social standing there could be no question, though her immediate family situation might well raise certain doubts: she was a Roosevelt, after all, and a niece of the President of the United States. Moreover, she was a sweet thing, rather pathetically so, eager to please and gratifyingly grateful for every kindness shown her. But she seemed not at all the kind of girl who would seriously attract Franklin, being quite easily classifiable, in the metaphorical botany of the day, as both wallflower and potential clinging vine. She was certainly not beautiful. Her large lustrous eyes were truly lovely, and she had a good figure and complexion, but all this was offset by her protruding teeth and slightly receding chin and by the self-conscious awkwardness she often displayed. She shared few, if any, of Franklin's active interests. She was not good at winter sports, she was a poor sailor, she couldn't swim, she played neither tennis nor golf (the only game she had ever played was field hockey, in England), and she had no special interest in nature nor any at all in collecting. She seemed old for her age, nineteen, and in unattractive ways, being excessively tense and earnest, as well as timid and retiring, with little evident force of mind or charm of personality. What, then, did Franklin see in her?

And how could he have arrived at his decision, through a process that must have extended through months of increasingly frequent meetings and growing intimacy, without his mother's having had the slightest inkling of what was going on?

It was with the latter question that the hurt began—the sense of loss accompanied by felt insult and outrage.

For there could be but one explanation of her complete surprise. Her son had been *deliberately* secretive, had taken pains to exclude her from knowledge of the most important development in his life thus far, and she could not but feel this as a derogatory and even a contemptuous commentary on herself and her relationship with her son. It was as if she were being cast aside—her love spurned, her authority flouted, her wisdom denied, her loneliness assured. And her first response, after the shock wore off, seems to have been a more or less calculated play for sympathy, an expression of hurt which was as a sword aimed at the tender heart and filial conscience of her son, at the faint heart and puritanical self-denial of Eleanor. This, at least, is the implication of two letters written to her immediately following the Thanksgiving vacation—letters which further testify that her swordplay had small success against her son's firmness of decision and Eleanor's strong yearning toward acceptance.

From Fairhaven she went with Franklin to New York City. He there brought Eleanor from 8 East Seventy-sixth Street, the home of the Henry Parishes, to his mother's apartment where, on Tuesday, December 1, "I had a long talk with the dear child," as Sara wrote in her diary.[6] On the following day, Eleanor wrote to her "Dearest Cousin Sallie" (one suspects she pondered the salutation) at Hyde Park: "I must . . . thank you for being so good to me yesterday. I know just how you feel & how hard it must be, but I do so want you to learn to love me a little. You must know that I will always try to do what you wish for I have grown to love you very dearly during the last summer. [She had spent much time visiting at Hyde Park and Campobello that summer.] It is impossible for me to tell you how I feel toward Franklin. I can only say that my one great wish is always to prove worthy of him." [7] Thus she indicated the price she believed she was willing to pay for her acceptance, sounding a note of abjectness that boded ill for her development of an independent individuality vis-à-vis either the imperious Sara or Sara's son. There was nothing abject about the letter Franklin wrote from Cambridge two days later: "Dearest Mama—I know what pain I must have caused you and you know I wouldn't do it if I really could have helped it—mais tu sais, me voilà! That's all that could be said—I know my mind, have known it for a long time, and know that I could never think otherwise: Result: I am the happiest man just now in the world; likewise the luckiest—" To which he added blandishment: "And for you, dear Mummy, you know that nothing can ever change what we have always been and will always be to each other—only now you have two children to love & to love you—and Eleanor as you know will always be a daughter to you in every way—" [8]

So she, the mother, changed tactics. She no longer employed her hurt as weapon, but, instead, her reasonable concern for their welfare, aiming no longer at soft conscience but at hard common sense.

Already it had been agreed that this engagement should be kept secret for the time being. Now she set about prolonging the "time being" into an indefinite but distant future, her grounds being that both Franklin and Eleanor were too young to know what they really wanted, much less to assume the grave responsibilities of marriage and children. She pointed out that her own father had not married until he was thirty-three, by which time he was "a man who had made a name and a place for himself, who had something to offer a woman." [9] What did Franklin have to offer that was truly his own? His inheritance from his father had been a relatively modest one; he must depend upon his mother's largess or his own earned income if he were to maintain the standard of living to which he and Eleanor were accustomed. And how was he to earn an income? He planned, tentatively and with no enthusiasm, to enter law school the following autumn. He could not complete his course work there and pass his bar examinations for nearly two years after that. Surely it was the part of wisdom to delay marriage until he was actually a bona fide member of some well-established law firm.

Nor was this all.

To the tactics of delay she added those of diversion. The real purpose of the proffered Caribbean cruise in early 1904 was to enforce his separation from Eleanor for many crucial weeks during which he, with Lathrop Brown, would be totally immersed in strange new scenes, new excitements, and would emerge with new perspectives whereby she hoped his mind would be changed. Both her son and Eleanor were fully aware of this purpose. Eleanor resented it. She resented not only Cousin Sallie's offer of the cruise, with all that it implied, but also Cousin Franklin's acceptance of it. And she may well have communicated some sense of her resentment to him as he bade her good-bye in New York. At any rate he began the cruise in a grumpy mood ("F. is tired and blue," wrote his mother in her diary on the day they sailed) and did not recover his spirits until they were well out to sea.[10]

II

As for Eleanor, if she watched him go with bitterness in her heart, if she was condemned now to a period of anxiety colored with despair, the experience was certainly not new to her. The tall, gawky adolescent girl who had been so miserable at Christmas holiday parties in New York had suffered a miserably unhappy childhood.

She had no later remembrance of her mother's calling her Granny during her first visit to Hyde Park when she was only two, but she did remember all her life other occasions when her mother did so and wounded her by doing it. She was the eldest child. She had two brothers: Elliott (Ellie), a couple of years younger than she; Hall (Josh), nearly six years younger. And she never forgot how, when the three children were with their mother for a children's hour in the late afternoons, she suffered always a sense of alienation from the others. Josh, the baby, cuddled and caressed, sat happily on his mother's lap. Ellie, adoring his mother and obviously adored by her in turn, responded with laughter and gay chatter to his mother's advances. But the little girl felt herself excluded from this circle of love by "a curious barrier." [11] They were together; she was alone. She knew that her mother not only did not love her as she did the others, but actually found her unattractive in appearance and personality; knew, or sensed, that the emotion she aroused in her mother was a mingling of pity with disappointment, irritation, embarrassment, even shame; and knew, too, that it was partly out of a sense of guilt for feeling this way that her mother "made a great effort" on her behalf. Such special effort could not but emphasize the felt alienation and encourage still further in the little girl a helpless and hopeless resentment. And all this came to a focus of pain on days when her mother, entertaining visitors, saw her hesitating in the doorway, a forbidden finger in her mouth, and called to her in a voice that had an edge of exasperation: "Come in, Granny!" Often then the mother would turn to her visitors and say, "She is such a funny child, so old-fashioned, that we always call her 'Granny.'" Eleanor on such occasions "wanted to sink through the floor in shame." [12]

The hurt was all the greater because she so admired her mother for the beauty and charm which were recognized throughout New York society, a society her mother deemed important. She slept in her mother's room. She could therefore watch her mother dress for going out in the evening. And she would remember always the great thrill this gave her. "She looked so beautiful, I was grateful to be allowed to touch her dress or jewels or anything that was part of the vision which I admired inordinately." She longed for her mother's affection and approval. She never received them. On the contrary, "I was always disgracing my mother." [13]

Often she did so through a "habit of lying" rooted in her fears, her insecurities, her craving for acceptance. When she was five, she was taken with brother Ellie to Europe by her parents, toured Italy with them, and was then placed in a French convent for several months while her father entered a sanitarium and her mother with Auntie Bye (this nickname for TR's sister, Mrs. Cowles, had by now largely replaced "Bamie") took a house in Neuilly, just outside Paris. She was placed there because her mother, expecting a baby (Josh was born that early summer), sought to protect her innocence against all knowledge of how children come into the world. She was terribly lonely and unhappy in the convent. She knew herself to be plain-faced and ill mannered, and she would have been isolated in any case from the other little girls by differences of language and religion. One day a girl there swallowed a penny and thereby made herself the focus of excited attention, arousing Eleanor's envy, and so, sometime later, she, Eleanor, went to the sisters saying that she herself had swallowed a penny. She hadn't, of course. The sisters knew she hadn't. But she persisted in saying she had until her mother was sent for and took her home in disgrace.[14] She acquired thus a label, an identity, by which her mother and she herself were horrified: she was a liar! And she was confirmed in this identity by being found out in other lies as the years of childhood passed—about not eating sugar and candy, for instance, when these were forbidden her by the family doctor.

The long, angry scoldings she received for these offenses were far more dreadful to her than "swift punishment of any kind," so dreadful that her fear of them sometimes encouraged the evil they were meant to correct. "I could cheerfully lie any time to escape a scolding, whereas if I had known that I would simply be put to bed or be spanked I probably would have told the truth," she later remembered.[15]

Almost the only warm, loving contact she ever had with her mother was when her mother took to bed with a sick headache. These headaches were frequent and severe—increasingly so as the years passed— and when they came, the little girl would sit at the head of her mother's bed stroking her mother's throbbing temples and forehead and neck for hours on end. She was grateful to her mother for being "willing to let me sit there," but at the core of her gratitude was the happy knowledge that this willingness was not merely permissive. She could feel her love flowing out through her caressing hands into her mother's beautiful head, alleviating pain, bringing peace; she knew that her presence was, for a change, truly welcome. She was being useful. And in her childhood the rare "feeling that I was useful was perhaps the greatest joy I experienced." [16]

Her mother had good reason to suffer nervous headaches: her marriage to Elliott Roosevelt, so joyously begun, grew tragic, and she was being subjected to intolerable strains.

Perhaps one root of the trouble was in Anna Hall's own upbringing, which seemed designed to destroy resilience of character, tolerance, and flexibility of mind. She had been raised in a family patriarchal to an almost pathological degree. Her father—never engaging in business, living wholly on the ample income from his inheritance—had indulged a profound interest in theology (he even had a clergyman live with him for purposes of learned religious discussion) while managing every aspect of the household, including the rearing of the children his wife brought abundantly into the world. This wife, born a Ludlow, a great belle and beauty in her day, was treated by her husband as essentially another child—more privileged than the others, pampered, even spoiled, but as helpless and ignorant as the children of her womb. So that when he suddenly died and left her with six children, all under seventeen years of age, she was wholly unable to cope with the heavy responsibilities thrust upon her. The four youngest children, two boys and two girls, suffered from this. But by that time the characters of Anna and her sister Elizabeth (Eleanor's Aunt Tissie), the two oldest children, had been largely formed through their father's discipline, which had been stern. He had impressed deeply upon them his own narrow view of a woman's proper role in that banal society into which they had been born, his own high and rigid standards of personal conduct, and also the religious piety by which these standards were allegedly sustained. The results, so far as Anna was concerned, would seem to show in photographs taken of her in her wedding year. These give the impression of a certain cold primness overlaying a beauty otherwise passionate, the latter manifested in her rather full pouting lips and enormous eyes. But passion is not all; there is also in those eyes a kind of tense, hurt look, as if they were windows opening on a soul drawn too painfully taut between poles of Right and Wrong, giving her a hard but brittle integrity.

It may have been this very coldness, sensed as being but the surface aspect of a profoundly sensuous nature whose sensuality, once aroused, would be all the greater for having been so rigorously repressed—it may have been this which first drew Elliott Roosevelt toward her. He was, from all accounts, a remarkably attractive young man, much more so than his brother Theodore. He was good-looking, spontaneous, sensitive, gay, and highly intelligent. But he had also rather more than his full share of the character defects that so often accompany great charm—and in his initial attraction to the beauteous Anna Hall a strong sexual desire may well have been linked with a sense of his own weaknesses, his own consequent inner needs, as he looked into her great eyes and saw not only the most exciting of promises, but also the possibility of her imparting to him some of that self-discipline, that capacity to keep emotions in check, of which he had so little and she so much. Instead, there would seem to have been a failure of the promises coupled with a shattering realization that what had appeared to him to be her self-control was in fact a deficiency of self *to be* controlled, the pout, the sultry look being but lingering traces of a passionate nature that had atrophied for lack of exercise or been destroyed through prolonged iron repression. Eleanor gave muted testimony to this years later. She wrote of her father: "He adored my mother and she was devoted to him, but always in a more reserved and less spontaneous way." [17]

There came, then, a recurrence of the mysterious illness, a failure of will and nerve, which had forced his withdrawal from prep school when he was in his teens. It began shortly after the birth of his first son. It was triggered evidently by a riding accident in which his leg was broken. (He was an ardent horseman; he and Anna had at that time, in addition to their city home, a country place at Hempstead, Long Island, where he could hunt and play polo.) The break was a very bad one and so poorly set that, later, after months of acute pain, the leg had to be rebroken and reset—an event that Eleanor, though a very little girl at the time, never forgot. ". . . I sensed that this was a terrible ordeal," she wrote a half century later, "and when he went hobbling out on crutches to the waiting doctors, I was dissolved in tears and sobbed my heart out for hours." [18] Amid this prolonged physical anguish, he began to drink heavily.

Soon he could not stop drinking.

There began then, for him, a long, hard, and ultimately futile "fight for . . . health [he never completely recovered physically from the effects of his accident] and power of self-control," a first step of which was his entrance into the sanitarium in France while his wife awaited the birth of Hall in Neuilly. He made no very satisfactory response to the medical treatment given him there, and his daughter remembered that when he came to the Neuilly house on temporary release from the sanitarium at the time of the baby's birth, he caused his wife and his sister "a great deal of anxiety," that he remained in the sanitarium when his family sailed for home many weeks after Hall's birth, and that finally "his brother, Theodore, had to go and get him. . . ." [19] He continued to drink. No "cure" brought more than temporary relief. And in a time and place when the label for such as he was not the neutral one of "alcoholic" but the opprobrious one of "drunkard," he was a disgrace to his wife and family—so great a one that his highly religious wife could not bear it. He was sent away, or went away, to a little town in Virginia, while his wife and children lived more and more with Eleanor's Grandmother Hall; they stayed in his New York house during the winter months but spent most of the warm seasons at Oak Terrace in Tivoli.

The effect of all this on the little girl, Eleanor, was devastating. Her father's love for her, joined to hers for him ("he . . . was the love of my life . . ."), constituted the one bright warm flame in the otherwise chilly gloom of her childhood. When he called her Little Nell, it was not as her mother called her Granny but, instead, as one speaks a term of endearment, and she knew this long before she knew (her father explaining it to her) that Little Nell was a character in Dickens' *Old Curiosity Shop*, a book he made her read when she was old enough. He never made fun of her, save in a teasing way that further indicated his love for her. With him she was always "perfectly happy." And when, in France, she was caught lying about swallowing the penny, her father, who was himself in disgrace (she sensed this from the tears and words and gloomy looks of her mother and Auntie Bye), "was the only person who did not treat me as a criminal!" [20] When he first went away, to Abingdon, Virginia, she was desolate. She couldn't understand why he had left her. She desperately needed the reassurance he gave her in a letter he wrote from his exile, saying, "My darling little Nell. . . . Because father is not with you is not because he doesn't love you. For I love you tenderly and dearly— and maybe soon I'll come back well and strong and we will have good times together, like we used to have." [21]

Alas, he never did come back "well and strong" to live with his family. Perhaps he was making definite progress toward that happy end when—suddenly, without warning—death struck down his beautiful young wife.

In early December, 1892, Anna Hall Roosevelt fell ill of diphtheria. Her little daughter was taken to stay with Mrs. Parish, her Cousin Susie. And it was there that she, Eleanor, was told, on the seventh of that month, that her mother was dead. She knew something horrible had happened, but she could not feel that she personally had suffered a great loss, and such sorrow as she did feel was more than overcome by the joy she felt when told that her father would soon come to Mrs. Parish's to see her. He did come, after a while. He took her driving, up Madison Avenue and over to Central Park. He was as charming, as kind and loving to her as ever. But she soon realized that this was, for him, a time of absolute tragedy. He was deemed incompetent—no doubt he deemed himself incompetent—to make a home for his children. They were taken, instead, to live with their Grandmother Hall, in the brownstone on West Thirty-seventh Street. And Eleanor never forgot his sadness as, in the gloomy library of that house, he, dressed all in black, took her in his arms and spoke of his bereavement and of how he had now only his children, of whom the two boys were too young for him really to talk to, so that it must be she and he together. Always they must remain close, even though physically separated, until someday they would live together, travel together, do all manner of interesting things together.

Thereafter she lived on the hope, the promise thus given her. She needed a bright future to look forward to, for her actual present life in her grandmother's house was, if anything, more gloomy and unsettling, more prolific of psychological insecurities than life with her mother had been. Two uncles, Vallie and Eddie, two aunts, Pussie and Maude, still lived in their childhood home. They were out of control, having grown up without guidelines or imposed standards of conduct. Their various storms and clashes of willful temperament, especially Vallie's and Pussie's, made the atmosphere of the house on Thirty-seventh Street and Oak Terrace in Tivoli anything but peaceful. And Grandmother Hall's reaction to this, so far as her grandchildren were concerned, was a determination that they "should have the discipline her own children had lacked," so that ". . . we were brought up on the principle that 'no' was easier to say than 'yes,' " as Eleanor later recalled.[22] Moreover, she was in the care of a French maid, Madelaine, who scolded her and pulled her hair and of whom she was desperately afraid.

Hence her yearning, her vital need for her father.

He came to the New York house for a second sorrowful visit in that same winter of his wife's death. Ellie and Josh had come down with scarlet fever, the latter recovering with no permanent ill effects; but Ellie, in his weakened condition, had caught diphtheria and quickly died. Eleanor, who was never seriously ill—she was practically never ill at all—was taken again to the Parishes, where she was quarantined.

During the next two years her father came to his mother-in-law's home for brief visits only, generally without prior notice. Nevertheless, his daughter, who seems always to have subconsciously waited for him, never failed to sense his presence from the instant he opened the front door; she did so even when (in the city house) she was in her room, two long flights of stairs above the front hall. Despite his prolonged absence, he "dominated all this period" of his daughter's life.[23] He took a great interest in her education, which her mother had been inclined to neglect, and she learned many things just to please him—most of *Hiawatha* by heart, for instance. She was by her own account a great physical coward, yet was frequently able to overcome her timidity when she was with him, because he so disapproved of it. He gave her puppies and a pony and loaded her down with presents at Christmastime and on her birthday. He wrote her often, and as she read his letters, she shared joyously in what she believed to be his life, which was evidently full of little children and fox terriers and horses. She lived with him in a dream-world.

Then he died.

On August 14, 1894, shortly before her tenth birthday, her Aunt Maude and Aunt Pussie came to her and told her that her father was dead. She wept for him—she was swept by a storm of tears and wept for a long time in her bed that night, before an exhausted sleep overcame her—but in her deepest self she would not, could not accept the fact that he was forever gone from her, that she would never see him again, and when she awoke the next morning, she "began . . . living in my dream world as usual." She was helped to do so by her grandmother's decision that neither she nor Josh should go to the funeral, for this meant that she had "no tangible thing to make death real to me." She knew in her mind that her father was dead, yet could not or would not *feel* that he was, so that for a long time ". . . I lived with him more closely, probably, than I had when he was alive." [24]

III

A thicker gloom than she had known before closed down around her.

For instance, while her father lived, a bright spot of almost every week in the city for her had been a Saturday visit with her father's aunt, Mrs. James King Gracie (Auntie Gracie), sister of her Grandmother Roosevelt. Auntie Gracie was a warm, vital, vibrant person, "much beloved by her greatnephews and nieces," of whom Alice Roosevelt and Teddy Robinson were generally with her at the same time as Eleanor was. Auntie Gracie talked to them by the hour, often about plantation life in the South, where she and her sister had been raised; took them sight-seeing in the afternoons to such educative entertainments as Mrs. Jorley's waxworks; and with them sometimes visited the Orthopaedic Hospital, which Grandfather Roosevelt had helped found and where the sight of "innumerable little children in casts and splints" aroused in Eleanor a great pity and desire to help alleviate the pain and suffering in the world. All week long, the little girl had looked forward to these rich Saturdays. Then—abruptly, with no reason given—they were forbidden her by her grandmother.[25]

Indeed, Grandmother Hall discouraged all contacts between her grandchildren and the Roosevelts. Perhaps she resented, as well as disapproved of, the family whose son had brought such great sorrow upon her daughter. Perhaps she feared that her grandchildren, if they were too much exposed to their lively and dynamic Roosevelt relatives, would escape or rebel against the rigid control she was determined to maintain over them. Whatever the reason, Eleanor was permitted no more than a couple of visits to the home of her Aunt Edith and Uncle Ted at Sagamore Hill, Oyster Bay, Long Island—visits that stood out so sharply, vividly from the dreary monotony of her average childhood days that she always remembered them in detail. She remembered her terror as she jumped off a dock into the ocean, upon her Uncle Ted's orders, despite her inability to swim (he insisted that this was the way to learn, but it didn't work). She remembered her almost equivalent terror when Uncle Ted lined her up with the other children atop a high, steep sandy bluff and had them all run pell-mell down it to a beach, most of them falling on the way and then rolling to the bottom—an exercise she rather enjoyed after she had learned that a fall wouldn't hurt her. Terrified or not, she always felt that she was alive with Uncle Ted. And she remembered with unalloyed pleasure being chased by him through haystacks, being read to by him in the house, and going with him and the others on a camping trip during which he "taught us many a valuable lesson"—especially "that camping was a good way to find out people's characters"; the selfish would reveal their selfishness by shirking their share of the work of the camp and by seeking for themselves the best food, the best bed.[26]

On West Thirty-seventh Street and at Tivoli she had almost no companionship with children her own age. She was much alone and in her solitude became an omnivorous reader. She had occasional good times with her uncles and aunts, especially with Uncle Vallie, who was gay and charming with her, and Aunt Pussie, who was an accomplished pianist, much interested in the theater. But these moments were more than balanced by tempestuous times with her uncles and aunts, especially with Pussie. For Pussie had what was called an "artistic temperament," meaning that she was highly emotional, made no effort to inhibit the expression of her feelings, and had a meager sense of responsibility. Once Pussie took Eleanor and Eleanor's governess to Nantucket, where, after a few days, she simply casually abandoned them, going off without telling them where she was going or leaving them any money with which to pay the inn bill or purchase tickets for transportation home. The frantic governess had finally to obtain the needed money through appeal to Grandmother Hall. Such treatment, coupled with her grandmother's inveterate habit of saying no ("I built up the defense of saying I did not want things in order to forestall her refusals and keep down my disappointments"), did nothing to build up the little girl's self-confidence or sense of security.[27] Small wonder that she entered adolescence as a shy, gawky creature who, at parties, was made painfully aware that she was "different from all the other girls," and in ways that were unattractive.

Not until she was fifteen and was enrolled in a school in England conducted by a remarkable Frenchwoman, Mlle. Marie Souvestre, did she again receive any such affectionate concern for her essential self as she had received from her father. The school was run on lines barely less austere than Peabody's at Groton. The girls were required to rise early each morning and walk on the common, no matter how cold and damp the weather, to take outdoor exercise each afternoon, to work hard at their studies; were given the plainest of food and lodging, with few luxuries or pleasures. And Eleanor thrived in this environment. She felt that she was set free of the past, with all its sins and terrors and repressions, and could begin anew. The result was that "for . . . the first time in all my life . . . all my fears left me," including those born of that "physical cowardice" of which she had formerly been ashamed. Required to play some game or other, she chose field hockey, the roughest of all, and managed to make the first team ("I think that day was one of the proudest . . . of my life"),[28] suffering proportionately as many hard knocks and bruises as Franklin Roosevelt had suffered in Groton football. She was accepted by the other girls, was even popular with them, and made friendships that would last a lifetime. All of which reduced the sense she had had of being utterly alone and helpless in a hostile world.

But it was from Mlle. Souvestre herself that she received the greatest boost to her morale. Mlle. Souvestre, in late middle age, had wavy white hair growing to a peak above a broad forehead that was faintly but permanently frown-furrowed between unusually piercing eyes, giving her an appearance of stern concentration. Her features were clean-cut, her face as a whole rather masculinely handsome above a thick neck and broad, stout body. She looked to be what she was—an executive temperament, a strong character, a powerful personality, a hard mind—and her pedagogical techniques and overall influence on the girls in her school were in several respects similar to those of Peabody upon the boys at Groton. Every night, for example, the girls were assembled in the library to bid good-night, one by one, to the headmistress whose "eagle eye," on such occasions, ". . . penetrated right through to your backbone and . . . took in everything about you." Therefore, it meant an immense amount to Eleanor that she should soon become one of Mlle. Souvestre's favorites. She was abruptly cured of her "habit of lying," knowing that she had nothing to fear from truth telling so long as she conformed to clearly defined rules and regulations. She was improved in her dress and manners by Mlle. Souvestre's expressed tastes in these things. And she was "shocked . . . into thinking" by Mlle. Souvestre's unorthodox views on politics and religion. In politics, the headmistress was a liberal; during the Boer War she was strongly pro-Boer, declining to join in those celebrations of British victories which she permitted her English pupils to hold in the gymnasium. In religion, she was an atheist, refusing to believe in a God who would bother Himself with insignificant individual human beings, and was convinced that religion in general was needed by only the weak. The effect of this last was especially salutary upon Eleanor, who had been so strictly raised in so gloomily a religious home. She was under the beneficent influence of this remarkable teacher for three school terms, plus many weeks of vacation, during which she and Mlle. Souvestre toured the Continent together.

But even during the years when this influence was being actively exerted, it was interrupted and counteracted by the influence on her of her mother's family.

She went home for the summer following her second term in the school. Her Aunt Pussie had come to Europe, and with Pussie she shared a cabin across the Atlantic. The boat was a slow one; the voyage seemed interminable. For Pussie, who had a penchant for violently unhappy love affairs, had just reached the end of one and spent most of each night sobbing and threatening suicide, adding an almost intolerable anxiety to the seasickness from which Eleanor always suffered. Nor did she escape Pussie's "artistic temperament"—wherein selfishness and self-indulgence were now streaked with a mean cruelty—during the weeks that followed. She went to stay for much of the summer with Mrs. Parish at Northeast Harbor on Mount Desert Island, Maine. Pussie stayed with a Ludlow aunt of hers nearby. And one day when she was furious with her adolescent niece for some reason, the ineffable Pussie plunged and twisted into the girl's sensitive soul the cruelest knife of words that could possibly have been devised at that time, in those circumstances. First she did her best to destroy the personal confidence, the mild self-esteem which the girl had begun to develop in Europe: she said flatly that Eleanor must never expect to have beaux as the Hall women had always had because she, Eleanor, was the ugly duckling of the family. Then she proceeded to tell the girl about Elliott Roosevelt's last years, giving his daughter ugly facts that had theretofore been carefully kept from her. Eleanor was cut almost to death; Mrs. Parish could do little to assuage the pain, much less to heal wounds that remained open and bleeding when the girl returned to her Grandmother Hall's house.[29] As for Grandmother Hall, she was too much preoccupied with her eldest son, Vallie, to give any sympathetic attention to Eleanor, for Uncle Vallie, after a brief period of exemplary young manhood, "was now beginning to sow his wild oats" with a vengeance and was well on his way toward chronic alcoholism.

He was definitely an alcoholic by the time Eleanor bade a final farewell to Mlle. Souvestre in England months later and returned to Oak Terrace in Tivoli. He continued to live with his mother. He was almost continuously drunk, often disgustingly so, sometimes terrifyingly so, as, driven violently insane by his prolonged excesses, he raged through the house. His sickness dominated the household and cut it off from the rest of the world: since he could never be trusted to behave decently when guests were present, few guests were ever invited—none "who was not so intimate that he knew the entire situation." With relief Eleanor took her young brother, Hall (the nickname Josh now fell into disuse), with whom her relationship from this time forward was less sisterly than maternal, out of that unhappy home in the early fall and journeyed with him and her grandmother to Groton for his enrollment in Endicott Peabody's school. She herself, with Aunt Pussie, moved not long afterward into the West Thirty-seventh Street house, leaving her Uncle Vallie with her grandmother at Tivoli—a move that somewhat decreased her misery.

But life was far from peaceful and happy with Pussie, whose "love affairs were becoming more serious" and who sometimes "shut herself into her room" for days at a time, "refusing to eat and spending hours weeping." Eleanor finally made attempts to discover the precise nature of her sorrowful aunt's troubles but was unable to do so; she was confronted, instead, "with many situations that I was totally unprepared to handle." Nor did she wholly escape her Uncle Vallie. Every now and then, despite her grandmother's desperate efforts to keep him in the country, he came roaring down the Hudson to the city house "for one purpose and one alone, . . . to go on a real spree" (as if his average drunkenness were not "real" enough), requiring of Eleanor (because Pussie was too preoccupied with herself to cope with the difficulties he imposed) a full exercise of strengths and braveries and managerial skills she had not theretofore known she possessed.[30] And Uncle Vallie was not the only sad, insoluble family problem which she had to face at this time. Her Uncle Eddie was now married but proved himself wholly incapable of handling this responsibility or any other; he, too, had become an alcoholic.

Thus Eleanor, in the season of her "coming out" and of an acquaintance with her cousin Franklin Roosevelt that grew toward intimacy, supped often on horrors in her most private life and, at some cost in terms of spontaneity and resilience, was strengthened by them in terms of essential character. She recognized the horrors to be the result of a complete loss of the power of self-control. She was determined, therefore, never to lose her own, but to increase it, building upon a habit of self-denial that had been forcibly impressed upon her from her earliest years. She developed what later appeared to her as an "exaggerated idea of the importance of keeping all of one's desires under complete subjugation."[31]

Her experience of life had made of her, by this time, a curiously mingled mind and personality. In many respects she was innocent and unworldly to a degree remarkable for one of her age and circumstances.

She had "painfully high ideals and a tremendous sense of duty entirely unrelieved by any sense of humor. . . ."[32] She knew virtually nothing about how most people earn their livings or about the handling of money; not until she was nineteen and living with the Parishes did she learn how to keep books and avoid expenditures in excess of income. She knew nothing through personal experience about sexual and other intimate relationships between man and woman; she was always rigorously chaperoned when with a man, had never been kissed by a man, and would have been insulted by the attempt of any man to kiss her or give her an expensive present who had not first proposed marriage to her and been accepted. But as regards other matters of which most women of her class were wholly ignorant—matters pertaining to what was then generally called "the seamy side of life"—she knew a great deal, thanks to her long and frequently bitter experience of Vallie and Pussie, plus the tragedy of her father.

By the quality of both her innocence and her sophistication, coupled with the sense she continued to have of herself as hopelessly unattractive and socially maladroit, she was unfitted for "success" in that formal society in which she was willy-nilly involved and which, because of the Hall women's teaching and example, she continued to deem important. She did her duty as she and the Hall family saw it. She went to the required dinners and dances night after night. But she greatly preferred the informal studio parties given by a famous woman painter to whom she was introduced by a bachelor friend much older than she, and she became engaged in other activities having nothing to do with society as such. The Junior League was then a new organization through which privileged girls undertook to earn their privileges to some degree through charitable and social work of various kinds. Eleanor became an active member. With Jean Reid, daughter of the Whitelaw Reids, she taught calisthenics and "fancy dancing" to slum children in the Rivington Street Settlement House. She also became active in the Consumers' League, going with an experienced older woman to investigate (and be shocked by) working conditions of girls in garment factories and department stores.

IV

And so she came to the autumn of 1903, to a memorable weekend spent in Groton, where she visited her young brother, Hall, and was visited by Franklin Roosevelt, who, after some weeks of increasingly ardent courtship, asked her to marry him.

She had evidently by then got over the astonishment, the incredulity with which she must have received his first intimations of a serious romantic interest in her. Perhaps she was even able by then to see herself a little through his eyes and realize that she was, if no beauty, by no means without physical, sexual attractiveness. For though awkward when tense, she had the tall, slender grace of a young willow when at ease and could not but feel, when her lover looked deep into her eyes, that this was so. She knew that her eyes were actually beautiful, that Franklin had been attracted to her in response to no conscious effort on her part, that he and she shared certain fundamental sympathies and antipathies—and from this knowledge had been born a warm sense of inner security greater than any she had known before.

It was so great, in fact, that his asking her to marry him seemed to her "an entirely natural thing." He was so absolutely sure of his feelings, so sure of what he wanted! She herself was not so sure. When she returned to the Parishes after that Groton weekend, she "asked Cousin Susie whether she thought I cared enough," a question that would hardly have occurred to her had she been deeply in love. And she herself later confessed that though she "solemnly answered 'yes' " when asked by her grandmother if she were "really in love," it was years afterward "before I understood what being in love was or what loving really meant." [33]

But if she was more certain of his feeling for her than of hers for him, she had no serene confidence that his desire for her was strong enough, tenacious enough to survive the covert, subtle, determined onslaught of her prospective mother-in-law. Hence, in proportion to her wish for marriage, she suffered anxiety during the weeks of Franklin's Caribbean cruise. He seemed so malleable in his mother's hands!

Fortunately, she was enabled to spend the weeks of waiting, not amid the banalities of New York society, which bored her, but in the much more interesting and less trivial society of Washington, D.C. She was in New York on February 16, 1904, when Pussie was married to W. Forbes Morgan—an occasion which made few of the bride's family and close friends "very happy," as Eleanor later wrote, because the groom "was a number of years younger than Pussie" and none who knew the latter well believed her capable of adjusting "to the complicated business of married life." [34] But Eleanor's Auntie Bye, who had asked her down for part of the winter of 1903, asked her down again for the winter months of 1904, and Auntie Bye—sister of the President, wife of an admiral—was not only very much in the mainstream of the capital's social affairs but was also a confidante and, on some matters of state, a respected adviser of Theodore Roosevelt. He, the President, came now and then to his sister's house, where he talked freely, and Eleanor was an overnight guest once or twice at the White House. Thus, she gained some inkling of the private life and self of a public man who had come to occupy an office of supreme power. She gained other knowledge as well. She accompanied her aunt on the latter's round of afternoon calls ("I was aghast at this obligation") and was a guest at almost daily luncheons, teas, and dinners where she met diplomats, high government officials, politicians, visiting celebrities—people who were actually doing important things in the great world and who had "charm and wit and *savoir faire*." [35] She found herself unwontedly at ease in this company. She further realized what she had begun to realize during her European schooling—namely, that she had a mind that was quick, capacious, and retentive and that she was an interesting conversationalist, able to use the smattering of information she had gained in various fields in such a way as to give her listener, frequently an authority in some one of those fields, the impression that she was far more knowledgeable than actually she was. This encouraged him to talk to her more frankly and seriously about his work than he would otherwise have done.

She blossomed in this environment. She gained swiftly in self-confidence and poise. So that she no doubt would have been able to bear the disappointment of her hopes for marriage to Franklin Roosevelt, had this been required of her.

It was not required.

Franklin with his mother left the cruise at Nassau and came up to the capital from Florida by train. Thereafter he spent most of his several days in Washington with Eleanor; he was as ardent and determined a lover as ever. Eleanor need not have worried even if she knew that his mother continued a relentless pursuit of her tactics of delay and diversion while in Washington, attempting there a new maneuver. Joseph Choate was President Roosevelt's ambassador to the Court of St. James's. He was in the capital at that time for White House and State Department consultations. He was known to be seeking a secretary who, presumably, would accompany him on his return to London. And Sara Roosevelt, a social friend of his in New York, requested that her son be given the secretarial post. One suspects that the ambassador was somewhat taken aback. Certainly he refused the request. He said that he had already engaged a secretary and that, in any case, Franklin, who had just turned twenty-two, was too young and inexperienced for so responsible a post.[36]

V

The engagement of Franklin Delano Roosevelt to marry Anna Eleanor Roosevelt was formally announced in late November, 1904.

By that time Franklin had been enrolled for more than two months as a student in the Columbia University Law School and was living with his mother in a house she had rented at 200 Madison Avenue in New York City. Some three weeks before he had journeyed to Hyde Park to cast his first ballot in a Presidential election. Despite his father's and his own lifelong Democracy, he had "voted for the Republican candidate, Theodore Roosevelt, because I thought he was a better Democrat than the Democratic candidate . . . ," as he said thirty-odd years later,[37] and whether or not this was actually his thought at the time, it would seem to have been historically justified. For the Democrats in that year repudiated the quadrennial candidacy of William Jennings Bryan and chose instead the calm and cautious Alton B. Parker, presiding judge of the highest court in New York, and Judge Parker was certainly less attuned to the reformist progressive mood of that time than Theodore Roosevelt was. The latter won election by a huge majority.

By that time, too, Franklin had informed Endicott Peabody by letter that his engagement to "my distant cousin . . . is about to come out" and had expressed the "hope," Eleanor's as well as his own, "that you will be able to help us in the ceremony—it wouldn't be the same without you." Of his own immediate occupation he wrote with something less than enthusiasm. He said he was in the Law School "trying to understand a little of the work," adding that "of course I am going to keep right on"—as if in spite of doubts, boredom, and a sense of personal inadequacy.[38]

And he did "keep right on," though with a bare minimum of that prolonged, concentrated study required of law students. Indeed, he evidently did less than the required minimum in two of his courses, one of them the highly important contracts, which he failed at the end of his first year, to his great surprise, for he had believed himself to be doing as well in the failed subjects as in the others, in each of which he received the very respectable grade of B. It became necessary for him to take makeup examinations the following fall if he were to stay with his class.[39]

His vital interests, during that first law school year, centered in the house on East Seventy-sixth Street—the Parish house—where Eleanor lived. He spent as much time with her as he possibly could, going often with her into New York society. On March 4, 1905, he and she were present by special invitation at the inauguration of Theodore Roosevelt as

President. They were very much at the center of the ceremonies and festivities of this historic event. They had come down to Washington in the private railway car of a cousin, George Emlen Roosevelt; they sat on the Capitol steps behind the Theodore Roosevelt family as the President took the oath of office and delivered his inaugural address; they lunched afterward at the White House before going out to the official reviewing stand to watch the inaugural parade; and they danced together at the inaugural ball that night.[40]

Thirteen days later, on St. Patrick's Day, which was also the birthday of Eleanor's mother, they were married.

The wedding took place, as Pussie's had the year before, in the home of Mrs. E. Livingston Ludlow, who was Pussie's aunt and Mrs. Henry Parish's mother. The Ludlow house adjoined the Parishes' on East Seventy-sixth Street, between Madison and Fifth avenues, and the drawing rooms of the two were separated only by sliding doors which could be opened for special occasions to make the two large rooms into one enormous one. This had been done for Pussie's wedding; it was to be done for Eleanor's wedding reception as soon as the ceremony itself, at which attendance was restricted to the two families and a few of the most intimate friends, had been completed.

The bride wore a long-sleeved dress of stiff white satin, with shirred tulle at the neck—a dress covered by her Grandmother Hall's rose-point Brussels lace, of which the long bridal veil was also made. Around her throat was a dog collar of pearls given her by her mother-in-law; in her arms was a huge bouquet of lilies of the valley. She was radiant, almost beautiful, and certainly graceful in her tall slenderness as she emerged from the upstairs bedroom where she had dressed, came down the stairway on the arm of her escort, and walked slowly along the aisle between the groom's assembled family and her own to the chancel of pink roses and palms which had been set up before the fireplace. The groom awaited her there, with his best man, Lathrop Brown, as did the Reverend Endicott Peabody, who performed the ceremony.

But the center of attention at this wedding and reception was not the bride. Not for her sake, nor that of the man she was to marry, did great crowds gather at both the Fifth and Madison Avenue entrances to that block, entrances cordoned off by more than seventy-five policemen who permitted none but invited guests to enter and so zealously checked the credentials of those that several did not get into the Ludlow-Parish houses until after the reception had almost ended. When the bride came down the stairs, she was less stared at even by that family assemblage than was the man who was the object of all this police guardianship—a bespectacled mustached man almost a head shorter than she, upon

whose arm she leaned—and the most memorable moment of the ceremony came, not when the Reverend Mr. Peabody pronounced Franklin
and Eleanor man and wife, but when he asked, "Who giveth this woman
to be married to this man?" and was answered by the stocky bespectacled man, in a loud voice, "I do!" For this man who gave the bride
away—this man for whose convenience the wedding date had been set
(in his official capacity he had reviewed the St. Patrick's Day parade up
Fifth Avenue before coming to the Parish-Ludlow houses)—was none
other than Eleanor's Uncle Ted, the President of the United States.

The sliding doors were opened. The throng gathered on the Parish
side of them, awaiting the reception, pressed toward the chancel where
the bridal couple stood. There the President of the United States was
heard to congratulate his niece and distant cousin, saying he was delighted that they were keeping the Roosevelt name in the family. Then
he strode into the Parish library, where refreshments were being served
and where he, one of the great trenchermen of that overstuffed age, par-
took heartily of them. The guests followed him. Soon the young married
couple stood all alone before the altar, gazing perhaps a bit ruefully at
each other, though Eleanor would later remember that neither she nor
Franklin was particularly surprised or dismayed by this desertion of
them. They simply followed the others into the library, where Uncle Ted
held forth with jokes and stories and where they listened and laughed
with the rest.[41]

After the President's departure and the reception's end, Franklin and
Eleanor slipped away, donned traveling clothes, and entrained for Hyde
Park, where they had a short week of honeymooning before moving into
an apartment they had rented in the Hotel Webster, on West Forty-fifth
Street. There they lived until Franklin completed his first year of law
school.

Seven

-»»×«««-

A Start in Life

THEN, in the summer of 1905, came their real honeymoon—a three-month grand tour of Europe. Everywhere they encountered friends and relatives; everywhere they were accorded special attention because of their relationship with the President of the United States. Sometimes this special attention was financially embarrassing. In London, in Brown's Hotel, they were assigned the royal suite and felt obliged to stay in it despite its costing them several times as much as they could afford. In St. Moritz, in the Palace Hotel, much the same thing happened: they were assigned a suite far larger and more expensive than they wanted.[1] Everywhere, too, but especially in London and Paris, Franklin indulged his passion for book collecting. It was a passion which his wife could not share. Nor could she share his love of mountain climbing—she would or could not really climb at all—and this provided the occasion for the first severe attack of jealousy in her marital life, for when they went to Cortina, in the Dolomites, they met a Miss Kitty Gandy, a "charming lady" whom Franklin already knew slightly and who was an enthusiastic climber with whom he climbed while Eleanor remained in the town below, helplessly fuming. She said nothing about it when her husband returned. Her tendency was always to retreat into a dead silence when she was hurt, "feeling like a martyr and acting like one" (years later an older friend told her frankly that her "Griselda moods were the most maddening things in the world"). She was "perfectly delighted when we . . . drove out of the mountains." [2]

The little episode measured her continuing shyness and insecurity, and so did other episodes during what was on the whole the happiest time in her life thus far. In England, when they were house guests of old friends of James and Sara Roosevelt, the wealthy and aristocratic Foljambes, she "suffered tortures" at dinner because, in accordance with upper-class English custom, nobody was introduced to anybody else, and she was utterly horrified after dinner to discover that she would have to play bridge, which she played badly, and for money, which outraged her principles! On another occasion, in another house, she sat alone at tea with her titled hostess, who suddenly asked her to explain "the difference between your national and state governments." She was terrified and ashamed because she didn't know the answer! When Franklin strolled in with the host at that moment, she referred the question to him, and he was able to answer it adequately.[3] She resolved that she would find out something about how her country's government worked when she returned to the United States.

In Scotland they were guests of old family friends, the Fergusons, whose younger son, Bob, had emigrated to America, had served as a Rough Rider in the Spanish-American War, and had subsequently, as a highly eligible but seemingly confirmed bachelor in New York, become one of Eleanor's closest men friends. He had greatly eased her way through New York society in the year of her coming out. He had introduced her to a Mrs. Tilden R. Selmes, of Kentucky and St. Paul, whose daughter, Isabella, an extremely beautiful girl some two years younger than Eleanor, had become among the closest of all of Eleanor's women friends. She, Isabella, had also become "one of the most popular debutantes New York has ever seen." Shortly after Franklin and Eleanor arrived in Europe, they received a cable from New York announcing that Isabella and Bob Ferguson were to be married very soon. Eleanor was greatly surprised—Bob was some eighteen years older than Isabella, and the marriage seemed "in some ways . . . incongruous"—but she was also greatly pleased.[4] And when she and Franklin were invited to come to Novar while the honeymooning Fergusons were at a small watering place nearby, she quickly accepted.

It was during the visit there, in the first days of September, that Eleanor had one of the strangest experiences of her honeymoon. She had already discovered that Franklin had nightmares and sometimes walked in his sleep—on the *Oceanic,* coming over, he had got out of bed asleep and started to walk out of the cabin, being halted by Eleanor's alarmed cry and begging request that he return to bed—but she was nonetheless startled and frightened by the nightmare he acted out in her presence on a night after he and a Ferguson son had tramped the moors all day and worn themselves out. His wild shrieks awakened her. He sat up in bed, pointing at the ceiling where he saw, with his nightmare eye, a revolving beam. "Don't you see it?" he cried, warning her that she was directly under it and would be crushed by it when it fell. Only with great difficulty did she prevent his getting out of bed and arousing the household.[5]

The Fergusons took a lively interest in public affairs and had as luncheon guests, while Franklin and Eleanor were at Novar, people of similar bent. One was a Miss Chamberlain, daughter of Joseph Chamberlain and sister of Neville, whom Franklin had seen at Groton, in 1897, when she was a house guest of the rector's and who had struck him as "evidently horribly learned." [6] Like Eleanor, she was a graduate of Allenswood, Mlle. Souvestre's school.* Other luncheon guests were identified by Eleanor in a letter as "Mr. & Mrs. Webb (they write books on sociology)," who were in fact the famous Fabian Society Socialists, Sidney and Beatrice Webb. ". . . Franklin discussed the servant problem with the wife!" wrote Eleanor.[7] She was astonished at how well informed everyone she met at Novar seemed to be on world affairs. Even the gardener seemed to know all about the international conference her Uncle Ted had convened at Portsmouth, New Hampshire, at which a treaty of peace ending the Russo-Japanese War was being drafted by envoys from St. Petersburg and Tokyo.

From the first to the last of this crowded tour, the bridegroom was tremendously active, much more so than his bride—an avid collector of experiences and information, as well as books. Six Japanese naval officers were aboard the *Oceanic* as the honeymooners sailed eastward. They were to take charge of two battleships being completed for Japan in British shipyards as the Russo-Japanese War, begun in 1904, approached its climax. Franklin had "several interesting talks with them," trying to find out about their country and its navy, but was forced at last to admit that he had found himself "giving out more information than I received." He had his camera with him always and took hundreds of pictures, including many that had, so far as Eleanor could see, no pictorial interest whatever (". . . some at the tops of passes where we were surrounded only by . . . snow") but that he was able to identify, with precise information on where and when each was taken, after they had been developed in America weeks and months later. (Eleanor was impressed. "That extraordinarily photographic mind of his never forgets anything he has once seen.") While with the Foljambes he had long discussions of "farming and cattle raising" with his host and others; at Novar, he visited and interviewed many of the tenantry; at Raith, where Sir Ronald Ferguson had a magnificent estate, he took an intense inter-

---

* Significant of the tightness, the smallness of that world of the elite in which the Roosevelts lived was the fact that Joseph Chamberlain, Miss Chamberlain's father and the father of a future Prime Minister, took as his third wife, after his second (Neville's mother) died, Mary Endicott of Salem, a first cousin of Endicott Peabody on his mother's side. The rector often stayed with Joseph Chamberlain when visiting England.

est in the scientific forestry practiced in the woodlands whereby these were rendered continuously beautiful while at the same time producing substantial annual revenue. (The same methods, he thought, might be profitably applied at Hyde Park. He indicated as much in a letter to his mother: ". . . the plans for Hyde Park now include not only a new house but a new farm, cattle, trees, etc." [8]) Of his purely recreational activities, mountain climbing was by no means the only one he engaged in without Eleanor. He went for long tramps across the moors without her, rode without her, golfed without her on the historic St. Andrews links.

Possibly significant of his general attitude toward her was the nickname he began to apply while they were abroad. He called her Babs, short for "baby." The nickname became habitual; he would continue to use it for the rest of his life.

The voyage home in the second week of September was a thoroughly miserable one for the bride. She was in general a poor sailor, though on calm seas sailing eastward she had "been a *wonderful* sailor" who hadn't "*missed* a single meal or *lost* any either," as Franklin bragged to his mother. She now suffered what she deemed at the time a seasickness more severe and prolonged than any she had suffered before. She was nauseated almost every mile of the way. And, surprisingly, she remained miserable even after their landing.

She consulted a doctor a day or so later. He examined her and told her she was pregnant.[9]

II

There was nothing passive about Sara Roosevelt's mother love. There had never been, and her acquisition of "two children to love & love you" simply multiplied the means and opportunities for maternal aggressions on her part. While the two "children" honeymooned in Europe and dutifully wrote her long letters detailing their experiences, she rented, redecorated, and furnished for them a little house at 125 East Thirty-sixth Street, just three blocks from her own house at 200 Madison. It was ready for them to move into when they returned; she had even hired the servants! And thus was set much of the pattern for the early years of Franklin and Eleanor's married life.

Sara never considered the possibility that these two young people, starting out in life, might well dispense with servants. Nor did her son or daughter-in-law. Years would pass before Eleanor became convinced that she and the children who had by then been born to her would have been far better off if she as a bride, in the total absence of servants, had been forced to learn to cook and perform all other essential household chores and had later been the sole nurse of her children. She would then have acquired the "knowledge and self-confidence" necessary for the efficient management of hired help, when she had it, and for her own independence. But an independent daughter-in-law was precisely what Sara did *not* want. She proposed to remain the actual head of the family. It served this end for "dear sweet Eleanor" to remain pretty much as she was—helpless, submissive, unsure of herself, undemanding and unassertive, grateful for every kindness, and content to have others make decisions for her.

"For the first year of my married life, I was completely taken care of," Eleanor would remember. "My mother-in-law did everything for me. I saw a great deal of Isabella Ferguson and a few of my other friends, and, like many other young women waiting for a first baby, I was sometimes nervous." [10]

The baby, a girl, was born on May 3, 1906. She was christened Anna Eleanor, after her mother and maternal grandmother, but was always called by her first name only. There came into the house at this time a trained nurse, Blanche Spring, with whom Eleanor formed at once a warm friendship; she was destined to be called back again and again into Roosevelt service and would do as much as any other one person, in these early married years, to help the young wife toward self-realization. Miss Spring was not well herself that year, yet managed beautifully her care of mother and child for the first few weeks, simultaneously teaching Eleanor a few of the rudiments of baby care. In the following year, Eleanor underwent a quite serious surgical operation, and Miss Spring became the nurse in charge of the case. The helpful friendship was reinforced.

In the summer of 1906, after the Columbia Law School term had ended, the young family moved out of the city, with the mother-in-law —first to Hyde Park (Sara's house), then to Campobello (Sara's cottage), where Eleanor's younger brother, Hall, spent much of his vacation with them (he thereafter made his home with the Roosevelts) while Sara was in Europe. Here the general pattern of the marriage relationship was further filled out: Franklin played golf and swam with friends and went for long sails with parties of men aboard the *Half-Moon*; the young wife stayed home and, with a nurse (not Miss Spring but a young and inexperienced one), looked after the baby. A good deal of special care was required as the summer drew to a close. The baby began to cry a great deal and stopped gaining weight as rapidly as she should have done. Not until they had returned to New York and consulted with a famous baby doctor was a regimen worked out under which Anna returned to normal health and growth.[11]

Not long after her operation, Eleanor discovered that she was pregnant again. Their second child was born on December 23, 1907. The boy, named James (as the eldest son) in accordance with Roosevelt family tradition, had a difficult infancy. No food could be found which agreed with him, he "cried every night all night," and not even Miss Spring, who was again "pressed into service," could discover what was wrong. Finally, he came down with pneumonia in the spring of 1908 and nearly died of it. Many months passed before he had caught up with the average child of his age in physique and mental development.[12]

By that time Eleanor was carrying her third child, another boy, born March 18, 1909, and named Franklin, Jr. He was, by her own account, "the biggest and most beautiful of all the babies," and his mother was much concerned to keep him well and strong. Accordingly she insisted that Miss Spring remain with her, even after they had gone for the summer to Campobello. No trouble occurred. But in the fall, after the children and their nurse were established at Hyde Park with "Granny," and Franklin and Eleanor were living weekdays in New York and weekends at Hyde Park, all the children came down with flu in their parents' absence. Franklin, Jr.'s illness became at once critical. Informed of this, a frantic Eleanor telephoned Miss Spring, who, when summer ended, had again left the Roosevelt employ. Miss Spring helped Eleanor persuade a New York doctor to accompany the two of them to Hyde Park, where they found Anna and James doing well. Baby Franklin's condition, however, had become desperate. His heart was affected. He was moved to New York, where the intensive care given him proved unavailing. He died on November 8, 1909, after something less than eight months of life.

Both parents watched in an agony of grief as the tiny coffin was lowered into wintry earth and frozen clods rained down upon it in St. James' churchyard at Hyde Park, but Eleanor was the more deeply affected. She could hardly tear herself away from the open grave. ". . . how cruel it seemed," she always remembered, "to leave him out there alone in the cold." [13]

Nor did this sharp anguish wear down to a dull ache during the weeks and months that followed. It was prolonged and rendered morbid by the feelings of guilt in which Eleanor indulged. She bitterly blamed herself for having left the baby too much in the care of others. She accused herself of not loving him as she should. And this misery was added to that of her fourth pregnancy all through the spring and summer of 1910, was carried with her to Campobello, was carried back down to the city in August, and was spread mercilessly to all around her, sometimes in her worst "Griselda" fashion. She focused bitterness on her young husband when he—who was making a crucial career decision that season, who may therefore have become more anxious about and exasperated by his young wife than he would otherwise have been—tried to reason with her and (as she recalled) "make me see how idiotically I was behaving." [14]

She continued in this sick mood almost up to the moment of her confinement. Always afterward she wondered, again with guilt feelings, if this "idiocy" of hers might not have exerted a sad prenatal influence upon her fourth-born. For this child, Elliott, entering the world on September 23, 1910, remained troubled and troublesome all through the years of his boyhood and adolescence. He was small for his age—as sickly a boy as his brother James had been as an infant. He was rickety, and for a long time he was required to wear iron braces to strengthen and straighten his bowed legs. And hardly had he been freed of these before he suffered a hernia. His physical infirmities were matched by psychological ones. He faced the world with a scowling pugnacity, and even his grandmother, who doted on all her grandchildren, found him the least attractive of the lot and showed it through a condescension that drove him to fury. His brother James remembered that he developed the "habit of sassing . . . [his grandmother] more than any of the rest of us ever dared." James also remembered that Elliott "was perhaps the only one of us whom Mother babied" [15]—as if to compensate for the hurt she may have given him during her self-indulgent misery as he lay helpless within her womb.

The radically different responses that Eleanor and Franklin made to the death of their child was expressive of a fundamental difference between them in attitude toward life and religious belief. He remained an optimistic fatalist whose fatalism had a simple Christian definition. Whatever happened that was against his wish or will, yet beyond his power to change—whatever present he saw as irrevocable, whatever future he saw as inevitable—was accepted by him without protest or complaint as the will of God. He would not permit himself the slightest doubt that this was so; as boy and youth he had shied away from any question that might open the way for doubt, and as a man he continued to do so. Eleanor's faith, on the other hand, was highly uncertain, with doubt at its very core. Her unhappy experience under her grandmother's professed Christianity, her pleasurable experience under Mlle. Souvestre's professed atheism, had encouraged skepticism, weakening the religious foundations for her rigidly puritan ethical standards. These last, however, she continued to maintain. And so, while it may have been "on the whole . . . very beneficial" for her to be "shocked . . . into thinking" by Mlle. Souvestre, as she later averred, the penalty she paid was a denial to her of the kind of optimism that sustained her husband.[16] He was serenely confident that all would be well in the end; his conscience, flexible in ways hers was not, was strongly rooted in his faith, whereas she was troubled and unsure, her excessive and even obsessive conscientiousness rendered all the more painful by her inability to accept blindly the orthodox definitions of good and evil, of right and wrong.

Once, during these early years, she asked him whether he felt their children should go to church and have Christianity inculcated in them or be left free to make up their own minds about religion as they grew older. She put the question to him with that solemn earnestness which seemed always to provoke in him a patronizing amusement. He replied that he thought the children had better attend church and receive the teachings he had received. These could do them no harm. But suppose the teachings were not true? she wanted to know. Did he himself believe all of them? He looked at her with an "amused and quizzical smile" and said, "I really never thought about it. I think it is just as well not to think about things like that too much." At the time she resented "heatedly" his manner of closing the subject—it seemed to her flippant and contemptuous—and for years afterward she continued to feel "a kind of virtuous grievance" whenever, in accordance with the wish *he* had expressed, *she* took the children to church while he played golf with friends, a fairly frequent occurrence in summer. Not until the older children were nearly grown and her "sense of humor came to the rescue" did she conclude that this attitude of hers was "utterly ludicrous," related in essence to the morbidity of her grief over the baby who died.[17]

III

Her own account of the early married years reads almost as a litany of her ineptitudes, humiliations, and recurrent "Griselda" moods.

She tried to ride her husband's horse Bobby at Hyde Park (". . . my mother-in-law felt we were not enough at Hyde Park to justify the keeping of two saddle horses"). She was terrified when the horse broke into a gallop at a certain point on the bridle path and continued to gallop at full speed, despite her efforts to stop him, until he reached another fixed point, as he had been carefully trained by Franklin to do. She then gave up riding altogether for many years, though she had ridden much as a

girl at Tivoli and had enjoyed it. One summer at Campobello she decided to learn to play golf, so that she might be a companion to her husband in the game he loved. After practicing for several days, she went
out with him on the course. He watched her for a few strokes, then "remarked he thought I might just as well give it up!" She was crushed and
never attempted golf again. That same summer she had trouble with her
young brother, Hall (Josh), who was at the rebellious boyish age and
had as one object of his rebellion the taking of daily baths. When she
scolded him severely, she was "sternly reproved" by Franklin for being
too hard on the boy, and then in her "most exasperating Griseldaish
mood . . . refused to take any further responsibility or to reprove him
for anything." Her Cousin Susie (Mrs. Henry Parish), who was a house
guest at the time, had to take Hall in hand and succeeded easily where
Eleanor had failed; soon the boy not only bathed daily without protest
but actually enjoyed doing so. In the summer of 1908—partly because
Baby James' precarious health made it advisable for them to be close to
their city doctor, partly because Franklin, for the first summer of his life,
was required to keep regular office hours—they did not move to Hyde
Park or have an extended vacation on Campobello but instead took a
beach cottage at Sea Bright, New Jersey, one of an endless row jammed
close together along the boardwalk. The cottage was set on stilts, to
avoid flooding when stormy seas swept in, and had a porch with no railing on it, yet Eleanor put the baby buggy with James in it out there. The
buggy was soon pushed off the porch by Anna, and though both buggy
and baby landed unharmed in soft sand, the mother was terribly frightened and angry with herself for not having foreseen what had to happen. That same unhappy summer (Franklin and Eleanor were unused to
middle-class accommodations; they could not adjust to them), while attempting to learn to drive a Ford car her husband had bought, she
promptly crashed it against a gatepost by the driveway and thereafter
refused for a decade or more to so much as touch a driver's wheel. Because her mother-in-law stressed the importance of fresh air for children
and Eleanor herself was a fresh-air addict, she ordered made for her "a
kind of box with wire on the sides and top" which could be suspended
outside a back window at 125 East Thirty-sixth Street. Anna was hung
out there for morning naps. But the little girl, chilled through on the
shady side of the house, slept little and cried much, a prolonged loud
howling, whereupon an irritated and outraged neighbor threatened to
report Eleanor to the Society for the Prevention of Cruelty to Children.[18]

The mother-in-law, who was seldom resisted on Eleanor's behalf by
Franklin (though he occasionally quarreled with her on his own behalf),

was often actively aided and abetted by him and continued to dominate every phase of the timid young wife's marriage.

At Christmastime, 1907, while Eleanor lay abed convalescing from the birth of James, she was shown a crude pen-and-ink sketch of a five-story house, made by her mother-in-law on Hyde Park stationery, with a notation below it in Sara's hand: "A Christmas present to Franklin and Eleanor from Mama, number and street not yet quite decided—19 to 20 feet wide." Thus was she informed of her mother-in-law's decision that the Thirty-sixth Street house was too small for this growing family and that a larger house must now be provided. A little later she learned that her new city home was to be even less distant from her mother-in-law's than the three short blocks separating 125 East Thirty-sixth from 200 Madison; indeed, there would now be no real separation at all. Sara bought a large costly plot on East Sixty-fifth Street and hired a well-known architect, Charles A. Platt, to design two houses for it, Nos. 47 and 49, one for Sara and one for her son, though Sara would keep title to them both. The houses would not be merely adjacent but actually interconnected, as the Ludlow-Parish houses were, the two dining rooms capable of being thrown into one, the two drawing rooms likewise, simply by opening wide doors. There would also be at least one connecting door in an upper hall.[19]

Construction of the two houses, begun in the spring, was completed by the fall of 1908. Both were decorated and furnished and ready to move into not long after Franklin and young Hall had returned from a hunting trip they took together in Newfoundland while a harassed Eleanor moved with the children from Sea Bright to Hyde Park for a visit, then back to the city with Franklin.

Throughout the whole of this enterprise, Franklin, who loved to design and build things, was happily involved, with his mother, in consultations with the architect, the builders, the decorators. He checked every detail. Eleanor was not consulted at all. Nor did she volunteer any opinion, express any desires of her own. ("I was growing very dependent on my mother-in-law, requiring her help on almost every subject," she later wrote, "and never thought of asking for anything which I felt might not meet with her approval." [20]) Her role was to appear humbly grateful for all that was being done for her. She seems to have played it well.

Nevertheless, there was a rebelliousness in her, a defiant resistance to being so utterly ignored as a person in her own right, and one day, soon after they all were settled into the new houses, her accumulated resentments broke through her self-control. She sobbed aloud as she sat before her dressing table. When her astonished husband asked her what was the matter, she blurted out that she didn't want to live in a house that was in no sense her own, its arrangements wholly inexpressive of her tastes, her personality. One senses that the moment was crucial. If he yielded to this assault on his emotions, he would be vulnerable to further similar assaults; he would be forced to take a stand with Eleanor in flat opposition to Mama. One also senses that his decision was not hard to make. For Eleanor's protest came too late, as a practical matter, the houses being already built; in any quarrel she was then a far less formidable opponent than Mama—this quite apart from Sara's control of purse strings—and, most important of all, there remained deep strong ties of affection between Franklin and Sara, an emotional interdependence which seemed to both of them a perfectly natural filial devotion and maternal love. (". . . my husband would never quite decide to make the break with his mother . . . ," was Eleanor's wry remembrance after both he and his mother were dead.) He now took, at any rate, the line of least resistance. Looking down upon his sobbing wife, he blandly pretended utter bewilderment. He told her "gently" that she must have gone insane but that the insanity was doubtless temporary. She would soon recover. He then left her alone to do so.[21]

Thus Sara continued to dominate what was now more than ever, to all intents and purposes, a single household. Her son had some money of his own from his father (Eleanor was sure Sara "always regretted" this), and Eleanor had from a trust fund, managed by Emlen Roosevelt and Henry Parish, an income of between $5,000 and $8,000 a year. At the outset of their marriage the young couple agreed to split household expenses fifty-fifty. Franklin set up account books, showed his bride how to keep them in an itemized way, and Eleanor did so for many years during which they managed to live "easily and comfortably if not luxuriously [employing always five or more servants] on $600 a month." [22] But their combined incomes was not enough to support the style of life they actually maintained—their living in three different houses at different seasons of each year, their yacht and smaller boats, Franklin's growing list of expensive clubs, their political and charitable contributions, their travels. The difference must be made up out of Sara's largess, which was just as she wished it to be. She could easily have arranged things differently. Without lowering in the slightest her own standard of living, she could have assigned her son a substantial portion of the property he would inherit when she died. She preferred instead to "help out" with gifts for which she expected, and received, thanks.

Moreover, in major instances, Sara's gifts consisted of the mere *use* of property to which she retained legal title, as in the case of the house on

East Sixty-fifth and of the house and land at Hyde Park, and the free use thus granted was by no means unlimited. When Franklin sought to apply at Hyde Park the scientific agriculture and forestry whose practice had excited him abroad, Sara stubbornly refused her permission—the property must be kept as James had left it, a gentleman's country estate —and Franklin was enabled to conduct forest conservation experiments only after he had bought land of his own on which to do so, adjacent to his mother's. To the general rule there was one important exception. The property next door to Sara's on Campobello consisted of several acres of shore land and a three-story "cottage" of thirty-four rooms, exclusive of baths, closets, and pantries, built in 1897 by the Kune family of Boston. Sara bought this and presented it to her "children" in 1909 as a belated wedding gift, and it was an outright gift, with full legal title vested in Franklin. It became in consequence the only place in which she lived, until she was well into middle age, that Eleanor could regard and feel as a home of her own, though even there she remained for years subordinate to Sara's rule.[23]

Indeed, she was submissive to a degree which she herself would regard as disgraceful in later years, after two more children had been born to her—a second Franklin, Jr., born in the Campobello cottage on August 17, 1914; a last son, John Aspinwall, born in Washington, March 13, 1916—and she had taken her first major step toward genuine individuality and independence.

We may as well anticipate the event here:

Sara, who had hired all of Eleanor's servants when the household was first established, continued to insist on choosing, if not actually paying the wages of, her grandchildren's nurses. Her preference was for traditional English "nannies," whose attitude toward their charges turned out to be always authoritarian, occasionally sadistic. Eleanor herself not only disliked, but also feared them, a fact which led them to order her about contemptuously, quite as if she too were in their charge.

The culmination of a succession of these martinets was a creature evidently psychotic. She once threw Anna down upon the floor and, kneeling on the little girl's chest, slapped her face back and forth for alleged unladylike conduct. When sickly Elliott pushed over Franklin, Jr.'s high chair with Franklin in it and laughed uproariously, the nurse tossed him into a closet and locked the door, turning the key with such violence that it broke off. Three hours passed before the little boy was extricated. The same thing happened later to young Franklin, whose terror-stricken hours in narrowly enclosed darkness gave him lifelong claustrophobia. She accused James of lying when he said he had brushed his teeth; he continued to deny that he had lied, whereupon she forced him to don

one of Anna's dresses and parade up and down the sidewalk in front of
the East Sixty-fifth Street house with a sign on his back proclaiming, I
AM A LIAR, while neighborhood children hooted and jeered at him.
Worst of all, enraged one day because James persisted in watching her
spread "hot" mustard over her food after she'd ordered him not to
watch, she forced him to eat a whole pot of it, spoonful by spoonful. He
became miserably ill. Decades later he was "certain that the experience
led to the chronic stomach ailment which I have suffered most of my
life." [24]

Eleanor was not ignorant of these atrocities, but lacking the courage
to intervene, she followed what she herself later described as the "silly
theory that you should trust the people with your children and back up
their discipline." Nor could Franklin plead ignorance. It was he who
rescued a howling Elliott from the three hours of imprisonment in the
locked closet, reportedly showing "livid anger" before his children as he
did so. Yet he continued to adhere to a hands-off policy as regards
"nurses and other household affairs"—an attitude reminiscent in its passivity of that he had taken toward the "Long-legged Duckling" of his
boyhood and a manifestation of that laissez-faire permissiveness which,
curiously, would always accompany his instinct for power and love for
the exercise of it. Not until Eleanor accidentally discovered a drawerful
of empty whiskey and gin bottles in the nurse's dresser was this virago
sent packing. For alcoholism, which had cast such a pall of misery over
her own early life, was one weakness that Eleanor would not tolerate in
her home—and on this subject she and her mother-in-law happened to
be in full agreement. As for Franklin, he "was as delighted as any of us
kids" (James would remember) over this forced removal of a woman
whose presence had long irked him.

But as regards the summary dismissal, the most important point was
that Eleanor did the deed herself without prior consultation with anyone. Sara could approve it only ex post facto. And this was a virtually
unprecedented decisiveness on Eleanor's part; in James' remembrance
it constituted "the first step in Mother's Declaration of Independence in
her relations with her mother-in-law." [25]

From that time forward, Eleanor selected her children's nurses herself. Moreover, she defended and supported those she hired against the
strictures of "Granny," who found constant fault with them. The children were delighted by the change now made in their guardianship.
They came actually to love dearly two of their mother's selections. One
was a young Swiss girl named Seline Thiel who had, among other en-
dearing qualities, a penchant for falling off boats at Campobello and
would do so at least twice in July, 1921, as Eleanor reported to her hus-

band (". . . I've just had to give her a little of your gin in hot lemonade as she has never warmed up since") in a letter written barely three weeks before Franklin himself fell from a boat into the Bay of Fundy's frigid waters. The other beloved nurse was a Scotswoman named Elspeth Connochie (Connie) who would become a confidante of Anna when Anna very much needed one, who would be of great help to Elliott during the boy's period of greatest physical difficulty, and who would in general become so popular with her charges that she provoked Sara's active jealousy. Once when Eleanor was away from home, Sara in a letter criticized Connie for a certain decision, adding in acid explanation, "Of course Connochie wants to have the children look back with pleasure on her time in charge. . . ." [26]

The "explanation" may well have been a psychological projection. For Sara herself was by no means averse to currying favor with her grandchildren by means of gifts that—often deliberately—subverted parental authority. She would do so increasingly as Eleanor, having asserted her independence, claimed to a greater degree than before her maternal prerogatives.

Of a multitude of examples that might be cited, two will suffice:

A couple of the boys once involved themselves in mischief so serious that drastic disciplinary action was called for. Accordingly, Eleanor and Franklin decided to deprive them for a summer of the pony which gave them immense pleasure at Hyde Park; the pony was taken to a family having two children on the other side of the town. And this discipline was proving effective, or so the parents believed, for the boys were much depressed and expressed bitter regret of their misdeed, when Granny, though fully informed of the parental decision and of the reasons for it, replaced the single pony with two horses, one for each boy! Franklin spoke "explosively" of this to a friend one afternoon as the two drove past a field in which the gift horses were grazing. "I don't know what I am going to do," he said. "How can I ever discipline those boys?" [27]

Franklin, Jr., upon graduating from Groton, was presented by his parents with a small cheap car, which he drove recklessly and soon smashed up. His parents then wisely decided he was too immature to own a car and had better be without one for a while. The matter was discussed in Sara's presence. Nevertheless, when young Franklin turned to her and pleaded for a new car, she promptly gave him one—a much larger, more expensive machine than the one he had wrecked. "When we objected," remembered Eleanor decades later, "she looked at us quite blandly and said she had not realized that we disapproved. She never heard anything she did not want to hear. . . ." [28]

IV

In the fall of 1907 Franklin Delano Roosevelt, already the father of one child and soon to have a second, made his entrance into the working world.

Upon his return from the European honeymoon, in September, 1905, he had taken makeup examinations in the two law courses he had failed the preceding spring and had easily passed them, having had the necessary books sent him abroad and having applied himself to them diligently, and so had been enabled to continue as a Columbia Law School student. He failed no more courses. He did not, however, complete his work for an LLB degree. Instead, having passed his bar examinations in the spring of 1907 and been admitted to the practice of law in New York, he dropped out of classes that had always bored him, devoted the next several months at Hyde Park and Campobello to gentlemanly leisure and physically active recreation, and then, in September, accepted the kind of job which came as a matter of course to one of his background. He became a clerk, unsalaried for the first year, as was customary, in one of the most distinguished and affluent law firms in the East, that of Carter, Ledyard, and Milburn, at 54 Wall Street. (He seems to have found it difficult to take himself seriously in his new role, for he announced it in a handwritten mock advertisement of himself as a "counsellor at law" who specialized in "unpaid bills," the chloroforming of "small dogs," the preparation of "briefs on the liquor question" for ladies, the prosecution of "race suicides," and the care of babies "under advice of expert grandmother. . . ." [29])

Carter, Ledyard, and Milburn, in prestige and in the type of business it handled, was similar to the Silliman firm in which James Roosevelt as fledgling lawyer had been briefly employed in the early 1850's. It had a large general practice, but its major source of income was corporation and admiralty law, the expert in the latter, Edmund L. Baylies, being the partner who personally hired Franklin Roosevelt and thereafter watched over him with a fatherly eye. ("Of all the people in the office . . . I felt that I could go to Mr. Baylies with my troubles . . . ," Franklin remembered a quarter century later.[30]) It numbered among its clients several of the greatest industrial combinations in the country. To these clients its most useful service in those years was the finding or shaping of means to circumvent the Sherman Antitrust Act or prevent the practical efficacy of court orders based upon it.

The firm, in other words, was a sworn and extremely active enemy of President Theodore Roosevelt's loudly proclaimed "trust-busting" policy, which would be continued and even intensified in the succeeding administration. (Taft's administration, as a matter of fact, would initiate nearly twice as many antitrust actions as Roosevelt's did, though the general public regarded conservative Taft as the very opposite of a "trustbuster.") Senior partner John G. Milburn, in whose Buffalo house William McKinley had died and Theodore Roosevelt had taken the Presidential oath of office, was counsel for Standard Oil of New Jersey in the highly publicized antitrust suit whose culmination, in 1911, would be a U.S. Supreme Court order that the giant combination be dissolved. Milburn and associates would then more than earn their huge fee by devising a legal scheme whereby the dissolution was rendered nominal for the most part, hence virtually painless to Standard's management stockholders. Senior partner Lewis C. Ledyard, enthusiastic yachtsman and friend of the great J. P. Morgan, whom he succeeded as commodore of the New York Yacht Club, was counsel for the American Tobacco Company in the famous antitrust action which paralleled simultaneously that taken against Standard Oil and which likewise culminated in a Supreme Court dissolution order (1911). He, too, would then earn his huge fee by "dissolving" the corporation in a way that appeased the government without actually increasing competition or effectively reducing single-management control.

Franklin continued to idolize his Cousin Theodore (or Uncle Ted, by marriage) and remained personally committed to most of the Roosevelt administration's major policies. He also remained on familiar terms with the President and the President's family: he had been among the guests at the wedding of Alice Roosevelt and Nicholas Longworth in the winter of 1906 (he'd gone by himself since Eleanor, miserably awaiting the birth of Anna, was unable to accompany him); he and Eleanor had visited two or three times with Uncle Ted in Washington or Oyster Bay since their marriage. It might be assumed, therefore, that the young man, by attaching himself to such a firm as Carter, Ledyard, and Milburn, must inevitably suffer a conflict of loyalties. This assumption, however, rests upon another—namely, that TR was absolutely on one side, with the giant trusts on the other, of an irreconcilable moral conflict, and Franklin had the means to know that this was simply not so.

He may or may not have known that the President was worried by the stock market's strongly negative response, in early 1907, to a threat that the White House might move under the Sherman Act against the E. H. Harriman railroad combination.* He may or may not have known that

---

* Harriman in the last month of 1906 had flatly told the Interstate Commerce Commission that, if it were legally possible, he would add the Santa Fe, the Northern Pacific, and the Great Northern to the Union Pacific empire. The President's rumored response to this was alleged in financial circles to have undermined public confidence not only in railroad securities but in industrial issues in general.

a continuing fear of financial panic had led TR in late August to order the Attorney General *not* to file the antitrust suit against International Harvester which had been planned. But he could hardly have failed to know something of the inside story of the financial panic which did, in fact, sweep Wall Street just a few weeks after he went to work there, for his own firm, especially Lewis Cass Ledyard, had much to do with halting it. He must have known, therefore, of the President's somewhat strange role in the matter and so have had confirmed what he was temperamentally, intuitively inclined to suspect—that TR, in his actual exercise of Presidential power, was less hostile to "malefactors of great wealth" (Morgan being publicly identified as one of these) than he gave public impression of being and that the Sherman Act must be regarded not as a law like other laws, which the executive was in duty bound to enforce consistently and indiscriminately, but instead as an instrument of executive authority, to be used or not used at the executive's discretion.

The story was as complicated as it was educative to a young man starting out in life.[31]

Ledyard was attorney for Colonel Oliver Payne, and Payne, a wealthy man, was member of a syndicate which owned a majority of the stock in the Tennessee Coal and Iron Company. Another member of the syndicate was Grant B. Schley, head of the prominent brokerage firm of Moore & Schley. Through Schley's firm the syndicate had bought its stock, largely with money borrowed through Moore & Schley from banks. To secure these loans, Moore & Schley had put up some $5,000,000 of Tennessee Coal and Iron stock certificates. Then came panic, triggered by the failure of a major brokerage house in mid-October and followed by the failure of the great Knickerbocker Trust Company, three others, and a national bank in New York. Banks that had lent money on the strength of the Tennessee stock began to wonder just how strong this stock might be on the market; it was seldom traded and there was good reason to fear that a large block of it thrown suddenly on a panicked market might bring but half the amount needed to cover the bank loans. Thus Moore & Schley—in desperate need of operating cash, its credit exhausted and its creditors clamoring—teetered on the verge of bankruptcy by the first weekend of November. Moreover, if this firm failed, it would, in all probability, set off a chain reaction that might bring down the whole flimsy financial structure erected with a considerable amount of peculation and speculation on Wall Street. Hence the prolonged anxious conferences in the library of a marble palace almost directly across the street from the house Sara Roosevelt lived in when Franklin and Eleanor were married, 219 Madison Avenue, at the corner of Madison and Thirty-sixth—the home of the elder J. Pierpont Morgan.

To this house on Saturday morning, November 2, 1907, came Lewis Cass Ledyard with a scheme that either he or Colonel Payne, or both of them together, had devised and that the great Morgan, who was the central figure throughout this whole crisis, promptly approved. Ledyard proposed that the United States Steel Corporation, the unprecedentedly huge combination of combinations which Morgan had organized a half dozen years before (Carnegie Steel had been its core component), acquire the Tennessee Coal and Iron stock now held, somewhat precariously, by the syndicate of which Payne and Schley were members. U.S. Steel could do so by exchanging its bonds for Tennessee stock; the price agreed upon was $45,000,000. Not only would this save Moore & Schley, for U.S. Steel bonds were as good as gold and no bank need worry about loans secured by them, but it would also enable U.S. Steel to eliminate a minor but nonetheless real competitor, adding to its holdings, at a rock-bottom bargain price, an immensely valuable property. (The U.S. Steel president, testifying before a Congressional committee less than a year later, would say that a valuation of $600,000,000 for the acquired property "is not very much too high" while others deemed a potential value of a billion dollars for the property a conservative estimate.)

There was to this happy solution but one major obstacle, which Judge Elbert H. Gary and Henry C. Frick, the top steel company officers, promptly set about removing. From Morgan's house on the night of Sunday, November 3, they went to the Pennsylvania Railroad station and thence by one-car special train down to Washington, having arranged an appointment with President Roosevelt for as early as possible on the morning of November 4. The President interrupted his breakfast to see them. He listened attentively, with Secretary of State Elihu Root at his side, as Judge Gary explained what U.S. Steel, in the goodness of its corporate heart, was prepared to do—buy the Tennessee stock at a "price somewhat in excess of its true value" in order to prevent a national financial collapse. Would the U.S. government penalize U.S. Steel for this act of altruism? Gary wanted to know. If the proposed deal went through, would U.S. Steel be prosecuted under the Sherman Antitrust Act? "I answered that, while of course I could not advise them to take the action proposed, I felt it no public duty of mine to interpose any objections," said the President in a memorandum dictated as soon as Gary and Frick had left the White House. The latter were elated. They immediately phoned the happy news to Morgan's offices at 23 Wall Street, from there it was spread as swiftly as possible up and down the Street, and it had its predictably bullish effect on the stock market when the exchange opened at ten o'clock. Bullish sentiment was further encouraged when, later that same day, news dispatches from Washington, obviously inspired by the White House, reported that the Bureau of Corporations investigation of the steel trust which had been under way for some time with a view to possible prosecution under the Sherman Act would, in fact, result in no such action. And so ended the Panic of 1907.

Great was the jubilation that day in the offices of Carter, Ledyard, and Milburn. Franklin Roosevelt, if only by virtue of his name and relationship with the President, may have shared in it. But it was seldom during the following three years that the firm's business aroused in him any excitement or even much interest.

As a lowly clerk he had nothing to do with high finance. He had said in a letter to his mother, shortly before his first day of work, that he was about to become a "full-fledged office boy," and that is pretty much what he was at the outset. He performed tedious, menial chores for the partners. He kept a docket of cases for them, looked up references in the law library, answered calendar calls in the Supreme Court when the firm had cases pending there, took deeds of property transfer to the county clerk's office for registration, ran all manner of errands. After a while he was assigned minor cases tried in the municipal courts, then was made managing clerk in charge of municipal cases.

In this latter capacity, he was brought into daily and sometimes harsh contact with people different from any with whom he had been associated before, save fleetingly and on a far different basis in his work with poor boys while at Groton and Harvard. For the most part, his court cases were defenses of the American Express Company or some other large corporation against petty claims pressed by people whose legal representatives were often themselves impecunious lawyers operating on a contingency fee basis. The experience was broadening. He rather enjoyed the rough-and-tumble courtroom tussles, the matching of wits with seedy, unscrupulous, sometimes thoroughly dishonest opponents in out-of-court settlements, the give-and-take of interviews with his own clients. He quickly learned a good deal about how ordinary people live and make their livings, how they think and feel. He learned, too, something about himself—about his capacity for getting along well in conflict situations with people of widely differing backgrounds and personalities, his ability to project his personality in such a way as to make of it a bridge between people otherwise unable to communicate with one another or even to make of it a solvent of hostilities out of which, by adroit management, he might precipitate workable fusions of interest.

After a year or so of this kind of work he was shifted, promoted to the firm's admiralty division, where he worked directly under Edmund Baylies' supervision. By that time it was abundantly clear to him and his superiors that he possessed no brilliant legal talent of any kind and, indeed, found his work often boring. (Once Ledyard in a hurry came out of his office into the clerks' room, where, seeing young Roosevelt dawdling, he asked him a question. The question called for a specific piece of information. The young man, however, merely replied in a dreamy voice, "Yes, yes." Ledyard was incensed. "You must be drunk!" he snapped, and stalked off.[32]) But it was also clear that Franklin could become a competent lawyer—Ledyard himself is said to have regarded him as "promising"—and in any case his generally attractive personality conjoined with his high social standing and family connections would make him a valuable asset to the firm. He could bring in business.

And so his future, if he chose to continue in the firm, was assured and perfectly predictable. He would climb steadily up the hierarchical ladder into a senior partnership where, handling lucrative corporate litigation, he would make a great deal of money and still have ample leisure for his club life (he was already a member of the exclusive New York Yacht Club and the Knickerbocker Club, among others), for the civic and charitable activities deemed proper for one of his class (he was now a director of the Seamen's Church Institute and the First National Bank of Poughkeepsie, a member of the Eagle Engine Company and the Rescue Hook and Ladder Company of Hyde Park), and for the pursuit of his gentlemanly hobbies of stamp collecting, book collecting, experimental forestry and agriculture, bird watching, yachting, golfing. It was a safe pleasant life that opened out before him, free of all serious strains, and to many of his acquaintances at that time he appeared ill suited to any other.

"Everybody called him Franklin and regarded him as a harmless bust," recalled one friend years later. "He had a sanguine temperament, almost adolescent in its buoyancy." [33]

V

Yet he himself, with the example of TR and the "strenuous life" constantly before him, never seriously considered following the conventional easy path. Moreover, there is clear evidence that, while most who knew him may then have looked upon him as a very ordinary young man, even a lightweight in intellect and emotion, not "everybody" did so by any means.

One idle day during his first year at Carter, Ledyard, and Milburn, he and his five fellow law clerks, each at his rolltop desk, began to talk of their personal ambitions. Franklin made a rare revelation of his inner self and a lasting impression on his listeners. He said candidly that he had no intention of making a career of the law. He was going into politics. He would run for office at the earliest opportunity. In itself, this was a sufficiently unusual ambition for one of his social class and background, despite the example of TR. But what might well have caused his listeners to laugh aloud in astonished disbelief was his further revelation that he intended to become President of the United States! He outlined the steps that would, he thought, lead him to his goal. He would begin with a seat in the State Assembly. After some years in the legislature he would win appointment as Assistant Secretary of the Navy. Then, still in the footsteps of TR, he would become governor of New York.

"Once you're elected Governor of New York," he said, "if you do well enough in that job, you have a good show to be President. . . ."

His listeners were all the same age, young and irreverent. The fact that they did not hoot at him or even smile in amused deprecation indicates that to them at least he seemed no "harmless bust" but a man of considerable abilities and rare personal force. He spoke "modestly enough" of his immodest ambition, a fellow clerk, Grenville Clark, recalled long afterward, and somehow managed to make it all seem "proper and sincere; and moreover, as he put it, entirely reasonable." [34]

Thus his years at Carter, Ledyard, and Milburn were for Franklin Roosevelt a meanwhile period, a time of waiting, during which he took far more interest in current political developments than he did in the practice of law. And indeed these developments, interesting to any politically knowledgeable citizen, could be little less than fascinating to a Democratic Roosevelt.

TR had made a grave error when on the evening of November 8, 1904, flushed with his election victory, he proclaimed his devotion to the "wise custom which limits the President to two terms" and his determination "under no circumstances" to become again "a candidate for or to accept another nomination." He had thereby given up a major instrument of control over the Congress during the latter half of his term; he could no longer coerce its members with the fear that he just *might* continue in office after March 5, 1909. The evidences of this error were beginning to multiply as Franklin entered upon his employment as law clerk. The financial panic of that fall was followed by a sharp, though temporary, economic depression. This increased the apprehension with which Congress looked toward the elections of 1908. It rose in revolt against executive domination. And, characteristically, instead of becoming more conciliatory as he felt power slipping from his grasp, TR became more truculent. By the end of 1907 there was open warfare between him and House Speaker J. G. "Uncle Joe" Cannon, between him and leading members of the Senate, with the result that precious little of the White House legislative program won enactment in 1908 and early 1909.

Cannon was a rock-ribbed conservative. TR moved now to the left, having adopted as his own one proposal after another made by Bryan in 1896 and 1900.

In June, 1907, he had told Congress that both an income tax and an inheritance tax "should be part of our system of federal taxation." In October, 1907, announcing a view that would have echoes in Franklin Roosevelt's future, he said in public speech that the U.S. Constitution should be "interpreted not as a strait-jacket . . . but as an instrument designed for the life and healthy growth of the nation." He added: "Sometimes executive and legislative officers are under temptation to yield too much to an improper public clamor. The temptation of the judge—the long term appointive or elective judge—is often just the reverse." A little more than two months later he voiced his displeasure when the U.S. Supreme Court declared unconstitutional (on the ground that it seemed to apply to intrastate commerce) the Employers' Liability Act of 1906. A few weeks after that, on January 31, 1908, he sent to the Congress a message in which he proposed a revision and reenactment of the liability law to take care of the Court's objections, legislation to eliminate the use of court injunctions to give unfair advantage to employers in labor disputes, a workmen's compensation law for federal employees (coupling his proposal with the hope that the "same broad principle" could be made to apply to "all private employees"), and, in a section particularly interesting to Franklin and outrageous to Franklin's employers, attacked "corporation lawyers" who strove, often successfully, to frustrate the executive's attempts to enforce laws for the regulation of business enterprise in the public's interest. TR boldly called for the "moral regeneration of the business world" and heaped contempt upon those who feared a destruction of business confidence if Congress' laws were vigorously enforced. "The 'business' which is hurt by the movement for honesty is the kind of business which, in the long run, it pays the country to have hurt," he declared. "It is the kind of business which has tended to make the very name 'high finance' a term of scandal." He expressed his conviction that responsibility for current "business distress" rested not with the acts of his administration but with "the speculative folly and flagrant dishonesty of a few men of great wealth." In July, 1908, he was confirmed in his strictures against corporation lawyers, and in his belief that the courts were in general bulwarks of reaction, when the circuit court of appeals in Illinois invalidated the spectacularly huge fine ($29,240,000) imposed on Standard Oil of Indiana by U.S. District Court Judge Kenesaw Mountain Landis for violations of the Elkins Act of 1903, an act whereby railroad rebates to favored firms were made illegal. On the day after the circuit court's action TR publicly fumed that there was "absolutely no question as to the guilt of the defendant nor of the exceptionally grave character of the offense," that it would be "a great miscarriage of justice if . . . the defendant escapes punishment which would unquestionably have been meted out to any weaker defendant guilty of such offense," that the government would therefore promptly institute new proceedings against the corporation for accepting railroad rebates (this last would come to nothing; Standard Oil in the end got off scot-free), and that there was "altogether too much power in the bench."

Dominant figures in the Congress were persuaded that there would be, if TR had his way, altogether too much power in the executive. One instrument of executive power had been the Secret Service: it was widely believed that Secret Service reports to the President had provided him with material that could be used to blackmail individual legislators into support of the White House program. So the Congress moved to blunt this instrument. In 1908 it voted to restrict the Secret Service to the protection of the President's person and to the detection of counterfeiting. In December of that year TR reacted in a message to the Congress asserting that the restriction was solely for the benefit of "the criminal classes" which might, he indicated, even infiltrate the Congress. He recognized the fact that "Congressmen did not wish to be investigated by Secret Service men," asserted that there had been little such investigation in the past, but added his belief that it was not "in the public interest to protect criminals in any branch of the public service." An outraged Senate refused to acknowledge receipt of this message. An outraged House actually, by a vote of 212 to 35, rejected the message in early January, 1909, as lacking in due respect for the legislative branch. All chance of favorable action on the Roosevelt program during that "lame duck" session was destroyed.

But if TR thus lost power over the Congress and enraged conservatives with his general policies and tactics, he gained in persuasive power over the electorate which became more than ever convinced that he was a champion of the people against predatory interests. His hold on the electorate enabled him easily to dominate his party's national convention in 1908, to dictate the nomination of William Howard Taft as his successor, and virtually to assure Taft's victory over William Jennings

Bryan, who, running for the third time as Democratic candidate, found his campaign fatally handicapped by TR's appropriation of key elements of the now-traditional Bryan program. Taft's victory margin, however, was less than half that of TR four years before—and a Democratic Roosevelt, young and inexperienced though he was, might see clearly enough that the margin depended on progressive votes and could easily be shifted to a Democrat in 1912 if the Taft administration failed to pursue at least with seeming vigor the policies TR had so loudly proclaimed. The country was in a progressive mood; everywhere, at all levels of government, reform was in the ascendant. The people clearly wanted strong creative leadership by the executive.

Taft was unable to supply it.

Immediately following the inaugural in March, 1909—animated in part by a laudable desire to give his protégé and successor a free hand— the ex-President embarked on a prolonged trip abroad. He spent a year in Africa bagging big-game specimens for the American Museum of Natural History, then made a tour of Western Europe lasting several months. It can hardly be said that he took himself out of the public eye. Under contract with *Scribner's Magazine,* he published widely read accounts of his African experiences that were later gathered into a book (*African Game Trails*). His European tour was a succession of triumphs unprecedented for a "private" citizen. In Italy, France, Belgium, Holland, Denmark, Norway, Germany, England, he was hugely feted; his role as honored guest of royal personages was greatly and proudly publicized in the American press. At Potsdam, seated astride a charger beside Kaiser Wilhelm II, he reviewed the emperor's guard for five solid hours. In London, as official representative of the United States government, he consorted on more than equal terms with nine kings and seven queens at the funeral of King Edward VII, an event whose solemn pageantry would be later nostalgically recognized as epitome-in-climax of a Western ruling order destined soon to end. He returned to America on June 18, 1910, his debarkation in New York being the occasion of yet another unprecedented triumph. Young Franklin Roosevelt personally witnessed it. And soon thereafter TR was plunged, or plunged himself, into national political controversy.

For by that time Taft and his administration were in serious trouble.

The corpulent President (he was physically the biggest man by far ever to sit in the President's chair) was an amiable, easygoing man of conservative instincts and judicious temperament. He had no flair for the dramatic. He was the opposite of bold. He had small talent for the subtleties of political give-and-take. He blundered incredibly on occasion. And he had much bad luck. His first fifteen months in office might well serve a politically minded young man as a case study in how *not* to succeed as President.

Hard upon his inaugural had come a special session of the Congress called to consider a revision of the tariff which, Taft had said during the campaign, should definitely be reduced. The session opened with a revolt in the House against the dictatorship of Speaker Cannon. Insurgents led by Nebraska's Representative George W. Norris seemed about to deprive Uncle Joe of his right to appoint standing committees when Taft gave the beleaguered Speaker his public support in return for the Speaker's promised support of the President's legislative program—and this despite Taft's personal wish that Uncle Joe's obstructive powers should be curbed. Taft thereby identified himself in the public mind with the old guard. Then came the Congressional battle between the old guard and the progressives over the Payne-Aldrich tariff bill, which, as finally passed in the late summer of 1909, was a clear victory for the former and an outrageous violation of the Republican platform pledge of 1908 as interpreted by Taft himself. Of the 847 changes it made in the tariff, 600 or so were revisions upward on major items; the downward revisions were on items of small importance, and the free list, as Finley Peter Dunne's Mr. Dooley pointed out in the newspapers, was a joke, comprising such things as "teeth, sea moss . . . , nux vomica, Pulu, canary bird seed" etc. etc. Thus the interests of Eastern industrialists were served at the expense of the agricultural Midwest, a traditional Republican stronghold across which angry rebellion roared as Taft, after vacillating awhile, ignored Progressive pleas for a veto and instead signed the bill into law. He then made a bad situation worse for himself by embarking on a speaking tour of the Midwest and Far West during which he actually eulogized Rhode Island's Senator Nelson W. Aldrich, leader of the old guard in the upper chamber, and (in Winona, Minnesota, of all places!) praised the Payne-Aldrich Act as "on the whole . . . the best tariff bill that the Republican Party ever passed."

There swiftly followed, in the fall and winter of 1909–10, another disaster for the administration—the famous controversy between Secretary of the Interior Richard A. Ballinger and Chief Forester Gifford Pinchot (the Forest Service was then a part of Interior; as a result of the controversy it would be shifted to the Department of Agriculture). Pinchot charged Ballinger with flagrant betrayals of conservation principles he was pledged to uphold, and during the uproar that ensued, Taft finally dismissed Pinchot, as he was perhaps in duty bound to do if he were to maintain the integrity of the executive's chain of command. But he stubbornly refused to dismiss Ballinger after a Congressional committee investigation of Interior, with the brilliant Louis D. Brandeis as committee counsel, fully exposed the Secretary's bias against conservation as the preceding administration had defined it and his untruthfulness concerning his relationships with the Guggenheims, who were interested in Alaskan coal lands that had been withdrawn from sale by TR but put back on the market by Ballinger. (Taft himself was caught in an outright lie during the investigation; he would at last have to accept, in March, 1911, Ballinger's forced resignation.)

Before the Interior investigation was completed, the ruin of the administration had been completed when a coalition of Democrats and insurgent Republicans, again led by Norris, won the fight against Speaker Cannon that had been lost the year before. Uncle Joe was stripped of his right to name members of standing committees, and a powerful Rules Committee was established from which the Speaker was ex officio debarred. Taft would have done well at this juncture to support publicly the insurgents' efforts since he privately approved their aims. He did and said nothing, however. The insurgents and the general public believed that this victory for House democracy had been won against the will of the President, that he was committed absolutely to the old guard. And, indeed, he soon was, to all intents and purposes. For the insurgents now declared open war upon the President, who, finding himself the target of incessant and often viciously unfair attacks, turned in anger to Cannon and Aldrich and with them shaped a highly organized and well-financed campaign, making full and ruthless use of the executive's patronage powers, to replace the insurgents with solid conservatives, all through the Midwest, in the spring primary elections. The railroads, the banks, the industrialists of the Midwest joined the President in this campaign, which, nevertheless, wholly failed in its purpose, for the insurgents had decisive popular support. The net result was a badly divided Republican Party, with disaffected Midwesterners already talking of splitting away from the Republicans and forming a new party if they were unable to block Taft's renomination in 1912. The leader to whom they turned was Theodore Roosevelt.

Nor was the Republican split limited to the Midwest. It was national. And nowhere was it more serious, or of greater immediate interest to young Franklin Roosevelt, than in the state of New York. There the old guard itself was split between a wing that found even Taft too liberal and a wing that supported the President, while a considerable segment of the party turned, as progressive Republicans elsewhere did, toward TR. The political prospect looked bright indeed for the New York Democracy as 1910 advanced from spring into summer.

VI

Dutchess County, like all the Hudson River counties, was overwhelmingly Republican. There was, however, a strong Democratic organization in Poughkeepsie, the county seat; the town, in fact, was controlled by Democrats in 1910. The mayor, John K. Sague, was a Democrat. So was the district attorney, John E. Mack. And naturally both men had looked upon Franklin Roosevelt as a possible future party candidate ever since he had made it clear that, though employed on Wall Street, he still regarded Hyde Park as home and intended to take an active part in local affairs.[35]

For young Roosevelt fitted perfectly into a pattern that had produced several local Democratic candidates in the past and even, on rare occasions, Democratic victories—that of Thomas Jefferson Newbold, for instance, who had gone to the State Senate in 1884 (Newbold remained the only Democrat to win that seat since 1856), or those of Lewis Stuyvesant Chanler, who had been elected Lieutenant Governor in 1906 and, following his defeat in a race for the governorship against Charles E. Hughes in 1908, had won election in 1909 as state assemblyman representing Dutchess County's Second Assembly District. Like Chanler and Newbold, Franklin Roosevelt was a wealthy man of old and distinguished family. If he ran for office he not only could bear the expenses of his own campaign but might well make substantial contributions to the campaigns of fellow Democrats. And to these attributes were added, as a major political asset, his name and relationship to the ex-President: any Roosevelt running as a Democrat for even a lowly office was bound to arouse popular curiosity, attract crowds, and garner more than his fair share of publicity.

Moreover, he was personally attractive. He was remarkably so in appearance, being tall and gracefully slender of figure, lithe and strong of physique, his facial features cast in that mold of level-browed, firm-jawed masculinity (an upper-class *American* masculinity) made fashionable by the drawings of Charles Dana Gibson and by the stories, the much-photographed person of Richard Harding Davis. He was somewhat less attractive in personality—on occasion a bit "snooty" (he had a way of tossing back his head and looking through pince-nez down his finely chiseled nose when challenged)—but generally able to hide whatever insecurities he felt, hence easy and affable of manner, seemingly poised and self-confident and outgoing in his interests, genuinely caring about other people and the situation "out there." Mack and Sague both liked him and Mack, at least, believed he might go far.

It was Mack who first broached to Franklin the subject of politics as an immediately possible career concern.

Early in the spring of 1910, the district attorney came to Roosevelt in New York City on some business matter which was quickly disposed of, whereupon the talk turned to the Dutchess County political situation. Mack believed Chanler gave signs of a waning interest in his Assembly seat; he might not run for reelection that fall, and if he didn't, would Franklin be interested in running? Franklin *was* interested. He frankly said so. Mack, delighted, at once started the wheels turning on Franklin's behalf within the Democratic machinery in Poughkeepsie, and Franklin began looking toward his first election victory. He could do so with some confidence; in the Second Assembly District he could count on Poughkeepsie Democratic votes.

But then, in the summer, Chanler decided to run again for the Assembly. The organization tried to persuade him to seek a seat in the State Senate instead. So did Franklin, who took Chanler out to lunch for that purpose. Chanler, however, thought with good reason that the chance for any Democrat to win the higher office was infinitesimal and had no desire to campaign in a hopeless cause. He may have pointed out that the lone Democratic victory in the Twenty-sixth Senatorial District, which comprised the three counties of Putnam, Dutchess, and Columbia fronting the east shore of the Hudson, in all the years since the Republican Party was first organized, had been a narrow one, made possible by a unique three-cornered race. There would be no three-cornered race this year. The Republican incumbent, Senator John F. Schlesser of Fishkill Landing, who would run for reelection, had won the last contest by so wide a margin that, clearly, a political earthquake of major proportions would be required to unseat him. No such earthquake seemed in the offing, despite Republican discontents which might well enable a Democrat to win the governorship that year.

Franklin Roosevelt was presented with what would appear to have been a difficult career decision at a time when his home life was perhaps less happy than it had ever been before.* His mother, others in his family, and Lewis Cass Ledyard had opposed his running for the Assembly —a contest he had an excellent chance to win. Now the Democrats of Poughkeepsie offered him the nomination for state senator—a contest in which the odds against victory appeared overwhelming. No one else was tempted toward so evidently futile a campaign. Mack himself had misgivings on the young patrician's vote-getting appeal to the dirt farmers who constituted a majority of the district's electorate and estimated

* See page 200.

Roosevelt's chances, if the young man chose to make the race, at no more than one in five. His running, though, would be a service to the party which might well reward him with nomination for the Assembly next year if Chanler, as seemed likely, declined to run again.

Franklin hesitated and pondered. One of his worries concerned Cousin (or Uncle) Theodore, who by midsummer had become a major active force in New York State politics, having declared open war on the old guard machine headed by Boss William Barnes, Jr. If TR were to speak in the Twenty-sixth District during the fall campaign and make a single derisive reference to Franklin's candidacy, the young Democrat's slight chance would be, in all probability, wholly destroyed. So Franklin asked Eleanor's Auntie Bye (Bamie) Cowles to find out if her brother planned to speak in the district; he indicated that his own decision might depend on the reply he received. The reply was noncommittal but not discouraging. "Franklin ought to go into politics without the least regard as to where I speak or don't speak," wrote TR to his sister on August 10, adding that Franklin "is a fine fellow" and a regret that his nephew-in-law was not a Republican. Franklin then decided to make the race.[36]

"I listened to all his plans with a great deal of interest," remembered Eleanor long afterward. "It never occurred to me that I had any part to play. I felt I must acquiesce in whatever he might decide. . . . I was having a baby [Elliott, born September 23], and for a time at least that was my only mission in life."[37]

The party's Dutchess County chairman was Edward E. Perkins, a Poughkeepsie attorney who was also a state committeeman and a follower of Boss Charles F. Murphy of Tammany Hall. Perkins had no enthusiasm for Sague and Mack's protégé. On the contrary, he thought he recognized in young Roosevelt a type he both despised and feared, the "dude-in-politics" who, born to wealth and privilege, hence freed of temptations that beset less-favored men, felt himself morally superior and hostile to professional politicians and to political machinery fueled by the needs of common folk. Yet Perkins, recognizing the usefulness of a candidate who would pay his own way and hoping for substantial contributions to the committee treasury from this well-heeled young man, went along with the choice.

But he was unable, or perhaps made small effort, to hide his personal antipathy, which was destined to last all his life. When the local Democratic chieftains gathered in his office on October 3, 1910, three days prior to the local nominating convention, in order to take a final look at prospective candidates and make a final decision concerning them, Franklin, summoned from Hyde Park, arrived bareheaded and clad in riding breeches and boots. He made a favorable impression on most of those assembled. His nomination was assured. Perkins, however, looked him up and down with ill-concealed distaste.

"You'll have to take off those yellow shoes," he said sourly, "and put on some regular pants." [38]

Eight

➤➤➤❮❮❮

The Emergent Definitions of 1910

I

I T WOULD appear in historical perspective that 1910, the year of Franklin Roosevelt's entrance into politics, was also a year of emergent definitions whereby his political future was patterned and, to a considerable degree, causally determined. A significant polarization began to occur that year within the general political movement of which young Roosevelt felt himself a part.

This movement was the Progressivism which, enlisting liberal minds of both major political parties, had succeeded and to a large extent grown out of the agrarian revolt of 1870–90, the Populism of the early 1890's, the Bryan Democracy of 1896–1900, and the social justice movement initiated by slum priests and preachers in the post-Civil War years but now increasingly focused on professional social workers and organizations. It was a movement that still embraced the farmer's concern for a reduction in the tariff on industrial goods. It continued to press for reform of the nation's financial structure (the 1907 panic sharply pointed the need for a system of flexible reserves of money and credit that would enable these to be rapidly distributed from areas where they were in excess at any given time to areas where the need for them was great); for taxation policies, especially graduated income and inheritance tax laws, that would more equitably distribute the tax burden and prevent excessive capital accumulations by a few individuals; and for railroad regulation, to bring rates down, halt wholesale corruption of state legislatures, and curb in the public interest the life-and-death powers which railroads, uncontrolled, exerted over the economy of any region. But the movement was no longer dominated, as it had been in Populist days, by the agrarian interest. For one thing, farmer unrest had subsided as the agricultural market improved (with the cheapening of gold) after 1897;

for another, the proportion of the total population living on farms had declined, and the migration from country to city continued at an accelerating rate. Between 1900 and 1910, as the national population increased from 76,000,000 to 92,000,000, the population of towns and cities as defined by census takers increased much more than the farm and small village population. In 1900, 40.5 percent of all Americans lived in towns and cities of 2,500 or more; by 1910, 46.3 percent did so.

Hence the leadership of Progressivism was shifted from representatives of the farmer to representatives of the small businessman, the professional man, the skilled artisan of town and city—what had once been an agrarian revolt was transformed into a revolt of the middle class—and there was a corresponding shift in the emphasis placed within the movement as a whole upon the various "causes" of which it was an unsystematized compendium. More emphasis was placed on purifying and increasing the efficiency of town and city governments (the commission form of municipal government, replacing the mayor-council system, was invented and vociferously promoted); on protection of the small borrower against usury and the small investor against the falsehood, fraud, and outright theft then characterizing much high finance; on woman's suffrage; on the problems of slums and poor relief. There was emphasis, too, on problems and grievances of the working class. This last, however, was not determined by representatives of the great mass of workers who, unskilled laborers of mass production and mass merchandising, were unorganized. It was only very partially determined by spokesmen for organized (craft union) labor. It was largely determined by middle-class exponents of the Social Gospel, the most effective of whom were men and women associated with Jane Addams' Hull House in Chicago, Lillian Wald's Henry Street Settlement in New York City, and settlement houses and similar organizations in other cities. These people pressed hard for the abolition of child labor and sweatshops; for wage and hour regulation, especially to protect women workers; for industrial accident insurance; for improved public health programs; and for various other laws to protect workers against hazardous working conditions and exploitive labor practices.

Simultaneously came the rise of a wholly new kind of journalism in such mass-circulation magazines as *McClure's, Munsey's, Everybody's, Collier's,* and *Cosmopolitan*—a journalism that focused revealing light upon theretofore secret recesses and dark corners of American industry, finance, politics, and the life of the poor. Ida M. Tarbell exposed to public gaze the unedifying details of John D. Rockefeller's achievement of oil monopoly in her *History of the Standard Oil Company*, which ran as a serial in *McClure's* before being published as a book. Lincoln Steffens, managing editor of *McClure's*, wrote a series of brilliant exposés of the corrupt alliance between business and politics which misgoverned virtually every city in the land, articles published first in the magazine he edited and later in book form as *The Shame of the Cities*. Also in *McClure's* appeared articles by Ray Stannard Baker exposing railroad evils, later published as a book, *The Railroads on Trial*. Thomas W. Lawson undertook to expose the wholesale fraud and thievery of the financial community in articles published in *Everybody's* and subsequently as a book, *Frenzied Finance*. There were others (Burton J. Hendrick, Ben B. Lindsey, John Spargo, Upton Sinclair, Charles Edward Russell, Robert Hunter, Frank Norris) who in magazines and books expressed and provoked a fact-supported indignation at flagrant betrayals of the American dream by greedy, power-lustful businessmen and their political allies—at the murderous exploitation of working women and children, as well as men, at the ugly miserable poverty of the masses who huddled in slums. Their work inspired and aided some of Theodore Roosevelt's most notable efforts at reform. Nevertheless, he as President viewed them with distaste, deprecating them in a public speech (1906) as people who focused always and only on filth, like "the man with the muckrake" in Bunyan's *Pilgrim's Progress*. He thereby bestowed upon them the name by which they are known to history and which they proudly bore in their own time: they were muckrakers.

And on such matters as the muckrakers exposed there was substantial agreement among Progressives.

But most of these "causes" were themselves effects of deeper causes: they were rooted in a fundamental historical process—namely, the application to economic operations of a scientific technology that advanced in continuous acceleration within a society committed to private profit. And it was with regard to a major manifestation of this fundamental process that Progressives in 1910 began to disagree and to define their disagreement in a way that polarized their movement.

This major manifestation was the gigantic business firm and its tendency to grow yet larger. Every advance in the size, efficiency, and cost of productive machinery seemed to place a greater premium on bigness of industrial organization, a greater competitive penalty on smallness, with the result that small firms were either absorbed or crushed. The obvious trend was toward monopoly or oligopoly—a domination of the market by one or a very few large firms—and it was viewed with alarm by the general public. The elimination of the free market meant destruction of a main source and guarantee of economic efficiency and justice; the whole process was dehumanizing and anti-individualistic, a contradiction of the principles of personal liberty and self-expression promulgated in the Declaration of Independence and the Bill of Rights. Such was the popular view. (Even within the top directorship of the great corporations themselves there was a diminishment of the importance of any one person as a determiner of economic activity. The unique gave way to the standardized, improvisation to routine, and increasingly, so far as policy-making was concerned, individual personality was submerged in committees, whose decisions were in turn largely grounded on studies and reports by technical experts. For already in 1910 it was becoming evident that the age of the mighty entrepreneurs—the Andrew Carnegies and John D. Rockefellers—was drawing to a close. Among the then-rising automobile manufacturing firms destined to survive, the Ford Motor Company was exceptional in its individualistic management and financial structure. General Motors was typical.) The popular conclusion was that the trend toward monopoly must be halted and free competition restored by federal statute.

Hence the Sherman Antitrust Act of 1890 forbidding combinations "in restraint of trade."

Progressive Senator Robert L. La Follette of Wisconsin regarded this law (in 1913) as "the strongest, most perfect weapon which the ingenuity of man could forge for the protection of the people against the power and sordid greed of monopoly," [1] but in point of fact it had proved a flimsy barrier against the flooding pressure toward corporate giantism. In 1895 a crucial antitrust case involving the American Sugar Refining Company (*U.S. v. E. C. Knight*) was ruled upon by the U.S. Supreme Court. By buying out four competing companies, the refining company had achieved control of at least 98 percent of the country's sugar-refining industry. None could deny, therefore, that it constituted an industrial monopoly. The Court made no effort to do so. But by asserting a rigid distinction between commerce and industry and implicitly holding that the Sherman Act applied only to the former, it found American Refining not guilty of conspiring to monopolize interstate commerce.* The Sherman Act appeared nullified.

And this greatly increased the practical efficacy of a famous state law enacted in 1889. New Jersey's governor, concerned to raise money for state expenses, had sought the advice of a corporation lawyer named James B. Dill, who suggested and drafted a bill legalizing the holding

---

* This same Court was quick to find that the Sherman Act applied to labor unions, even though no mention of labor combinations was made in the act. When Eugene Debs, labor leader, was sentenced to six months' imprisonment for refusing to obey a federal court injunction designed to break the Pullman strike of 1894, the Supreme Court upheld the sentence on the ground that Debs was obstructing interstate commerce and the government had an implicit power to remove such obstacles.

company—that is, permitting one corporation to hold the stock of other corporations. The device was not new. The Southern Railway Security Company of which James Roosevelt had been president in the 1870's was a holding company. But when Dill's bill was enacted by the legislature, it gave full legal sanction for the first time to what had formerly been deemed a highly questionable proceeding. The law did abundantly what Dill had promised the governor it would do: it increased the state's revenues as one large business combination after another was effected through holding companies incorporated in New Jersey.

The prime mover in most of these combinations, after 1900, was not the manufacturer or industrialist but the investment banker, the corporation lawyer, the promoter whose special genius was for manipulatory salesmanship. It was banker J. Pierpont Morgan who, in 1901, organized the two greatest combinations. One was the Northern Securities Company, which sought to institutionalize a "community of interest" (a favorite phrase of Morgan's) between the theretofore warring railroad interests of E. H. Harriman and Jim Hill. The other was the United States Steel Corporation. And as we have seen,* when Theodore Roosevelt, newly entering the White House, was anxious for political reasons to overturn the Knight decision, reviving the Sherman Act as an instrument of executive power, he chose as his target Northern Securities. The antitrust suit was instituted with dramatic flourish. Great popular excitement was engendered by it. And the five-four decision which the Court handed down (Justice Oliver Wendell Holmes was among the dissenters) fully accomplished the President's purpose. Northern Securities was declared illegal, and in language sweeping enough to constitute a reversal of the earlier ruling. "No scheme or device . . . could more effectively suppress competition," said Justice John Harlan, speaking for the majority. (Among his listeners in the courtroom on that March 14, 1904, was Mrs. Sara Delano Roosevelt. This was when she and Franklin visited Washington immediately after their Caribbean cruise, though her son did not accompany her that day.[2])

The decision did little, however, to halt or even seriously to slow the trend toward bigger and bigger business combinations, narrower and narrower concentrations of economic power. As a matter of fact, it had little effect on actual control of the interests Northern Securities would have formally combined. "What has been the result?" asked an angrily contemptuous Jim Hill. "To the owners of the properties, merely the inconvenience of holding two certificates of stock of different colors instead of one, and of keeping track of two different sets of securities. To

* See page 154.

the public, no difference at all except that it has missed the advantages which the simpler and more businesslike plan would have secured. . . ." Such astute corporation law firms as Carter, Ledyard, and Milburn were prolific of schemes to achieve the desired market controls without setting up formal institutions that seemed to be forbidden by Court interpretations of the law. Trade associations, for instance, were destined to become favorite devices for reducing competition and increasing cooperation, accomplishing many of the purposes of monopoly without incurring the legal wrath of the federal executive. And there was no consistent vigor in the Justice Department's movements against huge holding companies incorporated under New Jersey law. Morgan himself assumed that if either of his two great combinations of 1901 was illegal, the other must also be. But no action was initiated by the Theodore Roosevelt administration against U.S. Steel, and the President even, as we have seen, gave at least tacit approval to the corporation's acquisition of Tennessee Coal and Iron in 1907. Similarly with the International Harvester Company of New Jersey. Organized under Morgan's aegis in 1902, it comprised some 80 percent of all American manufacturing in its field. Yet (as we have also seen) a threatened antitrust suit against it, in 1907, never materialized.

II

Why the evident vacillations and inconsistencies of TR's war against the trusts? Political expedience was certainly part of the reason. The President felt no strong moral compulsion or official obligation to enforce the law willy-nilly; when facing a given citadel of corporate power, therefore, he could and did consult his conception of the immediate advantage to be gained or lost by his assault upon it. Often, on this ground alone, he refrained from the assault. But there was another and historically far more important factor in his motivation: he grew increasingly doubtful about the governmental approach to modern industrialism which the Sherman Act represented.

He had always had a temperamental aversion to Thomas Jefferson, whom he regarded as weak, shallow, sentimental, timorously desirous of popularity, possessed of a wholly mistaken conception of government— and he increasingly recognized the impulse behind the Sherman Act as Jeffersonian. It was an impulse that combined a blind faith in "little" people, "little" business, smallness of scale in general, with an irrational fear of strong men, big organization, the large-scale exercise of power— and this particular expression of it could not be justified, in TR's view, even in terms of a purely abstract morality, leaving aside the pressing claims of immediate practicality. Why, after all, should "littleness" be deemed inherently good, "bigness" inherently bad, in economic affairs? On what grounds must one conclude that "free competition" is superior to "planned cooperation" as a determinant of economic efficiency or of service to the general welfare? To such questions there were for him no convincing answers.

And in any case, the theory and purpose of the act were in hopeless opposition to the overwhelming tendency of the age—the act itself a sentimental gesture toward a dead past rather than a realistic design upon the living present or gestating future. One must boldly face rather than timidly shrink away from the fact that a huge technology implied huge companies to manage it, that the conscious ultimate aim in any single case of corporate growth was the achievement of a bigness sufficient to enable prices to be set and held by management decision rather than by a fluctuating relationship between supply and demand, and that the "inevitable" end of the process was precisely this achievement on the part of a few great firms in every major kind of enterprise. The so-called free market of former years was being contracted, perhaps even killed. But one must also recognize that both the individual corporate aim and the overall trend were only partially motivated by a "wicked" instinct for power through selfish acquisitiveness; they were also motivated by a "virtuous" instinct for order and a morally "neutral" instinct for self-preservation. The latter was fundamental. The costs of tooling up for a new product or for design changes in an old one, the time lag between the conception of these and their appearance on the market, grew with every technological advance. They increasingly added up to investments so great that responsible management, using other people's money, dare not risk them without some concrete assurance of prices high enough profitably to cover them. In other words, the conditions of mass production within a system of private profit made managed prices virtually a necessity of corporate survival, and survival was, of course, prerequisite to all other corporate aims. Finally, one had to recognize that the concentration of productive energy effected through the great corporations offered expanded opportunities for service of the public good—the new industrial organizations could plan and execute on an unprecedentedly large scale, greatly increasing the total output of goods while reducing per-unit costs and, hence, the price paid by consumers—provided only that the organizations be made submissive to a public authority that acted on behalf of the whole people.

TR would not have stated the case in precisely this way, but this way was certainly consistent with the reasoned attitude he had assumed by the time he left the White House. For he had by then developed his own fairly clear ideas of the proper relationships between large corporations and the other elements of private enterprise and between all these and the national government—a sense which resembled in essence the "concept of countervailing power" to be described by a famous American economist* more than four decades later. The right answer to the "natural" growth of large business organizations, concluded TR, was *not* an attempt to break them up (this, he soon asserted, was "futile madness") but, instead, the organization and power growth of other segments of the economy (labor, small business, agriculture) under the aegis of a national government strong enough to regulate any and all of them in the public interest. Traditional Jeffersonianism was wrong to regard concentrations of power as per se inimical to personal liberty. Only through such concentrations in industry could a full measure of the material blessings of modern technology be realized. Only through such concentrations in a central government could private power be made publicly responsible and kept subservient to the general will. Freedom, in other words, was threatened by great power concentrations only to the extent that some of these were not adequately checked and balanced by others within a whole whose aims were set and achieved through positive, but representative, government. So long as a proper countervalence of power was maintained, the concentrated growth of it would mean not merely the preservation of personal liberty, but an actual enhancement of it; men would be freed from crushing labor, from misery and want, and would gain in leisure, mobility, and a multiplicity of choices among material goods.

Two influences clarified and confirmed this overall conclusion in TR's mind after he left the White House. One was a book, *The Promise of American Life,* by Herbert Croly, published in November, 1909, and sent to TR in Africa by Learned Hand.[3] It struck at once a responsive chord in the ex-President with its assertion that Jefferson, a man of "intellectual superficiality and insincerity," had "perverted the American democratic idea" by insisting on egalitarianism in all fields of human endeavor. (Actually, argued Croly, the practice of "equal rights" at the outset always results in inequality in the end since "strong and capable men not only conquer, but . . . seek to perpetuate their conquests by occupying all the strategic points in the economic and political battlefield. . . .") The book went on to insist (a) that while giant trusts had

* John Kenneth Galbraith, *American Capitalism: The Concept of Countervailing Power* (Boston, 1952).

certainly been guilty of abuses, they in general "contributed to American economic efficiency" by substituting "cooperation for competitive methods," (b) that the Sherman Antitrust Act, far from being "impartial" in its application (no legislation ever is, Croly asserted), favored small business at the expense of big business and the general good, for (c) the new technology made it impossible for the small entrepreneur to function as efficiently as the big one in many fields, and where the former "is not able to hold his own, there is no public interest promoted by an expensive [and inevitably futile] attempt to save his life." The burden of Croly's message was a call for a "New Nationalism"—an almost mystical conception of an America "organized for its national historical mission," a state representing no mere "group of individuals" but "the nation of yesterday and tomorrow" whose elements were joined together in mutual obedience to "a morally authoritative Sovereign will." An immensely strengthened central government would permit and even encourage corporations to achieve their "natural" growth (if this ended in "harmful" monopoly, the corporation would be "gradually" nationalized) but would be empowered to regulate them rigorously in the "national interest," along with unions, agriculture, small business. He recognized dangers in this. He remained unquestioningly committed to democracy as the only "right" form of government, and obviously a corrupt officialdom possessed of immense powers could destroy democracy. But he was convinced that the risk was necessary. After all, he insisted, the "principle of democracy is virtue"; no basic reform could be accomplished without bringing "the feeling of human brotherhood . . . into possession of the human spirit," which meant that the inculcation of civic virtue, the promotion of brotherhood were of the very essence of the New Nationalism.[4]

The other clarifying and confirming influence on TR's conclusion was a man, George W. Perkins, erstwhile Morgan partner and leading organizer of giant combinations, who had long tried to effect some reforms in the public interest within the great corporations he helped control. Soon after TR departed for Africa, Perkins resigned from the House of Morgan, resigned most of his other directorships also, and embarked on a speaking and writing crusade to convince the American people that the age of competition was at an end—and a good thing, too, since ruthless cutthroat competition had been the root of most of the evils of capitalism. ("The Congressman who stands for a literal enforcement of the Sherman Act stands for the sweat shop and child labor," said Perkins.) "Cooperation must be the order of the day," he proclaimed, outlining a national program that was in close harmony with Croly's.[5] Corporations, far from being artificially curtailed in growth, should be encouraged to expand to "natural" limits but should be required to meet stringent federal standards as regards their financing, pricing policies, labor relations, etc., these to be enforced through a federal licensing of all corporations engaged in interstate commerce. The corporations themselves must become public-spirited. They should initiate programs and policies in the community interest, such things as profit sharing, old age pensions, social insurance. ("If regulation fails, then government ownership," said Perkins.[6])

Both Croly and Perkins were invited to confer with TR at Oyster Bay that summer as the ex-President subconsciously prepared to plunge again into elective politics. And both men were immensely pleased and excited when, on August 31, 1910, in Osawatomie, Kansas, where John Brown's men had fought Missouri proslavers in late August, 1856, TR fused their ideas with his own in a historic speech.

It raised a storm across the land.

For having been welcomed to the town as "the modern Tom Jefferson" (did he wince?) and having himself proclaimed to the assembled thousands that he stood for "the square deal," the ex-President went on to explain that by that phrase he meant "not merely that I stand for fair play under the present rules of the game, but that I stand for having those rules changed so as to work for a more substantial equality of opportunity and reward." He grew specific. Tariff schedules should be drafted by a commission of experts, freed of political pressures. Income and inheritance taxes should be used to prevent excessively "swollen fortunes." Corporations must be sternly regulated in the public interest. Measures must be enacted to protect labor, conserve natural resources, aid the farmer. And all this must be accomplished "mainly through the national government." What the American people demanded and were "right in demanding" was a "New Nationalism" which put "the national need before sectional or personal advantage" and looked upon the executive "as the steward of the public interest."

Then came the two sentences of the speech that would be most quoted during the next two years—sentences at once infuriating and terrifying to conservatives.

"We are face to face with new conceptions of the relations of property to human welfare," said Theodore Roosevelt. "The man who wrongly holds that every human right is secondary to his profit must now give way to the advocate of human welfare, who rightly maintains that every man holds his property subject to the general right of the community to regulate its use to whatever degree the public welfare may require it." [7]

To *whatever* degree!

III

The New Nationalism, however, represented but one side of the issue that in 1910 began to achieve divisive definition within the Progressive movement. TR might wish Jeffersonian Progressivism dead; it remained, nevertheless, very much alive. And not all its champions were as naïve and sentimentally attached to the past as TR believed them to be.

Their most effective spokesman was Louis D. Brandeis, who, after making a fortune as the most brilliant of corporation lawyers, had turned "people's advocate" and begun (in the 1890's) to argue cases, often without fee, for the purpose of effecting economic and social reforms. In 1908 he had made legal history by successfully defending before the U.S. Supreme Court, in *Muller v. Oregon,* Oregon's ten-hour day for women in industry. He had won this case with an argument, the famed "Brandeis brief," that unprecedentedly made use of a "logic of facts" (economic, sociological, and medical data were marshaled), rather than a logic of legal abstractions sustained by citations of precedents, to establish a "reasonable" relationship between the legislation in question and its stated objectives. Law in general, insisted Brandeis, was no expression of absolute and eternal verities, but a social instrument of living men who must continuously adapt it to the changing conditions of the real world. Modern limited liability corporations were themselves recent creatures of law—and in Brandeis' view, it was the purely legal devise of the holding company, coupled with the failure of effective antitrust legislation, which was largely responsible for the current trend toward monopoly. The alleged "necessities" of the new technology had little or nothing to do with it. Corporations were born of special privilege; they fed upon it and grew huge beyond the bounds of health or sanity.

On this ground, citing facts and figures, Brandeis shaped a vigorous and sophisticated counterargument to the Croly-Perkins-TR thesis regarding the "natural" and "inevitable" growth of corporate giantism and the proper governmental response to it. He did not deny that modern technology implied larger industrial organizations than had obtained at a simpler time. But he flatly denied that bigness, beyond a certain point, served economic efficiency. It did, in fact, just the opposite. While threatening the very structure of democracy, excessive size in business made for inefficiency, not only because the spur and checkrein of competition were removed, but also because the giant became incomprehensible, unmanageable by the individual men who presumed to direct it. In other words, the drive for corporate hugeness was motivated by no such impersonal economic-historical impulse toward maximum efficiency as Croly and Perkins and TR asserted but, instead, by the greed, the lust for power of men who cared little for the general welfare or for the human rights of their own employees.[8]

A glaring case in point was U.S. Steel. Its initial financial structure involved unprecedented amounts of capital but was otherwise typical and therefore revealing of how and why investment bankers interested themselves in the organization of such combines. U.S. Steel's initial assets had an actual value of $682,000,000. The corporation was capitalized, however, at $1.4 billion—$362,000,000 in bonds, $510,000,000 in preferred stock, $508,000,000 in common stock, $22,000,000 in cash—which is to say that half the total capitalization was water.*

Only three-fourths of the preferred stock and absolutely none of the common had any real backing whatever; thousands who bought common at the outset suffered dismay or worse when it soon fell to eight points, and a full fifteen years would pass before, through a combination of good luck and good management, all the original water was squeezed out. But the Morgan firm easily marketed the securities in 1901 and, according to investigators of the U.S. Bureau of Corporations (forerunner of the Federal Trade Commission), pocketed a fee of $62,500,000 for organizing and underwriting the enterprise. And did this consolidation of formerly separate firms increase actual operating efficiency? Far from it, argued Brandeis in testimony before a Congressional committee in 1911. Since the Steel Trust was formed, there had been a deterioration in product quality. The Interstate Commerce Commission had found, upon investigation, that a marked increase in train derailments was due to defective steel in the rails. The U.S. Department of Agriculture had been forced by farmer complaint to investigate a marked decline in the quality of fence wire. And American steel had claimed, since the trust was formed, a decreasing share of the world market. Nor had the consolidation effected improvement in the lot of steelworkers, despite George Perkins' much-eulogized pension and profit-sharing schemes. The former actually promoted "pensioned peonage," in Brandeis' view, since pensions were paid only for long service and could be denied a worker whose conduct displeased the management. Meanwhile, steelworkers toiled twelve hours a day and, often, seven days a week for wages that, in 65 percent of the cases, were less than the minimum cost of living. As for profit sharing, it was so nominal as to amount to a hoax; it had totaled $6 a year per worker on the aver-

* Andrew Carnegie insisted upon payment in 5 percent gold bonds ($225,000,000 of them) for his personal holdings in the Carnegie Company, around which U.S. Steel was built. He had a healthy distrust of Morgan and doubted the survival capacity of the vastly overcapitalized corporation.

age. In ten years the scheme had distributed $12,000,000 to employees, whereas, during that same decade, $435,000,000 had been added to the corporation assets and $220,000,000 had been paid out in dividends on watered stock.[9]

On the day of TR's New Nationalism speech, Brandeis in New York's Waldorf-Astoria Hotel was arguing on behalf of shippers before the Interstate Commerce Commission against a general rate increase sought by the railroads on freight east of the Mississippi and north of the Ohio and Potomac rivers. He pointed during the hearings to New York Central's acquisition of the Boston & Albany, which lost $1,000,000 a year, and to the Pennsylvania Railroad's proposed acquisition of the Northern Central. He strove to make it clear upon the record that neither of these acquisitions was motivated by a yearning for increased corporate efficiency, that both were part of the policy of "unsatiated aggrandizement" being followed by the great financiers who, though they knew nothing about the technical operations of railroading, controlled the lines. Brandeis, as a Bostonian, felt strongly on this matter. He viewed with outrage and dismay the use J. P. Morgan & Company was making at that time of the New Haven Railroad, which Morgan controlled. The line's capitalization of some $93,000,000 in 1903 was being multiplied; it would amount to some $417,000,000 in 1912; and the money obtained from this enormous overcapitalization (with *other* people's money) was being used, not for improvement of the New Haven or even for the acquisition of other railroad properties, but to achieve or attempt to achieve an absolute monopoly of New England's transportation facilities. For this megalomaniacal purpose, New Haven's directors were engaging in a wholesale corruption of state legislators, U.S. Senators and Congressmen, newspaper editors, and regulatory agency officials. The New Haven was destined never to recover from the crushing burden thus placed on its financial structure, and the whole New England economy was gravely injured.[10]

Obviously the proper governmental response to the challenge presented by this kind of enterprise was no supine abrogation of antitrust legislation. Instead, this legislation should be strengthened and expanded; the executive power should be fully used to restore and enforce competition. "We have been hearing constantly that the tendency to combinations is a natural economic law, that it is useless to attempt to stem the tide, that we ought to accept the Trust and undertake to regulate it," said Brandeis in 1912. "I believe that position to be absolutely unfounded. . . . Combination is not natural any more than any of the other things in life are natural which it is easier to do if you have no occasion to count the cost. The law may be made, to my mind, perfectly adequate to stem the growth of these organizations, and to say that it cannot is to declare the lawmaking power bankrupt. . . ." [11] Admittedly, competition must be regulated in the public interest, to prevent the evils against which Perkins inveighed, evils which in fact bred monopoly by enabling the most ruthless and unfair competitor to overwhelm the others. But the regulation of competition was far easier and more certainly productive of public good than the attempted regulation of monopoly could ever be. The latter implied a central government so strong as to endanger individual liberties, especially since it would almost certainly become in the end an instrument of the very trusts it ostensibly regulated. Competition, on the other hand, could be regulated in a much more decentralized fashion; it could be kept pure and wholesome and truly free without the development of a hugely powerful governing apparatus. No greater burden would be placed upon the wisdom and integrity of public servants than they, as fallible mortal men, could be reasonably expected to bear.

Inevitably, Brandeis, like myriads of Progressives who had voted for TR in 1904 and Taft in 1908, turned away from both Republican leaders in 1910 as he looked toward the Presidential election of 1912. Taft, said Brandeis, was a "wobbler" with "incorrigibly aristocratic leanings." Theodore Roosevelt was "not objective in his thinking" about giant corporations.[12] There remained, as the third leading figure of the party, Wisconsin's Senator La Follette, whose courage, tenacity, and consistency in battle for economic liberty against the threat of monopolistic tyranny had been abundantly demonstrated in his home state and in the halls of Congress. Brandeis—again like myriads of Progressives—turned toward him. He joined with influential men of like mind, Gifford Pinchot and William Allen White among them, in a National Progressive Republican League, formed in December, 1910, for the purpose of capturing the Republican Party for Progressivism and assuring the Presidential nomination of La Follette.

But as things turned out, the La Follette candidacy, which would almost certainly have won over Taft's if TR had supported it, could not survive competition with the ex-President's increasingly obvious and active bid for the Republican nomination. And when La Follette faded, Brandeis (yet again like myriads of Progressives) would turn away from the Republican Party altogether and toward Woodrow Wilson, former president of Princeton University, who erupted upon the national political scene in 1910 by winning election as Democratic governor of New Jersey.

Indeed, Brandeis was destined to play in Woodrow Wilson's political education a role analogous to that played by Croly in TR's, while a successful New York businessman named William Gibbs McAdoo would become Wilson's George Perkins. Born and reared in the South, McAdoo retained a Southerner's resentment and mistrust of Wall Street even after he, having come to New York as a youthful lawyer in the early 1890's, had demonstrated a genius for large-scale business organization, had headed an enterprise for tunneling under the Hudson River, and become president of the Hudson and Manhattan Railroad Company. He was as vehement as Brandeis in condemnation of the giant trusts. "These great corporations are not the *natural* outgrowth of new economic conditions and complex civilization," said he. "They are more likely the artificial product of the unrestrained activities of ambitious men of highly-developed acquisitive power." He was convinced that the national government should do all it could "to preserve competitive conditions" and that, though unregulated competition was preferable to regulated monopoly, "regulated competition is better than either." McAdoo, like Perkins on the other side of the Progressive issue, would become a major figure in the Presidential campaign of 1912.[13]

Thus the influence of both Brandeis and McAdoo, but of Brandeis especially, were to be manifested in the New Freedom that would become Woodrow Wilson's answer to the New Nationalism of Theodore Roosevelt in 1912.

Nine

➤➤➤《《《

First Flight: Education in Albany

I

MIDWAY through the afternoon of October 6, 1910, Franklin Delano Roosevelt made to the Democratic nominating convention in Poughkeepsie the first political campaign speech of his life. He had just been awarded his uncontested nomination for state senator, a three-man committee of escort (Edward Perkins was one of the three) had taken him to the speaker's platform, and from that platform he gave his address of acceptance. There was nothing at all remarkable about it.

"As you know, I accept this nomination with absolute independence," he said. "I am pledged to no man; I am influenced by no special interests, and so I shall remain. In the coming campaign, I need not tell you that I do not intend to sit still. We are going to have a very strenuous month. . . . We have real issues and an excellent platform . . . and with the aid of the independent thinking voters of these counties we have little to fear from the result on November eighth." [1]

But if there was nothing remarkable about the acceptance speech, there was much that was remarkable and revelatory of political astuteness in the campaign that followed. At the outset young Roosevelt dismayed most of the local Democratic organization by announcing that he would campaign by automobile, something no one had ever done before in that district. Campaign workers pointed out excellent reasons why it had never been done and should not be now. Automobiles in that year were still luxury items; this young patrician's use of one could only emphasize the social distance separating him from the average voter. Worse, automobiles were noisy contraptions, rarely seen on country roads, and farmers hated and feared them because they frightened horses, causing runaways. But the candidate was adamant. Election day was only a month away. Traveling by horse and buggy, he could not

possibly, in so brief a time, cover the three large counties as he was convinced they had to be covered if he were to win. Moreover, the very audacity of the stunt could be turned to his advantage if he took great care
not to frighten horses but instead stopped the car when he saw a buggy
or wagon approaching. As the farmer passed by, he, Franklin, would
greet him and introduce himself and thereby often gain a vote.

He owned no car at that time. So he hired for the month a Maxwell
touring car, painted bright red and topless—hired, too, the car's owner
to drive it, a man named Hawkey[2] whom Eleanor would remember as
"a delightful character"—and, with Richard E. Connell, perennial Democratic candidate for Representative from the Twenty-first Congressional District (it included the State Senatorial District plus a county
west of the Hudson), set out upon the campaign trail. Connell, through
a long succession of failed campaigns, had become something of a joke
to the electorate. He had a standard speech into which he injected whatever specifics he wished to present—a perfervid piece of patriotic oratory climaxed by an actual waving of the American flag (it was doubtless Connell who bedecked the red Maxwell with flags). But he was an
amusing joke, he was generally regarded with affection, he managed to
arouse a good deal of patriotic enthusiasm in most of his audiences, and
he gave Franklin some useful tips, especially about public speaking.

These last the young man needed.* He was not at ease before audiences as the campaign opened, and even after weeks of the most strenuous campaigning the district had ever seen, during which he spoke ten
to twenty times a day in all kinds of places and to all kinds of crowds, he
seemed to his wife "high-strung and . . . nervous" as he presented himself to watching eyes, listening ears. His words came slowly, haltingly,
"and every now and then there would be a long pause" during which Eleanor grew terrified lest he, paralyzed by shyness, was unable to go on.
He always did go on at last, however. The evident difficulty of his doing
so, the very fact that he was "no orator," seemed to endear him to
many, who felt his difficulty as their own, and to weight his words with
persuasive earnestness and sincerity.[3]

The words themselves, if never eloquent, were carefully chosen. The
campaign strategy in general was shrewdly shaped. He and Connell devoted little attention to such Democratic enclaves as Poughkeepsie and
Hudson but concentrated instead on the farmer vote, traditionally Republican; in appealing to the latter, they said relatively little about specific agricultural problems but concentrated instead on the issue of

---

* It was from Connell that young Roosevelt adopted the phrase "My friends," which always
afterward studded his public speech.

"bossism"; and while Connell attacked the bossism in Congress of Uncle Joe Cannon, Franklin concentrated fire on Lou F. Payn, who lived in Chatham in Columbia County, was Republican state committeeman from an area inclusive of the state senatorial district, and was a principal lieutenant of the Republican state boss, William Barnes, Jr. The burden of Franklin's complaint was that his opponent, Schlesser, took orders from Payn. Certainly Schlesser had bitterly opposed the reform program of Progressive Republican Governor Charles Evans Hughes whose acceptance of appointment to the U.S. Supreme Court in April, 1910, had (like TR's announcement he would not seek a third term) greatly lessened his strength in battle against legislative opponents. Schlesser had been one of a large majority of the legislature to vote against Hughes' direct primary bill on July 1—a measure that was anathema to machine politicians and that TR had strongly supported a few days before the vote was taken. Young Franklin Roosevelt was thereby enabled to capitalize to the fullest possible extent upon his namesake relationship to TR, identifying himself as an ally of the ex-President in a war against special privilege, graft, and corruption.

TR as governor of New York had fired Payn as state superintendent of insurance in early 1900 because, as TR then said, the superintendent "being a frugal man, out of his seven thousand dollars a year salary" had somehow "saved enough to enable him to borrow nearly half a million dollars from a trust company, the directors of which are also the directors of an insurance company under his supervision." * And in late September, 1910, as Republicans had gathered in state convention at Saratoga, Payn had publicly predicted that, if there were "any new party its nucleus will be the men who are making the fight now against Mr. Roosevelt . . . , a party of conservatism such as would appeal to the men who won't stand having the Republican Party handed over to a kind of Bryanism." [4] It was thus made obvious, and became increasingly so all through October, that though TR had succeeded in dictating at the convention the nomination for governor of Henry L. Stimson and the adoption of one or two progressive planks in the platform, there was every likelihood that Stimson's Democratic opponent, John A. Dix, himself a conservative, would be elected in November.

Roosevelt and Connell had good luck with the weather during the closing days of the campaign. Heavy rains fell. All out-of-doors work was brought to a standstill. Farmers having nothing else to do welcomed

---

* Payn had formerly been lobbyist for Jay Gould, among other financiers of doubtful ethics, and it was in reference to Payn's case that TR made his famous quotation of "the West African proverb: 'Speak softly and carry a big stick, you will go far.' "

the opportunity to attend political meetings, and Roosevelt addressed far more of these than did Schlesser, who made no effort to match his young opponent's energy. He returned to Hyde Park on the eve of election day and there, as he was to do many times in the future, he closed out the campaign with an informal talk to friends and neighbors. He spoke of his father (". . . you have known how close he was to the life of this town") and of his "desire always to follow in his footsteps." [5] The next morning he voted in Hyde Park's town hall, then returned to Springwood to await the election returns.

These proved to be in the highest degree gratifying.

As most observers had expected, Dix defeated TR's handpicked candidate for the governorship (he won by 67,471 votes). Less expected was Dick Connell's defeat of Republican Representative Hamilton Fish* for Congress; he carried the Twenty-first District by 517 votes. (Having achieved the ambition of a lifetime, Connell was destined to die before he could run for reelection.) As for Franklin Roosevelt, not unnaturally in what proved to be a Democratic "landslide" year (both houses of New York's legislature would be controlled by Democrats for the first time since 1892), he won the state senatorship. But if the fact of young Roosevelt's victory was not surprising in the circumstances, the size of it was and was remarked upon by politicians and reporters. He ran far ahead of his party's ticket, in Poughkeepsie, as well as in the rural areas. He defeated Schlesser by 15,708 to 14,568, or with a plurality of 1,140, whereas Dix's plurality in the district was only 663. His Hyde Park victory was overwhelming. He won the town by 406 to 205, whereas Dix carried it by only 22 votes.

The results clearly showed that Franklin Delano Roosevelt, in his first race for public office, had gained a handsome personal victory in addition to his proportionate share of the party's. This, of course, fully justified the nomination Perkins had only reluctantly endorsed, and then chiefly because he hoped and expected it would bring substantial funds into the party treasury. It hadn't done so. ("I guess several people thought I would be a gold mine," remarked Roosevelt later, "but, unfortunately, the gold was not there." [6]) Franklin, his mother, and a few friends contributed a little more than $2,500 to the Democratic campaign.

---

* Fish's namesake son, who would one day succeed his father as Representative from the Twenty-first District and be remembered in history for the bitterness of his political enmity toward his Hudson River neighbor, FDR, had been graduated the preceding spring from Harvard, where he was a classmate of John Reed, remembered in history for his *Ten Days That Shook the World.*

II

As he prepared to enter upon his duties as state senator, through the closing weeks of 1910, he had good reason to watch closely Woodrow Wilson's operations in neighboring New Jersey. For one thing, Wilson's victory had established him as a leading contender for the Democratic Presidential nomination in 1912, though the prize could be won only if he played with great care certain cards that had been dealt him during the campaign, and a Democratic President could provide young Roosevelt with opportunity to take the next step along the career road he had described to his fellow law clerks in 1908. For another thing, the battle in which Wilson became engaged immediately following his election triumph was similar in some ways to one that was shaping up in New York and that would require of Roosevelt a decision having, for him, fateful consequences. From Wilson's example, therefore, Roosevelt might learn much that would be useful to him in both the long run and the immediate future.

Prior to that year's gubernatorial campaign there had been no reason to regard Wilson as a strong Progressive Democrat or even as progressive at all.[7] In his multivolumed *History of the American People* he had written of "the crude and ignorant minds of the members of the Farmers' Alliance," he had publicly doubted that labor unions served the interests of individual workers, he had bitterly opposed Bryan in 1896 and 1900 and as late as 1908 refused to speak from the same platform with him, and he had been first brought to public attention as a Presidential possibility by a man in search of a candidate who would capture national Democratic leadership from the radical Bryan and restore the party to the orthodoxy of Grover Cleveland. This man, Colonel George Harvey, president of Harper & Brothers and editor of the then highly influential *Harper's Weekly,* had become immensely wealthy as an associate of Thomas Fortune Ryan and William C. Whitney in New York City public utilities and was a good personal friend of J. P. Morgan. It was Harvey who had persuaded the conservative James R. Smith, Jr., boss of the Newark-Essex County Democratic machine and the most powerful Democrat in New Jersey (his power derived from a typically corrupt alliance between corporate interests and politics), to support Wilson for governor. Without that support Wilson could not have been nominated. Without it he could not have won election.

But neither could he have won if he had not gained the support of Progressives of both major parties in his state, and it was after the crucial need for this support had become obvious during the campaign that he had committed himself unequivocally to workmen's compensation legislation, direct voting for all elective offices (New Jersey, like New York, still chose U.S. Senators by vote of the legislature), corrupt practices legislation, and other major elements of the Progressive program. He was consequently caught on the horns of a dilemma when Smith— his political benefactor, yet the bête noire of New Jersey Progressives— decided to enter the race for U.S. Senator, an office Smith had held without distinction for a term in the 1890's, when he and other right-wing Democrats had joined with Republicans to defeat Cleveland's tariff reform measures in 1894. There ensued a harrowing period for Wilson. He was on record in support of direct elections, and a Senatorial primary in late August (it was without legal effect) had been won against feeble opposition by a Bryan Democrat named James E. Martine, whom Wilson privately regarded as unfit for the office. If he now supported Smith against Martine, he not only would appear to be repudiating the principle of the direct primary but would also confirm in the public mind the charge made against him during the campaign that he had promised to support Smith for Senator in return for the Smith machine support of his own candidacy. On the other hand, how could Wilson emerge with any strength if, by supporting Martine, he branded himself an ingrate in the eyes of organization Democrats, split the New Jersey Democracy in two, and thereby made it impossible for him to push a Progressive program through the legislature?

Educative to a closely watching Franklin Roosevelt was Woodrow Wilson's triumphant solution of his problem. After weeks during which he maintained in public a neutral stance while vainly trying in private to persuade Smith to withdraw from the race, the governor-elect in early December issued a lengthy statement calling for the election of Martine, not because of Martine's personal qualifications (these went unmentioned since they were, in Wilson's view, nonexistent), but because the man personified the principle of the direct primary. Progressives cheered, all across the land. Everyone recognized that the open warfare which now flared between Wilson and Smith for control of the New Jersey Democracy had national implications. And the erstwhile college president proved to be a superb stump orator, able to shape and ruthlessly employ weapons of language that slashed and clubbed his opponents, able also to arouse huge audiences to a high pitch of moral indignation and idealistic fervor. He proved masterful in his mobilization of public opinion through appeals to a higher law—to principle, virtue, human nobility—and was but slightly less effective in persuading Smith's rank-and-file supporters, even some of Smith's lieutenants, to abandon their leader. To this end he used arguments that fused their desire to be on the winning side with their desire to be deemed honorable and public-spirited men. He appeared well on the way to victory as the old year ended, 1911 began, and the Franklin Roosevelts moved from Hyde Park to Albany.

Through most of January the battle raged. The climax came on the twenty-fourth. When the New Jersey legislature balloted for U.S. Senator that day, Martine emerged with more than four times the votes given Smith, nearly twice those given the Republican candidate, and only one less than needed for election. Thus his election on the morrow was absolutely assured. Smith did not stay in Trenton to see it. He issued a statement conceding defeat and left for his home in Newark, a broken old man, humiliated and embittered by the desertion of those he had long regarded as friends. "I pitied [him] . . . at the last," said Woodrow Wilson, who was now not only the master of New Jersey Democrats but a hero of Progressives everywhere, regardless of party lines.[8]

All this, to repeat, was educative to Franklin Roosevelt. But education was not all he derived from the spectacle. He derived also inspiration and courage and had need of them. For in the week before Wilson scored his great triumph, the political battle which had been shaping up in New York State ever since the November election broke in full fury. It, too, centered on the election of a U.S. Senator and was a battle against big city boss control of a state's Democracy. It, too, attracted national attention. And Franklin Roosevelt was in the thick of it.

Most members of New York's legislature were men of modest means who were in Albany only during those early days of each week when the legislature was normally in session or when special assignments required their presence in the capital. They stayed then in hotels or boardinghouses. Young Roosevelt rented for $400 a month a three-story house at 248 State Street, a short walk from the Capitol, and moved into it on the morning of January 1, 1911, with his wife, three children, and three servants "besides the nurses." The house was large, arranged in such a way as to provide ample room downstairs for entertaining large groups of people, and the neophyte senator's possession of it proved at once a political asset. There was nothing shy or retiring about the entrance he made upon the Albany scene. Some 400 of his constituents, accompanied by a brass band and the Hyde Park Fife and Drum Corps, came to the capital for Governor Dix's inauguration on January 2 (the din raised by his home town's fifes and drums in the street outside the Capitol nearly drowned out the opening prayer at the inaugural ceremonies), and the Roosevelts managed to entertain them all at a reception in their new home. For "three solid hours" they "wandered in and out" of the house, as Eleanor remembered, partaking of sandwiches, chicken salad, beer, coffee served by caterers in the dining room. That evening Franklin received a phone call from the governor inviting him and Eleanor to the Executive Mansion "for a little informal dancing." They accepted and "had a very delightful evening" at what turned out to be "almost a family party, only the military aides, two or three Albany girls and ourselves being there." [9]

The next day he attended his first Democratic caucus.

He already knew, for Governor Dix had told him the night before, that Tammany man Thomas F. Grady was to be deposed as Senate Democratic leader, a post Grady had held for eleven years. Dix had evidently requested this of Tammany chieftain Charles F. Murphy, who concurred in it. (Grady, the only senator who had been in the legislature when Theodore Roosevelt entered it in 1882, was famed for eloquence and parliamentary skill but had increasingly drowned his abilities in alcohol.) Hence it was no surprise to Roosevelt when Grady was shunted aside by the caucus and thirty-three-year-old Robert F. Wagner was chosen instead as Senate president pro tem. The caucus also chose the Democratic leader of the Assembly; he was thirty-seven-year-old Alfred E. Smith, then serving his seventh term in the lower house. The elevation of these two able and popular young men, if it aroused no enthusiasm in Roosevelt, provoked no opposition either—yet he could not forget that both were Tammany men who were subject to "the pressure of . . . [the] machine," as he wrote of Wagner in the diary he had begun to keep (and would soon abandon).[10]

The machine was very much on his mind. Boss Murphy, it seemed, was well aware of the sensibilities of upstate Democrats and anxious to defer to them when he could. He intended to drive the legislature's majority with as slack a rein as possible. He *did* intend to drive, however, and with regard to the first important business to be dealt with by the new legislature—the election of a U.S. Senator to succeed Republican Chauncey M. Depew, whose term expired March 4—it was already clear to Franklin that Murphy would use as tight a rein as necessary for the achievement of Tammany's purpose and would apply the whip, too.

What Tammany's purpose would be in this matter had not yet been fully disclosed, though it had been strongly indicated.

There were two leading contenders for the Senatorship. One was William F. Sheehan, known to all as Blue-eyed Billy, a standpatter who personified that alliance between business interests and conservative machine politics which all Progressives deplored. As a young Buffalo lawyer-politician in the 1880's, he had earned an unsavory reputation by his lack of personal scruple, his unconcern for the general welfare, as he fought against the then-rising Grover Cleveland and laid for himself the foundations of a fortune. He had become lieutenant governor, then moved to New York, where his fortune had grown large. With it had grown a considerable respectability—a rare amount of it for an Irish Catholic in the circles he now inhabited. The soubriquet applied to him in his young manhood no longer truly fitted. An urbane gentleman, he was law partner of the distinguished and conservative Alton B. Parker, Democratic Presidential candidate whom Franklin Roosevelt had declined to support in 1904, and was both counsel for and director of numerous railroad and public utilities companies. He had made large financial contributions to the last Democratic campaign, especially in doubtful districts, with the result that "at least half a dozen Democratic legislators elect" had "drifted into the capital bubbling over with gratitude to Mr. Sheehan," according to the Albany reporter of the·New York *Times*.[11]

The other leading contender was Edward M. Shepard, an independent Democrat, whose candidacy had been launched in late November by a group of Brooklyn and upstate Democrats. He was no flaming Progressive. His original sponsor in politics had been Boss John H. McCooey of Brooklyn; he was attorney for the Pennsylvania Railroad and was thoroughly orthodox in his economic views. Around him rallied the old-time Cleveland Democrats, such Democrats as James Roosevelt had been, who had never forgiven Blue-eyed Billy for his tactics in the 1880's and early '90's; around him, too, largely because of the alternative (Shepard *was* independent), rallied such Progressives as Franklin Roosevelt felt himself to be. "Shepard is without question the most competent to fill the position, but the Tammany crowd seems unable to forgive him his occasional independence and Sheehan looks like their choice at this stage of the game," young Roosevelt noted in his diary on the evening of the first day of the New Year. "May the result prove that I am wrong! There is no question in my mind that the Democratic party is on trial, and having been given control of the government chiefly through up-State votes, cannot afford to surrender its control to the organization in New York City." [12]

On the day after the caucus, January 4, 1911, Franklin Roosevelt presented his certificate of election to the State Senate's presiding officer, took his oath of office, and for the first time was seated in the large leather-upholstered chair, number 26, assigned him in the Senate Chamber. Two weeks later, when he was very much in the news, his appearance as he answered his first roll call was described in some detail in a feature article in the New York *Times*. The "young man" had "the finely chiseled face of a Roman patrician, only with a ruddier glow of health on it," said the feature writer. "Nature has left much unfinished in modeling the face of the Roosevelt of greater fame. On the face of this Roosevelt, younger in years . . . , she has lavished all her refining processes until much of the elementary strength has been lost in the sculpturing. Senator Roosevelt is less than thirty [he would be twenty-nine on January 30]. He is tall and lithe. With his handsome face and his form of supple strength he could make a fortune on the stage and set the matinee girl's heart throbbing with subtle and happy emotion." Another reporter described his face as "boyish" and went on to say, improbably, that "those who remember Theodore Roosevelt when he was an Assemblyman say the Senator bears a striking likeness to the Colonel." A woman reporter thought his face "a bit long" but conceded that his features were "well-modeled, the nose . . . Grecian in contour, and there is a glow of country health in his cheeks." She described his eyes as "deep set and gray" behind gold-bowed pince-nez spectacles and his chin as "aggressive and somewhat prominent." [13]

The occasion of all this personal publicity, rare indeed for a freshman senator, was the fulfillment of a prophecy allegedly made by old Timothy "Big Tim" Sullivan when he and Murphy went over a list of the new legislators together, shortly after election day. Big Tim, a thoroughly corrupt politician but also an amiable and warmhearted man, had long represented the Bowery in the Senate. As a Tammany stalwart he placed high value on party discipline and had small use for politicians who refused to work in harness. His aversion to wealthy young Harvard men who felt themselves superior to such as he, and showed it, was as strong as it was natural. And the story goes that when he and Murphy came to the name Roosevelt on their list and Big Tim was informed that Franklin was a cousin of Theodore, he said disgustedly that, having "caught a Roosevelt," the best thing they could do would be to "take him down and drop him off the dock." The Roosevelts "run true to form," Sullivan went on, "and this kid is likely to do for us what the Colonel is going to do for the Republican Party, split it wide open." [14]

Which is precisely what Franklin Roosevelt was helping do within two weeks after he had taken his seat.

III

There is no doubt that, as he pondered the course he should pursue in regard to the Sheehan-Shepard contest, he remembered the example set by Assemblyman Theodore Roosevelt a generation before. Brash young Theodore had made a shining reputation for himself as a reformer, while infuriating organization men in his own party, when during his first term as lowly assemblyman he forced an investigation of a financial scandal involving Jay Gould, Cyrus W. Field, Russell Sage, and a state supreme court justice. The example was reinforced in Franklin's mind by Woodrow Wilson's current battle against the Smith machine in New Jersey. He well knew that his district was almost certain to resume its Republican ways two years hence and that his chances of reelection were slim unless he managed somehow to make an outstanding personal impression on the public mind. An opportunity for doing so was presented by the Sheehan-Shepard contest.

But there is also no doubt that he was genuinely animated by a wish for reform when he learned of the system whereby this contest was scheduled to be settled. To win election as U.S. Senator, a candidate had to receive a majority of both houses of the legislature. There were 200 members of the legislature, and 114 of them, 13 more than a bare majority, were Democrats. On January 16 these Democrats were to caucus on the Senatorship, the majority decision at that time being binding on all who attended. Fifty-eight constituted a full caucus majority. This meant that it was technically possible for a mere 58 out of 200 legislators to make the decision, and since Murphy controlled many more than 58 Democratic votes, he had, in effect, the power personally to appoint a United States Senator! A few days before the caucus, Murphy passed the word: Sheehan was the man.

Young Roosevelt went for a long walk through Albany's wintry streets when he heard of Murphy's decision. During his walk he encountered William Church Osborn, who was a power in upstate Progressive Democracy and a leader of the Shepard movement, and he told Osborn emphatically that, caucus or no caucus, he would *never* vote for Sheehan.[15] He had learned by then (from Al Smith) that he could retain his freedom of choice in this matter simply by staying away from the caucus; its majority decision would not then be binding upon him. He had learned, too, that a group of Democratic assemblymen headed by Edmund R. Terry of Kings County were planning to boycott the meeting. If enough Democrats did so, they, with the Republicans, could block Sheehan's election by denying him the minimum of 101 votes he needed in the legislature to win. The ambitious young man carefully weighed the pros and cons as he swung along. By the time he arrived again at 248 State Street he had definitely decided to cast his lot with Terry's insurgents.

When the Democratic caucus assembled in the Capitol at nine o'clock Monday evening, January 16, Roosevelt, Terry, and eighteen other Democrats met in a hotel room, whence they issued a manifesto that made large headlines (Roosevelt's name was featured) in the next morning's newspapers. The manifesto explained that those who signed it had refused to attend the caucus because "they believed the votes of those who represented the people should not be smothered . . . ; and that the people should know just how their representatives vote . . . ; and that any majority secured for any candidate should be credited to the representatives in the Legislature and not some one outside the body." Roosevelt enlarged upon this when interviewed by reporters on the following day—a day when Sheehan received in the legislature only the ninety-one votes of those who attended the caucus (three Democrats who had not joined Roosevelt and Terry in the hotel room nevertheless stayed away from the caucus), or ten fewer than needed for election.* "We have decided to stand to a man and to the end against William F. Sheehan," Roosevelt declared, emphasizing that it was only upon this negative that the insurgents were unanimous and adamant. Some of them were for Shepard, others had other candidates, but all of them were "fighting against the boss rule system" and, on this matter of principle, would never yield.[16]

Nor did they—not for a long two and a half months during which their intransigency made it impossible for the legislature to conduct any business whatever.

At the outset, and perhaps for the duration of the struggle, Murphy was only mildly annoyed. He was by no means an essentially vicious man. A devout Catholic, he would have nothing to do with what he regarded as "dirty" graft; he would accept no money from organized vice and crime. He regarded himself as a "clean" boss. "If your taxes should be $5,000, he'd make them three, and you'd put up one . . . ," Arthur Krock of the New York *Times,* who liked him, once explained. "Anything of that kind was all right. That was called *clean* graft." [17] He kept his own counsel; his inscrutability was one of his strengths in machine politics. But the evidence was ultimately overwhelming that his assessment of political advantage rather than his private personal preference was what originally motivated his decision in favor of Sheehan. He personally would have liked to appoint as U.S. Senator his son-in-law and principal lieutenant, Daniel F. Cahalan, and he probably secretly hoped and believed that the net result of the insurgency, which would surely not be prolonged to a positively injurious extent, would be the elimination of both Sheehan and Shepard from the contest, enabling him to make the appointment of his desire.

* Big Tim Sullivan tried, before the balloting began, to make a deal with Boss Barnes of the Republicans whereby the latter would keep enough Republicans out of the chamber during the vote to enable Sheehan's ninety-one votes to constitute a majority. After all, Sullivan could point out, Sheehan represented essentially the same business interests as Barnes. But Barnes, eager to gain power for his organization from the quarrel among his party opponents, refused.

This, at least, would account for the rare good humor with which he personally met the challenge and the challengers, a humor that would have been unlikely had he felt that his basic authority was seriously threatened. When he had a private talk with Franklin Roosevelt on the latter's twenty-ninth birthday, he was affability itself. Instead of displaying anger or making threats, he "with a delightful smile" (according to young Roosevelt's own testimony) said, "I know I can't make you change your mind unless you want to change it. Is there any chance of you and the other twenty men coming around to vote for Sheehan?" Roosevelt said the opposition was not to Sheehan personally, but to the forced selection of a man who was not favored by "a great many of our Democratic constituents" and who was "too closely connected with the traction trust in New York City." (Sheehan was counsel for and director of the major traction and lighting corporations of the metropolis.) Murphy then urged the young man to tell Sheehan this to his face. Roosevelt promised to do so.[18]

As a matter of fact, he had already had a face-to-face meeting with Blue-eyed Billy, who, understandably, was considerably less affable than Murphy. The two had met in a private room of Albany's Ten Eyck Hotel on the day after the legislature first balloted on the Senatorship. Sheehan expressed angry resentment at what he deemed robbery and character "assassination." He would, he said, give up his law practice and devote full time to the vindication of his character. He threatened to "go into the counties where these men [the insurgents] live and show up their characters—the character in which they have accomplished this thing." [19] Nevertheless, no doubt at Murphy's urging and in the hope of effecting a compromise favorable to his ambition, he accepted an invitation to lunch on February 2 at 248 State Street. Eleanor never forgot the occasion. The lunch itself was "not so bad" since her husband and Sheehan carried the burden of the conversation, but afterward she had to entertain Mrs. Sheehan while the two men, in the privacy of Franklin's study, met in what both women well knew was "a really important fight." ". . . we sat and talked about the weather and anything else we could think of" until the two antagonists emerged, rather grim of face. The Sheehans then departed, to Eleanor's immense relief. Had any agreement been reached? she asked her husband. "Certainly not," said Franklin.[20] And since Sheehan stubbornly refused to withdraw, as Murphy (by February 1) obviously wished him to do, the fight went on.

Pressures brought to bear against the insurgents were predictably heavy and harsh, especially during the first weeks of the revolt. Some having mortgages on their property were suddenly threatened with foreclosures. Others found it suddenly difficult to obtain needed bank loans.

One whose livelihood depended upon government printing in the country newspaper and printing plant he owned was informed that this printing would be denied him next year if he persisted in rebellion. The insurgency was branded a revival of "Know-Nothingism" by no less a personage than the Catholic Bishop of Syracuse, who, in a statement especially hurtful to Roosevelt politically as well as personally, asserted that the rebels were motivated by anti-Irish, anti-Catholic bias. (Shepard was a Yankee Protestant.) And every insurgent suffered patronage losses and the threat of reprisal at the next election. Small wonder that many astute observers were convinced at the outset that the insurgency would collapse into utter futility before the month had ended.

But it didn't—and for this, Franklin Roosevelt deserved and publicly obtained a major share of the credit.

The magic name of Roosevelt, his relationship with TR were what originally propelled him into nominal leadership of a revolt actually under way before he joined it. He was personally the most newsworthy of the group, reporters came to him for statements as a matter of course, and so he was best fitted to serve as group spokesman. But from the first he was more than this. Despite his youth (the average age of the insurgents was forty-two; one was in his seventies), he was elected informal chairman of the group on the night of the caucus and thereafter presided over the deliberations, was the principal negotiator with the opposition, and, most important of all, was a main source and prop of morale. His personal charm in that year was still intermittent and variable in quality and quantity, but his geniality was generally sufficient to lubricate the group's operations. He proved skillful in garnering favorable publicity, he did much else to achieve public support, and he certainly sustained the others with his example of unflagging energy and optimistic courage. "Too much cannot be said of the untiring zeal and efforts of Senator Roosevelt to advance our cause," wrote Terry soon after the long fight ended. ". . . During the time when we were hounded and harassed, he was the shepherd of the flock, and his house was . . . a harbor of refuge. . . ." [21]

Indeed his possession of a house the insurgents could use as combined headquarters and social club proved of major importance to the insurgency and to the advancement of his own career. So did his possession of a wife who, rather surprisingly, swiftly adapted herself to her role as politician's helpmate.

Day after day, week after week, between twenty and thirty men gathered in the large library at 248 State Street at ten o'clock in the morning, marched from there in a body to the Capitol for the futile exercise of voting for U.S. Senator, and then (the legislature adjourned) dispersed to gather again at the Roosevelt home around five in the afternoon, remaining often until late at night. Eleanor spent the long evenings with them, learning much from their salty talk, so different from any she had heard before, and forming with them ties of mutual affection. Sometimes Terry, who wrote verse, brought his productions to read aloud to her. She understated the case when she said later that though the "rights and wrongs of that fight" meant little to her, she "probably contributed to its duration." Almost certainly she did so by helping make a pleasant social time out of what could otherwise have become an unbearable ordeal. Hers was the evening's closing gesture: ". . . I used to go into the pantry and bring out beer and cheese and crackers, which was a gentle hint that the time had come for everyone to eat, drink and go home." By then the library air would be blue and thick with cigar smoke. As a matter of fact the whole downstairs became soaked in the fumes of nicotine as the weeks passed. After a while the fumes seeped up the stairs and through air vents to such an extent that the Roosevelt children, in their nursery on the second floor, directly above the library, were being poisoned by them—or so their dismayed nurse asserted. The nursery had to be moved to the third floor.[22]

By March, when Sheehan at last gave up (Shepard had faded long before), nerves were frayed and tempers short in Albany. There was rising resentment against the insurgents on the part of many formerly sympathetic or neutral legislators. The excessively prolonged battle, requiring their continuous presence in the capital, worked financial hardship upon them. And this was true for most of the insurgents themselves. They grew restive. Roosevelt and Terry had to exert themselves to hold the group together while Roosevelt tried, with growing desperation, to gain Republican support for a suitable compromise candidate. Covert, complicated, and dubious maneuvers were engaged in.

Roosevelt had already tried to deal directly with Boss Barnes. The depth and strength of his economic Progressivism were indicated by his proposal to Barnes that the insurgents and Republicans agree upon some Democrat who was "conservative in regard to business interests and yet a man whose position can never be questioned by the radical element of society." Barnes said no. He then tried to deal with the Republicans through an intermediary, Francis Lynde Stetson—a strange choice for a Progressive to make. Stetson was a millionaire lawyer whose clients included J. P. Morgan and Thomas Fortune Ryan and whose Democracy was indistinguishable from the Republicanism of the old guard. One of Stetson's associates actually proposed that the insurgent group use its balance of power in the legislature to block New York State's ratification of the income tax amendment of the U.S. Constitution and to promote legislation favorable to business interests. Roosevelt refused any such commitment, which he could not have made on behalf of his colleagues in any case. Yet he seems to have turned to Stetson for advice when Mayor William J. Gaynor of New York City, after the announcement that a second Democratic caucus would be held March 27, proposed for the Senatorship a man whom Stetson's group was bound to oppose. The man was Samuel Untermyer. He had led a famous stockholders' revolt against the New York Life Insurance Company, had fought the shipbuilding trust, had engaged in many a battle in the public interest against Morgan interests, and was recognized by all as a brilliant lawyer and courageous man. Moreover, he was, if only nominally, a Tammany man and might therefore be accepted, however reluctantly, by Murphy. Yet Roosevelt, for reasons never satisfactorily explained, came out openly against him (the insurgents boycotted the March 27 caucus) and so made Untermyer's election impossible. The episode exposed Roosevelt and the other insurgents to the charge that they were mere tools of J. P. Morgan, with Stetson as Morgan's agent— that the whole of this alleged battle against bossism was in covert reality a struggle between rival New York City financial powers.[23]

The end came abruptly.

On the night of Wednesday, March 29, a fire (discovered by a newspaperman named Louis McHenry Howe) raged through the legislative chambers of the Capitol, forcing the legislature to meet the next day in Albany's City Hall and adding to the irritable impatience of legislators. On the morning of Thursday, March 30, newspapers carried Murphy's charge that the insurgency was a "plot" masterminded by Stetson; Roosevelt received a letter from Gaynor, enclosing a copy of one by Untermyer, wherein Murphy's charge was given support, with a threat to publish the Untermyer letter on Saturday unless a settlement was reached before then; and disaffection was spreading through insurgent ranks. Sometime during that day, Murphy proposed to Roosevelt, as compromise candidate for U.S. Senator, the name of State Supreme Court Justice Victor Dowling, and the insurgents, after considerable discussion, decided to accept it. But the next morning, Friday, March 31, as the insurgents gathered in the Roosevelt home to march in a body to the caucus, they were thrown into consternation by the news that Dowling had refused to accept nomination and that Murphy was substituting for his name the less acceptable one of Justice James Aloysius O'Gorman. Moreover, Murphy had already obtained, in the wee hours of that morning, the approval of this selection by Stetson!

O'Gorman, a former Grand Sachem of Tammany Hall, was a choice more pleasing to Murphy and to Tammanyites in general than ever

Sheehan had been. By sending O'Gorman to the Senate, Murphy would create a vacancy on the bench into which he could push his son-in-law, Dan Cohalan. Nor was it easy for opponents to find anything against O'Gorman, aside from his being indubitably a Tammany man; since going on the bench, he had stayed clear of politics and made, from all accounts, an excellent record. He was personally immensely popular with the Irish and highly respected by all who knew him.

The weary insurgents lost heart. Two of them left the Roosevelt home at once to attend the caucus. Those who remained in the library pondered a threat that Sheehan would win election after all if O'Gorman were denied; Boss Barnes was allegedly prepared now to join the Murphy forces with enough Republican votes to put over Blue-eyed Billy. They pondered a promise from Senator Wagner and Assemblyman Smith that if they now came to the caucus, they would be warmly welcomed back into the fold; there would be no reprisals. They pondered a message from Stetson in New York City saying that O'Gorman, in return for their vote, had promised to intercede for them with the Democratic regulars should the latter attempt reprisals. They pondered what seemed to Roosevelt the political necessity of their supporting an Irish Catholic (O'Gorman was one) for the Senatorship, in view of the charge that the insurgency was motivated by anti-Catholic and -Irish prejudice. Nevertheless, Roosevelt and ten others favored continuing the fight. The majority of the insurgents, however, had had enough. At a final conference in the Roosevelt house, late that afternoon, they gave in. Roosevelt was one of eleven who, though promising to vote for O'Gorman in the legislature, refused to go to the caucus. The other insurgents did so in a body, swelling the caucus attendance to precisely the 101 necessary to assure O'Gorman's election, no matter how Roosevelt and the others voted.[24]

Virtually every knowledgeable observer at the time, every reporter and editorial writer, was convinced that the insurgency, so bravely sustained for so long, had in the end suffered ignominious defeat at the hands of the wily Murphy. When Roosevelt and the ten other bitterenders entered the City Hall assembly room shortly after the caucus ended, they were greeted with a chorus of jeers and derisive laughter. Someone started to sing the Tammany victory song. Half the assemblage had happily joined in before the presiding officer could bring the session to order. Then the Republican minority leader, Edgar Brackett, in casual address, made sneering reference to Roosevelt, mentioning the "mysterious ways" in which God moves "His wonders to perform"— mentioning, too, the mountains that labor to bring forth mice. It required some hardihood for the young man to rise as he did from his seat, a little later, in an attempt to salvage whatever was left of dignity and respect. His words limped against a barrage of hisses and groans. "Two months ago a number of Democrats felt it was our duty to dissent . . . ," said he. "The Party had been restored to power after seventeen years of Republican misrule. We have followed the dictates of our consciences. . . . I believe that as a result the Democratic Party has taken an upward step. We are Democrats—not irregulars, but regulars. I take pleasure in casting my vote for the Hon. James A. O'Gorman." Thus did he contribute, on the sixty-fourth ballot, to O'Gorman's election victory over Depew by a vote of 112 to 80.

To reporters who interviewed him immediately afterward he put on a brave face. The initial purpose of the revolt had been the blocking of Sheehan, not the promotion of any other candidate. "The minority never assumed to dictate the choice of the majority." Once Sheehan was eliminated the whole aim of the insurgency had been the election of a "suitable man," and the "only credit" Murphy could now "claim in ending the . . . deadlock" was that he had finally named such a man. Had O'Gorman been put up in the first place there would have been no revolt, for "we all believe him to be a man of absolute independence" who "will truly represent the whole State." [25]

All the same, it was a nervous young politician who, as the legislature recessed for three weeks, rushed down to Hyde Park and Poughkeepsie to find out how his constituents viewed the outcome. He knew that while the battle raged, he had won rather than lost support among Republicans in his district, especially after Sheehan made the mistake of charging that the state senator was a tool of TR, carrying out TR's design to split the Democracy. He had had reason to believe that at the same time he was losing little Democratic support: Ed Perkins, despite his personal animosity toward Roosevelt, had responded with extreme caution to Sheehan's appeals for help, and a petition circulated by the Perkins group, calling upon Roosevelt to abide by the caucus result, had gained only a fraction of the number of signatures predicted for it. But if the end of the fight was regarded in the district as a Roosevelt capitulation, all was undone. Hence the young man's relief to learn that his constituency seemed pleased with the result and "did not feel that the victory belonged at all to Murphy." [26] Confidence flowed back into him. His public statements lost their defensive tone. He now boldly proclaimed victory for himself and fellow rebels—an unmitigated triumph of democracy and clean government over bossism and corruption.

And this was the view which ultimately prevailed throughout the general public, not only because Roosevelt so confidently reiterated it but also because it fitted perfectly into what most of the public wished to believe and later remembered of that year when a tide of Progressivism rose all across America toward the crest of 1912. After all, the Tammany tiger's tail *had* been twisted; Murphy had been taught that he could not run New York State as he was accustomed to running New York City; and the cause of direct election of U.S. Senators had been dramatized and advanced. Roosevelt himself emerged from the prolonged uproar famous in his home state and well known beyond its borders, a champion of Progressivism, his name sometimes linked in print with that of Woodrow Wilson—all this within six months after his formal entry into politics and before he had voted on a single bill!

IV

He continued to command far more public attention than any other first-term senator when the legislature reconvened in the first week of April. Among the items on the agenda was a resolution he had introduced as the term began, urging New York's Congressional delegation to support an amendment to the Constitution providing for direct popular election of U.S. Senators. (The Seventeenth Amendment, making this provision, would become effective May 31, 1913.) The resolution was now brought up for action, and Roosevelt led a successful fight for its adoption, 28 to 15, after five hours of debate. Four days later the Assembly adopted it. Next, he challenged Tammany on a bill to reorganize the State Highway Commission. The Murphy-sponsored bill was, he truthfully charged, a disgraceful hodgepodge of ineptitudes designed to encourage wholesale graft and corruption, and though it finally passed the Senate by a one-vote margin, young Roosevelt was singled out for editorial praise by the New York *Times* after garnering much favorable publicity in papers all over the state. He then joined and took a leading part in the fight for the direct primary. Machine politicians, Republican and Democratic alike, opposed this measure with a bitterness that would seem strange in future years, after repeated demonstrations of how easily organized politicians could control most primary results. Roosevelt seems to have had fewer illusions about the device than they did. He doubted that any high percentage of voters would participate in nominating elections; voter apathy would probably enable organizations to name their men almost as easily as before. On the other hand, the publicity attending primary contests would arouse public interest and *tend* to stimulate more popular participation in the choosing of representatives. So Roosevelt fought hard to obtain a good primary bill, voted for a poor one when the alternative was none at all, and prepared to join Progressive Republicans the next year in an effort to obtain an improved law.

Positive contributions were made by him through his chairmanship of the Senate's Forest, Fish and Game Committee. To the conservation of natural resources he was, and would forever remain, wholeheartedly committed. He called for advice from Gifford Pinchot. With Pinchot's help he initiated a revision and systematization of the state's fish and game laws and did what he could to promote forest conservation and protection against fire. He was all for the conservation of "moral" values, too, as defined by a majority of his rural constituency. With regard to Sunday baseball, liquor prohibition, legalized prizefighting, legalized horse racing he discovered in himself, and expressed in vote and statement, a degree of puritanism theretofore unsuspected, though consistent with his general opposition to "sinful" Tammany. He thereby further confirmed a public image of himself as the kind of Progressive most pleasing to prosperous farmers and small-town business and professional men—a clean-cut young man who stood for high ideals of personal conduct, as well as for honesty, justice, and efficiency in government.

He tarnished this image somewhat in the closing days of the 1911 session, after he had returned from his vacation on Campobello. A new charter had been proposed for New York City, supported both by Tammany and reform Mayor Gaynor. Roosevelt listened to the advice of his Harvard classmate Albert De Roode,* counsel for the Civil Service Reform Association, who with his organization opposed the charter on the ground that it would weaken the civil service, reduce the independent Democratic vote in the city, and strengthen Tammany's hold on state party conventions. Roosevelt then came out against the charter, though (having learned something of the practical limits of insurgency) he indicated a willingness to compromise and the forms such compromise might take. On this issue, however, Tammany was in no compromising mood; it countered with a threat, privately made, to reapportion Congressional districts in such a way as to put Dutchess County into a district so overwhelmingly Republican that no Democratic Congressman could be elected in it. This meant that Representative Dick Connell, to whom Roosevelt felt some personal obligation, would be denied all chance of reelection while Roosevelt himself suffered angry reprisals from Ed Perkins and the regular Democratic organization of Poughkeepsie. So he flatly reversed himself. He now announced that he

* See page 147. One provision of the proposed charter was that women teachers in public schools receive equal pay with men. Roosevelt was opposed to this.

favored the charter. The reapportionment committee simultaneously reported a district inclusive of Dutchess that was reasonably favorable to
Democrats. But then Roosevelt's own Progressive supporters, quick to
see the effect of Tammany threat-and-bribe, expressed anger at this
weak yielding by their champion. They denounced him so vehemently
that he again reversed himself: he switched back to his earlier opposition to the charter, whereupon the reapportionment committee also
changed its mind and reported out the hopelessly Republican district inclusive of Dutchess which had been earlier threatened. Embarrassed,
the young senator loudly denied that there was any connection whatever between his vacillation and these redistricting maneuvers. No one
was fooled. The upshot was that Roosevelt lost on both counts: the unsatisfactory New York City charter was finally adopted; the unfavorable redistricting went through.

Thus the 1911 session ended for him on a somewhat sour note,
though one that, after it ceased to waver, came into harmony with the
main theme of his politics. A few weeks later he was jarred and sobered
by the fate that befell most of his fellow insurgents in the Assembly elections. Of the two dozen rebel assemblymen who had used his home as
headquarters from January through March, only fourteen won renomination from their party, despite the promise of no reprisals; only four of
these fourteen won election at the polls. The party as a whole fared
badly with the New York electorate that year, losing thirty-seven Assembly seats and, with them, control of the lower chamber. When the
legislature met again in January, 1912, Republicans outnumbered Democrats 98 to 48 in the Assembly. But the percentage loss among insurgents was far higher than that among Democratic regulars, and the latter bitterly and publicly blamed the former for the swift reversal of party
fortunes.

In private, Roosevelt may well have had a queasy feeling that there
was at least a modicum of truth in what his critics said. In public, he
proclaimed that what had happened at the polls was not a Democratic
defeat but a Progressive triumph over machine politics in *both* parties.
"The good work has begun and it gathers momentum each succeeding
week," he said, naming Democratic chieftains who had "gone out on the
toe of a boot" or were "hanging on by the skin of . . . [their] teeth," but
naming, too, "Lou Payn and Odell, on the Hudson River," who were
"losing their grip on the Republican machines." The boss as type was
doomed. "Murphy and his kind must, like the noxious weed, be plucked
out, root and branch," he went on. "From the ruins of the political machines we will construct something more nearly conforming to a democratic conception of government." He made reference by name to Pat-

rick E. McCabe, clerk of the Senate, who would "be succeeded in the spring by a young Democrat who can defeat the Republican machine of Boss Bárnes." [27]

McCabe, stung, made acid reply. Roosevelt's speech was positively "bristling with the silly conceits of a political prig," said he. "Disloyalty and Party treachery is the political cult of a few snobs in our party who attain prominence through the exigencies of a turn-over in the politics of the State and who are simply political accidents. . . . Mr. Roosevelt admits he is the best-informed man in the Party in this State on obsolete and remote questions of government. . . . All this by contrast with my humble equipment . . . as my leadership in Albany depends absolutely upon human sympathy, human interest, and human ties among those with whom I was born and bred. . . ." McCabe blamed the "vigorous men of the Party" for "this embarrassing situation." They had "humored and coddled too much the . . . fops and cads who come as near being political leaders as a green pea does a circus tent." Other leaders of the party might stand "for the impudence and arrogance of these political prudes, but I won't." [28]

V

There is reason to believe that such words as McCabe's, echoed by many a Democratic regular, stung Roosevelt as sharply as ever his words stung the bosses, though he gave no immediate sign of it. He who had an actor's sensitivity to audience reaction could not but sense his unpopularity among his fellow legislators and that the coolness toward him was more a reaction to his personality than to his politics. He who had a natural politician's desire and need to be liked could not but be disturbed by the irritating effect he was evidently producing on others. And he whose ambition soared so high, recognizing personal relations as a prime ingredient of his success, could not but examine himself in the harsh light of this hostile criticism and strive to mend such flaws as it revealed to him.

He might expect and explain away the dislike of him by old-fashioned organization men who fattened on graft. They were accustomed to a politics of picnics and balls, with free beer and whiskey and cigars and a wide distribution of poultry among slum constituents at Christmastime.* They had no principles, no ideals. They would never understand

* For many years, Big Tim Sullivan gave away 2,000 pairs of shoes every year on his mother's birthday.

him, and he certainly made no effort, during his first political year, to obtain their goodwill. He seemed, in fact, to go out of his way to antagonize them. Thus, on a June day in 1911, when a bill he favored (it appropriated money for forest fire protection) was blocked in committee by Tammany men, he in a speech on the Senate floor, branded the act a criminal neglect of the public interest, made dire predictions of conflagrations raging through rich timberland, and pointed a dramatic finger at Senator Hugh Frawley as "one of the men responsible for this situation." Small wonder that Frawley loathed him—so much so that when Roosevelt boasted (inaccurately) of his boxing prowess, Frawley, a skilled amateur boxer, offered to meet him any time "in a pulpit or a rat pit" or anywhere else.[29] On another occasion that June, when voting for three Tammany appointments to high-paying political jobs, he took pains to explain that his vote was not spoilsmanship of the kind practiced by Senator Grady. "Senator Grady belongs to the old school of politics," he declared. ". . . I, on the contrary, am of the new school of politics which is assuming control of both parties." Small wonder that the alcoholic Grady loathed him. On yet another occasion he was involved in a verbal altercation with Sullivan, a man notable for personal warmth and kindness. Sullivan, while he did not actively loathe him, did say with strong distaste after clashing with the young man, "Awful arrogant fellow, that Roosevelt." [30]

But if he could defend his ego against such acid judgments by considering their contemptible source, the case was different with Al Smith and Bob Wagner. Both of them found Roosevelt insufferable and freely said so in private. Wagner, as presiding officer of the Senate, sometimes showed his feeling in public. "Senator Roosevelt has gained his point," said he with cold fury after Roosevelt had pointed his accusing finger at Frawley. "What he wants is a headline in the newspapers. Let us proceed to our business." Yet it was impossible for anyone to regard these two young men as contemptible corruptionists, devoid of decency or high intelligence. They represented what a Republican once described to Roosevelt, using them for examples, as "a new spirit in Tammany Hall," one by no means unconcerned with the general good. Indeed, Smith and Wagner demonstrated an informed interest, a grasp of public issues and of the techniques and resources of state government that exceeded Roosevelt's own. They could and did teach him far more in 1911 than he could teach them.

The case was different, too, with a slender, attractive bright-eyed girl named Frances Perkins who was in Albany that year as a representative of the National Consumers' League, having become a fervent convert of the social justice movement. She and Roosevelt had similar class and educational backgrounds (a Mount Holyoke graduate, she had just completed work for a master's degree at Columbia*), though she was far better informed than he in economics, sociology, political theory, and far abler than he to see the particular in terms of the general in the public affairs of that year. The two had moved in the same social circles in New York City (she first saw him at a tea dance in a private home in Gramercy Park), where he had impressed her as "just an ordinary, respectable, intelligent, correct young man" like "innumerable" others she knew "who had been educated in private schools and had gone to Harvard"—the kind of well-bred privileged youth for whom she had developed a certain contempt, measured by the challenges that had come to her through settlement house work. (She condemned such privilege for its cost in mass misery and exploitation; she blamed its possessors for being in general so soft, bland, and banal, unworthy and unaware.) Her opinion of young Roosevelt had not improved as she watched him operate in the Senate. She, too, was irritated by his "artificially serious" face, his small mouth that seldom smiled in public, his superior manner, his "habit of throwing his head back" and "looking down his nose." She was sure "he really didn't like people very much" and, in his "lack of humility," was deaf "to the hopes, fears, and aspirations which are the common lot." [31] The battle he had waged with Tammany over the U.S. Senatorship had made him no hero in her eyes. Such a battle seemed to her precisely the kind of heroics you might expect his kind to delight in, a spectacular sideshow accomplishing nothing of real importance but giving him abundant opportunity to reveal his moral and intellectual superiority while gaining for him an immense and favorable publicity.

With regard to truly substantive matters of social reform she and several others found him less knowledgeable and less interested than many a Tammany man to whom "reform" was a hateful word.

For instance, there was a ghastly fire in the top three floors of a ten-story building on Washington Place in New York City on March 25,

---

* She also studied under Simon N. Patten of the Wharton School at the University of Pennsylvania who argued in such influential books as *The Theory of Prosperity* (1902) and *The New Basis of Civilization* (1907) that Western society had passed from a "deficit" to a "surplus" civilization as a consequence of technological advances and that all that was necessary to achieve an economy of abundance for everyone was replacement of fighting individualism with a harmonization of interests through benevolent government planning. Especially needed was a radical reform of distributive economics. Patten regarded competitive struggle as destructive rather than invigorating of men and nations and had no use for the Social Darwinism, so popular among wealthy conservatives, whereby the possession of wealth was deemed *prima facie* evidence of an innate personal superiority, a "survival of the fittest." There were no general hereditary differences between rich and poor, he asserted, and this would be proved when scientific and engineering processes were properly applied to the economy. "Abolish poverty, transform deficit into surplus, fill depletion with energy, and the ascribed heredity of the poor will disappear with its causes," said he.

1911, as the long noisy struggle over the U.S. Senatorship was drawing to a close in the legislature. The three floors were occupied by the Triangle Waist Company; 148 of the company's employees, all but 15 of them girls and young women between the ages of sixteen and thirty-five, perished. Shock and horror swept city and state when it was revealed that the loss of life was less attributable to a deficiency of fire prevention and escape facilities, though these were gravely deficient, than to the company's practice of virtually imprisoning its employees during the long workday, locking them into a ninth-floor workroom and providing a single unlocked exit where they could be inspected when they left, to make sure they stole nothing. They could not escape downstairs through the single hall exit because the eighth floor, where the fire had begun, was a raging inferno. They could not escape to the tenth floor and then over the roof to a neighboring building, as employees on that floor had done, because the single up stairway was barred by a locked iron gate. They could not escape through windows because no fire escapes were there; some 40 of them jumped or were pushed from the window ledge to their deaths on the sidewalk 110 feet below. Rose Schneiderman of the Women's Trade Union League (she and the league would have strong influence upon Eleanor Roosevelt a decade hence) stated the case with bitter succinctness at a mass meeting held in Carnegie Hall in early April. "The life of men and women is so cheap and property is so sacred," she said, "there are so many of us for one job, it matters little if one hundred and forty-three [sic] of us are burned to death." [32] Nor could the company, under existing legislation, be penalized in courts of law; the owners and management were not even liable for damages. On all this, Franklin Roosevelt made no recorded comment, not even in private correspondence, and he took no initial part in the legislative furor which the tragedy soon produced.

Bob Wagner and Al Smith, on the other hand, were very much a part of that furor. They led in the establishment by the legislature of a Factory Investigating Commission consisting of two senators, three assemblymen, and four private citizens. Both of them served as members of that commission, which hired Frances Perkins as a principal investigator. In the following months Frances Perkins made sure that they saw with their own shocked eyes the horrors of an unregulated factory system—the children of five and six and seven shelling peas and snipping beans through long workdays in canneries; hollow-eyed men and women being literally worked to death for starvation wages, old at forty; the atrocious conditions of light and air and sanitation in which they were forced to labor; the tiny exits and flimsy or nonexistent fire escapes which made firetraps of numerous dirty factories; the unshielded wheels and belts of high-speed machinery which maimed and killed workers by the score every year.* They helped draft and then fought for passage by the legislature of no fewer than thirty-two bills designed to correct evils the commission had exposed—bills which, when enacted, made New York State a pioneer in social welfare legislation in America, a model for other states and for the federal government.

Not only did Franklin Roosevelt have no part in initiating this Progressive labor legislation, but he refused in 1911 to commit himself to bills already proposed to limit the workweek to fifty-four hours for boys between the ages of sixteen and twenty-one, to limit and regulate child labor in canneries, and to establish a fifty-four-hour week for women— the latter being the bill which the Consumers' League was sponsoring and which Frances Perkins had come to Albany to promote. It was not that such proposals were inconsistent with his personal attitude toward labor. They were, on the contrary, perfectly consistent with that attitude, which was one of benevolent paternalism. (He favored doing things *for* workers—he genuinely wished to improve their lot—but he was inclined to look askance at their own organization to force concessions from employers. He was, for example, strongly opposed to legalizing the boycott as an instrument of coercion by unions in labor disputes, yet took for granted the use of police or militia to enforce injunctions against strikers.[33]) What made him noncommittal was his awareness that the proposed bills were not popular with the farmers of his district.

There was, however, a significant shift in his approach to these matters and in his general personal attitude and manner toward his colleagues and the world of politics between the 1911 and 1912 sessions of the legislature.

In 1911 he had been noncommittal even on woman's suffrage. One would have assumed that his stand on this issue would be automatically and unequivocally affirmative; it was in line with his opposition to bossism, his wish to cleanse and purify government, his stated determination to increase popular participation in the political process. Instead, he angered the ardent suffragettes of Vassar in Poughkeepsie by saying that while personally "not opposed to female suffrage," he thought it "a very great question whether the people of the State as a whole want it or not" and that, therefore, the legislature should provide for a statewide referendum on the matter before a state constitutional amendment was submitted to the voters.[34]

---

* Some of "the vilest and most uncivilized conditions of labor in the State" were reportedly found in the Auburn factory of the Progressive Democratic leader, Thomas Mott Osborne.

But in 1912 he came out flatly for the women's suffrage amendment. He also, in 1912, came out flatly for labor bills he had shied away from the year before. Indeed, he is said to have been instrumental in obtaining passage through the Senate by a one-vote margin of the fifty-four-hour bill for women. He reportedly held the floor with a talk on birds until a supporter who had left the chamber to board the night boat for New York City could be brought back. When a Republican protested the irrelevance of his remarks, he is said to have replied that he strove "to prove that Nature demands shorter hours." But Frances Perkins, the person most intimately concerned with the bill, later remembered nothing of this, as she almost certainly would have done had the incident actually occurred. She remembered only that Big Tim Sullivan, of all people, was the savior of the bill. It was he who "came puffing up the hill after being pulled off the . . . boat" to cast the deciding vote. ("I seen me sister go to work when she was only fourteen," explained Big Tim to Frances Perkins, "and I know we ought to help these gals . . . to prevent 'em from being broken down while they're still young.") Roosevelt, she recalled, "did not associate himself actively with this bill. . . . I remember it clearly because I took it hard that a young man who had so much spirit did not do as well in this, which I thought a test, as did Tim Sullivan . . . [who was] undoubtedly corrupt. . . ."[35]

Roosevelt did actively support a workmen's compensation bill. He also personally investigated the work hazards of Adirondack iron mines and strove to establish improved safety standards for them. He later, at a legislative hearing, gave strong testimony in favor of the complete package of thirty-two bills which the Factory Investigating Commission proposed.

Another substantive matter on which he made a significant shift was that of public power. He had taken no active part in the battle over a proposal, put forward by private power interests during his first term, to permit the flooding of state forest preserves. A counterproposal reserved to the state exclusively the right to flood state land and provided that franchises, which might be granted private interests for fifty-year periods, must be paid for on a sliding scale and be accompanied by state-agency review of power rates every ten years. Roosevelt had merely voted for this countermeasure, which, supported by Tammany as well as by Progressives, was enacted. But in the 1912 session he was a strong advocate of a bill to permit the state to build and operate hydroelectric facilities, a bill which passed the Senate only to be lost in the now-Republican-dominated Assembly.

And as regards forest conservation itself, he went much farther in the direction of state regulation and positive action in 1912 than he had the year before. At the opening of the session he introduced a bill of radical import that went to the very root of questions on the proper relationship, in a modern democratic society, between private property and the public interest, between private enterprise and government activity. His bill, obviously influenced by Gifford Pinchot and by Charles Van Hise's *The Conservation of Natural Resources in the United States* (1911), provided not only for state inspection of private forests on watersheds, but also for compulsory reforestation of denuded watershed lands, the planting to be done according to state specifications at the owner's expense. The bill also provided for state regulation of the timber harvest—the time and manner of cutting—to ensure permanent cover and sustained yield. After public hearings in which private lumber interests proved more influential with lawmakers than did conservationists, the bill was drastically revised, its compulsory features being largely removed, and was then passed by both chambers and signed into law.

VI

It was through his deepening and widening concern with conservation that Roosevelt was led, early in 1912, to make what was for him a virtually unprecedented intellectual effort. He struggled to shape a general philosophy of economics and politics and government whereby he might deal, in a connected, organized fashion, with the central historical problems of his age. The occasion was an address to a People's Forum in Troy, New York, on March 3, 1912.[36]

His main argument began with confused echoes of Hegel and Marx.

"Conditions of civilization that come with individual freedom are inevitably bound to bring up many questions that mere individual liberty cannot solve," he said. "This to my mind is exactly what has happened in the past century." There had arisen "new sets of conditions of life" that required "for their solution" what he called a "new theory"—a theory which he rather curiously defined as a "struggle." "I have called this new theory the struggle for the liberty of the community rather than liberty of the individual. . . . Every new star that people have hitched their wagon to for the past half-century, whether it be anti-rebating, or anti-trusts, or new-fashioned education, or conservation of our natural resources, or State regulation of common carriers, or commission government, or any of the thousand and one other things that we have run after of late, almost without exception come under the same heading. They are all steps in the evolution of the new theory of the liberty of the community."

He blundered on into dangerous ground, saying that the "right of any one individual to work or not as he sees fit, to live to a great extent where and how he sees fit is not sufficient," his meaning in context being, evidently, that this "right" was no longer wholly operative. But he quickly recovered himself by putting it "another way," which was that "competition has been shown to be useful up to a certain point and no further. Cooperation must begin where competition leaves off and cooperation is as good a word for the new theory as any other."

He illustrated his thesis by reference to forest conservation. "One hundred and fifty years ago in Germany the individual was not restricted from denuding his lands of the growing trees," he said. "Today he must cut only in a manner scientifically worked out, which is calculated to serve the ends of the community and not his ends. They passed beyond the liberty of the individual to do as he pleased with his own property and found it was necessary to check this liberty for the benefit of the freedom of the whole people." The same necessity was evident in agriculture. "The two [forest production and food production] go hand in hand, so much so that if we can prophesy today that the State [in other words, the people as a whole] will shortly tell a man how many trees he must cut, then why can we not, without being called radical, predict that the State will compel every farmer to till his own land or raise beef or horses? After all, if I own a farm of a hundred acres and let it lie waste and overgrown, I am just as much a destroyer of the liberty of the community—and by liberty we mean happiness and prosperity— as is the strong man who stands idle on the corner, refusing to work, a destroyer of his neighbor's happiness, prosperity and liberty."

He tried, if only by flat assertion, to resolve the trust problem, and those of capital vs. labor, in terms of "cooperation" or "liberty of the community." Said he: "There is no such thing as a struggle between labor and capital. Not only is there no struggle, but there is and has always been the heartiest cooperation for neither can capital exist without the cooperation of labor, nor labor without the cooperation of capital." He said, too, in clear echo of Theodore Roosevelt: "The mere size of a trust is not of necessity its evil. A trust is evil if it monopolized [sic] for the benefit of a few and contrary to the interests of the community. Just as long as trusts do this is it necessary for the community to change this feature of them."

In all of which a retrospective vision can see, as in Croly's and TR's New Nationalism, grave dangers—a nascent totalitarianism, an implied corporate state—unless strongly qualified and modified (as actually it was in the developing Franklin Roosevelt) by a Jeffersonian emphasis on the sacredness of the individual person and of personal liberty.

*   *   *

He was learning, swiftly.

He was also growing as a person, breaking more and more out of the aristocratic mold into which his innately shy temperament had been cast during his most plastic years. And perhaps the most important thing he learned was that every categorical judgment of a human being or human institution is bound to be more or less wrong since it always leaves something out of account, often something vital to any adequate understanding. This is because no man or organization is all of a piece or altogether two-dimensional. Each has several dimensions, including that of living time, and each is in substance a various mixture, full of inconsistencies. Hence none is wholly visible from any one point of view or wholly measurable by any single standard. The part of wisdom in one's approach to human beings and human problems, therefore, is, as Roosevelt was learning, to fuse intuition and sympathy with logic and objective information, abjuring rigidities, maintaining always a degree of tentativeness in one's conclusions and a flexibility of total response.

Thus Roosevelt, in his thirtieth year, unbeknown to Frances Perkins at the time, began to comprehend and act upon what Pat McCabe had tried to say when he made invidious comparison between Roosevelt's alleged knowledge of "remote questions of government" and McCabe's own "human sympathy, human interest, and human ties." Tim Sullivan impressed this lesson upon him. Big Tim was as grossly corrupt in his private as in his public life. He had abandoned (though providing financially for) his wife, had fathered at least two illegitimate children, had contracted what then was euphemistically called a "social disease," and would a few months hence be confined to a mental institution, suffering from paresis.* [37] Yet Big Tim was also a warmly sympathetic human being whose feeling for the despised and rejected and exploited, of whom in his boyhood he had been one, was deep and sincere. It exceeded Roosevelt's own by far, as the young man dimly recognized even in that year and came vividly to acknowledge in the years that followed. Decades later, when Roosevelt was in the White House, Frances Perkins brought to him one day a problem of immigration policy on which she had strong views. She expressed them. He listened to her, then recalled for her something the old-time Bowery politician had said in 1912 about "people who had come over in steerage and who knew in their own hearts and lives the difference between being despised and being accepted and liked." There was a touch of sadness in his smile as he

---

* Hopelessly insane, he escaped from the mental institution one night in late August, 1913, stumbled onto some New Haven railroad tracks, and was there killed by a freight train. His mangled body lay in the public morgue for thirteen days before it was identified, and then by accident, though he had long been one of the best-known men in New York City.

added: "Poor old Tim Sullivan never understood about modern politics, but he was right about the human heart."

And the mature man who made this judgment of Sullivan would also pass judgment on himself as he had been in 1911. "You know," he said to Frances Perkins, with a wry grin, "I was an awfully mean cuss when I first went into politics." [38]

Ten

→>>⋘←

From Albany to Washington, 1912-13

I

FRANKLIN ROOSEVELT first met Woodrow Wilson personally in the autumn of 1911, a few weeks after the New York Assembly election and at the end of a year during which Wilson, having mastered his state's Democratic organization, had pushed through his state's legislature a spectacular series of reform measures. A corrupt practices law, an employer's liability law, a primary and direct election law, a law establishing a strong public utilities commission with rate-setting powers—all these, after having been agitated in vain for decades, were placed on New Jersey's statute books within four months after the governor's inauguration. In consequence, Wilson's position as front-runner for the next Democratic Presidential nomination was further advanced, and Roosevelt was but one of a great many ambitious Democrats who made pilgrimage to Trenton as 1911 drew toward a close. The two men talked first in the governor's office. Then, late in the afternoon, they with Wilson's personal secretary—an ebullient, impulsive, devoted Irishman named Joseph Tumulty—boarded a Pennsylvania railroad train and rode together through the ten miles or so separating Trenton's depot from that of Princeton Junction.* [1]

For young Roosevelt, the occasion was memorable. Seated opposite him in the railway carriage he saw a slender, rigidly upright figure topped by an austere ascetic countenance whose forehead was high and broad, whose gray-blue eyes looked out with cold directness through rimless pince-nez glasses, whose cheeks were thin and mouth stern and jaw excessively long and stubborn—in appearance the very type of ecclesiastical or academic intellectual. None looking at Woodrow Wilson without prior knowledge of him would think him likely to seek elective

---

* Wilson as governor continued to make his home, with his family, in Princeton.

office: he appeared to have the kind of aloof personal pride that would preclude his exposing himself to the critical gaze of a crowd of semiliterate strangers. Nor did this appearance wholly bely reality. Franklin Roosevelt could sense during their first talk together that Wilson did not easily give of himself or permit others to approach him closely. He was notably reserved; in this as in virtually every other essential respect he was as different from TR as one man can be from another. He had strong emotions. His, indeed, was a nature of imperious passions. But his emotions inclined toward the abstract, he was in general concerned more with ideas than personalities (it would be truly said of him that he loved mankind but liked few men), and consistent with this was the fact that though he had a rare persuasive power over men in crowds, he had relatively little over individuals in private conversation. The few objects of his affection (Tumulty was one of them that year) ran risk of being overwhelmed by the emotional demands he made upon them, especially his demand for absolute and unquestioning *personal* loyalty. This was a serious disability in a politician, who must necessarily regard every political associate as potentially expendable. It constituted a grave hazard for a public administrator, who must not permit personal loyalties to be placed above commitments to the public good. All the more remarkable, therefore, had been Wilson's demonstration of both political adroitness and administrative talent during the immediately preceding months. He was evidently far better equipped to be President of the United States than most who had occupied the office.

The obstacles that had to be overcome before that prize could be won, however, were certainly not fewer than they had been the year before. It was of these that the three men talked as their train rolled through the gathering dusk. Chiefly they spoke of the New York situation. Wilson wanted to know how many of New York's delegates he could count upon for support in the 1912 National Convention, which was to open in Baltimore late in the following June. He could count on none, Roosevelt had to say—not as things then stood. About a third of the Empire State's ninety delegates would be personally in favor of Wilson, the young man estimated, but the delegation would operate under the unit rule, the majority would be dominated by Tammany, and Tammany with Boss Murphy was understandably hostile to Wilson.[2] Conceivably, however, the situation could be changed during the next few months—and Roosevelt was firmly committed to an effort to change it by the time Wilson and Tumulty left the train.

But things did not go well for Wilson in New York during the weeks and months that followed. In early 1912 Roosevelt doubted that Wilson could win the nomination or that he himself could win reelection—so much so that he seriously considered not running again. The breach in the ranks of New York Republicanism which had been such a boon to upstate Democrats in 1910 was being closed and was not likely to recur unless there was a complete national split in the Republican Party. The New York Democracy, on the other hand, was now sharply divided between Murphy and anti-Murphy forces, with the former seemingly gaining in strength. The original Wall Street backers of Wilson, led by Colonel Harvey, had been increasingly alienated by the governor's Progressivism and were now conniving with Tammany to stop Wilson. In early January they published through their principal organ, the New York *Sun,* a letter Wilson had ill-advisedly written a Princeton University trustee in 1907, when the latter, a railroad president, made a speech attacking Bryan's proposal to nationalize the railroads. "I have read . . . [your speech] with relish and entire agreement," Wilson had then written and now read, to his dismay, in the newspapers. "Would that we could do something at once dignified and effective to knock Mr. Bryan once and for all into a cocked hat." Nonetheless, this tactic backfired. At a Jackson Day dinner, in Raleigh, North Carolina, arranged by Josephus Daniels, editor-publisher of the Raleigh *News and Observer,* Wilson with a remarkably eloquent and moving toast to Bryan, who was present, won his audience and the Great Commoner completely. He aroused far more audience enthusiasm than any of the other speakers, including Speaker of the House Champ Clark and Bryan himself.[3] Yet Bryan continued to refuse endorsement of Wilson's or any other candidacy. He held his political power in reserve for use in Baltimore, where his voice might well be decisive or, if the convention became hopelessly deadlocked, he might even win his fourth Presidential nomination.

Nor were Wilson's chances improved by April 12, when the Democratic State Convention met in New York City. Roosevelt arranged a dinner for Wilson supporters to be held in the Hotel Belmont the evening before the convention opened. He issued invitations by the dozen to upstate Democrats who were coming as convention delegates. Most recipients made no reply whatever, and of the twenty who did reply only three accepted. As for the convention itself, Murphy dominated it completely. A slate of ninety uninstructed delegates to the national convention was chosen, a decisive majority of them Murphy men, and Roosevelt was pointedly excluded from it, either as delegate or alternate.[4]

Nevertheless, he continued his efforts on Wilson's behalf. He took a month's vacation immediately following the convention. With his brother-in-law Hall Roosevelt, who was engaged to be married in June to Margaret Richardson of Boston, and with State Senator J. Mayhew Wainwright, a Republican friend, he sailed first to Jamaica and then to

Panama, where he saw the Panama Canal nearing completion and was enormously impressed by it.[5] But before he left New York, he joined with Thomas Mott Osborne and eighty-seven others, including the elder Henry Morgenthau, in a call for a "New York State Wilson Conference." A proclamation was issued asserting that the "true sentiment" of the State's Democratic Party could not be expressed "at the National Convention in Baltimore" under the unit rule and that this "sentiment" favored the Presidential nomination of Woodrow Wilson. "We, the undersigned," it went on, "call upon our fellow Democrats of New York who favor the progressive policies and the candidacy of Governor Wilson, to join in a CONFERENCE to be held in New York City, at a date to be fixed hereafter, for the purpose of appointing a Committee of representative Democrats who may appear on its behalf at the National Convention . . . ; there to cooperate with the friends of Governor Wilson upon the New York delegation in giving emphatic utterance to what we believe to be the true . . . desire of the New York Democracy." When he returned to New York in mid-May Roosevelt joined vigorously in the Wilson movement, working in New York City with William Gibbs McAdoo, Dudley Field Malone, and, somewhat surprisingly, Senator O'Gorman, whose conversion to Wilson had been confirmed at the Jackson Day dinner in Raleigh and whose defiant independence of Tammany now went far beyond any Roosevelt would have predicted.* Upstate he worked with Osborne, who became a principal source of funds whereby the Wilson Conference, of whose executive committee Roosevelt became chairman, carried out its proselytizing and propagandizing activities. To handle the latter he hired Louis McHenry Howe, Albany correspondent of the New York *Herald,* whose skill and industry impressed him and whose sardonic wit pleased him.[6]

It cannot be said that these preconvention activities of his were of any ultimate decisive importance. Roosevelt had good reason to continue to be pessimistic about his candidate's chances as spring gave way to summer. For one thing, all through the first half of 1912, Wilson was the target of a highly effective barrage laid down by William Randolph Hearst through Hearst's battery of sensational, mass-circulating newspapers. Hearst inflamed class and ethnic group passions against "Professor" Wilson, being abundantly supplied with ammunition for this operation by Wilson's own published words, notably the fifth volume of the *History of the American People.* One of Hearst's anti-Wilson allies, George Fred Williams, former leader of Populism in Massachusetts, summed up

---

* Malone was O'Gorman's son-in-law. O'Gorman had been toastmaster at the Raleigh affair.

the case with forceful eloquence, quoting extensively from this unhappy volume to prove fairly conclusively that Wilson's *magnum opus* was no objective history but "Toryism of the blackest type." It proclaimed an "admiration for everything which the radical democracy now seeks to change," it was studded with "sneers and insults to every class of men who have sought to alleviate the injustices of capitalism," it was wholly devoid "of sympathy for any suffering and protesting class," and it betrayed in general "a profound contempt for the Farmers' Alliance, the Populists, greenbackers, bi-metallists, trades unionists, small office seekers, Italians, Poles, Hungarians, pensioners, strikers, armies of unemployed." [7] This had undoubtedly hurt Wilson in state conventions and Presidential primaries across the country, in rural as in urban areas, while strengthening the Tammany-spearheaded animosity toward him in New York.

And Wilson had in fact done poorly in the race for instructed delegates. He would enter the convention with only 248 pledged votes as against 436 for his principal rival, Champ Clark. The latter had to gain only 109 votes to achieve a convention majority—and not since 1844 had a Democratic convention, operating under the two-thirds rule, failed to nominate the man who first gained a majority. Hence the seemingly crucial importance of Boss Murphy, who retained firm control of New York's 90 uninstructed votes despite the work of McAdoo, Osborne, O'Gorman, Roosevelt *et al.*

Then came the split in national Republicanism which Franklin Roosevelt had not really believed would occur but which, in his opinion, brightened somewhat the outlook for Wilson.

All through 1911 the quarrel between Cousin Theodore and President Taft had become increasingly personal and bitter. It was not without its ironies. For instance, Progressive TR was outraged by Old Guard Taft when the latter's administration, in late October, filed an antitrust suit against U.S. Steel, specifically citing that corporation's acquisition of Tennessee Coal and Iron in 1907 as a violation of the Sherman Act. TR, obviously uneasy about the permissive role he had played in that matter, took Taft's action as a personal affront. The final break came in February, 1912, when the President publicly denounced proponents of the New Nationalism as "political emotionalists" and "neurotics" who sought "to pull down the pillars of the temple of freedom and representative government." What rendered this unforgivable, in TR's view, was the fact that a campaign of loud whispers was then spreading abroad the allegation that TR had suffered a mental breakdown and was sliding into hopeless insanity. TR fumed for a few days. Then he announced that he himself was definitely a candidate for the Republican nomination for President. "My hat is in the ring," he said.[8]

There was no possibility of compromise between the two men when the Republican National Convention met in Chicago June 18-22, nor was there any possibility that TR could be nominated by that convention. He was the undoubted choice of his party's rank and file—the Presidential primaries had indicated as much—but Taft had the support of party bosses, and his forces were in control of both the machinery of the convention and a clear majority of the delegates. When TR realized this fact, he dramatically withdrew from the party organization (". . . we stand at Armageddon and we battle for the Lord!" he had cried before a huge mass meeting on the eve of the convention's opening), instructed his delegates to take no further part in convention work, and then, on Saturday night, June 22, 1912, in Chicago's Orchestra Hall, launched with his wildly excited supporters a third major party, the Progressive Party, laying plans for its formal convention in early August. Again proclaiming himself "strong as a Bull Moose," he would be the new party's Presidential candidate.

This was good news for Democrats. The overwhelming probability was that whoever the Democrats nominated in Baltimore would win election. The probability would become virtual certainty, in Franklin Roosevelt's opinion, if the convention nominated a strong Progressive (otherwise, he said, TR would "cut into the Democratic Progressive vote")—and obviously the strongest Progressive Democrat, despite his left-wing detractors, was Woodrow Wilson. Hence Roosevelt departed for the convention city in late June with his hopes for Wilson somewhat enhanced.

Eleanor Roosevelt accompanied her husband to Baltimore, leaving the children with his mother at Hyde Park. The couple took a house in the convention city, sharing it and its expenses with two other couples, Mr. and Mrs. Montgomery Hare of New York and Mr. and Mrs. James Byrnes of South Carolina, for the duration of the excitement. And this excitement was great for both of them, though considerably less for Eleanor than her husband. She "understood little or nothing of what was going on." She was frequently appalled by the lack of dignity and decorum, the outbursts of blatant vulgarity during demonstrations, that characterized proceedings which she felt should be conducted with sobriety, orderliness, and responsibility. It was all, for her, a vast noisy confusion. After a few days she had had more than enough of it. The constant humid heat was oppressive. She seldom so much as caught a glimpse of her husband; he was mysteriously occupied from early morning to late at night. So she bade him good-bye and left for Hyde Park, whence, with the children, she journeyed to Campobello.[9]

If her husband had departed at the same time, escaping with her to the island, it would have made no difference in the mainstream of convention events.

He came to Baltimore as leader of 150 members of the New York State Wilson Conference. He and they established a headquarters in Room 214 of the Munsey Building, presented a Wilson petition (Howe had been chiefly instrumental in gathering the signatures), issued a manifesto, obtained contiguous seats (through Senator O'Gorman) in the convention hall gallery, whooped it up for Wilson on every possible occasion, helped expand and prolong the Wilson floor demonstration, and buttonholed delegates by the score. He met and favorably impressed a good many nationally prominent Democrats, including sad-faced fiery-tempered Cordell Hull of Tennessee and round-faced sweet-tempered Josephus Daniels of North Carolina. He was ceaselessly busy, bustling to and fro and hither and yon, snatching but a few hours of sleep during a long hot week. But there is no evidence that his efforts changed a single delegate vote between the first ballot on the morning of June 28 and the finally decisive forty-sixth in the afternoon of July 2.

Certainly he had no effect on the delegate vote from his own state. For the first nine ballots, New York's 90 votes went to Governor Judson Harmon of Ohio, whose total of 150 or so placed him third among the candidates, well behind Champ Clark, who led with between 440 and 454, and Wilson, whose vote varied between 324 and 352. Then Boss Murphy made what he and others believed would be the decisive move: he switched New York's vote on the tenth ballot from Harmon to Clark, giving the Missourian a total of 556, 11 over a majority. This was supposed to trigger a Clark landslide. It didn't however. Senator Oscar Underwood of Alabama, whose support had amounted to approximately 120 votes during the first ten ballots, remained firm during the next three. And on the fourteenth ballot, Bryan, who with the Nebraska delegation had theretofore supported Clark, made a dramatic switch to Wilson, his stated reason being that he could not vote for any man "willing . . . to accept the high honor of the Presidential nomination at the hands of Mr. Murphy." He would withdraw his support from Wilson, too, he said, if ever the Tammany delegation cast its vote for the New Jersey governor. Thereafter, as ballots followed one another in weary procession, Wilson gained slowly in strength while Clark slowly faded. On the thirtieth ballot, Wilson's vote exceeded Clark's; on the forty-third, it exceeded a majority, whereupon Boss Roger Sullivan of Illinois switched his state's 58 votes to Wilson; on the forty-sixth, Woodrow

Wilson, with 990 votes, became the Democratic candidate for President of the United States. Thomas R. Marshall of Indiana became his running mate. Through all this, until the final token ballot, the New York delegation remained adamantly anti-Wilson.

Yet Franklin Roosevelt viewed the outcome as a personal victory of immense importance to his future. He was wildly happy. He promptly sent a telegram to Eleanor at Campobello: WILSON NOMINATED THIS AFTERNOON ALL MY PLANS VAGUE STOP SPLENDID TRIUMPH.[10] On the morrow of the convention's adjournment he was in Sea Girt, New Jersey, where Wilson as governor had a summer cottage and where he was one of many who conferred with the Presidential nominee about the forthcoming campaign. Nor was he mistaken in his estimate of the personal value to him of Wilson's convention victory. If his preconvention and convention activities had made no measurable contribution to the outcome in Baltimore, they had firmly established him in the public mind as the leading Wilsonian in upstate New York and had contributed to Wilson's national image as a foe of political bossism, whether Democratic or Republican. Wilson, if elected, seemed bound to reward his ardent young champion in ways that would substantially advance the latter's career. "I am especially pleased at the strong position it has placed you in," Montgomery Hare wrote to him a day or so after leaving Baltimore. And from Horseneck Beach in Massachusetts came a letter of hearty congratulations from Louis Howe. Its salutation was, "Beloved and Revered Future President!" [11]

II

He plunged at once into Wilson campaign organization work in New York. At that time, with the entrance into the field of TR's Progressive Party, there seemed little question that Wilson could carry the state even without active Tammany support, though there was equally little question that Tammany would *have* to give the party's nominee at least formal backing. The real question had to do with the state's Congressional delegation. Would it be sympathetic or hostile to a Wilson-Progressive legislative program? To ensure the election of a pro-Wilson slate became, therefore, a prime purpose of Roosevelt's organization work which, in cooperating with Osborne, resulted in the formation of a so-called Empire State Democracy as a "permanent" Progressive group.

It was launched with much fanfare in New York City on July 12, being strongly backed by Joseph Pulitzer's New York *World,* the New

York *Post,* and several influential upstate papers. Two weeks later it attracted about 200 Democrats to a meeting in New York's Hotel Astor, where Franklin Roosevelt was a principal speaker. He declared that the new movement represented "not a small minority," but "a big majority" of the state Democratic Party, that he and those who joined with him were therefore the true Democratic "regulars" whereas Tammany was a tightly organized group of "irregulars," and that 1912 was "the year to go ahead and strike" for freedom from the tyranny of Tammany. ". . . we've got the club," he asserted, adding his pious "hope" that "we don't have to use it." [12] Thus he broadly hinted that if the state and local party conventions were Murphy-bossed as earlier ones had been, resulting in the nomination of a slate of Tammany anti-Wilson candidates for state office and the Congress, the Empire Staters might put up a slate of their own, forming in effect a fourth party to run against the established Democratic organization, as well as against the regular Republicans and the New York TR Progressives. The fervent emotions animating others at the meeting are indicated in a report of the organization's temporary executive committee. "In imbecility, in greed and in suspected partnership in violence the small clique claiming control of the party organization has been bound to abhorrent criminal forces, to predatory special interests, to favored corrupt contractors and to unscrupulous patronage-mongers," charged the report. "If the party leaders throughout the State cannot release themselves from this bondage when October arrives, then the patriotism of self-respecting men requires, and the true party loyalty demands that, at whatever cost, that bondage shall be broken by the rank and file. If this be party treason, let those who are responsible for such conditions make the most of it." [13]

The threat was disturbing to Murphy: if carried out, the Democratic split in the state might be as disastrous to the party at the polls as the split resulting from TR's Progressivism would be to the Republicans. Progressive Party candidates might well sweep the state. But by that same token the threat was equally, if not more disturbing, to Wilson and his campaign managers, who would be unlikely to win the White House if they failed to carry New York. Nor was Roosevelt himself prepared to accept the consequences of this renewed insurgency, especially since one consequence would be the defeat of his own bid for reelection as state senator. Hence the veiled form of his own threat—a tacit admission to the astute Murphy that his brash young opponent was merely seeking a trading position on the political chessboard.

Roosevelt knew when he spoke that he personally was in a far from secure political situation. Three days before, in Poughkeepsie, he had had no pleasant time with Perkins and several others of the local Democratic committee. He had been forced to recognize that his leading role in the Empire State Democracy, coming atop his fight against Sheehan, might well be alienating more regular Democrats than it was attracting Independents and Republicans, especially in view of the fact that a TR Progressive, as well as a Republican, would be in the field against him. It appeared "that Tammany and the 'Interests' " were "really making an effort" to deny his renomination. He then spent a long day in an automobile tour of his district, seeing, as he reported in a letter from Hyde Park to "Dearest Babbie" in Campobello, "all the 'henchmen' in Claverack, Hillsdale, Copake, Ancram, Pine Plains, Bangall, Standardville, Clinton and Walt Point!" He found that the Columbia County "machine" opposed him "because of patronage troubles" and that "several agents" of Tammany were "trying to stir up the old Sheehan business and are taking advantage of the starting of the Empire State Democracy to howl about 'Discord' etc." But otherwise he could "truthfully say" that his day had been "really very pleasant—a change from the day before. . . ." He was encouraged. "The Enterprise, Eagle and two Fishkill papers have come out for me editorially, and none have dared to oppose me openly." He felt fairly confident that Perkins would not dare openly oppose him either. (". . . Perkins has no spine" and "knows now that if he listened to orders from 14th St. he will have a perfectly delightful little fight on his hands. . . ." [14])

Nevertheless, he moderated his rebellious stance in private talk and said no more in public about the possibility that the Empire State Democracy might put up a fourth ticket. Instead, as he campaigned vigorously for renomination, he stressed common denominators among otherwise dissident members of the party; he deplored intraparty feuds that gave aid and comfort to the party's enemies. And on August 24— though it had been previously "understood that Columbia County and two Dutchess committeemen were against him," as the New York *Times* reported—he was renominated by his district's Democratic Senatorial Committee. ". . . everything was harmonious," said the *Times,* "and the vote for Mr. Roosevelt was unanimous." His acceptance speech was conciliatory. "I realize that in places the Democrats are not in accord with one another as they ought to be, and to have success, I believe in unity," he said. He realized that he had won only half the battle, if that much; he would have to fight hard if he were to emerge victorious in November.[15]

Meanwhile, the Empire State Democracy had fallen on evil days. It had run out of money in mid-August when Osborne, its principal financial backer, decided he had spent all he wished to on it. It had failed to rally to its banner that "big majority" of Democrats which Roosevelt had claimed it represented at the outset: several other anti-Tammany factions were in the field, a division among Murphy's foes that favored a continuance of the boss' rule. Obviously, the Empire State organization was no vehicle that Wilson could mount with any assurance that it would carry him to victory in the state, and he, on advice of his managers, prudently refrained from mounting it.

In the immediately following weeks, both sides of the struggle for power in the New York Democracy made overly aggressive moves and were forced into defensive postures.

Murphy let it be known that he was determined to renominate Governor Dix when the Democratic State Convention met in Syracuse on October 3. This was met with cries of outrage from Progressive Democrats who, with good reason, had become thoroughly disgusted with the weak-kneed Dix and now saw him as a pliant tool of the boss. Then Murphy tricked Wilson into coming to the State Fair at Syracuse on September 12 to deliver what was announced as a nonpolitical speech at the fairgrounds. Not until the Presidential candidate arrived in the State Fair city did he discover that he was the guest not merely of the Fair Commission, as he had been led to believe, but of Murphy, Governor Dix, the State Democratic Committee, and associated Democratic county chairmen. His appearance under such auspices was obviously designed to give the impression that he had joined forces with the New York machine. Moreover, he was virtually forced into a locked room alone with Dix for ten long minutes during which Dix talked and he grimly listened. The tactic was badly mistaken. From his session with Dix, Wilson marched onto the platform of the Syracuse auditorium to address assembled leaders of the regular New York Democracy. Fuming, he seized the opportunity to snub Murphy: he castigated the boss and bossism, though without mentioning the Tammany chieftain's name or in any way acknowledging his presence in the room. What he said was prominently reported in the press.[16]

A week later the rank and file of the Empire State Democracy—emboldened by Wilson's expressed attitude at Syracuse, rebellious against their own official leadership, and recklessly disregarding their organization's lack of real strength—issued not only a public demand that Wilson repudiate Tammany wholly and unequivocally, but also a promise that they would put up their own full slate of anti-Murphy candidates for state and Congressional office. It was an action worse than futile; it merely called attention to the Empire Staters' political impotence while embarrassing their party's Presidential nominee. Wilson took no public notice of their demand. His managers privately but strongly deplored the announced strategy, causing a fair proportion of the latter's proponents to doubt Wilson's sincerity. And Franklin Roosevelt promptly dissociated himself from the "permanent" organization he had helped launch barely three months before. He announced in a letter to the papers of his district that, while the Democratic State Convention must of course be "open" and "fair," he personally had no intention of bolting the regular state party ticket.[17]

While these public moves were being made, Wilson and his campaign managers were engaged in behind-the-scenes maneuvers aimed at persuading Murphy to dump Dix in favor of "some unobjectionable Tammany man for Governor," to quote the diary entry for September 25 of Wilson's increasingly close friend and trusted adviser, Colonel Edward M. House. When the inscrutable Murphy gave no sign of yielding to this pressure but instead continued with seeming adamancy to sponsor Dix's renomination, Wilson on September 30, just three days before the Democratic State Convention, made a public move. He issued to New York newspapers a statement calling for an unbossed convention, asserting his belief that, "if only . . . [the party] be left free from personal control of any sort," it was "ready to choose a progressive man [for governor] of a kind to be his own master and to adopt a platform to which men of progressive principles everywhere can heartily subscribe. . . ."

The climactic move of this game and the last laugh were Murphy's. As at the end of the U.S. Senatorship battle, he bemused and outmaneuvered his enemies by seeming to yield to them while retaining the substance of his power. The state convention in Syracuse was in essence a rigged affair, characterized by a carefully managed "freedom," a calculated "spontaneity," an "openness" that was narrowly enclosed. As it began, Murphy seemed still stubbornly determined upon Dix's nomination. Then, as the balloting got under way, he abruptly "capitulated." The name of Congressman William "Plain Bill" Sulzer was brought forward as substitute for Dix. On the fourth ballot, Sulzer was named.

No one intimately acquainted with New York politics could regard Sulzer as a champion of Progressivism. He had often spoken as one, had sometimes even voted as one, but never on matters where the progressive stand conflicted with important Tammany interests. His deviousness was notorious. He had made the whole of his political career thus far out of a shrewd division of loyalties, playing both ends against the middle in ways disgusting to sincere reformers. And it was obvious to every knowledgeable observer that he had been handpicked by Murphy, though Murphy, as in the case of O'Gorman, would soon regret this choice. Yet Wilson saw fit to issue within hours after the nomination a statement praising the "freedom of action and of choice which the convention exercised . . ."—a statement that outraged many of the

most fervent Empire Staters. Thomas Mott Osborne, for one, thought it
betrayed an unprincipled expediency that would be "perfectly willing to
put the ten commandments to a popular vote and reject them if the vote
were adverse. . . ." [18]

As for Franklin Roosevelt, he was fortunately spared the necessity of
issuing any statement at all—and spared, too, the ignominy attending
the demise of the Empire State Democracy when, on the morrow of Syracuse, it withdrew its anti-Murphy slate. He was not present at the state
convention where Sulzer was nominated; instead, he was sick in bed.

As soon as possible after winning his battle for senatorial renomination, he had gone to Campobello, where he joined Eleanor and "the
chicks" (he always called his children that in his letters) for an abbrevi-
ated vacation before beginning his reelection campaign. The family returned by boat from the island and, during their voyage, thoughtlessly
brushed their teeth with water furnished them in pitchers in their staterooms, though they had been warned that it was unsafe to drink. De-
barking, they all went to Hyde Park, and there the children remained
when, after a day or two of work on his campaign plans, Franklin with
Eleanor came down to 47 East Sixty-fifth Street in the city. The house
there was empty and "entirely 'put up,' " as Eleanor later recalled. (One
result of the "splendid triumph" at Baltimore which had rendered "all
. . . plans vague" for him had been his decision *not* to keep the State
Street house in Albany another year, even if reelected, or to rent the
Sixty-fifth Street place to others for the time being.) They planned to
spend a single night in it.

Instead, they remained for weeks.

Franklin was already ill the night they moved in. He stayed bedridden during the following days, utterly miserable, with a low but ceaseless fever which their doctor could not explain. Then, after a week and a
half, Eleanor, who had been nursing him, fell ill herself. Her temperature was 102 degrees as she took to her bed, and it was easy to diagnose
her disease as typhoid; thereupon it was decided that her husband probably had typhoid also. The fact that he had had it as a child, developing
then a partial immunity to it, would account for the lowness of his fever.
But partial immunity or no, he was unable to shake off his sickness. For
many days after Eleanor, who was seldom ill and never for long, was on
her feet again, nursing him, he continued "in bed . . . feeling miserable
and looking like Robert Louis Stevenson in Vailima." [19]

At the outset, this was for him a time of despair.

He had anticipated that a formal support of his reelection was all he could expect from the local and state Democratic organizations; few, if any, of the party regulars would actively work for him. Indeed, he would be lucky if he were not covertly knifed by the Perkins crowd and by Tammanyites from outside his district. His problem was a small-scale replica of Wilson's. If he were to be victorious over his Republican opponent, Jacob Southard, a banker who was also a public utilities president, and over his Progressive opponent, George A. Vossler, he would have to capitalize upon the reputation he had made as a fighting independent, yet he could not afford to do so in ways that aroused the active opposition of his own party's organization men. Certainly his must be a *personal* campaign, as vigorous and dramatic as that of 1910. Hence his decision to make another month-long automobile tour of the district, visiting every remote corner of the three counties as he had done two years before. He had looked forward to it, remembering the pleasurable excitements of his encounters with farmers singly and in crowds, the sense of triumphant power that had come to him as he received their applause and felt that he had won their support—remembering, too, how beautiful the October countryside had been, with blue haze on distant hills and glorious colors everywhere, and how sweet the air had been to breathe, sharp with frost in the mornings and faintly pungent, almost always, with the smoke of burning leaves.

But now this planned tour was impossible. Personal activity of any kind was impossible. He must lie helpless in this narrow room staring at blank ceiling and walls while his defeat was inevitably accomplished at the polls and, with it, the end of a political career that had begun so promisingly. For how could he survive in politics if he failed of reelection in what seemed certain to be a big Democratic year, in the state as in the nation?

Desperately he cast about in his feverish mind for means of averting the disaster. And as he did so, he had an inspiration. It was perhaps the most fortunate inspiration of his entire political life since without it there might have been no such life at all in his future.

He called out to Eleanor. When she came, he asked her to send at once for Louis Howe.[20]

III

On that bright September day, Louis McHenry Howe was still with his family—wife, Grace; eleven-year-old daughter, Mary; ten-month-old son, Hartley—at Horseneck Beach, the southernmost point of mainland Massachusetts, where he had cheaply acquired four years before, as his summer vacation place, a plain, square, two-storied cottage with sand dunes behind it and ocean before it, with no road or telephone line leading into it and no neighbor nearby—a dwelling approximately as remote and isolated as any could be in that part of New England. He who owned it was grateful for its quiet solitudes. They were his escape from the constant deadline pressures of the political journalism by which he mainly made his meager and precarious living.[21]

He had no inkling that he stood upon the threshold of a new life as, on that sunny morning, he stood upon the threshold of his cottage and, through large and somewhat protuberant brown eyes, looked far out over the sun-glinted sea. His oversized nose sucked deep into asthma- and cigarette-tortured lungs the salt-tangy air which cleared them of phlegm and restored their resiliency as no other air ever did. Then he descended the steps and set off in a shambling walk along the beach and over the dunes toward Lulu Hammond's general store in the village a mile or so away, where telegrams and other messages were left to be picked up by him and his family. He was a man strange, even weird in appearance—among his defensive boasts in the years ahead would be an assertion that he was "one of the four ugliest men . . . in the State of New York"—and there would be those who, seeing him as a "medieval gnome" (a newspaper reporter would so label him), wondered if in actual fact there were three other New Yorkers who could equally share this distinction with him.* He was barely five feet tall. He was thin to the point of emaciation, weighing less than 100 pounds. When in public, he hid his scrawny neck, which was abnormally long, behind high stiff collars, and by contrast with it and his short narrow body his head appeared unusually large. His face was already growing "wizened in the Dickens manner," to quote his own later description of it—the face of a man approaching old age, though he was only forty-one. Deep lines curved from his lower jaw around his small, tight-lipped mouth. His hollowed cheeks were crisscrossed with seams, and there were pouches under his eyes. His forehead—a naturally high one that was further elevated by a receding hairline, for the whole front half of his skull above his large flaring ears was virtually hairless—was plucked together in a permanent frown above and between heavy shaggy brows. Everywhere his leathery facial skin was pitted with the small dark scars of wounds he suffered when thrown hard from a bicycle onto a graveled road while a boy. This gave to his face a perpetually dirty look, no matter how freshly he had scrubbed it, and so helped sustain the reputation for physical uncleanliness which he had acquired.

* He was "the ugliest thing you ever saw" according to a later co-worker of his in Washington, quoted by Frank Freidel in *Franklin Roosevelt: The Apprenticeship* (Boston, 1952), p. 161.

If this reputation was exaggerated, it was by no means wholly unjustified. He was the opposite of fastidious in personal bodily habits. He was inclined to wear shirts that were soiled, suits that badly needed cleaning and pressing, and to string around his high collar ties that were wrinkled and food-stained and carelessly knotted. Simultaneously he added to the general effect of messiness by scattering over himself and his immediate environment a steady shower of ash from the Sweet Caporal cigarette that was perpetually stuck to his lower lip. Thus, instead of attempting to offset or overcome the repellent effect his natural appearance might have had on others, he flaunted his ugliness. He went in this respect so far beyond the requirements of a defensive strategy as to suggest that his motive was a reverse or perverse vanity, an aggressive defiance whose cause was a fierce personal pride. He had received no quarter; he asked none; perhaps he would give none.

And indeed defiance had become his only alternative to an abject confession of defeat and failure. By harsh ways, through a world that was not merely coldly indifferent to him but often seemed to be actively malevolent, he had come to his present sorry pass.

His earliest memories were of Indianapolis. He was born there in 1871. But these memories were few and vague compared with those of Saratoga Springs, New York, where he was taken when five and had ever since regarded without affection as his principal home base. Saratoga was a curiously mingled town, a juxtaposition of incongruities. For two or three months out of every year it was an American version of a European spa, a resort for the wealthy, come ostensibly to drink the health-promoting waters of the mineral springs from which the town takes its name. But the wealthy were not all who came. Middle-class summer vacationers arrived in flocks sufficiently large to cause leading New York City stores to establish branches there; famous actors and actresses came to play on the local stage; horsemen came with accompanying trainers and jockeys and racetrack touts for the great annual race meeting; politicians of all kinds and both parties came for convention, as well as holiday; women of easy virtue came, and professional gamblers, to ply their trades in and around the Grand Union and other hotels and at Canfield's palatial casino. It was a community in which prospered a genius for quick impressions that make fast bucks; it encouraged, in those who grow up in it, an early sophistication, a lasting cynicism.

But this Saratoga, internationally famous, throve for only a part of each year and directly involved only a part of the local citizenry. Coexistent with it, a permanent sustaining core of the season's transient glitter, was a very different Saratoga, unknown to fame, composed of year-around residents who did not differ markedly in character and values from those of a dozen other upstate country towns. These sober citizens were thrifty, industrious, rural-minded folk who went to church, paid their taxes, revered the flag, honored their marriage vows, abhorred "loose conduct," and for the most part voted the straight Republican ticket. Among these it was that Louis' father, Captain Edward Howe, had made his uncertain way. The elder Howe had known affluence in Indianapolis, where he was an executive officer in an insurance company, but he came a bankrupt to Saratoga, having been ruined when his company failed following the Panic of '73. He came to live with relatives until he "got on his feet" again. By 1882 he had managed to scrape enough money together to buy a weekly newspaper, the Saratoga *Sun*, which was then struggling for survival. It continued to struggle after Captain Howe transformed it into a Democratic organ, a hotly partisan one, in a predominantly Republican town. Yet it not only survived but, with its accompanying job printing, was even moderately prosperous for several years, enabling the elder Howe to become prominent in the town, a leader of the local Democracy and Presbyterian Church. For the captain was, with his wife, as fervent a Presbyterian as he was a Democrat. Every Sunday he took his family to church; every day he stressed Christian patriotism in his home as he did weekly in the columns of his paper.

Hence Louis Howe, as boy and youth, was exposed to contradictory attitudes. On the one hand was the natural irreverence of the newspaper fraternity, especially in a gambling and racetrack resort town; on the other was the stern piety of Calvinistic religion. The former took. The latter did not, save to the extent that Presbyterian doctrine had helped confirm him in a view of Fate, or Christian God, in that order of probability, as Author of a drama on earth whose main events are all preordained and in which presumably he, like every other man, had an assigned role.

Certainly Calvinistic predestination was consistent with his tendency to see all the world as stage, all men and women merely players—himself included, himself *especially*. He was stagestruck as few men are. He had been from an early age. In his twenties he threw himself heart and soul into the local amateur theatricals which flourished more in Saratoga than in most communities, being stimulated there by the seasonal visitations of professional New York companies. Every element of the theater fascinated him. He had designed and built sets, painted scenery, experimented successfully with lighting effects, directed productions, even written plays. And he had acted. He loved to act. He handled himself well on stage, had a good speaking and singing voice and a rare capacity to feel himself into a part. But the parts assigned him had never been those noble heroic ones that he would like to play; always in the theater he had been given low-comedy roles; and during the black moods into which he often plunged, he asked himself if he were not similarly typecast in the drama of "real life."

His answer to this question, however, had been and remained an emphatic NO! He was convinced (the conviction was the essence of his continuing defiance) that in forty-one years of life and more than twenty of ceaseless striving and casting about he had not yet found his proper role.

He knew well that the range of roles it was possible for him to play was severely limited by certain salient facts about him. For instance, from early childhood he had suffered a variety of serious bodily ailments—bronchitis, asthma, a heart condition—and since early adolescence he had had constantly to wear a heavy truss. He was by nature shy, and when he was growing up, his tendencies toward withdrawal and introversion were encouraged by the solitudes imposed upon him by his illnesses. He had defied his physical infirmities with a more than average robustness of spirit—had bicycled, played golf and tennis, fished, and chain-smoked cigarettes despite the inescapable knowledge that they aggravated his respiratory difficulties and contributed to his almost constant hacking cough. He had defied his shyness, too, or sublimated it through creative disguise, by acting on the stage and by public speaking (his "impromptu speeches were much admired," writes Alfred B. Rollins, Jr.). Nevertheless, his disabilities had been limiting factors. He was too sickly a boy to attend public school, and his schooling, in consequence, was highly informal, haphazard, almost exclusively literary, most of it under his bookish father's tutelage, some of it in a seminary for young ladies (he entered by special permit) that was conveniently located across the street from his home. Ill health, his father's in addition to his own, combined with family financial difficulties to prevent his attending in his teens Saratoga Institute, the private day school where, according to plan, he was to prepare for Yale. As things turned out, he enrolled in no college at all. Instead, in his late teens, after taking a long cruise with his failing father through the West Indies, he entered the family business (now E. P. Howe & Son) as co-editor and -proprietor of the *Sun* and chief salesman of advertising and job printing.

He was probably by then as well informed as most college graduates, however. The voracious reading to which he was naturally inclined, encouraged and carefully guided by his father, had made him so.

Especially influential were the works of Thomas Carlyle, sustaining and expanding his sense of the world-as-stage and of Fate or Destiny as author, producer, and director of the Cosmic Drama. He felt a special affinity for the dyspeptic romantic Scot who had been so full of Calvinistic glooms while rejecting Calvinistic theology; so worshipfully admiring of the Hero and Heroic as personifying and acting out "the real tendency of the world"; so eloquent in his portrayals of Society as organism and History as organic growth and in his dangerous exaltations of feeling over thinking; so evidently, if unadmittedly, ambitious to become himself a Great Man of action, of power, and so soured because he could not realize this ambition in the bourgeois, industrial England of Queen Victoria. Louis Howe, with his love of the dramatic, had not been put off by the thunderously declamatory Carlylean style. He had vibrated to it—especially in those chapters of *Heroes and Hero-Worship* entitled "The Hero as Poet," "The Hero as Man of Letters," "The Hero as King." The first two of these describe a kind of greatness to which he himself might aspire; the third, as he had increasingly felt in his later years, described a kind of greatness he might promote or even, in some fateful sense, actually *create* in another.

He was generally recognized in his youth as the rising literary star of Saratoga. During his grade and high school years, a good deal of the competent verse he composed in the manner and mood of Whittier, Longfellow, Tennyson was published in his father's paper, some of it even in the rival *Saratogan*. In addition to his plays—most of which were farces and several of which were locally produced—he continued to write both light and serious verse after he became virtual head of the family business in his early twenties, when Cleveland was President and Captain Howe was for four years Saratoga's postmaster. At the same time he worked hard, as he always did, to become a first-rate newspaper reporter, not only for the *Sun* but also for the New York *Herald*, of which he was local correspondent. He became first-rate, too. He developed a distinctive reportorial style, bright and quick, and earned the sometimes fearful respect of competing newsmen through his skillful, stubbornly persistent pursuit of the facts, all the available facts, in any story to which he was assigned. He remained a meticulous researcher into whatever subject attracted his serious attention.

He now recognized the years of his young manhood as the happiest of his life. He had had then, intact and shining, a confidence in himself and a sense of security in the world which had since been sadly eroded by the acids of failure. The handicaps of poor health and unprepossessing appearance were then sufficiently overcome by his gaiety and sardonic wit to enable him to gain social acceptance by his contemporaries. He was enabled also to court successfully an attractive girl, Grace Hartley, who came from a prominent and prosperous Fall River, Massachusetts, family, had recently inherited money of her own, and was brought to Saratoga by a domineering and possessive mother in an effort to "save" her from a Fall River man, "a handsome Irishman" (says Rollins) who had been courting her. This mother approved no more of Louis Howe than she did of the Irishman. He seemed to her in every way an unsuitable match for her daughter. When the marriage took place in spite of her, she made a generous gesture of surrender: she gave to the bridal couple, as a wedding present, a fine house in Saratoga.

Within a few months after the wedding, the mother's forebodings proved justified. In 1899, E. P. Howe & Son added to an already heavy debt load by purchasing a color press, hoping to attract desperately needed new business, which failed to materialize. Creditors grew clamorous. To appease them, the wedding-gift house was heavily mortgaged, then Grace's inheritance was used up—and all in vain. In early 1900, E. P. Howe & Son ceased to exist. The new owner of the *Sun* hired Louis at the insultingly small wage of $10 a week for a year and a half, then ignominiously fired him, and since then the Howes had led a hand-to-mouth existence, with Grace and the children spending much of every year with her mother in Fall River. The struggling husband had been unable to support them continuously in a home of his own or even to support them at all at times without financial aid from a mother-in-law who did not hide her contempt for him.

He had known much contemptuous treatment during the last dozen years. Rejection, humiliation, frustration had been the bitter common bread of his spirit. Free-lance writing, journalism in New York City (his health broke under the pressures there), the secretaryship of a newly organized Saratoga Businessmen's Association, even gambling at cards and betting on horses (he briefly considered setting up as bookmaker at California tracks)—all these he had tried. For several months in 1909 and '10 he worked for the Saratoga Springs Commission and was sent to Europe to study the public operation of Continental watering places, returning to write a report which persuaded New York State to obtain control of the 163 springs at Saratoga. But his principal employers, independently of one another, had been the New York *Herald* and Auburn's mayor, the wealthy industrialist Thomas Mott Osborne. The newspaper he had served on a part-time basis, year after year, as a reporter covering Saratoga during the season, Albany during the legislative session, and, on occasion, upstate New York in general during election campaigns. Through his political reporting, from which he gained wide acquaintanceship among political figures and much shrewdness in political affairs, he had been led a half dozen years before into a spasmodic, uneasy working relationship with Osborne, whose ambition was to build an upstate Progressive Democracy strong enough to wrest control of the state party organization from Tammany but whose temper, alas for the success of such enterprise, was as erratic as his wealth was great. Howe had served Osborne on the latter's payroll, off and on at no fat wage, as combination idea man, ghost-writer, public relations counsel, publicist, secretary, and undercover political manipulator. He had had to flatter and cajole, even beg for jobs at times, had suffered rude rebuff often enough, and had never known with any certainty, in a dozen years, where or whether he would be employed a few months hence.

From all this he had emerged as a distinct "character," in the theatrical meaning of the term. He was conscious of himself as one. He conceived himself as a hard-bitten cynic whose every illusion had been shattered by prolonged harsh experience of behind-the-scenes realities, yet a cynic who had retained his loyalty to certain basic ideals—conceived himself as one contemptuously indifferent to mere appearances and to the tastes and values of fashionable society, yet quick to recognize solid worth and virtue and to respond to whatever of Truth, Goodness, Beauty came his way. (A favorite pastime of his at Horseneck Beach was the painting of subtle sensitive watercolors depicting the austere beauties of the seashore.) He was tough, abrupt of manner, uncouth, harshly honest, immensely shrewd, thoroughly sophisticated, yet romantic not only in his eagerness to attach himself to a "Beloved and Revered" Hero but also in his willingness to trust his intuition as a guide to action. (Grace complained that over the years, he had been both impulsive and indecisive, with sad effects upon his career.) A certain lugubrious self-deprecating humor was expressed in the expletive "Mein Gawd," used by him on every occasion of stress. He "played" himself to the hilt, standing at the same time outside himself and commenting on his performance, often with a "ghoulish chuckle" over the graves of so many dreams and hopes. It was with growing desperation that he now sought to attract the Author's personal attention.

Because he could not make on others an attractive personal impression, he put forth no effort in that direction. But he knew that he was deemed "the bane of every newspaperman in Albany" because of his alleged ability "to smell a story a mile off" and because he was reputed never to sleep. One irritated reporter dubbed him " 'the water rat' of the Capitol building" because, to supply background for his stories, he spent so many hours going over all records in the Capitol's musty basement. (His habit of painstaking research had not always proved an asset when applied in nonpolitical assignments. Covering a murder case in the summer of 1908, he spent so much time digging for facts that he failed to report those easily available until competitors had done so, eliciting from his paper a curt wire: SEND SOMETHING NEW FOR EACH EDITION. THIS IS *NOT* A POLITICAL CONVENTION.) Largely through his labors on behalf of Osborne, he had discovered in himself a rare talent for political intrigue and maneuver, for propaganda and promotion, along with an awareness of when, in what circumstances, and in what ways such talent might be profitably employed. He was convinced he could plan a political campaign and handle every phase of campaign publicity, that he had the capacity to shape long-term strategies into which immediate tactics could be fitted, that he was notably hardheaded and farsighted in such matters.

He had indeed within him, in his own conception, a veritable reservoir of powers that could become important in history were they properly harnessed and employed. They must be harnessed and employed in service of another. He now realized this clearly enough. But it was also clear to him that this "other," if ever found—some Right Man who was personally prepossessing, impressive as he could never be, possessed of leadership qualities which he wholly lacked—might become in a very real sense his own outer self, a being through whom and in terms of whom he would complete himself and come at last truly and wholly alive into the world.

Already it had occurred to him that the Right Man just *might* be Franklin Roosevelt. The young aristocrat from Hyde Park, with his Groton-Harvard education and his casual membership in the highest of high society, was in every outward respect the antithesis of Louis McHenry Howe, being tall, handsome, clear-complexioned, rich, vitally impressive, capable of immense charm. Yet he shared with Howe certain basic qualities which the "medieval gnome," watching him from the press gallery of the Capitol during the early rounds of the battle against Sheehan, at least sensed. Young Roosevelt was green, inexperienced. He made mistakes, aroused needless personal enmities, probably without knowing that he did so. He had, quite obviously to Howe's critical eye, no well-thought-out political program of his own. He could profit greatly from Howe's political knowledge and experience and talent. On the other hand, none as knowledgeable and appreciative of histrionic skills as Howe was could fail to admire the adroitness with which this political neophyte played to the galleries, captured headlines, maneuvered for advantageous position, gained credit for far more than he actually achieved, and, in times of adversity, maintained the boldest of fronts, seldom permitting even the smallest crack of doubt to appear in it. Young Roosevelt had an undoubted strong attraction to the dramatic and a personal flair for it. He seemed to appreciate more than most the uses of publicity. He exhibited a gambler's courage joined with a driving ambition. Such a man, properly helped and guided, could go far.

As a matter of fact, Howe came away from his very first personal interview with the young man believing that Franklin Roosevelt might one day be President of the United States. Every detail of that meeting would always be vivid in his memory. Over the fireplace in the library of the State Street house, where the interview occurred, was a carved coat of arms in which a clenched hand held a club. In the fireplace itself was a log fire. The tall handsome figure of Roosevelt was flame-lit as he strode up and down the large room, forcefully gesturing and talking in a richly resonant tenor voice. Whatever cynical reservations Howe had had about him were overcome. He found himself believing in Roosevelt's "seriousness, his earnestness, his firm dedication to his cause," and, above all, in Roosevelt himself.[22] Since then his initial suspicion that the young man was destined for greatness had hardened into conviction. He was by no means wholly facetious, he was in fact quite serious, when he addressed him, after Baltimore, as "Future President."

Yes, Franklin Roosevelt might very well be the Right Man, if only Roosevelt himself could be persuaded of it. There was no sign thus far that he was or would be.

And so, as Louis Howe walked through sand and waving dune grass beside the sea, he was nearly frantic. His very livelihood was in question again. Even the slender intermittent supports of the *Herald* and Osborne had latterly been withdrawn from him. His standard assignment from the *Herald*, to cover the autumn campaign, was given up when he accepted full-time employment, on Osborne's payroll, by the Empire State Democracy. "I notified the Herald as soon as Wilson was nominated," he had written Franklin Roosevelt, "and it made my boss very angry, as it upset his schedule." Then had come Osborne's abrupt withdrawal of financial support from the Empire State organization in mid-August. Howe was thrown out of a job; he was not even paid for work already done. "Now I am in a hole because there are five long months before Albany and the price of living has not gone down any," continued his letter to Roosevelt. "If you can connect me with a job during the campaign, for heaven's sake help me out, for this mess is bad business for me." His letter then presented evidence of the kind of service which he, with his fertile conspiratorial imagination, might render: "To my mind, now is the time to put that Young Men's Wilson Club idea through, using it as a blind to build up an anti-Murphy organization." [23] Weeks had passed, however, since this letter was mailed, and no campaign job had materialized. Deepest gloom therefore enshrouded him as he came to Lulu Hammond's store. He entered. A message was handed him across the counter.

And there and then, after he had forsaken the physical brightness of the out-of-doors for the comparative physical gloom of the building's interior, his private spiritual darkness was dissolved in the light of what he read, for what he held in his hand was Eleanor's telegram in behalf of Franklin, asking him to come posthaste to 47 East Sixty-fifth Street and indicating that he was to take charge of her husband's political fortunes until young Roosevelt was on his feet again. When he looked up from what he then felt to be his long-delayed cue for entrance upon the main drama of his life, the future was illuminated for him by a renewed flare of hope.

IV

None can doubt that he saved Franklin Roosevelt's political life, insofar as this depended upon reelection as state senator that year.

He rushed down from the seashore cottage to the Roosevelts' city house. He was warmly greeted there by Franklin, somewhat less warmly by Eleanor, and went at once into bedside consultation with the still fever-ridden candidate. It was quickly decided—indeed the conclusion was so obvious as hardly to require decision—that the basic campaign strategy should be in broadest outline the same as two years ago in that little attention would be given Poughkeepsie, where the Democratic organization must be counted upon to deliver the vote, while major effort was devoted to the normally Republican rural voter in the three counties. This agreed to, Howe found himself on Roosevelt's payroll at a salary of $50 a week and with virtual carte blanche for conduct of the canvass. He plunged at once into intense activity, moving his family into a boardinghouse near Vassar in Poughkeepsie, establishing his own headquarters in Poughkeepsie's old Morgan House, and, in a few days, planning and launching an election campaign every bit as dramatic and a great deal more substantial, as regards issues, than that of 1910.

Antibossism was an inescapable issue for so famed a warrior against Tammany as Roosevelt had made of himself, yet an issue requiring the most careful skillful handling if grave hazards were to be avoided. The young Progressive Democrat's opposition to Murphy had best be merely implicit for the time being, and Howe made no specific reference to Tammany or its chief in his campaign materials. He focused instead, as Roosevelt himself had done in 1910, on *Republican* bossism, moving boldly—more so, probably, than Roosevelt on his own would have done—to brand Jacob Southard as a "henchman" of Boss Barnes and a "bosom friend" of Jack Yale, the Putnam County Republican leader.[24]

Less clear-cut and also less well supplied with ammunition for Roosevelt's cause was the labor issue. Here, too, were hazards. The support of labor leaders must not be pursued in ways that reduced the support from farmers who felt their interests threatened by organized labor's demands. Howe avoided the hazards by calling attention to the senator's effort toward improved safety standards in mines, to the senator's responsiveness to the wishes of railway unions in his district, and to the senator's several public expressions of benevolent goodwill toward labor organizations. Shortly before election day, after consultation with the candidate, he pledged the senator to a reintroduction of the workmen's compensation bill on behalf of the State Federation of Labor, if reelected and if the federation wished it, thereby gaining for Roosevelt the federation chairman's heartiest endorsement.

But by all odds the most important and successful of Howe's stratagems was "a great farmer stunt" (as he called it), devised in close cooperation with his and Roosevelt's good personal friend, William Church Osborn of Putnam County.

Osborn, as chairman of the Market Committee of the State Food Commission, had become highly exercised over the wide spread between the price paid the New York farmer for his produce and the price paid by the New York consumer of this same produce. Both farmer and consumer were being cheated, Osborn averred. Commission merchants —middlemen who rendered relatively slight service in the economic structure—were obviously levying exorbitant service charges. The abuse must be stopped. And Osborn, at Howe's request, prepared an outline of proposed legislation for doing so. Howe used this in a way unprecedented in the district and nearly, if not wholly so, in American politics. He had the Osborn proposal set in type. Simultaneously he drafted for Roosevelt's signature a "personal" letter which, though multigraphed, had the appearance of being individually typed. In it, the senator pointed out that, if reelected, he would be chairman of the Senate Agricultural Committee, that he could be counted upon to fight for adoption of a law that would protect farmers against New York City's greedy commission men, but that he wanted such a law to embody the best thinking of his farmer constituents. The attached printed proposal was simply one suggestion. He hoped it would be discussed by the addressee and his neighbors at their local Grange meetings. "The matter so directly affects the farmers and is so important as to be above partisan politics. I trust you will help us in getting the right kind of bill drawn without regard to political considerations. I am sorry that my severe illness has prevented my talking this over with those interested in farming in my district personally but I hope you will write me what you think about it." [25] A stamped, self-addressed envelope was enclosed. The response was tremendous and tremendously gratifying. A flood of answering letters soon poured into the Morgan House headquarters.

Nor was this Howe's only use of the "personal" letter device. Shad fishermen along the Hudson were distressed by a hike in the fishing license fee recently imposed by the Conservation Commission. Each fisherman whose name and address Howe could obtain received a Roosevelt letter saying that the order increasing the fee would soon be rescinded. The senator's friend, Conservation Commissioner George Van Kennam, who actively supported the senator's reelection, had promised it would be. Yet another letter was designed to contrast the energetic concern for his constituents which Roosevelt manifested, despite severe illness, with the indolence and lack of concern manifested by his perfectly healthy Republican opponent, who conducted a McKinley-style "front porch" campaign. This "personal" missive went out to more than 11,000 of the district's voters.

Full-page advertisements in county newspapers were a further device, never before adopted in district politics, which Howe used with great effect. In them he listed the various issues mentioned above and added others. One of these last had to do with fruit barrels. Farmers who sold apples on a per-barrel basis were often cheated when buyers used oversized barrels to measure the fruit, so Howe pledged Roosevelt to the introduction of legislation providing for standard barrels. Support of woman's suffrage was also pledged in the ads. Howe, pressed for time, rushed a copy of the first ad down to Roosevelt by special delivery mail with a cover letter composed in his typically flippant, cynical style: "As I have pledged you in it I thought you might like to know casually what kind of a mess I was getting you into. Please *wire* o.k., if it is all right. . . ." [26]

To the preparation of all this written material, in itself a heavy work load, Howe added the organization and administration of a Roosevelt Committee with its volunteer workers; traveled incessantly by automobile through the district and to Albany, where he sought out jobs with which to reward such key supporters as demanded them; and engaged in a voluminous truly personal correspondence. He submitted daily reports of his activities to his employer, spicing them with the kind of broad "humor" to which Roosevelt himself was addicted. "I am jollying White, one of our workers, to wear a chauffeur's cap and leggings as we tour the district, so as to throw all the style we can," said one report. "Keep that temperature down, so that you can get on the job," said another, adding, "I am having more fun than a goat." He signed this last missive: "Your slave and servant, Louis Howe." [27] Only once or twice during these hectic weeks was he able to dash down to 47 East Sixty-fifth Street for personal consultation with the candidate.

Hence Roosevelt, though informed of what was being done on his behalf and enabled to approve in advance of most of Howe's major acts, found himself virtually as passive a spectator of his own campaign as he was of Woodrow Wilson's.

And we may be sure that he followed the Wilson campaign closely; he knew its success to be practically as important to his career as his own reelection.

V

In early August, the Presidential candidate had displayed an almost incredible naïveté regarding the necessities of a national campaign that would succeed for a Progressive Democrat in 1912. He had toploftily announced that he intended to make no long swings around the country, would not speak at all from the observation platforms of railway cars, would instead confine himself to a few major addresses in which he would "discuss principles and not men," and this "only in such debatable States where I accept invitations from Party leaders." [28] Nor had the candidate at that time any clear definition of the major issue between himself and Theodore Roosevelt, any national program of his own to set off against TR's New Nationalism. But by September the naïveté regarding the campaign's formal needs had been overcome, and the most serious deficiencies of its substance had been supplied—the former by Wilson's chief campaign tacticians, the latter by Louis D. Brandeis.

There was correspondence between Brandeis and Wilson in early August. Then, on August 28, at Sea Girt, the two men met for the first time, the lawyer coming to lunch and remaining in private conference with the Democratic candidate for three hours thereafter. The two agreed at the outset that Taft was not in the running.* The only real contest was with TR. And so Brandeis, at Wilson's behest, analyzed the events and platform of the Progressive Party's national convention, held in Chicago August 5–7, in order to contrast their inner meanings, their main purposes and direction, with Democratic Progressivism as Brandeis conceived it.

* Taft himself agreed with this. On July 22 he had written a friend: "I think I might as well give up so far being a candidate. There are so many people in the country who don't like me."

He found a sinister significance in the roles of George Perkins and publisher Frank Munsey at TR's side. Nothing in the known characters and careers of these two big businessmen justified a belief that they were now primarily concerned with human freedom. Their primary concern had always been for the rights of the giant corporations in which they had made their millions. And Brandeis was convinced that this remained their chief concern, that the economic policies of the new party were designed to promote it. True, the Progressive platform contained many a liberal plank. The long and detailed labor plank, for example, called for abolition of child labor, reduction of hours of labor for women in industry to eight a day, workmen's compensation, improved safety and health conditions in industry, a guaranteed one day's rest out of every seven, a minimum wage for women workers—all to be secured through federal legislation. The plank also said: "We favor the organization of the workers, men and women, as a means of protecting their interests and promoting their progress." But these proposals, in the overall context of the New Nationalism, constituted a false, Bismarckian type of "liberalism," according to Brandeis. He found special significance in the wording of the statement on labor organization: it left unclear *who* was to do the organizing; it did not specifically endorse labor's own *right* to organize. A right, pointed out lawyer Brandeis, was "something the law protects," and existing laws as interpreted by the courts gave no protection whatever to labor unions. Indeed, the Supreme Court had held in *Adair v. U.S.* that corporations had a right to discharge workers for joining a union—and one could be sure the corporations would fully exercise this right, since they were dedicated to the "extermination of organized labor." [29]

The crux of the matter was the new party's attitude toward the trusts. Perkins had seen to it that the printed Progressive Party platform contained no plank that even endorsed the Sherman Act, much less called for a strengthening of it. The party's contention, as Brandeis later put it in a memorandum to Wilson, was "that private monopoly may be desirable in some branches of industry, or at all events, is inevitable; and that existing trusts should not be dismembered or forcibly dislodged in those branches of industry in which they have already acquired a monopoly but should be made 'good' by regulation." [30] But in truth "no methods of regulation have been or can be devised to remove the menace inherent in private monopoly and overweening commercial power." The "liberal" proposals of the new party, therefore, in the design of the Perkins-Munsey wing of it, were essentially sops; they were aimed at soothing people into a passive contentment while their liberties were absorbed into a paternalistic all-powerful central government—a govern-

298 THE GREEN, YET RIPENING YEARS

ment closely allied, if not actually ultimately identical, with the directorships of a few giant trusts.

Here, then, was the central issue of the campaign. In contrast with the
Progressive platform, the Democratic called for a strengthening of antitrust law, making it enforceable by criminal as well as civil proceedings
and so specific that the Supreme Court could no longer interpret it with
trust-strengthening leniency. The Democratic Party insisted that competition be maintained or restored in every branch of private industry and
that "if at any future time monopoly should appear . . . desirable . . . , the monopoly should be a public one—a monopoly owned by
the people and not by the capitalists." What Democrats stood for, in
other words, was no foredoomed attempt to regulate monopoly but, instead, the *prevention* of monopoly through the regulation of competition.

Much of this was promptly echoed in the Labor Day speech which
Wilson made to a huge crowd in Buffalo—a speech that ridiculed TR's
notion of "regulating" giant trusts through a "Board of Experts," described monopolies as "so many cars of juggernaut" created by "unregulated competition," and demanded "remedial legislation" whereby
"the wrong use of competition" would be so restricted "that the right
use . . . will destroy monopoly." He conceded that the Progressive and
Democratic parties had the same broad aims as regards social justice
and improved living and working conditions for common folk, but he
was convinced that if these aims were achieved at all in terms of the
Progressive program, it would be at the expense of freedom. For the
Progressive program "legalizes monopolies and systematically subordinates workingmen to them and to plans made by the Government, both
with regard to employment and with regard to wages." (This last was a
reference to the Progressives' call for a minimum wage law for women.
Wilson opposed it on the ground that it would cause employers to lower
the wages of *all* their employees to the legal minimum.*) "By what
means, except open revolt," he went on, "could we ever break the crust
of our life again and become free men, breathing an air of our own,
choosing and living lives that we wrought out for ourselves? Perhaps this
new and all-conquering combination between money and government
would be benevolent to us, perhaps it would carry out the noble program of social betterment . . . , but who can assure us of that?" [32]

In the following weeks, as Wilson and TR both campaigned with utmost vigor, they made speeches remarkable in an American political

* To this, TR made prompt, cogent reply. Speaking in Spokane, Washington, on September
9, he branded the "objection" as "purely academic . . . formed in the school room." Anyone
experienced in practical economics would know that "these employers who now pay their low-
est-paid employees a starvation wage prove by that very fact that they are paying to all their
employees the very least that they can get them to take." [31]

campaign for their concentration on principles and programs to the virtual exclusion of personalities and appeals to passionate prejudice. Not that personalities, the vivid contrasts between Rough Rider and Schoolmaster, played no part in the campaign, or that the campaign was devoid of dramatic incident. It came close to tragic drama, as a matter of fact, when TR was shot by a fanatic while on his way to an auditorium jampacked with his followers in Milwaukee, on October 14. He insisted on making his scheduled speech anyway. Not until he had spoken for nearly an hour would he permit himself to be taken to a hospital, where it was discovered that his wound, though serious, was not dangerous. Yet even on this occasion of nearly hysterical crowd excitement and anxiety, the candidate's speech, after an opening of extemporized histrionics ("Friends, I shall ask you to be as quiet as possible. . . . I have just been shot; but it takes more than that to kill a Bull Moose . . ."), aimed to impress on the public mind the differences between the New Nationalism and the New Freedom.

In late September, addressing factory workers in Fall River, Massachusetts, Wilson had come out forthrightly for "the legal right of labor to organize," something the Progressive platform significantly failed to do. To this the wounded Rough Rider, on October 14, made tacit reply. "It is essential that there should be organizations of labor," he said. "This is an era of organization. Capital organizes and therefore labor must organize." He also answered Wilson's attack on the proposed expansion of federal powers as, at best, a paternalism inimical to freedom. ("The history of liberty is a history of the limitation of governmental power, not the increase of it," Wilson had declared in New York on September 16.) TR charged his opponent with a commitment "to the old flintlock, muzzle-loaded doctrine of States' rights" whereas the Progressives "are for the people's rights." If the latter "can be obtained best through the National Government, then we are for national rights." [33]

His was a brave show. But by that time it was clear to almost everyone, including TR, that the Bull Moose, however tough, was not strong enough to win election. His defeat was inevitable.

And it was also clear by then that the very process which sharpened the central issue between the New Nationalism and the New Freedom was defining a common higher ground between them, a ground where the two might conceivably meet and fuse. For as each candidate strove mightily to educate and persuade the public to his point of view, he also educated and persuaded his opponent to a significant degree. Each, in consequence, made important modifications of his original stand.

Thus the wounded Rough Rider, harassed by Wilson's charge that he defended the ruthlessly unfair competitive practices through which corporate giantism grew, issued from his hospital bed a statement which seemed to come close to an endorsement of strengthened antitrust legislation. Said he: "If . . . a corporation should be found crushing out competition . . . by underselling in districts, or in the dozen other ways that Congress should learn were being practiced and should say were illegal, I would have the statute say point blank, with no loophole for escape, that the corporation was guilty." [34] Similarly, Woodrow Wilson was forced to retreat somewhat from his original stand against big government. TR, pointing to his opponent's announced general agreement with the social objectives of the Progressive Party, demanded to know how these objectives could be achieved—or, indeed, how competition could be "regulated"—save through a strong national government. Said he: "We propose to use the whole power of the government to protect all those who, under Mr. Wilson's laissez-faire system, are trodden down in the ferocious, scrambling rush of unregulated and purely individualistic industrialism." Wilson, in reply, conceded that, "while we are followers of Jefferson, there is one principle of Jefferson's which no longer can obtain in the practical politics of America." No longer was it true, Wilson went on, "that the best government is that which does as little governing as possible. . . . America is not now, and cannot in the future be, a place for unrestricted individual enterprise." A federal industrial commission might be needed to regulate business enterprise, he admitted, echoing a Brandeis proposal (in a *Collier's Weekly* article) that a Federal Trade Commission be set up to define and enforce fair trade practices. . . .[35]

From all this, to the extent that he pondered it, a convalescent Franklin Roosevelt might derive clarification and amplification of that "new theory" of society which he had attempted to describe in his speech at Troy, New York, seven months before. Thesis and antithesis were defined with rare sharpness in this political dialogue. They clashed in ways that gave light. And out of their frictional clash emerged a tentative synthesis wherein "freedom" and "organization," "individualism" and "collectivism," were viewed, not as opposites with a "vs." between them, but as linked concepts, creatively modifying each other. The evident conclusion was that, in a modern industrial state, freedom must be given an organismic rather than an atomistic definition: it must be conceived, not as an individual quality or "right," not only as a private property, but also as a quality of society as a whole, a public enterprise, a function of community. It was toward this conclusion that young Roosevelt was groping when he spoke of the main historical movement of his time as a "struggle for the liberty of the community rather than liberty of the individual" and indicated that one aim of political leader-

ship should be to locate that "certain point" beyond which "competition" ceased to be "useful" and "cooperation must begin."

Decades later he would say that it was the duty of government to establish "a sense of community within a huge democratic industrial society."

As October gave way to November, 1912, however, Franklin Roosevelt's attention was riveted not on the national contest, where Wilson's
victory seemed assured, but on his own contest in the Twenty-sixth Senatorial District of New York, where the outcome was doubtful.

He knew that Louis Howe had done a superb job. The little man was
perhaps a bit careless about certain details. On one occasion, after Roosevelt had just been assured by his campaign manager that there remained plenty of money in the checking account, the bank informed
him that his account was overdrawn. It turned out that Howe, instead of
subtracting the amounts of checks on the stubs, had been adding them
—a mistake he would never be allowed to forget, by a mercilessly teasing Roosevelt, for the rest of his life.[36] But his overall operation was tremendously successful. All through October there were no signs of serious defection by Democratic regulars and many signs, including letters
from constituents to the candidate, that numerous Republicans who had
not voted for him in 1910 were now prepared to do so. Then came a
frightening development. In the opening days of November, so late in
the campaign that effective counteraction was impossible, the Republican opposition spread abroad the charge that the fight against Sheehan
had been motivated by anti-Catholic bias on Roosevelt's part—a reiteration of the charge made by the Catholic Bishop of Syracuse while the
fight was being waged. There was no question but that the tactic would
appreciably reduce Roosevelt's strength at the polls. The candidate was
furious; the injection of "any question of religion into politics" was, he
privately fumed, "un-American and un-Christian." [37] He was also seriously worried.

Hence the joyous relief with which, on the night of election day, November 5, he heard by phone from Howe that he had won reelection,
and by a wider margin over his Republican opponent than he had
achieved in 1910. He received 15,590 votes to Southard's 13,889 (the
Progressive candidate, Vossler, received only 2,628). Woodrow Wilson
carried the district. So did the Democratic gubernatorial candidate, Sulzer. Roosevelt's defeat, therefore, would have been as disastrous to his
political career, in all probability, as he had feared it would be when he
summoned Howe to his bedside. In the event, however, he outran both
the Presidential and gubernatorial victors and might claim that he
helped them, within the radius of his influence, far more than they

helped him. Since he had to bear most of the monetary cost of the campaign personally, he could be grateful that Howe had achieved this near miracle at remarkably small expense—a total of less than $1,800 out of the checking account assigned him, including $420.50 for his own salary and expenses, plus some $1,200 spent by or through the Roosevelt Committee.[38]

As for the national campaign, its outcome was, for Senator Roosevelt, wholly gratifying. Wilson was elected President of the United States with a popular vote of 6,293,019 to TR's 4,119,507 and Taft's 3,484,956. In the electoral college his triumph was overwhelming—435 to 88 for TR and only 8 for Taft. Further evidence of a fundamental shift in the direction of American politics was the impressive showing made by the Socialist candidate, Eugene V. Debs, who received 901,873 votes.

On the morrow of election day, Wisconsin's Senator La Follette, who might well have been elected President himself that year if only TR had remained quiescent and who as a nominal Republican had nothing to gain personally from Wilson's victory, published his interpretation of that victory's meaning. He saw "a nation of ninety million people demanding plain, simple justice, striving for educational, political and industrial democracy." The people, he said, "had seen the trusts grow and multiply, and the gigantic mergers and combinations welding Business into a Plutocracy, under Roosevelt. They had seen the special interests wax arrogant and the tariff wall raised by the hands of its pampered beneficiaries, under Taft. They demanded a change." [39]

VI

The months that immediately followed were, in Roosevelt's life, an interregnum, recognized by him as such even at the time.

On election day he was yet pale and weak from his long bout with fever, but thereafter, as he set about fulfilling his campaign promises to farmers, his old-time vigor swiftly returned to him. He called for help from the leaders of the State Grange and from the famous agricultural educator Liberty Hyde Bailey, head of the Agricultural College at Cornell University. With their aid he drafted five major agricultural bills— bills that would establish agricultural credit banks to make low-interest farm-improvement loans, facilitate the formation of farmer purchasing and marketing cooperatives, establish the office of Deputy Commissioner of Agriculture, give state aid to county farm bureaus, and provide state regulation of commission merchants through a system of licensing, bonding, and inspection. The chances for passage of these bills were enhanced by the fact that Democrats would again control both houses of the legislature and that the new Democratic governor, who planned to call the Executive Mansion "People's House," was clambering noisily aboard the Progressive Democratic, anti-Tammany bandwagon.

When the legislative session opened in Albany in January, 1913, two rooms in the capital's Ten Eyck Hotel sufficed for a state senator who, during his first term, had required a grand house on State Street. (Eleanor lived with him there three days a week, commuting from the New York City house, where the children remained.) With Roosevelt voting for him, Robert Wagner was again elected president pro tem of the Senate; Al Smith was elevated to the post of Assembly speaker; and Roosevelt was duly appointed chairman of the Senate Committee on Agriculture, in which capacity he promptly introduced his five agricultural bills and soon presided over public hearings on them.

They were hearings not devoid of headline-making controversy. Especially was this true of the hearings on the bill to regulate commission merchants. The merchants, predictably, organized strongly against this measure—they sent up from New York a whole trainload of spokesmen and partisans to jam the hearing chamber—and though farmers appeared in smaller number (most of them lacked the necessary train fare), they were no less vehement in their testimony and considerably more effective since they had by far the stronger case. They also had a strong political pressure group behind them. Louis Howe, filling in what he, too, may well have felt was a meanwhile period, went on the payroll of an organization called the New York State Markets League and prepared and mailed to local Grange leaders multigraphed letters rallying them behind the Roosevelt bill. Roosevelt himself was notably fair-minded and as conciliatory as possible to the opposition during the hearings. He readily agreed to technical modifications of his proposal when these seemed to him justified. But he would not retreat on essentials, and he well knew what these essentials were. He had taken pains to acquire firsthand information on how the present unregulated produce-marketing system worked. For instance, at two thirty one morning in New York City he was on an East River dock as a produce-bearing boat from Norfolk, Virginia, was unloaded and from there personally followed a crate of spinach as it passed through the hands of one middle merchant after another until at last it wound up in a Bronx grocery, whence it was sold to consumers. These consumers, he learned, paid at least $2.50 for spinach that had been bought from the grower for only 60 cents.[40] Eventually, after Roosevelt had left Albany, a bill calling for regulation of commission houses—not the precise one Roosevelt had introduced, but a similar one, containing the essentials of his—was passed and signed into law.

The young senator's strong and effective advocacy of governmental aid to agriculture was an important element of the foundation he was laying for his future career. He recognized this; he felt the satisfaction that derives from solid achievement and a measurable progress toward a definite goal. Nevertheless, Albany was no happy place for him during these early weeks and months of 1913. He had anticipated that it would not be. Soon after election day he had written a friend that the upcoming session of the legislature would be "difficult" and that "a good deal of tact and tenacity" would be required if he were "to come out of it with a whole skin." [41] He was virtually the sole survivor, in all the legislature, of the insurgency of 1911. As such he remained isolated from important leaders of his own party, several of whom continued to make open show of their personal dislike of him. Nor could he, in common prudence, permit himself to become linked in any way with the fortunes of the state executive, "Plain Bill" Sulzer, despite the latter's now increasingly assertive Progressivism. Sulzer's political judgment proved no better than his political morality as, recklessly, he moved toward a declaration of open war on Tammany. It was abundantly clear to Roosevelt and Howe that in making a full-scale attack on Tammany corruption, Sulzer laid himself open to devastating reprisals. His own past self and record made him vulnerable, and it was in the highest degree unlikely that the wily Murphy would have permitted Sulzer to achieve the governorship had he not retained the means of aggressive self-defense should Sulzer ever seriously threaten him.

But Roosevelt's political world, fortunately for him, no longer centered in Albany.

In mid-January he had received from Joe Tumulty a not unexpected telegram summoning him to Trenton for a conference with the President-elect. Patronage matters were discussed in the New Jersey governor's office, Roosevelt suggesting for preferment several of those who had worked with him in the Empire State Democracy. There is evidence that he mentioned his own desire to become a part of the new administration. No doubt he was given opportunity to do so, was asked direct questions on the matter by Tumulty; he may even have expressed his personal preference for the post of Assistant Secretary of the Navy and received assurances that, barring the unexpected, the post would be his. This at least would explain his otherwise almost inexplicable refusal to consider either the post of Assistant Secretary of the Treasury or that of Collector of the Port of New York (a powerful patronage position in which he might well have fought Tammany to a standstill) when these were offered him by the newly selected Secretary of the Treasury, William Gibbs McAdoo, a few days before the Presidential Inauguration, March 4, 1913.[42]

By that time, Roosevelt, who had come to Washington for the inauguration, knew that Josephus Daniels had accepted appointment as Secretary of the Navy. This seemed in some ways a strange appointment for the President to make. Daniels, a Southern small-town newspaper editor whose interests and tastes had always been predominantly agricultural, knew virtually nothing about the sea, ships, or sailors. He would certainly need as his top assistant someone who did, a recognition of which may well have lent warmth to the congratulations that Roosevelt tendered Daniels when the two encountered each other, quite by accident, in the lobby of the Willard Hotel on the night before the inauguration. As for Daniels, he had been strongly attracted to the young man when the two first met at the Baltimore convention. "I had charge of the distribution of tickets for editors at the convention," Daniels later recalled, "and Roosevelt came to my room with some up-State editors who wished seats in the press section. He was in a gay mood and I thought he was as handsome a figure of an attractive young man as I had ever seen." On the very day that he received Wilson's handwritten letter offering him the Navy post, Daniels had said to his wife, according to his later recollection, "I will ask the President to appoint Franklin Roosevelt as Assistant Secretary." And during this chance encounter in the Willard he did make the offer to the young man, subject, of course, to final clearance with the President and confirmation by the Senate. Roosevelt promptly accepted.

"All my life I have loved ships and been a student of the Navy," he reportedly said, "and the Assistant Secretaryship is the one place, above all others, I would love to hold." [43]

Eleven

⇶⇷

Assistant Secretary of the Navy, 1913-14

I

On MONDAY, March 17, 1913—his eighth wedding anniversary and less than seven weeks after his thirty-first birthday—Franklin D. Roosevelt was sworn in as the youngest Assistant Secretary of the Navy in history. A few hours later, in his office adjoining the Secretary's in the ornate State, War, and Navy Building across the street from the White House, he dashed off a note to his "Dearest Mama" saying he had been "baptized, confirmed, sworn in, vaccinated" (a smallpox epidemic was raging at the time), and was now "somewhat at sea," after having spent "over an hour . . . signing papers which had to be accepted on faith." He could only "hope luck will keep me out of jail." Absentmindedly he signed his note, as he had his dozens of unread official papers, with his full name, eliciting from his mother in her prompt reply a typical admonition. "Try not to write your signature too small, as it gets a cramped look and is not distinct," she urged in a missive dated March 18. "So many public men have such awful signatures. . . ." [1]

He lived then, and would continue to live through nearly all that spring and summer, as a single man in the Powhatan Hotel. Eleanor remained with "the chicks" in New York City, making frequent visits to Hyde Park after Sara moved there, and occasional ones to Washington, until she and Sara and the children all went as usual to Campobello. There, during the summer, they would be joined now and then by Roosevelt, though for shorter periods of time than theretofore.

The separation meant no lonely personal life, however, for the tall, handsome Assistant Secretary. Two days after being sworn in he wrote "Dearest Babbie" that he was "going some!" in a social way. On the preceding day, Tuesday, March 18, he had lunched with "Uncle Will" (Admiral William Sheffield Cowles, ret., husband of TR's sister, who was Eleanor's Auntie Bye) and Colonel and Mrs. Charles L. McCawley (the colonel, long one of the most popular figures in Washington society, was second-in-command of the Marine Quartermaster Corps). He had dined with "Nick and Alice" (former Republican Congressman Nicholas Longworth of Ohio, defeated last fall in his bid for reelection, and his imperious acid-tongued wife, "Princess Alice," TR's daughter). He had then gone with the Longworths to the theater for a performance of Pierre Loti's *The Daughter of Heaven*, returning to the Longworth house afterward for a late supper of eggs. On the day of his writing Eleanor, March 19, he again lunched with Admiral Cowles and would that night, he said, "give a dinner for Helen and Lathrop," these being his Groton-and-Harvard friend Lathrop Brown and Brown's wife, Brown having won election in 1912 as Democratic Representative from New York's First District.[2]

So it was that he plunged at once into the capital's social whirl. He remained in it, manifesting a taste for exclusive society and fashionable gaiety that varied markedly from the puritan tone set for the administration by the President when he refused to allow an inaugural ball to be held, by Secretary of State William Jennings Bryan when he banned wine and liquor from diplomatic functions, and by Secretary Daniels when he banned alcoholic beverages from all Navy ships and shore installations. Roosevelt joined the exclusive Chevy Chase Club and golfed there several times a week (Wilson's refusal of a proffered membership in this club offended its officers); he joined the even more exclusive Metropolitan Club and lunched or dined there every week (Wilson was the first President of the United States since the founding of the Metropolitan in the 1870's to whom the club's officers failed to extend an invitation to membership); and he was frequently entertained in the private homes of admirals, diplomats, Cabinet members, Congressional leaders, the members of the wealthy social and business elite.

In the autumn, when Eleanor and "the chicks" joined him in Washington, his social life became even more brilliant. They moved into one of the most famous houses in the capital, made so during TR's Presidency—Auntie Bye's "comfortable old-fashioned" place with "a little garden in the back and a most lovely rose arbor on the side" at 1733 N Street[3]—and formally entertained there, as Franklin's office and the Washington social system required them to do, with great frequency. Eleanor, under pressure of necessity as wife of the Navy's Assistant Secretary, made further conquest of her painful social shyness (she was required, for instance, to make as many as thirty formal calls in a single afternoon upon the wives of Navy officers and various dignitaries) and would be remembered as a poised and charming hostess, universally liked, if rather quiet and retiring, absorbed in maternal and household affairs, seemingly perfectly content to remain in the dim background while her brilliant husband occupied the center of the stage.[4]

By virtue of their relationship with TR, the young Roosevelts were warmly welcomed by the social leaders of the older generation who had been friends or friendly acquaintances of TR in the White House. Franklin and Eleanor were invited now and then to lunch or dine with widower Henry Adams, the intimidatingly acid, cynical, pessimistic historian whose house was across Lafayette Square from the Executive Mansion. (Eleanor would never forget how one day "after lunch with him, my husband mentioned something which at the time was causing him deep concern in the Government, and Mr. Adams looked at him rather fiercely and said: 'Young man, I have lived in this house many years and have seen the occupants of that White House across the square come and go, and nothing that you minor officials or the occupant of that house can do will affect the history of the world for long!' " [5]) TR's great friend (who was soon Secretary Daniels' enemy) Senator Henry Cabot Lodge of Massachusetts became the young Roosevelts' friend also. Supreme Court Justice Oliver Wendell Holmes and Mrs. Holmes entertained them, and Franklin went often to Holmes' famous Sunday afternoon discussion sessions for young men, where some of the most brilliant talk in Washington could be heard, though there is no evidence in his papers that he found the talk more than "interesting." Often they were guests in the British embassy (it was "one of the first houses to be opened to us," remembered Eleanor), because Sir Cecil Spring-Rice, the British ambassador, had been a particular friend of the TR family. So had been the French ambassador, Jean Jules Jusserand, and he, too, was their frequent host. Here they became special friends of the embassy's second secretary, M. de Laboulaye, and his wife, Marie.[6]

Their most intimate social friends, however, were Secretary of the Interior and Mrs. Franklin K. Lane; Lane's assistant, Adolph C. Miller,* and Mrs. Miller; and Mr. and Mrs. William Phillips, he being Assistant Secretary of State with an office only a few steps from Roosevelt's. The Roosevelts, Millers, and Phillipses were all of an age. The Lanes, being considerably older, naturally presided over the supper group which the four couples formed and which met every two weeks through Roosevelt's Washington years (the hostess on each occasion was permitted to invite one outside couple), though, as Eleanor later remembered, they "put formality behind us for these evenings, and did not even seat the

---

* When the Federal Reserve Board was established in 1914, Miller, a former economics professor at the University of California, was named to it.

Secretary of the Interior according to rank." [7] Lane was no stickler for formality in any case. A stout, jolly, convivial man with "a large white face" and bald, egg-shaped head (he reminded McAdoo "of Humpty Dumpty" [8]), the Secretary of the Interior loved to gossip, was the opposite of discreet in his talk, and was provided by his Cabinet post with an abundance of inside information on highly controversial matters. He formed a great affection for young Roosevelt. The latter, therefore, could not but have learned from him a great deal about Wilson's relations with his top advisers and about the interaction of personality and policy at the heart of the New Freedom.

Less purely social, but still primarily social so far as Roosevelt was concerned, was a luncheon group of some twenty administration officials and Progressive Democrats in the Congress, Roosevelt among them, which was organized in November, 1913, as the Common Counsel Club, one of its aims being the capture for Democracy of those Progressives who had been cast adrift by the failure of TR's third party in 1912.

Yet Roosevelt did not permit social activities to distract him from official duties or from the pursuit of his political ambitions. His position involved responsibilities which were, at the outset, intimidating. ". . . I will have to work like a new turbine to master this job," said his March 17 note to his mother, and in his letter to Eleanor two days later he announced, with evident pride, that in the absence from Washington of Secretary Daniels, who would be "away tomorrow also," he was Acting Secretary "and up to my ears." He "must have signed three or four hundred papers" that day, still largely on faith, but was, he felt, "*beginning to catch on.*" [9]

II

On that same day (Wednesday, March 19, 1913), evidently in pursuance of a promise tentatively made before he left Albany, he sent for Louis McHenry Howe.

"Dear Ludwig," he wrote, ". . . Here is the dope. Secretary— $2,000—Expect you April 1 with new uniform." Howe replied by telegram. He was "game," he said, though "it's going to break me"—which meant, as Roosevelt well knew (the two had already established a remarkable personal rapport), that Howe was more than pleased, was in fact delighted. Grace Howe was, too, and so was daughter Mary. As for Howe's fellow newspaper reporters in Albany, they received the news of his good fortune with hilarity. Much was made by them of the incongruous juxtaposition, as they saw it, of Howe and water. One of them proposed that all of them chip in to give the little man "a dozen cakes of soap" in the hope that, "exposed to water" with soap in hand, he might "finally come clean." [10]

It was a hope never realized, in the judgment of the naval officers with whom Howe was soon dealing, men whose disciplined notions of shipshape tidiness, bodily cleanliness, and proper office manners were outraged by him. One of them, a Navy captain, would warn Roosevelt one day that if Howe ever came aboard his ship, the crew would promptly "take him up on the foc'sle, strip him and scrub him down with sand and canvas"—a blunt expression of distaste which is said to have caused Roosevelt to "howl" with laughter.[11] (This response—hearty amusement rather than defensive resentment at aspersions cast upon an intimate friend and associate—is significant of the attitude Roosevelt often took toward those of whom he was most fond and who were most fond of him; he bantered them continuously, and there was a frequent wire edge of cruelty in his banter.) Howe himself seemed to derive malicious pleasure from the ill-concealed shock of high naval officers at their first sight of him sitting on a hot summer's day before his desk in the anteroom of the Assistant Secretary's office, his coat off, his shirt stained with sweat, his shirt sleeves rolled up, and his tie askew beneath his wilting, absurdly high collar, while ashes showered down and drifted across the desktop from the ever-present cigarette pasted on his lip. He spoke brusquely to them, often enough; he had no awe of rank. His one concession to Navy tradition would be the color of his tie: always it would be navy blue.

By his own admission, he was abysmally ignorant of the prescribed "duties of a secretary of the Assistant Secretary" when he entered his office for the first time. For several days thereafter, his sole contribution to the office's labors was his blotting of his superior's signature on official papers.[12]

He had at first to learn, as Roosevelt himself did, from a secretary who had served in the preceding administration, a young man named Charles H. McCarthy, who was efficient, hardworking, and thoroughly conversant with Navy Department routines. Simultaneously, often through simple naked assertion, Howe had to determine for himself the boundary lines between his and McCarthy's particular relationships with Roosevelt, had to assume certain functions in the office as peculiarly his own and measure for himself the limits of his authority. For Roosevelt gave neither of his secretaries any clear and firm definition of his job. In an early instance of an administrative habit that would later become notorious, he made very blurred delegations of authority, which

led inevitably to argument between Howe and McCarthy—argument
that was by no means always good-tempered. Sometimes it was so bitter
as to interfere with work, and Roosevelt had to arbitrate. That he did so
successfully, preventing the outbreak of open warfare and retaining for
himself the services of both men, was another early instance of lifelong
administrative habit. Few substantive changes in office organization or
procedure were made to accommodate either party to the quarrel. Specific objective causes of disagreement were seldom removed. Instead,
Roosevelt employed personal charm to soothe exacerbated feelings,
consciously using as the stuff of truce the personal devotion to himself
which each of his subordinates felt and which was their most important
common denominator. He needed both men and in a most engaging
manner he let them know that he needed them.

His need for one, however, differed radically from his need for the
other. "Howe goes to Newfoundland tomorrow and I shall try to clean
up his back work for him!" he would write to Eleanor in mid-September, 1916. "He is so wonderful on the big things that he lets the routine
slide. I need a thoroughgoing hack without brilliancy like the faithful
McCarthy to keep things running!" [13] And the "big things" on which
Howe was "so wonderful" were already looming large in the spring of
1913, so that there was from the outset no question that Howe was Roosevelt's principal subordinate.

One may question, however, whether a vocabulary of command, with
its precise ordering of "superiority" and "subordination," can be properly applied to what was in fact a relationship of mutual dependency.
The vocabulary of the theater seems more precisely applicable. Each
played a role indispensable to that of the other, since both were integral
parts of the drama in which they performed—in which they *chose* to perform because each of them felt *called upon* to do so. Certainly each fed
in the other a love of playacting and a sense of the world as theater. It
was in the mood of spectators of their own performance that they made
many of their jokes to each other, Howe needling Roosevelt (whom he
always called Franklin; few others did) about socialite playboy tendencies, Roosevelt needling Howe about general sloppiness of personal
habit and carelessness of office detail. Or, to shift metaphors, the two
played, not comedy or drama in a theater, but a game in a sports arena.
They made up a team—strong, resourceful, increasingly skillful. They
"played politics" as doubles partners might in a tennis tournament, with
political offices of ascending importance as the prizes of successive
rounds until, at last, they won the final round and gained, as ultimate
victory trophy, the Presidency of the United States. ("Even in 1913," Josephus Daniels would recall three decades later, "he [Howe] expected to

see Franklin occupy the White House, and to further that ambition he devoted his every effort." [14]) Yet this vocabulary of sport and theater is also, of itself alone, inadequate and distorting. It fails to describe the peculiar interpenetrative psychic intimacy of their relationship; it fails to indicate that to a limited but important degree, there was a virtual fusion of identities to create a double self. Large areas of Roosevelt's life, with a good many of his active interests, lay outside the range of this intimacy. To a much smaller extent the same was true of Howe. Yet as regards the central interest and purpose of their lives they were two minds with a single thought and two hearts that beat as one.

To Roosevelt, Howe became an extension of vital resource, an intelligent energy that operated in Roosevelt's interest without requiring any exercise of conscious will or thought on Roosevelt's part. Not a few projects and policies that added luster to Roosevelt's name were originally Howe's ideas. He contributed concepts, data, and language for Roosevelt's speeches. He mastered with astonishing swiftness and thoroughness the intricacies of Navy bureaucracy, made himself an authority on its internal workings and its external relations with business and labor. ("Always keeping himself in the background, he knew all the tides and eddies of the Navy Department . . . ," Daniels would remember. And a naval constructor at the New Orleans Navy Yard would write Roosevelt: "It is a source of wonder to me how a man not connected with the Naval Service can have obtained, in three years, the detailed knowledge of the situation that is possessed by Mr. Howe." [15])

He was guardian, promoter, and, to some degree, creator of Roosevelt's public image. He saw to it that Roosevelt received all the glory for whatever triumphs Howe's own efforts achieved; he also absorbed all he could of the blame for whatever acts proved mistaken or unpopular. He strove to dissociate Roosevelt in the public mind from those policies which caused the Secretary of the Navy to become the most controversial member of the Cabinet, cruelly ridiculed by sophisticates, most of them with axes to grind, as an absurd country yokel and hopeless landlubber. (Daniels was by no means unaware of Howe's operations in this respect. Howe, he once said good-humoredly, "would have sidetracked both President Wilson and me" to promote Roosevelt toward the White House.[16]) Not the least of his services was his spicing of his Roosevelt contacts with precisely the right kind of humor—a wry, ironical cynicism which Roosevelt hugely enjoyed but dared not openly indulge. When Daniels raised a storm by abolishing the officers' wine mess on ship and shore, Roosevelt was on an inspection trip to the West Coast. There he received a letter from Howe: "I know how greatly you regret not being here . . . to share some of the glory. As it is, of course, I can tell the newspapermen nothing except that you are away and naturally know nothing about it." Howe was also telling everyone that it was his own "wicked self," not Franklin Roosevelt, whose "wicked performances" had just provoked the wrath of the formidable *Army and Navy Register*. "Gillis tells me that it is part of the Bausch and Lomb-Steel Corporation publicity campaign, about which he warned the Secretary some time ago," Howe went on, in a psychologically revealing statement. "He may be right, but I am not inclined to believe in widespread conspiracies without considerable evidence, and I suspect it is more likely a case of toes trodden on of people who are friends of the management of the paper. I am sorry if I have trod on toes, but so far I have not considered going barefoot to avoid possible injuries from this cause in the future." [17] He was an ingenious contriver of strategies for Roosevelt's political advancement, employing his natural talent for intrigue and plot, a taste for indirection and devious manipulation that were similar to Roosevelt's and grew with their exercise. He became, too, a conserver and protector of qualities that were uniquely Roosevelt's own. He served as office doorkeeper. Only through him, with a few exceptions, which he invariably resented, could visitors gain access to the private office of the Assistant Secretary, and he screened applicants for this favor through a fine discernment of long-range political values.

Howe was as bold as he was shrewd in his stratagems and advice. He had also the strength to stand up against his friend when he thought him mistaken. He could and did press unwanted advice with tenacious stubbornness on occasion and was a generally effective naysayer against ill-considered words and deeds, helping thus to keep in check his friend's impetuosity. ("He was . . . the best adviser Roosevelt ever had, because he had the guts to say 'no,' " according to Admiral Emory S. Land, who knew him well during Roosevelt's Navy years. And Howe's own description of a major function of his, vis-à-vis the Assistant Secretary, was, "To provide the toe weights." [18]) Finally, he was not only a prodigious worker but also possessed of talents that Roosevelt lacked. From all this the conclusion is inescapable that Roosevelt could not have functioned anywhere near as well as he did if Howe had not been at his side; he would in all probability have blundered into traps fatal to his ambition or would have missed irretrievable opportunities for successes necessary to the ultimate election triumph. Nevertheless, *he* was the dominant one of these two always. Howe *wanted* Roosevelt to dominate; he *willed* it so after having invested all his romantic hero-worshiping energies in the handsome young man. But it would have been so in any case. There was no possibility at any time that Howe could use Roosevelt as a means to ends that varied from Roosevelt's own.

For though Roosevelt's need for Howe was very great, in personal as well as professional terms, it was a *partial* need always. Howe's need of Roosevelt, on the other hand, became virtually total. From 1913 on, Howe lived through Roosevelt—his life had practically no meaning for him apart from Roosevelt—so that one is justified in saying, as historians would always say, that "Roosevelt did this" or "Roosevelt did that" when the "this" or "that" were originally Howe's conceptions and the "doing" was of Howe's execution. Howe *was* Roosevelt (Roosevelt was never Howe), and a manifestation of his *necessary* acceptance of the other's domination was the fierce possessive jealousy with which he guarded his special relationship. He remained basically psychologically insecure and so was desperately fearful of rivals always. George Marvin was one who noticed this. A master of Groton during Roosevelt's last two years in the school, Marvin had become an editor of the influential magazine *World's Work* by the time Roosevelt entered the Navy Department. He sometimes came to see Roosevelt during office hours. And he remarked that it "always made Howe extremely sore when a few . . . , like myself, passed through his office, without any reference to him, on our way to see the Assistant Secretary." He added that Howe "was . . . vindictive, as well as extremely astute . . . and he never forgot his earlier inferiority complexes." Others would remember from those years that Howe was "frightfully self-conscious" and as ugly in disposition as he was in appearance.[19]

Indeed, Howe's general ill temper, expressed in frequent unnecessary rudenesses, a seeming deliberate courting of enmities, became an acknowledged fact among those who worked with him every day. "I am hated by everybody, I always have been hated by everybody, and I want to be hated by everybody," he reportedly once said to a friend.[20]

III

The job that Roosevelt was just "beginning to catch on" to on the day he sent for Howe was one that had never been precisely defined. Traditionally—while the Secretary worked with the White House on overall Navy policy, with the Congress on naval bills and appropriations, and with the State Department and the admirals on major movements of the fleet—the Assistant Secretary supervised the department's civilian personnel, handled the routine business of administration over the Navy bureaus, and negotiated most of the purchase contracts for coal, steel, oil (the Navy was just beginning to convert from coal to oil), naval stores, and the myriad other materials, bought in bulk, on which the

Navy ran. He had much to do with the shore installations (docks and yards), where he was responsible for a great deal of the Navy's labor relations—and here Howe's presence at his side was of particular importance to Roosevelt. It was Howe who insisted that he involve himself personally in negotiations with labor leaders regarding wages and hours and working conditions in Navy yards (earlier Assistant Secretaries had assigned subordinates to this task), partially filling what would otherwise have remained a serious gap in Roosevelt's education and garnering personal friendships that could be translated into votes on election days in the years ahead.

The Assistant Secretary's office was of course a functioning mechanism when Roosevelt was appointed to it: he inherited a trained staff and its procedures had been long established. Nevertheless, the post Roosevelt occupied was an administrative assignment whose proportions were huge (the annual appropriation of $143,497,000 for a Navy and Marine Corps of some 63,000 officers and enlisted men amounted to approximately 20 percent of the total government expenditures that year), and he was challenged by it and had to apply himself diligently to the mastery of it. Yet as early as June, 1913, he received a letter from one of the most prominent and powerful Congressmen (a Republican at that!) praising him as "the promptest and most efficient Assistant Secretary in any Department with whom we have dealt in our 11 years of service here." [21]

But he was not content to be known among a few insiders for the efficient performance of useful but mundane tasks. "I get my fingers into about everything and there's no law against it," he used to say.[22] Within days after his swearing in he had top administrative responsibility for the distribution of hundreds of thousands of Navy rations, blankets, and other items for relief of flood victims in Ohio and Indiana. Within weeks he was deeply involved in problems arising from the collapse of a huge dry dock under construction at Pearl Harbor, Hawaii; he would become responsible for the ultimate administrative decision to scrap the original construction plans for the project and substitute a method of employing floating caissons, as recommended by a Navy Bureau of Yards and Docks engineer. (This engineer was Lieutenant Commander Frederic R. Harris; he would become bureau chief two years later, and Roosevelt would find important use for his engineering genius three decades later.) Simultaneously, he tried to discover ways of profitably using the Navy's too-many shore installations, for the yards had long been grossly inefficient and many of them had no real use whatever. They were contradictions of the Daniels-Roosevelt commitment to economy. Similarly irritating was the overlapping of authority and function among departmental bureaus—a wasteful confusion great enough to overcome Roosevelt's personal penchant, which was not as marked then as it later became, for vagueness of definition in administrative organization. He and Daniels, during their first years together, devoted much attention to reorganizing the Navy bureaucracy, reassigning personnel and trying to see to it that each bureau's contribution to the department's operation was not duplicative of another's.

Also, in the spring of 1913, Roosevelt was much concerned with problems arising from attempts of efficiency zealots to introduce the Taylor system of scientific management into the Boston (Charlestown) Navy Yard—a story sufficiently significant in terms of Roosevelt's psychology and education to justify its brief telling here.

The Taylor system was named after its inventor, Frederick W. Taylor, an engineer who had been stimulated toward his revolutionary concepts by his experience as gang boss, during the 1880's, in a steel mill. He had subsequently made precise studies of "time-and-motion," "cost-and-time," work "routing" and the like in manufacturing and had published his findings and conclusions in epoch-making papers ("A Piece Rate System" and "Shop Management") in the early 1900's. They were carefully read by Louis D. Brandeis. And it is an element of the overall irony of American history that Brandeis, the archfoe of corporate giantism, should have played a key role in the rapid spread of Taylorism through American industry during the years of the New Freedom. In a much-publicized railroad rate case, as the decade opened, he argued with facts and figures that shippers would be enabled simultaneously to raise wages and increase profits if they applied the Taylor system to their operations. The argument was convincing not only to the Interstate Commerce Commission (he won his case), but also to leaders of American industry. Soon Taylor's ideas were being triumphantly applied by one industrial firm after another, most notably by the Ford Motor Company, which, in 1913, inaugurated the assembly-line manufacture of automobiles. The inevitable net effect, encouraged by the huge war market of 1914–18, was to place a greater premium than before on bigness of industrial organization and a greater competitive penalty than before on smallness.

Nor was the spread of Taylorism confined to private enterprise. The system was adopted by the Army's Watertown Arsenal, adjacent to Boston. The savings there in operating cost were substantial. And in the Hull Division of the Charlestown Navy Yard, in 1912–13, a partial application of the system by two assistant constructors, both of them youthful officers, was estimated by objective observers to have reduced costs by 35 percent, saving the Navy Department nearly a half million dollars a year.

Labor's response to Taylorism, however, was wholly and strongly negative. Workers feared and hated it as a relentless, soul-crushing speedup designed to transform them from human beings into virtual automata. Further, they were convinced that, to the extent of its actual increase in economic efficiency, it reduced the number of available jobs. Hence, in the Charlestown Yard, organized labor, backed by the commanding Navy captain who (typically) had no sympathy with "newfangled" notions that would require him drastically to modify his comfortably easy style of administration, protested bitterly the Hull Division innovations and threatened a strike if they were extended elsewhere in the yard. A letter containing this threat from the Boilermakers and Ship Metal Workers Union at the yard was personally delivered to Roosevelt by Democratic Representative James M. Curley of Massachusetts, who was then at the beginning of what would become one of the gaudiest careers in twentieth-century American politics.

Roosevelt, in mid-May, 1913, conducted a personal investigation of the yard, listened to labor and the commandant's complaints, and then issued a cautiously worded endorsement of labor's side of the case. He went so far as to promise tacitly that the two assistant constructors responsible for the Hull Division innovations would, as the commandant wished, soon be transferred elsewhere. But he had hardly arrived back in his Washington office before he received a letter from an old Harvard acquaintance who persuasively defended both the persons and official acts of the threatened young Navy engineers, a letter which confirmed a suspicion Roosevelt himself had formed during his inspection—namely, that the efficiency system did indeed "work" and, if widely applied, could enable him to make a remarkable record for efficient, economical operation of Navy installations. The letter was soon followed by a personal visit to Roosevelt from a brilliant recent graduate of the Harvard Law School, Felix Frankfurter, then an attorney for the War Department, who came armed with statistics on the savings made by Taylorism at Watertown. Frankfurter persuaded the Assistant Secretary to arrange for an unofficial study and report on the Charlestown Yard by an expert and to stop the threatened transfer of the two engineers.

When the expert's report firmly sustained the contentions of the efficiency engineers, Roosevelt temporized. Strongly attracted to the goals of increased efficiency, he was equally strongly repelled by the prospect of major labor trouble if "the Taylor system" or "any other" were "imposed from above on an unwilling labor force." [23] In the end, he made no clear-cut decision either way; he would still be "studying" and "considering" the matter in 1915, when a wholly politically motivated rider attached to a Navy appropriation bill, prohibiting the introduction of efficiency systems into naval installations, was approved by Congress.

Roosevelt thus ranged across the whole spectrum of departmental activity and intervened almost everywhere.

But he particularly aspired to become spokesman, representative, and figurative leader of the actual seagoing Navy with its Marine arm—himself a personification of the best in U.S. nautical tradition. He missed few opportunities for formal inspections of yards and ships, using these inspections not only to bring the Navy and the department's program before the general public but also to present himself in a dramatic light. He thoroughly enjoyed the elaborate ritual with which he, by virtue of his office, was welcomed aboard a naval vessel or upon his official arrival at a Navy yard—the thunderous salute of seventeen guns and four ruffles, the honor guard drawn up at stiff attention, the officers assembled in full dress uniform to greet him—and his enjoyment was not lessened by the fact that such inspections could be made to serve his personal political ambition. He produced headlines with them; he made useful contacts with the local powers of Democratic politics. Initially he was disturbed because there was no special Assistant Secretary's flag to be run up the mast when he boarded ship (the President and the Secretary of the Navy each had his special flag), but he ultimately remedied this unfortunate situation by designing a flag himself and seeing to it that it was properly flown.[24]

He was immensely pleased to be able to order a battleship, the USS *North Dakota*, to participate in the July 4, 1913, celebration at Eastport, Maine, he personally maintaining on this occasion a breezily informal "democracy" before his assembled family, friends, and neighbors of Campobello (he boarded the ship clad in summer flannels) while nevertheless receiving (he had prearranged this with the captain) his formal seventeen-gun salute. It gave him more than pleasure, it was for him a profound emotional experience, to review the fleet as he did in October, 1913, when nine battleships sailed from Hampton Roads, bound for a goodwill cruise among Mediterranean ports. He stood then atop the chart house of the *Dolphin*, which was the steam yacht assigned the Secretary of the Navy (though Daniels had so little use for it that he assigned it to other duties a few months later), stood there and watched the spectacle through binoculars. "The big gray fellows were magnificent as they went past, with all hands at the rail, and I only wish a hundred thousand people could have seen them," he wrote to "Dearest Babs" next day.[25]

Long a disciple of Mahan, he now had opportunities to translate Mahan's doctrines into practice, and he had not been a month in his new office before he publicly identified himself with the advocates of U.S. naval expansion. The Navy League of the United States was a "big navy" lobby whose leading members included top executives of corporations that would profit from an accelerated shipbuilding program. The chairman of the board of the International Nickel Corporation, Colonel Robert M. Thompson, was president of the league; Herbert Satterlee, son-in-law of J. P. Morgan, was a vice-president; and with both men young Roosevelt was on warmly friendly terms. He was quick to accept an invitation to address a Navy League convention in New York City, in April, 1913, where he endorsed the league's primary aim as emphatically as he could. He had, however, to take account of the mood of idealistic pacifism which then prevailed among Americans, especially in the ranks of Wilsonian Progressives, and therefore carefully phrased his expansionist doctrine. "This is not a question of war or peace," he averred. "I take it there are as many advocates of arbitration and international peace in the Navy as in any other profession. But we are confronted with a condition—the fact that our country has decided in the past to have a fleet and that war is still a possibility. We want the country to feel, too, that in this maintaining of a fighting force of the highest efficiency we are at the same time educating thousands of young men to be better citizens." [26]

One contribution to "education"—lifesaving physical education—he personally made not long afterward, when he was shocked to discover that a large proportion of the sailors on U.S. fighting ships, recruited from midland and Southern farms and towns, were unable to swim and that there had recently been several needless drownings because of this fact. With Daniels' concurrence, he promptly ordered that every new recruit thenceforward must qualify in swimming before going to sea, and every midshipman must do so before promotion to ensign. He also instituted an annual competition among Navy fighting ships to determine which could qualify the highest percentage of its crew in a test involving a dive of eighteen feet or more followed by a hundred-yard swim. He donated a cup, the "Assistant Secretary's Swimming Cup," to be awarded the winning ship.[27]

He soon convinced the naval officers he met that he did truly possess nautical knowledge and skill and was one with them in his feeling for ships and blue water. He loved to sail on fighting ships and did so whenever he could, preferring destroyers because they were so small and fast,

so swiftly responsive to the moods of the sea and hence so demanding of
those who sailed them. Once (this was in a later summer) he sailed on a
destroyer commanded by a young lieutenant named William F. Halsey,
Jr., to inspect naval installations in Frenchman's Bay on the coast of
Maine. They went from there to Passamaquoddy Bay, where the Assistant Secretary proposed that, because he was intimately familiar with the
channel, he should take the vessel through the strait between Campobello and the mainland. Halsey yielded reluctantly. He was keenly
aware of the great difference in skill required to "sail a catboat out to a
buoy" and "to handle a high-speed destroyer in narrow waters"; he
watched intently, fearful of disaster to his ship, and was proportionately
relieved and admiring when he saw that Roosevelt really "knew his
business"; this "white-flanneled yachtsman" took the ship safely
through the treacherous waters as easily as anyone could have done.[28]
He impressed Navy officers, too, with the decisiveness of his dealings
with matters they brought to him in his office—a decisiveness that contrasted favorably with Daniels' slow, cautious deliberation. They felt
that he understood their problems, as Daniels, a hopeless landlubber,
could never do. Soon they were going to the Assistant Secretary with
matters that should properly have been decided by the Secretary; sometimes they waited until Roosevelt was Acting Secretary, in Daniels' absence. He was encouraged to go close to the edge of insubordination, if
not well beyond it.

Daniels was aware of the threat to his authority posed by the younger
man and was prepared to check him, if far less narrowly and harshly
than many in his position would have done. He had expressed his attitude on this matter in conversation with Republican Senator (former
Secretary of State) Elihu Root of New York shortly before Roosevelt's
nomination for Assistant Secretary was sent to the Senate. Root, informed that the President planned to submit the appointment, raised no
objection but did raise his eyebrows. ". . . a queer look came on his
face" as he more than intimated that Daniels himself might soon regret
this choice. "You know the Roosevelts, don't you?" Root had asked.
"Whenever a Roosevelt rides, he wishes to ride in front. . . . You know
they like to have their own way. . . ." Daniels did know. He was unperturbed. He wanted a strong assistant, a man with a mind of his own who
would pull his full share of the load and possessed naval lore that Daniels lacked. "A chief who fears that an assistant will outrank him," he
said, "is not fit to be chief." [29]

He well knew that Roosevelt emulated TR, but his fatherly affection
for the young man was so totally devoid of envy or malice (one chapter
of his memoirs would be entitled "Love at First Sight—F.D.R. and

J.D.") that he more than sympathized with the latter's vaulting ambition. He did all he could to encourage it and facilitate its realization. "His distinguished cousin TR went from this place to the Presidency," he noted in his diary on the day of Roosevelt's swearing in. "May history repeat itself." Soon thereafter a photographer took a picture of the new Secretary and Assistant Secretary standing together on the east portico of the State, War, and Navy Building, the slender young man towering a full head above his paunchy chief. When developed, the picture showed both men smiling, but there was no such openmouthed exuberant grin on the Secretary's face as on that of his assistant. Daniels commented on this to Roosevelt. "Franklin, why are you grinning from ear to ear, looking as pleased as if the world were yours . . ." he asked. Roosevelt knew of no special reason; he was just trying to look his best. "I will tell you," said Daniels. "We are both looking down at the White House and you are saying to yourself . . . , 'Some day I will be living in that house.' . . ." [30]

Hence Daniels was neither surprised nor dismayed when, returning to his office on March 21, 1913, after a two-day absence, he read in the newspapers a remark his assistant had made to newsmen upon assuming for the first time the duties of Acting Secretary. Daniels, along with all America, remembered that in February, 1898, shortly after the blowing up of the U.S. armored cruiser *Maine* in Havana Harbor, Secretary of the Navy John D. Long had left Washington for a day, first warning Assistant Secretary Theodore Roosevelt to do nothing that affected administration policy "without consulting the President or me." Fire-eating TR, as Acting Secretary, had promptly disobeyed; he had dispatched the famous telegram ordering Commodore Dewey from Hong Kong to Manila Bay, where "offensive operations" against the Spanish Asian fleet were to be initiated "in the event [inevitable, as TR then believed and helped by his act to assure] . . . declaration of war Spain." His gross insubordination, abundantly publicized, had greatly added to his fame and pushed him another long step toward the White House he occupied four years later. Franklin Roosevelt made pointed reference to this. "There's another Roosevelt on the job today . . . ," said he to reporters with a wide grin. "You remember what happened the last time a Roosevelt occupied a similar position?" * [31]

The principal motive for the young man's remark was no doubt his boyish desire for personal publicity coupled with his politician's wish to capitalize upon his relationship with Cousin Theodore. But Daniels

* It is possible that FDR had by then received a letter from TR, mailed the day before, in which TR commented that it was "interesting to see . . . you in another place which I myself once held."

might well have contemplated the indicated possibility that FDR, in his heart of hearts, hoped to carry his emulation of TR to the point of personally profitable insubordination, should the opportunity ever present itself. If so, the Assistant Secretary was badly mistaken in his estimate of his superior's character.

IV

Josephus Daniels was no such vacillating mediocrity as John D. Long, nor was he any such comic figure ("the funniest looking hillbilly . . ." [32]) as Roosevelt at first saw him to be. He was a round-faced, blue-eyed, mild-mannered man who was addicted to black string ties and pleated linen shirts, plain and simple in his tastes, puritan in his morals, and magnanimous in his human relations. At fifty-one he seemed somewhat old-fashioned, but he fitted well into the general capital scene that year. Washington itself was old-fashioned. Wholly lacking in mass industry, its broad residential streets arched by great trees, dotted with government buildings and monuments executed in the Greco-Roman style, the city had the air of an overgrown country town whose permanent citizens looked more to the past than to the future, were more concerned to preserve traditions than to institute innovations. It retained much of the flavor and many of the customs of the Old South (its public facilities were racially segregated as a matter of course; much of its black population was jammed into back-alley slums so hideous that Mrs. Woodrow Wilson's first sight of them shocked her into ultimately effective social action). All in all, Washington bore not a few resemblances to Daniels' hometown of Raleigh, North Carolina, and the Secretary felt more at home there than the Assistant Secretary ever could.

For Daniels was himself invincibly rural—in his personal tastes, his manners, his mental attitudes, his slow but sure habits of work, his concomitant resistance to being rushed into a decision, and his political views. The latter were those of an old-line agrarian radical.* From early childhood he had absorbed from the farmers, small businessmen, and politicians of his acquaintance a profound antipathy for the "vested interests" of the East—the Tobacco Trust, the railroads—that had grievously exploited his home region, and this antipathy had been generalized, as he grew up, into reasoned antitrust, antiprotectionist,

* He shared to the full the Southern agrarian's racist views. His attitudes toward the Negro, expressed in the Raleigh *News-Observer* of those years, would seem outrageous when read in the 1960's and 1970's.

anti-tight-money convictions. By 1896 he had been ripe for conversion to Bryanism. And sixteen years later he remained as fervent a Bryan Democrat as he was a pious Methodist, his faith in the Common Man of a piece with his faith in a God of Infinite Wisdom and Loving Kindness. Loathing special privilege, he had none of his assistant's love of Navy protocol or ritual. He flatly refused to admit the necessity of social class distinctions between Navy officers and enlisted men, outraging the former by addressing the latter, in public speech, as "young gentlemen" instead of "sailors" or "my lads." He strove to democratize the Navy, opening the way for enlisted men to receive appointments to the Naval Academy and instituting an extensive basic education and technical training program for enlisted marines and sailors. He disliked big cities, feared big business, and distrusted big executives. Like Bryan—like Wilson, too, though in a quite different, far less egoistic way—he was a moralist in politics, measuring proposals by clearly defined standards of right and wrong. Yet this did not blind him to realities. He was, in his homespun way, an unusually shrewd judge of men and of the possibilities of effective action.

"Daniels," one of the Secretary's admirers recalled years later, ". . . had the exact combination of qualities needed to grapple with the Navy as it was in 1913. . . . He entered the Department with a profound suspicion that whatever an Admiral told him was wrong and that every corporation with a capitalization of more than $100,000 was inherently evil. In nine cases out of ten his formula was correct: the Navy was packed at the top with dead wood, and with politics all the way through, and the steel, coal and other big industries were accustomed to dealing with it on their own terms." [33]

The custom and terms were abruptly changed. Franklin Roosevelt's education was advanced thereby.

The Secretary had been only briefly in office before he advertised for bids for armor plate to be used in construction of a new battleship, the *Arizona*. When submitted by U.S. Steel, Bethlehem Steel, and Midvale Steel, which were the only three American companies making armor plate, the bids turned out to be identical to the penny—$454 per ton. This was not unexpected. Nevertheless, Daniels promptly summoned the responsible officer of each of the three companies to his office. He pointed out to each that all had sworn under oath not to confer, much less agree with one another while in the process of determining their bids. He charged the three with illegal collusion. They denied the charge, yet at the same time cited as precedent for their procedure the department's policy in the past of dividing each armor plate purchase equally among the three companies at whichever price was the lowest bid, a procedure that destroyed the *raison d'être* for competitive bidding. Daniels indicated his suspicion that this policy and procedure had been adopted at the behest of the three companies—certainly it "was very agreeable to them"—and also pointed out that at least one of the three, Bethlehem, was in the habit of selling armor plate to foreign governments at prices markedly below those charged their own government. ("In 1894 the Bethlehem Company sold armor-plate to Russia at $240 per ton and charged the United States Navy $616.14 per ton," Daniels would recall in his memoirs. "In 1911 they sold to Italy at $395 and charged Uncle Sam $420. Later they sold to Japan at $406.35 and to the United States at prices ranging from $440 to $540 a ton." [34]) He then refused to accept the bids and ordered a resubmittal on a genuinely competitive basis. He ordered in vain: the second bids were also identical, to the penny. Whereupon Daniels sent Roosevelt to New York City to consult with a British steel magnate who had just arrived there and who promptly submitted a bid so much lower than that of the three American companies that the latter were forced to drop their price substantially before the contract was awarded one of them. The Secretary saw to it that, through the press, the country was informed of all this; he told Congress that the enforced foreign competition had reduced the *Arizona*'s armor-plate cost by $1,110,084.

Roosevelt himself, with Howe at his side, entered with considerable enthusiasm into the campaign to save money for the Navy. In June, 1913, he was sufficiently concerned with cost savings to confer with President Wilson on what he called a "nice point" raised by competing bids from American and foreign firms for machines to be installed in a Navy yard. The lowest bidder was a German firm. An American firm, however, had submitted a bid only slightly higher—"so little that considering the cost of inspection etc. the American firm should have the award." But this left out of account the tariff duty of 15 percent which the German firm would be required to pay into the U.S. Treasury. "The President," as Roosevelt recorded, "took the view that the wage earners & capital of this country would gain more by award to the Am firm that w'd be saved to the gov. by award to the Germans." It was a view with which Roosevelt agreed—"but perhaps some day, pretty far off we may take a bigger view of economics than the purely nation wide one." [35] A little later, Bethlehem, Midvale, and U.S. Steel, uncowed in their exercise of monopoly power, submitted identical bids for turbine casings to be used in the *Arizona*. Roosevelt promptly sought bids abroad. He ultimately bought the casings from the Cyclops Steel and Iron Works of Sheffield, England, for only slightly more than a third of the price set by the American corporations.

Subsequently, the Assistant Secretary actively engaged in one battle after another against collusive bidding and monopolistic overpricing and against the strong tendency of old-line Navy bureaucrats to favor such practices.

One battle, a particularly important one, had to do with coal.

Roosevelt and Howe discovered that (a) the department's Bureau of Supplies and Accounts maintained a relatively short "accepted list" of coal companies able to supply fuel meeting the Navy's specifications and (b) the bureau customarily did not publicly advertise for bids but, instead, sent bid requests only to the listed companies. As for the specifications themselves, they were so rigid, so narrowly precise as to raise suspicion they had been drawn up in cooperation with the very companies that were listed, nearly all of whom mined coal in West Virginia. Suspicion was reinforced by the fact that the bids submitted by these favored few were always practically identical. They were actually identical, to the penny, in early 1914, when the department asked for bids on coal to be delivered at Hampton Roads, and were also much too high, in the judgment of Roosevelt and Howe. The bids rejected, Howe was assigned to rewrite the specifications, and a public advertisement for bids was then issued. A number of Pennsylvania firms now entered the competition with bids (a low of $2.57 a ton) considerably under the lowest ($2.80 per ton) of the new bids now submitted by any West Virginia firm. Substantial savings were made by the department.

But Howe, alas, though normally very astute and careful in such matters, evidently made mistakes in his respecifications. Several ship engineers later complained about the poor quality of some of the new coal in tones loud enough to be heard in Congress, which conducted an investigation. And Daniels, who was much more adept at dealing with Congressmen than was his assistant and who usually served as buffer between Roosevelt and Congressional hostility, declined in this instance, for whatever reason, to do so. Having taken full responsibility for rejection of the original, obviously collusive bids in his testimony before the House Naval Affairs Committee, the Secretary blandly protested a lack of any detailed knowledge of what subsequently happened: the whole thing had been handled by the Assistant Secretary. So Roosevelt was forced to endure very sharp questioning, especially from West Virginia Congressmen. He managed to weather the storm, partly through a truth-obscuring agility of testimony but mostly by convincing his interrogators that the mistakes had been made in a good cause and that, moreover, a measure of competition had indeed been restored to the market for Navy coal.

There was no major repetition of this kind of error, largely because a new and unusually competent Paymaster General, Samuel McGowan, was appointed in the general departmental reorganization of 1914. He with his assistant, Christian J. Peoples, became among the closest and friendliest working associates of the Assistant Secretary and the latter's top assistant. Daniels christened McGowan and Peoples the "Gold Dust Twins," to which Roosevelt added the soubriquet "Heavenly Twins." And in the end, Daniels and Roosevelt, with McGowan and Peoples, made a truly remarkable record of departmental economic efficiency.

But Roosevelt's battle, in his own view, was not essentially against the trusts; it had no such broad base in social morality as did his chief's. His dominant concern was to build a "Navy second to none." He saw economic waste as inimical to this end, maximum economic efficiency as conducive to it, and his battle was therefore against the former and for the latter. The Secretary of the Navy viewed the operations of the Navy in relation to the trusts as part of the overall New Freedom war for industrial democracy and—in his moral indignation against the chicanery that was obviously central to big business ethics—did not shrink from espousal of truly radical corrective measures. As a result of the armor plate controversy, he pressed for construction of a government plant in which the Navy would make its own armor plate and shell casings—a plant large enough to obviate the necessity for Navy dealings with private enterprise in these matters. He ultimately skillfully piloted through Congress a measure authorizing such a plant, which Wilson promptly signed.* Roosevelt was personally opposed to this. The most he favored was a small government plant which could be used to determine actual manufacturing costs, to experiment with armor improvement, and to serve "as a nucleus for great expansion in time of war." These three objects seemed to him "entirely legitimate" in that they did not contradict the principle of private enterprise; they would not, he said, ruin "anybody's legitimate business." [36]

Consistent with Daniels' political and economic philosophy, if somewhat incongruous with the Cabinet position he held, was his pacifism. Here the contrast between him and Roosevelt was particularly sharp. While Daniels had a healthy suspicion of the motives of the most ardent expansionists, Roosevelt was a "big navy" man, an activist and a militant in situations where Daniels, who loathed violence, was inclined toward conciliation. And in this, the Secretary was in much closer accord with the leading ideas of Progressivism in 1913 than Roosevelt was.

* The plant, located at Charleston, West Virginia, was only partially completed when the Wilson administration ended. The succeeding administration abandoned the project.

For 1913 marked the high tide of the peace movement which sprang from the late nineteenth-century conviction that the progress of moral education and scientific technology had made war wholly obsolete as a means of settling international disputes. Actively involved in it were such diverse Americans as Jane Addams and James J. Hill, Thomas A. Edison and Carrie Chapman Catt, Lyman Abbott (editor of *Outlook,* whose contributing editor was the far from pacifistic TR) and Andrew Carnegie. The last, whom Daniels much admired ("that interesting, delightful man," he called him[37]) was particularly active. No doubt influenced by the example of Alfred Nobel,* Swedish discoverer of dynamite, who dedicated to the advancement of peace and the arts of peace a fortune accumulated from the manufacture of explosives, Carnegie used his money, some of which had come from the manufacture of armor plate, to erect the Peace Palace at The Hague and the Pan-American Building in Washington and to establish a peace endowment bearing his name. He himself developed warm personal friendships with leading figures of the American peace movement, notably with Secretary of State Bryan who; in that first spring and summer of the Wilson administration, was making newspaper headlines with his Wilson-approved plan for a series of international treaties to assure a permanent world peace.

Signers of these treaties pledged themselves to submit all their international disputes to a permanent commission of investigation for a period of from six months to a year during which time they would neither resort to war nor increase their armaments. At the end of the "cooling-off" investigatory period each nation might accept or reject the commission findings and, rejecting them, was then free, without violation of her signature, to go to war. But Bryan—who asserted as a cardinal article of his faith that the "world is advancing in morals," being possessed of "a greater sense of kinship among men" and "more altruism" than ever before—was convinced that no nation would by that time elect to fight. "When men are mad, they talk about what they can do," said he when he announced his treaty plan in early May, 1913. "When they are calm they talk about what they ought to do. And it is the purpose of this plan to provide the time for passion to subside, for reason to regain its throne." [39] He was elated by the highly favorable response his proposal immediately received from the nations of the world.

---

* Carnegie shared with Nobel the then widely prevalent view of human nature as essentially reasonable—the same view which led Professor Seignobos (see page 88) to conclude that the "chemistry of explosives has worked in favor of peace" and led Nobel himself to express the wish that he "could produce a substance or a machine of such frightful efficacy for wholesale slaughter that wars would thereby become altogether impossible." [38]

No one of them rejected the proposal outright; all, including militaristic Germany and Japan, expressed warmest approval of the treaty aim; and no fewer than thirty—Great Britain, France, and Italy among them— would become actual signatories by August, 1914. Carnegie was one of millions who saw this as an unprecedented triumph of idealistic diplomacy, opening the way to a near future of universal peace and limitlessly expanding prosperity.

Josephus Daniels was only somewhat less enthusiastic. Upon Bryan's request, he willingly deferred activation of his own pet project of 1913, the calling of an international naval arms limitation conference, until the cooling-off treaties had been ratified. "The world took kindly to Bryan's plan," Daniels later recalled, "and I strongly favored it." He felt "that a long step forward had been taken." [40]

But he was well aware that others took a very different view.

TR was one of them, of course. The ex-President saw Wilson's Secretary of State as a "prize idiot . . . , a professional yodeler, a human trombone." He saw as worse than useless the Bryan-Wilson efforts "to procure universal peace by little arbitration treaties which . . . would not be worth the paper on which they are written in any serious crisis." [41] Such a procedure, he asserted, was positively dangerous insofar as it lulled the American people into a false sense of security and discouraged their taking realistic steps either to preserve the peace or to defend themselves in war.

And Franklin Roosevelt was in substantial agreement with his Cousin Theodore. He was perhaps less harsh than TR in his judgment of Bryan's personal qualities, though even here he was evidently in much closer agreement with his illustrious cousin than he was with Daniels. Witness the Assistant Secretary's hilarity, a hilarity not untinged with contempt, when he told how Bryan came to his office in a highly agitated state one day in 1913 crying, "I've got to have a battleship!" The battleship had to be in strife-torn Haiti within twenty-four hours, said the Secretary of State, to keep "white people" from "being killed." But when Bryan learned this was impossible because the nearest battleship was a full four days' steaming from the island, he was perfectly content to have a gunboat instead. "That's all I wanted," he said, then added a remark that Roosevelt could never quote without laughing uproariously. "Roosevelt," said the Great Commoner, "after this, when I talk about battleships don't think I mean anything technical." [42]

V

Given this difference in basic attitude, it was inevitable that Daniels and Roosevelt should flatly disagree about the proper Navy response to a dangerous international crisis which erupted only a few weeks after the new administration took office. The crisis reached a climax, ironically, on the very day (May 9, 1913) that Bryan explained his peace treaty plan to the American people, for it was then that the Japanese imperial government formally lodged with the U.S. government an "urgent and explicit" protest against an alien land bill, aimed at preventing Japanese from owning land in California, which had been almost unanimously passed by the California legislature six days before. The bill was "essentially unfair and discriminatory," said the protest statement; it was "not only prejudicial to the existing rights of Japanese subjects," but "inconsistent with the provisions of the treaty actually in force between Japan and the United States"; and it was "also opposed to the spirit and fundamental principles of amity and good understanding upon which the conventional relations of the two countries depend." This was strong language by the standards governing diplomatic exchanges in 1913 (the phrase about "conventional relations" might be construed as a threatened break in diplomatic relations), and its urgency was emphasized by huge and angry popular demonstrations against America in Japanese cities and actual calls for war in the Japanese press.

During the week of consternation and alarm which ensued in Washington, there developed a sharp difference of opinion among responsible officials concerning Japanese intentions and the consequent proper disposition of U.S. naval units in the Far East.

To a tense night meeting of the Joint Board of the Army and Navy,* General Leonard Wood (TR's great friend and commanding officer in Cuba) presented his view that war was inevitable and imminent, outlined the intensive Army preparations he planned to order for the defense of the Philippines, and strongly recommended that the Navy move five U.S. cruisers from the Yangtze River to Manila. Rear Admiral Bradley A. Fiske, aide for operations, needed no urging. That very night he addressed a memorandum to the Secretary of the Navy, with a copy for the Assistant Secretary, arguing that the Japanese, who had long coveted Hawaii and the Philippines, were so deeply offended by the land bill that they might attack without warning. ". . . I believe," he

---

* The board was the loosely organized top planning agency of the armed services at that time, but it had no power to act. Its function was advisory only.

wrote, ". . . that war is not only possible, but even probable." [43] The transfer of the cruisers to Manila was urgently necessary, he said, not only for defense of Corregidor, but also to save the ships themselves. Franklin Roosevelt thoroughly agreed with the admiral. It would be criminal folly to leave the Asiatic Squadron in so precarious a position at a time when hostilities could be initiated at any moment. He said so to his chief, either shortly before or shortly after the admiral and the Secretary conferred personally, on the morrow of the Joint Board meeting.

But Daniels disagreed emphatically when Fiske orally reiterated the argument of his memorandum and then added that Secretary of War Lindley M. Garrison, in hearty accord with General Wood's views, had already approved the Joint Board recommendations. This last was intended, no doubt, to clinch the matter. It had an opposite effect. Daniels bridled. "I suggested to him [Fiske] that it was unprecedented for an Army officer to be initiating Naval activities," he recalled in his memoirs, "and that if there were any movement of Naval ships, it could not be done without the order of the Secretary of the Navy or the Commander in Chief." He rejected the Joint Board's premise. He did not believe that the Japanese imperial government wanted war. On the contrary, he was convinced that the Japanese Cabinet in Tokyo was desperately trying to curb the rising war fever among the Japanese people while hoping that the United States government would make persuasive conciliatory gestures and was desperately afraid that the United States might instead act precipitously in ways provocative of warlike passions among the citizens of both countries. The fleet action recommended by the Joint Board might well precipitate an otherwise avoidable war (Daniels was privately of the opinion that "Admiral Fiske . . . , like General Wood . . . , really would like to have seen war with Japan" [44]).

Moreover, even if one accepted the Joint Board's premise, even if one were absolutely convinced that Japan intended to attack, the board's naval recommendation made no sense. The ships now in the Yangtze were "of an old type with guns of short range"; all five of them together were no match for a single vessel of dreadnaught class; and all five therefore could and would be sunk long before they reached Manila "if the Japanese were so minded." Nor did the other Joint Board recommendations make better sense. The blunt truth of the matter was that the Philippines, in case of war, were indefensible against a determined Japan. Our present force in the Far East was too small to be effective, and it was so far from an operating base that it could not possibly be reinforced nor even adequately supplied before Japanese forces overwhelmed it. (The whole sad situation "was proof of our country's unwisdom in embarking upon a colonial and imperialistic policy" in the first place, said Daniels in an aside; the error should be corrected by granting Philippine independence at the earliest possible moment.[45])

He repeated and amplified this argument a little later in crucial debate before a Cabinet session, followed by a private meeting with Garrison and the President in the White House rose garden. The debate's heat was heightened by the fact that the Joint Board's views and recommendations, the product of a supposedly secret meeting, had somehow been leaked to the press, had been printed that day under huge front-page headlines, and had thereby fomented an American war scare to match the rising war fever in Japan. Daniels was angrily certain that Fiske and Wood, hoping "to force the hands of the Commander in Chief," were responsible for the leakage. If so, the two militants badly overreached themselves. The untoward publicity rendered even more obnoxious to other Cabinet members than it might otherwise have been Garrison's overly forceful presentation of the Joint Board's case—a presentation in which he intimated that the question at issue, since it had to do with the disposition of military and naval forces during a crisis situation, was one for professionals only. It was beyond the competence of mere Cabinet members to decide. Bryan, in particular, was outraged by this. Secretary of Agriculture David F. Houston would always remember how the normally placid Secretary of State, red-faced with anger, "thundered out that army and navy officers could not be trusted to say what we should or should not do, till we actually got into a war; that we were discussing not how to wage war, but how not to get into a war; and that, if ships were moved about in the East, it would incite war." [46] Houston was one of a Cabinet majority that agreed with the Bryan-Daniels view. And in the end, Wilson agreed with it, too. Following the White House garden talk, the President as Commander in Chief ordered that no Navy "movement . . . be made at this time in the Pacific Ocean."

But the agitation by Army and Navy militants was not yet ended. There followed what in that year was an almost unprecedented challenge by professional warriors to civilian control over America's armed services.

Within hours after the Joint Board had been informed of the President's decision it met again. A memorandum strongly protesting the decision was prepared—it insisted that, at the very least, certain naval units on the California coast must be sent at once to Hawaii—and Fiske promptly presented this to an astonished and exasperated Daniels with the request that Daniels present it to the President. The Secretary of the Navy did so. Whereupon, as might have been predicted, Wilson was as astonished and exasperated as Daniels had been. ". . . these Army and Navy gentlemen . . . had no right to hold a meeting at all and discuss these matters," said he in high dudgeon. "When a policy has been settled by the Administration and when it is communicated to the Joint Board, they have no right to be trying to force a different course and I wish you would say to them that if this should occur again, there will be no General or Joint Boards. They will be abolished." He summoned newspaper reporters. Through them he reassured the nation by describing as "preposterous" the notion of war between Japan and the United States. He denied categorically that preparations for war were being made. Subsequently, he explicitly forbade the Joint Board to meet again without his permission—a permission he would, in the event, withhold until October, 1915, when Daniels himself requested it.[47]

Throughout this intramural controversy, Franklin Roosevelt was wholly on the side of the militants. Fiske, among the admirals, was a particular intimate of his. So was Rear Admiral William F. Fullam, aide for inspection, who came to him one day at the height of the crisis with a memorandum of things that the Navy should do immediately to prepare for war but could not do unless the Secretary of the Navy approved them. Of course the memorandum should properly have been addressed to the Secretary, "but . . . ," as Fullam himself explained to a Senate investigating committee years later, "I did not feel encouraged to take it to . . . [Daniels] because I had seen Admiral Fiske take papers like that to him, and he would not pay any attention to it." Roosevelt, on the other hand, "usually—always—took a lively interest in the Navy and in the cooperation of the Navy with the Army." On this occasion, having read the memorandum and told Fullam he agreed with "every bit of it," he acceded to Fullam's request that he present the memorandum's substance as his own personal recommendation, with no mention of Fullam, in a conference to be held in the Secretary's office later that same day. ". . . I remember so well," said Fullam to the Senate committee, "that he [Roosevelt] sat down in his chair, and he put this paper on the [floor] . . . between his feet, and he read off from time to time the items; and coming from him as a civilian to the Secretary of the Navy, it had some effect, and some of these things were done." [48]

The crisis had passed by June, 1913, though diplomatic relations between Washington and Tokyo remained strained—but Roosevelt, more than a year later, was still of the opinion that the decision against the Joint Board's recommendation had been badly mistaken. He said so in a letter to Admiral Mahan, dated June 16, 1914. "I did all in my power to have . . . [the ships anchored in Chinese waters] return nearer their base," he then wrote. ". . . Orders were . . . sent against my protest to

Admiral Nicholson, telling him not to move out of the Yangtze River." [49] His *public* statements at the time, however, prudently followed the policy lines laid down by Daniels and the President. He told reporters on several occasions that the Navy had no intention of mobilizing against Japan, that there was in fact "no Japanese scare" since "Japan doesn't want war and neither does this country. The trouble is not a national one," he went on, echoing the Jeffersonian-Wilsonian conception of states' rights. "It is a California question purely." [50]

He was less circumspect in his public statements during a crisis in U.S. relations with Mexico which became particularly acute in April, 1914, and during which there was again disagreement between Roosevelt and Daniels.

The Mexican trouble had deep and tangled historic roots. For decades the country had been under the iron dictatorship of Porfirio Díaz, who was supported by the immensely wealthy Catholic Church, by the few hundred great landholding families in the country, and by foreign business interests (mostly U.S.) to whom he granted mineral and other concessions on liberal terms. A "strong man" of the usual type, though more durable than most, Díaz maintained "law and order" on behalf of the privileged few by employing force, fraud, and violence against the impoverished many, and in usual fashion he had been greatly admired and actively aided by the U.S. Department of State. But, alas for the privileged, he grew old. He grew senile. And in 1911 he was at last driven into exile by an insurgency whose principal dynamic was the desperate land hunger and revolutionary wrath of millions of peons but whose leadership was a group of relatively mild middle-class reformers headed by Francisco I. Madero. Thus began the Mexican Revolution, destined to last for many a bloody year and to play an indeterminate part in Roosevelt's political education.

Madero's tenure as President was turbulent and brief. His attempts at reform, which did not go far enough to satisfy the revolutionaries, were nonetheless bitterly opposed by the landowners and foreign investors. They were opposed, too, by the U.S. Ambassador to Mexico, Henry Lane Wilson. The ambassador, who conceived his whole function to be that of diplomatic agent for American business and who personally hated Madero, went so far as to connive at last in a counterrevolutionary plot whereby General Victoriano Huerta drove Madero from office in February, 1913, proclaimed himself Provisional President, and then, a few days later, had Madero murdered in cold blood. European governments promptly extended full diplomatic recognition to Huerta's regime. Mexican revolutionaries in the north, led by General Venustiano Carranza, with Pancho Villa as lieutenant, rose as promptly against it. And Ambassador Wilson began to urge upon his government the importance not merely of recognizing Huerta but of actively aiding him to "restore order," since the fate of more than a billion dollars of American investments* and of 40,000 U.S. citizens residing in Mexico trembled in the balance.

For various reasons, none of which had anything to do with moral outrage, the Taft administration in its closing days failed to act as the ambassador wished. It was to the new Democratic administration that he had then to address himself. He did so in vain. For Woodrow Wilson *was* morally outraged. He was determined to abandon "dollar diplomacy" in Mexico and substitute for it an active encouragement of personal liberty and political democracy. In an almost unprecedented identification of diplomatic recognition with moral approval he flatly refused even a *de facto* recognition of Huerta's regime (the ambassador of course wanted it to be *de jure*), proclaiming instead a policy of "watchful waiting" while he bent every effort toward securing in Mexico a genuinely free popular election as prescribed by that country's constitution.

Months of confused and inept diplomacy followed, during which Wilson's attempts to translate idealism into practical action foundered repeatedly on faulty information, on misconceptions of the nature of the revolution, and on miscalculations of the character of the revolutionary leaders. The upshot was that by the spring of 1914 he found himself in a position where he felt he had to intervene forcefully in Mexico, if that were necessary to compel Huerta's abdication.

A pretext for doing so was provided in early April. Among U.S. naval vessels then in Mexican waters, sent there to protect American lives and property, was the USS *Dolphin,* from whose chart house roof Roosevelt had reviewed the departing fleet at Hampton Roads in the preceding October. The *Dolphin* was anchored in the Pánuco River at Tampico. From it to a Tampico warehouse dock, on April 9, went a whaleboat bearing the paymaster and seven crew members, to load supplies previously purchased—and at the dock the paymaster with two of the crew were arrested by an overly zealous Mexican colonel. They were released almost at once by order of the general in command of local Huerta forces. The general apologized profusely to them and to the American consul, and asked that his apologies be conveyed to the U.S. naval commander off Tampico, Admiral Henry T. Mayo. This, however, was not

---

* Hearings before a Congressional investigating committee a little later revealed that Americans in 1913 owned 78 percent of Mexico's mines, 68 percent of its rubber plantations, 68 percent of its railroads, 72 percent of its smelters, and 58 percent of its oil.

enough to satisfy the stiff-necked Mayo. He demanded that the hapless Mexican colonel be severely punished, that Mexican officers of suitable rank be sent to the *Dolphin* to present formal apologies in person, and that the local general, within twenty-four hours, "publicly hoist the American flag in a prominent position on shore and salute it with twenty-one guns. . . ."

When news of this exercise in quarterdeck diplomacy reached Washington, the Secretary of the Navy confessed himself "seriously disturbed" by the admiral's failure to consult with him (Mayo, after all, "was in easy reach . . . by wireless and telegraph" [51]) before issuing an ultimatum. Because the action seemed to Daniels ridiculously excessive, he was surprised when the President not only promptly backed Mayo's ultimatum, but also issued what amounted to an ultimatum of his own —a message to Huerta warning of "the gravest consequences" if the general at Tampico did not do as the admiral ordered. Nor would the President accept what seemed to Daniels adequate apologies conveyed in Huerta's reply;* Wilson professed to believe that the Tampico incident was part of a studied campaign of insult to the United States and continued to press for the flag salute until Huerta, infuriated, flatly refused to give it. Whereupon the President ordered the North Atlantic battleship fleet to sail for Tampico; ordered the Pacific Fleet to sail for the west coast of Mexico; went before Congress to ask for, and receive by a vote of 337 to 37, a resolution saying he was "justified in the employment of armed forces . . . to enforce demands made on Victoriano Huerta"; and, with Daniels, Garrison, and high Army and Navy officers, concerted an operational plan for the blockade of both Mexican coasts, the seizure of Tampico and Veracruz, and a march from Veracruz to Mexico City, if all this proved necessary to force Huerta's abdication. In public statement, he made sharp distinction between the Huerta government and the Mexican people: the United States was hostile to the former, friendly to the latter, he said.

While this was going on, Franklin Roosevelt was making an inspection tour of Navy installations on the Pacific coast. (He left Washington on April 2.) Neither privately nor publicly did he evince such misgivings as plagued Daniels during the crisis period. He welcomed the excitement. He became a dynamo of executive energy. At San Diego he doubled the work force on a big radio installation then under construction.

---

* Before he knew how Wilson would respond to Huerta's message, Daniels told newsmen: "I am inclined to believe that Admiral Mayo . . . will regard the apology of Huerta as sufficient. The greater includes the less, and if the Federal commander at Tampico should not actually salute the flag, Admiral Mayo will pass the matter, satisfied with what Huerta has said." [52]

At San Francisco he pledged a substantial expansion of naval bases on the Pacific coast and gave the public impression, perhaps inadvertently, that he was in personal charge of the Pacific Fleet movement toward Mexico. (San Francisco papers said flatly, on April 16, that the Assistant Secretary had been ordered by the Secretary to take charge of Navy mobilization on the West Coast; in reality, Daniels had merely asked Roosevelt to "make such suggestions . . . as you think wise.") In Portland, where he arrived just as Huerta refused compliance with the latest Wilson ultimatum, he told reporters grimly, "We're not looking for trouble, but we're ready for anything." In Seattle, in public speech, he excoriated the thirty-seven Representatives who had voted against the Mexican resolution, saying that "by their vote" they "put themselves in their true character," placing "party fealty" above "national fealty." (His contempt for such partisanship did not prevent his pointing out that two of the thirty-seven were *Republican* Representatives from the state in which he spoke.) "I know that the President and his Cabinet have come to . . . [their] decision with prayer, earnest thought and sorrow," he also said. " . . . But the day has come when studied insults are aimed directly at the nation." He went on to speak of an "administrative patience" that was near to being "exhausted," predicting that "when . . . the Administration has made up its mind, the thing will be seen through to the end." He neither doubted nor feared, as he spoke, that the "thing" would be war.[53]

A few hours later his prediction seemed abundantly justified. At two thirty in the morning of April 21, 1914, in Washington, D.C., the White House learned of the arrival in Veracruz of a German ship loaded with arms and ammunition for Huerta's forces. There followed a series of hurried and tense telephone conversations—between Wilson and Bryan, Wilson and Daniels, Wilson and Garrison—issuing in an order flashed from Daniels to Admiral Frank M. Fletcher at Veracruz: "Seize custom house. Do not permit war supplies to be delivered to Huerta government or to any other party." U.S. sailors and marines were promptly landed. The customhouse was promptly seized, the ship and arms impounded. But the action turned out to be no such bloodless affair as Wilson, misinformed about the Mexican temper, wishfully anticipated. Mexican troops fought back. Before they were finally routed, shortly before noon on April 22, they had killed 19 Americans and wounded 71 while themselves losing 126 dead and 195 wounded.

By then an excited young Roosevelt, eager to swing wide the door on which opportunity knocked so loudly, had applied his executive energy at the Bremerton base, across Puget Sound from Seattle, helping there to expedite the movements of fleet and Marine Corps units all along the

U.S. Pacific shore. He had also wired Washington for information concerning Navy Department plans for action on the west coast of Mexico. It was clear that he saw himself, and longed to have the public at large see him, in charge of organizing such action. The reply he received might well have come as a dash of cold water in the face of his eager ambition. It came not directly from Daniels to him, but indirectly through Roosevelt's own secretary in Washington, and it rather pointedly ignored the specific question Roosevelt had asked. "Secretary says," he read, "that as most of the vessels on the west coast will be down in Mexico and in view of the great help you can be to him in Washington, he thinks the wise course is for you to return as originally planned." [54]

Obviously, the Secretary of the Navy had no intention of risking a repetition of the Rooseveltian insubordination of February, 1898, especially since he at that very moment was doing all in his power to prevent the Veracruz episode from exploding into full-scale hostilities.

Daniels was allied in this effort with Bryan. He was opposed by Garrison, speaking for the same Army militants who had striven, a year before, to foment war with Japan. And he was aided by Woodrow Wilson's own shocked recognition that his "firmness" in backing Mayo and his forcefulness in attacking Veracruz had been disastrously mistaken. Neither action had achieved its stated purpose. The flag salute had not been given at Tampico, and would never be. The German merchantman's cargo of arms and ammunition had not been assuredly denied Huerta. Hardly had Admiral Fletcher acted upon his explicit instructions before lawyers in the State Department, responding to a protest from the German ambassador, insisted he had no right to do so under international law "as a state of war does not exist" between the United States and Mexico. While fighting yet continued in the streets of Veracruz, Fletcher was required to apologize to the German ship captain and to permit the vessel to sail for whatever port it pleased, its cargo intact and disposable to whomever the captain pleased. (The ship ultimately docked at Puerto Mexico, where the 200 machine guns and 15,000,000 cartridges it carried were delivered into Mexican hands, presumably Huerta's.) Nor was this the sum total of ill fortune. While failing to achieve their announced goals, the Tampico and Veracruz actions had greatly weakened the administration's moral position at home and abroad. Carranza, whom Wilson had decided to back against Huerta, demanded immediate U.S. withdrawal from Veracruz and threatened war if there were further interference by the United States in Mexico's internal affairs. Anti-American riots and demonstrations broke out in a half dozen Latin American countries. Liberal opinion throughout Europe was outraged. And it was at once evident that a large majority of the American people were not only strongly opposed to war with Mexico but also convinced that the danger of it was a consequence of administration bungling. Small wonder, therefore, that Wilson turned a sympathetic ear to Daniels' and Bryan's arguments, a deaf one to Garrison's, and leaped at a chance for withdrawal from his untenable position, presented to him on April 25.

On that date, Argentina, Brazil, and Chile, the ABC powers of Latin America, offered to mediate the quarrel. Wilson at once accepted, though doing so seemed tantamount to *de facto* recognition of Huerta's regime. Huerta accepted, too, a couple of days later. Carranza, however, who was in control of much of Mexico, accepted only "in principle"; he refused to suspend hostilities against Huerta at a time when his arms were everywhere victorious. Arrangements were then made for a mediation conference to open at Niagara Falls, Canada, on May 20.

Thus, even before Roosevelt boarded a train for his return to Washington, the threat of war with Mexico was in process of removal. He had no inkling of this. He was yet convinced that large-scale hostilities were about to be initiated when he talked to reporters in Butte, Montana, on April 24 and made there a show of calmness, of moderation. "We are merely engaged in the occupation of a city, it is not a war," he said. His belligerency thereafter increased, in inverse proportion to its objective justification. He was in Minneapolis on the evening of April 25. There, when a reporter asked him what the crisis meant, he replied unequivocally, "War! And we're ready!" He may not then have known of the ABC mediation offer. But he certainly knew that the offer had not only been made but been accepted by the administration when, in Milwaukee on the morning of April 26, he said to reporters: "I do not want war, but I do not see how we can avoid it. Sooner or later, it seems, the United States must go down there and clean up the Mexican political mess. I believe that the best time is right now." His belligerency—a response hugely disproportionate to its assumed immediate incitement—raged then at its maximum height: he seized the occasion to press for the absolute extreme of naval expansion. The United States needed dreadnaughts, he asserted ("You can't fight Germany's and England's dreadnaughts . . . with gunboats . . ."), and Congress should authorize the Navy Department "to buy and build dreadnaughts until our navy is comparable to any other in the world." A few hours later, in Chicago, he spoke of a "war spirit" that was "sweeping the West like a prairie fire." He went on: "The general opinion is that since the United States has finally started military activities they should be carried through to a finish with no compromise. Many persons and newspapers are openly advocating annexation as the only solution to the Mexican problem. The sentiment appears to be growing." [55] It was as if he could not bear to see closed in his face the door he had opened to what, in his belief, had been the knock of opportunity.

He detrained in a capital whose ruling personalities strove to limit the evils consequent upon the errors of Tampico and Veracruz. He conferred with a superior official who sincerely wished and earnestly sought to achieve a peaceful settlement of outstanding difficulties with Mexico. Daniels gave his ardent, impetuous young assistant a few words of fatherly advice, impressing upon him, kindly but firmly, the limits of an Assistant Secretary's authority. ("He was young then and made some mistakes," Daniels would recall in his memoirs. "Upon reflection, although I was older, I made mistakes too." [56]) And Roosevelt's press interviews on the Mexican trouble abruptly ceased.

VI

In all this, Franklin Roosevelt consciously followed the career script whose general outline he had described to his fellow law clerks at Carter, Ledyard, and Milburn, a half dozen years before.

As role player in that script he enlarged his personality to the extent that he was enabled to become another while remaining himself. Thus, on March 19, 1913—or on April 25, 1914—he, Franklin Roosevelt from Hyde Park, could *also* be TR, could *also* be Future President, thereby enhancing his sense of the historic meaning and importance of his every act on those days while heightening his personal enjoyment of it all. He could gain, too, in the kind of detached self-awareness that generates serenity of spirit and maintains a flexibility of response to outer challenge. Insofar as he felt himself an actor, he transformed himself into an object, a measurable element of his own environment—he became his own witness, his own audience—and could smile or frown upon his performance without taking it or himself-as-performer with utter seriousness.

Role playing, in other words, could help prevent the development in him of the concentrated and rigorously exclusive self-centeredness which flawed so dangerously the character of Woodrow Wilson. It could inhibit whatever tendencies he had toward such extremes of psychic tension as render men like Wilson cold and intolerant in their relations with people outside their own intimate circles, excessively self-righteous, censorious, and often incapable of understanding ideas differing at all widely from their own. Wilson's was a closed personality, as monolithic and essentially impenetrable as that of Endicott Peabody, the other great schoolmaster in Roosevelt's life, whereas Roosevelt was remarkably open to new experience, was sympathetic and empathic. Almost always he could see himself quite accurately as others saw him and could adapt himself, as manipulated image, to their preconceptions. He could do this swiftly and apparently without effort, almost as if the words and acts of others were cues for specific gestures and words already written down and rehearsed in his heart and mind. Moreover, as time went on, he became increasingly adept at glossing his responsiveness with a charm consisting in part of a calculated flattery: the self-esteem of modest men in inferior posts was pleasingly enhanced by a personal concern for them, a deference to their opinions, surprisingly manifested by a famous man in a seat of power. But there was more to it than this, especially as he gained experience. He was naturally attractive, and more and more he came genuinely to care for others and to derive pleasure from pleasing them, taking them as they were, not judging them or trying to change them. This bound them to him with ties of real affection and even, in not a few cases, of love.

In general, he as aspiring politician was well served by his role playing. It helped him fulfill the initial requirement of a successful politics—namely, the winning of votes.

There were, however, other effects which served him less well.

Yet alive in him, buried alive, was the shy child who had hidden behind his mother's skirts when she took him with her into the kitchen at Springwood; the pretty little boy whose girlish curls of blond hair were not shorn until after they had become an acute embarrassment to him; the son of a father who (as Sara wrote) "believed in keeping Franklin's mind on nice things, on a high level"; the adolescent whose passion for outward conformity was rooted in essential self-doubt, a deep-down fear of personal inadequacy. Role playing both disguised and encouraged a continuation of this shyness, this essential reticence and doubt; it discouraged or became a substitute for the rigorous self-examination which might have rationally defined his felt deficiencies and directed him toward the supply of them. It shut off introspection. Which is to say that his kind of objectification of the self was achieved at the expense of inwardness. By turning himself inside out, he increased the number of choices open to him in his environment. But at the same time and by the same process his *inner* capacity for truly decisive, creative choice was diminished. His range of intensive possibility was narrowed as his existential self was diluted.

There was also a shrinkage of his sense of personal responsibility for his acts. For to the extent that he became the role he was playing he was no longer a self-determining person but was instead moved from the outside; he was an effect of external causes, a focus of event but not a source or maker of it. He could act without thinking, since the necessary thought had already occurred in the mind of the Author. Nor was there need for him to worry overmuch about the moral rights and wrongs of indicated words and deeds, since the primary responsibility for these rested not with him but with the Author. There was encouraged in him, in other words, a certain kind of irresponsibility. It existed side by side with his peculiar *noblesse oblige* conscientiousness and interacted with it in ways that made him enigmatic, unpredictable.

Twelve

->>><<<-

Roosevelt and the New Freedom

I

THE New Freedom came to an end in November, 1914. Woodrow Wilson himself saw it so. Amid his disappointment over the outcome of midterm elections, during which the Democrats lost more Congressional seats than had been anticipated, though retaining control of both houses, the President looked back over the record of his first twenty months in office and comforted himself with the thought that, in any case, he had discharged the main burdens imposed on him by history. "The reconstructive legislation which for the last two decades the opinion of the country has demanded . . . has now been enacted," he wrote in a private letter as the 1914 election campaign drew toward a close. He saw as "practically completed" the political program which had been so vehemently pressed from the left since Populist days.[1] And he elaborated on this view, two weeks after 1914's election day, in a public letter addressed to William G. McAdoo* wherein he drew happy contrasts between the present state of the Union and that which had obtained when he took office. "We were living under a tariff which had been purposely contrived to confer private favors upon those who were cooperating to keep the party that originated it in power, and in that all too fertile soil the bad, interlacing growth and jungle of monopoly had sprung up," he said. "Credit, the very life of trade, . . . was too largely in the control of the same small groups who had planted and cultivated monopoly. The control of all big business, and by consequence of all little business, too, was for the most part . . . in their hands. . . . The legislation of the past year and a half has in very large measure done away with these things." [2] He therefore proposed no new major reforms; his administra-

* McAdoo was by then Wilson's son-in-law, having married Eleanor Wilson in May, 1914.

tion would thenceforward concentrate upon a consolidation of gains already made.

Three major battles for basic reform had been fought and won. On October 3, 1913, Wilson had signed the Underwood-Simmons Tariff bill, which effected the first general downward revision of tariff schedules since 1846 and, more important in terms of history, included a provision for a tax on all net personal and corporate annual incomes above $4,000—a graduated tax rising to a maximum of 7 percent. (The Sixteenth Amendment, giving Congress constitutional authority to impose an income tax, had been ratified in 1912.) On December 22, 1913, Wilson approved the Glass-Owen bill establishing a regionalized Federal Reserve System whereby the nation's credit resources were released from the stranglehold of Wall Street (though the Money Trust was in no way weakened by it) and rendered more flexible, more swiftly mobile in the service of all the people. On September 26 and October 15, 1914, Wilson signed, respectively, the Federal Trade Commission bill and the Clayton Antitrust bill. The first of these established an independent bipartisan board empowered to investigate and, through cease-and-desist orders, abolish "unfair competition," a term which the written law failed to define. (Court cases must in the end define it, all FTC rulings being subject to court review.) The Clayton Act strengthened the government's power to move against "combinations in restraint of trade," affirmed the legal right of workers and farmers to form organizations promoting their economic interests, and *seemed* to exempt labor unions from prosecution under the act by asserting that the "labor of a human being is not a commodity or article of commerce."

But none of these victories was complete enough to satisfy the advanced Progressives who fought hardest for them—and the President's open letter to McAdoo failed to please the leader of either wing of Progressive thought.

Louis Brandeis, champion of free competition among economic units small enough to be comprehensible by individual human intelligence, felt that Wilson claimed far too much and would quit the battle far too soon. The People's Advocate published in that year a book, *Other People's Money–and How the Bankers Use It,* in which he repeated and added to disclosures made by the House Banking and Currency Committee (the Pujo Committee, Samuel Untermyer its chief counsel) during a lengthy inquiry into the Money Trust in 1912 and 1913. The Pujo disclosures were scarifying enough to those who cared about economic individualism and personal liberty. They showed that a "community of interest" formed by a confederation of the Morgan and Rockefeller groups of financiers in the months following the 1907 panic held no fewer than 341 directorships in 112 of the nation's major banks, trust companies, insurance companies, transportation systems, manufacturing and trading corporations, and public utility corporations having resources and capitalization totaling well over $22 billion. Brandeis' further researches showed that, through interlocking directorates, three New York City banks—J. P. Morgan & Co., the National City Bank, and the First National Bank—had such control over the national money market that no major business enterprise of any kind could be launched against their disapproval or even without their participation. The mere contemplation of such "overwhelming power" had an "effect" akin to that produced by the Himalayas upon travelers among them, Brandeis had said in a public speech in November, 1913: ". . . man is cowed." And he resented this, feeling it an affront to personal dignity. "In a democracy it is the part of statesmanship to prevent the development of power which overawes the ordinary forces of man," he had gone on to say in his address. "Where such power exists, it must be broken. The privilege which begets it must be destroyed." In his book he proposed a total legal prohibition of interlocking directorates; direct sale of securities to the public, rather than through underwriting firms, whenever possible; a total divorcement of railroad ownership and management from that of corporations in every part of the economy. None of this had been accomplished. The Money Trust remained intact.

Herbert Croly, champion of a nationally planned and regulated "cooperation" among corporations of a maximally "efficient" size, was even more strongly displeased and, as editor in chief of the newly founded *New Republic* magazine, published his displeasure in trenchant prose. "Any man of President Wilson's intellectual equipment who seriously asserts that the fundamental wrongs of a modern society can be . . . righted as a consequence of a few laws passed between the birth and death of a single Congress casts suspicion either upon his own sincerity or upon his grasp of the realities of modern social and industrial life," he editorialized in his magazine's issue of November 21, 1914. "Mr. Wilson's sincerity is above suspicion, but he is a dangerous and unsound thinker upon contemporary political and social problems. He has not only, as he himself has said, a 'single-track mind,' but a mind which is fully convinced of the everlasting righteousness of its own performances and which surrounds this conviction with a halo of shimmering rhetoric. He deceives himself with these phrases, but he should not be allowed to deceive progressive popular opinion."

As for leading social justice reformers—the suffragettes, the national prohibitionists, the officers of such organizations as the National Consumers' League and the National Child Labor Committee—they made bitter reference to Wilson's failure (partly on ideological states' rights grounds, partly because of unadmitted personal prejudices) to press for, or even in some instances to endorse, federal measures prohibiting child labor, establishing woman suffrage, setting minimum wages for women workers, prohibiting liquor manufacture, and instituting federal health and educational programs. In the realm of race relations there had been actual retrogression. Wilson, born in Virginia four years before the Civil War began and reared in Georgia during that war and the Reconstruction, was wholly Southern in his race attitudes. (". . . a boy never gets over his boyhood," he once said, "and never can change those subtle influences which have become a part of him.") He therefore readily approved a reversal of the policy of nonsegregation in government offices which had been adhered to by preceding administrations. Soon after his inauguration there was a directed separation of the races in the offices and shops, the rest rooms and lunchrooms of the only bureaus employing considerable numbers of blacks, those of the Post Office and Treasury departments. When Oswald Garrison Villard, grandson of abolitionist William Lloyd Garrison and editor of the New York *Evening Post* with its weekly magazine, the *Nation,* inveighed in a public letter against this unprecedented "color discrimination" among government civilian employees, Wilson could make only the standard lame reply that he did what he did "as much in the interest of the negro as for any other reason, with the approval of some of the most influential negroes I know, and with the idea that the friction, or rather the discontent and uneasiness, which has prevailed in many of the departments would thereby be removed." He asserted that "the segregation of the colored employees" was "as far as possible from being a movement *against* the negroes"—whose national leaders nevertheless vehemently protested it.[3]

Thus Croly and Brandeis, though they continued to differ radically in their approaches to America's social and economic problems, were agreed that Wilson, instead of calling a halt to reform, should have demanded an acceleration of it on every major front. In this judgment the social reformers emphatically concurred. None would deny that the accomplishments of the administration's first twenty months were substantial (Croly was willing to "make allowances" for the President's "justifiable pride"), but none would accept, either, the President's seeming conclusion that the gains were sufficient. More, much more, remained to be done before the stated goals of the New Freedom were reached.

And it is another element of the continuing and increasingly bitter irony of American history that insofar as the New Freedom goals *were* ever actually achieved in Wilson's administration, most of them would be achieved by means which the New Freedom explicitly and emphatically repudiated. They would be achieved through the exercise of national governmental powers deemed proper and necessary in the political theory of Hamilton-Croly-TR, but *im*proper and *un*necessary, because inimical to personal liberty and the genius of democratic institutions, in the political theory of Jefferson-Brandeis-Wilson.

II

What was Franklin Roosevelt's opinion of all this, what his personal judgment on the administration of which he was a part? And what in general had he learned that would be useful to him in his own career? At nine o'clock in the evening of October 3, 1913, the President assembled some fifty leading Democrats, personal friends, and reporters to witness in the Executive Office the signing of the Underwood-Simmons Tariff bill. Roosevelt was one of them. He stood behind Woodrow Wilson as the latter, with two gold pens, transformed bill into act; he watched and listened as Wilson, the signing done, made a few graceful impromptu remarks. A line from Shakespeare's *Henry V* was quoted: "If it be a sin to covet honor, then am I the most offending soul alive." The President confessed himself at one with Shakespeare's king in this regard. The "honor" he "coveted," however, was not for himself alone but for his associates as well and for "the great party" of which he was a member. He concluded on a note loftier than most political leaders would have aspired to strike even in 1913, and which would be well beyond the range of effective communication with practical men a decade later. ". . . I feel tonight like a man who is lodging happily in the inn which lies halfway along the journey," said Wilson, "and that in the morning, with a fresh impulse, we shall go the rest of the journey, and sleep at the journey's end like men with a quiet conscience, knowing that we have served our fellowmen, and have thereby tried to serve God." Roosevelt, with the others, applauded.[4]

Roosevelt's very minor part in this scene would seem symbolically representative of the young Assistant Secretary's personal relationship to the New Freedom. He was very active in it, but only superficially, peripherally; he was never *of* it in such terms of intellectual and emotional commitment as Daniels was, with the other Bryan Democrats, or as Brandeis was, who continued as the President's chief economic adviser. From outer margins he looked upon inner workings, as from behind the seated President he witnessed the ceremonial bill signing, acutely aware of what he saw but, on the evidence, without any deep understanding of it.

Certainly his private letters and public speeches in 1913–14 give no sign that he ever made—on his own, as an inwardly directed effort—organic connections between what he personally was doing in the administration and what the administration as a whole was about. He often defended and praised the New Freedom in speeches, but he did so in "rather meaningless generalities," as Frank Freidel puts it. Typical was a Baltimore speech in December, 1913,[5] in which he said that America was "passing through" a "transition period" that was also "a period of idealism," under a President who "for the first time in the history of this country" had "gone before the people with a policy of ideal humanitarianism"—a policy which he did not specifically define. There was no repetition by him of the kind of thinking, relating the particular to the general, which he had attempted in his Troy, New York, speech in early March, 1912.

Insofar as connections were made in his mind between his individual role and the overall "plot" of the history play in which he acted, they were made from the outside. They were impressed upon him through his experience of conflict situations—situations wherein his private political ambitions came hard against the President's conception of larger purposes and of the strategies and tactics necessary to achieve them.

Thus:

Far from abandoning his active interest in New York politics when he moved from Albany to Washington, Roosevelt strove mightily to increase his personal political following in his home state by exercising the powers and privileges that became his as a ranking member of the national administration. Patronage power was of major importance to this enterprise. The trouble was that two other strong-willed New York Democrats in Washington, Senator James A. O'Gorman and Secretary of the Treasury McAdoo, had patronage influence considerably greater than accrued to Roosevelt by virtue of his relatively minor office and had also interests and ambitions of their own.

O'Gorman proved particularly troublesome. Daniels had been surprised by O'Gorman's response when, as a matter of courtesy, he (Daniels) consulted with the Senator concerning Roosevelt's nomination for Assistant Secretary before that nomination was sent to the Senate for confirmation. O'Gorman had made no objection. But neither had he expressed personal approval. "I expected him to show enthusiasm for the appointment of the young man chiefly responsible for his election to the Senate," Daniels later recalled. "The most I gathered was that it was agreeable."[6] Actually, as we know, O'Gorman had no such reason for personal gratitude to Roosevelt as Daniels believed. Certainly he felt none. And he did have reason to resent the ambitious Assistant Secretary's attempt, a few weeks later, to place in the crucially important patronage post of Collector of the Port of New York his friend and political mentor, banker-Mayor John K. Sague of Poughkeepsie. For in this attempt, whose success would have brought Roosevelt at one bound into the ranks of the most powerful in New York politics, O'Gorman was not even consulted.

McAdoo was. McAdoo, who was already aspiring that spring to become Wilson's son-in-law, also aspired to become Wilson's successor in the White House. To this end he needed and strove to build a Progressive Democratic organization in New York wherewith to wrest power for himself from Tammany. It was an effort in which he and young Roosevelt were natural allies, and since Sague's elevation, if promoted by McAdoo, would strengthen McAdoo's New York position along with Roosevelt's, the Assistant Secretary turned to him as a matter of course. He received McAdoo's endorsement, or believed he did (nothing concerning it was put in writing). He then went to the White House where he received (or believed he received) assurance that Wilson put Sague's name "at the top of the list." But Tammany's leaders were promptly informed of the proposal, and they moved promptly against it. They were enabled to block Sague's appointment with the aid of an angry and sulking O'Gorman, who at least tacitly threatened to invoke, if necessary, his personal privilege as a Senator. (Indeed and in general, despite his relationship with Dudley Field Malone and his preconvention support of Wilson, O'Gorman in Washington proved to be no Progressive Democrat. Essentially conservative, he soon developed a personal antipathy for Wilson, as Wilson did for him. "O'Gorman is always smiling and Jesuitical," Wilson once said of him.[7] With Tammany, on the other hand, the Senator, despite his independence, remained on friendly terms.) There followed a head-on clash between O'Gorman and Roosevelt. Neither would approve any of the other's candidates for the collectorship. Nor would the two agree to the appointment of a "compromise" candidate proposed by McAdoo, though this candidate was a Groton classmate and personal friend of Roosevelt's, Frank L. Polk, former chairman of the New York Civil Service Commission. McAdoo, in his turn, became adamant and even threatened to resign from the Cabinet when a harassed Wilson sought to end the impasse by appointing an eminently qualified man who just happened to be on O'Gorman's list of a half dozen nominees.

Ultimately, in early May, 1913, Wilson solved his problem by nominating for the collectorship a man whom neither of the warring factions had proposed but whom neither could oppose. This man was John Purroy Mitchel, president of the New York City Board of Aldermen, who, though unallied with either Roosevelt or McAdoo, was a strong anti-Tammany leader. He accepted the nomination with the understanding that he would resign in a few months to run for mayor of New York on a bipartisan fusion reform ticket. He was assured of Wilson's support in this race. And it is distinctly possible that Wilson, through Tumulty, his active agent in virtually all such matters, let O'Gorman know that when Mitchel resigned the collectorship, it would go to Malone, the Senator's son-in-law, who increasingly disagreed with the Senator in politics but remained on the warmest personal terms with him. O'Gorman may also have been informed that his close friend, wealthy State Supreme Court Justice James W. Gerard, a heavy financial contributor to the 1912 Democratic campaign, would be named ambassador to Germany. (Gerard was a Tammany man but nevertheless respected as personally upright and able.) At any rate, when both McAdoo and O'Gorman were informed of Mitchel's nomination a few hours before it was publicly announced, McAdoo merely acquiesced, as he had to do. Bitterly disappointed, he made no public comment. But O'Gorman professed great delight over the appointment. As a matter of fact, he seized the opportunity to obtain popular credit for it by publicly suggesting Mitchel's name himself shortly before the White House made its scheduled announcement.[8]

Wilson's dilemma in this case, as in others affecting Roosevelt's political fortunes, was a continuation of that faced by the Democratic Presidential candidate in 1912. He personally wanted to build a Progressive Democracy in every state by promoting Progressive Democrats into office whenever he could. In the opening days of his Presidency he proposed to devote the administration's patronage powers exclusively to this end. He said as much to his Postmaster General, Albert Sidney Burleson of Texas, an eminently "practical" politician who was ex officio the chief patronage dispenser and Presidential adviser on patronage matters. Burleson quickly dissuaded him. "Mr. President, if you pursue this policy, it means that your Administration is going to be a failure," the Postmaster General said flatly. "It means the defeat of the measures of reform that you have next to your heart." For though "it doesn't matter a damn" to the nation "who is postmaster at Paducah, Kentucky," such appointments mattered a great deal to Senators and Representatives. If their candidates for appointive office were "turned down, they will hate you and will not vote for anything you want," Burleson insisted. "It is human nature."[9] By the time the battle over the New York port collectorship reached its climax Wilson was acutely aware that he needed all the support he could get from O'Gorman, from Tammany and other organization Democrats, in order to pass the first major bill of his New Freedom legislative program, the Underwood-Simmons Tariff. (Chairman of the powerful House Appropriations Committee, for instance, was a Tammany man, Representative John Fitzgerald.) Hence the complicated compromise in the matter of this collectorship—a compromise that seemed to work. At any rate, O'Gorman did support the tariff bill. So did the Democratic House delegation from New York City and Brooklyn. And the tariff measure passed—though not before Wilson, in a dramatic move from which Roosevelt also doubtless learned, had forced exposure to public view of the activities of lobbyists who descended as a horde of locusts upon the capital that summer to prevent rate reductions on items of their special interest.

This, however, was but a single battle won in a war that continued without pause or abatement: Wilson's basic dilemma remained no less sharp than before. Already under way was the battle for banking and currency reform (the Glass-Owen bill), to be followed by battle against the trusts (the Clayton bill), so that Wilson's need for legislative support from New York's organization Democrats was no less in the winter of 1913–14 and in the summer of 1914 than in the spring of 1913. All through these months, the President's need seriously inhibited and even frustrated his desire to build a Progressive Democratic organization in Roosevelt's home state; it conditioned his every response to Roosevelt's open or tacit appeals for aid in furtherance of his (Roosevelt's) political ambition.

III

In these circumstances, Louis Howe's shrewdness, informed cynicism, and peculiar skills proved of inestimable worth to the team of Roosevelt and Howe.

The summer and early autumn of 1913 were a season of disaster for hapless and blundering "Plain Bill" Sulzer. Loudly proclaiming his devotion to Progressivism, the New York governor had declared by June his long-threatened open war on Tammany. It was a foolhardy move. Tammany, with Boss Murphy obviously prepared for such contingency, promptly instituted impeachment proceedings in the legislature, charging Sulzer with dishonest reporting of campaign funds and a misuse of them for personal speculations in Wall Street. (Roosevelt found "a certain grim, ironic humor in the spectacle of Tammany seeking to remove a Governor . . . [for] violating the election laws.") Sulzer countered with sensational but unspecific and unsubstantiated charges that Tammany had stolen millions from the state through corrupt public construction contracts of various kinds. ("I see where he [Sulzer] says the truth will prevail," was Howe's sardonic comment to the Assistant Secretary. "Such being the case, where will he get off?" [10]) The ensuing imbroglio was full of dangers for any New York Progressive. Roosevelt and Howe were of one mind on the importance of staying clear of it, and Howe greatly helped Roosevelt to do so, partly through his skill in drafting "nice pussy-footed" replies for Roosevelt to sign in response to Sulzer's many appeals for help. Shortly before the legislature voted on the impeachment charges, Roosevelt received a telegram from a desperate Sulzer beseeching him to obtain White House intercession, and there is evidence that Roosevelt did see Wilson on the matter. He could have made no urgent plea on Sulzer's behalf, however. He must have been more than content with Wilson's flat refusal to become involved.

For when the end came for Sulzer on October 17 (the legislature convicted him and removed him from office that day), the effect upon the New York Democracy seemed to favor Roosevelt's political fortunes. There was a wave of popular revulsion against Tammany. On the crest of it, John Purroy Mitchel rode to victory in the New York City mayoralty contest in November. Nor was the revulsion limited, in its object, to Tammany: state Democrats in general were suspect. It appeared that a complete reorganization of the party in New York along Wilsonian Progressive lines was required to stave off overwhelming defeat by the Republicans in 1914. Such at least was the highly plausible argument made to the President by McAdoo and by Malone, who succeeded Mitchel in the post of port collector as planned. It was an argument in which Roosevelt concurred.

Early in the new year he had high hopes of personal profit from plans shaped and presented for Wilson's approval by Colonel House, Malone, and McAdoo. They called for a total reformation of the party in Roosevelt's home state through an alliance between upstate Progressives and Mitchel's reform administration in New York City. An organization called the New Democracy (Wilson himself suggested the name) was to be formed for the purpose of capturing control of the state's party machinery, freeing it of Tammany bossism and making it into a trustworthy instrument of administration power. From this, young Roosevelt had, of course, everything to gain in terms of early and swift political advancement. The plans, however, were pierced and torn asunder on the sharp horns of Wilson's unresolved dilemma. For the President, though he strongly, if covertly, encouraged the efforts of House and the others at the outset, dared not risk the disaster to his legislative program which would come from a prolonged and bitter intraparty fight in the Empire State. He sought assurances that the proposed New Democracy could be quickly established with wide and solid popular support. He received none. He *did* receive veiled but unmistakable threats from New York's organization Democrats in Congress. And so he was receptive to a "compromise" suggestion put forth in February, 1914, by Tumulty, Martin H. Glynn who had succeeded Sulzer as governor, and William F. McCombs—the latter Wilson's campaign manager in 1912, who remained chairman of the Democratic National Committee. If not open enemies, McCombs and McAdoo were certainly not friends, being rivals for political power in New York, and the proposed "compromise," not unnaturally, favored McCombs at the expense of McAdoo. The administration was to recognize McCombs' leadership of the state Democracy, in partnership with Glynn—this in return for a "purge" of Tammany men and influence from key organization posts. What this really amounted to was an armistice between Tammany and the Wilson administration. The former promised to be good and to support the administration in Washington; the latter promised, in that case, to cease its support of efforts to destroy the New York City machine. The armistice was effected at a meeting of the Democratic State Committee in New York City on March 2, 1914. Boss Murphy, aided by Glynn's conciliatory stance, operated there with his usual behind-the-scenes adroitness, conceding overt victories to his enemies while retaining his power unimpaired. He connived in the election of William Church Osborn to the state chairmanship and in the election of other anti-Tammanyites to other committee offices. But he made sure that there was no truly meaningful reorganization. No knowledgeable person, said a gloomy Malone in a letter to House, could "have the slightest confidence in the . . . scheme which Glynn adopted, by the public acquiescence and approval of Murphy, and which merely means a change from one set of officers to another . . . , all the while the majority of the State Committee remaining in Murphy's control. . . ." [11]

Meanwhile, Roosevelt had been pressing for such advantage as might be gained from the intraparty turmoil.

In the closing weeks of 1913 there began to appear in the press political "dope" stories mentioning Roosevelt as a possible candidate for either New York governor or U.S. Senator in 1914, stories in whose preparation Howe may well have had a secret hand. The earliest and most prominent, appearing in the highly conservative New York *Sun* on December 10, 1913, described Roosevelt in flattering terms and predicted flatly that he would receive Wilson administration support for one or the other of the highest elective offices in his state if the new Governor

Glynn failed in office to be independent of Tammany. Roosevelt denied publicly and privately that he had any intention of running for office in 1914, yet did nothing to discourage speculations by others regarding his immediate political future. He made no attempt to achieve a working accord with Tammany, as he might easily have done. He tried instead to obtain Presidential approval of a contemplated foray by him into New York's political jungle war.

He tried this in typically indirect fashion, some four weeks after the State Committee "reorganization." On the last day of March he wrote Wilson a note saying that the New York *World* had "sent a special man to Washington to ask me to write an article on the New York situation." He had "steadfastly refused" theretofore "to be quoted about New York politics in spite of considerable pressure" because he did not wish "to be misconstrued as voicing the opinion of the Administration." But he found "the present situation . . . so critical that before I give a definite answer I would deeply appreciate a five minutes talk with you, as it occurs to me that if I do say anything it might help rather than embarrass the Administration." Wilson thought otherwise. Instead of granting the requested "five minutes," he sent the Assistant Secretary a note saying that in his judgment "it would be best if members of the administration should use as much influence as possible but say as little as possible in the politics of their several states. I think that just at the present time, particularly, it is difficult to comment serviceably upon the condition of affairs in New York, because while we may think we see the way they are unfolding themselves, the plot is not yet clear." [12]

Nor did it clarify as spring advanced into summer. Roosevelt had perforce to turn away from open warfare and, so far as his personal politicking was concerned, confine himself pretty much to the undercover patronage struggle—tedious, burdensome, intricate, interminable—which had all the while been going on. The brunt of it was borne by Howe, and it required the fullest exploitation of the little man's skill in covert personal politics.

Howe had a shrewd sense of how power is actually distributed through a chain of command as distinct from how it appears to be on an organization chart. He knew that the man at the top of a large and complex organization, the seemingly all-powerful man in whose name decisions are made and actions taken, is in reality very dependent on—is even at the mercy of—anonymous subordinates. If they happen not to respect him as a person or to be strongly antipathetic to his stated policies, they can frustrate him absolutely. Through procrastinations, "buck-passing," and calculated "mistakes"—the stuff of an unconquerable, virtually undetectable passive resistance—they can sabotage his every directive effort. Even of such archetypical pyramidal organizations as Army or Navy this is true. It is yet truer of the bureaucracy of a democratic government, where the bulk of the staff is composed of career people who remain "in place" while their elected or politically appointed heads come and go. In such bureaucracies, the foci of real rather than merely nominal power are very often individuals who occupy what, on the organization chart, appear very lowly and uninfluential posts. These are the ones whom the man at the top must win if he is to put his program through. And to them such shrewd operators as Howe, seeking influence, pay a great deal of attention. Hence he who was sometimes brusque to the point of rudeness in his dealings with admirals of the Navy and colonels of the Marines was cordial and solicitous in his relations with certain stenographers, personal secretaries, and assistants in the offices of bureau chiefs, Congressmen, Senators, and members of the Cabinet. Of these relationships he shaped a kind of private communications network through which he received confidential information that was invaluable to his patronage efforts.

The most important of his confidential relationships, however, was with a man nominally as high in the administration hierarchy as Roosevelt himself—a man who, though in the second or third echelon of power under the White House, had in fact more actual direct patronage to dispense than any other single official in Washington. He was Daniel C. Roper, the Assistant Postmaster General, whose office traditionally handled appointments to postmasterships in every town and hamlet— some 60,000 of them in 1913-14—and who, himself unversed in the complications of New York politics, was impressed by the detailed knowledge of these which Howe possessed and was willing to place (in a certain light, of course) at Roper's disposal. Moreover, Roper became convinced by Howe that the Assistant Secretary of the Navy truly wished to improve the caliber of appointees to postmasterships and that Roosevelt's candidates were generally better men than those proposed by O'Gorman and the Tammany men in the House. By the time Roosevelt and Wilson exchanged the notes we have seen, Roper was furnishing Howe with advance lists of postmastership openings and of the candidates proposed for them and was even conniving with Roosevelt and Howe on occasion in maneuvers and appointments that were strongly opposed by O'Gorman and, if less strongly, by his own chief, Postmaster General Burleson.

"I saw Mr. Roper again today," wrote Howe to Roosevelt in April, 1914, when Roosevelt was on his West Coast inspection tour. "We are getting what you might call chummy. Postoffice matters are going nicely and I think Ketcham is sure to win out in Orange County after my talk.

Mr. Burleson had his talk with the President and came back, according to Mr. Roper, undecided. Mr. Roper says he argued with him some more and that Mr. Burleson finally concluded to put it through and that he was going to break the news to O'Gorman in a few days. If you hear of that portion of the Postoffice Department roof sailing off into space accompanied by a violent explosion you will understand that the interview took place."[13]

Thus Roosevelt was enabled to win a number of victories over his political foes, including one of major importance to him since it concerned the postmastership of Poughkeepsie in his home county.

Ed Perkins of Poughkeepsie had threatfully advised Roosevelt in late December, 1913, "to keep out of the P.O. matter here. It will be a bitter fight," he had gone on, "and a good thing to leave alone for any one looking forward to future success in the party, not only here, but in the State." But even if he had not been temperamentally inclined to look upon this warning as a challenge, Roosevelt could not have stayed clear of what did indeed prove a bitter fight. Nor did the winning of it bring him unalloyed joy. He may even have wondered if it were not a Pyrrhic victory when an infuriated Perkins not only resigned as treasurer of the Democratic State Committee in protest against Roosevelt's methods, but also launched, through the Poughkeepsie *News-Press,* which he controlled, a viciously hurtful attack on Roosevelt's motives. These, charged Perkins, renewing charges made during the Sheehan fight, were a compound of "racial and religious prejudice" ("No Irish Need Apply") rather than "actual hostility to Tammany" as a political organization. Roosevelt, stung, hinted in a telegram to John Mack that he might take legal action against the paper, charging slander or malicious libel, if attacks of that nature continued. Another consequence was the temporary alienation of his political friend William Church Osborn, who, having completed a tour as state chairman of upstate New York, publicly reported that he had found his party in such disarray, largely because of quarrels over postmasterships, as to make likely its complete defeat in the upcoming November poll. He bitterly blamed certain "self-appointed little busybodies who had the President's ear and . . . , may have convinced him that many perfectly good Democrats are only Tammany heelers." Shortly thereafter, on July 24, 1914, the President himself, faced with a threatened revolt by twenty Democratic Representatives from New York City who had been consistent supporters of the New Freedom, felt compelled to deny in a public statement that he endorsed "the characterization of Tammany Congressmen as representatives of crooks, grafters, and buccaneers"—a characterization often implied by Roosevelt in public speech and loudly proclaimed by certain of his associates. The statement was tantamount to a White House repudiation of Roosevelt's gubernatorial candidacy. The Assistant Secretary promptly bowed to the inevitable. A few days before (July 19) he had said in a letter to "Dearest Babs," who was at Campobello awaiting the birth of the fifth Roosevelt child, that "the Governorship is, thank God, out of the question." He now, within hours after Wilson's announcement, issued a public statement of his own. He was not a candidate for governor of New York, he said. He would not accept nomination for that post if it were tendered. And he was saying this, "not . . . in diplomatic language, but seafaring language, which means it." [14]

His statement, however, did not free him of personal involvement in that year's elective politics.

Of some importance to the victory of Mitchel in the New York City mayoralty campaign of 1913 had been one John A. Hennessy, a colorful, histrionic, and emotional Irishman who, as a metropolitan newspaper reporter, claimed to have filled a "little black book" with names, dates, and descriptions of Tammany malfeasance. Presumably, the "little book" had been used on Sulzer's behalf during the latter's ill-fated war on the machine, for Hennessy had been the hapless governor's chief investigator; it had then notably failed either to convict Tammany or to acquit Sulzer of grievous charges. Nevertheless, it was still widely believed to be a potent political weapon, and Hennessy, in July, had placed it and himself at the service of the New York reform group of Democrats. He now became that group's declared gubernatorial candidate. Progressive Democrats then began to exert pressure upon thirty-two-year-old Roosevelt to declare himself a candidate for U.S. Senator. McAdoo seems to have joined in it: according to some accounts, the Treasury Secretary gave Roosevelt the *impression* that the President personally wished him to make the race, though no public administration support could be promised.* Such pressure was hard for one of Roosevelt's temperament to resist. As state senator he had championed the direct primary as a means of wresting power from the bosses; he had also been an early and leading upstate champion of Woodrow Wilson for President. The primary law was now in effect: for the first time in history, New York voters would go to the polls on September 28 to decide for themselves, in terms of their party preference, who their candidates would be. The Wilson administration of which Roosevelt was a part faced its first test at the polls. How could he, in these circumstances, re-

---

* If McAdoo did give this "impression," it was flatly contradicted by Daniels, who was probably as close a confidant of the President as McAdoo was in such matters, despite the latter's new family relationship with the White House. Daniels strongly advised his assistant not to run.

fuse the call to battle on behalf of his proclaimed principles, when the call was issued by national as well as state leaders of Progressive Democracy?

At any rate, he did not refuse. On the evening of August 12, responding to a telegraphic summons, he attended a conference of the reform group leaders in New York City. The next day, animated by a "stern sense of duty," as he put it in a note to Dudley Field Malone, he declared himself a Senatorial candidate. He offered himself in order that Democrats in his state could have a clear choice between "intelligent progress . . . in government" and "reactionary politics and politicians." [15]

A few hours later he departed sweltering Washington for cool, green Campobello to be with Eleanor during childbirth.

IV

One suspects he would have made a different political decision had Louis Howe been at his side. Howe wasn't, at this time. The little man was "drying out" (as he habitually described his vacations) at Horseneck Beach, and it was there that he read the rather rueful, half-apologetic message in which his friend, announcing the decision, asserted defensively that "my senses have not yet left me" and spoke of an "important political development" (unspecified) as a compelling reason for entrance into the race.[16] Howe could hardly have failed to deplore such rashness. He may privately have cursed his friend as a "damned fool." (He did so on not a few occasions, to Roosevelt's face.) But sharing as he did Roosevelt's penchant for daring gambles and being, like Roosevelt, determinedly optimistic, he would not permit vain regrets to inhibit his attempts to snatch victory from the jaws of seemingly inevitable defeat.

He immediately entrained for Washington, where his major efforts were devoted to plans and preparations for the primary campaign. Working through a headquarters opened in New York City under Stuart Gibboney, who was McAdoo's principal political assistant, he decided to employ much the same general strategy and several of the same tactics that had worked so well for Roosevelt in the campaign of 1912. He would "let . . . Hennessy look after the cities," he informed Roosevelt on August 29, "while I go gunning up in the rural districts which Tammany has never thought worth looking after." His detailed plans called for extensive and intensive cultivation of the goodwill of rural newspaper editors, the insertion of Roosevelt propaganda into "boiler-plate" copy distributed to these editors (the copy would proclaim in headlines as bold as they were false that Roosevelt ran as the national administration's candidate), the use of handbills passed out to workers at factory gates carrying endorsements from Navy yard labor union officials (this tactic backfired when the handbills were found not to carry the printers' union label), the placing of advertisements in several upstate papers, the mailing of "personal letters," and, of course, a speaking tour of the state by the candidate himself.[17]

Meanwhile, in the Roosevelt cottage on Campobello in mid-August, all attention was focused upon the impending arrival of the new baby. Miss Spring was in the house and Sara in her cottage next door when, near midnight of August 16, Eleanor awoke her husband to say, prematurely as it turned out, that her time had come. He hurriedly dressed and fetched the doctor from Lubec, crossing the dark narrow waters in his boat, the *Half-Moon*, but the child, a boy, was not born until the evening of the following day. He was named, as the dead baby had been, Franklin Delano Roosevelt, Jr. There were no complications. The new baby "progressed very satisfactorily," as Eleanor remembered years later, "and I never had a pleasanter convalescence. . . ."[18] The husband and father, freed of family anxieties, could turn his full attention again to politics.

He failed to do so, however, for the remainder of that month. He had been tired out by excessively long workdays in Washington's exhausting heat. ("I'm going home to bed after three nights at the various Departments up til nearly 3 a. m.," he had written "Dearest Babs" on August 7.[19]) Hence, while an increasingly exasperated Howe labored mightily and, for the most part, futilely to obtain administration backing and major newspaper publicity for his friend as candidate, Roosevelt lingered at Campobello, sailing and swimming, playing with his children and his stamp collection, golfing and hiking and picnicking, day after day.

During this period, he and Howe had a brief flurry of hope for their campaign. It was inconceivable that Murphy would willingly permit Roosevelt to enter the primary unopposed, but there was a chance that he might be forced to do so: the boss seemed to be having difficulty finding a suitable candidate of his own. "The truth is that they haven't a thing to say against you and no one is anxious to bell the cat," gloated Howe in a letter to Roosevelt, "—particulary when they have an idea that the President occasionally pats him on the back, calls him 'pretty pussy' and gives him a nice saucer of warm patronage milk to drink!" An Albany newspaper on August 21 published rumors that William Randolph Hearst, the publisher, might run (the prospect delighted Roosevelt; Hearst was, with good reason, one of the most hated men in America, and it "would be magnificent sport" as well as "magnificent service to run against him"), but four days later Hearst's New York *American* said the publisher had refused the invitation.[20] Nor did the Murphy-dominated preprimary conference of the party, in Howe's hometown of Saratoga, endorse a candidate. To do so would be improper, Murphy blandly explained, since the very purpose of the primary was to do away with the old system of nomination of party convention.

August gave way to September. Still Roosevelt dawdled on his "beloved island." He even failed to appear at Hennessy's side for the formal campaign kickoff, in New York City's Cooper Union, on September 2, thereby infuriating Howe and provoking newspaper speculation that he sought deliberately to dissociate himself from his running mate.

And indeed he would have liked to do this, had it been possible, when at last his own active campaign got under way in the second week of September. Hennessy's thick Irish brogue and florid campaign style were better suited to the amusement than the persuasion of a rural electorate, and it was soon clear that the picture of Tammany corruption which he drew from his "black book" would have the effect of alienating independent voters from the New York Democracy altogether rather than attract them to the reform wing of the party. Thus the gubernatorial candidate was but another liability upon a Senatorial primary campaign already crushed into hopelessness by the time Roosevelt, in this second week of September, began his personal speaking tour of the state.

For by then, in a stunning manifestation of the astuteness which had enabled him to survive all manner of assaults upon his position, Boss Murphy had found and named his Senatorial candidate—James W. Gerard, U.S. ambassador to Germany! This left Roosevelt with scarcely a leg to stand on, much less run. The ambassador could plausibly plead the necessity for his remaining in Berlin during a time of crisis; he was continuously and favorably in the news as he labored on behalf of Americans who had been stranded in Germany; and since he would make not the slightest gesture toward a personal campaign, he presented no target at which his opponent could shoot. Roosevelt could hardly attack as an administration enemy one who remained the President's personal representative in a most sensitive diplomatic post, nor could he even hint with any persuasiveness that he was *secretly* favored by the administration.

Not a single important administration leader would campaign for him. Malone wished to do so and was about to embark on a speaking tour when the President himself, still worried by the threatened defection of the New York and Brooklyn contingent in Congress, dissuaded him. "I feel extremely reluctant to have the administration as such constructively associated with the [New York] primary campaign because that would be so glaringly inconsistent with the position taken in other states," said Wilson in a message to Malone. "Hope you will think it best not to take part as a campaigner. You will inevitably be considered my spokesman. . . ." [21]

It is possible that a brilliant orator, armed with a compelling message and with the capacity to exert great personal charm over his audiences, could have overcome all these obstacles. Young Roosevelt was no such orator. He exerted no such charm. On his three-week speaking tour he made a generally pleasing impression on those who saw and heard him, but by no means a profound or especially vivid one, and his talks were tissues of generalities, lacking substance. There were published complaints that his listeners, at the end of his speeches, had no more idea where he stood on great questions than they had at the beginning.

On September 28, he cast his ballot in Hyde Park, then went to his boyhood home, where, only too early in the evening, he learned that he had gone down to crushing defeat. A day or two later he learned that his vote total was only 76,888 as compared with 210,765 for Gerard. He had run considerably stronger than Hennessy (he received 10,000 more votes than his running mate in New York City), but this was cold comfort in view of Hennessy's all-too-obvious deficiencies. Even in the circumstances, a defeat of these proportions was humiliating, and Daniels knew that it "hurt Roosevelt." Louis Howe sourly blamed the extent of the debacle on Hennessy, who, he said, "ruined us and will sink any ship on which he is a passenger." [22]

But Roosevelt managed to hide his chagrin from the public and even from his family and friends. He put on the boldest possible front, manifesting the same hardihood and truth-defying assertiveness he had displayed at the close of the Sheehan battle. He said the race had been "worthwhile" because it had "paved the way"—presumably for ultimate Progressive Democratic victory. He stressed the fact that he had carried a bare majority of the state's sixty-one counties, implying thereby that he had won a majority of the upstate vote ("I . . . was beaten only through the solid lineup in New York City," he wrote a friend), whereas actually, while losing the city four to one, he had been defeated elsewhere two to one. He sent a congratulatory cable to Gerard that was the opposite of humble, promising that he would "make active campaign for you if you declare unalterable opposition to Murphy's leadership and all he stands for." He added, "Please reply." Gerard, not unnaturally, took his time about doing so and then merely said that, if elected, he would "of course" represent all the people and not merely a "faction or individual." Roosevelt then announced his support of Gerard and even, during the last week of the general election campaign, made eight speeches in New York in support of the entire Democratic ticket, thus demonstrating his flexibility, as well as his hardihood.[23]

The predicted happened in November. Both Gerard and Glynn (the incumbent governor, who was Murphy's gubernatorial candidate) were overwhelmingly defeated. Republican James Wadsworth became U.S. Senator, Republican Charles S. Whitman became New York's governor, and even Murphy may privately have conceded that his Senatorial nominee ran less strongly than Roosevelt would have done.

Implicit in the returns was a political lesson that neither Roosevelt nor Murphy could afford to ignore and that they came gradually to accept—namely, that the continuing intraparty feud in New York must inevitably deny victory to the party when faced by a united opposition, whereas a coalition of Progressive and Tammany Democrats must almost as inevitably, in view of the city Democratic majorities, win victories. Actual coalition was at that time impracticable. Each side of the old quarrel had important interests vested in it. But neither thereafter would be as willing as before to wage open war on the other; each would seek increasingly to transform former battlegrounds into common grounds wherein enmities might be buried out of sight of the public and from which triumphs over the opposing party might be harvested. Already the astute Murphy—by pushing to the fore such remarkable young politicians as Bob Wagner and Al Smith and by assuring full Tammany support of the state's remarkable program of factory, welfare, and labor legislation—had done much to improve the Tiger's image in the eyes of Progressive reformers. The Boss would continue to promote young men of this sort (along with others who proved of different quality, such as the highly personable James J. Walker), and Roosevelt would do what he could to promote them, too. In his dealings with Congressman Fitzgerald, the Assistant Secretary would become "a very, very cooperative man" (the quotation is from Fitzgerald). He would speak on behalf of Al Smith in the latter's campaign for New York sheriff in 1915 and would actually persuade the President, a year later, to name Wagner to the postmastership of New York City—an appointment which the astonished Wagner would then decline because he aspired to become a justice of the State Supreme Court.*

---

* He became one in 1918 and remained on the bench until 1926, when he ran successfully for U.S. Senator.

And this burial of old enmities was encouraged by historic circumstances. Already in the summer and autumn of 1914, bossism as a political issue was losing force. Required for its continued vitality was a concentrated light of popular attention. Such light would from now on be denied it. For as never before in its national history—or not since 1815, at any rate—America had and would continue to have its attention riveted on events in Europe, events so stupendous and fearsome as to make all that was unrelated to them seem unimportant.

Book Three

✦

EDUCATION AMID WORLD CATASTROPHE

Thirteen

✦✧✦

Of Politics and War: Part One

I

I T WAS in the shadow of these events that Franklin Roosevelt waged his 1914 campaign. It was in part because of them that he entered the race with little enthusiasm and ran it almost halfheartedly, and because of them, too, he could more easily bear than he would otherwise have done the humiliation of his defeat. For these were events that presented to such an Assistant Secretary of the Navy as he, serving under such a Secretary as Josephus Daniels, far more challenging opportunities than would have been offered him as a first-term U.S. Senator. (In any case, as he confessed to Eleanor, he felt himself personally unsuited to a Senatorship: his was, he knew, an executive rather than a legislative temperament.)

No more than most other Americans had he heeded as an event of any world-shaking importance the murder of an Austrian archduke and his wife on a street in Sarajevo, capital of Bosnia, on June 28, 1914. The murdered Francis Ferdinand was a nephew of the octogenarian Emperor Franz Joseph and, as such, was heir apparent to the Austrian throne. Moreover, there was some suspicion that his youthful assassin, a fanatical Serbian nationalist named Gavrilo Princip, had operated as an agent of a conspiracy in which the Serbian government was implicated. Princip had been seized at the scene of his crime, and he and others of what was evidently a terrorist gang were being interrogated by Austrian authorities. If the investigation disclosed complicity by Belgrade in the affair, there would certainly be another Balkan crisis and might be another Balkan war. An American, however, could view this prospect without alarm. One had grown used to violence in the Balkans—a remote and semibarbarous region in which small nations were clustered along a political fault line between East and West, nations whose boundaries, largely determined by foreign rather than local interests, cut arbitrarily across natural ethnic communities. Each of the latter was caught up in a fever of nationalism. The result was turmoil and confusion atop a succession of political earthquakes as the balance of Great Power force in the area tipped first toward Asia, then toward Europe, back and forth, and found at no time a stable equilibrium. Thus far, however, the violence had been confined to the region itself, and one presumed that it would continue to be.

Two Balkan Wars had in fact been fought during the last two years—Bulgaria, Serbia, and Greece against Turkey in 1912; Rumania, Greece, and Turkey against Bulgaria in 1913—without causing general conflagration. True, the first of the two had generated a dangerous crisis when Russia strongly supported, and Austria adamantly opposed, landlocked Serbia's demand for an outlet to the Adriatic. Late in 1912 the two Great Powers had actually begun to mobilize against each other. But in the nick of time an alarmed England had exerted a moderating influence, Russia had withdrawn its support of the Serbian demand, and all concerned, with evident sighs of relief, had drawn back from the edge of the abyss. No similar crisis had attended the war of the following summer. The fighting had ended in a month with Bulgaria decisively defeated, and the peace treaties subsequently negotiated at Bucharest and Constantinople had made no local adjustments that affected in any important way the power balance between Russia and Austria.

Yet this balance remained precarious, the Balkans turbulent, all through the winter and spring of 1914, the principal trouble being a dispute between Greece and Turkey over possession of certain Aegean islands. By June the quarrel was about to erupt into the third Balkan war in three years, and Franklin Roosevelt was officially concerned with one aspect of it, the sale to the Greek government of two United States battleships, the *Idaho* and the *Mississippi*. Undersized, useless against dreadnaughts, they had been "orphans" in the U.S. Navy from the day they were placed in commission (1908), but they were perfectly suited to Greece's immediate needs in the Mediterranean. A dreadnaught being built in England for the Turks was yet several months from completion, and in the meantime the two ships would give to the Greeks a naval preponderance sufficient, perhaps, to deter their enemy from threatened attack. The transaction was, therefore, consistent with the pacific aims of Wilsonian diplomacy. It was also unprecedented, requiring for its conclusion a special act of Congress, and Roosevelt was so much involved in the business that he was unable to get away from Washington for a planned "surprise" visit to his mother at Hyde Park on Saturday, June 27. The sale was approved by Congress in a rider to the Naval Appropriations Act on June 30. Arrangements for prompt delivery to the Greeks (the *Idaho* was in Villefranche, France; the *Mississippi* at Newport News, Virginia) were then completed, despite urgent protests from Constantinople.* [1]

In the month following Sarajevo Roosevelt saw no reason to be worried over the European situation. Nor did any other member of the government. No important repercussions of the murders were reported in the press, or in diplomatic pouches from Europe, or even in personal letters to the President from Colonel House, who in the last two years had become Wilson's most intimate friend, most confidential adviser. And House certainly was in a better position than any other American at that time to know what was going on behind the scenes of West European diplomacy.

For House had been abroad since May as the President's unofficial personal representative seeking, as his diary put it, "to bring about an understanding between France, Germany, England, and the United States regarding a reduction of armaments, both military and naval." His mission—a very quiet one, its purpose unknown to all save the White House, members of the Cabinet, and a few of the latter's top assistants—had included long and intimate conversations with the German emperor and Acting Foreign Secretary Arthur Zimmermann in Berlin, with Prime Minister Herbert Asquith and Foreign Minister Sir Edward Grey in London, and had not been barren of encouraging results. Because of them, the colonel,† when he sailed for Boston on July 21 was much more optimistic about the chances for a permanently peaceful European settlement than he had been two months before. (On May 29, from Berlin, House had written the President that the general attitude in Europe was one of "jingoism run stark mad," adding: "Unless someone acting for you can bring about a different understanding, there is someday to be an awful cataclysm. No one in Europe can do it. There is too much hatred, too many jealousies.") The Sarajevo double murder had not impressed him as a factor of major importance in the immediate situation; nothing had been said in any of his high-level conversations to indicate that it had other than purely Balkan significance, though a cautious message from Sir Edward, brought him on his last day in London, announced that "the Austro-Serbian situation was giving . . . [the Foreign Secretary] grave concern." [2]

---

* The U.S. ambassador to the Ottoman Empire at this time was the wealthy New Yorker Henry Morgenthau, who had made a fortune in real estate and had become a principal financial prop of the Wilson wing of the Democratic Party. His namesake son, an ardent agriculturist and conservationist, acquired an estate at Hopewell Junction in Dutchess County, a few miles from Hyde Park.

† The title, though literal-minded Germans feted their visitor as an Army officer, was purely honorific, bestowed on House by the governor of his native Texas.

One can therefore imagine the astonishment and dismay with which, through ship's wireless, House learned that Austria, on July 23, had presented Serbia with an ultimatum no sovereign state could possibly accept *in toto,* since acceptance would be tantamount to surrender of all sovereignty, and had given Belgrade a mere forty-eight hours in which to concur. The colonel was still at sea when Serbia, whose government was indeed culpable in the matter of the assassinations (though Austria did not know this at the time), made its conciliatory but, on crucial points of sovereignty, necessarily unyielding reply. By the time House arrived at his summer home in Prides Crossing, north of Boston, the whole fragile structure of European international relations, erected on foundations laid at the Congress of Vienna, was splitting apart.

Franklin Roosevelt was on a train en route to Campobello when the Serbian reply to the Austrian ultimatum was delivered. He was asleep on the island when, in Vienna, a telegram was dispatched to the Serbian government on July 28 notifying it that war had been declared. He remained on Campobello through that day, though crossing to the mainland in the afternoon to obtain the latest news. This was sensational and ominous. Austrian troops invaded Serbia. Russia prepared to mobilize. Germany moved to honor its treaty obligations to Austria, and France moved to honor its treaty obligations to Russia, whose rulers it rashly encouraged toward "firmness." England—only loosely bound militarily to the Paris government through an ambiguously worded mutual defense covenant—awaited the turn of events, refusing to declare either its neutrality or its support of France.

On the following day, Wednesday, July 29, according to Eleanor's recollection, her husband "had a telegram to return to Washington because war seemed so imminent." [3] Such a telegram, however, could not have been delivered at Campobello, for Roosevelt was not there. He had previously been committed to make a speech at the formal opening of the Cape Cod Canal, a ceremony scheduled for the twenty-ninth, and in pursuance of this he had left by train from Eastport on the evening of the twenty-eighth, arriving in Boston the next morning. There he boarded a destroyer, the *McDougal,* which sailed as part of a flotilla containing ten or so large yachts and a half dozen other destroyers, from Massachusetts Bay around the Cape to the mouth of the canal in Buzzards Bay. Up the length of the canal and back down it again sailed the flag-bedecked ships—a pageantry witnessed by a "great many thousand people" who "lined the banks of the way," as he wrote his wife—and he found "the return trip . . . exciting enough as the current running against us was altogether too strong for safe navigation by a destroyer at low speed." (From the Danube, Austrian monitors shelled Belgrade that day. In Petrograd there was a great patriotic demonstration on Nevsky Prospekt, where a procession was formed to march "with banners flying" to the Serbian legation, then to the French and British embassies. Impassioned speeches were made; there was much cheering and singing of patriotic songs.) Going ashore at the village of Buzzards Bay in the waning afternoon, Roosevelt was one of five prominent men who made dedicatory speeches to a huge crowd. Then came an adventurous night of travel by motor launch, auto, and train as he strove to reach Washington at the earliest possible moment. He felt, he confessed, "very much like P. Revere." [4]

But when he arrived at the Navy Department early in the afternoon of Thursday, July 30, he was astonished and disgusted to find that "nobody seemed the least bit excited about the European crisis!" (Austria and Russia both ordered full mobilization; Germany responded with the gravest warnings to Petrograd; a proclamation of "a state of imminent threat of war" was prepared in Berlin for the Kaiser's issuance next day.) He therefore "started in alone to get things ready and prepare plans for what *ought* to be done by the Navy end of things." Twelve U.S. battleships were still anchored off Veracruz. The rest of the fleet was "scattered to the four winds." The ships must be brought together and prepared for any emergency. Who could say when U.S. policy might urgently require the "moral" support of a "fleet in being"?

He worked late in the office that night, was early in the office next morning, and again remained there until late at night. (Germany issued two ultimatums that Friday. Russia was given twelve hours within which to demobilize and "make us a distinct declaration to that effect." France was given eighteen hours in which to say whether or not it would remain neutral in case of war between Germany and Russia. England, speaking through Sir Edward Grey, who justified his name by shying away from black-or-white distinctions, continued to be vague and ambiguous, seemingly incapable of decision.) On the morrow, Saturday, Roosevelt was compelled by prior arrangement to go to Reading, Pennsylvania, and there dedicate, as a gift to the city from the Navy, an anchor salvaged from the wreck of the *Maine* in Havana Harbor.

In the afternoon of that August 1 he spoke to a crowd of 5,000 in the park, reviewing the anchor's history (cynical doubts had been cast upon its authenticity) and proclaiming in typical banalities the aims of the New Freedom. "The administration in Washington believes in . . . the fundamental theory that the success of a government depends upon the freely expressed consent of the governed," he said. "It is seeking so to handle the affairs of the nation that no man, no group and no class shall have privilege to the exclusion of any other man or group or class to the end that there may be equal opportunity for all." His written speech, prepared before he went to Campobello, did not refer to the European crisis, nor did he make any impromptu remarks concerning it.

But his mind was certainly full of the crisis as, on the train returning to Washington, he dashed off a note to "Dearest Babs."

"The latest . . . is that Germany has declared war on Russia," he wrote. "A complete smashup is inevitable, and there are a great many problems for us to consider. Mr. D. totally fails to grasp the situation and I am to see the President Monday a.m. to go over our own situation. . . . These are history-making days. It will be the greatest war in history." [5]

II

It would also be the end of an era most middle- and upper-class Americans would view in retrospect as a happy Golden Age—an era of stable institutions and assured values, of general peace and high idealism, and of a psychological security that would come to seem almost incredible by contrast with what followed.

Never again in Roosevelt's time, nor in our own, could there be a generally prevailing, unquestioned faith in man's essential decency and rationality and in his resultant movement, under God, toward the ever-higher, the ever-better. After 1914, in fact, nothing of major importance in the world where Roosevelt must make his way or play his part would ever be as it had been in his childhood, his youth, his young manhood. All would be consequent upon the "awful cataclysm" that was itself reflective of profound contradictions among Western man's scientific technology, his vital needs as a human person, and the largely preindustrial economic, social, and political patterns which he persisted in maintaining.

Bismarck had predicted, the year before he died, that the great European war would one day come out of "some damned foolish thing in the Balkans." [6] The event would place the German Empire in grave danger, and he assigned a large share of the responsibility for it to his emperor, Wilhelm II. He had reasons for doing so that have since recommended themselves to many historians.

The whole of the Iron Chancellor's foreign policy had been aimed at maximizing German power while at the same time preventing a general war in which Germany, by virtue of its central position on the Continent, would be forced to fight on two fronts. His fear of this had caused

him to curb the desire of German expansionists for a world empire rival-
ing England's. "The risk is too great for me," said Bismarck to an Afri-
kander who sought to persuade him into a colonial venture on the Dark
Continent. ". . . my map of Africa lies in Europe. There is Russia, on
the other side is France, we are in the middle; that is my map of Africa." [7] Similarly motivated had been his Three Emperors' League (Germany, Austria-Hungary, Russia), and his flat refusal to side with Vienna
when the league was shattered in 1885 by the conflicting interests of
Austria and Russia in the Balkans. He had then moved to guarantee the
Balkan status quo. "If Russia should make any aggression . . . ," he
said, "we are prepared to support Austria with all our forces; but if war
with Russia should ensue because Austria invades Serbia without previous understanding with us . . . , we shall not be prepared to represent
this to Germany as the occasion of making war on Russia." [8]

But Bismarckian policy had been discarded along with the Iron
Chancellor himself when Wilhelm II mounted the throne. The young
Kaiser, with his inept ministers, proceeded to wreck without ever understanding the careful system of checks and balances which Bismarck had
erected for Germany's external security over many decades. At the same
time (the effect of Mahan upon his disordered brain was catastrophic),
he permitted and even encouraged, by personal word and example, as
well as by dangerous shifts in domestic policy, a release of those inward
drives toward imperialist expansion which Bismarck had suppressed.

But even Bismarck, despite his bitterness toward Wilhelm II, would
not have assigned to the second Wilhelm the whole of the responsibility
for impending catastrophe. Indeed, before his death in 1898, there were
moods in which he was inclined to place much blame upon himself for
what was beginning to happen. For instance, when Czar Nicholas paid a
much-publicized visit to Paris in the fall of 1896 and portions of the
German press blamed Bismarck for the drawing together of Russia and
France in common cause against Germany, the ex-Chancellor resented
the charge with a public vehemence that suggested private unease. The
responsibility lay with the new regime, he said; it had failed to renew, as
St. Petersburg wished to do, the reinsurance treaty with Russia. Yet as
he said this, he well knew that what rendered the reinsurance treaty crucial was the Dual Alliance of 1879, and for *this* he himself was almost
solely responsible. In 1879 he had had a choice between the Austrian alliance and a strengthening of friendly ties with Russia. He could more
easily have chosen the latter, since this is what his own sovereign wished
and even sought to compel him to do. Against such august opposition,
his choice of Vienna had required for its practical realization the most
stubborn will, the most adroitly forceful political maneuvering on his

part. And in every respect his linkage of Germany's fortunes as a vigorous and rising world power to those of Austria-Hungary, a decrepit and
declining monarchy, had proved ominously fateful. It had greatly lessened the chances for a general settlement of Europe's quarrels through
peaceful conference and had greatly increased the chances that "some
damned foolish thing in the Balkans" would indeed incite general
conflagration, once the Iron Chancellor's restraining hand (as in 1885)
had been removed from Austria's Balkan ambitions.

Whatever Bismarck's reservations about the Dual Alliance, however,
they were minor and superficial compared with others he more than
hinted at as his life drew toward a close. He developed deep-seated
doubts about the constitution of the German Empire itself.

The empire, too, was largely his creation and, therefore, as he seemed
now inclined to believe, his "fault." He more than anyone else had
thwarted in Germany the democratic forces which in other Western
countries had achieved governing power in what seemed a natural political corollary of the Industrial Revolution. But for him, the movement
toward German unity, in the aftermath of 1848, might well have issued
in a federal union whose government was a constitutional monarchy on
the English model. Parliamentary democracy would then have prevailed. Instead, chiefly through Bismarck's will and genius, the German
union had been formed on the Prussian monarchical model. The fatherland's chief executive was a Prussian All Highest whose personal control
of the national military and bureaucratic apparatus was only feebly
checked by an elected Reichstag. Moreover, it was Bismarck more than
anyone else who, in creative defense against a rising Socialism, had in-
congruously grafted onto this divine right anachronism an ultramodern
welfare state powered by the best organized, the most scientific, the
most efficient and explosively expansive industrial and agricultural
economy in Europe.

Profound and far-reaching had been the effects of the economic and
social policy shaped by the Iron Chancellor into a coherent program in
the late 1870's and then forced through the Reichstag, item by item.
From it was growing the New Germany whose order, efficiency, and nationalistic fervor were much admired by the young TR (he liked and admired the young Kaiser, too), and whose conservation policies had been
cited by State Senator Franklin Roosevelt in 1912 as an example of the
"liberty of the community" that must now take precedence over the
"liberty of the individual," because of "new sets of conditions." In several important respects, as a matter of fact, the New Germany would
serve as model for the New Nationalism of 1912—and in the latter year
a Brandeis or a Wilson, a Bryan or a Josephus Daniels might point to

German authoritarianism, national egotism, and aggressive militarism as a forecast of America's own character, a loathsome example of what the United States must become, if the New Nationalists were permitted to have their way.

For already in the Germany of Bismarck's last years the activities of government and big business were so tightly intertwined and even interpenetrative as to make the two virtually indistinguishable when viewed overall. Under the aegis of the protective tariff of 1879 (Bismarck had formerly espoused free trade principles) and of an accompanying system of export premiums, cartels had been formed which grew ever more gigantic, dominating by the late 1890's all major portions of the economy save textile manufactures and agriculture. Simultaneously, the nationalization of railway, telegraphic, and postal communications; the establishment of a Reichsbank to serve as national clearinghouse for German credit, enabling private banks and the state (four huge private banks came to dominate the money market) to collaborate in the financing of specific commercial and industrial enterprises; the establishment also of a network of state-supported technical academies whose central purpose was to supply trained personnel, new products, and new production techniques to the national economy—all these acts ensured that government would be an active participant and not merely a regulatory force in every phase of German economic life. With the cartels had risen a new class of entrepreneur—namely, the managers, as distinct from the owners (the dispersed shareholders) of the huge combinations. In addition, the big business community was organized in associations—a Union of German Mining and Ironworks Owners, a General Federation of German Industrialists, a Bankers' Association, etc.—which operated not only as pressure groups upon government but also as an effective defense against worker organizations that, in any case, were rendered relatively docile by Bismarckian state welfarism. Indeed, to all intents and purposes, the officers of these big business organizations were officials of government as well, for they nearly always had seats in the Reichstag and were the highly influential consultants of the imperial ministries or even, in several instances, of the Kaiser himself. Not a few of the most powerful businessmen were ennobled by their emperor and thereby entered the hereditary aristocracy.

The empire, so constituted, had made spectacular economic gains. The virtual fusion of big business and the imperial government at the top policy level had facilitated national economic planning and the raising of capital for specific industrial and commercial enterprises, at home and abroad, on a scale much larger than would have been otherwise possible. By 1895, when Wilhelm II announced in typically strident tones that his country was now "a world power" whose "future . . . lay upon the water," Germany, after less than a quarter century of national existence, had become the second nation in Europe in industry and commerce and was rapidly overtaking England, the leading European country at that time, in the production of coal, raw iron, steel, and fabrics. It led the world in the new chemical industry. Simultaneously its population had grown at a rate considerably faster than that of other Continental powers, increasing from a little more than 40,000,000 to 52,000,000, and had become more and more concentrated in urban centers. (Berlin's population, 500,000 in 1860, was three times that in 1895.) A lesser prescience than Bismarck's could foresee that within the next two decades, at present rates of growth, Germany would become by far the leading industrial power in Europe and, in all the world, would have only the United States as a surpassing rival.[9]

But if such expanding prosperity gratified the ex-Chancellor as a justification of his economic and social policy, his pleasure in it was more than offset by anxieties and guilt feelings regarding the political context in which it occurred. This vast and growing power was now in such reckless, foolish hands! And he himself was in no small part to blame! Germany's industrial growth generated pressures toward an expanding foreign market for its industrial goods and toward the development of foreign sources of raw materials. The concentration of a growing worker population in urban centers generated pressures toward a democratization of German society, a socialization of the economy. And the political constitution of the empire, for which Bismarck was so largely responsible, ensured that these economic and popular forces would now result (through reaction by the ruling class) in precisely the kind of unlimited militaristic imperialism which the Iron Chancellor had been at pains to prevent.

Belatedly he recognized as sadly mistaken the "dutiful" attitude toward the Crown, the implacably hostile attitude toward parliamentarianism, which had animated his earlier years. He saw that the real enemies of his work and person, the destructive opponents of his deepest commitments, were not "the people" whom he had so contemptuously spurned but their rulers, whom he had elevated, and he bitterly regretted the abject servility of the former in their relations with the latter throughout his beloved fatherland. "Perhaps my dutiful behavior has been the cause of the deplorable lack of backbone in Germany, and for the multiplication of place-hunters and time-servers . . . ," he admitted, adding in a revisionist view of his own past that he had "invariably thought it better to obey no one, rather than try to command others," and so had always been essentially "a republican" rather than a monarchist. "The most important thing is to strengthen the Reichstag," he said, "but this can only be done by electing thoroughly independent persons."

Face to face with death, knowing his own future on earth to be a matter of only a few months, he strove to recognize and balance the factors of freedom against those of necessity as determinants of the future for others. He regarded as inevitable "the final victory of labor" in "the fight between labor and capital," as probable the "coming of a republic" in Russia within a few years, and as distinctly possible "a second era of decay" for Germany "followed by a fresh period of glory" that would be "certainly . . . upon a republican basis."

Sometimes he spoke of "the coming war" as if it, too, were inevitable —as if the tide of technological force, flowing toward catastrophe through channels of political and economic organization he himself had shaped, were already so hugely swollen, had already developed so terrific a momentum, that it could not be rechanneled or in any way diverted this side of the abyss.

At other times he took a less sweeping and doleful view. "If the country is well-ruled, the coming war may be averted . . . ," he said, though doing so would require a radical revision of the German constitution. There must be a major shift of governing power from the Crown to "the people." [10]

The Germany of Wilhelm II during the years after Bismarck's death manifested more intensely than did any other nation a central theme of Western civilization since the collapse of the medieval synthesis into the creative chaos of Renaissance and Reformation. Here were farther advanced or carried to a greater extreme than anywhere else two great cultural tendencies that have, through divergence and interaction, largely shaped modern Western man's world view and determined his historic acts. One tendency is commonly labeled "Romanticism," the other "Scientific Materialism."

No other people placed as great an emphasis on the physical sciences, on technology, on rational method and system in general. Significant of this was the fact that, by the 1900's German had virtually become the international language of science, a working knowledge of it a prerequisite to the serious study and practice of physics, chemistry, and even biology on both sides of the Atlantic. Nor had any other people gone as far in their economic life toward the design and establishment of an efficient machine state whose operations, directed by a scientifically informed and methodizing intelligence, could be aimed at achieving specific goals. In short, no other people, when operating in the realm of means as distinct from ends, were more purely and determinedly intellectual, more inclined to subordinate the feeling to the thinking self.

But at the same time no other people were as inclined to a ponderous emotionalism, an orgiastic sentimentality, a passionate "thinking-with-the-blood," and no other were as prone individually or collectively to an assertive, overweening egotism. This last could be heard in their music (Wagner, Strauss), read in their philosophy (Fichte, Hegel, Nietzsche), and seen in the strutting goose step of their constantly parading soldiers; but its most vivid expression and symbol was the person of Kaiser Wilhelm II himself. To the eyes of most rational liberal minds, especially those watching from abroad, the emperor with his upturned mustaches and theatrical uniforms appeared incredible as the head of an advanced Western state in the twentieth century. And to the ears of such minds he sounded no less so in his public speech. Fifteen hundred years after the collapse of ancient Rome he could say that "Germany, like the spirit of Imperial Rome, must expand and impose itself" by armed force. A thousand years after the last bloody-handed tribal god of the Nordics had given way to Christianity he could speak with patronizing affection of "our old God" as his own "Divine Ally" in that "work of civilization" which was Germany's historic mission. Centuries after gunpowder had made medieval armor obsolete he was constantly speaking of a Germany "clad in shining armor" that could impose its civilizing will with a "mailed fist" whenever and wherever necessary. And clearly, in striking such verbal attitudes, however absurd they seemed to non-Germans, he struck sympathetically responding chords among the great mass of his compatriots. In short, no other people, when operating in the realm of ends or values, were more inclined toward a pure emotionalism, a defiant "letting go" of rational controls, a willful subordination of the thinking to the feeling self.

Here, then, was a potentially disastrous discrepancy of ends and means. The two general cultural tendencies—romantic, scientific—produced two very different kinds of power. One kind was personal, individual, fervidly emotional. It was the power of heroic leaders, demagogues, tyrants, of ancient kings and feudal lords, each aspiring to and ultimately mantled by his own particular "glory." Of it the Kaiser was representative and expressive. The other kind of power was impersonal, social, and coldly rational. Derived from science and technology, it was realized through large organizations in which multitudes of men were themselves objectified in their working lives as elements of economic process. The two streams of power were as naturally divergent as their cultural sources and substances. Yet in Germany they were not permitted to proceed more or less independently of each other along the lines natural to them within the broad confines of a loosely organized, plural-istic state. Instead, they were narrowly confined, were bound together and even interwoven within the very fabric of a tightly organized, virtu-ally monistic state whose supreme government was almost wholly and darkly romantic. It was as if two highly reactive, mutually antagonistic chemicals were forcibly and concentratedly intermingled in an area where sparks were flying. An explosion, sooner or later, was inevitable.

Thus Germany became, in certain essential respects, an epitome of the West. It became, also, a cautionary tale for all Americans who were truly, deeply committed to human freedom and determined to maintain it in their own land. For more intensely present in Germany than in any other country at the opening of the second decade of the twentieth cen-tury were the fatal dangers of a "progress" that was nowhere more ar-dently embraced than in the United States.

This "progress," wholly Western in its conception, was almost exclu-sively concerned with the realization of material, external possibilities. Great stress was laid upon machine extensions of the human body; slight heed was paid to the effects of these, or the demands they im-posed, on the human spirit. In fact, many of those most committed to "progress" were inclined to deny reality to man's inward, existential self—they deemed themselves realistic materialists in philosophy— though in Germany this did not often prevent their passionate devotion to emperor and fatherland. The result was physical power divorced from humane intelligence in society at large, intellect split off from emo-tion in the individual soul. There was an increasing failure of nerve on the part of those who wished to continue to believe that the human per-son is the center and measure of all value. There was a growing sense of a loss of control over human destiny, a sense of being wholly at the mercy of socioeconomic forces as vast and impersonal as those of earth-quakes and hurricanes. How small and weak the individual person, how huge and mighty the machine, and how awesome this world-shattering and -building "progress" which, all agreed, was "inevitable"!

Nor was the sense of lost control an illusion. There was an actual, vis-ible diminishment: machinery and technical process more and more re-placed decisive human wills and minds in the determination of great events. One could trace and even measure this to some degree through the succession of crises in European Great Power relations that began with the German Fleet Law of 1900 and was conditioned by the naval arms race with Britain that "inevitably" followed. There was a Moroc-can crisis (with Germany threatening France) in 1905, a crisis over the Austrian annexation of Bosnia and Herzegovina (with Germany threat-ening Russia) in 1908, a second Moroccan crisis (Germany threatening

France again, with Britain unexpectedly declaring its firm support of France) in 1911, besides the Balkan crisis of 1912. Each was largely instigated by Germany's compulsive drive toward what the Kaiser described as its "place in the sun," each was given its dominant shape and color by the German conception of "economic necessity" joined to a peculiarly Germanic "will-to-power," each augmented the fearful hostility between two increasingly adamant Great Power blocs, and each was more "inevitable" than the last in the sense of being less determined or controllable by the nominal masters of national affairs.

When at last the final blowup came, sparked by Sarajevo, virtually all human control of events was lost. Machines and technical procedure overwhelmed the decision-making capacities of heads of government.

Witness, as significant instance, a scene in the palace of the German emperor late in the afternoon of Saturday, August 1, 1914. The time limit in the ultimatum to Russia has expired with no reply from Petrograd. Germany's general mobilization has been ordered, and a massive westward movement of German forces is under way in accordance with the long-laid Schlieffen Plan, as revised in 1913—a plan that involves the violation of a solemn treaty guaranteeing Belgium's neutrality. No formal declaration of war by Germany has yet been made,* however, when, through the Foreign Office, a decoded message from the German embassy in London arrives saying, mistakenly, as will be later learned, that England is prepared to guarantee French neutrality in case of war between Germany and Russia, provided, of course, that Germany refrains from hostile acts in the west. Pandemonium ensues in the palace. The All Highest, who for days has been jittery and anxiety-ridden over the prospect of a two-front war, is elated. He promptly telegraphs his acceptance of the alleged proposal and orders his Chief of the General Staff, Helmuth von Moltke, to halt the western drive. "Now we simply march the whole of our Army to the East!" he cries, almost tearful with relief. But Moltke is horrified. He emphatically shakes his head. "Sire," says he, flatly, "it cannot be done. The deployment of millions cannot be improvised." The Schlieffen Plan is the only one that has been thoroughly updated, with all its complicated railroad and other transportation schedules worked out. No fewer than 11,000 trains are being used! "The arrangements took a whole year to complete!" Once so intricate an operation is launched on so massive a scale, it becomes as irreversible as an avalanche—which is to say that, to all intents and purposes, hostilities against France have *already* begun. Thus argues Moltke with

---

* The declaration of war on Russia was announced at 7 P.M.

bitter vehemence, not only against the emperor but also against the Chancellor, Theobald von Bethmann-Hollweg. He says he can "undertake no responsibility for the war" if there is any political interference whatever with execution of the plan. And in the end, both Kaiser and Chancellor are forced to yield. They agree that the advance upon France must proceed "for technical reasons"! [11]

The scene presaged all too accurately the machine war which followed. Not long afterward, of course, Moltke himself found it possible to alter the Schlieffen Plan after the battle was joined. As the mighty right arm of Germany swung down through Belgium and northern France toward Paris, sweeping all before it, seemingly invincible, he weakened it by removing two corps and dispatching them eastward to strengthen defenses against the Russians, who, to the dismay of all Germany and especially of the All Highest ("—our lovely Masurian Lakes!" cried Wilhelm II), had invaded East Prussia. But this tampering with the machinery proved disastrous, from Moltke's point of view, insofar as it deprived Germany of the margin of victory on the Marne. And certainly machines and technical procedure took over completely thereafter. The very possibility of a battle of maneuver in which tactical and strategical skills might be employed was lost on a western front that reached in continuous opposing lines of muddy ditches, separated by a shell-churned, blood-bespattered no-man's-land, all the way across northern France and Flanders, from Switzerland to the sea. Barbed wire, machine guns, rifled cannon, high explosives, shrapnel, poison gas, flamethrowers—these dominated the battlefield and used up living men as if flesh and blood were fuel.

Generalship, rendered impotent by weapons technology, became crudely statistical. It was reduced to ordering repeated mass assaults against machines that mowed men down by the thousands, the hundred thousands, year after year, with no decisive result; it measured its "victories" in a few miles or even only a few hundred yards of ruined earth and in the presumed excess of enemy casualties over one's own. Moreover, significantly, this generalship was exercised at a safe, comfortable distance. The stench of death, the screams of men in agony, the monotonous filthy misery of trench life, the terror of going "over the top," the horror of shell storms that preceded enemy attacks—none of this actual living-and-dying experience of bloody stalemate penetrated to the pleasant houses, often with gardens behind them, where the generals slept in beds or to the pleasant rooms, on whose walls large maps traced the abstract pattern of battle, where these generals kept office hours with the regularity of business executives. Here a commander of armies could endure the slaughter of his troops with perfect calm, the casualties having no more meaning to him than that assigned them through an exercise in double-entry bookkeeping. And what was true for generals in this respect was true also for the politicians and statesmen, who, farther still from the battlefield, in the capitals of warring nations, surrounded by all the comforts of urban civilization, pretended to control what were in reality machine-controlled events—events by which, in actual fact, they themselves were driven.

Could not this whole arrangement be viewed as a gigantic outward projection of the inward division, that schism of the individual soul, which is characteristic of modern Western man? Was there not manifested here on a terrifyingly huge scale the growing separation of heart from mind, of the felt from the thought in the Western world—a widening gap between, on the one hand, fervent emotions engendered by actually experienced, concrete realities and, on the other, coldly calculated responses by the intellect to problems rendered abstract and statistical by the machine? Did not the overall pattern of violence demonstrate the deathly hostility of the thinking self toward the feeling self, and vice versa, once the two are divorced? Finally, and in sum, did one not see in this ghastly conduct of war the ultimate madness of a "progress" whose "inevitability" is allowed to work itself out to its "logical" conclusion without regard for the vital needs and ultimate yearnings of the human spirit?

III

To most of the key members of the Wilson administration, especially to those most committed to the New Freedom, news of the events in Europe in August, 1914, came as a numbing shock. The cumulative warnings, the flat prophecies of the great war to come, the clamor of successive European crises had come muffled by distance to American ears and been blocked from any convincing penetration of the American mind by a strong will to disbelieve. Much more persuasive was the argument of British author Norman Angell, who in his *The Great Illusion* (1910) proved beyond the possibility of successful contradiction that modern war did not "pay" and could therefore not occur between major powers in the twentieth century. David Starr Jordan, president of Stanford and director of the World Peace Foundation, reached the same conclusion in his *War and Waste* (1914). "What shall we say of the Great War in Europe, ever threatening, ever impending, and which never comes?" he wrote. "We shall say that it will never come. Humanly speaking, it is impossible." The editors of *Review of Reviews* agreed. The

January, 1914, issue of the magazine said flatly: "The world is moving away from military ideals; and a period of peace, industry and world-wide friendship is dawning." Amid the general acceptance of such views in this country, most Cabinet members, like most U.S. citizens, paid far more attention to the continuing troubles with Mexico all through July, 1914, than they did to the developing crisis in Europe.

Typical in this respect was Secretary of Agriculture David F. Houston. He was a thoroughly orthodox classical economist and no pacifist. His will to disbelieve in the possibility of major war was consequently far less strong than Bryan's or Daniels'. Nevertheless, he watched European developments almost with indifference that summer, as he later confessed, until he read in the papers of August 3 that England had served an ultimatum upon Germany, threatening war by midnight unless German troops were immediately withdrawn from Belgium. (In Berlin on August 3, Bethmann-Hollweg, referring to the treaty guaranteeing Belgian neutrality, expressed outraged astonishment that England would go to war over a mere "scrap of paper." In London, near midnight, Sir Edward Grey looked out into the darkness through the open windows of Whitehall and saw lights being extinguished as a precaution against possible zeppelin raids. "The lamps are going out all over Europe," he said sadly; "we shall not see them lit again in our lifetime.") Houston was thunderstruck. All at once it was borne in upon him that the world as he had known it was collapsing. "I had a feeling that the end of things had come. . . . I stopped in my tracks, dazed and horror-stricken." [12]

For Woodrow Wilson, the sense of everything ending, of darkness closing down upon the whole of earth, was stronger still. For him, the tragedy of Europe coincided with the greatest tragedy he had ever known in his personal life: his beloved wife, Ellen Axson Wilson, main source and prop of his private happiness, was dying of an incurable disease. On Tuesday, August 4, the day England declared war on Germany—the day, too, on which Wilson as President issued a formal proclamation of U.S. neutrality in the war—Dr. Cary T. Grayson, White House physician, suggested to Wilson that the family be gathered together because, for the First Lady, the end was near. On Thursday morning, August 6, at about the time Austria declared war on Russia, the dying woman whispered to her husband her last wish—that Congress would pass the Washington back-alley slum clearance bill which she personally had sponsored.* A few hours later, Joe Tumulty, whom Mrs. Wilson had warmly befriended and to whom he was devoted,

* See page 322.

brought news that passage of her bill was now assured. The dying woman smiled faintly before sinking into a coma. The end came at five o'clock in the afternoon. Her husband, who had been holding her hand as her life ebbed away, rose abruptly and went to the bedroom window. He looked out across the White House lawn, saw with grief-darkened vision that flowers yet bloomed, that birds yet darted and sang among the leafy boughs of elms, and cried aloud: "Oh, my God! What am I going to do?" [13] How could he possibly bear the immense burdens of his public office atop his private woe?

Others wondered, too, and worried. Daniels did, and Colonel House. So did Franklin Roosevelt. "It is too terrible about Mrs. Wilson," wrote the Assistant Secretary of the Navy to "Dearest Babs" on Friday, August 7. "We knew on Wednesday afternoon that there was little hope. . . . The President has been truly wonderful, but I dread a breakdown." [14]

The breakdown did not occur, however, and for this, paradoxically, the very weight of the Presidential burdens was responsible. "I never dreamed such loneliness and desolation of heart possible," Wilson wrote a friend soon after his return from the funeral services in Rome, Georgia, but under the "compulsion of necessity and duty," as he put it to another friend, he was forced to look outward, was forced to act in the great world. He was not permitted to withdraw into some hidden corner and there indulge his grief. His "salvation," as he said, was "the business of a great country that must be done and cannot wait, the problems that it would be deep unfaithfulness not to give my best powers to because a great people has trusted me. . . ." [15]

And as he looked abroad, shaping policy in terms of what he saw, his overriding concern was to prevent in the United States, as in himself personally, that divorcement of feeling from thinking, that loss of human control over events, which the western front would come so horribly and bloodily to manifest. He knew himself to be a passionate man, able to function for effective good in the real world only through the most rigid discipline of his feeling self. "All his life long," writes his official biographer, [16] "Woodrow Wilson had been fearful of emotion as a controlling influence on conduct. It was with complete sincerity that he had written, as a young man: 'Hearts frequently give trouble. . . . They must be schooled. . . .' "* Schooled, curbed, disciplined—but *not* crushed, *not* destroyed! What he aimed for in public act and private life was the Greek ideal of self-mastery, a balanced integrity of heart and

---

* Woodrow Wilson kept a framed copy of Rudyard Kipling's "If" upon the library table at which he did much of his work as President.

mind wherein cold logic freezes fluid emotions into rigid forms, giving them shape and direction, while emotions inspire, inform, and become ultimately the meaningful substance of ideas. His own heart was as strongly attracted by the British democracy as it was repelled by the Prussian autocracy. Yet he was intellectually convinced that the United States could truly serve its national interests and international ideals only through the strictest impartiality in its dealings with the warring nations. Hence his issuance on August 19 of a special "appeal by the President of the United States to the citizens of the Republic, requesting their assistance in maintaining a state of neutrality during the present European war"—the neutrality he had formally proclaimed two weeks earlier. He spoke "a solemn word of warning" against "passionately taking sides." In "these days that are to try men's souls," he said, "we must be impartial in thought as well as in action, must put a curb on our sentiments as well as upon every transaction that might be construed as a preference of one party to the struggle before another."

And there can be no doubt that he spoke the predominant wish and will of the American people not only to stay out of the war now, but to suppress the "sentiments" which might lead to participation later on, if the war were long-continued. (That it *would* long continue was the opinion of Franklin Roosevelt. In a letter to Eleanor written on August 2 he saw as "a most unlikely occurrence" a "sharp, complete and quick victory by one side." There remained the possibility of "a speedy realization of impending bankruptcy by all, and cessation by mutual consent, but this too I think unlikely as history shows that money in spite of what the bankers say is not an essential to the conduct of war by a determined nation.") At the same time, of course, few Americans found it possible to be truly "impartial in thought." Most shared with their President sympathy with the Allies, antipathy toward the Germans (Franklin Roosevelt hoped on August 2 that England would "join in and with France and Russia force peace *at Berlin!*" [17]), and the antipathy was swiftly augmented by the calculated "frightfulness" employed by the German invaders against the Belgian and French people whenever and wherever civilians took arms against them. Especially shocking and hate-provoking was the deliberate sacking and burning, in late August, of the lovely medieval city of Louvain with its world-famous Cloth Hall, town hall, university, and library containing a priceless collection of manuscripts and incunabula. Yet this vicious crime caused no influential American at the time to raise his voice in favor of American intervention.

If anyone might have been expected to do so it was the bellicose TR, from whom Franklin Roosevelt continued to take so many of his cues. Instead, for more than two months after hostilities began, TR gave strong public support to Wilson's neutrality stand and refused publicly to condemn the President's failure to protest Germany's violation of the Belgian treaty. Indeed, he went so far as to write in the *Outlook* of August 22, "I am not now taking sides one way or the other as concerns the violation. . . . When giants are engaged in a death wrestle, as they reel to and fro they are certain to trample on whomever gets in the way of either of the huge straining combatants." A month later, after a Belgian commission had arrived in the United States to plead for aid, TR actually *defended* the treaty-violating invasion on the ground of "necessity," asserting that "disaster would surely have attended her [Germany's] arms had she not followed the course she actually did follow" and adding that there could be "nothing but . . . praise and admiration due a stern virile and masterful people, a people entitled to hearty respect for their patriotism and far-seeing self-devotion." He further wrote, in the *Outlook* for September 23: "We can maintain our neutrality only by refusal to do anything to aid unoffending weak powers which are dragged into the gulf of bloodshed and misery through no fault of their own. . . . I am sure the sympathy is compatible with full knowledge of the unwisdom of uttering a single word of official protest unless we are prepared to make that protest effective; and only the clearest and most urgent National duty would ever justify us in deviating from our rule of neutrality and non-interference."

But what the ex-President said in public contradicted much that he simultaneously said in private. In his library at Sagamore Hill a few hours before England declared war he burst out to a British visitor: "You've got to go in! You've got to go in!" And by his own account, he and a group of visitors later that same day "all . . . sympathized with Belgium, and therefore with England and France" but *also* "felt that the smashing of Germany would be a world calamity, and would result in the entire Western world being speedily forced into a contest with Russia." On August 22 he said in a private letter: ". . . it seems to me that if I were President I should register a very emphatic protest, a protest that would mean something, against the levy of the huge war contributions on Belgium. . . . The Germans . . . trampled on their solemn obligations to Belgium and on Belgium's rights. . . ." On September 5, in conversations with two political friends, he exclaimed: "Germany is absolutely wrong. Her own White Paper [just issued] places her squarely in the wrong. . . ." [18]

A few weeks later he began to bring his private sentiments and public declarations into closer accord. In October, during his futile campaign for Progressive Party candidates in the midterm elections, he came out strongly for great and rapid increases in the nation's armed strength.

IV

Step by step, point by point, all through the late summer and fall of 1914, Franklin Roosevelt's developing attitudes toward the war closely paralleled those of Cousin Theodore.

Like TR, he felt no such numbing shock of disillusion as struck down for a time Bryan and Daniels, among other pacifistic idealists in the administration. TR had never believed a great war impossible or that war per se, ensuring and testing the "heroic qualities" of "the race," was undesirable. He was inclined to say "I told you so"—as in a statement on August 15 wherein he spoke of the events of the last "fortnight" as providing "fresh proof of the worthlessness of treaties, of names signed to pieces of paper, unless backed by force." Similarly, Franklin Roosevelt, in his letter to Eleanor of August 2, spoke contemptuously of "Mr. Daniels feeling chiefly very sad that his faith in human nature and civilization and similar idealistic nonsense was receiving such a rude shock." He went on: "These dear good people like W.J.B. and J.D. have as much conception of what a general European war means as Elliott [then four years old] has of higher mathematics. They really believe that because we are neutral we can go about our business as usual." [19] Though he rhetorically deplored it, as conventional piety required him to do, he was not at all depressed by the European tragedy. On the contrary, as a TR-emulating Assistant Secretary of the Navy, he was enormously exhilarated by the challenges and opportunities which were now presented to him. He reveled in the excitement of it all. He became, as he had been on the West Coast in April when war with Mexico seemed imminent, a dynamo of executive energy. "Alive and very well and keen about everything," he wrote "Dearest E." on August 5. "*I* am *running* the real work, although Josephus is here! He is bewildered by it all, very sweet but very sad!" Two days later he began a letter to Eleanor with "Gee! But these are strenuous days!" and went on to say that he had "been serving on two boards appointed by the President and representing our Department [his colleagues were of Cabinet rank] as Mr. D. didn't seem anxious to do it himself." One was a "Relief Board" set up to assist Americans stranded in Europe; the other "had to do with neutrality— you will read of the 'Varrington' holding the Kronprinzessin fast in Bar Harbor." * He added: "Most of the reports of foreign cruisers off the

* In his letter to Eleanor of August 2 he confessed his worry over the fact that his half brother Rosy and Rosy's new wife, the former Elizabeth R. Riley, were aboard the German

coast have really been of *my* destroyers!" He closed: "Everybody here feels that this country as a whole sympathizes with the allies against Germany." [20]

One doubts that Daniels was quite as helplessly "bewildered by it all" as he seemed to Roosevelt to be. In retrospect it would appear that the Secretary was not abdicating his authority so much as passively delegating it, permitting it to be exercised by an assistant whose possession of superior knowledge in the technical, professional aspects of the Navy had been a factor in his initial selection. But it is certainly true that Daniels was profoundly dismayed and distressed by the turn of events— he had not really believed that such calamities were possible—and he had no conception of what the Navy's role should now be. He was no student of Mahan. He outraged his young assistant when on August 1 he told newspaper reporters that he was inclined to favor employing the fleet to rescue Americans stranded in Europe. "Aside from the fact that tourists (females etc.) couldn't sleep in hammocks and that battleships haven't got passenger accommodations," exploded Roosevelt in a letter to Eleanor, "he [Daniels] totally fails to grasp the fact that this war between the other powers is going inevitably to give rise to a hundred different complications in which we shall have a direct interest." [21]

Roosevelt's conviction that the moment's most urgent necessity was the gathering together of scattered naval forces to create a fleet in being —a conviction derived from Mahan's strategic doctrines and concurred in by the General Board—was promptly supported by a personal and unsolicited letter from Mahan himself. Mahan had never met Roosevelt. (He never would: he hoped to do so on a late November day, 1914, when he called at the Navy Department, but Roosevelt happened to be absent then [Mahan talked with Daniels] and, a week later, the great sea-power theorist, aged seventy-four, was dead.) So it is indicative of the general reputation Roosevelt had acquired among the admirals—it was also implicitly denigrating of Daniels—that Mahan should say to him on August 18, in a letter advising the immediate return of battleships stationed in Mexican waters: "I write to you because I know of no one else in the Administration to whom I should care to write." [22] Obviously, Roosevelt was not alone in his estimate of his own importance at this time.

---

ship *Kronprinzessin Cecilie,* in mid-Atlantic, bound for Plymouth. (Rosy had recently undergone a serious operation; his European trip was partly for convalescence, partly a delayed honeymoon.) The ship would have been a rich prize of war for the French or (upon England's entrance) British since she carried toward Germany some $13,000,000 in gold and silver. In the event, while yet a thousand miles from Plymouth, the ship was ordered by German officials in Bremen to return to America and did so in what the New York *World* described as a "desperate four-day run" during which, each night, "every light on board [was] covered." It docked at Bar Harbor, Maine, in a dense fog, on August 4.

Largely through his executive energy "most of the preliminary fundamentals of neutrality both as to radio communication and as to ships
and cargoes" had been "worked out" by August 10, as he said that day
in a letter to Eleanor. Policy had been determined and implemented for
the "relief of Americans in Europe," and a fleet in being as strong as a
prudent handling of the Mexican situation would permit was in process
of concentration. His own staff was bursting with pride in him. "The
Boss has been the whole Cheese in this European business and is going
along great," wrote Charles McCarthy to vacationing Louis Howe on
August 8. By mid-August, when Roosevelt, on the eve of his departure
for Campobello announced his ill-fated candidacy for the U.S. Senate,
the Navy's emergency tasks, insofar as they could be handled by a civilian department head, were virtually completed.[23]

Having come out in October for increased American armaments, TR
in November flatly reversed himself regarding Belgium. He now asserted that the United States should at once have strongly protested the
German violation of the Belgian treaty and begun to prepare itself with
the armed force necessary to make the protest "effective." Thereafter his
verbal attacks upon the President's policies and person were unremitting and increasingly savage. He became the most influential of the
three leading political spokesmen for "preparedness" in the great debate
on that subject which began in the fall of 1914, the other two being his
longtime friend, Republican Senator Henry Cabot Lodge of Massachusetts, ranking member of the Senate Naval Affairs Committee, and
Lodge's son-in-law, Republican Representative Augustus P. Gardner,
also of Massachusetts, who was chairman of the House Military Affairs
Committee.

The debate was in some respects a continuation of the 1912 confrontation between the New Freedom and the New Nationalism, with the
latter stripped of Progressive reform features. A National Security League, an Army League, and various other pro-Preparedness organizations were formed to wage, along with the already established Navy
League, a massive campaign to capture American public opinion. All
these organizations were based in the Northeast. At the outset, the Preparedness movement had as its principal dynamic the economic interests of industrialists and financiers joined to the professional interests of
high-ranking Army and Navy officers, and its chief journalistic voice
was the Eastern metropolitan press. It received no support from the agricultural interests of South, Midwest, and West. Wilson could therefore
recognize in it the face of an old enemy, as could Bryan, Daniels, and
every other dedicated New Freedom Progressive. A huge military estab-

lishment would hugely profit big business at the taxpayer's expense—it would enlarge and strengthen giant trusts beyond the possibility of their restraint by a government which ultimately might even be taken over by them—and it therefore posed a far graver threat to American democracy than Germany did in 1914 or was likely ever to do. Indeed, one had only to look at Germany to see the outlines of the America of tomorrow if, yielding to fears and passions, we now permitted ourselves to be hustled down the path of militarism.

Portentous of this Prussianized America might be TR's great and good friend the politically ambitious General Leonard Wood, former Chief of Staff, who was now chief Army agitator of the armaments issue. His activities intensely irritated his civilian Commander in Chief. ". . . I do think," wrote the President to the Secretary of War in late 1914, "that General Wood is pursuing a questionable course hardly consistent with the right spirit of the service. . . ." When Colonel House, fresh from conference with the general, urged upon the President the need to "make the country too powerful for any nation to think of attacking us"—this in early November, 1914—Wilson replied with some acerbity that "immediate action" of that kind was *not* needed because, "no matter how the great war ended, there would be complete exhaustion; and, even if Germany won, she would not be in a condition seriously to menace our country for many years to come." [24] He spoke at that moment specifically against Wood's proposal greatly to expand the Army, but what he said also applied to a lesser degree, to proposals for expanding the Navy.

With this line of reasoning, Franklin Roosevelt emphatically disagreed.

Neither privately nor publicly did he express any concern over the effects a vast expansion of armaments might have upon the American economy and political tradition or even any recognition of these as factors in the overall problem. What did urgently concern him—as disciple of Mahan, emulator of TR, and ambitious occupant of a high Navy post—was the wide discrepancy between America's overseas commitment and the naval power now at its disposal. The two *ought* to be in balance; instead, our commitment was great, our power small. Roosevelt may or may not have known that the Monroe Doctrine's proclamation in 1823 had been contingent upon assurances from the British that they would actively implement it with their fleet if necessary, but he certainly did know that America had never had enough naval strength to defend the whole Western Hemisphere against European imperialism, as the Doctrine required us to do. From the first, enforcement of the Doctrine had depended on the British Navy's dominance in the Atlantic. The German threat to this dominance therefore endangered the security of the United States, as Roosevelt acutely realized, and it could be guarded against only through a policy which helped Britain while simultaneously strengthening our own sea arm greatly.

The latter was rendered doubly important by the fact that in 1898 we had undertaken a vast commitment in the mid and far Pacific, where Japanese naval power now exceeded our own. Others might inveigh, as Daniels did, against the "unwisdom" of our embarking in the first place "upon a colonial and imperialistic policy" in the Pacific. Franklin Roosevelt himself had done so as a schoolboy, it may be recalled, when at Groton he was assigned to uphold the negative in a debate upon the question "Resolved, that Hawaii be promptly annexed." But as a man, with freedom to choose his position on public questions, he asserted a precisely opposite view. He asserted with Mahan that a great power's greatness depended on overseas empire and a large foreign trade, and he was not at all troubled as Daniels was by the human and material costs of a "greatness" so defined. "In time of war would we be content like the turtle to withdraw into our own shell and see an enemy supersede us in every outlying part, usurp our commerce and destroy our influence as a nation throughout the world?" he asked rhetorically in a magazine article of January, 1914. "Yet this will happen just as surely as we can be sure of anything human if an enemy of the United States obtains control of the seas. . . . Our national defense must extend all over the western hemisphere, must go out a thousand miles into the sea, must embrace the Philippines and over the seas wherever our commerce may be. To hold the Panama Canal, Alaska, American Samoa, Guam, Porto Rico, the naval base at Guantánamo and the Philippines, we must have battleships. We must create a navy not only to protect our shores and our possessions but our merchant ships in time of war, no matter where they go." [25]

All this seemed to him so self-evidently true that he had slight patience with those who held a different opinion. And this meager patience became more meager still after the great war broke out. In the present highly explosive situation, a skillful diplomacy *might* secure our vital interests, *might* obviate the necessity of our fighting, but it could do so only if our potential enemies knew we were prepared to fight if we had to. The Navy had to be made strong enough to stave off a powerful and determined foe for the eighteen months or so that would be required for our raising, training, and arming the immense land forces which, as the European struggle showed, modern war demanded.

So it was that, simultaneously with TR's public shift of policy in the fall of 1914 and in continuation of the "big navy" policy he had publicly espoused from his first days in office, the Assistant Secretary of the Navy began to make himself known as a champion of Preparedness within a generally anti-Preparedness administration. His fervency had as its concomitant a tendency to regard Preparedness opponents as so many brute obstacles to be circumvented or overcome, insofar as they could not be moved by persuasion. And so he marched his banner to the very frontier of official insubordination, skirting it continuously and sometimes actually crossing it.

V

It was predictable that Senator Lodge and Congressman Gardner would be severely critical of the Secretary of the Navy. And so they were. They had nothing to do with him socially; they were inclined, as a matter of fact, to look down upon him as a rustic social inferior; and though Daniels felt that the Senator, being knowledgeable about the Navy and sincerely devoted to its welfare, tried always to be just in criticism, he had no such feeling about the Congressman. With rare rancor he spoke of Gardner in his memoirs, three decades later, as "the most vicious assailant of the Naval establishment in Congress . . . a blatant and bitter critic." [26] Yet both Gardner and Lodge, with their wives, remained among the cordial social friends of the Roosevelts, and the Assistant Secretary was also on the most amiable and cooperative terms with them in his official capacity.

In mid-October, 1914, Gardner made an alarmist speech on the House floor charging that the nation's defenses were appallingly deficient and calling for establishment of a National Security Commission to investigate the matter. Amid the furor this speech aroused, and on a day (October 23) when Daniels was absent from Washington, Roosevelt as Acting Secretary handed to the press a lengthy memorandum, prepared in cooperation with Admiral Fiske and other Navy militants, which substantially contradicted Daniels' position that all was well with the Navy and provided Gardner with ammunition to use in his attacks on the administration's defense policy. (Among other things, the memorandum asserted that thirteen of the Navy's second-line battleships were out of commission because manning them would require 18,000 more enlisted men than were permitted by Congress.) Sending a copy of the memo in a letter to Eleanor, Roosevelt wrote: "The enclosed is the truth and even if it gets me into trouble I am perfectly ready to stand by it. The country needs the truth about the Army and Navy instead of a lot of soft mush about everlasting peace which so many statesmen are handing out to a gullible public." [27] He *did* encounter a certain amount of trouble when, among the papers which reported his memorandum under large headlines, a Republican organ pointedly contrasted his contentions with those Daniels had published. It would appear the Secretary had once again to remind his subordinate of the limits of an Assistant Secretary's authority. At any rate, Roosevelt three weeks later issued a second memorandum in which, without retracting his earlier statement, he asserted that he had not and did not *recommend* the enlargement of the Navy by 18,000 men. He would not, he said, "consider it within my province to make any recommendation on the matter one way or the other." [28]

But he was by no means cowed or deterred from further emphatic public statements of positions markedly at variance with those of the administration. He came out strongly for universal military training. In early December, he and pacifist David Starr Jordan both addressed an annual meeting of the National Civic Foundation in New York's Hotel Astor. Jordan, who spoke first, called for disarmament and branded its opponents warmongers. Roosevelt retorted that compulsory military training was "just plain common sense" in a quarrelsome world and went on to assert, in language reminiscent of TR: "An able-bodied boy is better from every standpoint than a wretched runt, including the standpoint of the man at war." He denied that, in advocating military training and an expanded Navy, he was advocating war. "Many of us who want to keep the peace believe that $250,000,000 a year for the Navy, which amounts to only one-half of one percent of our national wealth, is merely good insurance," he said.[29]

Three days later, the President of the United States, in his annual message to a Congress whose overwhelming majority cheered him for his stand, came out flatly *against* compulsory military training. He also opposed by implication any such large and rapid naval building program as Roosevelt (with the Navy League and the admirals) favored, indicating that while a "powerful navy" was desirable as our first line of defense, its development should await expert studies in the light of the experience of modern war. "We never have had, and while we retain our present principles and ideals we never shall have, a large standing army," Wilson said. The "National Guard of the States should be developed and strengthened," he continued. ". . . More than this, proposed at this time . . . , would mean merely that we had lost our self-possession, that we had been thrown off our balance by a war with which we have nothing to do, whose causes cannot touch us. . . . But I turn away from the subject. It is not new. . . . We shall not alter our attitude toward it because some amongst us are nervous and excited." This last was an obvious thrust at Representative Gardner, who, it was observed by a New York *Times* reporter, sat "silent and solemn-faced" while Democrats in the chamber burst into loud laughter.[30]

The next day Daniels testified before the House Naval Affairs Committee, accompanied by two admirals who had been selected for the purpose because almost alone among their colleagues they were in sympathy with the administration. The gist of their testimony was that the Navy was in a high state of efficiency and "ship for ship" was "as good as the navy of any other nation." Daniels indicated that ships then in reserve could be readied for action within a few days and that the addition of fewer than 5,000 trained men would enable the Navy fully to man these vessels and the others which were now only partially manned. Roosevelt appeared before the same committee on December 16. He came prepared with a thoroughly digested mass of technical information on the basis of which he substantially contradicted key points of his superior's testimony while carefully refraining from "recommendations" that obviously conflicted with Daniels' statements of policy. He cited Naval War College estimates that between 30,000 and 50,000 additional men would be needed to man fully the Navy's vessels. He quoted the professional opinion of Navy captains that no less than three months was required to transform a reserve vessel into an efficient fighting ship. He said that the Navy had indeed gained in efficiency during the present administration, as Daniels had testified, but referred to technical studies showing that other navies had enlarged and improved at a faster rate so that, relatively, we were less strong than before: the U.S. Navy now ranked no higher than third (behind Britain and Germany) and might well rank fourth among the navies of the world. He was impressive. Committee members complimented him and newspaper editorials praised him for (as the New York *Herald* put it) "his promptness in answering questions" and "his candor." "He showed that in the short time he has been Assistant Secretary . . . he has made a most complete study of the problems of naval defense." [31]

He also showed, a few months later, that he agreed with the militant admirals' view that they and not Congress, no matter what the Constitution said, should be the final arbiters of naval defense policy. In March, 1915, he conceived the idea (though Fiske later claimed credit for it) of casting that year's spring naval maneuvers in the form of a war game in which an invading "red" fleet met a defending "blue" fleet off Narragansett Bay. Such an exercise would serve a dual purpose—the usual one of training fleet personnel and the additional one of "educating" the American public to the need for a U.S. Navy strong enough to meet and defeat a major enemy on the high seas. "The maneuvers should make a definite impression on the minds of the men in the streets," urged Roosevelt upon Daniels. Daniels assented. And in mid-May the assembled Atlantic Fleet, on the eve of the war games, was given a gala reception by New York City as it anchored in the Hudson. Daniels and Roosevelt both addressed a Navy League banquet in New York on that occasion. The Secretary's speech was full of praise for the "forward-looking Sixty-third Congress." The Assistant Secretary's speech was as full of implicit censure of that same Congress for its failure to provide an adequate naval defense. "Most of our citizens don't know what national defense means," he said. ". . . Let us learn to trust the judgment of the real experts, the naval officers. Let us insist that Congress shall carry out their recommendations." [32] (The "red" fleet of course "won" the war games that followed.)

The discrepancy between the Secretary's and the Assistant Secretary's judgments on the current Congress did not go unnoticed in the Eastern press. At least one important daily editorialized upon it in a way unflattering to the Secretary, calling him "self-satisfied." Roosevelt confessed to Eleanor some anxiety over the effect this might have upon his relations with Daniels and was relieved when the Secretary chose to ignore the incident. Returned to Washington, Roosevelt wrote to Eleanor, who was in Hyde Park with Sara and "the chicks," saying gratefully: "The Sec'y is back . . . and he seems cheerful and still glad to see me!" A day or so later (on May 20) he wrote of "dinner at the Daniels', who were cordial (!) but no reference was made to the New York episodes." [33]

In late summer of that year, when for several weeks during Daniels' vacation he was Acting Secretary, he announced "plans of the Navy Department" to create a National Naval Reserve of 50,000 men, the bulk of this number to consist of civilian volunteers. He did so with trepidation. "I . . . trust J.D. will like it!" he wrote to Eleanor on September 2, 1915. "It is of the utmost importance and I have failed for a year to get him to take any action, though he has never objected to it. Now I have . . . pulled the trigger myself. I suppose the bullet may bounce back on me. . . ." [34] It didn't, however. The Reserve became a reality in the summer of 1916. One result was the building to department specifications of a number of privately owned small boats (forty feet long, twenty-one knots top speed) for use in the patrol of harbors and coastal waters. Another was a four-week training cruise for volunteers (they turned out to be well-heeled young men for the most part, yachtsmen and speedboat enthusiasts, despite Daniels' objections to this and his efforts to obtain enrollment only of men possessing special skills that would be of use to the Navy in war)—a cruise making use of nine reserve battleships.

Instead of raising any personal objection to the repeated use by the Massachusetts Congressman of his committee testimony, with his name prominently attached, Roosevelt actively aided and abetted Gardner's efforts along this line. For instance, Daniels was inclined to encourage the popular view that the relative strength of the U.S. Navy among the navies of the world had been substantially increased by the naval losses which the belligerent powers had sustained since the war began. Gardner was anxious to disprove this view. Accordingly, in April, he addressed a letter to Daniels requesting U.S. naval intelligence statistics on British and German ship losses. Roosevelt as Acting Secretary answered it. He did not content himself with supplying the requested information. He wrote a cover letter in which he stated his "forced" conclusion that the losses sustained had been more than offset by the rapid construction of warships by all the belligerent powers, with the result "that our navy probably stands fourth in the list at the present time." Moreover, he seems to have given Gardner permission to quote him "in citing the facts," withdrawing it only when Daniels flatly ordered him to do so. He then suggested in private conversation that Gardner have Lodge request the information from Daniels, since the Secretary might feel obliged to give it to the ranking member of the Senate Naval Affairs Committee. Lodge made the request. Daniels promptly supplied the intelligence figures on losses but, in implicit rebuke of Roosevelt, stated unequivocally that the department had *no* solid information regarding British and German naval construction.[35]

VI

Aware of Roosevelt's tactics in this case, Daniels must by then have suspected, if not discovered, other instances of what most administrators would deem an intolerable insubordination. It is remarkable that he did not object far more strenuously than he seems to have done to Roosevelt's airing of his disagreements in ways that encouraged published reports of "friction" within the department. It is more remarkable still that he did not openly resent such things as Roosevelt's "killing" imitations of him, of his rustic manners and speech, before urbane fellow members of the aristocratic Metropolitan Club. (But perhaps he never learned of these: Roosevelt was soon shamed into discontinuing his mimicry by his good and older friend, Secretary Lane, who deemed such behavior dishonorable.[36])

Others knew, and Daniels must at least have guessed, that Roosevelt —wholly on the side of the militant admirals in virtually all their policy disputes with the Secretary—did nothing to reduce and on occasion a good deal to increase the personal displeasure, contempt, and even harsh enmity which several of these admirals felt toward their civilian chief. Nor did the Assistant Secretary discourage the expression of similar attitudes by other ardent activists who came to him complaining of the Secretary's dilatoriness, his "Southern" reluctance to expend energy, his habit of postponing decisions on matters they felt required prompt expedition. He himself shared this impatience. "I have any amount of work to do and J.D. is too damned slow for words," ran one of his outbursts to "Dearest Babs" (November, 1916), "—his failure to decide the few big things holds me up all down the line." [37] And sometimes when complaining activists were in his office he would remark in offhand fashion, but with a wink or significant grin, that Daniels was to be out of town on such-and-such a day; he, Roosevelt, would on that day be Acting Secretary, with all the privileges and powers appertaining thereto.

Often Roosevelt showed directly to his chief his exasperation with the latter's chronic "slowness." "Dear Mr. Daniels," began one of his hastily scrawled notes, "*Do please* get through two vital things *today.*" On another occasion, Daniels was handed a Roosevelt memorandum, addressed to a third party, which opened: "The *actual present* danger of this situation should be explained to the Secretary and he must understand that *immediate* legislation is necessary—" [38] And Daniels seems not to have resented overtly these implicit and explicit strictures upon him. Possibly he recognized a certain justice in Roosevelt's impatience with him, his strictures upon him. He, Daniels, *was* slow, cautious, deliberate, disinclined to take any long step until he was absolutely sure of the ground. He lacked dash. He was no gambler. He had little empathic understanding of the professional attitudes and aspirations of naval career officers.

But the Secretary did not lack courage or strength or a capacity for anger, nor was he ineffective in a fight when the need for fighting arose. And it *did* arise. Far from protecting him against embroilment in public quarrel, his pacifism and moralism tended in his special circumstances to involve him in conflict. He came under constant vicious attack from "profiteers waving the flag" (his phrase) because of his exposure and stern resistance of big business's penchant for corrupt bargaining with the Navy Department. He earned the bitterest enmity of powerful oil interests through his stubborn and successful resistance to their efforts to obtain drilling rights on naval oil reserves in California, efforts that were supported by Secretary of the Interior Lane.* His concern for the moral

---

* Lane would resign his government post in 1920 to become vice-president of the Pan-Amer-

well-being and "democratic rights" of enlisted men, opening to them
Annapolis doors that had theretofore been closed, outraged the Navy's
officer corps. He provoked anger among the liquor interests when he imposed prohibition on all Navy ships and shore installations. He was, all
in all, from first to last, the most controversial member of Wilson's Cabinet—more so even than pacifist Bryan or militarist Garrison during
their periods of service—and embroiled, he pressed his causes with a
righteous zeal that was sometimes indistinguishable from an actual zest
for battle.

A famous instance of this was his feud with the Navy League. From
the first, he was suspicious of Navy League purposes and had as little to
do with it as a Navy Secretary could. He could not be surprised, therefore, when the league, while professing a wholly disinterested patriotism
in its campaign for a big navy, "showed . . . its true colors" (again Daniels' phrase) in August, 1917, when it publicly charged that the department was permitting labor leaders to block investigation of an accidental explosion in the Navy yard at Mare Island. Daniels promptly issued
a public letter to Colonel Robert M. Thompson, the league president,
asserting that, in view of the "treasonable action by the League toward
the government and a gross slander of patriotic workers in the Navy
Yard," Thompson and his fellow officers should resign "from what . . .
[has] become an unpatriotic organization." He issued orders banning
league officials and representatives from all Navy ships and reservations. He requested "patriotic women not to send gifts [to enlisted men]
through the Navy League" but to do so instead through a special
women's organization, whose formation for that purpose he encouraged. And he refused to rescind these actions even after the Mare Island
investigation report, proving the original league charges unfounded, had
elicited from league officials a "grudging apology." Thereafter, not unnaturally, it was "war to the knife," as Daniels said, between the Navy
Secretary and the Navy League, with the latter's leaders missing no opportunity to cast aspersions publicly on Daniels' character and capacities.[39] Sometimes they made or inspired public statements in which invidious comparisons were made between Daniels' alleged bumbling
incompetence and Franklin Roosevelt's swift, shining efficiency. Always
they did what they could to advance the popular impression that young
Roosevelt was in fact, as in his privately asserted belief, *running* the
real work" while Daniels dawdled or dissipated his energies on matters
peripheral, if not wholly irrelevant, to the Navy's major concerns.

---

ican Petroleum Company, headed by Edward L. Doheny. Lane's reputed starting salary was
$50,000 per annum.

Through all this, Roosevelt remained on warm friendly terms with Colonel Thompson. He continued to cooperate with the league after he learned of Daniels' distaste for it, accepting, for instance, an invitation to address its annual meeting in the spring of 1916, a meeting Daniels boycotted. Nor did he do anything effectively to discourage the league's use of his league-bolstered prestige as a club with which to strike at Daniels—at least, he did not until it became clear to him that Daniels' forced retirement, which the league strove to accomplish, would almost certainly mean his own as well. He bore a famous name, he had famous friends, his membership among the social elite was unquestioned; but his position in the administration was at all times far more precarious than Daniels' ever was. The Secretary, as a matter of fact, was practically invulnerable: he enjoyed close personal ties with the President, a firm support from Congress, and (despite or because of the enemies he made) great national popularity. Roosevelt's support, on the other hand, was not of a kind that could shield him from dismissal, nor could it provide him with effective means of reprisal save at the expense of his own career, since so large a proportion of it came from enemies of the administration. In his own party, in his own state, many an influential friend of the administration was cool to him, and some were actively hostile. What all this boiled down to was the fact that his maintenance in office depended almost entirely on the very man whom so many of his Preparedness friends wished to destroy and to whom his own loyalty was imperfect. And Roosevelt seems to have been jarred into a realization of this during the weeks immediately following the 1916 Presidential election. He then privately and convincingly protested efforts to promote him into Daniels' post (the Navy League's wishful thinking apparently led to the absurd conclusion that Wilson, at this juncture, was about to replace Daniels), writing to one overly zealous supporter: "Personally I have no use for a man who, serving in a subordinate position is continually contriving ways to step into his boss's shoes and I detest nothing so much as that kind of disloyalty. I have worked very gladly under Mr. Daniels and I wish the public could realize how much he has done for the Navy. I would feel very badly indeed if friends of mine should unwittingly give the impression that I was for a minute thinking of taking his place at the head of the Navy." [40]

In general, it would appear that Roosevelt's personal feeling about his chief was a curiously mingled one.

Long years before, it may be recalled, the boy Franklin, introduced to some of the ideas of Christian Socialism by Mlle. Sandoz, had reacted to them with an assumed "toughness." * In assigned written compositions,

* See pages 75–76.

he had then poked fun at the earnestness, the moral fervor, with which his diminutive teacher had preached the Social Gospel to him. Thus early did he manifest a determination to be a "realist" in his approach to public questions—one who did not blink at "hard facts," one who eschewed "soft sentimentality," one who was sophisticatedly aware of the real world as much more complicated and various and difficult to change than it seemed to such good kind simple honest folk as Mlle. Sandoz. Yet he was very fond of her. He respected her spirited firmness. He admired her Christian concern for the general welfare. He may even have envied her, to a degree and in a certain way, for the very qualities of simplicity and directness which he viewed with contempt.

And all these discerned and surmised elements of his feeling for Jeanne Sandoz were evidently present in his feeling for Josephus Daniels, as they would be, decades later, in his feelings about Wendell Willkie. His frequent irritable impatience with Daniels' deliberate ways; his sometimes amused, sometimes angry contempt for what he regarded as Daniels' rustic simplemindedness and naïveté; his absolute conviction that Daniels' approach to the problems of national defense and foreign policy was wrong; his evident willingness on occasion to risk hurting his chief deeply, in order to further his own ideas—all these were underlain by great affection for Daniels personally, by great respect and admiration for the strength and sweetness of Daniels' character, and by a growing recognition of Daniels' political shrewdness whereby the Secretary could assess, more accurately than Roosevelt at that time, the popular temper and the limits it imposed upon the possibilities of government action.

As for Daniels, it is inconceivable that he could have borne with Roosevelt as he did had he not sincerely loved him or that he could have so loved him had not Roosevelt been both lovable and loving in return. Daniels was certainly not unique in his response to the younger man's personal force, charm, and physical attractiveness or in his belief in Roosevelt's basic moral goodness and generosity of purpose. Many others shared both the response and the belief. Among them was an aristocratic young Englishman, a Cambridge graduate, who came to the United States (on the *Lusitania*) in November, 1914, to join the war-expanded staff of the British embassy in Washington. His name was Nigel Law. He became a close social friend of the Roosevelts. And his regard for the Assistant Secretary, who was eight years his senior, grew almost worshipful. "I found him the most attractive man whom it was my good fortune to meet during my four years in America," he wrote long afterward to Josephus Daniels' son Jonathan. "One was first struck by his gaiety and kindliness. He always seemed to be considering the feelings of others and doing all he could to make those in his company happy and cheerful. He was intensely interested in other people. . . . He was intensely patriotic, but . . . during the period of American 'neutrality' he never disguised his strong pro-Ally sympathies. . . . He was a fine physical specimen . . . , delighting in all sorts of outdoor activity. But he was not just a gay athlete, for he had a deep understanding of politics and a sound knowledge of history and foreign affairs, strong convictions and ideals and a strong desire to serve his country. . . ." Young Nigel Law accorded his hero "the highest praise an Englishman can give a man, that he was a perfect example of the English Country Gentleman. . . ." [41]

There was a mutuality, a kind of equivalence of give-and-take, in the relations between Roosevelt and Daniels. The instances of it were numerous. "My most prized Christmas present was a painting of the U.S.S. *North Carolina* which Franklin Roosevelt had ordered for me," wrote Daniels in his diary on December 25, 1913. "It is the work of a famous artist. Franklin had the record showing that it was the first American line-of-battle ship to cross the Atlantic. She made that voyage in 1825. . . . She was the largest and most formidable vessel that had made the Atlantic crossing up to that time." [42] A gift so individual, requiring so generous an expenditure of thought and effort, as well as money, bespoke far more than a routine desire to please or to fulfill an obligation. A bantering camaraderie characterized some of their scrawled notes to one another, as in an exchange (much quoted in later years) wherein "SCNAV" was informed by "ASTNAV" that the latter had "just signed a requisition (with four copies attached) calling for the purchase of eight carpet tacks," eliciting from Daniels a rebuke of "this wanton extravagance." ("I am sure two would suffice." [43]) On July 1, 1915, at a time when policy disagreements between the two men were at their widest and the department's work load at its heaviest, Roosevelt was suddenly struck down by appendicitis. Rushed to the Washington Naval Hospital, he underwent emergency surgery. (His mother, coming down from Hyde Park, was at his bedside within hours; Eleanor could not arrive from Campobello until some days later.) Daniels promptly rearranged his own summer vacation plans and redistributed, so far as he could, the Assistant Secretary's work load so that Roosevelt, upon his release from the hospital, could go in mid-July to Campobello and there convalesce for several weeks. He then ordered the Secretary's yacht, the *Dolphin,* to take Roosevelt north. And on his beloved island, Roosevelt received letters from his chief in which Daniels spoke of his "love and happiness that you are coming on so finely." [44] Such kindness evoked sincere gratitude.

Fourteen

->>><<<-

Of Politics and War: Part Two

I

BUT Roosevelt's personal qualities and their interaction with those of Daniels, his adroit footwork in ticklish situations, his family name and influential friends, the address which enabled him to communicate with anyone, including the President of the United States, on terms of personal equality—all these would not have sufficed to save him from eventual dismissal had not history moved in the direction pointed by his pro-Preparedness, pro-Allied views. Step by reluctant step the administration was forced to accept policies which he, with others, had long since advocated and which the administration initially opposed.

They were policies logically implied by a negative decision taken by Wilson himself, despite Bryan's contrary urgings, in the opening weeks of war. He decided then not to attempt to implement his neutrality proclamation with effective restrictions upon the sale of American goods or the extension of American credits to the belligerents. The effect was an increasingly heavy economic investment in the Allied cause by the most powerful manufacturing and banking interests in the United States. For though both sides in the conflict had in theory an equal right to buy and borrow from American firms, in actual practice only the Allies could do so to any important degree. The Central Powers could not obtain delivery of American goods: Britain employed its still-great superiority in surface sea power to impose a naval blockade upon its enemies, violating as it did so rules governing neutral shipping that had been long established in international law.* Wilson protested the violations. He was, however, persuaded by Colonel House and by his own

---

* U.S. trade with Germany and Austria-Hungary declined from approximately $170,000,000 in 1914 to less than 1 percent of that in 1916. Simultaneously trade with the Allied nations increased from $825,000,000 to nearly four times that.

sympathies to moderate the language of his protests in such a way as to avoid a truly serious crisis in the relations between Washington and London. By early 1915, in the face of Britain's adamant determination to impose it, he had virtually acquiesced in the new maritime system. Germany's response was an attempted counterblockade, making use of a weapon that had not even been developed when the major tenets of international sea law had been established and whose unprecedented use violated what Wilson called the "laws of humanity." This weapon was the submarine. Since a submarine could not rise to the surface and apprise its prospective victim of coming attack without risk of being itself destroyed by armed merchant ships, since even passenger liners were being used by the Allies to transport contraband, and since British merchantmen not infrequently sailed under false colors, including the flag of the United States,* Germany felt compelled to adopt the tactic of unrestricted submarine warfare, torpedoing ships without warning at whatever cost in neutral and civilian lives. On February 4, 1915, the imperial German government made the following announcement: "The waters around Great Britain, including the whole of the English Channel, are declared hereby to be included within the zone of war, and after the 18th inst. all enemy merchant vessels encountered in these waters will be destroyed, even if it may not be possible always to save their crews and passengers." [1]

The tactic was perfectly consistent with the German belief in the efficacy of "frightfulness" in war, and it had the psychological effect that "frightfulness" always has, even upon temperamentally pacific people. It fomented a flaming anger, and in this case the effect on American popular opinion was unmitigated by any general recognition of Germany's side of the story. A single telegraphic cable had directly joined the United States to Germany at the outbreak of the war. The British immediately severed it, reducing virtually all the telegraphic news that reached America from Europe to Allied censorship. Often enough it was "news" strongly colored or even actually manufactured by professional Allied propagandists who capitalized to the full upon the advantages inherent in a common language, a shared democratic tradition, the proximity of Canada, natural sympathies with violated Belgium, traditional sympathies with a France that had aided us in past quarrels with England, and revulsion against the national egotism and aggressiveness which the German Kaiser personified.

*   *   *

* This was authorized by a British Admiralty order on January 31, 1915. When the United States protested use of the American flag as a *ruse de guerre,* Sir Edward Grey replied (February 20, 1915) that flying neutral flags to escape enemy attack was a time-honored practice among the merchantmen of warring nations. It had been done by Union ships to escape Confederate attack in our own Civil War, Grey said.

The frequency of private social contacts between the Roosevelts and the Spring-Rices (British ambassador), the Jusserands (French ambassador), and the Laboulayes (second secretary of the French embassy) was not affected by the European war. Indeed, so far as the war had any effect at all upon the friendship between the Assistant Secretary of the Navy and the British ambassador, the effect was one of increase—an enlargement of shared sympathies. The two families often dined together at the embassy. The two men often lunched together at the Metropolitan.

They did so at the time America's neutrality policy was suffering the first shocks of Germany's declared submarine warfare. The occasion was rendered memorably dramatic by the presence at the next table of the German ambassador, Count Johann von Bernstorff, who seemed to an outraged Roosevelt to be "trying to hear what we were talking about!" The young man sensed the hostility pulsing as an electric current between the two diplomats. (For many weeks, Bernstorff had been trying to stimulate and promote an American public opinion in favor of an embargo on arms shipments.) "Springy and von B. would kill each other if they had a chance!" he wrote to Eleanor, who was in New York City. He added: "I just know I shall do some awful unneutral thing before I get through!" [2]

But the dangers attending such "unneutrality" were certainly reduced by America's reaction to the German war zone proclamation. Roosevelt was gratified by the outburst of indignation with which the American press denounced the proclamation and by the firm tone in which the administration warned the German government that it would be held to "strict accountability" for any loss of American life. Obviously public opinion and administration policy were being nudged closer to Roosevelt's position. His gratification was increased when, during the following weeks, it became apparent that, for the time being, the submarine threat was mostly bluff (Germany did not yet have enough submarines to do great damage), and a disastrous bluff since it enabled Britain to impose, without serious political reaction in America and without provoking effective American challenge at sea, the last and most stringent element of its new maritime system, a close offshore blockade of Germany that was patently illegal.

There had been no sinkings of importance to U.S.-German relations when, in mid-March, Roosevelt and Eleanor, together with their friends the William Phillipses, accompanied the Vice President of the United States, Thomas R. Marshall, with Mrs. Marshall, on an official visit to the Panama Pacific Exposition in San Francisco. It was a gala occasion and, for the Roosevelts, a highly sociable one, made especially so by the fact that Secretary and Mrs. Lane and Mr. and Mrs. Adolph Miller came out to California at the same time. When the fleet was reviewed at San Francisco, the flagship ran up a flag especially designed by Roosevelt for the Vice President (there had never been a Vice President's flag before), along with the Assistant Secretary's flag, of course, and salutes were fired both for the Vice President and for the Assistant Secretary. As his West Coast visit drew to a close, Roosevelt was handed a dispatch saying that the American submarine F-4 had failed to surface after a dive off Pearl Harbor, killing all aboard. A shocked American public was told by Roosevelt that, "sad" though the accident was, it was something "that must be expected in any great navy." He was in Los Angeles at the time. He promptly boarded a submarine in Los Angeles Harbor, went down in it beneath a wave-heaped sea, and emerged safely to say to reporters in ebullient TR fashion that the experience was "fine" and that "for the first time" since leaving Washington he had felt "perfectly at home." Immediately afterward he boarded a destroyer and sailed for San Diego through seas so heavy that the ship, when in the troughs of huge waves, was hidden "time and again," as a Los Angeles reporter put it, from the sight of those watching on shore.[3]

And on that very same day (March 28) occurred the first incident of the submarine war that directly affected U.S.-German relations. A German U-boat torpedoed a small British liner, the *Falaba*, in the Irish Sea, killing several crew members and passengers. Among the latter was a U.S. citizen, a mining engineer bound for his post in West Africa. His name, Leon C. Thrasher, was in the headlines, and his case the subject of earnest discussion in the highest administration circles when Roosevelt arrived back in Washington. American press reaction was violent: editorials in every section of the country cried out against German "barbarism," "bloodthirstiness," and "vicious cruelty." No official action whatever was taken, however, as the weeks passed. There was not even a protest note—to Roosevelt's displeasure.

Then, on May 1, an American tanker, *Gulflight*, out of a Texas port, was torpedoed without warning in the Irish Sea. Three American lives were lost. On that same day there appeared in the American press a notice from the German imperial embassy addressed to "travellers intending to embark on the Atlantic voyage" reminding them of the formal proclamation of a war zone around the British Isles and of the liability of "vessels flying the flag of Great Britain . . . to destruction in those waters." Also on that day the great British passenger ship *Lusitania*, pride of the Cunard Line, sailed from New York City, bound for Liverpool. Most, if not all, of the Americans booked for passage on her received telegrams that morning, signed with obviously spurious names, urging them to cancel their trips. A single passenger did so. The standard reaction was one of anger at the "insolence" of the Germans in suggesting that an American citizen was not free to go where and when he pleased, in safety, upon the high seas—this coupled with a conviction that the Germans were bluffing. There were 1,257 passengers aboard, or nearly 2,000 human beings altogether, when the huge, 30,396-ton ship steamed past the Statue of Liberty.

Franklin Roosevelt and his Cousin Theodore found themselves in essential agreement about these events when they met face to face a few days later at a nationally publicized trial in Syracuse, New York, where TR was defending himself against a charge of libel brought by New York Republican Boss William Barnes, Jr. In July, 1914, TR had published a statement that Barnes and Democratic Boss Murphy could "always be found on the same side openly or covertly, giving one another such support as can be safely rendered" whenever "the issue between popular rights and corrupt and machine ruled government is clearly drawn." The statement, with its repercussions, was among the factors that decided Franklin Roosevelt to enter that year's Senatorial primary race—and among the repercussions had been Boss Barnes' prompt filing of this libel suit. Roosevelt, coming to Syracuse in defense of his Cousin Theodore, testified on May 4 that there had been collusion between Barnes and Murphy during the Sheehan fight, garnering much newspaper publicity as he did so and making, as TR wrote his wife next day, "the best witness we had yet, bar Davenport." (TR won acquittal on May 22. When Franklin sent congratulations on the verdict, TR wrote back gratefully: ". . . you were a part of it. I shall never forget the capital way in which you gave your testimony and the impression upon the jury." [4])

Three days later, on May 7, a German U-boat in the Irish Sea fired a torpedo into the starboard bow of the *Lusitania*. There were two explosions, whose violence surprised and puzzled the U-boat commander. The huge ship sank in just eighteen minutes with the loss of nearly 1,200 lives, 124 of them American—and from her downward plunge spread a shock wave of horror through all the Allied and neutral world. In America, pacifist and militant alike were outraged by what both regarded as "wanton murder on the high seas."

Colonel House was in London when the sinking occurred. He had come to Europe for the second time as Wilson's personal peace emissary,* and for the second time his belief that a negotiated settlement of

---

* House had himself crossed on the *Lusitania* as he began his mission, being aboard at the time of Germany's war zone proclamation (February 4). On the following day, as the ship sailed into the Irish Sea on her run to Liverpool, her captain broke out the American flag as an antisubmarine precaution.

the European quarrel might be possible was shattered by Teutonic aggression. "We shall be at war with Germany within a month," he confidently predicted to fellow dinner guests of Ambassador Walter Hines Page in the American embassy in London. By cable next day he advised the President to demand assurances from the Germans that there would be no further crime of this kind, a demand accompanied by an at least implied threat of war. "America has come to the parting of the ways, when she must determine whether she stands for civilized or uncivilized warfare," he asserted. "We can no longer remain neutral spectators." Ambassador Page more than agreed. In a dispatch purporting to interpret, for Washington, British public opinion he said: "The United States must declare war or forfeit European respect. So far as I know, this opinion is universal." [5]

TR was in the Syracuse courtroom when the first news of the tragedy was brought to him. He made no immediate comment. But that night, when a New York City editor phoned him, he denounced the sinking as "piracy on a vaster scale of murder than old-time pirates ever practiced. . . . It seems inconceivable that we can refrain from taking action in this matter, for we owe it not only to humanity but to our own national self-respect." [6]

Newspaper editorials all across the land expressed a shocked disbelief that any supposedly civilized nation could commit such an atrocity. Many called for immediate drastic action by this government to compel Germany's cessation of submarine barbarism. They demanded reparations, abject apologies, abject promises of future good behavior. But they were for the most part vague or silent about the action which the government should take. A stern protest was obviously indicated. But *how* stern? How threatful, if threatful at all? Of the many hundreds of editorials there were very few (though it is significant of a shift of national mood that there were any) that flatly indicated a willingness to go to war.

II

Thus Woodrow Wilson faced the first crucial test of his neutrality policy. Dazed by the first news of the tragedy, he slipped out of the White House without warning his Secret Service guards and walked for several blocks, seemingly unaware of the rain that fell or the startled stares of passersby, before returning to his study.[7] There his secretary saw "tears . . . in his eyes" as further details of the sinking came in. But he refused to act precipitously. Soon he refused even to read eyewitness accounts of *Lusitania*'s death. "If I pondered over those tragic items . . . I should see red in everything," he said to Tumulty, "and I am afraid that when I am called upon to act . . . I could not be just to anyone. I dare not act unjustly and cannot indulge my own passionate feelings." For three days he isolated himself from other top administration officials while he mastered his emotions, measured various possibilities against basic principles, and sought to determine the actual mood of the country. His sole public comment during this period was made through his secretary on the evening of May 8. "Of course the President feels the distress and gravity of the situation to the utmost, and is considering very earnestly, but very calmly, the right course of action to pursue," said Tumulty. "He knows that the people of the country wish and expect him to act with deliberation as well as firmness." [8]

On the evening of Monday, May 10, he had for weeks been scheduled to deliver an address in Philadelphia's Convention Hall before an audience that included 4,000 newly naturalized citizens. He made the address, knowing that the *Lusitania* crisis weighted his every word with a special significance. What he said was revelatory of his effort to fuse reason and emotion on the highest plane of idealism. "The example of America must be a special example, and must be an example not merely of peace because it will not fight, but peace because peace is a healing and elevating influence in the world and strife is not," he said. *"There is such a thing as a man being too proud to fight. There is such a thing as a nation being so right that it does not need to convince others by force that it is right."* * The last two sentences, in the special circumstances, provoked instant, widespread, and loudly expressed disapproval. TR in public statement poured angry scorn upon such cowardly, womanish sentiments; in private he said that, much as he disliked Boss Barnes, "I infinitely prefer him to Wilson and Bryan," who were "cordially supported" by "every soft creature, every . . . weakling . . . and every man who has not got in him . . . the sterner virtues. . . ." Others, many of them actively involved in a now well-organized peace effort (for instance, Jane Addams had launched a Women's Peace Party in January of that year), found the President's words inspiring and viewed the President himself as a new Lincoln, a "man of prayer, discretion, courage," Christlike in his moral leadership. Wilson himself at once regretted his words as "foolish" in the immediate context of event. To his press conference on the morning of May 11 he insisted that the controverted sentences had no reference to "any specific thing" and that he had certainly had no intention of giving "any intimation of policy on any special matter." He had been "expressing a personal attitude, that was all." [9]

* Italicized by history.

A few minutes later he read to his assembled Cabinet the protest note to Germany that he had composed without consulting anyone. It was firm but by no means belligerent in its reiteration of the "strict account-ability" phrase and in its confident expectation that the German govern-ment would "disavow the acts of which . . . the United States com-plains, . . . make reparation as far as possible for injuries which are without measure, and . . . take immediate steps to prevent the recur-rence of anything so obviously subversive of the principles of war-fare. . . ." The nearest it came to threatfulness was in its concluding statement: "The Imperial German Government will not expect the Gov-ernment of the United States to omit any necessary representation or any necessary act in sustaining the rights of its citizens or in safe-guarding the sacred duties of international obligation." The Cabinet unanimously approved this, with slight changes. It went to Berlin on May 13. It was published in the American press on the following day and was overwhelmingly approved by the American public. "It repro-duces with remarkable skill the mean of American opinion," editorial-ized Mr. Croly's *New Republic*. ". . . American public opinion has co-alesced around this note and the extremists of both sides have been si-lenced." [10]

But Secretary of State Bryan had signed the note "with a heavy heart" and with the understanding that the protest to Germany would be promptly balanced in truly neutral fashion (as in the event it was not) by equally strong protests against Britain's continuing violation of America's neutral rights under international law. Bryan pointed out that the *Lusitania* had carried contraband (4,200 cases of cartridges, 1,250 cases of unloaded steel shrapnel shells), that it was immoral, if not ille-gal, to use American passengers to attempt to ensure the safe passage of munitions with which Germans would be killed, and that the British constantly misused the American flag in ways that augmented the dan-ger of German attack upon authentically American vessels. He awaited with trepidation the German response to a communication which seemed to him to be, of itself alone, an expression of pro-Ally bias on the part of his government. Nor were his anxieties allayed by the Ger-man reply when it arrived on May 31—a reply that further inflamed American majority opinion against Germany with its assertion that the sinking (which had involved the slaughter of 270 women and 94 chil-dren) was an act "in just self-defense." The German note not only failed to give the assurances which the United States had requested, but also rejected the premises of the American position, arguing along much the same lines that Bryan had followed in his futile attempts to shape ad-ministration policy. The second of the two explosions that caused the

Lusitania to go down with such incredible rapidity may actually have been an explosion of ammunition the ship carried, said the reply note, which went on to cite an American law prohibiting the transport of explosives and passengers in the same vessel. Obviously, the Cunard Line bore major responsibility for the loss of American lives. In conclusion, the German government reserved its final statement on the matter until the American government had conducted an investigation and submitted, on the basis of it, a second note.

This second note, again of Wilson's personal composition, made no concession whatever to the German argument. It did not indicate, as Bryan wished to do, that a final settlement might be postponed until a later date—this in accord with the Bryan-sponsored arbitration treaties wherein cooling-off periods had been specified. The note was unaccompanied by any U.S. government action to prevent U.S. citizens from sailing on Allied ships bearing contraband or by any protest of Britain's illegal offshore blockade, whose intended effect, after all, included the starvation of German women and children. The note simply reiterated the "representations" of the "note of the thirteenth of May" and, in stronger language than before, made clear the American view that the *Lusitania*'s destruction had been a crime "against humanity" for which this government held the German government responsible. It called, in effect, for abandonment of the submarine war.

Bryan argued with a passionate earnestness that such a communication in such circumstances could only result in a break in diplomatic relations with Germany ("You are all pro-Ally," he accused his colleagues at the Cabinet meeting in which the note was discussed, incurring sharp Presidential rebuke), with war all too likely to follow. He could not sign it in good conscience. He *would* not. He resigned instead as Secretary of State on the morning of June 8, 1915, after long days and sleepless nights of a strain that brought him close to nervous collapse.[11]

Josephus Daniels and Roosevelt's plump, jolly, urbane friend Secretary of the Interior Lane—despite their great differences in personality and outlook and public philosophy—were agreed in their recognition of moral grandeur in Bryan's act. Both saw it as deliberate political self-immolation having the highest and purest of motives. On June 8, following the last Cabinet meeting he would ever attend, Bryan invited the Cabinet members to lunch with him in a private room of the University Club. Daniels and Lane were two of the five who accepted. Both were profoundly impressed by the magnanimity with which their host, his face drawn and pale, spoke his conviction over luncheon that the President was as anxious to stay out of war as he himself was, that they dif-

fered only in the amount of risk of war they were willing to run; he resigned because he was convinced he could "do more on the outside to
prevent war than . . . on the inside." He could "help the President
more." Lane, who had sided with Garrison against Bryan and Daniels
on defense policy, was moved to tears. "You are the most sincere Christian I know," he blurted out. This was too much for Bryan's strain-
weakened self-control. "I go out into the dark," he said brokenly. "The
President has the prestige and the power on his side." He fought for self-
possession. Then he added, huskily: "I have many friends who would
die for me." [12]

But there were few among the chief molders of American public opinion who saw Bryan's act as one of noble self-sacrifice or were willing
publicly to admit it if they did. Most proclaimed it an act of "unspeak-
able treachery, not only to the President but to the nation" (so said the
New York *World*), and ascribed to it motives of cynical self-promo-
tion.[13] Bryan, it was charged, hoped to capture from Wilson the Democratic Presidential nomination in 1916. "Men have been shot and be-
headed, even hanged, drawn and quartered, for treason less heinous,"
raged the famed "Marse Henry" Watterson in his Louisville *Courier-
Journal*. Others fumed publicly against Bryan's "colossal vanity," his
"crazy fanaticism," his "yellow streak."

And with those who thus denounced the Great Commoner, Franklin
Roosevelt was in full agreement. He had always regarded Bryan as an
absurd "hillbilly" who lived in a fantasy world of "idealistic nonsense."
"What d' y' think of W. Jay B.?" he now exploded in a letter to Eleanor.
". . . I can only say I'm disgusted clear through." (He added, cryptically: "J.D. will *not* resign!") To the President he dashed off a longhand
note. "I want to tell you simply that you have been in my thoughts during these days and that I realize to the full all that you have had to go
through," he wrote in terms revelatory of his self-importance and of his
personal relations with Wilson. ". . . I feel most strongly that the Nation approves and sustains your course and that it is *American* in the
highest sense." Wilson's longhand reply, on June 14, was also revelatory. "Your letter . . . touched me very much . . . ," wrote the President. "Such messages make the performance of duty worth while, because, after all, the people who are nearest are those whose judgment we
most value. . . ." [14]

III

Two weeks later, on a Wednesday morning, June 23, 1915, Roosevelt,
glancing out his office window, could have seen his poised, handsome

lawyer friend Robert Lansing—Counselor of the State Department under Bryan; Acting Secretary since June 9—crossing the street to the White House, where, in the President's office, he was to accept appointment to the Cabinet post Bryan had vacated.* (Roosevelt subsequently made invidious comparisons, not devoid of social snobbery, between Bryan and Lansing. "Last night I attended the official dinner of the Lansings . . . ," he wrote Eleanor in late August, "and it was a delight to see a Secretary of State who is a gentleman and knows how to treat Ambassadors and Ministers from other civilized countries." [15])

In Berlin, at about that same hour, Admiral Gustav Bachmann, head of the German Admiralty, and Admiral Alfred von Tirpitz, German Naval Secretary, submitted to the German Chancellor their draft of a proposed reply to the second *Lusitania* note. It made no important concessions to the U.S. position. None could be made, the two admirals argued, without destroying the effectiveness of the U-boat campaign—and they had the firm backing of several of the most powerful industrial and agricultural organizations in the empire, Tirpitz having worked hard to obtain it. Thus was reached a climax in the political quarrel between the Chancellor and the admirals, the Chancellor acting under the pressure of increasingly serious warnings from Bernstorff in Washington that a stubborn persistence in unrestricted submarine attacks could result in a U.S. declaration of war on Germany.

The fear of such a declaration weighed heavily upon the heart and mind of Josephus Daniels, though he would not admit even the possibility of our going to war as he spoke his troubled thoughts to Roosevelt that day. During the noon hour, the two men walked together to a hotel where they were to lunch with the Secretary of Commerce, William C. Redfield, and on the way Daniels raised the question of what the United States could do if Germany "refused . . . ever so politely" to abandon her submarine war. He seemed to Roosevelt "worried and bewildered," not daring "to suggest to himself" the answer to his question which sprang at once to Roosevelt's mind. Instead, Daniels said: "Why, as a matter of fact we couldn't do anything . . . except withdraw Gerard, and what good would that do?" Roosevelt asked whether Daniels thought the "people would stand for raising an army," and Daniels replied emphatically: "No, it would create terrible divisions of opinion."

---

* The new Secretary of State dealt irritably that day with a dispatch from the fervently pro-British Ambassador Page, who, in London, wanted to know on behalf of John Singer Sargent whether that famous painter might use State Department channels to return a German decoration he had accepted before the war. Lansing was disgusted. The matter was not one "with which the Department or its officers abroad can have any connection," he cabled. "Sargent should reimburse Embassy for your telegram and this reply, five dollars."

This reminded Roosevelt of a conversation he'd had with Garrison the day before in which the Secretary of War quoted Daniels as saying, perhaps during a Cabinet meeting: "I hope I shall never live to see the day when the schools of this country are used to give any form of military training. If that happens it will be proof positive that the American form of government is a failure."

Then Daniels said something Roosevelt would always remember. He had spoken of Garrison's "kind of mind, the mind of a lawyer," which insists upon "working things out to an ultimate conclusion," thus raising "a whole lot of unnecessary bogies." He now indicated that Bryan, too, for all his great differences from Garrison, had a somewhat similar kind of mind. "You know it was just that that made Bryan resign," he said to Roosevelt, "—the fear of the next step. . . ." He, Daniels, repudiated this way of thinking. He shared Bryan's principles; he, too, was concerned to act honorably, as a Christian. But he had had too much experience of the unforeseen, the unexpected contingency whereby the most careful and total calculation is thrown awry, to believe that any man is morally responsible for the ultimate consequences of any act, any decision. Morality is a quality of the inward intention, not the outward effect, and an excessive worry about the latter can prevent or distort needed moral initiatives. "It is a mistake to look too far ahead," he said, "to cross bridges before we get to them; it is sufficient to take . . . each step as it comes up." *

The Roosevelt of future years would accept this point of view and act in terms of it on many a historic occasion. But the Roosevelt of 1915, lumping Bryan and Daniels together in his mind, heard only moral and intellectual timidity in Daniels' words. After lunch, back in his office, he wrote out his thoughts on the subject. "My one regret is that the Cabinet has not more Garrisons," he said, "—the President is not getting real information because the Daniels & Bryans prevent the discussion of the future steps because it is a disagreeable subject." He knew "for a fact" that not "a single officer of the Army or Navy" had been enabled to give the President advice on "what we could do to carry out our declared policy." There were things that *could* be done—"military and economic steps"—and they should be carefully considered and then enacted "unless we go on negotiating by notes & more notes." Of the latter "there is a limit—witness the War of 1812." [16]

Precisely a week later, Roosevelt underwent his appendectomy, and precisely a week after that Germany made argumentative reply to the

---

* "It is a mistake to look too far ahead," said Winston Churchill to the House of Commons upon his return from Yalta in early 1945. "Only one link in the chain of destiny can be handled at a time."

second *Lusitania* note without giving the definite pledges that the United States had called for. Then, on July 21, while Roosevelt was convalescing on Campobello, Woodrow Wilson made two fateful decisions. He dispatched to Germany his third *Lusitania* note (his "last word" on the matter, said the Eastern press), which contained the ominous statement "that repetition by the commanders of German naval vessels of acts in contravention of . . . neutral rights must be regarded by the Government of the United States, when they affect American citizens, as deliberately unfriendly." Simultaneously, in the privacy of his "official family," he committed himself irrevocably to the Preparedness policy he had previously opposed, ordering Garrison and Daniels to prepare Army and Navy expansion programs for presentation to the next session of Congress. The order delighted Roosevelt when, on Campobello, he was told of it in a communication from Daniels which asked him to consider ways and means of using the Navy yards most effectively in pursuance of the new Preparedness goals.

The immediate effect of these decisions was a lessening of hostile tensions between Washington and Berlin.

When Roosevelt returned to his desk in Washington on August 16, he found "things in the Department . . . fairly quiet" and the general atmosphere of the capital much more relaxed than it had been in June. He lunched with Lansing that day and no doubt learned from him that the third *Lusitania* note seemed to be having its desired effect: no formal reply to it was expected or wanted, now that Germany had indicated in other ways its intention to abide henceforth by the long-established rules of cruiser warfare.[17] Then, on August 19, came the shocking news that a large British White Star liner, the *Arabic,* had been torpedoed without warning off Ireland's southern coast, with forty-four killed, including two Americans—news that again outraged the nation. And again Wilson refused to act precipitously. He turned down Lansing's suggestion that a special Cabinet meeting be summoned on August 20 to emphasize, for German consideration, our view of the gravity of the situation. He calmly told reporters that this government would make no definite move on the matter until all the facts about it were at hand. Nevertheless, Germany's top civilian leaders immediately realized that in view of the third *Lusitania* note, and as Bernstorff promptly cabled, it would "not be possible to prevent rupture this time if our answer about the *Arabic* is not conciliatory." (Roosevelt, after talking with Lansing on August 21, wrote Eleanor: "I . . . am worried about the Arabic and I think the President will really act as soon as we can get the facts. But it seems very hard to wait until Germany tells us her version and I personally doubt if I should be quite so polite." [18] As for the President, his "politeness" derived in large part from "two things" which, as he wrote Colonel House on that same August 21, were "plain" to him: "1. The people of this country count on me to keep them out of war; 2. It would be a calamity to the world at large if we should be drawn actively into the conflict and so deprived of all disinterested influence over the settlement." [19]) In Berlin, the issue between the German Chancellor and the German admirals was now so sharpened, so fraught with danger to the empire, that the Kaiser was forced to decide it. He decided in favor of the Chancellor.

On September 1, Bernstorff informed Lansing in writing that the instructions he had received from Berlin, in response to the third *Lusitania* note, had contained "the following passage: 'Liners will not be sunk by our submarines without warning and without safety of the lives of noncombatants, provided that the liners do not try to escape or offer resistance.'" Five weeks later (October 5), the ambassador deliberately exceeded his instructions (but was subsequently backed by his government) when he assured Lansing in writing that Germany "regrets and disavows" the sinking of the *Arabic* and was "prepared to pay an indemnity for the American lives which . . . have been lost." He also wrote: "The orders issued by His Majesty the Emperor to the commanders of the German submarines . . . have been so stringent that the recurrence of incidents similar to the *Arabic* case is considered out of the question." [20] Washington accepted this so-called *Arabic* Pledge with joy and thanksgiving. So did the American people, who had made it abundantly clear to Congress and White House, during the crisis, that their overwhelming wish was to stay out of war. They were assured that the President had achieved a rare triumph of diplomacy: without threat or bluster, but simply through patience, firmness, negotiating skill, and moral suasion he had forced a major reversal of German war policy.

Actually, the prime cause of Germany's backdown in 1915 was the failure of its underseas arm to accomplish what its overly eager admirals had claimed it would. Its growing submarine strength was not yet great enough to destroy a truly significant percentage of Allied commerce, and the fear of attack that the admirals had supposed sufficient by itself to reduce that commerce drastically had had no such effect. The final confrontation with the United States over "freedom of the seas" was therefore postponed.

Not until that confrontation came could retrospective vision assess the full importance of Wilson's decisions for Preparedness and against the U-boat campaign, accompanied as they were by a continuing failure to act against the illegal British blockade. For these decisions had the effect of nudging this country once and for all off the knife-edge ridge of "neutrality" onto a slope where the gravitational forces of history (a chief such force being our dependence on British sea power) must pull us at an accelerating rate into war on the Allied side. From then on, there would be for Woodrow Wilson, as there had been for European chiefs of government during the preceding years, a growing loss of control over events.

IV

On September 3, 1915, the President released for publication the letters he had written on the preceding July 21 to Garrison and Daniels. On November 4, in an address in New York City, he presented the Army and Navy expansion proposals which would be submitted to Congress—proposals much too modest to please ardent Preparedness advocates (TR dismissed them contemptuously as a "shadow program," a "half-preparedness") but provocative of violent protest from antiwar groups that included a majority of Progressive reformers. On December 7 his Preparedness message to Congress was received with a coolness that presaged grave difficulties in the way of his program's passage. Simultaneously his courtship and marriage (on December 18) of Edith Bolling Galt, widow of a Washington jeweler, were the subject of a huge publicity that would, Wilson's supporters feared, outrage the electorate,* coming so soon after the death of his first wife. By January, 1916, he seemed to have lost so much of his prestige and authority that his reelection was unlikely.

This was of course depressing to all whose political fortunes were tied to his. And for Franklin Roosevelt, the depression born of the political prospect was linked to that born of physical disability. He had been going at a very hard pace, driving his body to the limits of its strength, ignoring or defying its frequent protests, ever since his return to his office following his appendectomy convalescence. He had felt himself driven by the demands which history-in-the-making imposed upon his ambition. He was convinced that Preparedness lagged farther than ever behind the national need, despite the President's belated commitment to

---

* So fearful of this were Democratic politicians that a conference of several of the most influential of them, using Postmaster General Burleson as their emissary, called upon Daniels to go see Wilson and, as a personal friend, "acquaint him with the situation and urge him to think of the Party's success and not to jeopardize victory for next year" by marrying before November, 1916. This was in the early fall of 1915. An astounded and amused Daniels flatly refused to do anything of the kind.[21]

it; that it was unlikely, at the present rate, to achieve even the administration's far-too-limited goals; and that a principal reason was the lack of planning and coordination of the defense effort on a national scale. What was urgently needed, Roosevelt had been persuaded,* was a Council of National Defense with broad powers to place orders for war matériel and in general to mobilize America's industrial, scientific, and labor resources. He had said so to the President himself in a long conversation on August 27, 1915. The next day he had written Eleanor: "It seems that I can accomplish little just now as the President does not want to 'rattle the sword' while Germany seems anxious to meet us more than half way, but he was interested and will I think really take it up soon." [22] (Actually, of course, Wilson had a built-in, ideological resistance to the kind of "nationalism" which the Defense Council represented.) Since then, the Assistant Secretary, in addition to his assigned duties, had strenuously agitated for the council's establishment, but the President gave no sign of moving on this matter as the new year opened and a physically worn-out Roosevelt developed a throat infection that resisted medication. Roosevelt was still vainly treating this infection and stubbornly refusing to give in to it when, in late January and early February of a Presidential election year, the newly married Wilson set out to restore depleted political fortunes—his own, his party's.

The spectacle, though Roosevelt saw it with an illness-darkened vision, was impressive and inspiriting. With an apparently bold decisiveness that bade fair to gain for him a wider political support than he had had before, Wilson asserted a leadership which only the most probingly analytical could discern as a false appearance. The cardinal choices had, in fact, already been made. No more than a weather vane can determine the wind by pointing its direction could Wilson now determine the main course of events—though his own implicit metaphor, especially as regards his dealings with national defense, was that of a ship in dangerous waters, himself the captain on the bridge. He sought, he said, to steer a "middle course" between the rocklike "extremes" of pacifism and militarism.

He took his Preparedness case to the country in a series of addresses,

---

* By Alfred L. P. Dennis, a professor of history at the University of Wisconsin. The idea was by no means original with Dennis. Germany had had such a body, to achieve and administer total industrial mobilization, long before the World War began, and the countries Germany most threatened had perforce followed suit. When Dr. Hollis Godfrey, president of Philadelphia's Drexel Institute, visited England in 1906, he was impressed by the Committee of Imperial Defense which Prime Minister Balfour had instituted during the 1905 Moroccan Crisis. He became the leading promoter of the Defense Council idea for the United States in 1915–16, working through Colonel House, Secretary of War Garrison, and the chairmen of the Senate and House Military Affairs committees.

the first of them on January 27 in New York City. He spoke with force and eloquence before huge and wildly enthusiastic audiences. But what he essentially said ("boldly facing reality," as his official biographer puts it) was that he was helpless to do as he wished, could no longer act in accord with principles he held dear. "We live in a world which we did not make, which we cannot alter, which we cannot think into a different condition from that which actually exists," he said at the outset, admitting that he reversed himself on the armaments issue. ". . . I would be ashamed if I had not learned something in fourteen months. The minute I stop changing my mind with the change in all the circumstances of the world, I will be a back number." In Pittsburgh he told his hearers they could "count upon my heart and resolution to keep you out of war, but you must be ready if it is necessary that I should maintain your honor." He pleaded there for the means of defense "against things . . . I cannot control, the action of others." In St. Louis, even his self-control was momentarily lost. During this last address of his tour, carried away, as he later confessed, by the "exuberance" of his own "verbosity," he spoke sentences Franklin Roosevelt might have written and certainly applauded. "Have you ever let your imagination dwell upon the enormous stretch of coast from the Canal to Alaska,—from the Canal to the northern corner of Maine?" he cried. "There is no other navy in the world that has to cover so great an area of defense as the American navy and it ought, in my judgment, to be incomparably the greatest navy in the world." ("Most adequate" was substituted for "greatest" in the subsequent official printing of this speech.[23])

Roosevelt was still vainly treating a sore throat when the President, well pleased with the immediate popular reactions to his tour, returned to the capital. It appeared that public opinion was being mobilized solidly behind a defense policy whose "middleness" was emphasized, a few days later, by a Cabinet resignation neatly offsetting that of the pacifistic Bryan. On February 10, 1916, Lindley Garrison, the ardent militarist, refusing to retreat from his stand in favor of a Continental Army and compulsory military training, gave up his post as Secretary of War.

There was immediate newspaper speculation, encouraged by Louis Howe, that Franklin Roosevelt might be appointed to the vacated post. Roosevelt himself could read of it in the papers and letters delivered to him in Atlantic City, where, having at last been forced to yield to his rebellious body's demands, he went in mid-February to take the "cure" for ten days or so along the boardwalk. (He loathed the place. "This 'health resort' is purgatory, the place of departed spirits," he wrote Eleanor irritably on February 21. ". . . I fail to understand . . . how anybody can stay here more than 24 hours without wanting to murder somebody.") [24] The speculation was not without some factual basis. High-ranking Army officers, civilian officials of the War Department, powerful members of the business community, and many labor leaders (the latter a significant incongruity for which Louis Howe could claim large credit)—all these let it be known that the Assistant Secretary's elevation to the Cabinet would greatly please them. But Wilson seems never for a moment to have considered it. Instead, at about the time Roosevelt (his throat infection at last under control) returned to Washington, the President appointed as War Secretary Newton D. Baker of Cleveland, a famed Progressive Democratic reformer who had only recently expressed himself as a pacifist who opposed Preparedness! [25]

If Roosevelt felt any personal disappointment over this outcome—as almost certainly he did not, having had no expectations—he quickly forgot it: events crowded upon one another in his private as in his public life. On March 13, 1916, his youngest child, a boy whom his parents named after Franklin's uncle John Aspinwall, was born in the easiest of all of Eleanor's confinements. A few days later five-year-old Elliott came down with a severe cold which soon developed into a dangerous illness and from which he was destined not to recover for months, returning even then only to what Eleanor called "comparative health." The spring of 1916 was a season of private, personal anxieties for the Assistant Secretary.

He was also involved in the anxieties provoked by a German submarine's torpedoing without warning, in the English Channel on March 24, of a ferry steamer, the *Sussex,* en route from England to France. The explosion, killing several passengers, injured four of the twenty-five Americans aboard. Wilson was compelled by his *Lusitania-Arabic* stand to serve an ultimatum upon Berlin, declaring in his note of April 18 that "the Government of the United States . . . [must] sever diplomatic relations with the German Empire" if the imperial government did not "immediately" abandon "Its present method of submarine warfare against passenger and freight-carrying vessels." It was another instance of lost control masquerading as a firm decisiveness, and it achieved another diplomatic "triumph" of the sort that now added up to a virtual certainty of our going to war. Germany, its submarine strength still not great enough to conduct a truly effective blockade, acceded to the American demands in a note dated May 4, though retaining full freedom to adopt a different course of action in the future if the United States failed to bring Britain into an equivalent compliance with international law.

And the latter, which Roosevelt would in any case have opposed, was now a practical impossibility, as Wilson acutely realized. The President's handling of the *Sussex* crisis had made his reelection more likely, but all chance of this would now be lost if the country were plunged into the economic depression that would abruptly ensue if the administration (two years too late) embargoed shipments to the Allies and closed our ports to them. There was pressure for such action in some quarters. Allied blockade restrictions grew increasingly harsh and flagrant in their violations of international law. Congressional and Presidential tempers flared as the British blacklisted American firms, seized neutral mails on the high seas, even interfered with International Red Cross shipments of hospital supplies. Moreover, England's claims to moral superiority over the Germans were greatly depreciated by the British Army's ruthless suppression of the Irish Easter Rebellion that spring, followed by the executions in Dublin of Roger Casement and other Irish nationalist leaders.

Wilson could regain a measure of actual control over America's foreign affairs only through a successful mediation of the European conflict. He returned to this effort with renewed vigor on the morrow of his *Sussex* triumph. He recalled Sir Edward Grey's insistence, in a letter to Colonel House last fall, that a major objective of the belligerents was security against future aggression and that there was no chance of initiating peace negotiations unless they definitely pointed to this end. "How much are the United States prepared to do in this direction?" Grey had asked. "Would the President propose that there should be a League of Nations binding themselves to side against any Power which broke a treaty; which broke certain rules of warfare on sea or land (such rules would, of course, have to be drawn up after this war); or which refused, in case of dispute, to adopt some other method of settlement than that of war?" [26] Wilson also recalled that he had refused, in mid-April, an invitation to address a mass meeting, to be held in Washington on May 27, of the League to Enforce Peace. (This influential organization, launched a year before, was a rather strange amalgam of liberal peace movement leaders and political conservatives—ex-President Taft, Harvard's A. Lawrence Lowell—whose aim was to establish an international organization that could employ force, if necessary, to keep the peace.) The President now told the league's officers that he had changed his mind: he would address the great meeting, after all.

The event was memorable and historic.

Franklin Roosevelt was among the 2,000 who gathered that evening in the New Willard Hotel to listen, first, to an address by Henry Cabot Lodge. The Massachusetts Senator uttered words that, two years later, would seem strange indeed, coming from him. He asserted that the "limit of voluntary arbitration" had "been reached," that "the next step" was "to put force behind international peace," and that Washington's warning "against entangling alliances" did not mean that "we should not join with other civilized nations of the world if a method can be found to diminish war and encourage peace."

Then the President of the United States spoke.

"We are participants, whether we would or not, in the life of the world, and the interests of all nations are our own," he said; "henceforth there must be a common agreement for a common object, and at the heart of that common object must lie the inviolable rights of people and of mankind." He said "that the principle of public right must henceforth take precedence over the individual interests of particular nations, and that the nations of the world must in some way band together to see that right to choose the sovereignty under which they shall live . . . , that the small States of the world have a right to enjoy the same respect for their sovereignty that great and powerful nations expect and insist upon," and "that the world has a right to be free from every disturbance of the peace that has its origin in aggression and disregard for the rights of peoples and nations."

There followed words weighted with destiny.

". . . the United States," said the President, "is willing to become a partner in any feasible association of nations formed in order to realize these objects and make them secure against violation." [27]

V

Personal anxieties did not cease for Franklin Roosevelt during the long hot summer that followed, a summer during which he was able to spend only a few days at a time in the coolness of Campobello.

There was an infantile paralysis epidemic, the worst the country had ever known, beginning in New York City in June and spreading along the eastern seaboard. Roosevelt was almost morbidly afraid of it, for his children's sake. While establishing his wife and "the chicks" on Campobello during the first days of July, he spent hours, literally, swatting flies in the cottage because they were believed to spread the dread disease. "*Please* kill all the flies I left," he wrote Eleanor on July 7, upon his return to Washington. "I think it really important." His fear intensified when infantile paralysis cases began to appear in Poughkeepsie, in every village in Dutchess County, and "even in Rockland and other *Maine* points," as he wrote on August 18. He would not permit Eleanor and the children to travel southwestward by train or auto when summer ended; he kept them on the island until, in early October, he was able to sail with them from Eastport on the *Dolphin**—a two-day voyage, delightful for the children, along the coast to New York City and thence up the Hudson to Hyde Park to stay for a time with his mother. And in anticipation of their arrival, he ordered elaborate precautions to be taken at Springwood, where the three-year-old child of his mother's coachman had contracted the disease in mid-September. He wanted everything fumigated. Even so, "I think the children ought not to go in any of our own autos or carriages," he wrote his mother on September 30. He wanted "Rosy or his man" to come "down to the River to bring up" Eleanor, the nurse, and the two babies. "The rest of us can walk!" [28]

Another source of private worry that sweltering summer was a series of daring burglaries of large estates along the Hudson, between Hyde Park and Rhinebeck, the first of them in early July. Members of what the Poughkeepsie *Eagle* called "the millionaire colony" joined police in futile efforts to apprehend what everyone assumed to be a well-organized band of thieves. When Roosevelt visited Hyde Park during the first weekend of August, he "was up till three a.m." on Sunday morning "waiting for burglars!" as he wrote Eleanor, adding, "I wish they had come!" Two nights later, after Roosevelt had returned to Washington, a man named Fred Cramer, found trespassing on Vincent Astor's estate north of Rhinebeck, was shot to death in a running gun battle along a wooded road. With his death, the burglaries ceased. But Roosevelt could not be certain that the cause of this anxiety had been removed before he was presented with another. On August 14, upon his return from the New York State Democratic Convention in Saratoga, he found that his chauffeur, one Golden, had been badly injured in an accident that had wrecked the Roosevelt car. The next day he discovered that Golden had been "joy-riding" when the wreck occurred and had injured others in the wreck ("so . . . I get no insurance" for damage to the car that "looks like at least $500") and that the chauffeur had also pocketed some $250 in cash given him by Roosevelt to pay garage bills that remained unpaid. When the "weak, miserable wretch" was released from the hospital, Roosevelt discharged him.[29]

Anxieties continued to cluster, too, around his public life in that election year.

---

* Daniels had been reluctant to permit the official Secretarial yacht to be used for this private purpose that year. "The Sec'y was accused in Congress of intention to use *Dolphin* to campaign in Maine—hence he is scared blue and *Dolphin* won't be allowed within 100 miles of Maine till after September 11," Roosevelt wrote Eleanor disgustedly on August 18. September 11 was Maine's election day.

The administration, as regards Preparedness, did now move definitely in the direction he had pointed since the fall of 1914 (on June 14, Flag Day, when a huge Preparedness Parade was held in Washington, he was photographed standing near the President on the reviewing stand), but he himself had by then moved so much farther in the same direction that he was, if anything, less in accord with the administration's defense and foreign policy than before. The administration-sponsored National Defense Act, passed by Congress on June 3, failed to provide adequately for the nation's land force needs, in his opinion, and he was actively dissatisfied with the naval bill in the form in which it passed the House on June 2. Daniels' original proposal, in the drafting of which Roosevelt had had a minor role, called for a five-year naval construction program, with the building of two dreadnaughts to be started at once. In his testimony before the House Naval Affairs Committee in March, Roosevelt had boldly called for a considerably larger building program than this. But the House in its initial action, to Roosevelt's disgust, refused even to endorse the five-year program and struck out the proposal for immediate construction of two battleships, while adding two riders aimed at the private-profit armaments industry. (One of the riders appropriated funds for Daniels' government-owned armor-plate manufacturing plant, already approved by the Senate; the other, in implementation of Wilson's May 27 speech, pledged the United States to participation in a postwar conference for discussion of disarmament and the setting up of international machinery for the arbitration of international disputes.) "The Sec'y is still busy with the Naval Bill," wrote Roosevelt to "Dearest Babs" in early July, "and I am trying though I fear in vain to eliminate a number of fool features in it and to get into it a few more really constructive items." However, all at last came out well in this matter, from his point of view. The Senate, dominated by "big navy" men, passed by overwhelming majority a bill that crowded Daniels' five-year program into three years and ordered construction to begin within the next fiscal year on *four* dreadnaughts, four battle cruisers, thirty submarines, twenty destroyers, and sundry smaller vessels. When the two versions of the bill went into joint House-Senate conference, Wilson, concerned to develop a Navy "equal to the international tasks" in which "this Nation hopes and expects to take part," actively intervened in favor of the Senate version, which was then enacted without important change. Wilson signed it into law in another greatly publicized White House ceremony on August 29.[30]

Also established that August, through a rider on the Army appropriations bill, was the long-agitated Council of National Defense, composed of the Secretaries of War, the Navy, Agriculture, Commerce, Labor, and the Interior, with a seven-member Advisory Commission appointed by the President (October 11, 1916) and consisting of recognized leaders of various phases of American life. Roosevelt, in his private talk and correspondence, claimed large personal credit for this event, and though there were several others whose roles in the bill's passage were at least as great as his, he had certainly played an important part. He could be gratified.[31]

And he would have been even more gratified to know that by September the President had been driven to accept the basic tenets of Mahan's doctrine, the foundation for Roosevelt's own war-policy views. By then, too, ironically, after the possibility of a true neutrality of action had disappeared, Wilson personally was closer to a true neutrality of feeling and thought vis-à-vis Germany and Britain than he had ever been before. He more and more resented Britain's use of its sea power to close off options he must exercise, or at least keep open, if he were to prevent his country's active involvement in the war. He looked upon his naval expansion policy as a renewed Declaration of Independence. He said to Colonel House (September 24): "Let us build a navy bigger than hers [Britain's] and do what we please." [32]

VI

Meanwhile, the Presidential campaign, its outcome increasingly in doubt, constituted the major concern of Roosevelt's public life as the long summer yielded at last to the coolness of autumn. Preparedness was the issue on which the electorate's final decision seemed more and more to turn, and it was an issue on which Roosevelt found himself in closer agreement with the Republicans than with his own party!

Other differences, sharp in 1912, had since become blurred almost beyond recognition. In large part this was because Wilson, along with his change of direction in defense and foreign policy, had made an equally drastic shift on the domestic front. As he shrewdly appraised his chances for reelection in January, 1916, he was acutely aware that his victory in 1912 with 42 percent of the popular vote had come because TR's Bull Moose had gouged more votes out of the Republican Party than out of the Democratic. The Bull Moose was now moribund. It had been fatally injured in the midterm elections of 1914, and TR, wholly absorbed in his campaign for Preparedness, was obviously determined to return to the Republican fold. If he carried with him a majority of the independents who had followed him down the trail of the Bull Moose, Wilson's defeat in November would be overwhelming. It behooved the

President, therefore, to convince the electorate of three things: *one,* that the administration, though realistic in its assessment of defense requirements, was less likely than a Republican one to involve the country in war; *two,* that the administration was far more concerned with the general welfare, far more determined to redress the balance between big business and other segments of the economy, than a Republican administration could possibly be; but, *three,* that the administration was by no means hostile to the legitimate interests of business, but was on the contrary eager to adjust to the changing needs of the business community. The upshot was that he, who had announced the completion of the New Freedom two years before, abandoned a lifelong commitment to states' rights, his antipathy to the protective tariff, and his opposition to any federal action on behalf of "special" groups or classes or interests, in order to embrace virtually every key proposal of the New Nationalism of 1912.*

The reversal of position was as abrupt as it was drastic. On January 24, having been informed that his reelection might depend on his espousal of the "non-partisan scientific Tariff Commission" which TR had proposed in 1912 and which Wilson had then ridiculed, the President told the House majority leader that he now favored legislation to create a Federal Tariff Commission. The legislation was dutifully introduced in the House a week later. (Another Presidential action at this time juxtaposed incongruities in a way that contributed to the irony of American history. On January 28, Wilson appointed Louis D. Brandeis, archfoe of corporate giantism, archchampion of truly free and private enterprise, to be Associate Justice of the Supreme Court. There followed a long and bitter confirmation struggle centering on the appointee's Jewishness and "radicalism." Not until June 1 was Brandeis finally confirmed, though the final vote was overwhelmingly in his favor.) Ultimately, the Tariff Commission proposal was incorporated in the Revenue Act of 1916, along with a provision for the protection of the U.S. chemical industry against Germany's I. G. Farben by raising high tariff walls against imports of dyes, synthetics, and medicines.† Wilson also

* "In order to resurrect the Democratic party," wrote Herbert Croly in the *New Republic* for October 21, 1916, announcing his support of the President's reelection, "Mr. Wilson has been modifying the Democratic creed. . . . The New Freedom has been discarded. . . . The party program no longer seeks the restoration of a regime of incoherent, indiscriminate, competitive, localistic individualism. It fore-shadows rather a continuing process of purposive national reorganization determined in method by the realities of the task but dedicated to the ultimate enhancement of individual life within and without the American commonwealth. For the first time in several generations the party has the chance of becoming the embodiment of a genuinely national democracy."

† This Revenue Act was historically significant in ways important to Franklin Roosevelt's future. The administration had proposed some $300,000,000 additional taxes to provide for

gave his support to a measure, the Webb bill, which revised the antitrust law to permit theretofore illegal combinations of American manufacturers for the purpose of export trade—another action echo of Bismarck's New Germany. (The measure did not pass that year. It was adopted in January, 1918.)

In 1914 and '15, Wilson had blocked passage of a rural credits bill requiring federal underwriting of loans to farmers and farm cooperatives, his stated reason being that extension of "the credits of the Government to a single class in the community" was "unwise and unjustifiable." But in 1916 his support was decisive of the passage in mid-July of a Federal Farm Loan Act, whereby a Federal Farm Loan Board was established to organize and supervise a system of Federal Land Banks. Similarly with regard to legislation on child labor and workmen's compensation. Without overt Presidential backing, both measures had passed the House easily by mid-July, 1916, but they faced extinction in the Senate, where Southern and NAM pressure against the child labor bill was powerful, unless the President intervened actively in their behalf. Wilson gave no sign of doing so until, on July 17, Josephus Daniels and the chairman of the National Child Labor Committee jointly urged upon him the crucial political importance which attached to both measures in that election year. "I know that many Southern Senators oppose . . . [the child labor bill] but I believe that the failure to pass . . . [it] will lose us more votes in close States than our Southern Senators appreciate," said Daniels. "Besides, I strongly feel that it is essential to protect child labor and that such protection is the very basis of the social legislation which gave the Progressives [in 1912] hold on the conscience of that portion of their Party that . . . [was not] controlled by [George W.] Perkins." [34] Wilson then abruptly overcame whatever lingering doubts he may have had about the constitutionality of the bills. He *did* intervene, strongly and effectively. He signed both measures into law in August. And the Child Labor Act, especially, would prove of major importance to Franklin Roosevelt's future public career in that, for the first time, it made Congress' legislative authority over interstate commerce a means of federal control over employment conditions in factories, mines, quarries.

Preparedness, the bulk of them to be paid by middle- and lower-income classes. Progressives in Congress, from the West and South, rebelled. They substituted for the administration's tax bill one of their own whereby much of the new revenue was raised by a marked percentage rise in the tax on higher incomes, undistributed profits, and inheritances. These provisions were adopted. "It was a landmark in American history," writes Arthur S. Link, "the first really important victory of the movement, begun by Populists in the 1890's and carried on by Progressives in the early 1900's, for a Federal tax policy based upon ability to pay. . . . Wilson, insofar as we know, had had no part in this, one of the most significant achievements of the Progressive movement." [33]

Another instance of Wilsonian New Nationalism, this one directly born of the exigencies of European war, was the Shipping Act, which passed Congress that year only because the President insisted on it. Damned as a "socialistic scheme" by American shipping interests, it aimed to make up the difference between available bottoms and those needed to handle the war-expanded overseas trade by authorizing a U.S. Shipping Board of five members to spend as much as $50,000,000 for the purchase, construction, leasing, and operation of merchant ships. Outside shipping circles, however, it attracted little attention.

Far different in this respect, and more far-reaching in its consequences, was the Adamson Act, which imposed an eight-hour workday, in place of the former ten-hour day, upon all workers employed by railroads engaged in interstate commerce. It was pressed through Congress by the President under threat by the four railroad brotherhoods of a nationwide strike. It was signed into law barely twenty-four hours before the strike deadline. And it at once became the only specific domestic issue of any importance between the President and his Republican opponent in the fall election campaign.*

This opponent was Charles Evans Hughes, former governor of New York, who resigned as Associate Justice of the Supreme Court in order to accept nomination by the Republican National Convention, in Chicago, on June 10.

His choice was dictated by the same felt need as had dictated Wilson's shift to the New Nationalism—namely, the Republicans' realization that they had to capture as many as possible of the independent votes that in 1912 had gone to TR. This necessity was pointed up by the fact that the diehards of the Progressive Party met in national convention, in Chicago, simultaneously with the Republicans. TR personally disliked Hughes intensely—for one thing, Hughes, stamped with a reputation for Progressivism ever since his famous exposure of graft and corruption in New York life insurance companies in the early 1900's, had publicly charged George Perkins with business practices of highly dubious ethicality—but the ex-President's hatred of Wilson was by far the stronger motivating emotion. In TR's angry opinion, the Republican coterie who persuaded their party convention to nominate Hughes were "a sordid set of creatures" (TR would have liked the Republican nomination for himself that year), but he found them "a trifle better than the corrupt and lunatic wild asses of the desert who seem most influential in

---

* On March 19, 1917, the U.S. Supreme Court decided by a single vote (five to four) that the Adamson Act was constitutional—a decision of major importance in American political and economic history. Louis D. Brandeis voted with the majority.

Democratic councils, under the lead of that astute, unprincipled and physically cowardly demagogue Wilson." When the Progressive Party Convention nominated TR for President, therefore, he, knowing full well that his running would absolutely ensure Wilson's reelection, refused the nomination and threw his support behind Hughes. The dying Bull Moose was thus stabbed to death and buried amid much bitter recrimination.

Four days later, at high noon on Flag Day, while Franklin Roosevelt was involved in the great Preparedness Parade in Washington, the Democratic National Convention opened in St. Louis.

Wilson, his nomination by acclamation a certainty, ordered that "Americanism" (spelled out with bold explicitness in terms of Progressive Nationalism) be made the central theme of the convention as it was of the platform—the latter largely of the President's personal composition. "Americanism" would thus become the theme of the whole campaign. And certainly Franklin Roosevelt was in favor of this strategy. In his own campaign speeches, in September and October—in Maine, New York State, Rhode Island, all of which went Republican that year—Roosevelt concentrated on the increase in naval efficiency since Taft left office, on the progress being made toward a "Navy second to none," and on "the really great accomplishments" in domestic legislation "during the last four years." He said little about Wilsonian diplomacy or foreign policy. But his party in general, from the opening day of the convention, took a very different campaign tack. To the platform plank endorsing Wilson's reelection someone appended a sentence about "the splendid diplomatic victories of our great President, who has preserved the vital interests of our Government . . . and kept us out of war." It was this, not "Americanism" as Wilson had defined it, that became the theme of the keynote speech, delivered with magnificent effectiveness by ex-Governor Glynn of New York. And "He Kept Us Out of War" became the chief Democratic Presidential campaign slogan, to Franklin Roosevelt's unease.

Yet Roosevelt, like Wilson, could not but recognize the political potency of this theme. TR went raging across the land, damning as "the spiritual heirs of the Tories of 1776" those "who now with timid hearts and quavering voices praise Mr. Wilson for having kept us out of war." He asserted that had he been President, a U.S. declaration of war would have immediately followed the sinking of the *Lusitania*. He attacked the "hyphenated Americans" (the German-Americans, the Irish-Americans) who were pro-German or anti-British. He poured acid ridicule over Wilson's "too proud to fight" statement. But it was obvious that he spoke on this issue for a distinct minority of the electorate ("the jingoes and the Munitions Trust," as the St. Louis *Post-Dispatch* put it) and had slight persuasive power—indeed, his efforts were largely counterproductive—with the remainder. Josephus Daniels, upon whom the Republican concentrated much hostile fire, aroused considerably more enthusiasm than TR did among motion-picture audiences when their respective pictures appeared in newsreels.[35]

As for Hughes, his election by a substantial majority had at the outset seemed probable, even almost certain. He proved, however, to be a remarkably poor campaigner. He was a glacial personality, stiff, aloof, forbidding, his coldly calculating temperament unqualified by any zest for combat or, indeed, enthusiasms of any kind. TR, prior to Hughes' nomination, dismissed him contemptuously as just "another Wilson with whiskers." [36] But Hughes wholly lacked Wilson's oratorical powers. In public speech, his vague and lofty generalities had the effect of dampening rather than enhancing the initial ardors of his strongest partisans. And he was severely handicapped by Wilson's drastic shifts in governmental policy during the preceding year. He would not echo TR's bitter attacks on the "weakness" and "cowardice" of Wilson's response to the submarine threat: the most he would permit himself to say was that the President should have been (he himself would have been) "firmer" in his dealings with Germany during the *Lusitania* crisis. Yet TR's belligerent campaigning inevitably imposed on him some of the stigma of a "war party" leader determined to wrest power from an administration committed to "peace with honor." Nor could he find serious fault with major Democratic domestic policies, since these were essentially those of the Progressives whose wooing had largely determined his own nomination. He was reduced to carping criticisms of alleged ineptitudes and inefficiencies, criticisms offset by no constructive proposals of his own.

Thus he was a candidate in increasingly desperate search for a truly viable issue when he seized upon the Adamson eight-hour law as, in his proclaimed view, a craven submission by the government to forceful coercion by the railroad workers. "Transcending every other issue," he said on September 7, "is the issue . . . [of] whether the Government shall yield to force. . . ."

In this he certainly spoke the opinion of the big business community, whose outrage was augmented on that same September 7 by the signing into law of the Revenue Act with its "soak-the-rich" tax provisions. Henry Morgenthau, Sr., chairman of the Democratic Party's Finance Committee, was perturbed by the abrupt stop which the Adamson Act and the Revenue Act put to large contributions that had earlier flowed, at a fairly satisfactory rate, into the party's campaign treasury. Simultaneously, as Morgenthau suspected at the time, the flow of "big" money into the Republican treasury was increased. Not since 1896 had party lines so nearly coincided with economic class lines. (Later careful investigation would disclose that the Republicans raised and spent upwards of $15,000,000 during the 1916 campaign, nearly all of it coming in sizable contribution from businesses and businessmen.)

But Wilson was not dismayed. He was not even put upon the defensive. On September 23, in public speech, he boldly proclaimed that the eight-hour law, far from being a surrender to force, was a triumph of administration policy. The eight-hour day should not be limited to railroad labor, he asserted; it should be extended to *all* workers, "because a man does better work within eight hours than he does within a more extended day, and the whole theory of it . . . which is sustained . . . by abundant experience, is that his efficiency is increased, his spirit in his work is improved, and the whole physical and moral vigor of the man is added to." [37] The Adamson Act, in other words, was model legislation.

Hughes then fell silent about his "transcendent" issue.

And all through October—as Wilson reiterated his commitment to U.S. membership in a "society of nations" to keep the peace; as the potency of the "He Kept Us Out of War" slogan increasingly manifested itself, in reaction to TR's bombast—the Republican candidate lost ground to his opponent.

On election day, November 7, however, professional gambling odds still stood at ten to six in Hughes' favor.

VII

That Tuesday evening, Franklin Roosevelt was one of a large dinner party given by the elder Henry Morgenthau in New York's Biltmore Hotel, where the Democrats had their headquarters. The evening started gaily. The assembled Democrats were full of hope. But by midnight, when Roosevelt left the Biltmore in company with Secretary Lane, all was gloom. The Republicans had obviously won the East by large majorities (only New Hampshire seemed doubtful), and both the New York *Times* and the New York *World*, strong supporters of Wilson, had conceded the election to Hughes. When Roosevelt went to bed in the early morning, on a Pullman bound for Washington, it was in the belief that his days as Assistant Secretary were numbered. Well-founded rumor had it that Wilson was resolved, in case of defeat, to appoint Hughes Secretary of State in place of Lansing and then resign his office, with the Vice President. This would enable the President-elect to move into the White House at once. The constitutional interregnum of four long months was too dangerous for the country in such crisis times, Wilson was said to feel.[38]

But when he arrived at his office in Washington next morning, Roosevelt was astonished to learn that what had appeared to be an overwhelming victory for Hughes only a few hours before was actually a narrow and narrowing one, if indeed it proved to be a victory at all. To the traditionally Solid South, Wilson appeared to be adding one after another of the closely contested states in the Mid and Far West. By noon of the "most extraordinary day of my life," as Roosevelt scrawled in a note to "Dearest Babs" (she was at Hyde Park), the situation actually looked "hopeful." Thursday, November 9, was "another day of wild uncertainty" as counting continued, with often a difference of only a few hundred votes between the two candidates' totals in crucial states.[39] Not until the following morning was it certain that Wilson had carried the decisive state of California by some 3,000 votes and won reelection as President of the United States.*

The electoral vote was 277 for Wilson to 254 for Hughes. The popular vote was 9,129,606 for Wilson to 8,538,321 for Hughes. Some 819,000 votes were distributed among the candidates of the Socialist, Prohibition, and Socialist Labor parties, rendering Wilson still a minority President. The Democrats retained control of the Senate, 54 to 42. They were outnumbered by the Republicans 217 to 213 in the House, where, in consequence, a vote on strict party lines might be decided by the two Progressives, one Prohibitionist, one Socialist, and one Independent who had won election.

Roosevelt was, of course, jubilant over the outcome. He told Eleanor that he planned to send a telegram to arch-Republican Warren Delano in Barrytown saying, "The Republican Party has proved to its own satisfaction I hope that the American people cannot always be bought." (He added, to Eleanor, in evident reference to Delano's politics, "I hope to God I don't grow reactionary with advancing years.") A few days later he laughingly told an audience, as reported in the press, that, according to rumor, "a certain distinguished cousin of mine is now engaged in revising an edition of his most noted historical work, *The Winning of the West*." [40]

But he was by no means easy in his mind about the terms on which this amazing victory had been won. From a pro-Preparedness position he had now moved into a frankly pro-interventionist one. Between late

---

* Hughes did not send his congratulations to Wilson until November 22. They arrived "a little moth-eaten . . . but quite legible," was Wilson's private comment.

February and the fall of 1916, there had been four gigantic collisions in the European war—three on land (Verdun, the Somme, Brusilov's offensive on the eastern front); one at sea (Jutland). They had killed and maimed millions of men, had destroyed billions of dollars' worth of matériel and ships, without effecting a decision of any kind. They had, instead, established the fact of hopeless stalemate, the fact that no decision was possible so long as the gigantic war machines (now gone completely out of human control) and the stockpiles of flesh and blood by which they were fueled remained so evenly matched in power. Only active intervention by the United States on the Allied side could accomplish the defeat of the Central Powers. "We've got to get into this war!" said Roosevelt to Daniels, over and over again, that fall. To which Daniels always replied, with deep feeling, "I hope not!"

As for Woodrow Wilson himself, he could have borne an overwhelming election defeat with far more mental ease than he did a victory whose narrow margin depended on "He Kept Us Out of War," with the promise that this implied. Indeed, he had given every evidence of personal relief as, on the night of election day, he said "laughingly" to Tumulty over the phone that "it begins to look as though we have been badly licked." To Tumulty he had "talked like a man from whose shoulders a great load had been lifted and now he was happy and rejoicing that he was a free man again." His immediate family had gained the same impression from him. But regrets and division of mind were part and parcel of his mood in the immediate aftermath of victory. "I can't keep the country out of war," he grumbled to Daniels. "They talk of me as though I were a god. Any little German lieutenant can put us into the war at any time by some calculated outrage." And a week after the election he said to Colonel House that the United States must "inevitably drift into war with Germany upon the submarine issue" unless he somehow managed to persuade the combatants to stop fighting and negotiate a peace settlement. To the mediation effort, therefore, he now turned in near desperation.[41]

Fifteen

→»)«←

America Enters the War

I

ON JANUARY 1, 1917, Franklin D. Roosevelt, that avid collector of Americana, addressed a letter to Woodrow Wilson, enclosing a memorandum he had found "while going over some papers I acquired many years ago. It is in the handwriting of James Monroe and was evidently written in 1814 when the Congress of Vienna was about to meet." He had been unable to determine, he said, whether or not the memorandum had been "actually used" in any official document, "but it is in many ways so interestingly parallel to the events of the day that I thought you would like to add it to your collection of historical material." [1]

Composed by the Secretary of State (also of War) in Madison's Cabinet in a year when British troops, occupying Washington, burned both Capitol and White House and when, at year's end, the Treaty of Ghent closed out the futile War of 1812 on a basis of *status quo ante bellum,* the memorandum said in part: "A war in Europe, to which Great Britain with her floating thunder, and other maritime powers, are always parties, has long been found to spread its calamities into the remotest regions. Even the U.S., just and pacific as their policy is, have not been able to avoid the alternative of either submitting to the most destructive and ignominious wrongs from European Belligerents, or of resisting them by an appeal to the sword: or to speak more properly, no other choice has been left them but the time of making the appeal; it being evident that a submission too long protracted, would have no other effect than to encourage and accumulate aggressions, until they should become altogether intolerable; and until the loss of honor being added to other losses, redress by the sword itself would be rendered more slow and difficult."

There can be no doubt of Wilson's interest in this document or of his understanding of the motives that impelled Roosevelt to give it to him at that particular moment. Shortly before Christmas and shortly after Germany had put out a formal offer to negotiate peace terms with the Allies, Wilson had dispatched to all the major belligerents an identical note, reminding them "that the objects which the statesmen . . . on both sides have in mind in this war are virtually the same, as stated in general terms to their own people and to the world." Each belligerent had said it wanted to secure "the rights and privileges of weak peoples and small states" against aggression; that it wanted for itself only security "against the recurrence of wars like this and against aggression and selfish interference of any kind"; that it "would be jealous of the formation of any more rival leagues to preserve an uncertain balance of power amidst multiplying suspicions"; but that it was "ready to consider the formation of a league of nations to insure peace and justice throughout the world." In the latter noble endeavor, the people and government of the United States were eager to join. First, however, must come a cessation of hostilities. What, therefore, were the *specific* objects for which the nations were fighting and what the terms on which they were willing to lay down arms? On New Year's Day, no formal reply to the Wilson note had yet been received from the Allies (when it came, nearly two weeks later, it emphatically repudiated the President's statement that the Allies and Germany fought for the same objects), but Germany had politely rebuffed the implicit offer of mediation, saying that direct negotiations with the Allies were preferable. In these circumstances, Wilson could easily recognize Roosevelt's gift as an item of pro-Ally interventionist propaganda, and he acknowledged its receipt rather perfunctorily. "It was most generous of you to send me the Monroe manuscript," wrote the President to the Assistant Secretary of the Navy on January 3. "It is unusually interesting and I shall value it highly." [2]

But if the document was without influence of the sort Roosevelt wished to exert upon Wilsonian policy, it had influence of another kind.

An unexpected and disturbing repercussion to the appeal to the governments of the warring nations had been a rise of opposition in the Senate to the President's statement about America and a league of nations. The President, with good reason, had assumed that this proposal enjoyed overwhelming bipartisan support. The most virulent of his political and personal enemies, Theodore Roosevelt and Senator Lodge, both were publicly committed to the idea of international organization as expressed through the League to Enforce Peace. Wilson's address to the mass meeting sponsored by that bipartisan organization, in May, 1916—the address announcing U.S. willingness "to become a partner" in an "association of nations"—had been enthusiastically received not

AMERICA ENTERS THE WAR

only by its immediate audience, but also by the nation at large. Nevertheless, a proposed Senate resolution endorsing the President's December note to the belligerents had run into difficulties. Senator William E. Borah of Idaho vehemently opposed it, because this country's participation in a league of nations would, in his opinion, constitute an "entangling alliance" of the kind the Founding Fathers, in their wisdom, had urged us to avoid. Simultaneously, TR, writing an article for the January issue of *Metropolitan Magazine*, suddenly discovered reasons for opposing American participation in any organization that impaired U.S. sovereignty in the slightest or U.S. hegemony over the Western Hemisphere as proclaimed in the Monroe Doctrine. And on the day Wilson wrote his note of thanks to Roosevelt, Senator Lodge, addressing the Senate, contradicted the argument he had made in public speech to the same meeting Wilson had addressed the preceding May. He now professed the gravest doubts about the wisdom of our "abandonment of the policy we have hitherto pursued of confining ourselves to our own hemisphere. . . ." [3]

Yet Colonel House, calling upon the President that same day, found his friend far from dismayed by the unexpected turn which Senate debate on the endorsement resolution had taken. Wilson viewed it as a tactical opportunity. The questions raised by Borah and Lodge called for answers from the President. In the course of answering them, Wilson, without the appearance of officious meddling in the affairs of the warring sovereignties, could state the terms on which he felt a peace settlement should be arranged. [4] He promptly set about doing so.

And as he wrote, during the next few days, the great speech which he presented to the Senate on January 22, the Monroe memorandum which young Roosevelt had given him was on his desk and in his mind. Its influence is evident. As if in echo of the terms on which the War of 1812 was ended, the President called for a "peace without victory" because victory would mean "a victor's terms imposed upon the vanquished" and "only a peace between equals can last." He called for "not a balance of power, but a community of power; not organized rivalries, but an organized common peace" through a league of nations. "I am proposing . . . ," he said, "that the nations should with one accord adopt the doctrine of President Monroe as the doctrine of the world: that no nation should extend its polity over any other nation or people, but that every people should be left free to determine its own polity, its own way of development, unhindered, unthreatened, unafraid, the little along with the great and powerful. I am proposing that all nations henceforth avoid entangling alliances which draw them into competitions of power. . . . There is no entangling alliance in a concert of power. When all unite to act in the same sense and with the same purpose, all act in the common interest and are free to live their own lives under a common protection. I am proposing government by the consent of the governed; that freedom of the seas which . . . the United States have* urged with the eloquence of those who are the convinced disciples of liberty; and that moderation of armaments which makes of armies and navies a power for order merely, not an instrument of aggression. . . . These are American principles, American policies. . . . They are also the principles and policies of forward-looking men and women everywhere. . . . They are the principles of mankind and must prevail."

The words would echo—sometimes hollowly, sometimes mockingly, sometimes as a rich sad music of loss and regret—down the corridor of years along which Franklin Roosevelt would make his way. But they could have no effect on the immediate event. Germany had made a peace offer on the preceding December 12. It had done so from a position of strength, Austro-German forces having just conquered most of oil-rich, wheat-producing Rumania. The secret German plan had been to encourage Wilson to lead or force the Allies to the conference table, from which the American President would then be excluded, and there impose terms confirming Germany's mastery of the Continent. By the time of Wilson's speech, however, the Allies had replied to the German offer and to Wilson's earlier appeal in such a way as to slam shut every door through which mediation efforts or direct negotiations might proceed. The German admirals and generals, in consequence and at last, had won their long argument against Bethmann-Hollweg and Bernstorff regarding the use of submarines: on January 19, three days before Wilson spoke, Bernstorff had received official notice from his government that unrestricted submarine warfare "in a zone around Great Britain, France, Italy and in the eastern Mediterranean" would begin on February 1. The German ambassador was instructed to inform the American government of this fact on January 31. And Wilson's response to this move had, of course, been already determined by his *Sussex* memorandum of the preceding April.

The inevitable occurred on February 3, 1917. On the afternoon of that day, the President appeared before a joint session of Congress to announce that diplomatic relations with Germany had been severed. The American ambassador, Gerard, was being withdrawn from Berlin; the German ambassador in Washington had been handed his passports.

* The verb choice seems itself reflective of Monroe's memorandum wherein "the U.S." was used as a plural noun ("the U.S. . . . have"). Ordinarily, in earlier statements, Wilson wrote the United States "is" or "has."

II

Franklin Roosevelt was not on hand to witness in person this historic event. He was on an inspection tour of Haiti and Santo Domingo.

From the beginning of his service as Assistant Secretary he had taken a lively interest in Caribbean affairs. A frequent visitor to his office had been the Bryan-appointed Chief of the State Department's Latin American Affairs Division, Boaz W. Long, with whom he discussed Cuban, Haitian, and other Caribbean problems.[5] The discussions could not have been informed by any expert knowledge of the psychology, the economics, the turbulent politics of the Latin countries. Roosevelt possessed none. Neither did Long—a businessman whose single experience of Latin America, prior to his appointment to office as a "good Democrat" deserving of reward, had been through a Mexico City branch of the large commission house which he headed. Nor did Roosevelt's interest have as principal motive an intellectual curiosity about the islands or any strong urge to improve the lot of island natives. No, his primary concern, à la Mahan, was for America's strategic defenses and imperial power. It was greatly intensified by the outbreak of European war. And it focused on Hispaniola, where Haiti and the Dominican Republic were in constant revolutionary turmoil—turmoil encouraged by commercial rivalries between American and European business interests—and where a military strategist must see intervention by any European power as a threat to the strategically vital Panama Canal.

The President and top officials of the State and Navy departments, including Assistant Secretary Roosevelt, had been perturbed in late March, 1915, by news that the French, German, and Italian governments had recognized with suspicious alacrity a newly and precariously established revolutionary regime in Haiti. Perturbation was increased a day or so later when the administration was privately informed that French interests not only had gained control of the National Bank of Haiti but were also plotting with German interests to drive American investors away and then take over a Haitian harbor which the U.S. had been eyeing as a possible naval base. On the face of it, the report was highly dubious—Germany and France were at war with each other at the time—and its source was equally so. The man who presented it in a "Confidential Memorandum" to Secretary of State Bryan was Roger L. Farnham, a longtime business friend of Boaz Long, through whom he became also a friend of Roosevelt. Farnham was a vice-president of the National City Bank of New York, which had investments in Haiti and was eager to augment them. He was an affable, forceful, open-seeming man who had managed to gain the full confidence of the Great Commoner, despite his Wall Street connections, and Bryan promptly passed on to Wilson the gist of the Farnham memorandum, saying that "American interests" were "willing to remain" in Haiti "with a view of purchasing a controlling interest" in the National Bank of Haiti, making it a branch of the New York bank, "provided this Government takes the steps necessary to protect them." Otherwise, Bryan went on, the Americans would be forced to "retire from the field." [6] A prudent skepticism, recognizing Farnham's special pecuniary relationship to Haitian affairs, would have suggested that the accuracy of the banker's ominous tidings, unconfirmed by any official observer, should be carefully tested before any decision to act on them was taken. Instead, the administration promptly chose to do as the banker wished, awaiting only a propitious moment.

This quickly came.

In late July, 1915, the five-month-old Haitian regime, threatened in its turn by insurrection, torture-killed nearly 200 political prisoners in Port-au-Prince. As news of the atrocity spread, a maddened mob swept through the streets, seizing and brutally killing both the governor of the capital city and the President of Haiti. The latter was dragged from a room in the French legation, where he had sought refuge, and literally hacked to pieces. A few days later U.S. marines were landed* to "restore order" and "protect American lives and property," though the Haitian revolutionaries had been very careful not to threaten these last.

By mid-August the U.S. Navy was ruling the country.

The Navy Department, however, was responsible only for the *execution* of Haitian policy—or so Daniels wished to believe; he insisted in his memoirs that "the decisions of policy were made by the State Department, sometimes with and sometimes without consultation or Naval approval." [8] They were decisions highly profitable for National City Bank and the businessmen who were allied with that institution. Against rising native resentment and opposition, a convention empowering the United States to collect Haitian customs and administer Haitian finances for twenty years, or as much longer as the United States deemed necessary, was forced through a puppet Haitian Assembly. The Haitian National Bank, whence issued all Haitian paper currency, did in fact become a property of the National City Bank of New York, and R. L. Farnham, without relinquishing his vice-presidency of that bank, was firmly established as the principal, if unofficial, policy-maker and agent of the State Department in Haitian affairs. A revised Haitian constitu-

---

* This was while Roosevelt was convalescing on Campobello. He wrote Daniels from there: "It is certainly a curious coincidence that as soon as I go away we seem to land marines somewhere." [7]

tion, repealing a former prohibition of alien ownership of Haitian land, was then imposed upon the republic by force, though with a marine-contrived show of popular approval. By mid-1920 the National Rail-ways of Haiti, several sugar mills, some electric light plants, and thou-sands of the most fertile Haitian acres were owned or controlled by U.S. business interests.

Much the same thing for much the same reasons, and to much the same effect (though different business interests were involved), hap-pened simultaneously in the neighboring Dominican Republic. Not until May, 1916, however, did U.S. marines seize control of the capital city there. Moreover, leading Dominican politicians then proved less malleable than were their Haitian counterparts. When the Dominican legislature refused to comply with certain U.S. demands, the whole of Santo Domingo was put, in late November, 1916, "in a state of Military Occupation." It was ruled thereafter by the Navy Department, execu-ting State Department policies, in essentially the same way as Haiti was but directly, openly, with no pretense of local self-government.

Roosevelt thoroughly approved of all these forceful measures, of course, and not solely on grounds of military strategy. He took it for granted that American military rule, conjoined with forward-looking American business enterprise, was uplifting the black French-speaking Haitians, the white Spanish-speaking Dominicans: it was civilizing and democratizing them while improving their material standards of living. Daniels was far less sure of this. The Secretary believed the occupation justified in terms of U.S. security. He applauded the road building "and other improvements" which the occupation forces initiated. But not a few of the State Department decisions which his own department was charged with carrying out seemed to him "tinged with imperialism and . . . high-handed," so that in general the Haitian-Dominican adventure was for him "a bitter pill," as he indicated to Roosevelt at the time. His distaste discouraged his taking a close critical look at the operation's local detail; he was inclined by wishful thinking to accept without ques-tion the reports of the commanders on the scene; and he visibly flinched when, entering the Cabinet Room, he was often loudly hailed by a poker-faced Secretary Lane as "the Emperor of Haiti," his discomfiture naturally adding to the hilarity of his colleagues. He would have been more than willing to transfer the whole of the responsibility for the oper-ation to his Assistant Secretary, had such a transfer been possible.[9]

And Roosevelt would have been more than willing to accept it.

He seized enthusiastically upon a chance to make an inspection tour of the island when Daniels presented this to him at the opening of the new year, 1917. In addition to the Commandant of the Marine Corps,

Major General George Barnett, and the chairman of the U.S. Civil Service Commission, John A. McIlhenny, who would soon resign this post to become American financial adviser to Haiti, he took with him a Harvard classmate, aristocratic Livingston Davis, whom Eleanor was inclined to disparage as a sybaritic "lightweight" but whose gay-hearted companionship her husband thoroughly enjoyed.

They left Washington on January 21, going first to Cuba, an American protectorate at that time, where his former Groton master, George Marvin, now editor of *World's Work*, joined them and where Roosevelt was much impressed by the U.S.-sanctioned Cuban President under whom the country was making "orderly progress" and who was himself "distinctly the gentleman" and a "business man," as Roosevelt wrote in his diary.[10] He obviously gained no inkling of the smoldering discontents which flared into open revolt a few days after the Roosevelt party had left and to which Washington, ascribing the revolt to the machinations of "German agents," responded by sending U.S. troops that remained on the island for five years.

Into the days that followed, in Haiti, Roosevelt, dominating everything in his party but accepting without question the general arrangements and schedules that had been shaped for him, crowded enough speeches (he spoke French to the Haitians), reviews, inspections, banquets, long horseback rides through tropic heat over jungle trails, even mountain climbing, to exhaust his companions while he himself remained seemingly as fresh and full of energy at the end as he had been at the beginning of his tour. In holiday mood he was delighted by virtually every person he met, everything he saw.

Especially was he taken with the colorful "treat-'em-rough" Marine General Smedley Butler. He later told, in a personal account headed "Trip to Haiti and Santo Domingo," how Butler with a mere 18 marines had crawled through a drainpipe into a fort held by some 300 Haitian "bandits" (every native who forcibly opposed the occupation was *ipso facto* a "bandit"), achieving total surprise, after which there "ensued a killing, the news of which put down all insurrections we hope for all time to come." It was evidently a massacre of unarmed or ineffectively armed men (more than 200 Haitians were killed without a single reported Marine casualty), but Roosevelt was full of admiration for the deed. "I was so much impressed by personal inspection of the scene of the exploit," he said, "that I awarded the Medal of Honor to . . . Butler." [11]

And this general who was so efficient a killer of men was an equally efficient builder of roads. Under his command, a highway was constructed from Port-au-Prince to Cap-Haïtien with remarkable speed and at remarkably small expense. The Assistant Secretary, personally viewing the project in its initial stage, derived from the sight a full glow of American pride; and when the project was completed in December, 1917, he would radio a "Well done!" to the general. Butler would then reply with an effusive personal letter to Roosevelt boasting that the "road to date has cost not over $250.00 a mile" (!) and adding, with coy slyness, that "it would not do to ask too many questions as to how we accomplished this." [12] Thus Butler indicated his knowledge that Roosevelt was already privy to the secret and, as a fellow hardheaded realist, was not disturbed by it.

Others would be, however, when the secret, long kept by the strictest kind of local Navy censorship—kept from the Secretary of the Navy himself, it would appear—was at last revealed.

Butler built his roads so cheaply because he employed what amounted to slave labor. Having prevailed upon the puppet Haitian government to invoke an almost forgotten law of *corvée*, an import from the *ancien régime* of France, where it had been a major incitement of the French Revolution, Butler used it as an "excuse for kidnapping thousands of Haitians from their homes" and "forcing them to live for months in camps, insufficiently fed, guarded by Marines, rifles in hand," as journalist Herbert J. Seligman would report in the *Nation* magazine in the summer of 1920. "When Haitians attempted to escape . . . they were shot," Seligman continued, in a report confirmed by other investigators. "I heard ugly whispers in Haiti of the sudden accumulation of funds by American officers of the Haitian Gendarmerie who had the responsibility for providing food for these slave camps." And indeed the Gendarmerie was an organization whose nature rendered plausible the ugliest of whispers concerning it. Established by the Marines to impose "law and order" upon the populace, its rank and file were native and—according to the principle of self-selection inevitably operative in such circumstances—comprised many of the most violent and brutal of all Haitians, including known criminals. Its officers were marines, with Butler as initial commandant, who willingly accepted, if they did not actually volunteer for, this detached duty, and a perhaps disproportionate number of them were Southerners.

Alas for Roosevelt's "hope" that Butler's brave killing of the "bandits" in Fort Rivière would prevent "all insurrections for all time," a large-scale rebellion of Haitians broke out in 1918. Its leader was Charlemagne Peralte, a man of great pride and courage who had held high office in a former Haitian government but whom the Gendarmerie saw fit publicly to humiliate by forcing him, a political prisoner, to work in prison garb as a common convict upon the streets of Cap-Haïtien. He managed to escape. He soon rallied around him thousands of embittered countrymen, who, had they been adequately armed, might well have seized Port-au-Prince and overwhelmed the marines before the latter could be reinforced. As it was, Peralte, until killed from ambush by a marine who sneaked into his camp, proved a dangerous embarrassment to the occupation.

Roosevelt himself would be forced to take responsive action when Peralte raided to within a few miles of the Haitian capital in the spring of 1919. As Acting Secretary, after an urgent State Department appeal, he would then order an additional 400 marines to the island. He also at that time requested from his friend McIlhenny in Port-au-Prince a confidential report on the behavior of the Gendarmerie, whom the Haitian minister in Washington held largely responsible for his country's revolutionary discontent. McIlhenny's reply was predictably reassuring. Whatever wickedness had flawed the Gendarmerie's performance under its former commandant was now cast out, he said, and in any case, Peralte's "bandits" were no longer a serious menace. Roosevelt accepted this with obvious relief and no further checking: his primary concern was to protect the name of the Navy and Marine Corps against besmirchment. "I do not know what was back of all the smoke," he wrote McIlhenny, "but my own guess has been that some people are causing trouble for purely personal reasons. . . ." [13]

Thus, Roosevelt, if aware in a general way of the use of forced labor and willing to close his eyes to it in jovial winks, was enabled to remain unaware of the sickening details of the *corvée*'s operation. He could and doubtless did remain unaware, too, of other sordid elements of the occupation which would be revealed in the series of eyewitness reports—reports by Lewis Gannett and James Welden Johnson, as well as Seligman—published in the *Nation* in the summer of 1920. [14]

Both Seligman and Johnson would assert that 3,000 Haitians, including women and children, had been slaughtered by American machine-gun and rifle fire in five years, as compared with a total American loss of fewer than 20 killed and wounded. Seligman would further assert, and Johnson confirm, that marines habitually called Haitians "gooks," regarded them as subhuman, and often spoke of killing them as a sport (for a time any native suspected of bearing arms was shot on sight); that captured "gooks" were not infrequently "allowed to escape" so that they could be used as moving targets for rifles; that some marines "were themselves sickened by what they had to do"; and that what they "had" to do included the deliberate maltreatment of helpless captives in the process of interrogating them. "I have seen prisoners's faces and heads disfigured by beatings," wrote Seligman, ". . . and have heard officers discussing these beatings; also a form of torture—'sept'—in which the victim's leg is compressed between two rifles and the pressure against the shin increased until agony forced him to speak."

Somewhat less murderous, perhaps because the Dominicans were white, was "The Conquest of Santo Domingo" as described by Lewis Gannett. Here too had been much killing of unarmed or poorly armed people; Dominicans by the hundreds had been shot down in 1916 by Americans whose own losses totaled seven dead, fifteen wounded. Dominican jails and prison camps were crowded with political prisoners, whose maltreatment was common, and an iron military dictatorship, headed first by Captain H. S. Knapp of the USS *Olympia*, promoted rear admiral in 1919, and then by Rear Admiral Thomas Snowden, suppressed all freedom of speech, press, and assembly while preventing the dispatch abroad of any news report that failed to jibe with the "official line."

Roosevelt on Hispaniola in 1917 saw what his hosts wished him to see, which coincided with what he himself wished to see. Personally kind and courteous in all his public and formally social dealings with Haitians, showing (because he felt) no color prejudice whatever, he seems to have made a highly favorable impression on them. He, of course, knew that some Americans were making or hoped soon to make a good deal of money out of this armed intervention, but this did not strike him as reprehensible: he shared in full the prevailing and comforting belief that American business profits, exacted at gunpoint in an alien land, were a just recompense for risks and enterprise that brought "progress" to the island, especially to Haiti. As a matter of fact, he himself, in 1917 and later, considered, in a desultory way, investing some of his family's money in the development of a vacation resort at Sans Souci or in a chain of variety stores across Hispaniola.[15] It was therefore easy for him to become convinced that "ninety-nine percent of the inhabitants were not only satisfied with what has been done for them by the United States," as he told a reporter in mid-February, 1917, "but . . . would look with terror on an abandonment by this country of its interest in their welfare."[16]

Nor would he change his mind about this—at least not in public—after the aforementioned revelations by liberal journalists in a Presidential election year had made U.S. "imperialism" in Haiti-Santo Domingo a topic of heated, if limited, public debate. In 1915 (so he would assert in 1922), 95 percent of the Haitian population lived in a state of primitive savagery "in mud and wattle huts" and Haitian politics was characterized by an "almost unbelievable butchery and barbarism." Upon this awful scene the U.S. Marines had descended as a blessing from heaven. If they made "mistakes" on occasion, if there were instances of injustice or even cruelty, if Butler was fairly ruthless in his use of native labor, all this was as nothing compared to the evils that had theretofore prevailed or compared to the immense popular benefits that had ensued. These last comprised an unprecedented domestic tranquillity enriched by new modern highways, paved streets in leading cities, vastly improved medical and sanitation facilities, and, as others claimed, new schools and great improvements in public education.[17]

(Doubt was cast upon each of these alleged accomplishments by observers who were more disinterested, if not more accurately informed. The proclaimed "tranquillity" was achieved by means of violent repression, these critics said. The new highways, if impressive as engineering feats, were of slight benefit to the great mass of Haitians, who owned no motor transport, and were positive evils to those who lived beside them since the speeding automobiles killed chickens, donkeys, and other livestock. Though much was made of the fact that Port-au-Prince's streets, mudholes in 1915, were all paved by 1920, this was in fact no result of the occupation: the paving contracts had been let and work on them begun before the marines were landed. The health of Haitians in the larger cities was safeguarded by a more rigorous enforcement of certain sanitation regulations, and there had been a great improvement in the public hospital at Port-au-Prince, but the benefits of all this were less than might be supposed because Haiti under native rule, or misrule, had always been an unusually healthy country. As for the alleged improvements in the country's educational facilities, they were wholly mythical. Not a single school had been built, not a single teacher trained, and indeed nothing of any kind had been done by occupation authorities to improve popular education in Haiti.)

III

Certainly no harsh sound of anguish, no ugly sight of violence, no stench of evil assailed the senses of the Assistant Secretary of the Navy on the evening of February 3, 1917. He and his party dined alfresco in a flower-scented courtyard of a centuries-old palace in Santiago, Dominican Republic—guests of the local Marine commandant and his wife. As lanterns swayed above good food and good wine, there was much talk of the morrow, when the Roosevelt party, having just completed a five-

FDR: The Beckoning of Destiny, 1882–1928

Franklin Delano Roosevelt with his wife Eleanor and their children in 1919, while he was Assistant Secretary of the Navy; the children, by age, are Anna, James, Elliott, Franklin D., Jr., and John (Bachrach).

A Son
is Born:
1882

Three-year-old Franklin and "Budgy" go for a donkey ride.

Franklin's parents, Sara Delano and James Roosevelt, in a photograph he took of them at St-Blaise, Switzerland, during the family's trip to Europe in 1896, when he was fourteen.

Springwood, the home overlooking the Hudson River at Hyde Park north of Poughkeepsie, as it looked when Franklin was growing up; it was remodeled to its present appearance in 1915.

(LEFT) Franklin's generation-older half-brother, James Roosevelt Roosevelt, known as "Rosy," with Franklin's Scotty "Sandy" at Hyde Park in 1906. (BELOW) Franklin (right) with Rosy's two children, James R., Jr., known as "Taddy," and Helen, at a house rented in England, Summer 1889.

Theodore Roosevelt, Franklin's idolized "Cousin Theodore" of the Oyster Bay Roosevelts, with his family while in his last year as President, 1908.

Relatives: Father's and Mother's

The Warren Delano clan gathers to celebrate "Papa's" 81st birthday, July 1890. Franklin, his father, his mother, and her father are in the center, surrounded by aunts, uncles, cousins, and "present in spirit only," Sara's dead sister Laura.

Boyhood of a Patrician

Young Franklin and his aristocratic hobbies: (RIGHT-TOP) As a six-year-old, taking the helm in a stiff breeze on the Bay of Fundy. (RIGHT-MIDDLE) Snow-shoeing on a family outing to Loon Lake in the Adirondacks, 1895. (RIGHT-BOTTOM) Romping with "Monk," one of his many dogs, on the Hyde Park grounds, 1898. (BELOW) A life-long camera buff, photographed himself at the Delano home near New Bedford.

Groton: 1896–1900

A shy only son becomes an all-around preppy: (ABOVE) The second-string football player (lower left) shows his pride at having worked his way up from the seventh string, 1899. (LEFT) Franklin in the school play, "The Wedding March," acts "Uncle Bopaddy, a deaf gentleman," and all agree is "very funny." (BELOW) The graduate poses with his parents at their summer home at Campobello Island.

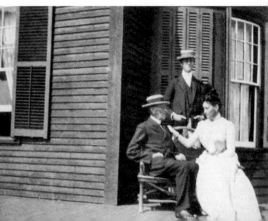

(LEFT) Franklin recuperates from his first year at Harvard by touring Europe with his mother and his cousin, Teddy Robinson, TR's nephew. They arrived home to the news that their famous relative had become President.

(ABOVE) Franklin and his fifth cousin Eleanor, secretly wooed and newly engaged to the shock of his mother, shyly look happy at Campobello, Summer 1904.

(BELOW) F. D. Roosevelt, new President of the Harvard *Crimson,* with its Senior Board, 1904.

Enter,
Eleanor

A Small Family Wedding,

St. Patrick's Day, 1905

Franklin and Eleanor were married in a relative's New York apartment on March 17, 1905. The bride was given away by her uncle Ted, whose inauguration as President they had attended two weeks before. TR was coming to New York to review the St. Patrick's Day parade and wished to give his niece away, so the date was hurriedly arranged. (Unfortunately, no photographs have been found of this eminently photogenic occasion.) The newlyweds spent a week's honeymoon at Hyde Park, then returned to New York for the rest of Franklin's first year at Columbia Law.

(LEFT) In May, Eleanor, Franklin, and his mother paid a visit to the Warren Delano home, "Algonac," at Newburgh, and these two charming photos were taken.

In the summer of 1905 came the proper honeymoon—a grand tour of Europe. Franklin visited model farms and forests, went moor-tramping and mountain-climbing, and photographed everything. (BELOW) Venice, captured in his panoramic camera. Meanwhile, Eleanor stayed behind. (OPPOSITE) They posed together before the Alps, but he went climbing with another woman. (OPPOSITE, TOP) In the Papadopoli Gardens, their matching expressions showed the result.

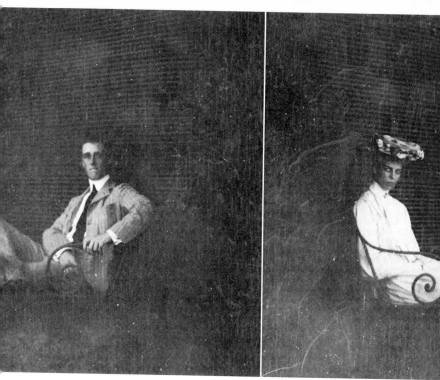

The First Child

On the sea voyage from Europe Eleanor was constantly seasick, and reaching home found she was pregnant. Anna was born in May of 1906, and (BE-LOW) posed the next year with her pleased parents.

On June 18, 1910, former President Theodore Roosevelt and his wife returned from their triumphal tour of Africa and the capitals of Europe. On the cutter that took them from the ship to the Battery were a crowd of well-wishers that included (far right, in front of the funnel) TR's niece Eleanor and her husband, Franklin, then a 28-year-old Wall Street law clerk.—Brown Brothers.

A Start in Life: Education in Albany, 1911–1912

A Republican county finds a Democratic Roosevelt: (BELOW) In this placid-looking sail off Campobello in the summer of 1910, Franklin actually is debating an offer to run for the State Senate, against the opposition of his mother (front, left) and despite the serious illness of his wife (front, right). (RIGHT) The new State Senator in Albany, 1911.

Franklin relaxes wit his family at Campo bello after a six-mont effort on behalf o Woodrow Wilson's non ination as the Demo cratic Presidential car didate, 1912.

1 April of 1912, after e State Senate session d State Democratic onvention, Franklin ok a month's vacation d with his brother-in- w Hall Roosevelt and a low State Senator visi- d the Panama Canal. ormously impressed, made a comprehen- e photographic study it. (RIGHT) His cross- tion of Gatun Locks, m the top of the tem- ary dam.

Assistant Secretary of the Navy, 1913–1920

As a reward for his services, Roosevelt was appointed by President Woodrow Wilson as Assistant Secretary of the Navy under Josephus Daniels. (LEFT) The new official and his wife visit the New York Navy Yard (UPI).

(ABOVE) Flag Day celebration, 1913: speaking before the State, War, and Navy Building is Josephus Daniels, while seated behind him are (L.-R.) Secretary of State William Jennings Bryan, President Woodrow Wilson, Assistant Secretary of War Henry Breckinridge, Assistant Secretary of State William Phillips, and FDR.

(LEFT) While a New York State Senator, FDR had been a leader of the anti-Tammany Democrats. On July 4, 1917, he officially made his peace with his old foes, Charles F. Murphy and John A. Voorhis, at Tammany Hall.

(RIGHT) The Secretary and Assistant Secretary of the Navy are caught looking longingly at the White House.

(OPPOSITE, BOTTOM) The family in the fall of 1917, riding at Hyde Park after the house had been remodeled.

(LEFT) Frustrated at being kept from active service in World War I by being considered indispensable at the Navy Department, FDR persuaded his chief in early 1918 to send him to Europe on an inspection tour of the war zones. Here he dashingly alights from a plane at the U.S. Naval Air Station at Pauillac, France.

(LEFT) The family, com
plete with Sara, look dis
gruntled at Campobello
Summer 1920.

*The
Campaign
of
1920*

In 1920, when the Democrats nominated Governor James M. Cox of
Ohio as their Presidential candidate,
FDR became the logical choice for
Vice President "to balance the
ticket." (ABOVE) The formal notification ceremony at Hyde Park, August 9, 1920. To the candidate's
right are his wife and Josephus
Daniels, President Wilson's daughter Eleanor and her husband William Gibbs McAdoo (Wilson's Secretary of the Treasury), Henry Morgenthau, Jr., Governor Al Smith
and his wife, and George White, the
Democratic National Chairman.
(RIGHT) The Roosevelts set out on
their first campaign trip.

Darkness at Campobello: 1921

(BELOW) FDR with his sons James and Elliott at Campobello in 1920 in their sloop *Vireo*, in which they went sailing on the day the next August that he fell victim to polio. (RIGHT) FDR with his sons Franklin, Jr., and John, in the first photo taken after his illness, 1922.

Return to Politics: 1924

FDR, home at Hyde Park after the 1924 Democratic presidential convention, poses for a unity picture with John W. Davis, winner of the nomination, and (right) Al Smith, the loser despite FDR's dramatic appearance at the convention to give his famous "Happy Warrior" speech (F.P.G.).

In 1928, FDR again nominated Al Smith for the Democratic presidential nomination and this time won. Al Smith then persuaded the still-crippled Roosevelt to run for governor, to carry New York. Thus did Destiny beckon (UPI).

Franklin D. Roosevelt, candidate for governor of New York, sits for a campaign portrait with his family (including Anna's husband) at Hyde Park, 1928.

Fateful Cue—
Fated Respon.
1928

day ride across Haiti, was scheduled to begin a five-day ride from Santiago to Santo Domingo City.

It was a trip destined never to be made. Roosevelt's orderly entered the courtyard as the dinner drew toward its close. He handed his superior a cryptic message from "SECNAV" to "ASTNAV" which Roosevelt read with a mingling of disappointment and anticipatory excitement. "Because of political situation please return to Washington at once," Daniels had written. "Am sending ship to meet you and party at Puerto Plata tomorrow evening." [18]

Since Germany had already announced a renewal of unrestricted submarine warfare, Roosevelt assumed that his summons to Washington meant that war was imminent. After boarding USS *Neptune*, a collier, on the evening of February 4, having by then been informed that Bernstorff had been handed his passports, Roosevelt and his party remained in a state of nervous excitement during three days and four nights of what he later wryly described as "a wild dash north" with "no lights showing, the guns . . . manned and . . . complete air silence." Everyone kept a sharp lookout for German submarines.[19]

Then the letdown: the whole experience became reminiscent of the one Roosevelt had had in August, 1914, when, feeling like Paul Revere, he had rushed down to Washington from Cape Cod.

He disembarked at Fortress Monroe on the morning of February 8. All was calm and peaceful there. The colonel commanding the fortress was aware of no national emergency, was "utterly surprised" by the sense of urgency which animated the Roosevelt party. And the colonel's mood was an accurate reflection of Washington's, as Roosevelt found when he arrived in the capital in the afternoon. He "dashed to the Navy Department," where there was, to his disgust, "no excitement" whatever. As in 1914, his sense of the first importance of concentrating the fleet at the earliest possible moment was shared by none in a position to issue the necessary orders. The warships at Guantánamo, which should by then have been ordered to return to their home yards on the East Coast, remained at the Cuban base. There was nothing Roosevelt could do to move them.

And this was but the first of a series of intensely irritating frustrations for activist Roosevelt during the weeks and months that followed.

Newspapers on February 8 carried a statement by Secretary of State Lansing in response to a request made by P. A. S. Franklin, president of the American (steamship) Line, for government advice on whether or not two of the line's ships should, in view of the German proclamation, be permitted to sail for England. The government could not give such advice, Lansing's statement said. "It, however," Lansing went on, "asserts that the rights of American vessels to traverse all parts of the high seas are the same now as they were prior to the issuance of the German declaration, and that a neutral vessel may, if its owner believes that it is liable to be unlawfully attacked, take any necessary measures to prevent or resist such attack." In other words, Franklin might, with his government's approval, arm his company's vessels for defense against submarine or other attack. But where was he to obtain the needed guns with men trained to handle them? He turned to the Navy Department. Roosevelt had been but a few hours in his office, on the morrow of his return from Hispaniola, when he received from Franklin an urgent plea that the Navy supply not only six-inch guns, but also gun crews for ships which must sail through war zones. The Assistant Secretary was eager to do so. The Navy, he found, possessed a half dozen of the needed unmounted guns. He also discovered an old statute, never repealed, which would permit the requested action to be taken by executive order. He incorporated this information in a memorandum to Daniels and urged the Secretary to take up the matter with the President. Daniels then enclosed Roosevelt's memorandum with one of his own, addressed to the White House, on February 10.[20]

Wilson, however—though hotly pressed to do so by most of his Cabinet, especially by Houston, Lane, and McAdoo—refused to issue the desired order. He clung desperately to the wishful belief that Germany, despite its proclamation, would avoid pressing its U-boat action to the point of forcing a U.S. declaration of war. He was in any case determined to commit no overt act which might be judged by the Germans, or by history, as a justification for retaliatory hostilities. Moreover, as President, sworn to uphold the Constitution of the United States, he had, he felt, no moral right to assume through legal trickery a warmaking authority which the Founding Fathers had very properly vested in the Congress. Instead, Wilson prepared reluctantly to ask Congress for specific authority to arm merchant ships.

There then came a disclosure of German duplicity which at first utterly dumbfounded the President and subsequently, when thoroughly authenticated, virtually destroyed his last lingering hope for peace. On February 24, through Ambassador Page in London, he received a copy of a telegram that had been dispatched by German Foreign Secretary Arthur Zimmermann* to the German minister in Mexico on the preceding January 19—a telegram that had been intercepted and decoded by

* Zimmermann had replaced Gottlieb von Jagow as Foreign Secretary in late November, 1916.

British Intelligence. It informed Germany's minister of Berlin's decision to commence "unrestricted U-boat war" on February 1. If this brought the United States into the conflict, Zimmermann went on, "we propose Mexico an alliance upon the following terms: Joint conduct of war. Joint conclusion of peace . . . and an agreement on our part that Mexico shall gain back by conquest the territory lost by her at a prior period in Texas, New Mexico, and Arizona." The German minister to Mexico was also instructed to suggest that Mexican President Carranza "mediate between ourselves and Japan" so that Japan could switch from the Allied to the German-Mexican side of the conflict and "take part at once" against America.

In the face of this, Wilson went ahead with his plan to ask Congress for emergency powers with which to implement a policy of "armed neutrality," especially the arming of merchantmen. He did so in an address to a joint session on February 26. The requested legislation was promptly introduced in both House and Senate. Two days later he released the Zimmermann telegram for publication in the morning papers of March 1. On the crest of the wave of fury which at once swept through Congressional halls, the armed ships bill rode to victory in the House by a vote of 403 to 13 before that day had ended.

The story was different in the Senate.

Favored by an overwhelming Senate majority, the measure was adamantly opposed by a handful, of whom (to Roosevelt's immense disgust) O'Gorman was one. Four of these opponents managed to take and hold the Senate floor, blocking all decisive action, from the morning of March 3 until the Sixty-fourth Congress came to its constitutional end at noon of the following day. The four were La Follette of Wisconsin, George W. Norris of Nebraska, Albert B. Cummins of Iowa, and A. J. Gronna of North Dakota, and Wilson was seething with anger against them when, a few minutes after the Senate's adjournment sine die, he was unceremoniously sworn in for his second term. (March 4, 1917, was a Sunday; the formal inauguration was therefore postponed till March 5.) A few hours later the President issued a public statement excoriating the four obstructionists as a "little group of willful men, representing no opinion but their own," who had "rendered the great Government of the United States helpless and contemptible" amid a "crisis of extraordinary peril."

Roosevelt shared to the fullest extent this bitter view. Wilson's expression of it made a far greater impression on him and on the general public than did the noble phrases of the Second Inaugural Address, delivered next day. The latter, in fact, made no impression at all upon the Assistant Secretary at the moment of their utterance. The day of the formal ceremonies, following two days of heavy rain, was gloomy, wet, and cold. The President shivered in a raw wind as he stood upon the platform at the Capitol's east front. (He would be forced to bed by a heavy cold a few days later.) And that same wind whipped most of his words away before Roosevelt, seated far from the platform, could hear them. The address aroused "little enthusiasm" in the crowd of 40,000, Roosevelt observed; it aroused none at all in himself when, hours later, he perused it in the newspapers.[21]

For by March, 1917, the war issue had blotted out all else in his conception of public life and duty; he had grown as impatient with Wilson's basic attitudes, as angrily irritated with Wilson's reluctance to act, as he had long been with Daniels'.

His closest personal affinities of feeling and thought were now definitely with the most active, vociferous enemies of Wilsonian Democracy—with Robert R. "Bertie" McCormick, for one, the publisher of the Chicago *Tribune* whom he had known as a schoolboy at Groton, to whom he had long fed information and advice on the "line" which that notably reactionary organ should take in its advocacy of naval Preparedness, and with whom he was on the most cordial of "Dear Bert-Dear Frank" terms. When he talked off the record to the Eighty-fifth Convention of Harvard's Fly Club, in Baltimore, four days before Wilson's second inauguration, he was as vehemently critical of the administration's defense and foreign policy as were arch-Republican Medill McCormick and "Gussie" Gardner, both of whom also addressed the meeting. When he dined at the Metropolitan Club in New York City on the weekend following the inauguration, he found himself in complete rapport with his Wilson-hating table companions—J. P. Morgan, TR, General Wood, and Elihu Root, among others. During that dinner, as he recorded in his diary next day, there was discussion "of 1 how to make Administration steer clear course to uphold rights 2 how to get active increase army & navy," from which issued an agreed decision "to use Governors' Conference to demand this." He further recorded that when Root displayed an inclination "to praise Administration's present course," TR objected that there should be "less indorsement of past" and "more vigorous demand about future course." Added Roosevelt: "I backed T.R.'s theory. . . ."[22]

He may or may not have known that Colonel House, in cahoots with the second Mrs. Wilson and a New York stock market speculator named Bernard Baruch, had tried in typically secret and devious ways, during the spring and summer of 1916, to force Daniels' dismissal or resignation from the Cabinet. He certainly *did* know that the confidential colonel had no love for "the good Josephus" (so House contemptuously dubbed him), that the Navy Secretary thoroughly disliked and distrusted the colonel, and that the latter, strongly pro-Ally, now threw all the weight of his influence with the President on the side of immediate U.S. entrance into the war. Hence, it required less of daring than of disloyalty for Roosevelt to complain to House privately of "J.D.'s procrastination" and Admiral William S. Benson's "dislike of England" (Benson was Chief of Naval Operations)—an alleged combination of lethargy and narrow prejudice which resulted in a most lamentable "failure to make plans with France & England & study their methods." [23]

He himself, according to his own account of his activities during this period, pressed far beyond his legal authority to get the Navy ready for imminent war.*

In the preceding fall, when Daniels was devoting most of his energies to the election campaign and Roosevelt in consequence was Acting Secretary often for days at a time, Louis Howe, as the Assistant Secretary's alter ego, had taken a great chance in the purchase of sodium nitrate from Chile for use in gunpowder manufacture. [24] He had bypassed the single American company which, because of the way in which Navy specifications had been drawn up, had a monopoly upon the import of this commodity and was charging an excessive price for it. He had also bypassed the State Department. In violation of several of the sternest government regulations, he had gone personally to the Chilean embassy and there negotiated on his own highly dubious authority a contract to buy 5,000,000 pounds of nitrate direct from the government of Chile, waiving all specifications, at a price considerably below that demanded by the American commercial importer. He and Roosevelt had already instituted the practice of using Navy colliers to transport to the United States purchases made abroad, thus saving hundreds of thousands of dollars in shipping costs, and it was by collier that the purchased nitrate was moved from the Chilean port of Antofagasta to Norfolk, Virginia. Howe arranged to have it tested immediately upon its arrival. Had it failed to meet specifications, he would have been in serious trouble. It didn't, however. It turned out to be "the finest nitrate ever shipped to the United States," as Howe was informed by telephone. Roosevelt's reputation for bold red-tape-slashing efficiency was thus augmented.

There was evidently a splurge of this kind of gambling on the part of

---

* Daniels privately resented but did not publicly contradict later published statements by Roosevelt implying that the latter's procurement activities were undertaken without Daniels' knowledge. In his diary, February 2, 1920, he recorded that Admiral Ralph Earle, chief of Navy Ordnance, had assured him (in response to Daniels' question) that "all orders had been made after conference by me."

Roosevelt and Howe immediately following Roosevelt's return from his tour of Haiti. ". . . I took the chance of authorizing certain large expenditures before Congress had actually appropriated money," Roosevelt would confess, or boast, in 1920. "I felt confident that Congress would pass the emergency appropriations for which we asked." In March, 1919, he would be quoted in the Boston *Globe* as saying that he and his fellow Navy activists had, between February 6 and March 4, 1917, "committed acts for which we could be, and may yet be sent to jail for 999 years. We spent millions . . . which we did not have—forty millions on one contract for guns alone to be placed on ships to fight subs. We had only 100 ships and 1,000 were needed. . . . We went to those whom we had seen in advance and told them to enlarge their plants and send us the bills." [25]

Simultaneously, his personal relations with his immediate superior became strained almost to the breaking point. Daniels would later speak of experiencing "the agony of a Gethsemane . . . in the first four months of 1917." Roosevelt's "agony" was of a wholly different kind during those same months. He suffered no anguish of crucial moral choice, no pain of indecision in the face of fatal challenge. He *knew* what must be done. He had absolute confidence in his ability to perform the role assigned him by the Author of the script. His suffering arose altogether from the frustration of his impulse to act—from his sense that the Author's text was being corrupted by the administrative consequences of the President's and the Navy Secretary's troubled consciences.

Sometime during the first week of March, by his own account, on a day when he was Acting Secretary, he went to the White House to plead with Wilson for permission to "bring the Fleet back from Guantánamo" and send the ships to yards where they could be prepared—"cleaned and fitted out"—for war. Wilson said no flatly. Roosevelt continued to press until Wilson again said no, this time with a curtness tantamount to rebuke. But as the young man started to leave the room, the President called him back. "I owe you an explanation," said Wilson, and proceeded to give one which, if unpersuasive at the time, would be a vividly meaningful memory of Roosevelt's a quarter century later. Wilson said that having "tried every diplomatic means to keep out of the war," he was determined now to do nothing "by way of war preparations" that "would allow the definitive historian" of the future to say that the United States "had committed an unfriendly act against the Central Powers." He wanted history "to show that war has been forced upon us deliberately by Germany." [26] All of which mollified Roosevelt only to the extent of its indication that the question in the President's mind was no longer *whether* the United States should go to war but, instead, when and how it should do so. The question's answer, however, was so perfectly obvious to Roosevelt that he continued to be exasperated with the President's failure to act upon it.

He made not the slightest effort to understand in any sympathetic way the reasons why Wilson and Daniels were so reluctant to accept the inevitable. The President and his Navy Secretary were drawn close together at this time. Wilson confided in Daniels as in none other of the "official family." Back in January, for instance, following a Cabinet meeting in which Daniels had stood firmly beside the President against those who argued vehemently for war, Wilson had talked with rare intimacy to him about what going to war must "inevitably" do, in his opinion, to the American body politic. He feared that "every reform we have won since 1912 will be lost." He mentioned the new currency, tariff, shipping, and trust legislation, saying that these had not yet had time enough to become "thoroughly set" as national policy and were therefore vulnerable, in case of war, to destruction or serious distortion by hostile special interests. "We will be dependent in war upon steel, oil, aluminum, ships, and war materials," he went on, according to Daniels' diary. "They are controlled by Big Business. Undoubtedly many captains of industry will be patriotic and serve the country, but when the war is over those whose privileges we have uprooted or started to uproot will gain control of government and neither you nor I will live to see government returned to the people. Big Business will be in the saddle. More than that—free speech and other rights will be endangered. War is autocratic." [27]

This last point was later stressed by Wilson in private talk with Frank Cobb, editor of the New York *World.* "Once lead this people into war," said the President to the newspaperman, "and they'll forget there ever was such a thing as tolerance. To fight you must be brutal and ruthless, and the spirit of ruthless brutality will enter into the very fabric of our national life, infecting Congress, the courts, the policeman on the beat, the man in the street." Moreover, U.S. entrance into the war would destroy any chance of that "peace without victory" which Wilson continued to believe prerequisite to the construction of a just, permanently peaceful world order. Germany would be beaten "so badly . . . that there would be a dictated peace." It would be dictated in accordance with "war standards"—there would be "no bystanders with sufficient power to influence the terms"; there would be no "peace standards left to work with" [28]—and so it was bound to be a temporary peace, a mere truce, fatally flawed by the vindictiveness of the victors and the hatred this provoked in the vanquished.

Such considerations weighed not at all in Roosevelt's calculations.

IV

And in Wilson's own mind, they were offset by others which, in the rush of events through the first weeks of March, gained rapidly in weight.

On March 8, the newly created Federal Reserve Board—of which Roosevelt's maternal uncle Frederic A. Delano was vice-governor; of which Roosevelt's good "supper club" friend Adolph C. Miller was member—learned that Allied gold reserves approached total exhaustion, that it was simply impossible for Britain to continue shipping gold to this country in cash payment for purchased goods, and that an earlier board warning against unsecured loans to the Allies by private investors had come close to drying up British credit in America.

Simultaneously, the rate of U-boat sinkings rose sharply. The full extent of the losses was not revealed by London to Washington, but there was no hiding the fact that ships were going down by the score every week and that American goods piled up in American ports because unarmed merchantmen refused to sail into the ever-more-dangerous seas.

The Wilson administration's response to this was twofold. First, the Federal Reserve Board issued a statement designed to encourage private purchases of Allied securities by implying that the U.S. government would take whatever action was necessary to protect such investments. Second, the President effected by executive order, on March 12, what the Senate's "little group of willful men" had prevented—namely, the arming of U.S. merchantmen with Navy guns and gun crews. ("White House statement that W has power to arm & *inference* that he will use it," wrote Roosevelt irritably in his diary on March 9. "J.D. says he will by Monday. Why doesn't the President say so without equivocation[?]." [29])

Three days later, on March 15, came news that the czarist regime in Russia, always an acute embarrassment to those who claimed the Allies fought for freedom against despotism, had been overthrown by liberals who sought to establish a constitutional democracy, while promising to continue the fight, though now for "democratic" aims, against the Central Powers. As soon as this news was authenticated, Wilson prepared to extend formal diplomatic recognition.* He could not but feel that a

* The United States recognized the new regime on March 22—the first nation to do so.

major moral or ideological obstacle to U.S. participation in the war had been removed.

Then, on Sunday, March 18, came news that German submarines had sunk three American ships within the preceding forty-eight hours, two of them without warning and one of these two with heavy loss of life. After this, there could be no slightest doubt that the German government was determined to press the U-boat war to the utmost, regardless of what the United States might do. On March 20, TR issued a statement saying that there was no longer "any question about 'going to war'" since Germany was obviously "already at war with us." The only remaining question, said TR, was "whether we shall make war nobly or ignobly." About 600 leading Eastern Republicans, including Charles Evans Hughes and Elihu Root, meeting in the Union League Club in New York City that day, thoroughly agreed. They adopted a resolution saying so.

Even now, however, there was no irresistible demand for war on the part of the American people as a whole. The peace movement, led by Bryan, David Starr Jordan, Jane Addams, and Socialist Eugene V. Debs, increased rather than slackened its efforts against intervention. The Midwest remained generally opposed to war, and Wilson himself, on March 20, took note of the fact that, while the East seethed with bitterness and indignation against Germany, much of the rest of the country seemed "apathetic." In New York City on that same day, Colonel House, talking confidentially with the British naval attaché, Captain Guy Gaunt, said that the response of Congress remained "uncertain" and there was anxiety in the administration "about danger of cooling down of public feeling." [30]

It was precisely such cooling down, of course, that Wilson had always stressed as a prerequisite to wise decision-making. Only by applying a refrigerant intellectualism to his own fervent feelings, then channeling them by ruthless logic into a pattern of idealism that was itself sustained by his deepest and highest emotions, had he been able to shape and act upon his conviction that a stalemated war would better serve the interests of his country and the future of all mankind than could a military victory by either side. And at this juncture, every bit of solid evidence at his disposal indicated that the war *was* stalemated. (Not until later would he learn that U-boats were achieving such destruction of Allied shipping as must bring England to its knees in a few months, if it continued; that both France and England now dug deep into the last stockpiles of flesh and blood with which they could fuel the war machine; and that the Russian Revolution had barely begun its course and would soon be captured by doctrinaire Bolsheviks, whose first major act would be to take Russia out of the war. Many hundreds of thousands of German and Austrian troops would be thereby freed for transfer to the west.) All clear indications were that the balance of power would remain much the same in the autumn as it now was, the only difference being that the antagonists might by then be forced by mutual exhaustion to negotiate what Wilson had repeatedly called for—namely, a "peace without victory," a "peace among equals." And certainly Wilson's expressed personal attitude, on March 20, was that of a man who had yet a choice between immediate full belligerency and a trial of the "armed neutrality" which he had finally implemented barely a week before.

March 20 was a Tuesday. The President met with his Cabinet, in regular session, that afternoon.[31] He had already, on March 9, summoned the new Congress to meet in extra session on April 16, having been forced to do so by the failure of the Sixty-fourth Congress, because of the "armed ships" controversy, to pass essential appropriation bills. He now placed before his Cabinet two questions: First, should he ask Congress to assemble at an earlier date? Second, what should he ask Congress to do? He called in turn upon the Secretary of the Treasury, the Secretary of Agriculture, the Secretary of Commerce, the Secretary of War, the Secretary of State, the Secretary of Labor, the Attorney General, the Postmaster General. Each of these, in his turn and way, expressed the conviction that Congress should be assembled at the earliest possible moment and asked to declare war on the Central Powers. Then the President turned to the Secretary of the Navy.

"Well, Daniels?" he said.

An intense hush fell upon the room. The response of every other Cabinet member to recent events had been generally predictable; that of the Navy Secretary was not. And all felt that a change of mind on his part—a shift away from Bryan pacifism—would have a wide significance.

For a long moment, Daniels was unable to speak. When at last he did, his voice trembled, his eyes filled with tears. He said that, in the circumstances, he could see no alternative to the course the others had urged. He had "hoped and prayed" that this black hour would not come, but the imperial German government seemed bound and determined to force it upon us, "do what we will." And so, as he wrote long afterward in his memoirs, "after a . . . conflict that had torn me for months . . . I gave my voice and vote for war."

The Secretary of the Interior, last of the Cabinet to speak, then added his predictable vote for war.

"Well, gentlemen, . . . there is no question what your advice is," said the President coolly. "I thank you."

*   *   *

What went on in Woodrow Wilson's mind during those crucial hours? *

We may be sure that a major factor in his decision, outweighing at last his dark fears of what war would do to the American way of life, was his forced conclusion that he could play an important part in the making of the peace, could work effectively to realize his dream of a democratic world order sustained through a league of nations, *only* if the United States became an active ally. Jane Addams had visited him in the White House on February 28, as one of a delegation from the Emergency Peace Federation, and had then heard him say that "as head of a nation participating in the war, [he] . . . would have a seat at the peace table, but that if he remained the representative of a neutral country he could at best only 'call through a crack in the door.' " [32] Such motivation was, of course, far from being wholly selfless: it was conjoined with no small ego, no dearth of imperious will.

We may be sure, too, that the Zimmermann telegram played its part in finally convincing him that the imperial German government was wholly dominated by a ruthlessly and limitlessly aggressive Junker militarism which must menace world peace, justice, and freedom for as long as it remained in power. He expressed to Colonel House, at this time, his belief "that no real peace was possible so long as the Prussian ideals remained."

Undoubtedly he was impressed by the closely reasoned lawyer's brief in favor of immediate American participation which the Secretary of State presented to him in a letter on the morning of March 20—especially by closing words that had been shrewdly chosen and artfully arranged in the light of Lansing's knowledge of the Wilsonian mentality, the Wilsonian temperament. "It is my belief," Lansing had written, "that the longer we delay in declaring against the military absolutism which menaces the rule of liberty and justice in the world, so much the less will be our influence in the days when Germany will need a merciful and unselfish foe." He had carefully added that his views were "in no way influenced by any bitterness of feeling toward Germany or by any conscious emotion awakened by recent events." He had earnestly "tried to view the situation coldly, dispassionately and justly." [33]

Finally, underlying all the conscious elements of Wilson's mind, there

---

* Writes Winston S. Churchill in his *The World Crisis, 1916–18* (abridged and revised edition, page 680): ". . . it seems no exaggeration to pronounce that the action of the United States with its repercussions on the history of the world depended, during the awful period of Armageddon, upon the workings of this man's mind and spirit to the exclusion of almost every other factor. . . ." This *does* seem an exaggeration to the present writer, but certainly what went on in Wilson's mind was important to history.

must have been a feeling of driven helplessness, an all-pervasive sense of lost control over events that now carried him beyond the last brink of apparent choice. He was hurled willy-nilly into the abyss. All that now remained for him was to try with every ounce of his strength to salvage something of basic value, something alive and capable of growth into a new and better world, out of the blood-soaked wreckage of the nineteenth century. *God helping me, I can do no other!*

At any rate, it seems clear in retrospect that Woodrow Wilson had already made his decision when the Cabinet met and that the unanimity of his advisers' opinion merely confirmed it. Within minutes after the session ended, he asked Daniels to consult with the Navy's General Board (it now met again, regularly*) on the best means of defense against submarines, and when Daniels reported to him the General Board's conclusion that there was *no* effective defense, he on that same March 20 ordered Daniels to arrange for confidential liaison with the British Admiralty to work out, initially, the "best routes to be followed" and the "safest possible approach" to British ports by ships sailing from the United States. (Daniels, in consultation with Roosevelt, decided to send to London, as liaison officer, Rear Admiral William S. Sims, president of the Naval War College at Newport—an aggressively opinionated, tactlessly outspoken Anglophile for whom the Secretary had small personal liking but whom he recognized as a highly effective professional, with "attractive qualities which drew young men to him.") Wilson also summoned the Council of National Defense to meet three days hence—the council having already made a major move toward war industrial mobilization by establishing, on March 17, a Munitions Standards Board—and took other steps leading definitely toward full-scale belligerency.[34]

On the following day, March 21, he made his purpose clear to all who knew of the Tuesday Cabinet discussion—and most of the country knew, since the gist of it had, through some unknown "leak," been accurately reported in the press. He called Congress into special session on April 2 "to receive a communication concerning grave matters of national policy."

V

Everyone in the city, it seemed, was determined to witness in person the historic event, and at first it appeared unlikely that the Assistant

* See pages 331–332.

Secretary of the Navy could obtain a seat in the House chamber for his wife. He finally did so, however. The two were tense with excitement when, early on that Monday evening, they left the pleasant house at 2131 R Street where they now lived,* entered their chauffeured automobile, and were driven to the Capitol. A light rain was falling. Pale shapes of mist drifted ghostlike along chill dark streets.[35]

But the House chamber was warm and brilliantly lighted as members of the Senate, received formally as guests by the Speaker, entered. Then filed in the Justices of the Supreme Court, to be seated in a half-circle before the Speaker's dais. Finally, at precisely 8:32 P.M., the President of the United States arrived.

Everyone stood up, applauding, and many cheered as Woodrow Wilson made his way to the lectern. He was darkly clothed. He seemed taller and thinner than ever before. His face was pale and unsmiling as he waited for the ovation to end.

And when, after three minutes or so, absolute silence fell, he did not even look at his audience but kept his gaze fixed upon the reading copy of his speech, which he had received from the hand of the Public Printer only a few hours before. He began his speech in a rather low, matter-of-fact tone.

"I have called the Congress into extraordinary session," he said, "because there are serious, very serious, choices of policy to be made. . . ."

Swiftly, succinctly he reviewed the submarine controversy. He asserted that the "German submarine warfare . . . is a warfare against mankind," that "armed neutrality, it now appears, is impracticable," and that the alternative choice of "submission" was one "we cannot make."

Then the crucial words:

"With a profound sense of the solemn and even tragical character of the step I am taking and of the grave responsibilities which it involves . . . I advise that the Congress declare the recent course of the Imperial German Government to be in fact nothing less than war against the Government and people of the United States; that it formally accept the status of belligerent which has thus been forced upon it. . . ."

Nearly all in the chamber, Franklin and Eleanor Roosevelt among them, rose to their feet, following the lead of Chief Justice Edward D. White, a Confederate veteran of the War Between the States, who had been long zealous in the Allied cause and down whose furrowed cheeks great tears now rolled. They clapped, shouted, stamped their feet,

* The N Street house of Auntie Bye (Mrs. Cowles), crowded by a family with four children, was overcrowded by a family with five. In the fall of 1916, some six months after the birth of John Aspinwall, the Roosevelt youngest, the family moved to the considerably larger R Street house.

caught up by such a storm of emotion as had seldom, if ever, before swept through that chamber.

Woodrow Wilson stood tall upon the dais, still pale, still unsmiling. He waited in seeming impassivity for the storm to subside.

"We have no quarrel with the German people," he said, when he could be heard again. "We have no feeling towards them but one of sympathy and friendship." Our quarrel was with the German government, a small group of privileged, powerful, ambitious men accustomed to using their fellow human beings as tools and pawns; our object was "the ultimate peace of the world and . . . the liberation of its peoples, the German peoples included." All nations "great and small" and all men everywhere have the right "to choose their way of life and of obedience," he said, and it was for this right that the United States would now fight.

"The world must be made safe for democracy," he said.

His wonderfully vibrant voice then throbbed and sang its way through some hundreds of other noble words, some dozens of other noble phrases. The emotions of his audience were lifted to the highest plane of self-sacrificial idealism by the time he reached, a half hour after he had begun to speak, his peroration.

"It is a fearful thing to lead this great peaceful people into war, into the most terrible and disastrous of all wars, civilization itself seeming to be in the balance," he said. "But the right is more precious than peace, and we shall fight for the things which we have always carried nearest our hearts,—for democracy, for the rights of those who submit to authority to have a voice in their own Governments, for the rights and liberties of small nations, for a universal dominion of right by such a concert of free peoples as shall bring peace and safety to all nations and make the world itself at last free. To such a task we can dedicate our lives and our fortunes, everything that we are and everything that we have, with the pride of those who know that the day has come when America is privileged to spend her blood and her might for the principles that gave her birth and happiness and the peace which she has treasured."

He looked up and out over the heads of his breathless audience.

"God helping her," he closed, "she can do no other." *

La Follette of Wisconsin stood motionless, his arms ostentatiously folded high across his chest, a "sardonic smile" upon his face (he was chewing gum), but around him surged a cheering, applauding throng.

---

* *"Ich kann nicht anders* [I can do no other]," said Martin Luther, refusing to recant in 1518, as Mark Sullivan points out in Vol. 5 of his *Our Times* (New York, 1933).

The Roosevelts' friend Senator Lodge approached the President as the latter was leaving the dais. Grasping the Presidential hand, the frostily aristocratic Bostonian spoke with rare warmth to one whom he had long hated with a bitter personal hatred.

"Mr. President," said Senator Lodge, "you have expressed in the loftiest manner possible the sentiments of the American people." [36]

No greater tribute could have been paid the power of Wilson's oratory.

As for Franklin Roosevelt, he returned home with Eleanor—who had "listened breathlessly," who remained "half-dazed by the sense of impending change"—and there wrote out a comment on the speech for release to the newspapers. In evident, if poor, imitation of Wilsonian eloquence, he wrote that "no statement about American national honor and high purpose more clear or more definite . . . could be made. It will be an inspiration to every true citizen no matter what his political faith, no matter what his creed, no matter what the country of his origin." [37]

Senate debate on the war resolution began in the morning of Wednesday, April 4, and continued far into the night. Only 5 Senators raised their voices against it—La Follette, Gronna, Norris (". . . upon the command of gold . . . we are about to put the dollar sign upon the American flag"), Stone of Missouri (". . . to prevent [this mistake] . . . I would gladly lay down my life"), Vardaman of Mississippi. Only 6 voted against it (the sixth was Lane of Oregon) while 82 voted for it when it won Senate adoption in the last hour of the day. In the House, 20 Representatives spoke against it, led by Claude Kitchin of North Carolina, chairman of the Ways and Means Committee, while some 80 spoke in favor of it; and the House vote, taken shortly after three o'clock in the morning of Good Friday, April 6, 1917, was 373 for, 50 against.

Some ten hours later, at about one twenty in the afternoon, Daniels' naval aide, Byron McCandless, ran out of the Executive Offices of the White House and, on the White House lawn, stood with arms upraised in a prearranged signal to a Navy officer posted at one of the department's windows. The President had just signed the War Resolution and would shortly issue the formal proclamation of a state of war.

Within minutes the news had been flashed to every Navy ship and shore installation.

Soon thereafter, a message went to every flagship, signed by Josephus Daniels: "Mobilize for war in accordance with Department's confidential mobilization plan of March 21st." [38]

Sixteen

➤➤➤×◄◄◄

Of Desk Warfare and a Secret Passion

I

THE SCRIPT, as Roosevelt had theretofore understood it, called now for his resignation as Assistant Secretary. He must don the uniform of an officer in the U.S. Navy, enter combat at the earliest possible moment, then perform such brave deeds as would make him a national hero by war's end. And this course was immediately urged on him, with great personal force, by none other than the man whose public career was the model for his own.

TR was now fifty-nine years old, blind in one eye, his hearing impaired, his general health undermined by the strains and injuries and fevers he had suffered during an exploratory expedition up a wild Brazilian river three years before. But his martial ardor was in no wise diminished. He wished to raise, for transport to France before summer ended, a volunteer division of infantry, of which one brigade would be cavalry, certain other units would be "mounted infantry," and he himself would be commanding general. His proposal had received no encouragement from Secretary of War Baker, with whom he had been in correspondence on the matter since early February.* Nevertheless, he was in Washington on the day war was declared, determined to persuade or, through public opinion, force the administration to grant his wish. When Franklin Roosevelt, with Eleanor, visited him in the home of his daughter, Alice Longworth, where he was staying, they found him so full of his project that he could talk of little else. He did, however, intersperse excited talk about his own plans with emphatic and succinct advice to his nephew-in-law.

---

* At one point, after Baker had stated that top commanders of any "volunteer forces" were to be "drawn from the regular army," TR was moved to remind the Secretary that he, TR, was "a retired Commander-in-Chief of the United States Army and eligible for any position of command over American troops. . . ."

"You must resign," said TR to Franklin Roosevelt. "You must get into uniform at once!"

It was admonitory advice that would be reiterated again and again in the months ahead ("Uncle Ted was always urging Franklin to resign," Eleanor told Frank Freidel long afterward),[1] and the younger man was eager to follow it. He would soon let Daniels and the White House know of his eagerness. But he was destined to be frustrated in this endeavor by essentially the same hard fact against which TR's last hope of martial glory was now dashed to bits—namely, that this was a machine war whose outcome depended far more upon huge organization and the abilities of an efficient administrator than it did upon battlefield heroics. As Woodrow Wilson put it, the "business now in hand is undramatic, practical, and of a scientific definiteness and precision"; there was no room in it for such brave shows as the legendary charge up San Juan Hill. Indeed, there was little room for any truly *personal* heroism on fields churned by shells, swept by machine-gun fire, strung with barbed wire, and flooded by poison gas nor on seas where the principal weapon of attack was an intricate underwater machine designed for furtiveness, sneak approaches, and indiscriminate slaughters from ambush.

On April 7, Franklin Roosevelt went to the office of the Secretary of War and told Baker how anxious TR was for conference with him, whereupon (at Roosevelt's suggestion) Baker called upon the ex-President at the Longworth mansion, where he listened, amiably but noncommittally, to TR's argument. A day or so later, humbling himself as never before in his life, the ex-President went to the White House to make a personal plea to the President of the United States—an interview outwardly cordial on the part of both men, but inwardly tense with dislike, resentment, distrust. Wilson, pointedly remarking that the war on the western front was no "Charge of the Light Brigade," told TR of the administration's plan for a conscript army to be raised under a "selective service" law ("selective service" was deemed psychologically more acceptable than "draft") and officered at all the higher echelons by Army professionals. TR promised to support the required legislation. But, he went on, this did not obviate the need for a volunteer division, swiftly formed and sent abroad as an earnest of our intention. "I could arouse the belief that America is coming," he urged; "I could show the Allies what was on the way." * Wilson said he would give the proposal

---

* TR's plea was echoed and amplified by none other than Georges Clemenceau, soon to become Premier of France. In a greatly publicized open letter to Wilson, Clemenceau said that among Frenchmen, TR's was "the one name which sums up the beauty of American intervention" and urged the President to "send . . . Roosevelt" as an inspiration to the "soldiers of France."[2]

careful consideration. When TR returned to the Longworths, he was "in a very unhappy mood," as Eleanor later recalled. He sensed "that his proposal was not going to be accepted." [3]

And it wasn't.

General John J. Pershing, named commander of the American Expeditionary Force in early May, wanted none of TR in his theater—and none of TR's politically ambitious friend Leonard Wood either. Aloof, austere, single-mindedly and coldly ambitious, as rigidly martial in character as in appearance, Pershing had been commander of a punitive expedition into Mexico, chasing, though never catching, Pancho Villa after that erstwhile lieutenant of Carranza's had made a murderous raid upon Columbus, New Mexico, in March, 1916. He was a comparatively junior officer (some five major generals outranked him at the time of his elevation), hence more jealous of his authority than he might otherwise have been, and he had reason to fear the effect upon his command efficiency of so imperious and irrepressible a "subordinate" as TR was bound to be. But Pershing had also larger reasons. "There could be no experimenting with volunteer commanders, no matter how great their valor, how pure their motives, or how eminent their positions in the nation," wrote Joe Tumulty three years later. "To make an exception of Colonel Roosevelt would have been to strike at the heart of the whole design." [4] Pershing thoroughly agreed.

As for Wilson, in whose view the "Roosevelt Division" would have been an anachronism as politically dangerous as it was militarily absurd, he was convinced his duty required of him an absolute support of the AEF commander. And to this conviction was evidently joined as motivating force a vindictive self-righteousness. It pleased him to reject TR's plea in a way coldly calculated to inflict a maximum of hurt upon the colonel personally and upon the colonel's popular image. (TR was desolated. "I think the decision was a bitter blow from which he never quite recovered," remembered Eleanor.) He, the President of the United States, would like to pay TR the "compliment" of a volunteer division, he said in published statement, but "this is not the time for compliment or for any action not calculated to contribute to the immediate success of the war." [5]

He was kinder but no less emphatic in his rejction of Franklin Roosevelt's wish for combat service. He reverted to the principle of "selective service." "Neither you nor I nor Franklin Roosevelt has the right to select the place of service . . . ," he said to Daniels, because that "place" had been already "assigned" by the country. "Tell the young man . . . to stay where he is." When Roosevelt came to him to plead in person for permission to resign, the permission was refused. Daniels, who now felt the need for Roosevelt's special qualifications as never before in office, was equally firm in the expressed conviction that Roosevelt's patriotic duty was to remain at his post.* And so were several of the most prominent of Daniels' and Wilson's political enemies. Leonard Wood, for instance, convinced that the "real work" in Navy was indeed being done by the Assistant Secretary, despite and against the ineptitudes and resistances of Daniels, disagreed with his friend TR's advice to nephew-in-law Franklin. The general asserted that "Franklin Roosevelt should under no circumstances think of leaving the Navy Department," that the young man's departure would be "a public calamity." [6]

II

And so the script, or Roosevelt's understanding of it, was changed. His career departed for the first time, in a major way, from the TR model. He remained at his civilian post, knowing well that the actual contribution he could there make to victory was greater than he could have made as admiral on the bridge of a flagship, but believing that only an astute management of his personal publicity, his public relations, would ensure that the popular prestige he gained would be as great and easily translatable into future election votes as that he might have gained as admiral. For this, as for so much else, he would have to count heavily upon Louis Howe.

He had, at any rate, the satisfaction of knowing that the single standard he had long employed in his official life as a measure of value and a determinant of priorities was now that of the administration and virtually the whole nation. "Germany has . . . said that force, and force alone, shall decide . . . ," Woodrow Wilson would assert on the first anniversary of the declaration of war. "There is . . . but one response possible from us: Force, Force to the utmost, Force without stint or limit. . . ." The standard, therefore, was that of efficiency in the development of physical force and in its application to the destruction of opposing force. Two questions only need be asked of any proposal: Is it feasible? Does it contribute more to the war effort, and more immediately, than any other possibility? If the answer to both questions was

---

* That a selfless patriotism was not Roosevelt's prime motive for seeking combat service was clearly recognized by Daniels and others in the department at that time. "Around the Department," says Daniels in *The Wilson Era: Years of Peace—1900–1917* (Chapel Hill, N.C., 1944, p. 130), "it was said that, inasmuch as his cousin Theodore left the position of Assistant Secretary to become a Rough Rider, later Governor of New York and then President, and both had served in the Legislature of New York, Franklin thought actual fighting in the war was the necessary step toward reaching the White House."

yes, the proposal had to be accepted; if no, it had to be rejected, and without regard for other effects which might be deleterious even to the point of catastrophe.

A premium was placed on precisely those qualities which the thirty-five-year-old Roosevelt possessed in greatest abundance—on his immense and zestful energy, his nimbleness of mind, his boldness, his talent for improvisation and persuasion, his tactical flexibility in pursuit of tenaciously held strategic purposes, his self-confidence (great in reality, greater still in appearance) within wide and various areas of competence, all joined to an instinct for power and the courage of a gambler who is exhilarated by games in which the odds are incalculable and the stakes of an unprecedented magnitude.* The President in a remarkable speech to the fleet, made from the quarterdeck of the USS *Pennsylvania* on August 11, 1917, advised the men of the U.S. Navy to strike the word "prudent" from their vocabulary; he urged them to "do the thing that is audacious to the utmost point of risk and daring . . . and you will win by audacity of method what you cannot win by circumspection and prudence." [7] Roosevelt needed no such advice. He continued impatient or uncomprehending of abstractions while focusing on particulars that were vividly, concretely present. He was therefore as little inclined toward circumspection as he was toward introspection. He had no lack of audacity. He was quick to break with hoary traditions when they would prevent the achievement of immediately overriding ends in view, regardless of possible long-term and wide-range side effects. His belief that the qualities he possessed in such abundance were lacking in many of his Navy colleagues, especially those in a position to overrule him, gave rise to his own greatest fears, his own continuing sense of frustration.

If only he himself had more authority, more freedom to act decisively! If only he could gather into his own hands some of the power now exercised by the Secretary and by the Chief of Naval Operations, Admiral William S. Benson! These two, having been major obstacles to a proper Preparedness, were now major obstacles to a proper prosecution of the war, in young Roosevelt's fervent belief. Benson was far too slow, cautious, suspicious of Britain, was in general too much of Daniels' mind and temperament, to direct war plans, preparations, and fleet operations as they *ought* to be directed.

On the first day following the declaration of war, the same day on

* During poker sessions (and he was fond of poker), Roosevelt often evoked loud groans from fellow players by calling for the weirdest and wildest of wild-card games.

which he went to Baker on behalf of TR, Roosevelt brought to Daniels, for the latter's signature, a special order prepared by himself. He badly needed help to handle the increased work load which the war was bound to impose, he said. The Secretary agreed. But when Daniels read the order placed on his desk, he drew back in astonishment. Roosevelt was proposing to bring to Washington, as his personal assistant, Rear Admiral Cameron M. Winslow, retired, former commander of the First Division of the Atlantic Fleet, an outspoken "big navy" man who had long been of one mind with the Assistant Secretary about both Preparedness and intervention. The idea of a flag officer's serving as assistant to an Assistant Secretary was absurd on the face of it, thought the Secretary.[8] Roosevelt must have an ulterior motive! Moreover, as he thought about it, Daniels suspected what the motive was.

Some years before, the Secretary had considered Winslow for the very post that Benson now held. This was when the department was in process of reorganization. The Council of Aides, inherited by Daniels from his predecessor, was being abolished. The office of Chief of Naval Operations was being created. And the militant Admiral Fiske, in partnership with equally militant Congressman Richmond Pearson Hobson of the Naval Affairs Committee, was making a determined effort to "Prussianize the American Navy," as Daniels put it, by imposing upon it a General Staff system modeled after imperial Germany's. Fiske wanted to transfer to the new office of Operations Chief so many of the decisive functions theretofore assigned to the civilian Secretary as to make the latter, in Daniels' view, "a supernumerary" * with "little power except to draw his breath and . . . salary." Daniels then firmly resolved to name as Operations Chief no officer who subscribed to the "Fiske-Hobson plan"; he therefore asked Winslow if he, Winslow, so subscribed, and when Winslow, "the soul of frankness," said he did, "that eliminated him from consideration, much as I liked him." [10] Similarly eliminated was every other admiral who was otherwise suitable for the new post. Finally, at President Wilson's suggestion, Daniels, who was in any case the least rank-conscious of men, lowered his sights to the level of captain and from it plucked Captain Benson, then in command of the Philadelphia Navy Yard. He had never regretted his choice. Benson was as deeply committed as Daniels to what the Secretary called the "American System" of civilian control over the military ("It is folly to talk of or

---

* When Fiske showed him a chart ("drawn by an artist") of the proposed department reorganization, Daniels praised it as "beautifully drawn . . . as perfect a diagram as I ever saw." But he had, he said, one objection: ". . . you have put the Secretary of the Navy on the top of the Washington Monument and denied him even telephonic communication with any officer or official of the Department except through Operations." [9]

to advocate clothing a Chief of Staff or a Chief of Naval Operations with authority independent of the head of the Navy," he said); he was honest, forthright, hardworking, intelligent, and unusually selfless and reluctant to bear grudges. The latter quality proved especially fortunate. His scrupulous adherence to the spirit, as well as the word, of the Secretary's policy cost him much in terms of the goodwill of "big navy" zealots, of many of the officers subject to his orders (he was often damned as "Daniels' toady"), and of department activists in general, including the Assistant Secretary. In such circumstances, forebearance became not only a virtue, but a necessity of survival.

But it was also essential that he recognize threats to his position and, on occasion, take defensive measures. When the Secretary told him of the Roosevelt request, he promptly confirmed Daniels' shrewd guess on Roosevelt's motive. "This is aimed at me!" he said, in some agitation. He and Daniels had a long talk about it on the night of April 7. They agreed that the request was a calculated bureaucratic power play and that a granting of it would be bound to lead—was *meant* to lead—to a division of authority over operations between Benson and the Assistant Secretary. So Daniels told Roosevelt, the next day, that the proposed assignment simply "would not work." There could be "no division of power as to operations." What Roosevelt really needed as assistant, said Daniels, was *not* a flag officer but a man "of business experience." [11]

This rebuff did not cause him to relax in the slightest his efforts, circuitous as well as direct, to compel Daniels and Benson to act as the crying needs of the hour demanded or else stand aside and let others do so. He struggled to reorganize department procedures along lines of greater efficiency—to speed up crucial decision-making and the carrying out of decisions, to speed up procurement and vastly enlarge its scale, to impart his own sense of urgency to all ranks, in general to slash red tape and remove or bypass obstructionists—this to meet challenges he estimated as huge even before high-ranking British and French missions arrived in late April to apprise the Americans of Allied requirements. The British mission, headed by former Prime Minister Balfour, arrived on April 23. The French, headed by Premier René Viviani, arrived two days later and was officially met by the Assistant Secretary, aboard the Presidential yacht *Mayflower,* at Hampton Roads. He and Eleanor were much involved with the official and social life of both missions. Members of the two delegations were entertained several times in the Roosevelt home, and the Roosevelts were a part of most of the other social and ceremonial events honoring the distinguished visitors during their long month in the capital. The news which the missions brought of ships lost to the submarine, of manpower lost on the western front, was shocking. If things continued the way they had been going for the last months, the Allies would lose the war. Many in the administration were dismayed by the magnitude of the effort which the Allies now asked of the United States. Roosevelt was not. He was only confirmed in his belief that the administrative deficiencies of Daniels and Benson could be catastrophic to the Allied cause and that it was up to him to compensate for them by whatever means were effective.

One means presented itself initially in a letter that came to him on the very day he was rebuffed in his effort to obtain an admiral as personal assistant. The letter was from Winston Churchill—not the British Winston Spencer Churchill, latterly First Lord of the Admiralty and soon to be Minister of Munitions in the British Cabinet, but the then-famous American novelist, a graduate two decades before from the Naval Academy at Annapolis, who had written several immensely successful historical romances (*Richard Carvel, The Crisis,* etc.) before turning to modern "problem" novels (*Coniston, Mr. Crewe's Career*) sentimentally dealing with themes central to the Progressive movement. The author, although a Progressive Republican, was nevertheless a personal friend of Woodrow Wilson—on successive summers the President had taken brief vacations in Churchill's house at Cornish, New Hampshire—and he would be listened to with respect on Navy matters by the President, as Roosevelt knew, not only because he was knowledgeable about them, but also because he was completely disinterested politically, bureaucratically, and financially. Hence, Roosevelt was quick to accept Churchill's offer to place his writing talents at the service of the Navy; he also hinted that the novelist need not confine himself to "mere 'write-ups' or recruiting posters of Navy life." [12]

And Winston Churchill took the hint. Beginning in May, he gathered material by personal interview with Navy people and through a perusal of Navy documents for several syndicated newspaper pieces and for an article on Navy administration that was published in the August, 1917, issue of the *Atlantic Monthly.* He was increasingly disturbed by what he saw and heard about low morale, endless delays, and bitter criticism of Daniels. The Navy Department, he told Roosevelt, was "suffering from hookworm—certainly not through any fault of yours." And it was with Roosevelt's hearty approval, if not at Roosevelt's direct suggestion—it was with information and opinion supplied by Roosevelt in addition to what Churchill had gained elsewhere—that the novelist prepared a carefully written, highly circumstantial, scrupulously fair statement, for the President's eye only, of what he could not but regard as a serious impasse for the Navy and consequently the country. This led to a personal conference with Wilson. (". . . am just back from lunch with Winston

Churchill," wrote Roosevelt to "Dearest Babs" on Thursday, July 26. "He saw the President yesterday and apparently had a pretty satisfactory talk." [13]) Wilson then talked the whole thing over with Daniels, though obviously with no thought of dismissing or even reprimanding the Navy Secretary, and followed this up with a memorandum, typed by himself, suggesting that certain personnel changes—an infusion of younger blood into procurement and operations—might improve matters. Roosevelt was gratified. In mid-August, when he himself had a talk with the President on another matter, he was "encouraged to believe" that the President "has *begun* to catch on, but . . . it will take lots more of the Churchill type of attack." [14]

Meanwhile, he fumed at Benson's alleged dealing with "little questions . . . cautiously and slowly" while matters "of real moment" were delayed "from 24 hours to 24 days." He fumed also at Daniels' tendency to procrastinate. (On June 26, in a memo reporting "thoroughly unsatisfactory" conditions found in his inspection of the Second and Third Naval Districts: "As I have many times recommended, the organization of the Naval District Defense should be radically changed. I have for nearly two months insisted that the work was going badly, and certain officers of the Division of Operations have admitted as much, but these officers frankly have failed to remedy the conditions. . . . Meanwhile the days, and the weeks and the months, are adding up and I should very much like to see some definite action taken." On July 27, in his diary: "I happened into the Secretary's office . . . and found him signing a batch of Bureau of Navigation mail . . . dated July 5th." On September 7, in a memo reporting "a second inspection trip" to the Second and Third Naval Districts: ". . . over two months after my first trip, I am sorry to say that the conditions are to all intents and purposes no better. . . .") He fumed at delays in drawing up contracts for destroyers and wooden submarine chasers. (On April 18, in a memo to Daniels: ". . . I want to call your attention to the fact that it is two weeks since the awards were made to private companies for building the 110-foot patrol boats, and I am told today by Naval Constructor Furer and the Bureau of Supplies & Accounts that not one single contract has been signed. . . . Today is . . . nearly three months after the definite need became evident and . . . practically not a timber that will go into their construction has been sawed." On July 12, in another memo to Daniels: "If we are going to build any more destroyers, no matter what type, *the estimates should go in now, whether the number be 50, or 100, or 200. . . .* If the Department is going to build any additional wooden chasers, *contracts should be let before September 1.*")[15] He fumed with a special fervency against the reluctance of Daniels, sustained by Admiral David W.

Taylor, chief of the Bureau of Construction and Repair, to build and buy 50-foot motorboats for patrolling harbors in defense against submarines.

In the spring and summer of 1917 he regarded as very real the possibility that U-boats would invade New York Harbor and others crowded with shipping and there exact a fearful toll of desperately needed vessels. He even worried a little about a submarine attack on Campobello! ". . . I meant to tell you," he wrote Eleanor on July 19, "that if by any perfectly wild chance a German submarine should come into the bay [of Fundy] and start to shell Eastport or the Pool, I want you to grab the children and beat it into the woods. Don't stay to see what is going on. I am not joking about this, for though it is 500 to 1 against the possibility, still there is just that one chance. . . ." [16]

The same consideration of remote possibility weakened somewhat Daniels' resistance to the small-boat proposal. On March 21, the day after the President's decision for war, the Secretary noted in his diary: "Franklin Roosevelt urged more motor boats be used for patrol. Will order many but are they valuable? How much of that sort of junk should we buy?" [17] He would later recall that both Admiral Taylor, "ablest naval construction officer in the world," and Captain Hugh Rodman of the General Board were unimpressed by Roosevelt's argument.* It was at a conference of naval experts called by Roosevelt himself, the preceding February, that the decision had been taken to use all available steel to build destroyers, supplementing these with hundreds of 110-foot wooden craft powered by three gasoline motors. The latter, usable for harbor patrol, were also usable upon the open sea and were large enough to cross the ocean under their own power, whereas the 50-foot craft would be useless outside protected waters. Taylor and Rodman, therefore, opposed diverting money for the purchase, and resources for the construction, of the smaller craft. Roosevelt's counterargument was that the 50-footers could be obtained by the many hundred within a few weeks or months, whereas the 110-footers, especially in view of red-tape delays in the assignment of contracts, would not be available in truly significant number until 1918. Taylor and Rodman remained unimpressed. "In my heart I agreed with Taylor and Rodman," Daniels remembered. "But suppose U-boats should enter our harbors and we lacked patrol boats, what then? Contrary to my belief in their worth I told F.D.R. to go ahead and buy a number." [18]

The number, however, was far too small to satisfy Roosevelt. He con-

* In his memoirs, *The Wilson Years: Years of War and After* (Chapel Hill, N.C., 1946), p. 254. He here amplified from memory his actual diary entry, identifying Rodman as an admiral, a rank Rodman did not attain until later that spring.

tinued to do all in his power to speed up the construction of 110-foot sub chasers. But he also continued to press with at least equal force for the 50-footers. He appeared before the General Board on March 24 to argue that since it would be impossible to obtain more than 200 or so of the larger craft by the end of the year, large orders should at once be placed for the smaller draft, on which delivery could be obtained in the summer and autumn. The 50-footers, in other words, were a necessary stopgap. He was persuasive, for the moment. The board orally approved his proposal. But the next day the board members changed their minds, having learned from bureau experts that more than twice as many of the 110-foot craft could be built by January as Roosevelt had estimated. The Assistant Secretary heatedly protested this reversal. He stubbornly persisted in his promotion. He later went so far as to issue a contract for construction of a number of the controverted craft, according to Daniels' remembrance, though he had no real authority, not even as Acting Secretary, to do so. At one very low point, Louis Howe—perhaps without Roosevelt's knowledge, certainly without Roosevelt's explicit permission—went to Rodman to suggest or broadly hint that the captain's career would be more certain to prosper if he withdrew his opposition to the small-boat project. Rodman at that time was anxiously awaiting sea duty. He was hopeful of promotion to command of a battleship squadron, with rank of admiral.* But this only increased the vehemence with which he rejected the tactfully proffered bribe. He was furious. Reportedly, he cursed out the Assistant Secretary's confidential assistant in the strongest of sea captain's language.[19]

Why this persistence, on Roosevelt's part?

For one thing, he had always had a special fondness for fast small boats. He loved their swift maneuverability, the physical excitement of their wave-slapping, wind-blasting speed. And he was sincerely convinced they would perform many useful functions of short surveillance that were impossible for craft of deeper draft.

Moreover, it was his nature to persevere. His frequently charming deference of manner, his eagerness to please cloaked a fundamental bulldog tenacity.

But in this particular case several of his colleagues believed that no small part of his persistence was due to his personal friendship with one Arthur Patch "Pat" Homer, of Boston. Certainly Roosevelt and Howe were much taken with Homer, who was American representative of Britain's Sterling Motors—an attractive man in appearance and person-

---

* He was subsequently named commander of Battleship Division Nine (five dreadnaughts) which operated as the Sixth Battle Squadron with the British Grand Fleet in European waters.

ality, an excitingly dramatic talker and letter writer, a man fertile of schemes and stratagems remarkable for ingenuity and daring and optimistic faith, a man possessed of an abundantly exercised talent for investing himself and his every activity with an aura of romantic adventure. He appealed strongly to the histrionic, the theatrical elements of the Roosevelt-and-Howe temperament.[20] He was not without practical energies and abilities: twice he had been sent by Roosevelt to England to gather information about aircraft motors for Navy use, doing an excellent job on both occasions. Primarily, however, he was a promoter, a supersalesman. In 1916 and '17 his most enthusiastic promotion was the 50-foot boat for which, by happy coincidence, a Sterling motor would supply the power.

III

But if the small-boat episode measured defects of Roosevelt's virtues, those virtues were very great by wartime standards. Their exercise contributed far more to the success of the war effort than was detracted from it by the rashnesses and lapses of moral scrupulosity that were rooted in his impatience, his willful assertiveness, and the driving ambition that seldom flagged in him and never on his behalf in Louis Howe.

His virtues were especially manifested in what he himself always regarded as his major contribution to the winning of the war—namely, the North Sea mine barrage.[21] The essential idea was an obvious one. A U-boat sailing from its home base had to traverse one of two stretches of narrow sea before reaching the open Atlantic. The narrowest, of course, was the English Channel: a mere 20 miles or so separated English Dover from French Calais. The other was a 240-mile stretch of the North Sea between the northeastern tip of Scotland and the coast of Norway. If both passages could be somehow closed, the U-boat threat and, with it, Germany's best chance for victory would be ended. Hence: "Daniels, why don't the British shut up the hornets in their nests?" Wilson asked the Navy Secretary "at Cabinet meetings several times" months before the United States entered the war. The President evidently had in mind no specific plan or project. He was simply, as he later said, "greatly surprised at the failure of the British Admiralty to use Great Britain's great naval superiority in an effective way" against the submarine, especially in the waters adjacent to major U-boat bases. "We are hunting hornets all over the farm and letting the nest alone," he complained.[22] Surely some concentrated combination of patrol vessels, minefields, and underwater obstacles of various kinds could be employed to fence in the North Sea!

Roosevelt was convinced of it. His general idea was to use vast numbers of mines to make a wall so deep no submarine could go under it, so dense that none could penetrate it, at either end of the North Sea. He discussed this on April 4 with Admiral Frederick R. Harris, who as a lieutenant commander had solved the problem of dry dock construction at Pearl Harbor in 1913* and was now chief of the Bureau of Yards and Docks. Harris, who had been thinking along the same lines, was encouraged by Roosevelt's enthusiasm to draw up a tentative project plan, with estimates of the material requirements. These last proved stupendous. Harris was staggered by them. Not so Roosevelt. He promptly presented the plan with its estimates to the Bureau of Ordnance, where, he learned, the head of the Mines Section, Commander S. P. Fullinwider, was already at work on a similar plan of his own. A major technical difficulty, Fullinwider stressed, was the lack of a suitable mine—one that did not require direct and solid contact with its body in order to explode—but he did not regard this difficulty as insurmountable. Necessity was the mother of invention, and so great an immediate need would probably be soon supplied. Even if it were not—even if the mine types then available had to be used—an effective barrier could be constructed, the commander believed. His section was hard at work on the problem. Soon thereafter Roosevelt learned that Major E. Lester Jones of the Coast and Geodetic Survey was also working on a barrier plan, one that made use of nets.

On April 15, in accordance with Roosevelt's wish, a conference to consider the proposal was assembled in Navy, including the Secretary, Assistant Secretary, Chief of Operations, Chief of Ordnance, Chief of Yards and Docks, and various technical specialists. Daniels was moved by it to send "with the President's hearty approval" a cable of inquiry to Admiral Sims in London, on April 16. "Is it not practicable to blockade German coast efficiently and completely, thus making practically impossible the egress or ingress of submarines?" he asked. "The steps attempted or accomplished in that direction are to be reported at once." Sims' reply was discouraging (he cabled, April 19, that to "absolutely blockade" against the arrival and departure of submarines from the German and Belgian coast "has been found quite infeasible"),[23] and Roosevelt was by no means alone in his refusal to accept it as conclusive. He was, however, in a key Navy administrative position, with personal access to the White House. He was the only man in such position

* See page 315.

who was ardently *for* the scheme since both Daniels and Benson had grave doubts about it. And had he been even slightly less active in his promotion of it the project would almost certainly have died a-borning in mid-May, 1917.

As it was, he presented strong oral arguments for the proposal to Lord Balfour and Admiral R. D. S. De Chair of the British mission when they were in Washington in May, also to Admiral Chocheprat of the French mission, and remained stubbornly unconvinced by their negative counterarguments. He was probably instrumental in moving Daniels to cable Sims again on May 9: "Much opinion is in favor of concerted efforts by the Allies to establish a complete barrier across the North Sea, Scotland to Norway . . . , to prevent egress of German submarines. The difficulty and size of the problem is recognized, but if it is possible of accomplishment, the situation would warrant the effort." [24] He was undeterred by Sims' reply to this, which was more emphatically discouraging than his earlier reply had been, its tone suggesting, as later communications confirmed, that he was more concerned to represent the British Admiralty to the U.S. Navy than he was to represent the latter to the Admiralty. (The barrier proposal, said Sims, had been "previously considered and abandoned." It was deemed by the Admiralty "quite impracticable.") Roosevelt then wrote out a lengthy and detailed memorandum for De Chair's presentation to the Admiralty, copies going to the Secretary and to various key officers of the department and to Sims in London. In it, he undertook to answer Balfour's principal diplomatic objection, which was that an effective barrier must necessarily violate the three-mile limit of Norway's territorial waters. "The use of territorial waters of neutrals by belligerent warships," wrote Roosevelt, "is carefully guarded [against] by . . . international law, and if Norway fails to carry out her direct obligation to prevent the use of a narrow line along her coast . . . by German submarines it would seem perfectly fair to carry out this duty for her." [25] He guessed (extravagantly, as it turned out) that the barrier of nets and mines might cost as much as $500,000,000—an enormous amount by 1917 standards—but the alternative could mean a continuation of the present rate of Allied shipping losses and a consequent loss of the war.

On the afternoon of June 4 he had a lengthy talk with the President during which the two reviewed the various North Sea "fence" suggestions. Roosevelt proposed establishment of a commission to make an authoritative report upon the feasibility of the general idea and of the alternative technical specifics. Wilson approved,[26] stipulating that the commission include representatives of the Coast and Geodetic Survey of the Department of Commerce (Redfield, the Secretary of Commerce, was an early and enthusiastic promoter of the barrier) as well as Navy, so there ensued, predictably, a bureaucratic squabble between those on the commission who would concentrate on nets (Jones and his colleagues of Commerce) and those who would concentrate on mines (Fullinwider and his colleagues of Navy), with the latter a decisive majority. The President himself was forced to take note of it when Jones angrily protested what seemed to him a cavalier rejection of his ideas by Navy officers. On July 3, Wilson sent Daniels a "Personal and Confidential" communication with which he enclosed a letter, dated June 28, received from the irate major. "I would be very much obliged if you would read the enclosed," wrote Wilson. "I am afraid from the evidence on the surface that professional jealousy has operated to sidetrack this important matter [the building of nets], or at least check the serious consideration of it." [27]

In this controversy, Roosevelt refused at first to take sides. He initially favored a weaving together of the two general approaches—a combination of various types of nets and mines—and he toyed with other schemes also, some of them farfetched indeed. But then there came to his office, one day in late May, an inventor, Ralph C. Browne of Salem, Massachusetts, who had with him a small-scale model of what he called the Browne Submerged Gun for use against submarines.[28] Roosevelt was at once greatly impressed, not by the gun itself but by Browne's device for firing it. This last was a copper antenna thrust downward into the water by a buoy in which was an open electrical circuit. If a metal object brushed the antenna, the circuit in the buoy closed, triggering the gun. Earle and Fullinwider were similarly impressed; and Fullinwider, with Browne, was soon at work adapting the antenna device for use on mines. The result was a new mine model which underwent highly successful tests at New London, Connecticut, on July 10. Roosevelt thereupon lost interest in Jones' net scheme and decided to concentrate exclusively on mines.

Meanwhile, the British Admiralty continued to oppose, first on one ground, then another, the very idea of fencing in U-boats. Only recently and with difficulty had the British been converted to the use of convoys (groups of merchantmen and transports escorted by fighting ships) for moving troops and matériel across submarine-infested seas. Sims had played a key role in this conversion. One may legitimately doubt that he would have attempted to do so, however, in view of his general attitude, had he not been very strongly pressed by Washington and had he not found many of the Royal Navy's younger officers already in favor of the idea by the time he arrived in London. Certainly he now fully shared the Admiralty's resistance to the new idea. He marshaled all the negative arguments which the Admiralty recruited and sailed them with the full weight of his forceful personality westward across the Atlantic.

After all, Sims wrote to Washington in late June, "the people over here are fighting for their very existence and . . . they know that this depends upon their success or failure in putting down the submarine." They had naturally thought of everything, had "examined . . . every scheme," and it ill became the inexperienced Americans "to be dogmatic in their opinions as to what could and should be done" when these ran counter to the Admiralty's. As for the proposed barrier, it would certainly be immensely costly. It would almost as certainly be ineffective. Nets tried off the English coast and at entrances to New York Harbor had performed poorly. High North Sea tides moved mines out of position, which meant that minelayers and escorts would have to operate continuously in great numbers, far from home bases, to maintain an effective barrage. The number of mines of the prevailing type that would have to be manufactured was huge beyond the bounds of feasibility, and while an effective antenna mine would have a much wider area of destructiveness than the older type, thereby drastically reducing the number of mines that must be laid, there was slight chance that the new mine would work in actual practice. London discounted to the point of nullification the New London tests. ". . . the British Admiralty has had a very serious and very bitter experience with every new mine that they have designed and developed. . . ." [29]

By such arguments, presented in an attitude almost worshipful of alleged Admiralty omniscience, Roosevelt was unpersuaded and Wilson coldly angered. The Admiralty had done nothing to justify any great faith in its judgment or any profound admiration for its fighting efficiency, so far as the President could see. Quite the contrary. "In the present submarine emergency, they are helpless to the point of panic," he said in a "strictly confidential" cable to Sims on July 4, 1917. "Every plan we suggest they reject for some reason of prudence. In my view this is not a time for prudence but for boldness. . . . I would be very much obliged to you if you would report to me, confidentially, of course, exactly what the Admiralty has been doing, and what they have accomplished, and, added to the report, your own comments and suggestions, based upon independent thought of the whole situation, without regard to the judgment of any one on that side of the water. . . . I believe . . . that you will give me such advice as you would give if you were handling the situation yourself, and if you were running a Navy of your own." [30] Sims, however, had no "independent thought" about the mine barrier. He continued to represent London to Washington rather than the other way around. And the President continued angry about it.

". . . I take it for granted that nothing I say here will be repeated and therefore I am going to say this," said the President to assembled U.S. Navy officers aboard the *Pennsylvania* on August 11: "Every time we have suggested anything to the British Admiralty the reply has come back that virtually amounted to this, that it had never been done that way, and I felt like saying, 'Well, nothing was ever done so systematically as nothing is being done now. . . .'"

Daniels and Benson, on the other hand, remained dubious about the mine barrage. Only after the event did Daniels see it as "the most daring and original naval conception of the World War," whose delay of execution "was, in my opinion, the greatest naval error of the War." At the time—at the very moment of final decision, as a matter of fact—he spoke of the barrier in his private diary as a "stupendous undertaking . . . of doubtful practicability. North Sea too rough," he went on, "and will necessitate withdrawing all our ships from other work and then can we destroy the hornet's nest or keep the hornets in?" [31]

Hence, Roosevelt's persistence in this matter, though but one of several factors essential to the outcome, became decisive. "If Roosevelt had not been there, the North Sea Barrage would never have been laid down . . . ," said Admiral Harris years later. "Certainly my own interest in it was due to his enthusiasm and encouragement." [32] The U.S. Navy, Roosevelt insisted, should go ahead with the project whether or not the Admiralty cooperated—and it was a major item in the reassessment he made of Wilson at this time, of the admiration he developed for Wilson as a strong courageous war leader, that the President at least tacitly agreed with him. The Assistant Secretary proceeded on his own authority to sign on October 3 an order for 100,000 of the new firing devices; hundreds of contractors and subcontractors were at work on their manufacture a few weeks later. Meanwhile, Daniels, despite his private doubts, continued to exert strong pressure on Sims to obtain project approval from the Admiralty. When Sims failed in this, the Secretary ordered to London Admiral H. T. Mayo, of Mexican flag-salute fame,* for the sole purpose of obtaining this approval. And Mayo, at long last, succeeded. In late October, 1917, came a cable from Sims: "Admiralty has approved mine barrier and now confirms approval."

Roosevelt then took steps, not only to expedite the actual laying of the barrage, but also to make sure that his own part in the enterprise was recorded for the eyes of posterity. He addressed to the Secretary, on October 29, a quite lengthy memorandum labeled "Confidential" and formally headed "Proposed measures to close English Channel and

* See pages 334–35.

North Sea against submarines by mine barrage." [33] Referring to the
project's final administrative clearance, it began: "This is, of course,
nothing more nor less than a resurrection of my proposition, which with
all earnestness possible, I called to the attention of the President, the
Secretary of the Navy, the Chief of Operations, the General Board (etc.
etc.) . . . during the months of May and June past. . . . I reiterated the
need for haste. I know how unseemly it is to seem to say 'I told you so,'
but it is a literal fact that, while the British Admiralty may be blamed in
part, our own Navy Department is at least largely responsible for failing
to consider this proposition seriously through all these months—May,
June, July, August, September and October—which have gone over the
dam beyond recall." He went on to stress "that the same need for immediate haste exists today as existed last May. . . . We have done altogether too much amiable 'consideration' of this matter," he said. "If it is
to be carried out at all it must be carried out with a different spirit from
any of the operations up to now. It will require prompt decision all
along the line. . . . To accomplish the above it should be placed in the
hands of one man on our part and one man on the part of the British."
These two men should operate under flat general orders "simply . . . to
carry out the plan" and "*should have all the authority requisite to do this.*
This is a bigger matter than sending destroyers abroad or a division of
battleships, or building a bunch of new destroyers—it is vital to winning
the war."

To make doubly sure that this accusatory and peremptory missive
was effective of its purpose, Roosevelt sent a copy of it to the President.
("I know you will not mind . . . , as I have discussed it with him several times," was the Assistant Secretary's bland concluding sentence.)
And in his cover letter to the President, of which Daniels, then or later,
obtained a copy, he said in part: [34] "I am very sorry to bother you, but
in view of our several talks during the summer I am sending you a copy
of a memorandum which I have just given to the Secretary. As you
probably know, Admiral Mayo reported on his return that the British
Admiralty would like 'serious consideration' of the . . . barriers, and a
week or so later we telegraphed Admiral Sims to ask whether the . . .
Admiralty really approved. . . . We received an affirmative reply a few
days ago and now our General Board has also approved. This much has
been accomplished in six months, but it is my duty to tell you that if the
plan is put into execution with the same speed and method employed in
the past other priceless months will be wasted and the success of the
plan will be jeopardized. . . . I dislike exaggeration, but it is really true
that the elimination of all submarines from the waters between the
United States and Europe must of necessity be a vital factor in winning

the war." (Wilson's reply to this was brief and noncommittal. "Thank you for your letter of yesterday," wrote the President to the Assistant Secretary on October 30. "I am interesting myself in the matter." [35])*

In a letter he wrote to "Dearest Babs" on that same October 29, Roosevelt clearly indicated that his memorandum was at least as expressive of his view of himself as a major role player in history's drama as it was of his sense of immediate and urgent need. "I . . . have given the Sec'y a very stinging memorandum, and sent a copy to the President," he told his wife. *"Some day they will be interesting reading."* †[36]

Thereafter, Roosevelt had little to complain about in the project's handling. Within a few months, 22,000,000 pounds of TNT and 50,000,000 feet of wire cable, along with the casings for nearly 100,000 mines, were manufactured in America and transported via a special fleet of two dozen cargo vessels to two Scottish ports, thence by a special transportation system across Scotland to two large assembly plants, at Inverness and Invergordon. The actual North Sea mining, under the command of U.S. Rear Admiral Joseph Strauss, was started in June, 1918, and by mid-August it had begun to have some physical effect and a very considerable psychological one upon Germany's submarine fleet, coming as it did atop the highly successful convoy system with the concomitant use of aerial patrols, subchasers and destroyers armed with depth charges, Q-ships (fighting craft disguised as helpless merchantmen), and other antisubmarine devices that had by 1918 cut Allied ship sinkings well below the rate at which ships were being built. By late October the North Sea barrage was virtually completed. More than 70,000 mines had by then been laid, each containing 300 pounds of TNT, at a total cost of about $80,000,000. The barrage destroyed at least seven submarines and damaged at least as many others during the few short weeks that it was in full operation; it became a factor, perhaps a major factor, in inciting mutiny in the German Navy during the first week of November, 1918.

---

* That Daniels' memory of the entire episode was a rankling one seems evident in the way he tells the story of the barrage in two of his published works, *Our Navy at War* and *The Wilson Era: Years of War and After*. In the former, published in 1922, he makes no mention whatever of Roosevelt in connection with the barrage. In the latter, published in 1946, he gives the Assistant Secretary credit for early advocacy of the general idea, but only as one of several who were, the most important of these being Woodrow Wilson. As regards the above-quoted memorandum, Daniels in the latter work makes a possibly significant, deliberate mistake in date: he has Roosevelt sending "a copy" of "his memorandum" to the President in "October, 1916," with no indication said memo was addressed to the Secretary—this amid an argument designed to show Wilson as a master naval strategist who saw what should be done about the submarine "months before we entered the war." Many historians and biographers have been confused by this error.

† Italicized by the present author.

IV

Roosevelt as desk warrior made other contributions to the war effort which, if somewhat less dramatic than his fight for the North Sea mine barrage, may in sum have been of greater overall importance.

On the same crowded Saturday, April 7, 1917, in which he made his futile effort to obtain an admiral as personal assistant, he swore into the Navy as a lieutenant commander in the Civil Engineering Corps a New York City building contractor named Elliott C. Brown. In the fall of 1915, having with some difficulty persuaded his mother to permit it, he had carried out plans long and carefully made for a drastic remodeling of the house at Hyde Park. Wings had been added to the north and south sides of the original structure, from which the tower was removed; extensive changes were made in the interior arrangement (a large library-living room was created on the first floor); and the house front was completely altered in appearance. What had been a typical specimen of Hudson River Bracketed was transformed into a handsome Georgian mansion. Brown had been the contractor in charge of this work and had greatly pleased Roosevelt with his imagination, initiative, and capacity to "get things done" with a minimum of waste motion. He was now given a remarkably free hand, by Roosevelt, for the employment of his special abilities on large Navy construction jobs.

Brown, years later, gave Ernest K. Lindley several examples of how this arrangement worked.[37] One day in mid-June, 1917, Roosevelt told Brown to find a site and make preliminary arrangements for constructing a Navy cantonment for several thousand men in New York City. On June 27, Roosevelt went up to New York to view the site Brown had selected in City Park, Brooklyn. On June 28, Admiral Harris gave Brown oral orders to proceed. Detailed planning began on June 29, ground was broken on July 5, construction was virtually completed on August 4, and the cantonment was occupied by 6,800 men on August 11. Not until October were official contracts for the job issued through prescribed channels! Similarly with regard to a medical building urgently needed in another camp. There were standard plans for such structures, and Roosevelt told Brown to follow them and go ahead at once with the construction. Weeks later Brown received through channels an official request that he submit his plans for the "proposed" project. A lengthy form was provided for this. Brown filled it out in every required detail, then gleefully attached to it a photograph of the completed building. Roosevelt was delighted. According to Lindley, Brown built an addition to the Pelham Bay camp in New York City for 10,000 men "without contractors" and completed it "two months ahead of schedule at a cost approximately one-third less than that of other large naval cantonments." In the process, he committed "holy murder . . . hourly" so far as regulations were concerned, as he said in a letter to Roosevelt. "You will have some beautiful requisitions to sign some-day," he went on, "but I'm getting everything bought before sending them in! So it makes no difference what anyone does with them." Roosevelt said he'd be glad to sign them "with my eyes closed." [38]

Of crucial importance to the whole construction program—not just the building of cantonments but also the building of ships, the manufacture of guns, of ammunition, of torpedoes and mines and matériel of all kinds—were the department's relations with management and labor and the latter's relations with each other. Here Roosevelt's contributions were of special importance—his and Howe's, one must add, for labor relations were Howe's particular province, and Howe was now promoted from his former position to that of Special Assistant to the Assistant Secretary at what seemed to him the huge salary of $400 a month. In the first weeks of the war, Roosevelt played a leading role in renegotiating numerous Navy fixed-fee contracts which were rendered obviously unfair and impracticable by war-boosted price and wage rates. Navy contracts, like practically all other government war contracts, were placed on a cost-plus basis: the government paid the private contractor the cost of production plus a fixed percentage (generally 6 percent) of profit. This was an arrangement that speeded up immediate production, but it had the obvious grave defect of abolishing the businessman's incentive to keep costs to a minimum (an actual *increase* of cost was to his profit advantage) and of inciting a general inflation of prices. Wages were in general the major cost item. To keep them within reasonable bounds, Roosevelt favored the establishment of labor boards for special areas and industries with authority to set wage scales on the basis of all available and relevant objective information. In the summer of 1917 he became the Navy's representative on an Arsenal and Navy Yard Adjustment Committee, appointed by the Secretaries of War, Navy, and Labor (Walter Lippman represented the War Department), which collected wage information and recommendations nationwide, established thereon a wage scale 10 percent higher than had theretofore prevailed, and induced labor union executives to sign one-year agreements to abide by this scale, despite their protests that it was not high enough. He worried thereafter lest union leadership cite cost-of-living increases as a justification for canceling the agreements before the year was up. The departments of Labor and of Agriculture should develop a living standard index by which cost-of-living changes might.be objectively measured, he suggested, thus transforming an arguable matter of opinion into a solid matter of fact.

Later he became convinced that Felix Frankfurter, who continued as a War Department adviser on labor matters, was right in his assertion that the prevailing piecemeal approach to labor problems, with each department handling its own labor relations independently of other departments, could not do what desperately needed to be done. There should be a national Labor Administration with authority to establish and enforce standard wage scales, he argued in a personal appearance before the Council of National Defense. His proposal "was vetoed by the Labor Department," whose sovereign domain it would have invaded, but it helped lead to a National Defense Council recommendation which, when followed, transformed the Labor Department into a near equivalent of the suggested administration. There were then set up, in May, 1918, a National War Labor Board and a War Labor Policies Board—agencies which would serve as guides to Roosevelt's dealings with labor problems a decade and a half later.

By that time Daniels had been persuaded to concentrate all Navy labor administration in Roosevelt's office. And because Howe remained far closer to labor leaders in outlook than Roosevelt was and had a far more acute awareness of their actual and potential importance to the Roosevelt political future than Roosevelt did, he continued to operate more extensively as Roosevelt's alter ego in the area of labor relations than in any other area. The Assistant Secretary was Navy's official representative on the Shipbuilding Labor Board, but Howe often substituted for him at this board's meetings. Howe himself represented Navy on the War Labor Board. He became intimate with the most important labor leaders having dealings with the department, notably the presidents of the International Machinists Union and the Metal Trades Council. He handled the bulk of the correspondence on labor matters and personally dealt with most of the complaints (there were no important work stoppages on Navy installations or among Navy contractors throughout the war). He encouraged Navy adoption of several constructive proposals made by labor. Roosevelt, for instance, made his own a union proposal that cost-of-living adjustments be included in wage formulas The Assistant Secretary was also instrumental in reducing the number of separate pay ranks among Navy employees, these having become so numerous and closely spaced as to constitute, so the unions complained, an instrument of employee coercion and a fomenter of needless jealousies. Such policy changes contributed not only to general labor peace, but also to Roosevelt's reputation as one of the best friends that organized labor had in the whole administration.

Howe's belief in the future importance of labor unions to an aspiring national politician was encouraged by the development of the administration's wartime labor policies. The War Labor Policies Board, guided by Frankfurter, took unprecedented inventory of the nation's labor resources and needs, established the standard nationwide wage-and-hour scales Roosevelt had favored, and promoted the establishment in the Department of Labor of a U.S. Employment Service, upon whose rolls were soon listed well over 5,000,000 workers of whom about 3,700,000 were placed where most needed for war production. Labor's right to organize and bargain collectively was officially recognized (AFL membership increased from a little over 2,000,000 in 1916 to something over 3,250,000 by war's end), and the eight-hour workday became standard. The government also assumed responsibilities for the improvement of working conditions for those employed by manufacturers having government contracts, especially for women and children, and tried to match increased living costs with increased wage rates. Of all this, Roosevelt thoroughly approved, but if he would permit no worker to be discharged from a plant with large Navy contracts for engaging in union-organizing activities, neither would he permit any union in any specific dispute to dictate terms "along lines different from the regular agreement" between the government and the AFL.

Techniques which Roosevelt and Howe had developed in earlier years for speeding up procurement and preventing profiteering were now refined and applied on an expanded scale. When bids were obviously too high, persuasion and cajolery were used in an effort to bring them down. This failing, a competent firm which had not submitted a bid was sought out, and effort made to persuade it to provide the needed articles at a reasonable price. If this was not possible, resort was made to commandeering orders. Between February and May, 1917, Roosevelt attempted to buy yachts and fishing craft and small steamers for use by the Navy in coastal defense. Outraged when a majority of the owners of suitable vessels refused to sell to the government save at exorbitant prices, he asked of Congress specific authority to commandeer all such craft, paying for them whatever price the government itself adjudged "fair." Congress granted this authority on May 14; Roosevelt made effective use of it. When he found no plant in existence which could manufacture hollow shafts for destroyers in the quantity required, he arranged with the Erie Forge Company of Erie, Pennsylvania, to build that company a plant at government expense, the plant to be operated by Erie during the war and then bought by it or else, as Daniels was inclined to favor, retained by the Navy. And when the lack of an electric generator of required capacity threatened to delay the opening of this plant, whose production was desperately needed, Howe acting for Roosevelt used a commandeering order to acquire a generator that was intended for use in the then-building Hotel Pennsylvania in New York City. (The Statler Hotel Company later informed the Navy Department [in "a good-natured letter," says Lindley][39] that this operation had delayed the opening of the new hotel by three months.) A more amiable method of procurement, equally effective, was employed by Roosevelt to obtain binoculars needed at once in great numbers by the expanding Navy. He launched with a great fanfare of publicity an "Eyes for the Navy" campaign, asking private owners of binoculars to donate them to the Navy for the duration. They were promised one dollar for each pair and the return of each pair when the war ended. Some 50,000 pairs of glasses were received, more than 95 percent of which were found usable by Navy lookouts. They were ultimately returned, as promised, to their owners, and returned in a way that did no harm to Roosevelt's personal fame. Each owner received with his returned glasses a handsomely engraved certificate signed in facsimile by Franklin D. Roosevelt.

V

In his private personal life, as in the vivid popular impression he consciously made, Roosevelt became during this period a significant blend of old and new fashions in young American manhood.

TR remained a model, especially as regards the "strenuous life." So did the Richard Harding Davis hero* who had loomed so large in American fantasy life during the first decade of the century—the aggressively handsome, jut-jawed Gibson Man, who, though a Christian gentleman, virtuous and idealistic, was also romantically exciting, dashing, virile, ceaselessly zestful, a fine athlete as a matter of course, and gracefully efficient in whatever he chose to do. "As he stood in front of a cheerful wood fire, his arm resting on the marble mantle, a bronze bust of John Paul Jones peering over his shoulder, he was an engaging picture of young American manhood," reported one newspaper feature writer who interviewed him on a January afternoon in his office. "Through the wide windows rays of dazzling light, reflected from the snow-clad expanse of the White House grounds across the street, caught the clean lines of his face and figure and threw them into sharp relief. They, the air of alertness they conveyed, the natural pose, were the sort

---

* One of Davis' leading fictional characters, Van Bibber, resembled in several respects—in Dutch ancestry, inherited wealth, social prestige, personal chivalry, Christian "idealism," and attitudes of *noblesse oblige*—the Roosevelt who married a President's niece in 1905.

of thing one sees in the work of leading American illustrators more often than in real life. The face was particularly interesting. Breeding showed there. Clearly cut features, a small, sensitive mouth, tiny lines running from nostrils to the outer lines of the lips, a broad forehead, close-cropped brown hair, frank, blue eyes, but, above all, the proud, straight, upstanding set of the head placed the man. And as he stood there he talked of war. . . ." [40] It was reported that the "hearts of girl stenographers fluttered" at the sight of Franklin Roosevelt striding down the broad corridors of the State, War, and Navy Building to and from his office where newsmen normally saw him twice a day and, over the months and years, reported him the most vigorous and vital of young Washington executives. Anna Roosevelt (Bamie) Cowles, Eleanor's Auntie Bye, spoke of him in the summer of 1917 as "debonair . . . , so brave and so charming" while her husband, the admiral, doting on him, was sure "the girls" would "spoil" him "soon enough." The young English bachelor, Nigel Law, third secretary of the British embassy, was by no means alone in regarding him as "a fine physical specimen." Walter Camp, the famous Yale coach, who was encouraged to come to Washington by the Navy's Assistant Secretary to inaugurate a Navy physical fitness program and who three mornings each week led setting-up exercises for desk-bound executives, Roosevelt among them, described his sponsor as "a beautifully built man, with the long muscles of the athlete." Moreover, said Camp, young Roosevelt's "spirit is resilient, and his effect upon others is . . . salutary in that he imparts some of his own vitality." [41]

But for all this, he was no flat echo or unqualified continuation of the recent past, in either inward feeling or outward impressions. Far from it.

The American nineteenth century which reached its climax in the first decade of the twentieth—the complex of interweaving tendencies that culminated in, say, 1912—was already beginning to seem, across the widening gulf of war, far away and long ago. Many of its dominant ideas now seemed naïve. "Victorian" had already acquired the denigrating connotations which would become virtually the adjective's sole meaning a few years hence. And such Populist-Progressive figures as Daniels and especially Bryan, who indeed had appeared old-fashioned on the eve of the war, now seemed almost ludicrous anachronisms to many. Not so Franklin Roosevelt. He was vividly contemporary, shiningly modern and up-to-date. He gave no sign of looking back with regret and longing upon the world the war had destroyed but, instead, gave every sign of embracing the present with ardor while looking eagerly toward a future in which his own part would be, as was everywhere recognized, prominent, if not great. The nineteenth century that remained alive in him was joined and often ruled by attitudes wholly novel and unprecedented in him, and not a few of these were profoundly disturbing to his traditionalist mother, who saw them as subversive of the only "right" moral and social order. She feared they caused in her son's personal life (there was perhaps more reason for fear than she knew) an erosion of character.

Being the kind of person she was, Sara Delano Roosevelt did not keep her opinions to herself. She inveighed with regal force against the "new ideas," becoming quarrelsome with her son on several occasions.

One such occasion was on October 14, 1917. Something of this particular quarrel's nature and vehemence is indicated by the rather incoherent letter which Sara wrote upon her return from Washington to her New York City house. Addressing herself to "Dearest Franklin and Dearest Eleanor" but doubting "if you will have time dear Franklin to read this," she said:[42]

". . . I am sorry to feel that Franklin *is* tired and that my views are not his, but perhaps dear Franklin you may on second thoughts or *third* thoughts see that I am not so far wrong. The foolish old saying 'noblesse oblige' is good and 'honneur oblige' possibly expresses it better for most of us. One can be as democratic as one likes, but if we love our own and if we love our neighbors, we owe a great example. . . . After I got home, I sat in the library for nearly an hour reading, and as I put down my book and left the delightful room and the two fine portraits, I thought: after all, would it not be better to spend all one has at once . . . , and not think of the future; for with the *trend* to 'shirt sleeves,' and the ideas of what men should do in always being all things to all men and striving to give up the old fashioned traditions of family life, simple home pleasures and refinements, and the traditions some of us love best, of what use is it to *keep up* things, to hold on to dignity and all I stood up for this evening. Do not say that I *misunderstood,* I understand perfectly, but I cannot believe that my precious Franklin really feels as he expressed himself. Well, I hope while I live I may keep my 'old fashioned' theories and that *at least* in my own family I may continue to feel that *home* is the best and happiest place and that my son and daughter and their children will live in peace and keep from the tarnish which seems to affect so many."

She added a sentence which may or may not have been admonitory and remonstrative in its direct, immediate, and personal implications.

"Mrs. Newbold's theory that children are 'always just like their parents' is pretty true," she wrote, "as *example* is what really counts."

The suspicion of shocked remonstrance derives from our knowledge that the summer and autumn of 1917 were a peculiarly nerve-racking period in Franklin and Eleanor's private lives. We know that there was initiated at this time an emotional involvement that would weave its way through all the rest of Franklin Roosevelt's secret life, and of Eleanor's also, profoundly affecting their marital relations and undoubtedly affecting, too, in ways indeterminate, their public lives and historic deeds. The details are not known. Probably they will never be. A rigorously maintained conspiracy of silence on the part of all who had vital knowledge of the matter protected the principal protagonists while these yet lived, and it is likely that whatever solid documentary evidence may once have existed—letters, diaries, and so on—has been long since destroyed. What remains is only the broad outline, its gaps to be filled, if at all, by conjecture and surmise.

The broad outline, however, is clear enough, and definitely enough established for any historian, most of its key facts having been published in Jonathan Daniels' *Washington Quadrille* and in the numerous newspaper and magazine articles stimulated by it and an earlier book of his, *The Time Between Wars*.

When Eleanor came to Washington as wife of the Assistant Secretary of the Navy, she "tried at first to do without a secretary," as she later wrote, "but found that it took me such endless hours to arrange my calling list, and answer and send invitations, that I finally engaged one for three mornings a week." In the spring of 1913 she had turned to her Auntie Bye ("I dashed to Auntie Bye, who was in Farmington, Connecticut") to find out "what were the duties of an Assistant Secretary's wife," [43] and it was very probably to her Auntie Bye that she turned for advice on whom she should employ as her social secretary, once she had decided that such a secretary was needed. At any rate she did employ precisely "the kind of girl old Bye always saw with a sympathetic eye," as Jonathan Daniels has written.[44]

The girl was Lucy Page Mercer. She was abundantly qualified to help her employer through the ritualized intricacies of formal Washington society. She knew everyone in it, and she herself was of it, though she was poor and came from a broken home.

Lucy's mother, Minnie Tunis Mercer—daughter of wealthy John Tunis of Norfolk, Virginia, and of Carolina Elizabeth Henderson, who came from one of the oldest, most distinguished families in North Carolina—had been a reigning beauty in Washington society in the eighties and nineties. Now well into her fifties, Minnie Mercer was a remarkably handsome woman and still socially prominent, being listed in the highly exclusive Washington *Social Register,* despite the fact that the fortune she had inherited from her father had been long since dissipated, apparently through sheer reckless extravagance, and that she herself was viewed askance by the more rigorously straitlaced as a woman with something of a past who, moreover, defied present convention, as did Alice Roosevelt Longworth, by smoking cigarettes in public. Minnie had been twice married. Her first husband had been an Englishman, Percy Norcop, whom she divorced in 1886, when she was twenty-three, on grounds of his adultery. She had by then met Carroll Mercer, whom she married in London on July 30, 1888.

He on his wedding day was a tall, blond, handsome man of thirty-one, possessed of great charm, an impeccable family social standing, a well-earned reputation for hard-drinking "wildness," and, alas, no money at all. He was Catholic in religion—a direct descendant of those English Catholic gentlemen and their ladies who, under Cecilius Calvert, the second Lord Baltimore, founded Maryland colony in the 1630's. His ancestors on both sides had been notable in colonial and early U.S. history. ("Remember Carroll's sacred trust" is one of the lines in the official state song, "Maryland, My Maryland!", and both a Mercer and a Carroll were members of the Second Continental Congress.) But his father, Dr. Thomas Swann Mercer, had somehow lost the whole of a very considerable inheritance before the son was out of his teens, so that this son, unequipped by education or temperament for any gentlemanly profession save that of arms, had at age twenty-three obtained, by use of family connections, a commission as lieutenant in the U.S. Marine Corps. He was still a lieutenant (in June, 1885, he had been suspended for more than a year on half pay by sentence of a general court-martial, for drunkenness on duty) and was stationed on a U.S. gunboat anchored in the Thames at the time of his marriage. Barely eight months after the wedding, on March 31, 1889, he became the father of a girl, Violetta. A little more than two months after that he resigned his commission and came to live on, and use up, Minnie's money in Minnie's luxuriously furnished house at 1744 P Street in Washington, near Dupont Circle.

It was there that Lucy Page Mercer was born, the second and last child of the Mercers, on April 26, 1891.

From the first she was the child of no happy home. On the evidence, she was subjected to some of the same kinds of emotional strain as Eleanor Roosevelt had undergone while growing up, especially after a dark cloud of financial trouble closed down upon the Mercers' glittering social life sometime toward the end of the Gay Nineties. Carroll and Minnie Mercer quarreled often and bitterly. They were enabled to separate without causing talk when Carroll obtained a commission as captain in the U.S. Army in June, 1899, and went off to serve as a supply officer in

Cuba, Puerto Rico, and the Philippines, rising to the rank of major before his honorable discharge in June, 1901. But there was much gossip soon after he had rejoined his family, in 1903. The Mercers then lived in a house at 1761 N Street, NW, in Washington, only a few doors from the Cowles house at 1733 N Street (TR's "Little White House") into which the Franklin Roosevelts would move in 1913, and no more than before did they live together peacefully, joyously. Nor did they live together long. Within a few months, Minnie and Carroll were again separated, and this time forever, though there was, for religious reasons probably, no divorce. Minnie moved with her two daughters to New York City, became an interior decorator, and managed to live quite comfortably for a decade at fashionable addresses (one of them was the Holland Apartments, 66 West Forty-sixth Street) and to maintain her social standing. Perhaps she had financial help from relatives, added to vestiges of her former affluence; certainly she was aided in her quest for wealthy clients by her family connections.

But if Lucy Mercer, like Eleanor Roosevelt, had a scapegrace father and much family trouble, she had never to suffer as a child and adolescent such utter loneliness and inward insecurity as embittered Eleanor's growing up. Not for a moment need the child Lucy feel herself ugly, awkward, a ridiculous little "granny," unloved because unlovable. She knew that she was loved by those closest to her. She knew, she could not help knowing, that she was a pretty child, who blossomed during her teens into what many regarded as a radiant beauty. Naturally poised and graceful, she had great dignity and, even as a child, was reserved, quiet of manner, yet according to those who knew her best, she was also a naturally warm, generous personality with a capacity for great passion. In all vital matters she was sustained, her essential life given lyrical meaning, by the Catholic faith and ritual in which she was reared and which she seems never, as a girl, at least, to have questioned. There was far more gaiety in Minnie's house than ever there was at Tivoli. Yet Lucy was as strictly brought up as Eleanor, if in different fashion, and she evidently had much less contact with the "seamy side of life" than was forced upon Eleanor by Pussie's amorous instability and Uncle Vallie's orgiastic drinking. When Lucy at age seventeen was being educated as boarding pupil in a convent, a nun shook her head disapprovingly over the girl's frilly nightgowns. They were indecent, the nun averred; they were such as a prostitute might wear. Lucy was puzzled. What, she asked, was a prostitute?[45]

This convent, where both Lucy and Violetta were educated, was in the ancient Austrian town of Melk beside the Danube, not far from the family seats of Count Maximilian Esterházy and Count Anton Heussenstamm, both of whom had married maternal relatives of Carroll Mercer. The Countess Esterházy was Carroll Mercer's Aunt Sallie Carroll, whose first marriage to Captain (later General) Charles Griffin in 1861 (President Lincoln attended the wedding) ended with Griffin's death in 1867. Her marriage to the Austrian count had come soon afterward and had no doubt pointed the way toward the marriage years later of Agnes Carroll of Carrollton to Count Heussenstamm. It was the Countess Heussenstamm, Carroll Mercer's cousin, who brought the girls to Austria, chose for them the convent school, and provided them their home away from home until, early in the second decade of the century, they returned to New York City.

Then, in 1912, they moved back to Washington with their mother. The move revived a certain amount of gossip in society circles. There was a published rumor in a Washington scandal sheet quoted by Jonathan Daniels that Minnie had "forgiven Carroll," who, after a decade of obscure poverty, dissipation, and ill health, still lived in Washington. The Mercer family, it was said, was being reunited. The rumor was wholly false. Carroll and Minnie continued to live apart, and though his daughters occasionally visited and corresponded with him (he needed their affection; he was now desperately ill), there is no evidence that his estranged wife ever did. When he died in mid-September, 1917, it would be remarked that the sparse attendance at his funeral did not include his widow. Nor would she or her daughters be listed as his survivors in Washington's two leading newspapers. But there were other published rumors following Minnie's return to the capital which had the ring of truth. One of them, also quoted by Daniels, was that Minnie had found employment in "an art establishment" somewhere in Washington, NW. Another was that "Mrs. Mercer has placed both her daughters in self-supporting positions; one [Violetta] a trained nurse; the other [Lucy] an inside decorator." [46]

Nonetheless, Lucy Mercer had no full-time position satisfactory to her in early 1914, when she was either offered or applied for the post of social secretary to Mrs. Franklin Roosevelt. Soon thereafter her name began to appear now and then, casually, in Eleanor and Franklin's personal correspondence. Thus, an undated letter from Franklin to "Dearest Babs," probably written in late May, 1914, begins: "Arrived safely [in Washington] and came to house and Albert [the Roosevelt chauffeur] telephoned Miss Mercer who later came and cleaned up." [47] From which it would appear that Lucy's status in the Roosevelt household at that time (she continued to live with her mother at the Decatur Apartments, 2131 Florida Avenue, NW) was almost, if not quite, that of servant.

It did not remain so. The social secretary immediately made herself highly useful to her employer, who had begun her duty calls "under poor auspices, for I was feeling miserable again, as another baby* was coming along the following August." [48] Lucy was energetic, efficient, tactful, and thoroughly knowledgeable about the matters with which her job was concerned. She was also personally sympathetic. Serving her employer well through three crowded years whose events, for the Roosevelt household, included Eleanor's final pregnancy (with John, born in March, 1916), the subsequent move from the N Street house to 2131 R Street, and hundreds of social calls, luncheons, dinners, balls, and theater parties, Lucy became established as almost one of the family. By early 1917 Franklin Roosevelt had long since ceased to issue instructions to "Miss Mercer" through a chauffeur and was, in fact, arranging bachelor escorts for Lucy now and then (Nigel Law was one of them) so that she might join in his recreational outings.

Indeed there was nothing of servility, ever, in Lucy's appearance, manner, or character. There was much that commanded a wholehearted respect from women, as well as men. Her unhappy circumstances were well known to the Roosevelts when she entered Eleanor's employ and gave her an appealing quality she might not otherwise have had. But the appeal had in it no abject plea for help or sympathy, and such pity as her misfortunes aroused was more than offset by admiration for the uncomplaining gallantry with which she bore them. She was twenty-three years old in the spring of 1914. Her figure was not unlike Eleanor's at the same age. She was tall, slender, erect, with a bearing often described as "stately," though there was evidently a more consistent bodily grace in her than there was or had ever been in the often tense and self-conscious Eleanor. Lucy was far prettier than Eleanor. Her complexion was no better (they both had perfect complexions of the transparent kind through which an inner light seems to shine), nor were her blue eyes (they both had lovely eyes of the kind through which, also, an inner light seems to shine); but her features were more regular, her teeth did not protrude, her chin did not recede. Her speaking voice was warm and rich, in marked contrast with Eleanor's, which was normally high-pitched and tended to climb into "shrill arpeggios" under stress or excitement. Her smile, from all accounts, was especially attractive: a Henderson cousin of hers described it to Jonathan Daniels as "the most beautiful and winning that I have ever seen." [49] She had gaiety and wit, and under the tutelage and with the example of a mother who placed a considerable value on such things, she had acquired not a little of that

* Franklin Roosevelt, Jr.

intensely feminine charm of manner, that ability to attract and please a man in social situations, which traditionally characterizes the Southern belle. Yet one senses across the years, on the testimony of those who knew her and from her photographs, that her attractiveness was not primarily or essentially physical, sexual. It was more abstract, intangible. She remained religiously devout; she kept her passions normally under tight rein; she maintained her dignity, almost always; and her special kind of beauty was cool, poised, a little remote, with virtually nothing in it of the sultry or voluptuous. The proper background for her portrait might be a Northern formal garden, with clipped shrubs and flower beds laid out along graveled paths in geometric design; it could never be a lush, opulent, Rosseau-ish jungle, with tigers lurking in it.

But this detracted not at all from her attractiveness to Franklin Roosevelt. Quite the contrary. He, whose sexual development seemed to lag somewhat behind that of most of his contemporaries at Groton and Harvard, had always been and would always be most strongly drawn to women of stately mien and great dignity, like his mother, if generally quieter, less assertive, or at any rate more submissive to him—and Lucy Mercer, as time passed, delighted him more and more. As for her, she was no doubt immensely impressed from the very first by her employer's husband, who was so greatly admired a figure on the Washington scene and so very kind to her, as he was to everyone, so warmly friendly and interested, as well as interesting. He may well have seemed to her from the first, as he did to others, an unlikely mate for the plain, excessively dutiful, and excruciatingly conscientious Eleanor, who appeared wholly dedicated to childbearing and rearing and household management. He was so handsome a man, so dashing and fun-loving! He had so rare an ability to impart vitality to those around him! And though his energy might often seem inexhaustible, Lucy could not but discover that it was very far from being so, knowing him as she did through months adding up to years of his home and family life. He must on frequent occasion be renewed, recharged, re-created. He *needed* a feminine companionship within which he could relax and have fun and forget for a time the heavy tasks and demands of his office, his ambition; he needed precisely the kind of gay, warmly intimate companionship which she, Lucy Mercer, could supply.

Thus it began, in all probability.

Later they must both have wondered at what precise moment their initial pleasure in each other's company became dangerously delightful and then, almost at once, something more, an emotional attachment so wide and deep that it absorbed much of their essential beings and secret lives and required of them, if it were to be expressed at all in the prevailing circumstances, a nauseating furtiveness and deceit. There must then have come to him, amid hectic days and restless nights, moments of pure horror when he recoiled in shocked disbelief from what he was doing. This, surely, was no part of the script! It deranged the whole scheme of priorities by which his career had been guided thus far. And it had to lead to the gravest injury, if not the actual destruction of good, innocent people whom he still loved and to whom he was bound by the most vital ties. And for Lucy, too, with her religious commitment and personal pride, the situation must have been horrible, if perhaps less so than for him because she had, after all, apart from the scruples and terrors born of her Catholicism, much less to lose from the dreaded issue, and more to gain. She was twenty-six years old in 1917. She had no money, no husband, no prospects. She need be no Becky Sharp to consider the advantages that would accrue to her from marriage to the man she loved, should his divorce and marriage to her become possible.

There is evidence of unprecedented tensions in Roosevelt in the growing and increasingly open irritability of his dealings with Daniels, among others who disagreed with him, and in the increased incidence of his bouts with ill health (colds, throat infections, sinus headaches), beginning with his return from Haiti in early 1917. There is clear evidence, too, that Eleanor, by the early summer of that year, had sensed a change in him which he was at pains to hide and that she was profoundly disturbed by it.

She was reluctant to leave with the children for Campobello. She delayed her departure by some days beyond the usual annual time for it, evincing in the interim a hurt suspicion that he was impatient to have her gone. "I had a vile day after you left," he wrote her from the office on Monday, July 16, "stayed at home, coughed, dozed, tried to read and work and failed even to play Miss Millikin. . . . * I really can't stand that house all alone without you, and you were a goosy girl to think or even pretend to think that I do not want you here *all* the summer, because you know I do! But honestly *you* ought to have six weeks straight at Camp, just as *I* ought to, only you can and I can't! I *know* what a whole summer here does to people's nerves and at the end of the summer I will be like a bear with a sore head until I get a change or some cold weather—in fact as you know I am unreasonable and touchy now —but I shall try to improve." On the following day he wrote: "It seems years since you left and I miss you horribly and hate the thought of the empty house. Last night I thought I heard a burglar and sat at the head of the stairs with the gun for half an hour, but it turned out to be the cat." [50]

* A game of solitaire of which he was fond.

But a few hours later he was evidently absolved of guilt feelings, if only temporarily, by an article based on an interview with Eleanor published on July 17 in the New York *Times*. It asserted that the "food-saving program adopted at the home" of the Assistant Secretary of the Navy had "been selected by the conservation section of the Food Administration as a model for other large households," there being, according to Mrs. Roosevelt, "seven in the family, and . . . ten servants . . . employed." Mrs. Roosevelt did "the buying, the cooks see that there is no food wasted, the laundress is sparing in her use of soap; each servant has a watchful eye for evidences of shortcomings in others, and all are encouraged to make suggestions in the use of 'left overs.' " Eleanor was quoted directly. " 'Making the ten servants help me do my saving has not only been possible, but highly profitable,' said Mrs. Roosevelt. . . . 'Since I have started following the home-card instruction prices have risen, but my bills are no larger.' " [51] Her husband read this with an emotion that mingled anger with disgust and a certain relief, for he was now enabled to turn the tables on Eleanor. The accused became accuser. On July 18, in a scathing letter that omitted his usual salutation of "Dearest Babs" (it bore in fact no salutation at all), he wrote: "All I can say is that your latest newspaper campaign is a corker and I am proud to be the husband of the Originator, Discoverer and Inventor of the New Household Economy for Millionaires! Please have a photo taken showing the family, the ten cooperating servants, the scraps saved from the table and the handbook. I will have it published in the Sunday Times." He averred with heavy irony that she had "leaped into public fame" to the extent that "all Washington is talking of the Roosevelt plan and I begin to get telegrams of congratulations and requests for further details from Pittsburgh, New Orleans, San Francisco and other neighboring cities." [52]

It was as though he had lashed an open wound. Eleanor was in agony. "I do think it was horrid of that woman to use my name in that way," she wrote him from Campobello on July 20, "and I feel dreadfully about it because so much is not true and yet some of it I did say. I will never be caught again that's sure and I'd like to crawl away for shame." [53]

Thereafter, boldly, as if to dissimulate through an ostentatious parade of innocence, he mentioned Lucy several times in his letters to Campobello. On July 25, for instance, he told of a cruise up the Potomac in the *Sylph*, a Presidential yacht seldom used by Wilson but often by the Secretary and Assistant Secretary of the Navy. "The trip . . . was a joy and a real rest . . . ," he wrote. "Such a funny party, but it worked out wonderfully! The Charlie Munns, the Gary Graysons [Rear Admiral Grayson, the President's personal physician, had been named medical director of the Navy], Lucy Mercer and Nigel Law, and they all got on splendidly." On the following day, he wrote: "Kiss the chicks. I do miss you so *very* much. . . ." [54]

But Eleanor remained uneasy, if not definitely suspicious. When she learned, a few days later, that Franklin's throat infection had recurred* and he was going into the hospital for its cure, she promptly boarded a train and came down to Washington to be with him. He was well on the way to recovery before she arrived and she could not, because of the children, remain with him long. Returned to Campobello, she received further letters from her husband in which Lucy Mercer was mentioned. On August 20 he told of an auto trip to an estate near Harpers Ferry. "Lucy Mercer went and the Graysons and we got there at 5:30, walked over the farm—a very rich one . . .—had supper . . . , left at nine and got home at midnight!" On September 9 he wrote of the denouement of the quarrel between Daniels and the Navy League† as it affected the Comforts Committee, adding in words that could hardly have been comforting to Eleanor: "*You* are entirely disconnected and Lucy Mercer and Mrs. Munn are closing up the loose ends." [55]

A climax to all this was reached sometime during the year that followed. Decades later there were several published versions of what occurred, and variant versions have been communicated orally to the author.

According to newspaper columnist Drew Pearson, "Eleanor Roosevelt discovered the romance rather abruptly when, driving through Virginia, she saw her husband and Lucy in a parked car." *Time* magazine, reporting Pearson's story, promptly concluded that the car was probably parked "in Arlington, roughly where the Pentagon now stands, in an area popular during World War I . . . as a trysting spot." This story is rendered dubious, however, by the fact that Eleanor at that time could not drive a car, having been discouraged from any attempt to do so by the accident she had had with the Ford at Sea Bright, New Jersey, in 1908. She could have been a passenger in a car driven by someone else, of course. More likely—indeed, almost inevitable—was the spread to her already suspicious ears of some of the gossip stirred by her husband's being seen so often in the company of "another woman" or, if not in Lucy's company, at least at the same social events and outings, while the mother of his five children was hundreds of miles away for months at a time.

* Josephus Daniels was convinced that the strenuous early morning exercises in which Roosevelt engaged, under Camp, lowered Roosevelt's resistance to infections. Daniels himself steadfastly refused to exercise at all and remained in perfect health throughout the war.

† See page 396.

But it is certain that "her worst fears were confirmed" in the autumn of 1918, shortly after her husband had returned, seriously ill, from a European mission which will be told of in its proper place. Joseph P. Lash, who had the story from her own lips, writes in his *Eleanor and Franklin* that she at that time "took care of his mail, and in the course of doing so she came upon Lucy's letters." The hurt she suffered was profound and everlasting.* There was a confrontation of the wife, the husband, and Lucy. The earliest published account is that of Olive Clapper, wife of a famous newspaperman, Raymond Clapper, in her book *Washington Tapestry,* issued in 1946. She, who obviously had little liking for Eleanor, does not name Lucy Mercer but speaks of "a persistent rumor" that the Roosevelt marriage was threatened in 1917–18 by Roosevelt's love for another woman. "Mrs. Roosevelt was supposed to have called her husband and the enamored woman to a conference, at which she offered to give her husband a divorce if the woman wished to marry him. A Catholic, the woman could not marry a divorced man. When she expressed these sentiments, Mrs. Roosevelt issued an ultimatum that they must stop seeing each other—to which they promptly acquiesced." According to one of Lucy's Henderson cousins, Mrs. Lyman Cotton of Chapel Hill, North Carolina, quoted by Jonathan Daniels, Lucy's Catholicism was *not* the decisive factor. "Eleanor was not willing to step aside," Lucy reportedly said to her cousin. The acid-tongued Mrs. Alice Roosevelt Longworth, in an interview printed verbatim in the *New York Times Magazine* in 1967, told of "doing imitations of Eleanor" one day while visiting her Auntie Corinne (Mrs. Douglas Robinson, TR's youngest sister, who was of course Eleanor's Auntie Corinne, too) "and . . . [she] looked at me and said: 'Never forget, Alice, Eleanor offered Franklin his freedom.' And I said, 'But, darling, that's what I've wanted to know all these years. Tell.' And so she said, 'Yes, there was a family conclave and they talked it over and finally they decided it affected the children and there was Lucy Mercer, a Catholic, and so it was called off.' " Other accounts cite Roosevelt's political ambition as the decisive factor; there can be no doubt that it was a major one. "Mrs. Roosevelt was not one to give up easily," wrote Drew Pearson. "And she knew that her dashing young husband had more than his wife and children to sacrifice—his political ambition. 'If you want to be President, Franklin,' she told her husband very sweetly, 'you'll have to take me with you.' " [56]

*   *   *

* For instance—a trivial, yet significant instance—Eleanor in her later years, though on a friendly first-name basis with Jonathan Daniels, would never address his wife by *her* first name, as she did many others whom she knew less well. Mrs. Jonathan Daniels' first name is Lucy.

Eleanor's sufferings at this time can be imagined. Over and over again in her life her great need to love and be loved had been denied—and in ways that seemed specifically designed, by some malevolent fate, to crush utterly her spirit. Over and over again she, in her painful shyness, knowing herself to be not beautiful and feeling herself to be more unattractive than actually she was, had had added to this feeling a sense of being ridiculed, laughed at or pitied or both together by people to whom she was deeply attached. Over and over again in her married life, in her relations with her domineering mother-in-law, she had been treated with a contempt all the more deeply hurtful for being unconsciously expressed. And now this! This culminating betrayal!

One can imagine, too, the protestations and avowals with which her husband accompanied his renunciation "forever" of Lucy Mercer and how Eleanor's eager yearning to believe them stumbled and fell upon jagged rocks of doubt. The doubts would persist. They could never be wholly dissolved or surmounted or even ignored. For though she would never claim to understand the deepest workings of her husband's mind, was never absolutely sure of what went on in the hidden recesses of his being, she did know of his seemingly fundamental aversion to final, clear-cut decisions. Thus he had never made and would never make a sharp distinction between the loyalties he owed his wife and the loyalties he owed his mother or even between the emotions centered on his mother and those centered on his wife, much less a clear-cut decision as to which loyalties and emotions had priority. And so it would probably be with regard to Lucy Mercer. In his conception of living Time there was almost nothing of Eternity, virtually nothing that could be labeled "never" or "forever," so that it was more than likely, as Eleanor could not but suspect, that his renunciation of Lucy was made with secret reservations at whose core were secret hopes.

Eleanor, writing of this crisis period in her life, twenty years later, ascribed the great change which was then made in her existence to the "variety of war activities" with which she "completely filled" her time following her return to Washington in the fall of 1917. She knitted and supervised a knitting project in which others were involved; she worked "two or three shifts a week" in a Red Cross canteen in the railroad yards; she came bearing gifts once a week to the Navy Hospital, where she became the confidante of many a lonely homesick wounded boy; and she took an especially active interest in St. Elizabeth's Hospital, the federal hospital for the insane, after the Navy had taken over a wing of it for sailors and marines suffering from shell shock (she herself was outraged by the conditions that prevailed in St. Elizabeth's, because of inadequate appropriations, and prodded Secretary Lane [the hospital was under Interior] into an investigation that produced some improvements)—all this while administering a large household and seeing to it that her three school-age children, Anna and James and Elliott, led reasonably normal lives. Every bit of her "executive ability, which had been more or less dormant up to this time, was called into play," she wrote, and she began "to have a certain confidence in myself and in my ability to meet emergencies and deal with them." She also learned then, largely, in her words, from the "many tragedies" she saw "enacted" in the hospitals, "that practically no one in the world is entirely bad or entirely good, and that motives are often more important than actions." She who had "spent most of my life in an atmosphere where everyone was sure of what was right and what was wrong" became "a more tolerant person, far less sure of my own beliefs and methods of action, but I think more determined to try for certain ultimate objectives." [57]

Seventeen

➤➤❂❮❮

Roosevelt and the Birth of Leviathan

I

Iᴛ WAS not only in his private personal life that Roosevelt during these years became a significant blend of old and new, transitional. Ambivalence and a dichotomy of concept that verged on the contradictory characterized his attitude toward public affairs and the acts and patterns of his administrative procedure.

On the one hand, he was strongly attracted by huge concentrations of administrative power whereby public questions could be answered or rendered obsolete by bold and sweeping action. (None delighted more than he in the triumph of "fact" over "theory.") He pressed for creation of the Council of National Defense, for a national Labor Administration, for a single authority over the mine barrier project, and his administrative strategy within the Navy Department generally aimed toward a centralization and unification of decision-making powers. He also pressed in speeches and articles for compulsory national service applicable "to all men and women and not only to the actual men in the Army and Navy." He privately admitted that he would have been hard put to find useful service in the Navy for drafted business and professional people aged forty and over.[1] But universal conscription would certainly have gone far to solve or obviate the necessity for solution of the myriad individual labor-management problems that now crossed his desk and Howe's.

On the other hand, he was "a great trial and error guy," as Emory S. Land once said of him,[2] whose wide-ranging empiricism must have space around it, an area of indefinition containing a multiplicity of free choices, if it were to express itself or even remain alive. Blanket solutions, heavy with compulsion, would smother it. He continued thoroughly conventional in the realm of abstract ideas, insofar as he operated in that realm at all. His general ideas were orthodox, his mental attitude one of passive subservience to the established order in philosophy and religion; but in his dealings with the external world of concrete particulars he was unorthodox, experimental, and, by willful temperament, insubordinate. He had shown over and over again how impatient he was with rules and regulations that inhibited efficiency or prevented needed innovations—how willing he was to cut corners in matters of procurement and construction and manufacture, ignoring established channels and prescribed procedures in order to get things done. And in his actual handling of labor relations, he was addicted to individual rather than blanket solutions, relying much on personal face-to-face negotiations. He "believed that a perfectly frank talk over matters of this kind will in nearly all cases obviate difficulties," as he wrote to a manufacturer who, troubled by a labor controversy, appealed to government authority. Alfred B. Rollins, Jr., cites an instance in which Howe "laid bare the dynamics of his approach" to the labor problem. Union leaders had asked the department to announce a standard policy applicable to all Navy yards on the basis of a decision reached through controversy at one particular yard. Howe demurred. "He suggested that comprehensive changes in policy were sometimes 'misunderstood,' while much could be done with individual cases as they arose." [3]

And viewing it in historical perspective, one may see in this dichotomy of Roosevelt's public attitude, administrative acts and patterns a more than personal significance. It was expressive, by it he was rendered symptomatic and representative, of America as a whole during those same years—an America in transition, war-forced and -speeded into the final phases of transition, from an economy-and-culture that was predominantly agrarian (Jeffersonian) to one that was predominantly industrial and urban (Hamiltonian). His very lack of *conscious* reflection made his mind a remarkably accurate mirror of prevailing trends. He became the epitome, in his official capacity, of the culminating process by which the New Freedom was transformed into the New Nationalism.

II

The success of the nation's "grand effort" in 1917–18 and indeed the effort itself were the result of "the very remarkable leadership" exercised by "Wilson and his Cabinet." So said Roosevelt in 1925, when a writer seemed to suggest that the effort had been a vast people's movement to which the administration merely responded. The "American organization for war" was "carefully thought out," he protested, and "was created *from the top down,* NOT *the bottom up.* This is very important." [4]

The center of this organization was the Council of National Defense, which turned out to be as crucially important as ever Roosevelt had argued it would be. Not that it did very much, of itself alone: composed of a half dozen Cabinet Secretaries, each with a war-burdened government department to administer and a war-burdened President to advise, it was an almost purely formal body, its function the passive legitimatization of deeds performed by others. But the Congressional act which authorized it also authorized the setting up of "subordinate bodies of specially qualified persons . . . capable of organizing to the utmost the resources of the country," as Wilson explained. When these subordinate bodies began to function, the council, itself inert, became the focus of gigantic organized energies, a pivot on which turned the whole mighty movement whereby America's economic power, as never before in history, was mobilized on a national scale and applied to the achievement of a national purpose.

Even a cursory review of the way in which this happened, however, belies the assertion that it had been "carefully thought out" and then imposed by an executive as decisively forceful as it was foresightful and forethoughtful.

There assembled in Washington for the first time on December 7, 1916, an innocuously named Advisory Commission to the Council. On it were seven men appointed by the President and serving, as he announced, "without remuneration, efficiency being their sole object and Americanism their only motive." [5] ("Dollar-a-year men," the press dubbed them in recognition of the token payment which legality required; there were hundreds of their ilk in government by war's end.) The seven were a railroad president; the president of an automobile manufacturing company; the head of a great mail-order house; the president of the Drexel Institute of Philadelphia; the president of the American College of Surgeons; Samuel Gompers, president of the American Federation of Labor (his inclusion marked a significant advance in the power of labor organization); and Bernard M. Baruch, who frankly called his business that of Wall Street "speculator." Baruch was the sole Democrat; all the others were Republican.*

At the outset, these men had no clear idea of what it was they were called upon to do. No one knew what authority they had, if any, to go beyond advice in the setting and executing of policy. The necessary first

* Though often cited by the President's partisans as evincing a patriotic statesmanship that eschewed politics, the preponderance of Republicans over Democrats in key government economic posts during the war simply reflected the fact that, in the big business community from which most of the choices had to be made, there were few Democrats.

step was obvious; they took it months before war was declared. Hiring employees as needed for the task, they made an unprecedented inventory of the nation's industrial plant, gathering masses of data essential to intelligent national economic planning. The second step, equally obvious, was taken a week before war was declared: there was created a Munitions Standards Board, to set uniform standards for ammunition manufacture. But these steps were the merest preliminaries to the major tasks of industrial mobilization. Almost at once it was necessary to reorganize the Standards Board and, renaming it the General Munitions Board, assign to it broad responsibilities for coordinating the purchase of ammunition for the fighting forces.

Certainly coordination, and not only with regard to munitions, was by then a crying need whose insistent voice grew louder with each succeeding week. Anarchy prevailed over the whole field of procurement and distribution of war matériel as the Army, the Navy, and Allied purchasing commissions bid and fought with one another for scarce supplies. Sometimes the squabbles went all the way to the White House. Roosevelt liked to tell in later years how his own highly successful procurement activities on behalf of the Navy, during February and March, 1917, caused him to be summoned to the White House in mid-April and there told by the President, in the presence of Army Chief of Staff, General Hugh Scott, that he had "cornered the market for supplies" and must "divide up with the Army." [6] But of course, the White House could not possibly operate as a general clearinghouse for purchases or as the final arbiter of myriad procurement disputes.

Nor was the General Munitions Board able to do so. The responsibilities assigned to it were as vaguely defined as they were broad, and they were unaccompanied—in the prevailing legal context they *could* not be accompanied—by a commensurate coercive authority. The professional Army and Navy proved especially recalcitrant: as agencies of force, knowing only the language of force, they would submit voluntarily to no outside controls. In late July, therefore, having notably failed to establish by persuasion or bold assertion the authority it required, this General Board was disbanded and replaced by a War Industries Board whose assigned responsibilities were broader and more explicit. Not only was the new board to serve as a clearinghouse for purchases, it was also to assume responsibilities for the allocation of raw materials, for controlling production, and for general supervision of labor relations. It had, however, no more direct authority over the procurement activities of the Army and Navy than its predecessor had had, and again this proved to be a fatal weakness. There was a near breakdown of industrial mobilization in the late autumn and early winter of 1917. Exceptionally severe winter weather was partially responsible: heavy snows blocked railroad lines, causing fuel shortages through the East and contributing thereby to a decline in steel production. But this merely pointed up the inadequacy of existing arrangements.

And so, at the end of the old year and the beginning of the new, sweeping changes in national economic organization were made in response to urgent necessities. Unprecedented government controls, direct and indirect, began to be exerted over every phase of industrial activity.

On December 28, 1917, by executive order under his emergency war powers, the President took over all the nation's railroads, placing them under a Railroad Administration of which the director general was William G. McAdoo, who resigned from the Treasury to accept this appointment. On January 16, 1918, the original chairman of the WIB resigned, some said "in disgust." Three days later the chairman of the Senate's Military Affairs Committee, a Democrat, charged on the basis of his committee's investigations that the "military establishment of America" had "almost stopped functioning" because of gross mismanagement and incompetence "in every Department of the Government." Within hours thereafter, leading Republicans were calling loudly for creation of a coalition War Cabinet to take over from the White House supreme direction of the war effort. Wilson's typically bold response was to draft and have introduced in Congress (by Senator L. S. Overman of North Carolina) legislation conferring upon himself, as a temporary war measure, almost limitless powers to "coordinate and consolidate" government agencies and organize the nation's war economy. ("We might as well abdicate!" certain Senate leaders were quoted as saying.) Nor did he await passage of this bill, which was not finally enacted until May 20, to employ the powers it explicitly conferred. On March 4, he named Bernard Baruch chairman of the WIB and assigned to that agency not only the long-needed authority over purchases, but also authority to set price guidelines and establish and enforce priorities of industrial production and distribution.

The forty-seven-year-old Baruch had had no executive experience whatever when he entered government. But he had a forceful personality and supreme self-confidence; he was a man of impressive physique, well over six feet tall and beautifully proportioned; he charmed with the courtly manners of his native South Carolina, manners whose seeming and certainly winning deference was enhanced by the deafness of one of his ears—and as a professional gambler on a huge scale he had developed a quick calculating shrewdness of judgment in his dealings with men and situations. He gathered around him some hundred men accustomed to the management of large enterprises (principal lieutenants were Alexander Legge of International Harvester, George N. Peek of the Moline Plow Company, Brigadier General Hugh S. Johnson, retired, of the U.S. Army's cavalry*), and they all set to work at a furious pace. By midsummer of 1918 order had fully emerged from, and had at last largely replaced, the preceding chaos. America's industrial plant, harnessed to a single purpose and centrally planned and administered, was achieving miracles of production.

Meanwhile, there were roughly similar developments with regard to food and fuel production and distribution.

On the day after war was declared, the Council of National Defense voted to request Herbert Hoover to accept the chairmanship of a committee on food supply and prices. A mining engineer and company manager who, having made a fortune in international operations, was residing in London at the outbreak of the war, Hoover, forty years old in 1914, had assumed the administration of the Belgian Relief Commission, a task of large scope and formidable difficulty which he had performed with admirable efficiency. In May the President published his intention to establish a Food Administration, to be headed by Hoover, with authority to exert controls over food production and distribution. He was unable to do so, however, until Congress, on August 10, 1917, after prolonged and bitter debate, passed the White House-sponsored Lever Act, which gave the President a broad grant of power over fuel production and distribution, as well as over agricultural production and the manufacture and distribution of foodstuffs.

The Food Administration, popularly known as the Hoover Administration, was set up within hours after the Lever Act was passed and at once began to put into effect programs already planned for greatly increasing food production while decreasing food consumption in America, especially of wheat, pork, and sugar. A United States Grain Corporation was set up to buy and distribute wheat at $2.20 a bushel—a price deliberately set so high above the free market level that it stimulated an immense increase in the acreage planted to wheat for 1918–19, especially of hard red winter wheat across the western Great Plains. A Sugar Equalization Board was established to buy the whole of Cuba's and the United States' sugar crop at a fixed high price, for resale to American refiners and the British government. Pork production for 1918 and '19 was almost doubled after the Food Administration, in November, 1917, set a price of $15.50 per hundredweight for hogs. Every food manufacturer and dealer doing a business of more than $100,000 a year was re-

---

* A few months before, Johnson had had charge of preparations for the first draft call, preparations virtually completed by the time Congress had passed and the President signed (May 18, 1917) the Conscription Act.

quired to obtain a license to operate from the administration, a license which could be revoked if regulations were disobeyed. Simultaneously, through a vast propaganda campaign of which the central theme was "Food Will Win the War," householders were stimulated to plant "war gardens"; to observe "wheatless" Mondays and Wednesdays, "pork-less" Thursdays and Saturdays, "meatless" Tuesdays; and in general to "Hooverize"—that is, practice "food conservation." As a result of all this, America was enabled nearly to triple in 1918–19 the total quantity of food shipped to the European Allies in normal prewar years. Without it, the British could not have survived.

Two weeks after the Food Administration was created, the President established a Fuel Administration and appointed a longtime personal friend, Harry A. Garfield, president of Williams College,* to head it. Authorized to do so by the Lever Act, the Fuel Administration set a price for coal high enough to bring marginal mines back into full pro-duction and took other steps to increase fuel production and decrease its non-war-industrial use. When rail transportation virtually broke down during the winter crisis of 1917–18, Garfield issued orders, much-protested but obeyed, to all manufacturing plants, save those engaged in vital war production, to limit their operations to a specified percentage of normal for five consecutive days (from January 18 through January 22) and for nine consecutive Mondays thereafter. Other Fuel Adminis-tration orders at various times shut down 170 silk-manufacturing plants in Paterson, New Jersey; banned the use of coal or oil on pleasure yachts; limited business hours to from 9 A.M. to 5 P.M.; closed all thea-ters and other places of entertainment at 10 P.M.; and ordered "lightless nights" for several days each week throughout the nation.

As for the crucial problem of shipping, whereby American war pro-duction and fighting men could reach the war zone across dangerous seas, this problem was solved, after many failures, by government action as direct, as authoritarian as any taken domestically by the rulers of Germany. There was chartered as a subsidiary of the U.S. Shipping Board, in April, 1917, an Emergency Fleet Corporation, whose assigned task was to build new ships faster than U-boats could sink them. A bit-ter quarrel at once broke out between the head of the board and the head of the corporation, whose respective areas of authority were vaguely defined, causing the President to remove them both in late July, 1917, and consolidate all administrative authority over shipping, its ac-quisition and employment, in a newly appointed head of the Shipping Board, Edward N. Hurley. Hurley moved at once to initiate con-

---

* Wilson's son-in-law, Francis B. Sayre, was a professor on the faculty of Williams.

struction of new shipyards designed to produce 15,000,000 tons of new shipping, but for various complicated reasons this colossal program failed dismally. By September, 1918, the Emergency Fleet Corporation had managed to deliver a mere 466,000 tons of new shipping altogether, and not a single ship had yet come down the ways of the greatest of the new shipyards, at Hog Island. The Shipping Board, however, had by then acquired a barely adequate merchant fleet by the simple, ruthless means of commandeering. Ninety-seven German ships in U.S. harbors were put into service. Some 3,000,000 tons of shipping being constructed in private yards was seized. A half million tons of Dutch shipping in U.S. ports was seized.

In the handling of this merchant fleet at sea, strong disagreement developed between the Shipping Board and the Navy, with Roosevelt as chief spokesman for the latter. The Assistant Secretary argued that the crews of merchantmen sailing into the war zone should be enrolled in the Naval Reserve, given Navy training for convoy duty, and remain subject to Navy discipline. He could point to numerous incidents in which merchantmen captains had disobeyed the orders of the Navy convoy command and in which lax discipline on the part of crews produced needless dangers and, on occasion, actual sinkings. But the Shipping Board for a long time said no. Not until early July, 1918, was it agreed that all merchantmen exclusively engaged in war zone shipping would be manned by the Navy.[7]

All this was enormously stimulating to Franklin Roosevelt, and educative of him. He learned much about how Presidential power may be enhanced and employed in national emergencies and about how great governmental enterprises can best be set up and managed, though it must be added that he, for various reasons, would repeat most of the Wilson administration's initial errors when he faced similar organizational problems two decades later. He was fascinated by the magnitude of the power concentrated in the executive and had, as a member of this executive, a heady sense of himself making things happen on a colossal scale, of personally shaping the course of history.

But surely, looking at what happened overall, in historical perspective, one can see in it little evidence of prescience, purposeful intelligence, and executive will as the *prime* movers, the actual initiators and molders, of stupendous events. One sees instead visible echoes of the process by which imperial Germany's political economy was given its final form, and by which the Great War itself came to happen—a process of human inadvertence and machine compulsion, of conflict between individual selfishness and communal necessities—a process, in sum, of losing control or failing to gain control over the vast energies which scientific technology was releasing in increasingly potent forms. Far from being imposed "from the top down" by a wise and forceful executive, the American war organization was generated "from the bottom up" by the very forces it seemed to organize. Its administrative structure was the necessary pattern or "natural" shape of these forces when applied to war. The men who, under the aegis of the Council of National Defense, came ultimately to exercise a government dictatorship over the national economy had the means and imperatives for doing so literally thrust upon them—and thrust upon them against their respective wills. For were they not, for the most part, men of big business? Were they not committed, in theory, to "free enterprise," with a bare minimum of federal controls? Similarly with regard to Woodrow Wilson personally and his political administration in general: a principled, purposeful intelligence was repeatedly overwhelmed or overruled by the events it sought to avert or to control. "In a democracy it is the part of statesmanship to prevent the development of power which overawes the ordinary forces of man," Louis Brandeis had said. And Wilson—the Jeffersonian Democrat, author of *Congressional Government* and advocate of decentralized administration—had thoroughly agreed. Yet under his Presidency there were heaped up such "mighty Himalayas" (Brandeis' phrase) of concentrated power as had never been before in his native land, and heaped up, moreover, through his own acts in large part, acts he felt compelled by circumstance to perform.

Or, if we may change metaphors, he whose natural love was for small familiar things, and not at all for bigness—he who had been intellectually convinced that a genuinely free society must be a loosely organized, atomistic one—was required by ironic fate to preside over the Birth of Leviathan.* The metaphor is peculiarly apt. For as he made his compelled responses to the challenges of war, the Calvinistic, idealistic Woodrow Wilson obviously strove to believe what the atheistic, materialistic Thomas Hobbes so emphatically asserted—namely, that the central authority of the state is created (not in historical fact, but in symbolic truth) by a social contract, an irrevocable "covenant" as Hobbes called it; which is to say that he, Wilson, as War President was a creature of sacred covenant. His every act was its expression. In Hobbes' theory, the authority thus granted the "sovereign" (his name for the single central governing power he deemed essential to social stability) was absolute and unlimited. In Wilson's sovereign practice, it almost became so.

* John Dos Passos uses this phrase as a subtitle in his *Mr. Wilson's War* (New York, 1962).

III

And nowhere was the irony more bitter than in the area of civil liberties, nowhere more "tragical" than in that life of the mind with which as a professional educator he had been chiefly concerned through most of his adult life.

The "inevitability" by which America was forced actively into the war included no truly overwhelming tide of popular opinion. In fact, considerable opposition to the war was expressed in the very last hours of decision. Wilson well knew that the minority for whom such men as Debs, La Follette, and Norris spoke was by no means insignificant, either in numbers or in persuasive prestige. And as academic idealists so often do in crisis situations wherein they must exercise power, he responded to this challenging fact by becoming the most cynically realistic of realists, the most ruthlessly practical of practical men. He created or permitted the creation of governmental machinery for manufacturing a public opinion that met precise specifications. He simultaneously acquired and employed executive powers whereby dissenting opinion was forcibly suppressed, with dissenters jailed when "necessary."

One week after war was declared, Wilson established by executive order a Committee on Public Information, nominally under the supervision of the Secretaries of State, War, and Navy. Its Presidentially appointed chairman, George Creel, was a prominent crusading journalist from Denver, Colorado, who had served Wilson well and gained the President's rarely bestowed personal affection during the 1916 election campaign. A man of fertile imagination, emotional combative temperament, and prodigious energy, his first-rate talents as a publicist uninhibited by any excessive concern for strict truth telling, Creel proposed a government war information policy of "unparalleled openness." The policy should be carried out, he said, as "a vast enterprise of salesmanship, the world's greatest adventure in advertising." [8] And he was given his way. With some $5,000,000 assigned him from a special $50,000,000 President's Fund, this in addition to an appropriation of $1,250,000 from a Congress that came to hate him for his openly expressed contempt for it, he built an unprecedentedly huge publicity organization (some 150,000 people became actively involved in it as employees or volunteers) which flooded the nation and reached into the remotest corners of the world with American war and peace propaganda. A Division of Pictorial Publicity, headed by Charles Dana Gibson, was set up. It recruited eminent painters, illustrators, cartoonists, and designers, who produced all manner of posters, placards, billboard signs, lantern slides, and illustrations for magazines and newspapers and books. A Motion

Picture Divison directly produced several one-reel and full-length feature films and guided the production of numerous others. Actors, actresses, singers, celebrities of all kinds were called upon or volunteered to make personal appearances by the thousand. Famous novelists, distinguished historians, educators, and ministers of the Gospel were enlisted to produce magazine articles, leaflets, and pamphlets, each issued in printings of hundreds of thousands, sometimes many millions, of copies. The Creel Committee also produced many hundreds of canned speeches for use by local orators, men and women of standing in their respective communities. By Creel's own estimate, about 75,000 Four-Minute Men (so called because they spoke "four minutes on a subject of national importance") delivered about 7,555,190 speeches in motion-picture theaters and other places of crowd assembly, speeches heard by an aggregate total of 314,454,514 people.

The tactical aims of this assault on the mind were many and various, including the development of popular pressures for passage of the much-controverted Conscription (Selective Service) Act, the prevention of effective resistance to the draft, the stimulation of the sale of Liberty Bonds to the public (much of the war was financed by loans thus obtained from citizens), the stimulation of industrial and agricultural production, food conservation, and the encouragement of voluntary enlistments in the armed services. The overall strategic aims became, under Wilson's leadership, two in number. The first was the obvious one of arousing a perfervid American patriotism having a passionate hatred of the national enemy at its core. The second was to arouse popular support in all the warring nations, including Germany, of Wilsonian proposals for a "just peace" permanently maintained through international organization—this being the great object which, in Wilson's tensely anxious heart and mind, justified all the viciousness needed to attain it.

And certainly the obverse of Creel's propaganda operation, if not this operation itself, was vicious in the extreme by the standards Wilson himself had always formerly maintained. The forcible effort by government to prevent the expression of views that contradicted those Creel promoted subverted the first principles of a democratic society.

On June 15, 1917, Congress passed a White House-sponsored Espionage Act, which, though ostensibly aimed at overt acts of war obstruction, was so drafted as to become a tool for the suppression of all dissent. It became a crime punishable by a fine of $10,000 and imprisonment for twenty years to circulate "willfully" false reports helpful to the enemy, to incite rebellion in the armed forces (what precisely constituted "incitement" was left unclear), or in any way to "obstruct" voluntary recruitment or the draft. The Postmaster General was empowered to bar from the mails any material which, in his judgment (and Burleson's was a far from liberal one), advocated treason, insurrection, or disobedience of U.S. laws. On October 6, 1917, Congress passed a White House-sponsored Trading-with-the-Enemy Act, which not only prohibited trade with the Central Powers (the restrictions upon the shipment of gold established a legal precedent that would become important to Franklin Roosevelt sixteen years later), but also gave the President censorship powers over international communications and the Postmaster General censorship powers over the domestic foreign language press. With these legal weapons in hand, the government made a determined effort to prevent "disloyalty" by crude force (a kind of "love-me-or-I'll-kick-your-teeth-in" campaign on the part of police and federal prosecutors), which resulted in the jailing of some hundreds of citizens who openly expressed a principled opposition to war in general, to this particular war, to conscription, to government restrictions on civil liberties. But the Attorney General, T. W. Gregory, was not satisfied with this. Nor, it would seem, was the President. They felt that federal prosecutions were unduly limited by the fact that the government was required to prove, under the Espionage Act, that specific "seditious utterances" did actually have consequences injurious to the war effort or *would* have if their repetition were permitted. So the executive sponsored and, on May 16, 1918, the President signed Congressional legislation (the Sedition Act) which removed this disability. Seditious utterance, which included "scurrilous" or "abusive" statements about the flag or the form of government or the uniform of the armed forces of the United States, became a crime per se, regardless of consequences. The Postmaster General, at his discretion, could deny use of the mails to anyone on the grounds that that person would violate the act.

Precisely one month after the signing of the Sedition Act, whose terms were more stringent than those of the notorious Act of 1798 which Jefferson so vehemently protested, Eugene V. Debs, former and future Socialist candidate for President of the United States, speaking to a convention of his party in Canton, Ohio, gave full and frank expression of his opposition to the war and the effect it was having on the American body politic. Promptly arrested, tried, and convicted, he was sentenced to ten years in a federal prison. And this was but the most notorious of many hundreds of cases of court-denied free speech (more than 1,500 citizens were arrested for speaking their minds or feelings; one teen-aged girl was sentenced to twenty years) which, in turn, were but a tiny fraction of the number of instances in which citizens were socially ostracized, dismissed from clubs, deprived of employment, even subjected to physical violence—there were whippings, tar-and-featherings, mutilations, fatal lynchings—by fellow private citizens, sometimes because they were merely suspected of having disloyal thoughts or unpatriotic attitudes. The formerly small Federal Bureau of Investigation of the Justice Department was abruptly expanded into a powerful organization with thousands on its payroll and a budget of many millions. Joined to it by secret voluntary enrollment were more than 200,000 patriots, who, with no questions asked about their qualifications for such delicate work (their motives, honesty, training, intelligence), undertook to spy upon their neighbors and report to FBI agents "dangerous" and "suspicious" words or deeds. There were also established secret or semi-secret intelligence agencies within the departments of State, War, Navy, and the Post Office. And all this formidable apparatus of repression, so reminiscent of czarist Russia, was primarily devoted *not* to the discovery and punishment of overt acts that gave aid and comfort to the foreign enemy, but to the discovery and punishment of "radicals" and alleged "revolutionaries," especially on the faculties of educational institutions and in the ranks of organized labor.

The worst instances of official and private violence in the name of Americanism occurred in the West and had as victims the leaders of the radical Industrial Workers of the World which, repudiating the craft union negotiating principles of Sam Gompers and the AFL, proposed to organize *all* workers in One Big Union and employ direct action (ultimately, the general strike) to "overthrow the capitalistic system." The open proclamation of such an aim was in itself frightening to the American employing class during and in the immediate aftermath of the Bolshevik take-over in Russia. The violent practice which accompanied it provoked even more violent counteraction. In September, 1917, when copper production was drastically reduced by IWW strikes in the West, federal agents raided the union's offices and seized its leaders, nearly 100 of whom were subsequently sentenced to long prison terms. In February, 1918, the government of Montana, dominated by Anaconda Copper, enacted a drastic criminal syndicalism law providing that anyone who spoke contemptuously or disrespectfully of flag, Army, Navy, Constitution, or the American form of government was guilty of treasonable utterance and subject to fine and imprisonment. IWW leaders and members suffered under it. In April, 1918, Congress passed and the President promptly signed a Sabotage Act specifically aimed at the IWW, making "willful sabotage" a federal crime when its objects were transportation facilities, war materials, utilities, or war plants. The legalized repression that ensued was supplemented by the activities of vigilante groups who staged impromptu raids on IWW headquarters and beat up those they found there.

The consuming flames of war hysteria, fanned and fed by Creel's incessant and ubiquitous propaganda, rose higher and higher as the war months passed. It became imprudent to conduct conversations in German, or indeed in any foreign language, in places where it might be overheard by zealous citizens for whom English was the only language of patriotism. The teaching of German was banned from many schools and colleges (sauerkraut became "liberty cabbage," German measles became "liberty measles"). Fritz Kreisler, the famous violinist, and Madame Schumann-Heink, the famous contralto, were denied concert engagements because they were, respectively, of Austrian and German birth. All German-Americans became suspect, subjected to frequent humiliations and abuse whenever they departed the areas where they were in a majority.

And if Woodrow Wilson privately deplored these excesses, he gave no public sign of it. Indeed, the final, the ultimate tragical irony for him personally was the effect all this had on his own psychology.

For as unadmitted, yet unavoidable doubts and guilt feelings spread through his spirit, he acted as if determined himself to fulfill the dire prophecies he had made about the entrance of "a spirit of ruthless brutality . . . into the very fabric of our national life." He became himself a victim of the machinery of repression and thought control he had done so much to create. The process was evidently one of an intensifying anxiety neurosis. The end *must* justify the means, since the means themselves were so atrocious: if the great object for which he strove were not achieved, only the viciousness would become his permanent contribution to history, and as he grew increasingly anxious about his chances for achieving this object, he made an increasing use of the machinery of propaganda and repression. The Creel Committee was at least tacitly encouraged by him into a campaign of personal glorification that was conducted on a scale and with a skill not seen before on earth. Every art of publicity and advertising, every resource of communications technology were devoted to exalting Woodrow Wilson and spreading his word throughout the world, as if it were the Word of God. Mark Sullivan quotes messages typical of those received by Creel from his agents abroad.[9] "The Wilson cult is truly making astonishing progress [in Spain]," said one; "newspapers devote innumerable columns to his career, his views, his present actions, personal details." Said another: "I have seen a new understanding of President Wilson come into the minds of the Danes so that they place him on a plane beside their greatest national heroes; I have known them to cut out photographs of him sent out by us which appeared in Danish papers and place them in a sort of family shrine." Small wonder that in America, where the "Wilson cult" was as assiduously promoted (if less effectively, because of counter publicity), George Creel became known to hostile Congressmen as Wilson's personal press agent. Simultaneously, the measures curtailing civil liberties and forcibly suppressing dissent became more and more harsh. Wilson's assumption, of course, was that this propaganda and repression removed obstacles in the way of shining Good while enhancing his own power to achieve the shining Good, but it was an assumption whose dubiousness could not but add to the weight of his unacknowledged feelings of guilt, his basic inward insecurity.

A major cause of his anxiety was the discovery, soon after America entered the war, that the Allies had entered into a number of secret treaties with one another—treaties which defined a peace very different from that Wilson had called for, and wholly different, too, from the noble aims implied by Allied war propaganda.[10]

A first hint of this came to Washington from the U.S. ambassador to Russia a little over three weeks after the abdication of Czar Nicholas. The Allies had "binding agreements to negotiate no separate peace and also probably agreements as to the nature of that peace and perhaps specific agreements or understandings between some of the Allies concerning territory and other subjects," cabled the ambassador to the Secretary of State in April, 1917, and in mid-May, under pressure from Wilson, the British disclosed to Washington under a pledge of absolute secrecy some of the various agreements they had entered into. (They significantly failed to mention Anglo-French agreements concerning the postwar disposal of Germany's African possessions or Anglo-Japanese agreements concerning Germany's possessions in the Pacific and Far East.) Then, on November 11, 1917, only a week after the Bolsheviks had seized power from Kerensky's Provisional Government, came news that the All-Russia Congress of Soviets had issued a call to all the belligerents to lay down their arms immediately and negotiate a peace settlement without indemnities or conquests or annexations (obviously, Bolshevik Russia was leaving the war) and had also voted to publish the secret treaties entered into by czarist Russia, treaties now declared null and void. Consternation spread through the corridors of power in London, Paris, Rome. Censorship, overt and covert, might deny this news to the masses, but there was no way by which it could be kept from the eyes of Woodrow Wilson, who from the first had been suspicious of British, French, and Italian war aims.

From Russia, too, and through George Creel's propaganda machine, came the specific suggestion which led to one of the great historic events of the war—the enunciation of Wilson's Fourteen Points. Creel's man in Petrograd was a newspaperman named Edgar G. Sisson. If Wilson would "restate anti-Imperialistic war aims and democratic peace requisites" in "almost placard paragraphs," cabled Sisson to Creel, "I can get it fed into Germany in great quantities in German translation, and can utilize Russian version potently in army and elsewhere. . . . Need this for external evidence that the President is thinking of German and Russian common folk in their situation and talking to them." Creel took this message to the White House, where Wilson, with the aid of Colonel House, reduced his long, long thoughts about the peace into fourteen capsule statements.[11] These he incorporated in a speech to Congress on January 8, 1918. Within hours thereafter the Fourteen Points were known in the farthest corners of the Allied and neutral world. Within days they were as well known among the peoples of the Central Powers.

The first five of them were general in nature. They called for "open covenants . . . openly arrived at," absolute freedom of the seas, the removal of trade barriers between nations "so far as possible," the reduction of national armaments "to the lowest points consistent with domestic safety," and the adjustment of all colonial claims in accordance with the principle of the "self-determination of small peoples."

The next eight points dealt with specific matters. They called for the evacuation of Russian and Belgian territory, the restoration of Alsace-Lorraine to France, the readjustment of Italian frontiers "along clearly recognizable lines of nationality," the "freest opportunity of autonomous development" for the "peoples of Austria-Hungary" (in other words, a splintering apart of the Habsburg Empire), the evacuation of the then-occupied Balkan states, the "autonomous development" of "nationalities . . . now under Turkish rule," the opening "permanently" of the Dardanelles to the "free passage" of the ships of all countries, and the creation of an independent Poland with "a free and secure access to the sea."

The most crucial proposal was stated last. Said the Fourteenth Point: "A general association of nations must be formed under specific covenants for the purpose of affording mutual guarantees of political independence and territorial integrity to great and small states alike."

There can be no doubt of the efficacy of the Fourteen Points as propaganda: they were shrewdly designed to appeal to great masses of people in the German, Austrian, and Turkish empires, weakening their will to continue the fight. And not only the people but also the rulers of Germany were moved by Wilson's later flat promise, in a speech to Congress on February 11, 1918, that there "shall be no annexations, no contributions, no punitive damages" at war's end. Nor were the Allied governments loath to join the Creel Committee in its use of the proposals as weapons of psychological warfare.

They gave no clear and definite assurances, however, that they would in fact establish the peace on the basis of these proposals. It behooved Wilson to create a world public opinion so strongly in favor of his conception of the peace, a peace organized and permanently maintained through the League of Nations, that none of the erstwhile belligerent governments could stand against it. He redoubled his efforts in this direction through the spring, the summer, the early autumn of 1918.

IV

Franklin Roosevelt, active attendant at the birth of the American Leviathan, expressed no aversion to its mental or spiritual aspects. The suppression of dissent, the denial of civil liberties, the ugly vigilante violence against "radicals," which accompanied and was encouraged by the Creel Committee's propaganda barrage, provoked from him no word of protest, private or public. On the contrary he stated strong approval of the Espionage and Sedition acts and of the jailing of people who distributed literature opposing the war. "Pamphlets of this kind are undoubtedly attacks not on the individuals who make up the Government but on duly constituted government itself," he wrote to a U.S. district attorney who had obtained the conviction of four persons for distributing a Socialist antiwar publication, "and I cannot help feeling that in certain parts of the country especially every effort should be made to stamp them out." He himself, in public speech, inveighed against "slackers," a term then applied to all who failed for whatever reason to conform to the government's war program (who failed, for example, to meet an assigned quota of Liberty Bond purchases), asserting ominously that they would "soon learn the fundamental principle of liberty" because it would "be taught them," presumably by force.[12] However, he personally manifested no vigilante spirit. He had no compulsion to inflict pain on anyone; in general, he would go to great lengths to avoid doing so. He therefore simply went along with prevailing trends in the realm of the national spirit, uninhibited by any strong ideological commitment to the Bill of Rights.

He seems not to have questioned the factual accuracy of the Creel Committee's propaganda—the manufactured reports, for instance, of German atrocities. He acquiesced in Creel's simplistic portrayal of the war as a struggle between Democracy and Despotism, Civilization and

Barbarism, Good and Evil. He made propaganda contributions of his own, in speeches and articles, asserting that he had personally witnessed German penetrations into the Caribbean that were intended to throw a noose around the neck of the United States, a noose which, tightened, would "choke us" if Germany won the war. He encouraged the executive secretary of the American Historical Association to search Navy archives for allegedly suppressed dispatches from Admiral Dewey in Manila Bay, dispatches that would reveal Germany's evil designs upon the Far East in 1898, and was disappointed when none was found, none having ever existed. He pressed Secretary of State Lansing to expedite the immediate translation from the French of a reportedly authoritative book about German atrocities since its publication "would have an excellent effect at the present time." [13]

He *did* caution, now and then, against a too-literal acceptance of certain propaganda slogans, especially in cases where such acceptance would have a deleterious effect upon his own interests. For instance, he strongly advised his mother not to liquidate profitable long-term investments in order to increase her immediate "patriotic" purchases of Liberty Bonds—though it seems highly unlikely that his mother could have been persuaded to do this, in any case, by Creel Committee sloganeering. When he wrote his thanks to her for the Liberty Bonds she had bought for his children ("It is too dear of you . . ."), he added that he did "*not* think it wise to sell out anything you now have in order to take more" bonds since she "would get a low price" for her stocks at that time and "if others did this it would upset things." Though one might not suspect it from the speeches and posters of Liberty Bond salesmen ("Buy until it hurts!" was the burden of their plea), Roosevelt knew and told his mother that the war loan "is intended primarily for uninvested or liquid assets." He was similarly cautionary about the "Food Will Win the War" posters; taken literally, they denigrated the role of the Navy and Army. Of course, it wasn't true that food would actually "win the war," he told a Springfield, Massachusetts, audience in May, 1918; the actual victory must be won—it could only be won—by "the men in khaki and blue on the other side." [14]

Even more heavily did he discount—indeed, he virtually repudiated—the propaganda slogan, emanating from Woodrow Wilson, that this was a "war to end wars." If he acquiesced in the view of the struggle as one of Good against Evil, he stubbornly persisted in identifying the Good with the sovereignty, interests, and physical might of the United States. "People have talked much of internationalism," he said to a graduating class of the Drexel Institute in May, 1918, ". . . of the day when nation will no longer rise against nation. But until that day is here, we must

recognize existing conditions." Nor did he foresee or indicate that he favored a fundamental change in these "existing conditions." The United
States must maintain its armed strength after the present war ended;
universal military training must become a permanent element of national life, for "the national life can never be called free from danger
even in the most unruffled periods of peace. The fight [evidently for national security] is constant and will be never ending as long as the nation endures." [15] Thus he remained a "hard-headed realist," impervious
to "idealistic nonsense"—and if Wilson's Fourteenth Point made any
particular impression upon him at all, it was solely as an adroit stratagem of psychological warfare.

"Realistic," too, in a way that seemed a virtual repudiation of his
former stance as a Progressive reformer, was his changing personal relationship to New York politics during this period. We have told* of the
process of burying the hatchet between himself and Tammany that was
initiated in the aftermath of the 1914 election, disastrous for the New
York Democracy largely because of the Progressive-Tammany feud. In
the summer of 1917 this process culminated in what appeared to be an
actual rapprochement. Roosevelt accepted Boss Murphy's invitation, issued through a third party, to be the principal speaker at Tammany's
great 1917 Fourth of July celebration. He gave a quite lengthy patriotic
address, which was favorably received by a large audience. He posed for
a picture with Boss Murphy, though it must be said that he did so with
no show of pleasure: his mouth was set in a grim line, his forehead
plucked together in a frown, his tall form slightly bent in a posture of
unease. (Murphy, on the other hand, appeared perfectly relaxed. Wearing around his neck the broad ribbon and medal of his Tammany office,
he wore upon his face a rather wicked-looking little half-smile.)[16] Subsequently, several prominent Tammany figures suggested that Roosevelt
become candidate for governor in 1918, a proposal warmly endorsed by
many upstate Democrats, but of course publicly disparaged, with
proper expressions of gratitude, by Roosevelt himself.

Actual pressure was put upon him to run, in the spring and early summer of 1918. The President himself joined in it, in mid-June, asking
Daniels to "tell Roosevelt he ought not to decline to run for Governor if
it is tendered to him." [17] Roosevelt's (and Howe's) political instinct had
told him, however, and continued to tell him, that 1918 was not the year
for his next office-seeking move. Actively to campaign for elective office
at the expense of his duties in the Navy, while war yet raged, would be
either a tacit admission that these duties were of minor importance or

* See page 361.

an admission of his willingness to subordinate his public obligations to his private ambition. Either admission would be harmful and, if he lost the election, might be fatal to his long-term designs. Only on the assurance of a final Allied victory before election day could such risk be practically justified.

And in June of that year the war appeared far from over, an Allied victory far from certain, despite America's entry on the Allied side. On March 3, Bolshevik Russia, soon to become the Union of Soviet Socialist Republics, had signed with Germany the Treaty of Brest-Litovsk, which formally ended the war on the eastern front; gave the Ukraine into the hands of the Central Powers to serve as granary, thereby offsetting to a considerable degree the effects of the Allied blockade; and enabled the completion of the massive transfer of German troops from Russia to the West that had been under way throughout the winter. On March 21, the German General Erich Ludendorff, now *de facto* political dictator of his country, as well as supreme commander of its armed forces, having at his disposal for the first time a clear numerical superiority in troops over those of his opponents and having also the advantage of a unified command whereas his opponents remained divided among separate and competing nationalisms, had launched the first of a series of terrific assaults intended to overwhelm the British and French before America's strength became effective on the battlefield. These had failed of their strategic purpose while forcing the Allies to establish, at long last, a supreme command (though an imperfect one) exercised by the French General Ferdinand Foch. At Château-Thierry and Belleau Wood, on the Marne, American troops (notably a Marine brigade with the U.S. Second Division) had fought their first important battle of the war, blocking Ludendorff's main thrust toward Paris in late May and early June. But the Germans were still on the offensive, their troop morale seemingly as high as ever. The French, on the other hand, were dispirited. In 1917, after a huge Allied offensive had totally, bloodily failed, there had been actual mutinies in sixteen French Army corps. These had been ruthlessly suppressed, as had been an actual armed revolt by some thousands of Russian infantry who had been sent to France under the czarist regime and naturally wished to return home after the czar's overthrow.* Disaffection remained, however, to an indeterminate degree, and seemed to Allied leaders increasingly ominous amid the long

---

* The Russians were ringed about by French artillery which then slaughtered them with a prolonged bombardment, the few survivors surrendering when the fire ceased. All news of this, as of the French troop mutinies, was of course denied the French, British, and American publics by the most rigorous military censorship. Not until after the war was the story told, in many books, *e.g.,* Winston Churchill's *The World Crisis,* p. 705 of 1931 one-volume edition.

red shadows cast westward by the Bolshevik Revolution. Hence, there were few among the most knowledgeable who believed that a final solution in favor of the Allies could be reached in 1918. Even if massive Allied offensives had driven the Germans out of France and Belgium by year's end, there would remain the task of crushing them as they stood upon a narrowed front in their own country—a formidable project that would require severe fighting through the whole of 1919.

Roosevelt, therefore, resisted the pressures put upon him to enter New York's gubernatorial election campaign. According to his own later account, Boss Murphy sent an emissary to him who, in oral communication, urged him to run, promising full Tammany support if he did so. He refused on the grounds that his war service was too important, though he well knew that the President did not share this view. A few days later Murphy's emissary returned to ask him to suggest a suitable upstate candidate. Instead, Roosevelt, by his own later testimony, offered the name of Al Smith, who was then president of the New York City Board of Aldermen. But if this story is true, Roosevelt was playing a devious political game, for he *publicly* called for the nomination of William Church Osborn, knowing well that Osborn had no chance of winning it against Tammany's adamant opposition. Moreover, after Osborn's candidacy had been blocked by Tammany in the state convention, which endorsed Al Smith, and after an angered Osborn then decided to oppose Smith in the primary, Roosevelt refused the public support which Osborn asked of him. He was enabled to do so gracefully by the fact that he was at that time unavailable for public comment of any kind. He was on war service overseas.[18]

He had known that he would be, when he announced his support of Osborn's candidacy.

V

By the end of the first year of America's war, the pressure of desk work upon the Secretary and Assistant Secretary of the Navy was considerably eased. The department was as well organized to administer the Navy effort as it was likely to become, and Roosevelt began to insist on the necessity for a personal inspection of Navy and Marine operations in the war theater by either Daniels or himself. Otherwise, each of them was as "a chess player moving his pieces in the dark," he said. Daniels finally agreed. But he was unable to make the trip himself, as Roosevelt had doubtless anticipated. ("Wilson wished me to remain in Washington for frequent conferences," said Daniels in his memoirs.) Hence, it was Roosevelt who sailed on July 9, 1918, embarking then upon what he ever afterward considered one of the great adventures of his life.[19]

He could have sailed three days later aboard a relatively safe and comfortable British Admiralty transport, the *Olympia*. Most of the small personal staff he chose to accompany him did so sail. (This staff included his lighthearted friend Livingston Davis, who for some months had been his civilian aide, and his contractor friend Lieutenant Commander Elliott Brown.) He, however, accompanied by Captain Edward McCauley, Jr., who was his chief of staff, and a Marine sergeant orderly, boarded a brand-new destroyer, the USS *Dyer,* which was making its first crossing into the war zone. He had an exciting voyage. He recorded its details in a lengthy diary-letter addressed to Eleanor, a diary marked here and there by the lyricism that ships and the sea often evoked in him. He wrote of the great transports silhouetted against the western sky at evening, showing neither light nor life nor motion, "yet peopled like a city and moving on . . . —moving on" through a night in which they became "dim looms in the darkness abeam of us" toward a dawn that might be literally blood-red for them since dawn was the "critical period" for submarine attack. He wrote of "the good old Ocean . . . — sometimes tumbling about and throwing spray . . . —sometimes gently lolling about with occasional points of white . . . —but always something known—something like an old friend of moods and power. . . . But now though the Ocean looks unchanged, the doubled number on lookout shows that even here the hands of the Hun False God is [*sic*] reaching out to defy nature; that ten miles ahead of this floating City of Souls a torpedo may be waiting to start on its quick run; that we can never get our good Old Ocean back again until that God and the people who have set him up are utterly cut down and purged." Yet he gloried in the danger, wished there were more of it for him personally, and would in later years claim that there had been. Once, during gun drill, "a green youngster pulled the lanyard of the port gun when it was trained as far forward as it could go," sending a four-inch shell "only a few feet outboard" from the bridge on which Roosevelt, McCauley, and Captain Fred H. Poteet (the *Dyer*'s commander) were standing. Once a lookout thought he saw a submarine periscope, and the *Dyer,* heading for it "at full speed about a mile away . . . fired three shots at it." Alas, "it turned out to be a floating keg with a little flag on it, probably thrown over by a passing vessel as a target to train the gun crews." Once, after the *Dyer* had left the convoy it helped protect in order to refuel in the Azores, the ship's two engines overheated and required a stop of a half hour or so six miles outside the breakwater at Ponta Delgada, on São Miguel. These were waters in which a German submarine *might* have been, and the temporarily disabled *Dyer* would have been an easy mark; but nothing happened.

After two days on São Miguel, Roosevelt aboard the *Dyer* sailed for England, where, at Portsmouth on July 21, he was grandly met by a large party of naval officers headed by Vice Admiral William S. Sims and the British Rear Admiral Sir Allan Frederick Everett, naval secretary to the First Lord of the Admiralty. "I am told that it is a very great honor to have had Everett sent down to meet me," he recorded a few hours later, having been driven to London "in one of the Admiralty's Rolls-Royces." He added: "Personally, I think it is because they wanted to report as to whether I am house-broken or not. We went straight to the Ritz Hotel and have a magnificent suite as the guests of the British Admiralty." That Sunday evening, in the Ritz, he met Livingston Davis, Elliott Brown, and others of the party who had come over on the *Olympic* and had with them a "happy reunion, dinner and went to a big entertainment for all American and Canadian Officers and men in uniform. House packed with khaki and a few of my [sic] Navy men." (A few days later, writing of the counterattack in the Rheims salient, he said: "One of my Marine Regiments has lost 1200 and another 800 men.")

Thus auspiciously began an English week of which every waking moment was crowded with significant event. He had several long, confidential, and fruitful conferences with the First Lord of the Admiralty (Sir Eric Geddes) and the First Sea Lord (Admiral of the Fleet Sir Rosslyn Wemyss), during which he was impressed by the magnitude and ingenuity of the British naval effort. He learned that certain large British fighting ships were being fitted out as "airplane ships," with cleared decks for the takeoff and landing of wheeled aircraft; that a new antisubmarine net barrier had been designed for closing the English Channel to U-boats; that 6,000,000 tons of shipping a month was being convoyed by British escort vessels, which was twenty-four times the amount convoyed by all other Allied navies, including that of the United States. He spent three highly interesting and educative days with Geddes on an inspection trip to Queenstown, Ireland, headquarters of an Anglo-American naval command that supplied more than 90 percent of the escorts for 360 convoys during the war.[20] ("At lunch time Geddes took me aside and asked what I felt about the success or otherwise of Admiral Sir Lewis Bayly [the notoriously irascible but highly effective British officer in command at Queenstown]. I told him frankly that our people from Sims down to the youngest destroyer officers felt that he was the ideal man to command this station. In the afternoon Geddes again took me aside and told me that he had decided to retain Bayly in command. This is a very unusual compliment as Bayly has already been here three years in command . . . and the usual tenure is two years.") Returned to England, he made further inspections of British and American installations and had further conferences with British and American officers at the Admiralty and at the U.S. Navy headquarters in London. After a two-hour meeting with the British Navy's chief intelligence officer he recorded that the British "Intelligence Department is far more developed than ours and this is because it is a much more integral part of their Office of Operations." The U.S. Navy would do well to emulate the British in this, he said. He listened carefully to suggestions, which he then transmitted to Daniels, for coordinating British and American naval construction plans for 1919. He learned of a controversy between Sims and British Admiral Sir David Beatty, of Jutland fame, regarding the laying of the North Sea mine barrage. Beatty, in command of the Grand Fleet, had little liking for the barrage (it limited the Grand Fleet's mobility) and wanted extensive gaps left in it for the passage of his ships. Sims, now fully converted to the North Sea project, insisted that the line of mines run unbroken from Norway to Scotland. Washington, said Roosevelt, should firmly support Sims in this stand.

He spent the weekend of July 27–28 as guest of the Waldorf Astors in their great country estate, Cliveden, finding "Mrs. Astor . . . the same, enthusiastic, amusing, and talkative soul as always. . . . I particularly like Waldorf Astor, who is doing wonderfully well and is now the Parliamentary Secretary of Ministry of Food. . . . Of course this place is wonderful and I am so glad to see it. They live in the big house with only women servants—everything comfortable, food about like ours, only a scarcity of sugar and butter. Within a five-minute walk is the big hospital which they started in the tennis courts building but which the Government took over and enlarged to 1100 beds. It is not much more than a quarter full just now but of course will be again when another batch comes over. . . . Down on the bank overlooking the Thames, the Astors have turned an Italian Garden into a really perfect little cemetery for the overseas men who die in hospital."

Early Monday morning, July 29, he motored from Cliveden to London to begin the most memorable two days of his stay in England—indeed, two of the most memorable days of his life. European royalty had always had, and would always have, a peculiar fascination for him. He was therefore delighted and flattered by the private audience he had with King George V at ten thirty that morning, in Buckingham Palace. "The King has a nice smile and a very open, quick and cordial way of greeting one," he wrote to Eleanor. "He is not as short as I had expected, and I think his face is stronger than photographs make it appear." When Roosevelt "remarked something about having been to school in Germany and having seen their preparation for the first stages of the war machine," the king said "with a twinkle in his eye" that he too had gone to school in Germany, for a year, adding, "You know I have a number of relations in Germany but can tell you frankly that in all my life I have never seen a German gentleman." The king had just had "a nice letter from Uncle Ted" which led him to speak with much sympathy about the loss of Quentin Roosevelt, TR's youngest son, who had gone to France as a lieutenant in the U.S. Army Air Corps and had been shot down and killed behind German lines on July 17. Roosevelt recorded proudly, next day, that though "this type of interview is supposed to last only fifteen minutes, . . . it was nearly three-quarters of an hour before the King made a move." There followed a luncheon given him and Geddes by the Anglo-American Luncheon Club, at which both he and Geddes spoke; then, in the afternoon, a visit to London's principal YMCA Hut, where he spoke "to a great gathering of American soldiers, with a sprinkling of Canadians, Anzacs and our Blue-jackets." That evening he attended, as prominent guest, "one of the famous Gray Inn's dinners, a really historic occasion in honor of the War Ministers," at which he heard Lord Curzon speak "most wonderfully for an hour," and, after listening to responses to Curzon by a Canadian and by General Jan Smuts of South Africa, was himself unexpectedly called upon to speak "to my horror."

Present at this Gray Inn dinner was the British Winston Churchill, then at a low ebb of his political fortunes as a result of the blame attached to him for the tragic Dardanelles fiasco. If he made any impression on Roosevelt or Roosevelt on him, it went unrecorded at the time.

The next day, at a luncheon given him at the American embassy, he had "a very good time" with Prime Minister David Lloyd George, who "is just like his pictures; thick set; not very tall; rather a large head; and rather long hair; but what impressed me more than anything else was his tremendous vitality." They talked about "the labor situation here and at home," strikes being then threatened at "a number of munition plants and shipyards" in Britain. The Prime Minister "said of course the weakness of the British Government's position was all come from the failure to adopt conscription at the outbreak of the war and I suggested to him that in the same way we should have had vastly more trouble if we had not had the selective draft law as the final lever to insure continuation of the work." Roosevelt also gave it as his opinion that "the British Unions would obtain no sympathy from our Federation of Labor in any action involving a tie-up of war work and that on the contrary a firmer attitude on the part of the British Government would receive hearty applause from the United States." Lloyd George "seemed . . .

greatly pleased and intimated that he had decided on a firmer stand in the future."

That evening he was guest of honor at a small dinner party at the House of Commons, after which he had a "long talk with Mr. Balfour . . . while we walked up and down the terrace in the dark." They talked of how well the war was now going ("The past month has I think clearly marked the turning point . . .") and of how everyone was beginning to "realize that the American troops are to be the deciding factor." They also discussed a proposal which Geddes had originally made to Roosevelt—namely, that Roosevelt go to Rome, while on this trip, and there try to persuade the Italians to join with the British and French in active naval operations in the Mediterranean, the Italian Navy having been thus far totally inactive. The British wished to establish a unified command for *all* Allied naval forces in the sea, an admiralissimo to match the generalissimo on the western front (Sir John Jellicoe was suggested for the post), and Balfour now told Roosevelt that the War Cabinet, having discussed the matter, "heartily approved" of Roosevelt's "going to Italy." Roosevelt himself was eager to do so, provided Daniels approved.

Then, at long last, France! The western front!

At noon on Wednesday, July 31, he and his party arrived at the Dover headquarters of Admiral Sir Roger Keyes, commandant of the naval district through which the great bulk of troops and matériel were poured from the British Isles into Belgium and France. ("Admiral Keyes' operations room was of tremendous interest . . . this station is of course far and away the most active . . . of all.") After lunch with Sir Roger and Lady Keyes he boarded a new British destroyer ("As I came over the side my flag was broken out at the main, the first time this sort of thing has ever happened on a British ship") and began the two-hour run to Dunkirk, during which he and his party witnessed a special demonstration of Britain's new "artificial fog," laid by high-speed P-boats. At Dunkirk he had his first direct view of the actual fighting war, for the town had "been bombed every night that flying was possible for three years" and, moreover, lay within long-range shelling distance of the front ("There is not a whole house left in this place"). That night he slept in a chateau outside Calais, which was also heavily damaged by bombs, the chateau being "the headquarters of one of our night bombing squadrons." By evening of the following day, August 1, he was luxuriously housed in the Hôtel Crillon, in Paris, as a guest of the French government.

The French week which followed was even more strenuous than his English week had been. He attended a luncheon at the Élysée Palace in honor of Herbert Hoover, who had arrived in Paris several days before, and there met President and Mme. Raymond Poincaré. He was formally called upon at the Crillon by the chief of the French General Naval Staff, with whom he later dined, and himself made a formal call upon M. Georges Leygues, the Minister of Marine. (During the latter call he was immensely impressed by the fact that a wall from which a famous tapestry had been removed for sakekeeping when the long-range Big Bertha shelling of Paris began had been covered with damask. "In London or Washington they would have left untouched the bare wall. . . . It is the same spirit which enabled the French during the 'touch-and-go' days of 1914, when the Government had gone to Bordeaux and the Germans were literally outside the gates, to keep on with the planting of the flower beds in the Tuileries. . . . They seem to lose their heads even less than the Anglo-Saxons—very different from what we thought four years ago.") He conferred with M. André Tardieu, who had "succeeded in creating a new position for himself in the French cabinet" and "might now be called the Liaison Minister" who facilitated cooperation between French and Americans. Roosevelt called also upon Marshal Joseph Joffre, and had a dramatic visit with "the greatest civilian in France," the 77-year-old Premier Georges Clemenceau. The famed Tiger told Roosevelt "of an episode he had seen while following just behind the advance—a Poilu and a Boche still standing partly buried in a shell hole, clinched in each other's arms, their rifles abandoned, and the Poilu and Boche were in the act of trying to bite each other to death when a shell . . . killed them both—and as he told me this he grabbed me by both shoulders and shook me with a grip of steel to illustrate his words, thrusting his teeth forward toward my neck." With Joffre the conversation, if considerably less dramatic, was more significant in terms of Roosevelt's personal history. "We had a delightful and intimate talk about the days of May 1917 when our decision to send a really great army to Europe hung in the balance. He was quite frank in telling me of his discouragement during his first visit to Washington, . . . and he kept insisting that the friendly advice I had given him from the very first day when I met him with the *Mayflower* at Hampton Roads had in the end enabled him to obtain the answers for which he had come to America. . . . I think he felt, and rightly so, that only a small part of the million and a quarter Americans now in France would be here had it not been for his mission. . . ."

During the crowded Parisian days, Roosevelt also found time to look up his relatives. On Saturday, August 3, he "went for Aunt Dora at noon and with her went out to Neuilly to see Cousin Hortense Howland, then back to pick up Cousin Charlie Forbes Gaston . . . for

luncheon at a neighboring restaurant. . . . I went out at tea time to see
Ted and Eleanor [Lieutenant Colonel and Mrs. Theodore Roosevelt, Jr.]
and found them in a nice little house just beyond the Arc de Triomphe.
Archie [TR's third son] was there also, looking horribly badly." Both
Theodore, Jr., and Archibald had been wounded in battle and were convalescing. "They both have really splendid records," wrote Roosevelt
enviously.

He lusted for danger and glory.

On Sunday, August 4, the fourth anniversary of the beginning of the
war in the west, he left with his party for "the front." Upon reaching
French Army Headquarters at Château-Thierry he learned, to his angry
disgust, that his naval attaché had carefully arranged a travel schedule
calling "for late rising, easy trips and plenty of bombed houses thirty
miles or so behind the front." He promptly scrapped this schedule and
thereafter "for four days I ran the trip," to the "visible annoyance" of
the naval attaché.

He moved then across ruined landscapes dotted with legendary
names, and the names became the ghastly fascinating places themselves,
became the ridges and ravines of Belleau Wood covered by a tangle of
stripped and broken trees where no birds sang and the shell holes full
of water stank of death; became the shattered walls and rubble heaps of
Châlons-sur-Marne, Châtillon-sur-Marne, Cierges and Sergy, and again
the stink of death "horrid . . . to our sensitive naval noses"; became
wide fields pocked with shell holes, covered with battle debris, where
men living only two days before lay in shallow graves ("rusty bayonets,
broken guns, emergency ration tins, hand grenades, discarded over-
coats, rain-stained love letters, crawling lines of ants and many little
mounds, some wholly unmarked, some with a rifle stuck bayonet down
in the earth, some with a helmet, and some, too, with a whittled cross
with a tag of wood or wrapping paper hung over it and in a pencil
scrawl an American name"); became a small straggling village along a
stream where only a few of the houses were damaged by shells, the village of Mareuil, through which the Germans had hurriedly retreated less
than twenty-four hours before (there "were a number of dead Boche in
the fields and in one place a little pile of them awaiting burial") and
where he fired toward the German lines one of a battery of 155's (did he
kill a man?). Then Château-Thierry again at nine o'clock for "an excellent dinner" with French General Jean Degoutte and his staff, everyone
exhausted who had gone with him ("The members of my staff have
begun to realize what campaigning, or rather sight-seeing, with the Assistant Secretary means . . ."), and a drive through "inky darkness and
winding streets" to one of two houses "still intact," where, with electric

torch, he climbed a "rickety stairs" to bed ("I managed to get my boots and leggings off and fell in—1:00 A.M. and a thoroughly successful day").

He inspected a battalion of the famous Fifth Marines in a village near Nancy next day and was impressed by the number of replacements lined up beside the survivors of earlier battles. The replacements were easily recognized by the standard Marine olive drab uniforms they wore; the others wore Army khaki, "their own olive drab having been worn out long ago." He wrote: "It gave one a pretty good idea of the heavy casualties . . . in the last fighting near Soissons." He was disturbed by the fact that "his" Marines were now, for the most part, indistinguishable by uniform from Army troops. When "General [John A.] Lejeune suggested that the Marine corps button could be worn on the collar points of their army shirts, but that he lacked the authority to allow this, I told him that I would assume responsibility, and then and there issued" the necessary order. He spent that night in General Lejeune's headquarters.

Early the next morning he departed for "another breakneck motor spin . . . through Toul and Void and Ligny-en-Barrois, where we turned right and ran into Bar-le-Duc," thence northward on the famed *Voie Sacrée* to Verdun, arriving shortly before noon at "the citadel crowning the hill" above the ruined town. There, as he went to lunch "in the tiny underground dining room" with the citadel's commandant, Colonel de Hay, who had commanded there during the great battle of 1916, the "first thing that met our eyes on one of the walls was the . . . original signboard which was posted near the entrance of the citadel during the siege, and on which thousands of troops going forward to hold the line read the words . . . 'ils ne passeront pas' [they shall not pass]." That afternoon, wearing a French helmet and carrying a gas mask, he crossed the Meuse, was driven with his party across the shell-churned killing grounds of Verdun, and there came again under fire. While they were in the Valley of Death before Fort Douaumont (". . . over a hundred thousand men were . . . killed in this little stretch of valley"), he and his party paused to photograph the site of the village of Fleury, now totally obliterated by shells (there was "not even a brick on the tumbled earth"), but were hurried on by Colonel de Hay. Boche observation balloons had spotted them, said the colonel. The road would be shelled "in a minute or two." And it was. "We passed on to the south slopes of Fort Douaumont, a quarter of a mile beyond, and sure enough the long whining whistle of a shell was followed by the dull boom and puff of smoke of the explosion at the Dead Man's Corner we had just left." He spent that night in a tunnel room of the citadel. ("Personally, I should not care to be permanently stationed in the citadel," he wrote to Eleanor. "All of the air for the tunnels has to be forced in by pumps and last night I could not help the feeling that it is the same air being breathed over and over again.")

On the following day, Wednesday, August 7, he was driven back to Bar-le-Duc over the *Voie Sacrée* and then on to Paris, "getting back to the Crillon at 4, just in time to hear the last few shots from the long range gun. One of them exploded just north of the Louvre, and the report is that a number of people were killed in a restaurant." A few hours later, accompanied by McCauley, he boarded a train for Italy, his official mission to that country having been approved by Daniels.

His five days in Italy may have been less exciting to him than his four at and immediately behind the western front, yet they were filled with fascinations. He engaged in war diplomacy at the highest level, a diplomacy not untouched by international intrigue, on a matter that then seemed of prime importance, striving both to persuade the Italians into offensive naval operations against the Austrians in the Adriatic and to obtain agreement upon a supreme Allied naval command in the Mediterranean.

He strove in vain.

The Italians had no such love of battle danger and glory as animated Franklin Roosevelt. Prime Minister Vittorio Orlando; the Minister of Marine, Admiral Del Bono; the Navy Chief of Staff, Admiral Thaon di Revel were clearly determined "to keep their capital ships intact to the end of the war" in order to have bargaining power over Mediterranean matters at the peace table. Particularly revealing of the official Italian attitude was a lengthy conference with the Marine Minister and the Staff Chief which Roosevelt had on Saturday August 10. During that conference he "remarked to them . . . that the Italian Battleship Fleet had not gone outside of Taranto Harbor for over a year, that they had had no fleet drill and target practice. Thaon di Revel leaned forward and said, 'Ah, but my dear Mr. Minister, you must not forget that the Austrian Fleet have not had any either.'" Roosevelt was disgusted. "This is a naval classic which is hard to beat," he wrote in the diary-letter, "but which perhaps should not be publicly repeated for a generation or two." [21]

As for the proposed unified Mediterranean naval command, it foundered on the jagged question of who or of which nationality should be the Supreme Commander. Roosevelt got into trouble with his own government over this question. He told the Italians in Rome that the United States favored appointment of a British admiral to the Supreme Command post. To this the French and Italians flatly refused to agree.

He then proposed a complicated compromise solution—"a plan for the creation of a General Naval Staff in Mediterranean, Adriatic and Aegean waters, to be composed of a Britisher, probably Jellicoe as senior member or chairman, and one member each from the French, Italian, American and Japanese Navies," as he wrote in his letter-diary. "This obviates the Italian and French objections to a British Commander-in-Chief," he went on, "and while it does not give complete unity of command it would be a distinct step toward unity of action and a policy directed more along the lines of an offensive." He was mistaken about the French reaction, however. The French were unwilling to submit even to the nominal command of a British admiral and soon communicated their displeasure to Washington through the French ambassador there, Roosevelt's good social friend Jean Jusserand. What authority did Roosevelt have, asked Jusserand of Secretary of State Lansing, to say that the United States favored a British officer for top command in the Mediterranean? He had none, Lansing replied, after consulting with Daniels, who asserted he had told Roosevelt that "our country favored allied command but declined to say who would command." [22] The President, when informed of the matter, grew angry over Roosevelt's evident assertion of an authority he did not have. He ordered the Secretary of the Navy henceforth to submit to him the names and the precisely defined missions of any civilians whom the department proposed to send abroad and to do so *before* the names and missions were officially designated. ". . . too many men go over assuming to speak for the Government," said Woodrow Wilson. [23]

But by that time, September 20, Roosevelt was in another and wholly different kind of trouble, one which protected him against whatever official wrath he might otherwise have had to face from his superiors.

He returned to France on Tuesday, August 13, arriving in Paris at noon. He conferred in the early afternoon with Admiral de Bon, telling him of the Roman negotiations. Then, with his whole party, he left for Bordeaux and the beginning of a month whose incessant strenuosity was even greater than that of the month just ended.

At the port of Pauillac, near the mouth of the Gironde, he inspected with severely critical eye the assembly plant where seaplanes shipped in parts from the United States were put together. He then drafted and dispatched a long cable to Daniels in which he complained bitterly, bolstering his complaint with horrendous examples, of planes shipped without inspection and arriving in such deplorable condition that hundreds of skilled man-hours of overhauling could not make them airworthy. ". . . one [Liberty] motor," he wrote in his diary-letter, "which was passed as ready to run was found to contain two pounds of sand in the cylinders. Then, also, many parts are lacking entirely; for instance, we have in France over a hundred seaplanes but only two self-starters." His cable to Daniels, he recorded, was "made . . . somewhat vigorous" in order to "make the office of aviation and the different Bureaus . . . so mad that they will get busy and correct the trouble. . . ." But his cable attempted more than this; it also tried to get at the root cause of the "scandalous conditions," which he blamed on the faulty administrative organization of the Navy air arm in Washington, an organization against which he had earlier protested "verbally and in writing" to Daniels as lacking any real concentration of authority and responsibility. Hence no one could determine who deserved blame for work done poorly and who praise for work done well. ("Just as long as the present indistinct and indefinite relationship exists between the Office of Aviation and the different bureaus concerned," Roosevelt wrote later, in his full report of his trip, "the same trouble will continue." As a result, the department might lose control of naval aviation altogether, and there might be established the equivalent of an Air Ministry, with control over all military and naval planes.)

He then spent "a frightfully busy week—on road each day from 6 A.M. to midnight," as he wrote "Dearest E" from Brest on August 20. ". . . we have done all manner of interesting things all the way from south of Bordeau [where he inspected the radio station being erected by the U.S. Navy for the French government] to here—all by auto—flying stations, ports, patrols, army stores, receptions, swims at French watering places, etc. etc." [24] On the way to Brest he had visited St.-Nazaire on the Loire, where 14-inch guns of the U.S. Navy, designed for battle cruisers, were being mounted on railway carriages for use in long-range bombardment (they could hurl a 1,400-pound shell nearly 25 miles) on the western front. Commanding these naval land batteries, which the Assistant Secretary had done much to promote in Washington, was Rear Admiral Charles P. Plunkett, USN. Plunkett wore an *Army* uniform. This suggested to Roosevelt a solution to what had been for him a troublesome dilemma. He was now determined to get into uniform as soon as he returned to America—a President who had wished him to run for elective office that year could hardly protest, any longer, his enlistment—and he wished to do so as a Navy officer. But he also wished to serve at the front, and this was something a Navy officer could not ordinarily do. In this war, as a matter of fact, few U.S. Navy officers saw action of any kind. Plunkett and his men, however, were going to the front! Roosevelt promptly asked if he might join them. Plunkett countered with a question of his own: Could Roosevelt curse well enough in

French "to swear a French train onto a siding" when the admiral needed the line for his big guns? Roosevelt then "with certain imaginative genius . . . handed him a line of French swear words, real and imaginary, which impressed him greatly," whereupon Plunkett promised to take Roosevelt on "with the rank of Lieutenant Commander."

There was no letup in his activities. They became, if anything, even more hectic.

In Paris again he conducted, at the behest of the Creel Committee, a large press conference for French newspapermen during which, in his admittedly atrocious "Roosevelt French," he announced Allied successes over the submarine. After breakfasting with Clemenceau next morning (the Tiger complained that French newsmen now demanded that he, the Premier, hold press conferences; he'd resign first!), he departed for his second tour of the front, this time westward through the British sector (he paid a brief courtesy visit to the British Commander in Chief, General Douglas Haig) into the tiny portion of Belgium that had remained in Allied hands. There he watched an exciting encounter between destroyers and U-boats in the Channel, came under prolonged long-range artillery bombardment, experienced two air raids in the night, and lunched the next day with King Albert. On the morning after that, he was back in Paris, having driven all night to get there—a nerve-racking trip since headlights could not be used on dark and often crowded roads. In Paris, Pershing called upon him. He called upon Foch. He conferred for an hour with the Allied Supreme Commander over the use to be made of Plunkett's batteries, though, as Roosevelt learned and admired, Foch in his lofty post normally refused to concern himself with this kind of "detail." Then Roosevelt was off for Britain, crossing the Channel on a destroyer which was twice attacked by bombing planes before reaching port.

In England, too, he conferred, he traveled, he inspected. He went to Scotland, to the Firth of Forth, visiting there the U.S. Navy's Battleship Division Nine which operated with the British Grand Fleet as its Sixth Battle Squadron. He talked at length with Admiral Rodman, the squadron commander; he lunched with British Admiral Beatty, the fleet commander. He went on to the north of Scotland to inspect very thoroughly the North Sea mine barrage and was, naturally, greatly pleased by its effectiveness. Returned to London, pointing to the success of the barrage and (by implication at least) to the ineffectuality of the Italian Navy, he urged the laying of a mine barrier at the base of the Adriatic, across the Strait of Otranto, to keep the Austrian Fleet out of the Mediterranean. His proposal was favorably received. He spent long hours in his London headquarters office working on reports and letters and holding conferences. Then he recrossed the Channel to France.

This crossing was the most difficult, the most dangerous of all. A great storm was raging. The seas were mountainous. One huge wave, breaking across a steeply slanted deck, swept a man overboard, and for fifteen hours the ship pitched and rolled before it completed a trip normally accomplished in less than a third of that time.

He was ill when he landed in France—and not from seasickness. For weeks on end he had been driving his body beyond its capacity for self-renewal, using up every reserve of its strength in reckless disregard of the protests it made. On the all-night ride from Flanders to Paris, for instance, some ten days before, he had developed a fever of 102 degrees, greatly alarming Livingston Davis, but had refused to go to bed the next day. Nor would he now yield to his body's demands. He ached from head to foot. There was a continuous dull roaring in his ears. Weird tricks of space and time were played upon his perceptions. Yet he continued to work at top speed for several days more. It was as if denied exposure to shot and shell at the front, he were determined to earn a wound stripe in other ways.

On September 8 he was again in Brest. Tied up at dock in the harbor there was the largest ship in the world—a coal-devouring, smoke-belching thousand-foot-long monster named *Leviathan**—and Roosevelt boarded her for his return to America. Hardly had he done so when he collapsed into his cabin bed, his imperious will at last overwhelmed by a red rage of fever and by a congestion of lungs and bronchial tubes that threatened suffocation. Within the iron walls of *Leviathan* he lay helpless and miserable through all his long voyage home, suffering from a combination of double pneumonia and influenza. The influenza, moreover, was of that especially virulent type called Spanish which, then sweeping toward the height of a world pandemic, would claim 20,000,000 lives in a few months, more than a half million of them American. Roosevelt, in mid-Atlantic, came near to death.

At journey's end in New York City he had to be carried down the gangplank on a stretcher. An ambulance, arranged for by his wife and mother, waited for him at dockside. He was taken to his mother's city home, his own adjoining house having been rented.† [25]

*   *   *

* She was originally the *Vaterland,* a product of the New Germany's fusion of imperial government and big business, having been launched as a Hamburg-American liner in the spring of 1914. She was interned in New York Harbor in August, 1914, then seized by the United States in April, 1917. Renamed *Leviathan,* she was fitted out as a transport capable of carrying 12,000 troops at a crossing.

† In 1914–1917, FDR's tenant was Thomas W. Lamont of Morgan and Company, 23 Wall Street, who paid an annual rent of $4500.

His condition aroused grave anxieties among his family and friends, though to Eleanor he "did not seem . . . so seriously ill as the doctors implied." Josephus Daniels expressed deep concern for him. So did TR, writing from Oyster Bay on September 23. "We . . . trust you will soon be well," said TR. "We are *very* proud of you."

But by then the crisis of his illness had passed, and he was beginning his recovery. It was slow. Weeks passed, the last two of them spent in Hyde Park, before he was strong enough to return to Washington—and he was still pale and weak when he went again to his office in mid-October. His period of home convalescence was by no means idly spent, however. During it he drafted a lengthy report of his overseas mission, describing in vivid detail the things he had seen and done, summarizing succinctly his many important conferences and inspections, and making a number of specific recommendations for improving the department's overseas operations. Daniels was greatly impressed by it. He spoke of it in his own annual report to the President as "clear, concise . . . , illuminating."

Eighteen

➹➹✠⬤⬤

The End of the Crusade

I

MEANWHILE, world-shaking events had occurred and continued to occur.

While Roosevelt was yet in France, there had been launched under Foch's supreme direction a series of coordinated Allied assaults on the western front. These at last shattered the trench stalemate, restoring for the first time since 1914 a battle of movement and, to a severely limited degree, of strategic maneuver. Most of the large salients pushed into the Allied line by the great German assaults of late spring and early summer had been flattened by the end of August in actions that convinced the Kaiser and First Quartermaster General Ludendorff that Germany had now no chance to win the war, and while Roosevelt lay desperately ill aboard *Leviathan*, on September 12 and 13, the St.-Mihiel salient was pinched out by American forces. There swiftly followed the simultaneous battles of Ypres (a British thrust) and the Meuse-Argonne (an American thrust primarily) designed by Foch to be two prongs of a pincer movement that would cut the enemy's main lateral communications and force a general withdrawal. By mid-October neither drive had made the gains originally scheduled for it. The Americans, badly mismanaged at the top command level, were struggling in the Argonne Forest, where terrain greatly favored the defense. But the continuing offensives, joined to the sudden total collapse of Bulgaria, which signed Allied armistice terms on September 30, were shattering German morale both at the front and at home.

The German General Staff had transported Lenin from Switzerland across Germany in a sealed railway car in 1917, so that he might foment Bolshevik revolution in Russia and take it out of the war. The generals now paid a bitter price for their myopic pragmatism. Soviet money financed the revolutionary Sparticist movement in Berlin, and Leninism seemed to be spreading as a virus disease among German factory workers. Everywhere were signs that a rising popular disgust with German leadership was being used by organized revolutionaries as the fuel of insurrection. There was an ominous increase in German Army desertions; soldiers on leave returned to duty with sullen reluctance. Actual mutiny threatened in the imperial Navy. And all this, piled atop the increasingly irresistible pressures upon the German fighting front, broke the martial courage of the Kaiser and Ludendorff.

The latter, as a matter of fact—though this remained unknown in Washington—suffered a spectacular failure of nerve at an evening meeting of his staff on September 28. He foamed at the mouth and fell to the floor in a convulsive fit after screaming imprecations against those (they included virtually all Germans save himself) who had betrayed the fatherland through cowardice and stupidity. Later that night, white-faced and trembling, he told Paul von Hindenburg, who agreed with him, that even the possibility of ultimate military stalemate no longer existed. Germany, already decisively defeated, teetered on the verge of total collapse. It must *at once* sue for peace, while it yet retained the appearance of being able to prolong the struggle. Even a delay of forty-eight hours might be too long! The next day, Sunday, September 29, the Supreme Army Command formally dispatched to the Foreign Office an urgent request that a peace proposal "to our enemies" be "issued at once." Ludendorff reiterated this through the Foreign Office's representative in the Supreme Headquarters a few hours later. "Today our troops are holding their own," he said; "what may happen tomorrow cannot be foreseen." [1]

Immediately the Chancellor and all the ministers through whom Ludendorff had been exercising his dictatorial powers resigned their offices. A Liberal, Prince Max of Baden, was named Chancellor and Foreign Minister, his coalition support in the Reichstag comprising Socialists, Progressives, and Centrists, as well as Liberals. Prince Max, however, was understandably reluctant to assume a post of dubious honor and much danger. He did not do so until October 4, having by then had a telegram from a Foreign Office observer at Supreme Headquarters in which Ludendorff was reported to have said that, though "the troops still hold their ground today . . . , the line might be broken at any moment. . . . He said he felt like a gambler, and that a division might fail him anywhere at any time." (The observer added, "I get the impression that they have all lost their nerve here. . . ." [2]) Within hours after he became Chancellor, Prince Max issued the peace proposal. But he did *not* address it to "our enemies," as the generals asked him to do.

He was too shrewd for that. He suspected that France and Britain's response would be a demand that Germany surrender unconditionally, and he knew that Ludendorff and associates would reject such a demand—would feel *forced* to reject it, even in the existing parlous situation, since acceptance would be tantamount to a destruction of their professional, if not their actual personal, lives. The new Chancellor therefore addressed himself to the President of the United States. He called for "the immediate conclusion of an armistice on land, on water, and in the air" in order "to avoid further bloodshed" and accepted, "as a basis for the peace negotiations, the program set forth by the President . . . in his message to Congress on January 8th [the Fourteen Points message] and in his later pronouncements [notably that of February 11, 1918, saying there should be at war's end "no annexations, no contributions, no punitive damages"]." This "program," to the extent that the Allies actually accepted it, would at least protect Germany somewhat against the vengeful wrath and cupidity of France and Britain.

It is a measure of Wilson's corruption by the arbitrary powers he had been wielding, a corruption encouraged by his Calvinistic self-righteousness and naturally imperious temper, that he initially chose to regard Prince Max's message as a private personal communication. He did not at once inform the Allied governments of it. He did not even inform his own military advisers and commanders, who had to join with Allied and enemy commanders in the actual armistice arrangements. Instead, through his Secretary of State, he entered into correspondence with the German Chancellor, seeking "clarification" of the German proposals in terms of his own conditions for an armistice. These explicitly included "the consent of the Central Powers immediately to withdraw their forces everywhere from the invaded territory" and, implicitly (the hint to this effect was too broad to be mistaken), the abdication of Wilhelm II followed by establishment of a German constitutional democracy.[3] The Kaiser's abdication, though obviously ultimately inevitable, was a condition that Prince Max had no legal authority to accept, and it remained the stumbling block to any cease-fire agreement for several weeks. Notes continued to be exchanged.

Indeed, the correspondence between White House and Berlin Chancellery which now ensued was reminiscent of the note writing about the *Lusitania* and *Arabic* sinkings of 1915 and '16, and like these earlier exchanges, it culminated in what appeared to be a great personal diplomatic triumph for Woodrow Wilson.

When Roosevelt returned to his Washington office on October 15, Wilson had just got off to Berlin—still without having officially informed London and Paris that negotiations were under way—a virtual demand that "the power which has hitherto controlled the German nation" be overthrown as a "condition precedent to peace, if peace is to come by action of the German people." [4] He wrote thus sternly in reaction to two particularly atrocious U-boat sinkings on October 10—one of a passenger ship off the Irish coast, the other of a mail boat—in which more than 800 people, many of them women and children, lost their lives and which, since they occurred many days after Berlin had sued for an immediate armistice, seemed proof that Prince Max's government had little or no control over the imperial Navy. Berlin's reply was prompt (October 20) and conciliatory to the point of abjectness. It announced the end of unrestricted submarine warfare; it protested, as if pleading for belief, that the present Berlin government, supported by "an overwhelming majority of the German people," was "free of any arbitrary and irresponsible influence." [5]

Wilson then proceeded to press his advantage to the very limit. He at last officially informed the "Governments with which the Government of the United States is associated as belligerent" * that Germany sued for peace, he transmitted to them copies of his correspondence with Berlin, and he accompanied these with "the suggestion" that the Allied governments, "if . . . disposed to effect peace upon the terms and principles indicated," ask "their military advisers and the military advisers of the United States" to draw up "the necessary terms" of an armistice, *provided* "they [the military advisers] deemed such an armistice possible from a military point of view." [6] At the same time, October 23, he dispatched a note to Berlin saying bluntly "that the nations of the world do not and cannot trust the word of those who have hitherto been the masters of German policy" and that "the United States cannot deal with any but veritable representatives of the German people who have been assured of a genuine constitutional standing as the real rulers of Germany." He threatened that if the United States "must deal with the military masters and the monarchical autocrats of Germany . . . it must demand, not peace negotiations but surrender." He also told Berlin of his transmittal of correspondence to the Allied governments and of the "suggestion" he had made to them. [7]

Upon receipt of this communication, which had the earmarks of an ultimatum, Prince Max, though he still lacked both the power and the nerve to request or even suggest the Kaiser's abdication, served upon

---

* It was a major tenet of Wilsonian policy that the United States was *not* one of the Allies but was only "associated" with them in belligerency against the Central Powers. His legal justification for this was that the United States was not joined to Britain and France by any such treaty ties as bound them to each other.

the All Highest an ultimatum of his own. From the moment the new Chancellor assumed office the chief domestic hazard to his conduct of foreign affairs had been the insufferably arrogant and hypocritical Ludendorff. The First Quartermaster General, recovered somewhat from his panic of late September and early October, bitterly blamed the new government for the policy which that panic had precipitated. He damned the civilian authority for cowardice. He was incensed by "the sacrifice of the U-boat warfare without any counter-concession." [8] He sought to prevent any peace concession that would effectively reduce German militarism. He more than hinted at treason in high places. And of this vicious obstructionism, rooted in a neurotic egotism of colossal proportions, Prince Max had had more than enough. Armed with the latest Wilson note, he now told the Kaiser flatly that Ludendorff must be dismissed *at once*—either that or he himself would immediately resign. The Kaiser had no choice. Nor had he any love for Ludendorff. He promptly did what he had to do, whereupon the heroic general fled the country disguised in beard and dark glasses. Prince Max was thereby enabled to cite seemingly conclusive evidence that "a government of the people" did "actually and constitutionally" have the "authority to make decisions" in Germany, as he wrote to Wilson on October 27—an authority to which not only the "military powers" but also the Kaiser himself were subject.[9] The end of the line for the Hohenzollerns as even a nominally ruling house was obviously very near.

And so, by October's end, Wilson's forceful skillful personal diplomacy, taking full advantage of the opportunities opened before it, had effected a revolutionary change in the German government while ensuring that the structure of the peace would rest on Wilsonian foundations and be raised according to Wilsonian designs. Or so it appeared. When Franklin Roosevelt came to the White House to request permission to resign his office in order to go overseas as a Navy officer (he had already received Daniels' permission), the President, triumphant, was able to tell him it was now "too late," the fighting would "in his judgment" be over "very soon." [10] Roosevelt received this news with decidedly mixed feelings. Like his cousin TR and a vociferous portion, perhaps even a majority, of the American public, maddened as it was by a propaganda-fed hatred of the Hun, he would have preferred the utter crushing of Germany on the battlefield followed by a merciless peace dictated by the victors in Berlin. There was nothing mixed, however, about the President's feelings as he viewed the outcome of his diplomacy. He felt he had now definitely won much of the great object for which so much had been sacrificed. He had successfully championed world peace and world democracy at a most crucial juncture of world history and had within his grasp an end of such transcendent importance that it justified every means "necessary" for its attainment. He deserved the acclamation he would now receive from every quarter of the globe.

II

How true in actual fact was this appearance of overwhelming personal triumph? Measured by Wilson's own historic purpose, what of solid worth had he achieved that would not have been achieved had he at once apprised the Allied governments of Prince Max's overture and given them opportunity to advise him concerning it?

One must suppose he shared at the outset Prince Max's fear that the British and French leaders would refuse an armistice during which peace terms were negotiated and would insist instead upon unconditional surrender, thus depriving him of his chance to establish his Fourteen Points, with his "later pronouncements," as the basis of the peace. But would this have happened? *Could* it have happened against his stubborn will and a negotiating strategy that made due allowance for the *amour propre* and special political problems of the British and French heads of government? In the first place, the President of the United States, whose armies were well on the way to becoming the strongest, as well as freshest, on the Continent and upon whose economic resources the very survival of Western Europe depended, was by no means compelled by sheer power politics to yield to the wishes of the Allied leaders. In the second place, Prince Max's original communication *was* addressed to him alone, which meant that the reply was his to draft. And in the third place, the German note was addressed as it was because Wilson had made policy proclamations in which the Allied leaders, acutely aware of their potency as underminers of the enemy's fighting morale, had tacitly acquiesced—proclamations that were enthusiastically approved by the most influential liberal and labor groups in every country of the world. Hence, the Allied leaders, faced by the German offer, were not free to originate terms of their own, as preconditions of a cease-fire, that differed importantly from the Fourteen Points. Wilson would have done well to assume, and to act upon the assumption, that his explicit policy statements had *to this extent* become implicit Allied commitments.

Clemenceau himself assumed as much. He even claimed later that his commitment to the Fourteen Points as conditions for an armistice had been explicitly made in early 1918. "Mr. Wilson, when he sent us the American army, had put to us his famous Fourteen Points," wrote the

Tiger of France in his book *The Grandeur and Misery of Victory.* "Were we prepared to cease fighting on the day the Germans accepted these various proposals? If I had refused to reply in the affirmative it would have been nothing less than a breach of faith. . . . We, like our Allies, were unanimous for acceptance. . . . After I had promised, with everyone's approval, to agree to President Wilson's conditions . . . was I likely to confront him with a refusal at the moment [October–November, 1918] when he asked us to fulfill our engagements? I was not the man to turn traitor to myself as well as to my country. . . ." [11]

Nothing of value, then, was gained by the exclusiveness of Wilson's highly personal diplomacy. Much, if not all, was lost by it.

Weeks before they were officially informed of the fact, Clemenceau and Lloyd George of course knew all about the President's and the Chancellor's negotiations. Many differences of national and personal interest and of philosophic outlook divided the French from the British Premier; they became as one in their resentment of Wilson's high-handedness, his evident assumption of a wisdom and morality superior to theirs. Who was he to treat them as trivial-minded, inherently naughty schoolboys who must be guided into right conduct by the wise firmness of a schoolmaster? And their shared antipathy toward this schoolmaster served as a highly effective lubricant of their relations with each other, greatly reducing what might otherwise have been harsh frictions between them. By the time Colonel House arrived in France on October 26 as Wilson's personal agent, armed in writing with what amounted to full power of attorney "in matters relating to the war," they were prepared to meet him with a united front.

In their first meeting, October 29, with the President's emissary in Paris—a meeting of the Supreme War Council in which they were joined by the Foreign Ministers of Britain (Arthur Balfour), France (Stéphen Pichon), and Italy (Sidney Sonnino)—the French and British Premiers made it abundantly clear that their tacit acquiescence in the Fourteen Points had constituted no genuine agreement with them or any acceptance of them as bases of a final settlement. Their acquiescence had been in Wilson's original proclamation, and the subsequent worldwide dissemination of it, as a remarkably shrewd and effective stroke of propaganda. Had not the original statement been drafted at the behest of a professional propagandist, for a propaganda purpose? They balked at being now forced to regard its "various proposals" as the terms of an actual treaty.

"Have you ever been asked by President Wilson whether you accept the Fourteen Points?" asked Clemenceau of Lloyd George, adding, in a statement contradictory of his later published remembrance: "I have never been asked." [12] The British Prime Minister said he had "not been asked either" and, turning to the President's emissary, put a question of his own. A crucial question. "What is your view, Colonel House? Do you think that if we agree to an armistice we accept the President's terms?" "That is my view," was House's prompt reply. One can imagine the abrupt increase of tension in the room. Clemenceau grew truculent. "Then I want to hear the Fourteen Points," said the Tiger, who would later acidly remark that fourteen commandments, for as commandments they were now presented, seemed to him an excessive number; the Good Lord had been content with ten. Pichon then prepared to read off the Fourteen Points, the ministers prepared to object to them, and Colonel House prepared to answer these objections. Fortunately the colonel, in anticipation of this confrontation, had designated a group of experts called the American Inquiry to draft a detailed interpretative commentary upon each of the points.* Approved by the President, this became the "official" interpretation. House had it on the table before him when Pichon began.

The very first point, calling for "open covenants openly arrived at," was objected to by both Lloyd George and Clemenceau on the grounds that it would make diplomatic negotiations impossible. House, referring to the commentary, explained that "openly arrived at" did not really mean what it said, that the whole purport of the point was to ensure full publication of the "final covenant" *after* it had emerged from negotiations which, of course, must almost always be conducted privately, confidentially. The two premiers seeming to accept this, Pichon then pressed on to Point Two, calling for "absolute freedom of navigation upon the seas, alike in peace and war." Lloyd George at once announced that the British could not accept this "under any circumstances" since it meant "that the power of blockade goes." "Germany has been broken almost as much by blockade as by military methods," said the Prime Minister. "If this power is to be handed over to the League of Nations, and Great Britain were fighting for her life, no League of Nations could prevent her from defending herself." If and when an actual and potent League were established, he "might be willing to discuss the matter"—but not now. Not as a condition of the armistice *or* of the peace. And Clemenceau backed him in this to the hilt. "It is impossible to make an armistice if doing so commits us to these conditions," summed up Lloyd George with a flatness that caused House to

---

* The actual drafting was done by Frank Cobb of the New York *World* and Walter Lippmann. It was a truly masterful exercise in the translation of glittering generalities, whose logical relationship to one another, if it existed, was far from clear, into the items of a reasonably coherent program.

bridle. The confidential colonel resorted to threats. "The discussion is leading to this," said he, coldly, "—that all negotiations with Germany and Austria up to this point will have to be wiped off the slate." If this happened, the President "would have no alternative but to tell the enemy that his conditions were not accepted by the Allies" and would be forced to consider taking "up these matters directly with Germany and Austria." The tension in the room was now palpable. Said Clemenceau, in disbelief: "That would amount to a separate peace between the United States and the Central Powers!" Colonel House remained outwardly cold and hard as ice. "It might," said he. Whereupon the fiery Welshman David Lloyd George flared up angrily. If the United States should make a separate peace, "we would be sorry," he said, "but we would not give up the blockade, the power which enabled us to live." Britain, he said, would "fight on." Then rose to his feet the most skillful and experienced diplomatist in the room, the imperturbable Balfour, himself a former Prime Minister, who sought to smooth ruffled feelings and restore a reasonable sense of proportion to the discussion. In calm and measured tones he reminded the others that there were "large areas of agreement contained in the President's Fourteen Points" on the basis of which, he was convinced, "we can arrive at a workable compromise." Obviously, he went on, Germany was "intent on driving a wedge between the Allies and the Associated Powers, and we should make every effort to avoid that trap." Lloyd George quickly responded to this cue. He had no objections to raise, he said, except to Point Two. He suggested that they all "go on with the terms of the armistice" and that, in the meantime "each of us, France, Great Britain, and Italy make a draft of our reservations . . . and see tomorrow whether we cannot agree on a common draft." On that highly tentative note, after further desultory discussion (Sonnino objected to Point Nine, calling for a readjustment of Italy's boundaries "along clearly recognized lines of nationality"; Clemenceau wished for clarification of Point Three, dealing with the "removal of trade barriers" and the "establishment of an equality of trade conditions"), the meeting ended.

Colonel House, in anticipation of a complete open break which Balfour's calming influence had but postponed, slept fitfully that night. At three o'clock in the morning he came wide awake. There occurred to him "a way out of the difficulty" he was in. He decided he would tell the hostile ministers "that if they did not accept the President's Fourteen Points and other terms enunciated since January 8, I would advise the President to go before Congress and lay the facts before it, giving the terms which England, France, and Italy insisted upon, and ask the advice of Congress whether the United States should make peace with

Germany now that she has accepted the American terms, or whether we should go on fighting until Germany had accepted the terms of France, England, and Italy, whatever they might be. . . ." He cabled his inspiration at once to the President. "The last thing they [the prime ministers] want is publicity . . . ," he added. "Unless we deal with these people with a firm hand everything we have been fighting for will be lost." [13]

Lloyd George, too, spent a restless night. Hours of it were consumed in conference with Balfour during which was drafted a "proposed answer to the President" to be signed by all the Allied governments—an answer derived from a "careful consideration to the correspondence which has passed between the President . . . and the German Government."

The next morning Lloyd George, Clemenceau, and House met alone for forty-five minutes in the office of the Minister of War. As they entered the room together, the British Prime Minister handed the colonel his "proposed answer." House read it with pleased surprise. Its tone contrasted sharply with the one Lloyd George had taken yesterday afternoon. It announced that the Allies were willing "to make peace . . . on the terms . . . laid down in the President's address to Congress of January 8, 1918, and the principles of settlement enunciated in his subsequent addresses," with only one reservation and one clarification. The *reservation* had to do, of course, with Point Two. Since "what is usually described as freedom of the seas" was "open to various interpretations," some of them absolutely unacceptable, the Allies "must . . . reserve to themselves complete freedom on this subject when they enter the peace conference." The *clarification* was of the President's declaration "that invaded territories must be restored as well as evacuated and freed." The Allied governments wanted clearly understood "what this provision implies"—namely, "that compensation will be made by Germany for all damage done to the civilian population of the Allies and their property by land, by sea and from the air." [14] House seems to have realized that this might lead to demands for reparation payments beyond Germany's capacity to pay without excessive hardship—might lead, in other words, to the "punitive damages" which the President had foresworn—for he at once suggested insertion of the word "illegal" between "all" and "damages." Clemenceau, however, "preferred that the draft be left as it was," and House did not press the point. To have done so at that moment would have been unpolitic, to say the least. Clemenceau, having indicated that he was preparing an elaborate brief of France's objections to the Fourteen Points, had just abandoned that project in the face of House's threat to expose the whole disagreement to the decision of Congress. (". . . it would doubtless be necessary for the President . . . to place the responsibility upon Congress for further continuation of the war by the United States in behalf of the aims of the Allies," House had said. "As soon as I . . . said this George and Clemenceau looked at each other significantly." [15])

And so the British memorandum became the agreed basis for the armistice; Wilson accepted both the reservation and the clarification which it contained. ". . . we have won a diplomatic victory," cabled House to the President exultantly, "in getting the Allies to accept our principles. . . . This was done in the face of a hostile and influential junta in the U.S. and the thoroughly unsympathetic personnel constituting the Entente governments." [16]

III

But surely, even in that moment of exultation, there must have lurked in House's mind, and Wilson's, an ugly fear that the "victory" would prove Pyrrhic.

This whole situation, so largely of Wilson's making, mingled the ludicrous with the tragic. While German and American soldiers killed one another on the battlefield, the President of the United States and the Chancellor of Germany had, in effect, made common cause against the Prime Ministers of the Allied governments whose troops fought side by side with the Americans and still bore the brunt of the battle in which the Americans were involved. In effect, Chancellor and President were joined together in an effort to ram down the throats of the premiers, as a *fait accompli,* the Fourteen Points and the various "complementary" and "explanatory" points. And despite its immediate appearance of success, the effort was bound to fail, thereby providing plausible grounds on which a resurgent German militarism could rest claims that Germany had *not* been defeated militarily but had been tricked into laying down its arms. Cowardly civilian ministers (so the argument would run), elevated to their posts by treasonable elements of the home front, had permitted themselves to be duped by the false promises of Germany's enemies.

Nor was this the limit of Wilson's folly. The errors in his conduct of foreign policy were compounded at this same time by an incredible blunder in the conduct of domestic affairs—and the root cause of the blunder, lying deep in his psychological nature, was the same as that of the errors.

All the while that he as head of state engaged in prearmistice negotiations, he as party leader was necessarily concerned with the American midterm election campaign. Not a few of the grave anxieties among many Democratic candidates were due to the obviously approaching end of the war. Large portions of the electorate could now feel free of any urgent patriotic duty to support the administration, free to register instead their blind resentments of high taxes, of business restrictions, of a price ceiling on wheat when none had been placed on cotton, upon a dozen and one inequities and irritations which resulted from wartime government regulations. Moreover, the chauvinism which the Creel Committee had done so much to foment while simultaneously glorifying Woodrow Wilson now threatened to become a potent political force against his administration. Its rallying cry was "On to Berlin." Its fear was that the President would deny our righteous arms this triumph by accepting a "soft" peace with the vicious Hun. And the fear was one on which Republican politicians were prepared to play in their bid for votes. ("Let us dictate the peace by the hammering guns," cried TR, "and not chat about peace to the accompaniment of the clicking of typewriters!" [17]) These signs and portents, added to the fact that traditionally there was a midterm loss of Congressional seats by the party in power, were ominous for Democrats running in close races and worrisome to Vance McCormick, chairman of the National Democratic Committee. There were cries for help from the White House. Demands that Wilson endorse specific candidates or issue a call for the election of Democrats in general became more and more insistent as October advanced.

Wilson resisted them. He had excellent, indeed conclusive reasons for doing so, which his Attorney General indicated in private statement. "For more than a year there has [sic] been in Washington thousands of loyal Republicans, working under Wilson's leadership for the country, at $1.00 a year, and sacrificing their private interests and forgetting their political affiliations," said Thomas W. Gregory. "There . . . [are] scores of Republicans in the Senate and House who . . . [have] voted consistently for Wilson's policies and held up his hands during the struggle, at a time when many of his own party were hamstringing him." [18] Legislation which placed sweeping war emergency powers in the President's hands, for instance—particularly the power of control over food and fuel—was bitterly opposed by influential Congressional Democrats and could never have been enacted had not Republicans fought for it. In these circumstances, the "worst political mistake" that Wilson "could make," said the Attorney General, would be to issue a blanket statement which "seemed to stigmatize everyone who was not a member of the Democratic party."

Yet this is precisely what Wilson proceeded to do, to the utter surprise and consternation of nearly all his closest associates. Alone in his study one late October night he typed out on his portable typewriter an appeal to "My Fellow Countrymen" which was issued in midafternoon of October 25 to the press. ("I . . . read it with horror in the morning paper," said Gregory later.[19]) It said, in part: "The Congressional elections . . . occur in the most critical period our country has ever faced or is likely to face in our time. If you have approved of my leadership and wish me to continue to be your unembarrassed spokesman in affairs at home and abroad, I earnestly beg that you will express yourself unmistakably to that effect by returning a Democratic majority to both the Senate and the House of Representatives. . . . I have no thought of suggesting that any political party is paramount in matters of patriotism. . . . I mean only that the difficulties and delicacies of our present task are of a sort that makes it imperatively necessary that the nation would give its undivided support to the Government under a unified leadership, and that a Republican Congress would divide the leadership. . . . The return of a Republican majority to either House of Congress would, moreover, certainly be interpreted on the other side of the water as a repudiation of my leadership." [20]

The immediate public reaction to this statement was stupendous, and may well have dismayed the very politicians who had urged Wilson to make it. Republican politicians pounced upon it with gleeful malice. Will Hays, the Republican national chairman, proclaimed it an "insult to every loyal Republican in the land." TR, exultant, wrote Senator Lodge of his delight that "Wilson has come out in the open; I fear Judas most when he can cloak his activities behind a treacherous make-believe of non-partisanship." [21] Eleven days later (November 5), the Republicans captured control of both houses of the Sixty-sixth Congress, winning 237 seats in the lower house, compared to 190 for the Democrats, and a Senate majority of two.

The damage done Wilson's prestige and effectiveness was immense. Out of his own mouth came the interpretation of the election result as a repudiation of him—and this interpretation was hammered into the public mind by Republican spokesmen. TR, for one. A few days after the election, the ex-President's wounded, broken, overstrained body—a bullet lodged near one lung, a chronic abscess in one thigh—finally collapsed under the demands he imposed on it. He was taken in great pain to Roosevelt Hospital in New York City, and from his bed there he issued a statement. "Our Allies and our enemies and Mr. Wilson himself should all understand that Mr. Wilson has no authority to speak for the American people at this time," said TR. "His leadership has just been emphatically repudiated by them. . . . Mr. Wilson and his Fourteen

Points and his four supplementary points and his five complementary points and all his utterances every which way have ceased to have any shadow of right to be accepted as expressive of the will of the American people."

The irony—the bitter, bitter irony for Woodrow Wilson—was that his partisan appeal of October 25 probably changed few votes, one way or the other. It simply rendered personal a defeat that would otherwise have been seen as a natural, relatively superficial shift of political sentiment, a shift determined in no small part by the fact that the Sixty-fifth Congress was widely regarded as less competent than most.

Thus, through strategic, psychologically caused mistakes of diplomacy and domestic politics, was lost an opportunity to forge, in the furnace heat of continuing battle and under the unifying effect of Germany's plea to end the slaughter,* a genuine agreement on the terms of the peace, along with a common strategy for implementing it at the negotiating table.

In retrospect it appears that public opinion might have forced the Allied leaders into substantial agreement with Wilson's position—if indeed these leaders were not themselves persuaded toward it—had Wilson at this critical juncture (from October 5 on) made use of an open and cooperative diplomacy instead of an exclusively personal and coercive one. By actively officially involving London, Paris, and Rome in pre-armistice decision-making, by exchanging communications with them on a basis of mutual respect and trust *prior* to his every communication with Prince Max, and by ensuring that the general public was accurately informed of each stage of solid agreement in the negotiations (the German military front would in that case almost certainly have collapsed in mid-October), the President might have largely shaped and become the spokesman of a consistent international policy which, though differing in detail from the Fourteen Points, effectively affirmed their essential spirit and culminating purpose—namely, the establishment of a League of Nations strong enough to make general war impossible.

It is true that the chauvinism then rampant among the most vociferous elements of the Allied and American populations militated against rational solutions. Clemenceau was personally animated by it. Lloyd George and his supporters in England, like the Republicans in America, were prepared to exploit it for partisan advantage in that fall's elections.

* Between the time Prince Max made his original proposal and the hour the guns fell silent, hundreds of thousands were killed and maimed on the western front. The fighting was approximately as intense, the casualty rates as high in October and early November, 1918, as they were in any six-week period of the war.

But it is also true that there was everywhere present a profound war weariness and disgust, a determination to prevent future wars at almost any cost, a compassion born of enormous communal suffering, a desperate hope for the emergence of great good out of immense evil. This vast emotional energy was focused on Woodrow Wilson. By the great masses of Europe the American President, thanks in part to Creel Committee efforts, had come to be worshiped almost as the New Messiah, and his prestige was but slightly less among millions of his fellow countrymen.

Here, then, was a world force that awaited only a clear and definite opportunity to express itself in effective international action, and here was a man who stood at the door of this opportunity, his hand upon its knob. If only that man had admitted to himself that the great vision which stirred him was not his alone but was shared with myriad millions! If only he had seen that his proper historic function was not to *make* things happen according to his private vision but to *enable* them to happen according to the best collective vision of mankind! If only, that is to say, he had been content to act the humble part of doorman! The upcoming peace conference might then have become as harmonious an enterprise as the Congress of Vienna in 1814 but dedicated, as the congress emphatically was not, to the realization on a global scale of liberal, humanitarian, and scientific principles. Instead, Woodrow Wilson saw *himself* as the Messiah. He was even bound and determined to achieve his own crucifixion and resurrection—or so it would later seem. Consequently more and more obstacles were placed in the way of any true settlement—liberal *or* conservative, punitive *or* conciliatory—of the international issues by which the war was ostensibly caused.

As for a rechanneling of the fundamental historic processes upon which these issues rode as chips upon a dark river flowing toward doom, all chance of this was now lost.

IV

Franklin Roosevelt had very little to do, directly or indirectly, with the great international events of late October, but that little was on the side of the hardest possible armistice terms for Germany, even at the risk of Germany's refusing them and prolonging the conflict.

Josephus Daniels was frequently away from Washington during this period, campaigning for Democrats in the midterm elections. In his absence, Acting Secretary Roosevelt was involved in what he described to a friend as "an immense number of important telegrams and operations, including conferences with the President." One of the telegrams, reaching Roosevelt's desk on October 29, was from Admiral Benson, who had gone to France as one of Colonel House's party aboard the USS *North Pacific* and had since been meeting the Inter-Allied Naval Council in Paris. The telegram contained the council's proposed naval conditions for an armistice. The conditions were harsh—all submarines were to be immediately unconditionally surrendered; all battleships, cruisers, and destroyers were to be interned in neutral ports with only maintenance crews aboard—and Captain William V. Pratt, Acting Operations Chief, believed them needlessly harsh, going beyond the President's specifications. Rather than accept them, the German admirals might order out the High Seas Fleet for a last desperate action—a violence that would kill and destroy to no purpose whatever. Pratt expressed this opinion in a memorandum that also reached Roosevelt's desk on October 29 and with which the Acting Secretary emphatically disagreed. The naval terms should be every bit as severe as the military terms, Roosevelt believed. He said so in a letter of his own to the President, covering his transmittal of both the Benson cable and the Pratt memorandum. The terms he favored were those ultimately imposed.

He took no active part in the election campaign. Al Smith had won the nomination for governor of New York which Roosevelt had refused. Roosevelt, of course, endorsed him in public statement. But he made no campaign speaking trips on behalf of Smith or anyone else. Partly this was because he had to remain in Washington when his chief was away campaigning, but it was also for reasons of health. Still very weak when he returned to Washington, he soon thereafter suffered a relapse and had to take to bed for several days—this at a time when all five of the Roosevelt children and three of the servants were down with the flu. Only Eleanor, of all the household, remained on her feet. ("We succeeded in getting one trained nurse from New York, as Miss Spring was not available," she later recalled. "This nurse was put in charge of Elliott, who had double pneumonia. . . . There was very little difference between night and day for me. . . .")[22] Thus Roosevelt was pushed by household conditions as he was drawn by office duties to return to work without an adequate period of convalescence from his relapse. He was back at work when the President issued the public appeal for a Democratic Congress, and shook his head over it with Louis Howe. They both suspected that the President had blundered badly.

The election day news was, of course, generally depressing to Roosevelt. It contained one bright spot. In his home state, the peace he had made with Boss Murphy, helping heal the split between Tammany and the Progressives, seemed justified by the election of Al Smith as governor of New York—a victory which not only removed Charles S. Whitman from the governor's chair, but also removed him from further consideration as Republican candidate for President in 1920. Otherwise, the immediate political prospect was gloomy for a high official of the administration, and Roosevelt, with Howe, swiftly calculated the probable or possible effects upon his own career of a Congress controlled by the opposition party. There would be postwar Congressional investigations of the Navy Department's conduct of war business—of procurement, the building of installations, contractual arrangements of all kinds—and these investigations would be by Republican-dominated committees whose principal purpose would be to provide political ammunition for party candidates in the next national election. The department, Roosevelt realized, would be particularly vulnerable to attacks upon its handling of business operations overseas, where millions had been spent under loosely drawn, manifestly faulty contracts with French, British, and Italian interests. Some installations had been built and turned over to the Allies without any contracts being drawn up at all! The chances for wholesale graft as these overseas operations were liquidated were very great.

But at any rate the war *had* been won, and under this administration. Its end now swiftly came.

On November 3, German Admiral Reinhard Scheer did as Captain Pratt had feared he might; he ordered the High Seas Fleet to come out and fight until sunk. Instead, as had happened at Kiel in late October, German crews mutinied and killed many of their officers. A mob of sailors wearing red brassards attacked and wrecked the headquarters offices of the Hamburg-American Line. Herr Albert Ballin, head of that line, to whom Bismarck had made his gloomy prophecy (in 1897) that the great European war would someday come from "some damned foolish thing in the Balkans," was savagely beaten by revolutionaries who invaded his office, then swallowed a fistful of sleeping tablets and staggered to his death in the street. Two days later (election day in America), the German government was notified that Marshal Foch would "receive properly accredited representatives . . . and . . . communicate to them the terms of an armistice." On November 9, Prince Max in Berlin proclaimed the abdication of the Kaiser, though in actual fact the Kaiser at Spa had stubbornly refused Max's repeated pleas that he do so. The next day the Kaiser fled in his personal train to Holland (there, interned by the Dutch, he would live out his ruined life), and Prince Max retired to Baden after the establishment of a German republic under Socialist leadership had been announced in Berlin.

A few hours later, at five o'clock in the morning of November 11,

1918, in Marshal Foch's railway train in the Forest of Compiègne, the formal armistice documents were signed. Orders went out to all military units: the fighting was to end in the eleventh hour of that eleventh day of the eleventh month of the year. At 11:55 A.M., French time, the last shot was fired. All was quiet on the western front after 1,563 days of a war that had killed 10,000,000 men in battle and wounded 20,000,000 more, that had cost, directly and indirectly, an estimated $300 billion, and that had inflicted such injuries upon Western civilization as generations of men could not repair.

News of the armistice arrived very early in the morning in Washington, D.C. Four days before, Roy Howard of the United Press, eager to achieve the greatest "scoop" in newspaper history, had on the basis of unchecked rumor signaled from Brest the end of the war, setting off wild celebrations all across America before his announcement was proved to be false. Would this abortive jubilation of November 7 blunt the celebration of the real armistice, when it came? Many had thought so, feared so. They were mistaken. Franklin and Eleanor Roosevelt awoke on November 11 to a din of screaming whistles, honking automobile horns, ringing church bells, shouting people in the streets. Hastily they dressed and were soon in the streets themselves, joining there a happy throng that sang, cheered, threw confetti ("or anything else they could find at hand," Eleanor would remember), and formed impromptu parades behind brass bands under streaming flags.

"The feeling of relief and thanksgiving," remembered Eleanor long afterward, "was beyond description." [23]

Among Franklin Roosevelt's most remarkable abilities, of great value to him in politics, was that of adjusting almost instantaneously and seemingly without pain to a total change in circumstances.

On the day following the armistice he was at odds with Daniels because the Secretary did not at once recognize and respond to one of the demobilization problems which now loomed large, that of providing warehouse space in America for surplus naval war supplies. He felt strongly enough about his disagreement to record it in a handwritten memorandum placed "for the record" in his personal files. And during the days and weeks that followed he pressed the Secretary with increasing vehemence for authorization to go again to Europe, to direct the demobilization of U.S. Navy installations and the disposal of naval matériel. He fumed at Daniels' decision to let Admiral Sims administer this complicated business. Congress, he pointed out, would hold the department's civilian administration responsible for whatever mistakes were made, and he for one was not willing to place his political fortunes in the hands of Navy career officers. Finally, in early December, when he was again stricken by a head cold, he penned from his sickbed an irritable missive to the Secretary in which he threatened to dissociate himself publicly from the demobilization operation, so that the whole burden of public responsibility for it would rest upon Daniels, unless the latter permitted him to make the requested trip abroad.[24]

Perhaps the threat was effective, or perhaps Daniels had by then concluded that his assistant's argument was indeed a valid one. At any rate, Roosevelt's second European mission was now authorized. It was also decided that Eleanor, who certainly was eager to do so, should accompany her husband abroad, ostensibly to protect his yet-precarious health against the wintry frosts and glooms of England and France.

They sailed from New York on January 2, 1919, aboard the USS *George Washington*,* of which Roosevelt's good friend Captain Ed McCauley, who had been the Assistant Secretary's chief of staff during last summer's European mission, was now in command.

V

For Christmas of 1918—a holiday always before spent by the Roosevelts at Hyde Park but this year celebrated in Washington—Eleanor gave her husband a book that had been privately printed in an edition of one hundred copies in 1906 but had only just been issued for general purchase. It was *The Education of Henry Adams*, it had an "Editor's Preface" by Henry Cabot Lodge, and the Roosevelts took it with them aboard the *George Washington*. Eleanor read it during a crossing in which her husband was occupied with calisthenics (Walter Camp was aboard), shuffleboard, ship inspection, and socializing with Livingston Davis, whom he took with him as special assistant (to Eleanor's regret), and such fellow passengers as Charles Schwab and Bernard Baruch.

She found the book remarkably like the crusty, rather intimidating old gentleman whom she and Franklin had come to know moderately well on Lafayette Square during the last years of his life. She was both impressed and disturbed by the labored ironies of Adams' involuted style, his world-weariness and ostentatiously paraded sense of personal failure and despair: these were harshly incongruous with the yet-prevailing, if diminishing, mood of idealistic optimism. They were, however, perfectly congruous with the mood that would become culturally dominant in postwar America—and Eleanor might have been com-

---

* Like *Leviathan*, the *George Washington* was a former Hamburg-American liner.

menting upon the America of the decade to come as well as upon Henry
Adams when, having finished the book, she wrote: "Very interesting,
but sad to have had so much and yet find it so little." [25]

There is no evidence that she was impressed by the theoretical roots
of Adams' peculiar sadness as outlined by him in the last chapters of his
book, chapters wherein he sketchily presented a Dynamic Theory of
History and attempted, with dubious success, to define a historical Law
of Acceleration. Yet she must have been impressed by the metaphorical
image through which he, in his closing pages, reiterated his sense of the
human effects of the enormous and constantly accelerating release of
usable energy resulting from the evolving scientific technology. Education could not keep pace with the demands made on it by changes so
swift and so huge. Virtually every major premise, every cherished
human value, every religious certainty of that eighteenth century whose
child Adams felt himself to be, had been destroyed by the end of the
nineteenth century, and nothing had been put in their places that could
give a comparable feeling of security and direction in an amiable, reasonable world. The world was no longer amiable *or* reasonable. Power
had gone out of control. An anarchy of stupendous forces raged
through the city of man. And of all this the New York City skyline as
seen from the deck of a steamer entering the harbor on November 5,
1904, had seemed to Adams symbolic. "The outline of the city became
frantic . . . ," he wrote. "The cylinder had exploded, and thrown great
masses of stone and steam against the sky." [26]

But if this were the effect upon Adams of the skyline of 1904, how
much greater in the same direction would have been the effect on him of
the skyline that Eleanor and Franklin Roosevelt looked back upon as
they passed the Statue of Liberty, outward bound, on January 2, 1919!
Its highest point was the top of the Woolworth Building, completed a
half dozen years before. This was unmistakably an office building; it
had, essentially, an office building's functional design. Yet Cass Gilbert,
the architect, had managed also to give it a soaring Gothic quality so
that—a Cathedral of Commerce—it thrust its way sixty stories and 792
feet toward heaven as if uplifted by the fused energies of Dynamo and
Virgin. It was the tallest habitable structure in the world. It was in fact
the tallest structure of any kind erected up to that time, with the single
exception of the Eiffel Tower in Paris. And in a way it ordered the scene
by providing a central focus for what was otherwise a mere jumble of
towers that more than doubled in height those Adams had seen—a jumble whose jagged outlines might well present themselves to a poet of history as a chaos of irrational drives rendered rigid in steel and concrete,
the postures of a mass hysteria.

Or perhaps one should say that the Woolworth Building sharpened the sense of chaos by suggesting, faintly, the possibility of order. It stood up as a finger of admonition above a skyline that—lacking any meaningful general pattern, hence manifesting no overall planning intelligence—did indeed appear an outburst, an upthrust of solidified energies that had escaped rational controls, like so many shrieks frozen into the upper air. And what these silent shrieks seemed to call for across the widening gap of wintry sea was a "new type of man," deemed by Adams urgently necessary in 1904—a type having "ten times the endurance, energy, will and mind of the old type" whose failure to master the "new forces" had, in Adams' phrase, "become catastrophic." Obviously this "new type" had not yet appeared—not at least in sufficient numbers in positions of ruling power—nor was there any sign of him on the urban-towered horizon of 1919.

Upon and beyond that horizon, as a matter of fact, what was happening at the moment of the Roosevelts' sailing was the opposite of what Adams had seen as a hysterically crying need fifteen years before. Demobilization was in full swing, and nothing could have more clearly indicated how little the organization of Leviathan had derived from men's free choices and controlling intelligence, how much it had been dictated by those "new forces" whose anarchical growth Adams had so greatly feared, than the abrupt, unplanned way in which Leviathan was dismantled. "The moment we knew the armistice to have been signed we took the harness off," said the President in his annual message to Congress, December 2, 1918. A more nearly accurate metaphorical description would have said that the "harness" was shaken off by the energies which had originally forced its imposition, now that these energies were released from between the drive shafts of war.

Millions of soldiers who had been in training camps were being summarily dismissed and sent home. Other millions who had gone overseas were being returned as swiftly as available transport and the needs of the German occupation would allow. Wartime regulations and restrictions were being relaxed or abolished as the special agencies through which the national economy had been directed, now abandoned by the dollar-a-year men who had administered them, were drastically reduced or eliminated altogether. Here and there attempts were being made to keep the "harness" on, in service of the general welfare. During the war, the U.S. Navy had developed a worldwide radio network, and Daniels pressed for continued government ownership and operation of it. There were voices raised—not many, but a few—on behalf of a government-owned and -operated merchant marine, making use of the vast fleet of merchantmen built or otherwise acquired as a war necessity by the Shipping Board. There was pressure for a nationalization of the railroads. McAdoo, retiring as head of the Railroad Administration, acutely aware of the gains in economic and operating efficiency effected by a nationally unified management of rail transport, was urging a five-year peacetime experiment in government operation. But these "Socialistic" measures were so strongly opposed by doctrinaire conservatives, by the business community in general, and by most union leaders that the likelihood of their being adopted diminished day by day. In the event there would be, to the wholesale shaking off of "harness," a single major exception: the Espionage and Sedition Acts continued to remain in full force; the war-swollen powers of the Attorney General (notably the greatly expanded FBI) remained intact.

Woodrow Wilson had paid slight heed to the problems of demobilization in the weeks immediately following the armistice. As regards railroad policy, for example, he was indifferent, saying to Congress in his December 2 message that he had, on this subject, "no confident judgment of my own." He had loftier concerns. And these had wholly absorbed him for a month before that wintry day when the Roosevelts stood together, at ship's railing, looking back upon the diminishing towers of Manhattan. Aboard this same *George Washington* the President had sailed from this same port on December 4, headed for the Preliminary Peace Conference which would open in Paris in January; had stood then with his wife beside Captain McCauley on the captain's bridge as the ship moved out through the mouth of the Hudson into the harbor, escorted by five destroyers which fired a twenty-one-gun salute and by two airplanes and a dirigible overhead; had seen the Battery packed by an immense, wildly cheering throng, the harbor crowded by tugs and launches jammed with people; had heard every ship in the harbor blast the sky with its steam whistle as the ship moved on toward and past the Statue of Liberty. The mass applause had been heartwarming to him. It was in marked contrast with the chilly reception Congress had given his official announcement, in his annual message two days before, that he intended to attend the Paris Conference in person.

Most of his advisers had begged him not to do so. His old friend Dr. Harry Garfield, the fuel administrator, spoke for many when he said to the President: ". . . if you go . . . you will have to descend from your present position as world arbiter. You will necessarily become a combatant in the hurly-burly. You will become a contestant in the struggle . . . of which you are the only possible referee." Frank Cobb made the same point in a memorandum to Colonel House, which House transmitted to Wilson. "The moment President Wilson sits at the council table with these Prime Ministers and Foreign Secretaries he has lost the power that comes from distance and detachment," argued Cobb. ". . . in Washington the President has the ear of the whole world. . . . If his representatives are balked by the representatives of other Powers in matters which he regards as vital to the lasting peace of the world, he can go before Congress and appeal to the conscience and hope of mankind. He can do this over the head of any Peace Conference. This is a mighty weapon, but if the President were to participate personally in the proceedings, it would be a broken stick." [27] Such argument was of no avail against Woodrow Wilson's messianic compulsions. "The gallant men of our armed forces on land and sea have consciously fought for the ideals . . . I have sought to express . . . ," he had told a grimly silent Congress; "they have accepted my statement of them as the substance of their own thought and purpose as the associated governments have accepted them; and I owe it to them to see to it . . . that no false or mistaken interpretation is put upon them, and no possible effort omitted to realize them."

And it was in the same egoistically messianic mood that he had picked the American delegation which accompanied him to the conference. Before any treaty negotiated in Paris became binding upon the United States, it must be ratified by two-thirds of the U.S. Senate, and the Senate after March 4 would be controlled by Republicans. Simple common sense would therefore seem to require the President to include at least one politically potent Republican among his delegation appointees. He was urged to do so by Tumulty, Lansing, Hoover, several others. Why not Elihu Root? they asked. Or Charles Evans Hughes? Or William Howard Taft? All three were publicly committed to the League of Nations idea. Instead, Wilson appointed House, Lansing, General Tasker Bliss (the Army Chief of Staff), and Henry White, a distinguished but overaged career diplomat whom he would consult now and then on procedure and protocol but almost never on substantive matters. White was nominally a Republican, but he was not and had never been strongly partisan; he had no influence whatever with Congress. In effect, then, as editor George Harvey wrote in his bitterly anti-Wilson *Harvey's Weekly*, the commission consisted of Woodrow Wilson accompanied by three shadows and a cipher. For whom did House represent? asked Harvey. "The Executive," he answered. Whom did Lansing represent? "The Executive." Whom did Bliss represent? "The Commander-in-Chief." And whom did White represent? "Nobody." By his very nature as Messiah, Wilson was denied the companionship of equals, was condemned to isolation at the pinnacle of the highest hopes and aspirations of mankind, and he refused to mitigate his solitude even to the extent of taking with him a personal staff adequate to cope with the load of paper work which would descend upon him when the conference began. He had embarked upon a journey which purposed nothing less than a reordering of the whole world's international relations on democratic principles, yet his personal entourage consisted of his wife, his physician (Grayson), two stenographers, and no one else at all! He lacked even a personal secretary. Having left Tumulty behind, because he didn't trust him, he had refused to take on a substitute in Paris, despite House's urgings, because doing so "would break Tumulty's heart."

But however isolated he was as a personality, he was by no means alone in his exalted view of himself and his mission. The Roosevelts, like all other Americans, but with a greater interest than most, had perused the glowing newspaper accounts of Wilson's reception on Friday December 13 at that French port, Brest, toward which the Roosevelts themselves now sailed and of his reception in Paris on the following day. Nor had there been any diminution in the hysterical greeting of him in the days that followed, during which he made one ceremonial public appearance after another in the French capital and in England also, for he paid a state visit to that country in the last week of 1918. On the day the Roosevelts sailed from New York City, the Wilsons were riding the Italian royal train southward from Paris toward Rome, where the President was accorded a triumph equivalent to those he had received in Paris and London and probably greater than any Caesar had been able to command in all that ancient city's years of imperial glory. Larger still were the roaring crowds at Milan a few days later. Wounded soldiers there tried to kiss his clothes when he appeared among them. And at Turin, on the day after that, Wilson's hand was kissed as worshipfully as a cardinal's ring by several of the thousand Piedmont mayors gathered to honor him.

Three days before landing at Brest, in a speech to a gathering of American Inquiry experts aboard the *George Washington*, the President had said that the Americans "would be the only disinterested people at the peace conference" and, with a lack of truth as well as of acumen, that "the men whom" the Americans "were about to deal with did not represent their own people." At that very moment there had been under way in England a general election in which the rival party candidates faced crowds animated by a veritable frenzy of hatred for Germans and Germany, a hatred long fanned by lurid propaganda. Lloyd George's opening campaign speeches had been Wilsonian in tone and substance; but he soon yielded to the prevailing sentiment, and on December 19 he and his partisans won a huge majority of the votes after a campaign whose central slogans were "Hang the Kaiser" and "Squeeze the German lemon till the pips squeak." Two days later Clemenceau, advocate of the harshest possible terms for Germany, won an over-whelming vote of confidence in the French Chamber of Deputies. These events plunged Colonel House into gloom. ". . . taking into considera-tion the result of the recent elections in the United States," wrote House in his diary, "the situation strategically could not be worse." Of the heads of the governments of Italy, France, England, and the United States, only the latter had been rebuffed by his electorate.

Yet Wilson, with the cheers of countless thousands of French, Eng-lish, and Italians ringing in his ears, persisted in the belief that he repre-sented not only the great masses of his own country but also those of Western Europe, and these last far more accurately than did their own elected officials. The optimism sustained by this belief was certainly not diminished by news which came to him on the morning of January 6, 1919, when he was on his way back to Paris from Italy. It was news he evidently interpreted as further proof that he, Woodrow Wilson, was in-deed an angel of the Lord, placed on earth to accomplish a divine mis-sion. His train paused briefly at Modena. Newspaper correspondents got out to stretch their legs on the station platform. From there they saw, through the railway carriage window, Wilson reading a telegram just handed him, and they were fascinated, so two of them later told Henry F. Pringle, by the play of contradictory emotions across his coun-tenance. ". . . first . . . there was surprise," writes Pringle. "Then came pity. Then came a look of transcendent triumph." [28] What in the world was this message? the newsmen wondered. Obviously it was of immense personal importance to the President. A few minutes later their eager curiosity was satisfied: the telegram announced the death of Theodore Roosevelt.

This same news came at almost precisely the same time, through ship's radio, to Eleanor and Franklin Roosevelt aboard the *George Washington*. It came as "in every way a great shock," said Roosevelt in a letter to Josephus Daniels three days later, "for we heard just before leaving that he was better—and he was after all not old." Released from the hospital, TR had returned to Oyster Bay just before Christmas, had resumed his massive correspondence and journalism, had seemed to be making a good recovery from his illness. On January 5 he had written an editorial for the Kansas City *Star*, of which he was a contributing ed-itor, saying that, while a League of Nations was a desirable objective, "Mr. Wilson's utterances" upon the subject were "still absolutely in the stage of rhetoric." Why not "begin with the League which we actually have in existence, the League of the Allies," he had asked, and then "agree to extend the privileges of the League as rapidly as their conduct warrants it to other nations?" He went to an early bed that night, and an early sleep. He never awoke. A coronary thrombosis killed him at four o'clock in the morning. "I knew what this loss would mean to his close family," remembered Eleanor long afterward, "but I think I realized even more keenly that a great personality had gone from active participation in the life of his people. The loss of his influence and example was what I seemed to feel most keenly." [29]

Four days later the Roosevelts disembarked at Brest.

They remained in Europe for thirty-five crowded days, during which Roosevelt was occupied in his official capacity with the settlement of numerous claims against the Navy on the part of private citizens; with the disposal of Navy overseas property, including the Lafayette Radio installation near Bordeaux, by far the largest in the world (the French bought it for the cost of its construction, after Roosevelt had threatened otherwise to dismantle it and ship it home); and with various other problems of overseas demobilization. His special and indispensable function in all this was that of high-level negotiator. The detailed work, frequently complex in the extreme, was skillfully handled by Commander John M. Hancock of the Navy Supply Corps, brought to Europe for that purpose as a member of the Assistant Secretary's party. Hancock was so efficient, as a matter of fact, that Roosevelt was "really not overworked," as Eleanor remarked in a letter to her mother-in-law.[30] And he stayed healthy; there was no recurrence of his flu.

It was Eleanor who, for one of the very few times in her life, became ill, "picking up some kind of germ . . . the day before we left for London." She was "running quite a temperature" and had a stabbing pain in her side when, on the way to the Channel by motorcar, she toured with her husband the shell-churned battlefields of the Somme, the ruins of Cambrai, Bapaume, Albert, Amiens. But she refused to remain in bed even after ordered to do so by a London doctor who diagnosed her illness as pleurisy and mildly frightened her with his voiced suspicion that she might be tubercular.[31]

She was still weak and unwontedly irritable when, after two weeks in London, her husband's work there was completed. He left then for a trip through Belgium into the American-occupied Rhineland, while Eleanor eventually went directly from London to Paris. She happened to arrive in the lobby of the Ritz Hotel simultaneously with Livingston Davis who had accompanied Roosevelt to Belgium, had then motored down to the French capital, and at the hotel had "found that for 12 hours he must occupy a room without a bath" because of a government requirement that the manager retain a certain number of rooms for the use of officers who might arrive unexpectedly. His reaction to this provoked in

Eleanor, irritable as she was from her late illness, an angry contempt. (". . . I thought the poor manager's head would be blown off!") ". . . Livy is lazy, selfish and self-seeking to an extraordinary degree with the outward appearance of being quite different," she wrote her mother-in-law disgustedly. "Franklin is too loyal ever to change his feelings but I am deciding more firmly every day that the estimate I've been making of him for over a year is not far from right." [32]

The Paris Conference had by this time (February 8) been formally convened for twenty-one days.[33] Its first order of business, at Woodrow Wilson's insistence and against strong initial opposition from the French, was the drafting of the Covenant of the League of Nations. The French, supported by the British, had wished this matter to be taken up as the concluding act of the conference, after agreement had been reached on the peace terms to be imposed upon the Central Powers; but Wilson's stated belief was that the establishment of the League should be "the center of the whole program," that everything else "should revolve around" it, and that "once it is a *fait accompli* nearly all the very serious difficulties will disappear." In his anxious eagerness to achieve this *fait accompli*, however, he made a major concession to Britain, France, and Japan concerning the disposal of former German colonies —a concession which set at naught the prescription of Point Five of the Fourteen Points that there should be a "free, open-minded, and absolutely impartial adjustment of all Colonial claims, based upon a strict observance of the principle that . . . the interests of the populations concerned must have equal weight with the equitable claims of the Government whose title is to be determined." Against Wilson's initial wish, the conference was organized in such a way as to enable the five major Allied and Associated Powers (Britain, France, Italy, Japan, and the United States) to control its proceedings and dictate its conclusions. There was set up a Supreme Council, or Council of Ten, composed of Lloyd George and Balfour, Clemenceau and Pichon, Orlando and Sonnino, Wilson and Lansing, and the two chief delegates from Japan. At a meeting of this council Wilson, on January 13, had forced an agreement upon a "list of subjects for discussion" of which the League of Nations was first and "colonies" last. But on January 23, Lloyd George suddenly proposed that colonial matters be now discussed, a proposal immediately backed (one suspected connivance) by Clemenceau and Italy's Sonnino, and proposed also (again with the support of France and Italy) that none of the colonies Germany had held at the outbreak of war should be returned. The next day British Dominion premiers appeared before the Council of Ten to press their claims to the colonies their forces had captured. And to this pressure, Wilson yielded. He said "that he thought all were agreed to oppose the restoration of the German Colonies." He balked at Lloyd George's proposal that the former German colonies be frankly and openly annexed by the powers (chiefly the British Dominions) which had seized them, but conceded that these conquests should be administered by the conquering powers as League of Nations "mandates." The League, once established, would set everything right! And it was upon the League's establishment that the Council of Ten had concentrated ever since.

They did so in utter secrecy. Members of the press assigned to cover the conference—and some 500 of the world's most skilled journalists were assembled in Paris for that purpose—protested bitterly this violation, as they saw it, of the very first of the Fourteen Points, the point calling for "open covenants for peace, openly arrived at" and asserting that "diplomacy shall proceed always frankly and in the public view," but their protests broke vainly against what the prime negotiators deemed an iron wall of necessity. It would simply have been impossible, asserted the negotiators, to arrive at necessarily compromise solutions within the full glare of instant publicity. So the special correspondents were reduced to dealing in their dispatches with rumor, gossip, and anecdote, drawing cold comfort from the fact that many high government officials in the French capital—virtually all of them, in fact, not directly involved in League deliberations—were kept as much in the dark as they were.

Franklin Roosevelt, for instance.

The Assistant Secretary was engaged in important government business involving several of the principals of the Peace Conference. He and Eleanor were social friends of these, in many cases, as they were of such Presidential intimates as Admiral Grayson. And certainly Roosevelt had no lack of active curiosity concerning the conference; he was eager to become at least a witness, personally present, in the rooms where world history was then being made. Yet as his days in Paris drew toward a close, and he with Eleanor prepared to sail for home on February 15 aboard the *George Washington*, which was also to carry President and Mrs. Wilson back to America, he had no more solid information about what was happening in the Council of Ten than had the porters of the Ritz. He was not in the Salon de l'Orlage on February 14, when the President of the United States reported to a plenary session of the conference the Covenant upon which the League Commission, representing fourteen nations, had unanimously agreed and which the conference as a whole then promptly and unanimously approved. He read of this as others did in the late-afternoon papers. Not until he and Eleanor were aboard the boat train bound for Brest that evening (their train ran twenty minutes ahead of the President's) did he see a copy of the Covenant, brought to him by a correspondent of the New York *Times*. "I remember our great excitement . . . ," wrote Eleanor long afterward. "What hopes we had that this League would really prove the instrument for the prevention of future wars, and how eagerly we read it through!" [34]

The Covenant in its initial form was a loosely drawn document (Wilson had bluntly rejected precisionist Lansing's drafting efforts, saying he "did not want lawyers to engage in that") consisting of a preamble and twenty-three articles. It prescribed the establishment of a Body of Delegates "representing the High Contracting Parties"; an Executive Council comprising representatives of the United States, the British Empire, France, Italy, and Japan, together with the representatives of four other member states, the selection of these four to "be made by the Body of Delegates on such principles and in such manner as they shall see fit"; and a permanent Secretariat, headed by a Secretary-General, to be located "at the Seat of the League." Admission to membership in the League required a two-thirds assenting vote of the Body of Delegates and was "limited to fully self-governing countries, including Dominions and Colonies." Article VIII called for "the reduction of national armaments to the lowest point consistent with national safety and the enforcement by common action of international obligations," this "lowest point" to be determined by the Executive Council and "not . . . exceeded without the permission of the . . . Council." This same article directed the Executive Council "to advise how the evil effects attendant upon" the manufacture by private enterprise "of munitions and implements of war" could be prevented. Article X, upon which great controversy would center in the United States, said in part: "The High Contracting Parties undertake to respect and preserve as against external aggression the territorial integrity and existing political independence of all States members of the League." In Article XII the "High Contracting Parties" agreed that disputes between them that could not "be adjusted by the ordinary processes of diplomacy" should be submitted "to arbitration or . . . inquiry by the Executive Council" and that there could be "no . . . resort to war . . . until three months after" the Executive Council had acted. And "even then," Article XII went on, there could be "no resort to war as against a member of the League which complies with the award of the arbitrators or the recommendations of the Executive Council." [35]

A few hours after the Roosevelts had perused this document, they arrived in Brest.

Their voyage home was rendered memorable for them chiefly by two personal contacts with the Covenant's principal sponsor. In general, Wilson aboard the *George Washington* kept himself severely aloof from his fellow passengers. When forced to appear on a few ceremonial occasions, he did so stiffly, sternly, and he flatly refused to appear at all at the boxing matches arranged for Washington's Birthday, saying "that he neither cared for boxing nor had the time to waste," as Eleanor later remembered. ("He seemed to have very little interest in making himself popular with groups of people whom he touched . . . ," she further remarked.) All the greater, therefore, was Roosevelt's pleasure when the President one day summoned him to the Presidential suite and there talked to him privately, with great earnestness, about the League and what it meant for the future of mankind. A day or so later the Roosevelts were included in a small luncheon party given by the Wilsons and having among its other guests McCauley, Grayson, and David R. Francis, U.S. ambassador to Russia from 1916 through the fall of 1918, returning now from that strife-torn land. For the most part, the luncheon conversation was trivial. The President said two things, however, which both Eleanor and Franklin always remembered afterward. He said that he had read no newspapers at all since the war began, had instead counted upon Tumulty to summarize for him the news stories and editorials he should review—a procedure that struck both Roosevelt and his wife as most unwise, since it gave to Tumulty a power of censorship that no personal secretary ought to have. Wilson also spoke of the League of Nations. "The United States must go in," he said, "or it will break the heart of the world, for she is the only nation that all feel is disinterested and all trust." [36]

At the end of this westward voyage came a narrow escape from disaster.

The President was scheduled to speak in behalf of the League in Boston's Mechanic Hall on the afternoon of February 24. On the morning of that day the *George Washington* slanted southward along the Massachusetts coast in heavy fog toward her Boston docking. Suddenly there loomed through the mist, upon the startled vision of lookout and steersman, a huge gray shape where assuredly no land ought to be! It was directly before the prow! Shouts were raised. Bells rang. The engines stopped. The great ship, palely enshrouded, lay abruptly silent. Roosevelt was below when the alarm was sounded. He dashed at once to the bridge, where he found a white-faced Captain McCauley peering anxiously at the gray shape ahead, while a chart was consulted in vain effort to determine their location. Eleanor had often remarked in her husband an almost uncanny physical sense of place and direction. (She would never forget how once when they were being driven in an automobile across a desert in New Mexico—an utterly flat and featureless plain which they had traversed but once before, with someone else at the wheel, several days in the past—they came to a crossroads, where the driver stopped. This driver, though he lived in that country, did not know which road to take. "You go straight ahead," Roosevelt had unhesitatingly said. He remembered the contour of certain mesas on the far horizon.) So Eleanor was not at all surprised to learn a little later that her husband, on the Presidential flagship's bridge, responding to his friend McCauley's anxious question, made a remarkably accurate guess on their position. They were not far from Marblehead, he said. Shortly thereafter the fog lifted enough to reveal that the ship had very nearly run aground on Thacher Island, which is only a few hundred yards from Cape Ann's easternmost tip and a bare seventeen miles northeast of Marblehead.

VI

A future historian might make of this episode a metaphor full of neat symbolism.

Thus:

The *George Washington* is America westwarding away from the European "entanglements" against which the Founding Father, after whom the ship was named, had allegedly warned his fellow countrymen for all time. The fog enshrouding the meeting of land and sea is the confusion of cross-purposes, wills, and ideas that always characterizes a sharp break in the continuity of human affairs or a change of phase in history. The rocks that loom through the mists are disasters narrowly averted by the ship of state at that historical moment, if only for the time being. As for Franklin Roosevelt's active presence upon the captain's bridge, where he displays an acute sense of place and direction while Woodrow Wilson remains isolated in his cabin and oblivious to the change of circumstance, this expresses a fundamental difference between the two men as personalities and as political leaders.

Certainly Woodrow Wilson did prove to be, during the weeks and months that followed, oblivious to the change in public mood and cultural tone that had begun even before the war was ended and would become drastic by 1920. Franklin Roosevelt seemed to sense, on the very morrow of the armistice, the beginnings of this shift of mood. Wilson, returning from Paris, had no sense of it at all, and in America, as in Europe, the immediate crowd response to his public appearances and to the words he spoke bemused him, blinding him to realities that did not accord with his preconceptions.

In Boston, for instance, on the Monday of his landing, he was greeted by a huge crowd which lined the streets all the way from the dock to the Copley Plaza Hotel. The Roosevelts rode in a car behind the President's. "We could see the President and Mrs. Wilson . . . ," Eleanor remembered long afterward, "the President standing up and waving his hat at intervals. . . . Everyone was wildly enthusiastic. . . ." [37] At the formal luncheon that day, Eleanor had as her companion the sour-faced remarkably laconic Republican governor of Massachusetts, Calvin Coolidge, whose one memorable remark during the meal (perhaps his only remark) was that he felt "sure the people would back the President" on the League. A little later, in Mechanics Hall, Wilson's address was repeatedly interrupted by applause as he spoke of national duty, honor, obligation, stressing in these idealistic terms the crucial importance of the role which the war had thrust upon the United States. "I say that America is the hope of the world," said he, and had no inkling that his eloquence (". . . the President's speech . . . was one of the best I ever heard him make," remembered Eleanor[38]) was addressed to a fading past rather than a brightening future. Soon thereafter he boarded the special train that would take him and the Roosevelts to Washington. A great crowd was gathered at the railway station. Wilson spoke to it. He said that the question of membership in the League of Nations presented the country with a momentous issue but that he was absolutely certain the right answer would be made. "I have no more doubt of the verdict of America," he declared, ". . . than I doubt the blood that is in me."

He did not know, would not permit himself to know, that the blood that was in him had already betrayed him.

The original suggestion that he land in Boston rather than New York had come from Tumulty: his doing so "would make ovation inevitable throughout New England and would center attack on Lodge," Tumulty had cabled him on January 6.[39] But it was a suggestion that accorded perfectly with Wilson's predilections, and its acceptance was a continuation of a long series of grave strategic errors—especially since the President had asked that Congressional debate on the League be deferred until his return to the capital. The senior Senator from Massachusetts, who very soon would be chairman of the Foreign Relations Committee, was perfectly aware of Wilson's motives. He was infuriated—so much so that he considered canceling his acceptance of an invitation to dine at the White House, with other members of the Senate and House Foreign Affairs committees, on February 26, an invitation Senator Borah had refused outright. He didn't cancel. He was notably unresponsive, however, to the President's belated attempt to win Congressional goodwill, and the next day he indicated that though the dinner had been "pleasant," the President, during the question-and-answer period following it, had seemed singularly ill informed on what the Covenant meant in concrete detail. On the day after that, on the Senate floor, Lodge delivered a long-prepared set speech against the Covenant (other League opponents spoke against it also). Then, at midnight of Monday, March 3, a bare dozen hours before the Sixty-fifth Congress must constitutionally adjourn sine die, he proposed a resolution saying, first, that it was "the sense of the Senate" that the League's constitution "in the form now proposed . . . should not be accepted by the United States" and, second, that a peace treaty with Germany should be signed before consideration was given to a League of Nations. Democrats blocked a vote on this, but Lodge, still holding the floor, added "by way of explanation" that thirty-seven Senators who would still be Senators after March 4, all of them Republican, "would have voted for the foregoing resolution . . . if they had had the opportunity." Thus his round robin bore the signatures of more than enough Senators to defeat any treaty the President might submit to the Sixty-sixth Congress—and other Senators promptly indicated their willingness to sign.

Came then high noon of March 4. The session was ended and, with it, six years of a Democratic Congress. The power to organize the new Congress was in the hands of Republicans. Many thought that a conciliatory gesture toward his Republican opponents would have been a wise one for the President to make at this point. He could at least tacitly concede, in public statement, that the draft Covenant might be something less than perfect, that his opponents might have at least a modicum of good sense and goodwill in their criticism of it, and that these criticisms would cause, as in the event they did, revisions that generally improved it. Instead, Wilson chose, compulsively, the path of defiance. On the evening of March 4 he was in New York City. There, in the Metropolitan Opera House, he addressed a mass meeting presided over by Governor Al Smith and made reference to the signers of the round robin as men who, alas, had "never felt the great pulse of the heart of the world." He was due aboard the *George Washington* again at midnight. He would sail then for France, there to resume his stellar role at the Paris Conference. And the "first thing" he would "tell the people on the other side" was that "an overwhelming majority of the American people is in favor of the League of Nations," for this majority realized there could be no

real peace without the Covenant. He pledged, therefore, and prophe-
sied: "When . . . [the peace] treaty comes back, gentlemen on this side
will find the Covenant not only in it, but so many threads of the treaty
tied to the Covenant, that you cannot dissect the Covenant from the
treaty without destroying the whole vital structure."

Nine days later he was again in Paris.

And there the tragedy, its central characters and final acts now set
beyond the possibility of revision, was played out to very near its bitter
end. Before leaving Paris in mid-February, Wilson had agreed with
Colonel House that a "preliminary" treaty of peace, exclusive of the
Covenant, was to be drafted in order to expedite a formal end to hostilities. There would then be shaped the "real," the "final" treaty of which
the heart and soul would be the League Covenant. But Wilson, returned
to France, suddenly realized that the negotiating strategy in which he
had concurred and which House as his agent had been pursuing in his
absence, was essentially the very thing proposed by Senator Lodge. He
further realized (it seems not to have occurred to him before) that this
"preliminary" treaty no less than the "final" one would have to be ratified by a two-thirds vote of the U.S. Senate to become effective. This
done, the end of hostilities finally assured, the American people might
with relative ease be persuaded or cajoled into giving up on the League.
Wilson was dismayed, outraged. He blamed House bitterly. ("House
has given away everything I had won before I left for Paris," he said to
his wife. "He has compromised on every side, and so I have to start all
over again, and this time it will be harder." [40]) As soon as he arrived in
Paris, he phoned Ray Stannard Baker, his press secretary, and ordered
him to release, March 15, a public statement: "The President said today
that the decision made at the Peace Conference at its plenary session,
January 25, 1919, to the effect that the establishment of a League of Nations should be made an integral part of the Treaty of Peace, is of final
force and there is no basis whatever for the reports that a change in this
decision was contemplated."

He won his way. The price he paid, however, was ruinously high.

Late March was for him a horrible time. Increasingly anxious, confused, exhausted, ill, solitary (for he now coldly estranged himself more
and more from Colonel House, and there was no one who could take
House's place)—his sore spirit and aching mind continuously gnawed
by guilt feelings and self-doubts he could never openly acknowledge—
he was forced to meet in secret session day after day with Lloyd George,
Clemenceau, and Orlando (the Big Four were now the vital center of the
conference), each of whom made demands for territory, indemnities,
and formal humiliations of Germany that flagrantly violated the spirit

THE END OF THE CRUSADE

and letter of the Fourteen Points. Especially outrageous were Clemenceau's demands for French annexation of the Saar, French occupation
of the Rhineland for thirty years, and reparations payments to France
so enormous Germany could not possibly make them, even if it retained
the full productive capacity of the Saar, or even seriously attempt to do
so without depressing the market, at home and abroad, for Allied and
American goods. Wilson made desperate attempts to budge the Tiger
from these demands. He tried conciliation: he went so far as to join
Lloyd George in pledging a treaty of alliance guaranteeing that the
United States, with Britain, would come to France's aid if Germany attacked her! He tried persuasion, describing with impassioned eloquence
the Brave New World which it was in their power to ensure through a
just and lasting peace. Nothing worked: Clemenceau remained adamant. March ended with the conference in total deadlock and Wilson
threatfully hinting that he might "go home" if the others continued to
refuse to "make peace on the principles laid down and accepted."

A horrible time!

But April was the cruelest month.

On the night of April 3, Woodrow Wilson suffered a complete breakdown, with high fever, nausea, catarrh, a racking sleep-preventing
cough. Even more alarming were certain symptoms he developed (one
side of his face became numb, taut; one eye began to twitch continuously) of a cerebral hemorrhage—a minor one to be sure but sufficient
perhaps to affect adversely his personality, his mental processes. While
bedridden, he made a fateful decision: unless the Allied premiers
yielded within a few days, he would destroy the secrecy in which Big
Four deliberations had been enshrouded; he would make an open fight
for the peace he had envisaged, with direct appeals to the hearts and
minds of the world's peoples. And he was still confined by his illness
when he acted upon this decision, ordering the *George Washington* to be
returned at once to Brest, prepared to take him home, and ordering the
Secretary of the Treasury to refuse further credits to Britain, France,
Italy.

Almost at once, however, came a reversal of mood and tactic.

The immediate popular reaction to his new stance was disheartening
to him. Tumulty cabled from America that the "ordering of the *George
Washington* to return to France" was "looked upon here as an act of impatience and petulance on the President's part and not accepted . . . in
good grace by either friends or foes." [41] The same reaction, magnified,
was evident throughout Western Europe; many who had worshiped him
as the New Messiah a few short weeks ago now angrily reviled him. Nor
was this all. In his misery he also felt the heat of conflagration raging on

the eastern horizon, in whose increasingly lurid light the Paris negotiations were being conducted. High into the heavens rose red flames of Russian Bolshevism, and from them came riding on the east wind a shower of sparks and embers. They fell on highly combustible social stuff in Germany, in the Balkans, amid the ruins of Austria-Hungary, in Italy, and in the very streets of Paris, just outside the sick man's house. Hence peace and social order must be restored at the earliest possible moment, else all Europe be consumed by atheistic Communism.

Wilson's Calvinistic soul shuddered at the prospect! "Europe is on fire," he now said. "I can't add fuel to the flames."

So he capitulated. Beginning on April 8 and all through the rest of the month, he capitulated, making one crucial concession after another (more than House had been willing to make) to Allied premiers who knew precisely what they wanted and quickly learned the best way to get it from Wilson. They had only to seize and use against him the sword he had forged for use against domestic foes of the League. Repeatedly they reminded him that, since the Covenant was now integral to the treaty, a failure to agree on treaty terms would mean an end to the League. Thus he was forced to agree that the treaty would set no limit on German reparations payments, after having earlier insisted on a specific total figure. He agreed to Italian annexation of the German-speaking Tyrol, to the carving of a Polish "corridor" out of Prussia, to French control of the Saar and the east bank of the Rhine for fifteen years, to Japanese exploitation of the Shantung Peninsula, to a dozen other designs that served the special interests of Allied powers at the expense of other peoples and were, by that token, certain to cause international frictions dangerous to the peace. And he justified these concessions on the grounds on which they were forced on him, namely, the supreme importance of establishing the League of Nations. Once established, he said to himself and others, the League would render null and void all decisions now made in violation of the Fourteen Points—an assertion hurled against hostile fact, as even he could not but feel. For the League, according to the revised Covenant approved by the conference in plenary session on April 28, was to have no real supranational authority at all and no structural capacity for growth into an agency strong enough to revise the conference's work. No sovereign power was to be vested in it. The only permanent members of its Executive Council would be delegates of the very nations which made the treaty, and since the "principle of unanimity" was to prevail over the Council's decision-making, each of these nations could veto any policy statement, any action proposal, with which it happened to disagree.

By April's end the main work of the conference was complete. The

German plenipotentiaries had been summoned to receive the victors' terms after having been kept waiting for weeks as virtual prisoners in the Hôtel des Reservoirs at Versailles, their quarters surrounded by a barbed-wire barricade and guarded by French soldiers. They waited one week more. Then, on May 7, the anniversary of the sinking of the *Lusitania*, the draft treaty was ceremoniously presented to them in the Trianon. They read it with dismay and ugly helpless anger. So, a little later, did their superiors in government. Berlin loudly proclaimed that Germany had been cruelly tricked, for "on essential points the basis of the Peace of Right, agreed upon between the belligerents," had been "abandoned" and demands made which "no nation could endure." Said the president of the National Assembly at Weimar: ". . . it is incomprehensible that a man who had promised the world a peace of justice, upon which a society of nations would be founded, has been able to assist in framing this project dictated by hate." [42]

Nor was this angry dismay confined to the Germans. Ranking members of the American and Allied delegations in Paris shared it. Lansing, White, and Tasker Bliss were harshly critical. Herbert Hoover has told how a copy of the treaty came to him by special messenger at four o'clock in the morning of May 7, how he at once read it through in bed, and how he became so agitated (he feared "the economic consequences alone would pull down all Europe and thus injure the United States") that he got up, dressed, and went for a long walk through the deserted Paris streets. At sunrise he met General Smuts of South Africa and a brilliant young Englishman, John Maynard Keynes, whom Lloyd George, who disliked him, called the "Puck of Economics." They had been similarly driven from their beds. "We agreed that it was terrible," writes Hoover, "and we would do what we could among our own nationals to make the dangers clear." [43]

Violently negative were the reactions of some of the younger members of the British and American delegations—idealists who had been swayed by Wilsonian eloquence, to whom Wilson personally had been a hero, who were committed to the kind of peace envisaged in the Fourteen Points, and who now felt betrayed. Among them was a wealthy, exuberant, willful twenty-eight-year-old Philadelphian named William C. Bullitt. Roosevelt, who had had a few contacts with him in Paris, thought him a bit absurd. ("I really want to . . . see for myself whether you are still the same . . . or have taken on the manners and customs of a Billy Bullitt," he would write a friend returning from Paris in the fall of 1919.[44]) But Colonel House, finding him useful, recommended him to Wilson.

And so, in late February, with the blessings of Wilson and Lloyd George, young Bullitt had gone on an exploratory mission from Paris to Moscow to discover, if possible, the terms on which the new Soviet regime, under Lenin, would make an accommodation with the West.[45] He had been accompanied by an older man, the famous muckraking journalist Lincoln Steffens. At that time, Allied and American expeditionary forces totaling many thousands of troops, side by side with Russian counterrevolutionaries, were "engaged in fighting the foul baboonery of Bolshevism" * in North Russia and Siberia. Nevertheless, Bullitt and Steffens were warmly received in Moscow, had frank and lengthy conversations with Lenin and other Soviet leaders, and returned to Paris with highly favorable impressions of the Communists and their regime.† ("I have been over into the future, and it works!" said Steffens to Bernard Baruch.) They returned, too, with a Soviet draft of terms which would be accepted by the Soviets if the Allied governments would formally propose them before April 10. The terms, in the circumstances, were astonishingly favorable to the West: if all Allied troops and military aid to the anti-Communists were withdrawn and the Allied blockade lifted, Soviet leaders would arrange an immediate armistice on all fronts, would grant *de facto* recognition to the anti-Communist governments established in various areas of the former empire, and would declare a general amnesty for Russians who had supported the Allies. Young Bullitt, convinced he had become the agent of a profoundly important and beneficent historical development, was in ecstasy. All the greater, therefore, was his dismay and personal humiliation when the British and American authorities refused even to consider the document he had brought back! Indeed, Lloyd George, returning briefly to London in mid-April and there facing in Commons angry questions from Conservatives to whom any dealings with Communists were anathema, blandly denied having any personal knowledge whatever of the Bullitt mission or of the document with which the young man was alleged to have returned. And when Bullitt called at the President's house on April 6, hoping to obtain a Presidential decision on the Soviet proposal before its time limit expired, Wilson refused to see him. The President gave a

* To quote a February 19, 1919, Mansion House speech by the British Winston Churchill.
† Among those taking special note of the Bullitt mission, when reports of it appeared in the press in mid-March, was a brilliant American radical journalist named John Reed, two years Bullitt's elder, who had been in Petrograd during the Russian "October" and whose vivid pro-Bolshevik eyewitness account of that event, *Ten Days That Shook the World*, was published on March 19, 1919. After Reed's death, in 1920, and his burial as a hero of the Soviet Union under the Kremlin wall (there is evidence he was becoming disillusioned with the Bolsheviki at the time of his death), his widow, the former Louise Bryant, married Bullitt (1923). Bullitt divorced her in 1930 for "personal indignitites."

sick headache as his excuse, and this was certainly plausible enough, for his nervous and physical collapse had occurred just three days before. Nevertheless, Bullitt was deeply offended and, taking note of the President's continued use of the Bolshevik "menace" as one justification for outrageous concessions, lost all faith in the sincerity, the moral purpose of Wilsonian idealism.

Hence, Bullitt was already thoroughly disaffected when a copy of the treaty first came into his hand. He was disposed to regard it as not only a violation of solemn pledges to the world, but also an affront to him personally. And his reaction to it epitomized that alienation of young intellectuals, even that revolt of youth in general, which was soon to become a salient feature of the Western world.

He was the most passionately embittered of a group of generally likeminded young Americans, all attached to the U.S. Peace Commission, who gathered in a Crillon apartment to vent their hurt and anger on the morrow of the treaty's printing. He proclaimed himself utterly disillusioned and saw no glimmer of hope upon the horizon, only a black wall of cloud shot through with flame and dripping blood. The millions dead had died in vain, the vast slaughter and misery of war would come soon again—and all because a false prophet of rare eloquence but little faith or courage had joined with a handful of selfish, lying, hypocritical old men to commit this travesty of justice and honor! He personally could see no point in further effort. He would go down to the Riviera, lie on a sun-warmed beach, and watch the world go to hell.[46]

First, however, he would quit the commission in a way that would register his disgust—and two of the others in the room agreed to do likewise. On May 15, 1919, these two, Adolf Berle and Samuel Eliot Morison, submitted resignations, with stated reasons of protest, to the Secretary-General of the U.S. Commission, Joseph C. Grew. Bullitt, typically, was more flamboyant. Having sent his resignation to the Secretary of State, he, on May 17, addressed a bitter letter to the President of the United States, releasing copies for publication. It caused a furor in many countries and became a factor of some importance in the great debate over the League which was now well under way in America.

He wrote:

"I was one of the millions who trusted confidently and implicitly in your leadership. . . . But our Government has consented now to deliver the suffering peoples of the world to new oppressions, subjections, and dismemberments—a new century of war. . . . Unjust decisions . . . in regard to Shantung, the Tyrol, Thrace, Hungary, East Prussia, Danzig, the Saar Valley, and the abandonment of the principle of the freedom of the seas, make new international conflicts certain. It is my conviction that the present League of Nations will be powerless to prevent these wars, and that the United States will be involved in them by the obligations undertaken in the covenant of the league and in the special understanding with France. Therefore the duty of the Government of the United States to its own people and to mankind is to refuse to sign or to ratify this unjust treaty, to refuse to guarantee its settlements by entering the League of Nations, to refuse to entangle the United States further by the understanding with France."

He said he was convinced that if Wilson had made his fight in the open instead of behind closed doors, he would have carried with him the public opinion of the world.

"I am sorry," he closed, "that you did not fight our fight to the finish and that you had so little faith in the millions of men, like myself, in every country who had faith in you." [47]

VII

On Saturday, June 28, 1919, the fifth anniversary of the assassinations at Sarajevo—in the Hall of Mirrors at the Palace of Versailles, where in 1871 Bismarck had proclaimed the birth of the German Empire—the treaty was signed by thirty-two nations* with great pomp and ceremony. General Smuts, signing as a British delegate, simultaneously issued a press statement denouncing it and demanding revisions. Herbert Hoover watched gloomily from his seat among the American delegation. ". . . I had difficulty keeping my mind on the ceremony," he writes. "It was constantly traveling over the fearful consequences of many of the paragraphs which these men were signing . . . , and then going back to the high hopes with which I had landed in Europe eight months before." [48]

A few hours later Woodrow Wilson boarded his train for Brest and the voyage home aboard the *George Washington*. He talked with Colonel House just before he left. "I urged him to meet the Senate in a conciliatory spirit," noted House in his diary next day; "if he treated them with the same consideration he had used with his foreign colleagues here, all

* A last-ditch German attempt to sign with reservations (Berlin balked especially at being forced to assume sole responsibility for starting the war) was blocked by Clemenceau. The chief German delegate to Versailles then resigned, the government he represented fell, a new government was voted by the Reichstag, and this government sent to Versailles a new German Foreign Minister with permission from the Reichstag to sign "under duress." This permission was granted barely three hours before Allied troops, poised on the west bank of the Rhine, were scheduled to march upon Weimar and Berlin.

would be well." Wilson's reply was "not reassuring." He said with asperity that he had "found one can never get anything in this life that is worth while without fighting for it!" And this was, literally, Wilson's last word to his former intimate, the man whom he had once characterized as his own "independent self." The two never met again.

On July 8, 1919, the *George Washington* docked in Hoboken. In Manhattan, wildly cheering crowds welcomed the President home—lining the streets through which he was driven in an open car, jamming Carnegie Hall where he briefly spoke, massing around the railway station where he boarded his train for Washington. In the capital that evening, the crowds were also huge and cheering. "After what I have seen today," said Wilson to his wife on the night of their return to the White House, "I believe that eighty percent of the American people are behind me and the League." [49]

On July 10, he presented the treaty to the Senate, urging its immediate ratification as a moral imperative. He asserted that the statesmen of Europe had come to see the League of Nations "as the main object of the peace. . . . the hope of the world. . . ." He asked: "Dare we reject it and break the heart of the world?"

Nineteen

➜➤🔆❰❰

The End of Idealism

I

AND indeed all signs were that a large majority of the American people did then favor ratification of the treaty—did favor, in other words, U.S. membership in the League. But there were also clear signs that the tide of popular enthusiasm for the League was less high now than it had been in late February and early March, when Wilson first returned from Paris. At that time, American entrance into the League had appeared a foregone conclusion. Senatorial opposition to it had seemed but a minor eddy in the massive flow of opinion, caused mostly by careless drafting of the proposed Covenant and easily dissipated by a tightening up of loose language and a writing into the document of specific guarantees of the Monroe Doctrine. This had been done in Paris in April. Nevertheless, what had seemed almost an absolute certainty in early March now seemed only a great probability, and a probability that might be reduced to nothing by the heat of a prolonged controversy.

Franklin Roosevelt's public speech, from the moment of his return with the President to the moment of the President's second return, was revealing of his intuitive sense of the fluid popular mood. In a series of addresses he made on the subject in early March, he paid serious attention to the critics and their arguments against the Covenant's central purpose. He undertook to answer them, so far as possible, on their own ground.

He was careful to point out that he himself—a realist, a patriot—had viewed the League as "merely a beautiful dream, a Utopia" until very recently. But now, having witnessed something of the war at first hand and seen among the peoples of Europe "a growing demand that out of it all must come . . . something greater" than mere defeat of "the Hun," he believed the League to be as practical as it was desirable. He made a few perfunctory gestures toward Wilsonian idealism. "This is a time of idealism," he said, "a time when more ideals are properly demanded of us, and over there on the other side, every man, woman and child looks to us to make good the high purpose with which we came into this war." But it was upon the League's practical efficacy, even its practical necessity, that he concentrated his argument in March and during the months that followed. He made no claim that the League's organic document was perfect; his approach in this respect differed radically from the one Woodrow Wilson later made. He admitted that the League, as a new departure in human affairs (he likened its shaping to that of the U.S. Constitution), was necessarily experimental in detail, and many of these details might therefore be changed or rejected. But the "general plan" was sound, and the "important" thing right now was "not to dissect the document," but to "approve the general plan." "I have read the draft of the League three times," he declared, "and always find something to object to in it, and that is the way with everybody. . . . Personally I am willing to make a try on the present instrument." [1]

Certainly any attempt "to go backwards towards an old Chinese wall policy of isolation," he said in late June, would do "grievous wrong" to us "and to all mankind." As a world power we were inextricably involved in world affairs. By joining the League, we would be able to help lead toward world peace and harmony instead of toward world war and chaos. If, on the other hand, we failed to join, the League would become "a new Holy Alliance" hostile to the American democracy. Moreover, the League's effectiveness against the spread of Communism from revolutionary Russia would be greatly reduced. Communism fed on hopes frustrated, expectations denied. "Among all the peoples of the Allies, and I believe Germany, too, there is a demand that out of this war we shall get more than a mere treaty of peace. . . . If this demand is not fulfilled many of these people will throw up their hands and say, 'Well, if the forms of government existing today cannot give us the answer, some kind of answer, why not try some other form?'" [2]

His own experimentalism stopped far short of this. He was convinced that the "existing forms of government" in Western Europe and even more so in America *could* "give us the answer" and, in any case, were immensely preferable to any proposed alternative to them. He was willing to experiment with new social and economic devices only to the extent that these might enable the "existing forms" to function more efficiently. He was opposed to any major substantial changes, such as the extension of government ownership or strong governmental controls into areas formerly reserved exclusively to uninhibited private enterprise. He favored, in these areas, only such government activity as would encourage private enterprise. And this essential conservatism of his was abundantly expressed, that spring and summer, in public words and deeds having nothing to do with the League.

For instance, he opposed any use of government-owned merchant vessels which would compete with private shipping interests. According to his own account, he submitted to the White House in early 1919 a memorandum proposing that the war-created Shipping Board and Emergency Fleet Corporation be abolished and that the government retain only "10 or 12 of the best passenger vessels" to be operated by the Navy "on trade routes not served by private American companies." As soon as these routes were sufficiently developed to be profitable for private enterprise, the Navy was to withdraw its ships from them, perhaps disposing of them to whatever "American company offered to provide the same service." ("The plan, of course, got nowhere," he commented in 1924, "but I am sure it was fundamentally sound." [3])

He also opposed establishment of an air force separate from the Army or Navy because, among other reasons, it might lead to government manufacture of airplanes and thereby "paralyze the entire [aviation] industry at its source." He waxed lyric in praise of America's "competitive genius" as the "key to the manufacturing world," adding that, "stifled by over-regulation, or confiscated by law, industry dies." He was quoted in the New York *Times* as saying, "In Heaven's name, do not brain industry with the club of politics, especially the youthful and growing industry of aircraft manufacture. Let us give the manufacturers and experimentalists full scope. The bread of encouragement cast upon the waters of industry will return a thousand-fold in the guise of progressive development and productive economy." [4]

From mid-March until mid-May, 1919, Daniels was in Europe on official Navy business. Roosevelt was Acting Secretary for a more extended period than ever before. (He gloried in it, boasting to friends of the vast difference in efficiency between his administrative operation and Daniels'. He was, he said, "running things with a high hand and getting things done that were never done before." For one thing, the mail was "signed at regular hours, and absolutely cleaned up every day, with the result that nothing is taken home, mislaid, lost, et cetera!" However, on policy matters he followed very specific instructions which Daniels had taken care to give him before departing.[5]) It was as Acting Secretary, therefore, that he conferred in April with Owen D. Young, head of General Electric, on a policy decision whose effects would prove of no small importance to the economic and cultural history of the United States.

General Electric research had developed much of the basic technology for long-range radio transmission. A key element of it was the Alexanderson alternator, commandeered by the Navy when America entered the war. British Marconi wished to buy it, and GE had been about to sell it when Admiral W. H. G. Bullard, who had just returned from Paris to take over direction of Navy communications, called upon Young with a plea that the sale be halted. Bullard stressed that ownership of the alternator would give to the British as complete a control over world radio communications as they had long had of cable communications; he spoke for the President when he said this would *not* be in the best interests of the United States. He suggested, instead, the formation of an American company to which the Navy could sell its radio rights and facilities. Young was easily persuaded: such a company—presumably exempt from the antitrust laws, since the government itself proposed it—would have a huge profit potential. He quickly moved to form a Radio Corporation of America.[6]

His conference with Roosevelt had to do with the sale of Navy radio facilities to RCA. The negotiations foundered when Roosevelt was informed that the American Marconi Company, a branch of the British firm, would have a major, if not controlling, interest in the new corporation. The department, he told Young, "could not even consider the sale of any of its war-acquired patents or stations to any company which was not wholly under American ownership." He cabled Daniels for advice, was told to defer action until Daniels returned. And when Daniels came back to Washington, it was with the conviction that radio communications were of such vital importance to national security that control of them must remain firmly in government hands. The Navy should continue to operate the network. A bill providing for this was introduced in Congress. It predictably got nowhere against strong Republican opposition. Eventually, Daniels was forced to approve the sale of Navy radio facilities to an RCA which, by that time, had acquired ownership-control of American Marconi.[7]

Among the specific instructions given by Daniels before he left for Europe was that Roosevelt as Acting Secretary not pay an exorbitant price for steel rails, on which bids had been let, or for any other Navy steel, no matter what the recommendation of the Bureau of Supplies and Accounts. Roosevelt obeyed. When steel companies submitted their usual practically identical and excessively high bids on steel needed to begin construction of a couple of new battleships, he at first rejected them. Shortly thereafter, however, because the immediate need was overwhelming, he was forced to reverse himself. He placed an order for 14,000 tons of steel with the Carnegie Steel Company, explaining, according to the New York *Times,* that "that company was the only complete bidder on the entire schedule of requirements" so that "better service and a more convenient and economical inspection" could be assured by dealing solely with that company.

But his repetitious experience of steel price gouging and of the steel executives' flouting of the law requiring truly competitive bids did not convert him to Daniels' view that the government should manufacture its own steel for use in armaments. He continued to believe that the armor-plate manufacturing project which Congress had authorized at Daniels' behest and which was now under construction should presage no more than a price "yardstick" operation on the part of the government—and even within this limit he was highly dubious of it. Nor did his unhappy experience with the steel executives cause him, in reaction, to espouse labor's cause in a year in which capital and labor, unprecedentedly organized for such battle, fought as never before in American history.

II

The voice of labor had been loud in the corridors of power during the war years. Samuel Gompers, president of the American Federation of Labor, had been among the mighty in Washington's councils, and union membership had multiplied as obstacles to union organization were reduced by federal policy and consequent management concessions, in return for what amounted to pledges by the unions not to strike until victory was won. But with the armistice in France came an end to the armistice between employers and organized labor. Many of the former were determined not just to hold the line, but to force a relinquishment by the unions of ground gained during the war. They resisted the demands for higher wages that inevitably accompanied the abrupt and steep rise in the cost of living—rents, transportation fares, taxes, the prices of food and clothing—in 1919. Labor, on the other hand, was determined not only to hold the gains it had made, but to increase them. Its leaders sought to expand union membership, mounting organization drives into fields formerly barred to them. The result was a huge wave of strikes, all across the country—some 2,665 of them for the year as a whole, involving more than 4,000,000 workers.

The most ambitious of the labor organization drives—indeed, the most ambitious project that had ever been attempted by the AFL—had to do with the iron and steelworkers, whose need for collective bargaining power was obvious and dire. Half of them were forced to work an eleven- to fourteen-hour day, another 25 percent worked a ten- to twelve-hour day, and a significant percentage worked, in addition, an unbroken twenty-four-hour shift every other Sunday. Yet their hourly wage rates were so low that even with this life-destroying excess of working hours, some 60 percent of them lived with their families at or below a bare subsistence level. In August, 1919, the new steelworkers union presented to Judge Elbert H. Gary, head of U.S. Steel, demands for union recognition, an eight-hour workday, reinstatement of workers discharged for union activity, and "an American living wage." Gary, his corporation's coffers stuffed with war profits, flatly refused to negotiate. The strike which followed (it began on September 22 in U.S. Steel plants; Bethlehem Steel workers struck on the twenty-fifth) was marked by murderous violence, with eighteen strikers killed.

The strike's leader was William Z. Foster. Gompers had named him to head this organizing effort in 1918, though Gompers was essentially conservative while Foster was a former syndicalist who became a founder of the American Communist Party in 1919—a necessarily underground operation in that year, because of the wartime antisedition legislation. In Foster's conception the great steel strike was by no means exclusively concerned with the classic issues of wages and hours. He fought to establish a tightly organized industrial union which, unlike the loosely federated craft unions, would be powerful enough to bargain on even terms with such corporate giants as U.S. Steel. Hence the strike had some of the nature of a social revolution. It aimed to effect a basic change in the power structure. And it was fought against by the steel managers as a revolutionary movement and was portrayed by them in public statements as an insurrection incited by Bolsheviks and directed by Bolsheviks, whose real aim was not to better the working conditions of steel employees but to overthrow the government of the United States.

This assertion of subversive conspiracy became, in fact, a standard tactic of employers as they warred against striking workers in every area of the economy that year, and they were aided in their use of it by open avowals of left-wing political objectives on the part of several strike leaders. Thus the United Mine Workers, initiating a massive coal strike a few weeks after the steel strike began, demanded immediate outright nationalization of the mines. The normally conservative railroad brotherhoods called for Congressional enactment of the Plumb Plan, whereby the railroads would be nationalized and labor given a voice in their management. As for the Industrial Workers of the World, it became a frankly Marxist-Leninist revolutionary movement. The Wobblies, as they were called, convening in Chicago in 1919, issued a manifesto saying: "The working class and the employing class have nothing in common. . . . Between these two classes a struggle must go on until the workers of the world organize as a class, take possession of the earth and the machinery of production and abolish the wage system." They were convinced "that the centering of the management of industries into fewer and fewer hands makes the trade unions unable to cope with the ever growing power of the employing class." The only answer was "One Big Union" of all workers everywhere, its "banner" inscribed with "the revolutionary watchword, 'Abolition of the wage system.'" Naturally, this outraged and terrified the business community, especially since the IWW translated its words into deeds whenever possible, employing the tactic of mass violence while proclaiming solidarity with the Communist revolutionaries of Russia.

It was easy in these circumstances to convince millions of Americans that their liberties, if not their lives, were endangered by a vast Communist plot. Employers fed and exploited to their advantage the fears thus engendered, making full use of the business-dominated press. So did A. Mitchell Palmer, a man of paranoid tendencies and aggressive political ambition whom Wilson had named U.S. Attorney General in March, 1919, succeeding T. W. Gregory. By the autumn of 1919, the Great Red Scare, as it became known to history, was raging through America—literally a Reign of Terror for the political left, marked by such gross infringements of civil liberty, personal freedom, and minority rights, all in the name of "Americanism," as the nation had not known since the close of the eighteenth century.

Roosevelt was relatively little infected by it. He contributed nothing to it in the way of inflammatory public speech. He deplored "the element of trying to get something for nothing, of trying to rush law and order off its feet, of seeking to put into effect new doctrines without . . . thought . . . [or] consideration of the whole mass of the people" which seemed to him evident in the current "unrest," but he identified this "element" not with deliberate wickedness, but with impatience at the slowness of needed social improvements. "Every one of us would like to see a state of perfection on earth . . . ," he said. "But we know too that every great reform takes time and good judgment." Excessive haste, he said, "often defeats its own ends." He had never been a stalwart defender of free speech as a matter of principle. He was not now. In his view, the commandant of the Boston Navy Yard was right to discharge a machinist who "actually circulated revolutionary literature in the shop, literature which advocated the Soviet form of government and which, therefore, constituted, in my judgment, an attack upon our form of government." But he chided this same commandant for discharging men simply because they were Socialists, and in this he manifested a greater tolerance than did the New York state legislature that year: a few months later, this legislature refused to seat five duly elected members solely because they were members of the Socialist Party.[8]

Nor did Roosevelt display an eagerness to grab easy headlines for himself as a defender of Americanism when opportunities for this were presented to him. On September 11, 1919, he was Acting Secretary. A telegram came to his desk from Governor Coolidge of Massachusetts, who was preparing to move, as soon as all political danger had been removed from his doing so, against an unprecedented, nationally alarming strike by Boston policemen. The policemen had serious legitimate grievances. Grossly underpaid and overworked in a period of rapid price inflation, subjected to continuous harassment from a harshly authoritarian police commissioner, they had been driven to form a union and, in defiance of a commissioner order, had affiliated with the AFL. When the commissioner then suspended nineteen of them, the whole force walked out on September 9. Coolidge, in his telegram, asked for assurance that the U.S. Navy was prepared to help break the strike if he, as governor, asked the President for federal assistance. Acting Secretary Roosevelt replied mildly that of course the Navy would do whatever it was ordered by the President to do.[9]

(The President himself proved less reluctant to gain publicity as an advocate of law and order on this occasion. On September 12, Coolidge called the state militia into Boston's streets. Two days after that he made terse reply to a telegram from Gompers. The AFL president had protested the firing of the nineteen police union officials simply for exercising their "right to strike." Replied Calvin Coolidge: "There is no right to strike against the public safety by anybody, anywhere, any time." The words, which struck a responding chord in the fearful public mind and made the Republican governor a national hero overnight, called for no public comment from the Democratic President. Nevertheless, Wilson did so comment: he greatly praised the governor's stand.)

Roosevelt steadfastly refused to identify dissent per se with un-Americanism or union leadership with alien "radicalism," though he strongly opposed the latter in public statement.

The flames of outrage had been further fed when sixteen parcels containing dynamite bombs, triggered to explode upon being opened, were found in New York City's General Post Office April 30. They and some twenty others already in the mails, subsequently discovered, were addressed to such men as Justice Oliver Wendell Holmes, who on March 3 had delivered the Supreme Court's majority opinion in the case of *Schenck v. United States,* justifying the wartime abrogation, under the Espionage Act, of constitutional guarantees of free speech; Postmaster

General Burleson; Federal Judge K. M. Landis, who had sentenced a group of IWW members to long prison terms; and A. Mitchell Palmer. Palmer lived directly across R Street from the Roosevelts in Washington. A month later, on the night of June 2, 1919, a powerful bomb blasted the front of Palmer's house. Eleven-year-old James Roosevelt (he was the only Roosevelt child at home at the time; the others were in Hyde Park) narrowly escaped injury. The windows of his bedroom were shattered, and bloody pieces of the bomb thrower, blown up with his bomb, rained down with other debris upon the Roosevelts' front steps. Franklin and Eleanor might have been blown to bits, too, had they returned a few minutes earlier than they did from a dinner party they had attended. They were garaging their car a block or so away when the blast occurred.[10]

Nor was this the only social violence that came close to Roosevelt personally during the summer of 1919. In late July there was a bloody race riot in Washington, sparked by reports of sexual attacks by black men upon white women. It was less sanguinary than a race riot that occurred almost simultaneously in Chicago, but it was sanguinary enough. A mob comprising hundreds of white servicemen and a thousand or more civilians initiated the violence, roaming the streets and savagely beating every black they could get their hands on. The blacks retaliated with violence of their own; for several days there was virtual civil war between black and white in the capital, with hundreds hurt and many killed. Army Reserve troops were at last called in to stop it. "The riots seem to be about over today, only one man killed last night," wrote Roosevelt to "Dearest Babs" on July 23 (she was at Fairhaven; she and the children had not gone to Campobello that year). "Luckily the trouble hasn't spread to R Street. . . . It has been a nasty episode and I only wish *quicker* action had been taken to stop it." [11]

In this same letter he wrote that he had "troubled to keep out of harm's way" (nevertheless, he had "heard occasional shots during . . . the night," he added), and this seems a fair description of his general attitude toward the turbulent domestic scene of that year.

For if he, with Howe, was concerned to retain the union goodwill which they had gained during the war, he was equally concerned to avoid antagonizing the business community to any important degree. He deemed it probable that the postwar period would be marked, as the post-Civil War period had been, by conservatism, materialism, and business dominion over American politics. But he sensed that such conservatism, having among its chief dynamics a disappointment of high hopes, was bound to pass in a decade or so and be followed by a resurgence of Progressivism—this at a time when he, with luck and proper care, would be in his prime as politician. He therefore began to play in 1919 a kind of meanwhile politics. He strove to occupy a neutral ground high above the economic battlefield, a ground on which he could stand against "radicalism" and for the general public interest. This last, he stressed, included the special interests of both capital and labor, and he strove to be *for* it in modern, practical progressive terms.

He became a fervent champion of government efficiency: the lessons of organization learned during the war should result in permanent reforms and innovations. Both the legislative and executive branches of the federal government should be reorganized along more businesslike lines. Before a House Select Committee on the Budget, on October 1, 1919, he gave strong testimony in favor of a bill destined to become, with revisions, the National Budget and Accounting Act of 1921. This proposed legislation provided for the preparation of an annual national budget, an integrated balanced plan for federal expenditures, and created a Bureau of the Budget as the instrument for achieving this. It would greatly strengthen the office of the President, who would be enabled to gather into his own hands powers that had been scattered and energies that had been dissipated through excessive departmental self-determination. Roosevelt, consistent with his former stands on this matter, pressed also for greater centralized controls within the departments themselves, especially the Navy Department, where bureaus had tended to become almost sovereign powers, wastefully competing with one another for appropriations and increased authority. A concomitant of his commitment to a streamlined executive was an impatience with the fumbling and bumbling of the legislative process, though he was of course careful not to express this in his hearing testimony. In a public address he did condemn Congress for "running its business in such a way that if it was a private business it would be in the hands of a receiver within a week." He recommended that the members of Congress "forget prerogative, precedent, parliamentary law and the Magna Carta, to put into effect—any businessman could do it—a system by which [it] would move along [modern] American lines." [12]

On this matter of efficiency he was forthright and emphatic. He was far less so in his publicly expressed attitudes toward the steel and coal strikes. Here his statements were essentially prudently noncommittal, though their balance tipped toward the management rather than the worker side of the controversy.

"If conditions in the steel industry are not right they will be improved," he said, "but the improvement ought not to come by means of a strike." When Attorney General Palmer obtained a federal court injunction against the calling of a strike by John L. Lewis and his fellow

UMW officers, Roosevelt backed the action. He made what must have seemed to labor leaders a weird, hypocritical distinction between "public" and "private" employment, asserting that "employees of railroads, in the mines, in the public service corporations" were in "public" employment; he then more than implied that they had, therefore, no right to strike. (They "must understand they owe a duty to the people and that they cannot of necessity be the same free agents as those working for private interests.") He continued wholly paternalistic in his labor attitudes. "We wish to give labor a larger share of the profits, successes and improved conditions of the country, but we can't stand for any small group in a community holding up a community." And the "small group" to which he referred was obviously composed of the workers who struck, not of the employers who refused to bargain. The country needed "a constructive program in labor matters," he said; he wished to continue into the postwar period, in strengthened form, the labor arbitration and adjustment machinery of the war years. He suggested the establishment of labor courts having legislative as well as judicial powers.[13]

III

Indicative not only of Roosevelt's strategy but also of his remarkable political sensitivity—of his quick responsiveness to slight changes in the temperature and pressure of public opinion—is the fact that he whose public advocacy of the League of Nations had been strong and active in the late winter and spring of 1919 said almost nothing on the subject, publicly, from July through the autumn of that year, when the political battle over the League raged toward a final decision.

It was of course as obvious to Senator Lodge and his anti-Wilson colleagues on the Foreign Relations Committee as it was to Roosevelt that American majority opinion favored U.S. membership in the League. But it was also clear to them, as it seems to have been to Roosevelt, that this majority opinion, far from being solidified, remained fluid, shallow. In no major part of it was there any great depth of factual information or ideal commitment. It was liable, therefore, to evaporation. The indicated strategy for League opponents was to delay final Senate action on the treaty for as long as possible.

And this is what they proceeded to do.

After a long month of inaction, during which more and more verbal fire was centered on the Covenant's Article X and Wilson's anxiety became unbearable, the President asked the Foreign Relations Committee to meet with him in the White House for a "conversation" about the treaty. The meeting, on August 19, was not a happy one. Wilson was not at his best when he entangled himself in acrimonious argument about the difference between a "moral" and "legal" obligation, with regard to Article X; when he displayed a notable lack of candor in response to questions about how certain of the conference decisions had been arrived at; and especially when he made the astonishing statement, easily proved false, that until he arrived in Paris he personally had known nothing about the 1915 secret treaties between the Allies, virtually every term of which, save as regards Russia, had become a term of the Versailles Treaty. At the meeting's end it was clear to others, if not to him, that his signature of the treaty would never be ratified unless he agreed to numerous revisions of the Covenant and of its specific treaty applications.

He would not, could not so agree.

Instead, against the protests of his wife, who knew he was far from recovered from his April breakdown, and in the face of Admiral Grayson's warning that his life might be forfeit, he decided, compulsively, to take his case to the country. "I know I am at the end of my tether," he said to Tumulty, "but . . . in the presence of the great tragedy which now faces the world, no decent man can count his own personal fortunes in the reckoning." [14] On September 3 he entrained for a national speaking tour, to rally the people behind his stand for treaty ratification with *no* amendments, *no* reservations, and during the next three weeks he traveled some 8,000 miles, delivering dozens of set speeches in twenty-nine cities, plus innumerable impromptu talks.

He was, as always, remarkably effective with his immediate audiences. His passionately earnest delivery was persuasive to most of those who saw and heard it. When read in cold print by men who knew or shrewdly guessed what had actually transpired in Paris, however, his words revealed an appalling failure of his sense of reality and proportion— a loss of control, not only of events, which now drove him more helplessly than ever before, but also of his own feelings and perceptions. He made prophetic statements. In Kansas City: "As soon as you have a military class, it does not make any difference what your form of government is; if you are determined to be armed to the teeth, you must obey the orders and directions of the only men who can control the great machinery of war. Elections are of minor importance." In Omaha: "I tell you, my fellow citizens, I can predict with absolute certainty that within another generation there will be another world war if the nations of the world do not concert the method by which to prevent it." But these flashes of prescience shone out of a deepening murk of fantasy and conceptual confusion. With each passing day his speeches became more emotional, his assertions more extreme.

Meanwhile, the Senate Foreign Relations Committee conducted deliberately prolonged hearings on the treaty. Young Bullitt was asked to testify. He did so with alacrity and devastating effect, if with something less than absolute truthfulness and concern for the human rights of men who had believed him their friend. He reported a private, confidential talk with Secretary of State Lansing which he had had on the preceding May 19, two days after his protest resignation from the Peace Commission. At that time, he told Lodge and other delighted foes of the treaty, Lansing had not only condemned the Shantung agreement but had also severely criticized the League Covenant. If the American people ever understood what entrance into the League would mean to them, Lansing had said, according to Bullitt, they would summarily reject the treaty. "The press representatives aboard the train called Mr. Bullitt's testimony to the President's attention," writes Tumulty. "He made no comment, but it was plain from his attitude that he was incensed and distressed beyond measure." [15] Nor was he mollified by Lansing's immediately telegraphed "explanation." Convinced that the Secretary of State had betrayed him, he intended (of this Tumulty was convinced) to demand Lansing's resignation as soon as he returned to Washington.

Perhaps it was not purely coincidental that, from that moment on (September 12), a severe headache that had been recurrent since the trip's beginning became for Woodrow Wilson a constant throbbing anguish. His speeches ranged farther and farther beyond the boundary of Fact into the misty realm of Wish and Dream. "An illumination of profound understanding of human affairs shines upon the deliberations of . . . [the Paris] conference that never shone before upon the deliberations of any other international conference in history," he said in San Francisco on September 17. The meetings of the Big Four—meetings that had been characterized by a harsh friction of cross-purposes and by a mutual dislike and mistrust which flared, often enough, into bitter quarrel—were described by him as "a very simple council of friends" whose "intimacies" were those "of men who believed in the same things and sought the same objects." He said that the hearts of Clemenceau, Lloyd George, and Orlando "beat with the people of the world as well as with the people of their own country" and had the rhythm of a gloriously hopeful destiny for all mankind. The Versailles Treaty now became, to his speaking mind, a perfect instrument. On September 24, in Cheyenne, Wyoming, he eulogized it as "the most remarkable document . . . in human history" because it made "a people's peace," and he challenged "any man to find a contradiction of that statement in the terms of the great document." He went on to declare that the "peace" that had been made was "so much of a people's peace that in every portion of its settlement every thought of aggrandizement, of territorial or political aggrandizement on the part of the Great Powers was brushed aside, brushed aside by their own representatives."

On September 25 he spoke in Pueblo, Colorado. Pale, drawn taut by aches and pains (he had told Tumulty he feared he would have to cut his speech short, he was so ill), he addressed to a huge throng the most passionately eloquent speech of the tour. Tears flowed down his cheeks, and hundreds in his audience wept, as he made his peroration. He told of going on last Decoration Day to the cemetery of Suresnes, near Paris, "a cemetery given over to the burial of the American dead." Behind him on a slope stood "rank after rank of living American soldiers." Before him on the level field lay "rank after rank" of the slain. And beside him as he spoke "was a little group of French women who had adopted those graves, had made themselves mothers of those dear ghosts by putting flowers every day upon those graves, taking them as their own sons, their own beloved, because they had died in the same cause. . . ." He fervently wished that the "men in public life who are now opposing the settlement for which these men died could visit such a spot as that," for they might then "feel the moral obligation that rests upon us not to go back on those boys, but to see the thing through, to see it through to the end and make good their redemption of the world." But he was sure that the American people as a whole *did* so feel and *were* so determined. They had, as always before in their history, risen up to embrace "the truth of justice and of liberty and of peace." And having "accepted that truth . . . we are going to be led by it, and it is going to lead us, and through us the world, out into pastures of quietness and peace such as the world never dreamed of before."

Thus he ended on a throbbing note of affirmation.

A few hours later he collapsed in excruciating pain in the drawing room of his special train as it carried him, through black night, toward his next scheduled speech, in Wichita, Kansas.

Thereafter the loss of control was total.

Against his will and despite his protests ("Senator Lodge . . . will say I am a quitter and . . . the Treaty will be lost" [16]), the rest of Wilson's speaking tour was canceled by order of his wife, his doctor, and his secretary, three who now banded together to protect him from the world and to deceive the world about his true condition. He lay behind drawn curtains in his drawing room as his train sped across half a continent. His condition was slightly improved when he arrived in the capital; he was able to walk unaided from his train to the automobile which carried him to the White House. But on the third morning after his arrival there his collapse became complete. He fell unconscious upon the bathroom floor, struck down by a cerebral thrombosis which paralyzed permanently the whole of his left side, and he lay then abed for many weeks, shattered, utterly helpless, tears flowing often down his cheeks, his mind often wandering, unable even on his best days to concentrate for more than a few minutes on any subject or to speak above a whisper.

And the treaty was indeed lost.

When Lansing, in early October, suggested to Tumulty and Grayson that they certify the President's incapacity so that the Vice President could take over, as provided by the Constitution,* he was angrily rebuffed. (". . . while Woodrow Wilson is lying . . . on the broad of his back I will not be a party to ousting him!" cried Tumulty.[17]) And thus an emotional devotee of erratic judgment, a narrowly specialized doctor of medicine, and a foolish distraught woman whose decisions were made in terms of personalities became in effect the nation's executive triumvirate. No message could reach the sick President save through these three. None could reach the outer world from him save through them.

Colonel House, arriving in New York from Europe that early autumn, sent Stephen Bonsal, a mutual friend of his and Lodge's, to plead the case of the treaty with the Massachusetts Senator. Bonsal found the Senator in an unwontedly mellow mood. Perhaps out of some human sympathy for the suffering man in the White House, Lodge indicated a willingness to modify his reservations to the treaty (he had formally introduced fourteen of these, in mocking deference to the Fourteen Points), and he made penciled note of the suggested modifications upon a printed copy of the Covenant. They seemed to provide a solid basis for accommodation between Wilson and his opponents. House was delighted and excited. He promptly sent the marked copy to the President, with a cover letter of his own, and then waited with anxious impatience, as did Senator Lodge, for Wilson's reply. None was received. Mrs. Wilson, whose hatred for House was now virulent, refused to disturb the crucified Messiah with any missive from the Judas colonel. Lodge, naturally, was incensed by what seemed to him a personal insult from the President and was thereby hardened in his determination, from that time forth, to accept no compromise whatever.[18]

---

* The man who in that case would have become important in American history, Thomas R. Marshall, a former governor of Indiana, is now chiefly remembered for a remark he made during a Senate debate. "What this country needs," he said, "is a really good five-cent cigar."

But probably Mrs. Wilson's interference made no real difference in the outcome. Woodrow Wilson would, in any case, have refused to accept the modifications, none of which, in point of fact, amounted to a really crucial revision of the Covenant. All fourteen could have been accepted without effect upon the League's structure and without interfering in the slightest with its workings. So said no less an authority than David Hunter Miller, who had done much of the drafting of the Covenant.[19] So said Herbert Hoover, who was among those (they included Ray Stannard Baker, Bernard Baruch, nearly every Cabinet member, and several pro-League Senators) who personally begged the White House to accept a treaty ratification upon Lodge's terms. But Wilson, now barely recovered enough to be seriously consulted on major policy questions, was adamant. Even his wife could not move him toward compromise. On November 18, according to her memoirs, she went "in desperation" to her bedridden husband. " 'For my sake,' I said, 'won't you accept these reservations and get this awful thing settled?' He turned his head upon the pillow and stretching out his hand to take mine answered in a voice I shall never forget: 'Little girl, don't you desert me; that I cannot stand. . . . Better a thousand times to go down fighting than to dip your colors in dishonorable compromise.' " [20] He then dictated a letter to Senator Gilbert Hitchcock, the Democratic leader, expressing his sincere "hope that the friends and supporters of the Treaty will vote against the Lodge resolution of ratification."

His letter was decisive. Republicans and Democrats who favored the League joined together next day to defeat it. The Lodge resolution to ratify with the listed reservations was defeated by fifty-five votes of which forty-two were Democratic, thirteen Republican. A motion for unconditional ratification, submitted by Senator Oscar W. Underwood of Alabama, then failed by seven votes of the needed two-thirds majority.

Nor did this fundamental division of expressed opinion change during the weeks that followed, weeks during which every effort at accommodation or compromise continued to be frustrated by the personal enmity between Lodge and Wilson. The latter, isolated in his sickroom, a ghost of his former self, hovering just this side of death, clung stubbornly to the belief that he could still *force* ratification on his own terms when Congress met again.

IV

Of all this Franklin Roosevelt was a silent spectator, so far as the general voter was concerned. His public stance was increasingly that of a political independent whose concerns were not with strictly partisan issues (the League was well on the way to becoming one, thanks to Lodge and Wilson) but with matters on which all men of goodwill had to agree. His working energies were absorbed into Navy business and into his speaking and writing on behalf of increased government efficiency. Now wholly withdrawn from the League controversy, he had no direct dealings with the White House.

All the same he was soon personally involved, not merely in the general malaise which emanated from the White House sickroom and spread over the whole of the administration, but also in the specific quarrels that became integral to the League question at the very summit of decision. His involvement was unwitting. It was nonetheless painful for him and dangerous to his political career.

In late October he went on a hunting trip into the wilds of New Brunswick with Livy Davis and Richard E. Byrd.* Returned to Washington at the end of the month, he with Eleanor took part in the formal entertainments of the King and Queen of the Belgians, whom he had met on both his European missions and who now paid a state visit to the United States. A few days later came the Prince of Wales—the future King Edward VIII, the yet more future Duke of Windsor—and in the boyish prince's entertainments, too, the Roosevelts took part. (Eleanor even managed to obtain introductions to him for two of the Roosevelt household employees who were British subjects—an English nurse named Ada Jarvis and the Scot governess, Elspeth Connachie, who was much beloved of the Roosevelt children.† [21]) Simultaneously they became close social friends of the new British ambassador, who had been a great friend and admirer of Eleanor's Uncle Ted and whom they entertained several times on R Street.

The ambassador was Viscount Grey of Falloden, who in 1914, as British Foreign Secretary Sir Edward Grey, had watched the lights go out all over Europe and who, a year or so later, had suggested to House and Wilson the idea of a league of nations. An old man, weary, almost blind, Grey had come out of retirement to accept this embassy because he and the British government were greatly disturbed by rising opposition to the League in America and greatly afraid that Wilson's refusal of any and all compromise would lead to Senate rejection of the treaty. His mission, for which he had obviously special qualifications, was to inform the President that Britain regarded America's entrance into the League of paramount importance and, like France and the other Versailles sig-

---

* Byrd, destined for world fame as explorer and aviator, had been assigned as Navy officer to the *Dolphin* early in the war and had at that time become a friend of the Assistant Secretary.
† See page 207.

natories, was more than willing to accept whatever treaty reservations were necessary to secure that membership. He landed in New York City on the very day of the President's collapse east of Pueblo. He came with an old friend, Sir William Tyrell, of whom the Roosevelts became very fond. But he also brought with him as an accredited attaché, to the astonishment of all official Washington, a certain Major Charles Kennedy Crauford-Stuart, DSO, who had been secretary to Lord Reading when Reading was ambassador and had at that time caused a scandal in Washington society.

He was a worldly man of parts, was Crauford-Stuart—a war hero (he had been badly wounded at Gallipoli), an excellent polo player, a fine shot, an accomplished pianist, and a composer of popular music ("Make-Believe Land" and "At Gloaming Tide" were two of his successful songs). He was also, alas, a reckless gossip, and in late 1918, at a party whose guests numbered many of Washington's highest society, he had made unforgivable remarks about the First Lady, remarks of which she had been promptly informed.* She had tried at that time to have him declared *persona non grata* and sent home in disgrace. Soon thereafter, however, she and the President departed for Paris, and Lord Reading, his embassy at an end, departed also, taking Crauford-Stuart with him. None expected to see the offensive major again in Washington diplomatic circles.[22]

It was inevitable, therefore, that his reappearance would cause talk and predictable that Mrs. Wilson would react to it in hurt fury. She refused to believe that Lord Grey and the British Foreign Office could have permitted the major's return out of simple ignorance. Certainly their want of knowledge, if it existed, was quickly supplied. Grey had barely settled in at the embassy when he received word from the White House through the State Department that Crauford-Stuart, whom he happened personally to like, was unwelcome in Washington. No reason was given. He asked for one. When told the major had slandered the President's wife, a charge the major flatly denied, and being convinced that the ill President knew nothing of the matter, Grey tried to shrug it off as too trivial for serious attention. Soon thereafter, however, the State Department under pressure from Dr. Grayson as White House emissary threatened to declare formally that the major was *persona non grata,* whereupon Grey himself seems to have lost his head. He refused to send Crauford-Stuart home. Instead, he removed the major from the accredited attaché list and made him a member of the ambassador's

* Crauford-Stuart allegedly slandered the First Lady with the following riddle: *"Question,* What did Mrs. Galt do when the President proposed to her? *Answer,* She fell out of bed."

personal household, thus rendering him immune to American official displeasure—a diplomatic blunder of the first magnitude, since Mrs. Wilson was in a position to deny him all access to the President. And that is what she did, of course, all through October and November (everyone remarked that the ambassador was not invited to accompany the Prince of Wales when the latter visited the White House) and through December also.

In these circumstances, Grey was no doubt more appreciative of the warm friendship of Franklin Roosevelt, an important member of the Wilson administration, than he might otherwise have been. He was quick to accept Eleanor's invitation to come with Sir William Tyrell and share the Roosevelts' Christmas dinner that year (in 1919 as in 1918, the Roosevelts had their Christmas in Washington instead of Hyde Park)—an otherwise family affair that included Franklin's mother and Louis Howe with his wife and children (the Howes were now practically "family") and that "went very well," as Eleanor later remembered, despite the sudden feverish illness, amid the festivities, of young James.* [23]

A few weeks later, it having become obvious that he would not be received at the White House, Grey resigned his embassy and returned to London. There, too, he blundered. One of his first acts was to address to the London *Times* a letter indicating that much too much was being made of the Lodge reservations, that they could be accepted *in toto* without important effect whereas a refusal to accept them, if it prevented U.S. entry into the League, would be a world catastrophe. The letter added to the anger felt toward him by Wilson and Mrs. Wilson. From the President's sickroom the First Lady brought a curt statement for the press, dictated by him, written in her own hand: "Had Lord Grey ventured upon any such utterance when he was still in Washington as Ambassador, his Government would have been promptly asked to withdraw him." [24]

Clearly, the White House was in an ugly mood—so viciously ugly that many, even among Wilson's friends, began to wonder about his sanity. Especially did they do so after Wilson, in early February, abruptly dismissed Lansing as Secretary of State, replacing him with Bainbridge Colby, allegedly because Lansing, as ranking Cabinet member, had called informal Cabinet meetings without express Presidential permission. But Lansing had been doing this since early October, as everyone knew, without a word of protest from the sickroom! Why this drastic action at so late a date? "I *hate* Lansing!" said Mrs. Wilson to Josephus

---

* After the guests had left, a doctor diagnosed James' illness as German (Liberty?) measles. Eleanor, much perturbed, promptly phoned Lord Grey to apprise him of his exposure. He soothed her fears. He doubted that he was "subject to childish diseases."

Daniels when the Navy Secretary, who was among the few former intimates remaining on friendly terms with the Wilsons, called at the White
House one February day.

She also "hated" Franklin Roosevelt, Daniels learned. So did the
President. Roosevelt's continued cordial relationship with Lord Grey
after it was known that Grey had incurred White House displeasure—
and especially his entertainment of the ambassador at Christmastime—
had been disloyal in the White House view. It had planted seeds of
angry suspicion. And these, by Roosevelt's own further act, a reckless
and ruthless gambler's act, had quickly sprouted and grown into an enmity whose magnitude and intensity were, to Daniels, almost frightening.[25]

V

This reckless act of Roosevelt's was a major public speech delivered
on February 1, 1920, at the Brooklyn Academy of Music. It was rendered grievous by a context very largely of Admiral Sims' making.

The intermittently brilliant and frequently childish Sims had become,
since his return from Europe to the presidency of the Naval War College at Newport, in April, 1919, a determined troublemaker for Daniels.
He bitterly protested both the brevity and composition of the list of
Navy personnel to whom medals for heroism and exceptionally meritorious service during the war were to be awarded—a list published in an
appendix to the Secretary's Annual Report in December, 1919. To point
up his protest, he refused to accept the Distinguished Service Medal
awarded him. And his stand on this matter was one with which Roosevelt—still a lover of Navy pomp and circumstance, still inclined to side
with the natty warrior admirals against the homespun and invincibly civilian Secretary—agreed. "Strictly between ourselves," he wrote the admiral's wife on December 24, 1919, "I should like to shake the Admiral
warmly by the hand." [26] But Sims did not let things rest there. He saw to
it that news of his protest was published in the *Army and Navy Journal*,
where Senate Republicans eager to discredit the administration seized
upon it. They promptly set up a special subcommittee of the Naval
Affairs Committee to hold investigative hearings upon the medal
awards, summoning Sims to appear as a witness on January 17. Meanwhile, a lengthy memorandum of Sims' entitled "Certain Naval Lessons
of the Great War," addressed to the Secretary on January 7, was conveniently leaked to the press. It made sensational front-page news in the
Washington *Post* on January 14, being reported as "a frank and fearless

exposé of the hopeless . . . maladministration, mistakes, and blunders into which the American Navy has fallen as a result of Mr. Daniels' policies"—and there was an equally sensational followup story next day. This enabled the Republican chairman of the investigating committee to broaden the scope of the inquiry far beyond the medals question. It became an inquiry into what Sims, during his testimony of January 17, called "the question of the morale of the service," and the admiral happily accepted the chairman's invitation to read the whole of his memorandum into the hearings record. More black headlines over "sensational disclosures" ensued. The Navy had been woefully unprepared in April, 1917, though long forewarned of war; thereafter the department had moved so slowly, reluctantly, inefficiently that the Navy was not on a true war footing until five or six months after the war declaration; and for this (Sims would later assert that it cost the Allied cause 2,500,000 tons of shipping, a half million lives, and $15 billion!)—for this, Daniels' administration of the department was to blame.[27] Such were the drift and substance of the admiral's complaint, to be further spelled out when the expanded investigation opened on March 9.

And such was the setting for Roosevelt's address of February 1.

On its face, the speech was an excessively bold, badly miscalculated risk, taken wholly in terms of Roosevelt's sense of the shifting popular mood with no due regard for his own special, highly vulnerable position. He chose to make it a continuation of his campaign for efficient government. During that campaign he had already run risks enough, but these risks were as nothing compared to those he ran in corroborating, as his Brooklyn speech essentially did, the two main charges Sims had made. The Navy had indeed been inadequately prepared in 1917, said Roosevelt, had indeed been too slow and cautious at the top decision-making level as it dealt initially with the problems of war. He himself, as Assistant Secretary, had done all he could to supply the deficiency. Without precisely saying so, he gave the clear impression that his wholehearted commitment to the Allied cause, his eager militancy, his swift efficiency were in sharp contrast with the hesitancies, the doubting timidities and "idealistic nonsense" of both Daniels and Wilson.[28]

All in all, it was a speech which even the long-suffering and -forbearing Daniels deemed traitorous and which came closer perhaps than Roosevelt ever knew to crippling his political career. For the only time, Daniels seriously considered an open break with his assistant, forcing the latter to resign his post. He indicated as much in a diary entry. And it is distinctly possible that he would have done so, despite the great personal pain this would have caused him, had he not encountered at precisely that moment the White House's enmity toward the brash young man. The enmity, by its very extremism, seems to have provoked in Daniels a defensive reaction. At any rate, there appears in the Daniels diary entry for February 21 the following cryptic note: "FDR persona non grata with W. Better let speech pass." [29]

Roosevelt himself publicly regretted his speech within hours after delivering it; he issued to the press an "explanation" of it, designed to mitigate its bad effects. But of course, the explanation received far less publicity than the speech itself. And if Roosevelt was unaware of the full danger during the weeks that followed, he was certainly aware of danger. He knew that his relations with Daniels were severely strained, more so than at any other period since America's entry into the war—knew also that he was out of favor with the White House.

Nor was this his only trouble. It was, in fact, but one strand in a heavy net of troubles that closed about him in early 1920—a net in which his normally buoyant, often soaring spirits became for a time almost hopelessly entangled. Seldom, if ever, before had he been dragged down for so long to a bleak and wintry earth.

VI

There were family illnesses as the new year opened. Several of his children came down with chicken pox. James, barely recovered from his Christmas fever, was laid low by appendicitis. Roosevelt himself fell ill again with a severe cold, developed tonsilitis, and had to have his tonsils out—an operation of some seriousness for a man of nearly thirty-eight. Small wonder that an old close friend of his, Mrs. Charles Sumner "Bertie" Hamlin,* meeting him as he walked along R Street in the second week of January, found him looking "rather poorly" and unwontedly depressed. "He had two of his boys and a dog with him," she noted in her diary for January 10, "and we walked along together." There had been speculation, at the outset of an election year, that he might run for the Senate. He dismissed the possibility with a show of irritation. "He said . . . that even if he wanted it or could get it—he thought it stupid." There were financial troubles, too, at this time. As often happened during his Washington years, his expenses for several weeks greatly exceeded his income. He would not have been able to pay his bills for the month, on their due dates, if his mother had not sent him an extra-large check for his birthday. He thanked her with the abject

* The wife of a Federal Reserve Board member, she was the former Huybertie Pruyn of the Hudson River aristocracy, her Dutch ancestry similar to Roosevelt's, and she had known him since he was a boy growing up at Hyde Park.

effusiveness she expected. "You are not only an angel . . . but the kind that comes at the critical moment of life!" he wrote. "For the question was not one of paying Dr. Mitchell for removing James' insides, the Dr. can wait, I know he is or must be rich, but of paying the gas man and the butcher lest the infants starve to death, and your cheque which is much too much of a Birthday present will do that. It is so dear of you." [30]

On the morning of February 4, he and Eleanor were shocked by a telegram to her from Forbes Morgan saying that her Aunt Pussie—beautiful, charming, jangled, self-indulgent Pussie, she of the "artistic temperament" streaked through with a careless cruelty that had come close to destroying the adolescent Eleanor—had just died, horribly. Pussie's marriage to the considerably younger Forbes Morgan, though it produced three children, had turned out as unhappily as all who knew her well had thought it would. She simply "could not," said Eleanor, "make life . . . an easy matter" for herself or those around her. Latterly, after a long stay in California, she had acquired an old stable that had been expensively converted into a house on Ninth Street in the heart of New York's Greenwich Village. This house she made her home. On the bitterly cold night of February 3, 1920, it caught fire, and she died in the flames, with her two little girls. (Her son, William Forbes, Jr., was away at boarding school.) Eleanor at once entrained for New York City, arriving there during a raging blizzard and before her Aunt Maude Gray, Pussie's sister, could come down from her home in Portland, Maine. "It was one of those horrors I can hardly bear to think of . . . ," she wrote long afterward. "To this day I cannot bear any funeral parlor." With Maude, Forbes, and Forbes, Junior, "a sad little group," she went up to Tivoli, that gloomy home of her childhood.[31] There the three charred bodies in their coffins were placed in a vault where, on an August day only six months before, her Grandmother Hall had been laid while she and Franklin stood by. It was as if a large portion of herself—most of the Hall past that had remained vital in her present being—were now dead. She returned to Washington feeling lost and empty, in no mood to lift her husband's spirits.

And these now drooped lower than before as new strands were woven into his net of troubles.

Perhaps he had kept close track of Lucy Mercer's movements during the two years that had passed since the breaking off of his relations with her, but future historians would find few clear traces of them. She visited relatives in North Carolina for extended periods. In 1919, she seems to have lived for a while in a Toronto apartment. She certainly at some point became involved in the household affairs, probably as an employee, of a wealthy New Yorker, Winthrop Rutherfurd, whom she had known casually in society since she was a girl. Roosevelt and Eleanor knew him, too, of course; he was very much a part of that closed circle of interrelated elite in which they had both been reared. He had married Alice Morton, daughter of former Vice President Levi P. Morton,* who with her sisters, Edith and Mary, had grown up on their father's Hudson River estate at Rhinebeck, only a few miles from Springwood. The Levi Mortons had been good friends of the James Roosevelts during Franklin's boyhood, and their daughter Edith, who was now the wife of William Corcoran Eustis and lived in the famous old Corcoran House at 1607 H Street in Washington, remained one of Roosevelt's close social friends.† Hence he had been personally touched when Alice Morton Rutherfurd died in June, 1917, leaving her bereaved husband with six children, the eldest a teen-aged boy, and it is conceivable, though there is no evidence, that he at some time in 1918 or '19, through Edith Eustis, recommended Lucy Mercer as one who, needing to earn her way, possessed special qualifications for service to the wealthy widower and the widower's brood. At any rate, she *did* become of service, whether formally employed or not; she was indispensable to Rutherfurd during the fatal illness of his eldest child, the teen-aged Lewis Morton, who died in early February, 1920.

Only a few days later, on Friday, February 13, just a week after Eleanor's return to R Street from Pussie's funeral, there appeared in the Washington *Post* a social item which said: "Mrs. Carroll Mercer announces the marriage of her daughter, Lucy Page, to Mr. Winthrop Rutherfurd of New York. The ceremony took place yesterday morning at the home of Dr. and Mrs. William B. Marbury, the latter [Violetta] a sister of the bride. On account of deep mourning, only the immediate family were present." [32] (There were certain curious similarities between this new marriage and that of Roosevelt's mother and father. Like James Roosevelt, the handsome, poised Rutherfurd, of distinguished old American stock on both sides of his family, was a country gentleman and horseman who took his pleasure-filled leisure as his proper due, traveled much in Europe, and had in general the tastes and outlook of England's landed aristocracy. Like James Roosevelt, he was a widower

---

* Morton, having been governor of New York, was Vice President during Benjamin Harrison's administration, 1889–93. One of the strongest emotions of his last years was a violent antipathy toward Theodore Roosevelt.

† Edith Eustis, several years older than Roosevelt, was a glamorous figure to him when he was a Groton schoolboy and Harvard undergraduate, and she in her turn was a great admirer of his when he was Assistant Secretary. She was a friend of Henry Adams and, like Adams, if to considerably less effect, wrote a novel about Washington society and politics. It was entitled *Marian Manning* (New York, 1902) and had infidelity as a central theme.

who, after many years of happy marriage, mourned the loss of a beloved wife. And like James Roosevelt he now, aged fifty-six, took for his second wife a woman more than young enough to be his daughter—a tall woman of stately mien who, in her cool formal dignity, was not unlike Sara Delano in 1880.)

Upon this social item, however, Roosevelt had little time in which to brood during February and March. He remained a public man. And if he was wearied of the role, as Mrs. Hamlin surmised—if there was a flagging of his ambition, a temporary want of self-advancing energy, which Louis Howe had to do his best to supply—he was nonetheless absorbed in public matters. Out of these were spun new strands of trouble: everything was going wrong!

Significantly, the center or source of many of these troubles was in Newport, Rhode Island, where Admiral Sims was headquartered.

At the Naval War College, headed by Sims, was a Captain Joseph K. Taussig, who had made a name for himself as commander of a destroyer division based at Queenstown during the war and had subsequently become the Navy's director of personnel. In the latter capacity he had become distressed by what he deemed the pernicious effects upon enlisted men of reforms instituted, at the behest of Daniels and Roosevelt, in the operation of the Portsmouth, New Hampshire, Naval Prison. Daniels had been shocked by the harsh "archaic . . . practices" that prevailed at the prison when he first saw the place—especially since most of the inmates were guilty of no criminal offense. ". . . we ought to mend, not break prisoners," said the Secretary as he turned for help to Roosevelt's old political friend Thomas Mott Osborne.[33] Osborne, since Roosevelt's years in the New York legislature, had become famous, and controversial, for his enlightened administration as warden of Sing Sing, and controversy followed him to Portsmouth when he took over there in the summer of 1917 with a mandate from Daniels and Roosevelt to transform the prison from "a scrap heap" into "a repair shop" of humanity, as he put it. He encountered strong opposition from old-line Navy officers. Taussig, for one, was outraged by the "softness" of Osborne's methods. Why, confinement at Portsmouth was being made more pleasant than sea duty! And Osborne's insistence upon returning to service instead of dishonorably discharging men who had served time was having disastrous effects on Navy discipline! Taussig felt so strongly about this that when Daniels and Roosevelt continued to back Osborne, he requested a transfer from the personnel directorship to Newport. There, soon after his arrival, he read an article in the *Army and Navy Journal* saying that the younger Navy officers, especially those on destroyer duty, were heartily in favor of the practice of returning former Portsmouth inmates to duty. Furious, he dispatched a letter to the service magazine editor saying, in effect, that the article lied: he was himself a "younger officer," had held a destroyer command, had been director of personnel, and he knew absolutely that there was general disapproval among such as he of the returning of ex-convicts—including homosexuals—to duty. The letter was promptly printed, in January, 1920. It was accompanied by an editor's note saying that the author of the challenged statements was none other than the Assistant Secretary of the Navy, Franklin D. Roosevelt! [34]

And Roosevelt in his turn, at this low point of his spirits and fortunes, became incensed. Taussig had publicly challenged his veracity; he publicly challenged Taussig's. Defending the policy Taussig had attacked, he said that the captain's letter gave "a wrong impression of the actual facts" and was therefore harmful to the service. For instance, only two men convicted of "morals offenses" (homosexual practices) had been restored to duty, and for each of these there had been very special extenuating circumstances. Roosevelt could only hope that Taussig had "made a false statement" wholly "through a lack of knowledge." [35] Taussig's response, encouraged, if not suggested, by Sims, was twofold. He addressed to the Secretary a formal request for a court of inquiry into the charges and countercharges (he asserted that scores of moral offenders, not two only, had been restored to duty, that Roosevelt himself while Acting Secretary had signed an order restoring ten of them). He also took his quarrel to one of Sims' good friends, John Rathom, editor of the Providence (Rhode Island) *Journal,* who, a lover of controversy and a highly partisan Republican, soon gave it the widest publicity he could.

Through Rathom, hence for Roosevelt, the Taussig quarrel became closely intertwined with another strand of trouble, spun out of Newport, having homosexuality as a central theme. The naval training base at Newport had long been more seriously plagued by vice problems than most, if not any, of the other Navy installations. The town was notorious for its "zones of rottenness" (the shocked language is Daniels') maintained through a corrupt alliance among politicians, policemen, vice merchants—districts wherein virtually every house was a "festering place of ill fame." And when "irrefutable evidence" of "immoral conduct" on the part of a Navy chaplain at the base was flatly and publicly contradicted by that chaplain's Episcopal bishop, Daniels sent Roosevelt to Newport to investigate.[36] The Assistant Secretary was as outraged as the Secretary by what he learned. He joined in ordering and pressing an intensive drive against Newport vice in 1917. The problems, however, remained acute in the spring of 1919, when Roosevelt as Acting Secretary signed an order establishing a secret vice squad, officially

designated "Section A—Office of Assistant Secretary," to gather Newport evidence. Some months later he learned that certain members of
the squad, in the process of collecting their evidence and allegedly for
that sole purpose, had themselves engaged in sodomy on several occasions. He was shocked. He was also alarmed and had reason to be. For
though he promptly ordered a halt to Section A activities, though a
court of inquiry was established for secret investigation, and though
strong efforts were made to keep the whole sordid business out of the
public prints, Roosevelt in January and February, 1920, found himself
pilloried in Rathom's paper and subsequently in others across the land
as the initially anonymous "high Navy official" who was responsible for
this officially perpetrated moral outrage. That Sims aided and abetted
Rathom in this enterprise seems almost certain, but Rathom was also
soon motivated by a personal enmity toward the Assistant Secretary.
Roosevelt was forced to counterattack vigorously, while at the same
time trying to persuade newspaper editors not to reprint the articles Rathom sent to them, not to publicize the charges made. He could and did
put his request on patriotic grounds: the continuing nauseating publicity was bound to have deleterious effects upon Navy recruitment. What
fond parent would permit his offspring to enlist in a Navy that was, according to the Rathom-inspired publicity, a "pretty rotten institution,"
on the whole? [37] Finally, he asked the Senate Naval Affairs Committee
to conduct a full-scale investigation, to cleanse the stains from his and
the Navy's honor.

Taussig's quarrel with the Assistant Secretary came to nothing, in the
end. Roosevelt was badly worried by it, following as it did upon the
aftermath of his Brooklyn speech. He summoned Taussig to Washington and tried to smooth things over in a two-hour face-to-face conversation during which he exercised all his personal charm. He then released
to the *Army and Navy Journal* what was supposed to be a joint statement
by the two of them but which Taussig had not in fact signed and which
he promptly repudiated because it failed to say, unequivocally, that he
had *not* made a false statement or given false impressions. He emphatically renewed his demand for a court of inquiry. Roosevelt simply ignored it. Daniels declined to act upon it. And so the quarrel, unresolved,
petered out in frustration for the helplessly fuming captain.

Nor did anything come, for the time being, of Roosevelt's request for
a Naval Affairs Committee investigation of the Newport vice scandal.
When he made it, the committee's investigative energies were absorbed
by preparations for the hearings on Sims' charges against the Secretary
and department—and they continued so absorbed for nearly three
months after the hearings opened, in a glare of sensational publicity, on

March 9, before the subcommittee of three Republicans, two Democrats.

Sims initiated the hearings testimony in the role of aggressive prosecutor. Soon after his public protest against the medals awards, the admiral had written a friend that his action had "created a unique opportunity for the Navy to . . . definitely turn down Mr. Daniels and his exploitation of the Navy for political purposes." Daniels, he thought, might be forced to resign. But for one ostensibly on the defensive, Daniels must have seemed, from Sims' point of view, rather disturbingly eager to join battle. "We are so well fortified," said the Secretary to the press, "not with perfect wisdom but in things accomplished . . . , that the more people learn about the work of the Navy in the war the more satisfied they will be. . . ." [38] Certainly Sims must ultimately have regretted, sharply, if secretly, his provocation of so formidable an antagonist into a battle for public opinion. Daniels' personal appearance before the investigators was a masterful exercise of the politician's art, particularly the art of "handling" Congress; his aggressive purpose, very largely achieved, was to destroy Sims' credibility while painting for the public a glowing picture of Navy war accomplishments. By direct statement and obvious implication, he portrayed Sims as an egoistic prima donna type, who loved "glitter" and intrigue, was more British than American in basic attitude, and even "aspired" to become a member of the British Board of Admiralty, whose opinions carried more weight with him than did the clearly expressed desires of his Washington superiors. In this connection, much was made of the admiral's initial opposition to the North Sea mine barrage. When the hearings at last ended on May 28—an event that went almost unnoticed by a press which for several weeks had relegated all hearings news to small items on back pages —it was Sims, not Daniels, who had suffered a great loss in popular esteem and professional prestige.[39]

And this outcome might easily have become disastrous for Franklin Roosevelt. The approach of the hearings opening was a source of anxiety for him all through February and early March. He knew that the Republican majority planned to ask him to appear. He had every reason to dread doing so. He had publicly disagreed with the Secretary on all too many occasions over the years—most recently upon the very point at issue between Sims and Daniels. He had inveighed against confusions and inefficiencies in the department's operations and had called for a procedural reform that would enable it to conduct its business in a businesslike way. This seemed to put him in the same camp with Sims, whose "Certain Naval Lessons of the Great War" argued for a departmental reorganization that would enable Navy professionals to plan and wage war far more effectively than the Navy had done in 1917–18. Many must know, too, of Roosevelt's fervent admiration of such Navy militants as Admirals Fiske and Fullam, in former years, contrasted with his expressed contempt for the procrastinating, pacifistic Daniels. (Predictably, Fullam, Fiske, and Captain Taussig testified on Sims' side during the hearings; Admirals Benson and Rodman testified in behalf of Daniels.) Some members of the Naval Affairs Committee or its staff might even know of the memoranda Roosevelt had covertly prepared and filed for use in dissociating himself from some of Daniels' acts and decisions should this be advantageous to his career at a future date. Republican investigators would naturally be eager to spread the substance of such memoranda across the hearings record. All in all, he was in no position to face safely a hostile interrogation. If Republicans armed with accurate information about certain of his past words and deeds managed to publicize that information while he was out of favor with the White House and while his relations with Daniels were strained near the breaking point, his Navy career might end in disgraceful dismissal.

But it didn't happen.

In the weeks before the hearings opened he repeatedly proclaimed, in public speech and private communication, his allegiance to Daniels and the administration, his pride in the Navy record, his contempt for those who sought to besmirch it. He strove in this and other ways to heal the breach between himself and the Secretary. Boldly dissimulating his reluctance to testify, he boasted he would make the subcommittee's Republican chairman sorry he had ever been summoned to the witness chair—and saw to it that his boasts reached the chairman's ear. He made sneering reference in public speech "to what we call 'three-to-two history' in Washington, written by three Republicans and two Democrats," pointing out that "ninety-seven investigations costing more than $2,000,000" had failed to uncover a single instance of corruption matching the "embalmed beef and paper shoe" scandals of the Spanish-American War, which was fought under a Republican administration.[40] And as it turned out, to his immense relief, he was *not* required to make a personal appearance before the investigators, *not* required to answer questions face to face. Instead, he was asked to submit in writing his proposals for Navy Department reorganization—and he managed to make this statement as much an indictment of prevailing Congressional methods of passing naval laws and appropriations bills (he spoke of the "pork barrel") and of Sims' administration of the War College (he spoke of the "tendency to build up a 'holier-than-thou' . . . aggregation of officers at Newport" who were not in "close contact with the actual life of the Navy") as it was a reiteration of his views on the need for more centralized intradepartmental controls. He also referred to certain "gold-laced gentlemen" who wished to have the department run by a general staff, with the civilian Secretary as their representative, or puppet, in dealings with Congress and public. This last made for him a fortunate hit, as perhaps it was deliberately aimed to do. Released to the press, which gave it wide publicity, it provoked a counterattack that accentuated in the public mind his allegiance to Daniels, his repudiation of and by Daniels' enemies among the militant Navy professionals. One of the latter, an admiral, angrily resentful, addressed to the *Army and Navy Journal* a letter, reprinted in many newspapers, charging Roosevelt with two-facedness and double-dealing in his relations with labor unions and Navy brass. High officers were "gold-laced gentlemen" to the Assistant Secretary when he was seeking "to ingratiate himself with the workingmen," said this admiral; they were not so "scorned . . . when he meets them in rich clubs of New York and Washington." [41]

VII

Thus, by the end of May, aided by good luck, Roosevelt had succeeded in extricating himself from the most serious of the troubles that had enmeshed him. In the process, he had gained integrity—a greater integrity than he had had at any earlier time, perhaps, since his entrance into politics. Lucy Mercer's wedding, painful though it may have been for him, restored integrity to his private life insofar as it absolved him of certain guilt feelings, removed from him certain temptations, that must inevitably focus on her as long as she remained unmarried. The integrity of his public life was promoted by his publicly declared and demonstrated loyalty to the Secretary. This last was now wholehearted. A calculating self-interest had certainly helped determine his choice of the Secretary over the "gold-laced gentlemen" when he was forced at last to decide, as a flat either/or, between the two. That choice, however, was sustained by gratitude for the Secretary's tacit forgiveness of his sins during his time of troubles; by the sincere affection he had always felt for Daniels personally, which his gratefulness augmented; and by a respect for Daniels' official operations which had been growing, despite himself, through the last seven years and was now at last full-grown. Never again would there be between these two men any such differences as had often divided them, with more or less ill feeling, in the past. Eleanor remarked her husband's changed attitude. He had "learned . . . to have a deep admiration for the qualities of character and to value the high ability of Mr. Daniels," she wrote decades later. "It was his own experience that taught him it was one thing to understand and get on with naval officers, and another and perhaps even greater quality that enabled Mr. Daniels to understand and get on with Congress." [42]

There was one more factor which may have encouraged the growth of integrity, and that was the dimness of the immediate political prospect for any Wilsonian Democrat in that springtime of a Presidential year. The impasse between White House and Congress remained, as Wilson's illness continued to deprive the Republic of executive leadership. On March 19, the Versailles Treaty with the fourteen Lodge reservations attached (plus a fifteenth, calling for Ireland's self-determination) came again to a Senate vote and was again voted down. The tally was 49 for ratification, 35 against—a failure by 7 votes to obtain the needed two-thirds majority—and again the sick President's command that all loyal Democrats vote "nay" was decisive. (A mere 12 Republicans voted against ratification; 23 Democrats did so.) Wilson now staked all his hopes on the upcoming Presidential election. This would be, he proclaimed, a "great and solemn referendum" upon the League question. But it seemed clear to others that the decisive issue of 1920 would probably be Wilson himself as a personality, Wilsonianism as a political creed and attitude, and that on this issue the chances for Democratic victory were virtually nil. Everywhere were signs of a popular revulsion against the President. His most fervent former supporters were forsaking him—or were convinced that *he* had forsaken *them*. Liberals found it difficult to forgive the compromises he had made in Paris, more difficult still to forgive such actions as his refusal to pardon Eugene V. Debs, still imprisoned at Atlanta for wartime "seditious utterance," * or to repudiate and halt the Red witch-hunting excesses of Attorney General Palmer. Much or most of the electorate seemed sick and tired of the schoolmaster's approach to public problems, sick and tired of the constant harping on High Ideals, Moral Obligations, Duty and Honor and Righteousness. All signs were that the American people wanted now to relax and pursue again their private interests, to the virtual exclusion of public affairs, without feeling guilty about doing so. In such circumstances, a still-young Democratic politician did well to curb his ambition for the time being: there was consequently no strong incentive for him to play both ends against the middle, to make deals, placate oppo-

---

* "I will never consent to the pardon of this man," said Wilson to Tumulty when the latter brought him a formal recommendation for Debs' release. ". . . While the flower of American youth was pouring out its blood to vindicate the cause of civilization, this man . . . stood behind the lines, sniping, attacking, and denouncing them. Before the war he had a perfect right to exercise his freedom of speech, but once the Congress . . . declared war, silence on his part would have been the proper course to pursue. . . . This man was a traitor to his country. . . ." [43]

nents, and equivocate on issues, in order to gain an immediate political objective.

And Roosevelt himself shared to a considerable degree in the changing mood he had sensed in the general public since the summer of 1919. He shifted personal attention and energies away from public to private concerns. In March, 1920, he formed a law partnership with two friends of about his own age, Langdon Marvin and Grenville T. Emmet, so that he would have some place to land when he came down from the heights of Washington bureaucracy. The practice of law, however, especially so conservative a practice as that of Emmet, Marvin & Roosevelt promised to be, was no more attractive to him now than it had been in 1910. In the spirit of the opening 1920's, he craved action, excitement, a gambler's chance to make a great deal of money quickly. With Howe, then and later, he considered investing in numerous highly speculative business ventures (the infant radio industry, a scheme to establish zeppelin passenger service between New York and Chicago, the proposal for a chain of variety stores in Haiti and Santo Domingo, a scheme for harnessing the huge tidal flows of Passamaquoddy Bay to generate electricity, a scheme for selling bond certificates to small investors through banks) and did actually invest in some of them.

One of these last was the Washington Oil Syndicate, formed by Roosevelt and Howe's friend Pat Homer, the affable, daring, dramatically exciting promoter who had formerly represented Britain's Sterling Motors in the United States.[44] The syndicate was to buy property in Oklahoma to speculate in oil drilling, and Homer had little trouble persuading Roosevelt to buy 500 shares of its stock at $10 a share, in the fall of 1919. A few weeks later Homer, comparing the cheapness of crude oil in Mexico and the expensiveness of refined oil in the United States (crude sold for $12\frac{1}{2}$ cents a barrel in Mexico, refined for well over $3 in Boston), concocted a scheme for building a refinery on the Mexican coast and transporting its product to the Northeast via tanker. Roosevelt was excited by it. He tried and failed to interest his friend and Hyde Park neighbor Henry Morgenthau, Jr., in the project (Morgenthau objected that the cost of building a refinery in Mexico would be excessive and that the needed tankers were absolutely unavailable); he then, at Homer's urging, proposed that the U.S. Navy finance the building of a refinery to be operated by Homer's company at Fall River, Massachusetts (Grace Howe's hometown), and also obtain the tankers needed to bring up the Mexican crude. His argument was that this would be an excellent stroke of business for the Navy, which was currently unable to obtain all the oil it wanted even at the prevailing inflated prices, nearly double those of 1917. The huge savings in the cost of refined oil would soon pay for the Fall River plant; the Navy would have the oil it needed and would, thereafter, be relatively independent of a market currently managed by Standard Oil and a few other giants of the oil industry. The argument failed to move Daniels (he had doubts about Pat Homer; he preferred to commandeer the needed oil), but it or the charm and persistency of Roosevelt's advocacy finally persuaded the other officials and officers having a voice in the matter, whereupon Daniels permitted the deal to be made. Homer then organized the New England Oil Corporation, merged the Washington Oil Syndicate with it (Roosevelt seems to have disposed of his syndicate stock at this time, though the record here is far from clear*), and proceeded to implement his promotional idea.

The outcome was in every respect unfortunate. Roosevelt boasted in 1920, in public speech, of what the new refinery would mean to New England (". . . that is what the Government has done right here to help you—I think I might almost say what I have done to help you," he told a New Bedford audience in September of that year, "because this whole matter came under me as Assistant Secretary of the Navy"),[45] but he had nothing to say about it in 1921 and after, when Homer's capacities as corporation executive failed to match his capacities as promoter. By the time New England Oil was in actual production, the managed market for refined oil had collapsed. The price per barrel on that market had fallen well below the price which Homer and the Navy had agreed upon, so that in the end the Navy paid a good deal more for its oil, because of the Homer deal, than it would otherwise have had to do.

* Louis Howe, at about this time, sent his wife 500 shares of syndicate stock for safekeeping, telling her that, if anything should happen to him (death was always close to him), she should send the shares to Roosevelt, who would sell them for at least $5,000. See Alfred B. Rollins, Jr., *Roosevelt and Howe* (New York, 1962), p. 124. Frank Freidel, in his *Franklin D. Roosevelt: The Ordeal* (Boston, 1954), p. 38, says in a footnote that Roosevelt's receipt for the $5,000 he invested in the Washington Oil Syndicate bears the notation "Sold 1920" on one corner. "A very careful search by the staff of the Roosevelt Library of all the pertinent Roosevelt papers there has failed to turn up any evidence that Roosevelt ever had any financial interest in the New England Oil Corporation," writes Freidel.

Book Four

✦

THE CRUCIAL YEARS:
CHALLENGE AND RESPONSE

Twenty

➸➤❯❮❮

The Campaign of 1920 and Its Aftermath

I

I N EARLY 1920 Franklin Roosevelt's public image gave to his career
an energy and direction which he of himself alone—his vitality abnormally low, his spirit troubled and distracted—would not have been able
to supply. As his inward self and private life diverged more widely than
ever before from his public role, the latter took over, propping up the
momentarily fumbling, faltering actor while sheer momentum, assisted
by Louis Howe, did the work of his enfeebled ambition.

Much of this momentum had been generated by a speech Roosevelt
made at a banquet of the Democratic National Committee in Chicago
on May 29, 1919. It was the most important speech of his career thus far
and an inspired performance, struck white-hot from his mind with a
minimum of merely shrewd calculation (he did not begin its composition until a few hours before he gave it) at a time when his commitment
to Wilson and Wilsonian idealism was at its strongest.

For twenty-five years, he said, a battle between liberals (progressives)
and conservatives (reactionaries) had been waged within each of the
major political parties, but now in each party a decision had been
reached. Conservatism and reaction had triumphed in the Republican
Party, liberalism and progressivism in the Democratic. The Republicans
had cast out of their ranks the soldiers of enlightenment, the servants of
the general welfare; they now devoted themselves "to the principles of
little Americanism and jingo bluff, to the old hypocrisy of Penrose and
Mark Hanna and Blaine." Their primary concern in the new Congress
was to reduce taxes for "those unfortunate individuals who have incomes of $1,000,000 a year or more" and to raise tariffs for the benefit of
"pet groups of manufacturers." As for foreign policy, Senator Lodge
shaped it for the Republicans in his own image, out of vindictive hatred

for Woodrow Wilson. "When Mr. Lodge reads his morning paper . . . and sees what the President has said or done, his policy for the next twenty-four hours becomes the diametrical opposite." In magnificent contrast with all this stood the Democracy! After going "too far in one direction perhaps in 1896 and 1900" (though "we must remember that many of the ideals and principles enunciated by Mr. Bryan . . . are now the law of the land"), the Democratic Party had tried "to reconcile the conservative wing of the party" in 1904, with disastrous consequences at the polls. And "from that day on, it became evident that the Democracy of the United States was and is and must be a progressive democracy," a fact made manifest in the Congressional elections of 1910, confirmed by the Presidential election of 1912, and gloriously demonstrated by a Democratic administration which in its first four years "carried through more great measures for the good of the whole population than any other party in any similar period" and then, in its next two, led the nation to victory in "the most stupendous war in history." Narrow partisanship had not been permitted to interfere with this beneficent process: the "best brains in the country, irrespective of party," had been called upon. He summed up: "So we are approaching the campaign of 1920—approaching it with the broad principles settled in advance; conservatism, special privilege, partisanship, destruction on the one hand—liberalism, commonsense idealism, constructiveness, progress on the other." [1]

Tremendously effective with those who heard it, much more so than Attorney General Palmer's keynote address to the same meeting, Roosevelt's speech also attracted far more newspaper attention across the country than Palmer's did. It was warmly praised by Democratic editors, angrily assailed by Republicans, and the chain reaction it set in motion continued through the months that followed. There was talk in New York of "Roosevelt for Senator" (if Al Smith ran as expected for a second term as governor) or "Roosevelt for Governor" (if Smith declared for the Senate). There was even a minor "Roosevelt for President" boom, some of whose organized manifestations he felt obliged to discourage. "Being early on the job is sometimes wise and sometimes not," he wrote one overzealous promoter in November, 1919. "I sometimes think we consider too much the good luck of the early bird, and not the bad luck of the early worm." [2] But the talk had continued, growing in volume as the election year opened. Thus, in early 1920, Roosevelt's standing as a political figure was higher with the general public than it had ever been before at precisely the time when his spirits and his personal standing with his administrative superiors were lower than they had ever been before.

It was on one of the gloomiest of his days—the very day in fact when Mrs. Hamlin, meeting him on R Street, remarked how "poorly" he looked and how harassed he seemed to be—that Roosevelt was called upon in his office by a friend of his from college days, Louis B. Wehle, a nephew of Louis Brandeis. Wehle, general counsel of the War Finance Corporation, had been a co-editor with Roosevelt of the Harvard *Crimson*, had worked with Roosevelt (and Walter Lippmann) on war labor problems while associated with the General Munitions Board, and came now to his old friend with the idea that the Democrats, at their national convention in San Francisco in July, should nominate Herbert Hoover of California for President, Franklin Roosevelt of New York for Vice President, and at the same time announce that the Vice President would sit as a member of the President's Cabinet. This would do much to assure a Democratic victory in two populous doubtful states. It provided the best, if not the only, chance for the Democrats to win in a year when the tide of public opinion flowed heavily against them. Wehle had already discussed this proposal with several leading Democrats, who enthusiastically endorsed it. With Roosevelt, he argued that a Vice Presidential campaign, whether won or lost, would greatly benefit Roosevelt's career. For one thing, "in your campaign tours you would make a great number of key acquaintances in every State" and afterward "if you would methodically build on them . . . would come to have such a personal following in the Democratic Party that it would probably lead you eventually to the Presidency." [3] Roosevelt listened smilingly, but with no great show of enthusiasm, finally telling Wehle to "go ahead" if he wished.

Wehle did so. He conferred with Colonel House, who agreed that Hoover-Roosevelt could be a winning ticket and sent Wehle to sound out Hoover. Hoover was noncommittal, obviously unable to decide between the Democrats and the Republicans, then and for weeks thereafter. Not until the last of March, after it had been announced that Republicans wishing to nominate Hoover for President would soon meet in Chicago, did he clearly state that he was a Republican, not a Democrat, and would under certain conditions accept a Republican nomination. But this made Roosevelt's place on the Democratic ticket, in order to carry New York, more important than ever, in the opinion of many.

By that time a good deal of Roosevelt's natural optimism and buoyancy had returned to him as he emerged from his net of troubles. He and Howe drew up a long list of "platform recommendations" for presentation to the national convention. They expressed the liberalism, the progressivism he had proclaimed as his party's tradition and purpose. One of them called for federal action to eliminate "speculative middlemen" (an echo of his New York legislature crusade) whose market operations boosted the cost of living. Others called for further development of federal farm loan policies and their extension to urban homebuilders; for a "complete reorganization" of the railway system, more federal aid to highway construction, encouragement to consumer cooperatives, guarantees of labor's right to organize, and "active participation by labor with employers in the management and profits of all industry." Yet others called for tax law revision to distinguish earned from unearned income (taxing the latter at a higher rate), prevent "profiteering," and impose heavy inheritance taxes; for the selling of Liberty Bonds on a government market at par; and for government borrowing to finance public works as a safeguard against economic depression. This last was to be accomplished through the sale of " 'Prosperity Bonds,' * or short term notes, to be issued by the President whenever he declares a state of acute industrial depression to exist," the proceeds of such sales to "be spent on an authorized program of economic-defensive works, such as intercoastal canals, roads, reclamation and land-resettlement projects, and administered by the army." Said Roosevelt and Howe, "We believe such policy to be the constructive preventative of acute depression otherwise almost certain to come, providing a way of 'taking up the slack' and probably forestalling the hysteria and manipulation which leads to panic and untold public suffering." [4]

Consistent with this liberal-progressive stance and indicative of his personal politics in playing for the future was the fight he made against Tammany in early May for abolition of the unit vote rule over the New York delegation at the national convention. He knew before he began that he had no chance to win this fight (in the event, at a conference of New York delegates on May 7, his proposal was defeated 64 to 8). He knew also that the Rules Committee of the convention itself would almost certainly vote down the unit rule, as had happened in preceding conventions. But his fight reestablished him in the public mind, particularly that of upstate New York, where he had his political base, as a foe of Murphy bossism and a progressive idealist willing to sacrifice personal ambition upon the altar of principle, for an effect of this battle gesture was to halt all talk for the time being of "Roosevelt for Senator."

Yet his seeming quarrel with Tammany was not so serious as to destroy or really damage to any significant extent the wary rapprochement that had been publicly effected between him and Murphy in 1918. He remained on good, although not intimate, terms with Al Smith, who

---

* Daniel R. Fusfield points out that the "prosperity bond idea was not original with Roosevelt" or Howe but had been suggested by Herbert J. Davenport in his *Outlines of Economic Theory*, published in 1896.

would be proposed, instead of McAdoo, as New York's "favorite son" Presidential candidate, and during the long, incessantly busy train ride from New York City to San Francisco in late June, he did his charming best to improve his personal relations with the Tammany men. If the talk of him for Senator had waned, that of him for Vice President continued among key Democratic decision- and opinion-makers. He went to the convention city prepared not only to seize the opportunity, should it present itself, but also actively to encourage such presentation. With him upon his arrival were his old Groton-Harvard friend Lathrop Brown; the two Dutchess County friends, John Mack and Tom Lynch, who had done most to launch his political career in 1910; his law partner Grenville Emmet; and his current personal secretary, Renah F. Camalier. In his camp also, in effect, was Josephus Daniels, whom he had urged to come when Daniels had seemed reluctant to do so. Daniels was probably personally the most popular of high Wilson administration officials in San Francisco; liked and respected by nearly all the delegates, Tammanyites as well as Bryanites, he would, as Roosevelt had argued, exert upon the convention a unifying influence.

The immediate prospect now seemed somewhat less bleak for Democrats than it had been a few weeks before, thanks to the Republican National Convention in Chicago in early June. William Allen White, the Emporia, Kansas, newspaperman and author, thought he had never seen before a convention "so completely dominated by sinister predatory economic forces"—oil interests particularly.[5] A cynical Ohio courthouse politician of unsavory local reputation, Harry M. Daugherty, had predicted the convention's course and outcome. Daugherty had long been the political manager of a handsome, amiable, weak-willed mediocrity named Warren Gamaliel Harding, publisher of a small-town Ohio newspaper (the Marion *Star*), who in 1920 was completing a totally undistinguished first term as U.S. Senator. It was Daugherty who had pushed the torpid, doubting Harding into announcing his Presidential candidacy in mid-December, 1919, and Daugherty was virtually alone in believing that Harding had a chance to win the nomination. He gave newspaper reporters his reason why, some days before the convention opened. None of the leading contenders—General Leonard Wood, Governor Frank Lowden of Illinois, Senator Hiram Johnson of California, Herbert Hoover—would be able to win a majority on the early ballots, he said. Days of balloting amid torrid heat would end in hopeless deadlock. Then "some fifteen men, bleary-eyed from lack of sleep, and perspiring profusely," meeting in a smoke-filled hotel room "about 2:11 in the morning," would agree upon Harding as the nominee. And that was approximately what had happened, the "smoke-filled room" being a suite on the thirteenth floor of the Blackstone rented by George Harvey —he who ten years before had launched the political career of Woodrow Wilson. Harding won nomination on the tenth ballot. (When the customary motion to make the nomination unanimous was offered, a stocky, clamp-jawed Chicago delegate named Harold Ickes sprang to his feet shouting "No!" Others echoed him. The convention chairman, Senator Lodge, then declared the nomination unanimous.)[6] Calvin Coolidge of Massachusetts was named as Harding's running mate.

But if less bleak, the prospect before the delegates at San Francisco was far from rosy. There were few signs of optimistic enthusiasm as the Platform and Rules committees completed their work (the platform, moderately progressive, contained a pro-League plank; the unit vote rule was abolished) and the convention formally opened. The one moment of wholly authentic excitement came at the opening session. Franklin Roosevelt was at the center of it. The unveiling of a huge oil painting of the President sparked a Wilson demonstration, predictable an event but unexpectedly fervent, during which one state delegation after another left its seats and, bearing aloft its banner, paraded around the hall to the sound of martial music. The New York delegation remained conspicuously seated, under orders from its Tammany chairman. But when the demonstration was at its height, Roosevelt, leading a contingent of New Yorkers, went to the Tammany man who held the state standard, seized it from him after a brief scuffle (no blows were struck, though some newspapers said there were), and then bore it triumphantly into the parade to the cheers of thousands. Thus did he testify dramatically to his Wilsonianism, his independence of Tammany bossism.[7]

Yet when Tammany's Al Smith received his "favorite son" nomination, lithe, tall, handsome Franklin Roosevelt, looking younger than his thirty-eight years, strode down the aisle to the platform to deliver a seconding speech. Though he spoke briefly, he was interrupted five times by enthusiastic applause—once when he said that the "nominee of this Convention will not be chosen at 2 A.M. in a hotel room"—and made a personal impression upon the assembled delegates that "could not have been better," as Emmet wrote Langdon Marvin a few hours later.[8] When the balloting began, he, of course, voted for Smith until, after seven ballots, Smith withdrew. Thereafter ballot followed ballot in seemingly endless succession, as nearly always happened in Democratic conventions, where the two-thirds rule prevailed. There were three leading contenders: McAdoo, handicapped by the fact that his father-in-law, the President, had refused to endorse him; A. Mitchell Palmer, whose Red-baiting had made him a formidable candidate but had simultaneously aroused adamant labor-liberal hostility; and Governor James M. Cox of Ohio, a Progressive whose personal stand on the League question was unknown and who was the candidate of Murphy and the other anti-Wilson city machine bosses. After Smith's withdrawal, Roosevelt voted steadily for McAdoo, though he seems to have been prepared to push for the nomination of John W. Davis if the leaders became hopelessly deadlocked. "Dark horse" Davis, a wealthy corporation lawyer, had formerly been a Congressman from West Virginia and was currently Wilson's ambassador to the Court of St. James's. Meanwhile, Roosevelt's friends were active on his behalf, moving discreetly among the delegates on the convention floor and in hotel rooms and lobbies, promoting him for Vice President and being everywhere warmly received.

In the end, the threatened deadlock did not occur. Palmer faded, then McAdoo, while Cox slowly gained, until at last, on the forty-fourth ballot, Cox won nomination. Roosevelt was a logical candidate for Vice President, to balance the ticket. Even Murphy, if reluctantly, agreed to this—and indeed Roosevelt's candidacy for the second spot had been among the bargaining counters in the complex series of behind-the-scenes maneuvers which had enabled Murphy to shift votes from McAdoo to Cox on the closing ballots. Others, including Cox's campaign manager, were inclined to favor Secretary of Agriculture Edwin T. Meredith, a publisher of farm and home periodicals in Des Moines, Iowa. Cox himself, however, preferred Roosevelt, whom he had never met but who, as a New Yorker, "met the geographical requirement, . . . was recognized as an Independent," and bore "a well-known name." So Roosevelt's selection was a forgone conclusion by the time Judge Timothy T. Ansberry of Ohio appeared at the rostrum to place his name in nomination. Al Smith was among those making seconding speeches. So was Joseph E. Davies of Wisconsin. And by the time the seconding speeches had been concluded, the three Vice Presidential candidates previously placed in nomination (they included the California oilman Edward L. Doheny) had withdrawn from the race. Roosevelt was nominated by acclamation.[9]

There were cries from the floor for a speech from the Vice Presidential nominee, but Roosevelt had hurriedly left the hall when told that his name was about to be placed in nomination. Josephus Daniels, being called upon, appeared in his place. He spoke words designed to dispel any suspicion of bad feeling between him and the Assistant Secretary. Said Daniels, all Democrats should rejoice "that we have nominated a ticket of young, able, and efficient men. . . . I wish to say that to me, and to five hundred thousand men in the American Navy, and to five million men in the Army, it is a matter of peculiar gratification that this Convention unanimously has chosen as candidate for Vice President that clear-headed and able executive and patriotic citizen of New York, the Assistant Secretary of the Navy, Franklin D. Roosevelt. And I wish to add that his service during this great war . . . was chiefly executive only because, when the war began, and he wished to go to the front, I urged him that his highest duty was to help to carry the millions of men across and to bring them back. . . ." [10]

II

Roosevelt's vitality, at so low an ebb a few months before, was now in flood. The last lingering effects of the long series of illnesses (influenza, pneumonia, head colds, clogged sinuses, tonsillitis) which had plagued him from early autumn of 1918 into early 1920 had disappeared weeks before he went to San Francisco. There the general impression he made was of boundless energy, a youthful zest sustained by unusually good physical health. Frances Perkins, who attended the convention, remembered him as "tall, strong, handsome" and incessantly active, "one of the stars of the show," always "in the thick" of things. "I recall how he displayed his athletic ability by vaulting over a row of chairs to get to the platform in a hurry." [11]

And he had need of all his buoyant strength as he set out to capitalize upon his great opportunity. On his way East from San Francisco, he made several stops—in Utah, Colorado, Kansas, Missouri—to confer on issues and strategy with local Democratic leaders. At Salt Lake City, he indicated to reporters that he planned a strenuous "speaking campaign," not a "front porch affair" of the kind what had been announced for the new McKinley, Warren G. Harding. At Glenwood Springs, Colorado, he welcomed the support of the Republican mayor, who said he would bolt his party's ticket this year in order to support the League of Nations. In Columbus, Ohio, he met Governor Cox for the first time—a man not unlike Josephus Daniels in general appearance and manner, if less homespun and more briskly businesslike. Cox had no remarkable physical presence. He was a bit thick of body, inches shorter than Roosevelt, and no one would have described as handsome his round, pleasant, open countenance. But he had personal force and high ability (he had been thrice elected governor of a normally Republican state; he had made an excellent progressive record), and his visual appraisal of Roosevelt, through pince-nez spectacles like Roosevelt's own, was quick and shrewd. He liked what he saw. And heard. Roosevelt struck him as alert and realistic, "keenly alive to the conditions that would bear on the campaign," though he could not agree to Roosevelt's proposal (a little brash perhaps in its time and place) that the Vice President should sit with the Cabinet and that an announcement to this effect should be issued now by the Presidential candidate. Congress would be antagonized by this, Cox believed; the Senate, ever jealous of its prerogatives, would resent having its deliberations presided over by a "White House snoop." In general, however, the two men agreed on the nature and issues of the campaign. It must be vigorous on the part of both of them, and it must not, *could* not be divorced from the administration and its record. Before the two parted, Cox invited Roosevelt to join him in a call upon the President at the White House on the coming Sunday, July 18.[12]

This last would prove an event of major political importance. By the time Roosevelt and Cox conferred each of them had received hundreds of congratulatory telegrams and letters. Walter Lippmann, returned to his editorship on the *New Republic* after war service in Washington (he and Roosevelt served together in 1917 on the Wage Scale Committee), wired that Roosevelt's nomination was "the best news in many a long day . . . , that when parties can pick a man like Frank Roosevelt there is a decent future in politics." Numerous others, including Robert H. Jackson, wired or wrote Roosevelt that his selection revived in them a theretofore waning interest in politics. Herbert Hoover offered him the "personal congratulations" of an "old friend," saying that he was "glad to see you . . . in such a prominent place" and that, though a Republican could hardly wish a Democrat success in the election, he "nevertheless" considered Roosevelt's nomination "a contribution to the good of the country" in that it would "bring the merit of a great public servant to the front." No such congratulations came from Woodrow Wilson, however, to either Cox or Roosevelt. A perfunctory single-line wire went from the White House to Cox: "Please accept my hearty congratulations and cordial best wishes." The single-line wire to Roosevelt was less enthusiastic still: "Please accept my warm congratulations and good wishes." And even these conventionally required messages must have cost Wilson a pang. For when the news of Cox's nomination was first brought to him, he startled and even frightened his valet, who was with him at the time, by exploding into a white-faced rage: a torrent of profanity interspersed with obscenities poured from him, who very rarely employed the mildest of curse words.[13] Like much of the public, he interpreted the convention's action as a personal slap in the face, a repudiation of his administration, Cox having been chiefly sponsored by notorious anti-Wilsonites. And the news of Roosevelt's selection next day did nothing to soothe him: he suspected the truth—namely, that Roosevelt's nomination had been helped rather than hindered by the fact that the Assistant Secretary was not in the White House's good graces. The sick President could not but anticipate further prolonged insult and humiliation as the Democratic nominees paid no more than lip service to the League of Nations while remaining as aloof as possible from him personally. Certainly this advice was pressed strongly upon Cox by several who had done most to promote his candidacy. Cox's request for permission to call may therefore have come to Wilson as a surprise, and he must have wondered if the visit would be, was intended to be, anything more than a noncommittal gesture of courtesy.

Sunday, July 18, was a clear pleasant day in Washington. Cox came to the White House in the afternoon wearing a conventional three-button business suit of sober brownish gray, his sole clothing concession to the season being a flat, wide-ribboned straw hat. But Roosevelt came nattily, nautically attired (a yachtsman sailing summer seas) in white shoes, white trousers, dark-blue double-breasted jacket, and navy blue tie. He was in high spirits (". . . young Roosevelt . . . was bright and boyish and a little silly in his exuberance—the thing has gone to his head," wrote a Republican observer to Senator Lodge a few days later*)[14] as he waited with Cox in Tumulty's office until the President was prepared to receive them. The two waited for fifteen minutes. Then they were taken out of doors onto the south portico facing a wide, lushly green south lawn—and there they came upon shocking contradiction of all else around them, all vital summer and warmth. Woodrow Wilson, huddled in his wheelchair, was frozen winter, a figure of rigid, bitter mortality. His long, narrow face, its left side wholly dead, leaned slack-jawed upon his sunken chest. A concealing shawl was draped over his left shoulder and arm. Not until Cox stood over him, greeting him warmly, did he look up. Then he said in a weak, whispery voice, "Thank you for coming. I am very glad you came." Roosevelt, moved almost to tears (he had not realized the President was so desperately ill), saw actual tears in Cox's eyes. Said Cox: "Mr. President, I have always admired the fight you made for the League." Wilson then drew himself up as straight as he could, with obviously painful effort. "Mr. Cox," he said, "that fight can still be won!" And Cox replied for Roosevelt as for himself when he said, "Mr. President, we are going to be a million percent with you, and your Administration, and that means the League of Nations." Wilson nodded. His long, lean jaw sank again upon his chest. "I am very grateful," he whispered. "I am very grateful." Then Cox and

* Lodge replied, "He is a well-meaning, nice young fellow, but light. . . . His head [is] evidently turned and the effect upon a not very strong man is obvious."

Roosevelt said good-bye and went again into the Executive Offices, where Cox wrote out a statement for the press, saying that the paramount issue of the upcoming campaign was the League of Nations and that he (with Roosevelt) would campaign for America's entrance. Roosevelt, too, issued a press statement. "I wish that every American could have been a silent witness at the meeting of these two great men," he said. "Their splendid accord and their high purpose are an inspiration." [15]

Roosevelt's own campaign had already had its informal beginning. There had been a rousing "welcome home" celebration for him in Poughkeepsie and Hyde Park on July 13. And already he and Howe had laid out in a general way the itineraries of the speaking tours he would make and had recruited the key members of his campaign staff. His campaign headquarters would be in New York City. His former secretary, Charles McCarthy, would be in charge of it. Howe for the time being would remain in Washington, filling in temporarily as Acting Assistant Secretary. Traveling with Roosevelt in his railroad car, the Westboro, which was to be attached to regular trains according to a precisely planned schedule, would be Marvin McIntyre, a veteran newsman, hollow of cheek, lantern-jawed, mild-mannered, who had latterly been the Navy Department's public relations director and would now serve as the candidate's chief speech writer and publicity man. Working in close cooperation with McIntyre would be another veteran newsman, hard-boiled and highly efficient Stephen T. Early, who had been covering Navy for the Associated Press. Early's name was as his function in that campaign: he was to be the advance agent, traveling some days ahead of the campaign train in order to gather and send back to McIntyre information about local personalities, local issues, local attitudes—information that would enable the candidate to maximize the effectiveness of his appeal for votes. Also on the train, at least part of the time, would be Tom Lynch, to act as disbursing agent and bill payer. This would prove a worrisome job: Roosevelt would put $5,000 of his own money into the campaign, his mother would put in $3,000 more, but the national Democratic treasury was, as usual, much smaller than the Republican, and the candidate was often short of funds.

Eleanor had not accompanied her husband to San Francisco, nor was she in Washington when he returned: she was on Campobello with her children and mother-in-law. (He wrote her there, rather plaintively, on July 17: "I miss you so so much. It is very strange not to have you with me in all these doings.") But he was with her and his family again on Sunday, July 25, when he himself came to Campobello for a few days of "rest." (He remained, in fact, very busy with campaign preparations.)

Then, with Eleanor, Anna, and James, who was to enter Groton that fall, he came back to Washington where, amid sweltering heat, Eleanor "made the arrangements for giving up the house and Franklin resigned as Assistant Secretary of the Navy. . . ." [16]

He submitted his written resignation to the President on August 6, saying to Wilson "personally" that he would "never fail to remember the unselfish service which you have given us as example." (Wilson's formal reply to this was as coolly perfunctory as his wires to San Francisco had been; he expressed "sincere regret" that Roosevelt was resigning his administration post. He asked Daniels to draft for his signature the formal resignation acceptance, dated August 30.) On that same August 6, Roosevelt was ceremoniously presented with an inscribed silver loving cup, the gift of department employees, some 2,000 of whom were assembled to witness the event. He then, as his last act at his old desk, dashed off a heartfelt letter to "My dear Chief," saying: "This is not goodbye—that will be always impossible after these years of closest association. . . . You have taught me so wisely and kept my feet on the ground when I was about to sky-rocket—and in it all there has never been a real dispute or antagonism or distrust. . . . We will I know keep up this association in the years to come—and please let me keep on coming to you to get your fine inspiration of real idealism and right living and good Americanism." Daniels replied next day: "Dear Franklin:—Your words of sincere friendship were very grateful to me. . . . I always counted on your zeal, your enthusiasm, your devoted patriotism and efficient and able service, and always found you equal to the big job in hand. My thought and feeling has been that of an older brother . . . and we will be brothers in all things that make for the good of our country." [17]

As Daniels wrote these words, Roosevelt, with Eleanor and Anna, was arriving in Dayton, Ohio, for the formal notification of Governor Cox—"a very colorful ceremony" during which, and in the festivities surrounding it, Anna, as Eleanor would proudly remember, "was quite a success. She was pretty, her light golden hair, which at that time was long, attracted a good deal of attention. . . . For her the day was over far too quickly." But even greater excitements swiftly followed for the girl. The next day she with her father and mother arrived in Hyde Park for Roosevelt's formal notification, a ceremony arranged under the local chairmanship of Henry Morgenthau, Jr., and held on August 9. Sara Roosevelt was there, too, of course, and, said Eleanor later, "I sympathized with my mother-in-law when I saw her lawn being trampled by hordes of people." [18]

More than 5,000 people, most of them doubtless Republican, were gathered on that lawn to hear the candidate's acceptance speech, delivered from the front steps. It was a long speech, logically organized. It had been labored over (Franklin K. Lane had helped him polish its phrases) as no earlier speech of his had been. And it made a strong impression on those who heard it, on most of those who later read it. "Two great problems will confront the next Administration," he said: "our relations with the world and the pressing need of organized progress at home. . . . In our world problems, we must either shut our eyes, sell our newly built merchant marine to more far-seeing foreign powers, crush utterly by embargo and harassing legislation our foreign trade, close our ports, build an impregnable wall of costly armaments and live, as the Orient used to live, a hermit nation, dreaming of the past; or, we must open our eyes and see that modern civilization has become so complex and the lives of civilized men so interwoven with the lives of other men in other countries as to make it impossible to be in this world and not of it. . . . As for our home problem, we have been awakened by this war into a startling realization of the archaic shortcomings of our governmental machinery and of the need for the kind of reorganization which only a clear-thinking business man, experienced in the technicalities of governmental procedure, can carry out. Such a man [Cox] we have." He declared again for the League of Nations. "The League will not die," he said. "An idea does not die which meets the call of the hearts of our mothers. . . . War may be 'declared;' peace cannot. It must be established by mutual consent. . . ." He made oblique reference to a much-quoted speech Harding had given in Boston in mid-May, a speech proclaiming that "America's present need is not heroics but healing; not nostrums but normalcy; not revolution but restoration; . . . not surgery but serenity." Said Roosevelt: "Some people have been saying of late: 'We are tired of progress, we want to go back to where we were before; to go about our own business; to restore "normal" conditions.' They are wrong. This is not the wish of America. We can never go back. The 'good old days' are gone past forever; we have no regrets. For our eyes are trained ahead—forward to better new days. . . . We cannot anchor our ship of state in this world tempest, nor can we return to the placid harbor of long years ago. We must go forward or flounder." Woman's suffrage had just become, by constitutional amendment, the law of the land; in 1920, women would vote for the first time in a national election; and the candidate, of course, made reference to this. ". . . the women of this nation . . . will throw their weight into the scale of progress and will be unbound by partisan prejudices and a too-narrow outlook on national problems." [19]

Two days later, as Eleanor, James, and Anna returned with his

mother to Campobello, Roosevelt set out on his formal campaign. Stephen Early would later complain to Harold Ickes that the Roosevelt of
1920 had a "playboy" approach to life, that he did not take his campaign seriously enough, treating it as though it were all a great lark; but
the campaign statistics and the substantial quality of his speeches and
quoted interviews seem to belie this. Between August 11 and election
day he traveled incessantly. In two long speaking tours of the Midwest
and West, plus a two-week tour of New England and upstate New York,
he appeared in virtually every state outside the South, delivered upwards of a thousand set speeches and innumerable impromptu talks,
and met personally with warmth and charm many hundreds of locally
important, as well as state and nationally important, Democrats. As
promised, he made the League, concerning which Harding was notably
vague and evasive, a central theme of most of his speeches. When Republican Elihu Root sought to clarify the issue by declaring that the
Covenant's Article X was the crux of the matter—Cox would accept it;
Harding would not—Roosevelt made trenchant reply: "Mr. Root
knows that the question of force of arms would not be raised unless . . .
other measures . . . had first wholly failed. In other words, force of
arms . . . would only be recommended in case of a threatened world-
conflagration such as that through which we have just passed. Every
sane man knows that in case of another world war America would be
drawn in . . . whether we were in the League or not." But he stressed
efficient government as well and took issue with Calvin Coolidge when
the latter seemed to claim that the legislative rather than the executive
branch of government was responsible for American progress. "As I recall history," he said, "most of our great deeds have been brought about
by Executive Leaders, by the Presidents who were not tools of Congress
but were true leaders of the Nation. . . ." He also stressed, now and
again, in ways most future historians would deem deplorable, the
"Americanism" of the superpatriots of that year. Thus, when he spoke
at Centralia, Washington, where an unprovoked attack by American
Legionnaires upon IWW headquarters a year before had resulted in
fatal battle, he described his visit as a "pilgrimage to the . . . graves of
the martyred" Legionnaires who "here gave their lives in the sacred
cause of Americanism" and said that their death "was not in vain for it
aroused the patriotic people of the Great Nation to the task of ridding
this land of the alien anarchist, the criminal syndicalist and all similar
un-Americans." He was a highly effective campaigner, was now an excellent public speaker (who had fumbled so in 1910), "with a tenor
note" in his voice "which rings—sings, one is tempted to say—in key
with" an intangible but "utterly charming . . . quality," as one enthusi-

astic reporter put it.[20] His physical presence was described even by political opponents as "magnificent," "superb," and by the afore-quoted reporter as "the figure of an idealized college football player, almost the poster type. . . ." He was so effective, in fact, that the Republicans soon sent Theodore Roosevelt, Jr., to dog his steps through the West, denouncing and disowning him. ("He is a maverick," said TR, Jr., at Sheridan, Wyoming, in a statement that did his distant cousin no harm. "He does not have the brand of our family.")[21]

He made one serious blunder. At Butte, Montana, on his first swing through the West, he endeavored to answer "realistically" the charge that in the League of Nations Assembly the United States would have a single vote whereas the British Empire would have six. Actually, he said, the United States would have a dozen votes in the Assembly, for "does anyone suppose that the votes of Cuba, Haiti, San Domingo, Panama, Nicaragua, and of the other Central American States would be cast differently from the vote of the United States?" He went on to say, according to an Associated Press dispatch: "I have something to do with the running of a couple of little Republics. Until last week, I had two of these votes in my pocket. Now Secretary Daniels has them. One of them was Haiti. I know, for I wrote Haiti's Constitution myself, and if I do say it, I think it was a pretty good little Constitution." [22] Obviously he, as he spoke his utter falsehood, was unaware of the series of exposé articles on American imperialism in Haiti and Santo Domingo which the *Nation* was publishing that summer*—but others were aware of them. Roosevelt soon found himself denounced, not only in the liberal press, but also by the Republican Presidential nominee. (Said Harding in mid-September: "Practically all we know is that thousands of native Haitians have been killed by American Marines, and that many of our own gallant men have sacrificed their lives at the behest of an Executive department in order to establish laws drafted by the Assistant Secretary of the Navy, to secure a vote in the League. . . .") He was forced to fall back on the lame defense, which no one believed and which was in fact untrue, that he had been misquoted. The readers of the liberal press, however, were a tiny minority of the voters; the blacks whom Roosevelt's statement would outrage were, for the most part, Republican where they voted at all; and so the brief furor which his foolish boast provoked did, probably, no important harm to his cause at the polls.

Eleanor boarded the special campaign car for her husband's second Western tour—the first campaign tour she had ever been on. Louis Howe was then with the party, too, and he undertook, during the in-

* See pages 440–41.

credibly crowded four weeks of travel (they went as far west as Colorado), to overcome Eleanor's felt disapproval of him and to educate her in the intricacies of politics and in "the standards and ethics" of newspaper reporting. She found herself beginning to like him.

III

Dark clouds were gathered over Hyde Park on Tuesday, November 2, 1920, and from them fell a cold rain as Franklin Delano Roosevelt, brisk and smiling, seemingly unfatigued by the long ordeal of his campaign, waved cheerily to the small crowd gathered at the village Town Hall, then entered the polling place to cast his ballot for Cox and himself. Rain continued to fall—the evergreens were black with it, the naked boughs of elms were darkly silvered by it, the far shore of the great river was hidden behind misty curtains of it—as he came back to his mother's house and, still wearing a smile for all to see, went in to await in warm physical comfort the election returns.

He expected defeat—had deemed it overwhelmingly probable months before the nominating conventions were held. Only rarely and briefly amid his strenuous campaigning had he believed he glimpsed the possibility of a different outcome. Hence, the actual emergent fact of defeat came to him as no surprise. The proportions of it did, however; they were unexpectedly huge. Harding and Coolidge were elected by 61 percent of the popular vote (16,152,200 to 9,147,353), carrying thirty-seven states and gaining an electoral college triumph of 404 to 127. Not since James Monroe's defeat of John Quincy Adams precisely a century before had any Presidential candidate scored so lopsided an electoral triumph. Even more disastrous, viewed from Hyde Park, were the results in New York State. To many an observer it appeared at the moment that Roosevelt's home base, on which he must build his political future, had been shattered beyond repair, for his party had won not a single state office and carried not a single county. Harding-Coolidge had garnered twice the vote of Cox-Roosevelt, and a large majority of those voting for the first time had gone Republican. Obviously this was not merely a lost election for the Democrats; it was an expression of popular revulsion against the administration, its policies and party candidates, so massive as to constitute a contemptuous repudiation.

Yet to none around him did Franklin Roosevelt give the slightest sign of dismay or even of the temporary depression that would normally follow so great an expenditure of energy in a lost cause. Indeed, it was his mother's impression, recorded in her diary, that he was "rather relieved not to be elected Vice-President," and his wife remembered that the "overwhelming defeat . . . was accepted very philosophically by my husband, who had been completely prepared for the result." In apparently high good humor on the morrow of election day he wired his congratulations to Calvin Coolidge, simultaneously issuing the traditional statement of a defeated candidate calling upon all Americans, of whatever party, to unite in support of the new administration.[23] And in personal letters written in the immediately following days he asserted that he had no regrets about either the conduct of the Democratic campaign ("It seems to me that everything possible was done . . .") or the decision to make the League of Nations the campaign's central issue ("no other [course] would have been either honorable or successful").[24]

Actually he was already beginning to doubt that the League, though the central theme of his and Cox's speeches, had been the decisive issue so far as the voters were concerned. Ultimately he would become convinced that it was not. Even while the campaign was under way, he had been informed by local newspapers and politicians that most voters had but the vaguest notion of what the League Covenant meant and hence of what the United States would lose or gain by formally subscribing to it; they were neither for nor against it in itself. They could have no clear idea, either, of where Warren Harding stood on the matter, for the Republican candidate and party had deliberately blurred the issue, sometimes seeming to favor League membership (or membership in *a* league), sometimes to oppose it. For instance, when Harding in a Des Moines speech implied that he was opposed to the League, his party managers pointed to a statement issued by some thirty-odd of the most prominent Republicans, including Herbert Hoover, saying that they strongly favored the League and, as if for that very reason, would vote for Harding. What the voters were against, then, was not the League or the Democratic nominees who espoused it but, instead, Woodrow Wilson the man ("He hasn't a friend," wrote Steve Early to Louis Howe from South Dakota[25]) and Wilsonianism as a political creed and attitude.

For the President—broken, partially paralyzed, soon to die—the election outcome was a final personal tragedy. He had convinced himself that the Senate's repudiation of the League had been wholly the work of petty-minded malicious politicians who would themselves be repudiated, as he and his cause were vindicated, when the people had their chance at the polls. The ears of his mind were deafened, the eyes of his mind were blinded by his memory of the vast throngs who had cheered him, who had hailed him almost as the New Messiah on both sides of the Atlantic only a year and a half before. "Daniels, you haven't enough faith in the people!" he had flared out angrily when his Secretary of the Navy, during the campaign, had predicted that "of course" Cox would lose. On election day itself, when one of those at the White House Cabinet meeting confessed a fear of Democratic defeat, the stricken President had said confidently, "You need not worry. The American people will not . . . elect Harding. A great moral issue is involved. The people can and will see it." [26] Hence the debacle came to him as a shock that virtually destroyed his will to live. He was made at last aware of his terrible isolation from his countrymen and from the turning stream of current history, of his utter loneliness at the edge of the grave of his great dream. He refused all public comment. In private he spoke bitter words. The American people, he said, had "repudiated a fruitful leadership for a barren independence" and had turned away from their historical and moral obligations. Soon, he grimly predicted, "we will see the tragedy of it all." Of Harding personally he spoke with weary contempt: "How can he lead when he doesn't know where he is going?" [27]

Franklin Roosevelt's private comments were very different in tone. He spoke of Harding's riding to victory on the "tidal flow of discontent and destructive criticism" that was inevitable following a great war. "Every war brings after it a period of materialism and conservatism," he wrote philosophically; "people tire quickly of ideals. . . ." The defeat, therefore, however regrettable, was not disgraceful. Nor was it proper cause for despair. He himself, he declared, was "not the least bit downhearted." Even the vast proportions of the opposition's triumph had, as spectacle, a bright side, in his view. "As long as the other people were going to win I am glad they have such a clear majority," he said. "The whole responsibility will be theirs. . . ." [28]

Nor was this outward show of sunny disposition, amid the dreariest of weather, merely a façade behind which lurked a damp, drizzly November in the soul. He had entered the contest knowing that he had personally little to lose and much to gain from it, both as a political figure and in terms of private income-producing prestige, regardless of the outcome.* What counted for him was the quality of the effort he had made, the manner and substance of his campaign inseparably joined with his personality. These, impressed upon the collective memory of the electorate, or of leading opinion-makers, would remain a latent political force to be activated at some future date. And from this point of view, looking

---

* During the campaign, he had indicated his determination to change the character of the Vice Presidency, should he win it. On September 18, 1920, he had written a friend: "The old idea about the vice-presidency is going to be knocked into a cocked hat this time if our ticket is elected . . . ; four years from now the vice-presidency is going to be a highly respected and live-wire office." [29]

back over the last crowded months, he was gratified by what he saw. He had made only one blunder that was at all serious; he could reasonably expect it to be forgotten. Meanwhile, it was certain that he who had been a second- or third-echelon official in what had become a decidedly unpopular administration, he whose major asset so far as national politics were concerned had been a name made famous by another, was now a national political figure in his own right, possessing potent political allies in every corner of the land. This conviction was strengthened in his mind by the numerous letters he received (and promptly answered) during the following weeks from politicians of the West and Midwest and South, as well as of the East, who expressed a warm liking and admiration of him personally. The energies he had so lavishly expended had bought for him intangible but precious commodities that were bound to appreciate in value, provided he carefully maintained and prudently handled them.

He had also gained a highly tangible asset—namely, a large file of yellow cards whose political value, great to him right now, would also appreciate vastly as he kept it up to date and added to it through the years. Louis Wehle had said to him in January, 1920, that if he built "methodically" upon the acquaintanceship he would make through a Vice Presidential campaign, he would "come to have such a personal following in the . . . party that it would probably lead . . . eventually to the Presidency." He and Louis Howe had acted on this suggestion. They had jotted down on index cards the names, addresses, occupations, connections, and in many cases the unique personal characteristics of the many hundreds of men he had met during his travels. This information would facilitate a vast and politically rewarding personal correspondence in the years ahead.[30]

He confessed, in that hour of overwhelming conservative triumph, to but a single fear. It was, as he wrote a friend, "that the old reactionary bunch will so control things that many Liberals will turn Radicals. . . ." To friends in Europe he wrote of his "hope" that the Republican administration would not prove to be "so tremendously reactionary as to fan the flames of Radicalism."[31] The statements were determined by, and revealed, his deepest political instincts and intuitions. By temperament, as well as conviction, he was committed to the tactics of moderation and tolerance and compromise within an overall strategy of the golden mean or middle way. His tacit assumption was that a democratic society generally demands as the price of its survival the acceptance of halfway measures and imperfect solutions and that its survival is an absolute value well worth the sacrifice of relative ones. Hence his abhorrence of extremism, whether of left or right. It was a concomitant of his essential conservatism, however, that his abhorrence was imperfectly balanced between its opposing objects. Communist revolution continued in Russia. It was echoed by the continuing Red Scare in the United States to which he was by no means wholly immune. Hence, though he deplored right-wing extremism, he did not fear it as much as he did the extreme left, even in a year when blind insensate reaction posed by far the greater immediate threat. Indeed, his chief stated fear of the extreme right was that its excesses might strengthen the far left.

But his fear was outweighed by optimistic hope. He did not seriously doubt the brightness of the ultimate future for him and for the country.

This was one of the times in his life when, external props collapsing around him, he was inwardly sustained by his serene faith in a beneficent Providence working through history, a Providence which shone with a special radiance upon him personally as it heaped and drew the great tides of event. For there was a rhythm to the Providential history of his conception, a rhythm like the treacherous sea off Campobello, ebbing and flowing in alternation, requiring of him who would sail upon it an accurate discernment not only of its tidal movements but also of the rocks, the shoals of time around which it swirled. The tide now ebbed for such as he. He was as one stranded upon a barren shore. But this was not forever; it was only for a period, if perhaps quite a long one. ("Thank the Lord we are both comparatively youthful!" he wrote Steve Early shortly before Christmas that year. To Cox he indicated that the Democrats, in his opinion, might not again win the White House until there was a serious economic depression.[32]) As certain as moonrise would come a turning of the tide, bringing again a surge of waters whereby those now cast down upon dry sands could be raised up, if only they were ready for such elevation, were prepared with the right craft in the right positions.

He himself intended to be so.

Meanwhile, after a decade in public office at meager salaries and with five children to educate in expensive schools, he must substantially increase his private income.

In January, 1921, he would assume his regular duties as partner in the New York City law firm of Emmet, Marvin & Roosevelt, the firm he had arranged to form with his friends Langdon Marvin and Grenville T. Emmet in the spring of 1920. He looked forward to this with scant enthusiasm; his liking for the law as a profession had not increased in the years since he had last engaged in active practice, and it seemed evident that the new firm's business would consist mostly of wills, estates, private trusts, "all of which," as he later confessed to his partners, "bore me to death." [33] He was much more interested in the position he had accepted as vice-president in charge of the New York City office of the Fidelity and Deposit Company of Maryland—a position whose far from onerous duties he would also enter upon in January.

This company, one of the largest surety bonding concerns in the nation, was headed by Van Lear Black, a millionaire Baltimore financier and sportsman who shared with Roosevelt several common interests and personality traits. Like Roosevelt, he was a fervent Democrat, an enthusiastic yachtsman, a devotee of the strenuous life in general, and had a controlled taste for the dramatic and venturesome in both his business and recreational activities. He was persuaded—he easily persuaded his fellow company directors—that the Roosevelt name and personality, just in themselves, would constitute a valuable asset for their firm, and to this asset were added Roosevelt's membership in the highest society, his contacts with labor unions, business leaders, and government officials (especially valuable might be his contacts with New York State's Banking Department), and his demonstrated abilities as an effective, if often unorthodox, administrator.

As for Roosevelt, he was more than satisfied with the vice-presidential salary of $25,000 per annum, which, though smaller than some that had been offered him, was by several times the largest he had ever received and required of him in return nothing that would jeopardize his present or future political standing. Indeed, it was understood if not formally agreed between him and Black that his company duties would not be so demanding as to prevent his active participation in party politics and in the kind of civic affairs that would add prestige and authority to his name. After all, it was in large part the use of his name that Fidelity and Deposit was buying.

Between election day and January the weeks were filled by him in typically strenuous fashion—and it was during this period that he formed a close working relationship with a remarkably charming, tactful, efficient, and attractive young woman who would remain among the most important members of his "official family" for more than two decades. Her name was Marguerite LeHand. Everyone called her Missy. She was slender, delicate-appearing, fair-complexioned, with large and unusually beautiful blue eyes, and these qualities, in addition to her competence as a stenographer, recommended her highly to Charles McCarthy when he was secretary of the Emergency Fleet Corporation. She became his personal secretary, going with him into the office of the Secretary of the Navy when he transferred there and accompanying him also to the Democratic National Committee headquarters in New York when he, at Roosevelt's request, became manager of the Vice Presidential campaign in 1920. She and Eleanor Roosevelt met at the headquarters. They became warm friends. And at a dinner which Franklin and Eleanor gave all the campaign workers soon after election day, the latter asked Missy to come to Hyde Park for "a few weeks" to help Franklin deal with the vast piles of correspondence and other paper work that had accumulated there. She worked so well with him that he asked her to stay on as his personal secretary, and after some hesitation (she had to be assured that he would not be "merely" a lawyer; the legal profession seemed as boring to her as it did to him) she accepted.[34]

He had, during these weeks, numerous business conferences in New York and Washington, including one in the latter city which shocked some of his ex-colleagues in the Navy Department by its seeming attempt to use his former official position for private business advantage. (He himself did not realize that this interpretation might be placed on his action when he went to Daniels on behalf of the New England Oil Corporation which, as Daniels noted in his diary, wanted the Navy Department "to take bonds on secured mortgage and release our first mortgage." Daniels sent him to Gordon Woodbury, Roosevelt's successor as Assistant Secretary, and Woodbury hurt and angered him by treating his request with cold curtness. ". . . I really think that Woodbury person is either crooked or pin-headed!" he wrote Eleanor next day.*)[35] He took a brief vacation in late November and early December, going down with his brother-in-law Hall Roosevelt to the Louisiana marshes, where for a few days, some of them rainy and chilly, he and Hall shot ducks, as houseboat guests of the Louisiana conservation commissioner. It was not the kind of vacation that would relax a tired body and taut nerves: it involved long train rides (during which he wrote letters) with numerous changes and close connections, interspersed with a diligent cultivation of local political contacts. He was back in Washington for more conferences in mid-December; he was in Hyde Park with his mother, wife, and children for the Christmas holidays, handling there a good deal of accumulated personal correspondence.

Then began his new life. In the first week of 1921, in a move as expressive of a shift in the center of national force as (in a different field) had been William Dean Howells' move from Boston to New York in the 1880's, the former high government official in Washington became a lawyer and financier on Wall Street, devoting each workday morning to

* Woodbury, of a distinguished New Hampshire family, had edited a newspaper in Manchester and was admired by Daniels for his intelligence and probity. He "held office until the Wilson Administration ended and served with ability, loyalty and devotion," Daniels wrote in his The Wilson Era—Years of War and After (Chapel Hill, N.C., 1946), p. 271.

Fidelity and Deposit and each afternoon to the new law firm. "The two varieties of work seem to dovetail fairly well," he wrote Felix Frankfurter on January 7.[36] The family was established at 47 East Sixty-fifth Street from Monday through Friday of every week, going up Friday evening to Hyde Park for the weekend. Hyde Park continued to be "home."

His move, his change of occupation did not go unpublicized. On the evening of the day of his letter to Frankfurter he was given a large testimonial dinner at Delmonico's, attended by many of the greatest names of business and industry. Edward R. Stettinius of U.S. Steel and Owen D. Young of General Electric were there. So were Adolph S. Ochs of the New York *Times*, Daniel Willard of the Pennsylvania Railroad, and Frank A. Munsey of the Munsey publishing empire, among others. The principal speaker of the occasion was the governor of the Federal Reserve Board, whose thesis, reported in the New York newspapers next day, was that American business had now grown up and assumed the temper, the habits of maturity: there would no longer be wild fluctuations between "orgies of extravagance" and "irrational pessimism," he predicted.

As for Roosevelt himself, he seemed to conform as completely to the standards and values of the Wall Street of that year as he had to those of Groton a quarter century before. Already he had publicly delivered himself of thoroughly orthodox opinions concerning the abrupt and steep price decline which had begun in the latter half of 1920 and continued into 1921, causing many business bankruptcies, farm mortgage foreclosures, and millions of unemployed. Roosevelt was unperturbed. Deflation, he indicated, was an inevitable, but temporary, phenomenon. To a newspaper reporter he said, "It requires more than a few months for the vast industry and commerce of this country to resume prices which compare favorably with the pre-war values. The entire cycle of revision must be accomplished before business will again function normally." [37] Certainly none among his business colleagues could take exception to this statement, it being their own standard reply to the complaints of the dispossessed about the workings of an allegedly "free" market. Obviously this new man on Wall Street was fundamentally sound.

Thus auspiciously was Roosevelt launched upon his career in what had become and would remain for a decade and more the effective center of the governing power of the United States.

Meanwhile, Louis Howe was facing difficult career decisions.
Daniels had kept a place for him in the Navy Department after he re-

signed to join Roosevelt's campaign staff. He had returned to Washington gratefully and was rendering such valuable technical service that Harding's appointee as Secretary of the Navy, Edwin N. Denby, would keep him on for a while to help smooth the way for the new Assistant Secretary. He would still be working, in that capacity, under a Roosevelt: Franklin's successor as Assistant Secretary was none other than Theodore Roosevelt, Jr. Several attractive job offers would come to him. A New York newspaper wanted him as city editor. The New England Oil Corporation wanted him as an executive. And he was forced by his circumstances to consider such offers seriously. His living expenses had greatly increased during his Washington years. His daughter, Mary, was now a junior in Vassar; his eleven-year-old son, Hartley, was in a private school. But in the end, in the month of Harding's inauguration, he would decide (the decision would later seem to have been inevitable) to remain at Roosevelt's side.

At that time, his plan would be to wind up his Navy duties in the summer of 1921, take several weeks of vacation, and in September enter Fidelity and Deposit as the New York vice-president's special assistant.

IV

". . . we are now repeating history." So wrote Franklin Roosevelt to a friend as he prepared his move from the capital to Wall Street.[38]

His obvious reference was to the period of crass, cynical materialism that had followed the Civil War in America—and he would have little reason to change this judgment during the years immediately ahead. After the World War, as after the Civil War, came an accelerated surge toward industrial and financial giantism. Now, as then, came a breakdown of ethical standards in government, an explosion of graft and corruption at every level: the Harding regime would prove a match for Grant's in this respect. Now, as then, special interests organized and conspired to raid the treasury, plunder the public domain, circumvent inhibiting laws, and gain all manner of governmental preference for themselves. And now, as then, it could be stated as a general rule that no private interest regarded as iniquitous any government interference with the free play of economic forces from which it itself profited.

Business interests in general were better organized to promote such self-benefiting interference in 1920 than they had been in 1870; they would become increasingly so as the new decade advanced. Trade associations would be actively encouraged by the federal executive during the twenties, despite their initially dubious legality under the Sherman and Clayton Antitrust laws. (Not until 1925 would the Supreme Court rule them legal, on the ground that they did not overtly engage in production controls and price-fixing.) Franklin Roosevelt was to become a leading figure in one of them. There was the increasingly powerful National Association of Manufacturers, formed in 1895. There was the Chamber of Commerce of the United States, formed in 1912. There was an influential, specifically business press to supplement the mass-circulating newspapers and magazines which, being themselves corporate enterprises, naturally stressed in their columns the attitudes and views and values of the general business community. Through all these devices, with their inherent capacities for rewarding or punishing public servants, formidable pressures could be brought to bear upon a Congress and executive already disposed to regard business and businessmen as the principal, if not the sole, authors of American prosperity. There would be inevitably a plethora of federal policies and legislation of the kind business wanted—as regards taxes, credit, tariffs, special subsidies, and the enfeeblement of regulatory agencies.

No equivalent pressures could be exerted in the 1920's any more than in the 1870's by the two other major segments of the economy—namely, labor and agriculture. None of the great strikes of 1919, with the possible exception of the bituminous coal strike, achieved its objectives. Nor did most of the minor ones. And union membership, totaling something over 5,000,000, or 12 percent, of the total labor force in 1920, would decline almost steadily until, at decade's end, it stood at only 3,400,000, or 7 percent, of the labor force. Major reasons for this were obvious. Government did nothing to encourage union growth; quite the contrary. Employers effectively promoted the "American Plan"—a grandiose name for the old-fashioned open shop—and made wide use of yellow dog contracts, whereby employees, as a condition of their employment, pledged themselves *not* to join a union. The AFL, meanwhile, wedded to the craft union concept and opposed to government interference in labor-management relations, made no real effort to organize the workers of the bourgeoning mass-producing industries. (The assembly-line workers of the automobile industry, for example, remained wholly unorganized.) Hence labor's relative ineffectiveness as economic bargainer or political pressure group.

Equally disadvantaged economically, if not more so, were the nation's farmers. Here, too, the parallel with the post-Civil War period was clear —though, because there was no longer a Western frontier, it was far from exact. In the 1920's, while industrial production was concentrated in fewer and fewer hands, agriculture remained divided among many millions of competing units. While industry was being Taylorized, with machines increasingly replacing muscle power in every aspect of production, agriculture continued to rely primarily on horse and human muscle. And though the fact was not yet generally recognized, it was impossible for agricultural production to begin to approach the mechanized efficiency of industry so long as its basic unit was the traditional family-sized farm. This unit was much too small; of itself alone it could neither pay the initial costs nor make profitable use of the farm machinery that was beginning to come on the market. Combinations of acreages similar to combinations of industrial plant would be required—especially since, unlike manufacturing, agriculture was at the mercy of uncontrollable weather factors.

The immediate and long-to-be-continued economic problem for agriculture, however, was not under- but overproduction. During the war, farmers—deemed so essential to the war effort on the home front that they were exempt from military draft—were encouraged by government to expand greatly their crop acreages. Land formerly in grass was plowed and planted. Much of the high plains, for example—a land of little rain, flat and treeless, and formerly an open range—was transformed into a vast wheat field. To finance this expansion, many a farmer had gone recklessly into debt and was therefore peculiarly vulnerable to the collapse of the foreign market, which immediately followed the war; he began the new decade in acute economic depression; and the farm prices which plunged downward in 1919 and 1920 were destined never to rise, during the coming decade, to anywhere near parity (meaning a just relationship between agricultural and other prices).

Agriculture's sad plight, consequent upon having to buy in a managed market while selling in a free one, would be revealed in census figures at the decade's end. Farm acreage would increase by more than 3 percent in the 1920's; total agricultural production would markedly increase. Yet the market value of all farm products would fall from $21.4 billion in 1919 to well under $12 billion ten years later—this during the years of widely publicized prosperity! Meanwhile, there would be significant increases in farm mortgages and tenancy. The former would rise from 37.2 percent of all farms to 42 percent, the latter from 38.2 percent to 42.4 percent. And as a sign and portent of the developing impact of technology upon the last major stronghold of truly competitive individualism, there would be during the 1920's, for the first time in history (despite the increase in total acreage), an actual decrease in the number of farms. There would be 2.5 percent fewer of them in 1930 than in 1920.

The perennial "farm problem" would become a major item on the country's political agenda throughout the decade, placed and kept there by approximately a score of Senators and perhaps twice that many Representatives, nearly all from the Midwest and South. They constituted the so-called Farm Bloc and would prove effective in forcing through Congress much legislation presumably beneficial to their agricultural constituency. But every legislative attempt to get at the root cause of the farmer's distress—his inability to exercise any control over the prices of his produce either through a curtailment of supply or an expansion of demand—would be frustrated by the Farm Bloc's inability to muster the Congressional strength necessary to override Presidential vetoes.

Gradually, reluctantly, bitterly the depression-ridden farmer was forced to recognize that America was no longer a predominantly rural community with agriculture its chief economic activity and that the economic strength of agriculture relative to business and industry steadily waned.

The trend was already clearly visible in the census figures for 1920.

Ten years before, a majority of Americans had lived on farms or in rural communities of fewer than 2,500 inhabitants, the latter dependent for livelihood on agriculture. Now, for the first time in history, more than half the national population lived in towns of 2,500 or more—and the movement from country to city, accelerated during the war, grew apace. In 1910 there had been forty-nine cities with populations of 100,000 or more; in 1920 there were sixty-seven; in 1930 there would be ninety-six, and the number of people living in them would approach half the total population. Moreover, as a general rule, the larger the city, the faster its growth if one took into consideration, as 1920's census takers had not yet begun to do, its ever more extensive suburbs. This was reflective of the expansion and concentration of mass-productive manufacturing whose goods had a gross value nearly three times that of agriculture's in 1920 and which, with associated "mechanical industries," employed fifty-four persons for every forty-six engaged in agriculture.

V

But the actual physical shift of population from country to city and of occupation from agricultural to industrial and commercial pursuits was not accompanied by an equivalent shift in cultural values and outlook. These last remained predominantly rural for the country as a whole.

A principal reason was that millions born and reared on farms or in villages remote from urban centers carried with them into the cities the rural pieties instilled in them during their formative years. Their bodies thronged the city pavements. City dust and smoke stung their eyes.

Their ears were constantly assailed by city noise, their minds by ugly, vivid, socially dangerous contrasts between the lives of the very rich (who were few) and the very poor (who were many). Their working days, whether prosperous or impecunious, were spent in narrow places, enclosed by walls, floors, ceilings. Yet the dwelling place of their essential thought and feeling was still an America of open fields and hard but healthful labor under skies unstained by factory smoke; an America of country schools with their spelling bees and country stores with their cracker-barrel philosophers; an America of quiet tree-shaded streets along which all the houses were set in grassy yards and had front porches on which people sat in swings and rocking chairs through the long summer evenings, their murmurous talk and laughter mingling with insect sounds; a stable America where human lives could remain rooted from birth to death in a single landscape over which changes crept slowly enough to permit a painless adjustment to them; an America characterized by intimate neighborliness, as well as by self-defining spaces and solitudes, sustained by strong, simple, unquestioned religious faiths and codes of ethics; an America in which "nobody was rich, nobody poor" (as Mark Sullivan remembered his boyhood Pennsylvania) and in which (as Albert Shaw remembered his boyhood Iowa) there was no need for any public welfare program because "every neighborhood could . . . take care of any family or individual who through illness or other misfortune needed assistance";[39] an America so safely isolated by wide oceans from Europe and Asia that it was able freely to choose whether or not to participate in world affairs and generally wisely chose not to. This, for them, remained the only *real* America, the source and vital repository of all genuinely American virtues and freedoms, the essential body politic across which the city spread as a cancerous growth, corrupt and corrupting, wicked and deathly. ("It is when I go to the city that I am afraid for America," said Ray Stannard Baker, friend and authorized biographer of Woodrow Wilson, who perforce spent much time in cities. "Thousands and thousands of faces with no light in them!" [40]) And so their lives became ironical—literally, increasingly. Contradictions, ambiguities, ambivalences would grow in them year by year as the gap widened between the world they actually lived in and the world they were emotionally committed to and, out of their commitment, strove to believe to be true. Thus, though the pasty-faced raucous newsboy of the pavements was daily before their eyes, they never saw him as typically American; they saw instead the barefoot boy with cheek of tan who whistled along a country lane—such a lad as they might not have so much as caught a glimpse of, actually, in a dozen years.

They refused to accept the fact that Currier and Ives were dead.

It was indeed a resistance to this sad news on their part as well as on the part of millions who yet remained in country places—it was the stubborn nostalgic effort to preserve a beloved rural organic America against the onslaught of a hated urbanized inorganic one—which had generated much of the motive force behind the Populism and Progressivism that had fused in the formation of Wilson's New Freedom. The impulse toward trust-busting had had in it a vague but strong longing for a simpler age when manufacturing was yet in the skilled hands of individual cobblers, cabinetmakers, ironmongers, coopers, gunsmiths, blacksmiths, and the like. The proclaimed impulse toward conservation was the felt need to preserve against urban-industrial ruin the open landscapes of the past—the natural world of field and pasture and wood, the beauties and solitudes of yet-virgin lands. Threading through the declarations of war on big-city bossism was a yearning toward the pure democracy of the old-time farming community and country town where every governmental transaction was openly discussed in town meeting and every governmental officer could be held directly accountable for his acts. Certainly the impulse behind the temperance crusade had been and yet remained essentially a rural one—prohibition was an attempt not only to preserve and protect the purity of country life against urban wickedness, but also to force the city into country purity —and it was but another of the abundant ironies of American history that this crusade should culminate in an Eighteenth Amendment which went into effect (January 17, 1920) in the very year when, for the first time, the national census showed a majority of Americans no longer living on farms or in villages but in towns and cities.

Ironical, too, was the fact that amid the confusions and disillusionments following hard upon the war, much of what had been the motive force behind Populism and Progressivism—this nostalgia for a rural America, this commitment to Jeffersonian democracy—was channeled into the political party most dominated by an urbanized and urbanizing big business. When Warren G. Harding asserted in his incredible prose that what the country needed was "not nostrums but normalcy, . . . not surgery but serenity, . . . not submergence in internationality but sustainment in triumphant nationality," his primary appeal was to a widespread longing to "return" to a rural America, isolated from quarrelsome foreigners, genuinely individualistic, pious and virtuous in the ways traditional for those who work on and with the soil. When he, a small-town newspaperman, campaigned from his front porch in his Ohio town, he seemed the kindly patriarchal embodiment of the old America. And this impression, along with its nostalgic appeal, was reinforced by the choice for his running mate of Calvin Coolidge, the archetypical taciturn Yankee, born and reared in a Vermont crossroads village approximately as remote from the big city and its ways as one could get. No comparable appeal could be made by Cox and Roosevelt, either in their persons or in the issues on which they had been forced by Wilsonian circumstance to campaign.

And in this last was irony compounded to the extent that Franklin Roosevelt personally—though he had none of the obvious typicalities of the American farmer or of the small-town professional or businessman —was as strongly biased in favor of country and small-town life, as strongly averse to what seemed to him the corrupting antivital influence of great cities, as any man prominent in national politics. He retained in that year many of the attitudes of the typical Progressive Democrat. He was more tolerant of economic bigness than some, but was still largely Jeffersonian in outlook and more inclined than most to translate his country bias into state and national policy. He had revealed as much during his service in the State Senate, where he fought Tammany, promoted conservation, and vigorously sponsored advanced legislation to aid agriculture. He continued to love country living. Only out of felt necessity, in service of his ambition, was he now become a Wall Street lawyer and executive, residing in Manhattan. His true home remained Hyde Park, where he spent every possible weekend and holiday, and in public speech he sounded and reiterated over and over again a note of lyric feeling for trees and fields, along with the fear he had of an overly urbanized America.

This fear was underlined in a speech he made, June 20, 1921, on "The Danger of Big Cities" in Lenox, Massachusetts. Addressing the Berkshire Bankers' Association, he deplored the finding of 1920's census that more than half of all Americans now lived in cities. The trend must be halted, he said. The "growth of cities while the country population stands still will eventually bring disaster to the United States." The national health requires a "nice balance" between industry and agriculture. And to this end he advocated a program of agricultural aid. Better farm-to-market roads were needed, better rural schools, and improved marketing systems (here he reiterated a favorite theme of his state senatorial days) whereby the farmer would retain some of the profits now going to middlemen. But Jeffersonian in mood, he did not advocate state or federal action. The effort should be made by local communities. "Legislation will not do it," he asserted in phrases more pleasing to his banker audience than consistent with his earlier statements of needs and aims; "paternalism in Washington or Boston or Albany will give no panacea. We have more than enough laws—what we need is action." [41]

*   *   *

A concomitant of urbanization, soon to be much influenced by the multiplication of automobiles, was a revolution of morals and manners that was to a considerable degree identical with a revolt of youth against their elders.

Parents born and reared in country places bore children, wholly reared in towns and cities, whose tastes, attitudes, beliefs, and standards of conduct arose not out of their parents' rural conditioning and nostalgic commitments, but out of their own very different experience—an experience that inclined them toward the traditional city view of farmers and villagers as rubes, hayseeds, country bumpkins. Nor were the young of town and city the only young who, if they did not challenge the old ways, at least questioned them. Country-bred youths called into the Army, sent to camp by the million and to France by the 100,000, returned to their homes ill disposed to accept uncritically all the values, the mores of their upbringing. A popular song of the war years expressed a very real parental fear when it asked, "How are you going to keep them down on the farm after they've seen Paree?"—and in 1919 and '20 this fear, often enough, was being realized. For though the farm-bred soldier might return to the plow, he was likely to do so with a difference of outlook that contained the seeds of rebellion, his present world seeming to him harshly limited in its possibilities compared with the larger, freer, far more various one of which he had had a taste abroad.

The watchword of this as of all revolutions was "freedom," the goal an emancipation from the past, a release of "inhibitions" (then a new psychological term), a repudiation of "hypocrisy" in every realm of human conduct. And the revolution most shocked, even terrified the older generation in its dealings with the "problem" of sex. Suddenly, after long cloakage in silence and darkness, the pursuit of sexual pleasure was everywhere in open evidence. New fashions of dress for women (skirt hems rose; necklines plunged downward; stockings were rolled sometimes below the knee) seemed designed to attract the sexual attentions of men. Cosmetics (rouged lips, rouged cheeks, eye shadow) were now quite generally used as only harlots had used them before the war. The new dances had almost the appearance of sexual intercourse performed in public: boys and sparsely clad girls (they now refused to wear corsets; they would not risk being dubbed "Old Ironsides" by their partners) clung to each other cheek to cheek and loin to loin as they moved in time to barbaric African rhythms. All of which provoked public cries of outrage from religious leaders, business leaders, college presidents, conservative politicians, and leaders of the highest society. Among the latter was Mrs. James "Rosy" Roosevelt, Franklin's half-sister-in-law, who joined with a distinguished group of Episcopal churchwomen in New York (Mrs. J. Pierpont Morgan, Mrs. Borden Harriman, Mrs. E. H. Harriman, and others) to propose an organization that would actively oppose "improper ways of dancing" and an "excess of nudity" in female attire.[42]

The sexual revolution had its rationale, of course—a "scientific" justification that was, if anything, more shocking to most of the older generation than were the revolutionary acts themselves. Sigmund Freud provided it. He had been publishing books and articles on psychoanalysis for more than twenty years, but it was only now, in the disillusioning aftermath of the war, that his name (often mispronounced to rhyme with "lewd") was suddenly on everyone's lips. Freud was said to hold that the sexual realm was basic to all others of human experience in that it contained virtually the sum total of human motivation; that all creative energy was in essence sexual; that all mental illness had sexual "repression" as root cause; that only through a new liberty of speech and action as regards sex could a genuinely healthy people, a genuinely sane society, be attained.

Two novels published in 1920 epitomized the new cultural mood and, by so doing, further stimulated that mood's development, helping set the tone for a whole decade. One was Sinclair Lewis' *Main Street.* It was not without fictional antecedents. Ed Howe's *The Story of a Country Town* (written in the 1880's), Hamlin Garland's *Middle Border* autobiographies, Edgar Lee Masters' *Spoon River Anthology,* Sherwood Anderson's *Winesburg, Ohio*—all these had portrayed farm and village life as bleak, stultifying, often corrupt, in flat contradiction of the popular view of it as inherently healthful, happy, virtuous. But the earlier books had not been conceived as outright attacks on country values and ways of life. *Main Street* was. It openly sneered at Gopher Prairie where "dullness is made God," it made fun of the good citizens of the village, and it provoked a storm of controversy. The other novel was F. Scott Fitzgerald's *This Side of Paradise,* which, though its total sale was less than 10 percent of *Main Street*'s, was at least equally influential of manners and morals. In it and the books he wrote in the immediately following years, Fitzgerald created the consciousness or self-consciousness of a whole generation of "flappers" (*Flappers and Philosophers,* 1920) and "sad young men" (*All the Sad Young Men,* 1926) who were both "beautiful and damned" (*The Beautiful and Damned,* 1922) as—disillusioned, flippant, defiantly gay, sentimentally cynical, or cynically sentimental— they roamed the wastelands of the "jazz age" (*Tales of the Jazz Age,* 1922). His first novel was most disturbing to the older generation in its revelation that "petting parties" were now a common indoor (or parked car) sport among the young, who were, as one feminine character said, "hipped on Freud and all that" and whose night life and "talking [of theretofore forbidden subjects] . . . with a furtive excitement" seemed even to Amory Blaine, Fitzgerald's protagonist, to represent "a real moral let-down."

But if this rebellion of youth shocked and outraged the older generation, it also aroused a grudging admiration in many and even, in not a few, an open approval of those parts of it which did strip away cowardly Victorian hypocrisies and substitute for them candor, frankness, honesty, courage. Representative members of the older generation—themselves sadly, if secretly, disillusioned, their attitudes rendered ambivalent and ambiguous—were weakened from within as they faced the youth revolt. Thus, the closing scene of Sinclair Lewis' *Babbitt* (1922) wherein Zenith's banal real estate operator, the epitome of scared conformism, backs his son, who has just violated the mores, against those who would "try to bully you, and tame you down." Says George F. Babbitt: "Tell 'em to go to the devil! . . . Don't be scared of the family. No, nor all Zenith. Nor of yourself, the way I've been."

To face facts, calling them by their plain unvarnished names, was the loudly proclaimed order of the new day. Millions of average Americans and all the "intelligentsia" (this Russian term was just beginning to gain wide currency in the United States) had grown suspicious of the motives behind elevated words and phrases that Woodrow Wilson and Theodore Roosevelt had habitually, confidently used in public speech—words and phrases like "honor," "high ideals," "moral light," "force of principle," "sound values," "right conduct," or simply "the right" as something to be preserved or achieved. People felt or knew that such words had often been used deliberately to deceive them, especially by the government's war propagandists; they were inclined to insist that from now on, as the price of their belief, all high-sounding words must be defined in terms of the concrete situations that evoked them. This insistence was in line with the general cultural movement whose literary expression was "naturalism" or "realism" in revulsion against "romanticism" and an allegedly sentimental "idealism," and it meant that significant portions of the vocabulary of Progressivism and the New Freedom were lost from the political dialogue.

Franklin Roosevelt adapted himself with seeming ease to the changed cultural climate. He had been substituting "realism" for "idealism" in his support of the League of Nations when he fell into his trouble over the Haitian constitution during the 1920 campaign. And in the spring of 1921 he who had made his initial political reputation as a reformer dropped all reference to "reform" from his public utterances. He advised others to do the same. "The word 'reform' . . . brings visions of pink tea artists who dabbled in politics one day a week for perhaps two months in the year," he said as he warned the National Civic Federation that it would "get off on the wrong foot" if it called its new political committee a "Department of Political Reform." [43]

VI

He was tremendously busy that spring, even feverishly so. He engaged in a bewildering number and variety of activities in addition to his law practice and his duties as Fidelity and Deposit vice-president. He was president of the Boy Scout Foundation of Greater New York, chairman of a fund drive for Lighthouses for the Blind, member of the executive committee of the National Civic Foundation, member of the Board of Overseers of Harvard University (he had been elected in 1917, reputedly the youngest man ever to be so chosen), member of the Near East Relief Committee. He took a leading part in establishing and was chairman of the fund-raising committee for a Woodrow Wilson "Memorial." Simultaneously he led an active social and club life. It was during this period, again possibly in emulation of Cousin Theodore, that he sought to add to his list of prestigious club memberships that of the Century Association of New York.*

Nor did he neglect purely political matters. Through a voluminous and ceaseless correspondence—through conferences, speeches, press interviews—he sought to rebuild the shattered state Democratic organization along the lines of the triumphant Republican organization which Will Hays, who became Postmaster General in Harding's Cabinet, had created in Indiana in just four years. Hence, despite his strong personal bias in favor of country over city, he did all he could to remove from between the two in New York State the vs. that had been in part responsible for the huge majorities (three to one, even five to one) by which the Republicans had carried upstate districts. His whole stress now was on party unity and careful party organization from precinct to state level in preparation for 1922's midterm elections when he, it appeared, might well win his party's nomination for U.S. Senator. Long gone were the days and attitudes of his insurgency. No more did he challenge the sachems of Tammany. Instead, he refused to take part in any alliance

---

* It was certainly not difficult for him to secure nomination to this club. His father had been a member, his half brother Rosy was a member, his Uncle Frederic was among a half dozen Delanos who were or at their death had been members. Franklin Delano Roosevelt was himself duly elected a Centurian in 1922.

against his onetime political enemy, Boss Murphy, even when an at least tacit request for his aid was made by his old upstate political friend William Church Osborn, now joined in opposition to Murphy (such are the complex shifts and reversals of practical politics) by Al Smith. (Roosevelt did, however, and at the same time, support Osborn's bid for chairmanship of the State Committee.) Clearly, if the choice must be between a defeat-assuring schism in New York and a victory-prόducing unity under Boss Murphy's iron rule, his choice would be the latter, but his hopeful aim was to prevent, through compromise, cooperation, and a strict avoidance of confrontations, the necessity for decision between alternatives so distasteful.

His political efforts, his political horizons, were by no means limited to his home state. Having become a national figure, he proposed to remain one, simultaneously using his influence to achieve party unity everywhere in the country. And to this end he made some significant shifts in his stands on national issues, while at the same time carefully avoiding any such flat repudiation or contradiction of his earlier positions as might prevent his return to them.

For instance, it seemed clear that his national reputation as a "big navy" man and fervent advocate of the League could in present circumstances become for him a serious political liability. None could doubt that President Harding played upon the fears and patriotic sentiments of an overwhelming majority of Americans when, at his inauguration on March 4, 1921, he addressed himself to international affairs in his unique rhetoric. "America builded on the foundations laid by the inspired fathers can be party to no permanent military alliance," he said. "Since freedom impelled and independence inspired and nationality exalted, a world supergovernment is contrary to everything we cherish and can have no sanction by our Republic. This is not selfishness, it is sanctity." His evident implication was that the League of Nations was designed to become a "supergovernment." And Franklin Roosevelt may well have taken his own policy cue from Harding's following assertion: "We are ready to associate ourselves with the nations of the world, great and small, for conference, for counsel, to seek the expressed views of world opinion to recommend a way to approximate [sic] disarmament and relieve the crushing burden of military and naval establishments." ("We must strive for normalcy to reach stability," he added.) At any rate, a few weeks later Roosevelt let it be known that, since there was obviously no hope of America's signing the Versailles Treaty with the League Covenant written into it during the present Republican administration, and though he personally continued to favor U.S. entry into the League, he now felt that the best possible policy for us was to seek a separate peace with Germany and follow this with efforts toward international agreements that would reduce "the terrible burden of armaments from which all nations are suffering." He was, he now said, "wholly out of sympathy with this talk about our having the greatest Navy in the world." [44] He proposed instead that the Democratic Party ask President Harding to call a conference of the three greatest naval powers—the United States, Britain, and Japan—for the purpose of halting the hugely expensive naval construction race in which they were involved.

(In the summer of 1921, Harding acted on this suggestion, not as a proposal of the Democratic Party but as one by Republican Senator William E. Borah of Idaho supported by Secretary of State Charles Evans Hughes. On August 11, Hughes issued invitations to Britain, Japan, France, and Italy for a five-power Arms Limitation Conference, which opened in Washington on November 12 and concluded three months later with drafts of two major treaties and five minor ones, all subsequently ratified by the Senate. Of the two major ones, a naval limitations treaty pledged the United States, Britain, and Japan to keep their ratio of capital ships at 5-5-3 for the next fifteen years and not to engage in new capital ship construction, not even for replacements, for the next ten years. The other major treaty was an agreement among the United States, Britain, France, and Japan to respect one another's Pacific possessions and to consult among themselves if any of their Pacific rights were threatened by an outside power. It was to remain in force ten years. Josephus Daniels was among the minority who, at the time, doubted the wisdom of the naval limitations proposal, but Roosevelt thoroughly approved of it.)

His major anxiety, as spring gave way to summer, was the continuing investigation of the Newport scandal that was being conducted by the subcommittee of the Senate Naval Affairs Committee. In mid-February, 1920, early in the hearings, he had appeared before the subcommittee (it was composed of two Republicans, one Democrat) to present with others what he called "a preliminary outline of what the Navy Department knew of the Newport case." He had at that time been promised that before the final report was released, he would be given an opportunity to review the full testimony and to present in open hearing a rebuttal of whatever portions of it were derogatory of himself and the department. But more than a year had passed, and there had been no word to him from the subcommittee's chairman. Then, in mid-July, after Eleanor and the children had been for a week or so at Campobello and he had either joined them there or was on the verge of doing so for a long-needed vacation, he was informed by Howe, who had it from friends in Washington, that the majority report had been filed with the full committee on July 5 and that it contained a scurrilous attack upon himself.[45]

He rushed down to Washington. He arrived on Monday, July 18, a sweltering hot day. He demanded the promised right to see the testimony and be heard in reply to it. His demand was at first flatly refused by the subcommittee majority, who blandly claimed that his earlier testimony had sufficed for the investigation's purposes, but then the two Republican Senators relented to the extent of turning over to him the 6,000 pages of testimony, bound in fifteen volumes, and giving him until eight o'clock that night to prepare an answering statement! Taut with anger, streaming with perspiration in the humid heat, he went to his old office in the Navy Building, where, with the help of Steve Early and Missy LeHand, he studied relevant portions of the testimony and prepared his refutation.

The majority report alleged that the Newport vice investigators had been under Roosevelt's "direct supervision" when some of them engaged in sodomy to obtain evidence against homosexuals and that his actions constituted "a most deplorable, disgraceful and unnatural proceeding." His anger at this became a white-faced fury when, at four o'clock that afternoon, he learned from "the newspaper boys" that "the majority report was in the hands of all the papers for release the next P.M. and that Senator Ball [the subcommittee chairman] had declined to hold it back or amend it in any way." There could no longer be the slightest doubt that the Republicans were out to get him, to smear him out of political life if possible. This of course increased the urgent importance of a well-prepared, well-publicized rebuttal; he and Early continued their feverish labors, whose results were swiftly typed by Missy LeHand. And at eight o'clock, bone-tired from prolonged tension in the smothering heat, he went before the subcommittee with his statement.[46] In it he denied all responsibility for the scandal. "Emphasis was placed by the Newport officers on the need for secrecy . . . ," he said, "and for this reason the squad was placed for purely technical purposes . . . first under Naval Intelligence and later under my office. Their work . . . was at no time supervised by me personally. . . ." As soon as he had learned that some of the squad were using "highly improper and revolting methods in getting evidence," he had issued "orders . . . to stop it," and there was "no charge that any wrong-doing occurred after that." He then switched to the attack. "Throughout their report I accuse them [the two Republican Senators] of deliberate falsification of evidence, of perversion of facts, of misstatements of the record, and of a deliberate attempt to deceive," he said. "This business of using the navy as a football of politics is going to stop. People everywhere are tired of partisan discussion of dead history. . . . I only ask fair play." He then requested an

open hearing before the whole Naval Affairs Committee—though he
knew as he made it that his request would be ignored by the committee's
Republican majority.

Distraught, oppressed by fearful anxieties amid the continuing heat
wave, he remained in Washington for another day and night, awaiting
the newspapers' handling of the whole affair. And the front page of the
New York *Times* for Wednesday, July 20, did nothing to soothe him.
The prominent headline on a story which seemed to him grossly and deliberately unfair said:

LAY NAVY SCANDAL
TO F. D. ROOSEVELT

with the addition in a lower deck of the tantalizing words "Details Are
Unprintable." The press as a whole, however, gave his own statement
and the Democratic Senator's minority report fairly prominent display;
he was assured by his newspaper and political friends that the majority
report was so obviously a partisan smear that it would not be effective;
and by the time he arrived in New York that evening and saw that the
afternoon papers weren't taking up the matter at all his worry was much
reduced. He slept that night at 47 East Sixty-fifth Street—the first good
night's sleep that he had had in several days.

But there was to be no relaxation for him in the days that immediately followed. As he wrote Eleanor, he had to prepare and file with the
whole Naval Affairs Committee "a complete statement in answer to
every paragraph of the Majority Report." He planned to compose it
over the weekend, in Hyde Park. Also, he had found "lots of mail and
work on both desks" which would require him to be "very busy" for
some time to come. In addition to his law and business duties were numerous meetings and consultations in connection with the civic and
charitable organizations of which he was an officer. He was tired and
knew it. He yearned for Campobello. And since he could have only two
weeks there in August, according to plan (Grenville Emmet was in Europe, Langdon Marvin was to begin his vacation in mid-August, so
Roosevelt must then return to New York to man the law office), he resented demands that prevented his immediate departure. Eleanor and
the children had now been joined on the island by the Howes (Louis,
Grace, and son Hartley; daughter Mary was not with them) for what
was planned to be a stay of several weeks at the cottage. "Tell Louis I
expect those boats to be all rigged and ready when I get there," wrote
Roosevelt, "and I am greatly put out not to be there now." [47]

Twice during the next ten days, activities of his were given minor publicity in the newspapers. On July 27 he, as president of the Boy Scout Foundation for the city, went with New York's police commissioner and several other notables to the Scout camp on Lake Kanowahke in the Palisades Interstate Park for a fun-filled, but far from relaxing, day during which, in addition to ceremonial public appearances, he engaged in a good deal of elaborate horseplay with others in his group. A news photograph taken that day showed him in white trousers and dark coat—tall, slim, rigidly erect, his thin face rather grim, the whole somehow expressive of fine-drawn tension—walking with two others of his party at the head of an apparently casual procession, though Scout standard-bearers walked immediately behind him. On August 5, as reported in next morning's New York *Times,* he was a leading participant in a meeting of what was now called the Woodrow Wilson Foundation. (The name had been adopted after the ailing ex-President had written Roosevelt, on the preceding July 4, protesting in jocular fashion the use of the word "Memorial" to describe the fund which Roosevelt was raising. "Memorial" implied that he, Woodrow Wilson, was dead whereas he hoped "in the near future to give frequent evidences" that he was not.[48]) This was evidently Roosevelt's last duty in the city before embarking, at last, upon his vacation.

He did literally embark.

Van Lear Black had brought his 140-foot power yacht, the *Sabalo,* into New York's harbor. Roosevelt was easily persuaded to sail on her to Campobello instead of taking the train, for it meant that he would have fun all the way and would arrive refreshed, relaxed, and clean instead of weary, cramped, and soiled.

But that isn't what happened.

The *Sabalo* ran into dirty weather off the coast of Maine. Fog closed down on a roughening sea, and since the yacht's captain was unfamiliar with what he knew to be increasingly treacherous waters, as they coasted northeastward past Frenchman Bay and Machias Bay and into Grand Manan Channel, he asked Roosevelt to take the wheel. Roosevelt was more than glad to do so, of course; he took pleasure not only in the exercise of his nautical prowess, but also in its display before admiring spectators. He stood at the helm hour after hour, his ears measuring distances by the sound of buoy bells and foghorns, his eyes straining to discern the shapes of possible disaster through the swirling mists, his hands at once strong and sensitive upon the handles. He did not doubt his ability to navigate safely the dangerous Lubec Narrows with their terrific currents, fog-shrouded though they be. He reassured the nervous Black. Had he not taken a high-speed destroyer through these same narrows a few years before? But it was tense, fatiguing work all the same, and there was a note of relief as well as of triumph in his tenor voice when he sang out at last: "Welshpool Harbor, dead ahead!" [49]

Twenty-one

➺➤❮❮

Darkness on Campobello

I

A TIRED man had come to a remote green isle. He could loaf there and invite his soul.

He might lie abed as late of a morning as he pleased and then go solitary into wood or treelined open grassland away from the sight and sound of men or even of anything men had made. He could stroll at ease along narrow paths under pine and fir, through groves of aspen that whispered in mild breezes and twinkled green and gold in the sun, while he idly watched for birds he knew and breathed deeply the pine-scented salty air that flowed in from the sea. Or he might go out onto a rocky point above the sea and there sit or lie for hours on a sun-warmed rock, hearing the cries of gulls as the hiss and slap of waves upon the pebbled beach below lulled him into slumber. Or he could go out upon the sea itself, gliding under sail over safe waters that imposed no strain on either attention or muscle and let him rest, rest, rest. A succession of such mild sweet days coupled with cool nights of sleep would soak the bone-deep tiredness out of him.

But he didn't loaf. He didn't let up for a moment.

Van Lear Black had "quite a party with him" aboard the *Sabalo,* as Eleanor later recorded. The party was met by a crowd. Eleanor and the five children were at the dock along with Miss Jean Sherwood, tutor of the younger Roosevelt children, her mother, Mrs. Sidney Sherwood, the three Howes, and several servants. His mother was not on the island— she was on a European trip and was not due back until the last of August—but at the cottage were other servants and outside employees, in addition to those who had come to the dock. Hence there was continuous noise, ceaseless bustle, and he did nothing to escape it. Instead, he added to it, plunging at once into activities initiated by himself and involving as many of the others as possible.

His wife's memoirs suggest that on that first night after his arrival the weir extending out into the sea from the Roosevelt shoreline was seined by local fishermen who were summoned by a watchman's horn and worked in the reddish light cast by flares against the misty dark. If so, we may be sure that Franklin Roosevelt was among the crowd who watched, explaining everything to Black as the nets were drawn up full of squirming herring and dumped into the small boats (the fishermen "in their rubber boots, sweaters and sou'westers" looked to Eleanor "like pictures in the Bible stories" [1]), and that, nearly exhausted though he must have been following his long stretch as helmsman in foggy narrow waters, he did not go to bed until the seining was completed.

Certainly he did not sleep late next morning. He was up at dawn or soon thereafter to eat a hasty hearty breakfast and then go out into the Bay of Fundy on a deep-sea fishing expedition he had planned with Black and members of Black's party while on the voyage up from New York. The weather had turned fine during the night, and it was actually hot by midday. The sun's was not the only heat that warmed him. For as they fished for cod from the *Sabalo*'s motor tender and he performed the strenuous task he as host had set himself, that of baiting hooks for his guests, he was required to move from the fore cockpit to the aft, back and forth, crossing on a three-inch varnished plank close beside the tender's hot engine. He became bathed in perspiration. Sometime during the hot afternoon his foot slipped as he made his precarious passage; he fell overboard. He was astonished, even a little alarmed, by the magnitude of the shock of frigid water (the bay's water is always frigid) upon his overheated body. "I'd never felt anything so cold . . . !" he would recall a decade later. "I hardly went under, hardly wet my head, because I still had hold of the side of the tender, but the water was so cold it seemed paralyzing." [2] Almost at once, as helping hands reached down to him, he scrambled back aboard, laughing with the others at his discomfiture. But he perforce spent most of the rest of that afternoon in wet clothes, only slowly drying out in sunlight and engine heat, and he still felt a little strange—dull, heavy, achy—when they at last returned to the cottage.

Nor did he feel well when he awoke the following morning. He made no concessions to what he deemed a slight indisposition. He continued without pause a round of activities that some of Black's party had already found far too vigorous for their tastes, causing them to receive "most opportune telegrams . . . which made it imperative that they should start back to N.Y.," as Grace Howe wrote her daughter, Mary.[3] And sometime on that Tuesday, perhaps prodded by those "telegrams," perhaps driven only by his own restlessness (he was as compulsively active as Roosevelt), Van Lear Black did sail away on the *Sabalo,* taking his party with him. The departure relieved Roosevelt of any further special obligations as host: in addition to the Roosevelts and their servants, there remained at the cottage the three Howes and the Sherwood mother and daughter, but these all were virtually part of the family. He could easily have spent the remainder of that day, and all the next, in relaxing pursuits.

He didn't, of course.

When he awoke on the morning of Wednesday, August 10, 1921, he felt no better, he felt worse, if anything, than he had the day before. But the weather remained fine. It beckoned him to outdoors exercise. And instead of limiting his exertions in deference to his dull achiness, he put in the most strenuous day thus far in his vacation.

He had been eager for a long sail in his *Vireo,* the fast and sturdy 24-foot gaff-rigged keel sloop he had acquired ("in order that the boys might learn to sail," according to Eleanor[4]) after he had given up the *Half-Moon* during the war. He took Eleanor and the children out in her that morning, finding her as always a joy to handle. They sailed for hours. Early in the warm afternoon they were homeward bound when they spotted a forest fire on a small island and at once made for that island and went ashore to fight the fire. With evergreen branches they beat out flames that spread through the brown needles and low-growing shrubs of the forest floor. It was the hardest kind of work, hot and dirty. They kept at it for hours. Not until late afternoon was the fire brought at last under control. "Our eyes were bleary with smoke," Roosevelt recalled long afterward; "we were begrimed, smarting with spark-burns, exhausted." [5]

His exhaustion, however, did not prevent his proposing, as soon as they set foot again on Campobello, that he and the children refresh themselves with a swim. They all donned bathing suits. They jogged two miles along a narrow dirt road, the sunlight warm on their bare heads, the road's dust warm on their bare feet, until, perspiring, they came to a small freshwater lake, Glen Severn, which is narrowly locked away from the ocean on the east shore of the island by a few dozen yards of low ridge and sandy beach. They plunged in. Glen Severn's water was warm, and Roosevelt was accustomed to topping off a swim in it with an icy dip into the ocean. He did so that late afternoon. But he did not, when he had emerged, "feel the usual reaction, the glow I'd expected." He wondered a little about this as, with the others, he jogged back to the cottage. There he found that the mail had arrived, including "several newspapers I hadn't seen," and he sat for a while on the porch in his wet bathing suit reading them, "too tired even to dress." It was no ordinary tiredness, but very strange. "I'd never felt quite that way before," he later remembered.[6]

Suddenly, he felt a violent chill. Somewhat alarmed, thoroughly annoyed, he got shivering to his feet. He told his wife he feared he might be catching cold and had better not eat supper with her and the others. He would, instead, go straight to bed.

Eleanor sent up a tray with his supper on it. He ate some of it, lying in bed, but he wasn't hungry, and later he couldn't really sleep. He'd drop off, then come wide awake again, feeling more and more ill. He kept shivering, despite the heavy wool that blanketed him. When morning came and he tried to swing his legs out of bed in his usual fashion, he found that he could not, that his left leg dragged and almost collapsed under him when he stood up. Only with difficulty, and in pain (his legs ached, every bone and muscle in his body seemed to ache), did he shave himself and then stagger back to bed, where, however, he managed a cheerful smile and even a little joke when his daughter, Anna, bringing up his breakfast tray, asked anxiously how he was. He seemed to have a touch of lumbago and a bit of fever, he said.[7]

Actually, when Eleanor took his temperature a little later, the thermometer registered 102 degrees, whereupon she abruptly canceled her plans to start out that morning on a three-day camping trip on the mainland "with the children who were old enough to go, such elders as wanted to go, and Captain Calder [an island native, long a summer friend of the Roosevelts], who was to take charge of the party," as she wrote in her memoirs.[8] All arrangements for this trip had been completed. She now insisted that the trip be made by the others who had planned to make it, for it would be best to have them out of the house for the time being. They left. The house grew unwontedly quiet. And as the pain in her husband's back and legs increased and it became increasingly difficult for him to move, she sent an islander in a motor launch to fetch their summer doctor from Lubec. He, Dr. E. H. Bennett, having questioned and examined the patient, was frankly puzzled by the symptoms but finally concluded that they must be those of an unusually heavy cold. He prescribed for that.

The patient himself knew better—or worse. He had had a great many colds in his life, more than most, and he was convinced that this was something else, something far more serious. The pain was much greater than any he had ever suffered from lumbago; it was different in kind from any he had ever felt before. He indicated as much to Louis Howe when Howe came up to the sickbed. His face was white and etched in lines of pain as he looked up at his friend in a bewildered way.

"I don't know what's the matter with me, Louis," he muttered, over and over again. "I just don't know." [9]

II

What *was* the matter? What had happened, what was continuing to happen, in that lithe, slender, graceful, and formerly immensely vigorous and vital body of his?

Sometime during the preceding three weeks—perhaps in sweltering Washington, perhaps on crowded Wall Street, perhaps amid the dust of the Boy Scout encampment—he had breathed in or transferred by touch to his mouth myriad thousands of pale spherical bodies so tiny that their very existence had to be inferred, by the science of that day, from the effects they produced on gross living tissue. No microscope was then powerful enough to make them visible;* no porcelain filter was fine enough to prevent their passage through it. But their effects were often violent and were such as to cause scientists to designate them a "filterable virus"—*virus* being Latin for "poison." Franklin Roosevelt, then, had taken poison into his system. And that was the beginning.

What was the nature of this poison? The science of 1921 could not say with much definiteness. It could not even say for sure whether these mysterious substances were alive or dead. They seemed to flicker on the borderline between the animate and inanimate. In some respects they were as inert as clustered molecules of pure protein, and it would be demonstrated in a later year (1935) that they could be crystallized—that is, rendered as rigidly, fixedly ordered in their structure as iron or ice—and then redissolved into their original state without any change in their original properties. The man who first made this experiment was convinced by it (since no living thing had ever been crystallized) that viruses *were* merely dead protein.[10] It was true that they manifested some of the most distinctive characteristics of life. They could absorb nutrients and grow from the inside, rather than from the outside only, by simple accretion, as some crystals do in some solutions. Still more significant was their ability to reproduce themselves, multiplying their populations. But it was of the essence of their toxicity that they could do these things only by intimately involving themselves in the affairs of indubitably living matter, to the detriment of the latter. Hence the ques-

---

* Not until the invention of the electron microscope in the late 1930's would anyone see objects as small as these—spheres having diameters of approximately 0.022 micron, a micron being one-millionth of a meter or one twenty-five-thousandth of an inch. Not until 1953 would the polio virus (or viruses), magnified 77,000 times, be photographed.

tion remained of whether a virus, of itself alone, could be properly classified among the living.

Years would pass following the first virus crystallization experiment before an answer satisfactory to most scientists could be made. It would then be discovered that viruses have much the same chemical composition and capability as genes—and genes, the repositories of a living cell's most distinctively "living" properties, must surely be deemed the most vital of vital matter. Like genes, viruses are nucleoproteins, consisting of about 94 percent protein and 6 percent nucleic acid. Like genes, they can undergo mutations, forming new replicating strains that differ in character and virulence from the originals. And in general they act very much as genes that have been somehow loosed or forced from the cells that should normally contain them and over which they would normally rule in a strictly orderly, legal fashion.[11] Evil comes of this seeming displacement. Imperious executive types by nature, viruses require subjects to command, organizations to direct, and being deprived of these they behave as if frustrated to the point of madness. They roam the world as angry outlaws, dangerous in their enmity toward the established order, preying generation after generation on alien hosts, invading the host cells, forcing out or killing the genes that lawfully rule these (unless killed themselves in the attempt), and then using as their own the cells' vital chemistry. Upon cells the effect is disastrous. The attack always hurts them; the conquest, if achieved, destroys them.

All this would become known in two decades' time. In part (thus mysterious are the ways of Destiny) it would become known *because* of what happened now on Campobello. And once it was known, few would deny that those myriad tiny blobs of matter that invaded Franklin Roosevelt's respiratory tract on a day in July or early August, 1921, were living creatures.

This particular virus had a marked partiality for nerve tissue. Indeed, the general belief of medical science at that time was that it could grow *only* in nerve tissue, for since its first isolation in a laboratory barely a dozen years earlier (by Dr. Simon Flexner, 1909), no trace of it had been observed in living blood, and every effort to grow it in non-nerve tissue had failed. The belief was mistaken, however. The virus that lodged in Roosevelt's throat and intestines after entering his body was able to grow there, if slowly. Armies of antibodies were mobilized against it. But because of the nervous anxiety and fatigue that characterized the host organism as a whole and affected the operation of every part of it, these defending armies were less strong, less effective than they would otherwise have been. The virus survived their onslaught and continued to grow, until the myriad thousands of infinitesimal spheres became myriad millions and found their way into the bloodstream. There, as they coursed the whole of the host body, the battle against them became more desperate, producing effects so gross they impinged forcibly upon Roosevelt's consciousness. They were warnings.

But Roosevelt had more than his full share of the kind of willful pride which stubbornly resists outer checks upon inward assertions; he was accustomed to ruling his body absolutely, driving it to do his will without regard for its protests; and insofar as this body now became alien to his felt essence, an obstacle to his desire, he treated it with his usual contempt, ignoring signals which, had he heeded them, might yet have enabled him to escape with symptoms no more serious than those of a cold or mild influenza. Instead, the virus was enabled to force its way at last into precisely the environment most congenial to it, the nerve cells of the spinal column, and there, as Roosevelt's resistance to infection in general was reduced by a cumulative physical exhaustion and as his resistance to this particular infection was reduced by two nerve-numbing plunges into frigid water, the virus multiplied rapidly. Then it was that he knew chills and fever and first felt an unprecedented heaviness in his limbs, a reluctance of his legs, especially, to do his bidding.

Had it been possible to make a microscopic examination of his spinal cord at that time, marked changes from its normal state would have been observed. Blood vessels, particularly those feeding the anterior horn, were dilated, congested, and so were the capillaries, many of which had burst, spilling their contents. Tissue that would normally have been serenely pale, a calm grayish white, was become furiously red and swollen—an inflammation and edema that seriously inhibited the transmission of motor impulses.[12] But this was by no means the sole inhibiting factor. More important and far more disastrous was the inflammation's inciting cause—namely, the activities of the now explosively growing virus populations as these swarmed through the nerves, focusing on connective tissue in the cord. There motor nerve cells were being attacked, conquered, devoured by the scores of thousands all through the first days of Roosevelt's agony—a massacre that transformed into permanent injury (since nerve tissue is nonregenerative) what might otherwise have been a temporary symptom.

The paralysis increased and spread. By the evening of Thursday, August 11, 1921, Roosevelt was barely able to stand; his right leg had become as weak and unresponsive to his will as his left had been at daybreak. The next morning, Friday, he could not stand up at all. A dozen hours later, as evening shadows fell, he had lost the capacity even to move his legs. He had to ask Eleanor or Louis Howe to shift the position of his legs in bed, and he had to do this often because, though they felt essentially numb and dead, they also ached deeply, steadily, and were more acutely, painfully sensitive to touch than they had ever been before. A shift in their position relieved the pain, at least to the extent of breaking its monotony. Nor was the paralysis by that time confined exclusively to his legs. His back muscles were becoming affected, and so were those of his shoulders and arms, and even of his fingers; when he tried to sign a letter sometime in the late afternoon, he found that he could not because his thumb muscles were too weak.[13]

Meanwhile, the fever raged. His temperature climbed at times to heights that would have been alarming in a child of five or six and were terrifying in a man of thirty-nine. Still more terrifying, both to him and to those who watched him day and night, was the black despair, the utter despondency, that now settled down upon him—a mood so completely different from any he had revealed before, or even experienced, that there seemed no way to cope with it.

When the three-day campers returned on Saturday, August 13, they entered a house of fearful anxiety, a house with the feel of death in it, though every effort was made to hide this from the children.

III

A worried Dr. Bennett confessed on Saturday morning that his tentative initial diagnosis had been wholly mistaken. The symptoms baffled him. He decided with Eleanor that another physician should be called in for consultation as soon as possible, and since there was no telephone in the cottage, he and Louis Howe went back to his office in Lubec, where they made a phone survey of nearby resorts seeking "the best available diagnostician."

They soon found that Dr. W. W. Keen of Philadelphia, a nationally famous doctor, though now also an elderly one, was vacationing at Bar Harbor. They talked with him. He agreed to drive up at once and spend the night at the cottage, and he did so, arriving at seven thirty Saturday evening. Immediately he made "a most careful, thorough examination," repeated it next morning, and concluded that "a clot of blood from a sudden congestion . . . [had] settled in the lower spinal cord, temporarily removing the power to move though not to feel," as Eleanor wrote her brother-in-law Rosy on Sunday afternoon.[14] A complete but probably slow recovery was predicted: it might be months before the clot could be entirely reabsorbed. To maintain muscle tone and circulation in the meantime, Keen prescribed heavy massage. This, he insisted, "was vital," along with all the skillful nursing that could be given. So Eleanor wired New York at once for a trained masseuse but did not wait to begin the treatment; she and Howe began massaging that very day, taking turns.[15]

This was an excruciating torture for Franklin Roosevelt. His legs had become so sensitive to touch that even the weight of the bedclothes was often painful to him. A sweat of agony glistened on him (despite the continuing fever) as Eleanor or Louis Howe kneaded his muscles. Now and then a groan escaped through gritted teeth. Otherwise, he bore the torture without complaint. Nor did he overtly challenge the optimistic assurances given him about his immediate future—that his illness was not really dangerous, that the symptoms would soon disappear—though he could not believe them.

His spirits were low in inverse proportion to his fever, which remained very high. His paralysis, far from diminishing, had now spread to his bladder and rectal muscles and into the muscles of his back to such an extent that he could no longer sit up.[16] He was utterly helpless. Thus was added to his physical suffering a personal humiliation rendered especially harsh by his kind of physical pride. The nursing of him grew more difficult, more nauseating of detail: he had to be catheterized; he had to be given enemas; he had to be fed and bathed like a baby. And he sensed on the third and fourth days that if his present condition was temporary, it was probably not because he would soon be well but because soon he would die. In his deepest self he knew that he was very close to death, that indeed a gray death actually raged now within him, virulently cruel, wholly ruthless, seemingly invincible.

A crisis of the soul accompanied this crisis of the body.

Years later Roosevelt confessed to Frances Perkins, one of the very few to whom he ever made deliberately a profoundly intimate revelation, that during these first days of his illness his despair was absolute. At the vital core of his being had been his uncomplicated faith in God as beneficent Creator of the universe and in himself as a chosen instrument of God. Part and parcel of his faith was the conviction that in the great drama of history, with Almighty God its author and producer, he had been assigned a major role. Now, for the time being, he lost this faith, this conviction. In their absence, as he lay hour after pain-soaked hour in that second-story bedroom, he felt loneliness of a kind that could not be alleviated by wife or friend—an utter solitude shot through with moments of pure naked animal terror. He stared at the blank ceiling, noting its every slight crease and stain, and at the wallpaper, actually seeing for the first time the paper's design of delicate yellow flowers and green leaves against a creamy background, and he felt himself as one already entombed. He said that during those awful days, he felt that God had abandoned him.[17]

Probably the ultimate crisis, body and soul, was reached during the dark hours of Sunday night, August 14, or the early morning of Monday, August 15. This, at least—the fourth day following an acute attack —is the time normally most fatal to sufferers of the disease that afflicted him. And certainly, in the hours that immediately followed, his temperature began to fall and his spirits to rise correspondingly. By Wednesday his temperature was normal (though he was destined to have flare-ups of fever for many weeks to come), and there had come riding back into his soul, on a tide of relief, some of the faith he had temporarily lost. He had been dragged to the very edge of the abyss. Why? And why had he been finally spared? Was there a reason for it beyond his knowing, beyond any man's knowing, since it lay in the realm of divine purpose? He began to wonder if the whole of this shattering experience might not have been designed by God to chasten him, purify him, test him, and thereby prepare him for his great task. He could hope again, intermittently.

Eleanor and Louis Howe noted gratefully the change that came over him. ". . . I think he is getting back his grip and a better mental attitude," she wrote Rosy on Thursday, the eighteenth, "though he has of course times of great discouragement. We thought yesterday he moved the toes on one foot a little better which is encouraging." [18]

But she did not dare tell him of a long letter she had just received from Dr. Keen in which he, having reflected on the symptoms after his return to Bar Harbor, revised his original diagnosis. He was now "inclined to believe" that the root of the trouble was not a blood clot but a "lesion of the spinal cord"—a more serious matter, which meant "a longer business" than he had at first envisaged. ("He also sent his bill for $600!" wrote Eleanor.) "I dread the time when I have to tell Franklin," she said in her letter to Rosy, "and it wrings my heart for it is all so much worse for a man than a woman. . . ." [19] Which indicates strong doubt on her part, despite brave assertions, that her husband would ever completely recover. She could have no real confidence in the diagnosis, the prognosis made by Dr. Keen.

Nor could Louis Howe.

These two, the sick man's wife and his most devoted friend, were drawn close together during this crisis. He had liked and admired her from the first, despite her coldness toward him in Albany and the early Washington years, her evident resentment of his influence over her husband, her initial revulsion (he, a sensitive man, could not but have felt it) against his person. He had sensed in her a growth potential of which she herself was unaware and had begun, during the 1920 campaign, to help her realize it. Now his admiration of her grew immense. The nursing her husband required would have taxed the skill of the most highly trained professional, but since no professional was available, she did it all, with Howe's help, during the first crucial weeks. She slept on a couch in the sickroom at nights. She applied with native art (she had always had "healing hands") such science as she had learned from Blanche Spring during their long years of association.[20] Simultaneously, she managed a large household, ordering its routines in such a way as to protect the sick man absolutely without making of his condition a greater source of anxiety for the others, especially the children, than it had to be. She was patient, cheerful, knowledgeable, seemingly indefatigable, and wonderfully self-reliant.

But she was acutely aware that she could not do all that needed to be done. She would have been overwhelmed if Louis Howe had not been at her side. She was profoundly grateful to and for him. (". . . thank heaven . . . [he] is here, for he has been the greatest help," she said in her letter of the fourteenth to Rosy.) And as the anxious days passed, she became more than grateful: she came to love as a dear friend this untidy, unclean, unhealthy little man whose sour visage and harsh cynicism masked a kindness, a sweetness of spirit, a capacity for selfless love all the more intense for being so exclusively and narrowly focused.

In former years she had doubted that there was much disinterestedness or any deep personal devotion in Howe's relationship with her husband. She could doubt no longer. He revealed an anguished regard for Franklin's welfare that matched her own, and the service he now rendered, the total commitment of his future he now made, went far beyond the requirements of self-advancement and even, in some respects, contradicted these. It never occurred to him to reconsider the career decision he had made in March. "From that time on he put his whole heart into working for my husband's future," Eleanor would remember. Most surprising of all, when he relieved Eleanor in the sickroom, he displayed a rare empathy and even a good deal of nursing skill, manifesting precisely the mixture of toughness and tenderness most likely to maintain or restore the sick man's morale.[21]

In all this he was perhaps aided by his personal experience of dangerous illness, he whose chronic heart condition and asthma had made virtually the whole of his physical life a fending off of imminent death. Certainly the experience had taught him slight respect for the professional competence of doctors. He had never forgotten or forgiven the doctor in Albany who, in 1908, had examined his heart and solemnly predicted his death within two months. Two years later, November, 1910, he had watched helplessly, and been outraged by the equal help-lessness of the doctors, as his firstborn child, a boy, died horribly of meningitis only a week after birth. And if this tragedy had caused him to "research" the subject of nerve diseases as he normally did subjects which interested him, his skepticism regarding Dr. Keen's diagnosis in the present case could not but have been increased. At any rate he wrote long letters to Frederic A. Delano in New York describing Franklin's symptoms in great and accurate detail so that Uncle Fred could relate them to New York specialists. The specialists suspected infantile paraly-sis.[22] Delano then insisted that Eleanor arrange a consultation with Dr. Robert W. Lovett of Boston, the leading American authority on this dread disease. Eleanor did so through Dr. Keen, though Keen still clung to his "spinal lesion" theory.

Lovett came to Campobello on Thursday, August 25, two weeks after the first acute symptoms had appeared, ten long days after the agonizing massage treatments had begun. He made at once a definite diagnosis of poliomyelitis.

The diagnosis initially threw Eleanor into a panic, not so much on her husband's account as on that of the children—the Howe boy, as well as her own sons and daughter. The doctor was happily able to soothe these terrors. No one knew how the disease was communicated, he told her, but it was certainly not highly contagious in the way that scarlet fever was, or smallpox. Generally it struck but one child in a large family, even at the height of an epidemic, and in the present instance, the fact that none of the children had developed symptoms weeks after exposure would seem to indicate that all were immune.[23] Besides, he told her, her husband's attack seemed to him a relatively mild one, indicating that it was no especially virulent virus that infected him. A complete recovery was probable.

Recovery, however, would take months, and there was little that med-ical science could do to help the process along. The massaging must be stopped at once; it could only "prolong hyperaesthesia and tenderness" and further injure already-damaged muscles. (Bitter it was to learn that she and Louis Howe had been torturing their helpless beloved for naught, and worse than naught, hour after hour, at the behest of a pro-fessional who thought $600 a fair fee for less than a day of his vacation time and a mere guess of a diagnosis.) Drugs were "of little or no value, and not worth giving if they impair appetite," though "bromide for sleeplessness may be useful." He recommended "the use of hot baths . . . as it is really helpful and will encourage the patient, as he can do much more under water with his legs." He laid heavy stress on the need for encouragement of the patient. "There is likely to be mental depression and sometimes irritability in adults . . . ," he said.[24] In general, save for the tragically mistaken massage, the care given thus far had been excellent and would be hard to improve upon. The doctor, in fact, as Eleanor remembered with a pardonable pride, was "so flattering as to certain aspects of my husband's care, not knowing that I had been the only nurse on the case, that it was decided that I should continue a certain amount of the nursing" even after a registered nurse, a Miss Rockey from New York, arrived a day or so after Lovett's departure.[25]

It was decided that the sick man would be moved by boat to New York in mid-September and there placed in the Presbyterian Hospital under the care of Dr. George Draper, who was Roosevelt's age and was in fact an old school friend, now a protégé of Lovett's.

IV

There began what all realized must be a long, grinding struggle for health whose outcome was in doubt and in which mental factors were of immense importance. A psychological strategy was agreed upon, tacitly for the most part, that anticipated to a degree the formula Émile Coué would soon (in early 1923, when he lectured in America) make famous: "Day by day in every way I am getting better and better." All were resolved to speak and act as if the sick man's full recovery were a foregone conclusion, as if his present helpless anguish were only a bad joke (wry laughter its proper response), as if he were able even now to continue functioning as a public man.

The sufferer's paralysis was at its most extensive. Even his arms were affected by the time Lovett arrived; they remained so for some time thereafter. Every shift of his body's position had to be made by others at the cost of excruciating pain to himself, for his tactile sensitivity increased at least in proportion to the failure of his motor nervous system. Ultimately it became so great as to seem to radiate from him, threading with naked quivering extensions of his nerves the very air around him, the very sheets he lay between. To fan this air, to touch these sheets, was to hurt him. Yet he had to be frequently touched, handled in most intimate ways; for instance, it continued to be necessary to catheterize him and remained necessary until September 8. With all this came wider and more abrupt fluctuations of body temperature than he had ever experienced before. Sometimes his fever raged as high as it had during the first few days; at other times his temperature was markedly subnormal, with all that that meant in terms of general depression. Yet he seldom permitted even a hint of discouragement to break through the cheerfulness he and the others determinedly maintained in the sickroom. Eleanor would later claim that he *never* did. Morever, at a time when he could barely sign his name, he allowed Howe to commit him to various public activities.[26] He accepted membership on a committee to raise money for Vassar College (August 22); he accepted membership on the New York State Democratic Committee (September 12); and after Missy LeHand arrived from New York in the last week of August he did some dictating each day himself, referring to his sickness in a casual, lighthearted way and striving to keep himself actively involved in business, legal, and political matters, though it would be impossible for those who studied these letters decades later to determine which were actually composed by him and which were written in his name by Howe.

A few days after Missy's arrival on Campobello, Sara Delano Roosevelt, returning from Europe, debarked in New York. Eleanor's anticipation of this event had contained elements of dread. The mother in Europe had not been informed that her son was ill—there had seemed no point in alarming her; there was nothing she could have done—and Eleanor and Howe feared the response her imperious, possessive nature might make to the shocking knowledge that her son was crippled, perhaps for life. The response would almost certainly be at variance with the psychological strategy which the sick man's wife and friend and the sick man himself were so determinedly pursuing. It might well destroy the good this strategy had thus far achieved. Hence Eleanor's arrangement to have her mother-in-law met at the boat by Uncle Fred, and her statement to Rosy in a letter of August 23 that there was "no hurry" as regards the mother's inevitable trip northward since "no change can occur here." Hence, too, the rather curious tone (in the circumstances) of the brief letter she wrote "Dearest Mama" on August 27, after Sara had sailed, which therefore could not be received until the boat had docked. "Franklin has been quite ill and so can't go down to meet you . . . , to his great regret, but Uncle Fred and Aunt Kassie both write they will be there so it will not be a lonely home coming. We are all so happy to have you home again dear, you don't know what it means to feel you near again." She added remarks about the children and the weather, closing with: "Franklin sends all his love and we are both so sorry he cannot meet you." [27]

Early in the afternoon of September 1, the anxious mother arrived at the cottage. The next day she described her experience in a letter to her brother Fred. "I . . . at once . . . came up to a brave, smiling, and beautiful son, who said: 'Well, I'm glad you are back Mummy and I got up this party for you!' " she wrote. "He had shaved himself and seems very bright and *keen*. Below his waist he cannot move at all. His legs (that I have always been proud of) have to be moved often as they ache when long in one position. He and Eleanor decided at once to be cheerful and the atmosphere of the house is all happiness, so I have fallen in and follow their glorious example. . . . Dr. Bennett just came and said 'This boy is going to get all right.' They went into his room and I can hear them all laughing. Eleanor in the lead." [28] It was laughter that may have had relief in it. Eleanor, at least, was forever grateful for the manner in which her mother-in-law entered into the forced spirit of the occasion. ". . . I am sure that, out of sight, she wept many hours, but with all of us she was very cheerful," wrote Eleanor in her memoirs, though she also then referred, in a muted way, to other less admirable parts of her mother-in-law's response to the prolonged crisis.[29]

Sara Roosevelt stayed at the cottage only a few days, spending much time with her grandchildren, whom she continued to indulge in ways Eleanor was sure was bad for their characters. Then she returned to New York to get the twin East Sixty-fifth Street houses ready for the family's arrival.

Franklin Roosevelt left Campobello for New York on September 13. He left by train, not by boat as had been originally planned. Frederic Delano had been able to arrange for a private car to be sent to Eastport and for the switching of this car from one line to another in Boston; the sick man, once aboard, need not be moved from his berth until he arrived in Grand Central Station.

It was necessary, however, to move him from his upstairs bedroom down to a motor launch at the Roosevelt dock, then across the channel to Eastport, and finally from the launch at its Eastport docking to the parked and waiting car. For Roosevelt this meant excruciating physical suffering and, unavoidably, a certain amount of public humiliation. For Howe it meant a crisis in public relations.

From the moment that the seriousness of the illness became known, Howe had been concerned with the effect that public knowledge of it might have on Roosevelt's future. He had determined to keep all news of it out of the papers until the initial announcement could include an optimistic medical report. And by trading heavily upon the confidence reporters had learned to place in his word, he had succeeded. Inevitably rumors of the illness reached newspaper offices soon after the initial attack. Correspondents had thereafter come over from Eastport almost every day, but Howe had given them nothing substantial to report for more than two weeks. Not until August 27 did the first news story appear, and its main thrust was that Roosevelt was "now improving" from what had been a serious illness. The words "paralysis" and "polio" were not mentioned.

And now, on September 13, Howe engaged in deliberate subterfuge. Word had, of course, got about that the famous sick man was being moved that day. A small crowd of the curious, including newsmen, was gathered in Eastport to witness the operation. But they gathered at the wrong place because Howe had let it be known that the launch with Roosevelt aboard would dock at the far end of town, whereas in fact it docked at the near end.

There were few—none save family, servants, a handful of friends— who saw a helpless suffering man, pale and feverish, being carried on an improvised stretcher down the slope and then carefully laid out of sight upon the motor launch's bottom. He was in agony. Every step the stretcher-bearers took was felt by him as a bone-deep stab of knives into his back and legs. Yet when he saw his seven-year-old son Franklin, Jr., watching him tensely, anxiously, he managed "a tremendous sunny smile" and a cheery wave of his hand, convincing the boy that his father "couldn't be so sick after all." [30]

On the other side of the channel he was loaded into a luggage car whose lack of springs on a rutted road and along poorly paved streets made the uphill journey to the railway car at least as agonizing to him as the initial journey to the launch had been. He was passed on his stretcher into the car through an open window. By the time the crowd found out where he was and gathered at the car, he lay in bed smoking a cigarette and smiling, seemingly perfectly at ease. He responded cheerfully to reporters' questions. "Mr. Roosevelt . . . said he had a good appetite," reported the correspondent for the New York *World*. "Although unable to sit up, he says he is feeling more comfortable."

Eleanor had asked their old Poughkeepsie friend Tom Lynch to meet the train at Grand Central, and as the stretcher was being taken out of the car through the window there, the sick man heard his old friend's voice warning the porters to be particularly gentle and careful. "Why, hello, Tom!" he called cheerily, with no hint in his tone of the hurt that came to him with every slightest shift or jolt of his body. When he was on the platform, he asked Lynch to ride with him in the ambulance to the hospital. "There are some things I want to talk to you about," he said. But the sight of that figure, so lithe and strong and graceful and full of life when last seen, lying now broken and helpless, was too much for Lynch's emotional equilibrium. He muttered something noncommittal and turned away. Later he asked Eleanor to tell her husband that he, Lynch, would visit him in the hospital on the morrow.[31]

*　　*　　*

He had been for twenty-four hours a patient in New York's Presbyterian Hospital on Park Avenue when, at last, the press was told the nature of his illness. The New York *Times* carried the story on page one, September 16, 1921, under the headline:

F. D. ROOSEVELT ILL
OF POLIOMYELITIS

Brought on Special Car from Campobello,
Bay of Fundy, to Hospital Here

Recovering, Doctor Says

Patient Stricken by Infantile Paralysis
A Month Ago, and Use of Legs Affected

The opening paragraph of the story said Roosevelt had lost the use of both legs below the knees "for more than a month." But Dr. Draper was quoted as saying "definitely he will not be crippled" and that no one "need have any fear of permanent injury from this attack."

When Roosevelt read this, he was stimulated to dictate a jaunty little note to the newspaper's publisher, Adolph S. Ochs, saying that while formerly possessed of "the usual dark suspicion" that doctors were merely "trying to make me feel good" when they told him he would recover completely, he could no longer have any doubt that he would; the authoritative *Times* had said so. He added that he was "in the best of spirits" and was already being "allowed to take up part of my somewhat varied interests." [32]

Actually the doctor, who deemed the morale of his friend and patient more important at this juncture than absolute scientific accuracy of public statement, was by no means as certain of the final effects of the illness as the direct quotation of him indicated—and he became less so in the following days and weeks. To a large degree, his initial optimism had been based on a long letter he had received from Dr. Lovett, whose medical judgments he profoundly respected, soon after Lovett's visit at Campobello. "There was a scattered weakness in the legs, most marked in the hips when I saw him, very few muscles were absent, and in those that were recovering there was a pretty fair degree of power at the end of two weeks," Lovett had written.[33] "No deformities were present, and the general aspect of the thing was a mild, rather scattered attack without excessive tenderness, coming on promptly and not in a sneaking way, with spontaneous improvement beginning almost at once and progressing. It seems to me that it was a mild case within the range of possible complete recovery." But Draper must soon have wondered if Lovett had not been misled by the sick man's amazing outward cheerfulness, the incredible stoic courage which enabled him to bear fierce pain with a smile, the general impression he gave of euphoria—a psychology utterly at variance with that usual to sufferers of this disease.

For the blunt truth of the matter was that the sick man remained very sick indeed, in almost constant pain, often feverish, and only slightly less paralyzed than he had been when Lovett examined him. "There is a marked falling away of the muscle masses on either side of the spine in the lower lumbar region, likewise the buttocks," wrote Draper to Lovett on September 24.[34] ". . . The lower extremities present a most depressing picture." The paralysis of the legs was, Draper indicated, virtually total. "What I fear more than anything else is that we shall find a much more extensive involvement of the great back muscles than we have suspected and that when we attempt to sit him up he will be faced with the frightfully depressing knowledge that he cannot hold himself erect." Draper wondered if it would be possible for Lovett "to devise some kind of support for him which we can put on while he is in bed, just preparatory to getting him up in a chair for the first time, so that he will not realize too suddenly that his back will not hold him." There was a weakening, too, of Roosevelt's arms, a "marked weakness of the right triceps; and an unusual amount of gross muscular twitching in the muscles of both forearms." But Draper had, he said, "studiously refrained from examining his upper extremities because he believes them to be untouched by the disease." He went on: "It is fortunate that one does not have much opportunity in the recumbent position in bed to call upon the deltoids or the triceps—the biceps are fortunately pretty good so that he is able to pull himself up by the strap over his head and so help himself to turn in bed. This of course gives him a great sense of satisfaction."

None was permitted to visit the hospital room save family, close friends, and intimate working associates, people with whom Roosevelt might be expected to be frankly himself, and they all were astonished by the hearty manner with which he brushed aside their at least tacitly offered condolences. Josephus Daniels was one who came. He had always been especially appreciative of his young friend's physical attractiveness; he may now have revealed, in consequence, a special lugubriousness. At any rate, having been beckoned to the bedside, he was suddenly sent reeling backward by a blow of Roosevelt's fist against his chest, Roosevelt laughing up at him: "You thought you were coming to see an invalid. But I can knock you out in any bout." Others told Ernest K. Lindley "eagerly and with tones of wonder" more than a decade later how they were "sent . . . away [from the hospital room] more cheerful than they could make a pretence of being when they arrived." The letters he dispatched from that room maintained the tone. To a note from Walter Camp he replied that he had "been given every reason to expect" that his "somewhat rebellious legs" would permit him, in the future, "to join in another course of [physical] training." To a note from the supervisory force of the Washington Navy Yard he replied that "the doctors consider me a prize patient and are much gratified at my progress toward recovery." [35]

Draper—an astute man gifted with rare empathy; a man, too, whose upper-class background and education were similar in several respects to his patient's—was aware that much of this was an exercise of self-defense and profound courtesy on Roosevelt's part. It was the proper conduct for a well-bred gentleman in such circumstances to erect and maintain a pleasant façade behind which were hidden whatever feelings he might have of humiliation, outrage, injustice, and sheer terror. But Draper was also aware that Roosevelt did indeed delude himself—deliberately, even assertively—and being unable to measure the width or depth of this delusion, the doctor could not but fear the effect of eventual inevitable disillusionment. "I feel so strongly . . . that the psychological factor in his management is paramount," wrote Draper to Lovett. "He has such courage, such ambition, and yet at the same time such an extraordinarily sensitive emotional mechanism that it will take all the skill we can muster to lead him successfully to a recognition of what he really faces without crushing him." [36]

Certainly no doctor would permit assertive optimism to hide the fact that his patient's progress toward recovery was unexpectedly slow. Only gradually, belatedly, did Roosevelt emerge from the general nervous prostration that inevitably follows acute polio. Only gradually, belatedly, was his tactile sensitivity sufficiently reduced to permit doctors to manipulate him as extensively as a thorough physical examination required. Such an examination was given him on October 2. It allayed fears that his bladder and prostate might be affected; they were found normal. But it revealed no sign of power returning to the muscles of his legs and only a slight improvement in the condition of the great muscles of his back, though his arms and shoulders grew stronger as he constantly exercised them, lifting and turning himself in bed.

During the next four weeks there was little evident change of any kind.

On October 28, 1921, he was discharged from the hospital. He was still unable to sit up under his own power. But he was able, with help, to swing himself from bed into wheelchair by means of the strap with ring suspended from the ceiling, and he was able to wheel himself about in the chair. The final note written on his hospital chart was a sad one. "Not improving," it said.[37]

He was taken in an ambulance to 47 East Sixty-fifth Street, where he was installed in the quietest part of the house, a back bedroom on the third floor.

V

This house, it will be recalled, though four stories tall, had narrow frontage and was by no means too large for ordinary Roosevelt family needs. It was now badly overcrowded.

Four of the Roosevelt children were at home—all of them save James, who was at Groton. The trained nurse, Miss Rockey, was in the house from early morning till late evening, with time off in the afternoons, taking meals there, and had to have a room to sit in during the day. Louis Howe had moved in because he had to be close by and his wife had been unable to find an apartment that was both satisfactory and cheap enough for the severely limited Howe budget. (Mrs. Howe, with son Hartley and daughter Mary, took a house in Poughkeepsie, where Mary continued at Vassar; Louis spent weekends with them.) There was a nurse for the two youngest boys, Franklin and five-year-old John. There were house servants, too, who lived in.

Managing so crowded a household in the prevailing conditions of anxiety required all of Eleanor's executive talent and energy. She arranged to have the two little boys and their nurse use rooms on the fourth floor, where there was a connecting door with the adjacent house of her mother-in-law. She gave fifteen-year-old daughter Anna a choice between sharing with Miss Rockey, during the afternoons and evenings, the large sunny third-floor room which had always been Anna's, a room that had a bathroom attached, or moving out of it into a small fourth-floor room, next door to eleven-year-old Elliott's, where she would have complete privacy. The girl chose the latter. The third-floor room was then assigned to Howe: he was downtown most of every day attending to Roosevelt's business, leaving this room free then for Miss Rockey's use. No room at all was left for Eleanor. She slept in a bed in one of the little boys' rooms and dressed in her husband's bathroom. "In the daytime I was too busy to need a room," she later remembered. She added that "various members of the family thought it their duty to criticize the arrangements which I had made" but that this "never troubled me greatly, for I realized that no one else could plan our very complicated lives." [38]

The latter statement was not wholly truthful. She herself contradicted it in other of her published memories of this "most trying winter of my entire life." [39] For the chief critic of her arrangements was her mother-in-law, and her mother-in-law's critical attitudes, the manner and above all the purpose of their expression, troubled Eleanor greatly indeed, adding immensely to burdens that would in any case have been hard enough to bear.

Sara Delano Roosevelt had become somewhat stouter of body with the passing years, but in her inner being she had changed not at all. She was not one who *could* essentially change. She remained absolutely rigid in every basic attitude and belief and idea—quick to judge and unwavering in her judgments, certain of her knowledge of right and wrong and of proper personal conduct in general, iron-willed, essentially thoroughly selfish—and was therefore as incapable of growth as she was of shrinkage. She was simply, undeniably there, a solid center of radiating force. She remained insistent upon her own dominating matriarchal power over the only world she cared about or that seemed to her important, the private world of her family; she was adamant in her resistance to any circumstantial development, any decisive act by others, that could reduce it. She had liked having Franklin and Eleanor dependent on her financially because it gave her means of control over their lives. ("She was most generous in her gifts," wrote Eleanor, "when she wanted to make any. She gave her son and me . . . anything she felt was essential, but she did not like any of us to have regular incomes of our own." [40]) She had derived no pleasure, therefore, from the abrupt and drastic increase of private income that had accompanied her son's move from Washington to Wall Street or from the independence of spirit that Eleanor developed as her children grew older and she broadened her active interests.

From all this it was predictable that Sara Roosevelt would seize upon her son's illness as an opportunity to regain power she had lost or was in process of losing.

Almost at the moment she first saw him on his bed of pain at Campobello she made up her mind that he was condemned to lifelong invalidism. He must give up all idea of ever returning to active public life. He must retire to Hyde Park and there live out his remaining years. But surely this need be no unalloyed tragedy, for he had already had a sufficiently brilliant career and the life of a country gentleman in easy circumstances was a graceful and pleasant one. Nor was it socially useless insofar as it maintained valuable standards and a way of life that were in danger of being destroyed by a rising tide of egalitarianism. At Hyde Park he could indulge his hobbies, building his stamp and other collections as never before; he might write the books he had always said he wanted to write; he would visit or at least be visited by cultivated people of his own class. And all the while, until she died, he would be under her loving care in much the same way as his father, her "beloved invalid" James, had been for so many years.[41]

This end became her ruling purpose. Toward the achievement of it she launched a relentless, ruthless personal campaign, employing every psychological weapon in her formidable arsenal and aided by that inescapable physical propinquity she had imposed when she built these twin houses. She was unaware, of course, that she was animated by any but the purest, most disinterested of motives: she believed her sole concern to be the welfare of Franklin, who, in his helplessness and grave danger, must be protected against the exploitive ambition of Louis Howe, the unwisdom of "poor dear Eleanor," the refusal of the doctors to admit failure. And if no close observer, then or later, was likely to see anything truly selfless in the aggressive, crippling mother love she now exerted, it must be admitted that the sick man's condition when he came home from the hospital and developments during the following weeks added plausibility to her basic contention.

On November 19 and 20, after nearly three weeks of seeming improvement, he went into a sudden relapse as mysterious to the doctor as it was terrifying to them all. His fever flared up. His eyes began to pain him. For a day or so there was fear that his vision was impaired. Then, as mysteriously as it had come, the fever and pain departed.[42] There was no recurrence. He resumed a recovery that became, perhaps, a bit more rapid so far as his general condition was concerned, though there was no improvement in his legs. When son James came home from Groton for Christmas holidays he found his father still unable to sit up (he was propped up on pillows) but greatly strengthened in his arms and shoulders and chest by continuous exercise on the trapeze arrangement over his bed. Giving way to sudden tears, the youth was reassured not only by his father's verbal heartiness, but also by a rib-cracking hug. His father got out of bed every day during these holidays and crawled around on the floor for physical exercise to assure himself that he was not utterly helpless, that he had a chance to escape in case of fire (a concomitant of his crippling was the development of a morbid fear of being trapped in a fire). He dragged his useless legs behind him. He Indian-wrestled on the floor with his eldest son and easily put down his son's hand every time. In January, 1922, however, came a new and truly horrible complication. As the nerve- and blood-starved muscles of his legs atrophied, the tendons behind his knees contracted. His right leg almost jackknifed under him, and his left leg was also bent backward. It became necessary to put both legs in thick plaster casts and then, every day, drive a wedge a bit farther into these casts behind the knees, forcibly stretching the tendons. The process was agonizingly painful, almost as if the sick man were being stretched on a rack in a medieval torture chamber, and it continued for two full weeks before the legs were straight again. Roosevelt bore it all (remembered Eleanor) "without the slightest complaint." [43]

He never complained about anything.

But Sara did on his behalf. She complained about the care given him, that he was being permitted, even encouraged to do far more than was good for him, complaints that led to "discussions . . . somewhat acrimonious on occasion," as Eleanor later understated it. [44] She, his mother, was sure she knew what was best for her son, regardless of what Draper said, or Eleanor, or Louis Howe, or Franklin himself. With every passing week it seemed to her more obvious that she was right in her contention that he could never be well enough to resume his career. Certainly he could never achieve the full measure of whatever recovery was possible so long as he remained in this overcrowded, overly noisy city house into which too many visitors brought too many problems of business and politics, keeping him stirred up when he desperately needed peace and quiet. She pressed continuously and openly for his removal to Hyde Park and less openly but just as persistently for Howe's removal from the household altogether.

Everything about Howe's person and habits and attitudes outraged her—his brusque manners, his sardonic wit at the expense of values and institutions she held dear, his sloppy dress, his chain-smoking, his scattering of ashes over clothes and carpets and furniture, his apparent unconcern for bodily cleanliness, his constant asthmatic cough, his burning of incense in his room. *His* room! By what right was it his? He was a usurper. Her granddaughter, her own flesh and blood, had been forced out, banished to a dark cell in a remote part of the house, to accommodate this "dirty, ugly little man" (she so described him to Franklin on occasion, provoking her son to cold fury[45]), and there was no justice in it. She said as much to Anna herself, fanning the girl's sense of being rejected, unloved. She encouraged Anna to go to Eleanor with the demand that a switch be made, that Anna have her old room back and Howe (whom the girl, too, disliked) be moved into the fourth-floor rear. A bitter scene ensued. The demand was curtly refused, the girl sternly rebuked. She retired in tears.

No longer child and not yet woman, Anna was often in tears that year. Her mother had placed her in Miss Chapin's School, after visiting several, because of a fancied resemblance between Miss Chapin's personality and that of Mlle. Souvestre. Eleanor's hope had been that Anna and Miss Chapin would develop much the same kind of relationship she had had with her own great teacher. But this hadn't happened. The school was "set and rigid" in its ways, its teaching methods were strange and bewildering to Anna, and as regards personal relationships with other students, she was in somewhat the same situation as her father had been when he entered Groton two years late. The others all knew one another, had formed their friendships. Anna was an outsider. And the teachers, too—Miss Chapin and the others—largely ignored her. Her grades were low, she pretended not to care, and in general the flip, harsh manner she put on to hide her hurt loneliness had the effect of increasing it, for it put off any friendly interest she might otherwise have attracted. She had always adored her father, and he her, but even he in this anxious painful time often found her so annoying that he sharply scolded her. There was a scene once in the library, there were several scenes at the dinner table, from which she fled weeping.[46]

An actual, psychologically dangerous enmity grew out of the almost total failure of communication between mother and daughter that winter. Eleanor was unaware that "Granny" encouraged the girl's rebellious mood, she was acutely aware of all she herself had done and continued to do to keep the family going through this seemingly endless ordeal, and she was deeply hurt by what seemed to her an inexcusable lack of appreciation on Anna's part. But she didn't say so out loud. That was not her way when things went badly for her. She "shut up like a clam." And to the troubled girl it was as if her mother slammed doors in her face, over and over again. She longed to become her mother's confidante, longed for a useful adult role in the home; instead, she was treated as an obnoxious child. She began to believe, as the bitter months wore on, that she hated her mother.

Meanwhile, there was no letup in the war over the issue of Franklin's present activity and future career—a war in which Eleanor was firmly allied with Dr. Draper and Louis Howe, and, most important, with Franklin himself. He who had confidently predicted that he would walk out of the hospital on crutches at the end of three weeks had instead been carried out on a stretcher at the end of six. After weeks of suffering in the Sixty-fifth Street house there was no clear sign he would ever be able to sit erect again; not until early 1922 did sufficient strength return to his back muscles to enable him to do so. And this, virtually completing his recovery above the waist, was the last retreat of his paralysis: as winter gave way to spring, the muscles of his legs were visibly atrophied. (The sight of his once remarkably handsome legs withering, shrinking to ugly skin and bone, was harder for him to bear than almost anything that had happened to him since the first black days of his despair.) But still he did not for an instant, by gesture or choice of words or shifting tone of voice, reveal any doubt of his ultimate complete recovery, and he blandly ignored for the most part his mother's more-than-hints that he was permitting other people to impose on him, was trying to do too much and endangering himself with excessive tiredness. His displays of stoic courage had been notable on several occasions during his boyhood and youth. He had manifested an iron determination, a stubborn will in pursuit of his main purpose on many occasions in his adult life—as collector, as political campaigner, as promoter of projects—while seeming "light," a "featherduster," a "playboy" to some who thought they knew him well. But he now drew upon a courage and strength that he himself may not have known he possessed. Hope deferred was never, for him, hope denied—at least not openly. He minimized the significance of every setback, maximized the importance of every improvement.[47] Triumphantly he faced the severest possible tests of his ability to maintain intact that wall of reserve which he had already raised around his essential self by age fourteen and which had been, it would seem, greatly reinforced over the years.

The wall, peculiarly made, was as peculiarly maintained. His most profound reticences wore often the outward aspect of a voluble frankness—a frankness seemingly so utterly open as to be sometimes, as regards his physical condition, actually a little shocking to family and friends and working associates. Always, though, the initial shock had in the end a disarming effect. It relieved tensions; it put others at ease, and, above all, it put *himself* at ease insofar as it demonstrated to himself (the presence of witnesses being necessary to the demonstration) that there was nothing, absolutely nothing pitiful or shameful in what had happened to him. Thus he would throw back the covers of his bed to display to his sons his withered legs, pointing out and naming in Latin the shrunken muscles, as if they were those of an anatomical specimen, and leading his children in cheers "as if at a football game" (so son James remembered) when he reported what he believed to be "a slight improvement in the muscles leading to the *gluteus maximus*." [48] While he was yet confined to his bed, he often showed visitors what he could do by means of the trapeze arrangement suspended from the ceiling. Later he would, on occasion, suddenly push himself out of his chair at the dinner table when guests were present, would flop down on the floor, crawl around the table at a speed surprising for one who had to do it all with his arms, and then, with help, hoist himself back into his chair again, beaming with pride at this proof of his agility. He would sometimes crawl upstairs, too, while friends and family watched from the lower hall, sweating profusely as he lifted himself step by exhausting step, yet keeping up all the while a steady line of bright, cheerful talk. When atrophy was so complete that his legs were light as sticks, he one day discovered that he could pick up one leg by the crease in his trousers, the crease pinched between thumb and forefinger, and cross it over the other; he promptly did so before others, calling attention to it, as if with pride.[49]

By the spring of 1922, despite her extraordinary reluctance to accept facts at odds with her wish, Sara must have realized that she had lost her war. Her son was not going to become her "beloved invalid," though her recognition of this did not cause her to cease her various unconsciously motivated efforts to persuade him to be. True, he was then preparing to go to Hyde Park, as she had for so long urged him to do. But this move was to be simply a continuation of a long-established pattern —winters in the city; springs, summers, autumns in the country—and he made it clear that, far from relaxing his strenuous efforts to recover the use of his legs and strengthen his body in general, he proposed to increase them.

Sometime in March he put on for the first time the steel leg braces which must forever after (though he would not then admit the possibility of it) serve as substitute for dead muscles whenever he stood erect. They were heavy, cumbersome, even painful if worn for long periods; he hated them from the first. They had to be locked at the knees, making iron stilts of his nether extremities, before he could so much as get to his feet, an operation that required assistance or the most exhausting effort on his part; but without them he could not safely use the crutches which were given him at the same time and which did at least enable him to move himself, without having to crawl, outside his wheelchair. He now proposed to learn to walk. He had by this time become something of an authority on polio, through hours of quizzing his doctors and reading medical literature. He knew that if the initial attack was a mild one (he remained convinced that his had been!), not all the motor nerve cells controlling the muscles of the legs were destroyed. There remained clusters in the spinal column which, by means of prolonged "education," could be made to perform the functions of those motor nuclei that the raging virus had killed. Such "education" was to be achieved through unremitting exercise, and as the leg muscles were reanimated, this exercise would cause them to grow back to normal size and strength, as the once-paralyzed muscles of his back had done. So he arranged to have sets of parallel bars put up in the garden at Hyde Park, one set hip-high, the other higher. On these he could move back and forth, supporting most of his weight on his hands but swinging his steel-braced legs from the hips, feet on the ground, in simulation of a striding man.[50]

And whether or not he succeeded in restoring the muscles of his legs (he, of course, never admitting the possibility he would not), his career would continue along the lines he and Louis Howe had set years ago. He had not in fact dropped out of public life for even a little while or from his private income-producing life either, not even when confined helpless to his bed. A highly able and willing Louis Howe was there to serve. Missy LeHand was proving to be a more than competent personal secretary, as well as a warm friend, and she, too, could serve. He was thereby enabled to retain his office as vice-president and director of Fidelity and Deposit of Maryland (he had offered his resignation as soon as he knew the nature of his illness; Van Lear Black had refused to accept it); to retain many of his numerous offices in civic and charitable organizations, including the Woodrow Wilson Foundation and the Boy Scouts; and to continue, virtually without interruption, his extensive political correspondence. He was writing and receiving letters on state and national Democratic politics within a week after his removal from the hospital to East Sixty-fifth Street, and this correspondence had increased in volume during the months that followed.

VI

Howe wished to enlist the aid of Eleanor in keeping alive her husband's political career—to help at least until it was possible for Franklin to appear again in public. He kept prodding her to participate in Democratic Party affairs in order that she, serving to a degree as her husband's legs and eyes and ears, could report to him what was going on, maintaining his informed and active interest. She, however, was unable to think of anything she could do along that line. Indeed, she had no time or energy with which to do it so long as the issue of the household war for her husband's health and independence remained in doubt.

But in the spring, as they were preparing to move to Hyde Park for the summer, she met two women, Marion Dickerman and Nancy Cook, who had long been friends of each other and with whom Eleanor now formed what was destined to become a long and close working relationship, as well as the warmest of friendships. Miss Dickerman was then assistant principal of the Todhunter School, a private school for girls from the primary grades through high school. She was interested in politics. She was also interested in bettering working conditions for women, an interest Eleanor had developed in girlhood; Eleanor was easily persuaded by her and others to attend a luncheon of the Women's Trade Union League and to become an associate member. Nancy Cook was a leader of the Women's Division of the Democratic State Committee. She persuaded Eleanor to chair a luncheon for women political workers, introduced her to other able and forceful Democratic women, and soon had her enlisted in party work on the state level.[51]

Thus, as she emerged from that long hard winter, tested and tempered, she widened her horizons, multiplied her active interests, and laid firm foundations for a rich, full future life. Her present life at home, however, continued tense and unhappy. Partly this was because of the continuous "small personal irritations" inflicted on her by her mother-in-law, but mostly it was because of her estrangement from her rebellious and increasingly difficult daughter.

One April afternoon, as she was trying to read to her two little boys, she suddenly burst into tears. She didn't know why she cried; she only knew she couldn't stop. The little boys left her. She sat on a sofa in the sitting room "and sobbed and sobbed." When Elliott came home from school, he took one look at her and fled. She still sat there when Louis Howe came in from his day's work downtown, tried in vain to find out what was the matter, then (helpless) left her. Finally, she went weeping into an empty room in her mother-in-law's house, locked the door, and applied a towel soaked in cold water to her flushed and streaming face. Gradually she brought her sobs under control. "That is the one and only time I ever remember in my life having gone to pieces in that particular manner," she recorded, as if still in wonderment, fifteen years later.[52]

But she also recorded that her breakdown had upon Anna and upon her relationship with Anna a salutary effect. It surprised the fifteen-year-old girl with the knowledge that her mother was, after all, a human being, not a perfectly controlled and efficient machine. She came to her mother in a new mood. Soon she was telling her mother of her troubles at school and confessing that she had been wrong ever to believe she was unloved. Eleanor responded. She for the first time took the girl into her full confidence, spoke frankly of the difficulties and problems arising from her husband's illness, and established thereby a rapport with her daughter that nothing afterward could destroy.[53] She was even enabled, sometime later, to confide in Anna the most profound hurt of her personal life—that of Lucy Mercer—though she again burst into tears as she did so.

That summer, at Hyde Park, she made herself learn to drive a car, persevering even after she had driven into one of the stone gateposts at the entrance to the mansion drive and, on another occasion, had backed off the road and down a steep slope into a tree. She had become a competent driver by fall: in the next fifteen years she would have not a single accident. She drove voters to the polls on election day, having by then, initially through her interest in the League of Women Voters and the Women's Trade Union League, begun to engage in the kind of political activity which Howe had urged upon her. She became a regular worker, ultimately a leading figure, in the Women's Division of the Democratic State Committee, establishing, with Howe's professional assistance, a printed newspaper which she endeavored to make self-sustaining through the sale of advertising and subscriptions. During the winter she "found time . . . to go with Miss Dickerman and Miss Cook to the Y.W.C.A. to learn to swim," and in the following summer, when her mother-in-law took Anna and James to Europe, she with Miss Dickerman and Miss Cook took young Franklin and John, with two other small boys, on a memorable camping trip, leaving her husband at Hyde Park. The trip took them, via automobile, through northern New York into Canada, then down through the White Mountains in New Hampshire, and finally across Maine to Campobello, where they remained for a couple of weeks. She had not seen the island since her husband's illness; she found it, "in spite of all our trials, . . . still serene, beautiful and enjoyable." [54]

Twenty-two

➤➤❮❮❮

The Road Back

I

Of GREATER life-affirming courage and fortitude in a political leader of the first rank, all history affords few examples.

He lived now into times diseased, lived into an increasingly febrile world of brittle unrealities behind whose brightly various façade the shapes of greed and fraud grew monstrous and the very possibility of human nobility seemed more and more denied, yet though himself crippled by disease, spread around him a glow of good health, good cheer, optimistic faith, and essential decency. Moreover, as he did so, he maintained a plain and simple way of life, without glitter of any kind, that was of itself alone a tacit rebuke to the ostentatious materialism of his age. He was at ease in the world. He made others feel at ease. And often in hours of gloom, when dark clouds lowered ominously and every breath stank of despair, his effect on those around him was as a burst of sunlight, a cleansing sweep of wind off sea or prairie.

Become a hero, he would bring many gifts to his fellowmen. Some would prove worthless or worse in the end. But this first gift of all—his laughter in the face of doom, his gay defiance of all dire adversity, his constant implicit insistence on life against death and that life is meant to be lived to the utmost—this gift was a priceless boon.

II

Much would be written in future years about the presumed effects of Roosevelt's desperate illness and permanent bodily injury upon his interior life.

He imposed on himself in the summer and autumn of 1922 a physical regimen harsh and painful beyond the bearing of most men. He spent hours between his parallel bars in the garden at Hyde Park, strenuously "walking"; once, losing his grip, he fell heavily to the ground and suffered the rending agony of a torn ligament that required weeks of healing. He spent hours upon his crutches; he tried almost every day to negotiate the whole of the long drive from the Hyde Park house to the highway, heaving, sweating, gasping for breath as he lifted and swung himself along, but laughing too, keeping up a bright line of chatter with those who accompanied him until, arms and shoulders exhausted, he collapsed into his wheelchair. He was unable for many weeks to go all the way to the stone posts at the gate, but he went farther as he grew stronger until at last, when the days grew short, the evenings chill, he now and then reached the trafficked road. He might wave there, with sunny smile, at neighbors driving by. He spent hours swimming, too, in Vincent Astor's heated indoor pool at nearby Rhinebeck, exercise from which he could derive some physical pleasure and mental satisfaction, for it gave him the illusion of control of his legs in addition to a meager actual control by means of the water's buoyancy. ("Water got me into this fix!" he sang out from the pool one day to his mother's chauffeur. "Water will get me out again!" [1])

There would grow up about him, inevitably, a legend of mortal agony and transfiguration, of spiritual rebirth and purification through suffering. The legend would have it that he became compassionately philosophical, who had formerly had a playboy approach to life; it would be said of him that a formerly swift but shallow intellect, a mind of wide focus but slight penetration, was greatly deepened and strengthened in its grasp, he becoming a student of the causes of things who had formerly been but a superficial observer and manipulator of effects. It would even be said that through lonely sessions of silent thought during this enforced retreat he shaped the grand design of a future he would impose upon his state and nation.

The legend has some measure of truth and the truth is attested to by several who knew him in those years, especially by two women who understood him as well, perhaps, as anyone was permitted to do. One of these was Frances Perkins. "Franklin Roosevelt underwent a spiritual transformation during the years of his illness," she wrote decades later. ". . . the years of pain and suffering purged the slightly arrogant attitude he displayed on several occasions before he was stricken. The man emerged completely warmhearted, with humility of spirit and a deeper philosophy." When she saw him for the first time after his illness (it was on a summer's day in 1922, after he had published an open letter to Al Smith), she "was instantly struck by his growth. He was young, he was crippled, he was physically weak, but he had a firmer grip on his life and himself than ever before. He was serious, not playing now. He had become conscious of other people. . . ." [2] His wife's testimony, if less dramatic in its contrast of before with after, is generally corroborative of Madame Perkins'. "Franklin's illness was . . . [a] turning point, and proved a blessing in disguise; for it gave him a strength and courage he had not had before," Eleanor would remember in the late 1940's. "He had to think out the fundamentals of living and learn the greatest of all lessons—infinite patience and never-ending persistence." [3]

But it would be easy to mistake the nature and exaggerate the amount of interior change in him. Even Eleanor and Frances Perkins may have done so to a degree. The testimony of Roosevelt's son James does not flatly contradict Eleanor's, but he obviously doubts that polio was a "turning point" or a "blessing in disguise" in quite the way Eleanor implies. James believes that polio had little effect on his father's character. Had not his father demonstrated often before an unusual patience, persistence, stoic courage, strength of will? Were these now rendered actually greater than before? Or were they merely revealed and exercised as they need not have been had he remained cloaked by good fortune in easy country? ". . . I believe it was not polio that forged Father's character but that it was Father's character that enabled him to rise above his affliction." Nor did polio have any important effect on his father's career, in James' opinion. Headed for the White House when crippling disease struck, Roosevelt continued in that direction, perhaps with a greater "understanding of human suffering" than he would otherwise have had but, for the most part, in much the same way he would have gone "regardless of polio." ". . . I cannot accept the theory that Father would not have been a great man and a great public figure had he not gone through his personal Gethsemane." [4] Most historians, after studying the evidence, would be inclined to agree. Indeed, it appears to at least one of these that the actual essential change wrought in Roosevelt by his prolonged physical anguish and disability—the percentage increase of seriousness, integrity, tenacity, understanding of self and others between, say, 1921 and 1924—was little, if any, greater than that which occurred during his time of troubles in early 1920 and the subsequent campaign for the Vice Presidency. From this point of view, if polio was a "blessing in disguise," it was largely for reasons having nothing to do with interior change. The reasons were environmental, circumstantial. He was kept from immediate office-seeking efforts that might well have failed in the unpropitious circumstances of the Harding-Coolidge years, a failure that might have denied him the golden opportunity which later came. He also gained admiring sympathy from common folk who, insofar as they were aware of his disability, could identify with him, eschewing envy and malice, as they might never have done with a perfectly healthy, handsome, wealthy Hudson River aristocrat, a stranger to all misfortune. His jaunty self-assurance now could, and later would be, seen by them not as a manifestation of personal conceit born of privilege, but as the badge of a triumphant courage tested and proved by calamity.

As for the "spiritual transformation" that Frances Perkins asserts, the phrase seems excessive—a grandiose, if not actually false, label for what really happened. It suggests the creative mystic's withdrawal into a desert place, his agony and ecstasy and inward illumination there, his return with a redemptive vision for mankind. But Roosevelt notably lacked the mystic's lyric temperament. He lacked the tragic sense of life. He was essentially a practical man, matter-of-fact, bleakly prosaic of mind, with little natural talent or taste for poetry, music, painting, or, indeed, the esthetic in general, and though his intuitions were often remarkable, they were rarely flashes of insight into the heart of things. They were not, for him, ends in themselves. They were means to ends which were practical, he using his intuition as a tool of politics. Similarly with regard to the histrionic in him. He loved to act a part. He derived from his various role playing something of an artist's delight in the exercise of his art. But this of itself alone was seldom a motive. His conscious "acting," when not merely a game played for fun—a "fooling," a species of practical joke—was almost always an exercise of power, its purpose the production of calculated audience effects that might help him toward concrete goals. And as he lacked the lyric temperament, so too did he notably lack the mystic's compulsion to go to extremes, to explore the outermost limits of experience, in order to arrive at ultimate apocalyptic meanings. His compulsion, his vital strategy were in fact precisely opposite to this. By temperament and conviction he was a moderate, a gradualist, a *both/and* man in the sense in which Kierkegaard employs this phrase.* His whole tendency was toward a blurring of definitions which, remaining sharp, must have conflict between them. In private as in public life he normally went to greater lengths than most men do to *avoid* flat confrontations, with the necessity they impose of totalitarian either/or decisions. He sought instead consensus and compromise upon a middle ground. This was an aspect of his kind of patience; it was of the essence of his politics. And insofar as he succeeded in this strategy, in his interior life, he was denied the mystic experience, the consequent inward illumination.

---

* One says so in the present context without necessarily subscribing to the Kierkegaardian dictum that "*both/and* is the road to hell"! See reference to Roosevelt's abhorrence of extremism on pp. 625–26.

For the mystic *as* mystic must operate upon the principle of limits. Driven to seek out what is most *really* real in terms of experience, he acts upon the knowledge that, experientially, reality is most real at the margins of things—that everything becomes itself most intensely at its outermost edge. Where land meets sea, there is the land most solidly earth, the sea most liquidly water. Where forest meets field, you sense the nature of forest most keenly, and the nature of open field. It is when you come to the edge of a town or to a border country with wilderness beyond that you are most conscious of the human community behind you and the solitudes ahead. Surely none who walked the Roman Forum or strolled the gardens of Canton in centuries past could have been as intensely, self-consciously Roman or Chinese as the centurian patrolling Hadrian's Wall or the captain of Han Wu-Ti upon the Great Wall at Tingpien: on such far ramparts, at the ultimate limit of empire, looking out over the wild hills of Pict or Scot, or across the desert landscapes of the Hun, the homesick warrior must often suffer as an ache of his spirit the double-sense of barbarism and civilization, knowing the latter, *feeling* it, with an acuteness impossible for those who remained safely ensconced at the empire's heart. And is not silence most silent at the instant noise ceases, as when the engines of the *George Washington* suddenly stopped off Cape Ann? Is not peace most peaceful, violence most violent, at the times and places of their meeting, as when the last shells killed the last men to die on the western front and the survivors came out of the trenches—wonderingly, strangely subdued—into no-man's-land? Is not one's sense of life, *his* life, unique and isolate, raised to its highest pitch at the moment he faces, in full consciousness, his imminent death, as when Roosevelt in the blackest night on Campobello knew himself to be at the point of annihilation?

No doubt Roosevelt's confession to Frances Perkins of his total despair, in that dark hour, of his feeling that God had abandoned him, encouraged her to speak in retrospect of his "spiritual transformation." So did his further revelation of belief "that Divine Providence had intervened to save him from total paralysis, despair, and death"—a belief that, as Frances Perkins went on to say, "was a solid basis for his future inner security in times of stress." [5] All this seems to fit the religious mythic pattern of death and resurrection, of dying *in order* to be born anew (his Uncle Fred Delano described him years later as "a twice-born man"); it has echoes of Christ's despair in His ninth hour upon the cross ("My God, my God, why hast Thou forsaken me?"), His giving up of the ghost, His triumphant rise out of the sepulcher on the third day. The fit, however, is far from perfect, and the echo but a feeble one. What one derives from such experience depends on what one brings to it, and

Roosevelt brought the moderation of a Christian gentleman as wary and disdainful of religious enthusiasms as ever was John Locke. Neither saint nor devil did he aspire to be. He had in him none of the dark pride of a Captain Ahab who, sensing an "inscrutable malice" at the heart of the universe, would risk all, dare all, defying God Himself, to strike at it through its outward and visible forms. He was much more closely akin to Starbuck, "no crusader after perils," but a calm practical man in whom "courage was . . . a thing simply useful . . . and always at hand upon all mortally practical occasions." (Perhaps there was in him, too, something of the Stubb who saw "in all your horribles" a "waggish leering" and, "come what will," was determined to "go to it laughing.") As for the Christ of Roosevelt's belief, He remained the Jesus of Endicott Peabody—no burning-eyed zealot, no radical death-seeking revolutionary, but the supreme moral aristocrat whose most significant cry from the cross was an ultimate expression of *noblesse oblige* and *noblesse honneur:* "Forgive them, Father, for they know not what they do!"

Hence the conclusion that "spiritual transformation" is a misleading description of what happened to Roosevelt upon his bed of agony. At this crucial juncture his vital strategy seems to have been, as always before and after, a blurring of the ultimate issue to the greatest possible extent (". . . I think it is just as well not to think about things like that too much," he had said to Eleanor; he resigned the event into the hand of God)—and he himself remained essentially the same as before. He maintained uninterrupted the pattern of character and behavior whose outlines could already be traced in him when he was fourteen years old. He was only further confirmed in vital principles, traits, tendencies already firmly established—was only *somewhat* more serene of spirit, *somewhat* more patient and tenacious, *somewhat* more serious, *somewhat* more thoughtful. Probably the greatest quantitative change in his character, though of its extent no one can speak with certainty, was an increase of his essential emotional reticence, a further thickening of that already thick wall of reserve which wore the aspect of a remarkably open cheerful frankness but behind which his innermost self, his deepest feelings, were hidden from even his closest intimates.

III

Dr. Draper greatly worried about what would happen to Roosevelt's "extraordinarily sensitive emotional mechanism" when the sick man was forced at last to face the fact that he would never walk again. So did Louis Howe and Eleanor, whose rage against his mother, during the bitter winter of 1921–22, had had this worry at its heart. But on the evidence one may doubt that he ever did actually face it, flatly confront it, as a stark reality. He continued his strategy of blurring the ultimate issue. He deferred a final consideration of it while concentrating upon treatments and exercises designed to strengthen his legs. He continued to insist, on the basis of no evidence, that he made marked improvement; he continued confidently to predict his ultimate complete recovery; and as he did so, he developed one psychological cushion after another with which to absorb and thereby prevent a brutal shock of recognition when at last even he had to admit that he had reached the full limit of possible recovery.

On May 2, 1922, he wrote General Leonard Wood, in blithe defiance of obvious fact, that his shrunken leg muscles "are all coming back." To his lifelong friend Mrs. Bertie Hamlin, with whom he was more genuinely self-revelatory than with most of his friends, he asserted in early June, 1922, that, though his leg muscles were sadly atrophied, he was "gaining very surely." A month later, to one who wished him to run for governor, he wrote that he was "very much better and improving every day," though he was "still forced to get about on crutches and could not possibly run a campaign this fall." To Richard E. Byrd he wrote on November 21, 1922, "By next Autumn I will be ready to chase the nimble moose with you." And not until more than a year after that, on December 15, 1923, some twenty-eight months after the onset of his illness, did he ask an executive of the Dutchess Golf and Country Club to remove his name from the club's list of active members. Since he was still on crutches, he could not "possibly play golf . . . for a year or two," he wrote. Eleanor once said that after he was stricken, he never mentioned golf in her presence—he who had loved that game above all others and had spent a large percentage of his happiest hours on green and fairway. Yet as late as late October, 1924, he continued to say to others that it was but a matter of time before he could discard not only crutches, but leg braces, and "try my hand at golf again." [6]

By no accurate assessment of objective realities could such optimism be sustained. His doing so was, in part, an exercise in stubborn self-deception. But even so it manifested rare courage, it required great strength of will, and if far different in kind from the creative mystic's daring, this courage was wholly admirable when measured in its own terms, the terms being those of the aristocratic, profoundly courteous, and hence, on painful private matters, profoundly reticent gentleman.*

---

* ". . . the essence of plebeianism, that which separates vulgarity from aristocracy, is perhaps less a defect than an excess, the constant need to animadvert upon matters which for the aristocratic temperament do not exist," writes William James in his *Principles of Psychology*. "To ignore, to disdain to consider, to overlook, are the essence of the 'gentleman.' "

For though he would not admit it, he could not wholly blink the harsh actual truth that from the autumn of 1921 to that of 1924—that is, through three full years of incessant painful exercises and treatments of various kinds—his legs showed little, if any, improvement whatever.

But he improved physically in other ways to a very marked degree between the spring of 1922 and the summer of 1923, and he increased this compensatory improvement thereafter. The Roosevelt whom Frances Perkins would have seen in, say, July, 1923 (she says she saw him but once between 1921 and 1924), could not have been accurately described as "physically weak" save in his poor withered legs. From his hips up, his hips remaining perfectly normal, he was much stronger than ever before. The stern physical regimen he imposed upon himself broadened and deepened his chest; armored with heavy muscle his once-lithe, slender torso; developed the iron-hard arms and shoulders of an old-time blacksmith, the thick neck of a professional wrestler. He grew proud of his muscular development, liked to display the huge pushing and hauling strength of his arms and the crushing grip of his big hands, bragged often that from the waist up he had the physique of a Jack Dempsey— and, indeed, by actual measurement, his chest expansion became greater than Dempsey's. Despite the fact that his legs grew light as sticks, he gained in total weight, eventually reaching 187 pounds, which was 30 more than he had weighed in college. And his general health was improved: he continued susceptible to head colds and sinus trouble, but less so than before.

There were other compensatory gains. In sum, these may have more than offset the loss of physical mobility—especially since the latter could be kept at a minimum by fortunate financial circumstances. Roosevelt had ample means to hire long-distance transport for himself by train or ship; it was not for lack of means that he made no trips abroad during this period. He could hire healthy legs as substitutes for his own useless ones: a servant to push his wheelchair (he liked to be pushed at almost a trot, five miles an hour), strong men to carry him when need be (Howe early issued the strictest orders against Roosevelt's being carried anywhere in public, *ever!*), chauffeurs to drive his car. He even could and did buy a car he could drive himself, a Ford which could be operated wholly with hand controls and which he drove skillfully at what sometimes seemed to others a reckless speed over country roads (he never drove in the city). He could and did rent a houseboat, the *Weona II*, in early 1923 and, with parties of friends, spent weeks upon her cruising and fishing in the Florida sun, off the keys; could, in the following years, in partnership with a friend, John S. Lawrence, actually buy a houseboat, christened *Larooco* (short for "Lawrence, Roosevelt, and

Co."), and spend long winter vacations upon her in Florida waters on three successive years, being assured by doctors that warmth and sunlight were the best medicine possible for his sick legs. The one thing he could *not* do was "run around," and he himself "soon began to find that . . . [even this] inability . . . had advantages," according to the astute Ernest K. Lindley—advantages "which, in time, became a really powerful asset." Lindley, in analysis of close personal observations and much conversation with Roosevelt, wrote: "He had always been a restless worker, frequently jumping up and down and dashing here and there through sheer excess of physical energy. . . . Now that he was compelled to sit in one spot, all of his energy was of necessity concentrated upon the work before him. A bit removed from the hurly-burly, he was relieved of many petty irritations. . . . He had an excellent excuse not to do what he did not wish to do; and at the same time, he could not resort to the normal human impulse to run away from a difficult problem. Everyone came to see him; he spent neither time nor energy moving from this conference to that." [7]

It seems hardly possible to doubt that the physical fact of enforced sedentariness had far more to do with the evident increase in his thoughtfulness than did the spiritual experience and spiritual effects of his nearly fatal anguish.

IV

And in any case the increase was of modest proportions.

In no deeply intellectual sense did he become "philosophical." He made no known effort even to become aware of, much less understand with any profundity, the general ideas determinative of the intellectual life of the 1920's—gave no sign, then or later, that he ever read so much as a page of Marx, Freud, Spengler, Ortega y Gasset, Lenin, Dewey, Bergson, Whitehead, Veblen, Russell, Parrington, Beard, the Webbs, Keynes, Henry Adams, or even of such best-selling popularizers of ideas, in those years, as Will Durant and H. G. Wells and Sir James Jeans. He took a somewhat more active interest in American history than before, but his interest continued to be that of the collector of historical items, the antiquarian who is a standard sustaining member of state and local historical societies, rather than of the serious student of historical processes and significances.

Thus:

Having acquired at auction the original minutes of the Council of Appointment of New York from April 4, 1778, to May 3, 1779, he persuaded the New York Historical Society to publish it as a volume of its collections. Having become chairman of the publication committee of the Holland Society, he raised and subscribed to a fund of several thousand dollars with which to publish a book of photographs and accompanying historical text entitled *Dutch Houses in the Hudson River Valley Before 1776*. Having a family interest in his hometown's history, wherein his grandfather and particularly his father had figured with some prominence, he edited and published *Records of the Town of Hyde Park, Dutchess County*. He also continued to build his collections of naval prints, of books of Americana, of historical memorabilia, and he gathered a good deal of material for a projected biography or biographical novel about John Paul Jones.

Yet when he reviewed his friend Claude G. Bowers' *Jefferson and Hamilton* for the New York *World* in late 1925, he revealed a poverty of elementary historical ideas, along with a lack of intellectual sophistication, that were amazing in one of his interests, experience, and educational advantages. Apparently it was news to him, as he approached his forty-third birthday, that the oppositions of Jefferson and Hamilton in the earliest years of the Republic had defined what had ever since been a central theme of American history as process—a theme that, redefined during the controversies of the New Freedom-New Nationalism years, was manifest in the politics of La Follette Progressivism and of the Farm Bloc in the 1920's. Roosevelt, reading Bowers' "thrilling" book, "felt like saying 'At last' . . . ," having never heard, evidently, of Beard's *An Economic Interpretation of the Constitution* or any other work explanatory of the issues between Federalists and Anti-Federalists. He confessed to "a breathless feeling as I lay down this book." He had in his mind, he said, "a picture of escape after escape which this nation passed through in those first ten years; a picture of what might have been if the Republic had been finally organized as Alexander Hamilton sought." He was "breathless" also with "wonder if, a century and a quarter later, the same contending forces are not again mobilizing." ("Hamiltons we have today," he concluded. "Is a Jefferson on the horizon?") The book provided him with a vocabulary and pattern of interpretation, applicable to the current scene, which he promptly used. Writing to a fellow Democrat just a week after the review appeared, he explained: "We are approaching a period similar to that from 1790–1800 when Alexander Hamilton ran the federal government for the primary good of the chambers of commerce, the speculators and the inside ring of the government. He was a fundamental believer in an aristocracy of wealth and power—Jefferson brought the government back [*sic*] to the average voter, through insistence on fundamental principles and the

education of the average voter. We need a similar campaign of education today, and perhaps we shall find another Jefferson." [8]

In general, the stubborn stoic courage, the spartan self-discipline, the
remarkably persistent strenuosity with which he pressed his struggle to
walk again were notably lacking from his response to purely intellectual
challenges. He could become utterly absorbed for hours on end in his
numerous hobbies—his stamp collection, his several other collections,
his making and sailing of small model boats on the Hudson.* He spent
hours on an elaborate "Log of the House Boat Larooco," illustrated by
Howe, and hours enjoying the skits and spoofs of the Cuff Links Club
each year. (The "club" was made up of those of his 1920 campaign entourage to whom, the following Christmas, he presented gold cuff links.
Its meeting to celebrate his birthday became traditional.) But it was
only rarely, overcoming a great reluctance, that he made himself even
begin any of the literary works he said he wished to write, and he
finished none of them. "In regard to my own actual pen-to-paper possibilities," he wrote with cheerful frankness to his editor-friend George
Marvin in September, 1922, "I am always in the delightful frame of
mind of wanting to say 'Yes' to anything in the way of writing, be it a
magazine article or a 12-volume history of the Navy—always provided
that the writing is to be done next week, or the week after. (Miss Le-
Hand who is taking this is nodding her head and saying 'too true—too
true!')" A month earlier he had written Marvin to say "how glad I am
that you are writing again," adding, "Nevertheless, I can't help feeling
that you are built a bit like me—that you need something physically
more active, with constant contact with all sorts of people in many
kinds of places." He managed to produce barely five handwritten pages
of his projected "little volume" about John Paul Jones, less than fourteen dealing with the discovery and early exploration of America. (He
subscribed, interestingly enough, to a species of historical determinism
in this brief beginning. "Many . . . factors contribute to the thought
that the period itself was the discoverer of America, and Columbus the
agent of his time," he wrote. ". . . It is perhaps not stretching the point
to assert that definite knowledge of America to the European world was
bound to come at the end of the 15th Century.") He managed to write

---

* The model boat hobby was especially absorbing during his Hyde Park summers, he striving to answer in practice the question "How fast can a small boat be made to sail?" Having
settled on a standard overall length of 38 inches, as he wrote in a letter published in a hobbies
magazine in 1923, he used "balsa wood for the hull, balsa or oiled silk for the deck and aluminum for the spars," simultaneously experimenting with different designs of hull and rigging.
He was immensely proud of the speed he achieved. "The first year the boats took nearly 16
minutes to cross the Hudson, a distance of ⅜ths of a mile. Since then some of them have done
it in 10 minutes and 11 seconds." [9]

only a few pages of the preface to a projected book-length critique of the way the American executive and legislative branches did their work—a book, to be entitled "The Machinery of Government," that would have continued the personal campaign for increased government efficiency which he had launched as the substance of his neutralist meanwhile politics in 1919-20. ("If American governments were private corporations they would go into the hands of a receiver in about twenty-four hours," he reiterated in this preface.)[10]

He did manage to complete a magazine article on U.S.-Japanese relations, his immediate incitement to this rare effort being his disagreement with an editorial in the ultraconservative Boston *Transcript,* but he did so only under the continuous prodding of Marvin, who gathered much of the material for it, went over Roosevelt's dictated rough draft with much care, and added to that draft considerable writing, factual in nature, of his own. Published in *Asia* magazine for July, 1923, the article's chief interest for historians would lie in its revelation of Roosevelt's total change of mind, since 1913, with regard to America's Pacific and Far Eastern policy. In 1923, despite the naval limitations agreements reached at the Washington Conference, many Americans, especially on the West Coast, spoke loudly about the "inevitability" of war between the United States and an aggressively militaristic, thoroughly untrustworthy Japanese Empire. Their answer to the question asked by the title of Roosevelt's article, "Shall We Trust Japan?," would have been an emphatic "No!" Roosevelt's answer was an emphatic "Yes!"

It was technologically impossible for Japan to threaten, militarily, the Panama Canal or the U.S. Pacific coast, he argued; it was equally impossible for the United States to threaten Japan militarily or even to hold the Philippines if Japan was determined to conquer them. Neither nation, therefore, had the capability to achieve a quick military decision over the other. "Economic causes would, without doubt, become the determining factor, after the first year or two of war. Japan and the United States would be sitting five or six thousand miles away from each other making faces and showing their teeth. Some brilliant genius might at that time arise and ask the simple question of what it was all about anyway. . . ." For there was no outstanding difference between the two powers that could not be readily resolved through peaceful commonsense negotiation, now that Japan had demonstrated its faithfulness to its treaty obligations. The Open Door policy for China, "the only definitely expressed foreign policy of the United States," was a sore point, of course. But surely Americans could now "appreciate . . . a little more readily the Japanese point of view," recognizing "the greater necessity to Japan of the markets and raw materials of the Chinese mainland contiguous to her island shores." Restrictive immigration policies aimed by the United States against the Japanese were another sore point. But surely the Japanese had to realize that they themselves would oppose a mass American emigration to the Japanese home islands as strongly as Americans opposed the mass Japanese immigration which threatened to inundate the West Coast unless bars to it were raised. Undeniably, there were strong commercial rivalries between the United States and Japan; undeniably, these would continue and even increase. But our long experience of economic competitions with England and other European countries surely demonstrated that such rivalry, of itself alone, was no sufficient cause of war.[11]

Even more revelatory than this article of Roosevelt's change of heart and mind were his responses, published and private, to critics of his argument. He now repudiated imperialism almost as emphatically as Daniels had always done—though it must be added that he did so with reservations as regards the United States in the Caribbean and the Philippines, continuing vehemently to defend the use of marines in Haiti and Santo Domingo, the highhanded policies of Governor-General Leonard Wood in the Philippines. "The whole trend of the times is against wars for colonial expansion," he wrote. "The thought of the world leans the other way. Populations themselves have a say." And the United States agreement not to fortify Guam or the Philippines manifested neither cowardice nor stupidity, in his opinion, but, instead, simple common sense. It was a decision taken "with our eyes open" to the disastrous folly of armaments increases and "defensive" moves that were bound to provoke counterincreases and -moves by the other side, back and forth, until inevitably there was armed conflict. He condemned "England's new fortifications at Singapore, Holland's new fleet for the Dutch East Indies," as "gestures not in accord with the spirit of the day"; they would "result in the same old vicious circle." [12] He even spoke, on at least one occasion, of the new era of international relations in which "spirituality" supplanted "materialism"—as if he had become at last a heart-and-soul convert to the very essence of Wilsonianism.

And indeed his commitment to the kind of international organization which Wilson had espoused—his concomitant opposition to the rising tide of American isolationism—was stronger and more firmly grounded in genuine understanding than it had ever been before. His personal relations with Wilson, though necessarily maintained by an infrequent correspondence only, were warmer and more cordial in tone, having been greatly improved following his polio and because of his polio. A bond of sympathy was created between the two stricken men.

When the first news of Roosevelt's infantile paralysis appeared in the press, Wilson, now living (dying) in a four-story Georgian house at 2340 S Street in Washington,* promptly wired the sick man his "heartfelt sympathy." Two months later Wilson wrote Eleanor that he was "greatly relieved" by reports of her husband's improvement, and a month after that, having received birthday best wishes sent by Roosevelt on behalf of the Woodrow Wilson Foundation, the ex-President wrote: "I am exceedingly proud of the proofs of friendship and confidence which the progress of the Foundation affords me, and your own friendship and unselfish devotion to its objects gives me, as I hope you know, peculiar gratification." Commenting on a typically optimistic report of Roosevelt's progress toward complete recovery, Wilson wrote (April 30, 1922): "I am indeed delighted to hear you are getting well so fast and so confidently, and I shall try to be generous enough not to envy you." Yet another S Street communication to Roosevelt said there was now a race between the two invalids to determine which would first play golf again.[13]

In 1923, Roosevelt devoted much time and energy to two educational projects which, like the Wilson Foundation, would promote Wilson's kind of internationalism. One was the establishment of a Walter Hines Page School of International Relations at Johns Hopkins University—a graduate school that was endowed by Owen D. Young, among others, and in which, Roosevelt privately suggested, Senator Lodge ought to be forcibly enrolled.[14] (His antipathy to Lodge, with whom he had been on the friendliest social terms for so many years, became acute following the 1920 campaign and was personal, as well as ideological.) The other project was one in which he became involved through his wife.

Eleanor continued to serve her husband along the lines she and Howe had laid out in the spring of 1922. She was constantly on the move, helping organize the new League of Women Voters, attending innumerable public luncheons and dinners and meetings of all kinds, and taking an increasingly important part in the activities of the new Women's Division of the state Democratic Party. She learned to give very full and accurate reports to her husband of what she saw and heard. She brought to the house people whom she thought her husband should meet or people already known to him who had things to say which he, in her judgment, ought to hear. But she also did and became much more than this. She was now very much a person in her own right—an independent, increasingly forceful, increasingly *public* person. She was even learning, at

* Ten prosperous friends of Wilson subscribed $10,000 each for purchase of a suitable residence for the ex-President's retirement. Bernard Baruch, one of the ten, also bought a vacant lot next door, to insure privacy. Built in 1917, the house cost $150,000 to buy—an enormous price in 1920.

Howe's insistence and under his tutelage, to give a reasonably effective public speech, conquering a nervous self-consciousness that was visible in awkward postures and audible in an unpleasantly high-pitched, wavering voice. (Howe sometimes sat in the back row of meetings at which she spoke and afterward criticized mercilessly her performance: "Why did you talk so fast? Why didn't you look at your audience? Why do you keep giving that silly little giggle?")[15] No more did she appear to others a mousy, passive creature in the background of her husband's public life. No longer was she wholly subordinate, if subordinate at all, in her dealings with him, whether on private or public matters. When she disagreed with him, she said so frankly and often argued her opposing case with fervor. She fed his mind out of her own increasingly well-stocked one; she sharpened his conscience against her own rigid one, often through frictions more or less harsh; she had some influence on his opinions, though she could never be sure how much; and she took initiatives which, now and then, determined his activities.

She did so when Edward Bok, the famous magazine editor, offered through the Bok Foundation in 1923 a substantial prize, in a competition open to all, for the best submitted plan to preserve world peace. Eleanor's good friend Esther Lape, with whom she had worked in the League of Woman Voters, was the competition's manager, and Eleanor not only joined in planning and organizing the project, but also served as a member of the award jury. The latter fact, indicative of her growing stature as a public person, prevented her husband's actual competition for the prize. But he was stimulated by its offer, and by his conversations with Esther Lape and Eleanor, to work out a peace plan of his own, which became the basis for all his future thinking about international organization.

There was little that was truly creative in this labor of his. There was virtually nothing new in its end product. His "Plan to Preserve World Peace" was but a draft revision of the League of Nations Covenant, and a revision, moreover, whose primary aim was *not* the improvement of the peacemaking capability of the international organization, but the overcoming of political objections to America's participation in that enterprise. Roosevelt was as convinced as Woodrow Wilson that no international peace-keeping machinery could work unless the United States was a part of it. He was more willing than even Wilson in Paris had been to sacrifice other considerations to the achievement of what seemed to him a supreme object. ("I don't care how many restrictions or qualifications are put upon our [participation]," he would write in a private letter two years later. ". . . I seek an end and do not care a rap about methods of procedure." [16]) And a consequence of this willingness to divorce means from ends was that his "Plan," like the Covenant, either blurred or ignored every aspect of the clash between national sovereignty and world government: he did not espouse with any consistent clarity even that minimal supranational authority essential to the actual making and keeping of world order. Yet his was a useful effort at public as well as self-education, for he managed to obtain for his "Plan," and himself in connection with it, a considerable press publicity, stimulating thereby a further public questioning of the major premises of American isolationism.

At the very outset, in his foreword to the "Plan," he deliberately blurred the issue.[17] "We seek not to become involved as a nation in the purely regional affairs of groups of other nations," he wrote, "nor to give to the representatives of other peoples the right to compel us to enter upon undertakings calling for or leading up to the use of armed force without our full and free consent, given through our constitutional procedure. Nevertheless, we believe that the participation of the United States with the other nations in a serious and continuing effort to eliminate the causes of war is not only justifiable but is called for by the record of our history, by our own best interests, and chiefly by our high purpose to help mankind to better things." To this end he proposed that in "the place and stead of the League of Nations there shall be created a new permanent and continuing International Conference to be known as the 'Society of Nations.' " Its members would be signatory "national governments," any one of which might, "after three months' notice [instead of the two years required by the League Covenant] withdraw from the Society. . . ." He proposed one significant change in the structure and operational procedure of the organization. In place of the League Council he would establish an eleven-member Executive Committee "representing eleven different members of the Society." The United States, the British Empire, France, Italy, and Japan would be members of this committee by virtue of their Great Power status, but for an assured period of ten years only "from the date of the first meeting of the Assembly of the Society." He explained that the "ten-year limitation follows the theory of the Washington [Naval] Conference of 1921, i.e., that after ten years a further determination of the subject can properly be arrived at." The other six members of the committee "shall be selected by the Assembly from time to time in its discretion." He also stipulated that, during the initial ten-year period, "no representative of a dominion or colony" could sit upon the committee. As regards voting procedure, he made what he described as "a radical departure from Article V of the Covenant . . . which, in general, requires unanimous agreement of the Assembly or of the Council" before action could be taken. Instead: "Decisions at any meeting of the Assembly or the Executive Committee shall require the approval of two-thirds of all members of the Society represented, except that matters of procedure may be decided by majority vote." To the objections raised against the Covenant's much-controverted Article X, his answer was essentially a yielding; he would further weaken the already feeble powers of the international organization to deal with any overt act or threat of war. League members in Article X pledged themselves merely to "undertake to respect and preserve as against external aggression the territorial integrity and existing political independence of all Members of the League." The Council, "in case of any such aggression" or threat of it, was to "advise upon the means by which this proposal shall be fulfilled." Roosevelt eliminated the words "as against external aggression" from his formula, offsetting this somewhat by providing that "the Assembly, if in session, or if not, the Executive Committee, shall make recommendations to the members of the Society upon the means by which this undertaking shall best by fulfilled."

In sum, his "Plan" made no more provision for an actual pooling of sovereign powers in the international body than did the Covenant, and he deplored proposals made a little later to provide the League with an air force of its own with which to police the peace. He did so on stated grounds of expediency. ". . . to speak at this time . . . of the use of warlike implements by the League" was, he declared, "a pity," for the world was "going through a period of national sensitivity that must wait until people come back to a more normal perspective." [18]

In all these years of private life, the nearest he came in his writing to anything actually "philosophical" in the usual meaning of the term was a commencement address he gave at Milton Academy in May, 1926— and though it was so unwontedly felicitous in style as to make one wonder if a hand other than his own had not had a large part in its composition,* it was typically Rooseveltian in its essential incoherence, its presentation of a glittering collection rather than a true organization of ideas. He mentioned many important things—the scientific revolution; the rhythmic pattern of conservatism-liberalism in American political history (he echoed here a conversation he once had with Woodrow Wilson); the relative ease of achieving cohesiveness among conservatives, whose minds are by definition inert; the difficulty of achieving it among

---

* Houghton Mifflin Company of Boston was sufficiently impressed by it to publish it between hard covers in the late summer of 1926. The tiny book was little noticed by reviewers, though Walter Lippmann and others praised it in letters to the author. It had no success at all in the marketplace, selling fewer than 350 copies.[19]

liberals, whose minds are by definition active; the grave dangers in a time of swift change of a prolonged governmental conservatism, dangers much greater than four to eight years of liberalism or even radicalism would engender—but he explored none of these things in depth and wholly failed to relate them internally one to another. He had no under-lying unifying theme with which to do so.

V

The same restlessness which characterized and vitiated his intellectual life—the need for variety and excitement that limited his attention span—was evident in his business and legal activities. He was quickly, easily bored. He shied away from any project requiring prolonged, concen-trated attention. And one must add that his quest for various excite-ments in the business world, joined to his impatience to make a great deal of money very rapidly (his current personal income scarcely sufficed to pay the costs of his struggle for recovery added to the costs of educating his children in expensive private schools), was uninhibited by any excessive scrupulosity. He accepted with no more question than he had the National City Bank's operations in Haiti the ethical standards generally prevailing among businessmen, especially big businessmen, in the 1920's.

After his illness, he did his first strokes of business for Fidelity and Deposit in late January, 1922. He had then barely emerged from the two weeks of medieval torture which the stretching of his cramped knee ten-dons required, and he was still in much pain. But from his home, he could handle business correspondence, use Howe as his mobile agent, conduct telephone conversations, and hold conferences. And even as a semi-invalid he continued to be worth more than his salary to the firm, in the opinion of Van Lear Black, because of the business brought in by his name and connections. He now, very actively, exploited the latter. He and Howe had no aversion to reminding industrial and labor union executives of the relations he had with them when he was Assistant Sec-retary of the Navy or even of favors done them at that time, asking for their business in return. Typical was a letter he wrote in the late spring of 1922 to the executive of a company just awarded a Navy contract for "some 8-inch gun forgings." Roosevelt had learned of this from "one of my old friends in the Navy Department," he wrote, and the news had "brought to my mind the very pleasant relations we held during my term as Assistant Secretary . . . , and I wondered if you would feel like letting my company write some of the contract bonds that you are obliged to give the government from time to time." He would, he said, "like very much to have one of our representatives call." Howe capitalized as much as he could upon his relationships with officials in the Washington headquarters of the AFL. "Some of my good friends at the head of the Federation of Labor," wrote Roosevelt to a Fidelity and Deposit officer, in January, 1922, "have been kind enough to pass the word along the line generally that the Federation considered me an old friend, and suggesting that whenever possible bonds should be placed with the company. . . ." [20] The AFL business eventually went elsewhere (the home office of Fidelity and Deposit refused to lower its interest rate to that offered by another bonding firm), but in general the Roosevelt-Howe efforts paid off. The volume of business done by the New York office increased more rapidly than did that of rival firms; it would more than double by 1928.

One of Roosevelt's attempted exploitations of formerly official connections, in the spring of 1922, brought him into marginal contact with what would soon become one of the great scandals of American political history.

Of the defensive battles waged against predatory business interests by Daniels as Navy Secretary, the most stubbornly difficult had been what he described in his memoirs as an "eight-year fight to preserve the Navy oil reserves." The Navy decision to convert from coal to oil as fuel had been contingent, in 1912 and '13, upon firm assurance that enough oil would be available, in the event of war, to fuel an oil-burning fleet. Portions of the public domain in which oil was known to be were then set aside for the exclusive use of the Navy. Two of the most important were the Buena Vista and Elk Hills reserves in California. Administration of the reserves remained under the Department of the Interior, whose staff, notoriously in the Ballinger-Pinchot case but on many other occasions as well, had demonstrated a greater sympathy for the acquisitive designs of special interests, chiefly Western interests, than for the general welfare as conservationists saw it. Hence, when Secretary Lane refused to exempt the naval reserves from provisions of a General Leasing bill which he sponsored in the Congress of 1913, he seemed to Daniels to be following a malodorous Interior tradition, and Daniels, with Roosevelt's help (this despite a continuing friendship with Lane), fought the measure tooth and nail. The two succeeded in blocking the measure's passage until the naval reserves were not only specifically exempted but also transferred from the jurisdiction of Interior to that of the Secretary of the Navy. Moreover, as war raged in Europe and the submarine menace

grew, Daniels continuously pressed Interior to discover, through its geologists, new oilfields on government land with which to augment the
Navy's reserve supply. He was delighted when, in mid-April, 1915, the
Interior Secretary, through an executive order signed by Wilson, transferred to Navy 2,481 oil-rich acres lying some 50 miles north of Casper,
Wyoming[21]—a tract whose distinguishing landscape feature was a sand-
stone dome that had been carved by erosion into roughly the shape of a
teapot. It became known as the Teapot Dome Reserve. Its acquisition
relieved much of the Navy's anxiety, during and immediately following
the war, regarding future oil supply.

But the oilmen continued their fight for the reserved oil, and they increasingly employed a device for stealing it which was highly effective
and difficult to guard against. This device was the drainage of the oil
through wells drilled just outside reserve boundaries. When Daniels
learned to his outrage and alarm, in 1920, that most of the Buena Vista
oil had already been drained away and that the Elk Hills reserves were
being rapidly depleted, he advertised for bids for the drilling of twenty-
one "offset" wells along the western edge of Elk Hills, to tap the drainage—bids that were still pending when he left office. He also proposed
that the whole of the nation's petroleum resources be nationalized.

But there was no chance of the latter's happening in the America of
1920. Instead came the take-over of government by business.

Harding's Secretary of the Navy, Edwin Denby, who had made a million as an automobile dealer in Detroit, was a man far different in every
respect from Josephus Daniels—vacillating, weak-willed, small-minded,
and, in the literal sense of the word, unprincipled. His chief subordinate,
Assistant Secretary of the Navy Theodore Roosevelt, Jr., proved considerably less astute, knowledgeable, and hardworking, if not less committed to the Navy and the general public's welfare, than Franklin Roosevelt had been in that same position, with Howe under him and Daniels
over him. The new Secretary of the Interior, Albert B. Fall, was a sour-
visaged land-poor New Mexican rancher and politician, heavily in debt
in the spring of 1921, who was actively opposed to the principles and
practices of conservation. His chief business in the past had been an uninhibited exploitation of natural resources (he had prospected for silver
in Nevada with Edward L. Doheny in the 1880's, had lost a small fortune in Mexican gold and silver mines when Díaz was overthrown in
1911, had ever since advocated U.S. annexation of northern Mexico),
and he swiftly acted to remove inhibitions from a further private exploitation of the public domain. He had not been in office a month before
he managed to persuade Denby, who was easily persuaded, that the

Navy oil reserves should be transferred from Navy back to Interior. The change was then promptly effected through a secret, or at least highly unpublicized, executive order.

Events thereafter marched swiftly in the direction oilmen wished. Complicated arrangements were made in utmost secrecy for an opening of the naval reserves to private drilling, without competitive bidding and on terms highly favorable to the drillers. By late spring of 1922 contracts had been signed with Edward L. Doheny's Pan-American Petroleum and Transport Company, giving Doheny unlimited drilling rights at Elk Hills for fifteen years. Similar contracts had been signed with Harry F. Sinclair's recently formed Mammoth Oil Company, giving Sinclair a twenty-year lease on the entire Teapot Dome Reserve. Simultaneously, Fall's financial status was elevated from virtual bankruptcy (he had been ten years in arrears on some of his property taxes) to an affluence that surprised and puzzled his New Mexican neighbors. Later they and the world would learn that Fall had received unsecured "loans" of something over $300,000 in cash and Liberty Bonds from Sinclair, this in addition to gifts of expensive livestock for Fall's ranch, and that Doheny had "lent" him $100,000 in cash, the cash having been conveyed to him by Doheny's son, on November 30, 1921, in what was destined to become a nationally renowned "black satchel."

But to the oilmen in 1921 and early 1922, the danger of embarrassment through an indecent exposure of these transactions did not seem great. They had taken out insurance policies against it by involving in their operations men or names of political potency. Sinclair, at the personal request of TR, a few months before TR's death, had provided the war-wounded, convalescing Archibald B. Roosevelt with a well-salaried sinecure vice-presidency. (Archie would resign from Mammoth Oil within hours after he allegedly first learned, from Sinclair's confidential secretary, that "somebody might have lent Mr. Fall money," and would appear as a voluntary witness before the special Senate committee investigating the matter.) Doheny, who had been among the leading exponents of the Great Red Scare, charging that a "majority of the college professors of the United States are teaching socialism and Bolshevism" and that "most of those one hundred historians Wilson took abroad with him" were outright Bolshevists, had nevertheless provided lucrative employment to no fewer than four former members of Wilson's Cabinet: ex-Secretary of the Interior Lane, who died in June, 1921; ex-Secretary of War Lindley M. Garrison; ex-Attorney General Thomas W. Gregory; and, as principal attorney, Wilson's son-in-law, ex-Secretary of the Treasury William Gibbs McAdoo.*

---

* Doheny had also on his payroll, briefly, as publicist, Wilson's wartime propaganda chief, George Creel.

It was to the latter that Franklin Roosevelt addressed on April 13, 1922, a chatty personal letter, simultaneously arranging for a personal call upon McAdoo by one of Fidelity and Deposit's West Coast vice-presidents. McAdoo, his Presidential aspirations disappointed in 1920 by his father-in-law's refusal to endorse him, now had his hopes fastened upon the Democratic Presidential nomination in 1924, and most of Roosevelt's letter was composed of political gossip. Only casually, incidentally did it mention the surety bonding business. Doheny, wrote Roosevelt, "is a good friend of mine and I feel sure he will be very glad to have you place the business our way." [22]

It will be recalled that at the outset of Roosevelt's New York business career, he regarded his vice-presidency of Fidelity and Deposit and his law partnership with Emmet and Marvin as elements of essentially the same operation. "The two varieties of work seem to dovetail fairly well," he had written Felix Frankfurter in January, 1921. But in point of fact they did *not* fit well together, even in the months preceding his polio. He devoted precious little of his time and energy to the law work of Emmet, Marvin & Roosevelt. He spent most of his hours in the law office writing the great number of letters and holding the numerous conferences entailed by his political activities and his various offices in foundations, charitable organizations, and clubs. He brought little business into the firm—far less than his partners had expected him to do. After his polio, though he continued publicly to classify himself as a lawyer rather than a businessman, he practiced no law whatever for a long time.

In part, this was because it was physically difficult for him to get to his law office at 52 Wall Street, whose front entrance had before it a flight of stone steps. He could not mount these on his braced legs and crutches. He had to be carried up. This not only was a personal humiliation, which he felt keenly, though he hid his feeling behind wisecracks and laughter, but was also "bad politics" insofar as it was witnessed by street crowds, violating a Howe edict in which he fully concurred. When 52 Wall Street was remodeled in 1924, the flight of steps was removed, but two steps up remained and, as Roosevelt wrote one of his partners, in a rare reference to his disability, "the question of even two steps is a very difficult one as I have to be actually lifted up and down them." [23]

But this physical hazard was not the only or even the most important of his objections to his law partnership. More important was his continuing, deepening dislike of the kind of sedate and intricately tedious practice in which the firm was engaged—the establishment and management of trust funds, the drawing up and execution of wills, and similar operations. "He didn't like to study too much—he liked to act and he was therefore sometimes rather impulsive in his acts," Langdon Marvin would recall years later.[24] And he himself was perfectly frank about this. The law per se had no interest for him whatever, but "I have accomplished practical things along the lines of business administration," as he said in a letter to Emmet in September, 1924, adding that his "whole training in the Navy Department was just that and in the Fidelity & Deposit Company also everything relates to the practical management of business of one kind and another." Almost nothing of that activist kind could he do in partnership with Emmet and Marvin. They were "dear delightful people," he said to Van Lear Black, but their "type of law business" bored him to distraction, and he received "not one red cent out of my connection with them, whereas, if I were with some real live people working along other lines I could be of material assistance on reorganizations, receiverships, etc. pulling my weight in the boat and incidentally making some money out of it." Moreover, his law practice in that case would be helpful to his work on behalf of Fidelity and Deposit "as our connections would be with the type of corporations and companies which would help in the bonding end of the game." [25]

And so, in that September, 1924, he ended his partnership with Emmet and Marvin (it is a measure of his personal warmth and charm that he was able to do so without harm to his friendships with them); three months later he formed a new partnership, with a successful corporation lawyer almost precisely ten years his junior—a man whose approach to the law and to life was as vigorously activist as his own, if very different in kind, and whose office (this was a point of importance) was in the same building as Fidelity and Deposit.

The new partner, who became a close lifelong friend, and one active in Roosevelt's career, was D. Basil O'Connor. Short, thin-faced, slightly built, his movements as quick and precise as his gaze was quick and sharp through rimless spectacles, he was as widely different from Roosevelt in family background, educative experience, and personality as he was in appearance. The son of an impoverished tinsmith in Taunton, Massachusetts, he had had to earn all his own way from childhood, doing so through an unusual combination of musical talent, mental brilliance, superb self-confidence, immense capacity for work, and almost incredible drive. Entering Dartmouth College at age sixteen, he had earned his way playing violin in a dance orchestra he promptly organized. He had also organized a social fraternity, made high grades, excelled in debate and public speech, and been voted Most Likely to Succeed of his class. He had then entered Harvard Law School, where, under incessant strain, his eyesight had failed, leaving him totally blind for a while. Medical treatments restored his vision, but even while he was blind, he had continued with his studies, having students read to him, and ever since, he had justified his college nickname Doc, which continued to be applied to him, by taking a greater than usual layman's interest in the medical profession and in the problems of the physically handicapped.

Since leaving law school, he had moved into a Boston law firm; had even in his mid-twenties taken the place of its senior partners when they went to France in the war (his weak eyes kept him out of the armed services); had "married an understanding girl," as Turnley Walker has written; had then moved to New York City and, with a breathtaking boldness fully justified by his success, opened a one-man law office of his own, specializing in contractual arrangements between crude oil producers and the refining companies. His was an international practice. He worked ten- to fifteen-hour days, had no time for hobbies, and, an urban type by temperament as well as upbringing, evinced no desire for country living or particular love of nature.

He would never forget his introduction to Franklin Roosevelt.

One chill October morning in 1922, a few days after Roosevelt, returned from Hyde Park, made his first post-polio visit to Fidelity and Deposit, O'Connor happened to enter 120 Broadway as Roosevelt was doing so. With a sympathetic concern which soon became anxiety, he watched the big, smiling man, so dreadfully crippled, heave himself on his crutches, with the panting help of a chauffeur, up the one step from sidewalk to entrance and through the door and then—slowly, painfully, precariously—across the polished marble floor toward the bank of elevators. Suddenly, despite the chauffeur's bracing efforts, the left crutch slipped. Roosevelt crashed down full-length upon the floor. He at once managed with great effort to thrust himself into a sitting position, but the chauffeur, though he tried, was not strong enough to lift him upright.

And Roosevelt laughed!

The big man, helpless on the floor, looked up at the people watching him but offering no aid, and he laughed into their abashed faces as though this were all a great joke. Without the slightest sign of embarrassment he asked a brawny young man to help lift him, and the brawny young man did so, of course, and then Roosevelt, with the crutches under his arms again, was on his way to the elevator, smiling and speaking to people whom he recognized as if nothing at all untoward had happened.

In the elevator, Basil O'Connor introduced himself.[26]

Official announcement of the formation of the new firm of Roosevelt and O'Connor was made on New Year's Day, 1925. Neither of the partners ever regretted this arrangement, despite the fact that Roosevelt's part in it consisted chiefly of giving legal advice to a relatively few clients while O'Connor did the actual work on contracts, receiverships, reorganizations, and the like. The law office not only was in the same building as the insurance firm office, but was actually next door to the latter, so that physical propinquity combined with a commonality of interests to ensure that Roosevelt's "two varieties of work" did now actually "dovetail" in ways prospering to both.

VI

But his activities in the business world were by no means confined to his salaried activities on behalf of Black's company conjoined with his legal work.

In the spring of 1922, when he was just beginning to devote himself strenuously to body-building exercises, he became involved in the founding of a national business organization called the American Construction Council. This was an organization actively encouraged, even promoted by Herbert Hoover, Harding's Secretary of Commerce, who continued to be a personal friend of Roosevelt's.* Its twofold aim was described by Hoover in early May: first, "to place the construction industry on a high plane of integrity and efficiency and to correlate the efforts toward betterment . . ."; second, "to stabilize the entire construction industry by eliminating 'peak and valley' conditions, to the advantage of capital, labor, and the public in general." [27] This smacked of "Socialism" to Roosevelt's friend Elliott C. Brown, the contractor who had rebuilt Springwood and then served the Assistant Secretary of the Navy so well as a lieutenant commander in the Civil Engineering Corps

* The promotion of cooperation between government and business by encouraging the formation of trade associations was the major policy of the Department of Commerce under Secretary Hoover. In 1923, the department issued a handbook entitled *Trade Association Activities* which extolled such organizations' virtues: product standardization, establishment of uniform credit policies, elimination of "unfair trade practices," settlement of trade disputes, etc. The Supreme Court and the Federal Trade Commission were inclined at that time to regard the associations as combinations in restraint of trade, hence illegal. In a 1923 ruling, Chief Justice William Howard Taft declared the "manifest purpose" of the members of one association "was to defeat the Sherman Act without subjecting themselves to penalties." Hoover was undeterred. Soon the FTC was packed with appointees who had no wish to engage in antitrust activity, and in 1925, the Supreme Court reversed its earlier stand by declaring two important associations to be legal. There followed a tremendous surge of business combination—the greatest since the earliest 1900's.

during the war. How could these announced aims be accomplished without national regulation? asked Brown. And who in the end would do the regulating? Obviously the federal government. ". . . the moment a combination is formed," the contractor wrote Roosevelt in mid-May, "the Government will assert an interest and will express that interest through the medium of some clerk in the Department of Commerce, who will approve or disapprove of many matters. . . ." [28] Roosevelt could agree that this was a danger to be guarded against. ". . . government regulation is not feasible," he said in a published statement a few weeks later. "It is unwieldy; it is expensive. It means employment of men to carry on this phase of the work; it means higher taxes. The public doesn't want it; the industry doesn't want it. . . ." But for that very reason, with an administration in Washington dedicated to as little government as possible, the danger of federal regulation seemed remote. The problems facing the construction industry, on the other hand, were immediate and acute. Chaos reigned. "Muddling through has been the characteristic method employed by the construction industry for the last few years," said Roosevelt. "There has been no system, no cooperation, no intensive national planning." The leaders of the industry also had good reason "to feel that the confidence of the public . . . [was] slipping away" from them. Hence the "time was ripe for an organization such as that being formed." [29]

Roosevelt became president of the council. Announcement of that fact was made in June amid a fanfare of national publicity. His new role was likened to that of Will H. Hays as "czar" of the motion-picture industry, of Judge Kennesaw Mountain Landis as "czar" of professional baseball. And there was indeed a certain superficial resemblance between the processes that resulted in the baseball and movie "czardoms" and the events leading up to the Construction Council's formation. When eight players of the Chicago Black Sox baseball team were indicted by a grand jury for accepting bribes from gamblers to throw the 1919 World Series to the Cincinnati Reds, the public outrage was such as to convince major-league team owners that drastic steps had to be taken to ensure future public confidence in the honesty of the sport if the sport itself were to survive. Hence the creation of the post of Baseball Commissioner with Judge Landis as its initial occupier. When one Hollywood film after another violated the sexual mores of small-town America, provoking demands for censorship from churchmen—demands that grew louder as scandalous disclosures were made of the private lives of certain movie performers and directors—worried producers joined together to hire Hays, who had been Harding's Postmaster General, to set and enforce upon their product standards of morality and taste. Similarly, the construction industry, especially that of New York City, had become an object of public indignation and demands for regulation. Construction costs had soared to unprecedented heights in 1920, accompanied by rumors of widespread graft, corruption, and racketeering in the building trades. The New York legislature had established an investigating commission, whose probing was directed by the veteran antitrust lawyer Samuel Untermyer. What Untermyer exposed to the public gaze was ugly indeed: instance after instance of graft paid to the Building Trades Council, of honest contractors forced out of business because they refused to go along, of other contractors remaining in business only at the price of extortion payments, of local unions dominated by hoodlums. And his disclosures coincided with that sudden drastic decline in building activity which was a major element of the postwar depression. It was upon and against this sea of troubles that the American Construction Council was launched. Its basic purpose was "building public confidence in the . . . industry," said Roosevelt, primarily by helping its members "to keep their own house in order." If they failed to do so, he warned, "an exasperated public will some day regulate their house for them." [30]

But with this similarity of originating process and of general purpose ended all resemblance between Roosevelt's new role and that of Landis or Hays. The latter two received large salaries (Hays was paid $150,000 a year) for full-time employment; Roosevelt received no salary for services that occupied but a small portion of his time. Both Landis and Hays operated with large grants of executive authority; they could actually rule the members of their organizations to an important degree. Roosevelt had no executive authority whatever. His was essentially a public relations function. He exhorted and advised and issued pronouncements, but the only certain effects of all this were to keep his own name favorably before the public, to educate him in some of the intricacies and problems of the industry he spoke for, and to develop into somewhat more definite form certain ideas which he had first vaguely outlined at Troy, New York, in 1912, and which were destined to flower into a major experiment in national government in the years ahead.

The council over which he presided was a loosely organized association of some 250 trade associations and professional groups within the building industry. "All branches of the industry," said Roosevelt, "are represented . . . : Architects, engineers, general contractors, sub-contractors, construction labor, material and equipment dealers, financial, bond and real estate interests, public utility construction departments, and the construction divisions of Federal, state and municipal governments." [31] There was, however, no administrative machinery through which these very different groups could achieve the kind of "cooperation" and do the kind of "planning" that Roosevelt repeatedly called for and that was clearly necessary on a national scale if efficient use was to be made of the industry's resources. Instabilities plagued the industry. There was instability owing to excessive seasonal fluctuations, with too much building in summer, too little in winter, though, as Roosevelt pointed out, this was not technically necessary: the Navy during the war had had no slackening of construction activity or efficiency in the bitterest winter weather. There was instability owing to a grossly uneven distribution of building activity geographically, resulting in excessive demands upon the labor and other building resources available in some areas, a drastic underemployment of them in others. There was a general shortage of skilled labor in the building trades—a shortage so serious that Roosevelt during his six years as council president would try again and again, in letters and public relations maneuvers, to persuade college graduates that they would do better for themselves and their country by entering the ranks of skilled labor than they could do in low-salaried white-collar positions. (In one letter he deplored the fact that "we bring our boys and girls up to look up at white collars and down on overalls. . . ." [32]) Simultaneously, in cooperation with Secretary Hoover, he pressed the trade unions for a relaxation of the numerical limits they persisted in placing upon apprenticeships and pressed contractors to improve facilities for apprentices.

One argument he made was that college-trained men in overalls would not be as content as less educated men with the antiquated methods of building that prevailed in the industry; they would insist, he thought, upon "eliminating manual drudgery from their job, and substituting improved mechanical processes," devoting "much of their spare time to devising means" for accomplishing this.[33] No doubt he was less naïve than his argument indicates. He could not but have some realization of the root causes of the industry's stubborn conservatism, some sense of those solidified, narrowly exclusive self-interests which made craft unions and contractors resistant to technological changes and large-scale cooperation. Certainly he had a generalized sense of the council's failure, in terms of its own announced purposes. At the very first annual meeting of the organization's board of governors, held in his home on May 16, 1923, he bluntly told his colleagues that the council "has not done one darned thing" except collect dues.[34] Before any planning could be done that would alleviate any of the industry's ills, accurate data descriptive of the industry nationwide had to be gathered. None had been. There ought to be a standardization of building codes throughout the country, but not even a start had been made upon a detailed study of these varying codes in order to determine common denominators. And the crying need for a national building index remained unsatisfied throughout the six years of Roosevelt's council presidency.

VII

Among the construction industry evils that Roosevelt inveighed against in his public pronouncements was that of "speculative building" on the basis of which mortgage bonds were issued and promoted by "fictitious statements of earnings at abnormal interest rates." [35] But though he publicly opposed risky speculations as a general practice, especially in the building field, he personally, in his own business activities, participated in one risky venture after another.

Stimulated for a time, after his polio, by his and Howe's continuing warm friendship with the dramatic and exuberant Pat Homer, he continued with three promotional schemes to which he had committed himself before his illness—the ill-fated New England Oil Corporation; the almost equally ill-fated Compo Bond Corporation, formed to sell bonds through banks to small investors in the pattern established by the Treasury's Liberty Bonds and savings stamps during the war; and the proposal to establish lighter-than-air craft passenger lines between major American cities.

The latter was a particular enthusiasm of his in the early 1920's. He was sure that the future for long-distance air transport depended not on the airplane, but on the dirigible—and there was a psychological significance in his thinking so. He *wished* to think so. The same love of the "natural" and dislike of the "artificial" which caused him to prefer sail to motorboating and country to city living led him to prefer a relatively quiet device for riding the natural buoyancy of air to a roaring machine riding an artificial wind blasted against a rigid wing, especially since the latter was at that time hazardous in the extreme. (He was "horrified" to learn that his mother on her European trip in the summer of 1921 had flown in a plane from London to Paris. "Wait until my dirigibles are running," he wrote to one of his law partners at that time, "and then you will be able to take a form of transportation which is absolutely safe." [36]) When the syndicate he had joined in 1919 managed to acquire American rights to basic patents held by the German inventor Dr. Johann Schuette, he became, in February, 1923, one of the incorporators (with R. B. Mellon, Owen D. Young, Marshall Field, and others*) of the Gen-

---

* One of the others—indeed, a principal instigator of the whole enterprise—was Lewis Green Stevenson of Bloomington, Illinois, son of the Adlai E. Stevenson who had been Vice

eral Air Service. The company, it was announced, would soon initiate travel in helium-filled dirigibles between Chicago and New York. It didn't, of course. Prospective investors, including several of the original incorporators, were soon convinced that the airplane was destined to outstrip lighter-than-air craft as a means of transport, so that what was to have been a soaring enterprise never got off the ground.

In March, 1922, despite the fact that the New England Oil Corporation was in deep trouble because refined oil prices were falling, Roosevelt became majority stockholder in another Pat Homer speculation, Witham Bros., Inc., whose profits were to derive from expected rises in lobster prices. The original Witham enterprise was a lobster-packing plant at Rockland, Maine, operated by three brothers. Homer (he was named president of the new corporation; Roosevelt and Howe became directors) proposed to expand this into big business by acquiring pounds in which to keep huge numbers of lobsters until the price was right for a highly profitable sale of them, the sales to be made not only to the already assured market in the great restaurants and hotels of New York City, but also throughout the country. (Homer's marketing ideas were always expansive.) Alas, as in the case of refined oil, the expected price rise did not occur. Instead, lobster prices fell; the Witham brothers, quarreling with Homer's management, resigned as employees of the firm, though retaining stock in it, and Roosevelt as majority stockholder found himself obliged to pour out good money after bad in payment of endlessly mounting costs until, when the company finally failed in 1926, he had lost some $26,000 in it. Long before that time, his formerly warm friendship with Homer had markedly cooled.[37]

More fortunate—indeed, almost uniquely so among Roosevelt's numerous speculations—was the United European Investors, Ltd.,* whose formation was announced in New York City newspaper advertisements on September 14, 1922. The new company's president was Roosevelt himself. Its purpose was "to exchange its shares for German marks held by American investors and to invest these marks in actual values in Germany. Carefully selected investments will be made in real estate, mortgages, securities and participation in industrial and commercial enterprises. The company's facilities and connections enable it to secure attractive and sound investments; the directors will take advantage of the present money stringency in Germany and of the purchasing power of the mark which is far greater than is reflected by exchange quota-

President of the U.S. during Cleveland's second term and father of the Adlai E. Stevenson, then a Princeton undergraduate, who in the 1950's would twice be Democratic nominee for President.
* It was incorporated in Canada.

tions." [38] Buyers of the company's stock, in other words, paid for it in German marks, which were then exchanging at the rate of about 1,500 per dollar, and the stock's par value was set at 10,000 marks per share. Roosevelt announced on that same day that his company had invested in nineteen German firms, including the Nobel Dynamite Company of Hamburg and the German Edison Company. These and other investments, to an ultimate total of approximately $100,000 in marks, did very well for the American stockholders while helping supply desperately needed capital to the sick German economy. When United European Investors was liquidated in August, 1924, by which time the acute German financial crisis had come to an end, it was with an announced profit of 200 percent for its investors. Roosevelt himself made a profit of around $5,000, according to his own later recollection, his investment having been of typically modest size.[39]

In most of his other speculative ventures he lost money. There were a number of schemes that died aborning into which he put some money and a good deal of time and energy. One was a proposal to merge several small shipping lines into a corporation which, acquiring some of the surplus ships of the war-born and still-operative Emergency Fleet Corporation, would transport freight between the East and West coasts through the Panama Canal. Another was to plant and raise a 10,000- or 15,000-acre pine forest, the harvesting to begin in twenty years, when, since pine was being cut faster than it was being grown, lumber prices would surely be greatly advanced. A third would have sold advertising space in taxicabs. A fourth would have organized a National Resorts, Inc., to establish and operate a string of resorts between Lake Placid, New York, and Warm Springs, Georgia. In the summer of 1927 he made a second foray into the now rapidly recovering German economy when he became an incorporator and director of the International Germanic Trust Company, which was to invest American capital in German securities. The company offered its shares for sale on August 25, 1927, at $170 a share (Roosevelt owned seventy-five of them), and for a few weeks the price shot up. Then it went down as precipitously as it had risen. Roosevelt resigned his directorship in early 1928, and not long thereafter the company went into receivership. He invested in an ephemeral company which wildcatted for oil in Wyoming but struck sulfur instead (Howe suggested he "go into the sulphur bath industry— look at Hot Springs!" [40]) and lost everything he had put into it.

Viewed in historical perspective, the most interesting of all the enterprises in which he speculated was Camco (the Consolidated Automatic Merchandising Corporation), formed in 1928. Camco's brief and unprofitable existence, the criticisms it aroused at the time, and the repercussions that followed its demise were expressive of basic dilemmas created by technological advances within a private profit society—and there is a further symbolic significance in the fact that Roosevelt's involvement in it, which he later regretted, was largely inadvertent. Certainly such decisions as he made about it were narrowly focused on its presumed profit-making potential and contained no element of concern about general social consequences.

Some time before, he and Henry Morgenthau, Sr., had become two of the directors of the Sanitary Postage Company, whose business was the dispensing of stamps through machines and whose promoters claimed that one such machine in a large retail outlet would "do about one clerk's work, releasing human labor for more constructive purposes." Sanitary Postage was doing fairly well when it became, with Roosevelt's directorial acquiescence, one of five vending machine companies which merged to form Camco, a holding company. Roosevelt became one of the original directors when he exchanged his Sanitary Postage stock for stock in the new corporation. He resigned this directorship a few months later, for political reasons. He later claimed that he also disposed of his Camco stock "as soon as he could." But the evidence is that he shared at the outset, and for some time thereafter, in the great tide of optimism concerning future profits on which Camco was launched, with a flourish of financial-page publicity. The corporation proposed to introduce some 1,500,000 vending machines into stores across the nation within the next five years. It would open three wholly "clerkless" stores in New York City. Its robots would sell not only stamps, candy, cigarettes, but many other kinds of small-item merchandise, eliminating the need for thousands of clerks (these would be freed from "the deadening monotony of a mechanical job," said one of Roosevelt's fellow directors), whose wages would be converted into Camco dividends. The dividends would swiftly multiply, according to the projections made in Camco stock-promotional literature. Every dollar invested in 1928 would earn $1.50 in dividends in 1933 as share values increased 3,000 percent.

But Camco, in its zeal to replace men with machines, failed to reckon with outraged "human nature," as journalist Alva Johnson later put it, and "human nature struck back." Too many of the "silver coins" thrust into robot mouths turned out to be lead slugs. Too often the robot, through mechanical failure, denied customers the goods they had paid for, provoking machine-wrecking reprisals. (Human beings had soon to be hired to guard the machines against human beings.) Too many potential customers refused even to enter the "clerkless" stores. So that Camco, instead of earning a projected $2,200,000 in 1929, lost $458,000, lost nearly twice that in the following year and more than $1,000,000 in 1931, when it was supposed to earn $7,800,000. It went into receivership, to the accompaniment of angry lawsuits, two years later, having lost some $3,200,000 instead of earning, as it was supposed to do, well over $43,000,000. By that time the very idea of displacing men with machines was anathema to the American people, and Roosevelt heartily wished he had never heard of Camco.[41]

Less hazardous in this way to his political career, but only because much smaller in scale, was another automation speculation in which Roosevelt engaged. This was Photomaton, Inc., of which he and the younger Morgenthau became directors in 1927 and of whose shares Roosevelt owned 500, purchased for $3 a share. Its business was quar-ter-in-the-slot photographing machines, its projected profits of $1,000,000 a year were to consist of the money saved in photographers' salaries, and its stock shot up in price in the great bull market of 1928. In December of that year, Roosevelt sold his 500 shares for $17 apiece. Two years later Photomaton went into receivership.[42]

In general, Roosevelt seems to have "played" business, including his salesmanship for Fidelity and Deposit, as if it were a game, in much the same way as his father had done, for excitement rather more than for profit, though he certainly wished and felt the need for quick profits. It will be remembered that he described his work for Black's company, in a letter to Black himself, as "the bonding end of the game." Moreover, he "played" it as a game of chance rather than skill: he even seemed de-termined to maximize the role of chance in many cases, proportionately reducing the amount of skill involved, as he did at the poker table when, given dealer's choice, he called for variations so wild that the odds be-came incalculable.

Yet it is evident that the excitement he craved and sought to gain through this gambling was not that of great risk or peril. He tempered his enthusiasms, his seemingly unquenchable optimism, with a fair measure of Dutch prudence and frugality.

He seldom staked much on a single gamble—never enough to endan-ger his financial security. Sometimes he risked a few hundred dollars only; an initial $5,000 seems to have been about his limit, though his seventy-five shares of International Germanic, if he paid the list price for them, cost him $12,750. He ran far greater risks with his reputation, his good name. "I have noted with a great deal of concern the use of your name to further the sale of stocks in new promotions that . . . are business risks of the more hazardous type and I am wondering if your attention has been called to the fact that these securities are being

offered for public subscription as 'safe investments,'" said a letter to
him in July, 1923, from the executive officer of the Society for Promoting Financial Knowledge, who went on to express his sense of "pity that
a distinguished and honored name should be commercialized in this
manner. . . ." [43] But such risk of honor was not run deliberately in
order to enhance a thrill of danger. It was run almost unconsciously, out
of a certain moral irresponsibility, an insensitivity to the nicer moral distinctions. (For instance, his conscience seems not to have been troubled
by the fact that Compo Bond, of which he was a well-publicized director, prominently displayed "The United States of America" at the
top of the certificates it sold, with the evident purpose of conveying to
the unwary the impression that these certificates were a species of U.S.
Treasury bond; he was only relieved when, in a court ruling by a lenient
judge, the display was deemed legal. Nor did he have qualms about attempting to influence government shipping policy in ways that would
profit his private interest, though a public revelation of the latter might
have rendered less persuasive than it was a letter of his published in the
New York *Times* in the spring of 1924 deploring the cost to taxpayers
[$40,000,000 to $50,000,000 a year] of the continued operation of the
Emergency Fleet Corporation. If the corporation had disposed of "the
dozens of ships . . . now tied up in the Hudson, Potomac, the Chesa-
peake, etc. . . . for whatever they will bring," as he advocated in a private letter at that time, it would certainly have been a boon to the new
shipping corporation he was striving to form.) [44]

No, quite clearly the excitement he sought was not that of danger. It
seems instead to have been an excitement of vital curiosity regarding his
particular luck, suspenseful across the time interval between his placing
of a bet and the culmination of a particular game—a curiosity whose climactic satisfaction would be the revelation, at game's end, of a portion
of that luck's special nature and dimensions. This, in turn, in his doubtless unconscious belief, would reveal something of the divine intent in
general. For, as has been often before remarked, he had an acute sense
of himself as a vital element in the ongoingness of the universe, a major
actor in the drama of history, and it was of the essence of his living faith
that a cosmic purpose—continuously and, in the long run, benevolently
determinative of events, especially of events having to do with him personally—underlay all appearance of random, meaningless chance. "He
felt that human beings were given tasks to perform and with those tasks
the ability and strength to put them through," Eleanor Roosevelt has
written. "He could pray for help and guidance and have faith in his own
judgment [thereby informed by divine will] as a result." [45] Hence, his
chance taking might be described as a kind of praying or, if not truly

prayerful, since it was deficient in piety, as at least an operation teleologically motivated. It was a question asked about his personal relationship with fate at a given time, in a given context.

Consistent with this interpretation is the fact that Roosevelt was genuinely, if mildly, superstitious. He was inclined to consult trivial things, insignificant happenings, for signs and portents, when forced to make choices among alternatives of seemingly equal merit. He could become addicted to a certain article of clothing as lucky—an old felt hat, an old sweater—and averse to others as unlucky. He disliked dining at a table set for thirteen and took pains, sometimes very considerable pains, to avoid beginning any long journey on a Friday the thirteenth. He never lighted three cigarettes from the same match; he was annoyed when others did so in his presence.[46]

Twenty-three

❧❧❧❧❧

Return to Politics: 1924

I

VERY different from his approach to business-as-game during these interim years was his approach to politics.

Politics was more a game for him than it was for such idealists and ideologists as Bryan, Daniels, La Follette, Wilson, Hoover. Each of these men had clearer, more definite, more rigid ideas of what America ought to be than he had. Each had stronger commitments to certain specific programs and policies. Each evinced in general a greater willingness than he to sacrifice election victories to the goals for which, in their lofty conceptions, the whole of the political process ought to work. As a consequence, the proportion of pure fun was less, of earnest endeavor more, in their politicking than in his.

But if, and to the extent that, politics was a game for him, he played it not as a game of chance, but as a game of skill. He had a basic plan to which he adhered through thick and thin with rare persistence and consistency. He did everything he could to minimize the role of accident and maximize that of the controllable as determinants of the outcome. Indeed, he knew intuitively so precisely what he was doing—there was so little of random inadvertence in it, so much of careful calculation— that the game metaphor seems less adequate to describe his enterprise than the metaphor of the architect-builder who, presented with a specific site and functional purpose, proceeds to design and erect a structure that fits well into its environment, is efficient, and in the construction of which the materials closest at hand are used flexibly, creatively.

The main outlines of the blueprint he followed may be traced by the historian back to those two of his speeches which, of all he had given prior to the 1920 campaign, had the highest intellectual content. The first of these was his speech of March 3, 1912, before the People's Forum of Troy, New York, wherein he groped toward a solution of the problem of individual freedom within a technologically advanced society, concluding that "new sets of conditions" required that a "new theory" of the "liberty of the community" take precedence over the "old theory" of the "liberty of the individual." His vague but strong feeling at the time, since somewhat clarified and rigidified, was that a community is no mere collection of individuals externally related to one another and to the collection as a whole but is, instead, a kind of organism substantially composed of the *internal* relations of its members. The New Freedom, therefore, differed from the "old" freedom in that it was not an isolate individual natural "right"—a private property right—but was a function of community. To some indeterminate degree it must be planned, it must be organized in socioeconomic terms, if it were to survive in the modern world.*

The other speech was that of May 29, 1919, before the Democratic National Committee in Chicago, wherein he announced that the twenty-five-year struggle between liberal and conservative forces within each of the major political parties had now been resolved in such a way that "the Republican party is the conservative party of the United States and . . . the Democratic party is the progressive or liberal party." † He had by that time developed, and had since very definitely clarified, a conception of what "conservatism" and "liberalism" meant in America in terms of political party composition and program. He sent on December 27, 1921, a letter to be read to the next Jackson Day gathering of Democrats in Portland, Oregon. In it he indicated that Andrew Jackson's "earnest determination to keep the control of our government out of the hands of the professional moneymakers and to keep it, as was always the intention of our forefathers, in the hands of the people themselves" had a special relevance to the America of the 1920's.[1] "Conservatism," then, was to be identified with "professional moneymakers," "liberalism" with "the people themselves."

The Republicans were essentially a single-interest party—a party of business, especially big business so far as national policy-making was concerned. Farmers, other small entrepreneurs, workingmen, professional people were attached to it by relatively slender ties, often merely traditional, which could be broken by the million in times of stress. The Democracy, on the other hand, was very distinctly a multiple-interest party. Its membership included the whole spectrum of religious faiths,

* See pages 265 and 300.
† See pages 607–8.

regional differences, and economic, social, and cultural interests. There were large numbers of Catholics and Jews and a wide range of ethnic groups in the Democracy; the Republican Party was much more exclusively Protestant and Anglo-Saxon, or North European, in descent. There were big businessmen and scions of inherited wealth in the Democratic Party—Doheny, William Randolph Hearst, McAdoo, Gerard, banker Herbert H. Lehman, Baruch, the Morgenthaus, Roosevelt himself—but their economically interested influence, insofar as they strove to exert it, was offset by that of the millions of "common people" for whom William Jennings Bryan remained a spokesman. Of such offset, the Republican Party had relatively little. There were Southerners, white Southerners by the million in the Democracy, whereas the Southern interest was but feebly represented, if at all, in the highest Republican councils.

And Roosevelt was sharply aware of the tactical and strategic advantages and disadvantages which accrued to each party, in relation to the other, out of this alignment, this difference of composition.

On the face of it, the long-run strategic advantage in the electoral wars should lie with the new Democracy. It was much more representative, much more a fair cross section of America as a whole, than was the party of McKinley-Taft-Harding. Its programs and policies ought, therefore, to be more responsive to general needs, more expressive of the general welfare than those of the Republicans. But this long-run advantage required for its successful exercise the overcoming of very grave and immediate tactical disadvantages. The Republicans, by virtue of their single overriding interest, were much more naturally cohesive and far wealthier as an organization than the Democrats. They could easily make up their collective mind on almost any issue of importance, being predominantly of the same mind to begin with, and having made up this mind, they could finance a campaign on its behalf with an abundance of money, swiftly and easily raised. Democrats, on the other hand, could decide on national candidates and issue stands only through prolonged, wound-dealing controversies. Conflicting interests must be either reconciled or put to one side. Widely divergent views must somehow be harmonized. Wholly different systems of value must be brought into a viable relationship with one another. And this had proved increasingly difficult since the second of the Bryan campaigns. It had proved impossible in 1920, when Tammany and other Democratic city machines had not lifted a finger to help Cox and Roosevelt, when no major part of the national campaign had been efficiently coordinated with any other part or with the efforts made in state and local contests. So long as this situation prevailed, the Democracy was doomed to national defeat, for it had

to fight its battles under a weak and compromised leadership, upon issues ill-chosen and ill-presented, and with a campaign war chest smaller
by far than the Republican.

Indeed, there was a serious question in many informed minds whether
the Democracy could now survive at all on a national scale. It seemed
to be falling apart, its internal factional divisions being wider than its
overall division from the Republican Party. But Roosevelt's political intuition told him that this seemingly imminent dissolution simply meant
that the process whose end he had so confidently announced in his 1919
Chicago address was in fact still under way. It had not yet been completed. The Republican Party, with men like Norris, La Follette, Johnson, and Borah at least nominally in it, was not yet quite the "conservative" party it was destined to become under its present leadership. The
Democratic Party, with men like Hearst and Doheny in it, was not yet
quite the "liberal" party which *it* was destined to become when it had
found its proper leadership. In other words, there were elements of nominal Republicanism which belonged in the new Democracy, elements of
nominal Democracy which belonged with the Republicans, and since
the former elements were numerically greater than the latter, the Democracy had much to gain and little to lose by developing a unity of
effective agreement on certain broad general progressive principles,
even though this meant a sloughing off of all who would not so agree.

To the task of achieving this unity Roosevelt had consciously addressed himself even before the 1920 campaign. He continued to do so,
with an intensified consciousness of definite aims and possibilities, in
the aftermath of his polio. In October, 1921, for instance, when he was
still dangerously ill in bed, he, or Howe in his name, sent to the Democratic National Committee a proposal for party reorganization—one
that would establish full-time administrative machinery at a national
headquarters, provide for periodic national conferences in which the
party rank and file would participate in policy-making, and in general
shape the Democracy into an army fighting under the banner of liberalism against Harding-Coolidge reaction.

II

Both a cause and a symptom of the Democracy's disarray in New
York State, in the summer of 1922, was an especially acute recurrence of
publisher William Randolph Hearst's perennial lust for high elective
office.

Hearst and Al Smith were sworn enemies. Through his ownership of

the New York *American* and New York *Evening Journal,* the most sensational of yellow journals, and of a string of similar papers reaching all
across the country, each staffed by men utterly subservient to his will
and whim, the unscrupulous demagogic publisher could so amplify
whatever lies he chose to tell that the truth was often drowned out by
them. He used this power with utter ruthlessness in the service of his
ambition and of that peculiarly virulent form of "patriotism" which had
caused him to foment the Spanish-American War and now caused him
to hate Woodrow Wilson and the League of Nations. He had backed
the successful campaign of John F. Hylan for mayor of New York in
1917; Hylan, a man of monumental stupidity, had ever since acted as
the publisher's hireling. Hearst had evinced a willingness to shape accommodations with Smith when Smith was elected president of the
Board of Aldermen of New York in 1917. But when Smith, having easily
bested him in competition for the Democratic gubernatorial nomination
in 1918, curtly refused as governor to heed any of his requests or recommendations, Hearst set out to destroy him. Huge headlines in the *American* and *Evening Journal* proclaimed in early autumn of 1919 that Governor Smith was directly responsible for the scarcity, high price, and
unsanitary quality of milk in New York City, though in point of fact
Smith had tried in vain to persuade a Republican legislature to grant
him the executive powers he needed to cope with an increasingly serious
"milk crisis." BABIES ARE DYING IN NEW YORK, screamed a *Journal* banner headline. A *Journal* front-page editorial, printed in large type, was
addressed to the governor: "You have sold the babies to the Milk Trust,
as that other Judas, President Wilson, has sold the world to British tyranny." Smith struck back. He challenged Hearst to a face-to-face debate
of the issues between them and, when Hearst contemptuously refused,
appeared alone in a jampacked Carnegie Hall on October 29, 1919, to
deliver a slashing attack on Hearst as a vicious liar, guilty of "breeding
the seeds of anarchy"—an attack so effective with the general public (it
was very fully reported in all newspapers save Hearst's) that historians
would deem it the beginning of the final decline, slow but inexorable, of
the publisher's political power and influence.[2]

But Hearst in 1922 gave no sign of awareness that such decline had
begun. Smith's defeat in his campaign for reelection in 1920 had been
by a margin so narrow as to constitute a tremendous personal triumph
in that year of Republican tidal wave.* There was little doubt of his re-

* While the Cox-Roosevelt ticket lost New York to Harding-Coolidge by an almost incredible 1,200,000 votes, Smith lost to his Republican opponent, Judge Nathan L. Miller of Syracuse, by a mere 75,000. Smith, in other words, ran some 1,090,000 votes ahead of the Democratic national ticket in his home state.

turning to elective office. But he had taken a high-salaried position as board chairman of the United States Trucking Company, which handled some four-fifths of New York City's trucking business, and Hearst may have been among those who believed that Smith, with a large family to support, would not consider giving up his $50,000 a year as trucking executive until 1924 at the earliest. At any rate, the publisher, encouraged by the reelection of Hylan as New York mayor in 1921, quietly launched early in the year a personal campaign to capture the Democratic gubernatorial nomination for himself. Judge Samuel Seabury, Democratic candidate for governor in 1916, gave public warning of it in May; an "alleged demand for Hearst" was being "drummed up," he said in an open letter to Smith, through lavish expenditures of Hearst money.[3] By late June it was apparent that only Smith, by running himself, could prevent Hearst's domination of the state convention, though it was equally apparent that Hearst, running against the incumbent Governor Nathan Miller, would lead the state Democratic ticket to ignominious defeat.

Roosevelt watched this development with growing perturbation. Polio had not interrupted in the slightest his close attention to Dutchess County Democratic politics and his effective leadership of them, a leadership he continued to exert in alliance with such men as Tom Lynch and John Mack against the continuing personal hostility of Ed Perkins. He had little fear of Hearst inroads upon his home county's organization. But, as he wrote Smith, "there are some dreadfully weak sisters upstate" to whom "the promise of the Hearst iron men looks mighty good." Roosevelt acted. To state Democratic leaders scheduled to meet in conference in early July he, physically unable to attend the meeting himself, addressed a letter urging them to reject "false gods and political nostrums" and to call upon Smith to run again. He was sure, he said, that Smith would respond to "the need of the State of New York for his services" despite the "rest from public service in order to attend to his personal affairs" which the ex-governor certainly wanted and deserved. The letter received wide publicity. Smith, however, remained silent, and Hearst continued to gain ground. It was not until a week before the final day for filing nomination petitions that Smith, responding to now-frantic pleas from upstate anti-Hearst Democrats, agreed to make the race, provided he was directly and publicly called up to do so by a leading Democratic spokesman. Roosevelt became that spokesman. On August 13, he addressed an open letter to "Dear Al," saying in part: "Many candidates for office are strong by virtue of what they promise they will do. You are strong by virtue of what you have done. . . . I am taking it upon myself to appeal to you in the name of countless citizens of upstate New York. . . . You represent the type of citizen the voters of this state want to vote for for Governor. . . ." He added that the "decision must be made now." The letter was front-page news in the state and nationally. So was Smith's prompt reply, an open letter to "Dear Frank," saying: "I appreciate your kindly sentiments, and they compel me to talk to you from my heart. . . . It has been and still is my desire to remain in business life—but during the past twenty years I have been so honored by my party that even the members of my family would be dissatisfied if I did not answer the call. . . ." He closed with "kind regards to your mother and Mrs. Roosevelt and all the children," signing himself, "Sincerely yours, Al." [4]

And that was the end for Hearst.

Roosevelt hosted a reception for Smith at the Hyde Park house in early September. This was his first occasion to display before a considerable group of state party workers the degree of his physical recovery and of his return to political activity. It was also an occasion of vivid social contrasts. Sara Delano Roosevelt would entertain for her son's sake this crude man of the streets with his brown derby and tobacco-stained teeth, his rasping voice and Lower East Side accent, his self-asserted plebeianism (he proclaimed himself a graduate of the Fulton Fish Market) which in her presence was perhaps a little more assertive than normally; but she could never accept Al Smith as a social equal, could no more approve of him as a man than she did of Louis Howe or, as Eleanor would remember, "believe that . . . [he] could have any ability." [5] Her usual *grande dame* manner became grander still when she greeted him, conversed with him. He could not but know precisely how she felt about him. Yet though it was Eleanor's impression that he respected her mother-in-law, he obviously did not take her seriously enough to be intimidated by her. He seems to have accepted her as an interesting anachronism, admirably strong of will and personality, and to have wondered if the son of such a mother, raised in such a home as this and still obviously bound to his mother by economic as well as emotional ties, could ever become more than a dilettante, however brilliant, in elective politics.[6] Certainly his experience of Sara Roosevelt did nothing to remove from his attitude toward her son whatever residue there was of the dislike, mistrust, and essential contempt he had felt, in 1911 and 1912, toward a state senator from Dutchess County who had seemed to him, and to Bob Wagner also, insufferably supercilious and arrogant.

A few days after the reception, Roosevelt sent a written formal endorsement of Smith to be read before the county committee meeting at which delegates to the state convention were selected and was gratified when a strong pro-Smith delegation, including his wife and Morgenthau, Jr., was sent to that convention. There "Al" was nominated "with great enthusiasm," as Howe wired Roosevelt, adding that "Morgenthau and your missus led the Dutchess delegation with the banner three times around the hall." [7] Hearst, tacitly conceding that he had no chance against Smith for the gubernatorial nomination, had been pressing, ever since Smith's announcement of availability, for nomination for the U.S. Senate. He had sent emissaries to promise Smith the support of the Hearst press—prominent Tammany men who urged Hearst's case with vehemence, out of their fear of what Hearst's hostile publicity and Hylan's mayoralty power might do to them and their organization. Boss Murphy favored a rapprochement between Smith and Hearst. But Smith was adamant. He flatly refused to run on the same ticket with the hated publisher.

At this juncture, a mild combination of Roosevelt "luck" and Roosevelt adroitness enabled him mildly to advance his cause of party unity. Smith had wanted him to run for the Senate himself. This being a physical impossibility, Roosevelt had pressed for the nomination of a leading liberal upstater instead, George Lunn, a former Socialist who had won the Democratic Senatorial nomination in 1920 and seemed eager to run again. But while Howe and others were working toward this end at the convention, Lunn suddenly accepted a proffered nomination for lieutenant governor. Howe was a bit chagrined.[8] Roosevelt, however, saw in the event an opportunity to heal somewhat the breach with Hearst and with those Murphy Tammanyites who had favored Hearst for the Senate. He indicated a more than willingness to back for the Senatorial post Royal S. Copeland, MD, whose fame rested upon a medical column he wrote for Hearst's newspaper syndicate and who was a personal friend of the publisher's. Copeland was given the nomination. Roosevelt then accepted the honorary chairmanship of Copeland's campaign committee.

He played no active part in the campaign that followed. Eleanor did, however. Smith's campaign manager was a tall, red-haired Jewish lawyer named Joseph M. Proskauer, a friend of the matronly, brilliant Mrs. Belle Moskowitz upon whose utter personal devotion to him, joined to very formidable executive and political talents, Smith had heavily leaned during his 1919–21 term as governor. Proskauer wrote many of Smith's speeches, gathered together a group of intellectuals to serve as expert advisers in various fields, and made extensive use of that new arm of the Democratic Party, the Women's Division. Especially did he make use of Frances Perkins and Eleanor, both of whom toured the state making speeches and organizing local Democratic women's groups. The outcome was a heartening triumph. Al Smith, running on a progressive reform platform which he insisted was a "promissory note" that must and would be paid in full to the people, won election over his respected conservative opponent with a plurality of almost 400,000—the largest ever won up to that time by a New York governor. He carried with him to victory, though by a narrow margin, Royal S. Copeland.

And he then proceeded to pay rich dividends on Roosevelt's investment in his career, encouraging further such investment, by making in his second gubernatorial term a record more brilliant than he had made in his highly successful first term.

Freed of binding obligations to Murphy and Tammany Hall by the manner in which his victory had been won, convinced that efficient and dedicated public servants through their day-by-day efforts would do more to secure his reelection than could party hacks who were rewarded with state jobs for "getting out the vote," he replaced the latter with the former when and where he could. He thereby did more toward developing a state employment merit system than had any other New York governor since Grover Cleveland. Proskauer, whom he appointed to fill out an unexpired term on the New York Supreme Court and who then won election to a full term as Supreme Court judge, continued as one of his two most intimate advisers, the other being Belle Moskowitz, and he continued to draw upon the knowledge and intellectual skills of the "college people" whom Proskauer had recruited during the campaign. There would be echoes of this in Roosevelt's future career. Smith's chief labor adviser was Frances Perkins, whom he appointed to the three-member Industrial Board. This board had quasi-legislative, quasi-judicial functions in the detailed application of the general statutes emergent from the Factory Investigating Commission of 1911–15, and Miss Perkins became at once its dominant member. Very largely due to her was the fact that the Labor Department, of all the state's executive units, became the one of which the governor was most proud.

Even before his inauguration, Smith moved decisively to redeem a major campaign pledge—namely, to conserve and develop on behalf of all the people the state's hydroelectric resources. This, too, would have echoes in Roosevelt's future. The power resources of the St. Lawrence, the Niagara, the Upper Hudson were enormous and, because of a long-deadlocked struggle between the proponents of private and those of public power, remained little developed, though the need for them was growing. Immediately following the 1922 election, certain giant private interests—the Aluminum Company of America (ALCOA's Andrew Mellon was now Harding's Secretary of the Treasury), the DuPonts, General Electric—moved, through a holding company called the Frontier Corporation, to grab some of the best power sites before the new

Democratic administration took office. A meeting of the State Water-power Commission was quietly scheduled for November 23, 1922. All five of the commission members were Republican officeholders, including the attorney general, the president of the Senate, and the speaker of the Assembly, H. Edmund Machold, who functioned as legislative agent of the private power interests.* It could be expected, therefore, that the commission would act favorably upon Frontier's application. Smith, however, on November 22, in a telegram to the attorney general, bluntly asked the commission, "in view of the decision of the people at the polls following the campaign, in which this subject was a distinct issue, not to grant any licenses to private corporations . . . for waterpower resources that belong to the state and permit the subject to be dealt with by the incoming administration in accordance with explicit promises made during the campaign." The telegram was released to the press in a way that would assure its receiving top news coverage on the morning the commission met, and in the spotlight of publicity thus focused upon them, the commissioners perforce did as the governor-elect requested. No licenses were issued.[9]

And this preinaugural instance of publicity used as an instrument of government was duplicated again and again after Smith took office. With Belle Moskowitz managing his public relations and influencing his policy, he managed to get through the legislature, of which the Democrats controlled the Senate while Republicans controlled the Assembly, a substantial portion of the progressive measures he had called for at the opening of the 1923 session, including an extension of rent control and a provision for public housing corporations, both bitterly opposed by real estate interests. Narrowly defeated (it would be enacted four years later) was the bill for the forty-eight-hour workweek for women. He also made a remarkable record of reorganizing and increasing the efficiency of state administration. Well before the end of 1923 he had become a hero to myriads of liberals and workingmen across the land, was regarded by these as the outstanding Progressive of the national Democracy, and was being boomed for his party's Presidential nomination in 1924, a boom adroitly managed by Belle Moskowitz and Proskauer.

III

Roosevelt, of course, watched with close attention the growth of

* Machold would give up his speakership a few years later to become a banking partner of the chairman of the board of the Niagara-Hudson Power Corporation.

Smith's fame. But he would have nothing to do publicly with the governor's Presidential boom or with the activities on behalf of any of the other all-too-numerous Democratic aspirants in 1923. He deplored this early promotion of potential nominees because it encouraged the party's besetting sin of factionalism. It prevented the kind of unity upon agreed general liberal principles which was necessary for persuasiveness over a majority of the electorate and in the absence of which there could be no effective partisan attack upon Republican "government by selfish interests or powerfully entrenched individuals." What good was done, he asked, even for the candidates themselves, by all this promotion of "personal candidacies" so many months before the national convention? Such "candidacies . . . rarely develop into anything tangible," he had written to a friend shortly before Christmas, 1922. "In our own Party for the last 30 to 60 years the nomination has been nearly every time a matter of luck, or of some eleventh hour opportunity boldly seized upon." * [10] Far better would it be, for party and candidates alike, to declare a moratorium on all talk of personalities until the spring of 1924 at the earliest! Then, in the interim, everyone could devote his attention and energy to the shaping of progressive party policies, the building or rebuilding of effective party organizations.

He was especially concerned at this time lest "personal candidacies" become fused with opposite sides of the Prohibition issue. This was an issue much more likely to divide disastrously the Democrats than it was the Republicans, since the Democracy could function successfully at the polls only as a coalition of the overwhelmingly "dry" rural South with the overwhelmingly "wet" urban North. He doubted the issue's intrinsic importance, relative to other matters; he wondered, in fact, if it were not being cynically exploited by special interests to divert popular attention from truly basic social and economic problems—problems which the Republican leadership wished to have ignored. Eleanor, who had suffered so greatly from her father's and her uncles' alcoholism when she was growing up, was a convinced dry. If she did not quite regard drinking as sinful per se, she was inclined to regard Prohibition as a *moral* question. Roosevelt could not see it so—but even if it was, that was all the more reason why it should not and must not become a partisan political question. A device for removing it from politics altogether should be found. Until then the issue should be straddled. And he personally did straddle it, as a bridge does an abyss, addressing himself to opposite sides with a seeming equivalence of affirmation and emphatic

---

* Of course, his and Howe's deep handling of his own candidacies, all through these years, evinced his realization that the "luck" he referred to, like a lightning bolt, was likely to strike only a prominent object in the political landscape.

weight. The time was ripe, he said in 1923, for a national referendum on the Volstead Act, which was the implementing legislation of the Eighteenth Amendment. To fervent wets he indicated that such a referendum would result in modifications of the act that would at the very least legalize light wines and beer and protect individual rights of privacy and property from the excessive zeal of Prohibition agents. To fervent drys, notably William Jennings Bryan, he indicated that the proposed referendum would result in endorsement of the present act by an overwhelming majority, thus encouraging a much more rigorous enforcement than had thus far obtained.[11]

To Bryan, also, he gently hinted his belief that the Progressivism to which Bryan was committed and to which the Democratic Party must be recommitted for victory over the Republicans was in danger of being sidetracked by the furor over liquor.

The Great Commoner remained an epitome of a way of life and politics which was dying out of the increasingly industrialized, urbanized country—dying more from a lack of intelligently creative leadership, one suspects, than from a lack of essential vital relevance to the current scene. What Bryan stood for, essentially, was an America that a great many, if not most, Americans of the early 1920's, given a free choice, would have preferred over the America which "progress" was making. Indeed, the disease of the times would appear to have been in large part an anxiety neurosis born of the frustration of deeply felt needs by this "inevitable progress"—a neurosis that was only increased by a vague suspicion that the loudly proclaimed "inevitability" might actually be a misnomer. *Why* was such "progress" absolutely necessary? Why was the old America utterly at the mercy of the new technology? Could there not be a creative interaction between the two, enabling the best of the old to be carried intact, and even enhanced, into the new world? These questions, unexpressed, wrapped about with a sense of human failure, gave rise to sick confusions of mind and spirit, especially in those who sought simply to face down the future with willful assertions of the past. Hence the symbolism of Bryan's being, at sixty-three, old beyond his years, physically ill and soon to die of diabetes, mentally so confused as to be the laughingstock of all the bright, cold, brittle wits of the city. For Bryan was not only a fanatical dry, but also a fanatical Fundamentalist (he actually believed that Eve was made of Adam's rib, that a Great Flood once drowned all life on earth save that aboard Noah's Ark, that the divergence of languages began at the Tower of Babel), while continuing to be an advanced political progressive—advanced, in many respects, even by the standards of the early 1920's. It was as a liberal intellectual of the Brandeis stamp that he responded to the challenge of

Harding-Coolidge conservatism. Farmers were caught in a squeeze between depressed prices for the produce they must sell and inflated prices for the goods they must buy: "something must be done" to raise the former or lower the latter. The Federal Reserve banking system had been "captured by Wall Street": it must be re-formed into a credit system for all the people. The antagonistic rift between labor and capital dangerously widened: a governmental means of adjudicating the disputes between the two must be devised. Larger and larger combinations of industry were being formed, with "the masses" their "victims": the government must act forcefully against them. But of course, none of these things could happen, indeed the evils were actually fostered, under the present administration, whose dominant figure, and Bryan's bête noire, was Secretary of the Treasury Andrew Mellon, author of "the most reactionary revenue bill ever enacted." [12]

It was in recognition of this weird juxtaposition of commitments—Prohibitionism, Fundamentalism, Progressivism—in the Great Commoner's mind that Roosevelt in the late spring of 1923, in a letter to Bryan, made an improbable identification of political "reactionaries" with wets in the Democratic Party. He warned Bryan that these "reactionary forces" were seeking to make New York City the 1924 Democratic National Convention city because, "hopeful idiots" that they were, they believed this wet environment might enable them to write into the party platform a plank calling for repeal of the Eighteenth Amendment or, failing that, might at least enable them to block the nomination "of a real progressive democrat or an outspoken dry. . . ." [13]

Yet Roosevelt as he wrote this well knew that the real and growing danger to the political values for which Bryan stood was not of a linkage of wets with reaction but rather of a tacit working alliance between the drys, who maintained a very powerful lobby in the Anti-Saloon League, and the Ku Klux Klan.

The latter brutal secret society of Reconstruction days in the South had been revived or refounded in 1915 * and, animated by a blindly ignorant nativism and by the most vicious racial and religious bigotry, was prospering immensely in postwar isolationist America. It represented the dark ugly side of the Populism which lived into the third decade of the century. It fed hugely at first upon the white Southerner's fear of "uppity" blacks returning from the armed services, but soon it fed everywhere upon a white Protestant "old-American" fear and ha-

---

* The specific inspiration of this revival seems to have been D. W. Griffith's classic motion picture of 1914, *The Birth of a Nation,* based on a virulently racist, hate-ridden "historical" novel of Reconstruction days in the South, entitled *The Clansman,* by Thomas Dixon.

tred of such "foreign" elements as Catholics, Jews, "radicals," Southern European immigrants, and intellectuals in general. It was essentially a terrorist organization. In the darkness of night, under its sign of the burning cross, its anonymous hooded members perpetrated thousands of acts of violence upon helpless men and women—whippings, tar and featherings, maimings, fatal lynchings. But it was also increasingly a nonpartisan or bipartisan political movement. It throve as such in the Midwest and along the Pacific coast, as well as in the South, actually ultimately capturing control of the state governments of Oregon and California, of Ohio and Indiana, of Oklahoma, Arkansas, Texas. And New York was by no means immune to it in 1923. Across the state's farmlands and through its smaller towns, the KKK swept in indeterminate strength to the very gates of cosmopolitan New York City.

The Klan's New York presence, in conjunction with the Anti-Saloon League, increased the hazard for Al Smith of a dilemma into which he was deliberately maneuvered by his Republican opponents in May, 1923, and concerning which Roosevelt offered him carefully considered advice.

In 1921 the Republican legislature had passed and Republican Governor Miller had signed into law the Mullan-Gage bill, which added state to federal enforcement of the Volstead Act. It authorized state police and deputy sheriffs to engage in the same search and seizure activities as did federal Prohibition agents. Al Smith had denounced it as a redundant measure whose net effect would be the exposure of state law enforcement officers to the same corrupting influences as were already playing havoc with the federal enforcement agency—though in point of actual fact the new law was *not* redundant insofar as the Volstead Act could not be enforced by federal agents alone in New York unless their number were greatly increased. Highly effective of Republican purpose, therefore, was a reversal of ground by Republicans in the legislature as the 1923 session drew to a close. Suddenly, unexpectedly they voted for a bill to repeal the Mullan-Gage Act. Smith was dismayed when news of this first came to him. "They have me down and out!" he cried to his associates. For if he signed the bill, he would face the wrath of drys all over the country, formidably organized through the Anti-Saloon League, and would greatly reduce his chances for Presidential preferment. If he vetoed it, he would outrage the wets of his own party in his own state and do violence to his own integrity, his own self-respect, for he was personally thoroughly wet on principle.

Roosevelt commiserated with him. "I am mighty sorry for the extremely difficult position in which you have been placed over this darned old liquor question," he wrote on May 21, 1923, going on to suggest a complicated maneuver whereby the governor might placate both sides somewhat while shifting from his own shoulders to those of President Harding the blame for failures of Prohibition enforcement. Smith should veto the bill, said Roosevelt, announcing that he did so because the state was bound to aid in the enforcement of federal law; but at the same time he should call the legislature back into special session to enact a new state Prohibition law in place of the vetoed one—a law that would simply require state officers to cooperate with federal authorities when specifically called upon to do so, relieving them of any obligation to initiate enforcement proceedings. This would call attention to the fact that the Harding administration was spending only a fraction of the amount of money, was hiring only a fraction of the number of special agents needed for adequate enforcement of the Volstead Act.

Smith may have wished to accept such advice but was unable to do so. Forthright by nature (in politics he knew no other way than "to be exactly as I am" [14]), he seldom dissembled, almost never on matters he deemed important. He was a devout Roman Catholic who was repeatedly informed, in various ways, that his religion was a political liability nationally; his response was to stress rather than deemphasize his Catholicism. (When his daughter married, a cardinal conducted the ceremony, increasing the event's newsworthiness.) He was convinced that Prohibition should be at once modified to permit the sale of light wines and beer. He said so. And as regards Mullan-Gage he was under extreme pressure from Boss Murphy, who said he would never again support Smith for elective office if Smith did not sign the repeal. Smith did sign it, on June 1, 1923, simultaneously issuing a public statement reiterative of his belief that there was no need for a state law duplicative of federal law, reminding New Yorkers that they remained still subject to the federal law, and asserting that he as governor would cooperate with federal authorities in the enforcement of it. "Much has been said with respect to the effect my action on this bill may have upon my political future," he said. "I have no political future that I am willing to obtain by the sacrifice of any principles or any convictions." [15]

The expected howls of outrage went up from drys. The wet label was ineradicably stamped upon Smith's candidacy, evidently greatly weakening it relative to that of the Democratic front-runner, William Gibbs McAdoo, who, a dry and a Protestant, had growing support, though he would never publicly acknowledge it, from the Ku Klux Klan.

IV

But what, after all, would a Democratic Presidential nomination be worth to the man who won it in 1924? That it would lead that man into the White House seemed unlikely in the extreme to both Roosevelt and Howe in the late summer and autumn of 1923.

In June, Roosevelt had believed that a continuing decline in the export market "due largely to the complete failure of the American government to help other nations get back on their feet" threatened a "serious depression at home." If this happened, the Democrats should win in 1924. But in the weeks that immediately followed, Roosevelt inclined more and more to the belief that the Harding administration would probably succeed in its efforts "to bolster up general prosperity for another year." [16] The "prosperity" was "false," he insisted. Farmers, for instance, had no share in it, and labor's share, outside the ranks of skilled craftsmen, was disproportionately small. But it was sufficiently distributed, and more than sufficiently publicized, to make the national political prospect bright for Republicans, dim for Democrats, in 1924. He seems to have had no more definite information than did the general public of the graft and corruption which, under Harding, besmirched major operations of the Veterans' Bureau, the Alien Property Custodian, the Attorney General's office (with Daugherty's friend William J. Burns in charge of the FBI), and the office of the Interior Secretary. He had, however, been thoroughly convinced during the 1920 campaign that Harding was a "weak sister," and he had heard rumors of moral laxness in the private lives of Presidential intimates. Two of the White House inner circle—Charles Cramer, general counsel for the Veterans' Bureau, and Jesse Smith, close friend of both Daugherty and the President—were recent suicides, and another, Charles R. Forbes, director of the Veterans' Bureau, had resigned under a cloud in January, 1923. Forbes' administration of his bureau was under Congressional investigation, as was Fall's leasing of the naval oil reserves, Fall himself having resigned his Interior post on March 4. There were also signs of a waning of Harding's general popularity over the country. But all these things added up to no grave disadvantage for the Republicans as the quadrennial election was viewed in the summer of 1923—and at least one of the seeming liabilities appeared on the way to removal when, leaving Washington in late June, the President journeyed across the country, making numerous public appearances before sailing from the West Coast for a tour of Alaska. Harding's personal popularity, it appeared, was being revived.

On July 27 the President arrived in Seattle on his return trip from the northern territory. That night he fell ill. His personal physician made light of it in public statement—the President had suffered "a slight attack of ptomaine" with "no serious aspects" after eating spoiled crabs—and Harding continued his journey by train to San Francisco, where he insisted on walking unaided from railway car to limousine. A small crowd watched silently. Reporters noted that he looked old and tired, his shoulders slumped, his normally olive complexion paled to a sickly green. In his suite in the Palace Hotel he went at once to bed, critically ill of bronchial pneumonia. That was on Sunday morning, July 20. Monday night the crisis of his acute illness was reached and passed. The next day and on following days he made seemingly strong recovery.

Then, suddenly, without warning, at seven thirty in the evening of Thursday, August 2, 1923, Warren Gamaliel Harding died of what his personal physician promptly diagnosed as cerebral hemorrhage. (Other doctors disagreed. The official bulletin said "death was apparently due to some brain evolvement, probably an apoplexy." The widow would permit no autopsy.)

The nation, caught wholly by surprise, was swept by a shock wave of grief.

But the same newspapers that told of the collapse of this presumed pillar of society told also, reassuringly, of a homely scene enacted at two thirty in the morning of Friday, August 3, in a remote hill village of New England where the Vice President of the United States had gone on vacation to his boyhood home. It was a scene whose significance aimed at the future, yet was out of the past, straight out of the old, quiet, green rural America that was being done to death by iron-roaring, fume-belching machines and cities. The Vice President had gone to bed at his usual early hour the night of August 2 in his father's house in Plymouth, Vermont. He was awakened in the darkest of early-morning hours to be told of Harding's passing. Shortly thereafter, in his father's small, plainly furnished living room, by the light of two kerosene lamps, his hand resting upon a Bible that had belonged to his dead mother, Calvin Coolidge took the oath of office as President of the United States, the oath being administered by his aged father, a notary public. And the transfer of such awesome power and majesty by so simple a ceremony in so humble a rural setting struck deeply responding chords of nostalgia in the American people.

Franklin Roosevelt sensed at once that no new President could have assumed office, in that year, under circumstances more auspicious. This succession further brightened the prospects for national Republicanism in 1924. "I cannot help feeling that Harding's unfortunate taking off has helped rather than hurt the Republican Party," he said in a letter three weeks later. "Coolidge . . . is not a world beater, but in his past career he has been clever enough to take advantage of situations after the other fellow has done all the work—witness the Boston Police Strike, where Andrew Peters [Boston's mayor in 1919] practically settled things before Coolidge made any move. It looks to me now as if he would be nominated next year. He will be considered, of course, a Conservative, and that means that we must nominate a Progressive without fail." [17]

Roosevelt did not say who the Progressive Democrat should be, but at that time, and for months afterward, it certainly looked to him as though McAdoo would be the convention's choice. Roosevelt's own interests would be better served by the nomination of Al Smith, he (Roosevelt) having been the chief instigator, in the public eye, of the movement to return Smith to the governorship in 1922. Smith, however, was "not yet regarded as a truly national figure," having not yet spoken out on any national question "except . . . the Volstead Act," though Roosevelt had urged him to do so. Consequently "many people wonder if his knowledge . . . [is] sufficiently broad to handle international affairs." McAdoo, on the other hand, had been prominent nationally for more than a decade and had labor union support (the railroad brotherhoods had prospered under his wartime administration of the rail lines), in addition to that of the drys and a majority of the rural Democracy in, probably, all regions—certainly in the South and Midwest. Yes, it definitely looked like McAdoo as 1923 gave way to 1924.

Nevertheless, early in the new year, Roosevelt formally publicly committed himself to Smith's candidacy. So did Eleanor, despite certain qualms about Smith's wetness and parochialism.

But then, abruptly, simultaneously with Roosevelt's open endorsement of Smith, came a dramatic change of circumstance. From it, McAdoo's candidacy suffered grave injury.

In late October, 1923, after eighteen months of careful preparation, the Senate subcommittee that had been set up, as a result of a La Follette resolution, to investigate the naval oil reserve leases, held its first public meeting, under the chairmanship of Thomas J. Walsh, Democrat of Montana. Nothing of dramatic import was revealed in this first hearing or for weeks afterward. But Walsh was persistent. Patiently, stubbornly, he pursued his curiosity concerning the source of Albert B. Fall's sudden and obvious leap from near bankruptcy to affluence immediately following appointment to the Interior Secretaryship, until finally he forced a revelation of Doheny's unsecured "loan" of $100,000 in cash. The oilman, warned by his personal lawyer that he stood in some danger of criminal prosecution, mitigated this danger by describing the strange transaction factually, under oath, on January 27, 1924. He denied there was anything unusual about it. One hundred thousand dollars "was a bagatelle to me," he told the Senators; it was "no more than $25 or $50 perhaps to the ordinary individual." But what of Fall's side of the story? Walsh wanted to know. ". . . looking at it from Fall's side," said Walsh dryly, "it was quite a loan." The questioning continued. It grew harshly critical. Doheny, an irascible man long accustomed to the deference he felt due him for his great wealth, lost his temper. Soon he struck back at his Democratic Senatorial tormentors with boasts of his ability to buy the services of men high in Democratic Party councils. He named several of them. What services had he bought? "I paid them for their influence," he bluntly said.[18]

And one of them, the most newsworthy of all of them, was William Gibbs McAdoo. The blackest of black headlines in the nation's press proclaimed that McAdoo, over a period of years, had received some $250,000 in payment for services rendered Edward L. Doheny. He subsequently testified before the investigative body that he had had absolutely nothing to do with the naval reserve leases, his professional concern having been with Doheny's Mexican petroleum interests. Those who listened to him believed him. Nevertheless, his political potency was permanently diminished.

V

On Friday, February 1, 1924, Franklin Roosevelt was en route by train to Florida when word went out from 2340 S Street that Woodrow Wilson had collapsed. It was announced that "the end is near, there is no hope." McAdoo, with Nellie, his wife, Wilson's daughter, had been summoned to the deathbed, along with the rest of the family.

The news was brought to Roosevelt at a station stop—and as the train moved on again, ever more deeply into the South, he recalled that Wilson was a Southerner by birth and breeding and that it had been upon a train moving through a countryside not unlike the landscape now sliding past his window that he, Roosevelt, more than a dozen years ago, had first conversed with Woodrow Wilson, had first looked closely upon the long, lean, ascetic Wilson countenance. Out of the dozen intervening years leaped to mind a dozen scenes of which Roosevelt had been a part

and Wilson a central figure, the most vivid being perhaps the excruciatingly sad scene upon the White House's south portico on a bright warm
summer's day in 1920, with Wilson in a wheelchair, shawl-enwrapped,
cold as death, looking up at Roosevelt and the tear-blinking Cox standing over him. What ghastly mental anguish the sick man must have
suffered that year! And since! And suffered right now if one of the
newspaper accounts was true—namely, that Wilson in delirium relived
his battle for the League of Nations, believing himself back in the White
House in 1919. Ghastly! Roosevelt wrote out a statement—"Woodrow
Wilson in his life gave mankind a new vision of pure democracy" [19]—
while in Washington a small crowd gathered in wintry gloom and chill
across S Street from the house of the dying man to keep silent vigil.
Doctors came and went. One who came to Wilson's bedside went also
that day to the Wardman Park Hotel, a few miles away, to call professionally, with two colleagues, upon a haggard, ailing Albert Fall. The
ex-Secretary had claimed he was too ill to appear next day before the
Walsh Committee, which had subpoenaed him. The three doctors decided he was well enough to do so.

On Saturday, February 2, 1924, arrived at Jacksonville, Florida,
"F.D.R. went on board and put Larooco in commission" for her first
winter cruise, the houseboat being tied up at a dock in the St. Johns
River. "Sailing-master Robert S. Morris and Mrs. Morris spent the day
getting provisions, and the trunks etc. were unpacked, fishing gear
stowed and Library of the World's Worst Literature placed on shelves,"
said the initial entry in the log of the Larooco.[20] Missy LeHand was one
of the party (Roosevelt gave her dictation almost every day), soon to be
joined by a Dutchess County neighbor named Maunsell S. Crosby,
whom Sara Roosevelt had recommended to her son for this trip and
who was an amateur ornithologist of note. To Edith Bolling Wilson in
Washington's S Street, where Woodrow Wilson [said Admiral Grayson
to reporters] was "just slowly ebbing away . . . not talking to anyone
but . . . still conscious," went a Roosevelt telegram, one of hundreds
delivered by uniformed messenger boys who pedaled their bicycles up
the S Street hill that day. "Deeply distressed," the telegram said. "Am
hoping for the best. You are both constantly in my thoughts." Again a
chilled and silent crowd was gathered in S Street, to keep vigil. Many
knelt in silent prayer upon the cold ground, the colder sidewalk pavement. Meanwhile, on Capitol Hill, a flabby, broken Albert Fall, leaning
heavily upon a cane, walked from his car into the Capitol corridors, into
the Walsh Committee hearing room, and almost collapsed into a witness
chair. There he read in a dead, flat voice the statement his lawyer had
prepared for him. "I decline . . . to answer any questions," the state-

ment said, "on the ground that it may tend to incriminate me. . . ." [21]

On Sunday, February 3, 1924, at about nine o'clock in the morning, Roosevelt "gave all hands" aboard *Larooco* "opportunity to go to Church." There were "no takers." So preparations were made to cast off, while, in distant Washington, Woodrow Wilson lay in a coma, his pulse so weak, his breathing so shallow, that Grayson, bending over his bed, could scarcely perceive them through his stethoscope. At eleven fifteen, precisely, all such perception ceased: the weary heart stopped beating.* It was just fifteen minutes later, according to the *Larooco* log, that Roosevelt's houseboat "left dock . . . proceeding down St. John's River" toward the canal that had been dug a few miles inland from the sea due southward toward St. Augustine. At sundown, after a lazy day, they were moored to an old piling upon the canal bank "2 or 3 miles short of the Toll Chain." [23] They were solitary there, and no sound came to their ears from beyond the boat that might not have been heard 10,000 years ago. Night closed down. The stars came out, thick and brilliant in the subtropic sky.

On Monday, February 4, 1924, in the morning, at nine thirty, *Larooco* was untied from her mooring and chugged on down the canal "into a marshy river—strong head wind," while in Washington President Coolidge proclaimed thirty days of national mourning and the Senate suspended all business, including the Walsh Committee hearings, for three days. McAdoo and a weeping Nellie Wilson McAdoo arrived at S Street. There, to Edith Wilson's angry outrage, the son-in-law of her dead husband received in the library directly above the death room one group after another of his Washington supporters, all badly frightened by the Doheny disclosures. (The widow upbraided weeping Nellie: "You care more about getting your husband elected President than you do about your dead father!") OIL SCANDAL SMEARS MC ADOO CANDIDACY, said headlines in the early afternoon papers. . . . At 2:30 P.M., *Larooco* "anchored at St. Augustine," where those aboard "saw the flags at half mast" and learned that Wilson had been dead for twenty-seven hours. "Our own ensign will remain at half mast for 30 days," wrote Roosevelt into the *Larooco* log.[24]

For him there followed days adding up to weeks, weeks adding up to

---

* William Allen White pecked out on his battered typewriter that day, in the office of his Emporia (Kansas) *Gazette,* a four-line epitaph:

> God gave him a great vision.
> The devil gave him an imperious heart.
> The proud heart is still.
> The vision lives.[22]

months, of loafing, swimming, fishing, sunbathing, and exercises to strengthen his legs on the houseboat deck, bird watching with Maunsell Crosby, playing with his stamp collection—a long period of mental and physical recreation, during which he made his abortive attempt at a history of the United States but was otherwise far less concerned with national affairs than he was with *Larooco*'s chronic engine troubles, the leaks that developed in her cabins and staterooms during hard rains, the question of what colors to paint her interiors, the struggles to land big ocean game fish, and the navigational difficulties resulting from "unusual" Florida weather. ("This year has been considered a very poor one as to weather down here," said one log entry, "—a lot of wind, large temperature changes, etc.") Missy LeHand received word of her father's death on February 10 and entrained for Boston from Daytona Beach next morning; she returned two weeks later. At Palm Beach, Roosevelt, "not having been here since 1904, . . . found the growth of mushroom millionaire's houses luxuriant" and repellant. "The women we saw went well with the place—and we desired to meet them no more than we wished to remain in the harbor even an hour more than necessary." At Miami he motored to Miami Beach to see the wintering James M. Coxes, "who were out," then to Cocoanut Grove to visit briefly with William Jennings Bryan, "who came out to the car" in which Roosevelt sat. (The Great Commoner, who had moved his permanent residence from Nebraska to Florida for reasons of health, his own and his wife's, conducted in Miami a famous Bible class which attracted an attendance of 4,000 to 5,000 people every Sunday; he also, fusing capitalism with the Protestant ethic, lent his oratorical talents and national prestige to the promotion of Florida's then burgeoning and soon to become wholly incredible real estate boom.) He maintained before others, with rarely the slightest crack of it, his façade of cheerfulness. Perhaps only Missy LeHand knew of the moods of black depression which occasionally overwhelmed him in the early morning hours and kept him solitary in his room, sometimes until noon. But at noon he would appear before the many guests he had aboard the boat bright and eager for fun, exuberantly gay.

Livingston Davis joined the houseboat party in mid-March "weighted down with sundry wet and dry goods," looking "like a sick child" and provoking from Roosevelt the hyperbole he often employed when speaking of or to people who delighted him. Livy Davis, he reported in the log, "is recuperating from shingles, boils, bunions, and cold in the head." But the next day Davis provoked a very different reaction by exercising "on the top deck a la nature" and then coming back from a fishing expedition "minus trousers—to the disgust of the two ladies" (*i.e.*, Mrs. Morris and Missy LeHand), and of Roosevelt, too. So intense was his irritation that he confided it to the *Larooco* log that evening. "Why do people who *must* take off their clothes go anywhere where the other sex is present?" he wrote in the entry for March 17. "Capt. Morris remarked that some men get shot for less." And this unprecedented reaction to a young man whose companionship had always before given him unalloyed pleasure—a reaction akin to that Eleanor had had to Livy Davis in 1919—seems to have faded only slightly if at all in the following days.* "L. Davis waved from the train departing for Key West at 8:30 A.M.," said the log entry for April 3. "He was seen by Mrs. Morris who shook a towel at him in reply." Eight days later the *Larooco,* moored at the Royal Palm dock in the Miami River, "went out of commission" at sundown, ending "Cruise No. 1." At ten thirty that night of April 13, a Sunday (he would not have begun the journey had it been a Friday), "½ owner F.D.R. left for N.Y." [25]

Arrived at his Sixty-fifth Street house—refreshed, relaxed, zestful, his general health better than it had ever been before (he had not had a single illness, not even a slight head cold, for months)—he was at once plunged into hectic political activity.

Within a day or two, his old enemy, Tammany's Boss Murphy, moving quietly as always behind the scenes, came to his house to discuss with him and Howe the lining up of convention delegates from other states behind Al Smith. Smith, who on April 15, before the New York State Democratic Committee, had formally announced his candidacy for the Presidential nomination, receiving then the committee's unanimous endorsement, had gained much strength relative to McAdoo since January. There had been a head-on collision between the two in early April, when the governor's name was entered, allegedly without his prior knowledge, in the Wisconsin primary. McAdoo was entered also. The outcome had been a thumping victory for Smith, who captured twenty-three of Wisconsin's twenty-six delegates, to the surprise of most national observers. Evidently the oil smear across McAdoo's name, in La Follette's home territory, joined to the appeal of Smith's wetness to the multitudinous beer and wine drinkers of Milwaukee and other Wisconsin cities, had had marked effect, and Smith's Catholicism, if not a positive asset there, had done no harm. Further advantage had been gained for Smith, in Murphy's opinion, when Murphy and his colleagues succeeded in their effort to have New York chosen as the convention city, with Madison Square Garden as the convention hall. This

---

* It did fade thereafter, however. Davis was soon restored to Roosevelt's good graces, though never to the same extent as before.

assured Smith of vociferous support from the galleries. "They [the Tammany men] are demanding thirty-five hundred seats," Howe had written Thomas Mott Osborne April 1, "and the plan is to pack the house when the psychological moment arrives with Smith rooters." [26] But Howe and Roosevelt and Smith himself were by no means as sure as Murphy was that this was a sound tactic or even that New York City was the environment most conducive of Smith's nomination. The effect would be a further stressing of Smith's ties with Tammany and of his wholly urban personality, and this could be a severe handicap to him among Democrats from the South, the West, the Midwest, many of whom hated big cities and were accustomed to looking upon the metropolitan Tiger as a hopelessly depraved and vicious animal.

No doubt this was among the topics of conversation between Murphy and Roosevelt that day, with Roosevelt tactfully suggesting the need for moderation of overt Tammany zeal on Smith's behalf. Possibly discussed also was the question of who should be named chairman of the Citizens' Committee for Smith, then in process of formation. Proskauer, able manager of Smith's 1922 gubernatorial campaign, was unavailable for this new post, now that he was a State Supreme Court justice, though he would play an important part in the campaign. Murphy, as he himself must have recognized, was disqualified by his Tammany connection, his national notoriety as a "machine boss." Who, then?

The question, if raised, was left hanging as Boss Murphy—smiling, affable, soft-voiced as always, still the gentle grafter who ruled and robbed by covert stratagem rather than overt force—arose to take his leave. He seemed in the best of health.

But a few days later, on the morning of April 25, 1924, he was struck dead by a heart attack.

The event, coming as it did barely two months before the convention's opening, spread consternation through the ranks of Smith supporters. ". . . New York has lost its most powerful and wisest leader," said Roosevelt's public statement, which was less perfunctory, more disregardful of the past, than might have been expected of him.[27] There was a great outpouring of grief mingled with dismay by Smith associates at a great funeral in St. Patrick's Cathedral. Belle Moskowitz, however, said in private talk that the Boss' death, though sad in itself, was politically "the best thing that could have happened for the Governor" [28] at this juncture. It removed all plausibility and every vestige of truth from the charge that Smith was "boss-ridden." Smith himself was now in command of the state Democratic machine, his authority unchallenged. (Judge George W. Olvany of Court of General Sessions was chosen to succeed Murphy as Tammany Hall chieftain, after Surrogate James

Foley, Murphy's son-in-law, had refused the office: Olvany would prove far less astute, less able in general, than the wily Murphy.)

Roosevelt, too, profited from this death politically.

Belle Moskowitz and Judge Proskauer called together upon him at 47 East Sixty-fifth Street. They described to him the kind of man needed to head the Citizens' Committee for Smith. That man should be a New Yorker of national repute who was not a Tammanyite, not a Catholic, not exclusively urban in "tone" or orientation, not sharply identifiable as either wet or dry, yet a man who was on good terms with all major factions of the national party and able to function as a medium of friendly communication between them, an agent of unity among them. None other fitted this description as closely as did Franklin Roosevelt— and the need for him in this post was increased, while an obstacle to his acceptance of it was removed, by Murphy's passing. Would he take on the job? He referred to his physical disability, as he was bound in this case to do, since the chairman of the committee would be, in effect, manager of the campaign. He obviously could not dash about, as campaign managers are wont to do, from one meeting to another. His visitors assured him that this didn't matter, they "would do the work." [29] And so, with an outward smile that showed no awareness, much less any resentment, of the contempt implicit in their request (they thought him "light" enough to be lightly manipulated, a handsome piece of window dressing and little more), but with an inward smile of a wholly different nature (it was wry in its humor, a trifle grim in its determination), he did accept the post. No doubt his decision to do so had been made before his visitors arrived, he having discussed the matter with Howe, the two of them considering it carefully from every angle.

VI

Neither he nor Howe had any real belief that Smith would win nomination. Still less did they believe that the eventual nominee, whoever he might be, could win election that year, their conclusion on this matter remaining the same as it had been the year before.

McAdoo would enter the convention with far more committee delegate votes than Smith, despite the latter's gains in recent weeks. On the other hand, McAdoo's strength fell far short of the 732 votes needed to nominate if the two-thirds rule were retained—and there was little doubt the convention *would* retain it against the efforts of the McAdoo people to change it. What Smith's gain in relative strength actually meant, therefore, was the probability of a deadlocked convention. Howe anticipated a situation akin to that of the Republican conclave of 1920. "A general guess is that the leading candidates will be trotted out one after another for enough ballots to make it evident that they cannot secure the nomination," he had written with cheerful cynicism in his letter to Osborne of April 1, "and that after that they will hold a conference in a back room among the leaders of the largest blocks of votes at which some unguessable . . . John Smith will be picked as the man whom every Democrat has really been yearning to see as the standard bearer of his party. . . ." [30] (He added that Roosevelt was "sitting perfectly tight and not even talking about a second choice in case Smith does not go through.") Both Roosevelt and Howe, therefore, must now face the fact that their activity on Smith's behalf, to the degree of its effectiveness, would further increase the probability of deadlock. This did not unduly disturb them. What *did* disturb them was their recognition of the *kind* of deadlock which might develop. If Smith's principal support became a rigidly solidified coalescence of wet with city machine, if McAdoo's became a similarly solidified coalescence of dry with rural Democracy, and if the active influence of the Ku Klux Klan stirred into the broil a bigoted, nativistic, virulent anti-Catholicism, the party might become so deeply, widely, acrimoniously divided that its very survival was threatened. At the least all chance would be lost for that year of developing the issues of progressivism vs. reaction in debate with the Republicans.

The Republicans, it was clear, wanted no debate at all. They certainly didn't want to talk about the Harding scandals. Further exposures of these had come thick and fast in February and March. In mid-February, Secretary of the Navy Denby, under heavy Congressional fire for his part in the transfer of the oil reserves to Interior, resigned his office. On February 20, ex-Director Forbes of the Veterans' Bureau was indicted by a grand jury for defrauding the government of an estimated $250,000,000 through purchasing and construction contracts and the equally corrupt sale of deliberately acquired surpluses of clothing, bed sheets, floor wax, etc., for veterans' hospitals. In March the Senate adopted a resolution for an investigation of Attorney General Daugherty's handling of his office—an investigation during which particular attention would be paid to Daugherty's working relationships with Colonel T. W. Miller, Alien Property Custodian, who, like Fall and Forbes, was destined to go to the penitentiary for conspiracy to defraud the government. (Though the circumstantial case against him was damning, Daugherty would escape conviction in his criminal trial after he refused to take the stand in his own defense on the ground, unmistakably implied in his statement to the court, that his testimony and answers to questions "might tend to incriminate" not only himself, but also the dead Warren G. Harding, whose personal attorney he had been for twenty years.) Such matters, in the opinion of Republican leaders, were properly left to professional defenders of the public weal, professional law enforcement agents, and impartial courts of justice. They were no fit subject for partisan debate.

And with this opinion a large majority of the electorate seemed to agree. It was a measure of the mood and moral climate of the time—or, perhaps, of the degree of control which Republican businessmen had of the means of mass communication and opinion-making—that there was actually more angry public denunciation of Walsh, in the early months of 1924, and of Walsh's Montana colleague, Democratic Senator Burton K. Wheeler, who introduced the resolution to investigate Daugherty, than there was of the malefactors whose operations Walsh and Wheeler exposed. The two were dubbed "the Montana scandalmongers." They were "character assassins." The general feeling was that they needlessly rocked a boat that would otherwise sail through placid seas toward shores of peace and wondrous plenty. Roosevelt himself, sunning aboard the *Larooco*, had wanted above all else an even keel, a quiet sea, cloudless skies overhead, and he had reacted mildly, evincing no great moral indignation or sense of outrage, when called upon for comment upon the scandals by one of his correspondents. "I am so far away from base down here that I have seen only an occasional paper . . . ," said a letter of his, dated March 22. "All I know is that Daugherty's friends have never been what might be termed 'high class.' There was no question that poor old Harding was personally honest himself, but he was not the kind of man who could ever tell the difference between a real friend and a crooked one, and he allowed himself to be surrounded by a pretty rotten crowd." [31]

This expressed attitude of Roosevelt's was essentially that which Republican leaders adopted as a central theme of their reticence in 1924. They had something of a problem, these leaders. They had to persuade the public that their party as such was not responsible in the slightest for major operations of the Republican administration between 1921 and mid-1923, though in point of fact tainted oil money from Sinclair had been used in devious ways to pay off the national party deficit following the 1920 campaign. Moreover, three of Harding's Cabinet, two of whom remained Cabinet members, had been directly involved in the transaction. Fortunately the Walsh Committee had not yet discovered the fact.*

* Postmaster General Hays, Secretary of War John Weeks, and Secretary of the Treasury

"Poor old Harding," according to the Republican apologists, was a good man but a poor judge of other men. A kindly person (had he not pardoned Gene Debs and even invited Debs to the White House? Had he not personally persuaded the steel barons to cut the workweek for steel labor from twelve hours to ten?), he had been dogged by a cruel fate. He had trusted his friends absolutely, being himself of an honest, loyal, trusting nature. He could not conceive of their betraying him. Yet they had done so. When he found this out, the shock was fatal—itself proof positive of his personal integrity, his earnest wish to be and do good in his high office. What had happened was highly regrettable, even deplorable, and no Republican would say otherwise; but, the GOP insisted, it was totally irrelevant to the choice the electorate must make that year between Republicanism and the Democracy. After all, "poor old Harding" *was* dead. He was not running for reelection. And the man who *would* be running, the Republican successor to Harding in the White House, was wholly different from him in character and personality. Who could even imagine Calvin Coolidge—chilly, prim, prissy, frugal, cautious Cal Coolidge—sitting in shirt sleeves at a poker table, shouting and laughing with a group of coarse-mouthed, backslapping, whiskey-drinking machine politicians? (One could imagine McAdoo's doing so, despite McAdoo's avowed dryness; one knew Al Smith had done so.) Why, Silent Cal would wear a high starched collar and a carefully knotted tie while being photographed holding aloft a fish he had allegedly just caught in a Western trout stream! Never had he evinced any desire for great wealth or luxurious living or the exercise of great power; as a matter of fact, the very essence of his Presidency had been, would continue to be, a refusal of the exercise of power, and no breath of scandal had ever touched him personally. He was the personification of Puritan rectitude. Indeed, one looked upon his remarkably smooth, self-contained, tight-lipped countenance, his cold, wary eyes and doubted that he had enough hot, passionate blood in him to be even tempted toward any kind of sensual pleasure.

What he *did* have in abundance, as Roosevelt had noted, was a calculating Yankee shrewdness whereby he could "take advantage of situations after the other fellow has done all the work." He was even managing to take advantage of the Walsh Committee's work in that spring of 1924! For many weeks after the oil scandals became sensational news he refused all comment upon them, refused also to fire Daugherty after Daugherty's unfitness for his office was known to all. There was thus en-

---

Mellon were the three Cabinet members. Revelation of the transaction was not made until 1928, when the Walsh Committee uncovered it.

couraged in the public mind a suspicion that he was afraid to act, or too lazy, or could not without grave injury to his party and administration. But the very energies that fed this suspicion fed an inordinate admiration of him when at last he did demand Daugherty's resignation, appointed as Attorney General the impeccable, highly able Harlan F. Stone,* and made a public statement about Teapot Dome. It was a statement terser than his famous one during the Boston police strike. "Let the guilty be punished," was all he said. Simultaneously he initiated government proceedings to cancel the Teapot Dome and Elk Hills leases and appointed lawyer Owen J. Roberts, Republican of Philadelphia, and ex-Senator Atlee Pomerene, Democratic lawyer from Ohio, to prosecute the oil cases. Huge headlines at once proclaimed that Coolidge had hit hard at the "oil deals," having "quietly assumed control of situation" and "surprised his foes." Chief among the latter were Walsh and Wheeler! The President's prolonged silent passivity, it now appeared, had been determined by the very opposite of weakness and timidity. Strong, courageous, fair-minded, he had refused to be hustled into judgments that were premature, actions that might be unjust, and he now emerged as the *true* champion of honesty in government. Walsh and Wheeler were "politically" motivated, their object a personal and Democratic advantage, whereas Calvin Coolidge's sole purpose and stern resolve, in the implementation of which he appointed a bipartisan commission, was to find and punish wrongdoers.

The irony was sweet or bitter, depending on one's point of view, but the truth sustaining it was unequivocally clear to such a mind as Roosevelt's. Every stain of oil had now been washed from White House walls; the Harding scandals in general provided no ammunition that could be used with effect against Coolidge.

VII

Nor was much effective ammunition to be found in the general economic situation. This had markedly improved since the summer of 1923, when Roosevelt had seen the possibility of a "serious depression" consequent upon the collapse of the postwar European economy. He had sensed at the time that Europe's economic troubles were causally related to a mistaken American foreign economic policy and that high tariff

---

* Stone promptly and completely reorganized the Department of Justice. He brought in as Director of the FBI, replacing William J. Burns, young J. Edgar Hoover, who soon transformed his agency from the shoddy and corrupt thing it had been into one of the most efficient organizations of its kind in the world.

walls were a key element of the mistake,* though no published statement of his indicates that he had much explicit understanding of how this cause-effect relationship had developed or how it actually worked. Had he realized its implications for his future career he *might* have studied it with care.

The story, a tangled one, began with Woodrow Wilson's coldly moralistic rejection of a British proposal, in Paris in 1919, that all intergovernmental war debts be canceled—a proposal in which the French concurred. Most of these debts were owed by the Allies to the United States. There were, however, substantial complicating offsets. The British had lent about $4 billion to seventeen different countries, the French had lent many hundreds of millions to ten different countries, while borrowing from the United States something over $7 billion during the war, plus $3,250,000,000 in the months immediately following the armistice. Thus the cost of wiping out all debts would not have been borne exclusively by the United States. Even if it had been, the operation would have been justified, in the Allied view. The British argument was manifold: debt cancellation was essential to the restored good health of the international economy; it was morally just, since the United States and the Allies had been joined in common cause and the United States had made in that cause, in proportion to its total resources, very minor sacrifices of blood and treasure compared to those Britain and France had made; it was economically just, too, in view of the fact that practically every dollar borrowed by the Allies had been spent in the United States and so had gone into the pocket of an American industrialist, farmer, banker, merchant, worker. To all this, Wilson had turned a deaf ear. Allied leaders had then proposed that the Allied debt payments to the United States be formally linked to German reparation payments to the Allies, as in actual practice the former were inevitably dependent to a considerable degree on the latter. To this, also, Wilson had refused to listen. The Allies had to pay their full debt to this country, he insisted. Reparations were a wholly different matter with which the United States had no direct concern, since the United States made no reparation demands. From this position he could not be budged. He had yielded to Clemenceau, Lloyd George, and Orlando one point after another whose yielding dangerously increased international tensions and frictions—

---

* In December, 1922, he had written Governor Cox that though he was "not wholly convinced that the country is quite ready for a definite stand" by the Democratic Party "in favor of immediate entry into the League of Nations," the country *was* "beginning to recognize that national isolation on our part" was inimical to our own economic interests. It would, he said, "bring hard times" because it would "cut off exports etc. etc." Hence Democrats "should stand firmly against the isolation policy of the Harding Administration."

this because he deemed it necessary for the establishment of a League of Nations organization—but he stubbornly refused the slightest concession on this one point whose total concession would have been a positive contribution to world stability.*

The Harding administration had adopted Wilson's position on this matter. The Coolidge administration continued to maintain it. "They hired the money, didn't they?" was Coolidge's famous comment upon the debt and the justice of its full collection. And this position's hazardous falsity was augmented by Republican Congresses and a typically Republican Tariff Commission (Coolidge would appoint, as a matter of course, commissioners who represented special interests seeking protection) which reverted to traditional Republican protectionist policies. The Fordney-McCumber Tariff Act of 1922, opposed by Congressional Democrats, increased the protection which the Wilson administration's Revenue Act of 1916 had given the American chemical industry against the German dye trust.† It raised to prohibitive heights the duties on farm products—this as a result of the Farm Bloc's desperate economic nationalism. It raised to even more prohibitive heights the duties on many things (cutlery, chinaware, guns, certain textiles, etc.) which the Germans and Japanese produced more cheaply than Americans did. The tariff schedules as applied by White House and commission were conjoined with nationalistic U.S. shipping policies, thus preventing American acceptance of the foreign goods and services which were the only means, in the long run, through which the war debts could possibly be paid. The fact was pointed out to Washington with vehement gestures by London and Paris—to no avail. Consequently, the Allied war debt became a major obstacle to that reduction of Germany's reparations bill which the Allies might otherwise have made, which even France might have agreed to in the light of simple common sense, once the murky passions of war had somewhat cleared away.

Vicious indeed became the circle of action-reaction in Western Europe.

On May 1, 1921, sparked by a vengeful, fearful, hate-ridden France, the Reparations Commission presented to the Weimar Republic a bill for $33 billion, this to be paid *in addition* to the whole of the Belgian war debt, which Germany had been forced to assume, and the costs of main-

---

* He could not have conceded without a major effort to educate his fellow countrymen in the economic facts of international life. That effort, however, or so it appears to a historian, might have reduced by at least an equivalent amount the effort he made on behalf of the treaty's purely political arrangements and should, in any case, have been part and parcel of his pro-League battle.

† See page 423.

taining the armies of occupation! The demand, within the time limit imposed, was impossible. Behind the façade of a remarkably liberal written constitution, the Weimar Republic's government was precariously balanced considerably to the right of center, and this hearty shove from without brought it tottering to the very brink of collapse into a right-wing dictatorship. Desperately, futilely, it resorted to the printing press in an effort to stimulate production and supply the monetary deficiency. The Reichsmark had theretofore been valued at 4 to the dollar. By midsummer of 1921 it was valued at 75 per dollar and, a few months later, at 400. It officially exchanged at the rate of 1,500 per dollar when Roosevelt's presidency of United European Investors, Inc., was announced in late September, 1922,* and the rate climbed ever more steeply thereafter, reaching 7,000 per dollar by year's end. By that time the German government, in default on timber deliveries to France, was pleading for a reparations moratorium. Instead, in January, 1923, France and Belgium, against Britain's wishes, sent troops into the Ruhr Basin to collect at gunpoint from the richest mining and industrial region of the Reich, thereby preventing that rapid recovery of German strength which France mortally feared.

The event instantaneously united all Germans in common cause as they had not been since August, 1914. They fought back in the only way they could, through a planned, determined passive resistance. A general strike of Ruhr workers, financed by the government, halted all Ruhr production. France was denied the wealth it sought to expropriate, though at a cost to the Reich of some 4 billion gold marks. All efforts to stabilize the currency ceased. By deliberate government policy, primarily in order to sabotage the Ruhr occupation and the reparations program, the Reichsmarks were permitted to find their "natural" market level. And at this "natural" level they were utterly worthless. (The exchange rate shot up to astronomical heights: 18,000 per dollar in late January, 1923; 160,000 per dollar on July 1; 1,000,000 per dollar in August. In November, 1923, a single American dollar would buy a billion Reichsmarks!) The inflation benefited big industrialists, large landowners, and, to a degree, the government itself. All these were enabled to write off their bonded indebtedness with mere pieces of paper while retaining tangible property whose exchange value was vastly increased. But by the same token, this inflation was disastrous for the great masses of the citizenry. The lifetime savings of millions of the worker and middle classes, in bank accounts, war bonds, life insurance, annuities, and the like, were wiped out, while, simultaneously, many of these same mil-

* See pages 705-6.

lions were thrown into the increasingly disorderly ranks of the unemployed.

This chaos, this widespread misery, spelled political opportunity for extremists of both the left and right in Germany, but chiefly for those of the right. The workers were accustomed to being at the base of the economic pyramid, the bottom of the social hierarchy. They suffered now no shock of status loss; they were psychologically sustained by their long-defined class consciousness and the political orientation, generally mildly leftist, which derived from this. But for those of the bourgeoisie who were now suddenly ruined the case was very different. In addition to the loss of their savings, upon which they were more dependent economically than were members of the working class, they suffered a traumatic loss of class and personal identity. Their economic and political pieties—their lifelong commitments to industriousness, thrift, obedience to duly constituted authority—were mocked by this disastrous change in their circumstances. They felt betrayed. They were confused, embittered, instinctively conservative, yet politically naïve; they were easy prey for a demagoguery that would supply their double need, psychologically, for a savior and a scapegoat.

There resided in Munich, in that dark November, a politician of the extreme right who was eager to supply the need. He was an Austrian native who had become a fanatically nationalistic German—a dark-haired, thin-faced, burning-eyed, toothbrush-mustached man of thirty-four with a rare genius for rabble-rousing propaganda and public speech. He had served in the German Army through four years of war, during which he had been twice decorated for bravery but never promoted beyond the rank of corporal. He had been in a hospital recovering from poison gas when the armistice was signed. He had seen this event and the establishment of the Weimar Republic as elements of a swinish Jewish-Communist plot against pure-blooded Germans and the Aryan "race" in general; he had long been a rabid hater of Jews and democracy and intellectuals and all that was humane in humanity, an advocate and practitioner of violence as political tactic, and he now became a sworn enemy of the Weimar Republic, committed to its overthrow, to the establishment of a German dictatorship, to the scrapping of the Versailles Treaty, to the rearming of Germany, to the wreaking of dreadful vengeance upon the Allies, and to limitless German expansion. A few months after his release from the hospital he had joined a tiny and obscure political organization, the German Workers Party, becoming at once its dominant figure, and had shaped it since in his own image as a hate-driven, virulently racist, aggressively militaristic Nazi (National Socialist) Party, its leadership made up for the most part of rootless, declassed men, its growing rank and file of the embittered lower middle class. His name, then little known outside Bavaria, was Adolf Hitler.

With all the joy possible for one of his darkly passionate, humorless nature, Hitler welcomed the mass miseries which increased throughout the fatherland in 1923's spring and summer. In early autumn the Berlin government began to draw back from the brink of destruction to which the Ruhr strike and the official sabotage of reparation payments had brought the republic. Berlin, on September 26, decreed an end to passive resistance, a resumption of token reparations payments, this in order to facilitate negotiations for settlement with France, while in France influential voices were raised in favor of such negotiations. Hitler, furious, was thrown into a fever of fear that his chance to seize power might slip away, never to recur. (It is significant that left extremists of the Communist Party were similarly furious and afraid.) But joy and hope were renewed in him as the inflation continued, the mass miseries grew apace, and rightist officials of the Bavarian government refused to obey Berlin's decree. By November he was convinced, and convinced others, that the hour of decision had arrived. Social and economic conditions were probably at their worst. An improvement of them sufficient to save the republic might occur during the months ahead—*unless* the republic were toppled now. He moved to topple it. With the connivance of extreme rightists in the Bavarian government and with no less a figure than General Ludendorff as his front man, Adolf Hitler organized and, on November 8 and 9, 1923, launched what became known to history as the Munich Beer Hall Putsch, its aim the capture of dictatorial power in Munich, to be followed by a March on Berlin akin to Benito Mussolini's Fascist March on Rome of a year before.

The putsch failed, ignominiously.

Everywhere there was now a drawing back from the brink of catastrophe, not only among responsible leaders of government in Western and Central Europe, but also in the United States. Indeed, it was in Washington that this drawing back, this shift in the direction of international relations, was initiated—and initiated despite the fact that doing so was tacitly contradictory of the thesis, which the United States continued officially to maintain, that there was no connection between war debts to America and reparations payments to the Allies. At the very time when Roosevelt, in the summer of 1923, was condemning "the complete failure of the American government to help other nations get back on their feet," Harding's Secretary of State, Charles Evans Hughes, alarmed at the prospect of total German economic collapse, was beginning to intervene actively in the reparations quarrel. With Britain's blessing, he entered into long-drawn-out negotiations with France aimed at persuading it to moderate its reparations demands. And as events argued ever more persuasively on his side (even a Frenchman could see danger in a right-wing take-over of the German government), he won his way. The Berlin decree of September 26 was an early response to this Hughes initiative—or, rather, to its effect on the French attitude—and the general climate of opinion thereby generated was increasingly unfavorable to such ventures as Hitler now engaged in.

Even the Bavarian state commissioner who had conspired with Hitler against his own government drew back at the crucial moment. He betrayed Hitler; he gave police authorities Hitler's plan of action. So when a Nazi column of some thousands of armed men, headed by Ludendorff and Hitler, marched upon the center of Munich on November 9, it encountered a cordon of perhaps a hundred police placed at a strategic point, at the end of a street so narrow that the Nazis' firepower superiority was of no avail. There was a brief exchange of gunfire. When it was over, nineteen men lay dead or dying in the street—sixteen Nazis, three policemen—along with dozens of wounded, including a Hitler lieutenant named Hermann Göring who had been among the greatest of German air aces during the war. Hitler himself suffered a dislocated shoulder as he threw himself, or was thrown, to the pavement. He fled the scene in an automobile but, with some dozens of his followers, was soon arrested on a charge of high treason. And that, it appeared to everyone, including Hitler himself at the time, was the end of the would-be dictator's dream of power.*

For in the weeks and months that immediately followed there was a

_____

* But Hitler made a remarkably swift recovery from this blow. Within a few short months he had managed to transform a humiliating personal defeat into a personal triumph, manifesting as he did so a political genius and technique having elements in common with those Roosevelt had employed, in a very different key and on a much smaller scale, at the close of the Sheehan fight of 1911. He simply *asserted* a personal victory before a public which, as he well knew, *wished* to believe him. His trial for high treason opened before a special court, one highly sympathetic to him, in Munich on February 26, 1924. It lasted four weeks and, being covered as major news not only by the German press, but throughout the world, provided him with a forum of which he made the most effective possible use. He did not deny responsibility for the "events of 8 November"; he gloried in them. "I alone bear the responsibility," he declared. He proclaimed his dedication to the overthrow of the republic but claimed this was not traitorous because "there is no such thing as high treason against the traitors of 1918." "I feel myself the best of Germans who wanted the best for the German people," he said. Convicted (Ludendorff was acquitted), he was sentenced to five years' imprisonment, though the crime of high treason specifically called, in the code, for life imprisonment. He was released in less than nine months. During those months, comfortably ensconced with some forty of his followers in an old fortress at Landsberg, he dictated to one of his worshipful underlings, Rudolf Hess, the first volume of a combined autobiography and political tract entitled *Mein Kampf*, published in the fall of 1925.

marked and accelerating improvement in Germany's economic condition, thanks largely to the United States. Hughes persuaded the Reparations Commission to establish a special committee to work out a reparations payment plan that was in realistic alignment with Germany's capacity to pay. Two Americans were appointed to serve with this committee in November, 1923. One was Owen D. Young of General Electric, the other Charles G. Dawes, a Chicago banker whom Harding had chosen as the first Director of the Budget Bureau when this, for which Roosevelt had agitated in 1919 and 1920, was established by Congressional act in 1921. Technically the two Americans were not members of the committee—their service was "unofficial," since the United States was unrepresented on the parent commission—but they nonetheless dominated the deliberations of what became known as the Dawes Committee, and the plan which this committee proposed in April, 1924, and which the governments concerned agreed to, was called the Dawes Plan. It was effective of its immediate purpose. The total ruin of the German economy, which must inevitably have destroyed the Weimar Republic and involved all Europe in financial collapse, was prevented for the time being. Reparations demands were drastically reduced, complicated machinery was set up to collect and distribute the reparations payments, and a loan of $200,000,000 in gold was made to the German government through private financial institutions in the United States.

This last, the American loan, was of crucial and beneficent immediate importance. Within a week after Hitler's failed Munich Beer Hall Putsch, the government in Berlin had opened a new Rentenbank, and a special currency commissioner, Hjalmar Schacht, had been assigned the difficult task of establishing on a sound basis a new monetary unit, the Rentenmark, in place of the old worthless paper currency. He could not have done it without the American loan. With it, he placed the Rentenmark on the gold standard and so stabilized it.

But if this loan was in itself immediately beneficial to all concerned, the way in which it was made and the process of international finance which it initiated were hazardous to the future. The loan was not made by or through the government in Washington, though it went to the Berlin government. Instead, it was handled in America as a private transaction: the loan was floated by American bankers on terms favorable to themselves, and it was but the first of a series of such flotations whereby—in conjunction with investments in European industry by U.S. businessmen, tourist expenditures, etc.—a huge flow of American dollars overseas, chiefly to Germany, financed European recovery, bolstered the American export market, and so contributed to the prosperity of America's domestic economy. Altogether, approximately a billion dollars was annually exported to Europe during the 1920's, with European bankers and merchants actually piling up dollar surpluses by the hundred million every year. A complicated triangular arrangement obscured the fact that U.S. insistence on full payment of the Allied war debts, coupled with continued U.S. insistence that there was no necessary connection between these debts and German reparations payments, was dangerously unbalancing the whole structure of international economic relationships. In essence, the arrangement was this: American dollars were lent Germany, this enabled Germany to make reparations payments to the Allies, and this in turn enabled the Allies to make war debt payments to the United States—the whole process being dependent on a continuous supply of private credit for which the security offsets (since we refused to accept payment in goods and services) were every year more slender. The arrangement could work only so long as a day of reckoning, a settlement of real as distinct from fictitious accounts, could be postponed. The longer the postponement, the more difficult the settlement and the more painful the reckoning.

In the spring of 1924, however, only the short-term effects of all this were visible, and these, as Roosevelt noted, greatly favored the reelection that fall of a Republican administration. American agriculture remained depressed and farmers discontented, but the acute farm distress of 1920–22, which had led to the calling of a Midwestern Conference for Progressive Political Action in early 1922 and to the election of several Farmer-Laborites and insurgent Republicans to the House and Senate in the fall of that year, had passed. A second Progressive Conference had met and decided to try for the Presidential nomination of Senator La Follette by the Republicans in 1924. Failing that, as they were bound to fail, the Midwestern rebels intended to launch a new national Progressive Party with La Follette heading its ticket. But as convention time approached, the potency of this threat, whose realization would in any case be as damaging to the Democracy as to Republicanism, was waning. The total national income and the individual incomes of most Americans were going up. Taxes—especially on high incomes, but to a felt degree on smaller incomes, too—were going down or promised soon to do so. Never, it seemed to the broad middle classes, had a sun of prosperity shone more brightly upon a smiling America, out of a sky less troubled by clouds. It shone with a special glowing warmth upon the political fortunes of Coolidge, Mellon, and Company.

Republican policies of favoritism for business enterprise were responsible for the present economic happiness and the even greater such happiness which appeared to be in the offing. So said the President of the United States. So said the "greatest Secretary of the Treasury since

Alexander Hamilton." Americans were encouraged toward political passivity, were discouraged from active participation or interest in the processes of government, by the evident fact that very little government was now needed—none, in fact, beyond an exercise of police powers for the maintenance of public order plus a few simple devices to assure that private business was unhampered in its pursuit of private profit. American capitalism was a self-determining, self-regulating system to which the federal authority was quite properly subordinate. "The business of America," said Calvin Coolidge, "is business." The government itself, said Andrew Mellon, "is just a business." On this score, all a good American had to do was relax and enjoy the automatic beneficence of the marketplace.

VIII

But though committed to what he recognized as a probably doubly doomed cause (Smith could not be nominated; no Democrat could win the White House in November), Franklin Roosevelt was by no means downhearted.

Like Adolf Hitler in that year, he surveyed a scene of gathering gloom and saw personal opportunity shining out of it bright as burnished gold in a spot of sunlight. Like Adolf Hitler, he aimed to take political advantage of events of disunity, those present and those foreseen, to establish a new order of which he would become the central figure. But as the prospect before him differed greatly in character from that which presented itself to Hitler's vision, as the gold that glittered in his eyes was wholly different in shape and quality from that which Hitler aimed to acquire, and as his essential nature differed radically from Hitler's, Roosevelt made responses to what he saw so different from Hitler's as to amount, generally, to an oppositional contrast. It was a contrast definitive of spiritual differences between democracy and dictatorship. Hitler's political attitude was one of chaos-breeding intransigence, Roosevelt's one of order-creating compromise. Hitler saw egoistic selfishness, malicious envy, fearful hate, angry despair, and a sadomasochistic lust as prime human motivations and made his exhortative appeals to these; Roosevelt saw and appealed to goodwill, generosity, love, and hope. Where Hitler employed force and terror as major political tools, Roosevelt employed persuasion and trust. Hitler's ultimate, if unconscious, aim was simply to disrupt and destroy. Roosevelt's ultimate aim, wholly conscious, was to unite and preserve.

He would do nothing overtly to foment the party disunity which presented him with opportunity, for he recognized this opportunity to be one of making peace among currently warring factions. He was now offered a chance to demonstrate before a national audience that he was fighting his way back to full recovery and was already physically able to perform arduous public tasks—a chance also to wipe from his reputation the last vestigial stain of anti-Catholicism which remained from the Sheehan fight. That he fought in a losing cause would enable him to display, as he could not have done in any obviously prosperous enterprise, a graceful courage, a personal gallantry and integrity of purpose, a selflessness and broad-mindedness, which would recommend him in the highest terms to those who must decide the future leadership of party and nation.

When Roosevelt's appointment to head the Smith preconvention campaign was announced in May, the New York *Herald Tribune,* a Republican paper, editorialized: "What the campaign has lost in practical political ability through the death of Murphy it has now compensated for in prestige and principles." [32] Other papers made similar comment. This helped build for Roosevelt the kind of appeal to independents and liberal Republicans which he would need for future election victories. It also precisely fitted the prescription Belle Moskowitz and Judge Proskauer had made for the figurehead chairmanship of the Citizens' Committee. Thus the relationship between Roosevelt and Smith was at this juncture and to this extent a symbiotic one, each man feeding as he fed upon the other's ambition, and though the symbiosis was sympathetic on the whole, it contained elements of antipathy which might grow large in the future. Roosevelt had no intention of being a *passive* figurehead. With Howe, he promptly established an intensely active Smith campaign headquarters whence issued every day at least one news release and form letters by the hundreds, each designed to appear uniquely personal and each bearing Roosevelt's personal signature. A massive, truly personal correspondence was also handled, chiefly by Howe, while Eleanor labored as head of the Women's Division, one of her main chores being to chair a "committee to present to the resolutions committee of the convention some of the planks of interest to women," as she later recalled.[33] Roosevelt did his best to overcome the obvious and acute disabilities of the Smith candidacy. It was not his fault if, by doing so or through the manner of his doing it and through Smith's negative responses to his efforts, he piled up more political credit for himself than he did for Smith.

He strove in May and early June to present his candidate to the public as a champion of farm relief. He was forced to do so in glittering generalities. In actual fact, Smith knew and had said virtually nothing about national agricultural problems, and Roosevelt himself was opposed to the major farm relief proposal, the McNary-Haugen bill, then under consideration by the Congress. McNary-Haugen, which would have important repercussions in Roosevelt's future, was the brainchild of George N. Peek and Hugh S. Johnson, both of whom had been associated with Bernard Baruch and the War Industries Board during the war. They were now fellow executives of the Moline Plow Company in Moline, Illinois. Their ingenious proposal called for establishment of a federal farm board with authority to buy major American crops, such as wheat and corn, at a price approximately equivalent to the prevailing world price plus the tariff on those crops. This board-set price, representing what the bill called a "fair exchange value," would of course become the American domestic market price. The board would then sell on the foreign market the surplus production—that is, all that was produced beyond domestic market demand—and would assess the farmer for the board's loss in this transaction through an "equalization fee." Since the equalization fee would be less than the difference between the original board-set price and the foreign market price, there would be a net gain in American farm income. The bill had the enthusiastic endorsement of every major farm organization, of dozens of Midwestern and Northwestern chambers of commerce, and of several legislatures in predominantly agricultural states. It was strongly opposed by Eastern Republicans, representing nonagricultural manufacturing and finance, and by the Coolidge administration. It was defeated in the House on June 3 (agitation for it would continue), whereupon Roosevelt let it be known that he personally opposed it as an "artificial price-fixing scheme," thus manifesting his conservative's faith in the "natural" price-fixing of the prevailing market.[34]

He strove also to present Smith to Progressives and League advocates as a foe of isolationism in foreign policy, a champion of liberal internationalism, and as a champion of Progressivism in general. But Smith knew and had said almost as little about foreign as about agricultural policy. He had perforce supported the League of Nations during his gubernatorial campaign of 1920 but felt he had lost votes thereby (the urban Irish opposed the League as a scheme to perpetuate and strengthen the British Empire) and had since made no public mention of it whatever. Nor was Smith sympathetic to the kind of federalism with which Wilson had become identified through such measures as the Federal Reserve Act, the Federal Trade Commission Act, the Adamson Act, and for which McAdoo continued to stand. Progressive in his power policies and in matters pertaining to individual human welfare— persuaded by Belle Moskowitz, as well as by his own conscience, toward humanitarian as opposed to business-favoring legislation whenever the two were in flat opposition—he was invincibly conservative in his basic economic views and philosophy of government. He had now moved from his old Lower East Side home to a swank hotel suite uptown. His social and professional associations were more and more with wealthy businessmen. And he was as convinced as they were, as convinced as Calvin Coolidge, that governmental budgets must be kept in balance and that the trend toward the centralization of governing authority in Washington, the extension and strengthening of Presidential power which the Wilson administration had so greatly advanced, posed a grave threat to personal liberty and the private enterprise upon which American prosperity depended. The intermittently Jeffersonian Roosevelt was often more inclined than not to agree with the candidate on this score. Small wonder, therefore, that Roosevelt met failure in this as in other aspects of his effort to divert the electorate's prime attention from Smith's Catholicism and wetness and big-city parochialism, his effort to make the upcoming national campaign a dialogue between progressivism and conservatism.

No such private reservations and ambiguities hindered his attempt to keep the rivalry between Smith and McAdoo from splitting the party asunder at the convention. Here his efforts were wholehearted. He repeatedly urged the more rabid of Smith's partisans to moderate their factional passions. He promised McAdoo they would do so. "To argue as persuasively as we may the merits of our own man because of the faith that is in us, that is eminently proper," he wrote in a letter to McAdoo dated May 19; "to decry the merits of others, to misrepresent, to attempt to keep full knowledge of their just claims for consideration from the delegates, and most of all to inject a spirit of partisan bitterness into this weighing of candidates, is wrong, and everything which would leave scars behind in our own Party will be scrupulously avoided by the friends of Governor Smith." * [35] But he lacked actual authority either to make or to enforce this promise; it was a personal assertion flung in the face of onrushing realities and was doubtless recognized as such by McAdoo.

For the harsh truth was that Smith, increasingly bitterly angered by McAdoo-partisan attacks on his religion, leaned heavily upon Proskauer and Mrs. Moskowitz and New York Secretary of State Robert Moses for advice on issues but placed slight value upon the advice of Franklin Roosevelt and generally ignored it. When Roosevelt drafted

* The Gibbon-like balance and rhythm of this lengthy period strongly suggests that it was not penned by Roosevelt personally. It certainly expressed his sentiments, however.

for the governor a statement in which the Prohibition issue was described as a "red herring" and in which Smith was made to say that "a
temperate people are a happy and contented people, and to that end all
my acts and words will bend," the candidate refused to issue it. Instead,
Smith reiterated his stand in favor of an immediate repeal or modifica-
tion of the Volstead Act to permit the sale of beer and light wine.
Threatened then with reprisals from a dry pressure group, Smith wrote
and released for publication an angry letter in which he called again for
immediate legalization of beer and wine and said that "no committee or
any other power" could "prevent me from giving full expression to just
what I think about any public question." [36] Nor did Smith count upon
Roosevelt to handle the preconvention campaign's tactical and administrative detail. He recruited for this purpose Norman E. Mack, the Democratic boss of Buffalo, and George Brennan, the Democratic boss in Illinois, two men who had long been admiring friends of his and whose
political professionalism he respected, contrasting it with what seemed
to him the essentially dilettante approach of Roosevelt. He, of course,
had plausible excuse for doing this—namely, Roosevelt's physical disability and his, Smith's, humane concern for Roosevelt's health—but the
situation was inevitably humiliating in its immediate effects on the
younger man. The nominal campaign manager, manipulated as a piece
of lightweight window dressing and only too conscious that this was so,
could play his role with the necessary grace only if he continually reminded himself that "being used" was in this case a reciprocal relationship.
    He was only perfunctorily consulted, if at all, in May and early June,
on the important question of who should make the speech placing Smith
in nomination before the convention. In San Francisco in 1920, the
nominating speech which Roosevelt had seconded was made by the sil-
ver-tongued Tammanyite Bourke Cochran. Cochran's effort had mightily pleased Smith. But Cochran was now dead, and Smith, who actually
auditioned several prospective speechmakers, despaired of finding anyone who could equal Cochran's effectiveness. Finally, he turned to Roosevelt. According to Ernest K. Lindley, Roosevelt said he would "do it,"
provided Smith would "dispense with the tryout," whereupon Smith,
with a grin, "accepted the situation." [37] This has been interpreted by historians as a purely jocular exchange. It may have been instead, or also, a
covert adversary encounter, for it is more than possible that Smith, un-
warned, would have asked Roosevelt to try out for what, after all, was to
be an actor's performance, a reading of lines written by another. Roosevelt seems not to have realized this last at the outset. He retired at once
to Hyde Park to write his speech. He gaily boasted of his occupation to

his tenant farmer, Moses Smith, when the latter found him dictating out-of-doors to Missy LeHand one bright summer's day. Some swallowing of pride must have been required of him, therefore, when his script failed to pass muster with Al Smith. The draft speech which Smith approved was the work of Judge Proskauer.

The Republican National Convention opened in Cleveland on June 10. Three days later—having with perfect decorum adopted a platform promising government economy, tax reduction, and some unspecified form of farm relief; having nominated Calvin Coolidge for President on the first ballot, with Charles G. Dawes as his running mate—the Republicans adjourned to prepare a campaign in whose victorious outcome they had perfect confidence.*

Shortly thereafter, Roosevelt, Proskauer, and Herbert Bayard Swope of the New York *World* met together to go over the Proskauer manuscript line by line. Roosevelt suggested minor changes in phrasing here and there for greater ease of delivery. These suggestions were accepted. He insisted upon including a fervent plea against acrimonious factionalism, an appeal for party unity. The other two agreed. But they could not accept, and Roosevelt ultimately yielded, his initially quite strong objection to the device with which Proskauer had concluded the speech—a quotation from William Wordsworth:

> This is the Happy Warrior; this is he
> Whom every man in arms should wish to be.

That was much too "fancy," too "literary," said Roosevelt; it would not go down well with hardheaded delegates on the floor or with the kind of Smith-supporter who, thanks to Tammany, would pack the galleries.[38]

* The 1924 Republican National Convention was noteworthy in that, thanks to Coolidge, it was *directly* controlled by big business—notably William M. Butler, a Boston industrialist, who was convention boss, working closely with Andrew Mellon, among others of the elite of the business community. "Heretofore for fifty years . . . [the Republican] party had served business through the leadership of politicians," writes William Allen White in his *A Puritan in Babylon.* "They assumed to arbitrate between capital and government, between the people and organized plutocracy—government invisible and never quite brazen. Coolidge . . . wrecked that political liaison." He "destroyed the arbitration myth" by dispensing with the "mediation of the political machine." A principal casualty of this wholesale transfer of power was Senator Henry Cabot Lodge, who, in the process of destroying Wilson and the League of Nations, had made himself personally hated, even within his own party, as a vindictive mean-minded old man. Lodge had been both temporary and permanent chairman of the 1920 convention. He was not named to a single convention committee in 1924! He sat simply and solely as a delegate from Massachusetts—a shunned figure, lonely, powerless, snubbed day after day by men he had long despised.

IX

The 1924 Democratic National Convention formally opened in Madison Square Garden on June 24, chose Montana's Senator Walsh (he, too, was a Roman Catholic) to be its permanent chairman, and at once set about fulfilling the direst of the dire predictions that had been made for it.

First came a knock-down, drag-out floor fight over a proposed platform plank condemning the Ku Klux Klan by name. (The Committee on Resolutions had been able, fortunately, to avoid any incendiary mention of Prohibition.) When McAdoo arrived in the city from California, he infuriated the Smith camp and delighted his own by issuing from his headquarters in the Vanderbilt Hotel a statement denouncing the "sinister, unscrupulous, invisible government which has its seat in the citadel of privilege and finance in New York City." He made no mention of the sinisterly secretive Klan.* Smith did. The Klan, said he in public statement, was symptomatic of the prevailing "spirit of unrest" and must "in time . . . fall of its own weight" since it was "so abhorrent to intelligent thinking Americans of all denominations." It would do so, however, in his evident belief, only if this abhorrence were forcefully expressed by American leaders, each of whom was morally obliged to deal with it as a serious threat. (Said Smith of the Klan: "The Catholics . . . can stand it. The Jews can stand it. But the United States of America cannot stand it." [40]) The battle over the proposed explicitly condemnatory plank was therefore essentially a trial of strength between the candidacies of Smith and McAdoo. The latter won it, though by the narrowest of margins. There was a terrifying scene in the Garden on the sweltering night of June 29. William Jennings Bryan mounted the speakers' stand to plead against the proposed plank. He was angrily jeered and hooted from galleries packed by thousands upon thousands of Smith supporters. Only the active presence of a greatly augmented police contingent prevented a bloody riot. And passions thus aroused could not be soothed for either side by the roll call vote of $543\frac{3}{20}$ to $542\frac{7}{20}$ whereby the anti-Klan plank was finally defeated.

* The head of McAdoo's campaign organization in Nebraska, Arthur Mullen, wrote a statement repudiating the KKK for McAdoo's use, but, as Mullen wrote in a post-election letter, "Tom Love of Texas and others influenced him [McAdoo] by arguments about political expediency, to hold back from statement. He should have known Sen. Joseph Bailey's opinion of Tom Love, his fellow townsman. . . . 'In my travels I have seen in the galleries of the Old World seventeen different portraits of Judas Iscariot and every one looked like Tom Love.' McAdoo trusted him, though. . . ." [39]

Then came the balloting on nominees. On the first ballot McAdoo led with 431½ votes, followed by Smith with 241, the other votes being scattered among such nominees as Cox, John W. Davis, and Oscar W. Underwood of Alabama. Ballot followed ballot with no decisive shift of strength, McAdoo always leading but never coming close to the needed two-thirds majority—and in the bitter aftermath of the Klan battle there was no possibility of Smith's withdrawing in any way that would profit McAdoo or of McAdoo's permitting Smith to win. The deadlock was total and apparently unbreakable. After some scores of futile ballots, Catholics of the West who had been in McAdoo's camp came to Smith with the proposal that he throw his support behind Irish Catholic Senator Walsh as a compromise candidate. Smith refused. He refused also to make any deal with McAdoo when the latter proposed they both agree upon Edwin T. Meredith of Iowa, who had been Wilson's Secretary of Agriculture—this when the two met at the behest of desperate convention managers after ninety-odd ballots had failed to come anywhere near a decision. At this meeting Smith did acknowledge the impossibility of his own nomination and offered to withdraw if McAdoo would do so. But McAdoo would make no such promise, even after Smith's offer was announced to the convention by Franklin Roosevelt. The balloting went on ("Alabama casts twenty-four votes for Oscar W. Underwood" became a refrain of frustration as, day in and day out, the roll call of the states was made in alphabetical order) until finally, on July 9, negotiations behind the scenes focused on the man whom Roosevelt had been inclined to favor, as his second choice, in the Convention of 1920—John W. Davis, the urbane, handsome, and wealthy corporation lawyer who, a native of West Virginia, lived now in luxury at Locust Valley, Long Island. Accordingly, on the one hundred and third ballot, Davis won nomination with a vote of 839. To balance the ticket and appease so far as possible the enfeebled Bryan wing of the party, the convention nominated as Davis' running mate Charles W. Bryan of Nebraska, beloved brother of the Great Commoner.

So ended the most disastrous national political party convention since the Democratic assemblage of 1860, when the party broke completely in two, the North under Douglas, the South under Breckenridge, on the eve of the Civil War.

For Franklin D. Roosevelt, however, this long ordeal of anger and frustration was the means and circumstance of a great personal victory.

The high point of the convention was his speech placing Al Smith in nomination.[41] He was then the central figure of the only scene that would brightly shine, to a retrospective vision, out of the Garden's prolonged and gloomy turmoil. Thunderous were the cheers sweeping the great hall when he appeared, a gallant figure on crutches, at the rear of the platform. He was the personification of courage, defying pain and death with every forward swing of his braced legs, as he made his way slowly, carefully, across the stage, the whole of his attention concentrated on this physical effort, which was psychological also. The huge crowd felt the risk he took. How ghastly it would be if he fell down! His safe arrival at the rostrum, therefore, his casting aside of his crutches, his drawing himself erect with his hands gripping the lectern, his lifting high his handsome head and smiling triumphantly into the spotlights' glare constituted a moment of dramatic heroism. And there was no lessening of the excitement, there was rather a gain of it, as he began to speak. The words written on the page before him rang out over the hall in his wonderfully vibrant tenor voice and, fusing with the brave sight of him, became a personal expression. They were heard by millions over the radio, for the convention procedings were broadcast that year for the first time. "On our Governor for over twenty years in public office the white light of publicity has pitilessly beaten, and revealed only spotless integrity," said he, standing in white light. He dominated the hall as he cried out the words he himself had written, his fervent, though futile, plea for party unity: "You equally who come from the great cities of the East and the plains and hills of the West, from the slopes of the Pacific and from the homes and fields of the Southland, I ask you in all sincerity, in the balloting on that platform tomorrow, to keep first in your hearts and minds the words of Abraham Lincoln—'With malice toward none, with charity to all.'" He risked spoiling Judge Proskauer's carefully calculated climactic effect when he inserted into the body of his text a reference to "the 'Happy Warrior' of the political battlefield" (obviously he continued to have no faith in this overly "poetic" conclusion), but in the event he didn't spoil it. He sang out the Wordsworth lines, joined them to the name of Alfred E. Smith—and pandemonium reigned thereafter, thousands marching and cheering and singing "The Sidewalks of New York" over and over again, for more than an hour.

Al Smith was from that time forth the Happy Warrior.

But so was Franklin Roosevelt.

From every section of the country, from representatives of every shade in the political spectrum, came glowing published praise of the speech. "A noble utterance" that "belongs with the small list of really great convention speeches," wrote Mark Sullivan. Walter Lippmann spoke of it as "moving and distinguished." Other observers published their conviction, after the balloting for nominees had begun, that Roosevelt was "the one man whose name would stampede the convention were he put in nomination," to quote a political columnist in the New

York *Herald Tribune*. His attractiveness was vastly enhanced by his apparently selfless devotion to Smith. "From the time Roosevelt made his speech [nominating Smith] . . . he has been easily the foremost figure on floor or platform," said the *Herald Tribune* columnist on July 1. ". . . without the slightest intention or desire to do anything of the sort, he has done for himself what he could not do for his candidate." [42]

A week later, after Roosevelt's tireless double effort to gain delegate votes for Smith and to prevent a fatal party disruption had won personal admiration even from McAdoo's adherents, the New York *World* proclaimed that "Franklin D. Roosevelt stands out as the real hero of the Democratic Convention of 1924." Said the *World*: "Adversity has lifted him above the bickering, the religious bigotry, conflicting personal ambitions and petty sectional prejudices. It has made him the one leader commanding the respect and admiration of delegates from all sections of the land." (The "fine courage that flashes in his smile," the *World* went on, prevented his being "a pathetic, tragic figure.") On the day after Davis' nomination, the New York *Times* praised editorially Senator Walsh's performance of his difficult duties as the convention's permanent chairman and added: "Franklin Roosevelt is another man who succeeded in gaining . . . unanimous respect and admiration from the members of the Convention. . . . They [Walsh and Roosevelt] are the two outstanding personalities revealed by the Convention—the two who did, and did perfectly, what they tried to do and what they should have done." [43] Such publicity had, of course, a hopeful significance for Roosevelt's future. It was of less practical effect, however, than the highly favorable impression he made on men like Tom Pendergast, the notoriously tough-minded boss of Kansas City's Democratic machine and the most powerful single Democrat in Missouri. When Pendergast returned to Kansas City, he said to one of his supporters, who was also a friendly acquaintance of Roosevelt's: ". . . you know I am seldom carried away . . . but I want to tell you that had Mr. Roosevelt . . . been physically able to have withstood the campaign, he would have been named by acclamation in the first few days of the Convention. He has the most magnetic personality of any individual I have ever met, and I predict he will be the candidate on the Democratic ticket in 1928." [44]

One may be sure that Roosevelt had a very accurate sense of the impression he made and that this helped him bear with no show of resentment the tacit rebuffs he met with from Smith and Smith's inner circle of advisers. (Roosevelt's attempt to persuade the Smith camp to support an innocuous compromise resolution on the Ku Klux Klan had, for instance, been brushed aside.) As regards his psychological relationship with Smith, his major concern seems to have been to prevent the sprouting of such seeds of suspicious enmity toward him as might be sown in Smith's mind by published invidious comparisons between the candidate and the candidate's nominal manager. He was very careful to maintain toward Smith at all times an attitude of deference, of gratitude for the opportunities Smith "gave" him. He encouraged the older man to patronize him. It served his purposes for Smith to continue to regard him as too light a man to be taken very seriously, either in his present role as supporting friend or in his possible future role as political rival.

Not until the convention was over would Roosevelt, in private talk and correspondence, reveal just a little of the irritation he had kept hidden behind smiles. In response to one letter complaining that Smith had failed to take definite stands on major issues, Roosevelt would then explain that "Governor Smith positively forbade anything being done for his candidacy prior to May 1st," which "meant that anything after that time in the way of statements by him on national questions would have looked too much like campaign propaganda," and Smith personally "vetoed many suggestions that were made in regard to statements by him on the farm question and other national issues." Years passed before he revealed anything at all of the contempt, mingling irritation with amusement, which was occasionally aroused in him by Smith's gaucheries and ignorant parochialism. It was in 1928 that he told Claude G. Bowers, as recorded in Bowers' autobiography, how Smith allegedly met a group of Kansas delegates during the 1924 convention. The delegates were conferring with Roosevelt when, so Bowers writes, Smith entered "like a breeze, in a swallowtail coat, a silk hat at a rakish angle, and with the usual cigar in his mouth. 'Hello, hello, my boy, and how's things?' he said, addressing Roosevelt. The latter introduced his callers. . . . 'Hello, boys,' said Smith, shaking hands. 'Glad to see you. Y'know, the other day some boys were in from Wisconsin, and I learned something. I always thought Wisconsin was on the other side of the lake. It's on this side. Glad to know it. Glad to know more about the place where the good beer comes from.' And this to delegates from a strong Prohibition state." [45]

Twenty-four

➤➤➤◄◄◄

Warm Springs

I

H E LEFT the sweltering city and the sweat-soured, smoke-thickened air of the ironically named Garden, with all its ugly din, and journeyed north along the river to the garden and woods and wide green lawns of his boyhood home. Always the river flowed southward, slowly bringing fresh waters down from the mountain wilderness though open country to the sea, while he went upstream from city to country seeking refreshment, renewal, convinced in his heart that life was made possible in the city only by a continuous influx of fresh country nature. Never had Hyde Park seemed lovelier to him. Never had he been more eager to yield himself wholly to the peace and openness of country living.

And he could do so now for a time, for quite a long time, with no feeling that he ought really to be doing something else. Having emerged with greatly enhanced prestige from the convention's turbulence, having been shunted aside, as was natural in the circumstances, by Davis' campaign organization, having arranged his business activities in such a way as to require little of his time and energy, he served his ambition and his nation best by doing precisely what he now did, in almost full retreat from the hurly-burly.

There was talk of nominating him for governor of New York, it being then unknown that Al Smith would run for reelection. A letter urging him to accept such nomination came from a prominent New York Democrat who, like him, had suffered a crippling illness. He replied that he could not "consider it for a moment," and for reasons which his correspondent should understand "better than anybody else." He was, he wrote, "perfectly convinced that if you and I devote another two or three years to overcoming our disability, we will be in much better shape to render service than if we were at this time to enter actively into a campaign."

Glenn Frank, the brilliant editor of *Century Magazine*, soon to become president of the University of Wisconsin, thoroughly agreed with him. In the second week of August, John W. Davis was a guest at Hyde Park. Roosevelt had several influential people in to meet the Democratic Presidential candidate, Glenn Frank among them. The editor was much more favorably impressed by Roosevelt than he was by Roosevelt's guest of honor; he said so in his thank-you note. He, Frank, fervently hoped that Roosevelt would "sidetrack everything in the interest of the one thing of 'getting your legs back' by June 1928, for I want to be able to vote for a President with greater enthusiasm than I am able to muster this year." (Roosevelt wrote back in mild defense of Davis. The candidate would "grow as the campaign goes on," Roosevelt "honestly" believed, though there was obvious need for Davis "to be more dramatic.")[1]

It was to the "getting" of his "legs back" that Roosevelt now devoted his major attention and a physical effort as strenuous, almost as painful as the one of 1921 and 1922. He worked at recreation, a literal re-creation of physical self, and he worked very hard. The "progress" toward "full recovery" which he continually asserted he was making had been in fact far too slow to meet his time schedule—if, in fact, it was truly progress at all toward an actual walking. Rare and feeble were the signs of life's return to the muscles of his thighs and calves and toes. They remained atrophied, shriveled to the dimensions of strings; they had but slightly more rigid strength than strings; and they were seemingly nourished by the merest trickle of warm blood, so that his sticklike legs felt always cold, twenty or more degrees colder than normal body temperature, save when they were heated from the outside by sunlight or hot bath.

There entered into his physical effort a note of increasing urgency and impatience, if not of secret anxiety and desperation. Every day, for hours, he "walked" the parallel bars and walked on crutches, wearing only a single brace, sometimes his left one, sometimes his right, putting as much weight as possible upon his loosely swinging foot. He tried every new alleged recovery device that, called to his attention, had any plausibility at all. Invariably he was disappointed. His mother brought back from Europe a man-sized tricycle; he tried it, was briefly enthusiastic about it, then abandoned it as useless. Someone recommended horseback riding, a recreation he had particularly enjoyed in the past; it proved worse than useless—it was actually hazardous because, having been mounted with difficulty, hoisted into the saddle on the brawny shoulders of servants, he was unable to grip the horse's flanks with his dangling legs. (He wrote jocularly to a friend that what he required was an animal "constitutionally unable to trot, and which is also guaranteed against any sidewise motions.") Yet he knew that a "leg in a brace does not have a chance for muscle development"; such development "must come through exercise when the brace is not on—such as swimming. . . ." [2] And it was only through water—through his daily swimming and other water exercises—that his assertion he would walk again was actually sustained by some degree of objectively measurable truth.

Dr. Lovett in Boston encouraged his long-held belief in the efficacy of a water cure. Lovett assured him that many polio patients had made marked improvement as a result of swimming—told him, too, that the improvement was greater among those who swam in warm water than among those who swam in cold, as Roosevelt had surmised it would be. Obviously he, Roosevelt, should have a summer-sun-warmed pool of his own at Hyde Park, and he made tentative arrangements with Elliott Brown for the construction of one only a few yards from the house. But Eleanor, going now her own way, living her own life,.having only such relations with her husband as one law partner might have with another on matters effecting the firm, had a different and, she insisted, a better idea. Roosevelt good-humoredly conveyed it to Brown in a letter dated August 5, 1924. "My Missus and some of her female political friends [they were Nancy Cook and Marion Dickerman] want to build a shack on a stream in the back woods [it was Val Kill, a mile and a half east of the house] and want, instead of a beautiful marble bath, to have the stream dug out so as to form an old fashioned swimmin' hole," he wrote. "Apparently the girls think that this will get them more closely back to nature. . . ." The idea appealed to him; he canceled the arrangements he had made. Next year he would have a "shack" (actually a substantial stone cottage, costing many thousands of dollars) and a good-sized swimming pool built at the desired site by a Poughkeepsie contractor, working under his close personal supervision.

At about the time he was canceling his original swimming pool plans, he had talk and correspondence with a longtime friendly acquaintance, the white-haired and -bearded George Foster Peabody, an impressively tall, impressively wealthy, occasionally philanthropic New York City banker who had recently acquired financial control of a resort hotel with more than 1,000 acres of surrounding grounds near a village called Bullochsville,* in Peabody's native state of Georgia. It had been a famous and prosperous resort in the years before the Civil War and for some decades afterward but had been badly hurt by poor management,

* The village was named after the Bulloch family, one of whose daughters married the first Theodore Roosevelt, becoming then the mother of a President and paternal grandmother of Eleanor Roosevelt.

joined to the changed vacation patterns imposed by the automobile. It was now, admittedly, in deplorable shape.

The actual promoter and manager of the enterprise, Peabody explained, was a newspaperman named Thomas Wesley Loyless. Loyless had been part owner of the Columbus (Georgia) *Enquirer-Sun* when, in 1920, he organized the Warm Springs Operating Company, leased the resort for $9,000 a year, with an option to buy, and prepared to raise sufficient capital to restore it to profitable operation. Simultaneously, however, he continued an editorial war he had declared in his newspaper on the Ku Klux Klan. This was an extremely hazardous thing to do at that time, in that place, for the Klan was immensely powerful locally and ruthlessly vicious in its enmities. It retaliated with repeated threats upon Loyless' life and a boycott that drastically reduced the *Enquirer-Sun*'s advertising and circulation revenues. By late 1922 Loyless had been forced out of his partnership. He had gone then to New York City to edit an ephemeral periodical called *Tolerance*. It was there and then, in early 1923, that he met Peabody and at once tried to enlist Peabody's financial interest in the struggling Warm Springs Company.[3]

But the banker had been persuaded to buy into Loyless' enterprise less by the newspaperman's eager arguments than by his own assessment of the resort's central feature and principal asset. This was an outdoor swimming pool, one of the largest in the South, measuring 150 by 50 feet, fed by a thermal spring which gushed out of a huge fissured rock at an abundant rate (800 gallons a minute) which never varied, drought year or no, and, according to Indian lore, had been unvarying for centuries before the white man came. As Roosevelt with his avidity for facts would subsequently learn, the water source for the spring was rain falling upon a 1,400-foot ridge, called Pine Mountain, rising some 2 miles away to the south. This rainwater soaked into a permeable rock formation which geologists had named the Hollis and which carried it northward at a depth of a few hundred feet for a mile or so before plunging suddenly, at a steep angle, to a depth of 3,800 feet. Here the Hollis stratum came hard against impermeable rock. It then shot upward to the surface again, as if tracing the trajectory of a bouncing ball, carrying with it the original Pine Mountain rainwater, now heated by pressure and enriched by dissolved mineral salts.[4] The water issued from the emergent fractured rock at a constant temperature of 89 degrees Fahrenheit. And it seemed to have, said Peabody, remarkable therapeutic properties. The Creek Indians had used the spring for curative bathing since very ancient times, achieving, according to legend, miraculous cures of crippling illness. The waters were not only "a specific for all cutaneous diseases," but also a remedy "for chronic rheumatism, chronic diseases of the liver, kidney, and bladder," and "dyspepsia," according to the advertisements of nineteenth-century promoters. Such claims must be discounted, of course, for lack of concrete evidence in support of them. But there was no need to discount for this reason the most remarkable claim of all, made in a written testimonial which Peabody enclosed in a letter to Roosevelt—namely, that a young man named Louis Joseph had come to the resort three years ago almost totally crippled by polio (his back and abdomen had been affected along with his legs, which were useless) and, by constant swimming in the heated pool and walking exercises in the buoyant water, had so improved that he was now able to walk about the streets on unbraced legs, supported only by an ordinary cane! [5]

Roosevelt's hopeful interest was at once aroused. It was now the end of summer, a summer during which his legs had gained measurably, if slightly, in strength owing, he was convinced, to "sunlight and swimming." He had been unable to stand up unsupported, without making swimming motions with his hands, in water up to shoulder height when summer began. Now he could stand up on unbraced legs in water below shoulder height. He was unable to walk in water of that height, however, for all his struggle to do so, and soon the weather would be too chilly in the Hudson River Valley for further outdoor swimming exercise. He wrote to Loyless. He made arrangements to go down to the Warm Springs resort in the first days of October, accompanied by Eleanor and Missy LeHand. He believed that in the "natural highly mineralized" and nearly blood-warm water which was said to fill the pool he "could actually walk around at the shallow end with the water up to my shoulders," as he wrote one of his doctors. He could thereby achieve "the normal walking motion better than in any other way." He was particularly eager to meet and talk with Louis Joseph and was assured by Loyless that Joseph would be on hand; the Joseph family had built a house near the resort and lived there the year around.

II

His introduction to the place could hardly have encouraged optimism concerning the resort's future, even in so determinedly optimistic a man as he.[6] The branch line train that brought him and his party up from Columbus was made up of ancient, creaking, shabby cars, none too clean. The railway station at Bullochsville (the village would be officially renamed Warm Springs a few days later) was a small shabby structure with paint peeling off its sides. Many of the white people and all the blacks in the crowd of nearly a hundred which gathered at the station in the late afternoon to witness his arrival (word that a famous man was coming had spread through the village) were shabbily clothed, and the village itself, behind the station, was a shabby sleepy place whose evidences of a former relative affluence rendered it all the more lost-seeming and forlorn.

Beyond the village, the countryside through which Tom Loyless drove them in a borrowed automobile was of great natural beauty, dominated by Pine Mountain, but bore marks of a miserably impoverished human life. Stands of scrub pine were interspersed with erosion-scarred red clay fields where weeds grew tall along rows of sparse dead corn. Here and there, set down amid debris-littered yards of bare packed earth that was red as blood, were flimsy leaning shacks that had never known paint and were obviously devoid of sanitary facilities, yet in which large families of blacks or poor whites were living. Eleanor was shocked by the sight. It was a relief for her when they turned off the main highway onto a narrow road that wound, climbing, through a lovely stand of tall pine. Here the October early evening air was cool and sweet with the scent of pine needles, and here there were, on either side of the road, no ugly signs of human misery or enterprise. But this relief was brief. They came to a gutted broken driveway curving up to a hilltop—and there, towering high against the sky, stood the resort hotel, the Meriwether Inn. It was a sprawling multistoried monstrosity of the worst Victorian design, its porches and towers and cupolas fretful with gingerbread, its pretensions to grandeur mocked by flimsy construction. It was a gross contradiction of the natural beauty around it, and even Roosevelt, whose talk during the drive had been encouraging to Loyless' local pride and hope for the future, was taken aback by his first sight of it. Eleanor sensed that he was when he remarked, mildly, that fire insurance rates must be quite high on such a structure. Tom Loyless allowed that this was so.

They drove on through unkempt grounds to the cottage, tree-shaded, with a tangled garden at its back, assigned them for their stay. They were told it was the property of some people named Hart (Loyless and his wife lived next door) and were introduced to a black couple, Roy and Mary, who were to serve them during their visit as chauffeur-valet and cook-housekeeper. The cottage, too, they quickly discovered, though of attractive appearance, was of the flimsiest construction. The floors of wide pine board creaked noisily under the weight of Roosevelt's wheelchair, and Eleanor would never forget her "surprise that I could look through the cracks [in the walls] and see daylight."

She was not sorry, as she went to bed, that her Warm Springs stay would be brief. It had been agreed before she left New York that she must return in a few days for the concluding weeks of Al Smith's reelection campaign, in which she was intensely and importantly active, and her more-than-willingness to do so was in no wise diminished when, the next day, she drove with Missy to a nearby town to buy chickens for the table and found, to her "perfect horror," that the chickens must be taken home live, not killed and dressed. ". . . they ran around in our yard, until the cook wrung their necks amid much squawking and put them in the pot," she remembered a quarter century later. "Somehow I didn't enjoy eating them!" [7]

Her husband had no such squeamishness. He adapted at once to the slow, easy rhythms of Georgia rural life, was not put out by what seemed to Eleanor a prevalent and deplorable slovenliness, was regretful but not dismayed over the "neglect and poverty" he saw all around him, and was positively delighted by the hospitality shown him by everyone he met—a friendliness he found every bit as warm as Southern hospitality was traditionally supposed to be.

He was particularly taken with Tom Loyless, who was a vivid personality, a spendthrift of his energy and ideas, generous, impulsive, sentimental, youthful in his outlook despite a dozen more years of actual age than Roosevelt had, and despite signs of failing health. He was utterly fearless. Roosevelt encouraged him to talk of his experiences as editor and publisher of the Augusta (Georgia) Chronicle from 1903 until 1919, years during which he had fought relentlessly against the rabble-rousing former Populist, Tom Watson, whose championship of white supremacy had been coupled in the 1910's with a virulent, obscenely expressed hatred of Jews and Catholics. Especially notable had been Loyless' editorials during the notorious case of Leo M. Franks, a Jew convicted on dubious evidence of murdering a girl employee in his Atlanta factory; when Franks, his death sentence commuted by Georgia's governor to life imprisonment, was taken from prison by a lynch mob which hanged him at Marietta, Georgia, in 1915, most of the state's papers had condoned the deed, but Loyless' condemnation of it had been as bitter as the New York World's. With a wry humor streaked by angry contempt he told Roosevelt of his costly Ku Klux Klan battle. He had sold his interest in the Augusta Chronicle in late 1919, using the proceeds to buy the Enquirer-Sun in partnership with Julian Harris, son of the Joel Chandler Harris who wrote the famous Uncle Remus stories. Harris was no such adamant warrior against intolerance as Loyless was: as the KKK boycott took effect, he counseled a greater prudence of editorial utterance than Loyless was willing to agree to. Finally, in November, 1922, when Harris and Loyless "irrevocably differed" over an editorial the latter wished to run, Loyless resigned as editor and president, his published letter of resignation saying that, having been "free and untrammeled" in the exercise of his pen for twenty-eight years, he proposed to remain so for whatever time he had left of life.* [8]

But it was the huge T-shaped swimming pool that had drawn Roosevelt here. Everything depended on it. Nothing else could draw him back if it failed him; nothing else could prevent his return if it came near fulfilling his glowing anticipations.

He was introduced to it on the first morning of his stay by Loyless and Louis Joseph, a slender dark-haired young man whose simple story was soon told him in all necessary detail and whose degree of recovery from almost total paralysis did indeed border on the miraculous. Roosevelt's valet pushed him in his wheelchair to the edge of the pool. His valet and Loyless gently lowered him into the water, where Joseph was already swimming. At once a "heavenly warmth" and vitality flowed into his withered legs. "How marvelous it feels!" he cried out over and over again. "I don't think I'll ever get out!" Not only the warmth but also the remarkably energizing buoyancy of this highly mineralized water enabled one to remain in it, swimming, floating, exercising for hours on end, without excessive tiredness. On that first morning he remained in for more than an hour. Before he emerged, more refreshed than he remembered having been for years, he had met and talked at poolside with Joseph's attending physician of the last three years, Dr. James Johnson of the nearby town of Manchester. Johnson confessed that what little he knew about poliomyelitis came from his experience with Joseph's case, but it had been his observation that "about three weeks" of daily and prolonged immersion in the pool was required "to show the effects," as Roosevelt wrote that night to his "Dearest Mama." (". . . the pool," he wrote, ". . . is really wonderful. . . ." [9]) Actually, Roosevelt was convinced of a measurable effect during his very first dip: as he stood shoulder-deep in the water, he managed, with concentrated effort, to lift slightly his right foot. His right leg was the stronger of the two—it had been since that ghastly morning at Campobello when he first realized he was becoming paralyzed—but not since the morning of that day had he been able to make it move. He was overjoyed!

His life at Warm Springs fell into a pattern thereafter. It was "just the same day after day and there is no variety to give landmarks," he wrote in a letter to "Dearest E" a week after she had returned North. "The mornings are as you know wholly taken up with the pool and four of the

---

* In 1926, Harris as publisher of the *Enquirer-Sun* was awarded a Pultizer Prize for "meritorious public service," the basis for the award being the editorial opposition to the Klan which Loyless had initiated.

afternoons we have sat out on the lawn or as Roy calls it the 'yard,' and I have worked at stamps or cheques or accounts or have played rummy with Missy. The other three afternoons we have gone motoring with Mrs. Loyless and have seen the country pretty thoroughly. I like him ever so much and she is nice but not broad in her interests, but she chatters away to Missy on the back seat and I hear an occasional yes or no from Missy to prove she is not sleeping. . . . The legs are really improving a great deal. The walking and general exercising in the water is fine and I have worked out some special exercises also. This is really a discovery of a place. . . ." [10] His improvement, as undeniable as it was astonishing, continued apace. Before many days had passed he found that, for the first time since the tragic August, 1921, he could wiggle his toes! Soon, in that glorious pool, in water only four feet deep, he could "walk around . . . without braces . . . almost as well as if I had nothing the matter with my legs." He announced jubilantly in a letter to George Foster Peabody that in just three weeks at Warm Springs he had progressed farther toward recovery than he had in all the preceding three years! "I have had many talks with Mr. Loyless about the development of the property," he also told the banker.[11]

With some difficulty he persuaded Basil O'Connor to come down from New York City in the last week of October, his principal argument being that this would enable the two of them, then in process of forming their law partnership, to become better acquainted personally. O'Connor, hurried as always, jealous of his time, grumpily suspected ulterior motives and, upon arrival, said so. Roosevelt grinned and tacitly acknowledged the truth of the accusation. He wanted O'Connor's judgment on Tom Loyless and Loyless' ideas for this place, as well as on his own ideas about it. He had, he insisted, the greatest confidence in O'Connor's judgment—though when O'Connor strongly advised him *not* to become personally, financially involved in this enterprise, he indicated that he might or might not follow this advice. The net result was that O'Connor felt himself drawn to Roosevelt, charmed by Roosevelt as he had never been by any other man, and knew, deep down, that against his expressed wish and better judgment he would undoubtedly become involved in many a Roosevelt enterprise having nothing to do with the practice of law by Roosevelt & O'Connor. One such enterprise, a principal one, might very well be the transformation of this shabby, moribund Southern resort into a health spa—an enterprise to whose dubious attractiveness he was rendered personally vulnerable by the interest he had long taken in the special problems of the physically handicapped. ("When I get back I am going to have a long talk with Mr. George Foster Peabody . . . ," Roosevelt was writing his mother. "I feel that a great 'cure' for infantile paralysis and kindred diseases could well be established here." [12])

A day or so after O'Connor's arrival, a reporter came down on special assignment from the Atlanta *Journal*. He was a political reporter whose editor wanted reports of Roosevelt's views on the current campaign. The product of his visit, however, was a lengthy Sunday feature article whose large-typed headline proclaimed that FRANKLIN ROOSEVELT WILL SWIM TO HEALTH and which described in optimistic detail how Roosevelt "has the large swimming pool all to himself," swam in it for hours every day, then sunbathed for at least another hour, and was improving at a rapid rate. "So marked have been the benefits . . . [that] Mr. Roosevelt plans to return to Warm Springs in March or April to remain two or three months," the article said. "At that time he will build a cottage on the hilltop, so that he may spend a portion of each year there until he is completely cured." George Foster Peabody; his nephew, Charles Peabody ("a noted New York architect"); and Loyless planned "extensive developments" of the resort, "with the possible expenditure of several million dollars. . . ." Roosevelt himself had "made a great hit with the people of Warm Springs who have met him" and with a "number of Georgia's public men" who had "called to pay their respects." Georgians who attended the Democratic National Convention "have been especially cordial, because they appreciate the interest Mr. Roosevelt showed in them, and his courtesy in apologizing, as an Al Smith leader, for unfortunate and embarrassing incidents in connection with the convention." He was delighted with Georgia and Georgians. He described "everything in Warm Springs . . . [as] 'Great' or 'Fine' or 'Wonderful.' " This was "the spirit that has carried him to remarkable heights for a man just past his fortieth year," the article concluded, "and it is the spirit that is going to restore him to his pristine health and vigor, for political and financial battles and successes in the years that are to come." The story was illustrated with a photo of Roosevelt seated at poolside in his swimming suit, broadly smiling into the sun under a sloppy canvas hat, his legs so arranged (an opened newspaper largely obscured one of them) as to reveal that they were shrunken while minimizing the degree to which they were. Roosevelt cheerfully opined that the publicity, which he believed would be confined to the *Journal*'s circulation, would do some good for Tom Loyless; O'Connor growled that it might just as easily do harm by attracting patronage of a kind Loyless was wholly unequipped to handle.[13]

The last three days of the visit were crowded ones. "On Wednesday the people of Warm Springs are giving me a supper and reception in the Town Hall," Roosevelt wrote happily to his mother, "and on Friday evening, our last day, I am to go to Manchester . . . for another supper and speech. I think every organization and town in Georgia has asked me to some kind of a party, and Missy spends most of her time keeping up a huge and constant local correspondence." [14]

III

He returned to New York in time to cast his vote, on November 4, for John W. Davis as President of the United States, Alfred E. Smith as governor of New York.

A month or so before leaving for Georgia, he had written from Hyde Park to John Lawrence about his plans for "Cruise No. 2" of the *Larooco*, on which he expected to embark in early February, 1925. He was then preparing to make a couple of speeches on behalf of Davis' candidacy. (One of them was to be broadcast over radio, a still-novel device with which he felt at once peculiarly at ease; his intimate, conversational style of speech, the very opposite of the floridly oratorical, was naturally suited to it.) And because the political situation was very much on his mind he made passing reference to it in his Lawrence letter. The threatened third party, the Progressive, had been duly formed on July 4 with La Follette nominated for the Presidency, Montana's Burton K. Wheeler for the Vice Presidency, and Roosevelt, his judgment perhaps influenced by an inability to develop wholehearted enthusiasm for Davis and by his growing antipathy to Silent Cal, was convinced that the La Follette vote would be a large one. ". . . even through the East [it] is much larger than any of us have any idea of," he wrote Lawrence. "Of course this may change before the election, but my personal opinion is that if the elections were held tomorrow neither Coolidge nor Davis would obtain a majority in the electoral college and the election would be thrown in the House. This of course is highly confidential. . . ." [15] In his radio address on September 24 he praised Davis in warm, if not glowing, tones and was sharply critical of "old line Republican policies," but he said nothing against La Follette as man or political leader. It was understandable why many a Progressive would wish to vote for the Wisconsin Senator, he said; it was also obvious, however, that La Follette could not be elected. "Don't waste your vote!" he advised. In mid-October, writing Eleanor from Warm Springs, where he received almost daily letters and bundles of marked newspapers from Howe dealing with campaign developments, he had "a hunch that Davis' strength is really improving" but still thought "the election will go into the House." "Anyway," he went on, "I am philosophical enough to think that even if Coolidge is elected we shall be so darned sick of conservatism of the old money-controlled crowd in four years that we will get a real progressive landslide in 1928." * [16]

Certainly the national campaign bore little resemblance to that dialogue between conservatism and progressivism which Roosevelt had argued for, worked for. The Democratic Presidential candidate was a lawyer of immense ability. In private social situations he was charming, in public appearances attractive and sometimes impressive. He strongly favored American entry into the League of Nations. He made this a major theme of speeches that were uncommonly well written—logically organized and often beautifully phrased. But he presented to the electorate no real alternative to Republican "business government," being himself as conservative as his Republican opponent (his firm had been counsel for J. P. Morgan and Company,† a fact which did him no good in his quest for the farmer and labor vote), and he expended as much verbal ammunition upon La Follette "radicalism" as he did upon "Republican scandals." He gave no convincing reasons why the average voter should not "Keep Cool with Coolidge," as Republican sloganeers urged—did nothing to dispel the generally prevailing notion that there was no important difference between the two major parties, that the choice was one of tweedledum or tweedledee—and failed to generate any popular excitement whatever.

When election day came, barely half of those eligible to vote bothered to go to the polls. The national Republican victory was lopsided. Coolidge-Dawes won 15,724,000 of the popular vote to a little less than 8,400,000 for Davis-Bryan (the latter ticket received a quarter million fewer votes than Cox-Roosevelt received in the 1920 debacle) and won 382 of the electoral votes to Davis-Bryan's 136. The Republicans retained control of both houses of Congress, though, as before, the cooperation of Progressive Democrats and Progressive Republicans would keep Coolidge conservatism from having all its own way. As for the La Follette vote, it turned out to be considerably smaller than Roosevelt had thought it would be, if perhaps no smaller than he expected it to be when he cast his ballot: it was reduced by a sharp rise in farm prices during the two or three weeks immediately preceding the election. The

---

* Among the campaign songs sung that year was one entitled "A Democrat is Going to the White House," with words and music by Hugh Gordon. It inveighed in rhyme against the "rank corruption" of "the gang" in power and asserted that "a new deal is pending." [17]

† Davis was proud of his "fine list of clients," as he had frankly said in early 1924, listing the Morgan Company, the Erie Railroad, the Guarantee Trust Company, the Standard Oil Company, "and other foremost American concerns." So long as they "ask for my services for honest work I am pleased to work for them. Big Business has made this country what it is. We want Big Business. But it must be honest." [18]

Progressive candidate polled 4,823,000 votes, carrying only his home state of Wisconsin, with 13 electoral votes; he ran second, however, in eleven other states, all of them west of the Mississippi, a fact that was carefully noted and weighed in a balance of political judgment by Roosevelt and Howe.

Wholly different in character and outcome was the New York State gubernatorial campaign.

Al Smith ran hard on the platform of his accomplishments during his first two terms. Eleanor worked strenuously for him. She was convinced at the time that she "understood Governor Smith better than Franklin did." Perhaps this was because her husband did not reveal to her or anyone else all that he really felt and thought about the Happy Warrior, but she herself believed it was "because during my intensive work with the Democratic State Committee while Franklin was ill I had more opportunity to observe him [Smith] from different points of view." Her admiration of him was highly qualified. He had, in her view, "an extraordinary flair for government" and a truly "phenomenal" knowledge of his state's government, but he had slight "knowledge of the country as a whole," was abysmally ignorant of foreign affairs, was considerably "less of a humanitarian than most people thought," and was something less than wholly lovable as a personality. She gave Belle Moskowitz credit for the "social welfare plans for which . . . [Smith] was generally acclaimed" and which he carried out, she believed, largely "because he knew they were politically wise." * His personal humanitarianism was limited, she felt, by the "snobbishness . . . of the self-made man" who "glories in his success," who looks down upon "a man who had not met and conquered the situations he himself had—a man like Franklin," and who by that same token looks down upon those of his own native class who have not risen in life as he has done.[19] These were grave deficiencies, in Eleanor's eyes. Nevertheless, she "believed in him" and was convinced he was "a great man in many ways." She committed herself wholeheartedly to his reelection. The fact that his Republican opponent was her own first cousin, Theodore Roosevelt, Jr., seems only to have increased her ardor on his behalf—in part, no doubt, because she remembered that this cousin had worked against her husband during the 1920 campaign. She, with Louis Howe, joined delightedly in a de-

* Frances Perkins took a far more charitable view of Smith as humanitarian. She was convinced that he and Robert Wagner "never recovered" from the "firsthand look at industrial and labor conditions" which they had during their Factory Investigating Commission days. "They became firm and unshakable sponsors of political and legislative measures designed to overcome conditions unfavorable to human life," she writes in her *The Roosevelt I Knew* (New York, 1946), p. 17.

sign to keep the New York electorate continuously reminded that TR, Jr., had been Harding's Assistant Secretary of the Navy at the time the naval oil reserves were leased to Sinclair and Doheny. As she later described it, "we had a framework resembling a teapot, which spouted steam, built on top of an automobile; and it led the procession of cars which toured the state, following the Republican candidate . . . wherever he went!" This despite her conviction that her cousin "had had nothing to do" with the Teapot Dome scandal. "In the thick of political fights one always feels that all methods of campaigning are honest and fair," she would say a quarter century later, "but I do think now that this was a rough stunt. . . ." [20] Certainly TR, Jr., thought so at the time. He was infuriated by it. And his fury no doubt encouraged the numerous and grievous campaign blunders which he made.

The upshot was that on November 4 Smith won reelection by 140,000 votes over his opponent. This was a smaller margin of victory than he had enjoyed two years before but a more impressive one in view of the fact that Coolidge carried New York that year by 700,000 votes.

Pleased by Smith's victory, Roosevelt refused to be dismayed by the national defeat, though its nature and proportions destroyed that confidence he had expressed to Eleanor in "a real progressive landslide in 1928." Obviously the struggle between liberals and conservatives within the Democracy—announced by him as completed in May, 1919, but recognized by him as actually incomplete in the aftermath of 1920—was no nearer resolution in a liberal victory than it had been during the 1920 campaign. Which meant that the Democracy was not yet a truly national party: it remained a loose collection of state, regional, and local groupings having no common basis of understanding and working toward no clearly defined ends. In some of his letters and talk, Roosevelt now reiterated the view he had expressed in the autumn of 1920, that a Democratic President could probably not be elected "until the Republicans . . . have led us into a serious period of depression and unemployment"—and to one intimate he named 1932 as the year in which this might happen.[21]

Woodrow Wilson had once said to him that "conservative government is in the saddle two-thirds of the time" because "only once in a generation" could a people "be lifted above material things," and in his correspondence following the '24 election, Roosevelt elaborated on this theme. History did indeed show that conservatives found it "easy to control governments at least two-thirds of the time," he said, but this was not wholly because people "tire quickly of ideals"; it was also because conservatives were "united on the perfectly simple proposition of 'doing nothing' and of 'letting well enough alone' " whereas progressives and liberals "have necessarily a constructive program" on the details of which "they insist on dividing among themselves." He remained personally "convinced that the majority of the voters in this country are really progressive but are generally unable to control the government because of their subdivisions and unwillingness to agree as to method and machinery." [22]

IV

Again, as in the aftermath of the 1920 defeat, with Howe very active at his side, Roosevelt addressed himself to the task of removing "subdivisions" and achieving national party agreement on progressive aims and on the "method and machinery" required for their realization. This time, however, he need pay slight heed to the New York party organization which, under Al Smith's domination, was in excellent working order, if less strong upstate than it ought to be. It was the part of wisdom, as a matter of fact, for him to dissociate himself from Smith for a time, putting a distance recognizable by others between the governor and himself. This would help further develop his own position, now much stronger than it had been four years before, as a rallying point, a vital center of union for all factions save those so invincibly conservative that they properly belonged in the opposition party.

His first step was to send to each member of the 1924 Democratic National Convention a carefully worded circular letter reiterating his assertion that "we are unequivocally the party of progress and liberal thought," asking for opinions on the causes of the national party's election failure, and asking for ideas as to what could be done "to make the Democracy a stronger and more militant organization nationally." [23] The response was tremendous. Democrats of the rank and file, smarting under defeat, welcomed this unprecedented opportunity to air their grievances in a way that might influence national party policy. Nor were important national figures more reticent. New cards were added by the hundred to that index of names and personal data accumulated during the 1920 campaign and since constantly augmented: an immense network of correspondence was cast over the land, drawing goodwill and commitments toward Roosevelt from every section. And there emerged from his avid reading of this mail, carefully analyzed and summarized by Howe, an overview of the national political situation that was invaluable to any Democrat aspiring to national political office.

The losing campaign of 1924 had of course done nothing to reduce intraparty differences over Prohibition and the Klan. Quite the contrary.

These differences were given, in the letters, an expression often outrageous of Roosevelt's own sensibilities. Had he regarded them as basically important, he must have despaired of ever achieving the unity at which he aimed. But he had never regarded them so. Whatever longterm historical significance they had derived from the fact that they coincided roughly with differences in geographic region and that the latter coincided roughly with differences in economic interests joined, in some measure, to differences in ethnic background. The Klan and the Anti-Saloon League were but signs or symptoms of a distortion of fundamental process—a continuing process which, having led through Populism, Bryanism, Progressivism, and the New Freedom, pointed now, under the placid surface of things, toward a resurgence of political idealism and progressive-reformist zeal.

Admittedly the regional cleavage of the party was broad and deep. Many an Eastern Democrat called for a return of the party to the sound business policies of Grover Cleveland. One of them, Senator William Cabell Bruce of Maryland, proposed the drawing down of "an iron curtain between the East and the Bryan West," the difference between the two being, in his opinion, the difference between flatly opposed systems of government. Western and Southern Democrats often expressed an equivalent hostility to the East, blaming the conservatism of Eastern leaders for the debacles of 1920 and '24. Senator Walsh of Montana, writing his Progressive friend George Fort Milton in late December, 1924, was sure that hope for the party's success "lies only in concert of action between the South and West" exclusive of the finance- and industrial-dominated East. Walsh was also sure that the "bogy of Bryanism" was "a product of . . . Republican propaganda," as was the "industriously inculcated" notion "that the La Follette tail was wagging the Democratic dog" in the halls of Congress. Bryan's influence, said he, had reached "the vanishing point. . . . However seductive it may appear," he told Milton, employing much the same language he used in communications with Roosevelt, "I am confident that any attempt to secure a victory through a union of other forces, in either or both sections mentioned, with those of the highly industrial northeast, would result in the future as it has twice in the past, only in disaster." He admitted the possibility that "some dominating figure may arise in our ranks, having his home in that part of the country [the East], but harboring political views approximating those entertained by the remoter sections referred to, on whom all sections might enthusiastically unite." Wilson had been such a figure, "but no man like him can be scanned on the political horizon today, search it as we may," Walsh concluded.[24]

These latter sentiments, if he knew of them, could not have gratified

Franklin Roosevelt, who *was* gratified when several of those who replied to his circular expressed the belief that the Moses who would ultimately lead the wandering Democrats out of the wilderness might very well be himself.

In the first days of February, 1925, accompanied by Missy LeHand and his chauffeur, husky Montfort "Monty" Snyder, he journeyed from New York to Miami. On his way he had a long talk with Walsh, who, also Florida bound, boarded Roosevelt's train in Washington.

The responses he had received, said Roosevelt, indicated not only the crying need for a reconstitution of the party into a coherent and hence effective agent of Progressivism (his definition of the word was always studiously vague), but also a solid basis for such reconstitution, in terms of shared opinions, of general agreements. He proposed the calling of a national conference of Democratic leaders for the purpose of shaping a general party policy that was clearly opposed to Republicanism and a program of political action to implement it. He asked Walsh, as 1924's convention permanent chairman, to help promote such a conference. And the Senator readily agreed to do so—despite his expressed hostility to the "highly industrialized northeast" and his conviction that cooperation with that section's dominant Democrats could lead only to catastrophe. (Roosevelt, in a letter to Iowa's Edwin T. Meredith six weeks later, condemned as "wicked" and "destructive" the "talk of a combination between South and East or between South and West." There was, he insisted, "one common ground—Progressive Democracy—on which we can all agree." [25]) A general plan of procedure was worked out by the time the two men parted, it being understood that Louis Howe, as Roosevelt's personal agent, would perform most of the actual labor which carrying out the plan would require.

On February 4, Roosevelt arrived in Miami (". . . train just 24 hours late due to floods in Georgia and the vagaries of the Florida East Coast RR.") and at once boarded the *Larooco*. The next day, in the afternoon, "the Executive Council of the Am. Fed. of Labor with wives etc., thirty in all, came on board and I had an interesting talk with William Green, the President . . . ," as he wrote into the log that evening.[26] On Saturday, February 7, the *Larooco* "got underway at 12:30 P.M. and proceeded down Biscayne Bay" to start what would be described by him, on its last day, as "a very delightful 2nd cruise." On the fourth day, however, it came near being disastrous. He was returning to the anchored houseboat after a joyous afternoon's fishing for barracuda when a sudden "heavy squall of rain broke on us." In rough water he attempted to swing himself from launch to houseboat deck, missed his hold, fell heavily onto the launch's floor, and writhed there in agony. The ligaments of one knee were badly torn, and weeks passed before the injury was fully healed.

But he did not permit this to interfere with sunbathing and exercises on deck and beach designed to strengthen his other leg, or with his daily handling of a very considerable correspondence, or with the entertainment of a continuous series of guests. It is notable that Livy Davis, whose penchant for nudity had so outraged Missy, the Morrises, and Roosevelt last year, was not one of these guests—but others who had been invited before were invited again. Maunsell Crosby, for instance, soon came aboard and remained for much of the cruise. Henry Morgenthau, Jr., and Tom Lynch were guests for several days. So, with his family, was Henry C. de Rham, a Harvard classmate of Roosevelt's who was now a political as well as personal friend, being active on the Democratic Committee of Putnam County, New York. Julian Goldman, president of Julian Goldman Stores, Inc., the most notable of the clients of Roosevelt & O'Connor with whom Roosevelt personally dealt, was a guest on Sunday, March 8, when Eleanor arrived for her very first visit to the *Larooco*—and it was Goldman, a man prone to florid gestures, who recorded the event in the houseboat log. "Could we commence the Sabbath in any better way than to proceed to the Station to greet the Heavenly Mrs. Roosevelt . . . ," he wrote. "Mrs. Roosevelt upon her arrival [at the boat] . . . vindicated my high opinion of her by seizing the Heavenly deck for her sleeping quarters. Mosquitoes, flies etc. mean nothing to her so long as the Citronella holds out." Actually Eleanor didn't enjoy her visit much. "I tried fishing but had no skill and no luck," she later remembered (Missy LeHand, it may be remarked, loved fishing and frequently accompanied her employer on fishing expeditions). "When we anchored at night and the wind blew, it all seemed eerie and menacing. . . . The beauty of the moon and stars only added to the strangeness of the dark waters and tropic vegetation." [27] Nor did she stay long. She had departed before son James, now seventeen and a fifth former at Groton, came down for a week or so of spring vacation at the end of March. (Elliott was now also at Groton and hated the school virulently.)

Meanwhile, Howe, in New York and Washington, worked hard to implement the national conference idea. He sought and gained the support of Colonel House, Bernard Baruch, and other national figures. In late February, he dined with John W. Davis in the latter's apartment, happily reporting to Roosevelt thereafter that the party's titular head was enthusiastically in favor of this proposal and would tell Clem

Shaver so, Shaver being the man Davis had named as chairman of the Democratic National Committee. The groundwork thus laid, Roosevelt and Walsh exchanged public letters in early March. Roosevelt suggested that the conference be called. He asserted that the party leaders were "insistent that the Democratic party shall not, nationally, in the future confuse with basic principles those matters of momentary or temporary nature which are principally of local interest" but would instead confine itself "to those issues which the whole party, in every section of the nation, agrees to as fundamental." Thus "we shall not only present a united front, but shall cease to confuse the electorate." Walsh expressed in his reply his "entire harmony" with the conference proposal and said his own contacts since election day bore out Roosevelt's summary of the views of party leaders.[28]

Immediate editorial comment by leading Democratic papers was generally favorable. The New York *Times* opined on March 10 that any "rational plan for smoothing out the animosities" which, "with other causes, brought so signal a disaster to the Democratic Party last year deserves welcome and encouragement," and that the "correspondence between Mr. Franklin D. Roosevelt and Senator Walsh of Montana discloses such a plan. . . ." But there was opposition, too, and this achieved formidable proportions as the days passed. Despite the goodwill most of them felt toward Roosevelt personally, McAdoo supporters were naturally suspicious of a party-reforming proposal made by the man who had been Smith's floor manager at Madison Square Garden. Democrats in Congress feared a conference whose decisions might be binding on them or at least inhibiting of their actions, yet from which most of them would be excluded. Equally suspicious were Southerners and Westerners who, though not committed to McAdoo, were hostile to Smith and wanted no meeting whose ultimate aim might be the Happy Warrior's nomination for the Presidency in 1928. Dan Roper wrote Roosevelt pointedly (March 18) that the party had already gained enough publicity through its factional fights, implying that the proposed meeting would be but another such battle.

Nevertheless, when the *Larooco* docked at Miami on Monday morning, March 30, Roosevelt believed with good reason that all objections would be overcome and the conference held, with himself as at least temporary chairman. On the following afternoon he and son James went to Fort Lauderdale, made arrangements at a commercial yacht basin there for "care of Larooco during the summer," then "went down to Cocoanut Grove and spent $1\frac{1}{2}$ hours with Mr. and Mrs. William Jennings Bryan." He found the Great Commoner and wife Mary in sad

shape physically. She had been for years a wheelchair invalid, and
Bryan was unwontedly thin, the skin of his once-full cheeks and throat
now loose about his still-firm jaw, his eyes dull, weary.* But he brightened as Roosevelt talked with him about the proposed meeting. "He
was, at first, fearful that a conference, especially a large one, would result in more trouble than good," wrote Roosevelt a few days later.
"After we had talked for over an hour he agreed that if the conference
were kept small, as I outlined, it would accomplish very great things."
Bryan was, "of course, fearful of . . . domination . . . by the big cities
of the East and Middle West, but, as I pointed out to him, there are millions of really progressive.Democratic voters in these localities who cannot be read out of the Party policies and Party effort must be made national instead of sectional." [29] The next day, Wednesday, April 1, 1925,
Roosevelt "[p]laced 'Larooco' out of commission at 6 P.M. and took
train for Warm Springs, Georgia."

At Warm Springs, within the first ten days after his arrival, he learned
of the defeat of his conference plan.

It was significant in terms of that realignment of the two major parties
which he saw now in process and which he did all he could to encourage
that the men who dealt the death blow to his unity project were not
rural Progressives of the West and South but, instead, wealthy financiers
and industrialists of the party's conservative wing, concentrated in the
East. Clem Shaver flatly opposed the plan when Davis first presented it
to him. His reasons for doing so soon recommended themselves to
Davis. The party's titular head then backed away from it. Adolph Ochs
of the New York *Times* backed away from it, too, after having seemed
initially enthusiastic about it. "Mr. Franklin D. Roosevelt's well-meant
proposal for a harmony meeting of Democrats . . . has gone glimmer-
ing," said a *Times* editorial on April 10, 1925. "A conference of Democrats to discuss party reorganization could only result in greater disor-
ganization so long as the Democratic Party is divided into factions. The

---

* Only three months ahead lay the opening of the notorious Scopes "monkey trial" of Dayton, Tennessee. Asked to aid in the prosecution of a young high school biology teacher for
teaching evolution in defiance of Tennessee law, Bryan would foolishly accept and find himself
pitted in the courtroom against Clarence Darrow, a famous criminal lawyer, political radical,
and religious agnostic. The biology teacher would be found guilty as charged, but by then
Bryan would be convicted of an incredible poverty of general information, an appalling torpid-
ity of mind, at the bar of public opinion, the absurdities of his Fundamentalism fully exposed
when he foolishly permitted himself to be maneuvered onto the witness stand as a prosecution
"expert" on the Bible. Darrow's cross-examination of him would be merciless. All that he held
most sacred would be held up to ridicule; he himself would become the object of a mocking
laughter all across the land; and a few days later, on Sunday, July 26, 1925, he would die while
taking a nap following a noonday chicken dinner.

bitterness and disappointment of 1924 have not had time to cool. . . ."

And by this, the bitterness and disappointment of Louis Howe were heated to boiling wrath. He saw in it and described for Roosevelt a design devious and utterly cynical. Ochs represented the type of Democrat who insisted on a conservative as the party's Presidential candidate every four years, knowing full well that a conservative Democrat was bound to lose. ("Every time . . . [the party] nominates conservative candidates it loses the progressives and fails to get the conservatives," ex-Governor Samuel V. Stewart of Montana had written Roosevelt in reply to the circular.[30]) Ochs and his kind *wanted* the party to lose. Their aim was a Democracy strong enough and absorptive enough of popular discontents to prevent the growth to dangerous proportions of a radical third party, yet a party too weak to take federal executive power away from those who presently held it and exercised it on behalf of big business.

All of which provided final confirmation of the conclusions about party composition and his own personal political activity which Roosevelt had reached in late 1920.

V

It is evident in his every major political move from this point on that Roosevelt now very clearly perceived the central ingredients of a new coalition that could carry him into the White House. This coalition would emerge, it *was* emerging, from the Democracy's intraparty strife, but it would also come out of the palpable disaffection, the increasingly bitter alienation from the Coolidge administration, of those TR Progressives who, their judgments warped by the passions of war, had mistakenly returned to the Republican fold in 1916 and 1918. Its nuclear ingredients could be loosely classified under four headings: Labor (particularly organized labor), Agriculture (particularly the national farmer organizations), Big City Machine, and Solid South. The ground of common denominators on which the coalition would rest was the middle ground between the "radicalism" of a La Follette and the "conservatism" of a Davis—and this ground Roosevelt now cultivated more assiduously than ever before. He favored in late 1924 no open alliance with La Follette; he evidently feared that such an alliance might be in effect a capture of the party by the La Follette movement, as Populism had captured it in 1896, with a resultant defeat at the polls. "The Democratic Party is *the* Progressive party of the country," he wrote a La Follette supporter who had formerly been a Populist, "but it is not and I hope will never be the radical party of the country. . . ." [31] Thus far he agreed with Ochs. His fundamental difference from the *Times* publisher was that he intended a Democracy not merely strong enough to prevent the rise of "radicalism" but strong enough actually to capture the government, returning it to the traditional Americanism of Jefferson-Jackson-Lincoln-TR-Wilson. The party, said he, "must make it clear that it seeks primarily the good of the average citizen through the free rule of the whole electorate, as opposed to the Republican party, which seeks mere moneyed prosperity of the nation, through the control of Government by a self-appointed aristocracy of wealth and social and economic power." [32] This meant a Democracy considerably farther left than Ochs was willing to countenance but by no means as far left as several prominent Democrats now stood and far indeed to the right of Gene Debs or Debs' successor as head of the Socialist Party, Norman Thomas.

The time grew ripe for this coalition. History favored it. But Roosevelt did not count on historical necessity to bring it about automatically. God did not operate in that way—not the God of his father and Endicott Peabody, not the divine Providence which shone upon him with a special radiance, not the Author of that drama of history in which he was chief actor. God assigned tasks; imposed burdens, including that of free will; required choice and struggle as He tried and tested; helped only those who help themselves. And so, to the making of what would become known to history as "his" coalition, Roosevelt applied an endlessly patient, intensely conscious effort, guided by a manipulatory intelligence of high order, though very different in kind from that of the technician or scientist who deals with static things, with rigid concepts, and can put these together in purely logical design. Roosevelt dealt with living stuff, with fluid elements that were not mutually exclusive but, instead, flowed into one another. He must function, in consequence, less as a scientist than as an artist—must not so much think his way logically as feel his way intuitively toward his goal.

The Solid South, for instance, whose electoral vote was necessary to any Democrat's winning of the White House and whose long domination by the Democratic Party, conjoined with Congress' seniority system, ensured a Southerner's potent chairmanship of virtually every major committee in a Democratically controlled House and Senate— this South was very far from being an actually solid object. It was a living process, characterized by quite rapid change, in which a great number of tendencies were operating, tendencies that often grated against one another in harsh contradiction. (Consider, as example, the case of Tom Loyless vs. the Ku Klux Klan.) Roosevelt was acutely sensitive to this fact in the spring of 1925 and would become increasingly sensitive to it and informed about it as he had more and more experience of Georgia and Georgians at Warm Springs. Only in terms of central theme or major emphasis could the Solid South be sharply distinguished from the other major elements of coalition. In these terms it was a unique mixture of political traditions, economic interests, social patterns, cultural attitudes, shaped by the historical experience of slavery, Civil War, and Reconstruction, with an unsolved problem of black-white relations at its heart.

More easily defined conceptually, being elements of relatively single-minded interests, were Labor, Agriculture, and City Machine, but these also were fluctuating processes rather than solid objects. He courted political disaster who assumed a *precise* identity of interest and outlook among the corn-hog farmers of Iowa and Illinois, the winter-wheat farmers of the high plains, the cotton farmers of the Middle and Deep South, the sheep and cattle ranchers of the Mountain States, the corporate truck gardeners and fruit growers of the irrigated Southwest. Similarly with regard to the workers organized in the various craft unions, the miners of the UMW, and the unorganized laborers in steel, automobiles, textiles, chemicals, and other mass-production industries. Similarly, too, with regard to urban Democratic organizations: between Boss Pendergast's Kansas City machine and Boss Curley's Boston one, between Tammany and Boss Frank Hague's Jersey City machine, even between Tammany and Boss Edward J. Flynn's Bronx organization, there were significant differences in composition and in relative emphases among issues. Moreover, one who would shape a workable core group out of Agriculture, Labor, City Machine, and Solid South must never forget that actual farmers and workingmen were a major portion of the population of the South as actual geographic region; that Southern whites, as well as blacks, moved North and carried with them Southern attitudes; that those who moved into large Northern cities, as virtually all of them did, had modifying effects on the political organization of those cities; and that labor unions were highly important elements of the urban Democracy.

In other words, as he dealt with two orders of reality—a realm of conceptual category, a realm of concrete fact—and as he sought to translate the ideas of one realm into the voting blocs of the other, Roosevelt must keep the difference between the two clearly in mind. Only thus could the core group serve as nucleus for the other distinct voting blocs, each smaller than any of the initial four but all together as large as the nuclear four, wherewith he intended to complete his coalition. His politician's problem was one of accurately sensing the phase lines at which significant numbers of, say, the workers or farmers of the South would cease to think and vote in terms of the labor or agricultural interest and begin to vote as elements of Solid South, or, contrariwise, he must determine the lines at which a Southerner's purely regional commitments gave way to his functional economic interest as, say, a textile mill hand or a cotton farmer. And this was a problem in psychology—in individual as well as social psychology. It involved an assessment of human motivation that could only come out of a sympathetic understanding of how people felt about themselves and their circumstances, of what they wanted out of life, and of the ways in which this affected their group behavior, their patterns of voting.

He set out now deliberately to develop such understanding and collect the factual information on which it could feed. He was personally well equipped for this enterprise as few major politicians have ever been. The painful shyness of his earliest years had manifested an uncommon sensitiveness to people: he shied away from direct confrontations with them because he was so acutely *aware* of them, responsive to them, vulnerable to hurts from them. This sensitivity had evolved through the years into an empathic faculty of great range and subtlety, organically joined with his actor's ability to play many roles, assume many disguises, projecting through each of them a considerable force of personality. He used this latter ability not only for psychic defense (he continued, if in a now highly complicated fashion, to shy away from direct, naked confrontations), but also as a tool of his external will or purpose. He delighted in people, partially because they provided both the materials and the audience of his empathic, histrionic art, and he showed his delight in them, which flattered them and of course added to their willingness to talk to him in frankly self-revelatory ways. Hence he could establish rapport with virtually all kinds and conditions of men, and he did so, applying to this effect a rare vital zestfulness.

He summoned a young Jewish tailor from New York's Lower East Side to spend whole days with him on the Massachusetts seacoast in summertime, as Mrs. Hamlin has recorded,[33] during which "Franklin . . . felt he got to the bottom of situations that could and should be remedied—the scandalous housing conditions—labour—schools— churches and family life" in the crowded slums, and during which he felt his way into the psyche of that young Jew to the extent of actual identity with him in several respects. He himself then experienced to a degree the "unbearable tenement living—the lack of decent provisions for sanitary purposes—sometimes one faucet for a whole house," and felt, to a smaller degree, the helpless anger which the young Jew felt toward tenement owners who paid no heed to the human misery which profited them, having "left the care of their property to agents who had no interest but to extract the rent," though these absentee landlords were sometimes extremely wealthy. (The Astors, for instance, Roosevelt's friends and relatives through his half brother's marriage, owned whole blocks of some of the worst tenements in New York City.) And this struggling tailor was but one of hundreds of similar human explorations he made during his persistent, wide-ranging inquiry. From all with whom he came in contact, especially from those having backgrounds and stations in life wholly different from his own, he sought information about their special concerns. He asked friendly, yet pointed personal questions of his valet, his and his mother's chauffeurs, his secretaries, his tenant farmer, Moses Smith, at Hyde Park, and so on. He talked and corresponded about special fields of interest or knowledge with scores of leading authorities, especially those in the related fields of natural resource conservation and electric power development and distribution. Long afterward Eleanor Roosevelt would tell Frank Freidel how she, "whose own social horizons were broadening so rapidly in the 1920's, established a habit which she continued until her death," as Freidel has recorded.[34] "She would give him one or another book to read on some social or economic problem. If he expressed interest in it, she would bring the author around to talk with him. It was from such conversations that he learned the most, and with incredible rapidity." Nor were they only authors whom Eleanor brought to him. She continued to invite to the house, often as luncheon or dinner guests, men and women from widely various walks of life from whom she felt he might learn. And she continued to serve him as an extension of his sensory apparatus, reporting to him in great and concrete detail about the meetings she attended, the conditions she inspected, the people she met, the political situations she dealt with.

In general, this deliberate undertaking of his seems comparable in scope with Walt Whitman's effort to enfold all America within a single consciousness and personally identify with it. Approaching what was to be for him the year of crucial political career decision, Roosevelt, despite the absence of the lyrical from his temperament,* might feel that he could indeed "hear America singing, the varied carols" of merchants, professional people, coal miners, farmers, housewives, salesmen on the road, loggers, stevedores, factory workers, stenographers, the iceman, "each singing what belongs to him or her and to none else," yet all of them together forming a mighty chorus that might be conducted to

---

* But then Old Walt himself was no great shakes as a lyric poet. His, like Roosevelt's, was an essentially practical, prosaic, optimistic temperament. His, like Roosevelt's, was an ego of colossal proportions, curiously streaked with humility.

greater glory by one who understood its nature, as well as the general nature and limits of political leadership in any free society. Abundantly confirmed and augmented was that essential human knowledge of which he had gained his first inklings during and immediately following the Sheehan fight—namely, that no man is all of a piece, perfectly self-consistent; that every man is a various mixture, often self-contradictory; that every catagorical judgment on man in general is therefore certain to be partially false about any individual man; and that the great strength of democracy and of the politics of freedom is that they are shaped in recognition of this fact. They aim at a unity *of* diversity amid which sep-arate individual choices *must* be made; hence they are characterized by a high degree of tentativeness, looseness, openness to change. *E pluribus unum*, says the Great Seal of the United States. And Walt Whitman:

> One's-self I sing, a simple separate person,
> Yet utter the word Democratic, the word En-Masse

Whitmanesque, too, in a sense, was Roosevelt's mental handling of the facts and ideas and empathic experiences which his effort piled up in huge accumulations within his remarkably capacious memory. Whit-man, a collector, counted heavily on the automatic emergence of gen-eral poetic meanings, of general emotional effects, out of the mere listing of evocative names at great length, out of extensive catalogues of things and ideas and specifically labeled feelings. Roosevelt, a collector, counted heavily on the automatic emergence of general political mean-ings, of general concepts and programs of political action, out of an enormous number of specific items of information, loosely classified for ready reference in filing cases of memory.

No more at age forty-four than at age fourteen did he even attempt to shape the raw data he had accumulated into a coherent body of knowl-edge. If he had the natural intellectual capacity for doing so, he had wholly failed to develop it, and certainly he felt no need to do so. It was his tacit belief that basic principles, central themes, general concepts all were in the Divine Mind of the Author of the script which he followed and that, to the extent that he must know these generalities in order properly to play his assigned role, they would be impressed upon him by the information he gathered, impressed upon him as patterns or designs for action. His essential function was simply to recognize salient cues and then act upon these in character. The cues were to be recognized, for the most part, in terms of traditional values from which the current subordination of government to the single business interest was an ab-horrent departure. His acts would be these of a kindly Christian country gentleman of "constructive vision" whose vocation was the political leadership of his country toward the higher, the better. (It would be said of him with considerable truth, by both friends and enemies, that he tended to regard "his" America as a kind of vastly extended and complicated Hyde Park estate.)

In sum, though he heard America singing, though he intended ultimately to be the conductor of the mighty chorus, he did not hear this singing as a formalized melody. He did not write it down in his mind, would have no score to follow. He heard it as a continuously improvised variation upon a few traditional themes, and he would play it by ear.

VI

When Roosevelt arrived at Warm Springs in the late afternoon of April 2, 1925, accompanied by Missy LeHand, he had completely recovered from his fall, was tanned, fit, rested, and bursting with energy. He had need of it. Problems demanding active solutions awaited him, as he had known they would.

The Sunday feature article about his "swimming back to health" had been nationally syndicated following its initial publication in the Atlanta *Journal* and had sparked renewed hope in thousands of crippled polio survivors across the land. Not a few of them had been moved to write Roosevelt at Hyde Park and New York City. A veritable deluge of correspondence had descended upon Tom Loyless, who lacked the secretarial help to deal with it and, in any case, did not know what he ought to say in reply. He lacked the energy to deal with it, too, even if adequate secretarial help had been available to him, for his health, failing in the preceding autumn, had deteriorated sadly during the winter months. "I have neuritis and am in low ground of sorrow," he wrote Roosevelt soon after the latter had returned to New York from his first Warm Springs visit. ". . . I welcome a little sunshine; for, as the drunken fellow said as he rolled out of the street into the gutter, to get out of the way of a runaway team, 'I am in no condition to be runover.'"[35] And his "neuritis . . . or whatever it is" had grown steadily worse thereafter. He was in almost constant pain, and he had lost much weight and the last vestiges of that youthfulness which had characterized him when Roosevelt first met him. It was a weary, anxiety-ridden, aging man, uncertain of mind and bodily movement, with death's pallor on his shrunken cheeks and the dullness of death in his eyes, who shook hands with Roosevelt at the Warm Springs depot.

Roosevelt was shocked.

But he hid his shock, his suspicion that his friend's illness was mortal, as, with gaiety and swift effectiveness, he tackled the problems posed by the load of unanswered correspondence (he and Missy undertook to answer it); by Loyless' inability properly to direct the various crews at work upon the resort's physical rehabilitation (there were "two or three carpenter gangs . . . plumbers . . . roofers . . . painters . . . paper hangers . . . concrete workers . . . electricians . . . pipefitters . . . pump installers . . . roadbuilders," said Loyless[36]); and, most important, by the unexpected actual arrival at the resort of crippled polio victims, some dozen and a half of them in a few weeks.

There were no medical facilities whatever for the care of these patients. There was not even adequate housing for them at the resort, since the Meriwether Inn had not yet opened for the season and most of the few unoccupied cottages were under repair. Temporary housing had to be arranged. Then Roosevelt called for help from Dr. Johnson of Manchester, who "came and looked them [the paralytics] over and guaranteed that they did not have heart trouble or something from which they would suddenly die, and he recommended cream and fattening diets for some and he recommended very little food for . . . others," as Roosevelt would recall in 1934, indicating that he was concerned with the feeding, as well as the housing, of the patients. "And then I undertook to be doctor and physiotherapist all rolled in one. I taught Fred Botts to swim. I taught them all at least to play around in the water. I remember there were two quite large ladies; and when I was trying to teach them an exercise I had really invented, which was the elevating exercise in the medium of water, one of these ladies found great difficulty in getting both feet down to the bottom of the pool. Well, I would take one large knee and leg down until the foot rested firmly on the bottom. And then I would say, 'Have you got it?' and she would say, 'Yes,' and I would say, 'Hold it, hold it.' Then I would reach up and get hold of the other knee very quickly and start to put it down and then number one knee would pop up. This used to go on for an hour at a time; but before I left [in mid-May, 1925], I would get both knees down at the same time." [37] With Dr. Johnson, he began to prepare a chart of all the muscle groups in the body, a chart which, when completed a year or so later, had with it, as Turnley Walker has written, "a scale of markings to indicate functional strength from normal power to zero." [38] It would prove of great value to the devising of special water exercises designed for the strengthening of a specific set of damaged muscles.

Tom Loyless' sole source of income at this time was a thrice-weekly column written for the Macon (Georgia) *Daily Telegraph*. Its composition had become increasingly difficult for him; he wondered if Roosevelt might not "have fun" taking it over for a while, the pay for it going, of course, to Loyless, who so desperately needed it. He broached the subject to Roosevelt, diffidently. It would be an easy chore, he insisted; Roosevelt could dictate the column, saying whatever came to mind— and he must have a lot on his mind that he wished to say about current affairs. Roosevelt admitted that he did—agreed, also, to do the column while his good friend Tom took a much-needed rest.

"In addition to all this," he boasted in a letter to the uncritically admiring Livy Davis in late April, "I am consulting architect and landscape engineer for the Warm Springs Co.—am giving free advice on the moving of buildings, the building of roads, setting out of trees and remodelling the hotel. We, i.e. the Company plus F.D.R., are working out a new water system, new sewage plan, fishing pond, and tomorrow we hold an organization meeting to start the Pine Mountain Club which will run the dance hall, tea rooms, picnic grounds and other forms of indoor and outdoor sports." Revelatory of his attitude toward himself was his further statement: "I sometimes wish I could find some spot on the globe where it was not essential and necessary for me to start something new—a sand bar in the ocean might answer, but I would probably start building a sea wall around it and digging for pirate treasure in the middle." [39]

He wrote eight lengthy columns for the Macon *Telegraph*, all of them published on the editorial page under the heading "Roosevelt Says," the first of them on April 16, the last on May 5, 1925, and though he seems to have thought them good enough for syndication (they were offered for publication in other papers; none was accepted), they were no more than competently written and dealt only superficially with their various subjects. A historian would find them chiefly interesting as demonstrations of the politician's art of *seeming* to say more than was actually said, of seeming to offer with the left hand of mind what was in fact withheld by the right, and of glossing the whole with ingratiating good humor. He inveighed against the Republicanism of the press in upstate New York ("It isn't even intelligent Republicanism. . . . They are organized almost 100 percent to keep harping on and disseminating the carefully prepared propaganda of the Republican organization"), but he offered no suggestions for making journalism more responsible. He deplored the prejudicial statements being published by some of the opponents of any increase in European immigration quotas ("It goes without saying that no sensible American wants this country to be made a dumping ground for foreigners of any nation . . . [but] we lack a sense of humor and proportion if we forget that not so very long ago we were immigrants ourselves"). He called for a rationalization of the tax system

("Here in the United States, we have a hodgepodge of direct and indirect taxes . . .") and for federal civil service reform to increase government efficiency (". . . you could raise the pay of the men and women in the higher, more responsible Civil Service . . . positions 50 percent or even 100 percent, and still have the government cost no more . . . [provided there was established] with the increase in salaries a system of promotion based on merit and capacity only"). He opposed the current administration's isolationism. ". . . every American wants to see this country play the part of a man and lead in the advancement of civilization as a whole, and in the lessening, not only of the horrors of war, but of the chances of war itself," he wrote. But he also said, "No American, of course, wants any entangling alliance. . . ." [40]

Only when he dealt with "the matter of woods and trees and lumber in general" was he wholly unambiguous. "Yesterday afternoon I went up to the top of Pine Mountain," he wrote in his column for April 18. "There, stretching out for many miles to the horizon, was a large portion of Meriwether County. It was good looking country—and good to live in. In many ways it reminded me of the views I get from hilltops in my own Dutchess County, back from the Hudson River. . . . But there in front of me, in the middle distance, two thick columns of smoke were rising in the quiet air. 'Burning off the woods,' somebody said." He was outraged. "I suppose some of my Republican friends would call me a Socialist for asserting that the owner of land owes it to the community, and to the State, and to the nation, to use that land in the best possible way for humanity. It is fine talk . . . to think of the individual as complete master of his own home, at perfect liberty to do any old thing he wants with his own property . . . [but] the farmer who burns off his wood lot [ought to be sent] to the home for incurables!" There were echoes of the Troy, New York, speech of 1912. "Many of the nations of Europe found themselves, about 150 years ago, practically stripped of their forests," he wrote. "They learned that individuals are, as individuals, essentially selfish—that if it was left to the sweet will of the individual land owner he would not bother his head to plant new trees or protect young seedlings where he had cut off his original piece of timber. Over in Europe the timber shortage became so acute that the governments had to step in to create State forests. Like most Democrats, I am pretty thoroughly opposed to having the Federal, or even the State governments, embark on new enterprises which should be handled by individuals, but unless we, in the United States, take immediate steps to compel the growing of new timber by individuals, I prophesy that it will become a government enterprise in the next generation."

* * *

By the time Roosevelt left Warm Springs for New York, he had had several long talks with ailing Tom Loyless about the resort's future and had pretty definitely committed himself to a personal responsibility for it. Certainly he was emotionally committed. Already, as "Doctor" Roosevelt (so his "gang" called him; so he called himself), he had established among the eighteen or so paralytics what was destined to become nationally known as the Warm Springs Spirit. He had spun it out of his own buoyant, infectious optimism. It was a spirit of gaily defiant courage whereby the determination to get well and to work hard at doing so was sustained or increased by much fun and laughter. Serious had been the daily hours of exercise in the pool, exercise as arduous as the individual sufferer could bear, but these hours had been fun-flecked, too, and followed by hours of sunbathing during which there was much socializing, much joking back and forth. There had been impromptu picnics. There had been impromptu parties. And "Doctor" Roosevelt, upon whom focused the desperate hopes aroused by the article he had permitted, if not encouraged, had been the creative center of it all. These fellow sufferers had become warm personal friends. It was inconceivable by his emotional self that he could now abandon them.

Inconceivable, too, was his forsaking of Tom Loyless, whose obviously waning life now had as its sole meaning this Warm Springs development. It had been Loyless' idea last fall that the property might be developed as *both* a pleasure resort and a post-polio treatment center, with the former paying part of the cost of the latter. But he now had good reason to fear that the two kinds of development were incompatible. Moneyed people who wanted to relax and enjoy themselves and would pay for this at the Meriwether Inn were put off, rather than attracted, by the kind of publicity Roosevelt had brought to Warm Springs, and those who did come seeking pleasure, rest, and freedom from anxieties were almost certain to resent the constant presence of sick and crippled people. Loyless, talking to Roosevelt on the eve of the latter's departure, gloomily forecast troubles that would reduce revenues.

And this forecast proved only too accurate when the regular resort season opened. By that time or shortly thereafter some thirty "infantiles" had arrived—far too few to pay operating costs, far too many to be inconspicuous—and the other paying guests, who showed up in fewer numbers than had been hoped for, promptly let Loyless know that a hospital had not been their choice for a holiday spot. They objected to swimming in the same pool, eating in the same dining room with the lame and halt; they objected to the very sight of so many invalids about the grounds; and some of them abruptly canceled their reservations and went away out of fear they themselves might become infected by crippling disease. What could Loyless do about it? Could he ruthlessly expel the injured ones who came here with such desperate hope? Obviously he could not, who now realized that he himself suffered from something far more serious than neuritis—that he was, in fact, dangerously ill. Yet the cost of developing adequate separate facilities for the "infantiles" would be great, and it was clear that George Foster Peabody would not put up the money for it. The philanthropic banker's charitable impulses did not extend to Warm Springs, which, for him, was a purely business speculation. His design had been to sell out his interest at a substantial profit once Loyless had sufficiently developed the resort to attract a buyer, and he strongly disapproved of a management which was having an opposite effect.

Franklin Roosevelt was the only one to whom Loyless could turn, and Loyless had little faith that summer in Roosevelt's doing what must be done to save the Warm Springs Company. ". . . I have made mistakes, errors of judgment, miscalculations, etc. etc.," he wrote to an old friend at this time. "Some of them are my fault outright, some, possibly, the fault of others, though I recognize my own responsibility even for that, and some of it nobody's fault at all. I, it seems, who had to plan it all, and execute it, even to the point of undermining my health, and piling up a doctor's bill and drug bill of several hundred dollars . . . must forage for myself. In the meantime, I have had to give up my Macon *Telegraph* work, on account of my physical condition, and my last life insurance policy, on account of my financial condition, and I have now nothing else I can give up, except possibly my life." [41] His letters to Roosevelt were less despairing in tone. Their factual content, however, fed Roosevelt's growing sense of responsibility for what was happening to Loyless' enterprise, which in turn fed Roosevelt's maturing idea of taking over the resort himself and developing it as an infantile paralysis treatment center.

VII

To his implementation of this idea the chief or only obstacle was a financial one.

Evidence of the severe strain placed on Roosevelt's finances by his medical expenses, the *Larooco* and its cruises, his children's schooling, and the business gambles he lost is the fact that in January, 1925, he sold at auction in New York City's Anderson Galleries many of the historical English and early American marine and naval prints and paintings he had collected. He realized $4,537 from this sale, according to newspaper reports[42]—hardly enough to compensate him, in ordinary circumstances, for the anguish of parting with them. Further evidence of strain is the scrambling effort he made in those months to retain the indispensable services of Louis Howe without paying for them out of his own pocket. A part of Howe's scattered income during this period came from Fidelity and Deposit, on whose payroll he had been placed as assistant to the New York vice-president in March, 1921. Now, in the summer of 1925, Roosevelt associated himself with the National Crime Commission, a private organization set up to study and recommend solutions for the country's increasingly serious crime problem; he obtained Howe's employment as assistant to the commission chairman, a part-time job paying about $300 to $400 a month. Howe took it seriously and would work hard at it, becoming a national authority on crime and seeing to it that Roosevelt got most of the public credit for his work.

But Howe had no intention of working hard—indeed he lacked the time and energy with which to work at all—upon another paying assignment which Roosevelt obtained for him at about this same time. Or *attempted* to obtain for him. Having accepted appointment by Governor Smith as a member of a newly created Taconic State Park Commission, Roosevelt blandly announced to the president of the New York State Council of Parks that Howe would go on the state payroll as his secretary. He was sadly mistaken. The council president, who was head of the state park system out of whose budget Howe's pay must come, was the immensely capable, ambitious, hard-driving, often tactless politician and public works administrator Robert Moses, and Moses, whose standards of public morality were puritanical, rose up in righteous wrath against the suggestion that Howe be paid out of state funds for no work, simply because Roosevelt wished it. He bluntly told Roosevelt so. "If you want to pay personal debts and take care of your secretary, you can't do it in the park system," he said, according to his own account,[43] thereby incurring an enmity which he would have many occasions to regret in the future and which would prove unfortunate for the general welfare insofar as it denied to the nation services Moses was uniquely prepared to render.

Obviously Roosevelt would have made no such mistake had he not felt driven by financial need, a need magnified by the expense of building the cottage and swimming pool at Val Kill that summer, and by the far greater expense that was in the offing if he assumed the obligations at Warm Springs which he now seriously considered.

Moses would ultimately blame Howe far more than Roosevelt for the enmity which denied him great career opportunities. "He [Howe] was vindictive, and he got his revenge," Moses would write decades later. "I have no doubt . . . [he] believed he was protecting F.D.R. against . . . disloyalty, but as in the case of many other fierce, fanatical secretaries, Howe had his own cherished personal animosities and grudges and his own devious ways of passing them on to his chief." And Moses would go on to elaborate upon the crooked, evil impression which Howe made upon him in the summer of 1925 and which was never erased, was in fact deepened with the years—an impression resembling in some respects the historically inaccurate portrait Shakespeare drew of that Duke of Gloucester who became Richard III. He saw Howe as "a strange, ailing, gnomish little man" (Moses was himself physically large and handsome) who derived "immense advantages" over competitors for Roosevelt's favor from the fact that he was wholly free "from personal, political, and social ambition" and wholly indifferent "to public recognition and acclaim." Howe was content to wield "immense power from the sickroom and the shadows," where he could "plot, plan, brood." Howe had no "gay, friendly exuberance," was "like the NVKD men in the U.S.S.R." who "listened in and gathered secret information." He was "a second-story man." [44]

Yet at the very time he initially made this evil impression on Moses, Louis Howe was actively manifesting in his relations with the Roosevelts a very different character—romantically idealistic, sensitive to the sufferings of others, eager to alleviate those sufferings—which he kept hidden behind a harsh mantle of cynicism from all save a handful of intimates. None who knew him only as he showed himself to be in public —none who, knowing him better, was convinced he cared for absolutely nothing save making Roosevelt President—would have predicted any enthusiasm on his part for Roosevelt's personal and financial involvement in the development of Warm Springs. Such involvement was more likely to hinder than help Roosevelt along the road to the White House: it would mean a distraction of mind, a diversion of energy from the central purpose of Roosevelt and Howe. Nevertheless, Howe *was* enthusiastic about the Warm Springs project or indicated he would be if the decision to go ahead with it were made. He was delighted by the tonic effect which planning for the resort was having on his friend's spirits, was infected by it, too: his innate kindness and humanitarian sympathies vibrated to Roosevelt's creative vision. He was even more delighted by the obvious increase in the strength of his friend's legs (Roosevelt estimated he could now place twenty more pounds of weight on each knee than he had been able to do when he first entered the marvelous pool);[45] he began for the first time to believe that his friend just might actually *walk* through the White House door as President of the

United States on, say, March 4, 1937, leaning on no one and with his legs unbraced.

But there was no need to count on Warm Springs alone to accomplish this happy event. Howe had learned of a Dr. William McDonald, a neurologist, who had reportedly achieved amazing cures of polio paralysis through special exercises of his own devising, some of them involving a "walking board" he had invented, and who now devoted himself exclusively to polio treatment. McDonald had bought a cottage on the seacoast at Marion, Massachusetts, where he worked with only four patients at a time, giving to each of these a concentrated attention. Marion was but a few miles up Buzzards Bay from Horseneck Beach, where the Howe family would be going for their August vacation. Why didn't Roosevelt come, too? He could sun and loaf on the sand and bathe in the surf of Horseneck Beach; he could meet McDonald, be examined by him, and decide whether the doctor's treatments were worth their very considerable monetary cost.[46]

And so it was arranged.

Roosevelt was sitting on the porch of Louis Howe's summer cottage on a bright August day when, amid the mail brought him from Westport Point, he found a letter from Tom Loyless' daughter Margaret. It was as he had feared: Tom was mortally ill. An operation performed in Atlanta had discovered cancer so advanced that nothing could be done about it. Tom would be dead within two or three pain-racked months, according to the surgeon. But he had not been told of the cancer, and Margaret asked Roosevelt to say nothing about it in any letter he wrote her father. Roosevelt promptly wrote Tom a cheery note looking forward to his return to Warm Springs next April and the solution at that time, with Tom, of all the resort's problems.

Roosevelt was in Marion, Massachusetts, having become one of Dr. McDonald's four patients (the other three were teen-agers), when he received Tom's reply to his note. Poor Tom, lovable, idealistic Tom, was now indeed in low ground of sorrow. His suffering was greater than before his operation. ". . . I am hanged if I believe that Atlanta surgeon did any more than cut me a little and throw me back in the creek—at a cost to date of about a thousand dollars." He fretted helplessly about the paralytics who remained at Warm Springs (he had returned there from Atlanta but was soon to be taken to his daughter's home in Pennsylvania). "We have nothing to offer them; nothing to give them in the way of proper treatment—just groping blindly in the dark and trusting to luck." Roosevelt wrote back at once in a determinedly optimistic tone: Tom would be going full speed ahead by spring, and Warm Springs had a great future. Roosevelt himself profited greatly from the

McDonald treatments, he wrote. The constant exercise with the "walking board," whose principle was the same as that of his parallel bars at Hyde Park but which had the advantage of greater mobility, was doing a world of good. He had every reason to believe he would soon discard his leg braces forever. Tom, though he must by then have been stripped of illusions concerning his own condition, responded with the warm generosity that was natural to him. "You are bound to get on those legs of yours sooner or later," he wrote, "—because the world, the flesh, and the devil can't beat the sort of fight you are making." [47]

The original plan had been for Roosevelt to remain in Marion a month. Mrs. Bertie Hamlin's brother-in-law Edward lent him a cottage he owned just three doors from the doctor's house (Bertie Hamlin herself had a summer place at nearby Mattapoisett), and into this he moved on August 24 with his chauffeur and valet, beginning on that same day McDonald's strenuous course of treatments. They seemed to him so productive that he prolonged his stay, remaining more than three months. Missy LeHand was there intermittently, and Louis came often, so that he was able to keep up with his various business and political activities, and Eleanor visited in early autumn, upon her return from Campobello. ". . . the muscles continue to improve," he wrote "Dearest Mama" on November 1. "The walking progresses slowly but definitely . . . ," he wrote "Dearest Mama" on November 17.[48] And in early December, just before he left for New York and Hyde Park, where he would spend the Christmas holidays, he actually made his way upright—a brace on his left leg only, a cane propping up his right—from McDonald's cottage to the end of McDonald's wharf, a distance of almost a block. He was almost tearful with joy and exhaustion! (He could not know, of course, that this was the limit of the improvement he would make under McDonald's treatment, that this was in fact as close as he would ever get to walking on unbraced legs.)

He continued, all through this period, to write bright, cheery letters to Tom Loyless, full of happy ideas for the future—letters which literally kept Tom alive, in his daughter Margaret's opinion, well beyond the term which the Atlanta surgeon had set.

Tom still lived when Roosevelt set out again for Florida waters on the last day of January, 1926.

He, Roosevelt, had not intended a third *Larooco* cruise. ". . . on a houseboat it is very difficult to get the kind of exercise I need, i.e., swimming in warm water," he had written John Lawrence from Warm Springs last May. "The sharks made it impossible to play around in deep water for any length of time, and the sand beaches are few and far between. There is now no question that this Warm Springs pool does my legs more good than anything else." Heating facilities were being installed in the Warm Springs cottages, making it possible for him to live there and swim in the naturally heated pool even during the winter months and he would have liked to do so in early 1926 instead of going to Florida. He therefore tactfully proposed a dissolution of the Lawrence-Roosevelt partnership and a disposal of the *Larooco* by lease or sale. To this Lawrence, who had got very little use from the boat himself, promptly, good-naturedly agreed.[49] But when no buyer or lessee could be found, Roosevelt decided he'd better use the boat once more—he could hardly afford not to—and so the *Larooco* again "went into commission" on February 2.

Eleanor came down with her husband this time. She doubtless anticipated no great pleasure, and she had very little, during the week and a half of her stay. The cruise began in a fashion which could not but make her wonder how her husband could even pretend to enjoy this sort of thing. First storm, then engine trouble, then a running error which fetched them up on a sandbar, then more engine trouble, then the discovery that the port shaft had been bent when they ran aground, requiring dry dock repairs—all these delayed their departure from Miami until February 10.

During these days of waiting, Roosevelt had ample time to talk over with Eleanor his glowing ideas for Warm Springs. She threw on them all the cold water she could without damage to his basic morale. This was a much more serious undertaking than the purely business speculations in which he had risked and continued to risk modest amounts of money—modest in proportion to his total capital—and she felt she had not only the right but the duty to protest. Most of his personal fortune, about two-thirds of it, would be required for the purchase of the resort; if this investment turned out as most of his recent ones had done, he might find himself financially unable to put their children through college. He dismissed this argument out of hand. "Ma will always see the children through," he said.[50] He also pointed out what she herself knew to be true, that he was not a plunger inclined to incur needless risks on any scale that could be disastrous. Though mildly tempted at one point, he had refused even to speculate in Florida real estate and would continue to refuse, despite the fact that land offered him at $450 an acre on Boca Chica near Key West last year was now selling for $2,000! He looked upon the Florida land boom, then at its fantastic height, as a spectacle of absurdities, educative in its demonstration of the extremes of chicanery and gullibility to which Americans, in this era of crass materialism, could be carried in their pursuit of the almighty dollar. (The *Larooco* log

796 THE CRUCIAL YEARS: CHALLENGE AND RESPONSE

entry for February 9 told of Eleanor's being "motored . . . out to Coral Gables and other swindles"; the entry for March 21 would speak of "two excursion trains bearing 2,000 people from Miami to view the 'great' Key Largo development," an excursion in which a "free ride, free lunch, free motor trip, free lecture" led up to a "free chance . . . to buy a lot for $2,000 worth $20!") He insisted that the Warm Springs venture could not, in any case, be properly judged by the standards that applied to his speculations in oil, lobsters, shipping, et al. Of course, he hoped to make some money out of it, but profit was not his primary motive. He saw Warm Springs as a rare opportunity for humanitarian constructiveness, and he refused to concede that, given this premise, it could possibly fail.

Two days after the *Larooco* came off the ways at Vogal's Yard in Miami and at once proceeded down Biscayne Bay, Eleanor entrained for New York. She knew by then that her husband had made his decision—he would buy the resort if the price asked for it by the Peabody interests was not impossibly high—and she gracefully yielded to his decisive will. (In a letter revealing of their psychological relationship she would write on May 4: ". . . I know you love creative work, my only feeling is that Georgia is somewhat distant for you to keep in touch with what is really a big undertaking. One cannot, it seems to me, have *vital* interests in widely divided places, but that may be because I'm old and rather overwhelmed by what there is to do in one place and it wearies me to think of even undertaking to make new ties. Don't be discouraged by me; I have great confidence in your extraordinary interest and en-
· thusiasm." [51])

Following Eleanor's departure, things went much better with *Larooco*, and much the same as on earlier cruises. Several of the same people were involved. Maunsell Crosby was again there (it was he who had driven Eleanor to Coral Gables) and Missy LeHand came aboard at Key Largo on the day before Eleanor left. Tom Lynch visited for many days. Special guests this year were Sir Oswald Mosley, a prominent British MP, and his wife, Lady Cynthia, daughter of the famed Lord Curzon, former viceroy of India—"a most delightful couple," as Roosevelt noted in the *Larooco* log on February 19, the day after the Mosleys left the cruise in Florida Bay.* Five days later, William Hart of Columbus, Georgia, owner of the cottage in which Roosevelt had lived during his last stay in Warm Springs, and Charles S. Peabody, representing the Peabody interests, arrived, "and we began talking over the . . . pur-

---

* One assumes there was little political argument aboard the houseboat during the Mosley stay. Sir Oswald's admiration for Mussolini and growing contempt for democracy were already leading him toward his future dark role as head of the British Union of Fascists.

chase of Georgia Warm Springs," as the log entry said. When they left after three days, the price and general terms of sale had been agreed upon. Roosevelt wrote his mother: ". . . it looks as if I had bought Warm Springs. If so I want you to take a great interest in it, for I feel you can help me with many suggestions and the place properly run will not only do a great deal of good but will prove financially successful." To Tom Loyless, lying on a bed of agony far from home, his mind dulled by pain and sedatives, went a Roosevelt telegram: "We will see our dream carried out." [52] They were among the last words Tom Loyless ever read or heard. A few days later he died.

Elliott came on board the *Larooco* in mid-March for his spring vacation from hated Groton. He was "looking rather pale." By far the most difficult of the Roosevelt children, he was doing badly scholastically at Groton ("he struggled at or near the bottom of his Form"), where he was increasingly unpopular with both masters and students because of his ferocious temper and consequent tendency to engage in contact sports as if they were actual battles, their object the maiming of opponents. Roosevelt himself was convinced that the cause of this behavior was an "inferiority complex"; it made Elliott abnormally "sensitive to praise or blame" and required for him "special treatment" to build up his ego, as Roosevelt would write Dr. Peabody in late 1927—a treatment that might include "even . . . an occasional bit of over praise." [53] Roosevelt was especially delighted, therefore, when Elliott landed several of a "record catch of groupers" a few days after joining the 1926 cruise and then, on March 22, hooked and helped land what the log joyously described as "the record fish of all time, . . . a perfectly enormous Jewfish." It was more than seven feet in length, measured five feet around, and weighed close to 500 pounds!

This last cruise of the *Larooco* ended on Saturday, March 27, 1926, at Miami. "Completed all final arrangements and said farewell to the good old boat," said the log's final entry. "Elliott and I left on the evening train for Warm Springs."

The boat was at once again put on the market but was destined never to be sold. In a postscript to her log Roosevelt would later tell how, during the "violent hurricane" which "swept the East Coast of Florida" in September, 1926 (it brought to an abrupt end the great Florida real estate boom), the *Larooco*, moored two miles up the Fort Lauderdale River, was swept inland by the wind on a flood which, receding, deposited her in a pine forest a mile or more from the nearest water. She was "finally sold for junk in 1927." [54]

VIII

At Warm Springs, on April 29, 1926, Franklin Roosevelt signed an agreement to buy the resort—its thermal springs and pools, its ramshackle hotel, its cottages, and some 1,200 acres of land—for something over $200,000. He did so against the strong advice of Basil O'Connor, who thought the price too high (George Foster Peabody had held an option to buy at $100,000) but who, characteristically, at once engaged in the task of organizing the enterprise on the soundest possible business principles and giving as practical a form as possible to Roosevelt's developmental ideas. These ideas were expansive—and expensive. A small treatment pool for paralytics, already begun at Roosevelt's behest, was completed and a table installed in it a foot below the water's surface on which patients could perform special underwater exercises of Roosevelt and Johnson's devising. Two additional pools were built. More cottages were renovated. The driveways around the hotel grounds were repaired. A golf course was laid out. Ramps were installed for wheelchair use at the porch entrances to the Meriwether Inn, for whose management Roosevelt hired a young man who had studied hotel management at Cornell. Simultaneously, he set about obtaining a professional medical staff. He involved Dr. Johnson more and more deeply in the enterprise. He persuaded Dr. Leroy Hubbard of the New York State Board of Health to accept employment as physician in charge of the medical side of Warm Springs. A physical therapist named Helena T. Mahoney, a truly remarkable woman who had become dedicated to the virtually exclusive treatment of polio victims following her horrendous experiences during the 1916 infantile paralysis epidemic in New York City, was persuaded to come down as Hubbard's principal nurse-assistant.

The American Orthopedic Association held its annual convention in Atlanta that year. When Roosevelt learned of this, he wrote the presiding officers requesting permission to appear before the assembled specialists with a report on his experiments with underwater treatment of paralytics and to ask for professional guidance and approval of future treatments. The permission was curtly denied in a letter whose reading made Roosevelt pale with anger—he who was seldom angered. Roosevelt was not an association member, the letter pointed out, nor was he eligible for membership. He had no scientific standing whatever. And this was strictly a meeting of, by, and for professionals. Also, the convention's program was absolutely full; it had been for a long time. Roosevelt then put through a long-distance call to the hotel where the convention met, talked to a doctor there, was again rebuffed very flatly, whereby his "Dutch stubbornness" was thoroughly aroused. He ordered his car and had himself driven to the Atlanta hotel. Then, in his wheelchair, he went up and down the hotel corridors engaging doctors in conversation, turning on all his charm, until he had finally persuaded a decisive group of them to pay serious attention to him. He managed thus to obtain unofficial approval of a continuation of the Warm Springs medical treatments on an experimental basis while an appointed committee of orthopedists conducted an investigation of their effects and of the resort's actual and potential treatment facilities.[55]

The same never-say-die spirit became, through him, central to the now-established "Warm Springs Spirit." He made everything such exciting fun for people who, theretofore, had been shunted off, cooped up in back bedrooms. He was the laughing, zestful leader, devising and playing with the others special water games, directing their exercise, organizing picnics and parties with them. They hated to see him leave for New York as May drew to a close; they looked forward eagerly to his promised return in the fall.

He had that year a more than normally crowded summer and early autumn.

Last year his daughter, Anna ("Sister" he always called her), who loved country life and had thought she might become a farmer, had enrolled in agricultural courses at Cornell. But this year she had met and become engaged to marry a young Wall Street broker, Curtis B. Dall, who was employed by Lehman Brothers. Roosevelt gave her away at a wedding at Hyde Park in early June.

A few days later, in the offices of Roosevelt & O'Connor, an interim corporate setup was completed by Basil O'Connor for Roosevelt's new enterprise—the Georgia Warm Springs Foundation, incorporated under Delaware law—and in early July Roosevelt was named its president, O'Connor its secretary-treasurer, and Louis Howe one of its directors.

Shortly thereafter he went to Marion to take his second series of treatments under Dr. McDonald. This time he rented a large house in the town—large enough to accommodate the whole of his family, though not all the family came (Roosevelt's mother went as usual to Campobello)—and Eleanor was with him through all August. She felt at the time that her husband profited from his month in terms of basic morale. McDonald had, she would later say, "an extraordinary ability to give his patients confidence." [56] But she was not so sure of his physical gains under the doctor's strenuous exercise-treatments, and Roosevelt himself was disappointed by his failure to make any such improvement as he had made under McDonald the year before. By the end of August he had definitely decided not to return here but to spend all the time he could at Warm Springs instead. Meanwhile, he and Eleanor had little quiet time alone together. His treatments and the handling of his correspondence, now somewhat more voluminous than normal, absorbed strenuous hours of every day. There was an almost constant stream of New York politicians in and out of the house as Roosevelt prepared to deliver, at Al Smith's request, the keynote address at the New York State Democratic Convention in September, and to serve as the convention's temporary chairman.

Much pressure was being put upon Roosevelt at this time to accept nomination for the U.S. Senate while Smith ran for reelection to the governorship. Walsh was among those urging Roosevelt to run, and if he did run, he would almost certainly defeat his Republican opponent, Senator James W. Wadsworth. But it seemed equally certain to him and to Howe that such a victory would be less than worthless to him. It would cost him his chance to walk again and probably his chance for the White House; he would be denied the long months of work on his legs which he intended to engage in at Warm Springs and he would be forced to take sides on controversial issues, thereby becoming controversial when, for his ultimate triumph, he needed to be a focus of party and independent voter unity. Moreover, he was, as he had repeatedly said to Eleanor and others, "temperamentally unfitted" to be a U.S. Senator. "I like administrative or executive work, but do not want to have my hands and feet tied and my wings clipped for 6 long years." ("It is because of my three years in the State Senate that I have already twice declined to be the party nominee for United States Senator . . . ," he would say two years later. "I do not think I could endure the atmosphere of that verbose and eminently respectable social club." [57]) All the same, Louis Howe was uneasy about his friend's possible response to a possible convention development. "I have been warned," he wrote Roosevelt, "of a plan to get you up to make a speech and then demand you accept the nomination by a stampeded convention with everybody yelling 'We want Franklin!' . . . I hope your spine is still sufficiently strong to assure them that you are still nigh death's door for the next two years. Please try to look pallid and worn and weary when you address the convention so it will not be too exceedingly difficult to get by with the statement that your health will not permit you to run for anything for two years more." [58]

This speech was important—almost as important "career-wise" as the "Happy Warrior" effort had been. Because of the national stature he had gained at the 1924 convention and added to thereafter and also because Al Smith was a likely 1928 Presidential nominee, what he said would receive national press coverage. It would also be widely broadcast over radio, a fact he kept constantly in mind as he worked on the manuscript. He and Howe now knew that he shone superbly on radio (which he foresaw as a more important means of political communication than the press) while Al Smith, alas, did not. Smith's East Side accent—he could never be cured, for instance, of his pronunciation of "radio" as "raddio"—grated on the ears of most listeners, whereas Roosevelt's rich tenor voice was as music. He gave to the speech's composition, therefore, very serious attention. Ideas, information, even bits of language were recruited from such men as Walter Lippmann and Owen D. Young, and Louis Howe prepared a draft to be woven together with Roosevelt's own.

In the midst of this effort, Roosevelt found time to give Al Smith carefully considered advice concerning Smith's campaign for the 1928 Presidential nomination, this in a letter, dated September 17, that was not only revelatory of his personal relationship with Smith, but also of his sense of political tactics and strategy. "I have hesitated to make suggestions and, particularly, to criticize the strategy of others among your friends," he wrote, "but it is only right for me to tell you my own personal thoughts and even if you don't agree with them, I know you will understand that they come from my heart. . . . I am convinced that some of your friends are, without your knowledge or consent, giving you *aggressive* publicity in the south and west, where such publicity is at the present time harmful. You will have noticed from the papers that these people who are pushing you to the front as individuals, are stirring up opposition and giving the old McAdoo crowd a reason for organizing against you." He indicated the depth of his own deep game as he went on: "In every letter I have written I have taken the stand that no one can tell at this early date who the right man will be and that we should devote ourselves to building up a strong National Organization. More work along this line would have resulted in all the little booms for little candidates picking up courage and gathering a certain amount of local headway in all the McAdoo or similar delegates." In other words, Roosevelt's effort toward national party unity was one that served Smith's ambition. ". . . it is much better to encourage local candidates who would have delegates not unfriendly to you as second choice than to build up any strong anti-Smith feeling at this time." [59]

By the end of August Al Smith and Tammany had settled upon Smith's friend Robert F. Wagner as the Senatorial candidate. A German immigrant who as such was barred by the Constitution from any higher office than that of U.S. Senator, a hardworking, sober-minded man, devoid of any kind of brilliance, yet with an integrity and quiet personal charm that made him widely beloved, Bob Wagner had made an excellent liberal record as a State Supreme Court justice. He had not easily decided to abandon the bench in order to embark again upon the perilous seas of elective politics (he was just halfway through the fourteen-year term to which he had been elected in 1919), but once he had done so, even the Republicans recognized him as eminently qualified for the Senatorial post. His fellow Democrats were generally delighted.

Hence there was no danger of a delegate stampede to Roosevelt when, on September 27, 1926—his legs iron-braced, a crutch under his left arm, a cane in his right hand—he made his gallant way, while thousands cheered, to the convention rostrum. He stood straight, tall, and handsome, the personification of self-confident strength and courage, before the multitude and sang out his words with a perfect sense of timing. What he had to say and his way of saying it were as effective with the invisible audience reached through the microphone as they were with the audience he saw before him.[60] He provoked cheers and laughter with his jibes against Coolidge's failure to deal with the great coal strike of that year ("The people of the East have well learned . . . the hard meaning of the slogan 'Keep Cool With Coolidge' "), his jibes against the administration's subservience to the ultrawealthy ("Calvin Coolidge would like to have God on his side, but he must have Andrew Mellon"). And his eulogy of Smith as governor, his argument for Smith's reelection, was lengthy, eloquent, persuasive, and enthusiastically received.

The chief historic interest of his speech, however, lay in its indication of his developing basic ideas of government.

From his earliest years in politics he had thought of himself as a Jeffersonian as well as Progressive Democrat. There were several obvious similarities between his personal life-style and that of Thomas Jefferson. He loved country living and farming, and his Hyde Park estate was analogous to Monticello. He loved to design and build things— houses (here, too, Hyde Park was analogous to Monticello), boats, structures of all kinds. He disliked huge cities and feared the corrupting effect of their growth on the American democracy. As he came in contact with increasing numbers of them, he liked and trusted common folk of modest personal ambition far more than he did the kind of man who rose to the top in big business. His instinct was for a various, multiform, loosely connected world, full of surprise and accident, as against a uniform, tightly organized one directed by a single centralized authority. Consistent with this, in his own view, had been his opposition to proposed extensions of federal executive power to regulate industry or to engage directly in economic operations that competed with private enterprise. He had been against the original McNary-Haugen bill because it would permit the federal executive to set artificial prices for farm products. Like Jefferson, he had often expressed approval of an idea originally phrased by Tom Paine, an idea that had become central to orthodox Jeffersonian doctrine—namely, "That government is best which governs least."

Yet in his official acts in Washington during the war and in his later campaign for greater efficiency in government, he had worked toward a centralization of powerful authority in the federal executive, had sometimes expressed an impatience bordering on contempt for the fumbling and bumbling of the democratic legislative process. He had pressed for the act creating the Bureau of the Budget as a strong arm of the executive, greatly expanding the powers of the office of the President. During his 1920 Vice Presidential campaign he had insisted that "most of our great deeds have been brought about by Executive leaders, by the Presidents who were not tools of Congress. . . ." As president of the American Construction Council and in many of his other public activities, he had stressed the virtues of long-range national planning while deploring the chaotic consequences of unrestrained factionalism. Especially had he done so with regard to natural resource conservation and hydroelectric power development—a field wherein he had a strong bias toward direct, large-scale federal action.

In general, since 1920, he had evinced a greater and greater awareness of what such divergent liberal intellectuals as Croly and Brandeis, Lippmann and Beard, had long explicitly recognized—namely, that Tom Paine's expressed view of the proper powers of government, a view grounded in an eighteenth-century radical's passionate concern for individual liberty, was now integral to the basic credo of conservatives and reactionaries who had no concern whatever for the personal freedoms of anyone save themselves—who, indeed, were hostile to the liberties of the great masses of people insofar as the social expression of these was threatening to their own selfish privileges. In the mid-nineteenth century, Herbert Spencer had joined Paine's salient idea with Charles Darwin's in an unholy wedlock that distorted and falsified both partners. ("The struggle for existence" and "survival of the fittest" were Spencerian phrases.*) Measured in terms of impact upon politico-economic

* In point of fact, Darwinism was very much in the intellectual air of the nineteenth century long before Darwin's name became attached to it, in 1859, with the publication of *The Origin of Species.* Spencer himself presented the evolutionary idea in an essay, *The Development Hypothesis,* published in 1852, and it was in this essay that the famed phrases about "struggle" and "survival" first appeared.

history, the principal issue of this unfortunate marriage was Spencer's *Social Statics* and *Principles of Sociology*. These books had become a bible for conservatives, providing them with effective arguments against any power of government to regulate or control private business or indeed to engage in any activity at all beyond that required for the national defense and the maintenance of internal order. They also inadvertently provided a philosophical justification of the pillage and chicanery and corruption—the stealing, the lying, the ruthless exploitation of human and natural resources, even the killing of human beings—characteristic of the process whereby every single one of the greatest American fortunes (Astor's, Vanderbilt's, Morgan's, Rockefeller's, Mellon's, Harriman's, *et al.*) had been accumulated. Against the palpable consequences of this approach to government in the modern age—hence against the approach itself—Roosevelt had a strong visceral reaction.

"Here is a practical dilemma," he had written in a letter, April 16, 1925: "People of all parties believe we should have less governing from Washington with a decrease in the existing functions of the national government, and a decrease in the amount of legislation ground out by Congress each year. On the other hand, the complexities of modern civilization and the breaking down of state boundaries by public utilities, interstate commerce and through country-wide large corporations, seem in many cases to demand government to prevent abuses or extortion." [61]

A few months later his thinking along these lines had been greatly stimulated and clarified by his reading and reviewing of Bowers' *Jefferson and Hamilton*. He at once saw that the truly basic difference between Hamilton and Jefferson was not the former's espousal of a strong federal government and the latter's of states' rights. This merely manifested in the practical context of the late eighteenth and early nineteenth centuries the truly basic difference, which was Hamilton's desire for government by an aristocracy of wealth as against Jefferson's for government of, by, and for the people as a whole.

And so, in his keynote address to the New York Democrats in 1926, Roosevelt made a significant revision of earlier expressed views.

"If we accept the phrase that 'the best government is the least government,' " he now said, "we must understand that it applies to the simplification of governmental machinery, and to the prevention of improper interference with the legitimate private acts of citizens, but a nation or a State which is unwilling by governmental action to tackle new problems, *caused by the immense increase of population and the astounding strides of modern science,** is headed for decline and ultimate death." [62]

* Present author's italics.

Obviously—through his feeling self rather more than through his thinking self, out of a basic kindness and human decency rather than out of any abstract intellectualization, and in partial consequence of his experience of Wilsonianism in the light of the exemplary TR's words and deeds—Roosevelt had by this time gone far toward the conclusion that the Jeffersonian ends to which he subscribed could be achieved or maintained in the twentieth century only by Hamiltonian means. (Herbert Croly defined a "welfare state" as one employing Hamiltonian means toward Jeffersonian ends.) The great threat to the individual liberty of Americans in the 1920's was not the powerfully active central government feared by Tom Paine and Jefferson but the irresponsible, self-serving activities of giant corporations to which a weak, pliant government was currently subservient. The great hope for the maintenance or increase of personal freedom and welfare was the creation of a truly representative government powerful enough to keep any special interest in the economy from distorting the "whole picture."

Thus, Roosevelt would be prepared to understand the negative reactions of liberal intellectuals to the call Al Smith would make, in 1928, for the "unflinching application of Jeffersonian principles to the problems of the day"—could understand this despite the fact that he himself had repeatedly called for a "return" to "Jeffersonian principles" in the past. He could even share this negative reaction insofar as Smith assumed the "principles" to be those of laissez-faire. He might then read with a considerable measure of approval (though there is no evidence that he ever did actually read) the comment upon Al Smith's call made in the *New Republic* that year by a Columbia University professor of economics named Rexford G. Tugwell. "Cannot Governor Smith understand," Tugwell would write, "that . . . the stronghold of Jeffersonianism has shifted from the South to the Northeast and that its latterday prophet is Calvin Coolidge?" [63]

IX

Within a few days after the New York State Democratic Convention had ended, Roosevelt, accompanied by his mother and Missy, was back in Warm Springs, where he was most heartily welcomed by the patients. ("Have you been good boys and girls while Papa was away?" he called out to them, and at once plunged into the marvelous pool, the regimen prescribed by Dr. Hubbard and Mahoney, and the round of activities which brightened the lives of the patients.) He hoped to interest his mother in investing in the resort and to persuade her to build a cottage of her own there, as one of the "cottage colony" to be established during the next two years. Construction of his own cottage was about to begin. But when she returned to New York two weeks later, she had committed herself to no part of her son's enterprise but, instead, had done her best to curb his enthusiasm for it. She feared it would be ruinous to him financially. Something of her attitude and his response to it is revealed in the letter he wrote her a few days after she had left. "I miss you a lot and I don't have to tell you how I loved having you here," he said, "and I know you were really interested in seeing what I think is a very practical good to which this place can be put and you needn't worry about my losing a fortune in it, for every step is being planned either to pay for itself or to make a profit on." [64] His mother remained unconvinced. In the event, she would finally underwrite the cost of a year-around house on the resort hillside but would seldom, if ever, occupy it, would rent it out instead on an annual basis. She would once or twice engage in activities —benefit teas and the like—that helped raise money for Warm Springs, and she made some tax-deductible contributions of her own, but she would never invest any of her own money there.

Roosevelt remained in Warm Springs until after 1926's election day, casting an absentee ballot for Al Smith. During October he composed for public speech "A Parable on War Debts" that was in some ways even more significant of his basic attitudes toward government and of the role of the executive than was his state convention address. The parable told of "a little country bank surrounded by prosperous farms"—a bank whose president was "a man of sympathetic understanding . . . [who] had grown to be regarded as a sort of father confessor and disinterested and wise counselor for all the neighborhood." He was an old man when "there suddenly descended [upon the community] a terrible series of calamities—cyclones and sickness, death and famine." The desperate farmers turned to the bank. He responded. "Freely, almost to the point of straining the Bank's credit, loans were advanced or extended, and *what was far more important** words of cheer and hope and encouragement were given to every frightened Farmer who came to the Bank in his hour of need." But then, just as "the tide of misfortune turned" and "the Farmers set about to build their farms and their fortunes anew" with the encouragement of the Banker, "an inscrutable Providence" called this banker "to his reward." To replace him, "the Directors selected a man of far different type. A typical small town lawyer, of unquestioned honesty but without vision, and constructive capacity, that lacked sympathy and deep understanding of human nature

* Italicized by the present author.

which had made his predecessor so successful. A narrow, practical, un-
imaginative sort of man, who believed that a penny saved was a dollar
earned and who had no clear understanding that there were any moral
precepts other than personal honesty, regard of the ten commandments
—and thrift." The new bank president refused to extend loans when
these fell due at a time when the farmers could not pay. "He met [a delegation of farmers] with no words of hope, no assurance of support or
compassion, nothing but a demand to know what was the utmost that
could be realized on their possessions and announced to them that he
would send someone to investigate and make sure that by no possible
chance could one cent more of immediate cash be applied on their
notes." This sudden reversal of bank policy "bewildered, angered,
dumbfounded" the farmers, who protested bitterly. The banker was un-
moved. He "swung round to the papers on his desk with no reply but
this snarling question, 'Well, you hired the money, didn't you?' " And
Roosevelt reminded his listeners that these last words were almost a direct quotation of Calvin Coolidge's recent comment upon war debt collection. "Shall we place alongside the old words 'With malice toward
none, with charity to all' the newer saying, 'Well, you hired the money,
didn't you?' " [65]

Through the newspapers and letters written him from the North,
Roosevelt closely followed the New York election campaign. It was an
unedifying spectacle. Smith's Republican opponent was the exceedingly
wealthy, exceedingly conservative Ogden L. Mills, whose great Hudson
River estate was only a few miles north of Hyde Park, who was currently a Congressman and an intimate of Coolidge, and who accepted
as his main campaign issue Hearst's old discredited charge that Smith as
governor was responsible for "poisoned" and "watered" milk being sold
in New York City. For Mills, it was a hugely counterproductive issue.
Smith had no trouble disproving the charge, and among those it outraged with its nastiness was a top General Motors executive named
John J. Raskob, a co-religionist of Smith's. Raskob asked to meet the
governor and was so taken with him that he switched his party allegiance from Republican to Democrat, contributed $25,000 to the Smith
campaign, and became by election day one of the governor's closest,
most trusted friends. Wagner ran a disappointing campaign. He had as
speechwriter, Roosevelt was interested to learn, Claude G. Bowers, who
had recently come to New York City from Indiana to edit the *Evening
World,* but Wagner, evidently a much less effective public speaker than
Roosevelt remembered him to have been before he became a judge, delivered these speeches poorly.[66] He would undoubtedly have lost to
Wadsworth if the latter's forthright opposition to Prohibition had not

provoked the Anti-Saloon League and WCTU into organizing an Independent Republican Party of New York which, with the undercover encouragement of Tammany, put up a Senatorial candidate of its own. This candidate drew away from Wadsworth enough upstate Republican votes to assure Wagner's victory by a margin of 116,000 votes. Al Smith won election to his fourth gubernatorial term with a plurality of 257,000.

Roosevelt left Warm Springs for New York on November 8. He was living in his Sixty-fifth Street house, going downtown almost every day to his law office or his office at Fidelity and Deposit, when he learned, in January, 1927, that the investigating committee of the American Orthopedic Association had been favorably impressed by the work Dr. Hubbard was doing at Warm Springs: every one of the twenty-three patients who had received treatments for periods ranging from five to seventeen weeks had showed definite improvement! The association now recommended "the establishment of a permanent hydrotherapeutic center at Warm Springs."

At once the interim corporate setup which O'Connor had devised and which had been legally established six months before was replaced by a new, drastically revised one. The Georgia Warm Springs Foundation, Inc., became a nonprofit nonstock enterprise which operated a fully accredited Hydrotherapeutic Center and was legally qualified to receive tax-deductible charitable contributions. On its board of directors were Basil O'Connor, Louis Howe, Dr. Leroy Hubbard, and Roosevelt, plus names appealing to the affluent: George Foster Peabody (he was put on against O'Connor's protest; the "philanthropist," said O'Connor, would never contribute a dime to the project); bankers Russell Leffingwell and Harvey Gibson; Henry Morgenthau, Jr.; Herbert Straus; William H. Woodin. The purely business side of the project, established to operate the public pool and golf course and hotel with adjacent cottages, from which Roosevelt hoped to realize a profit, was run through a subsidiary called the Meriwether Reserve.[67]

Legally entirely separate from all this, but joined organically with it in Roosevelt's personal life in Georgia, was a 1,750-acre farm he purchased atop Pine Mountain—this despite or because of the dangerously large financial commitment already made. Perhaps he felt he was reducing rather than increasing the risk he ran. The purchase included acreage formerly owned by a farmer with whom he had made friends—a man named Ed O'Doyle, whose effort to make a good living for his family by raising cotton and corn had been a losing one but who was a good farmer, a good man, intelligent and hardworking. Roosevelt had often discussed the farm problem with him, and Roosevelt now employed him as farm manager at a wage that substantially improved his standard of living. "No cotton, though," ordered Roosevelt. Georgia's agricultural economy was far too dependent on that one crop, cotton. Why not try raising beef instead? Texas and Florida were raising beef with success. And so the Pine Mountain farm became primarily a cattle farm from which Roosevelt was destined to make little money but from which he gained much in education and recreative interest.[68] He laid out a road across his land to a lovely lookout point called Cowdell's Knob, which was thereby made easily accessible by car to the Warm Springs patients and would become, through the years, the scene of many a famous picnic.

This road and his hillside cottage had just been completed when Roosevelt, joyously energetic, full of plans for the foundation, arrived at Warm Springs in early February, 1927, having stopped off in Washington for the annual meeting of the "Cuff Links Club" on his forty-fifth birthday. "The new cottage is *too* sweet, really very good in every way, the woodwork covering all walls and ceilings a great success, and the new furniture fits perfectly and is just the right color," he gushed in a letter to "Dearest Mama" a day or so after his arrival. ". . . This morning I have driven with Mr. [Egbert T.] Curtis [the hotel manager he had hired months before] and Miss Mahoney over the 'Pine Mountain Scenic Highway'—five miles long . . . , marvelous views all the way and cost me only $1050. I've been in the pool each day and done all the exercises and stretching and am feeling finely. The weather is warm and bright, the peach blossoms coming out. . . ." He still clung to the original idea he had shared with Loyless, of developing the place as *both* a recreational resort and treatment center, with special facilities for patients and other facilities for the relatives of patients and for vacationers. "It ought to be a success as the doctors are most enthusiastic . . . ," he wrote Eleanor's Auntie Bye in late June, 1927. "Aside from the therapeutic value, we have so many natural resources for families or patients that the swimming, golf, riding and quail shooting ought to appeal to those in perfect health. The whole property I have under the . . . Foundation and am now busily engaged in trying to raise two or three hundred thousand dollars to carry out the improvements and pay the mortgage on the property. . . ."[69]

As part of the fund-raising effort, he ordered written and published a pamphlet containing a brief history of Warm Springs and a description of its present and proposed future development. Of the several thousand words of history, only a little over a hundred were devoted to Roosevelt's first coming to this place and subsequent involvement in it—a story told in bare-factual prose. This was sufficient, however, to arouse protest from his mother. She identified strongly with Dr. McDonald; he was "socially acceptable" by such as she, a doctor whose treatments only the affluent could afford. She regretted her son's attachment to Warm Springs; it further weakened her maternal hold upon him. Hence her letter to him, in the fall of 1927, saying "Dr. McDonald was much hurt that all accounts and circulars speak of Warm Springs as being the only place that had helped you" whereas "I consider that the first *real* improvement you made was with Dr. McDonald." Roosevelt made hot reply: "*No* circular about Warm Springs, no statement or authorized account has spoken of Warm Springs as being the only place which has helped me. . . . If Dr. McDonald is hurt I am sorry, but he has no cause to be. . . . Why Dr. McDonald's name should appear in literature about Warm Springs I really can't see—the literature is not about me. Furthermore Dr. M. has been constantly begged by me to come down here and look things over. Finally, as Dr. M. is not an orthopedist none of the orthopedists who are in touch with the work here would care to have him associated." [70]

In the months that followed, the original idea of combining a medical with a recreational resort was, perforce, abandoned. "You would love the informality and truly languid southern atmosphere of the place!" he had written Auntie Bye. "My one fear is that the gentle charm will appeal to some of our rich friends who are suffering from nervous prosperity and that they will come down here and ruin our atmosphere." His fear proved wholly unfounded. Roosevelt's rich friends wished him well. Some of them made charitable contribution to the foundation. In March, 1928, Edsel Ford of the Ford Motor Company sent Roosevelt a check for $25,000, used to build a glass enclosure for the largest of the treatment pools, so that patients could swim there every day of the year. But few, if any, of the rich could be persuaded to invest in Warm Springs as a business proposition or to spend their vacations there. From the outset, the Hydrotherapeutic Center was the only truly viable part of the project; it soon became virtually the whole of it; and the foundation's directors finally resorted to professional fund-raising personnel and techniques—the kind used by such organizations as the Red Cross—in order to place the enterprise on a sound financial footing.* It then became within a few short years the most famous and probably the most effective infantile paralysis treatment center in the world.

*   *   *

* Roosevelt's original investment in Warm Springs became a loan to the foundation when this was established as a charitable, nonprofit enterprise. On February 28, 1928, he received from the foundation a demand note for $201,677.83—an amount paid back in full, with interest, in installments of irregular date and various amount, during the next seventeen years. The last two payments were made to Roosevelt's estate after his death. See Eleanor Roosevelt's *This I Remember* (New York, 1949), pp. 44, 367, 368.

For Roosevelt personally, Warm Springs continued to be his one great hope of walking again—really walking, with new muscles grown in place of the atrophied ones. By 1928 he was able to discard his crutches and in public, when necessary, with the aid of a cane and the occasional arm of a companion skilled in such matters, swing himself along on iron-braced legs in a plausible imitation of true walking. He continued to say, and perhaps believe, that he'd be able to throw his braces away, too, in another few months, or next year, or two years hence.

Warm Springs also became his second home, as beloved as Hyde Park. In some respects, indeed, it was a happier place for him than Hyde Park, to which his vital ties were somewhat loosened when, on May 7, 1927, his half brother, James Roosevelt "Rosy" Roosevelt, bedridden with bronchitis following his return in late April from Bermuda, died in the house next door to Springwood at the age of seventy-three. ("It is very hard to realize when I am at Hyde Park that he is no longer there and in so many more ways than I had realized, I depended on his companionship and on his judgment," wrote Franklin Roosevelt to Auntie Bye seven weeks after Rosy's death.)[71] He was the master of his house and land in Georgia as he could never be of the house and land at Crum Elbow while his imperious mother lived.

Twenty-five

❧❧❧❧❧

Fateful Cue—Fated Response

I

APT IT was, therefore, that the most crucial single career decision in the whole of his life should be made at Warm Springs.

On a pleasantly cool midnight in the early autumn of 1928 he sat by an open window of the Meriwether Inn, telephone in hand. The receiver at his ear was a black cone of silence—of tense, waiting silence—and the whole world seemed to wait outside his window, softly breathing in the dark, as a gentle wind sighed through the pines. The silence lengthened. The dark grew darker still.

At last, hesitantly, he spoke fateful words into the phone.

II

In August, 1927, at about the time the Federal Reserve System encouraged the further flow of speculative money into the stock market by unexpectedly and abruptly lowering the rediscount rate from 4 percent to 3½, President Calvin Coolidge, on vacation in the Black Hills of South Dakota, unexpectedly and abruptly handed to each of the newspaper reporters assigned to cover him a typewritten slip of paper bearing a single cryptic ten-word sentence: "I do not choose to run for President in 1928." Characteristically, he refused, then or later, to amplify or explain his statement. He loved to mystify, loved to make himself the object of speculation; no doubt he enjoyed to the fullest extent of his meager capacity for joy the vast popular puzzlement that ensued over the precise meaning of "choose" in his declaration. Equally, if less obviously, characteristic of him was the hurt resentment he inadvertently revealed to his closest associates when, in following months, the businessmen in control of his party chose to interpret his statement as a flat *refusal* to run and indicated not the slightest desire to draft him. The net effect of his withdrawal was to clear the way for Herbert Hoover, whose campaign engines went at once into high gear. (Coolidge had no liking for his Secretary of Commerce. "That man has offered me unsolicited advice for six years, all of it bad!" he reportedly said to Secretary of Agriculture William M. Jardine when, in May, 1928, Jardine urged the President to support actively a farm bill Hoover favored.)[1] As the summer of election year approached, it was as certain as anything can be in politics that Hoover would become the Republican Presidential nominee when the party's national convention assembled in Kansas City in mid-June.

Less than certain but overwhelmingly probable, in that spring of 1928, was the Presidential nomination of Alfred E. Smith by the Democrats when they assembled for their national convention in Houston, Texas, during the last week of June. The cumulative blighting effects upon McAdoo's candidacy of the Doheny disclosures and the failure to rise of any equivalent rival of Smith's; the waning power of the Ku Klux Klan and the waxing popular revulsion against it; the growing disillusionment with Prohibition even in rural areas, coupled with the open repudiation of it in urban centers; the thumping election triumphs scored by Smith in 1924 and '26 and the excellent record made by him in his third and fourth gubernatorial terms; the grim determination of leading Democrats to avoid, at whatever cost in terms of personal or ideological commitment, any repetition of 1924's disastrous convention deadlock— all these factors worked strongly in Smith's favor. Also operating toward his nomination was the generally recognized unlikelihood that "any Democrat can win in 1928," as Roosevelt had written Josephus Daniels in late June, 1927. "It will depend somewhat on whether the present undoubted general prosperity of the country continues," Roosevelt had gone on to say. "You and I may recognize the serious hardships which the farmers in the south and west are laboring under, but the farmers in the south will vote the Democratic ticket anyway and I do not believe the farmers of the west will vote the Democratic ticket in sufficient numbers even if they are starving." [2] They were in fact slightly farther from starvation in June, 1928, than they had been the year before—there had been some improvement in the agricultural economy—and the country in general seemed more prosperous, and more convinced that prosperity would increase interminably, than it had ever been. An effect of this was to reduce the reluctance of Southern and Western Democrats to nominate Smith. He and what he represented was distasteful to them. But since there was so little chance of his winning election and since his nomination would serve that cause of party unity which was so persistently championed by Roosevelt, whom they generally liked and admired, they were increasingly willing to go along.

As for Roosevelt, he did all he could to encourage these feelings among dry, rural, Protestant Democrats. (His letter to Daniels, quoted above, evoked a response from Daniels in which the latter averred that never before had he "felt so perfectly at sea as to what we ought to do and what we can do." Daniels was convinced that the "liquor question," which Roosevelt wished to play down, was "much more acute" than it appeared "on the surface" to be. In addition, "the religious question, which ought not to exist but which does on both sides; and the hero-worship of Smith . . . ; and the lack of any other leader of commanding support, all combine to muddy the waters so that it will take a keener eye tha[n] I possess to see to clear water." [3]) By the spring of 1927, Roosevelt had again openly committed himself to Smith for President and was doing more than he had done three years before to promote the governor's candidacy and to reduce the liabilities imposed on it by Smith's parochialism, Smith's wetness, Smith's Tammany background, Smith's religion.

In early March of that year, Ellery Sedgwick, editor of the *Atlantic Monthly*, sent him galley proofs of "An Open Letter to the Honorable Alfred E. Smith," to be published in the magazine's April issue. Its author was a prominent New York City attorney and Episcopal layman who argued on highly legalistic grounds that a "loyal and conscientious Roman Catholic" must as a Catholic subscribe to "certain conceptions" that were wholly "irreconcilable" with the Constitution of the United States. Roosevelt found the argument "ridiculous"; its publication, he wrote Sedgwick, would serve no useful purpose, would serve only the waning cause of Ku Klux Klan bigotry. But obviously "the fool article" was going to be published no matter what he or anyone else said, and so, simultaneously, he wrote to Smith urging the governor "to answer it yourself" instead of letting it go or letting someone else (himself, for instance, as an Episcopalian of good standing) answer it for him. The governor could reply, said Roosevelt, "in such a way that people all over the United States will respect you even more than they do now." [4] Since the same advice was given by Proskauer and Belle Moskowitz, Smith, overcoming a strong initial reluctance, acted upon it.* His reply was

* He asked Judge Proskauer to draft the letter, in collaboration with the nationally famous Father Francis P. Duffy, chaplain of the "Fighting 69th" New York National Guard division during the war. This draft, carefully revised by Smith, was approved by Patrick Cardinal Hayes. Proskauer found it significantly amusing that he, a Jew, should be asked to reply to a Christian Protestant's attack, on religious grounds, upon the Presidential candidacy of a Roman Catholic. He said so to the governor.[5]

published in the May, 1927, *Atlantic*. It was a ringing affirmation of his devotion to the Constitution ("I believe in the absolute separation of Church and State"), a ringing denial that there was any inconsistency between such devotion and his Roman Catholicism, a ringing plea for religious tolerance (". . . I join with my fellow Americans in a fervent prayer that never again will any public servant be challenged because of his faith . . ."). Roosevelt applauded.

As for his personal relationship with Smith, there were subtle changes. As Smith's career need for his support increased while his own need for Smith's support decreased, Roosevelt became proportionately less deferent to the older man in act and attitude than he had been in 1924. Once, indeed, the two came close to actual quarrel.

In late December, 1927, Roosevelt protested to Robert Moses the meagerness of appropriations proposed for the Taconic State Park Commission in the coming fiscal year. At the time of his acceptance of the commission's chairmanship he and Howe had concluded that the commission's major task would be to plan and supervise the construction of a parkway extending northward from Westchester through Putnam and Dutchess counties to Columbia County. Subsequently he had led his fellow commission members to conclude with him that this project should be undertaken, not in some indefinite future, but at once. The proposed appropriations were, however, wholly insufficient to begin the purchase of right-of-way through Dutchess County, he complained in a letter to Moses. The latter did not reply for a month. He then said that available funds were limited and that first priority in their assignment must go to the development of parks and parkways "closest to population centers," where the need for them was greatest and the cost of land-taking rapidly rose to prohibitive heights.* This was logically persuasive. But the tactless Moses didn't stop there. He went on needlessly to say that, in any case, he "personally" had "never thought" of extending a parkway farther north than "some park area on one of the lakes in Putnam County." He knew, he said, "that the legislative leaders would not approve" any further extension.[6] Roosevelt, who still smarted from the rebuke Moses had administered him two years before and whose resentment was fed by Howe's, felt this as a slap in the face. He was infuriated. In a telegram, letters, even a personal interview in the Biltmore in New York City, he let Smith know how he felt. ("I wasn't born yesterday," he said; Moses was playing a "skin game.") The governor at last made sharp written response. "I know of no man I have met in my whole public career that I have any stronger affection for than

---

* In progress at that time was the Long Island park and parkway system.

yourself," he said. "Therefore you can find as much fault with me as you like. I will not get into a fight with you for anything or anybody. But that does not stop me from giving you a little tip and the tip is don't be so sure about things that you have not the personal handling of yourself. I have lived, ate [sic], and slept with this park question for three and one-half years. I know all about it. . . . When I told you . . . that the legislative leaders would not stand for these appropriations, I was telling you what I knew to be a fact and you were guessing at it. . . ." [7]

But this dispute was not quite a quarrel. It ended with Roosevelt's tacit acknowledgment that the governor did indeed know whereof he spoke and with the governor's saying that, "satisfied with all the park plans," including the Taconic Commission's, he expected "to see them all carried out" eventually.

And even while the dispute was going on, Roosevelt was showering advice about the forthcoming Presidential campaign upon National Democratic Chairman Shaver, National Finance Director Jesse Jones of Houston, Texas, and other National Committee members. He concentrated upon overcoming Smith's glaring deficiencies in the realm of foreign policy, sending the candidate letters of advice, memoranda by himself and others, foreign economic data, and the like. Among those he called upon for help in this enterprise were Colonel House and a longtime friend of his, a fellow Grotonian ten years his junior, named Sumner Welles.[8] The coldly, aristocratically handsome Welles, a career member of the State Department's Foreign Service, was highly critical of the current administration's Latin American policies, was also a strong advocate of U.S. adherence to the World Court,* and Roosevelt sent letters from him to the governor and also arranged to have Welles discuss the court question in personal interview with Judge Proskauer.

Roosevelt himself undertook to prepare what he intended to be, in effect, the foreign affairs plank of the 1928 Democratic Party platform when he accepted an invitation from Hamilton Fish Armstrong, editor of *Foreign Affairs*, to submit an article on Democratic foreign policy to that authoritative journal. He solicited information and ideas from others and devoted to the actual writing a most careful attention. The fruit of this labor, however, was as disappointing to League advocate John W. Davis as it was to liberal intellectuals and to editor Armstrong, for it lightly dealt with heavy matters, probed none of the depths of its sub-

---

* The Permanent Court of International Justice was an organ of the League of Nations but any nation, League member or no, could join it. Harding had proposed that America do so. Coolidge had, also. So did the prospective Republican candidate for President, Herbert Hoover. But isolationist sentiment had been and would remain strong enough in the Senate to defeat this proposal.

ject, and was determinedly equivocal in its handling of key issues. It did, however, reveal major revisions of its author's earlier foreign policy views. Nine years before, he as Acting Secretary of the Navy had approved and ordered the landing of additional marines in Haiti; he now condemned the Coolidge administration's recent landing of marines in Nicaragua ("Single-handed intervention by us in the internal affairs of other nations in this hemisphere must end . . ."). Fourteen years before, he had been sure that war with Japan was inevitable and had favored "strong" acts which might provoke it; he now, restating the opinions expressed in his *Asia* magazine piece of 1923, saw "no fundamental reason why our relations with Japan should not be on a permanent and cordial basis." Ten years ago he had been the most fervent of "big navy" advocates; he now condemned Coolidge for not calling for a ban on cruiser building at the recent disarmament conference in Geneva, this to match the limitation on battleship construction imposed by the Washington Naval Treaty, and for subsequently approving an extensive, highly expensive cruiser-building program proposed by the Navy. He who in 1919 and 1920 had actively campaigned for the League of Nations now said merely that the United States "should cooperate with the League . . . and without entering into European politics . . . take an active, hearty and official part in all those proceedings which bear on the general good of mankind." (Equally equivocal was his statement about the World Court: if the President had had the will, he and the Senate could have found a way by which the United States could adhere to the court "without loss of any real or even contingent sovereign right.") Fourteen years before, he had deemed dangerously absurd Bryan's active faith in formal declarations of a love of peace, on the part of national governments, as an actual insurance against war—and on *this* matter he remained of the same opinion still. Soon to be signed * by fifteen nations, including every Great Power save the Soviet Union (the Soviets and some fifty other nations would sign later), was the famous Pact of Paris whose instigators had been U.S. Secretary of State Frank B. Kellogg and French Foreign Minister Aristide Briand. "The High Contracting Parties," it said, "solemnly declare in the names of their respective people that they condemn recourse to war for the solution of international controversies, and renounce it as an instrument of national policy in their relations with one another." But such lofty pronouncements were of no practical effect in the absence of "machinery for the elimination of the causes of disputes before they reach grave proportions," Roosevelt declared. "Secretary Kellogg's plan . . . fails in

* On August 27, 1928.

two points," he went on. "It leads to a false belief in America that we have taken a great step forward. It does not contribute in any way to settling matters of international controversy." [9]

The article would be published, along with one on Republican foreign policy by Ogden Mills, now Undersecretary of the Treasury, in the July issue of *Foreign Affairs*. This would be too late to influence the platform builders at the Democratic National Convention which opened in Houston on June 26, but Roosevelt arranged to obtain advance reprints of it; he saw to it that a reprint was in the hands of every delegate and alternate.

Meanwhile, he continued copious of advice to Smith and Smith's pre-convention campaign manager, George R. Van Namee. To the latter he wrote, March 27, that Senator Cordell Hull of Tennessee "would make an excellent choice" as candidate for Vice President. "He has a splendid record, great experience, is universally liked and would be very helpful to the ticket in Tennessee and to a certain extent in Kentucky and Missouri. He is not a fanatic. Furthermore . . . [if he were called upon to succeed to the White House], Hull would make a fine President." On the following day, in a letter to be read at a Jefferson Day banquet in Oregon, he presented in the cautiously vague language he hoped the platform writers would employ, "the most vital of the many arguments" for a Democratic victory that year. As regards Prohibition: ". . . honest and effective enforcement of all laws, equally including whatever law the people decide on as a means of carrying out the eighteenth amendment." As regards farm relief: ". . . place agriculture on a parity with industry in making and carrying out our laws." * As regards protection: ". . . restore the tariff to an honest basis, so as to eliminate present favoritism." As regards the League and World Court: ". . . cooperation with other nations for the elimination of war and for the settlement of international problems and disputes. . . ." As regards conservation (here he was, as usual, somewhat more forthright): ". . . preservation of natural resources, particularly water power in the ultimate ownership of the people." In general: ". . . the substitution of a Democratic Government of practical idealism in place of an Oligarchy of gross materialism." [10]

He would be pleased when the convention adopted a platform built along the lines he suggested. This platform would be reasonably definite and progressive in its labor plank, endorsing the principle of collective bargaining and calling for passage of an anti-injunction act. It would be

---

* What farmers were demanding, of course, was a parity of *prices* for farm and industrial products.

definitely progressive in its demand for public control and development of hydroelectric power. Otherwise, it would be studiously vague. Newton D. Baker later complained to Roosevelt that "McKinley could have run on the tariff plank and Lodge on the one on international relations," to which Roosevelt made bland reply: "If you or I had been the candidate, we would have ordered it otherwise—and thereby insured our defeat in November." The "glittering generalities" were, said Roosevelt, the work of Smith's "advisors." [11]

III

For Roosevelt personally, the 1928 convention was a repetition of 1924's in several respects. Again he was Smith's floor manager. Again he made the speech placing Smith in nomination. Again he scored, with his speech, a great personal triumph.

On June 12, 1928, the all-too-predictable Republicans assembled in Kansas City for their national convention and proceeded to do precisely what they were supposed to do. With little argument, they adopted a platform approving Prohibition, the protective tariff (with a promised increase in the tariff on agricultural imports), and a "sane" program of farm relief, the latter being described in negative terms as one devoid of "artificial price supports." A single ballot was sufficient to nominate Herbert Clark Hoover for President by a huge majority. Another single ballot disposed of the Vice Presidential nomination, which went to a standpat conservative, Senator Charles Curtis of Kansas. Then, on June 15, serenely and justifiably confident of victory in November, the Republicans adjourned.

Twelve days later, the unpredictable Democrats, assembled for their convention in Houston, proceeded to do what they had seldom done before: they held a national convention that was characterized, on the whole or on the surface, by an efficient order and harmony.

To Roosevelt's delight, Claude G. Bowers had been selected to make the keynote address, and he proved as effective a political orator as he was a journalist and historian. How, he said derisively, could the Republican Party be equally devoted, as it claimed, to Alexander Hamilton and Abraham Lincoln? The political principles of the one flatly contradicted those of the other. "You cannot believe with Lincoln in a government 'of the people, by the people and for the people' and with Hamilton in a government of the wealthy, by the powerful and for the privileged," cried Bowers. To be both a Lincoln Republican and a Hamilton Republican one must "find some way to ride two horses going in opposite directions at the same time!" He went on to "demand," on behalf of the Democracy, "that privilege take its hands out of the farmer's pockets and off the farmer's throat." He was a bit surprised, as he later confessed, by the audience response to this sally. Delegates from the South, Midwest, and West sprang to their feet, cheering, and cynical observers were diverted by the spectacle of Smith's pale-faced, soft-handed Tammany supporters—wholly urban types, unable to distinguish a field of wheat from one of rye—joining with tanned, hard-handed farmer delegates, of whom the New Yorkers were normally openly contemptuous, in a wild demonstration reminiscent of Populist days.[12]

But the high point of this convention, as of the Madison Square Garden assemblage in 1924, was Roosevelt's speech nominating Al Smith.

For this effort, the first of his major addresses to be broadcast over a national radio network, he made careful preparation. The preparation was as arduously physical as it was mental. He was determined to demonstrate before the multitude the fullest possible extent of his physical recovery since he last appeared, on crutches, before the delegates—was determined, indeed, to give the impression of a greater recovery than had actually been achieved. He would show himself merely lame, not crippled, and to this end he practiced "walking" and standing (these remained for him precarious balancing acts as well as tests of strength and endurance) for many hours, day after day, in the living room of his cottage at Warm Springs. He had become expert in the use of his cane in such a way as to avoid danger of slippage while giving maximum support to his braced right leg. This enabled him to reduce the weight he must place upon the brace that propped his yet almost useless left leg and upon the strong right arm of Mahoney (everyone called her by her last name) which he grasped in his left hand.[13]

He then asked his son Elliott to come down for training in the techniques of assisting him and to accompany him as his page in Houston. There were family reasons for asking Elliott to do this. Son James was in Europe that summer as the traveling companion of Sara Delano Roosevelt, and troubled and troublesome Elliott, who would enter his last year in hated Groton in September, was already in full rebellion against the family tradition requiring his going from Groton to Harvard College. His father may have hoped that the Houston experience, followed by a promised two months on a Wyoming ranch, would put him into a happier, more reasonable frame of mind. ("Elliott was thrilled at the chance to be with his father," Eleanor would later remember, "but I had no desire to take part in the hurly-burly of a convention—the 1924 convention had given me all I wanted of that type of experience. In addition, our two youngest boys, Franklin, junior, and John, were at Hyde Park and I had to stay with them." [14]) Certainly it was important that Elliott *appear* happy as the two of them moved along hotel corridors, auditorium aisles, and across the spotlighted stage. The son must be a smiling foil for the joking, the laughing with which the father masked the painful strenuosity of his physical effort. Roosevelt impressed this upon Elliott, who responded readily enough, learning to do this as he learned to keep his right arm bent at a right angle across his abdomen, and his fist clenched there, so that his biceps bulged hard where his father tensely gripped and leaned, sometimes heavily, upon him.

Meanwhile, the nominating speech draft, closely parallel in tone and substance to the "Happy Warrior" speech of four years before, was put into final shape. The basic draft was again largely the work of Judge Proskauer, but several others made suggestions, and Roosevelt worked the whole of it over with great care, adapting it to his natural speech rhythms, simplifying it, sometimes cutting out Proskauer's words in order to substitute language of his own. He looked upon the enterprise as a "definite experiment . . . of writing and delivering . . . wholly for the benefit of the radio audience and press rather than for any forensic effect it might have on the delegates and audience in the convention hall," as he later wrote to Walter Lippmann. "Smith had the votes anyway, and it seemed to me more important to reach out for Republicans and independents throughout the country." [15] He rehearsed the speech aloud several times with this in mind.

In the event he was as hugely successful with the 15,000 people who saw and heard him in the auditorium as he was with the estimated 15,000,000 who listened to him on the radio. His movement across the platform to the podium with Elliott at his side was a triumphant progress, and he made it, holding his head high, smiling, with far greater confidence than he had felt upon his crutches in 1924. With his left hand gripping the lectern and his braced legs (hidden from the audience by the lectern's bulk) spread far apart, he seemed to stand perfectly naturally, perfectly at ease, nodding to the left and right and looking up at the galleries, even waving with his right hand, in acknowledgment of the applause. Again, as he spoke, he seemed the personification of the qualities he ascribed to Smith. Especially was this so when, having described the "mental and moral equipment without which no President can successfully meet the administrative and material problems of his office," he went on to speak of the "one thing more needed to make . . . a great President," a "thing" of which, he implied, Herbert Hoover had none at all. "It is," he said, "that quality of soul which makes a man loved by little children, by dumb animals, that quality of soul which makes him a strong help to those in sorrow or in trouble, that quality which makes him not merely admired, but loved by all the people—the quality of sympathetic understanding of the human heart, of real interest in one's fellowman. Instinctively he senses the popular need because he himself has lived through the hardship, the labor and the sacrifice which must be endured by every man of heroic mould who struggles up to eminence from obscurity. . . . [America needs] a leader who understands the human side of life, who has the force of character and the keenness of brain to take, instinctively, the right course and the real course toward a prosperity that will be more than material, a leader also who grasps and understands not only large affairs of business and government, but in an equal degree the aspirations of the individual, the farmer, the wage-earner—the great mass of average citizens. . . . America needs . . . a pathfinder, a blazer of the trail to the high road that will avoid the bottomless morass of crass materialism that has engulfed so many great civilizations of the past." Then, lifting his head very high, he sang out with superb effect the nominating words: ". . . one who has the will to win —who not only deserves success but commands it. Victory is his habit— the happy warrior, Alfred E. Smith!" [16]

Press comment was as glowing as in 1924, if not more so. Even Colonel "Bertie" McCormick's Chicago *Tribune*, the most virulently partisan of all right-wing Republican organs, praised the speech in an editorial entitled "The Twilight of the Silver Tongues," bestowing upon the speaker an accolade he might find somewhat dubious: Roosevelt, said the *Tribune*, was "the only Republican in the Democratic party." The New York *Times*, in an editorial headed "A High-Bred Speech," found an "eloquence" rare in "a political speech." Continued the *Times*: ". . . the entire address . . . is a model of its kind—limpid and unaffected in style and without a single trace of fustian. It was not fitted to provoke frenzied applause, but could not be heard or read without prompting to serious thought and sincere emotion. . . ." Al Smith, who had listened to the speech on his "raddio" in Albany, tore this commentary from the paper and mailed it to "Dear Frank," having written on the margin: "This must be right because it brought tears in the Mansion when you spoke it. Al." One suspects that Smith, if at all sensitive to nuances, was somewhat less pleased, and that Roosevelt himself was proportionately more pleased, by the eyewitness account filed from Houston to the New York *World* by philosophy-popularizer Will Durant. "Here on the stage is Franklin Roosevelt," wrote Durant, "beyond comparison the finest man that has appeared at either convention. . . . A figure tall and proud even in suffering; a face of classic profile; pale with years of struggle against paralysis; a frame nervous and yet self-controlled with that tense, taut unity of spirit which lifts the complex soul

above those whose calmness is only a stolidity; most obviously a gentleman and a scholar. A man softened and cleansed and illumined with
pain. . . . Nothing better could be said for the Governor of New York
than that Franklin Roosevelt loves him. . . . Hear the nominating
speech: it is not a battery of rockets, bombs and tear-drawing gas—it is
not shouted, it is quietly read; there is hardly a gesture, hardly a raising
of the voice. This is a civilized man. . . . For the moment we are lifted
up." [17]

Al Smith won nomination on the first ballot. Cordell Hull, whether or
no he wanted the Vice Presidential nomination, was removed from consideration for it by friends who had foolishly pushed him forward as a
contender for the Presidency. Instead, Smith chose as his running mate
Senator Joseph T. Robinson of Arkansas.

<h1 style="text-align:center">IV</h1>

From Houston, when the convention adjourned, Roosevelt went to
Warm Springs (Elliott entrained for Phoenix, Arizona, whence he was to
go "by airplane . . . to Salt Lake City over the Grand Canyon," then
northward to the Wyoming ranch*) but had barely begun to relax into
the recreative routine centered on his beloved pool when a telegram
summoned him to New York City for a meeting of the Democratic National Committee. There he learned with more distress than surprise
that Al Smith proposed to name John J. Raskob chairman of the committee—that is, manager of the national campaign. He found himself
virtually alone at that meeting in his opposition to Raskob for this crucial post. Belle Moskowitz and Judge Proskauer both argued against it
in private talk with Smith. Joe Robinson, with his rural Arkansas background, refused to commit himself when asked about it during the committee session. But everyone else in the conference room expressed ap-

---

* Elliott became, in effect, a runaway that summer. The plane he was supposed to take from
Phoenix had not been arranged for, as Eleanor thought it had been, by her brother Hall. Elliott
seized upon this as an excuse for wandering for weeks through Arizona, Idaho, and Wyoming,
ending up, not at the White Grass Ranch, where he was supposed to go, but at another Wyoming ranch, the Bar BC, near Moose. During these weeks he wrote not a line to his parents, who,
of course, grew increasingly anxious about him. Roosevelt, by inquiry through the New York
state police, finally tracked his son down, whereupon Elliott sent his mother an eleven-page letter of explanation and justification, she being at that time loaded down with the tense labors of
a Presidential campaign. The closing words of Elliott's letter are revealing: "I hope you really
will forgive me for no [sic] writing before. Of course I suppose you told everybody how terrible
I was and that I hadn't written so I suppose there is no use asking you to keep my defects and
faults quiet, but I do hate to have . . . that sort of thing told to people whom it does not concern." [18]

proval of a decision Smith had obviously already made and would have
changed only in the face of very strong committee opposition.

"Your hunch was right," wrote Roosevelt from Hyde Park to Josephus Daniels on July 20, commenting on a Daniels editorial in the
Raleigh *News and Observer.* "The appointment [of Raskob] was a bold
stroke to try to end the 99% of business (big and little) preference for the
Republican Party. I told Smith quite plainly that it would make the
whole situation far more difficult . . . in the south, but Smith felt that
we should take our chances on this as we would lose anyway if we did
not carry the big industrial states. Furthermore, I told the Governor that
if he decided on Raskob we should make it clear that it was a purely
personal appointment of an old friend and that Raskob would be
merely a business manager and have nothing to say about issues. Smith
would not agree to this last as he thought it would be disloyal to Raskob
to tie his hands." [19]

Everything was wrong with this choice and with the party strategy it
indicated, in Roosevelt's strong opinion.

He might understand, as Eleanor certainly did, the bond of personal
sympathy which tied the governor and the big businessman to one another. There was, of course, a shared fervent Roman Catholicism of a
kind favored by the church's hierarchy: Raskob, the father of twelve, a
generous donor to the church, had been named a Knight of St. Gregory
by the Pope. There was a shared antipathy to Prohibition: Raskob was
generally regarded as the leading wet in the nation. There was a sharing
of laissez-faire economic views so far as big business was concerned
(though Smith took exception to these views as applied to hydroelectric
power), joined to a strong attraction toward great wealth. There was
also the fact that Raskob, like Smith, was a self-made man. Born of poor
parents in a small New York town, he had worked as a youth at modest
wages in a number of jobs before becoming private secretary to Pierre S.
Du Pont of the Delaware family, whose corporation at that time was engaged almost exclusively in the manufacture of explosives. His shrewd
abilities were great enough to win him rapid promotion, overcoming the
obstacles of an appearance and personality far from attractive (he was a
small man physically, shy, introverted, with Machiavellian attitudes toward power and a manner many deemed furtive), so that by 1914 he
was sufficiently influential within the company to persuade Du Pont to
diversify interests on a grand scale by buying control of General Motors, this at a time when the creator of General Motors, William C. Durant, was overextended financially to the point of collapse. By 1928 Raskob headed the finance committee of a greatly prospering General
Motors, was a vice-president of E. I. Du Pont de Nemours, was a mem-

ber of the board of some of the largest banks in New York, and had become, reputedly, one of the wealthiest individuals in America.

But though all this endeared Raskob personally and recommended him professionally to Al Smith, it added up, in Roosevelt's view, to an immense liability for a national chairman in that election year—a grave hazard to Smith's candidacy and to the welfare of the Democracy. This appointment glaringly contradicted both the central thesis of Bowers' keynote address to the convention and that portion of Roosevelt's nominating speech which was most widely quoted. It represented another intraparty triumph of extreme conservatism and, as such, another repudiation of Roosevelt's long effort to build the Democracy into a national party unified on liberal-progressive principles. Gleefully pointed out by Smith's opponents, sadly noted by his partisan supporters, especially those of liberal persuasion, was the fact that Raskob in his last *Who's Who* entry had described his politics as "Republican," his occupation as "capitalist," and the listing seemed to Roosevelt all too significant of the direction in which the new chairman sought to guide, the party. The Democratic National Headquarters was promptly established in the General Motors Building at Fifty-seventh and Broadway in New York (the suggested capture of the party by the corporation seemed to Roosevelt utterly deplorable): from this headquarters, the new chairman pridefully announced that Arthur James, the copper and railroad multimillionaire; Rudolph Spreckels, the sugar multimillionaire; and multimillionaire Harkness of Standard Oil all were supporting Alfred E. Smith, which clearly meant that none of them "considers that his interests are in the slightest degree imperilled" by the policies Smith in the White House would pursue. He later let it be known that his benefactor, Pierre S. Du Pont, was also supporting Smith. And not only did Raskob thus woo rich businessmen, but he also proved remarkably effective at extracting from these rich men large contributions to the Democratic campaign chest.

This, too—this way of financing a political campaign—ran directly counter to ideas Roosevelt had expressed and sought to implement in the past. In mid-June, 1925, he had said in a letter: "Just as the idea of the professional Republican politicians is an endless chain of obtaining official office so as to grant special favors to wealthy corporations so that wealthy corporations will give them large sums to enable them to select their candidates so as to grant them more favors and so on indefinitely, the fundamental Democratic idea that a political party is a piece of machinery by which the ideals of its principles can be put into actual practice in government should be carried into the financial side by refusing to permit large contributions and make instead almost every

Democratic voter an equal partner through his subscription to our enterprise. If we believe in granting special favors to none, should we not be equally firm in refusing to accept special favors from none?" He had been sharply critical of Jesse Jones' dependence on "a mere handful of very rich or moderately rich gentlemen" to pay off the 1924 party campaign deficit and raise money for the upcoming campaign—had tried to persuade the National Committee into an arrangement whereby millions of people would be enabled to make individually small contributions through local Democratic organizations, thus raising an estimated $200,000 a year for the national treasury.[20] He had wholly failed in this.

And his failure was now emphasized by Raskob's fund raising and disbursing activities. Money was expended on a lavish scale unprecedented for Democrats; some students of the campaign would later claim that the Democrats actually outspent the Republicans that year ($5,324,000 to $3,429,000), and Raskob displayed no qualms over the fact that some of this money came from highly odoriferous sources—from Thomas Fortune Ryan, for instance, who was accustomed to harvesting in lucrative special favors a myriad of, if not a million, dollars for every hundred he invested in a politician's career. In the end, grown angry and desperate as he stared defeat in the face, Raskob would resort to ruthless, almost extortive means of raising money. It would later be charged that some of Smith's friends were actually financially ruined by the campaign obligations which Raskob imposed upon them.

As for the effect of Raskob's operations and the Smith-Raskob campaign strategy upon the presentation of issues to the electorate, it was wholly disastrous. On various fundamental questions the two parties, the two candidates differed less in 1928 than they did in 1924: even the traditional Democratic opposition to a protective tariff was wholly abandoned by Smith, whose advocacy of both the principle and practice of protectionism was almost as strong as Hoover's. Liberals were alienated. A young but already well-known professor of economics at the University of Chicago, Paul H. Douglas, normally a Democrat, spoke for many when he repudiated Smith because of the "sterile and corrupt groups" whom Raskob was mobilizing and called instead for support of Norman Thomas, the Socialist candidate. Thomas himself asserted that Smith "accepts Hoover's general philosophy . . . [which] reduces the battle between them to the comparatively insignificant question of power at Muscle Shoals and Boulder Dam."

Actually the question which Socialist Thomas seemed here to deprecate was by no means "insignificant," even "comparatively." It had to do with that growing loss of human control over human destinies, that widening gap between physical power and humane intelligence, which has been the essential tragedy of modern history. Its direct concern was with the problems born of an unhappy marriage of technology to private profit. The one partner was aggressively expansive, the other selfishly contractive; their offspring grew up as unruly monsters.

The Preparedness legislation which Woodrow Wilson, in his shift from the New Freedom to the New Nationalism, had sponsored in 1916 empowered the President and War Department to build a nitrate-manufacturing plant in order to relieve the United States of dependence on Chile and Germany for nitrate supplies. Two nitrate plants were built in 1918 at Muscle Shoals on the Tennessee River, and construction was then begun on a giant dam, the Wilson Dam, wherewith to harness the Tennessee's falling water for use in operation of the plants. When the war ended, both nitrate plants were completed, but the dam was not—it was only three-fourths done—and the Harding and Coolidge administrations opposed its completion unless or until the whole Muscle Shoals development could be leased on a long-term basis to private interests for the development of nitrate fertilizers and electric power. Henry Ford offered to do this. His proposal, if accepted, would have granted him a 100-year lease on property that had already cost the federal government between $100,000,000 and $200,000,000 to develop, he paying $1,500,000 in annual rent and guaranteeing to provide an annual minimum of 40,000 tons of nitrates (the combined capacity of the Muscle Shoals plants was 154,000 tons annually) for farmers' use in "cheap" fertilizer. Both Harding and Coolidge, along with Secretary of Commerce Hoover, heartily favored Ford's proposal. So, initially, did leading farm organizations. And legislation accepting it quickly passed the House of Representatives. In the Senate, however, the measure ran afoul of Nebraska's Senator George W. Norris, chairman of the Agriculture Committee, whose investigations soon convinced him that Ford's offer, loudly extolled for its "generosity" by the Republican press, was in effect a gigantic steal in that it would, for a paltry fee, transfer to private industrial and utility interests publicly owned hydroelectric sites in the Tennessee Valley whose potential value was of many billions of dollars. Norris, blocking Senate approval of the House-passed bill, proposed instead a bill of his own, providing for government development and operation of the Muscle Shoals facilities. Alabama's Senator Oscar W. Underwood countered with proposed legislation providing for private operation of these same facilities.

And so the issue was joined.

The Underwood bill, strongly backed by the administration, passed the Senate. A slightly different version of it passed the House. But when the proposal went to joint House and Senate conference, Norris managed by adroit parliamentary maneuver, including threat of a filibuster, to prevent final action upon it. His own proposal subsequently gained the support of House insurgents, who creatively revised it to provide for establishment of a federal corporation which would not only operate the Wilson Dam and the nitrate plants but also build at Cove Creek, Tennessee, a second large dam, augmenting the hydroelectric power supply and providing increased flood control down the Tennessee. Further, the proposal called for preferential rates to municipalities and other public bodies in the selling of the government-generated current and for the use of surplus current in experimental developments aimed at improved methods of nitrate production. An aroused public, unmistakably comprising a majority of those well informed on the issue, strongly favored the proposal—and Congress adopted it through a joint resolution of House and Senate on May 25, 1928. This, however, was only shortly before adjournment. Under the Constitution's ten-day rule, President Coolidge, without public comment upon it, was enabled to smother the measure by pocket veto instead of returning it to Congress with a veto message.

Thus it had been by the narrowest of margins and largely by the efforts of a single man, George Norris, that the people of the United States had managed to retain even the possibility of control, through their responsible representatives, of the development of hydroelectric power in the Tennessee Valley. And a loss of control in that valley would have meant a loss of it in many, if not all, other areas rich in waterpower resources.

For the electric light and power industry had grown into a monster of physical and economic power since the turn of the century. The total output of electricity had been increased from 6 billion kilowatt-hours in 1902 to approximately 117 billion in 1928, or by a factor of more than 19, and this expansion of productive capacity had been accompanied by the rise of a few giant corporate structures, replacing the relatively small companies which had originally generated and distributed light and power. The technology of electricity implied regional systems of distribution whereby hundreds of communities were linked together in regional power grids, and this, within the American system, implied mergers and mergers of mergers through unfettered use of the holding company device, until, by 1927, about 3,700 utility companies had been eliminated and a mere dozen holding companies legally controlled nearly three-fourths of the nation's electric power. These corporate giants were too huge to be regulated by the several states (the national executive, in Republican hands, had no wish to regulate them). They were too huge and complicated to be understood in actual operational terms even by their makers (Samuel Insull of Chicago, for example, "ruled" a utility empire extending into twenty-three states and was chairman of the board of no fewer than sixty-three subordinate firms). And, far from promoting the most efficient production and distribution of electricity for use, they seriously inhibited these in the interests of the private profit of their nominal managers. Rates were far higher than they ought to be, and a large segment of the population—virtually the whole of the farm population, for instance—was denied electricity altogether.

Herbert Hoover made no mention of Muscle Shoals—indeed, he said nothing specific about the power problem in general—in his speech accepting the Republican nomination. He contented himself with pointing out that water transportation, reclamation, irrigation, flood control, and waterpower development were interrelated and therefore required "coordinated" development.

Al Smith, on the other hand, in his acceptance speech, was specific and vehement in his condemnation of policies whereby "we . . . have allowed to run to waste or have given to private exploitation our public waters with their great potential power for the development of electrical energy." Said he: "The value of this heritage can best be measured when we consider the recent disclosures [through Congressional investigation, widely, if reluctantly, publicized] of the methods employed by private monopolies to wrest our remaining water resources from public control. No more dishonest or unpatriotic propaganda has ever been seen in this country. . . . Private utility corporations to gain control of public resources have procured the writing of textbooks for the public schools; have subsidized lecturers pretending to give to the country their own honest and unbiased advice; have employed as their agents former public officials and have endeavored to mislead public opinion by the retention of the services of leaders of the community in various parts of the country. Highly paid lobbyists penetrated into every State and into the legislative halls of the nation itself."

Came then Smith's statement of principle:

". . . The ownership of some of these great water powers is in the nation, of others in the several States. These sources of water power must remain forever under public ownership and control. Where they are owned by the Federal government they should remain under Federal control. Where they are owned by an individual State, they should be under the control of that State, or where they are owned by States jointly, they should be under the control of those States. . . . The Government—Federal, State, or the authority representing joint States—must control the switch that turns on or off the power so greedily sought by certain private groups without the least regard for the public good." [21]

V

Relatively few voters clearly recognized the electric power issue between Hoover and Smith, however. Every voter was forced to recognize the "false issues," as Roosevelt called them, of Prohibition and religion.

Immediately following his nomination, a whispering campaign of almost unparalleled scurrilousness was launched against Smith. Within a week, an estimated 10,000,000 pamphlets and handbills bearing such titles as "Alcohol Smith," "Convent Horrors," "Traffic in Nuns," and "Popery in the Public Schools" had been issued. One circular warned millions of Protestants that their marriages would be annulled, their children rendered illegitimate, if Smith won. Bishop James Cannon, Jr., of the Methodist Episcopal Church, South, inveighing against Raskob as "this wet Roman Catholic Knight of Columbus and chamberlain of the Pope of Rome," was organizing a passionate crusade of Protestant bigotry against Smith through the Southern states. In Smith's own state, Methodist Bishop Adna Leonard of Buffalo was asserting that "no Governor" who would "kiss the papal ring" could "get within gunshot of the White House." And even so enlightened a publication as the *Christian Century,* a nondenominational organ, was preparing to declare editorially its perturbation at the prospect "of a representative of an alien culture, of a medieval Latin mentality, of an undemocratic hierarchy and of a foreign potentate in the great office of President of the United States."

As always, Roosevelt was outraged by the scurrilousness and bigotry. The loathsome character of the opposition committed him more strongly to Smith than he would otherwise have been. Yet he could not but continue to blame the candidate for needlessly provoking such opposition while refusing to define and focus on issues that *ought* to divide Democrats from Republicans. "The campaign is working out in a way I, personally, would not have followed and Smith has burned his bridges behind him," said he in a letter on July 25. He indicated that he would not become "one of the 'yes men' at headquarters"—that he could "find little room for active work" in a campaign which was so largely run by "the General Motors publicity and advertising staff," as he complained to Van Lear Black. (In his letter to Daniels on July 20 he had said: "Frankly, I am more and more disgusted and bored by the thought that in this great nation, the principal issue may be drawn into what we do or do not put into our stomachs. Are there no great fundamentals of the science and practice of government left?") Nor was he encouraged by the candidate or the candidate's inner circle to play more than a minor role. Smith did not ask for his advice or accept it when it was offered unless it happened to jibe with that of the inner circle and with Smith's own predilections, while the triumvirate of Belle Moskowitz, Proskauer, and Raskob, having small use for him, effectively barred his direct personal access to the candidate. "I rarely get a chance to see the Governor himself and can communicate only by way of other people," he confessed to Senator Harry F. Byrd of Virginia. And so, having accepted with some reluctance the task of organizing a Division of Commerce, Industry and Professional Activities in the national headquarters, he did so with dispatch, then retired to Hyde Park, leaving Howe to work as his full-time representative in the General Motors Building. (Among the letters to businessmen which he signed as division head or to which he permitted his signature to be affixed was one critical of Secretary of Commerce Hoover's alleged penchant for excessive regulation of private enterprise. ". . . I think the policy of Governor Smith to let businessmen look after business matters is far safer for our country," he said!)[22]

He was so little occupied by the campaign that, in late July, he readily accepted when two of his oldest political friends invited him to become, for the second time in his life, a newspaper columnist. The friends were Morgan and Ferdinand Hoyt of Beacon, a town on the southern border of Dutchess County, directly across the Hudson from Newburgh. It was Morgan Hoyt who in 1910 had introduced Roosevelt for Roosevelt's first speech of the campaign for state senator, this in what was then the town of Matteawan (Matteawan and Fishkill were merged in 1913 to form Beacon), where Hoyt owned and edited the Matteawan (later the Beacon) *Journal.* In 1920, during the postwar recession, financial difficulties had forced the Hoyts to sell the *Journal* to chain-newspaper publisher Frank E. Gannett, but in 1927 they had returned to the newspaper business by backing a former reporter on the *Journal* in his acquisition and publication of the *Standard* in Beacon, self-identified as "The Southern Dutchess County Weekly Newspaper," of which Morgan Hoyt became the listed editor. Staunchly Republican theretofore, the *Standard* was abruptly transformed into a Democratic organ, one of the very few upstate, and it badly needed the boost in circulation and advertising which would accrue, the Hoyts insisted, from a front-page Roosevelt column.

The first of these columns, dated July 30, 1928, was published on August 2 under the heading of "Between Neighbors." It was a mild condemnation of extreme political partisanship (no longer could you "fool people into believing that the nation . . . is going to the dogs just because one political party happens to be in power . . .") and religious bigotry (". . . the time has come to prove definitely that . . . [religious bigotry] must not and cannot be a controlling factor in our national life"). In his second column he said that he had just received "four letters, two of them making wholly untrue insinuations about Secretary Hoover's personal habits, the other two about Governor Smith's," and that, since "I happen to be a personal friend of both of these gentlemen it makes me a little hot under the collar. . . ." He also spoke of unsigned letters coming in "every day in literally enormous numbers. . . . They are silly letters, foul, dirty letters, threatening letters—and of course they go promptly to the fire. The pity is that there are still so many gullible or unthinking people in our midst." In his column published September 13 he attacked Hoover's assertion, in the Republican candidate's acceptance speech of mid-August, that "an adequate tariff is the foundation of farm relief," whereas, in point of fact, "the so-called agricultural imports into the United States" consisted "almost wholly of things we cannot raise in this country," things like "rubber and sisal and bananas and in fact all of the products of the tropics." Obviously Smith was right to say that the tariff "is ineffective on commodities on which there is exportable surplus"—commodities on whose production, as it happened, the bulk of the farm population depended for livelihood. He came dangerously near an actual repudiation of the Smith-Raskob stand on protectionism when he went on to say "that the farmer sells his goods in a world-wide and therefore unprotected market and buys the machinery for his farm and the clothes for his family in a highly protected national market" and that this "in the final analysis" was a major cause of the farmer's woes. The tariff, he said, "ought to prevent him [the farmer] from being gouged by especially favored monopolies when he buys the necessary farm supplies." Two weeks later he dealt with "the problem of water power sites," but in such a way as to make it difficult to determine where he himself stood on the issue of private vs. public power development. ". . . it is worth while for us to give serious attention to the desirability of allowing the several governments [state and federal] to own and control the actual power sites, letting private companies do the distribution," he said, his chief argument being that "the government can raise the necessary money on a 4 percent basis or lower, whereas private companies can only raise money by paying 8 percent or more," and that "the operation of a power plant requires very few employees . . . and can be done just as cheaply and efficiently . . . by [the government] as by a private company." A week later, in the last of the ten columns he wrote, he compared Smith's record of "actual accomplishment" in consolidating state agencies, in increasing state government efficiency, with the lack of accomplishment along these lines by two Republican administrations in which Herbert Hoover had served as Cabinet officer. This "subject," said Roosevelt, ". . . happens to be an old pet of mine." [23]

It was customary from late July through early September for the *Standard*'s publisher to drive up to Hyde Park each Monday morning to pick up copy, neatly typed by Missy LeHand, for the column which was to appear in the coming Thursday's paper. The last two columns, however, were delivered by mail from Georgia. "I am off on Monday for Warm Springs . . . ," said a note from Roosevelt to Morgan Hoyt on Saturday, September 15. He had "prepared two other articles," he added, and would "send them in a few days." [24]

VI

While her husband made his unprotested withdrawal to the periphery of the Presidential campaign, Eleanor was plunged into the midst of it—and not merely as his representative. Her abilities as political campaigner had grown stronger with their exercise since her effective work in the gubernatorial campaign of 1924. In 1926, despite the fact that she had initially preferred Owen D. Young over Robert Wagner for the U.S. Senatorial nomination, she had worked so well for Wagner against Wadsworth (she described the latter as "a country squire of the seventeenth century" with a Marie Antoinette mentality) that Wagner had publicly given her much of the credit for his victory.[25] Equally recognized were her talents as an organizer, talents that involved a remarkable ability to stimulate the political consciousness and conscience of women primarily, but of men also. Governor Smith was no ardent feminist—he had old-fashioned prejudices against women in realms of activity that had formerly been exclusively masculine, was convinced that men who were really men would never submit to the order-giving authority of a female executive—but he welcomed the advice and assistance of forceful women (they had men's brains, in his view) so long as they acknowledged that he was the boss, and he had several times called upon Eleanor for assistance when his welfare bills ran into trouble in the legislature. She had freely given it, out of her deep commitment to the causes of old-age pensions, civil rights, minimum-wage guarantees, slum clearance, unemployment compensation, and the like.

It was a commitment she shared with bob-haired, chain-smoking, fast- and sometimes tough-talking Nancy Cook and with tall, sad-faced, gentle, and stately Marion Dickerman. Her friendship with these two had grown closer over the years, had become more variously and intensely active in pursuit of mutual interests. Especially had this been so since the Stone Cottage and swimming pool at Val Kill were completed. The cottage was home for Nancy and Marion. For Eleanor, too, it was home in many important ways—more her own home than was the big house at Hyde Park or the house on Sixty-fifth Street. It filled a place in her life akin to that of Warm Springs in her husband's. Like Warm Springs for Franklin, Val Kill had for Eleanor the great advantage that it was seldom visited by Sara. And like Warm Springs for Franklin, Val Kill became for Eleanor not only a place to live but also a vital working interest.

Nancy, who "had distinct artistic ability and could do almost anything with her hands," undertook to furnish the cottage with pieces of her own manufacture. She then conceived the idea of establishing a workshop at Val Kill for the production of authentic replicas of early American furniture—expensive pieces, necessarily, since they would be for the most part handcrafted—which might be sold by mail through the use of brochures, as well as through some large store in New York City. Roosevelt encouraged the project. He was eager to find ways in which to halt the continuous, accelerating drain of population from country to city and felt that Nancy's project might point the way toward an economically viable mixture of small local industries and family farms whereby a healthy rural-urban balance could be maintained. And so Val-Kill Industries was launched. It was largely financed by Eleanor. It was managed by Nancy, who continued as executive secretary of the Women's Division of the New York State Democratic Committee. It was staffed with local employees. ". . . we had to have a certain number of expert craftsmen, and were fortunate in finding some very fine cabinetmakers of Italian and Norwegian descent," Eleanor would later say.[26] By the spring of 1927 enough furniture had been made to enable the holding of an exhibition of it in the Sixty-fifth Street house—an exhibition which, though very favorably reported upon in the New York *Times,* produced no rush of advance orders. Nancy, Marion, and Eleanor continued to believe in the project, however, and to work hard on it.

Nor was this the only working interest with which the three women were concerned. By the time the furniture exhibition was held Eleanor was approaching the end of her first term as a part-time teacher of English, American literature, and American history to teen-aged girls in the Todhunter School in New York City. Miss Todhunter, founder and principal of the school where Marion Dickerman had been vice-principal when Eleanor and Marion first met, had some months before decided to return to her native England to live. She had offered the school for sale to Marion at a price considerably higher than Marion could afford. Marion had discussed the matter with Eleanor and Nancy. At Eleanor's suggestion, the three friends had then joined together to buy the school, which, she hoped, would become as inspirational and educative of its enrollees, most of whom came from *Social Register* families, as Mlle. Souvestre's Allenwood had been for her a quarter century before. Her approach to education was thoroughly progressive. With John Dewey—no doubt in reflection, conscious or no, of Dewey's *Democracy and Education*—she believed that education's primary aim is the discernment of relationships, vital relationships, and that, as Dewey said, "no relationships can become perceptible" save through "experience." The teacher must begin with the student's present interests, recognizing these as tentacles reaching out for connections with a larger and larger world. "It is the teacher's function," Eleanor would say in a later year, "to manage this relating process. . . ." The teacher must "seize all opportunities" to make specific subject matter "somehow akin to the things pupils are doing in their daily life." [27] When she taught a course in current events (she would call it, significantly, "Happenings"), she would take her girls to produce markets, to slum area settlement houses, to courtrooms where trials were in progress, to police stations at lineup time, and would make far more use of newspapers than of books, more use of classroom discussion than of teacher lectures.

Wife, mother, educator, business entrepreneur, Eleanor had also become, by the summer of 1928, a lecturer and writer for whose speeches and articles there was a steadily increasing demand. Louis Howe continued to provoke and inspire her into these enterprises, and she was initially astounded and remained always delighted by the size of the checks she received for such efforts—$500, for instance, for a 2,500-word contribution to *McCall's* magazine, checks of comparable size for a contribution to *Success Magazine* entitled "What I Want Most Out of Life" and one to Redbook entitled "Women Must Learn to Play the Game as Men Do." Far less lucrative, but more prestigious among intellectuals, and more directly contributory to her recognized effectiveness in politics were articles she did for the *North American Review* and *Current History*. To the former she contributed a piece entitled "Why Democrats Favor Smith," published in November, 1927, comparing Smith, who had "a practical knowledge of how to achieve political results," with Woodrow Wilson, who, lacking a "knowledge of practical politics," was unable "to translate his dreams into facts." To the latter magazine she contributed a piece, published in June, 1928, reflective of her own reading of Bowers' *Jefferson and Hamilton.* She distinguished among the Democrats of "today" who "trust in the people" (she meant "the plain, ordinary, every-day citizen . . . not one of the 'best minds' but the average mind," who was "neither superlatively rich nor distressingly poor"), the Socialists who "believe in making the Government the people's master," and the Republicans who "believe that a moneyed 'aristocracy' . . . should rule the Government." The Democratic Party, she implied, abhorred all class distinctions; "the Democrats believe that the whole people should govern." [28]

From all this, conjoined with a Christian selflessness and an objectivity which enabled her to work harmoniously and productively with all kinds of people, including the often arrogant and impatient Belle Moskowitz, it was inevitable that Eleanor would be called upon to play an important part in Smith's Presidential campaign. It was also inevitable that she would answer the call, despite the fact that she was no more taken with Al Smith personally than she had been four years before, regretted his failure to press for U.S. membership in the League of Nations, and continued to suffer pangs of conscience over his views on Prohibition. Her husband twitted her about the latter—laughed at an "awful picture" taken of her at some meeting or other wherein she was "apparently looking at a fly on the ceiling in the hope of finding out how to be wet and dry at the same time." [29] (A camera somehow always emphasized her most unattractive features while ignoring those which, in a face-to-face meeting with her, offset the ugliness of protruding teeth and receding chin.) No doubt her husband's attitudes and judgments helped her toward adoption of a scale of values by which Smith's deplorable stand on Prohibition was outweighed by his admirable stands on other matters. Civil liberties, for instance. When a Texas lady, speaking for a Southern organization known as the Women's Democratic Law Enforcement League, bitterly accused Smith of contempt for the Constitution because he opposed enforcement of the Eighteenth Amendment, Eleanor publicly wondered why this lady and her organization, if truly concerned with a rigid application of constitutional law, were not working as fervently "to enforce the 14th and 15th amendments relating to the right of all citizens to vote" as they did to enforce Prohibition. (Her published comment was applauded by George Marvin in a letter to her husband, the sad irony of this being that George Marvin had now become an alcoholic, rapidly going almost as far out of control as Eleanor's Uncle Vallie in a tragic waste of the talents that had made him an excellent Groton master and a successful magazine editor and writer.[30])

Eleanor headed the women's side of the campaign. "Mrs. Moskowitz and I worked together in full harmony from April to the end of the campaign . . . ," she later wrote, as if getting along with Mrs. Moskowitz were in itself an achievement, "and I have always been grateful to her for the opportunity." She "induced" Mary W. "Molly" Dawson, whom she had first known in 1924 as civic secretary of the Women's City Club,* to go out to St. Louis, where "the women in the Midwestern Headquarters of the Democratic National Committee" were said to be "fighting"—a mess which Molly Dawson cleaned up swiftly, transforming the St. Louis office into such an effective organization in the process that, as Eleanor said two decades later, "we knew that no future campaign should be conducted without her. . . ." Eleanor also worked closely with Mrs. Nellie Tayloe Ross, who in 1924, a month after the death of her husband, the incumbent governor, had been elected governor of Wyoming—the first woman in history to become governor of a state. Eleanor and Mrs. Mary Norton, Congresswoman from New Jersey, who headed the women's speakers bureau at headquarters, arranged for Mrs. Ross a speaking schedule heavy beyond the lady's bearing; it had to be reduced, whereupon Eleanor herself filled a few speaking engagements, including one requiring travel in company with the beauteous Mrs. Charles Dana Gibson, a Langhorne of Virginia who, having married the famous artist, had become his model for the "Gibson Girl." But speaking "was still something of an ordeal" for Eleanor.[31] She felt herself less effective in public speech than in fact she was. And so she remained for the most part at headquarters, where she put in twelve- and fourteen-hour days.

She handled a volume of correspondence and a mass of executive detail which soon overtaxed the formidable working capabilities of her secretary, Miss Malvina "Tommy" Thompson, a young woman whose shrewd practical common sense was guided by the sternest of New England consciences and who, employed by Eleanor part time since 1922, was destined to remain with her as her closest working associate for the rest of Eleanor's life. It became necessary to employ a second secretary —a pretty, vivid, vivacious Irish Catholic girl named Grace Tully, who had for many years been secretary to Cardinal Hayes and had been released by him, at her request, for work in the campaign. Miss Tully had "long ago resolved never to work for a woman," as she later recalled, and in her first workday with Eleanor she found herself wondering irritably why she had permitted that resolution to be broken. "In that first session she [Eleanor] charged through nearly thirty letters," then an-

---

* The Women's City Club had joined some years before with the Women's Trade Union League, the League of Women Voters, and several other progressive-minded women's organizations to initiate the Joint Legislative Conference, of which Molly Dawson was a leading spirit and in which Eleanor was active.

nounced that she "had an engagement, but . . . would be back later in the day to sign the finished products." But Grace Tully managed to get those first letters accurately typed within the allotted time, was pardonably proud of her achievement, was rewarded by Eleanor's warm appreciation of her work, and was soon devoted to her new, temporary boss. ". . . Mrs. Roosevelt was most considerate, never annoyed at being asked to repeat [when dictating] and never thrown off her own trend of thought by any form of interruption." [32]

In September, Eleanor resumed her teaching at the Todhunter School while maintaining an increasingly heavy load of work at the Democratic headquarters. It became necessary for her and her secretaries to work until midnight and after, night after night.

In September, too, she took Grace Tully with her to Hyde Park, where "the principal project for the weekend," as Miss Tully would remember, "was for Mrs. Roosevelt to get Johnny and Franklin, Jr., . . . packed for departure to Groton." John was to be enrolled for his first year at Groton, and Eleanor, who had always felt and would always feel that a twelve-year-old boy was far too young to be separated from his parental home, resented it bitterly. "The day I took each boy to school [for the first time], unpacked his clothes and settled him was always a terrible day for me, and when it came to the last child it was particularly hard," she later said. This was "because there was then no child left at home." She deemed it "fortunate . . . that I had a strenuous autumn to cope with. . . . I might otherwise have been a very disagreeable companion for my husband and my mother-in-law." [33]

VII

She *might* have been, for him, but she could not have been in the immediate future without traveling nearly a thousand miles. This was the distance separating her from her husband after she had returned to New York City from her sad farewell at Groton.

It was from a covert motive in addition to an overt one, it was as much to reduce massive pressures on his public life as it was to increase the flow of lifeblood into withered limbs, that Franklin Roosevelt journeyed to Warm Springs in the third week of September. He wanted to get away from importuning politicians who, ever since Smith's Presidential nomination, had been begging him to run for governor of New York—wanted sound excuse for absence from the New York State Democratic Convention, which met in Rochester on October 1. There, in Rochester, the mounting pressures would reach their climax and then, if he continued successfully to resist, be abruptly removed from him. Someone else would be nominated. And so, to bolster his health excuse for leaving his native state at that time, not returning until the nomination had been made, he arranged to make a speech in behalf of Smith's candidacy in Atlanta on September 25: another in Manchester, Georgia, on October 1; a third in Columbus, Georgia, on October 4. He would then move north and east, speaking in Cleveland on October 6, in Boston on October 12, and finally in New York City on October 15.

He had three reasons for not wanting to enter the gubernatorial race that year, any one of which, standing alone, would have been conclusive from his and Howe's point of view.

First and foremost was his openly stated reason of health. He had to admit to himself that the rate of improvement of his legs was now much slower than it had been in the year he first went to Warm Springs and then to Marion; but he did still improve, and so he continued to say he might walk again on unbraced legs in another two or three years, provided he went on uninterruptedly with his winter exercises at Warm Springs, his summer exercises at Hyde Park.

A second reason, which he of course could not openly state, was his realization that if he entered the race, he might very well be defeated. By mid-September he was more certain than he had been in the spring that this was another Republican year nationally. Nothing Al Smith had said or done, nothing Al *could* say or do within the framework of a Raskob pro-business campaign, matched in popular persuasiveness Herbert Hoover's boast, in his acceptance speech, that under Republican leadership "[we] in America today are nearer the final triumph over poverty than ever before in the history of any land" or the Republican sloganeers' promise of two chickens in every pot, two cars in every garage, if this leadership was continued. Why should the average voter wish to take power away from a party that seemed to have demonstrated its ability to generate prosperity in order to give it to a party which merely claimed it could do so and which, as regards basic principles and attitudes, presented no real alternative to current Republicanism? Inevitably, a tide that swept Hoover into the White House would carry many Republicans into the executive mansions of their respective states. The likelihood that this would happen in New York was increased by the New York Republicans' choice of a gubernatorial candidate. Their nominee (he had been decided upon shortly after the Republican National Convention, though he would not be formally named until September 29) was Albert Ottinger, who as attorney general had waged effective war in the public interest against dealers in phony stocks, dealers in adulterated foods, price gougers, loan sharks, and the like. Ottinger was a Jew, the first of his religion ever to win a gubernatorial nomination. His public record seemed to assure his hold upon the Republican majorities upstate; his Jewishness should greatly strengthen him in normally Democratic New York City, where the Jewish population was large; and he was reputed to be an excellent campaigner.

Roosevelt's third reason for not wanting to run that year was even more deeply buried in silence behind walls of reticence than his second one, to which it was closely related. He felt that 1928 was too early for him to run again for office. The timing was wrong, all wrong in terms of his and Howe's grand design upon the future.

In part from his awareness of current economic dislocations, in part from his feeling that there was a tidal ebb and flow in large-scale human affairs, he had derived his belief that the prevailing Republican prosperity could not last indefinitely, that it must ultimately collapse into a serious depression. But in the summer and autumn of 1928 it seemed unlikely that the collapse would come within the next four years. Certainly Roosevelt did not believe it would. He revealed as much through the kind of business speculations he engaged in that year (his Camco gamble, for instance), though a certain wariness about the immediate economic future seems implicit in the fact that he refused to gamble in common stocks, as so many of his fellow Americans were beginning to do—was no more tempted toward this kind of gamble than he had been toward speculations in Florida real estate three years before.

The long-rising stock market, supposed generally to reflect coming economic developments with fair accuracy, had shown signs of faltering last January. It had good reason to do so, in the judgment of perhaps a majority of economists. The flow of government money into the general marketplace had been reduced in recent years by the Mellon-Coolidge economic policies. Consumer spending for durable goods had declined in 1927. The agricultural depression continued. The rate of growth of the automobile industry had slowed during the last two years, and there were some who thought it might soon halt altogether—that the plant for automobile, gasoline, and tire production might even prove to be overexpanded in market terms within the next few years. The housing market was already glutted; it had been since 1926, though the speculative building of new apartment houses, hotels, and office buildings continued apace. These last two developments, having to do with cars and housing, were especially worrisome to those who realized how greatly America's prosperity depended on the construction and automotive industries. Hence had come warning from market analysts that stocks were overpriced, having been bid up by purely speculative buying; that anticipated progress had been heavily overdiscounted; that a drastic market readjustment was in the offing; and that, as both symptom and partial cause of the malaise, the volume of brokers' loans, enabling individuals to purchase stocks on exceedingly thin margin, was dangerously high. (Loans to brokers and dealers by the New York Federal Reserve member banks had in fact increased from $2,818,561,000 to $3,810,000,000 during 1927.)

But then, as always during the Coolidge years when there was a perceptible waning of bullish confidence, the administration had spoken reassuring words. This time the words had come directly from the President himself—he who was so addicted to silence on most matters of public concern. Though brokers' loans had "reached unprecedented heights . . . , President Coolidge does not see any reason for unfavorable comment . . . ," reported the New York *Times* on January 7, 1928. "The President, it was said at the White House today [Friday, January 6], believes that the increase represents a natural expansion of business in the securities market and sees nothing unfavorable in it." At once the market had resumed its advance. ". . . the stock market community," said the New York *Times* on January 8, ". . . concluded that . . . [the President's statement] invited heavy buying of shares." On that same day the *Times'* financial editor reported Wall Street's amazement that a President would intervene in "a controversy of just that character." There was no precedent for it. "The Chief Executive has traditionally avoided expressing opinion on subjects purely technical or which are surrounded with problems of speculative activities."

Then, in early March, sparked by huge purchases of General Motors stock by John J. Raskob and GM's Managers Securities Company, among others, the advance had become a leap upward so spectacular that the stock market was suddenly front-page news all across the country. General Motors had opened at 139¼ on Saturday, March 3, and closed after just two hours of trading at 144¼; it had "crossed 150" on the following Tuesday; it stood at 160 on March 10. On that same Saturday, the last trading day of the initial week of what would be known to history as the Big Bull Market of 1928–29, Radio Corporation of America stock had shot up from 107¾ to 120½, a gain of 12¾ points in two short hours. On Monday, March 12, Radio shot up another 18 points, then opened on the following morning at 160, an incredible leap of 21½ points overnight! Virtually every stock on the list was soon being driven upward in a veritable frenzy of buying "for the rise." Day after day the bull market roared on. It stumbled badly in early June—the break in the market was then as spectacular as the initial upward leap had been—but this decline proved of brief duration, thanks to the flood of bullish statements promptly issued by high administration officials and respected spokesmen for business and to the continued eagerness of bankers to make loans on little or no security. By the day of Hoover's nomination stock prices were rising again, and more rapidly than before. Since then, market speculation had become a mania that spread to the remotest corners of the land, actively involving hundreds of thousands of people—taxi drivers in Chicago, ranchers in Wyoming, stenographers in Des Moines, schoolteachers in Manhattan, Kansas—who a few months before would not have known how to go about buying a share of stock. They now borrowed to the hilt from all-too-willing bankers in order to invest in the market on the narrowest of margins, and brokerage offices were being opened to a profitable business in towns like Storm Lake, Iowa (population, 5,000).

The spectacle was absurd, fantastic, a little pathetic, and more than a little disgusting to eyes like Franklin Roosevelt's. Yet it could not but affect his psychology. It generated a euphoria, an eagerness to believe in the New Economic Era (so Hoover and contemporary economists had dubbed it), which few could wholly resist and to which a temperamentally optimistic nature must respond at least to the extent of doubting, emphatically doubting, that a deep depression was imminent or even possible for years to come. Roosevelt might even begin to wonder if it were ever coming. Did not commodity prices remain remarkably stable? Did this not indicate that no matter what happened in the stock market, the economy remained basically sound? And was not Herbert Hoover still "a wonder," as Roosevelt had called him in 1920, when, to Hoover's friend, diplomat Hugh Gibson, he had expressed the "wish we could make him President" because there "could not be a better one"? [34] More intelligent, immensely better informed, immensely more hardworking than Silent Cal, with a demonstrated genius for large-scale organization and administration, Hoover would doubtless prove equal to the challenges he would face if, as seemed more than likely, he won the Presidency. He might not be able to prevent the ultimate debacle, but he would at least postpone it.

In other words, once established in the White House, Hoover would probably remain there for eight years, in Roosevelt and Howe's opinion. Not until 1936 would the Presidency become a prize for which a Democrat could compete with much hope of success. It behooved Roosevelt, therefore, to postpone running for governor until 1932. He should devote his next four years to strengthening his legs as much as possible; to strengthening his personal organization within the party as much as possible; to enhancing his national prestige as a man dedicated to the general welfare, not merely to partisan advantage; and hence to the further development of that coalition among the voters at large, centered on himself, which would swell to a victorious majority when the conditions for it were right. Elected governor of New York in 1932, reelected in 1934, he would be ready to reach out for the White House two years later.

VIII

But though Roosevelt, by journeying to Warm Springs, had placed a thousand miles between his physical self and Rochester and emphasized by doing so his physical reason for refusing to run, he had by no means escaped further intense pressures upon him to accept the nomination. He had simply made these pressures somewhat more difficult to apply.

Four days before his departure for Georgia, an important meeting of some fourteen of New York's top democratic leaders was held in the Executive Mansion in Albany, with the governor presiding.[35] The state situation was discussed. It was taken for granted that Smith had to win New York's forty-five electoral votes if he were to win the Presidency. There was increasing, if unspoken, doubt that he could do so without the aid of a winning gubernatorial candidate. And all agreed that the strongest possible candidate would be Franklin Roosevelt. His name, however, was eliminated from consideration at the outset by Smith, who cited Roosevelt's need or wish to continue his health regimen for at least two more years.

Other names were then discussed.

One was Justice Townsend Scudder of the State Supreme Court; he was a prominent Mason, whose selection would give the lie to charges that Smith was a political tool of the church whom all good Masons were bound to oppose. Another was Colonel Herbert H. Lehman of Lehman Brothers (employers of Roosevelt's son-in-law), a political protégé of Belle Moskowitz's. He was one of the four multimillionaires handling the financial side of the national Democratic campaign under Raskob (the other three were James W. Gerard, Senator Peter G. Gerry, and Jesse Jones); he was greatly respected by all who knew him; and since, like Ottinger, he was a Jew, he would not only reduce religious opposition to Smith, but also remove the religious issue altogether from the gubernatorial race. A third name was Owen D. Young. A fourth, Senator Wagner. None of these proposals proved acceptable. Young was absolutely uninterested in running. So was Bob Wagner, who had four years still to go on his first term as U.S. Senator, was happy in that post, and, because of his foreign birth, could aspire to no higher office; Wagner's great dread, in fact, was that the party's desperate need would ultimately force him to run. Scudder's ability was everywhere recognized, but he had an aloof, forbidding manner which made him personally unpopular with many party politicians and would alienate voters. Lehman, though an unusually able administrator and though he had labor as well as business support in New York City, where he had successfully mediated labor-management disputes, was a novice in elective politics and virtually unknown upstate.[36]

Inevitably the conferees returned to Franklin Roosevelt. Was his a flat, total refusal or only a reluctance to run? Was the health factor truly decisive or only an excuse, a mask for other reasons which, exposed, might be overcome? Smith confessed he didn't know. Nor did any other in the room, not even Ed Flynn of the Bronx, who ever since the 1924 convention had had a warmer, closer personal relationship with Roosevelt than any of the others. So Smith, who was about to leave on a two-week Western speaking tour, delegated Flynn to communicate with Roosevelt, to probe Roosevelt's motives, to persuade Roosevelt to run if at all possible, and to report his findings to Smith directly and promptly by phone or telegram.

Flynn had some difficulty in carrying out this assignment. He learned that there was no phone in Roosevelt's cottage at Warm Springs. The only phone in the whole of the resort was in the Meriwether Inn. It was necessary to send a telegram to Roosevelt asking him to be at the inn phone at a certain time to take an important call, and when Flynn did get through to him, the initial conversation was, from Smith's standpoint, highly unsatisfactory. Roosevelt "was adamant in his refusal to run," the Bronx boss later recalled. Nevertheless, egged on by Smith, Flynn persisted. He was encouraged by the fact that Roosevelt did, after all, accept his calls in the following days when refusing them would have been easy, far easier physically than accepting them was. And when Roosevelt in "one of our conversations . . . spoke of the financial responsibilities he had assumed in establishing the Warm Springs Foundation" and of his felt need "to stay there [in Warm Springs] and manage the enterprise so that it eventually became a paying proposition," Flynn inferred that Roosevelt was significantly shifting ground, that a solution of the Warm Springs financial problem would make "the going . . . easy." He sensed (". . . I began to feel") that Roosevelt "was weakening in his opposition." [37]

Howe in New York City sensed this, too, or feared it, knowing Roosevelt as he did. He grew almost frantic with anxiety. All that the two of them had invested over the years in their quest for the White House—

the careful planning, the intricate tactical maneuvers, the endlessly patient effort—could so easily be lost, a futile sacrifice upon the sadly flawed altar of Smith's ambition, if Roosevelt did not now stand firm. Howe warned his friend that newsmen, interpreting his removal to Warm Springs as a bid for a draft, might say so under large headlines and thereby promote this dire eventuality. He urged Roosevelt to issue a public statement so emphatic, so unequivocal in its refusal of the candidacy that a draft would become impossible. "There is no answer to the health plea," he wired on September 25, "but any other reason will be overruled by the Governor himself." He followed this with a letter next day: "I do not believe your running will really induce anyone to vote for Al, but on the contrary some of your friends now voting for Al for your sake will vote for you and not for Al if you run. . . ." [38] He indicated that Eleanor was in thorough agreement with him in all this.

Was she?

To hard-pressing questions on her husband's "availability," put to her by Smith's inner circle, Eleanor returned soft, noncommittal answers. The decision was her husband's alone. She could not speak for him, would not presume to express an opinion of her own, on a matter of this nature. It had been agreed between them that she would never do so. She did indicate that so far as she knew, her husband's stated reasons for refusing to run were his real and only reasons. When Smith himself phoned her from Milwaukee just two days before the opening of the Rochester convention, she repeated these statements. She told Smith that she would not phone her husband, or write him, or make any other effort to influence him on this question, one way or the other. She suggested that Smith call him himself. [39]

The governor did so. He came hard against a mind now made up, it seemed, beyond any possibility of change. Roosevelt was again as adamant as he had been when Flynn first phoned him, and, as Howe had insisted he must do, he based this adamancy firmly upon the unanswerable "health plea." He was sorry he could not "even consider the possibility of running for Governor this year, especially if by doing so I could further help you," but he was convinced that Smith really did not need such help. ". . . your own record . . . is so clear to the voters that you will carry the State regardless of who is nominated for Governor and my nomination would make no difference to your success on the New York ticket." He himself, on the other hand, did need all the help that further exercise and treatment would give his legs. He was, after all, only forty-six years old; he had many active years ahead of him; he owed it to his family and himself "to give the present constant improvement a chance to continue," and his doctors were "very definite in stating that the continued improvement in my condition is dependent on my avoidance of cold climate and on taking exercises here at Warm Springs during the next two winters. . . ." Smith could and did argue his political need in contradiction of Roosevelt's assessment of it, but he could hardly argue against Roosevelt's statement of his own physical need. "Well," said the governor at last, "you're the doctor." And hung up.[40]

The next day, Sunday, September 30, Roosevelt wrote in a letter to his mother of the "difficult time" he had been having "turning down the Governorship," of the "letters and telegrams by the dozen" he had been receiving "begging me to save the situation by running." He could "only hope they don't try to stampede the Convention tomorrow and nominate me and then adjourn!" [41] He took steps to mitigate this danger. He dictated to Missy LeHand, who was as strongly averse to his running as Louis Howe was, a lengthy telegram to the governor "confirming my telephone message" and reiterating the arguments he had presented over the phone. This telegram should certainly give pause to any draft attempt, for if he were drafted and the wire were published, as it almost certainly would be, the draft would be made to seem a ruthlessly selfish exploitation of a crippled man, a sacrifice to Smith's ambition of Roosevelt's chance to walk again, and would thereby provide the opposition with deadly ammunition. But Roosevelt still remained uneasy about the convention. To double lock the door against unwanted opportunity, he arranged for the morrow a long afternoon of picnicking at the Knob, miles from the nearest phone, planning to return to his phoneless cottage barely in time to dress for the political speech he was to make that evening in Manchester, ten miles from Warm Springs. Thus he would be out of the reach of importuning messages from Rochester until after the convention had completed its slate-making.

Or so he hoped.

Smith was handed Roosevelt's telegram upon his arrival at Rochester's Hotel Seneca in the early morning of October 1; within an hour or so thereafter the gist of that wire was known to every interested person in town. Gloom and consternation ensued for all strongly committed to Smith's election; they were now more than ever convinced that a winning candidate for governor was essential to Smith's gaining of the state's electoral votes and that Roosevelt was the one man who, in a race against Ottinger, could win.

Smith, Raskob, Flynn, Lehman, Wagner, Tom Lynch—these were central figures of long, anguished meetings in a suite on the Seneca's fifth floor that day, meetings which absorbed the attention of every delegate and newsman. The actual formal convention was almost forgotten. Flynn presented to the other conferees his assessment of Roosevelt's situation, his expressed belief that the principal obstacle to Roosevelt's doing as they wished was his heavy financial commitment to the Warm Springs Foundation. Raskob promptly offered to remove this obstacle: he personally would underwrite the Warm Springs investment if Roosevelt consented to run. Eleanor was summoned for questioning. ". . . I wish I didn't have to go [to Rochester] for everyone makes me so uncomfortable," she had written her husband the day before. "They feel so strongly about your running and even good explanations can be made to sound foolish." (This last seems to indicate that she herself found the "good explanations" not wholly convincing, not utterly conclusive.) Nevertheless, she again loyally presented them and again firmly refused when Smith, Raskob, and Flynn joined in begging her to advise her husband to run. (Flynn gained from her manner, however, the distinct impression "that she was anxious that he should run, . . . that she would be happy if he would consent to it." Ernest K. Lindley, who covered the events of that day for the New York *World,* was later told by Eleanor herself that though she "knew how earnest . . . [Roosevelt] was in his refusal, . . . she thought . . . that if Smith should lose the Presidency by a few votes, or that if Smith should carry New York but the State Administration be lost, he would never forgive himself.") Raskob wanted to know if, in her judgment, it would change her husband's mind if he were relieved of all financial anxiety. She replied that she was sure it would not.[42]

So the conferees turned their attention to the evidently determinative health factor. The solution they proposed for this was akin in nature to the proposal Belle Moskowitz and Judge Proskauer had made when they asked Roosevelt to serve as Smith's nominal campaign manager prior to the 1924 convention. A certain contempt for him was at its heart—as if he were still to be regarded as handsome window dressing, a lightweight, showy but insubstantial. ("He will be a good candidate," said Robert Moses sourly, "but a lousy Governor." [43]) It was proposed that Lehman accept the nomination for lieutenant governor if Roosevelt ran. Admittedly, Lehman was too important and effective a person for what was normally a minor, largely ceremonial office, but in this case it was expected that his office would become executive: he would serve as a kind of assistant governor when Roosevelt was in Albany and as acting governor when Roosevelt went to Warm Springs to continue his treatments and exercises for months at a time. Lehman consented to this, though Howe had told them all emphatically that Roosevelt would never take an office he couldn't actively fill. Lehman also accepted the task of reaching Roosevelt by phone and explaining the situation to him.

This last assignment, of course, proved impossible through a long afternoon and evening. No one at Warm Springs could or would say where
Roosevelt might be. All efforts by phone operators to find him "somewhere in Georgia" failed. When he returned from the Knob to his cottage at dusk, he was told of the frantic efforts to get him on the phone.
He was handed a sheaf of telegrams, one of them from his daughter,
Anna, saying, "Go ahead and take it." (He replied to her next day,
"You ought to be spanked.") But his only manifested response to all this
was a boyish pleasure in having thus far won the game he was playing,
outwitting and discomfiting his opponents. Swiftly he bathed and
dressed for his evening engagement. He was driven to Manchester.
There he found to his dismay that the school auditorium where he was
to speak was three flights up. A prolonged physical ordeal that left him
panting for breath and drenched with perspiration was required for him
to reach the auditorium stage. And it was not until he sat upon that
stage awaiting his turn to speak that he was finally located, still inac-
cessible, by the now-desperate men of Rochester.

Obvious to them now was the fact that he had deliberately cut himself
off from communication with them. No doubt he would continue to do
so, would refuse any call they tried to put through to him.

But surely he would accept a person-to-person call from his wife!

Eleanor was again summoned to the Seneca's fifth-floor suite, where
Smith himself importuned her. Would she not please at least get her
husband on the phone for them? She needn't say a word to him beyond
"hello." All she had to do was get him on the line, hand the receiver to
one of them, and let them take it from there. Was that too much to ask
of a loyal Democrat who knew, as her husband could not possibly
know, precisely what the statewide situation was, as reflected here in
Rochester?

She must have hesitated long before answering. What they asked of
her was no neutral, noncommittal gesture; it was tantamount in the circumstances to an expression of conclusion on her part, a conclusion
that he should accept the nomination. He was bound to interpret it so.

But at last she said she would do as Smith wished.

Roosevelt took her call in a phone booth in a Manchester drugstore
after his speech in support of Smith's candidacy was ended. He was in
high spirits. "He told me with evident glee that he had been keeping out
of reach all day and would not have answered the telephone if I had not
been calling." [44] She broke in to say hurriedly that she must rush to
catch the midnight train to New York City (the Todhunter School

opened next morning). She had called because Governor Smith begged her to. Here was the governor. And handing Smith the phone, she rushed from the suite.

Not until the morrow would she learn through the newspapers what this conversation decided.

IX

He was too big a man to be so narrowly confined. He was most uncomfortably seated, his broad, thick shoulders wedged into a corner, his iron-braced legs rigidly extended through the phone booth door, as he heard through the receiver Al Smith's warm, loud, whiskey-voice saying, "Hello, Frank—" [45]

Then, providentially—or so it might and doubtless did seem to Franklin Roosevelt, who must have felt the need for more time in which to iron-brace his spirit against what would now be the maximum pressure Smith could bring against his resolve—providentially, the phone connection went bad. Though Smith seemed to hear Roosevelt clearly enough, the governor's voice came to Roosevelt as a meaningless roar. "It's no use, Al," he said at last. The phone operator suggested that he return to Warm Springs; she would put the call through to him there, at the inn.

He was unwontedly silent, withdrawn, as he was driven from Manchester back to the resort through the October night. All day, all through what he had believed would be the decisive hours in Rochester, he had acted in accordance with the conclusion he and Howe had reached. (If a sacrificial goat were needed, why not Wagner? Howe had asked in a wire Roosevelt had read shortly before taking Al Smith's call from Milwaukee. [46]) There was, however, a difference between Roosevelt's sense of ultimate realities, his way of dealing with them, and Louis Howe's. Louis, as Eleanor later said, "liked to feel that he dominated circumstances" and attempted therefore to "plan every move." Once he had finally made up his mind to a course of action he sealed it up with willpower; his purely personal will became thereafter the voice and arm of destiny, as befitted the "hero" and the "heroic" of Carlyle's conception. But Roosevelt was acutely aware that, as Eleanor also said, "one could not plan every move in this world, one had to accept circumstances as they developed." [47] It was a consequence of Roosevelt's religious faith, which was considerably stronger than Howe's—it was, in other words, a consequence of his sense of history as a drama conceived in the mind of God—that a measure of tentativeness was at the heart of his every decision.* And this difference between the two men now manifested itself. Howe in New York stubbornly refused to admit that unforeseen factors might indicate the wisdom of revising the design he and Roosevelt had made upon the future, whereas Roosevelt in Georgia that night was making precisely this admission, albeit with extreme reluctance. He gazed out into a darkness that was unrelieved by the light of any cabin, any house (all good countrymen had been long abed). He searched the night in vain for some visible sign. And so he was forced to turn inward—felt driven to admit that the matter he had thought settled once and for all in his mind had become again unsettled to the extent, at least, of requiring a reexamination of it in the light of new circumstances.

Of these new circumstances, a principal one, as she surmised it would be, was Eleanor's having permitted herself to become the agency through which the immediate and ultimate pressure was brought to bear upon him. Clearly this meant that she no longer stood, if she ever really had, on Howe's side of the question. What else did it mean? Having balanced her estimate of his chance to walk again against her estimate of the party's need, she must have concluded that the latter outweighed the former, and since Duty, the concept of Service, loomed large in all her calculations, she must believe that Duty, if the health factor were eliminated, required his acceptance of the nomination. Was she then truly, as she evidently believed, the agent of a larger purpose, perhaps even a divine one? Was her phone call a signal from a Providence which focused on him at that moment a concentrated attention? Was Providence now presenting him with a fateful cue, the most important in all the drama of his public life thus far?

Missy LeHand, sitting beside him, was respectful of his wish and need for silence all the way from Manchester, but she broke her silence as the car turned off the highway into the drive toward the inn.

"You're still not going to take it, are you?" she asked, anxiously.

And he said no, he was *not* going to take it.

"Don't you dare let them talk you into it!" she said fiercely.

No doubt she fervently hoped, probably they both hoped, that the phone connection to the inn would be as bad as the drugstore connection had been. It often was between New York and Warm Springs.

* Paradoxically, this tentativeness often served to increase rather than reduce his capacity for decision. It enabled him to avoid post-decision anxieties, thereby removing from him the inhibiting anticipatory dread of such anxieties. "Once you have made a decision, there's no use worrying about whether you were right or wrong," he said to one of his closest associates.[48] "Events will soon prove whether you were right or wrong, and if there is still time you can change your decision." The operative words here are "if there is still time." He believed that there would be, for the event was in the hand of God.

But this time (another sign?) the connection was perfect.

Beside the open window, looking out blindly into the soft-breathing night, Roosevelt heard first "clear as a bell" Raskob's "quiet voice" pleading the great need of the national party, begging him to run as an indispensable service to the national party, dismissing with a "damn the Foundation" his argument of moral and financial obligation to Warm Springs (Raskob said to Roosevelt, as he had to Smith, that he personally would "take care of it," underwriting Roosevelt's foundation investment). Then came Al Smith's loud voice saying that he, Roosevelt, need only "accept the nomination, . . . make a couple of radio speeches," be elected, then return to Warm Springs for a couple of months. He need come to Albany for only as long as required to "get your thirty days' bills out," going back then to Warm Springs for the summer. Roosevelt snorted. "Don't hand me that baloney," he said, to the delight of watching, listening Missy. ("Don't you dare!" Missy kept saying to him whenever, during this long conversation, he seemed to be weakening.) But it *wasn't* "baloney," Smith insisted. Herb Lehman had agreed to take the lieutenant governorship if Roosevelt ran, and Lehman, as Roosevelt well knew, was fully equipped to function as the state's top administrator whenever and for as long as Roosevelt wished to be absent from the state. Lehman himself then came on to say why he was willing to take this nomination—it was solely because the need for Roosevelt to head the state ticket was so desperate—and to promise to do everything he could to make possible Roosevelt's uninterrupted quest for full recovery of his legs. But when Smith came back on, Roosevelt still said "No!"— and perhaps more firmly than he would have done if the arrangement with Lehman had not been made. "Frank," said Smith at last, his tone now wholly pleading, "I told you I wasn't going to put this on a personal basis, but I've got to." The margin between victory and defeat for him in the national race might well be provided by a victorious Democratic gubernatorial candidate in New York, and it was a margin that Roosevelt and Roosevelt alone could assure. This fact could not be removed by Roosevelt's assertion that it wasn't so.

Perhaps now sensing a certain hesitancy in Roosevelt's responses ("Don't you *dare!*" cried Missy, more fervently than before), Smith hurried on to his final clinching maneuver.

"I have just one more question," he said. "If those fellows nominate you tomorrow and then adjourn, will you accept the nomination?"

Roosevelt's hesitancy was now palpable.

He had of course anticipated this question—his letter of yesterday to his mother indicated as much—and during the ride back from Manchester he must have evolved the strategy for dealing with it which he now employed, a strategy profoundly expressive of his psychology, his ultimate living faith.

Raskob's financial offer* and Lehman's offer of service had forced him to subtract something from the weight of his own side of the argument, though he had continued to say no as forcefully as he could, and to reiterate his reasons for saying it as forcefully as he could. Smith's placing of the matter on a basis of direct personal appeal forced him to subtract a great deal more: it clearly signaled the danger that, if he refused to help Smith now, he would lose the support of the Smith camp for his own bid for power when he made it later on, at his own convenience.

At this point, as he had anticipated, the oppositions were so closely balanced in the scale of final judgment that he could make no clear, definitely logical choice between them. Purely willful and capricious, therefore, would have been that flat yes or no which Smith's question explicitly demanded, and Roosevelt declined to make such answer. Instead he said at last, slowly, that he could not sanction the presentation of his name to the convention. But if this were done without his permission and if the delegates in full knowledge of his personal situation and wishes then nominated him, he couldn't say right now *what* he would do. He didn't know.[49]

Smith's reply was an exultant roar.

"I won't ask any more questions!" he cried.

Roosevelt, replacing the receiver on its hook, turned toward Missy's stricken countenance a face that was calm, abstracted. If he showed slight signs of regret and rueful resignation, of grim determination joined to an awakening zest for battle, he showed none at all of angry dismay.

He felt no dismay.

His decision had been, in form, a reluctant and passive yielding to the will of others—he thereby deferred, he felt, to a Higher Power—but its effect and felt essence were the same as if he thrust himself across his Rubicon with the boldness of Julius Caesar. The die was cast. He who had been standing upon a shore of safety stood now upon a shore of danger, committed to combat and cut off from every path of retreat by a narrow but very deep, swift flood of Time. He could only advance toward glory or disaster.

It is unlikely, however, that the metaphor of the Rubicon occurred to

* Raskob during the next few years gave something over $100,000 outright to the Warm Springs Foundation after Roosevelt had refused, with thanks, Raskob's proffered loan of $250,000.

him in that moment. More likely, for him as for Louis Howe, once Howe had adjusted his mind to the event, was the metaphor of the theater. Certainly the latter metaphor was the one they were both most inclined to apply, in a future time, to their remembrance of this October midnight in the forty-seventh year of Roosevelt's life, this decisive moment when he came to the end of his years of youthful plasticity and growth, of education in apprenticeship, the crucial years of bitter trial and testing. Heretofore he had been at best a minor figure in great historic scenes dominated by other actors. Often he had been mere spectator in the wings or orchestra when such scenes were played. Now destiny beckoned him to the very center of the stage.

Notes and Sources

--->>><<<---

The notes for the early chapters are fuller, including more commentary, than are notes for the later ones because I was dealing at the outset with materials that earlier biographers have paid relatively little attention to but which, for my purposes, were important. Later, going over ground long cultivated, I generally list sources simply by title and page. Full title and publication date citations are listed in the bibliography.

Prologue: HOUSES BESIDE A RIVER

1. M. W. Goodwin, *The Dutch and English on the Hudson*, pp. 46–47. Thomas A. Bailey, *The American Pageant*, p. 39.
2. Edward P. Cheyney, *The Anti-Rent Agitation in the State of New York, 1839–1846*. Carl Carmer, *The Hudson*, pp. 293–316.
3. Olin Dows, *Franklin D. Roosevelt at Hyde Park*, unnumbered front pages.
4. *Ibid.*, p. 10.
5. Nicholas Roosevelt, a second cousin of Franklin D. Roosevelt's paternal great-grandfather, made major contributions to the *Clermont*'s success—perhaps a greater contribution as inventor than did Robert Fulton. Born in 1767, dead in 1854, Nicholas was of all the Roosevelts the only one to manifest creative genius. See *Lost Chapter in the History of the Steamboat*, by John H. B. Latrobe; Richard Shelton Kirby, Sidney Withington, Arthur Burr Darling, Frederick Gridley Kilgour, *Engineering in History*, pp. 250–55; Allen Churchill, *The Roosevelts: American Aristocrats*, pp. 74–82; Karl Schriftgiesser, *The Amazing Roosevelt Family, 1613–1942*, pp. 125–32.

One: THE HOUSE AT CRUM ELBOW

1. Clara and Hardy Steeholm, *The House at Hyde Park*. Olin Dows, *Franklin D. Roosevelt at Hyde Park*.
2. Karl Schriftgiesser, *The Amazing Roosevelt Family, 1613–1942*, pp. 180–81.
3. Allen Churchill, *The Roosevelts: American Aristocrats*, pp. 3–15. Cuyler Reynolds, J. Collins, D. Dumpelly, John W. Jordan, *Annals of American Families*, p. 17. The latter source states flatly that Claes had married Jannetjke in Holland, before coming to New Amsterdam, but later students of the Roosevelt genealogy are uncertain of where the marriage took place. No official record of the marriage ceremony has been found.

4. Churchill, *op. cit.;* Schriftgiesser, *op. cit.;* Bellamy Partridge, *The Roosevelt Family in America;* Alvin Page Johnson, *Franklin D. Roosevelt's Colonial Ancestors;* Franklin D. Roosevelt, "The Roosevelt Family in New Amsterdam Before the Revolution," a 1901 manuscript.

5. Though Isaac Roosevelt was certainly the "most distinguished" Roosevelt in terms of fame and honor among his contemporaries, he is not included in the *Dictionary of American Biography.* His cousin Nicholas Roosevelt, the inventor, *is* included.

6. Johnson, *op. cit.,* pp. 26–27, says that Martinus Hoffman was born at Revel on the southern shore of the Gulf of Finland about 1625 and suggests that Martinus' father had been an officer in the army of Gustavus Adolphus and had settled in Revel after the Swedes conquered it. Martinus himself was of a "military nature," writes Johnson.

7. Notably Frank Freidel, *Franklin D. Roosevelt: The Apprenticeship,* p. 7.

8. Johnson, *op. cit.,* p. 29, says that New York had applied to the Continental Congress for a loan of 45,000 pounds and had been refused, whereupon Isaac Roosevelt was ordered to obtain an emission of paper money as soon as possible. The committee's order was confirmed by official act of the House of the Provincial Congress on May 5, 1776.

9. Schriftgiesser, *op. cit.,* p. 117.

10. The portrait now hangs in the living room of the Roosevelt house at Hyde Park. The New York Chamber of Commerce *Record* is quoted in *Annals of American Families,* p. 29: "In 1784, Mr. [Isaac] Roosevelt resumed his business of sugar refining, in partnership with his son, under the firm name of Isaac Roosevelt and Son. Mr. Roosevelt continued president of the Bank until 1791, when he retired and was succeeded by Gulian Verplanck. He was the fourth President of the Society of the New York Hospital, 1790–94. He died, 1794, aged 68, beloved and honored as a tried, true and constant patriot."

11. When the Revolution began, Abram (or Abraham) Walton was as ardent a Whig and patriot as Isaac Roosevelt, but when the British occupied New York, he, like most wealthy city merchants, took an oath of allegiance to the king and was pardoned by the British for his former "treason." After the war, A. Walton, again like most other wealthy New York merchants, was permitted to resume full property rights in all he had formerly owned and was pardoned for his Tory allegiance. See Johnson, *op. cit.,* section headed "The Waltons."

12. Churchill, *op. cit.,* p. 85.

13. Though the portraits of James I and Dr. Isaac are as expertly done as Stuart's of Isaac the Patriot, their painters are now unknown.

14. A. A. Aspinwall, *The Aspinwall Genealogy;* Schriftgiesser, *op. cit.,* p. 182.

15. Steeholm, *op. cit.,* p. 39.

16. Schriftgiesser, *op. cit.,* pp. 184–86. Schriftgiesser opines that Dr. Isaac was "undoubtedly . . . a frequent guest at University Place and at Tarrytown [this is an error; the Aspinwall estate was at Barrytown], and it is also quite likely that he entrusted W. H. [Aspinwall] with his and Rebecca's investments." The quotes are from p. 186 of *op. cit.*

17. Philip Hone, *The Diary of Philip Hone, 1828–1851,* Entry for February 17, 1846. Vol. 2, p. 270.

18. Steeholm, *op. cit.,* pp. 39–40. "Rosedale stood darkly in trees, with wide verandas somberly shaded," write the Steeholms. And indeed this almost funereal atmosphere still enshrouds the place. During my first visit in November, 1967, I was shown a secret cellar, cement-walled, on the river-facing side of the house which, the present owners told me, had been discovered by a plumber working in Rosedale's basement a dozen years before. Historical research had indicated (I was told) that this hiding place had been a station on that well-organized but necessarily highly secret Underground Railroad along which fugitive slaves had been helped from the South into Canada in the 1830's, 1840's, and 1850's. Whether or not Dr. Isaac was thus involved in history I have been unable to determine. No later Roosevelt said or wrote anything about it, despite the family's concern with its own history, but this, of itself alone, proves nothing. On the evidence, Dr. Isaac's peculiar psychology would have enabled him to engage in the alleged activity without ever saying a word about it to anyone.

19. Steeholm, *op. cit.,* p. 46.

20. *Ibid.,* pp. 41–42.

21. Miscellaneous papers of Isaac Roosevelt: holograph letters of which typewritten copies have been made, to James Roosevelt from his father, about 1842–49. Franklin D. Roosevelt Library.

22. Nott was a man of great energy and versatility—an inventor who held many patents for stoves, an ordained Presbyterian minister, a professor of moral philosophy, and an innovative college president who pioneered in the addition of technical and scientific courses to college curricula. He was also a leading temperance advocate. He was president of Union College from 1804 to 1866. See biographical sketch in *Who Was Who in America,* the *Dictionary of American Biography,* and Steeholm, *op. cit.,* pp. 43–44.

23. Steeholm, *op. cit.,* says on page 45 that "James finished his studies in the spring of the term of 1847, although the college records show that he did not receive his degree until 1848." But James himself recorded in a pencil-written and undated "Summary of My Life" now in the Franklin D. Roosevelt Library that he was "graduated from Union in July, 1847, and went abroad in autumn of that year."

24. Elliott Roosevelt, ed., *F.D.R., His Personal Letters, 1928–1945,* Vol. II, p. 1224.

25. Steeholm, *op. cit.,* pp. 54–55, say that a "search of the roster of commissioners and agents" of the commission "has failed to reveal his [James'] name" and that it "would have been more than likely that James Roosevelt, with his ever surer finger on the pulse of the nation's railroads, made his contribution to the cause . . . by assisting the government with the transportation problems." This, say the Steeholms, "would appear to be a reasonable surmise."

26. Charles E. Beachley, *History of the Consolidation Coal Company, 1864–1934.* Cited by Freidel, *op. cit.,* pp. 9–10.

27. George H. Burgess and Miles C. Kennedy, *Centennial History of the*

Pennsylvania Railroad Company, 1846–1946, pp. 279, 280, 357. Stuart Daggett, *Railroad Organization,* pp. 145–48. Cited by Freidel, *op. cit.,* p. 10.

28. Anonymous, *A Century of Progress: History of the Delaware and Hudson Company, 1823–1923.* On the flyleaf of this volume in the Franklin D. Roosevelt Library is the handwritten statement "My father, James Roosevelt, was for 25 years a director of the D&H and was for many years also the Vice President; and the President of the Champlain Transportation Co., and the Lake George Steamboat Co." It is signed "Franklin D. Roosevelt, 1925." The volume contains a short history of the Champlain company and of the Lake George company, acquired by D&H in 1871, but no mention is made of James Roosevelt's activities. He is listed as a manager of D&H from April 7, 1875, to December 8, 1900. John L. Aspinwall had been a manager from March 26, 1861, to May 12, 1868.

29. Freidel, *op. cit.,* pp. 12–13, speaks of James Roosevelt's speculative ventures into bituminous coal and Southern railways as "peripheral," adding that the "main thread of his business career involved no such spectacular efforts." Freidel opines that James Roosevelt "may have engaged in speculative ventures more in the spirit of a tremendous poker game than with any real hope of building a towering fortune."

30. Schriftgiesser, *op. cit.,* pp. 188–90. Steeholm, *op. cit.,* pp. 55–56.

31. One of his racing horses was Gloucester, the first to trot a mile in under two minutes twenty seconds. Leland Stanford of California bought the horse after its record-breaking performance; it was killed in a train wreck while en route to Stanford's estate. Its tail adorned the wall of Franklin D. Roosevelt's bedroom in the White House in the 1930's. See Schriftgiesser, *op. cit.,* p. 190 (he spells the name "Gloster") and Frances Perkins, *The Roosevelt I Knew,* pp. 66–67.

32. Steeholm, *op. cit.,* pp. 59–61. Minutes of meetings of the Dutchess County Board of Supervisors, 1871–72.

33. Among the miscellaneous papers of James Roosevelt, in the Roosevelt Library at Hyde Park, is a deed for cemetery lots No. 43, 44, 45, and 46 in St. James Church cemetery, to James Roosevelt, for $560, dated September 15, 1876—some two weeks after his first wife's burial. The deed is countersigned by him as clerk of the vestry.

34. Churchill, *op. cit.,* p. 129, Steeholm, *op. cit,* pp. 62–63. Harvey O'Connor, *The Astors,* pp. 211–12.

35. Steen Valetje, a town house in Colonade Row in Lafayette Place (New York City), and a $200,000 trust fund were wedding gifts of Laura's father, William Backhouse Astor, when the marriage took place in 1844. When Laura's father died in 1877, he left his daughter some $1,100,000 in cash and property. See O'Connor, *op. cit.,* pp. 74, 119.

36. Rita Halle Kleeman, *Gracious Lady: The Life of Sara Delano Roosevelt,* p. 83.

37. Steeholm, *op. cit.,* p. 36.

38. *Ibid.,* pp. 63–64.

39. Freidel, *op. cit.*, p. 5, based on personal interview with Mrs. Eleanor Roosevelt, May 1, 1948. James Roosevelt, with Sidney Shalett, *Affectionately, FDR,* p. 17.

40. Daniel W. Delano, Jr., *Franklin Roosevelt and the Delano Influence,* is the principal source of Delano genealogical information. The quote is from his p. 31.

41. According to Delano, *op. cit.*, Philippe "hunted and soldiered" for a decade after Priscilla refused him and did not seek admission to the Pilgrim community until 1633. His marriage, says Delano, broke an 800-year-old tradition during which the family "had not permitted their Norman-Flemish blood to be diluted by any alien strain." Through Hester Dewsbury, the bloodstream of Anglo-Saxon yeoman flowed into the Delano line. The ship on which Philippe came to America was the *Fortune,* which entered Plymouth Harbor on November 11, 1621, precisely one year after the signing of the Mayflower Compact.

42. Schriftgiesser, *op. cit.*, pp. 55–56.

43. Mrs. Susan Lesley, *Memoir of the Life of Mrs. Anne Jean Lyman,* is a principal source of information about the Robbins and Lyman families. On p. 438 a letter from Mrs. Lyman to her son Edward, dated Northampton, Massachusetts, October 13, 1843, is quoted: "I can hardly express to you my joy that you have found in Mr. Delano a friend that pleases you so much. We have from the first been delighted with him. He has such a composed and dignified air for a man of business . . . ; and then his warm-hearted promptings of every sort of kindness to every one he comes in contact with, where friendship is admissable, so necessarily prompts one to a reciprocation of the feeling he has expressed, that there can be nothing but pleasure in his society. . . ."

44. Mrs. James Roosevelt, as told to Isabel Leighton and Gabrielle Forbush, *My Boy Franklin,* p. 9.

45. Quoted by Kleeman, *op. cit.*, pp. 34–35.

46. Delano, *op. cit.*, tells of the opium trade defensively. When the book was published, it prompted a virulent column by FDR-hating Westbrook Pegler, who charged Warren Delano with "opium smuggling." Steeholm, *op. cit.*, bases its account of the trade on Delano's book and defends it, but adds: ". . . his opium associations were not very frequently spoken of by the family, probably because the very word had an unpleasant connotation." Kleeman, significantly, in her otherwise detailed biography of Sara (*op. cit.*), doesn't mention the opium trade at all.

47. The *World*'s account appeared on October, 1880. It and the account in the New York *Times* were used by the Steeholms in their detailed story of the wedding, *op. cit.*, pp. 66–68.

48. Kleeman, *op. cit.*, p. 104.

Two: A SON IS BORN

1. Rita Halle Kleeman, *Gracious Lady: The Life of Sara Delano Roosevelt,* pp. 109–10. Clara and Hardy Steeholm, *The House at Hyde Park,* pp. 69–72.

2. Steeholm, *op. cit.*, p. 72.

3. *Ibid*, p. 73. Steeholm obviously derives from Kleeman, *op. cit.*, pp. 110–20, which describes the long honeymoon in considerable detail, Kleeman having been given access to Mrs. Sara Delano Roosevelt's personal diary.

4. Kleeman, *op. cit.*, p. 118. Steeholm, *op. cit.*, p. 75.

5. Newspaper clipping, source unknown, dated simply 1888, in Sara Delano Roosevelt's scrapbook, quoted by Steeholm, *op. cit.*, p. 96. The newspaper reporter spoke of "the home of James Roosevelt, who dwells there in quiet happiness with his wife, a most estimable lady celebrated in both Europe and America, for her loveliness and goodness" and of "the grand residence of Archie Rogers—the stables cost $48,000 and the coachman's house $18,000."

6. The *Icicle* is now on display, with a legend recounting its history, along with newspaper stories and other material on iceboat racing on the Hudson, in the basement of the Franklin D. Roosevelt Library Museum.

7. This sleigh is also on display in the FDR Library basement.

8. New York *Times*, January 27, 28, 29, 30, 31, 1882, was source of information about current events and weather.

9. Steeholm, *op. cit.*, p. 81.

10. Mrs. James Roosevelt as told to Isabel Leighton and Gabrielle Forbush, *My Boy Franklin*, says, p. 12, ". . . I was given too much chloroform, and it was nearly fatal to us both. As a matter of fact, the nurse said she never expected the baby to be alive and was surprised to find that it was." Rudolph Marx, M.D., *The Health of the Presidents*, p. 353, describing the birth, writes: "Apparently the most primitive and efficient method of resuscitation was used on the infant: mouth-to-mouth breathing. After minutes—an eternity—the air, rhythmically blown in and sucked out, expanded the collapsed lungs, cleared the narcotized respiratory center of the brain, and awakened the newborn infant. He heralded his entrance into the world with a cry of anger and bewilderment."

11. The scribbled message is displayed in the museum of the Franklin D. Roosevelt Library.

12. Kleeman, *op. cit.*, p. 127.

13. Mrs. James Roosevelt, *op. cit.*, pp. 12–13.

14. James Roosevelt, with Sidney Shalett, *Affectionately, F.D.R.; A Son's Story of a Lonely Man*, p. 34.

15. Kleeman, *op. cit.*, p. 129, gives facsimile reproduction of the diary entry for Sunday, March 19, 1882, in which the naming of the child is described. It is quoted by Frank Freidel, *Franklin D. Roosevelt: The Apprenticeship*, p. 20.

16. Kleeman, *op. cit.*, p. 126. The first of the two direct quotes is Kleeman's paraphrase of what Elliott wrote; the second is her direct quote of his acceptance letter.

17. Kleeman, *op. cit.*, p. 137. Mrs. James Roosevelt, *op. cit.*, p. 18.

18. Anonymous, *Campobello Island*, a pamphlet published by Campobello Island Board of Trade, 1966 edition. Betty E. Barber, *A Guide Book to FDR's "Beloved Island,"* a pamphlet published by the Hammer Library for Regional Research, Vicksburg, Miss., 1962.

19. Steeholm, *op. cit.*, pp. 85–86. Kleeman, *op. cit.*, pp. 137–38 and p. 193.

20. Frank Davis Ashburn, *Fifty Years On: Groton School, 1884–1934*, pp. 7–16. Also the same author's *Peabody of Groton.*

21. Ashburn's *Fifty Years On* prints the original announcement of the school in full on p. 17.

22. Steeholm, *op. cit.*, pp. 88–89. Kleeman, *op. cit.*, p. 140.

23. Kleeman, *op. cit.*, pp. 152–53, quoting Mrs. Roosevelt directly.

24. Mrs. James Roosevelt, *op. cit.*, p. 11.

25. Steeholm, *op. cit.*, p. 97. Kleeman, *op. cit.*, pp. 153–55. Ismay was the J. Bruce Ismay who, as president and managing director of the White Star Line, sailed on the maiden voyage of the *Titanic* in 1912, behaved disgracefully aboard the sinking ship, and then saved himself (he was one of the few male passengers who did) by entering a lifeboat. The public opprobrium he thus earned forced his retirement from his office, and he died a virtual recluse in 1937. See Walter Lord, *A Night To Remember.*

26. Kleeman, *op. cit.*, p. 156, says Sir Cameron Gull taught Franklin to swim. Roosevelt and Shalett, *op. cit.*, pp. 47–48, tell how FDR taught his children to swim in a pond on the Archibald Rogers estate, describing the use of rope and pole. "It was really a wretched way to teach anyone to swim," writes James Roosevelt, "but it was the way Father had learned and—traditionalist that he was—it was the way he was going to teach us."

27. Steeholm, *op. cit.*, pp. 94–95. Kleeman, *op. cit.*, pp. 144–45.

28. Kleeman, *op. cit.*, p. 146.

29. Steeholm, *op. cit.*, p. 101.

30. Freidel, *op. cit.*, pp. 32–33, quoting FDR address, Chicago, October 2, 1932.

31. Kleeman, *op. cit.*, p. 147.

Three: BOYHOOD OF A PATRICIAN

1. Mrs. James Roosevelt, as told to Isabelle Leighton and Gabrielle Forbush, *My Boy Franklin*, p. 29.

2. *Ibid.*, p. 4.

3. *Ibid.*, p. 18.

4. *Ibid.*, p. 19.

5. *Ibid.*, pp. 5–6.

6. Elliott Roosevelt, ed., *F.D.R., His Personal Letters: Early Years*, p. 16.

7. Rita Halle Kleeman, *Gracious Lady*, pp. 188–89.

8. Mrs. James Roosevelt, *op. cit.*, p. 32.

9. Mrs. James Roosevelt, *op. cit.*, pp. 31–32. Note on FDR's dogs, prepared by staff of Franklin D. Roosevelt Library.

10. Mrs. James Roosevelt, *op. cit.*, p. 15.

11. Elliott Roosevelt, *op. cit.*, p. 6. The drawings are reproduced on the second and third pages of the illustrations in this book.

12. Franklin D. Roosevelt, Introduction to *Whaleships of New Bedford*, by Clifford W. Ashley, pp. iv. and v.

13. Elliott Roosevelt, *op. cit.*, p. 18.

14. Mrs. James Roosevelt, *op. cit.*, p. 26.

15. Elliott Roosevelt, *op. cit.*, p. 13.

16. Mrs. James Roosevelt, *op. cit.*, pp. 23–25. Kleeman, *op. cit.*, p. 160, identifies the discharged governess as a Miss Gerver and says it was her "Complacent competence" that Sara Roosevelt couldn't bear. "I do not believe I can stand her or that she is suitable," wrote Sara in her diary, quoted by Kleeman.

17. Constance Drexel, "Unpublished Letters of F.D.R. to His French Governess," *Parents Magazine*, XXVI (September, 1951), pp. 30–31, 80–84. Mlle. Sandoz was a paternal aunt of Mari Sandoz, the Nebraska author whose most famous work, *Old Jules*, is a wonderfully vivid biographical portrait of her father, Jeanne's brother.

18. Franklin D. Roosevelt Library, FDR Group 14, Box 1. School Records, Tutorial Papers, 1891–95.

19. Drexel, *op. cit.*, p. 30.

20. Franklin D. Roosevelt Library. FDR Group 14, Box 2.

21. *Ibid.*

22. Drexel, *op. cit.*, p. 30.

23. Elliott Roosevelt, *op. cit.*, p. 20. Kleeman, *op. cit.* pp. 160–62. Freidel, *op. cit.*, p. 33, identifies the German schoolmaster, in a footnote, as Christian Bommersheim, citing the New York *Times* of January 17, 1933, as source for the quote I use. Ernest K. Lindley, *Franklin D. Roosevelt*, p. 50, speaks of FDR's interest in the map reading and military topography taught at Bad Nauheim, and Freidel, *op. cit.*, p. 34, tells of FDR's citing this decades later, Freidel's source being an interview with Eleanor Roosevelt, May 1, 1948.

24. Drexel, *op. cit.*, p. 31.

25. *Ibid.*, p. 83. Kleeman, *op. cit.*, pp. 187–88.

26. FDR announced in a letter to "Aunt Doe" on April 10, 1891, that he had "begun to make a collection." Elliott Roosevelt, *op. cit.*, p. 18. Kleeman, *op. cit.*, p. 177.

27. Franklin D. Roosevelt Library. Group 14, Box 2.

28. Mrs. James Roosevelt, *op. cit.*, p. 16.

29. Letter from Marion B. Carr, keeper of memorabilia, American Museum of Natural History, New York, February 28, 1968, to George F. Mason, author and naturalist, Princeton, Massachusetts. Of the ten study skins, "two have disappeared—no one knows where—but our Bird Department still has eight skins," writes Mr. Carr.

30. Mrs. James Roosevelt, *op. cit.*, pp. 17–18. The house was that of Cecil G. S. Foljambe, a Liberal MP, according to Freidel, *op. cit.*, p. 27.

31. Freidel, *op. cit.*, pp. 27–28.

32. Lindley, *op. cit.*, pp. 50–51. This was the earliest publication of the story, obtained by direct conversation with FDR; it has since been retold in many books.

33. Kleeman, *op. cit.*, pp. 192–93.

34. *Ibid.*, p. 193.

35. Rexford G. Tugwell, *The Democratic Roosevelt,* seems to me especially insightful and convincing in his analysis of FDR's psychological development. See especially his pp. 29–30.

36. From opening sentences of F. Scott Fitzgerald's famous short story "The Rich Boy."

37. Kleeman, *op. cit.,* p. 190.

38. *Ibid.,* p. 189.

39. Mrs. James Roosevelt, *op. cit.,* pp. 15–16.

40. Kleeman, *op. cit.,* p. 192.

41. *Ibid.,* p. 191.

Four: THE GREAT WORLD AND GROTON

1. Frank Freidel, *Franklin D. Roosevelt: The Apprenticeship,* p. 36.

2. Henry Adams, *The Education of Henry Adams,* p. 469.

3. The translated edition was entitled *A Political History of Europe Since 1814.* The quotation of MacVane, which follows, is from his preface to this work, p. iii.

4. All direct quotations of Charles Seignobos are from *ibid.,* Chapter XXII, entitled "Transformations of the Material Conditions of Political Life."

5. Charles Carlisle Taylor, *The Life of Admiral Mahan,* p. 131. Quoted by Barbara W. Tuchman, *The Proud Tower,* p. 151.

6. Freidel, *op. cit.,* pp. 10–11. Freidel's sources were Nicaragua Canal Construction Company, *The Inter-Oceanic Canal of Nicaragua . . .* and Maritime Canal Company of Nicaragua, *The Nicaragua Canal.*

7. Ray Ginger, *The Bending Cross: A Biography of Eugene Debs,* p. 191. Louis W. Koenig, *Bryan,* p. 235.

8. Elliott Roosevelt, ed., *F.D.R., His Personal Letters: Early Years,* pp. 35, 37, 38, 40.

9. *Ibid.,* p. 30. Freidel, *op. cit.,* pp. 42–43, speaks of Franklin's accent, as mentioned in following sentences.

10. Franklin D. Roosevelt Library, FDR Group 14, School Records, Groton, 1896–1900.

11. Elliott Roosevelt, *op. cit.,* p. 42.

12. Interviews with the Reverend Philemon Sturges and Miss Marjorie Peabody, Princeton, Massachusetts, and Groton, Massachusetts, May, 1968.

13. George Biddle, "As I Remember Groton School, A Chapter of Autobiography, 1898–1904," *Harper's Magazine* (August, 1939), pp. 292–300.

14. Interview with the Reverend Philemon Sturges, Princeton, Massachusetts, May, 1968.

15. Biddle, *op. cit.,* quotes the Harriman letter, since quoted many times by Arthur M. Schlesinger, Jr., James MacGregor Burns, Freidel, etc.

16. *Ibid.*

17. Frank Davis Ashburn, *Fifty Years On: Groton School, 1884–1934,* p. 71.

18. *Ibid.,* pp. 72–73. Frank Davis Ashburn, *Peabody of Groton,* pp. 112–13.

19. Ashburn, *Fifty Years On,* pp. 74–77.

20. Elliott Roosevelt, *op. cit.,* p. 130.

21. *Ibid.,* p. 44.

22. *Ibid.,* p. 97.

23. *Ibid.,* pp. 40, 58, 60.

24. Biddle, *op. cit.*

25. New York *Times,* June 3, 1934. Quoted by Freidel, *op. cit.,* p. 35.

26. Ashburn, *Peabody,* p. 80.

27. *Ibid.,* p. 251.

28. *Ibid.,* p. 41.

29. Elliott Roosevelt, ed., *F.D.R., His Personal Letters, 1928–1945,* Vol. I, p. 522.

30. Ashburn, *Peabody,* p. 347.

31. Elliott Roosevelt, *Early Years,* p. 51.

32. Franklin D. Roosevelt Library. FDR, Group 14, Groton School Papers, 1896–1900.

33. Elliott Roosevelt, *Early Years,* pp. 78–79.

34. *Ibid.,* p. 78.

35. *Ibid.,* p. 82.

36. *Ibid.,* pp. 93, 96, 97.

37. *Ibid.,* p. 110, for Theodore Roosevelt talk. For quote from Sherrard Billings, Henry F. Pringle, *Theodore Roosevelt,* p. 33, derived from Roosevelt Memorial Association papers.

38. Elliott Roosevelt, *Early Years,* pp. 105, 112, 115.

39. *Ibid.,* pp. 122, 125, 210, 297, 298. In the FDR Library is an "Anthropometric Chart" for Franklin dated April 28, 1899, comparing him at ages 16.8 and 17.3 years.

40. Elliott Roosevelt, *Early Years,* p. 393.

41. *Ibid.,* pp. 184, 185, 186.

42. *Ibid.,* pp. 130, 131.

43. *Ibid.,* pp. 407–8.

44. *Ibid.,* p. 34.

45. *Ibid.,* pp. 242, 365, 368.

46. *Ibid.,* pp. 212, 213, 396, 387, 398.

47. *Ibid.,* pp. 253, 254.

48. *Ibid.,* p. 159.

49. *Ibid.,* pp. 160–65.

50. *Ibid.,* pp. 358, 378.

51. *Ibid.,* p. 378. The quotes on Professor Morse are from pp. 308, 310.

52. *Ibid.,* pp. 204–5. Ernest K. Lindley, *Franklin D. Roosevelt,* p. 52. Mrs. James Roosevelt, *My Boy Franklin,* pp. 42–46. (Mrs. James Roosevelt, strangely enough, identifies the disease as "old-fashioned measles.") Freidel, *op. cit.,* p. 48.

53. Elliott Roosevelt, *Early Years,* p. 136.

54. *Ibid.,* p. 401.

55. *Ibid.,* pp. 374, 375, 376, 384.

56. *Ibid.*, pp. 385, 387. Copies of the playbill and of tickets to the play are in Franklin D. Roosevelt Library, with copies of the Groton paper reviewing the performance.

57. *Ibid.*, p. 371.

58. *Ibid.*, p. 413. Ashburn, *Peabody*, 341.

Five: HARVARD

1. Elliott Roosevelt, ed., *F.D.R., His Personal Letters: Early Years*, pp. 423, 425, 426. The quotations which follow are in a copy of the printed booklet *The Consecration of St. John's Chapel, Groton School* (October, 1900), now in Franklin D. Roosevelt Library.

2. George Santayana, *Harvard Monthly*, 1892. Quoted by Samuel Eliot Morison, *Three Centuries of Harvard, 1639–1936*, p. 484.

3. George Santayana, *The Middle Span*, Vol. II, *Persons and Places*, p. 175.

4. Quoted by John Corbin, *Which College for Your Boy?* (Boston, 1908), p. 41. This (considering its title) is a surprisingly acute analysis of "Leading Types in American Education" made by a conservative mind and had its influence on my view of Eliot and Eliot's Harvard in the early 1900's.

5. The quotes are from *ibid.*, pp. 48 and 76.

6. Morison, *op. cit.*, pp. 104–5. Cleveland Amory, *The Proper Bostonians*, p. 295.

7. Amory, *op. cit.*, p. 300.

8. Frank Freidel, *Franklin D. Roosevelt: The Apprenticeship*, pp. 56–57. Freidel's cited source is the New York *Herald* (then a sensational paper) for October 19 and 20, 1900. Elliott Roosevelt, *op. cit.*, p. 430.

9. Elliott Roosevelt, *op. cit.*, pp. 432, 424, 425, 460, 461, 479, 480, 505, 506.

10. Freidel, *op. cit.*, p. 72.

11. The instructor was Philip G. Carleton, quoted in *ibid.*, p. 54.

12. L. L. Cowperthwaite, "Franklin D. Roosevelt at Harvard," *Quarterly Journal of Speech*, XXXVIII (February, 1952), pp. 37–41.

13. Rita Halle Kleeman, *Gracious Lady: The Life of Sara Delano Roosevelt*, p. 208.

14. Elliott Roosevelt, *op. cit.*, pp. 429, 433, 434, 437.

15. Kleeman, *op. cit.*, p. 209.

16. *Ibid.*, p. 209.

17. Elliott Roosevelt, *op. cit.*, pp. 427, 428, 430, 431.

18. *Ibid.*, p. 428.

19. Quoted by Henry F. Pringle, *Theodore Roosevelt*, pp. 167–68.

20. Charles W. Eliot, "Political Principles and Tendencies," *Outlook*, Vol. 66 (October 20, 1900) pp. 457–60.

21. Elliott Roosevelt, *op. cit.*, p. 430.

22. *Ibid.*, pp. 456–57.

23. Kleeman, *op. cit.*, p. 219.

24. Elliott Roosevelt, *op. cit.*, pp. 477–79. Freidel, *op. cit.*, p. 60. Kleeman, *op. cit.*, pp. 224–25.

25. Elliott Roosevelt, *op. cit.,* pp. 467–68.

26. Kleeman, *op. cit.,* p. 230.

27. John Gunther, *Roosevelt in Retrospect,* writes, p. 175, on basis of personal interviews: "FDR's classmates recall him today as a boy not particularly popular. . . . His desire to be universally liked repelled some of his fellows. . . ."

28. Arthur M. Schlesinger, Jr., *The Crisis of the Old Order,* pp. 322–23.

29. Ms. in Franklin D. Roosevelt Library, Hyde Park.

30. Elliott Roosevelt, *op. cit.,* p. 481.

31. *Ibid.,* pp. 465 and 469.

32. Gunther, *op. cit.,* p. 176. Freidel, *op. cit.,* p. 57. Amory, *op. cit.,* p. 304. Morison, *op. cit.,* p. 427.

33. Freidel, *op. cit.,* p. 59. Elliott Roosevelt, *op. cit.,* pp. 486, 487, 488. Jonathan Daniels, "Franklin Delano Roosevelt and Books," in *Three Presidents and Their Books,* pp. 89–105.

34. Elliott Roosevelt, *op. cit.,* pp. 487–88.

35. *Ibid.,* p. 504.

36. *Ibid.,* pp. 486, 489, 490.

37. *Ibid.,* p. 514.

38. *Ibid.,* pp. 518, 521.

39. *Ibid.,* p. 516.

40. Compton Mackenzie, *Mr. Roosevelt* (New York, 1944), p. 35.

41. Lindley, *op. cit.,* p. 64.

42. *Harvard Alumni Bulletin,* April 23, 1928. Quoted by Freidel, *op. cit.,* p. 66.

43. Elliott Roosevelt, *op. cit.,* p. 531.

44. Carleton Putnam, *Theodore Roosevelt: The Formative Years, 1858–1886,* pp. 140 and 166.

45. Kleeman, *op. cit.,* p. 233. Freidel, *op. cit.,* p. 71.

46. Frank Davis Ashburn, *Peabody of Groton,* pp. 176–77.

Six: ENTER, ELEANOR

1. Mrs. James Roosevelt, *My Boy Franklin,* p. 62. Rita Halle Kleeman, *Gracious Lady: The Life of Sara Delano Roosevelt,* p. 234. Eleanor Roosevelt, *This Is My Story,* pp. 9, 104.

2. Eleanor Roosevelt, *op. cit.,* p. 51.

3. *Ibid.,* p. 104. Kleeman, *op. cit.,* pp. 233–34.

4. Eleanor Roosevelt, *op. cit.,* p. 103.

5. Mrs. James Roosevelt, *op. cit.,* p. 63.

6. Kleeman, *op. cit.,* p. 235.

7. Elliott Roosevelt, ed., *F.D.R., His Personal Letters: Early Years,* p. 517.

8. *Ibid.,* p. 518.

9. Kleeman, *op. cit.,* p. 235.

10. Elliott Roosevelt, *op. cit.,* p. 523. Kleeman, *op. cit.,* p. 235.

11. Eleanor Roosevelt, *op. cit.,* p. 17.

12. *Ibid.,* pp. 17–18.

13. *Ibid.*, pp. 13, 17.

14. *Ibid.*, pp. 11–12.

15. *Ibid.*, p. 12.

16. *Ibid.*, p. 13.

17. *Ibid.*, p. 5.

18. *Ibid.*, p. 8.

19. *Ibid.*, pp. 8, 12.

20. *Ibid.*, pp. 6, 12.

21. Quoted by Archibald MacLeish, *The Eleanor Roosevelt Story*, p. 6.

22. Eleanor Roosevelt, *op. cit.*, p. 24.

23. *Ibid.*, p. 29.

24. *Ibid.*, p. 34.

25. *Ibid.*, pp. 28, 34, 35.

26. *Ibid.*, pp. 49–50.

27. *Ibid.*, pp. 43, 46.

28. *Ibid.*, pp. 65, 59.

29. *Ibid.*, p. 89.

30. *Ibid.*, pp. 101–2.

31. *Ibid.*, p. 98.

32. *Ibid.*, p. 110.

33. *Ibid.*, p. 111.

34. *Ibid.*, p. 114.

35. *Ibid.*, p. 113.

36. Kleeman, *op. cit.*, p. 240. Kleeman says that Sara "had entirely forgotten" this episode "until Miss Mabel Choate reminded her of it long afterward."

37. Samuel I. Rosenman, *The Public Papers and Addresses of Franklin D. Roosevelt*, 1938 volume, the Jackson Day Dinner speech, January 8, 1938, p. 38.

38. Elliott Roosevelt, *op. cit.*, pp. 532–33.

39. Elliott Roosevelt, *F.D.R., His Personal Letters, 1905–1928*, p. 73.

40. Eleanor Roosevelt, *op. cit.*, p. 123.

41. *Ibid.*, pp. 124–26; Kleeman, *op. cit.*, pp. 243–44; Freidel, *op. cit.*, p. 78, quoting the New York *Herald* for March 18, 1905.

Seven: A START IN LIFE

1. Eleanor Roosevelt, *This Is My Story*, pp. 127–38, pp. 130–31. Elliott Roosevelt, ed., *F.D.R., His Personal Letters, 1905–1908*, p. 10.

2. Eleanor Roosevelt, *op. cit.*, p. 130.

3. *Ibid.*, p. 137.

4. *Ibid.*, pp. 107, 134.

5. *Ibid.*, p. 135.

6. Elliott Roosevelt, ed., *F.D.R., His Personal Letters: Early Years*, pp. 130–31.

7. Elliott Roosevelt, *Personal Letters, 1905–1928*, p. 80.

8. *Ibid.*, p. 7.

9. The quote about Eleanor's being "a *wonderful* sailor" is from *ibid.*, p. 7. Eleanor Roosevelt, *op. cit.*, p. 139.

10. Eleanor Roosevelt, *op. cit.*, p. 140.

11. *Ibid.*, pp. 145–46.

12. *Ibid.*, pp. 150–51, 157.

13. *Ibid.*, p. 165.

14. *Ibid.*, p. 165.

15. James Roosevelt, with Sidney Shalett, *Affectionately, F.D.R.: A Son's Story of a Lonely Man*, p. 9.

16. Eleanor Roosevelt, *op. cit.*, p. 71.

17. *Ibid.*, pp. 149–50.

18. *Ibid.*, pp. 162–63 (for riding episode); p. 163 (for golfing episode); pp. 148–49 (for episode involving Hall); p. 157 (for episode of baby buggy at Sea Bright); pp. 157–58 (for episode of Ford car at Sea Bright); p. 151 (for episode of baby in box).

19. James Roosevelt and Shalett, *op. cit.*, pp. 37–38, has reproduction of Sara's sketch of house she proposed to build, with description. Eleanor Roosevelt, *op. cit.*, p. 152.

20. Eleanor Roosevelt, *op. cit.*, p. 152.

21. *Ibid.*, p. 162. Eleanor Roosevelt, *This I Remember*, p. 18.

22. Eleanor Roosevelt, *This I Remember*, pp. 14–15.

23. Rita Halle Kleeman, *Gracious Lady: The Life of Sara Delano Roosevelt*, pp. 246, 250. Eleanor Roosevelt, *This Is My Story*, pp. 177–78.

24. Roosevelt and Shalett, *op. cit.*, pp. 39–41.

25. *Ibid.*, p. 41.

26. *Ibid.*, pp. 41–43. Elliott Roosevelt, *Personal Letters, 1905–1928*, pp. 518–19.

27. Frances Perkins, *The Roosevelt I Knew*, p. 63.

28. Roosevelt, *This I Remember*, p. 11.

29. Franklin D. Roosevelt Library ms. Reproduced in facsimile, Robert D. Graff, Robert Emmett Ginna, Roger Butterfield, *FDR*, p. 47. Frank Freidel, *Franklin D. Roosevelt: The Apprenticeship*, p. 82.

30. Samuel I. Rosenman, *The Public Papers and Addresses of Franklin D. Roosevelt*, 1941 volume, pp. 457–58.

31. The story is told, from different points of view, by Henry F. Pringle, *Theodore Roosevelt*, pp. 310–13; by Frederick Lewis Allen, *The Great Pierpont Morgan*, pp. 202–7; and in several standard histories.

32. Noel F. Busch, *What Manner of Man?*, pp. 74–75.

33. Richard Harrity and Ralph G. Martin, *The Human Side of F.D.R.*, unnumbered pages, quoting anonymous FDR friend.

34. Grenville Clark, *Harvard Alumni Bulletin*, Vol. 47 (April 28, 1945), p. 452. A slightly different version, directly quoting Clark, is given in Graff, Ginna, Butterfield, *op. cit.*, p. 46.

35. Ernest K. Lindley, *Franklin D. Roosevelt*, pp. 69–76; Freidel, *op. cit.*, pp. 87–96; Kleeman, *op. cit.*, pp. 251–53; Eleanor Roosevelt, *This Is My Story*, pp. 166–68; Elliott Roosevelt, *Personal Letters, 1905–1928*, pp. 151–58.

36. Theodore Roosevelt, *Letters to Anna Roosevelt Cowles* . . . , p. 289. Quoted by Freidel, *op. cit.,* p. 88.

37. Eleanor Roosevelt, *This Is My Story,* p. 166.

38. Lindley, *op. cit.,* pp. 71–72.

Eight: THE EMERGENT DEFINITIONS OF 1910

1. Robert M. La Follette, *La Follette's Autobiography,* p. 478. Quoted by Arthur Schlesinger, Jr., *The Crisis of the Old Order,* p. 20.

2. Rita Halle Kleeman, *Gracious Lady: The Life of Sara Delano Roosevelt,* p. 239.

3. Eric F. Goldman, *Rendezvous with Destiny,* p. 189. Theodore Roosevelt described Croly's book as "the most profound and illuminating study of our national conditions which has appeared in many years," on p. 86 of Vol. XIX of his *Works of Theodore Roosevelt,* Hermann Hagedorn, ed.

4. The direct quotes and paraphrase are of Herbert Croly, *The Promise of American Life,* pp. 29, 189, 358–59, 369–88, 169, 279–88, 403–9. Goldman, *op. cit.,* discusses Croly's book in *op. cit.,* pp. 188–207.

5. Schlesinger, *op. cit.,* p. 21, quoting Perkins' addresses and articles.

6. Goldman, *op. cit.,* p. 206, quoting Harold Kellock, "A Pioneer of Big Business," *Century* magazine, Vol. LXXXIX (April, 1915), p. 953.

7. Hagedorn, *op. cit.,* Vol. XIX, pp. 16–27. Goldman, *op. cit.,* pp. 208–9.

8. Louis D. Brandeis, *The Curse of Bigness;* Alfred Leif, ed., *The Social and Economic Views of Mr. Justice Brandeis,* and *Other People's Money and How Bankers Use It,* by Brandeis, are expositions of the Brandeis position.

9. Alpheus Thomas Mason, *Brandeis: A Free Man's Life,* pp. 355–60. Mason quotes copiously from Brandeis' testimony in Hearings before the Committee on Interstate Commerce (1911), U.S. Senate, 62nd Congress, Sen. Res. 98.

10. Mason, *op. cit.,* pp. 316–23. Brandeis, *Financial Condition of the New York New Haven & Hartford Railroad Company, and of the Boston & Maine Railroad.* Arthur S. Link, *American Epoch: A History of the United States Since the 1890's,* pp. 53–54.

11. Brandeis address to Harvard undergraduates, "Social Justice and the Trusts," December 18, 1912. Quoted by Mason, *op. cit.,* p. 352.

12. *Ibid.,* pp. 366–67.

13. W. G. McAdoo, *Crowded Years,* pp. 104–5, and *Decent Treatment of the Public by Corporations and Regulation of Monopoly: A Speech Before the Chamber of Commerce, Boston, Mass., January 30, 1911* (an undated and unpaged pamphlet). Quoted by Schlesinger, *op. cit.,* p. 29.

Nine: FIRST FLIGHT: EDUCATION IN ALBANY

1. Ernest K. Lindley, *Franklin D. Roosevelt,* p. 72.

2. In the Franklin D. Roosevelt Library is a receipt, November 12, 1910, signed by H. T. Hawkey, Dr., dealer in Maxwell Motor Cars and Accessories,

acknowledging payment in full ($560) for "twenty-eight days service with automobile at $20 per day."

3. Lindley, *op. cit.*, pp. 73–74. Samuel I. Rosenman, *The Public Papers and Addresses of Franklin D. Roosevelt,* 1933 volume, p. 339. Eleanor Roosevelt, *This Is My Story,* pp. 167–68. Frank Freidel, *Franklin D. Roosevelt: The Apprenticeship,* pp. 92–93.

4. Henry F. Pringle, *Theodore Roosevelt,* pp. 149, 378.

5. Freidel, *op. cit.*, p. 94.

6. FDR letter to L. J. Magenis, August 15, 1928. Quoted by Freidel, *op. cit.*, pp. 87–88. To FDR, at the Wall Street office of Carter, Ledyard, and Milburn, came a letter dated November 1, 1910, from Ezra P. Prentis, chairman of the Republican State Committee, warning him of the dire consequences of a Democratic victory and asking him to "contribute $50 to the Republican campaign fund." FDR replied from Hyde Park on November 9, 1910: "I appreciate your courtesy in sending me the enclosed appeal. I have used it with great effect in my campaign as Democratic candidate for the State Senate in the Counties of Dutchess, Putnam, and Columbia." Group 9, Franklin D. Roosevelt Library.

7. Arthur S. Link, *Wilson, the Road to the White House,* pp. 173–237, gives a detailed account of Wilson's introduction to politics, the gubernatorial campaign, and the subsequent battle over the Senatorship.

8. Letter, Woodrow Wilson to M. A. Hulbert, January 29, 1911, in Ray Stannard Baker, *Woodrow Wilson, Life and Letters,* Vol. III, pp. 126–27.

9. Eleanor Roosevelt, *op. cit.*, pp. 168, 170. Freidel, *op. cit.*, pp. 98, 100, quoting FDR diary, January 2, 1911.

10. FDR diary, January 3, 1911, quoted in Freidel, *op. cit.*, pp. 100–1.

11. Lindley, *op. cit.*, p. 80. Pp. 77–97 is a history of "The Fight Against Sheehan." (Lindley, incidentally, misspells Lou Payn's name, adding an "e" to it, in his account of the FDR 1910 campaign—an error perpetuated by later writers.)

12. Freidel, *op. cit.*, p. 99, quoting FDR diary, January 1, 1911. For a pro-Tammany or anti-FDR account of the Sheehan-Shepard battle, see Oscar Handlin, *Al Smith and His America,* pp. 42–43.

13. Freidel, *op. cit.*, pp. 103–4. Lindley, quoting a New York *Times* feature article by W. Axel Warn, January 22, 1911, *op. cit.*, pp. 86–88.

14. Lindley, *op. cit.*, p. 78.

15. *Ibid.,* p. 81.

16. *Ibid.,* pp. 82–83. Freidel, *op. cit.*, p. 102.

17. Oral History Research Office, "The Reminiscences of Arthur Krock." See also Harold Zink, *City Bosses in the United States,* pp. 147–63.

18. Lindley, *op. cit.*, p. 92.

19. Freidel, *op. cit.*, p. 105.

20. Eleanor Roosevelt, *op. cit.*, pp. 174–75.

21. Edmund R. Terry, "The Insurgents at Albany," *The Independent,* Vol. 71 (September 7, 1911), p. 538.

22. Eleanor Roosevelt, *op. cit.*, pp. 173–74, 176.

23. Freidel, *op. cit.*, pp. 110–12. Alfred B. Rollins, Jr., *Roosevelt and Howe,*

pp. 29–31. Handlin, *op. cit.*, p. 43. In a letter to Wagner, March 24, 1911 (FDR Group 9, Box 37, File 354, Franklin D. Roosevelt Library), FDR states reasons for refusal to attend the upcoming second Democratic caucus: "The majority [of the Senate Democrats] has taken no collective action since Jan. 16 which would warrant us in assuming, as responsible men, that the new caucus would be held under substantially more favorable conditions and we therefore must consistently refrain, as we did before, from entering such a caucus. Should we enter the caucus next Monday night we would run the risk of stultifying our former action and sacrificing the very principle for which we have stood."

24. Freidel, *op. cit.*, pp. 112–14. Rollins, *op. cit.*, pp. 30–32. Lindley, *op. cit.*, pp. 94–96.

25. *Ibid.*, p. 97. Freidel, *op. cit.*, quoting Saratoga *Sun*, April 1, 1911, p. 115.

26. *Ibid.*, p. 15.

27. Lindley, *op. cit.*, p. 101. The speech was given in Buffalo on December 23, 1911.

28. New York *Times*, December 25, 1911.

29. Freidel, *op. cit.*, p. 119, quoting New York *Globe*, June 2, 1911.

30. *Ibid.*, p. 119. Frances Perkins, *The Roosevelt I Knew*, p. 11.

31. Perkins, *op. cit.*, pp. 11–12.

32. Handlin, *op. cit.*, p. 56. Perkins, *op. cit.*, p. 31. Freidel, *op. cit.*, pp. 120–21.

33. FDR letter to George Haven Putnam, March 17, 1911, quoted in Freidel, *op. cit.*, p. 111.

34. Freidel, *op. cit.*, p. 126.

35. Perkins, *op. cit.*, p. 14. Louis Howe is the quoted source of the story about FDR's "saving" the bill. See Freidel, *op. cit.*, p. 122.

36. The Franklin D. Roosevelt Library has (FDR Group 9) a typescript of this speech, with some of it in FDR's handwriting, indicating that it is undoubtedly and wholly his own work. (It is not easy to determine in most of his speeches and published writings how much or what portions are truly of his own composition.) The speech is extensively quoted by Daniel R. Fusfeld, *The Economic Thought and the Origins of the New Deal*, pp. 49–51; by Rollins, *op. cit.*, p. 40; and by Freidel, *op. cit.*, pp. 132–33.

37. Link, *op. cit.*, pp. 92–95. For a comprehensive journalistic account of Big Tim Sullivan and the tangled interrelationships of his career with those of Boss Murphy and two future governors of New York (and characters in our story of FDR), Republican Charles Whitman and Democratic "Plain Bill" Sulzer, see Andy Logan, *Against the Evidence*, dealing with the notorious Becker-Rosenthal murder case, 1912–1915. It must be cautiously used, however, for it contains many factual errors.

38. Perkins, *op. cit.*, pp. 12–13.

Ten: FROM ALBANY TO WASHINGTON, 1912–13

1. Ernest K. Lindley, *Franklin D. Roosevelt*, p. 102. Elliott Roosevelt, ed., *F.D.R., His Personal Letters, 1905–1928*, p. 178. Frank Freidel, *Franklin D. Roosevelt: The Apprenticeship*, pp. 134–35.

2. Freidel, *op. cit.*, pp. 134–35.

3. Arthur S. Link, *Wilson, The Road to the White House*, pp. 352–57.

4. FDR Group 9, Box 6, File 8 of Franklin D. Roosevelt Library, State Senatorship Papers, has carbons of the FDR invitations, all saying, "Will you give me the pleasure of dining with me at the Hotel Belmont in New York City on Wednesday evening, April 10th at seven-thirty P.M.? I am having a few democrats from all over the State. . . ." The three who accepted were Frederick Sheide, Alonzo McLaughlin, and John Trombly. Freidel, *op. cit.*, pp. 138–39.

5. Eleanor Roosevelt, *This Is My Story*, p. 181. Elliott Roosevelt, *op. cit.*, pp. 180–87.

6. FDR Group 9, Box 6, File 8, New York State Wilson Conference, April–June, 1912, Franklin D. Roosevelt Library. Lela Stiles, *The Man Behind Roosevelt: The Story of Louis McHenry Howe*, p. 34. Alfred B. Rollins, Jr., *Roosevelt and Howe*, pp. 48–49.

7. Link, *op. cit.*, p. 381, quoting letter published in New York *Times*, February 2, 1912.

8. Henry F. Pringle, *Theodore Roosevelt*, p. 556. William Henry Harbaugh, *Power and Responsibility: The Life and Times of Theodore Roosevelt*, pp. 404–9, 419–20.

9. Eleanor Roosevelt, *op. cit.*, pp. 187–89.

10. Elliott Roosevelt, *op. cit.*, p. 192.

11. The letter, on stationary of New York State Wilson Conference, is in FDR Group 9 of Franklin D. Roosevelt Library. It is undated. Stiles, *op. cit.*, has facsimile of it facing p. 25.

12. New York *Herald,* July 30, 1912.

13. A copy of the report is in FDR Group 9, Box 6, File 9, Empire State Democracy, July–August, 1912, Franklin D. Roosevelt Library.

14. Elliott Roosevelt, *op. cit.*, pp. 193–94.

15. New York *Times*, August 25, 1912. Quoted in Elliott Roosevelt, *op. cit.*, p. 196, and Rollins, *op. cit.*, p. 54.

16. Link, *op. cit.*, p. 495.

17. Rollins, *op. cit.*, p. 54.

18. *Ibid.*, p. 55., quoting letter of Thomas Mott Osborne to Thomas Ewing, Jr., October 7, 1912.

19. Eleanor Roosevelt, *op. cit.*, pp. 190–91.

20. Rollins, *op. cit.*, p. 402.

21. Sources for impressionistic portrait of Howe include Arthur Schlesinger, Jr., *The Crisis of the Old Order*, pp. 340–42; Rollins, *op. cit.*, especially pp. 63–84; Stiles, *op. cit.*, especially pp. 33–40; Eleanor Roosevelt, *op. cit.*, pp. 192–93; James MacGregor Burns, *Roosevelt: The Lion and the Fox*, p. 44; Elliott Roosevelt, *op. cit.*, p. 197; Elliott Roosevelt, "The Most Unforgettable Character I've Met," *Reader's Digest* (February, 1953), pp. 26–30.

22. Stiles, *op. cit.*, pp. 30–31.

23. *Ibid.*, pp. 34–35.

24. Rollins, *op. cit.*, p. 58, quoting Hudson, New York, *Register* clipping in Scrapbook, FDR Group 9, Franklin D. Roosevelt Library.

25. Freidel, *op. cit.*, p. 150.

26. FDR Group 9, Franklin D. Roosevelt Library. Undated letter Howe to Roosevelt (October, 1912). Quoted by Stiles, *op. cit.*, p. 37, and Rollins, *op. cit.*, p. 58.

27. Stiles, *op. cit.*, p. 37.

28. Quoted by Link, *op. cit.*, p. 487.

29. Alpheus Thomas Mason, *Brandeis: A Free Man's Life*, pp. 377–84.

30. The memorandum, headed "Suggestions for Letter of Governor Wilson on Trusts," is among the Ray Stannard Baker papers in the Library of Congress. It is quoted extensively by Link, *op. cit.*, p. 492.

31. Theodore Roosevelt, "The Minimum Wage," editorial in *Outlook*, Vol. CII (September 28, 1912), pp. 159–60. This is substance of the Spokane speech of September 9, 1912.

32. The New York *Times*, September 3, 1912, carries speech in full. Quoted by Link, *op. cit.*, pp. 487–91.

33. Harbaugh, *op. cit.*, pp. 448–49.

34. *Ibid.*, p. 448.

35. *Ibid.*, p. 447.

36. Eleanor Roosevelt, *op. cit.*, p. 192. Stiles, *op. cit.*, p. 38.

37. FDR letter to Eugene Wells, November 19, 1912. Quoted by Freidel, *op. cit.*, p. 152.

38. Freidel, *op. cit.*, p. 152. Stiles, *op. cit.*, p. 38. Rollins, *op. cit.*, p. 60.

39. *La Follette's Weekly Magazine*, Vol. IV (November 9, 1912), p. 3. Quoted by Link, *op. cit.*, p. 526.

40. Freidel, *op. cit.*, p. 144, quoting story in New York *Telegraph*, November 30, 1913.

41. FDR letter to Henry deForest Baldwin, November 19, 1912. Group 9, FDR Library. Quoted by Rollins, *op. cit.*, p. 87.

42. Josephus Daniels, *The Wilson Era: Years of Peace, 1910–1917*, p. 124. Lindley, *op. cit.*, p. 110. Freidel, *op. cit.*, p. 155.

43. All quotes in this and preceding paragraph are from Daniels, *op. cit.*, p. 433. In a brown, leather-covered *Standard Diary and Daily Reminder, 1913*, now in the Manuscript Division of the Library of Congress, Daniels recorded in his crabbed longhand on Thursday, March 6, that "this morning I went to the White House and told the President that I had decided upon Mr. Roosevelt. He said 'capital' and heartily approved. This was gratifying to me." In his entry for Saturday, March 15, 1913, Daniels records that FDR "arrived today, expecting to enter upon his duties, but the Senate not having acted, he returned to New York. . . . Mr. Roosevelt told me on the night before the inauguration that if he served in any place in the administration he preferred to be in the Navy Department."

Eleven: ASSISTANT SECRETARY OF THE NAVY, 1913–14

1. Elliott Roosevelt, ed., *F.D.R., His Personal Letters, 1905–1928*, pp. 199–200.

2. *Ibid.*, p. 200.

3. Eleanor Roosevelt, *This Is My Story* (New York, 1937), pp. 196–97.

4. Unpublished ms. of William Phillips, "Memoirs." Quoted by Frank Freidel, *Franklin D. Roosevelt: The Apprenticeship*, p. 170.

5. Eleanor Roosevelt, *op. cit.*, p. 237.

6. *Ibid.*, pp. 234–36.

7. *Ibid.*, pp. 199. Ernest K. Lindley, *Franklin D. Roosevelt*, pp. 118–19.

8. William G. McAdoo, *Crowded Years*, p. 182.

9. Elliott Roosevelt, *op. cit.*, p. 200.

10. FDR to Howe, March 19, 1913. Group 10, Box 2, Franklin D. Roosevelt Library. Alfred B. Rollins, Jr., *Roosevelt and Howe* (New York, 1962), p. 89. Frank Freidel, *op. cit.*, p. 161. Lela Stiles, *The Man Behind Roosevelt: The Story of Louis McHenry Howe*, p. 41.

11. Freidel, *op. cit.*, p. 162, quoting an interview with Joseph K. Taussig, June 7, 1947. Quoted by Stiles, *op. cit.*, p. 43.

12. Stiles, *op. cit.*, pp. 42–43.

13. Elliott Roosevelt, *op. cit.*, p. 330.

14. Josephus Daniels, *The Wilson Era: Years of Peace—1910–1917*, p. 128.

15. Freidel, *op. cit.*, p. 161.

16. *Ibid.*, p. 162, quoting a personal interview with Daniels.

17. Louis Howe to FDR, April 4, 1914. FDR Group 10, Box 2, Howe file, Franklin D. Roosevelt Library.

18. Stiles, *op. cit.*, pp. 49, 40.

19. Freidel, *op. cit.*, pp. 161–62.

20. Unofficial Observer (Jay Franklin), *The New Dealers*, p. 220.

21. Augustus P. Gardner to FDR, June 25, 1913. FDR Group 10, Franklin D. Roosevelt Library.

22. Josephus Daniels, *The Wilson Era: Years of War and After*, p. 253.

23. Unmailed letter, FDR to Robert G. Valentine, July 31, 1913, quoted by Freidel, *op. cit.*, p. 201.

24. The flag is displayed in the Franklin D. Roosevelt Library museum.

25. Elliott Roosevelt, *op. cit.*, p. 211.

26. Lindley, *op. cit.*, p. 119, quoting a newspaper clipping dated April 10, 1913, in FDR scrapbook.

27. *Ibid.*, p. 122. Daniels, *The Wilson Era: Years of Peace*, pp. 129–30.

28. William F. Halsey and Julian Bryan III, *Admiral Halsey's Story*, p. 18.

29. Daniels, *Years of Peace*, p. 127. In his diary, now in the Manuscript Division of the Library of Congress, Daniels in the entry for Thursday, March 9, 1913, says he "related the conversation to the President who expressed about the same opinion I had entertained."

30. *Ibid.*, p. 129.

31. New York *Sun*, March 19, 1913.

32. William D. Hassett, "The President Was My Boss," *Saturday Evening Post* (October 31, 1953), pp. 38–39.

33. Lindley, *op. cit.*, pp. 117–18, quoting anonymous source.

34. Daniels, *Years of Peace*, p. 351. In his diary (see note 29), Daniels (or Daniels' secretary, probably the latter since he is referred to as "the Secretary), records on Wednesday, August 27, 1913, that "at 12:00 M. the Secretary accompanied by his Aids and several of the bureau chiefs repaired to the Navy Library to witness the opening of bids on armor for Battleship No. 39. It was hoped that as a result of agitation in favor of a government armor plant, some material reduction and variations in bids might be disclosed." None was. ". . . the Secretary issued a scathing report on the subject in the afternoon and made arrangements for a conference on the morrow with the representatives of . . . Carnegie, Midvale, and Bethlehem to investigate the reasons of their submitting identical bids."

35. Freidel, *op. cit.*, p. 210.

36. FDR to Warren Delano, January 5, 1917. FDR Group 10, Box 81, Franklin D. Roosevelt Library. It should be noted that Warren Delano was "reactionary" in FDR's view, which may have caused the latter to tailor his expressed opinion to a pattern pleasing to Uncle Warren.

37. Daniels, *Years of Peace*, p. 356.

38. Barbara W. Tuchman, *The Proud Tower*, p. 270, quoting Baroness Bertha von Suttner, *Memoirs* (Boston, 1910).

39. Arthur S. Link, *Wilson: The New Freedom*, p. 282, quoting New York *Times*, May 10, 1913.

40. Daniels, *Years of Peace*, p. 413.

41. Theodore Roosevelt to Arthur Lee, August 1, 1914, quoted by William Henry Harbaugh, *Power and Responsibility: The Life and Times of Theodore Roosevelt*, p. 465.

42. Lindley, *op. cit.*, pp. 115–16, directly quoting FDR.

43. Admiral Bradley A. Fiske to Secretary Daniels, May 14, 1913, Daniels Papers, Manuscript Division, Library of Congress. Daniels' diary entry for Tuesday, May 13, 1913, records his reading to the Cabinet that day a letter from Fiske urging that three ships then in Chinese rivers—the *Saratoga*, *Monterey*, and *Monadnock*—be at once ordered to the Philippines. Fiske was somewhat less warlike in this epistle than he became next day. "While I do not believe that our present tension with Japan will result in war, while I realize the reasonableness of the belief of many people that Japan does not desire war, and while I earnestly hope that war will not result, yet I beg leave to present the following statement of facts," he began. The facts were that Japan needed Hawaii and the Philippines and could easily seize these if she "should decide to go to war" and then "stand pat." "In other words," Fiske closed, "it is conceivable that Japan may conclude—may already have concluded—that, if she should go to war . . . , she could, by enduring a period of privation and distress lasting about two years [owing to U.S. naval blockade, etc.], acquire possession of both the Philippine Islands and the Hawaiian Islands."

44. Both quotes are from Daniels, *Years of Peace*, p. 164.

45. *Ibid.*, p. 165.

46. David F. Houston, *Eight Years with Wilson's Cabinet*, Vol. I, p. 66.

47. Daniels, *Years of Peace,* pp. 166–67. Link, *op. cit.,* p. 299.

48. Freidel, *op. cit.,* p. 225. Theodore Roosevelt wrote FDR, on *Outlook* stationery, from New York City, on May 10, 1913, a personal letter: "It is not my place to advise, but there is one matter so vital that I want to call your attention to it. I do not anticipate trouble with Japan, but it may come, and if it does come it will come suddenly. In that case we shall be in an unpardonable position if we permit ourselves to be caught with our fleet separated. There ought not to be a battleship or any formidable fighting craft in the Pacific unless our entire fleet is in the Pacific. Russia's fate [in 1905] ought to be a warning for all time as to the criminal folly of dividing the fleet if there is even the remotest chance of war." Group 10, Box 137, Franklin D. Roosevelt Library.

49. FDR to Admiral Alfred T. Mahan, June 16, 1914. FDR Group 10, Box 137, Franklin D. Roosevelt Library. At that time, Roosevelt was concerned over the possibility that, with the opening of the Panama Canal, there would be renewed political pressure for a division of the fleet between the East and West coasts, and he was urging TR and Mahan to publicize, in magazine articles, the dangers of doing so. He referred to the situation in May, 1913, when his effort to get the ships "in the Yangtze" to sail "nearer their base" had been frustrated by diplomatic considerations. "This, to my mind, is an excellent example of what might happen in case half our battleships were at San Francisco and the other half at New York. To bring the two fleets together during critical diplomatic negotiations would be almost impossible and if the negotiations failed the time for a possible junction of the fleets would be gone."

50. Watertown (Massachusetts) *Standard,* May 29, 1913.

51. Daniels, *Years of Peace,* p. 188.

52. New York *Times,* April 12, 1914.

53. San Francisco *Bulletin,* April 16, 1914. Josephus Daniels to FDR, April 16, 1914, FDR Group 10, Franklin D. Roosevelt Library. Portland *Oregonian,* April 20, 1914. Seattle *Post-Intelligencer,* April 21, 1914. Freidel, *op. cit.,* pp. 230–31. Rollins, *op. cit.,* p. 120.

54. Howe to Roosevelt, April 22, 1914. FDR Group 10, Box 2, Franklin D. Roosevelt Library.

55. Freidel, *op. cit.,* pp. 231–32.

56. Daniels, *Years of Peace,* p. 129.

Twelve: ROOSEVELT AND NEW FREEDOM

1. Arthur S. Link, *Wilson: The New Freedom,* p. 469, quoting letter from Wilson to Powell Evans, October 20, 1914.

2. *Ibid.,* p. 470.

3. *Ibid.,* p. 251.

4. New York *Times.* October 4, 1913. Cited by Frank Freidel, *Franklin D. Roosevelt: The Apprenticeship,* p. 168.

5. Freidel, *op. cit.,* p. 168.

6. Josephus Daniels, *The Wilson Era: Years of Peace—1910–1917,* p. 494.

7. Link, *op. cit.*, p. 166. The New York *Times,* April 11, 1913, has a story datelined Washington, D.C., April 10, telling of a delegation of upstate Democrats, headed by FDR, calling on Wilson at the White House to urge him to "ignore Murphy" in making federal appointments. One of the delegation was FDR's Harvard roommate Lathrop Brown, now a Congressman from St. James, Long Island. "The newspaper statements that John K. Sague, former Mayor of Poughkeepsie, had a better chance than anyone else of being appointed Collector of the Port of New York, have caused a good deal of worry in Tammany Hall. There is now a disposition on the part of New York politicians here to believe that Mr. Sague's chances for appointment have been minimized."

8. Freidel, *op. cit.*, pp. 176–77. Link, *op. cit.*, pp. 165–67.

9. Link, *op. cit.*, p. 159.

10. Alfred B. Rollins, Jr., *Roosevelt and Howe,* p. 91.

11. Link, *op. cit.*, p. 169.

12. Woodrow Wilson to FDR, April 1, 1914. FDR Group 10, Box 137, Franklin D. Roosevelt Library.

13. Freidel, *op. cit.*, pp. 177–78.

14. *Ibid.*, pp. 181–83. Elliott Roosevelt, ed. *F.D.R., His Personal Letters, 1905–1928*, pp. 229–31.

15. Rollins, *op. cit.*, pp. 100–2. Elliott Roosevelt, *op. cit.*, pp. 230, 250. Freidel, *op. cit.*, pp. 183–84. Link, *op. cit.*, p. 169.

16. Rollins, *op. cit.*, p. 102.

17. *Ibid.*, pp. 102–3.

18. Eleanor Roosevelt, *This Is My Story,* p. 215.

19. Elliott Roosevelt, *op. cit.*, p. 245.

20. Freidel, *op. cit.*, p. 184. Rollins, *op. cit.*, p. 104.

21. Link, *op. cit.*, pp. 170–71.

22. Freidel, *op. cit.*, p. 186.

23. *Ibid.*, p. 188. Ernest K. Lindley, *Franklin D. Roosevelt,* pp. 132–33.

Thirteen: OF POLITICS AND WAR, PART ONE

1. Elliott Roosevelt, ed., *F.D.R., His Personal Letters, 1905–1928*, p. 221. Josephus Daniels, *The Wilson Era: Years of Peace—1910–1917,* pp. 382–83.

2. Arthur S. Link, *Wilson, The New Freedom,* pp. 314–18. Walter Millis, *The Road to War,* pp. 28–37.

3. Eleanor Roosevelt, *This Is My Story,* p. 215.

4. Elliott Roosevelt, *op. cit.*, pp. 237–40.

5. *Ibid.*, pp. 233–36.

6. Winston Churchill, *The World Crisis,* abridged and revised, p. 112.

7. Emil Ludwig, *Bismarck,* p. 541.

8. *Ibid.*, p. 536.

9. Fritz Fischer, *Germany's Aims in the First World War,* pp. 11–20.

10. Ludwig, *op. cit.*, pp. 632–33.

11. Fischer, *op. cit.*, pp. 86–87. But the scene is a famous one, described in virtually every history of World War I, popular or academic. For instance, S. L. A. Marshall, *The American Heritage History of World War I*, tells of it on p. 38.

12. David F. Houston, *Eight Years with Wilson's Cabinet*, p. 120. Quoted by Walter Millis, *op. cit.*, p. 41.

13. Link, *op. cit.*, p. 462.

14. Elliott Roosevelt, *op. cit.*, p. 245.

15. Link, *op. cit.*, pp. 463–65.

16. Ray Stannard Baker, *Woodrow Wilson, Life and Letters*, Vol. VI (Garden City, 1935), p. 334.

17. This parenthetical quote of Roosevelt and the one preceding it in the same paragraph are from Elliott Roosevelt, *op. cit.*, pp. 239–40.

18. William Henry Harbaugh, *Power and Responsibility: The Life and Times of Theodore Roosevelt*, pp. 467–69.

19. Elliott Roosevelt, *op. cit.*, p. 238.

20. *Ibid.*, pp. 243, 245.

21. *Ibid.*, pp. 238–39.

22. A. T. Mahan to FDR, August 18, 1914. The quotation is a postscript to a longhand letter written from Marshmere, Quogue, Long Island, in which Mahan expressed grave concern over the "sudden and ill-considered action of Japan" in decisively moving toward the declaration of war on Germany which Japan made on August 23, 1914, at which time Japan began to land forces in Shangtung. Mahan made several points: "1. First, from the first article of the Treaty between Great Britain and Japan, it would appear that Japan could not have taken this step, on the grounds alleged in the 'ultimatum,' without consulting Great Britain. Under this understanding, the utterly inadequate grounds alleged for the action cannot but arouse sympathy for Germany, militating against the pretty general feeling heretofore testified against her by our people. It seems to me our Government, in its neutral impartiality, should represent this to Great Britain; with the frank acknowledgment that, while it can answer for its own fairness, it cannot control the sympathies of the people, which are almost sure to swing around; for the ultimatum of Austria was reason [*sic*] they compared with the reasons advanced by Japan. 2. Japan, going to war with Germany, will be at liberty to take the German Islands, Pelew, Marianne, Caroline, and Samoa. The first three flank our Mercator course to the Philippines; and it is one thing to have them in the hands of a Power whose main strength is in Europe, and quite another that they should pass into the hands of one so near as Japan. The question is pertinent to Great Britain. 'If these islands are seized, will they henceforth be considered among these territorial possessions of Japan which the Treaty of Alliance guarantees?' Let Great Britain be brought at once to face the fact that the action of her ally thus seriously affects her relations with us, because of this military contingency; and also that the infallible effect of Japan's action will be to transfer popular sympathy in the present war

from Great Britain to Germany, because the latter, in a moment of extreme embarrassment and danger, has been wantonly and needlessly assailed, on a trumpery pretext. If the action goes beyond Kiai-Chau, to the above named German islands, Australia, New Zealand, and Canada will be offended equally with ourselves. 3. These considerations are so obvious that I doubt if Great Britain was consulted; but, article I being as it stands, she will be believed to have been, which amounts to the same thing. . . . My own sympathies have been strongly against Germany, because I have believed her ultimately the state responsible for the general war; but I love fair play, and I hate disingenuousness, which is written all over the Japanese ultimatum." On January 9, 1915, Ellen Lyle Mahan, widow of the admiral, wrote FDR on black-margined paper to thank him for sending her "the resolution passed by the British Navy Boards Society of their sympathy with us at this time." As a postscript she wrote: "Shortly after his arrival in Washington my husband went to the Department to pay his respect to you—he told me that he had not seen you and that his card had been returned to him. I mention this as I would like you to know that he tried to see you and was disappointed." FDR Group 10, Box 137, Franklin D. Roosevelt Library.

23. Frank Freidel, *Franklin D. Roosevelt: The Apprenticeship*, p. 239. Elliott Roosevelt, *op. cit.*, pp. 249–50.

24. Baker, *op. cit.*, Vol. VI, p. 7.

25. Josephus Daniels, *The Wilson Era: Years of Peace—1910–1917*, p. 165. Ernest K. Lindley, *Franklin D. Roosevelt*, p. 120.

26. Daniels, *op. cit.*, p. 537.

27. Elliott Roosevelt, *op. cit.*, pp. 256–57.

28. Freidel, *op. cit.*, pp. 241–42.

29. *Ibid.*, p. 242.

30. Link, *op. cit.*, pp. 139–40. New York *Times*, December 9, 1914.

31. New York *Herald*, December 17, 1914. Lindley, *op. cit.*, p. 124.

32. Elliott Roosevelt, *op. cit.*, pp. 269–70.

33. *Ibid.*, pp. 268, 269.

34. *Ibid.*, p. 291.

35. Freidel, *op. cit.*, p. 245.

36. William D. Hassett, "The President Was My Boss," *Saturday Evening Post* (October 31), 1953, pp. 38–39. Arthur Schlesinger, Jr., *The Crisis of the Old Order, 1919–1933*, p. 345.

37. Elliott Roosevelt, *op. cit.*, p. 339.

38. Freidel, *op. cit.*, p. 303.

39. Daniels, *op. cit.*, pp. 340–42.

40. Freidel, *op. cit.*, p. 291.

41. Jonathan Daniels, *Washington Quadrille: The Dance Beside the Documents*, pp. 88–89.

42. Quoted in Josephus Daniels, *op. cit.*, p. 134.

43. Elliott Roosevelt, *op. cit.*, p. 299.

44. Freidel, *op. cit.*, p. 253.

Fourteen: OF POLITICS AND WAR: PART TWO

1. New York *Times,* February 7, 1915.

2. Elliott Roosevelt, ed., *F.D.R., His Personal Letters, 1905–1928,* pp. 266–67.

3. Josephus Daniels, *The Wilson Era—Years of War and After, 1917–1923,* p. 256. Frank Freidel, *Franklin D. Roosevelt: The Apprenticeship,* p. 249.

4. Freidel, *op. cit.,* p. 189.

5. Arthur S. Link, *Wilson: The Struggle for Neutrality, 1914–1915,* p. 375. Burton J. Hendrick, *The Life and Letters of Walter Hines Page,* Vol. II, p. 2. Walter Millis, *The Road to War, 1914–1917,* pp. 170–71.

6. William Henry Harbaugh, *Power and Responsibility: The Life and Times of Theodore Roosevelt,* p. 476.

7. Link, *op. cit.,* pp. 217–18.

8. Joseph Tumulty, *Woodrow Wilson as I Know Him,* p. 232. Link, *op. cit.,* p. 380.

9. Link, *op. cit.,* p. 382. Tumulty, *op. cit.,* p. 236.

10. *New Republic,* May 22, 1915, p. 57.

11. Link, *op. cit.,* p. 211. David F. Houston, *Eight Years with Wilson's Cabinet, 1913 to 1920,* Vol. I, pp. 132–37. Josephus Daniels, *The Wilson Era: Years of Peace—1910–1917,* p. 429.

12. Link, *op. cit.,* p. 424. Houston, *op. cit.,* pp. 142–46. Daniels, *op. cit.,* pp. 431–32.

13. New York *World,* June 12, 1915. Cited by Link, *op. cit.,* p. 426.

14. Elliott Roosevelt, *op. cit.,* p. 270. Freidel, *op. cit.,* p. 250.

15. Elliott Roosevelt, *op. cit.,* p. 285.

16. Franklin Roosevelt penciled memorandum, June 23, 1915. FDR Group 10, Franklin D. Roosevelt Library. Cited by Freidel, *op. cit.,* pp. 251–52.

17. Elliott Roosevelt, *op. cit.,* p. 278.

18. *Ibid.* p. 283.

19. Ray Stannard Baker, *Woodrow Wilson: Life and Letters,* Vol. 5, p. 373.

20. Link, *op. cit.,* pp. 583–85.

21. Daniels, *op. cit.,* pp. 452–54.

22. Elliott Roosevelt, *op. cit.,* p. 288. Since what happened on this matter was in effect the birth of what would become notorious as the military-industrial complex in the aftermath of World War II—the "birth" of this, that is to say, insofar as it established the pattern of industrial and military relationships which would later develop—the correspondence between FDR and Dennis is of some historical significance. On May 29, 1916, on stationery of the University Club in Madison, Wisconsin, Dennis wrote longhand ("Confidential") to FDR: "I thank you for the copy of H.R. 15948 and your letter of May 26. I don't think I can ever tell you much about the bill. But, my dear man, I have only begun to fight. It was a great disappointment to me that the Secretary of State was not made chairman and that in general the [making?] of foreign policy with other things was not made more secure. [Dennis' concern on this point was to ensure a close relationship between foreign policy and war-making industrial potential.] As for J. D. [Josephus Daniels, and the reference is indicative of

FDR's expressed attitude toward his chief] biff-bang my letter of May 17 produced an answer which showed that he knew nothing of what was going on and which stated that he took only a 'perfunctory interest in such matters' and that I must 'count him out.' Poor man—he is a good chap; but there is no help to be had there. . . ." FDR did not reply until June 9, 1916, in a letter labeled "Confidential." He said: "I am of all sorts of mind about H.R. Bill 15948, the title of which, providing for a 'Council of Executive Information for the Coordination of Industries and Resources for the National Security and Welfare,' sounds like pure buncombe. In spite of the fact that I threw up both hands on first seeing it, I am beginning to come around to the opinion that we have accomplished something anyway, and there is no reason why we should not make further efforts to improve the bill. As it stands now the council itself consists of certain members of the Cabinet, the Secretary of State being left out and one or two unnecessary ones being put in. In this I think I see the hand of Mr. Lane who all along has told me he thought the Cabinet could handle the situation. In this I, and I know you, do not concur, *but the meat of the bill is Section 2, providing for an advisory commission.* [Italics mine.] As an offhand expression of opinion I would suggest roughly the following line of improvements on which we can concentrate: 1. Add the Secretary of State and leave out the Secretary of the Interior. I do not see where the latter comes in. . . . 2. *Increase the importance of the advisory commission in some way* [italics mine] by making them actual members of the council or by giving them compensation. I think the latter should be done anyway [a statement indicative of the innocence which characterized the whole initiation, on the "public" side, of this development]. And their terms of office should not be at the whim of any one Cabinet or Administration. [!]" Roosevelt gave it as his opinion that now was "an excellent time straight off to start work on Senators Chamberlain, Swanson, Underwood, Lodge, Stone, Tillman, and anybody else you think of value. I think there is an excellent chance at least of improving things, and, without intending to throw bouquets at myself I think I am the only person in Washington in the Administration who realizes the perfectly wonderful opportunities, nationally and politically, to accomplish something of lasting construction." On June 22, 1916, Dennis wrote from 12 Roosevelt Place, Montclair, New Jersey, where he spent his summers, a "Confidential" letter saying that "the [New York] *Times* and [New York] *World* have given special private instructions to their Washington men to help in every way [on the establishment of the proposed council]. There is a report that your chief spending the night with Edison gave promise of a special bill empowering the Navy Consulting Board or in some other way proposing a new game. I doubt this; but it would be a saving of time if your private secretary could collect for purposes of study any and all bills which in any way touch this matter. The *Times* says that the bill for a Council of Executive Information has been thrown into the melting pot of the Army Appropriations Bill. The *Times* says introduce a new bill and the *World* says amend the old bill. It might be a help to get all the information we could. . . ." FDR Group 10, Box 94, File, Dennis, Alfred L. P., Franklin D. Roosevelt Library.

23. Baker, *op. cit.*, pp. 26–29.

24. Elliott Roosevelt, *op. cit.*, p. 301. Eleanor Roosevelt, *This Is My Story*, p. 240. ". . . his mother met him" at Atlantic City, writes Eleanor.

25. Freidel, *op. cit.*, p. 259.

26. Arthur S. Link, *Wilson: Confusions and Crises, 1915–1916*, p. 103.

27. Arthur S. Link, *Wilson: Campaigns for Progressivism and Peace, 1916–1917*, pp. 25–26. Baker, *op. cit.*, Vol. 6, pp. 219–23.

28. Elliott Roosevelt, *op.cit.*, pp. 304, 325, 227.

29. *Ibid.*, pp. 314–16, 320–24.

30. Freidel, *op. cit.*, p. 262. Elliott Roosevelt, *op. cit.*, p. 304. Link, *Confusions and Crises*, pp. 334–38.

31. Link, *Confusions and Crises*, pp. 338–39. Baker, *op. cit.*, Vol. VI, p. 308. Freidel, *op. cit.*, p. 255.

32. Link, *Confusions and Crises*, p. 337. Quoting House Diary.

33. Link, *Campaigns for Progressivism and Peace, 1916–1917*, pp. 64–65.

34. *Ibid.*, p. 58.

35. Baker, *op. cit.*, Vol. VI, p. 283, quotes a statement from the Democratic National Committee chairman, that Daniels and the Navy were the Cabinet official and department most applauded by motion-picture audiences when a campaign film portraying achievements of the Wilson administration was shown.

36. Harbaugh, *op. cit.*, p. 491.

37. Link, *Campaigns for Progressivism and Peace*, pp. 140–41.

38. Baker, *op. cit.*, Vol. VI, pp. 291–92. Link, *Campaigns*, pp. 154–56.

39. Elliott Roosevelt, *op. cit.*, pp. 338–39.

40. *Ibid.*, p. 339. Freidel, *op. cit.*, p. 267.

41. Tumulty, *op. cit.*, p. 218. Link, *Campaigns*, pp. 156–57. Baker, *op. cit.*, Vol. VI, p. 258.

Fifteen: AMERICA ENTERS THE WAR

1. Ray Stannard Baker, *Woodrow Wilson: Life and Letters*, p. 415. Josephus Daniels, *The Wilson Era: Years of War and After*, p. 258. Frank Freidel, *Franklin D. Roosevelt: The Apprenticeship*, pp. 268–69.

2. Freidel, *op. cit.*, p. 268.

3. Baker, *op. cit.*, pp. 417–18. Arthur S. Link, *Wilson: Campaigns for Progressivism and Peace*, pp. 264–65 n.

4. Link, *op. cit.*, p. 250.

5. Freidel, *op. cit.*, p. 272. Arthur S. Link, *Wilson: The Struggle for Neutrality*, pp. 498–99.

6. Link, *Struggle for Neutrality*, pp. 518–19, 529–30.

7. Freidel, *op. cit.*, p. 277.

8. Josephus Daniels, *The Wilson Era: Years of Peace*, pp. 178–79.

9. Freidel, *op. cit.*, pp. 270–71.

10. FDR diary for January 20–25, 1917, entry for January 24. FDR Group 10, Franklin D. Roosevelt Library.

11. FDR, "Trip to Haiti and Santo Domingo 1917." FDR Group 10, Franklin D. Roosevelt Library.

12. Smedley Butler to FDR, December 28, 1917. FDR Group 10, Franklin D. Roosevelt Library. Quoted by Freidel, *op. cit.,* p. 282 n.

13. Correspondence between John L. McIlhenny and FDR, Group 10, Franklin D. Roosevelt Library. Cited and quoted in Freidel, *op. cit.,* pp. 284–85.

14. See "The Conquest of Haiti," by Herbert J. Seligman, *Nation,* Vol. CXI, No. 2871 (July 10, 1920), pp. 35–36; Lewis S. Gannett, "The Conquest of Santo Domingo," *Nation,* Vol. CXI, No. 2872 (July 17, 1920), pp. 64–65; James Weldon Johnson, "Self-Determining Haiti, I. The American Occupation," *Nation,* Vol. CXI, No. 2878 (August 28, 1920), pp. 236–38; Johnson, "II. What the United States Has Accomplished," *Nation,* Vol. CXI, No. 2879 (September 4, 1920), pp. 265–67; Johnson, "III. Government of, by, and for the National City Bank," *Nation,* Vol. CXI, No. 2880 (September 11, 1920), pp. 295–97. See also editorial comment in *Nation,* Vol. CXI, No. 2882 (September 25, 1920), p. 337; " 'Pitiless Publicity' for Haiti," *Nation,* Vol. CXI, No. 2884 (October 6, 1920), p. 366; "Murder Will Out," *Nation,* Vol. CXI, No. 2887 (October 27, 1920), p. 455; plus editorial comment in the issues of November 10 and December 15, 22, and 29, 1920.

15. Freidel, *op. cit.,* pp. 281, 284.

16. Boston *Transcript,* February 17, 1917.

17. FDR, "Memorandum in Regard to Hayti." Prepared in response to a bulletin of National Council for Reduction of Armaments issued April 8, 1922. FDR Group 11, Franklin D. Roosevelt Library.

18. FDR, "Trip to Haiti and Santo Domingo 1917," FDR Group 10, Franklin D. Roosevelt Library.

19. *Ibid.*

20. Carroll Kilpatrick, ed., *Roosevelt and Daniels: A Friendship in Politics* presents memorandum in full, pp. 31–32. Link, *Struggle for Neutrality,* pp. 310–13. Freidel, *op. cit.,* pp. 298–99.

21. FDR diary, March 5, 1917. FDR Group 10, Franklin D. Roosevelt Library.

22. FDR diary, March 11, 1917.

23. *Ibid.*

24. Ernest K. Lindley, *Franklin D. Roosevelt,* pp. 138–39; Lela Stiles, *The Man Behind Roosevelt: The Story of Louis McHenry Howe,* pp. 55–56.

25. Lindley, *op. cit.,* p. 140; Freidel, *op. cit.,* p. 294.

26. Samuel I. Rosenman, ed., *The Public Papers and Addresses of Franklin D. Roosevelt,* 1939 volume, p. 117.

27. Daniels, *Years of Peace,* pp. 581–82.

28. John L. Heaton, *Cobb of "The World,"* pp. 268–70. Quoted in Walter Millis, *The Road to War,* pp. 430–31; Baker, *op. cit.,* pp. 489–90; and Link, *Wilson: Campaigns for Progressivism and Peace,* pp. 398–99. Cobb himself said the conversation took place at one o'clock in the morning of April 2, and all historians save Link who mention it accept Cobb's statement as true. Link, however, is

convinced that the conversation took place on the afternoon of March 19, when Cobb certainly did have an interview with the President. "There is no evidence whatever that Cobb went to the White House" on the night of April 1–2, says Link.

29. FDR diary, March 9, 1917. FDR Group 10, Franklin D. Roosevelt Library.

30. Millis, *op. cit.*, p. 419.

31. The story of this crucial Cabinet session is told in detail by Robert Lansing in a "Memorandum of the Cabinet Meeting, 2:30–5 P.M., Tuesday, March 20, 1917" incorporated in the Lansing Diary and quoted in full by Link, *Campaigns*, pp. 401–8. See also David F. Houston, *Eight Years with Wilson's Cabinet, 1913 to 1920*, Vol. I, pp. 241–44; and Daniels, *Years of War and After*, pp. 22–25.

32. Millis, *op. cit.*, pp. 415–16, quoting Jane Addams.

33. Link, *Campaigns*, pp. 400–1.

34. *Ibid.*, pp. 408–9. Daniels, *Years of War and After*, pp. 67–68. Daniels, *Years of Peace*, p. 270. Freidel, *op. cit.*, p. 300.

35. Eleanor Roosevelt, *This Is My Story*, p. 245. Millis, *op. cit.*, pp. 436–37.

36. Baker, *op. cit.*, p. 515. Diary of Thomas W. Brahany, Chief Clerk, White House Executive Office, Typescript in FDR Group 10, Box 137, Franklin D. Roosevelt Library, entry for April 2, 1917.

37. Freidel, *op. cit.*, p. 300.

38. Daniels, *Years of War and After*, p. 39. Brahany, *op. cit.*, in his entry for Thursday, April 5, 1917, tells of letter (handwritten) from J. P. Morgan, 23 Wall Street, dated April 4, 1917, and addressed to the President. Brahany quotes: "Permit me to congratulate you and the country on your address to the Congress of April 2nd. It was a superb performance and in every way worthy of your country and the great occasion. Allow me also to say for myself and all my partners that we are most heartily in accord with you as to the necessity of the United States assisting the allies in the matter of the supplies of materials and of credits. To those matters we have been devoting our whole time and thought for the last two years. I write to assure you again that the knowledge we have gained in those two years of close association with the allies in these matters are [*sic*] entirely at the disposal of the United States Government at any time or in any way you may wish to use it." Brahany comments that according to his understanding, more than $2,000,000,000 had been disbursed by the Allies in this country by the advice and under the guidance of Morgan & Company since the war began, this being about 75 percent of the total purchases by the Allies of munitions and raw materials in America.

Sixteen: OF DESK WARFARE AND A SECRET PASSION

1. Eleanor Roosevelt, *This Is My Story*, p. 249. Frank Freidel, *Franklin D. Roosevelt: The Apprenticeship*, p. 301, quoting interview with Eleanor Roosevelt, May 1, 1948.

2. Quoted by William Henry Harbaugh, *Power and Responsibility: The Life and Times of Theodore Roosevelt*, p. 502.

3. Henry F. Pringle, *Theodore Roosevelt*, pp. 594–99. Harbaugh, *op. cit.*, p. 500. Joseph Tumulty, *Woodrow Wilson as I Knew Him*, pp. 285–88. Eleanor Roosevelt, *op. cit.*, pp. 249–50.

4. Tumulty, *op. cit.*, p. 289.

5. Quoted by Harbaugh, *op. cit.*, p. 501.

6. Josephus Daniels, *The Wilson Era: Years of Peace—1910–1917*, p. 130. Freidel, *op. cit.*, pp. 301–2.

7. *The Public Papers of Woodrow Wilson*, edited by Ray Stannard Baker and William E. Dodd, Vol. V, pp. 82–88. Quoted by Ray Stannard Baker, *Woodrow Wilson: Life and Letters*, Vol. VII, pp. 211–12.

8. Josephus Daniels, *The Wilson Years: Years of War and After*, p. 255. Freidel, *op. cit.*, p. 303.

9. Daniels, *Years of Peace*, p. 242.

10. *Ibid.*, p. 244.

11. Daniels, *Years of War and After*, p. 255.

12. FDR to Winston Churchill, April 18, 1917. FDR Group 10, Box 137, Franklin D. Roosevelt Library.

13. Elliott Roosevelt, ed., *F.D.R., His Personal Letters, 1905–1928*, p. 354. Revelatory of FDR's bitterness toward Daniels at this time and of his more than willingness to force Daniels' resignation is an unsigned and unaddressed memorandum (someone has dated it May 10, 1917) now in the Franklin D. Roosevelt Library. It was evidently written by FDR for the confidential information of Churchill and considers "the work of the Navy" at that time "from two points of view: 1. Errors already committed, which it is too late to remedy, but which are illustrative of existing troubles. 2. Pending matters which are not progressing in the right way and which can be remedied at the present time." There follow ten typewritten pages detailing FDR's charges of disastrous confusions and delays, a continuous postponement of decisions that should have at once been made, for all of which Daniels was directly responsible, in FDR's view. "The Secretary was told hundreds of times that in case we should need 150,000 men in the Navy to jump from 52,000 or even 70,000 to 150,000 in a month or two would absolutely upset the existing organization. The Surgeon General begged for reserve tents, hospital supplies, etc. etc. The Bureau of Navigation begged for additional training camp sites. The Bureau of Supplies & Accounts begged for additional clothing. It was not until *well along in March* of this year that they were able to obtain the authorization to spend the money to get these things even though the money was appropriated. The result has been a disgrace to the country. The conditions at the four regular training camps— Newport, Norfolk, Great Lakes and San Francisco—have been such that contagious disease of every form, from spinal meningitis to measles, has taken a large toll of men. The hospitals have been overcrowded and the actual training of the men has been put on a far less efficient basis. This is due not only to the delay of the past, but to the impossibility of getting a decision yes or no immediately."

As regards munitions: "It is absolutely true that the Secretary has saved the Government much money by dickering with the steel plants, shipbuilding companies, etc., etc., but it is an absolute fact that the saving caused by these long preliminary negotiations has been eaten up many times by the fact that when war actually came on *April 7th* the Government had to jump in and purchase millions of dollars worth of supplies at higher figures in order to make up for the deficiencies." FDR's conclusion was damning: "In the Secretary's office the least that can be said is that there is constant delay and lack of decision—so much, in fact, that the actual naval operations in this country by the United States have been seriously threatened. The delay of two months, which has already occurred, has, in all probability, meant the loss of many thousands of tons of merchant shipping. The same delay which is existing at the present moment and which will evidently continue to exist will mean the further loss of merchant shipping, and the further delay in solving the general submarine problem if it is going to be solved at all." FDR early on explained to Churchill the proposal for a mine barrage in the North Sea. FDR Group 10, Box 137, Franklin D. Roosevelt Library.

14. Elliott Roosevelt, *op. cit.,* pp. 356–57. FDR received a copy of the highly confidential letter Winston Churchill addressed to the President. Its tone was far less bitter than that of FDR's memorandum, but it was sharply critical (or reported sharp criticism) of Daniels as Secretary and suggested that the President "investigate what has been told me." "The chief, the universal comment concerning him [Daniels] from officers of all ranks who have had dealings with him, has been of his dilatoriness, of his unwillingness to act on great matters and small, the result of which has been to delay and at times almost to paralyze the activities of the Naval Service—a characteristic that has had cumulative effects and is leading to something like demoralization. . . . On the other hand, it is only fair to say that of late he seems to be arriving at a keener realization of the situation, that in certain important matters he is less obstructive, as gradually more and more concerted pressure has been brought to bear upon him. Whether this dilatoriness is inherent, or whether what psychologists would call Mr. Daniels's 'centre of energy' is gradually being turned in the proper direction, I do not pretend to say." Churchill expressed a warm personal liking for Daniels and praised the Secretary for his action on liquor, his building up of the War College, his kindness and courtesy which, Churchill said, were recognized throughout the Navy. FDR Group 10, Box 137, Franklin D. Roosevelt Library.

15. The quotes in this paragraph are from (in order), a memorandum cited by Freidel, *op. cit.,* in footnote on pp. 307–8; memorandum from Roosevelt to Daniels, reproduced in part in Carroll Kilpatrick, ed., *Roosevelt and Daniels,* p. 36; Roosevelt diary, quoted by Freidel, *op. cit.,* p. 307; Kilpatrick, *op. cit.,* p. 37; *ibid.,* p. 35; *ibid.,* pp. 36–37.

16. Elliott Roosevelt, *op. cit.,* p. 351.

17. Quoted in Daniels, *Years of War and After,* p. 254.

18. *Ibid.*

19. *Ibid.* Also Freidel, *op. cit.,* p. 312.

20. Something of Homer's temperament and the kind of excitement he stimulated is revealed in a letter he wrote FDR on February 1, 1915, from his State Street, Boston, office. Wrote Homer: "The writer was present Saturday afternoon when a remark was made by the Canadian Assistant Member of the Marine, which I think you should know about, as it shows conclusively how thin the ice really is. We were coming up Boston Harbor, and a remark was made jokingly, what a beautiful target the new Custom House would make. This man, in all seriousness, perfectly quietly said, 'Well, if your Government persists in the buying of German ships and putting them under the United States flag, I think the chances are good of its being used as a target in a comparatively short space of time. . . . I am sending this to you personally, and trust that you will regard the information as confidential, but I felt you should know it." FDR Group 10, Franklin D. Roosevelt Library.

21. The story is told in considerable detail by Ernest K. Lindley, *Franklin D. Roosevelt*, pp. 149–63.

22. *Public Papers of Woodrow Wilson*, Vol. V., p. 82. Quoted by Daniels, *Years of War and After*, p. 44.

23. Daniels, *ibid.*, p. 84.

24. *Ibid.*

25. Quoted by Freidel, *op. cit.*, p. 314.

26. Baker, *op. cit.*, p. 99. Freidel, *op. cit.*, p. 315.

27. Baker, *op. cit.*, p. 144.

28. Roosevelt on December 27, 1928, was quoted in the New York *Times* as saying that Browne was a "typical inventor," with "a beard" and "regular inventor's black bag"—a "crank" in appearance. A very similar account, directly quoting Roosevelt, is in Lindley *op. cit.*, pp. 155–56. The story, as Freidel pointed out (*op. cit.*, p. 315–16) is inaccurate, and Roosevelt apologized to Browne for it when Browne, who was in no sense a "crank" in either appearance or reality, protested this published description of him.

29. Elting E. Morison, *Admiral Sims and the Modern American Navy*, pp. 414–15.

30. Daniels, *Years of War*, pp. 85–86. Baker, *op. cit.*, pp. 144, 146–47.

31. Lindley, p. 160. Daniels' diary, quoted by Freidel, *op. cit.* in footnote, p. 316.

32. Quoted by Lindley, *op. cit.*, pp. 106–61.

33. Printed in full in Kilpatrick, *op. cit.*, pp. 39–40.

34. Elliott Roosevelt, *op. cit.*, pp. 366–67.

35. Baker, *op. cit.*, p. 334.

36. Elliott Roosevelt, *op. cit.*, p. 363.

37. Lindley, *op. cit.*, pp. 141–42.

38. Freidel, *op. cit.*, p. 327.

39. Lindley, *op. cit.*, p. 145.

40. Ashmun Brown, feature article, Utica (New York) *Saturday Globe*, January 23, 1915.

41. Freidel, *op. cit.*, p. 321.

42. Elliott Roosevelt, *op. cit.*, pp. 274–75.

43. Eleanor Roosevelt, *op. cit.*, pp. 195, 199.

44. Jonathan Daniels, *Washington Quadrille*, p. 63. For factual detail of Lucy Mercer's biography I rely heavily on Daniels' book.

45. *Ibid.*, p. 69, quoting a statement by Mrs. Lyman Cotten, Chapel Hill, North Carolina.

46. *Ibid.*, p. 70.

47. Elliott Roosevelt, *op. cit.*, p. 219.

48. Eleanor Roosevelt, *op. cit.*, p. 208.

49. Jonathan Daniels, *op. cit.*, p. 157.

50. Elliott Roosevelt, *op. cit.*, p. 347.

51. *Ibid.*, p. 350.

52. *Ibid.*, p. 349.

53. *Ibid.*, p. 350.

54. *Ibid.*, pp. 352, 354.

55. *Ibid.*, p. 361.

56. Drew Pearson, syndicated column, July 30, 1966.

57. Eleanor Roosevelt, *op. cit.*, p. 259.

Seventeen: ROOSEVELT AND THE BIRTH OF LEVIATHAN

1. Correspondence between Roosevelt and Arthur Train, November–December, 1917. Quoted by Frank Freidel, *Franklin D. Roosevelt: The Apprenticeship*, p. 331.

2. Quoted by James MacGregor Burns, *Roosevelt: The Lion and the Fox*, p. 63.

3. Alfred B. Rollins, Jr., *Roosevelt and Howe*, p. 141.

4. Letter FDR to Thomas G. Frothingham, October 16, 1925. Quoted by Freidel, *op. cit.*, p. 319.

5. Quoted by John Dos Passos, *Mr. Wilson's War*, p. 222.

6. Ernest K. Lindley, *Franklin D. Roosevelt*, p. 140.

7. Freidel, *op. cit.*, p. 332.

8. Letter from George Creel to Woodrow Wilson, April, 1917. Quoted by Mark Sullivan, *Our Times*, Vol. 5, p. 425.

9. Sullivan, *op. cit.*, p. 445.

10. Ray Stannard Baker, *Woodrow Wilson: Life and Letters*, Vol. 7, pp. 11–12, 74–75.

11. Sullivan, *op. cit.*, pp. 445–46.

12. Freidel, *op. cit.*, p. 335, quoting dispatch in New York *Telegram*, May 4, 1918.

13. *Ibid.*, p. 333.

14. *Ibid.*, p. 335.

15. FDR Commencement Address, Drexel Institute, Philadelphia, May 1, 1918. FDR Group 10, Franklin D. Roosevelt Library.

16. Photograph by Paul Thompson, in Franklin D. Roosevelt Library.

17. Josephus Daniels autobiography ms., quoted by Freidel, *op. cit.*, p. 340.

18. Freidel, *op. cit.*, pp. 341–43.

19. Josephus Daniels, *The Wilson Era: Years of War and After*, pp. 262–63. Freidel, *op. cit.*, pp. 341, 343–45. Roosevelt Diary, summer, 1918, printed in full (save for censor deletions) in Elliott Roosevelt, ed., *F.D.R., His Personal Letters, 1908–1928*, pp. 375–439. All the direct quotations from Roosevelt which follow, in the description of this trip, are from the letter-diary. See also Carroll Kirkpatrick, *Roosevelt and Daniels*, pp. 44–49.

20. *Summary of Activities of U.S. Naval Forces Operating in European Waters*, prepared in London office of U.S. Navy, 1919, p. 19.

21. Among those with whom Roosevelt talked in Italy was Captain Charles E. Merriam, director of the Committee on Public Information operations in that country. Merriam told him that there was a good deal of anti-American feeling among the Italians, who were encouraged by Italian socialists to regard the United States as a capitalist-imperialist nation having exploitive designs upon Italy.

22. Daniels, *op. cit.*, p. 264.

23. Daniels Diary, September 10, 1918, quoted by Freidel, *op. cit.*, p. 364.

24. Elliott Roosevelt, ed., *op. cit.*, p. 439.

25. Eleanor Roosevelt, *This Is My Story*, pp. 267–68. Freidel, *op. cit.*, p. 369. Daniels, *op. cit.*, pp. 265–66.

Eighteen: THE END OF THE CRUSADE

1. Dispatch from von Lersner to German Foreign Office, October 1, 1918, 1 P.M. In Ferdinand Czernin, *Versailles, 1919*, p. 2.

2. Brunau to German Foreign Office, October 1, 1918, 2 P.M. In Czernin, *op. cit.*, p. 3.

3. Robert Lansing to German government, October 8, 1918. In Mark Sullivan, *Our Times*, Vol. 5, p. 507. Czernin, *op. cit.*, printed dispatch in full, pp. 6–7.

4. Lansing to German government, October 14, 1918. In Sullivan, *op. cit.*, pp. 508–9.

5. German government to Lansing, October 20, 1918. In Sullivan, *op. cit.*, pp. 508–9.

6. Lansing to diplomatic representatives in Washington of nineteen Allied nations, October 23, 1918. In Herbert Hoover, *The Ordeal of Woodrow Wilson*, p. 43.

7. Lansing to German government, October 23, 1918. Printed in full in Hoover, *op. cit.*, pp. 37–39.

8. The quotation is from Hindenburg to imperial Chancellor, but expresses Ludendorff's views. Ludendorff himself demanded that the German note of October 20 include a statement to the effect that Germany would "be forced to have recourse to this weapon [the submarine] again unless an armistice goes into effect within a brief period." His demand was rejected by the Foreign Office as "impossible."

9. Czernin, *op. cit.*, p. 9. Quoted in Sullivan, *op. cit.*, p. 511.

10. Josephus Daniels, *The Wilson Era: Years of War and After, 1917–1923*, p. 258. Frank Freidel, *Franklin D. Roosevelt: The Apprenticeship*, p. 370.

11. Georges Clemenceau, *The Grandeur and Misery of Victory*, p. 117.

12. Minutes of Supreme War Council Meeting, October 29, 1918. Printed in Czernin, *op. cit.*, pp. 24–26. All following quotes in description of the meeting are from these minutes.

13. House Diary, October 26, 1918. Czernin, *op. cit.*, pp. 27–28.

14. Czernin, *op. cit.*, p. 31, prints the memorandum in full.

15. Cable from House to the President, October 30, 1918. Printed in full in Hoover, *op. cit.*, pp. 47–49.

16. Quoted in Czernin, *op. cit.*, p. 30.

17. Quoted by Thomas A. Bailey, *Woodrow Wilson and the Lost Peace* (New York, 1944), p. 40.

18. From a memorandum by T. W. Gregory in the Edward M. House Papers, Yale University Library. Reproduced in part in a footnote on p. 16 of Herbert Hoover, *op. cit.* Past has been changed to present tense.

19. *Ibid.*

20. Joseph P. Tumulty, *Woodrow Wilson as I Knew Him*, has on p. 331 a facsimile reproduction of the first page of this statement as typed by Wilson, with Wilson's inked deletions.

21. Quoted by Bailey, *op. cit.*, p. 60.

22. Eleanor Roosevelt, *This Is My Story*, p. 270.

23. *Ibid.*, p. 272.

24. Handwritten letter to Daniels from FDR, December 7, 1918. Freidel, *op. cit.*, pp. 5–6.

25. Eleanor Roosevelt, *op. cit.*, p. 275.

26. Henry Adams, *The Education of Henry Adams*, p. 499.

27. The full memorandum is printed in Hoover, *op. cit.*, pp. 62–63.

28. Henry F. Pringle, *Theodore Roosevelt*, p. 602.

29. Letter from FDR to Daniels, January 9, 1918, in Daniels Ms. Freidel, *op. cit.*, p. 4. Eleanor Roosevelt, *op. cit.*, p. 275.

30. Elliott Roosevelt, ed., *F.D.R., His Personal Letters, 1905–1928*, p. 464.

31. Eleanor Roosevelt, *op. cit.*, pp. 280, 282–84.

32. Elliott Roosevelt, *op. cit.*, pp. 466–67.

33. The summary description of the conference which follows is based on relevant portions of Czernin, *op. cit.;* Herbert Hoover, *op. cit.;* Winston S. Churchill, *The Aftermath, 1918–1928*; Ray Stannard Baker, *Woodrow Wilson and the World Settlement*; the same author's *Woodrow Wilson, Life and Letters*, Vol. 8; and Bailey, *op. cit.*

34. Eleanor Roosevelt, *op. cit.*, p. 288.

35. The first, second, and third (or final) draft of League Covenant are printed in full in Czernin, *op. cit.*, pp. 140–63.

36. Eleanor Roosevelt, *op. cit.*, pp. 289–90.

37. *Ibid.*, pp. 185, 290–91. Freidel, *op. cit.*, pp. 14–15.

38. Eleanor Roosevelt, *op. cit.*, pp. 292–93.

39. Tumulty cable to Wilson, January 6, 1919, printed in appendix to Tumulty, *op. cit.*, p. 517.

40. Edith Bolling Wilson, *My Memoir*, p. 246.

41. Tumulty cable to "Grayson, c/o President Wilson," April 9, 1919, printed in appendix to Tumulty, *op. cit.*, p. 525.

42. Quoted by Sigmund Freud and William C. Bullitt, *Thomas Woodrow Wilson: A Psychological Study*, p. 268.

43. Hoover, *op. cit.*, pp. 233–34.

44. Letter from FDR to Herbert Bayard Swope, September 30, 1919.

45. Divergent views are taken of the Bullitt mission by Lincoln Steffens in his *Autobiography*; Churchill, *op. cit.*, pp. 178–79; George F. Kennan, *Russia and the West*, pp. 130–35; and W. C. Bullitt himself, *The Bullitt Mission to Russia*.

46. Arthur Schlesinger, Jr., *The Crisis of the Old Order*, describes the Crillon episode on p. 14, basing his account on a letter from Adolf A. Berle to Upton Sinclair, December 27, 1919. Bullitt's remark about "watching the world go to hell" became a famous symptomatic remark of the 1920's.

47. The letter appears in full in Freud and Bullitt, *op. cit.*, pp. 271–72.

48. Hoover, *op. cit.*, p. 252.

49. Alden Hatch, *Edith Bolling Wilson*, p. 196.

Nineteen: THE END OF IDEALISM

1. Address, New York Bar Association, March 8, 1919; Washington *Star*, March 2, 1919; speech in Atlantic City, N.J., June 21, 1919, reprinted in Elliott Roosevelt, ed., *F.D.R., His Personal Letters, 1905–1928*, pp. 476–78. Frank Freidel, *Franklin D. Roosevelt: The Ordeal*, p. 17.

2. Commencement address, Worcester (Mass.) Polytechnic Institute, June 25, 1919. Elliott Roosevelt, *op. cit.*, p. 477. Freidel, *op. cit.*, p. 18.

3. Freidel, *op. cit.*, p. 19 n.

4. *Ibid.*, p. 19.

5. *Ibid.*, p. 22, quoting FDR letter to Livingston Davis, April 26, 1919.

6. Ida M. Tarbell, *Owen D. Young: A New Type of Industrial Leader*, pp. 130–34.

7. Freidel, *op. cit.*, p. 28. Josephus Daniels, *The Wilson Era: Years of War and After*, pp. 106–9.

8. FDR speech to Knights of Columbus Peace Convention, August 6, 1919. Letter from FDR to Samuel S. Robinson, December 30, 1919. Both cited by Freidel, *op. cit.*, pp. 30–31.

9. New York *Times*, September 12, 1919.

10. James Roosevelt with Sidney Shalett, *Affectionately, FDR: A Son's Story of a Lonely Man*, pp. 55–60.

11. Elliott Roosevelt, *op. cit.*, pp. 479–80.

12. Rochester (New York) *Post Express*, December 27, 1919, reporting FDR speech at Chamber of Commerce luncheon, Rochester, New York. FDR speech

before Harvard Union, Cambridge, Massachusetts, February 26, 1920. Typescript in FDR Group 14, Franklin D. Roosevelt Library.

13. Philadelphia *Record*, November 12, 1919, reporting FDR speech to Knights of Columbus testimonial dinner, Philadelphia, November 11, 1919.

14. Joseph Tumulty, *Woodrow Wilson as I Knew Him*, p. 435.

15. *Ibid.*, p. 441.

16. *Ibid.*, p. 447.

17. *Ibid.*, p. 444.

18. Stephen Bonsal, *Unfinished Business*, pp. 271–76.

19. Quoted by Herbert Hoover, *The Ordeal of Woodrow Wilson*, p. 284.

20. Edith Bolling Wilson, *My Memoir*, p. 297.

21. Eleanor Roosevelt, *This Is My Story*, pp. 304–5.

22. Jonathan Daniels, *Washington Quadrille*, tells the Crauford-Stuart story in detail, pp. 136–43, 179–83, stressing its interconnection with Bernard Baruch and a society girl whom both Baruch and Crauford-Stuart "found fascinating." Jonathan Daniels derived much of his information from letters written him by Sir Arthur Willert, former Washington correspondent of the London *Times*, and by Mrs. Charles Sumner Hamlin. The story is told in several other books, including Gene Smith, *When the Cheering Stopped*.

23. Eleanor Roosevelt, *op. cit.*, pp. 305–6.

24. Smith, *op. cit.*, pp. 142–43.

25. Jonathan Daniels, *The End of Innocence*, pp. 309–10, 316.

26. Quoted by Freidel, *op. cit.*, p. 40.

27. Elling E. Morison, *Admiral Sims and the Modern American Navy*, pp. 440–41. Josephus Daniels, *op. cit.*, pp. 492–507.

28. Speech at Brooklyn Academy of Music, February 1, 1920, reported New York *Times*, February 2, 1920, p. 1. Freidel, *op. cit.*, p. 40.

29. Freidel, *op. cit.*, p. 58.

30. Elliott Roosevelt, *op. cit.*, p. 486.

31. Eleanor Roosevelt, *op. cit.*, p. 308.

32. Quoted by Jonathan Daniels, *Washington Quadrille*, pp. 189–90.

33. Josephus Daniels, *The Wilson Era: Years of Peace—1910–1917*, p. 317.

34. *Army and Navy Journal*, January 3 and January 10, 1920. Freidel, *op. cit.*, p. 43.

35. *Army and Navy Journal*, January 24, 1920. Freidel, *op. cit.*, p. 44.

36. Josephus Daniels, *The Wilson Era: Years of War and After*, p. 199.

37. Letter, Roosevelt to Senator Carroll S. Page, ranking Democrat on Senate Naval Affairs Committee, February 16, 1920.

38. Quoted by Mark Sullivan, *Our Times, 1900–1925*, Vol. 6 (New York, 1939), p. 537.

39. Even Morison, *op. cit.*, is forced to indicate as much, albeit in tortured prose, on pp. 459–60 of his highly partisan (pro-Sims) book.

40. New York *Times*, March 27, 1930.

41. Appendix to Naval Investigation *Hearings*, 66th U.S. Congress, Senate Subcommittee of Committee on Naval Affairs (Washington, 1921), pp. 3391–95.

42. Elliott Roosevelt, *op. cit.*, pp. xvii–xviii (Eleanor Roosevelt's Foreword).

43. Tumulty, *op. cit.*, p. 505.

44. Alfred B. Rollins, Jr., *Roosevelt and Howe*, pp. 173–74. Freidel, *op. cit.*, pp. 37–39.

45. Franklin Roosevelt Vice Presidential Campaign Address, New Bedford, Massachusetts, September 16, 1920. Freidel, *op. cit.*, p. 39.

Twenty: THE CAMPAIGN OF 1920 AND ITS AFTERMATH

1. FDR speech to Democratic National Committee banquet, Chicago, May 29, 1919.

2. FDR letter to Henry Heymann, December 2, 1919. Group X, FDR Library.

3. Louis B. Wehle, *Hidden Threads of History: Wilson Through Roosevelt*, pp. 81–82.

4. Daniel R. Fusfield, *The Economic Thought of Franklin D. Roosevelt and the Origins of the New Deal*, pp. 74–75. "Platform Recommendations Emphasizing Home Affairs," typescript in FDR Group 10, Box 139, Franklin D. Roosevelt Library.

5. *Autobiography of William Allen White*, p. 584.

6. Francis Russell, *The Shadow of Blooming Grove: Warren G. Harding and His Times*, p. 395.

7. Josephus Daniels, *The Wilson Era: Years of War and After*, pp. 552–53. Frank Freidel, *Franklin D. Roosevelt: The Ordeal*, pp. 62–63.

8. Grenville T. Emmet letter to Langdon P. Marvin, July 8, 1920. FDR Group 15, Franklin D. Roosevelt Library.

9. Freidel, *op. cit.*, pp. 67–68. James M. Cox, *Journey Through My Years*, p. 232.

10. Daniels, *op. cit.*, pp. 554–55.

11. Frances Perkins, *The Roosevelt I Knew*, p. 27.

12. Cox, *op. cit.*, p. 238. Freidel, *op. cit.*, p. 73.

13. Walter Lippmann to FDR, July 8, 1920; Herbert Hoover to FDR, July 13, 1920; Robert H. Jackson to FDR, July 7, 1920—all in FDR Group 15, Franklin D. Roosevelt Library, Roosevelt Papers. New York *Times*, July 7, 1920. Edmund W. Starling and Thomas Sugrue, *Starling of the White House*, p. 157.

14. Charles S. Groves to Henry Cabot Lodge, July 24, 1920; Lodge to Groves, July 26, 1920. Quoted, Freidel, *op. cit.*, p. 74.

15. Cox, *op. cit.*, pp. 241–42, quoting a letter from Claude G. Bowers to Cox in which Bowers told of Roosevelt's reminiscence of visit to Wilson. Freidel, *op. cit.*, p. 74. Elliott Roosevelt, ed., *F.D.R., His Personal Letters, 1905–1928*, pp. 496–97.

16. Elliott Roosevelt, *op. cit.*, p. 494. Eleanor Roosevelt, *This Is My Story* (New York, 1937), p. 312.

17. Freidel, *op. cit.*, p. 75. Daniels, *op. cit.*, pp. 267–69. Elliott Roosevelt, *op.*

cit., pp. 489–90. In his diary entry of Friday, August 6, 1920, Daniels wrote: "He [FDR] left in afternoon but before leaving wrote me a letter most friendly and almost loving which made me glad I had not acted upon my impulse when he seemed to take sides with my critics."

18. Eleanor Roosevelt, *op. cit.,* p. 312.

19. The full speech is printed in Elliott Roosevelt, *op. cit.,* pp. 489–90.

20. Harold L. Ickes, *The Secret Diary of Harold L. Ickes: The First Thousand Days, 1933–1936,* p. 699. Writes Ickes: "In those earlier years, as Steve puts it, the President was just a playboy. When he was campaigning for Vice President, he couldn't be made to prepare his speeches in advance, preferring to play cards instead." *Literary Digest,* Vol. 67 (October 30, 1920), pp. 10–11. FDR address, Manchester, New Hampshire, September 13, 1920. FDR address, Centralia, Washington, August 21, 1920. Alfred B. Rollins, Jr., *Roosevelt and Howe,* p. 161.

21. New York *World,* September 18, 1920. Quoted, Freidel, *op. cit.,* p. 85; Rollins, *op. cit.,* pp. 159–60.

22. New York *Times,* August 9, 1920. Quoted by Rollins, *op. cit.,* p. 160. See also Freidel, *op. cit.,* pp. 81–83.

23. Eleanor Roosevelt, *This Is My Story,* p. 320. Freidel, *Franklin D. Roosevelt: The Ordeal,* p. 90.

24. Letter FDR to Mathew Hale, November 6, 1920. FDR Group 15, Franklin D. Roosevelt Library.

25. *Ibid.,* p. 89.

26. David F. Houston, *Eight Years with Wilson's Cabinet,* Vol. II, p. 93. Quoted by Gene Smith, *When the Cheering Stopped,* p. 169.

27. Cary T. Grayson, *Woodrow Wilson: An Intimate Memoir,* quoted by Alden Hatch, *Edith Bolling Wilson: First Lady Extraordinary,* p. 244.

28. Letter FDR to Mathew Hale, November 6, 1920.

29. *Ibid.,* p. 89.

30. Wehle, *op. cit.,* p. 108.

31. Letter FDR to Louis B. Wehle, November 6, 1920. Quoted by Wehle, *op. cit.,* p. 88, and Freidel, *op. cit.,* pp. 90–91.

32. Elliott Roosevelt, *op. cit.,* p. 514. Arthur M. Schlesinger, Jr., *The Crisis of the Old Order,* p. 366.

33. FDR letter to Langdon Marvin, December 19, 1924. Quoted, Schlesinger, *op. cit.,* p. 374.

34. Grace Tully, *F.D.R., My Boss,* p. 339. Unofficial Observer (Jay Franklin), *The New Dealers,* pp. 230–33.

35. Jonathan Daniels, *The End of Innocence,* p. 322. Elliott Roosevelt, *op. cit.,* p. 511.

36. Letter FDR to Felix Frankfurter, January 7, 1921. Quoted by Freidel, *op. cit.,* p. 93.

37. Unidentified newspaper clipping, 1920, in FDR Scrapbook. Quoted by Freidel, *op. cit.,* p. 93.

38. Letter FDR to Anna Henderson, November 9, 1920. Quoted by Schlesinger, *op. cit.,* p. 366.

39. Mark Sullivan, *The Education of an American*, p. 119. Albert Shaw, memorandum to himself, October 22, 1937. Shaw Mss. New York Public Library. Quoted by Otis L. Graham, Jr., *An Encore for Reform: The Old Progressives and the New Deal*, p. 71.

40. Notebook 53, Ray Stannard Baker, Mss., Library of Congress. Quoted by Graham, *op. cit.*, p. 72.

41. Berkshire Massachusetts *Evening Eagle*, June 21, 1921. Quoted by Daniel R. Fusfeld, *op. cit.*, p. 84.

42. Frederick Lewis Allen, *Only Yesterday*, p. 111.

43. Letter FDR to Ralph M. Easley, February 24, 1921. Quoted by Freidel, *op. cit.*, p. 94.

44. Letter FDR to E. J. Coleman, March 30, 1921. Quoted, Freidel, *op. cit.*, p. 95.

45. Rollins, *op. cit.*, p. 178.

46. *Ibid.*, p. 178. Roosevelt's statement is printed in Elliott Roosevelt, *op. cit.*, pp. 519–20.

47. Elliott Roosevelt, *op. cit.*, pp. 517–18. Langdon P. Marvin's Reminiscence, Oral History Project, Columbia University.

48. Letter Woodrow Wilson to FDR, July 4, 1921. Quoted by Daniels, *op. cit.*, p. 325, and Freidel, *op. cit.*, pp. 123–24.

49. Ernest K. Lindley, *Franklin D. Roosevelt*, p. 201.

Twenty-one: DARKNESS ON CAMPOBELLO

1. Eleanor Roosevelt, *This Is My Story*, p. 329. She tells of weir seining in the midst of her account of Van Lear Black's visit to the island.

2. Earl Looker, *This Man Roosevelt*, p. 111.

3. Letter, Grace Howe to Mary Howe, August 7, 1921. Howe personal papers, Group 36, Franklin D. Roosevelt Library, quoted by Alfred B. Rollins, Jr., *Roosevelt and Howe*, p. 179.

4. Eleanor Roosevelt, *op. cit.*, p. 329.

5. Looker, *op. cit.*, p. 111. James Roosevelt, with Sidney Shalett, *Affectionately, F.D.R.*, pp. 141–42.

6. *Ibid.*, p. 111.

7. Letter, FDR to William Egleston, MD, Hartsville, S.C., October 11, 1924. (A facsimile of this appears in Richard Harrity and Ralph G. Martin, *The Human Side of F.D.R.* (pages unnumbered). Looker, *op. cit.*, pp. 111–12. Anna Roosevelt, "How Polio Helped Father," *Woman*, July, 1949. Frank Freidel, *Franklin D. Roosevelt: The Ordeal*, pp. 98–99.

8. Eleanor Roosevelt, *op. cit.*, p. 331.

9. Lela Stiles, *The Man Behind Roosevelt: The Story of Louis McHenry Howe*, p. 76.

10. He was biochemist Wendell Meredith Stanley, an American, whose famous experiment won him a share of the Nobel Prize for chemistry in 1946.

11. Isaac Asimov, *The Intelligent Man's Guide to the Biological Sciences*, p. 186.

12. Ivan Wichman, MD, *Acute Poliomyelitis*, chapter on "Pathological Anatomy," pp. 18–19.

13. Anna Roosevelt, *op. cit.*, p. 54. Ross T. McIntire, *White House Physician*, p. 31. Freidel, *op. cit.*, p. 99.

14. Elliott Roosevelt, ed., *F.D.R., His Personal Letters, 1905–1928*, p. 524.

15. *Ibid.* James Roosevelt and Shalett, *op. cit.*, pp. 142–43. Jean Gould, *A Good Fight* (New York, 1960), p. 20. Gould derived much of her material from personal interviews with James Roosevelt, Margaret Suckley, and others.

16. Letter FDR to Egleston, *op. cit.*

17. Freidel, *op. cit.*, p. 100, based on a personal interview with Frances Perkins. Gould, *op. cit.*, p. 29, gives a circumstantial, imaginative account of an experience referred to obliquely in FDR and Eleanor Roosevelt letters. James Roosevelt and Shalett, *op. cit.*, write, p. 142, that FDR's "agony, both physical and mental, was acute."

18. Elliott Roosevelt, *op. cit.*, p. 525.

19. *Ibid.*

20. Eleanor Roosevelt, *op. cit.*, p. 332.

21. *Ibid.*, pp. 314–16, 333. Rollins, *op. cit.*, p. 180.

22. Rollins, *op. cit.*, p. 180.

23. Eleanor Roosevelt, *op. cit.*, p. 332.

24. Elliott Roosevelt, *op. cit.*, pp. 527–28.

25. Eleanor Roosevelt, *op. cit.*, p. 332.

26. Freidel, *op. cit.*, p. 101.

27. Elliott Roosevelt, *op. cit.*, p. 527.

28. Freidel, *op. cit.*, p. 100. Rita Halle Kleeman, *Gracious Lady: The Life of Sara Delano Roosevelt*, p. 276.

29. Eleanor Roosevelt, *op. cit.*, p. 335.

30. *Ibid.*, pp. 333–34. Rollins, *op. cit.*, p. 182. John Gunther, *Roosevelt in Retrospect*, p. 223. Ernest K. Lindley, *Franklin D. Roosevelt*, pp. 202–3. Freidel, *op. cit.*, pp. 101–2.

31. Lindley, *op. cit.*, p. 203. Eleanor Roosevelt, *op. cit.*, p. 334.

32. Letter, FDR to Adolph S. Ochs, September 16, 1921, FDR Group 11, Franklin D. Roosevelt Library.

33. Gunther, *op. cit.*, pp. 224–25, published this letter for the first time.

34. *Ibid.*, pp. 225–26. This letter, too, was published by Gunther, *op. cit.*, for the first time.

35. Lindley, *op. cit.*, p. 205. Elliott Roosevelt, *op. cit.*, pp. 530–31.

36. Gunther, *op. cit.*, p. 226. The report of the physical examination of October 2, 1921, in the following paragraph, is also from Gunther, p. 224. Gunther had access to theretofore unpublished medical records of Roosevelt's case.

37. *Ibid.*, p. 224.

38. Eleanor Roosevelt, *op. cit.*, p. 337.

39. *Ibid.*, p. 336.

40. Eleanor Roosevelt, *This I Remember*, p. 12.

41. The story of the "battle to the finish" between Sara and Eleanor "for

Franklin's soul" (Gunther's phrase) is told by him, *op. cit.,* pp. 227–28; Freidel, *op. cit.,* pp. 100–1; Rollins, *op. cit.,* pp. 184–85; Lindley, *op. cit.,* p. 204; Eleanor Roosevelt, *This Is My Story,* pp. 335–40 (in careful understatement; she is much franker about her mother-in-law in *This I Remember,* published after her husband's death); James Roosevelt and Shalett, *op. cit.,* pp. 147–49. Sara refers to it in her *My Boy Franklin* (as told to Isabel Leighton and Gabrielle Forbush), p. 101, saying: ". . . I arranged for his return to Hyde Park where I hoped he would devote himself to the restoration of his health. . . . But Franklin had no intention of conforming to my quiet ideas. . . ."

42. Gunther, *op. cit.,* p. 227.

43. Eleanor Roosevelt, *op. cit.,* p. 335. Gunther, *op. cit.,* p. 227.

44. Eleanor Roosevelt, *op. cit.,* p. 336.

45. James Roosevelt and Shalett, *op. cit.,* p. 148.

46. *Ibid.* Eleanor Roosevelt, *op. cit.,* pp. 335–37.

47. See, for interpretation, Rollins, *op. cit.,* pp. 182–83.

48. James Roosevelt and Shalett, *op. cit.,* p. 147.

49. Gunther, *op. cit.,* pp. 321–32, derived from personal interview with "one of FDR's secretaries."

50. Lindley, *op. cit.,* p. 208. Gunther, *op. cit.,* p. 229.

51. Eleanor Roosevelt, *op. cit.,* pp. 340–42.

52. *Ibid.,* p. 339.

53. *Ibid.,* p. 340.

54. *Ibid.,* p. 350.

Twenty-two: THE ROAD BACK

1. Interview with Louis A. Depew quoted by John Gunther, *Roosevelt in Retrospect,* p. 229.

2. Frances Perkins, *The Roosevelt I knew,* pp. 29, 30.

3. Eleanor Roosevelt, *This I Remember,* p. 25.

4. James Roosevelt, with Sidney Shalett, *Affectionally, F.D.R.,* p. 158.

5. Perkins, *op. cit.,* p. 29.

6. Letter, FDR to Leonard Wood, May 2, 1922; diary of Mrs. Charles Sumner Hamlin for June 10, 1922; letters, FDR to George Albert, July 20, 1922; FDR to Richard E. Byrd, November 21, 1922; FDR to J. P. Adriance, December 15, 1923; FDR to R. P. Davis, October 27, 1924. All in Franklin D. Roosevelt Library.

7. Ernest K. Lindley, *Franklin D. Roosevelt,* p. 207.

8. New York *World,* December 3, 1925. Letter, FDR to W. C. Martin, December 9, 1925, in Franklin D. Roosevelt Library.

9. Letter, FDR to J. W. Kean, December 8, 1923, FDR Library.

10. Letter, FDR to George Marvin, September 12, 1922, FDR Library; Elliott Roosevelt, ed., *F.D.R., His Personal Letters, 1905–1928,* p. 135, *ibid.,* pp. 545–52 (prints "history" in full); Frank Freidel, *Franklin D. Roosevelt: The Ordeal,* pp. 160–61.

11. Franklin D. Roosevelt, "Shall We Trust Japan?" *Asia* Magazine, Vol. 23 (July, 1923), pp. 475–78.

12. Letter, FDR to editor, Baltimore *Sun,* August 13, 1923. Freidel, *op. cit.* p. 134.

13. Woodrow Wilson to FDR, September 16, 1921; Wilson to Eleanor Roosevelt, November 9, 1921; Wilson to FDR, January 5, 1922; Wilson to FDR, April 30, 1922. Freidel, *op. cit.,* pp. 124–25. Gene Smith, *When the Cheering Stopped,* p. 216.

14. Letter, FDR to Livingston Davis, April 20, 1924. FDR Library.

15. Eleanor Roosevelt, "The Seven People Who Shaped My Life," *Look* magazine (July 19, 1951). Eleanor Roosevelt, *This Is My Story,* p. 352.

16. Letter, FDR to Thomas Amory Lee, undated but probably June, 1925. FDR Group 11, Franklin D. Roosevelt Library.

17. The whole of his "Plan" is published as Appendix I to Eleanor Roosevelt's *This I Remember,* pp. 353–66.

18. Letter, FDR to George Rich, February 7, 1923. FDR Group 11, Franklin D. Roosevelt Library.

19. Freidel, *op. cit.,* p. 227.

20. Letter, FDR to William E. Barton, January 18, 1922. Freidel, *op. cit.,* p. 140.

21. Josephus Daniels, *The Wilson Era: Years of Peace—1910–1917,* p. 379.

22. Letter, FDR to William Gibbs McAdoo, April 13, 1922. FDR Group 11, Franklin D. Roosevelt Library.

23. Letter, FDR to Grenville T. Emmet, September 24, 1924.

24. Langdon Marvin interview, Oral History Project, Columbia University, April, 1949.

25. Letter, FDR to Granville T. Emmet, September 24, 1924; letter, FDR to Van Lear Black, September 24, 1924.

26. Turnley Walker, *Roosevelt and the Warm Springs Story,* pp. 7–9, 41–42. Jean Gould, *A Good Fight,* pp. 95–96.

27. New York *Tribune,* May 5, 1922, quoted by Daniel R. Fusfeld, *The Economic Thought of Franklin D. Roosevelt and the Origins of the New Deal,* p. 102.

28. Letter, Elliott C. Brown to FDR, May 12, 1922, quoted by Freidel, *op. cit.* p. 152.

29. New York *Times,* June 4, 1922.

30. *Ibid.* Also New York *Post,* July 1, 1922.

31. New York *Tribune,* May 5, 1922.

32. Freidel, *op. cit.,* p. 156, quoting letter, FDR to Ellis F. Lawrence, January 9, 1924.

33. *Ibid.,* p. 157.

34. Minutes of Board of Governors of the American Construction Council, May 16, 1923. FDR Group 11, Franklin D. Roosevelt Library.

35. New York *Times,* May 12, 1923. Freidel, *op. cit.,* p. 157.

36. Letter, FDR to Emmet, July 26, 1921. FDR Group 11, Franklin D. Roosevelt Library.

37. Alva Johnson, "Mr. Roosevelt as a Businessman," *Saturday Evening Post,* Vol. 209 (October 31, 1936), p. 64 ff. Freidel, *op. cit.,* pp. 147–48.

38. New York *Times,* September 14, 1922. Johnson, *op. cit.*

39. Freidel, *op cit.,* p. 145, derived from "two confidential sources."

40. Quoted by Alfred B. Rollins, Jr., *Roosevelt and Howe,* pp. 196–97.

41. Johnson, *op. cit.* Freidel, *op. cit.,* pp. 150–51.

42. Johnson, *op. cit.* Freidel, *op. cit.,* p. 151. A recent (as of April, 1972) acquisition by the Franklin D. Roosevelt Library is FDR's Accounts and Investment Ledger for the years 1918–1927 inclusive—a ledger that had been in son John Roosevelt's possession since his father's death. In it FDR recorded at the first of each year, itemized, his holdings of stocks and bonds, their appreciation or depreciation during the preceding twelve months, the dividends paid, and the net gain or loss of his "Principal Account." He also itemized his total expenses and income for the year. His stocks and bonds had a total current market value of $269,387.75 on January 1, 1918; $276,490.25 on January 1, 1919; $272,971.00 in 1920; $269,249.94 in 1921; $288,324.55 in 1922; $313,850.68 in 1923; $299,742.06 in 1924; $310,203.10 in 1925; $323,804.29 in 1926; and $377,712.47 in 1927. In the nine years of 1918–26 inclusive, his income exceeded his expenditures in only four years, and the excess of income over outgo was modest compared to the net loss in other years. Thus, in 1918 his total income was $23,827.62, his expenses $22,860.12, giving him a net gain for the year of $967.50. In the following year his income exceeded his expenses by $2,324.32. But in 1920, owing in part to political expenditures, his expenses exceeded his income by $12,102.59. He gained $7,220.80 in 1921 and $2,109.44 in 1922, but lost $3,494.14 in 1923 (when his income was $40,054.51), $9,454.30 in 1924 (when his income was $39,692.85), $9,625.15 in 1925 (when his income was $52,594.61), and a whopping $20,821.79 in 1926 (when his income was $53,766.85).

43. Letter, Fred R. Andree to FDR, July 20, 1923. Franklin D. Roosevelt Library.

44. Johnson, *op cit.,* quoting New York *Times,* May 5, 1924. Letter, FDR to Kermit Roosevelt, May 9, 1924.

45. Eleanor Roosevelt, *This I Remember,* p. 69.

46. Grace Tully, *F.D.R. My Boss,* p. 22. Gunther, *op. cit.,* p. 95.

Twenty-three: RETURN TO POLITICS: 1924

1. Chicago *Tribune,* May 30, 1919. Letter from FDR to Harvey G. Starkweather, December 27, 1921, quoted by Frank Freidel, *Franklin D. Roosevelt: The Ordeal,* p. 112.

2. New York *American,* October 1, 1919. New York *Journal,* October 1, 2, 1919. Matthew and Hannah Josephson, *Al Smith: Hero of the Cities,* pp. 244–52. Richard O'Connor, *The First Hurrah,* pp. 110–16. Emily Smith Warner and Hawthorne Daniel, *The Happy Warrior,* pp. 112–14.

3. Josephson, *op. cit.,* page 267. Freidel, *op. cit.,* p. 117.

4. FDR to Al Smith, July 18, 1922. Freidel, *op. cit.,* p. 117. Josephson, *op. cit.,* pp. 267–69. Warner, *op. cit.,* pp. 131–33.

5. Eleanor Roosevelt, *This I Remember,* p. 16.

6. James Roosevelt, with Sidney Shalett, *Affectionately, F.D.R.,* pp. 54–55.

7. Louis Howe to FDR, September 29, 1922 (telegram). FDR Group 11, Franklin D. Roosevelt Library.

8. *Ibid.* Freidel, *op. cit.,* p. 118.

9. Josephson, *op. cit.,* pp. 282–83.

10. FDR to Byron R. Newton, December 20, 1922. FDR Group 11, Franklin D. Roosevelt Library.

11. Freidel, *op. cit.,* pp. 161–62. FDR to William Jennings Bryan, June 20, 1923. FDR Group 11, Franklin D. Roosevelt Library.

12. Louis W. Koenig, *Bryan,* p. 597.

13. FDR to William Jennings Bryan, June 20, 1923.

14. Josephson, *op. cit.,* p. 294.

15. Warner, *op. cit.,* p. 147. Josephson, *op. cit.,* p. 295.

16. FDR to Edward S. Moore, June 18, 1923. Quoted by Freidel, *op. cit.,* p. 163.

17. FDR to Abram I. Elkus, August 20, 1923. Freidel, *op. cit.,* pp. 163–64.

18. Mark Sullivan, *Our Times,* Vol. VI, p. 333.

19. FDR note, February 1, 1924, quoted by Freidel, *op. cit.,* p. 125.

20. The *Larooco Log* is in the Franklin D. Roosevelt Library. Its title page and "dedication page" are reproduced in Elliott Roosevelt, ed., *F.D.R., His Personal Letters, 1905–1928,* between pp. 596–97.

21. Gene Smith, *When the Cheering Stopped,* pp. 238–39. Sullivan, *op. cit.,* pp. 327–29.

22. Emporia (Kansas) *Gazette,* February 4, 1924. Reprinted in *The Editor and His People,* a collection of White editorials arranged by Helen O. Mahin, p. 213.

23. Smith, *op. cit.,* pp. 241–42. Elliott Roosevelt, *op. cit.,* p. 538.

24. Elliott Roosevelt, *op. cit.,* p. 538.

25. *Ibid.,* pp. 539–44, 555–60.

26. Alfred B. Rollins, Jr., *Roosevelt and Howe,* p. 211, quoting "typewritten note" in Franklin D. Roosevelt Library.

27. Quoted by Freidel, *op. cit.,* p. 168.

28. Denis Tilden Lynch, "Friends of the Governor," *North American Review,* June, 1928. Quoted by Josephson, *op. cit.,* p. 306.

29. Warner, *op. cit.,* p. 152. Josephson, *op. cit.,* p. 307. Freidel, *op. cit.,* p. 169.

30. Louis Howe to Thomas Mott Osborne, April 1, 1924. Group 36, Franklin D. Roosevelt Library.

31. FDR to David S. Hawkins, March 22, 1924. Quoted by Freidel, *op. cit.,* p. 166.

32. Ernest K. Kindley, *Franklin D. Roosevelt,* p. 222.

33. Eleanor Roosevelt, *This Is My Story,* p. 354.

34. FDR to James Norris, June 10, 1924. FDR Group 16, Franklin D. Roosevelt Library.

35. FDR to William Gibbs McAdoo, May 19, 1924. FDR Group 16, Franklin D. Roosevelt Library.

36. FDR letter for Smith's signature, FDR Group 16, Franklin D. Roosevelt Library. Quoted by Rollins, *op. cit.*, p. 214. New York *Times*, June 9, 1924.

37. Lindley, *op. cit.*, p. 222.

38. *Ibid.*, p. 223. Warner, *op. cit.*, pp. 159–60. Joseph D. Proskauer, *A Segment of My Times*, pp. 50–51. There was published in 1924, whether before or after the speechwriting I do not know, a biography of Theodore Roosevelt entitled *Roosevelt: The Happy Warrior*, by Bradley Gilman, who quoted the Wordsworth poem in a frontispiece. On March 7, 1915, Woodrow Wilson answered a letter received from his close friend, Mrs. Crawford H. (Nancy) Toy: "It was generous of you to think of any part of Wordsworth's Happy Warrior as applying to me. I seem to myself so unheroic a figure (just a man who intends right things and looks for them every day with a steady mind, uncommon in nothing except that it is at his command when he wishes, as the result of long discipline) and with none but common tools to work with."

39. Arthur Mullen, *A Western Democrat*, p. 242.

40. Smith statement. Quoted by O'Connor, *op. cit.*, p. 149.

41. New York *Times*, June 27, 1924; Elliott Roosevelt, *op. cit.*, p. 561; Freidel, *op. cit.*, p. 176; Warner, *op. cit.*, pp. 160–61.

42. Earl Looker's column, "Looker On," New York *Herald Tribune*, July 1, 1924. Quoted by Lindley, *op. cit.*, pp. 223–24. Walter Lippmann to FDR, June 27, 1924, FDR Group 16, Franklin D. Roosevelt Library.

43. New York *Times*, July 10, 1924.

44. Ike B. Dunlap to FDR, July 10, 1924. Quoted by Freidel, *op. cit.*, p. 180.

45. Claude G. Bowers, *My Life*, pp. 177–78.

Twenty-four: WARM SPRINGS

1. Glenn Frank to FDR, August 11, 1924; FDR to Glenn Frank, August 12, 1924. FDR Group 16, Franklin D. Roosevelt Library.

2. FDR to Dr. William Eggleston, October 11, 1924. Published in *Journal of the South Carolina Medical Association*, Spring, 1946. Quoted by Ross T. McIntyre, *White House Physician*, pp. 31–34.

3. Donald Scott Carmichael, editor with commentary, *F.D.R., Columnist*, pp. 6–8. Turnley Walker, *Roosevelt and the Warm Springs Story*, pp. 14–15.

4. Kenneth S. Davis, Luna B. Leopold, original ms. of *Water*, a volume in the *LIFE Science Library*.

5. Jean Gould, *A Good Fight*, pp. 120–21. Earl Looker, *This Man Roosevelt*, pp. 118–19.

6. Walker, *op. cit.*, pp. 17–25, and Gould, *op cit.*, pp. 119–20, present circumstantial accounts of Roosevelt's introduction to Warm Springs.

7. Eleanor Roosevelt, *This I remember*, p. 27.

8. Carmichael, *op. cit.*, pp. 7–8.

9. Elliott Roosevelt, *F.D.R. His Personal Letters, 1905–1928*, p. 564.

10. *Ibid.*, pp. 565–66.

11. FDR to George Foster Peabody, October 14, 1924. Quoted by Carmichael, *op. cit.*, p. 10.

12. Elliott Roosevelt, *op. cit.*, p. 568.

13. Carmichael, *op. cit.*, reprinted the Atlanta *Journal Sunday Magazine* article of October 26, 1924, in its entirety on pp. 160–64. Walker, *op. cit.*, gives circumstantial account of O'Connor's first visit to Warm Springs, pp. 42–48.

14. Elliott Roosevelt, *op. cit.*, p. 568.

15. FDR to John Lawrence, September 8, 1924. Quoted by Gould, *op. cit.*, pp. 118–19.

16. Elliott Roosevelt, *op. cit.*, p. 566.

17. Song published by Democratic Song Bureau, New York, 1924, with Words and Music by Hugh Gordon.

18. Quoted by Harold U. Faulkner, *From Versailles to the New Deal*, pp. 219–20.

19. Eleanor Roosevelt, *op. cit.*, pp. 49–50.

20. *Ibid.*, pp. 31–32.

21. FDR to Willard Salisbury, December 9, 1924.

22. FDR to J. A. H. Hopkins, April 8, 1925. Quoted, Freidel, *op. cit.*, p. 204.

23. Circular letter to some 3,000 Democrats, December, 1924. Ernest K. Lindley, *Franklin D. Roosevelt*, pp. 224–25, quotes letter as do Freidel and others.

24. Thomas J. Walsh to George Fort Milton, December 23, 1924. (Notes taken by Robert Campbell, Department of History, Clark University, for projected biography of Walsh.)

25. FDR to Edwin T. Meredith, March 17, 1925.

26. Log of the *Larooco*, in Franklin D. Roosevelt Library. Elliott Roosevelt, *op. cit.*, p. 571. Following quotes are from the log.

27. Eleanor Roosevelt, *This Is My Story*, p. 345.

28. FDR to Thomas J. Walsh, Walsh to FDR, March 8, 1925, as published in New York *Times*.

29. FDR to William A. Oldfield, April 11, 1925. Quoted, Freidel, *op. cit.*, p. 212.

30. Samuel V. Stewart to FDR, December 20, 1924, FDR Group 16, Franklin D. Roosevelt Library.

31. FDR to James A. Edgerton, December 12, 1924, FDR Group 16, Franklin D. Roosevelt Library.

32. FDR to Thomas J. Walsh, public letter, March 8, 1924. Quoted in Lindley, *op. cit.*, p. 225.

33. Mrs. Charles Sumner Hamlin's "Memories of Franklin D. Roosevelt." Franklin D. Roosevelt Library.

34. Freidel, *op. cit.*, p. 106. Based on interview with Eleanor Roosevelt, September 3, 1952.

35. Quoted by Carmichael, *op. cit.*, p. 16.

36. Tom Loyless' column in Macon (Georgia) *Daily Telegraph*, April 14, 1925. Printed in full in Carmichael, *op. cit.*, pp. 19–24. Loyless included in his column of that day three interesting Roosevelt letters on political matters.

37. Memorandum dictated by Roosevelt in White House, President's Personal File, 1934, in Franklin D. Roosevelt Library. Quoted by Carmichael, *op. cit.*, pp. 17–18, and many others.

38. Walker, *op. cit.*, p. 107.

39. FDR to Livingston Davis, April 25, 1925. FDR Group 11, Franklin D. Roosevelt Library.

40. Carmichael, *op. cit.*, prints all nine of FDR's *Telegraph* columns, pp. 27–70.

41. *Ibid.*, pp. 24–25.

42. New York *Times*, January 4, 1925, under heading "Naval Prints for Sale."

43. Robert Moses, *Public Works: A Dangerous Trade*, pp. 141, 142.

44. FDR to Van Lear Black, April 22, 1925. FDR Group 11, Franklin D. Roosevelt Library. Elliott Roosevelt, *op. cit.*, p. 578. Freidel, *op. cit.*, p. 195. James Roosevelt, with Sidney Shalett, *Affectionately, F.D.R.*, p. 167.

45. Elliott Roosevelt, *op. cit.*, pp. 585–87. Gould, *op. cit.*, p. 138.

46. Walker, *op. cit.*, p. 80.

47. Elliott Roosevelt, *op. cit.*, pp. 590, 591.

48. Donald S. Carmichael, "An Introduction to the Log of the *Larooco*," *The Franklin D. Roosevelt Collector* (November, 1948), p. 37.

49. Freidel, *op. cit.*, p. 197. Based on interview with Eleanor Roosevelt, September 3, 1952.

50. Elliott Roosevelt, *op. cit.*, p. 611.

51. *Ibid.*, p. 600.

52. FDR to Endicott Peabody, January 9, 1928. FDR Group 11, Franklin D. Roosevelt Library. Printed in James Roosevelt and Shalett, *op. cit.*, pp. 89–90.

53. Elliott Roosevelt, *op. cit.*, pp. 607, 609.

54. *Ibid.*, pp. 611–13. Walker, *op. cit.*, pp. 84–86.

55. Eleanor Roosevelt, *op. cit.*, p. 26.

56. FDR to Charles G. Burlingame, July 5, 1928. FDR Group 11, Franklin D. Roosevelt Library. Reproduced in part in Donald Day, *Franklin D. Roosevelt's Own Story*, p. 103.

57. Louis Howe to FDR, undated letter of late summer, 1926. Group 36, Franklin D. Roosevelt Library. Quoted by Alfred B. Rollins, Jr., *Roosevelt and Howe*, p. 224, and Freidel, *op. cit.*, pp. 216–17.

58. FDR to Al Smith, September 17, 1926. Freidel, *op. cit.*, p. 231. Day, *op. cit.*, pp. 95–96.

59. Press release, September 27, 1926, of FDR speech to New York State Democratic Convention, September 27, 1926. Freidel, *op. cit.*, p. 217.

60. Quoted by Day, *op. cit.*, p. 90.

61. Address to New York State Convention, September 27, 1926. FDR Group 11, Franklin D. Roosevelt Library.

62. Quoted by Richard O'Connor, *The First Hurrah: A Biography of Alfred E. Smith*, p. 185.

63. Elliott Roosevelt, *op. cit.*, p. 617.

64. Speech ms., October, 1926, FDR Group 11, Franklin D. Roosevelt Library.

65. O'Connor, *op. cit.*, pp. 162–66. J. Joseph Huthmacher, *Senator Robert F. Wagner and the Rise of Urban Liberalism,* pp. 51–52.

66. Walker, *op. cit.*, pp. 118–21, 141–42, gives circumstantial account of founding of Warm Springs Foundation.

67. *Ibid.*, pp. 134–35. Freidel, *op. cit.*, p. 198.

68. Elliott Roosevelt, *op. cit.*, pp. 620–21, 623–24.

69. *Ibid.*, pp. 628–31.

70. *Ibid.*, p. 623.

Twenty-five: FATEFUL CUE—FATED RESPONSE

1. William Allen White, *A Puritan in Babylon,* p. 400.

2. FDR to Josephus Daniels, June 23, 1927. Carroll Kilpatrick, *Roosevelt and Daniels: A Friendship in Politics,* p. 87.

3. Josephus Daniels to FDR, July 19, 1927. Kilpatrick, *op. cit.*, p. 88.

4. FDR to Al Smith, March 20, 1927, FDR Group 17, Franklin D. Roosevelt Library. Frank Freidel, *Franklin D. Roosevelt: The Ordeal,* p. 253.

5. Emily Smith Warner, with Hawthorne Daniel, *The Happy Warrior,* pp. 183–84.

6. Robert Moses, *Public Works: A Dangerous Trade,* pp. 147–48.

7. Al Smith to FDR, February 3, 1928. FDR Group 11, Franklin D. Roosevelt Library. Arthur M. Schlesinger, Jr., *The Crisis of the Old Order,* p. 379.

8. FDR had some part in launching Sumner Welles' career in the State Department when, in March, 1915, Welles wrote him from 493 Commonwealth Avenue, Boston: "In order to send in my application . . . for entrance to the Diplomatic Service it is necessary for me to have several letters of recommendation as you know. And I am in hopes that you may be willing to send me such a letter to go with my application blank. You probably know better than I what it is necessary to write. When William Phillips was here last week he encouraged me in my plan to enter the Service, and since the examinations are in June, I am anxious to get my application in quickly." He hoped he was "not causing you much trouble." FDR replied, March 15, 1915: "My dear Sumner:—I am delighted to learn that you are going to take the diplomatic examinations this Spring, and am gladly sending you a line to go with your application." The enclosed letter, addressed to William J. Bryan, Secretary of State, said: "I take great pleasure in commending to your good offices Mr. Sumner Welles, who desires to take the examinations for the Diplomatic Corps this Spring. I have known him since he was a small boy and have seen him go through school and college and I should be most glad to see him successful in entering the Diplomatic Corps. He has travelled extensively, speaks several languages, I think, and should give a very good account of himself in the service. . . ." FDR Group 10, Box 81, File: Patronage-General, 1913–1920, Franklin D. Roosevelt Library.

9. FDR, "Our Foreign Policy, A Democratic View," *Foreign Affairs*, Vol. 6 (July, 1928), p. 585.

10. FDR to George R. Van Namee, March 27, 1928; FDR to Carl C. Danaugh, March 27, 1928. FDR Group 17, Franklin D. Roosevelt Library.

11. FDR to Newton D. Baker, July 12, 1928; FDR to Clark Eichelberger, July 20, 1928. FDR Group 17, Franklin D. Roosevelt Library.

12. Richard O'Connor, *The First Hurrah*, p. 197, deriving from Claude G. Bowers, *My Life*.

13. Jean Gould, *A Good Fight*, p. 175.

14. Eleanor Roosevelt, *This I Remember*, p. 38.

15. FDR to Walter Lippmann, August 6, 1928. FDR Group 17, Franklin D. Roosevelt Library. Freidel, *op. cit.*, p. 243.

16. FDR speech nominating Al Smith, June 27, 1928. FDR Group 17, Franklin D. Roosevelt Library.

17. Chicago *Tribune*, July 1, 1928. New York *Times*, June 28, 1928. Elliott Roosevelt, ed., *F.D.R., His Personal Letters, 1905–1928*, p. 639. New York *World*, June 28, 1928.

18. James Roosevelt, with Sidney Shalett, *Affectionately, F.D.R.*, pp. 181–84.

19. FDR to Josephus Daniels, July 20, 1928. Kilpatrick, *op. cit.*, p. 94.

20. FDR to Myron D. Kings, June 15, 1925, quoted by Freidel, *op. cit.*, p. 221.

21. Alfred E. Smith, Acceptance Speech, Albany, August 22, 1928. See Arthur M. Schlesinger, Jr., ed., *History of American Presidential Elections, 1789–1936*, Vol. III, p. 269.

22. FDR to Van Lear Black, July 25, 1928; FDR to Josephus Daniels, July 20, 1928; FDR to Harry F. Byrd, August 20, 1928; FDR to Ward Melville, September 21, 1928. FDR Group 17, Franklin D. Roosevelt Library.

23. Donald Scott Carmichael, *F.D.R., Columnist*, pp. 81, 95–96, 103–45.

24. *Ibid.*, pp. 95–96.

25. New York *Times*, November 2, 1926. Tamara K. Hareven, *Eleanor Roosevelt, An American Conscience*, p. 27.

26. Eleanor Roosevelt, *op. cit.*, pp. 32–34.

27. New York *Times*, December 4, 1932. Joseph P. Lash, *Eleanor and Franklin*, p. 307.

28. Eleanor Roosevelt, "Women Must Learn to Play the Game as Men Do," *Redbook* (March, 1928); "Why Democrats Favor Smith," *North American Review*, Vol. 224 (November, 1927), pp. 472–75; "Jeffersonian Principles the Issue in 1928," *Current History*, Vol. 23 (June, 1928), pp. 354–57.

29. FDR to Stanley W. Prenosoil, August 23, 1928. FDR Group 17, Franklin D. Roosevelt Library.

30. George P. Marvin to FDR, February 2, 1928, quoted by Lash, *op. cit.*, p. 313.

31. Eleanor Roosevelt, *op. cit.*, pp. 40–42.

32. Grace Tully, *F.D.R. My Boss*, pp. 31–32.

33. *Ibid.*, p. 34. Eleanor Roosevelt, *op. cit.*, pp. 43–44.

34. FDR to Hugh Gibson, January 2, 1920. FDR Group 10, Franklin D. Roosevelt Library.

35. Ernest K. Lindley, *Franklin D. Roosevelt*, p. 14. Edward J. Flynn, *You're the Boss*, p. 47.

36. O'Connor, *op. cit.*, p. 215. Warner, *op. cit.*, p. 221. Matthew and Hannah Josephson, *Al Smith, Hero of the Cities*, pp. 372–73.

37. Flynn, *op. cit.*, pp. 67–68.

38. Howe to FDR, September 26, 1928. FDR Group 14, Franklin D. Roosevelt Library.

39. Eleanor Roosevelt to FDR, September 30, 1928. Elliott Roosevelt, *op. cit.*, p. 646.

40. Direct quotations are from telegram, FDR to Al Smith, September 30, 1928. Lindley, *op. cit.*, pp. 14–15.

41. Elliott Roosevelt, *op. cit.*, p. 645.

42. Eleanor Roosevelt to FDR, September 30, 1928. Flynn, *op. cit.*, p. 68. Lindley, *op. cit.*, p. 18. Eleanor Roosevelt, *op. cit.*, p. 45.

43. Warner, *op. cit.*, p. 239. Mrs. Warner, Al Smith's daughter, says Moses made the remark in her presence at the Rochester convention. She uses the adjective "poor" in her book. Others report the word as "lousy" and this seems more in line with Moses' usual language in such cases.

44. Eleanor Roosevelt, *op. cit.*, pp. 45–46.

45. Lindley, *op. cit.*, pp. 18–20, gives a circumstantial account of Roosevelt's "drafting" for the governorship, and I have followed it closely in my account. He was an eyewitness of the events in Rochester.

46. Louis Howe to FDR, September 26, 1928. (The exact quote is: "If they are looking for a goat, why doesn't Wagner sacrifice himself?") FDR Group 17, Franklin D. Roosevelt Library.

47. Eleanor Roosevelt, *op. cit.*, p. 46.

48. Samuel I. Rosenman, *Working with Roosevelt*, p. 36.

49. In a letter to his uncle Frederic A. Delano, October 8, 1928, FDR said he had told Smith, ". . . not that I would allow the use of my name before the convention, but . . . if, in the final analysis, the convention insisted on nominating me, I should feel under definite obligation to accept the nomination." FDR Group 17, Franklin D. Roosevelt Library. Lindley reports the conversation as I do in *op. cit.*, p. 20. See also James A. Farley, *Jim Farley's Story: The Roosevelt Years*, pp. 59–60. Doris Fleeson, "Missy—To Do This—FDR," *Saturday Evening Post*, Vol. 210(3) (January 8, 1938), pp. 8–9.

Acknowledgments

⇥⇥⤠⇤⇤

THIS book has been, of its kind, a more than normally solitary labor, which makes me all the more grateful to the few people who have helped me with it.

First and foremost of these is my wife, Florence Olenhouse Davis, whose criticisms and suggestions have often improved the quality of my prose and prevented lapses of judgment and taste as I dealt with complex personalities and events. She has been invaluable to me in the role of secretary. She has helped me organize my research, has repeatedly located misplaced notes and documents (I have a special talent for misplacing them), and has typed the manuscript with remarkable neatness and accuracy, some of it twice—a formidable task in view of the fact that the final typescript totaled nearly 1,400 pages.

My debt to Tilton M. Barron, director of the Goddard Library at Clark University, is much greater than these published thanks can repay. Without the special service he gave me—service far beyond a librarian's call of duty—it is probable that my wife and I could not have continued to live in the lovely New England countryside where this work is being done. And Mr. Barron's help in this regard has been augmented by that of the librarians of our home town of Princeton, Massachusetts. I owe special thanks to my Princeton friends and neighbors, the Reverend and Mrs. Philemon Sturges. He, a former master at Groton School, later rector of St.-Martin's-in-the-Fields, Chestnut Hill, Philadelphia, guided me on a tour of the school; facilitated an interview with Miss Marjorie Peabody, daughter of Endicott Peabody; and in general helped me understand Peabody and his school as I could not otherwise have done.

Upon the high professional competence of the staff as well as upon the rich resources (wonderfully well arranged for easy access) of the Franklin D. Roosevelt Library at Hyde Park, New York, every writer about FDR must heavily lean. If I have made less direct use of this special competence and these resources than earlier writers on my subject have done, it is only because these predecessors have used them so well

—and my direct use steadily increases as I deal with matters more recent and exclusively focused upon FDR than most of those in the volume here concluded. I am especially grateful for the personal kindnesses and professional assistance of Joseph W. Marshall, librarian and head of the Research Room Unit.

My thanks go also to Louis M. Starr, director of Columbia University's Oral History Research Office, for introducing me to the staff and rich resources of this project which pioneered in the application of tape-recorder technology to the development of historical materials. My use of these resources increases as my work on FDR proceeds.

Three friends have read parts of the book in manuscript.

Robert Campbell of Clark University's Department of History, an authority on the period of American history with which my book is concerned, read the whole of the manuscript up to and inclusive of the chapter dealing with FDR's polio and most kindly made available to me the research he has done for a projected biography of Montana's Senator Walsh, a project to which I hope he will return. He not only enabled me to avoid certain errors of fact and interpretation, but also sharpened my points of view by disagreeing with them, on occasion, as we talked of what I was doing.

William L. Shirer read portions of the manuscript with a critical eye and, with Martha Pelton Shirer, facilitated my meeting James MacGregor Burns in circumstances conducive of the friendship that has been formed between us. I am most grateful. Mr. Burns' *Roosevelt: The Lion and the Fox* and *Roosevelt: The Soldier of Freedom* are of course classics of American history and biography. His judgments on my work have therefore had a special value for me, and I am more thankful than I can say for his critique of the portions of my manuscript which he, though intensely and actively concerned with the politics of an election year, found time to read.

Marcus A. McCorison, director of the American Antiquarian Society, Worcester, Massachusetts, while in process of weeding out books not in the special field of Americana with which his great research library is concerned, assigned me on "permanent loan" a half dozen FDR books which have been useful to me and for which I thank him. He also gave me useful information about FDR's relations with the Antiquarian Society, of which FDR became a member in the 1920's, and in whose work FDR took an active interest for the remainder of his life.

Last but by no means least is my grateful acknowledgment of the support—spiritual, material, and professional—given me by my editor, Harvey Ginsberg of Putnam's. I must confess I have not always felt gratitude toward him for persuading me into this project; but it is certainly not his fault that the project has grown, as if with a perverse logic and will of its own, far beyond the bounds we originally set for it, and I have been and remain profoundly appreciative of his unwavering faith in my work, his patience with me during dark hours of despair, and his application of a critical intelligence and editorial talent of high order to every aspect of this labor.

Bibliography

➤➤➤◄◄◄

T O A LONG book intended for a general rather than specialist readership it has seemed unnecessary to append an extended bibliographical essay. Many such essays have been published over the years and are readily available to Roosevelt scholars.

Mention must be made, however, of two documentary compilations indispensable to any student of Franklin Roosevelt. *F.D.R., His Personal Letters*, edited by Elliott Roosevelt (New York, 1947, 1948, 1950), is in four volumes. Volume one is subtitled *Early Years*; volume two (edited with the assistance of James N. Rosenau), *1905–1928*; and volumes three and four (edited with the assistance of Joseph P. Lash), *1928–1945.* These volumes, it must be added, include but a tiny fraction of Roosevelt's total personal correspondence, and the student must take note of the stated principles of selection. The bulk of this correspondence may be consulted at the Franklin D. Roosevelt Library in Hyde Park, New York. *The Public Papers and Addresses of Franklin D. Roosevelt*, edited by Samuel I. Rosenman (thirteen volumes, New York, 1938–1950), is also a selection rather than a comprehensive compilation, and there are occasional significant differences between the speech as printed therein and the reading copy in the Franklin D. Roosevelt Library or the copy released to the press at the time the speech was given. For the present volume, however, such differences were unimportant since my concern here has been with the relatively few memoranda and notes scattered through the thirteen volumes in which Roosevelt reminisces of his early life and of things his parents told him of their lives.

Frequent reference was made to a compilation by Robert L. Jacoby, *Calendar of Speeches and Other Published Statements of Franklin D. Roosevelt, 1910–1920.*

The great pioneer of Roosevelt scholarship, upon whose work all subsequent scholarship has greatly depended, is Frank Freidel. My notes record my heavy debts to his *Franklin D. Roosevelt: The Apprenticeship*; *Franklin D. Roosevelt: The Ordeal*; and *Franklin D. Roosevelt: The Triumph.* These three volumes, with the three yet to come (they have been long and eagerly awaited), will constitute as near an approach to a truly definitive biography of FDR as we are likely ever to achieve.

I should perhaps add that Joseph P. Lash's remarkably fine and popular *Eleanor and Franklin* (New York, 1971) did not appear until the last chapter of the present volume had been written. My immediate careful reading of the book caused me to make a couple of revisions of my own account. One of them provided additional confirmation of a point already made. The other was more important. I had conjectured on the basis of available evidence that Eleanor Roosevelt had somehow discovered irrefutable proof of her husband's romantic involvement with Lucy Mercer in the fall or early winter of 1917. Mr. Lash, on the basis of personal interviews with Mrs. Roosevelt, tells us she found letters from Lucy Mercer to her husband in the fall of 1918.

What follows is a simple alphabetical listing of *only* those books and other materials actually used in the course of this work. Most, though by no means all, of these are cited as specific sources in the chapter notes. I trust it will be obvious to the interested reader how and for what purpose, and for what portion of my book, each of these was consulted. The reader is reminded that this bibliography is for a history ending with the year 1928.

I. GENERAL LIST: BOOKS USED FOR NARRATIVE HISTORY

AARON, DANIEL, *Men of Good Hope: A Story of American Progressivism.* New York, 1951.

ADAMS, SAMUEL H., *Incredible Era: The Life and Times of Warren Gamaliel Harding.* New York, 1939.

ALLEN, FREDERICK LEWIS, *Only Yesterday.* New York, 1931.

———, *The Lords of Creation.* New York, 1935.

———, *The Great Pierpont Morgan.* New York, 1949.

AMORY, CLEVELAND, *The Proper Bostonians.* New York, 1947.

ANGELL, NORMAN, *The Great Illusion.* New York, 1910.

ARMSTRONG, HAMILTON FISH, *Peace and Counter-Peace: From Wilson to Hitler.* New York, 1971.

ASHBURN, FRANK D., *Fifty Years On: Groton School, 1884–1934.* New York, privately printed, 1934.

———, *Peabody of Groton.* New York, 1934.

ASHLEY, CLIFFORD W., *Whaleships of New Bedford,* with introduction by Franklin D. Roosevelt. Boston, 1929.

ASIMOV, ISAAC, *The Intelligent Man's Guide to the Biological Sciences.* New York, softbound, 1964.

BAKER, RAY STANNARD, *Woodrow Wilson and the World Settlement.* New York, 1922. 3 vols.

———, *Woodrow Wilson, Life and Letters.* New York, 1927–1939. 8 vols.

BAKER, RAY STANNARD, and DODD, WILLIAM E., *The Public Papers of Woodrow Wilson.* New York, 1925–1927. 6 vols.

BAILEY, THOMAS A., *Woodrow Wilson and the Lost Peace.* New York, 1944.

———, *Woodrow Wilson and the Great Betrayal.* New York, 1945.

BLUM, JOHN MORTON, *Joe Tumulty and the Wilson Era.* Boston, 1951.

———, *Woodrow Wilson and the Politics of Morality.* New York, 1953.

———, *The Republican Roosevelt.* Cambridge, Mass., 1954.

———, *From the Morgenthau Diaries: Years of Crisis, 1928–1938.* Boston, 1959.

BOWERS, CLAUDE G., *Beveridge and the Progressive Era.* New York, 1932.

———, *My Life.* New York, 1962.

BRANDEIS, LOUIS D., *Financial Condition of the New York, New Haven & Hartford Railroad Company, and of the Boston & Maine Railroad.* Privately printed, 1907.

———, *Other People's Money, and How the Bankers Use It.* New York, 1914.

———, *The Curse of Bigness.* New York, 1934.

BRANDENBURG, E., *From Bismarck to the World War: A History of German Foreign Policy.* New York, 1927.

BROOK, W. F., *A Social and Economic History of Germany From William II to Hitler, 1888–1939.* New York, 1939.

BUCK, SOLAN J., *The Agrarian Crusade.* New Haven, 1921.

BURNS, JAMES MAC GREGOR, *Roosevelt: The Lion and the Fox.* New York, 1956.

BUSCH, NOEL, *What Manner of Man?* New York, 1944.

CARMICHAEL, DONALD SCOTT, editor and commentator, *F.D.R., Columnist.* New York, 1947.

CHURCHILL, WINSTON S., *The World Crisis, 1911–1918.* Abridged and revised edition. London, 1931.

COIT, MARGARET L., *Mr. Baruch.* Boston, 1957.

COMMAGER, HENRY STEELE, *The American Mind.* New Haven, 1950.

CORBIN, JOHN, *Which College for Your Boy?* Boston, 1908.

COX, JAMES M., *Journey Through My Years.* New York, 1946.

CROLY, HERBERT. *The Promise of American Life.* New York, 1909.

CZERNIN, FERDINAND, *Versailles, 1919.* New York, 1964.

DANIELS, JONATHAN, *The End of Innocence.* Philadelphia, 1954.

———, *The Time Between the Wars.* New York, 1966.

———, *Washington Quadrille.* New York, 1968.

DANIELS, JOSEPHUS, *The Wilson Era: Years of Peace—1910–1917.* Chapel Hill, 1944.

———, *The Wilson Era: Years of War and After.* Chapel Hill, 1946.

DAVIS, KENNETH S., *The Politics of Honor: A Biography of Adlai E. Stevenson.* New York, 1967.

DORFMAN, JOSEPH, *Thorstein Veblen and His America.* New York, 1934.

DOS PASSOS, JOHN, *Mr. Wilson's War.* New York, 1964.

DOWS, OLIN, *Franklin Roosevelt at Hyde Park.* New York, 1949.

FARLEY, JAMES A., *Behind the Ballots.* New York, 1939.

FAULKNER, HAROLD U., *The Decline of Laissez-Faire, 1897–1917.* New York, 1951.

———, *The Quest for Social Justice, 1898–1914.* New York, 1931.

———, *From Versailles to the New Deal.* New Haven, 1950.

FAY, SIDNEY B., *Origins of the World War.* New York, 1930. 2 vols.

FILLER, LOUIS, *Crusaders of American Liberalism.* New York, 1939.

FISCHER, FRITZ, *Germany's Aims in the First World War.* New York, 1967. Original German edition, Düsseldorf, 1961.

FLYNN, EDWARD J., *You're the Boss.* New York, 1947.

FOWLER, GENE, *Beau James: The Life and Times of Jimmy Walker.* New York, 1949.

FREIDEL, FRANK, *Franklin D. Roosevelt: The Apprenticeship.* Boston, 1952.

———, *Franklin D. Roosevelt: The Ordeal.* Boston, 1954.

———, *Franklin D. Roosevelt: The Triumph.* Boston, 1956.

FREUD, SIGMUND, AND BULLITT, WILLIAM C., *Thomas Woodrow Wilson: A Psychological Study.* Boston, 1967. *Note:* This book must be used with caution. It was published long after Freud's death, and it is impossible to determine what part of it is his and what part that of the listed junior author, whose repudiation of Wilson was highly emotional and personal. There are valuable insights, however, which can be checked for accuracy against other sources.

FUSFELD, DANIEL R., *The Economic Thought of Franklin D. Roosevelt and the Origins of the New Deal.* New York, 1956.

GARRATY, JOHN A., *Right-Hand Man: The Life of George W. Perkins.* New York, 1960.

GINGER, RAY, *The Bending Cross: A Biography of Eugene Debs.* New Brunswick, 1960.

GOLDMAN, ERIC F., *Rendezvous With Destiny.* New York, 1952.

GOSNELL, HAROLD, *Champion Campaigner.* New York, 1952.

GOULD, JEAN, *A Good Fight.* New York, 1960.

GRAHAM, OTIS L., JR., *An Encore for Reform: The Old Progressives and the New Deal.* New York, 1967.

GRATTAN, C. HARTLEY, *Why We Fought.* New York, 1929.

GUNTHER, JOHN, *Roosevelt in Retrospect.* New York, 1950.

HALSEY, WILLIAM F., and BRYAN, JULIAN, III, *Admiral Halsey's Story.* New York, 1947.

HANDLIN, OSCAR, *Al Smith and His America.* Boston, 1958.

HARBAUGH, WILLIAM HENRY, *Power and Responsibility: The Life and Times of Theodore Roosevelt.* New York, 1961.

HATCH, ALDEN, *Edith Bolling Wilson.* New York, 1961.

HEATON, JOHN L., *Cobb of "The World."* New York, 1928.

HICKS, JOHN D., *The Populist Revolt.* Minneapolis, 1941.

———, *Republican Ascendancy, 1921–1933.* New York, 1960.

HOFSTADTER, RICHARD, *The American Political Tradition and the Men Who Made It.* New York, 1948.

———, *The Age of Reform.* New York, 1955.

HOOVER, HERBERT, *The Ordeal of Woodrow Wilson.* New York, 1958.

———, *Memoirs.* New York, 1950–1952. 3 vols.

HOUSTON, DAVID F., *Eight Years with Wilson's Cabinet.* New York, 1926. 2 vols.

HUTHMACHER, J. JOSEPH, *Senator Robert E. Wagner and the Rise of Urban Liberalism*. New York, 1968.

ICKES, HAROLD, *The Secret Diary of Harold Ickes: The First Thousand Days, 1933–1936*. New York, 1953.

JOHNSON, GERALD W., *Roosevelt: An American Study*. New York, 1942.

JOHNSON, WALTER, *William Allen White's America*. New York, 1947.

JORDAN, DAVID STARR, *War and Waste*. New York, 1914.

JOSEPHSON, MATTHEW AND HANNAH, *Al Smith: Hero of the Cities* (a political portrait drawing upon the papers of Frances Perkins). Boston, 1969.

KILPATRICK, CARROLL, ed., *Roosevelt and Daniels: A Friendship in Politics*. Chapel Hill, 1952.

KLEEMAN, RITA HALLE, *Gracious Lady: The Life of Sara Delano Roosevelt*. New York, 1935.

KOENIG, LOUIS W., *Bryan*. New York, 1971.

KROCK, ARTHUR, *Memoirs: Sixty Years on the Firing Line*. New York, 1968.

LA FOLLETTE, ROBERT M., *La Follette's Autobiography*. Madison, Wisconsin, 1913.

LASH, JOSEPH P., *Eleanor and Franklin*. New York, 1971.

LEUCHTENBURG, WILLIAM E., *The Perils of Prosperity, 1914–1932*. Chicago, 1958.

LINDLEY, ERNEST K., *Franklin D. Roosevelt: A Career in Progressive Democracy*. New York, 1932.

LINK, ARTHUR S., *Woodrow Wilson and the Progressive Era*. New York, 1954.

———, *Wilson, The Road to the White House*. Princeton, 1947.

———, *Wilson, The New Freedom*. Princeton, 1956.

———, *Wilson, The Struggle for Neutrality, 1914–1915*. Princeton, 1960.

———, *Wilson, Confusions and Crises, 1915–1916*. Princeton, 1964.

———, *Wilson, Campaigns for Progressivism and Peace, 1916–1917*. Princeton, 1964.

———, *American Epoch: A History of the United States Since the 1890's*. New York, 1955. This is much more and better than a standard "textbook" history. It is written with a clear sense of underlying forces and has the sweep and power of great drama.

LOOKER, EARLE, *This Man Roosevelt*. New York, 1932.

LUDWIG, EMIL, *Bismarck*. New York, 1928.

MCADOO, WILLIAM GIBBS, *Crowded Years*. New York, 1931.

MCINTYRE, ROSS T., *White House Physician*. New York, 1946.

MACKENZIE, COMPTON, *Mr. Roosevelt*. New York, 1944.

MARX, RUDOLPH, M.D., *The Health of the Presidents*. New York, 1960.

MASON, ALPHEUS THOMAS, *Bureaucracy Convicts Itself: The Ballinger-Pinchot Controversy of 1910*. New York, 1941.

———, *Brandeis: A Free Man's Life*. New York, 1946.

MILLIS, WALTER, *The Road to War: America, 1914–1917*. New York, 1935.

MORISON, ELTING E., *Admiral Sims and the Modern American Navy*. Boston, 1942.

MORISON, SAMUEL ELIOT, *Three Centuries of Harvard*. Cambridge, 1936.

MOSCOW, WARREN, *Politics in the Empire State.* New York, 1948.

MULLEN, ARTHUR, *A Western Democrat.* New York, 1940.

NORRIS, GEORGE W., *Fighting Liberal, An Autobiography.* New York, 1945.

NORTH, DOUGLASS C., *Growth and Welfare in the American Past.* Englewood Cliffs, N.J., 1966.

O'CONNOR, RICHARD, *The First Hurrah, A Biography of Alfred E. Smith.* New York, 1970.

O'CONNOR, RICHARD, AND WALKER, DALE L., *The Lost Revolutionary, A Biography of John Reed.* New York, 1967.

PERKINS, FRANCES, *The Roosevelt I Knew.* New York, 1946.

PRINGLE, HENRY F., *Theodore Roosevelt.* New York, 1931. Revised edition reissued softbound, 1956.

———, *Alfred E. Smith.* New York, 1927.

———, *The Life and Times of William Howard Taft.* New York, 1939. 2 vols.

PROSKAUER, JOSEPH D., *A Segment of My Times.* New York, 1950.

PUTNAM, H. PHELPS, *Theodore Roosevelt: The Formative Years.* New York, 1958.

ROLLINS, ALFRED B., JR., *Roosevelt and Howe.* New York, 1962.

ROOSEVELT, ELEANOR, *This Is My Story.* New York, 1937.

———, *This I Remember.* New York, 1949.

ROOSEVELT, JAMES, WITH SHALETT, SIDNEY, *Affectionately, F.D.R.: A Son's Story of a Lonely Man.* New York, 1959.

ROOSEVELT, MRS. JAMES, as told to Leighton, Isabelle, and Forbush, Gabrielle, *My Boy Franklin.* New York, 1933.

ROSENMAN, SAMUEL I., *Working with Roosevelt.* New York, 1952.

RUSSELL, FRANCIS, *The Shadow of Blooming Grove: Warren G. Harding and His Times.* New York, 1968.

SCHLESINGER, ARTHUR M., JR., *The Crisis of the Old Order,* Vol. 1 of *The Age of Roosevelt.* Boston, 1957.

SCHRIFTGIESSER, KARL, *This Was Normalcy.* Boston, 1948.

———, *The Gentleman from Massachusetts: Henry Cabot Lodge.* Boston, 1944.

SEIGNOBOS, CHARLES, *A Political History of Europe Since 1814.* Translation edited by Silas MacVane. New York, 1900.

SEYMOUR, CHARLES, ed., *The Intimate Papers of Colonel House.* New York, 1926–1928. 4 vols.

SLOSSON, PRESTON WILLIAM, *The Great Crusade and After, 1914–1928.* New York, 1930.

SMITH, GENE, *When the Cheering Stopped.* New York, 1964.

———, *The Shattered Dream.* New York, 1970.

SOULE, GEORGE, *Prosperity Decade.* New York, 1947.

STEFFENS, LINCOLN, *The Shame of the Cities.* New York, 1904.

———, *Autobiography.* New York, 1931.

STILES, LELA, *The Man Behind Roosevelt: Louis McHenry Howe.* Cleveland, 1954.

SULLIVAN, MARK, *Our Times, The United States, 1900–1925.* New York, 1926–1935. 6 vols.

TAYLOR, CHARLES CARLISLE, *The Life of Admiral Mahan.* New York, 1920.
TUCHMAN, BARBARA W., *The Zimmermann Telegram.* New York, 1958.
———, *The Guns of August.* New York, 1962.
———, *The Proud Tower.* New York, 1966. Softbound edition, 1967.
TUGWELL, REXFORD G., *The Democratic Roosevelt.* New York, 1957.
TULLY, GRACE, *F.D.R., My Boss.* New York, 1949.
TUMULTY, JOSEPH P., *Woodrow Wilson as I Knew Him.* New York, 1921.
WALD, LILLIAN D., *The House on Henry Street.* New York, 1915.
WALKER, TURNLEY, *Roosevelt and the Warm Springs Story.* New York, 1953.
WARNER, EMILY SMITH, WITH DANIEL, HAWTHORNE, *The Happy Warrior.* New York, 1956.
WARREN, GAYLORD HARRIS, *Herbert Hoover and the Great Depression.* New York, 1959.
WEHLE, LOUIS B., *Hidden Threads of History: Wilson Through Roosevelt.* New York, 1953.
WHITE, WILLIAM ALLEN, *A Puritan in Babylon.* New York, 1938.
———, *Autobiography.* New York, 1946.
WICHMAN, IVAN, M.D., *Acute Poliomyelitis.* New York, 1913.
WILSON, EDITH BOLLING, *My Memoir.* Indianapolis, 1938, 1939.
WISH, HARVEY, *Contemporary America: The National Scene Since 1900.* New York, 1948. Revised edition, 1955.

II. SPECIAL LISTS

A. FOR FDR'S ANCESTRY AND FAMILY HISTORY

ANONYMOUS, *A Century of Progress: History of the Delaware and Hudson Company, 1823–1923.* Privately printed, 1923.
ASPINWALL, A. A., *The Aspinwall Genealogy.* Rutland, Vt., 1901.
BEACHLEY, CHARLES E., *History of the Consolidation Coal Company, 1864–1934.* New York, 1934.
BURGESS, GEORGE H., and KENNEDY, MILES C., *Centennial History of the Pennsylvania Railroad Company.* Philadelphia, 1949.
CHURCHILL, ALLEN, *The Roosevelts: American Aristocrats.* New York, 1965, 1966.
DAGGETT, STUART, *Railroad Reorganization.* Cambridge, Mass., 1908.
DELANO, DANIEL W., JR., *Franklin Roosevelt and the Delano Influence.* Pittsburgh, 1946.
HONE, PHILIP, *The Diary of Philip Hone, 1828–1851,* edited by Bayard Tuckerman. New York, 1889. 2 vols.
JOHNSON, ALVIN PAGE, *Franklin Roosevelt's Colonial Ancestors.* Boston, 1946.
LESLEY, MRS. SUSAN, *Memoir of the Life of Mrs. Anne Jean Lyman.* Cambridge, Mass., privately printed, 1875.
PARTRIDGE, BELLAMY, *The Roosevelt Family in America.* New York, 1936.
REYNOLDS, CUYLER; COLLINS, J.; DUMPELLY, D.; and JORDAN, JOHN W., *Annals of American Families.* New York, 1916.

SCHRIFTGIESSER, KARL, *The Amazing Roosevelt Family, 1613–1942.* New York, 1942.

B. FOR HISTORICAL SETTING, FDR ANCESTORS

BOYLE, ROBERT H., *The Hudson River.* New York, 1969.
CARMER, CARL, *The Hudson.* New York, 1939.
CHEYNEY, EDWARD P., *The Anti-Rent Agitation in the State of New York, 1839–1846.* Philadelphia, 1897.
GOODWIN, M. W., *The Dutch and English on the Hudson.* New Haven, 1919.
HACKER, LOUIS M., *The Triumph of American Capitalism.* New York, 1940.
NETTLES, C. P., *The Roots of American Civilization.* New York, 1938.
SCHLESINGER, A. M., *The Colonial Merchants and the American Revolution.* New York, 1947.

C. FOR BASIC THEMATIC DEVELOPMENT

ADAMS, BROOKS, *The Law of Civilization and Decay.* New York, 1896. Softbound edition, 1955.
ADAMS, HENRY, *The Education of Henry Adams.* Boston, 1918.
———, *The Degradation of Democratic Dogma,* containing Adams' prescient "A Letter to American Teachers of History." New York, 1919, 1947.
ARENDT, HANNAH, *The Origins of Totalitarianism.* New York, 1951. Its publisher asserts that "this book lays bare for the first time the roots of twentieth-century man's political and human tragedy: totalitarianism." It does no such thing. Incredibly, in view of its stated purpose, the book in all its 439 large-size, closely printed pages makes no reference to causal relations between the rise of scientific technology and the developing phenomena of nation-states, imperialism, and totalitarianism. Miss Arendt, a German whose doctorate was taken at the University of Heidelberg, where she majored in philosophy, theology, and Greek (Karl Jaspers was her major professor), has evidently had no exposure to or interest in the physical and biological sciences; this, in my opinion, virtually incapacitates her as a philosopher of modern history. She deals with historical phenomena brilliantly, but ignores their deeper roots.
ARON, RAYMOND, *Progress and Disillusion: The Dialectics of Modern Society.* New York.
BERLE, ADOLPH, *Power.* New York, 1969.
BERLE, ADOLPH, AND MEANS, GARDINER C., *The Modern Corporation and Private Property.*
CARTER, GEORGE R., *The Tendency Towards Industrial Combination.* London, 1913.
COMMONER, BARRY, *Science and Survival.* New York, 1965.
FROMM, ERICH, *The Revolution of Hope: Toward a Humanized Technology.* New York, 1968.
GALBRAITH, J. K., *The New Industrial State.* Boston, 1967.

GIEDION, SIEGFRIED, *Mechanization Takes Command.* New York, 1955.

LIPSET, MARTIN SEYMOUR, *Political Man: The Social Bases of Politics.* New York, 1960. Softbound edition, 1963.

MEIKLEJOHN, ALEXANDER, *What Does America Mean?* New York, 1935.

MORISON, ELTING E., *Men, Machines, and Modern Times.* Cambridge, Mass., 1966.

MUMFORD, LEWIS, *Technics and Civilization.* New York, 1934.

———, *The Myth of the Machine: I. Technics and Human Development.* New York, 1967.

———, *The Myth of the Machine: II. The Pentagon of Power.* New York, 1970.

NIEBUHR, REINHOLD, *The Self and the Dramas of History.* New York, 1953.

ORTEGA Y GASSET, JOSÉ, *The Revolt of the Masses.* New York, 1932.

RUSSELL, BERTRAND, *The Scientific Outlook.* New York, 1931.

———, *Power, A New Social Analysis.* London, 1940.

SCHUMPETER, JOSEPH A., *Capitalism, Socialism, and Democracy.* New York, 1942.

SPENGLER, OSWALD, *The Decline of the West.* New York, 1932. 1 vol. ed.

WHITEHEAD, A. N., *Science and the Modern World.* New York, 1923.

III. PERIODICALS, PAMPHLETS, OTHER MATERIALS

ANONYMOUS, *Campobello Island* (pamphlet, Campobello Island Board of Trade, 1966).

BARBER, BETTY E., A Guide to FDR's "Beloved Island" (pamphlet, Hammer Library for Regional Research, Vicksburg, Miss., 1962).

BERLIN, ISAIAH, "President Franklin Delano Roosevelt," *Political Quarterly,* Vol. XXVI (December, 1935). Compares Roosevelt with Wilson.

BIDDLE, GEORGE, "As I Remember Groton School, A Chapter of Autobiography," *Harper's Magazine* (August, 1939).

BOWER, CLAUDE G., Reminiscences, Oral History Research Office, Columbia University.

BRADEN, WALDO W., and BRANDENBURG, EARNEST, "The Early Speaking of Franklin D. Roosevelt," *Franklin D. Roosevelt Collector,* Vol. III (May, 1951), pp. 3–23.

BRAHANY, THOMAS W., Chief Clerk, White House Executive Office, Typescript of Diary, March 4–April 24, 1917. FDR Group 10, Box 137, Franklin D. Roosevelt Library.

BRANDENBURG, EARNEST, "The Preparation of Franklin D. Roosevelt's Speeches," *Quarterly Journal of Speech,* Vol. XXXV (April, 1949), pp. 214–21.

CARLSON, EARLAND I., "Franklin Roosevelt's Fight for the Presidential Nomination, 1928–1932," *Dissertation Abstracts,* Vol. XVI (February, 1956), p. 323.

———, "Franklin D. Roosevelt's Post-Mortem of the 1928 Election," *Midwest Journal of Political Science,* Vol. VIII (August, 1964), pp. 298–308.

CHAMBERS, CLARKE A., "FDR, Pragmatist-Idealist: An Essay in Historiography," *Pacific Northwest Quarterly*, Vol. LII (April, 1961), pp. 50–55.

COREY, ALBERT B., "Franklin Roosevelt—Local Historian," *New York History*, Vol. XXVIII (October, 1947), pp. 506–11.

COWPERTHWAITE, L. L., "Franklin D. Roosevelt at Harvard," *Quarterly Journal of Speech*, Vol. XXXVIII (February, 1952), pp. 37–41.

CROWELL, LAURA, "Roosevelt the Grotonian," *Quarterly Journal of Speech*, Vol. XXXVIII (February, 1952), pp. 31–36.

DANIELS, JONATHAN, a chapter, "Franklin Delano Roosevelt and Books," in *Three Presidents and Books* (Urbana, Ill., 1955). Originally a lecture.

DANIELS, JOSEPHUS, Diary, 1913–1920, Manuscript Division, Library of Congress.

DREXEL, CONSTANCE, "Unpublished Letters of FDR to His French Governess," *Parents Magazine*, Vol. XXVI (September, 1951), pp. 30–31.

ERIKSON, ERIK H., "Psychoanalysis and Ongoing History: Problems of Identity, Hatred, and Non-Violence," with commentary by Richard Hofstadter, *American Journal of Psychiatry*, Vol. 122 (September, 1965), pp. 241–53.

FABRICANT, NOAH D., "Franklin D. Roosevelt's Tonsillectomy and Poliomyelitis," *Eye, Ear, Nose, Throat Monthly* Vol. XXXVI (June, 1957), pp. 348–49.

———, "Franklin D. Roosevelt's Nose and Throat Ailments," *Eye, Ear, Nose, Throat Monthly*, Vol. XXXVI (March, 1958), pp. 179–85.

———, "Franklin D. Roosevelt, the Common Cold and American History," *Eye, Ear, Nose, Throat Monthly*, Vol. XXXVII (March, 1958), pp. 179–85.

FREIDEL, FRANK, "The Education of Franklin D. Roosevelt," *Harvard Education Review*, Vol. XXXI (Spring, 1961), pp. 158–67.

FRISCH, MORTON J., "Franklin D. Roosevelt and the Problem of Democratic Liberty," *Ethics*, Vol. LXXII (April, 1962), pp. 18–92.

———, "Roosevelt the Conservator: A Rejoinder to Hofstadter," *Journal of Politics*, Vol. XXV (May, 1963), pp. 361–72.

GALBRAITH, J. K., "On the Economics of F.D.R.: What a President Ought to Know," *Commentary*, Vol. XXII (August, 1956), pp. 172–73.

HAND, SAMUEL B., "Al Smith, Franklin D. Roosevelt and the New Deal: Some Comments on Perspective," *Historian*, Vol. XXVII (May, 1965), pp. 366–81.

HOYT, MORGAN H., "Roosevelt Enters Politics," *F.D.R. Collector*, Vol. I (May, 1949), pp. 3–9.

JOHNSON, ALVA, "Mr. Roosevelt as a Businessman," *Saturday Evening Post*, Vol. 209 (October 31, 1936), pp. 64 ff.

KOISTINEN, PAUL A. C., "The 'Industrial-Military Complex' in Historical Perspective: The Interwar Years," *Journal of American History*, Vol. LVI, No. 4 (March, 1970).

KROCK, ARTHUR, Reminiscences, Oral History Research Office, Columbia University.

McAVOY, THOMAS, "Roosevelt: A Modern Jefferson," *Review of Politics*, Vol. VII (July, 1945), pp. 270–79.

MARVIN, LANGDON, Reminiscences, Oral History Research Office, Columbia University.

MILLIS, WALTER, "Roosevelt in Retrospect," *Virginia Quarterly Review*, Vol. XXI (July, 1945), pp. 321–30.

NEVINS, ALLAN, "The Place of Franklin D. Roosevelt in History," *American Heritage*, Vol. XVII (June, 1966), pp. 12 ff.

PERKINS, FRANCES, "Franklin Roosevelt's Apprenticeship," *New Republic*, Vol. CXXXII (April 25, 1955), pp. 19–21.

POTTER, DAVID M., "Sketches for the Roosevelt Portrait," *Yale Review*, Vol. XXXIX (Autumn, 1949), pp. 39–53.

ROLLINS, ALFRED B., JR., "Young Franklin Roosevelt and the Moral Crusaders," *New York History* (January, 1956), pp. 3–16. Reproduced in Rollins' *Roosevelt and Howe.*

———, "Franklin Roosevelt's Introduction to Labor," *Labor History*, Vol. III (Winter, 1962), pp. 3–18. Also in Rollins' *Roosevelt and Howe.*

ROOSEVELT, FRANKLIN D., "The Roosevelt Family in New Amsterdam Before the Revolution," a 1901 ms. written for Harvard class assignment, now in Franklin D. Roosevelt Library.

ROSSITER, CLINTON J., "The Political Philosophy of F. D. Roosevelt: A Challenge to Scholarship," *Review of Politics*, Vol. II (January, 1949), pp. 87–95.

SCHIFFMAN, JOSEPH, "Observations on Roosevelt's Literary Style," *Quarterly Journal of Speech*, Vol. XXXV (April, 1949), pp. 222–26.

SHIPLER, GUY E., "Franklin Roosevelt and Religion," *Churchman*, Vol. CLXIX (May 1, 1955), pp. 10–11.

SILL, LEONORA, "Bird Lover of Hyde Park," *Audubon Magazine*, Vol. LVII (June, 1955), pp. 116–19.

STAFF OF FRANKLIN D. ROOSEVELT LIBRARY, "A Note on FDR's Dogs."

THORNTON, HARRISON J., "The Two Roosevelts at Chautauqua," *New York History*, Vol. XXVIII (January, 1947), pp. 33–65.

TUGWELL, REXFORD G., "The Fallow Years of Franklin D. Roosevelt," *Ethics*, Vol. LXVI (January, 1956), pp. 98–116. Reproduced in Tugwell's *The Democratic Roosevelt.*

Index

Roosevelt, John Aspinwall (FDR's uncle), 25, 45

Roosevelt, Maria Eliza Walton, 21

Roosevelt, Mary Rebecca Aspinwall (FDR's grandmother), 22–24

Roosevelt, Nicholas, 17

Roosevelt, Quentin (TR's son), 520

Roosevelt, Rebecca Brien Howland, 29–30, 32, 54

Roosevelt, Sadie Meisinger, 137

Roosevelt, Sara Delano (FDR's mother), 33–52, 123, 141, 142–43, 149, 151, 171, 172–76, 190, 197–200, 202–7, 228, 483, 660–61, 667–68, 669, 672, 717, 805-6, 820

Roosevelt, Theodore, 34, 54, 59, 116–17, 122, 124, 127, 137, 140, 144, 145–46, 147, 148, 149, 150, 153–55, 156, 164–66, 167, 183–84, 189–90, 191, 196, 208, 209–10, 211, 214–19, 222, 226, 229, 230–31, 232, 233, 235, 237, 241, 246, 248–49, 267, 274–75, 296, 298–300, 302, 321, 328, 383–85, 387, 389, 404, 405, 406, 414, 422, 423, 425–26, 427, 432, 433, 446, 451, 458–60, 463, 530, 542, 543–44, 555–56, 639

Roosevelt, Theodore, Jr. (TR's son), 621, 630, 695, 771, 772

Roosevelt, Theodore, Sr., 164

Roosevelt, Mrs. Theodore, Sr., 171

Roosevelt & O'Connor, 767, 799

Roosevelt & Son, Isaac, 20

Roper, Daniel C., 354–55, 777

Rosedale estate, 24, 45, 50

Rose Hill estate, 42

Ross, Nellie Tayloe, 837

Rough Riders, 124, 128, 145, 195

Royce, Josiah, 138, 139

Russell, Charles Edward, 226

Russell, Sturgis & Company, 38

Russell and Company, 42, 59–60

Russia, 92, 450, 510–11, 515, 568, 583

Russian Revolution, 451–52, 516, 531–32, 626

Russo-Japanese War, 196

Rutherfurd, Winthrop, 595–96

Rutland, Duke and Duchess of, 62

Ryan, Thomas Fortune, 243, 253, 826

Sabalo (yacht), 645–46, 647, 648, 649

Sage, Russell, 249

Sague, John K., 220, 222, 348

St. James Church, Hyde Park, 31, 32, 54, 73, 141, 199

St. Louis and San Francisco Railroad, 50–51

St. Mark's School, 58, 114

St. Paul's Academy, 34

Samuels, Thomas, 17

Sandoz, Jeanne (governess), 74–77, 152, 397–98

Santayana, George, 132, 138

Santo Domingo, 154, 435, 437, 441, 442–43, 621, 688

Saratoga *Sun,* 286

Sargent, John Singer, 108, 410 n.

Satterlee, Herbert, 319

Schacht, Hjalmar, 746

Schenck v. U.S., 579

Schlesser, John F., 221, 241, 242

Schley, Grant B., 210

Schlieffen Plan, 378, 379

Schneiderman, Rose, 263

Schopenhauer, Arthur, 87

Schuette, Johann, 704

Schumann-Heink, Madame, 509

Schwab, Charles, 549

Schwabe, Madame, 49

Scott, Hugh, 499

Scribner's Magazine, 217

Scudder, Townsend, 843, 844

Sea Bright, New Jersey, 202

Sea Girt, New Jersey, 277

Seamen's Church Institute, 213

Secret Service, U.S., 216

Sedgwick, Ellery, 814

Sedition Act, 552

Seignobos, Charles, 87–88, 327 n.

Seligman, Herbert J., 439, 440, 441

Selmes, Mrs. Tilden R., 195

Seventeenth Amendment, 257

Shaler, Nathaniel S., 138, 139

Shame of the Cities, The (Steffens), 226

Shaver, Clem, 776–77, 778, 815

Shaw, Albert, 634

Sheehan, William F., 246–47, 249, 250, 251, 253, 255, 256, 291

Sheer, Reinhard, 547

Shepard, Edward M., 247, 250, 252, 253

Sherman Antitrust Act (1890), 154, 208, 209, 210, 211, 212, 227, 228, 229, 232, 297

Sherman Silver Purchase Act, 97, 99, 114

Sherwood, Jean, 647

Shipping Act, 45

Shipping Board, U.S., 425, 502, 551–52, 574

Signet society, 157

Silliman, Benjamin Douglas, 27

Silver issue, 46, 99

Sims, William S., 454, 470, 471, 473, 475, 518, 591–92, 596, 597, 598, 599, 600

Sinclair, Harry F., 696

Sinclair, Upton, 226